DISCOVER MCGRAW-HILL NETWORKS FOR FLORIDA SOCIAL STUDIES

AN AWARD-WINNING SOCIAL STUDIES PROGRAM DESIGNED TO FULLY SUPPORT YOUR SUCCESS.

» Aligned to the Next Generation Sunshine State Standards with end-of-year assessments in mind

» Engages you with interactive resources and compelling stories

» Provides resources and tools for every learning style

» Empowers targeted learning to help you be successful

There's More Online!

(top to bottom) ©George Hammerstein/Corbis/Glow Images, Julia Goss/Flickr Open/Getty Images, National Aeronautics and Space Administration (NASA), NASA, Library of Congress Prints and Photographs Division [LC-DIG-ppmsca-08102], ©George Hammerstein/Corbis/Glow Images

W9-BYC-696

UNDERSTANDING IS THE FOUNDATION OF ACHIEVEMENT

Clear writing, real-life examples, photos, interactive maps, videos, and more will capture your attention and keep you engaged so that you can succeed.

You will find tools and resources to help you read more effectively.

networks™
There's More Online!

FOCUS YOUR TIME AND YOUR EFFORT

LEARNSMART®

No two students are alike! We built LearnSmart® so that all students can work through the key material they need to learn at their own pace.

YOUR TIME MATTERS

LearnSmart with SmartBook® adapts to you as you work, guiding you through your reading so you can make every minute count.

DISCOVER A PERSONALIZED READING EXPERIENCE

Every student experiences SmartBook differently. The interactive challenge format highlights content and helps you identify content you know and don't know.

RETAIN MORE INFORMATION

LearnSmart detects content you are most likely to forget and will highlight what you need to review.

STUDYSMART

StudySmart: Succeeding in Modern U.S. History will make it easy for you to review what you need to know to be successful on your chapter tests and end-of-year assessment.

» Print work text designed with you in mind

» Summaries and activities allow you to focus your study

» Build critical thinking and test-taking skills with activities designed around primary sources, political cartoons, maps, charts, and graphs

» Prepare for assessments using the chapter tests

Left page: (top to bottom) ra photography/Getty Images.; Library of Congress Prints and Photographs Division [LC-DIG-ppmsca-08102] ; Right page: ©Cultura Creative (RF)/Alamy Stock Photo

BE THE STUDENT YOU WANT TO BE.
STUDENTS WHO UNDERSTAND THE WORLD WILL BE THE ADULTS WHO CAN CHANGE IT.

DISCOVER IT ALL ONLINE!

1. Go to connected.mcgraw-hill.com

2. Enter your username and password from your teacher.

3. Click on your book.

4. Select your chapter and lesson, or explore the Resource Library.

Julia Coss/Flickr Open/Getty Images

networks
There's More Online!

GO ONLINE AND START EXPLORING!

MHEDUCATION.COM/PREK-12

FLORIDA EDITION

UNITED STATES

HISTORY AND GEOGRAPHY

MODERN TIMES

netw_rks

There's More Online!

Joyce Appleby, Ph.D.

Alan Brinkley, Ph.D.

Albert S. Broussard, Ph.D.

James M. McPherson, Ph.D.

Donald A. Ritchie, Ph.D.

Mc
Graw
Hill
Education

Cover Photo Credits: (bkgd)National Aeronautics and Space Administration (NASA); (clockwise from top)Julia Goss/Flickr Open/Getty Images;(2)Library of Congress Prints and Photographs Division [LC-DIG-ppmsca-08102]; (3)© George Hammerstein/Corbis/Glow Images; (4)NASA

www.mheonline.com/networks

Copyright © 2018 by McGraw-Hill Education

All rights reserved. No part of this publication may be reproduced or distributed in any form or by any means, or stored in a database or retrieval system, without the prior written consent of McGraw-Hill Education, including, but not limited to, network storage or transmission, or broadcast for distance learning.

Send all inquiries to:
McGraw-Hill Education
8787 Orion Place
Columbus, OH 43240

ISBN: 978-0-07-676843-1
MHID: 0-07-676843-0

Printed in the United States of America.

3 4 5 6 7 8 9 10 LWI 20 19 18 17

DISCOVER MCGRAW-HILL NETWORKS FOR FLORIDA SOCIAL STUDIES, AN AWARD-WINNING SOCIAL STUDIES PROGRAM DESIGNED TO FULLY SUPPORT YOUR SUCCESS.
- Aligned to the Next Generation Sunshine State Standards with end-of-year assessments in mind
- Engages you with interactive resources and compelling stories
- Provides resources and tools for every learning style
- Empowers targeted learning to help you be successful

AUTHORS

Joyce Appleby, Ph.D., is Professor Emerita of History at UCLA. She is the author of several books, including *Economic Thought and Ideology in Seventeenth-Century England,* which won the Berkshire Prize. She served as president of both the Organization of American Historians and the American Historical Association, and chaired the Council of the Institute of Early American History and Culture at Williamsburg. Dr. Appleby has been elected to the American Philosophical Society and the American Academy of Arts and Sciences, and is a Corresponding Fellow of the British Academy.

Alan Brinkley, Ph.D., is Allan Nevins Professor of American History at Columbia University. His published works include *Voices of Protest: Huey Long, Father Coughlin, and the Great Depression,* which won the 1983 National Book Award. He received the Levenson Memorial Teaching Prize at Harvard University.

Albert S. Broussard, Ph.D., is Professor of History at Texas A&M University, where he was selected as the Distinguished Faculty Lecturer for 1999–2000. He also served as the Langston Hughes Professor of American Studies at the University of Kansas in 2005. Before joining the Texas A&M faculty, Dr. Broussard was Assistant Professor of History and Director of the African American Studies Program at Southern Methodist University. Dr. Broussard has also served as president of the Oral History Association.

James M. McPherson, Ph.D., is George Henry Davis Professor Emeritus of American History at Princeton University. Dr. McPherson is the author of 11 books about the Civil War era, including *Abraham Lincoln as Commander in Chief,* for which he won the 2009 Lincoln Prize. Dr. McPherson is a member of many professional historical associations, including the Civil War Preservation Trust.

Donald A. Ritchie, Ph.D. is United States Senate Historian Emeritus. Dr. Ritchie received his doctorate in American history from the University of Maryland after service in the U.S. Marine Corps. He has taught American history at various levels, from high school to university. He edits the Historical Series of the Senate Foreign Relations Committee and is the author of several books, including *Press Gallery: Congress and the Washington Correspondents,* which received the Organization of American Historians' Richard W. Leopold Prize. Dr. Ritchie has served as president of the Oral History Association and as a council member of the American Historical Association.

Contributing Author

Jay McTighe has published articles in a number of leading educational journals and has co-authored ten books, including the best-selling *Understanding By Design* series with Grant Wiggins. Jay also has an extensive background in professional development and is a featured speaker at national, state, and district conferences and workshops. He received his undergraduate degree from The College of William and Mary, earned a Masters degree from The University of Maryland, and completed post-graduate studies at The Johns Hopkins University.

The **Florida Teacher Advisory Board** provided valuable feedback on this program. We thank these teachers for their hard work, creative suggestions, and commitment to their discipline.

Lauren Bernat
Manatee County Public Schools

Christine Disinger
Volusia County Schools

Ashley Hall
Santa Rosa County School District

Charles Lyles
Duval County Public Schools

Stacy Moser
Polk County Public Schools

Amy Parker
Santa Rosa County School District

Pamela Rose
Santa Rosa County School District

Rachel Slone
School District of Osceola County

Stacy Thompson
Leon County Schools

Theodore Wright
Polk County Public Schools

Clark Youngblood
Santa Rosa County School District

ACADEMIC CONSULTANTS

David Berger, Ph.D.
Ruth and I. Lewis Gordon Professor of
  Jewish History
Dean, Bernard Revel Graduate School
Yeshiva University
New York, New York

Steven Cunha, Ph.D.
Professor of Geography
Humboldt State University
Arcata, California

Linda Clemmons, Ph.D.
Assistant Professor of History
Illinois State University
Normal, Illinois

Neil Foley, Ph.D.
Associate Professor of History
University of Texas at Austin
Austin, Texas

Shawn Johansen, Ph.D.
Professor of History
Brigham Young University Idaho
Rexburg, Idaho

K. Austin Kerr, Ph.D.
Emeritus Professor of History
The Ohio State University
Columbus, Ohio

Jeffrey Ogbar, Ph.D.
Associate Dean for the Humanities
University of Connecticut, Storrs
Storrs, Connecticut

William Bruce Wheeler, Ph.D.
Emeritus Professor of History
University of Tennessee
Knoxville, Tennessee

Tom Daccord
Educational Technology Specialist
Co-Director, EdTechTeacher
Boston, Massachusetts

Justin Reich
Educational Technology Specialist
Co-Director, EdTech Teacher
Boston, Massachusetts

TEACHER REVIEWERS

Marsha Baugh
Montgomery Public Schools
Brewbaker Technology Magnet High School
Montgomery, Alabama

Terry L. Cherry
Garland Independent School District
Naaman Forest High School
Garland, Texas

Brian P. Dowd
Massapequa Public Schools
Massapequa High School
Massapequa, New York

Jennifer L. Flores
Francis Howell School District
Francis Howell High School
St. Charles, Missouri

Dr. Robert A. Handy
Bel Air High School
Bel Air, Maryland

Karl R. Johnson
Paradise Valley Unified School District
Pinnacle High School
Phoenix, Arizona

Mark Kuhl
School District #115
Lake Forest High School
Lake Forest, Illinois

Julie M. Lasowski
Orange County Public Schools
Olympia High School
Orlando, Florida

Kevin McCaffrey
Evanston Township High School
Evanston, Illinois

Michael McLaughlin
Hazelwood School District
Hazelwood East High School
St. Louis, Missouri

Kelly M. Machala
Harford County Public Schools
Patterson Mill Middle/High School
Bel Air, Maryland

James May
Harford County Public Schools
Patterson Mill High School
Bel Air, Maryland

Steven "Duff" Pace
Enterprise School District # 21
Enterprise High School
Enterprise, Oregon

Christa Martell Schneider
Francis Howell School District
Francis Howell High School
St. Charles, Missouri

John A. Toronski
Pinellas County
Lakewood High School
St. Petersburg, Florida

Heather McGraw Verdi
Consolidated School District of New Britain
New Britain High School
New Britain, Connecticut

Andrew White
Montgomery County Public Schools
Paint Branch High School
Burtonsville, Maryland

Brandon J. Woodrome, Ed.S.
Belleville Township High School District 201
Belleville West High School
Belleville, Illinois

CONTENTS

CONTENTS

The Granger Collection, New York

CHAPTER 6

The Progressive Movement, 1890–1920 .... **199**

Essential Question
Can politics fix social problems?

Underwood & Underwood/Bettmann/CORBIS

CHAPTER 7

World War I and Its Aftermath, 1914–1920 .... **229**

Essential Question
Why do nations go to war?

CONTENTS

Bettmann/CORBIS

CHAPTER **10**

Roosevelt and the New Deal, 1933–1941 ...... **307**

Essential Questions

Can the government fix the economy? • Is government responsible for the economic well-being of its citizens?

Library of Congress

CHAPTER **11**

A World in Flames, 1931–1941 ...... **331**

Essential Questions

Could World War II have been prevented? • Why do some people fail to respond to injustice while others try to prevent injustice?

CONTENTS

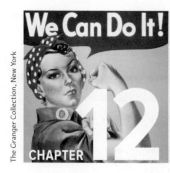

The Granger Collection, New York

CHAPTER 12

Bettmann/CORBI

CHAPTER 13

CONTENTS

Bettmann/CORBIS

CHAPTER **19**

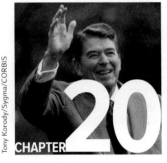

Tony Korody/Sygma/CORBIS

CHAPTER **20**

CONTENTS

Pete Souza/Obama Transition Team/Handout/Corbis News/CORBIS

CHAPTER **23**

Obama and Beyond, 2008–Present 641

Essential Questions

How is American culture shaped by a set of common values and practices? • How have disputes over ideas, values, and politics resulted in change?

Analyzing PRIMARY SOURCES

ANALYZING SUPREME COURT CASES

BIOGRAPHY

Connections to TODAY...

Thinking like a HISTORIAN

FLORIDA CONNECTION

FEATURES

POLITICAL CARTOONS

SKILLBUILDER

MAPS, CHARTS, AND GRAPHS

MAPS, CHARTS, AND GRAPHS

networks ONLINE RESOURCES

Interactive Slide Shows

Interactive White Board Activities

networks ONLINE RESOURCES

∨ Interactive Time Lines

∨ Analyzing Primary Sources

Interactive Charts, Graphs, and Tables

Interactive Analyzing Supreme Court Cases

Interactive Self-Check Quiz

PRIMARY SOURCES

PRIMARY SOURCES

PRIMARY SOURCES

PRIMARY SOURCES

CHAPTER 22

CHAPTER 23

TO THE STUDENT

Welcome to McGraw-Hill Education's **Networks** online student learning center. Here you will access your Online Student Edition as well as many other learning resources.

① LOGGING ON TO THE STUDENT LEARNING CENTER

Using your Internet browser, go to connected.mcgraw-hill.com.

Enter your username and password or

Create a new account using the redemption code your teacher gave you.

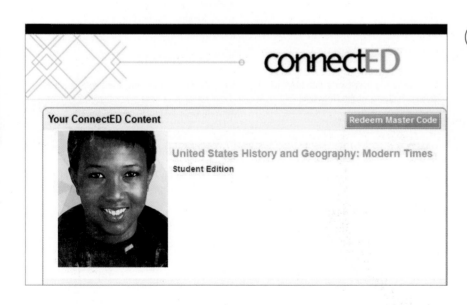

② SELECT YOUR PROGRAM

Click your program to launch the home page of your Online Student Learning Center.

HOW TO USE THE ONLINE STUDENT EDITION

Using Your Home Page

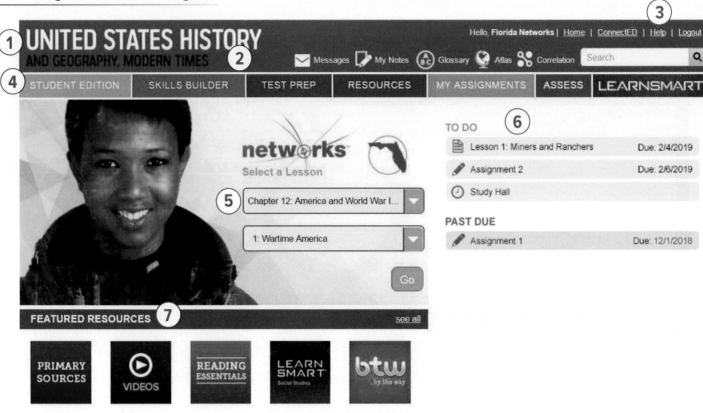

① ② ③ ④ ⑤ ⑥ ⑦

① HOME PAGE

To return to your home page at any time, click the Networks logo in the top left corner of the page.

② QUICK LINKS MENU

Use this menu to access:
- My Notes (your personal notepad)
- Messages
- Glossary
- Atlas
- BTW (current events website for social studies)
- Correlation

③ HELP

For videos and assistance with the various features of the Networks system, click Help.

④ MAIN MENU

Use the menu bar to access:
- The Online Student Edition
- Skills Builder (for activities to improve your skills)
- Assignments
- Resource Library
- Test Prep
- LearnSmart

⑤ ONLINE STUDENT EDITION

Go to your Online Student Edition by selecting the chapter and lesson and then click Go.

⑥ ASSIGNMENTS

Recent assignments from your teacher will appear here. Click the assignment or click See All to see the details.

⑦ RESOURCE LIBRARY

Click on the featured resources or click see all to browse the Resource Library.

Using Your Online Student Edition

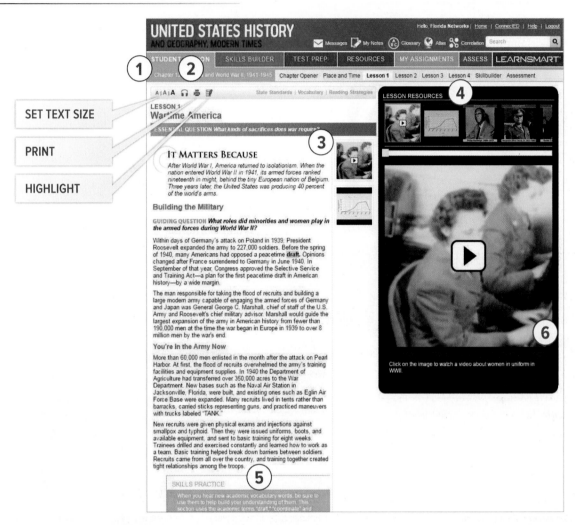

1. LESSON MENU

• Use the tabs to open the different lessons and special features in a chapter or unit.

• Clicking on the unit or chapter title will open the table of contents.

2. AUDIO EDITION

Click on the headphones symbol to have the page read to you. MP3 files for downloading each lesson are available in the Resource Library.

3. RESOURCES FOR THIS PAGE

Resources appear in the middle column to show that they go with the text on this page. Click the images to open them in the viewer.

4. LESSON RESOURCES

Use the carousel to browse the interactive resources available in this lesson. Click on a resource to open it in the viewer below.

5. CHANGE PAGES

Click here to move to the next page in the lesson.

6. RESOURCE VIEWER

Click on the image that appears in the viewer to launch an interactive resource, including:

• Lesson Videos

• Interactive Photos and Slide Shows

• Interactive Maps

• Interactive Charts and Graphs

• Games

• Self-Check Quizzes for each lesson

HOW TO USE THE ONLINE STUDENT EDITION

Reading Support in the Online Student Edition

Your Online Student Edition contains several features to help improve your reading skills and understanding of the content.

1 LESSON VOCABULARY

Click Vocabulary to bring up a list of terms introduced in this lesson.

VOCABULARY POP-UP

Click on any term highlighted in yellow to open a window with the term's definition.

2 MY NOTES

Click My Notes to open the note-taking tool. You can write and save any notes you want in the Lesson Notes tab.

Click on the Guided Notes tab to view the Guided Reading Questions. Answering these questions will help you build a set of notes about the lesson.

3 GRAPHIC ORGANIZER

Click Reading Strategies to open a note-taking activity using a graphic organizer.

Click the image of the graphic organizer to make it interactive. You can type directly into the graphic organizer and save or print your notes.

HOW TO USE THE ONLINE STUDENT EDITION

Using Interactive Resources in the Online Student Edition

Each lesson of your Online Student Edition contains many resources to help you learn the content and skills you need to know for this subject.

Networks provides many kinds of resources. This symbol shows that the resource is a slide show.

1 LAUNCHING RESOURCES

Clicking a resource in the viewer launches an interactive resource.

2 QUESTIONS AND ACTIVITIES

When a resource appears in the viewer, there are usually 1 or 2 questions or activities beneath it. You can type and save your answers in the answer boxes and submit them to your teacher.

3 INTERACTIVE MAPS

When a map appears in the viewer, click on it to launch the interactive map. You can use the drawing tool to mark up the map. You can also zoom in and turn layers on and off to display different information. Drag the scale onto the map to measure distances. Many maps have animations and audio as well.

4 CHAPTER FEATURE

Each chapter begins with a feature called *Place and Time*. They include maps, primary sources, and a time line to help you understand the place and time of the chapter's events.

The map and time line are both interactive. You can click on the map and the time line for an interactive version.

Assessment

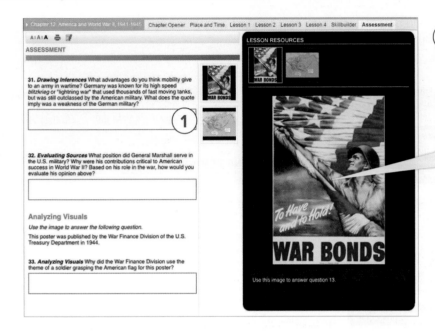

Use this image to answer question 13.

1 CHAPTER ASSESSMENT

At the end of each chapter is the assessment tab. Here you can test your understanding of what you have learned. You can type and save answers in the answer boxes and submit them to your teacher.

When a question uses an image or graph or map, it will appear in the viewer.

Finding Other Resources

There are hundreds of additional resources available in the Resource Library. Click the Resources tab to enter the library.

2 RESOURCE LIBRARY

Click the links to find collections of Primary Sources, Biographies, Skills Activities and the Reading Essentials and Study Guide.

You can search the Resource Library by keyword.

Click the star to mark a resource as a favorite.

A Guide for Students and Parents

Welcome to Grade 11 Social Studies and *United States History and Geography Modern Times*. Get ready to learn about the history of the United States. It will be an exciting journey.

This course focuses on the political, economic, and social events that have shaped modern America. You will be viewing and interpreting the period from various perspectives, including historical, geographical, political, economic, and cultural. Together these perspectives can help you understand how the past has led to our present and to appreciate your role in shaping our future.

The Grade 11 Florida Standards

On the following pages, you will find the Grade 11 Florida Standards. The Florida Standards contain the content and skills you will learn in Grade 11. You might want to review these standards before you begin the course. Many of the names, terms, and events might not be familiar to you at first. You will learn about these, however, as you study the course. You might also review these Florida Standards throughout the year to help you focus on the new information you will learn as you study the program.

The knowledge and skills found in these Florida Standards will help you beyond the classroom. To become an informed citizen, it is not enough to learn names and dates. You must prepare yourself for living in a complex, interdependent world. This course will help you view and interpret history from various perspectives. These perspectives can help you understand how the past has shaped the nation and the world we live in today. We hope this program will help you succeed as a student and a citizen.

Alex Gore/Alamy

Hoagen Key, Boca Grande, Florida ▼

English Language Development Standards

ELD.K12.ELL.SI.1   English language learners communicate for social and instructional purposes within the school setting.

ELD.K12.ELL.SS.1   English language learners communicate information, ideas and concepts necessary for academic success in the content area of Social Studies.

Health Standards

HE.912.C.2.4   Evaluate how public health policies and government regulations can influence health promotion and disease prevention.
Remarks/Examples: Seat-belt enforcement, underage alcohol sales, reporting communicable diseases, child care, and AED availability.

HE.912.C.2.7   Analyze how culture supports and challenges health beliefs, practices, and behaviors.

Language Arts Florida Standards, Reading Standards for Literacy in History/Social Studies 6–12

LAFS.1112.RH.1.1   Cite specific textual evidence to support analysis of primary and secondary sources, connecting insights gained from specific details to an understanding of the text as a whole.

LAFS.1112.RH.1.2   Determine the central ideas or information of a primary or secondary source; provide an accurate summary that makes clear the relationships among the key details and ideas.

LAFS.1112.RH.1.3   Evaluate various explanations for actions or events and determine which explanation best accords with textual evidence, acknowledging where the text leaves matters uncertain.

LAFS.1112.RH.2.4   Determine the meaning of words and phrases as they are used in a text, including analyzing how an author uses and refines the meaning of a key term over the course of a text (e.g., how Madison defines faction in Federalist No. 10).

LAFS.1112.RH.2.5   Analyze in detail how a complex primary source is structured, including how key sentences, paragraphs, and larger portions of the text contribute to the whole.

LAFS.1112.RH.2.6   Evaluate authors' differing points of view on the same historical event or issue by assessing the authors' claims, reasoning, and evidence.

LAFS.1112.RH.3.7   Integrate and evaluate multiple sources of information presented in diverse formats and media (e.g., visually, quantitatively, as well as in words) in order to address a question or solve a problem.

Courtesy National Gallery of Art, Washington

Washington at
Valley Forge,
Pennsylvania

LAFS.1112.RH.3.8 Evaluate an author's premises, claims, and evidence by corroborating or challenging them with other information.

LAFS.1112.RH.3.9 Integrate information from diverse sources, both primary and secondary, into a coherent understanding of an idea or event, noting discrepancies among sources.

LAFS.1112.RH.4.10 By the end of grade 12, read and comprehend history/social studies texts in the grades 11–CCR text complexity band independently and proficiently.

LAFS.1112.SL.1.1 Initiate and participate effectively in a range of collaborative discussions (one on one, in groups, and teacher-led) with diverse partners on grades 11– 12 topics, texts, and issues, building on others' ideas and expressing their own clearly and persuasively.

   a. Come to discussions prepared, having read and researched material under study; explicitly draw on that preparation by referring to evidence from texts and other research on the topic or issue to stimulate a thoughtful, well-reasoned exchange of ideas.

   b. Work with peers to promote civil, democratic discussions and decision-making, set clear goals and deadlines, and establish individual roles as needed.

   c. Propel conversations by posing and responding to questions that probe reasoning and evidence; ensure a hearing for a full range of positions on a topic or issue; clarify, verify, or challenge ideas and conclusions; and promote divergent and creative perspectives.

> **d.** Respond thoughtfully to diverse perspectives; synthesize comments, claims, and evidence made on all sides of an issue; resolve contradictions when possible; and determine what additional information or research is required to deepen the investigation or complete the task.

LAFS.1112.SL.1.2   Integrate multiple sources of information presented in diverse formats and media (e.g., visually, quantitatively, orally) in order to make informed decisions and solve problems, evaluating the credibility and accuracy of each source and noting any discrepancies among the data.

LAFS.1112.SL.1.3   Evaluate a speaker's point of view, reasoning, and use of evidence and rhetoric, assessing the stance, premises, links among ideas, word choice, points of emphasis, and tone used.

LAFS.1112.SL.2.4   Present information, findings, and supporting evidence, conveying a clear and distinct perspective, such that listeners can follow the line of reasoning, alternative or opposing perspectives are addressed, and the organization, development, substance, and style are appropriate to purpose, audience, and a range of formal and informal tasks.

LAFS.1112.SL.2.5   Make strategic use of digital media (e.g., textual, graphical, audio, visual, and interactive elements) in presentations to enhance understanding of findings, reasoning, and evidence and to add interest.

LAFS.1112.SL.2.6   Adapt speech to a variety of contexts and tasks, demonstrating a command of formal English when indicated or appropriate.

Language Arts Florida Standards, Writing Standards for Literacy in History/Social Studies, Science, and Technical Subjects

LAFS.1112.WHST.1.1   Write arguments focused on discipline-specific content.

> **a.** Introduce precise, knowledgeable claim(s), establish the significance of the claim(s), distinguish the claim(s) from alternate or opposing claims, and create an organization that logically sequences the claim(s), counterclaims, reasons, and evidence.

> **b.** Develop claim(s) and counterclaims fairly and thoroughly, supplying the most relevant data and evidence for each while pointing out the strengths and limitations of both claim(s) and counterclaims in a discipline appropriate form that anticipates the audience's knowledge level, concerns, values, and possible biases.

> **c.** Use words, phrases, and clauses as well as varied syntax to link the major sections of the text, create cohesion, and clarify the relationships between claim(s) and reasons, between reasons and evidence, and between claim(s) and counterclaims.

d. Establish and maintain a formal style and objective tone while attending to the norms and conventions of the discipline in which they are writing.

e. Provide a concluding statement or section that follows from or supports the argument presented.

LAFS.1112.WHST.1.2 Write informative/explanatory texts, including the narration of historical events, scientific procedures/experiments, or technical processes.

a. Introduce a topic and organize complex ideas, concepts, and information so that each new element builds on that which precedes it to create a unified whole; include formatting (e.g., headings), graphics (e.g., figures, tables), and multimedia when useful to aiding comprehension.

b. Develop the topic thoroughly by selecting the most significant and relevant facts, extended definitions, concrete details, quotations, or other information and examples appropriate to the audience's knowledge of the topic.

c. Use varied transitions and sentence structures to link the major sections of the text, create cohesion, and clarify the relationships among complex ideas and concepts.

Library of Congress Prints and Photographs Division [LC-DIG-ppmsca-09855]

The painting "American Progress" symbolized the idea of Manifest Destiny.

d. Use precise language, domain-specific vocabulary and techniques such as metaphor, simile, and analogy to manage the complexity of the topic; convey a knowledgeable stance in a style that responds to the discipline and context as well as to the expertise of likely readers.

e. Provide a concluding statement or section that follows from and supports the information or explanation provided (e.g., articulating implications or the significance of the topic).

LAFS.1112.WHST.2.4 Produce clear and coherent writing in which the development, organization, and style are appropriate to task, purpose, and audience.

LAFS.1112.WHST.2.5 Develop and strengthen writing as needed by planning, revising, editing, rewriting, or trying a new approach, focusing on addressing what is most significant for a specific purpose and audience.

LAFS.1112.WHST.2.6 Use technology, including the Internet, to produce, publish, and update individual or shared writing products in response to ongoing feedback, including new arguments or information.

LAFS.1112.WHST.3.7 Conduct short as well as more sustained research projects to answer a question (including a self-generated question) or solve a problem; narrow or broaden the inquiry when appropriate; synthesize multiple sources on the subject, demonstrating understanding of the subject under investigation.

LAFS.1112.WHST.3.8 Gather relevant information from multiple authoritative print and digital sources, using advanced searches effectively; assess the strengths and limitations of each source in terms of the specific task, purpose, and audience; integrate information into the text selectively to maintain the flow of ideas, avoiding plagiarism and overreliance on any one source and following a standard format for citation.

LAFS.1112.WHST.3.9 Draw evidence from informational texts to support analysis, reflection, and research.

LAFS.1112.WHST.4.10 Write routinely over extended time frames (time for reflection and revision) and shorter time frames (a single sitting or a day or two) for a range of discipline-specific tasks, purposes, and audiences.

Mathematics Florida Standards, Mathematical Practice

MAFS.912.S-IC.2 Make inferences and justify conclusions from sample surveys, experiments, and observational studies.

MAFS.912.S-ID.1 Summarize, represent and interpret data on a single count or measurement variable.

MAFS.K12.MP.1.1   **Make sense of problems and persevere in solving them.**

Mathematically proficient students start by explaining to themselves the meaning of a problem and looking for entry points to its solution. They analyze givens, constraints, relationships, and goals. They make conjectures about the form and meaning of the solution and plan a solution pathway rather than simply jumping into a solution attempt. They consider analogous problems, and try special cases and simpler forms of the original problem in order to gain insight into its solution. They monitor and evaluate their progress and change course if necessary. Older students might, depending on the context of the problem, transform algebraic expressions or change the viewing window on their graphing calculator to get the information they need. Mathematically proficient students can explain correspondences between equations, verbal descriptions, tables, and graphs or draw diagrams of important features and relationships, graph data, and search for regularity or trends. Younger students might rely on using concrete objects or pictures to help conceptualize and solve a problem. Mathematically proficient students check their answers to problems using a different method, and they continually ask themselves, "Does this make sense?" They can understand the approaches of others to solving complex problems and identify correspondences between different approaches.

MAFS.K12.MP.3.1   **Construct viable arguments and critique the reasoning of others.**

Mathematically proficient students understand and use stated assumptions, definitions, and previously established results in constructing arguments. They make conjectures and build a logical progression of statements to explore the truth of their conjectures. They are able to analyze situations by breaking them into cases, and can recognize and use counterexamples. They justify their conclusions, communicate them to others, and respond to the arguments of others. They reason inductively about data, making plausible arguments that take into account the context from which the data arose. Mathematically proficient students are also able to compare the effectiveness of two plausible arguments, distinguish correct logic or reasoning from that which is flawed, and—if there is a flaw in an argument—explain what it is. Elementary students can construct arguments using concrete referents such as objects, drawings, diagrams, and actions. Such arguments can make sense and be correct, even though they are not generalized or made formal until later grades. Later, students learn to determine domains to which an argument applies.

The Seminole, Osceola

Library of Congress Prints and Photographs Division [LC-DIG-pga-00467]

Students at all grades can listen or read the arguments of others, decide whether they make sense, and ask useful questions to clarify or improve the arguments.

MAFS.K12.MP.5.1 **Use appropriate tools strategically.**

Mathematically proficient students consider the available tools when solving a mathematical problem. These tools might include pencil and paper, concrete models, a ruler, a protractor, a calculator, a spreadsheet, a computer algebra system, a statistical package, or dynamic geometry software. Proficient students are sufficiently familiar with tools appropriate for their grade or course to make sound decisions about when each of these tools might be helpful, recognizing both the insight to be gained and their limitations. For example, mathematically proficient high school students analyze graphs of functions and solutions generated using a graphing calculator. They detect possible errors by strategically using estimation and other mathematical knowledge. When making mathematical models, they know that technology can enable them to visualize the results of varying assumptions, explore consequences, and compare predictions with data. Mathematically proficient students at various grade levels are able to identify relevant external mathematical resources, such as digital content located on a website, and use them to pose or solve problems. They are able to use technological tools to explore and deepen their understanding of concepts.

Bridge in the
Florida Keys

Dieter Melhorn/Alamy

MAFS.K12.MP.6.1 **Attend to precision.**

Mathematically proficient students try to communicate precisely to others. They try to use clear definitions in discussion with others and in their own reasoning. They state the meaning of the symbols they choose, including using the equal sign consistently and appropriately. They are careful about specifying units of measure, and labeling axes to clarify the correspondence with quantities in a problem. They calculate accurately and efficiently, express numerical answers with a degree of precision appropriate for the problem context. In the elementary grades, students give carefully formulated explanations to each other. By the time they reach high school they have learned to examine claims and make explicit use of definitions.

Social Studies American History Standards

Standard 1: Use research and inquiry skills to analyze American history using primary and secondary sources.

SS.912.A.1.1 Describe the importance of historiography, which includes how historical knowledge is obtained and transmitted, when interpreting events in history.

SS.912.A.1.2 Utilize a variety of primary and secondary sources to identify author, historical significance, audience, and authenticity to understand a historical period.

SS.912.A.1.3 Utilize timelines to identify the time sequence of historical data.

SS.912.A.1.4 Analyze how images, symbols, objects, cartoons, graphs, charts, maps, and artwork may be used to interpret the significance of time periods and events from the past.

SS.912.A.1.5 Evaluate the validity, reliability, bias, and authenticity of current events and Internet resources.
Remarks/Examples: Students should be encouraged to utilize FINDS (Focus, Investigate, Note, Develop, Score), Florida's research process model accessible at: http://www.fldoe.org/bii/Library_Media/pdf/12TotalFINDS.pdf

Mount Rushmore in the Black Hills of South Dakota

NPS Photo

SS.912.A.1.6 Use case studies to explore social, political, legal, and economic relationships in history.

SS.912.A.1.7 Describe various socio-cultural aspects of American life including arts, artifacts, literature, education, and publications.

Standard 2: Understand the causes, course, and consequences of the Civil War and Reconstruction and its effects on the American people.

SS.912.A.2.1 Review causes and consequences of the Civil War.
Remarks/Examples: Examples may include, but are not limited to, slavery, states' rights, territorial claims, abolitionist movement, regional differences, Reconstruction, 13th, 14th, and 15th amendments.

SS.912.A.2.2 Assess the influence of significant people or groups on Reconstruction.
Remarks/Examples: Examples may include, but are not limited to, Andrew Johnson, Radical Republicans, Jefferson Davis, Frederick Douglass, Ulysses S. Grant, Robert E. Lee, William T. Sherman, Buffalo Soldiers, Harriet Tubman, and Sojourner Truth.

SS.912.A.2.3 Describe the issues that divided Republicans during the early Reconstruction era.
Remarks/Examples: Examples may include, but are not limited to, the impeachment of Andrew Johnson, southern whites, blacks, black legislators and white extremist organizations such as the KKK, Knights of the White Camellia, The White League, Red Shirts, and Pale Faces.

SS.912.A.2.4 Distinguish the freedoms guaranteed to African Americans and other groups with the 13th, 14th, and 15th Amendments to the Constitution.
Remarks/Examples: Examples may include, but are not limited to, abolition of slavery, citizenship, suffrage, equal protection.

SS.912.A.2.5 Assess how Jim Crow Laws influenced life for African Americans and other racial/ethnic minority groups.

SS.912.A.2.6 Compare the effects of the Black Codes and the Nadir on freed people, and analyze the sharecropping system and debt peonage as practiced in the United States.

SS.912.A.2.7 Review the Native American experience.
Remarks/Examples: Examples may include, but are not limited to, westward expansion, reservation system, the Dawes Act, Wounded Knee Massacre, Sand Creek Massacre, Battle of Little Big Horn, Indian Schools, government involvement in the killing of the buffalo.

Standard 3: Analyze the transformation of the American economy and the changing social and political conditions in response to the Industrial Revolution.

SS.912.A.3.1 Analyze the economic challenges to American farmers and farmers' responses to these challenges in the mid to late 1800s.

Remarks/Examples: Examples may include, but are not limited to, creation of agricultural colleges, Morrill Land Grant Act, gold standard and Bimetallism, the creation of the Populist Party.

SS.912.A.3.2 Examine the social, political, and economic causes, course, and consequences of the second Industrial Revolution that began in the late 19th century.

SS.912.A.3.3 Compare the first and second Industrial Revolutions in the United States.

Remarks/Examples: Examples may include, but are not limited to, trade, development of new industries.

SS.912.A.3.4 Determine how the development of steel, oil, transportation, communication, and business practices affected the United States economy.

Remarks/Examples: Examples may include, but are not limited to, railroads, the telegraph, pools, holding companies, trusts, corporations, contributed to westward expansion, expansion of trade and development of new industries, vertical and horizontal integration.

SS.912.A.3.5 Identify significant inventors of the Industrial Revolution including African Americans and women.

Remarks/Examples: Examples may include, but are not limited to, Lewis Howard Latimer, Jan E. Matzeliger, Sarah E. Goode, Granville T. Woods, Alexander Graham Bell, Thomas Edison, George Pullman, Henry Ford, Orville and Wilbur Wright, Elijah McCoy, Garrett Morgan, Madame C.J. Walker, George Westinghouse.

SS.912.A.3.6 Analyze changes that occurred as the United States shifted from agrarian to an industrial society.

Remarks/Examples: Examples may include, but are not limited to, Social Darwinism, laissez-faire, government regulations of food and drugs, migration to cities, urbanization, changes to the family structure, Ellis Island, angel Island, push-pull factors.

SS.912.A.3.7 Compare the experience of European immigrants in the east to that of Asian immigrants in the west (the Chinese Exclusion Act, Gentlemen's Agreement with Japan).

Remarks/Examples: Examples may include, but are not limited to nativism, integration of immigrants into society when comparing "Old" [before 1890] and "New" immigrants [after 1890], Immigration Act of 1924.

SS.912.A.3.8 Examine the importance of social change and reform in the late 19th and early 20th centuries (class system, migration from farms to cities, Social Gospel movement, role of settlement houses and churches in providing services to the poor).

SS.912.A.3.9 Examine causes, course, and consequences of the labor movement in the late 19th and early 20th centuries.
Remarks/Examples: Examples may include, but are not limited to, unions, Knights of Labor, American Federation of Labor, Socialist Party, labor laws.

SS.912.A.3.10 Review different economic and philosophic ideologies.
Remarks/Examples: Economic examples may include, but are not limited to, market economy, mixed economy, planned economy and philosophic examples are capitalism, socialism, communism, anarchy.

SS.912.A.3.11 Analyze the impact of political machines in United States cities in the late 19th and early 20th centuries.
Remarks/Examples: Examples may include, but are not limited to, Boss Tweed, Tammany Hall, George Washington Plunkitt, Washington Gladden, Thomas Nast.

SS.912.A.3.12 Compare how different nongovernmental organizations and progressives worked to shape public policy, restore economic opportunities, and correct injustices in American life.
Remarks/Examples: Examples may include, but are not limited to, NAACP, YMCA, Women's Christian Temperance Union, National Women's Suffrage Association, National Women's Party, Robert LaFollette, Florence Kelley, Ida M. Tarbell, Eugene Debs, Carrie Chapman Catt, Alice Paul, Theodore Roosevelt, William Taft, Woodrow Wilson, Upton Sinclair, Booker T. Washington, W.E.B. DuBois, Gifford Pinchot, William Jennings Bryan.

Old State Capitol, Tallahassee, Florida

Ilene MacDonald/Alamy

SS.912.A.3.13 Examine key events and peoples in Florida history as they relate to United States history.
Remarks/Examples: Examples may include, but are not limited to, the railroad industry, bridge construction in the Florida Keys, the cattle industry, the cigar industry, the influence of Cuban, Greek and Italian immigrants, Henry B. Plant, William Chipley, Henry Flagler, George Proctor, Thomas DeSaille Tucker, Hamilton Disston.

Standard 4: Demonstrate an understanding of the changing role of the United States in world affairs through the end of World War I.

SS.912.A.4.1 Analyze the major factors that drove United States imperialism.
Remarks/Examples: Examples may include, but are not limited to, the Monroe Doctrine, Manifest Destiny, *The Influence of Sea Power Upon History,* Turner's thesis, the Roosevelt Corollary, natural resources, markets for resources, elimination of spheres of influence in China.

SS.912.A.4.2 Explain the motives of the United States acquisition of the territories.
Remarks/Examples: Examples may include, but are not limited to, Alaska, Hawaii, Puerto Rico, Philippines, Guam, Samoa, Marshall Islands, Midway Island, Virgin Islands.

SS.912.A.4.3 Examine causes, course, and consequences of the Spanish American War.
Remarks/Examples: Examples may include, but are not limited to, Cuba as a protectorate, Yellow Journalism, sinking of the *Maine,* the Philippines, Commodore Dewey, the Rough Riders, acqusition of territories, the Treaty of Paris.

Fort at St. Augustine, Florida

Henryk Sadura/Getty Images

SS.912.A.4.4   Analyze the economic, military, and security motivations of the United States to complete the Panama Canal as well as major obstacles involved in its construction.
Remarks/Examples: Examples may include, but are not limited to, disease, environmental impact, challenges faced by various ethnic groups such as Africans and indigenous populations, shipping routes, increased trade, defense and independence for Panama.

SS.912.A.4.5   Examine causes, course, and consequences of United States involvement in World War I.
Remarks/Examples: Examples may include, but are not limited to, nationalism, imperialism, militarism, entangling alliances vs. neutrality, Zimmerman Note, the *Lusitania,* the Selective Service Act, the homefront, the American Expeditionary Force, Wilson's Fourteen Points, the Treaty of Versailles (and opposition to it), isolationism.

SS.912.A.4.6   Examine how the United States government prepared the nation for war with war measures (Selective Service Act, War Industries Board, war bonds, Espionage Act, Sedition Act, Committee of Public Information).

SS.912.A.4.7   Examine the impact of airplanes, battleships, new weaponry and chemical warfare in creating new war strategies (trench warfare, convoys).

SS.912.A.4.8   Compare the experiences Americans (African Americans, Hispanics, Asians, women, conscientious objectors) had while serving in Europe.

SS.912.A.4.9   Compare how the war impacted German Americans, Asian Americans, African Americans, Hispanic Americans, Jewish Americans, Native Americans, women and dissenters in the United States.

SS.912.A.4.10   Examine the provisions of the Treaty of Versailles and the failure of the United States to support the League of Nations.
Remarks/Examples: Examples may include, but are not limited to, self-determination, boundaries, demilitarized zone, sanctions reparations, and the League of Nations (including Article X of the Covenant).

SS.912.A.4.11   Examine key events and peoples in Florida history as they relate to United States history.
Remarks/Examples: Examples may include, but are not limited to, the Spanish-American War, Ybor City, Josè Marti.

Standard 5: Analyze the effects of the changing social, political, and economic conditions of the Roaring Twenties and the Great Depression.

SS.912.A.5.1   Discuss the economic outcomes of demobilization.

SS.912.A.5.2   Explain the causes of the public reaction (Sacco and Vanzetti, labor, racial unrest) associated with the Red Scare.
Remarks/Examples: Examples may also include, but are not limited to, Palmer Raids, FBI, J. Edgar Hoover.

SS.912.A.5.3   Examine the impact of United States foreign economic policy during the 1920s.
Remarks/Examples: Examples may include, but are not limited to, the Depression of 1920-21, "The Business of America is Business," assembly line, installment buying, consumerism.

SS.912.A.5.4   Evaluate how the economic boom during the Roaring Twenties changed consumers, businesses, manufacturing, and marketing practices.

SS.912.A.5.5   Describe efforts by the United States and other world powers to avoid future wars.
Remarks/Examples: Examples may include, but are not limited to, League of Nations, Washington Naval Conference, London Conference, Kellogg-Briand Pact, the Nobel Prize.

SS.912.A.5.6   Analyze the influence that Hollywood, the Harlem Renaissance, the Fundamentalist movement, and prohibition had in changing American society in the 1920s.

SS.912.A.5.7   Examine the freedom movements that advocated civil rights for African Americans, Latinos, Asians, and women.

SS.912.A.5.8   Compare the views of Booker T. Washington, W.E.B. DuBois, and Marcus Garvey relating to the African American experience.

SS.912.A.5.9   Explain why support for the Ku Klux Klan varied in the 1920s with respect to issues such as anti-immigration, anti-African American, anti-Catholic, anti-Jewish, anti-women, and anti-union ideas.
Remarks/Examples: Examples may include, but are not limited to, 100 Percent Americanism.

SS.912.A.5.10   Analyze support for and resistance to civil rights for women, African Americans, Native Americans, and other minorities.

SS.912.A.5.11   Examine causes, course, and consequences of the Great Depression and the New Deal.

SS.912.A.5.12   Examine key events and people in Florida history as they relate to United States history.

Harriet Tubman, famous "conductor" on the Underground Railroad

Library of Congress Prints and Photographs Division [LC-USZ62-7816]

Remarks/Examples: Examples may include, but are not limited to, Rosewood, land boom, speculation, impact of climate and natural disasters on the end of the land boom, invention of modern air conditioning in 1929, Alfred DuPont, Majorie Kinnan Rawlings, Zora Neale Hurston, James Weldon Johnson.

Standard 6: Understand the causes and course of World War II, the character of the war at home and abroad, and its reshaping of the United States role in the post-war world.

SS.912.A.6.1   Examine causes, course, and consequences of World War II on the United States and the world.
Remarks/Examples: Examples may include, but are not limited to, rise of dictators, attack on Pearl Harbor, Nazi party, American neutrality, D-Day, Battle of the Bulge, War in the Pacific, internment camps, Holocaust, Yalta.

SS.912.A.6.2   Describe the United States response in the early years of World War II (Neutrality Acts, Cash and Carry, Lend Lease Act).

SS.912.A.6.3   Analyze the impact of the Holocaust during World War II on Jews as well as other groups.

Painting of the completion of the Transcontinental Railroad

GOLDEN SPIKE

Architect of the Capitol

SS.912.A.6.4   Examine efforts to expand or contract rights for various populations during World War II.
Remarks/Examples: Examples may include, but are not limited to, women, African Americans, German Americans, Japanese Americans and their internment, Native Americans, Hispanic Americans, Italian Americans.

SS.912.A.6.5   Explain the impact of World War II on domestic government policy.
Remarks/Examples: Examples may include, but are not limited to, rationing, national security, civil rights, increased job opportunities for African Americans, women, Jews, and other refugees.

SS.912.A.6.6   Analyze the use of atomic weapons during World War II and the aftermath of the bombings.

SS.912.A.6.7   Describe the attempts to promote international justice through the Nuremberg Trials.

SS.912.A.6.8   Analyze the effects of the Red Scare on domestic United States policy.
Remarks/Examples: Examples may include, but are not limited to, loyalty review program, House Un-American Activities Committee, McCarthyism (Sen. Joe McCarthy), McCarran Act.

SS.912.A.6.9   Describe the rationale for the formation of the United Nations, including the contribution of Mary McLeod Bethune.
Remarks/Examples: Examples may include, but are not limited to, the Declaration of Human Rights.

SS.912.A.6.10   Examine causes, course, and consequences of the early years of the Cold War (Truman Doctrine, Marshall Plan, NATO, Warsaw Pact).

Fishing on Florida's intercoastal waterway

Florida Images/Alamy

SS.912.A.6.11   Examine the controversy surrounding the proliferation of nuclear technology in the United States and the world.

SS.912.A.6.12   Examine causes, course, and consequences of the Korean War.
Remarks/Examples: Examples may include, but aren't limited to, Communist China, 38th parallel, cease fire, firing of Gen. Douglas McArthur.

SS.912.A.6.13   Analyze significant foreign policy events during the Truman, Eisenhower, Kennedy, Johnson, and Nixon administrations.
Remarks/Examples: Examples may include, but are not limited to, the Domino Theory, Sputnik, space race, Korean Conflict, Vietnam Conflict, U-2 and Gary Powers, Bay of Pigs invasion, Cuban Missile Crisis, Berlin Wall, Ping Pong Diplomacy, opening of China.

SS.912.A.6.14   Analyze causes, course, and consequences of the Vietnam War.
Remarks/Examples: Examples may include, but are not lmited to, Geneva Accords, Gulf of Tonkin Resolution, the draft, escalating protest at home, Vietnamization, the War Powers Act.

SS.912.A.6.15   Examine key events and peoples in Florida history as they relate to United States history.
Remarks/Examples: Examples may include, but are not limited to, Mosquito Fleet, "Double V Campaign", construction of military bases and WWII training centers, 1959 Cuban coup and its impact on Florida, development of the space program and NASA.

Standard 7: Understand the rise and continuing international influence of the United States as a world leader and the impact of contemporary social and political movements on American life.

SS.912.A.7.1   Identify causes for Post-World War II prosperity and its effects on American society.
Remarks/Examples: Examples may include, but are not limited to, G.I. Bill, Baby Boom, growth of suburbs, Beatnik movement, youth culture, religious revivalism (e.g., Billy Graham and Bishop Fulton J. Sheen), conformity of the 1950s and the protest in the 1960s.

SS.912.A.7.2   Compare the relative prosperity between different ethnic groups and social classes in the post-World War II period.

SS.912.A.7.3   Examine the changing status of women in the United States from post-World War II to present.
Remarks/Examples: Examples may include, but are not limited to, increased numbers of women in the workforce,

Civil Rights Act of 1964, *The Feminine Mystique,* National Organization for Women, *Roe* v. *Wade,* Equal Rights Amendment, Title IX, Betty Freidan, Gloria Steinem, Phyllis Schlafly, Billie Jean King, feminism.

SS.912.A.7.4 Evaluate the success of 1960s era presidents' foreign and domestic policies.
Remarks/Examples: Examples may include, but are not limited to, civil rights legislation, Space Race, Great Society, War on Poverty.

SS.912.A.7.5 Compare nonviolent and violent approaches utilized by groups (African Americans, women, Native Americans, Hispanics) to achieve civil rights.
Remarks/Examples: Examples may include, but are not limited to, sit-ins, Freedom Rides, boycotts, riots, protest marches.

SS.912.A.7.6 Assess key figures and organizations in shaping the Civil Rights Movement and Black Power Movement.
Remarks/Examples: Examples may include, but are not limited to, the NAACP, National Urban League, SNCC, CORE, James Farmer, Charles Houston, Thurgood Marshall, Rosa Parks, Constance Baker Motley, the Little Rock Nine, Roy Wilkins, Whitney M. Young, A. Philip Randolph, Dr. Martin Luther King, Jr., Robert F. Williams, Fannie Lou Hamer, Malcolm X [El-Hajj Malik El-Shabazz], Stokely Carmichael [Kwame Ture], H. Rap Brown [Jamil Abdullah Al- Amin], the Black Panther Party [e.g., Huey P. Newton, Bobby Seale].

SS.912.A.7.7 Assess the building of coalitions between African Americans, whites, and other groups in achieving integration and equal rights.
Remarks/Examples: Examples may include, but are not limited to, Freedom Summer, Freedom Rides, Montgomery Bus Boycott, Tallahassee Bus Boycott of 1956, March on Washington.

SS.912.A.7.8 Analyze significant Supreme Court decisions relating to integration, busing, affirmative action, the rights of the accused, and reproductive rights.
Remarks/Examples: Examples may include, but are not limited to, *Plessy* v. *Ferguson* [1896], *Brown* v. *Board of Education* [1954], *Swann* v. *Charlotte-Mecklenburg Board of Education* [1971], *Regents of the University of California* v. *Bakke* [1978], *Miranda* v. *Arizona* [1966], *Gideon* v. *Wainright* [1963], *Mapp* v. *Ohio* [1961], and *Roe* v. *Wade* [1973].

SS.912.A.7.9 Examine the similarities of social movements (Native Americans, Hispanics, women, anti-war protesters) of the 1960s and 1970s.

SS.912.A.7.10 Analyze the significance of Vietnam and Watergate on the government and people of the United States.

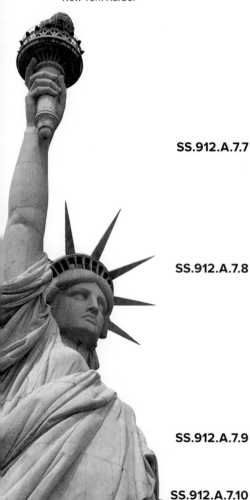

The Statue of Liberty on Liberty Island in New York Harbor

©TongRo Image Stock/Alamy

Remarks/Examples: Examples may include, but are not limited to, mistrust of government, reinforcement of freedom of the press, as well as checks and balances, *New York Times* v. *Nixon*.

SS.912.A.7.11 Analyze the foreign policy of the United States as it relates to Africa, Asia, the Caribbean, Latin America, and the Middle East.
Remarks/Examples: Examples may include, but aren't limited to, Haiti, Bosnia-Kosovo, Rwanda, Grenada, Camp David Accords, Iran Hostage Crisis, Lebanon, Iran-Iraq War, Reagan Doctrine, Iran-Contra Affair, Persian Gulf War.

SS.912.A.7.12 Analyze political, economic, and social concerns that emerged at the end of the 20th century and into the 21st century.
Remarks/Examples: Examples may include, but are not limited to, AIDS, Green Revolution, outsourcing of jobs, global warming, human rights violations.

SS.912.A.7.13 Analyze the attempts to extend New Deal legislation through the Great Society and the successes and failures of these programs to promote social and economic stability.
Remarks/Examples: Examples may include, but are not limited to, Civil Rights Act of 1964, Voting Rights Act of 1965, War on Poverty, Medicare, Medicaid, Headstart.

SS.912.A.7.14 Review the role of the United States as a participant in the global economy (trade agreements, international competition, impact on American labor, environmental concerns).
Remarks/Examples: Examples may include, but are not limited to, NAFTA, World Trade Organization.

SS.912.A.7.15 Analyze the effects of foreign and domestic terrorism on the American people.
Remarks/Examples: Examples may include, but are not limited to, Oklahoma City bombing, attack of September 11, 2001, Patriot Act, wars in Afghanistan and Iraq.

SS.912.A.7.16 Examine changes in immigration policy and attitudes toward immigration since 1950.

SS.912.A.7.17 Examine key events and key people in Florida history as they relate to United States history.
Remarks/Examples: Examples may include, but are not limited to, selection of Central Florida as a location for Disney, growth of the citrus and cigar industries, construction of Interstates, Harry T. Moore, Pork Chop Gang, Claude Pepper, changes in the space program, use of DEET, Hurricane Andrew, the Election of 2000, migration and immigration, Sunbelt state.

Social Studies Geography Standards

Standard 1: Understand how to use maps and other geographic representations, tools, and technology to report information.

SS.912.G.1.2   Use spatial perspective and appropriate geographic terms and tools, including the Six Essential Elements, as organizational schema to describe any given place.

SS.912.G.1.3   Employ applicable units of measurement and scale to solve simple locational problems using maps and globes.

Standard 2: Understand physical and cultural characteristics of places.

SS.912.G.2.1   Identify the physical characteristics and the human characteristics that define and differentiate regions.

SS.912.G.2.3   Use geographic terms and tools to analyze case studies of regional issues in different parts of the world that have critical economic, physical, or political ramifications.

SS.912.G.2.5   Use geographic terms and tools to analyze case studies of debates over how human actions modify a selected region.

Standard 4: Understand the characteristics, distribution, and migration of human populations.

SS.912.G.4.2   Use geographic terms and tools to analyze the push/pull factors contributing to human migration within and among places.

SS.912.G.4.3   Use geographic terms and tools to analyze the effects of migration both on the place of origin and destination, including border areas.

SS.912.G.4.7   Use geographic terms and tools to explain cultural diffusion throughout places, regions, and the world.

SS.912.G.4.9   Use political maps to describe the change in boundaries and governments within continents over time.

Social Studies Humanities Standards

Standard 1: Identify and analyze the historical, social, and cultural contexts of the arts.

SS.912.H.1.1   Relate works in the arts (architecture, dance, music, theatre, and visual arts) of varying styles and genre according to the periods in which they were created.

SS.912.H.1.2   Describe how historical events, social context, and culture impact forms, techniques, and purposes of works in the arts, including the relationship between a government and its citizens.

SS.912.H.1.3   Relate works in the arts to various cultures.

SS.912.H.1.4   Explain philosophical beliefs as they relate to works in the arts.

SS.912.H.1.5   Examine artistic response to social issues and new ideas in various cultures.

SS.912.H.1.6   Analyze how current events are explained by artistic and cultural trends of the past.

Poster from 1872 advertising land for sale

Standard 2: Respond critically and aesthetically to various works in the arts.

SS.912.H.2.5   Describe how historical, social, cultural, and physical settings influence an audience's aesthetic response.

Standard 3: Understand how transportation, trade, communication, science, and technology influence the progression and regression of cultures.

SS.912.H.3.1   Analyze the effects of transportation, trade, communication, science, and technology on the preservation and diffusion of culture.

SS.912.H.3.2   Identify social, moral, ethical, religious, and legal issues arising from technological and scientific developments, and examine their influence on works of arts within a culture.

Library of Congress American Memory Collection [rbpe.13401300]

SCAVENGER HUNT

NETWORKS contains a wealth of information. The trick is to know where to look to access all the information in the book. If you complete this scavenger hunt exercise with your teachers or parents, you will see how the textbook is organized and how to get the most out of your reading and study time. Let's get started!

1 How many chapters and how many lessons are in this book?

2 Where do you find the glossary and the index? What is the difference between them?

3 Where can you find primary sources in the textbook?

4 If you want to quickly find all the maps, charts, and graphs about World War I, where do you look?

5 How can you find information about civil rights activist Dr. Martin Luther King, Jr.?

6 Where can you find a graphic organizer that lists the causes of the Great Depression discussed in Chapter 9?

7 Where and how do you find the content vocabulary for Chapter 15, Lesson 3?

8 Where is the best list of those who have lived in the White House?

9 You want to read the Declaration of Independence. How will you find it?

10 What time period does Chapter 8 cover? How do you know?

(t)DEA / A. DAGLI ORTI/De Agostini Picture Library/Getty Images, (c)C Squared Studios/Getty Images, (b)© Comstock/PunchStock.

◀ This portrait of Christopher Columbus was painted by Sebastiano del Piombo after Columbus's death in 1506. Columbus's transatlantic voyage in 1492 opened the Americas to a flood of European exploration.

FROM BEGINNINGS TO 1877

Creating a Nation

The Granger Collection, New York

THE STORY MATTERS ...

Scientists believe the first people in the Americas arrived from Asia more than 10,000 years ago. Their descendants spread across the Americas, developing distinct cultures. Centuries later, Europeans began exploring overseas, hoping to find a new trade route to Asia. Sailing west from Spain, Christopher Columbus reached the Americas in 1492. This encounter initiated the European colonization of North America and South America.

ESSENTIAL QUESTIONS

- What characteristics define a society?
- Why do people form governments?
- How should societies settle disputes?

Place & Time: The Americas, Beginnings–1877

The arrival of the Europeans in the Americas set in motion a series of complex interactions between peoples and environments. These interactions, called the Columbian Exchange, permanently altered the world's ecosystem and changed nearly every culture around the world. The effects of this exchange still shape the world today.

Step Into the Place

Read the quotes and look at the information presented on the map.

DBQ **Analyzing Historical Documents** How did the arrival of Europeans affect both Native American and European cultures?

PRIMARY SOURCE

❝ This land is very populous, and full of inhabitants, and of numberless rivers, [and] animals: few [of which] resemble ours. . . . [T]hey have no horses nor mules . . . nor any kind of sheep or oxen: but so numerous are the other animals which they have. . . . The soil is very pleasant and fruitful. . . .
The fruits are so many that they are numberless and entirely different from ours. ❞

—Amerigo Vespucci, from *The First Four Voyages of Amerigo Vespucci,* 1505

PRIMARY SOURCE

❝ While the Spaniards were in Tlaxcala, a great plague broke out here in Tenochtitlán. . . . Sores erupted on our faces, our breasts, our bellies; we were covered with agonizing sores from head to foot. The illness was so dreadful that no one could walk or move.

A great many died from this plague, and many others died of hunger. They could not get up to search for food, and everyone else was too sick to care for them, so they starved to death in their beds. ❞

—an Aztec observer, from *The Broken Spears: The Aztec Account of the Conquest of Mexico,* 1959

Horses allowed some Native Americans to become nomadic hunters.

Horses

Peppers

PHOTO: **left page** (cl)Portrait of Amerigo Vespucci (1452-1512) (oil on canvas), Titian (Tiziano Vecelli) (c.1488-1576) (after)/© National Library of Australia, Canberra, Australia/The Bridgeman Art Library; (peppers)C Squared Studios/Getty Images; (horses)©Corbis; **right page** (1)Getty Images; (2, 16)Library of Congress, Prints & Photographs Division [LC-USZ62-242]; (3)Ingram Publishing/Alamy; (4)Brand X Pictures/PunchStock; (5)Burke Triolo Productions/Getty Images; (6)Alan and Sandy Carey/Getty Images; (7)Dynamic Graphics Group/IT Stock Free/Alamy Images; (8)Stockdisc/PunchStock; (9)PhotoAlto/Getty Images; (10)C Squared Studios/Getty Images; (11)Stockdisc/PunchStock; (12)©Corbis; (13)Siede Preis/Getty Images; (14)Image Source Pink/ Getty Images; (15)Iconotec/Alamy Images; (17)Westend61/Getty Images; (18)Ingram Publishing/Alamy; TEXT: The Broken Spears: The Aztec Account of the Conquest of Mexico by Miguel Leon-Portilla. Copyright © 1962, 1990 by Miguel Leon-Portilla Copyright. Reprinted by Permission of Beacon Press, Boston.

Step Into the Time

DRAWING CONCLUSIONS

Choose the event from the time line that you think had the most significant impact on growth in the United States. Write a paragraph defending your position.

THE AMERICAS

1492 Christopher Columbus reaches the Americas

1519 Hernán Cortés begins Spanish invasion of the Aztec Empire

1607 The English found Jamestown in Virginia

1500   **1575**   **1650**

WORLD

1498 Vasco da Gama sails around Africa to India, locating a water route to Asia from Europe

1518 First Spanish trade ship carries enslaved Africans directly from Africa to the Americas

1520 Ferdinand Magellan sails into Pacific Ocean

1707 Act of Union creates Great Britain

NEXT GENERATION SUNSHINE STATE STANDARDS
Students will understand the following benchmarks from the Florida NGSSS

LAFS.1112.RH.3.7: Integrate and evaluate multiple sources of information presented in diverse formats and media (e.g., visually, quantitatively, as well as in words) in order to address a question or solve a problem.

LAFS.1112.RH.3.9: Integrate information from diverse sources, both primary and secondary, into a coherent understanding of an idea or event, noting discrepancies among sources.

LAFS.1112.RH.4.10: By the end of grade 12, read and comprehend history/social studies texts in the grades 11–CCR text complexity band independently and proficiently.

SS.912.A.1.2: Utilize a variety of primary and secondary sources to identify author, historical significance, audience, and authenticity to understand a historical period.

SS.912.A.1.3: Utilize timelines to identify the time sequence of historical data.

SS.912.A.1.4: Analyze how images, symbols, objects, cartoons, graphs, charts, maps, and artwork may be used to interpret the significance of time periods and events from the past.

SS.912.G.4.2: Use geographic terms and tools to analyze the push/pull factors contributing to human migration within and among places.

SS.912.G.4.3: Use geographic terms and tools to analyze the effects of migration both on the place of origin and destination, including border areas.

SS.912.H.3.1: Analyze the effects of transportation, trade, communication, science, and technology on the preservation and diffusion of culture.

The Columbian Exchange

Native Americans introduced Europeans to new crops such as corn, cocoa, and tomatoes. Europeans introduced Native Americans to various grains, fruits, and other foods. Europeans also became familiar with Native American inventions such as canoes, moccasins, and toboggans. When Europeans arrived in North America, however, they brought with them infectious diseases to which the Native Americans had no resistance.

Pigs

European diseases and violence decimated Native American populations.

Disease

Citrus Fruit

Grains

Sugarcane

Millions of enslaved Africans were forcibly transported to the Americas to labor on sugarcane plantations.

Cattle

Honeybees

Bananas

Coffee

Potatoes

Potatoes increased northern Europe's population and changed Ireland's diet.

Corn

Beans

Squash and Pumpkins

Peanuts improved people's health in West Africa by providing protein.

Peanuts

Cocoa

Tobacco use killed tens of millions in only a few hundred years.

Disease

Tobacco

Tomatoes became popular in Europe and greatly changed the cuisine of Italy.

Tomatoes

1765 Parliament passes the Stamp Act, triggering protests throughout the colonies

1787 U.S. Constitution is drafted

1803 Louisiana Purchase doubles size of the nation

1850 Compromise of 1850 is adopted in an attempt to ease sectional tensions

1861 Fort Sumter is bombarded by Confederate forces; the Civil War begins

1865 Lee surrenders to Grant; Abraham Lincoln is assassinated

1877 Compromise of 1877 ends Reconstruction

1725

1800

1875

1789 French Revolution begins

1812 Napoleon invades then retreats from Russia

1821 Mexico declares independence from Spain

1839 Slave revolt occurs aboard the *Amistad*

1853 Crimean War begins, pitting Russia against Britain and Turkey

1868 Meiji Restoration begins Japanese modernization

LESSON 1

Origins of the American Nation

ESSENTIAL QUESTIONS

• What characteristics define a society?
• Why do people form governments?
• How should societies settle disputes?

READING HELPDESK

Academic Vocabulary

• eventually   • enforce

Content Vocabulary

• conquistador
• joint-stock company
• indentured servant
• committee of correspondence

TAKING NOTES

Key Ideas and Details

Organizing As you read about the colonization of America, use a graphic organizer similar to the one below to indicate ways in which the colonists defied British rule. **LAFS.1112.RH.3.7**

Colonists' Acts of Defiance

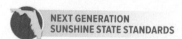

NEXT GENERATION SUNSHINE STATE STANDARDS

LAFS.1112.RH.1.3: Evaluate various explanations for actions or events and determine which explanation best accords with textual evidence, acknowledging where the text leaves matters uncertain.

LAFS.1112.RH.2.4: Determine the meaning of words and phrases as they are used in a text, including analyzing how an author uses and refines the meaning of a key term over the course of a text (e.g., how Madison defines faction in Federalist No. 10).

Continued on page 5

IT MATTERS BECAUSE

A number of civilizations flourished in the Americas before Europeans looking for trade routes colonized the region. Escalating tensions over British control of the colonies resulted in a revolt against British rule.

Pre-Columbian America

GUIDING QUESTION *How did geography influence the ways Native American cultures developed?*

No one knows exactly when the first people arrived in the Americas. Recent research suggests that they may have arrived between 15,000 and 30,000 years ago. In time, Native Americans learned how to raise crops. This shift led to the first permanent villages and to new building methods. Societies became more complex, and civilizations arose, marked by advanced knowledge of trade, government, the arts, science, and language.

Early Civilizations

Anthropologists think the first American civilization arose between 1500 B.C. and 1200 B.C. among the Olmec. They lived in Mesoamerica, the region that today includes central and southern Mexico and Central America. Later, the Maya and the Aztec also developed civilizations in Mesoamerica, building impressive temples and pyramids and establishing trade networks.

After A.D. 300, the Hohokam and the Anasazi began growing crops in North America's dry Southwest by building elaborate irrigation systems. People in the Eastern Woodlands were developing their own cultures. The Hopewell built geometric earthworks that served as ceremonial centers, observatories, and burial places. By A.D. 900, the Mississippian people had built Cahokia, one of the largest early American cities.

Native Americans of North America

By the 1500s, Native Americans had established an array of cultures suited to their environments. In the Eastern Woodlands, most Native Americans combined hunting and fishing with farming.

In the Southeast, many Native Americans built wooden stockades around their villages for protection. Southwestern peoples farmed corn, beans, and cotton. By the 1500s, the Apache and the Navajo had come to the Southwest. The Navajo settled in farming villages, but many of the Apache remained nomadic hunters. Hunting also sustained the Sioux and other peoples of the western Great Plains.

The Pacific Northwest was home to fishing peoples. In what is today central California, groups such as the Pomo trapped small game and gathered acorns. In the Far North region from Alaska to Greenland, the Inuit and the Aleut hunted sea mammals, polar bears, and caribou.

✅ **READING PROGRESS CHECK**

Explaining In what different ways did Native American cultures provide food for themselves?

Early Modern Europe

GUIDING QUESTION *What ideas and inventions encouraged Europeans to begin overseas exploration?*

As the people of Europe emerged from the Middle Ages, they wanted to find a quick trade route to Asia, the source of many luxury goods. Rulers of Portugal, Spain, France, and England wanted to find a water route to Asia that would bypass the Italian and Arab merchants and traders who controlled trade in the eastern Mediterranean.

Renaissance and Reformation

In Western Europe, an intellectual revolution—the Renaissance—was underway. The arts flowered amid a rebirth of interest in ancient Greek and Roman culture. Europeans rediscovered the works of ancient thinkers and began reading the works of Arab scholars. A renewed commitment to reason helped trigger a scientific revolution. Inventions such as the astrolabe and the compass made sea travel easier.

©Corbis

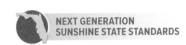

NEXT GENERATION SUNSHINE STATE STANDARDS

Continued from page 4

LAFS.1112.RH.3.7: Integrate and evaluate multiple sources of information presented in diverse formats and media (e.g., visually, quantitatively, as well as in words) in order to address a question or solve a problem.

LAFS.1112.WHST.1.1: Write arguments focused on discipline-specific content.

LAFS.1112.WHST.4.10: Write routinely over extended time frames (time for reflection and revision) and shorter time frames (a single sitting or a day or two) for a range of discipline-specific tasks, purposes, and audiences.

SS.912.A.1.2: Utilize a variety of primary and secondary sources to identify author, historical significance, audience, and authenticity to understand a historical period.

SS.912.A.1.4: Analyze how images, symbols, objects, cartoons, graphs, charts, maps, and artwork may be used to interpret the significance of time periods and events from the past.

SS.912.A.2.7: Review the Native American experience.

SS.912.G.1.2: Use spatial perspective and appropriate geographic terms and tools, including the Six Essential Elements, as organizational schema to describe any given place.

SS.912.G.4.2: Use geographic terms and tools to analyze the push/pull factors contributing to human migration within and among places.

SS.912.G.4.3: Use geographic terms and tools to analyze the effects of migration both on the place of origin and destination, including border areas.

Continued on page 8

The caravel was ideal for exploration. These small ships ranged from 70 to 90 feet (23 to 27 m) long, were highly maneuverable, and very fast. Their smaller size enabled them to sail along shallow coastlines and explore up rivers much farther than other ships.

▶ **CRITICAL THINKING**
Determining Cause and Effect
Why might the development of the caravel have encouraged European exploration? LAFS.1112.RH.3.7, SS.912.A.1.4, SS.912.H.3.1

PHOTO: British Library/HIP/Art Resource, NY
TEXT: The Broken Spears: The Aztec Account of the Conquest of Mexico by Miguel Leon-Portilla. Copyright © 1962, 1990 by Miguel Leon-Portilla. Copyright. Reprinted by Permission of Beacon Press, Boston.

Analyzing PRIMARY SOURCES

The Defeat of the Aztec

❝A thing like a ball of stone comes out of its entrails: it comes out shooting sparks and raining fire. . . . If it is aimed against a tree, it shatters the tree into splinters. This is a most unnatural sight, as if the tree had exploded from within.

They dress in iron. . . . Their deer carry them on their back wherever they wish to go. These deer, our lord, are as tall as the roof of a house.❞

—from *The Broken Spears: The Aztec Account of the Conquest of Mexico*, 1959

DBQ **IDENTIFYING** What do you think the Aztec are seeing for the first time? LAFS.1112.RH.1.3, LAFS.1112.RH.2.4, SS.912.A.1.2

This image depicts the battle for Tenochtitlán between the Aztec and the Spanish in 1519.

▶ **CRITICAL THINKING**
Drawing Conclusions What does this image tell you about the Aztec view of the battle? SS.912.A.1.2, SS.912.A.1.4, SS.912.H.1.3

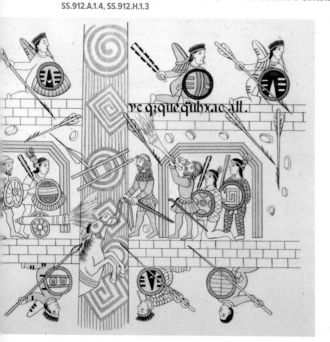

Religious changes were taking place as well. In 1517, the German monk Martin Luther called for the reform of the Catholic Church, launching the Protestant Reformation. New churches emerged in Germany and England, including a burgeoning movement known as Puritanism. Puritans hoped to "purify" the new Church of England, but faced challenges after King James I became the English monarch in 1603.

Overseas Exploration Begins

Portugal took the lead in searching for a sea route around Africa to Asia in the early 1400s. Later, Spain funded an expedition by Italian sea captain Christopher Columbus to sail west across the Atlantic. In August 1492, Columbus and his crew left Spain and landed two months later on an island in the Caribbean. Columbus's news that he had reached land on the other side of the Atlantic triggered a wave of European exploration. Soon people realized that Columbus had not reached Asia but instead a continent they did not know. They named the new continent *America* in honor of Amerigo Vespucci, who explored the South American coastline for Portugal.

☑ **READING PROGRESS CHECK**

Summarizing What drove some European rulers to send explorers in search of a water route to Asia?

The Spanish and French Establish Colonies

GUIDING QUESTION *Why did Spain and France establish colonies in the Americas?*

After sailing west from Spain, Columbus reached the Bahamas in October 1492. He then headed farther into the Caribbean, searching for gold. At about that time, Spain and Portugal both claimed control over the Atlantic route to Asia. The Treaty of Tordesillas resolved the rivalry in 1494, and recognized Spain's claim to most of the Americas.

New Spain

In 1519, a Spaniard named Hernán Cortés sailed from Cuba to explore the Yucatán Peninsula. He had heard reports of vast riches in that region and set sail with an army seeking glory and gold. After conquering the peninsula, Cortés, his troops, and Tlaxcalan warriors (enemies of the Aztec) destroyed the Aztec city of Tenochtitlán in 1521. On its ruins, the Spanish built Mexico City, which became the capital of the colony of New Spain. Cortés then sent several expeditions to conquer the surrounding regions. The men who led these expeditions became known as **conquistadors,** or "conquerors." Deadly diseases brought by the Spanish killed many native peoples and severely weakened their ability to resist the invaders. The Spanish soon controlled a territory stretching from Florida to California and into South America.

New France

France began exploring eastern North America, funding trips by Jacques Cartier and Giovanni da Verrazano in the early 1500s. In 1602, French king Henry IV authorized a group of French merchants to establish a colony in what is now Canada. They hired Samuel de Champlain to help them. In 1608, Champlain founded Quebec, the eventual capital of New France. The backers of the colony sought fur, and Frenchmen began a brisk trade with Native Americans. In the late 1600s, France began expanding the colony. Explorers Louis Jolliet and Jacques Marquette reached the Mississippi River, and René-Robert Cavelier de La Salle followed it to the Gulf of Mexico. La Salle named the newly claimed region Louisiana for King Louis XIV. The French went on to found Biloxi, Mobile, and New Orleans.

✓ READING PROGRESS CHECK

Contrasting How did Spanish and French relations with native peoples differ?

Settling the Thirteen Colonies

GUIDING QUESTION *For what reasons were the thirteen colonies founded?*

Soon after Columbus made his historic voyage, England began exploring the eastern part of North America, sending John Cabot on expeditions in 1497 and 1498. It was not until the 1600s, however, that England succeeded in establishing colonies in North America.

Jamestown

English business and government leaders saw colonies as sources of raw materials and as markets for English goods. In 1607, they established Jamestown, the first lasting English settlement, in Virginia. The settlement was funded by a **joint-stock company**—a group of private investors who supported major projects to gain profits. The Jamestown settlers overcame early troubles with the help of a group of local Native Americans known as the Powhatan Confederacy, and **eventually** prospered by growing tobacco.

Encouraged by the Virginia Company, more than 4,500 settlers immigrated to Virginia by 1622. Alarmed Native Americans attacked Jamestown. An English court blamed the company's policies for the settlers' deaths and revoked its charter. Virginia then became a royal colony.

The New England Colonies

Not all settlers came for economic gain. Some Puritans had decided the Church of England was too corrupt to be reformed. They were called Separatists. In 1620, a group of Separatists, later known as the Pilgrims, set sail from England on the *Mayflower* to escape persecution for their religious beliefs.

The Pilgrims finally settled near what is now Plymouth, Massachusetts. The colonists drew up the Mayflower Compact, a plan for self-government. Ten years later, facing increasing persecution in England, another group of Puritans arrived in Massachusetts Bay with a charter for their new colony. They founded several towns, including Boston.

Before long, Puritan efforts in Massachusetts to suppress other religious beliefs led to the formation of Rhode Island and Connecticut. Dissenter Roger Williams founded the town of Providence. Anne Hutchinson and others banished from Massachusetts settled in the area and eventually joined their towns to become the single colony of Rhode Island and Providence Plantations. Religious freedom became a key part of the colony's charter. Reverend Thomas Hooker and his congregation moved to the Connecticut River valley and founded the town of Hartford, marking the beginning of the colony of Connecticut, which adopted America's first democratic constitution in 1639. The territory north of Massachusetts was divided into Maine and New Hampshire, but claimed by Massachusetts. In 1679, New Hampshire became a royal colony. Maine remained part of Massachusetts.

Portrait of Anne Hutchinson (1591-1643), American School, (20th century)/Schlesinger Library, Radcliffe Institute, Harvard University/The Bridgeman Art Library

BIOGRAPHY

Anne Hutchinson (1591–1643)

Anne Hutchinson arrived in Boston in 1634. There, she held meetings with other women to discuss sermons, express her own beliefs, and evaluate the ministers. Hutchinson stirred up controversy with her views on how salvation could be obtained. She was tried for sedition and banished by the Massachusetts General Court in 1637. Hutchinson, her family, and some followers settled in what is today Rhode Island. She later moved to Long Island, where she was killed in an attack by Native Americans.

▶ CRITICAL THINKING
Identifying Central Ideas
Why was Anne Hutchinson banished from Massachusetts?

conquistador Spanish for "conqueror;" the men who led the expeditions to conquer the Americas

joint-stock company a form of business organization in which many investors pool funds to raise large amounts of money for large projects

eventually at an unspecified time or day; in the end

Atlantic Slave Trade

ATLANTIC OCEAN

EUROPE

NORTH AMERICA

New Orleans
Charleston
Gulf of Mexico
TROPIC OF CANCER
Santo Domingo

PACIFIC OCEAN

Cartagena

SOUTH AMERICA

Pernambuco
Bahia

Lisbon
Azores
Madeira
Canary Is.
Cape Verde Islands

AFRICA

WOLOF
Île de Gorée 19%
MALINKE
MANDINGO Accra
11% ASHANTI YORUBA
Elima Ouidah 27% HAUSA IBO
16% SEKE
BAKONGO
25% MBUNDU
Cabinda
Luanda

ATLANTIC OCEAN

EQUATOR

N
W E
S

0   800 miles
0   800 km
Miller projection

People of African ancestry as a percentage of the population
- 90–100
- 40–50
- 30–39.9
- Major slave-trade port

SLAVE TRADE DESTINATIONS

SOUTH AMERICA		CENTRAL AMERICA	
Brazil	3,650,000	Spanish	1,500,000
Dutch America	500,000	**NORTH AMERICA**	
WEST INDIES		British Colonies	500,000
British	1,660,000	**EUROPE**	175,000
French	1,660,000		
		TOTAL	9,645,000

GEOGRAPHY CONNECTION

The introduction of enslaved Africans to the American Colonies was part of the broader Atlantic slave trade.

1 **THE WORLD IN SPATIAL TERMS** *What sub-region of the Americas was the destination for most enslaved peoples?* SS.912.A.1.4, SS.912.G.1.2

2 **PLACES AND REGIONS** *What area of North America held the largest numbers of enslaved people?* SS.912.A.1.4, SS.912.G.1.2

NEXT GENERATION SUNSHINE STATE STANDARDS

Continued from page 5
SS.912.H.1.3: Relate works in the arts to various cultures.

SS.912.H.3.1: Analyze the effects of transportation, trade, communication, science, and technology on the preservation and diffusion of culture.

indentured servant an individual who contracted to work for a colonist for a specified number of years in exchange for transportation to the colonies, food, clothing, and shelter

The Middle Colonies

In 1609, Henry Hudson, a navigator hired by Dutch merchants, had discovered what is now the Hudson River valley in New York. The Dutch called the region New Netherland and established their main settlement of New Amsterdam on Manhattan Island. Charles II seized New Netherland from the Dutch and granted the land to his brother, the Duke of York. Much of the land was renamed New York. The rest became New Jersey, a colony that offered greater land grants, religious freedom, and political rights. In 1681, William Penn, wanting to help his fellow Quakers escape persecution in England, created the colony of Pennsylvania south of New York. The "lower counties" became Delaware.

The Southern Colonies

Farther south, tobacco helped Virginia thrive. Its neighbor colony, Maryland, was a proprietary colony that began in the 1630s to provide a refuge for Catholics who faced persecution in England.

In 1663, King Charles II gave eight friends a vast tract of land named Carolina. This region developed into two distinct areas: North Carolina, with scattered tobacco farms, and South Carolina, where a larger number of settlers established the community of Charles Towne (Charleston), exported deerskins, and grew rice. With a charter from King George II, James Oglethorpe founded Georgia as a place for English debtors to begin a new life.

Most colonists relied on agriculture for their livelihoods. Often, poor English people came to America as **indentured servants** who agreed to work for four or more years in return for ship's passage and basic needs. Southern landowners with large plantations also relied on the labor of enslaved Africans, taken from Africa by way of the Atlantic slave trade. This reliance on enslaved labor increased as land became cheap, more enslaved persons were forcibly transported to American, and fewer English settlers were willing to become indentured servants. Unlike indentured servants, enslaved workers were not freed at the end of a set contract.

☑ **READING PROGRESS CHECK**

Drawing Conclusions What is the historical importance of the Mayflower Compact?

The American Revolution

GUIDING QUESTION *Why did the colonists fight a war for independence against Great Britain?*

The American colonies experienced rapid population growth. In time, colonists revolted against what they saw as oppressive British rule. They established a new, independent government for themselves.

New Ideas Influence the Colonists

During the 1600s and 1700s, philosophers of the Age of Enlightenment stressed the use of reason and logic to understand natural laws. Enlightenment writer John Locke attempted to use reason to discover natural laws that applied to politics and society. He argued that governments existed because the people who were governed allowed them to exist: "For no government can have a right to obedience from a people who have not freely consented to it; which they can never be supposed to do, till . . . they are put in a full state of liberty to choose their government." Locke's ideas influenced Thomas Jefferson and other colonists.

Also in the 1700s, some Americans renewed their Christian faith in what became known as the Great Awakening. The new ideas of Baptists, Presbyterians, and Methodists won many converts. Along with the Enlightenment, this movement emphasized an individualism that inclined American colonists toward political independence.

The Growing Rift With Britain

In the 1750s, Great Britain and France began fighting for control of North America. Both countries relied on Native Americans as allies, and the war became known as the French and Indian War. The British victory in the war left Britain with steep debts and new territories to govern and defend. Many British leaders thought that the colonies should share in these costs. The American colonists, however, did not like the policies Britain adopted to solve its financial problems.

The Proclamation of 1763 tried to halt colonial expansion into Native American lands west of the Appalachians. King George III wanted to avoid another costly war with the Native Americans, but the colonists, who wanted access to the Ohio River valley, were enraged.

"No Taxation Without Representation" Colonists had been smuggling goods without paying customs duties, so Britain tightened customs and introduced unpopular taxes such as the Sugar Act and the Stamp Act—the first direct tax Britain had levied on the colonists. In October 1765, representatives from nine colonies issued the Declaration of Rights and Grievances, arguing that only representatives elected by the colonists—not Parliament—had the right to tax them. "No taxation without representation" became a popular catchphrase. Colonists boycotted British goods, and Britain repealed the Stamp Act in 1766. In 1767, the Townshend Acts put new customs duties on key British imports and **enforced** rules against smuggling. Colonial anger turned to violence in 1770, resulting in the Boston Massacre on March 5. Eventually Britain repealed the Townshend Acts.

enforce to urge or carry out using force

The resumption of smuggling soon led to strife. Colonists created **committees of correspondence** to communicate with one another about British activities. In 1773, colonists dumped hundreds of cases of tea off British ships in a protest called the Boston Tea Party. Outraged, Parliament passed the Coercive Acts to punish the colonists for their defiance and the Quebec Act, which extended the boundaries of what was then the Province of Quebec to include much of what is now Ohio, Michigan, Indiana, Wisconsin, and Illinois. Together these laws came to be known as the Intolerable Acts.

committee of correspondence a committee organized in each colony to communicate with the other colonies about British activities

This lithograph, titled *The Destruction of Tea at Boston Harbor,* was created by engravers Currier & Ives in 1846.

▶ **CRITICAL THINKING**

Interpreting What was the significance of the Boston Tea Party being a physical demonstration? LAFS.1112.RH.3.7, SS.912.A.1.4

Declaring Independence Opposition to British policies continued to rise. Fifty-five colonial delegates met at the First Continental Congress in Philadelphia on September 5, 1774. Soon after gathering, they learned that Britain had suspended the Massachusetts Assembly. The Congress responded by approving a plan to boycott British goods.

In the meantime, the suspended Massachusetts Assembly gathered secretly to create a new Massachusetts Provincial Congress and a Committee of Public Safety. They selected John Hancock to be President of the Committee and gave him the power to call up the militia, in effect making Hancock a rival governor to General Gage, whom the British had put in control of Massachusetts. In April 1775, Gage decided to seize control of the militia's weapons and supplies that were stored in Concord. As the British troops marched past the town of Lexington on their way to Concord, fighting broke out between the Minutemen militia and the British troops. The first shots of the revolutionary war had been fired.

Three weeks later, as fighting continued in Massachusetts, the Second Continental Congress gathered in Philadelphia. The appointed George Washington to command a new Continental Army made up of the colonial militias. Battles took place in Boston; near Norfolk, Virginia; in North Carolina; and outside Charleston, South Carolina. By July 1776, the Congress had decided the time had come to declare independence and appointed a committee to draft a declaration. The first draft of the Declaration of Independence was written by Thomas Jefferson, then edited and revised by others on the committee including John Adams, Benjamin Franklin, Roger Sherman and Robert Livingston. On July 4, 1776, the Continental Congress issued the Declaration of Independence.

John Hancock was the first person to sign, followed by 55 other representatives from the colonies. Among the signers were Thomas Jefferson,

©Bettmann/Corbis

Roger Sherman, John Adams, and Benjamin Franklin. Others included Benjamin Rush, who had helped organize the Sons of Liberty in Pennsylvania and assisted Tom Paine in writing *Common Sense;* John Witherspoon from New Jersey, who went on to help draft the Articles of Confederation; and Charles Carroll, the sole Catholic signer of the Declaration, and one of the leaders of opposition to Britain in Maryland. With the signing of the Declaration, the thirteen colonies had now become the United States of America and the American Revolution had begun.

The War for Independence

The Continental Army could not match the British army in size, funding, or experience. It was fighting on home ground, however, and used unconventional tactics.

The British enjoyed early victories, but the American win at Saratoga in 1777 was a turning point in the war. Morale improved, and the French signed a military alliance with the United States and recognized the new nation's independence.

American troops controlled the frontier, but the British won victories in the South. In 1780, Patriot forces regained control in the South after the Battle of Kings Mountain. The last major battle of the war was fought at Yorktown, Virginia. Trapped by Washington's forces and the French navy, General Charles Cornwallis and approximately 8,000 British troops surrendered on October 19, 1781.

Parliament then voted to end the war. Peace talks began in early April 1782, and the Treaty of Paris was signed on September 3, 1783. With the Revolutionary War over, a new nation began to take shape.

✓ READING PROGRESS CHECK

Identifying What factors helped the American colonists win their independence?

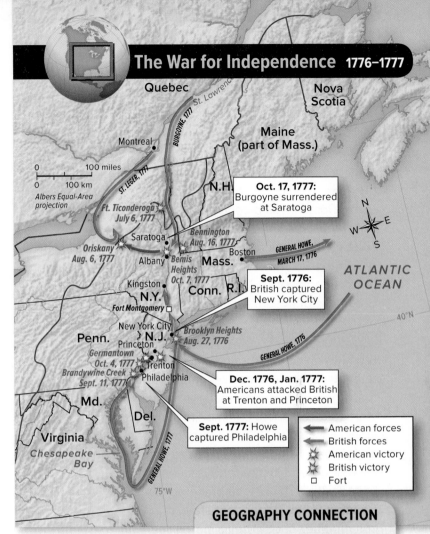

The War for Independence 1776–1777

Quebec

Nova Scotia

Maine (part of Mass.)

Montreal

0 — 100 miles
0 — 100 km
Albers Equal-Area projection

St. Lawrence

BURGOYNE, 1777

ST. LEGER, 1777

N.H.

Oct. 17, 1777: Burgoyne surrendered at Saratoga

Ft. Ticonderoga July 6, 1777

Oriskany Aug. 6, 1777

Saratoga

Bennington Aug. 16, 1777

Albany Bemis Heights Oct. 7, 1777

Mass.

Boston

GENERAL HOWE, MARCH 17, 1776

ATLANTIC OCEAN

Kingston

Conn. R.I.

N.Y.

Fort Montgomery ☐

40°N

New York City

Penn. N.J.

Princeton

Brooklyn Heights Aug. 27, 1776

Sept. 1776: British captured New York City

Germantown Oct. 4, 1777

Brandywine Creek Sept. 11, 1777

Trenton

Philadelphia

GENERAL HOWE 1776

Dec. 1776, Jan. 1777: Americans attacked British at Trenton and Princeton

Md.

Del.

Sept. 1777: Howe captured Philadelphia

Virginia

Chesapeake Bay

GENERAL HOWE, 1777

75°W

→ American forces
→ British forces
✸ American victory
✸ British victory
☐ Fort

GEOGRAPHY CONNECTION

In March 1777, General John Burgoyne proposed a three-pronged attack to isolate New England from the other American states.

1 **THE WORLD IN SPATIAL TERMS** *What are two colonial victories that occurred in New Jersey?* SS.912.A.1.4, SS.912.G.1.2

2 **THE USES OF GEOGRAPHY** *How did General Howe make his attack on the United States?* SS.912.A.1.4, SS.912.G.1.2

LESSON 1 REVIEW

Reviewing Vocabulary

1. *Explaining* What was the purpose of committees of correspondence? LAFS.1112.RH.2.4

Using Your Notes

2. *Summarizing* Use the notes you completed during the lesson to summarize ways that the colonists resisted British rule. LAFS.1112.RH.3.7

Answering the Guiding Questions

3. *Identifying* How did geography influence the ways Native American cultures developed? SS.912.A.2.7, SS.912.G.1.2

4. *Analyzing* What ideas and inventions encouraged Europeans to begin overseas exploration? SS.912.H.3.1

5. *Explaining* Why did Spain and France establish colonies in the Americas? SS.912.G.4.2, SS.912.G.4.3, SS.912.H.3.1

6. *Identifying* For what reasons were the thirteen colonies founded? SS.912.H.3.1

7. *Determining Cause and Effect* Why did the colonists fight a war for independence against Great Britain?

Writing Activity

8. **ARGUMENT** Take on the role of a Patriot trying to convince other colonists to support independence from Great Britain. Write a speech in which you explain why independence is the right choice. LAFS.1112.WHST.1.1, LAFS.1112.WHST.4.10

LAFS.1112.RH.1.1, LAFS.1112.RH.1.2, LAFS.1112.RH.1.3, LAFS.1112.RH.2.5, LAFS.1112.RH.2.6, LAFS.1112.RH.3.8, LAFS.1112.RH.3.9, LAFS.1112.RH.4.10

Boston: Hotbed of Revolution

The growing dispute between colonists and British authorities centered on the extent of Parliament's power over the colonies, particularly the power to levy taxes. Boston was a center of protest against British policies. When, on the night of March 5, 1770, British soldiers fired into a crowd, killing or injuring 11 people, colonists were quick to declare the event a "massacre," even though exactly what occurred is debatable.

POLITICAL ESSAY, 1767

From what has been said, I think this **uncontrovertible** conclusion may be deduced, that when a ruling state obliges a dependent state to take certain commodities from her alone, it is implied in the nature of that obligation; is essentially **requisite** to give it the least degree of justice; and is inseparably united with it, in order to preserve any share of freedom to the dependent state; that those commodities should never be loaded with duties, FOR THE SOLE PURPOSE OF LEVYING MONEY ON THE DEPENDENT STATE.

Upon the whole the single question is, whether the parliament can legally impose duties to be paid by the people of these colonies only, FOR THE SOLE PURPOSE OF RAISING A REVENUE, on commodities, which she obliges us to take from her alone, or, in other words, whether the parliament can legally take money out of our pockets without our consent.

—John Dickinson, "Letters From a Farmer in Pennsylvania to the Inhabitants of the British Colonies," *Pennsylvania Gazette,* December 10, 1767

VOCABULARY

uncontrovertible
indisputable

requisite
necessary to reach a goal or achieve a purpose

indulgence
allowing oneself the pleasure of having or doing something

palliate
to find excuses for

stipulates
demanding or insisting on something as part of an agreement

mode
a particular operating arrangement or condition

opprobrious
expressing very strong disapproval

conciliating
to gain the goodwill or favor of

provocation
the act of provoking

▲ *The Boston Massacre took place on March 5, 1770. When the smoke cleared, five were dead and colonists were angrier than ever.*

Universal Images Group/Getty Images

POLITICAL ESSAY, 1774

To suppose, that by sending out a colony, the nation established an independent power; that when, by **indulgence** and favour, emigrants are become rich, they shall not contribute to their own defence, but at their own pleasure; and that they shall not be included, like millions of their fellow subjects, in the general system of representation; involves such an accumulation of absurdity, as nothing but the show of patriotism could **palliate.**

He that accepts protection, **stipulates** obedience. We have always protected the Americans; we may therefore subject them to government.

The less is included in the greater. That power which can take away life, may seize upon property. The parliament may enact, for America, a law of capital punishment; it may therefore establish a **mode** and proportion of taxation.

—Samuel Johnson, *The Patriot*

LETTER, 1770

"[T]he Mob proceeded to a [S]entinel posted upon the Custom House and Attacked him. . . . Captain Preston . . . hearing the [S]entinel was in Danger of being Murdered, he detached a sergeant and twelve men to relieve him. . . . This Party as well as the [S]entinel was immediately attacked. Some [colonists] throwing Bricks, Stones, Pieces of Ice and Snow-Balls at them, whilst others advanced up to their Bayonets, and endeavored to close with them, to use their Bludgeons and Clubs; calling out . . . by the most **Opprobrious** Language.

Captain Preston [used] every **conciliating** Method to perswade [the mob] to retire peaceably. . . . All he could say had no Effect, and one of the Soldiers, receiving a violent Blow, instantly fired . . . and the Mob . . . attacked with greater Violence. . . . The Soldiers at length perceiving their Lives in Danger, and hearing the Word Fire all round them, three or four of them fired one after another, and again three more in the . . . Confusion. . . .

Some have sworn Captain Preston gave Orders to fire; others who were near, that the Soldiers fired without Orders from the **Provocation** they received."

—Thomas Gage, commander in chief of all British North American soldiers, explaining the events of March 5, 1770

DBQ Analyzing Historical Documents

1. **Paraphrasing** Using your own words, explain each narrator's argument over taxes.

2. **Argument** Do you agree with the patriot or the farmer? Write an essay defending your point of view.

3. **Explaining** According to Commander Thomas Gage, why did Captain Preston and his men go to the Custom House?

4. **Differentiating** On what specifics of the event did Captain Preston's officers disagree? Provide evidence from Gage's letter to support your answer.

5. **Using Context Clues** How does Gage use language to help make the case for his men?

6. **Predicting Consequence** The paper's account of the event claims Preston yelled "Damn you, Fire, be the consequence what it will!" How does this fact help or hurt the British cause?

PRIMARY SOURCES

LAFS.1112.RH.1.1, LAFS.1112.RH.1.2, LAFS.1112.RH.1.3, LAFS.1112.RH.2.4, LAFS.1112.RH.2.5, LAFS.1112.RH.3.9, LAFS.1112.RH.4.10

Declaring Independence

When the Declaration of Independence was written in 1776, with very few exceptions, the people of the world were governed by monarchs, emperors, and absolute rulers. Since Roman times, there had been very little development in the relationship between the individual and the government. A reexamination of government began in the Renaissance, and by the time of the Enlightenment in the eighteenth century, many new ideas had emerged. Those ideas culminated in the American Declaration of Independence.

VOCABULARY

endowed
provided, or born with

unalienable
cannot be taken away or given away

divests
gives up, or takes off

arbitrary
based on a person's opinion or preference, not following the rules

levying
imposing taxes or duties

THE DECLARATION OF INDEPENDENCE, 1776

The text of the Declaration of Independence has four parts. The first part is the preamble, which explains why it is being issued. The second part explains the idea of natural rights, and uses that idea to explain the legal justification for declaring independence. The third part, the list of grievances, charges the British with violating the rights of the colonies and gives examples. The fourth part is the resolution, where the colonies officially declare their independence.

The Declaration was written by Thomas Jefferson with the help of Benjamin Franklin and John Adams. It was then revised by Congress before being issued. The document draws on the new political theories of the Enlightenment. It summarizes these ideas when it states that people are **endowed** with **unalienable** rights. This was a revolutionary idea. It means that rights do not come from the government. People have rights no matter what their government says, no matter what laws it passes, and the government cannot take them away.

Second, the Declaration argues that the only reason people create government is to protect their rights. The only legitimate or just powers a government has are the powers it gets from the "consent of the governed." In other words, government exists to serve the people and when it fails to protect people's rights, the people have a right to overthrow it.

The Declaration of Independence is very important. It marks the birth of the United States, the first modern democratic republic. Its ideas and values have influenced people in other nations, and have helped to transform governments and societies around the world.

THE SECOND TREATISE OF GOVERNMENT, 1689

The political ideas behind the Declaration came from many sources, including Enlightenment writers and classical thinkers such as Aristotle and Cicero. But the greatest influence on American thinking was probably the 17th century English philosopher John Locke, who wrote "Two Treatises of Government" shortly after the English Parliament removed King James II from power and asked William and Mary to become the new monarchs of England:

Men being, as has been said, by Nature, all free, equal and independent, no one can be put out of this Estate, and subjected to the Political Power of another, without his own Consent. The only way whereby any one **divests** himself of his Natural Liberty and puts on the bounds of Civil Society is by agreeing with other Men to Joyn and unite into a Community, for their comfortable, safe, and peaceable living one amongst another, in a secure Enjoyment of their properties. . . .

Governments are dissolved from within . . . when such a single Person or Prince sets up his own **Arbitrary** Will in place of the Laws, which are the Will of the Society, declared by the Legislative. . . . Secondly, when the Prince hinders the legislative from . . . acting freely, pursuant to those ends, for which it was Constituted . . . Thirdly, When by the Arbitrary Power of the Prince, the Electors, or ways of Election are altered, without the Consent, and contrary to the common Interest of the People.

. . . In these and the like Cases, when the Government is dissolved, the People are at liberty to provide for themselves, by erecting a new Legislative, differing from the other, by the change of Persons, or Form, or both as they shall find it most for their safety and good.

THE ENGLISH BILL OF RIGHTS, 1789

The Declaration of Independence contains 18 charges against the king. This list of grievances were patterned after several documents, but the most influential was the English Bill of Rights issued by the English Parliament in 1689:

By assuming and exercising a power of dispensing with and suspending of laws and the execution of laws without consent of parliament. . . . By **levying** money for and to the use of the crown by pretence of prerogative for other time and in other manner than the same was granted by parliament.

DBQ Analyzing Historical Documents

1. **Evaluating Intent** Summarize the purpose of the Declaration of Independence.

2. **Analyzing Meaning** According to John Locke, who gives government its authority? What does the Declaration of Independence say is the source of government's power?

3. **Analyzing Text** What basic rights does the Declaration of Independence identify as belonging to all people? How do they differ from the rights Locke mentions?

By raising and keeping a standing army within this kingdom in time of peace without consent of parliament and quartering soldiers contrary to law. . . .

By violating the freedom of election of members to serve in parliament. . . .

And excessive bail hath been required of persons committed in criminal cases to elude the benefit of the laws made for the liberty of the subjects. And excessive fines have been imposed. And illegal and cruel punishments inflicted. . .

And thereupon the said lords spiritual and temporal and commons . . . declare that the pretended power of suspending of laws or the execution of laws by regal authority without consent of parliament is illegal.

That levying money for or to the use of the crown . . . without grant of parliament for longer time or in other manner than the same is or shall be granted is illegal.

That it is the right of the subjects to petition the king and all commitments and protections for such petitioning are illegal.

That the raising or keeping a standing army within the kingdom in time of peace unless it be with consent of parliament is against law. . . .

That election of members of parliament ought to be free. . . . That excessive bail ought not to be required nor excessive fines imposed nor cruel and unusual punishments inflicted. . . .

The said lords . . . do resolve that William and Mary, prince and princess of Orange, be declared king and queen of England. . . .

4. **Comparing and Contrasting** What are the similarities between the complaints in the English Bill of Rights and the Declaration of Independence? What are the differences?

5. **Explaining** What do all three documents agree is the most likely reason people's rights will be threatened? Which branch of government do all three documents imply is the source of the people's power?

THE DECLARATION of INDEPENDENCE

Words are spelled as originally written.

What It Means

The Preamble The Declaration of Independence has four parts. The Preamble explains why the Continental Congress drew up the Declaration.

impel: force

What It Means

Natural Rights The second part, the Declaration of Natural Rights, states that people have certain basic rights and that government should protect those rights. John Locke's ideas strongly influenced this part. In 1690, Locke wrote that government was based on the consent of the people and that people had the right to rebel if the government did not uphold their right to life, liberty, and property.

endowed: provided

In Congress, July 4, 1776. The unanimous Declaration of the thirteen united States of America,

[Preamble]

When in the Course of human events, it becomes necessary for one people to dissolve the political bands which have connected them with another, and to assume among the Powers of the earth, the separate and equal station to which the Laws of Nature and of Nature's God entitle them, a decent respect to the opinions of mankind requires that they should declare the causes which **impel** them to the separation.

[Declaration of Natural Rights]

We hold these truths to be self-evident, that all men are created equal, that they are **endowed** by their Creator with certain unalienable Rights, that among these are Life, Liberty, and the pursuit of Happiness.

That to secure these rights, Governments are instituted among Men, deriving their just powers from the consent of the governed,

That whenever any Form of Government becomes destructive of these ends, it is the Right of the People to alter or to abolish it, and to institute new Government, laying its foundation on such principles and organizing its powers in such form, as to them shall seem most likely to effect their Safety and Happiness. Prudence, indeed, will dictate that Governments long established should not be changed for light and transient causes; and accordingly all experience hath shown, that mankind are more disposed to suffer, while evils are sufferable,

Photodisc/Getty Images

than to right themselves by abolishing the forms to which they are accustomed. But when a long train of abuses and usurpations, pursuing invariably the same Object evinces a design to reduce them under absolute **Despotism**, it is their right, it is their duty, to throw off such Government, and to provide new Guards for their future security.

[List of Grievances]

Such has been the patient sufferance of these Colonies; and such is now the necessity which constrains them to alter their former Systems of Government. The history of the present King of Great Britain is a history of repeated injuries and **usurpations**, all having in direct object the establishment of an absolute Tyranny over these States. To prove this, let Facts be submitted to a candid world.

He has refused his Assent to Laws, the most wholesome and necessary for the public good.

He has forbidden his Governors to pass Laws of immediate and pressing importance, unless suspended in their operation till his Assent should be obtained; and when so suspended, he has utterly neglected to attend to them.

He has refused to pass other Laws for the accommodation of large districts of people, unless those people would **relinquish** the right of Representation in the Legislature, a right **inestimable** to them and formidable to tyrants only.

He has called together legislative bodies at places unusual, uncomfortable, and distant from the depository

despotism: unlimited power

What It Means

List of Grievances The third part of the Declaration is a list of the colonists' complaints against the British government. Notice that King George III is singled out for blame.

usurpations: unjust uses of power

relinquish: give up
inestimable: priceless

▼ *Declaration of Independence* by John Trumbull depicts the presentation of the Declaration of Independence to John Hancock (seated right), president of the Continental Congress.

©Francis G. Mayer/Corbis Art/Corbis

4562000561 0250

of their Public Records, for the sole purpose of fatiguing them into compliance with his measures.

He has dissolved Representative Houses repeatedly, for opposing with manly firmness his invasions on the rights of the people.

He has refused for a long time, after such dissolutions, to cause others to be elected; whereby the Legislative Powers, incapable of **Annihilation**, have returned to the People at large for their exercise; the State remaining in the mean time exposed to all the dangers of invasion from without, and **convulsions** within.

He has endeavoured to prevent the population of these States; for that purpose obstructing the Laws for **Naturalization of Foreigners;** refusing to pass others to encourage their migrations hither, and raising the conditions of new Appropriations of Lands.

He has obstructed the Administration of Justice, by refusing his Assent to Laws for establishing Judiciary Powers.

He has made Judges dependent on his Will alone, for the **tenure** of their offices, and the amount and payment of their salaries.

He has erected a multitude of New Offices, and sent hither swarms of Officers to harass our people, and eat out their substance.

He has kept among us, in times of peace, Standing Armies without the Consent of our legislature.

He has affected to render the Military independent of and superior to the Civil Power.

He has combined with others to subject us to a jurisdiction foreign to our constitution, and unacknowledged by our laws; giving his Assent to their acts of pretended legislation:

For **quartering** large bodies of troops among us:

For protecting them, by a mock Trial, from Punishment for any Murders which they should commit on the Inhabitants of these States:

For cutting off our Trade with all parts of the world:

For imposing taxes on us without our Consent:

For depriving us in many cases, of the benefits of Trial by Jury:

For transporting us beyond Seas to be tried for pretended offences:

For abolishing the free System of English Laws in a neighbouring Province, establishing therein an Arbitrary government, and enlarging its Boundaries so as to **render** it at once an example and fit instrument for introducing the same absolute rule into these Colonies:

For taking away our Charters, abolishing our most valuable Laws, and altering fundamentally the Forms of our Governments:

annihilation: destruction

convulsions: violent disturbances

Naturalization of Foreigners: process by which foreign-born persons become citizens

tenure: term

quartering: lodging

render: make

For suspending our own Legislature, and declaring themselves invested with Power to legislate for us in all cases whatsoever.

He has **abdicated** Government here, by declaring us out of his Protection and waging War against us.

abdicated: given up

He has plundered our seas, ravaged our Coasts, burnt our towns, and destroyed the lives of our people.

He is at this time transporting large armies of foreign mercenaries to compleat the works of death, desolation and tyranny, already begun with circumstances of Cruelty & **perfidy** scarcely paralleled in the most barbarous ages, and totally unworthy the Head of a civilized nation.

perfidy: violation of trust

He has constrained our fellow Citizens taken Captive on the high Seas to bear Arms against their Country, to become the executioners of their friends and Brethren, or to fall themselves by their Hands.

He has excited domestic **insurrections** amongst us, and has endeavoured to bring on the inhabitants of our frontiers, the merciless Indian Savages, whose known rule of warfare, is an undistinguished destruction of all ages, sexes and conditions.

insurrections: rebellions

In every stage of these Oppressions We have **Petitioned for Redress** in the most humble terms: Our repeated Petitions have been answered only by repeated injury. A Prince, whose character is thus marked by every act which may define a Tyrant, is unfit to be the ruler of a free People.

petitioned for redress: asked formally for a correction of wrongs

Nor have We been wanting in attention to our British brethren. We have warned them from time to time of attempts by their legislature to extend an **unwarrantable jurisdiction** over us. We have reminded them of the circumstances of our emigration and settlement here. We have appealed to their native justice and magnanimity, and we have conjured them by the ties of our common kindred to disavow these usurpations, which, would inevitably interrupt our connections and correspondence. They too have been deaf to the voice of justice and of **consanguinity**. We must, therefore, acquiesce in the necessity, which denounces our Separation, and hold them, as we hold the rest of mankind, Enemies in War, in Peace Friends.

unwarrantable jurisdiction: unjustified authority

consanguinity: originating from the same ancestor

[Resolution of Independence by the United States]

We, therefore, the Representatives of the united States of America, in General Congress, Assembled, appealing to the Supreme Judge of the world for the **rectitude** of our intentions, do, in the Name, and by Authority of the good People of these Colonies, solemnly publish and declare,

What It Means

Resolution of Independence The final section declares that the colonies are "Free and Independent States" with the full power to make war, to form alliances, and to trade with other countries.

rectitude: rightness

That these United Colonies are, and of Right ought to be Free and Independent States; that they are Absolved from all Allegiance to the British Crown, and that all political connection between them and the State of Great Britain, is and ought to be totally dissolved; and that as Free and Independent States, they have full Power to levy War, conclude Peace, contract Alliances, establish Commerce, and to do all other Acts and Things which Independent States may of right do.

And for the support of this Declaration, with a firm reliance on the Protection of Divine Providence, we mutually pledge to each other our Lives, our Fortunes and our sacred Honor.

What It Means

Signers of the Declaration The signers, as representatives of the American people, declared the colonies independent from Great Britain. Most members signed the document on August 2, 1776.

John Hancock
    President from
    Massachusetts

Georgia
Button Gwinnett
Lyman Hall
George Walton

North Carolina
William Hooper
Joseph Hewes
John Penn

South Carolina
Edward Rutledge
Thomas Heyward, Jr.
Thomas Lynch, Jr.
Arthur Middleton

Maryland
Samuel Chase
William Paca
Thomas Stone
Charles Carroll
    of Carrollton

Virginia
George Wythe
Richard Henry Lee
Thomas Jefferson
Benjamin Harrison
Thomas Nelson, Jr.
Francis Lightfoot
    Lee
Carter Braxton

Pennsylvania
Robert Morris
Benjamin Rush
Benjamin Franklin
John Morton
George Clymer
James Smith
George Taylor
James Wilson
George Ross

Delaware
Caesar Rodney
George Read
Thomas McKean

New York
William Floyd
Philip Livingston
Francis Lewis
Lewis Morris

New Jersey
Richard Stockton
John Witherspoon
Francis Hopkinson
John Hart
Abraham Clark

New Hampshire
Josiah Bartlett
William Whipple
Matthew Thornton

Massachusetts
Samuel Adams
John Adams
Robert Treat Paine
Elbridge Gerry

Rhode Island
Stephen Hopkins
William Ellery

Connecticut
Samuel Huntington
William Williams
Oliver Wolcott
Roger Sherman

(t & b) ©Bettmann/Corbis

LESSON 2
The Young Republic

ESSENTIAL QUESTIONS
- What characteristics define a society?
- Why do people form governments?
- How should societies settle disputes?

READING HELPDESK

Academic Vocabulary
- framework
- revenue

Content Vocabulary
- separation of powers
- enumerated powers
- implied powers

TAKING NOTES

Key Ideas and Details

Comparing and Contrasting As you read the lesson, use a graphic organizer like the one below to compare and contrast the Articles of Confederation and the Constitution. **LAFS.1112.RH.3.7**

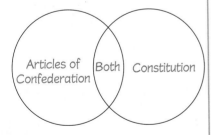

Articles of Confederation | Both | Constitution

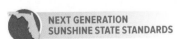

NEXT GENERATION SUNSHINE STATE STANDARDS

LAFS.1112.RH.2.4: Determine the meaning of words and phrases as they are used in a text, including analyzing how an author uses and refines the meaning of a key term over the course of a text (e.g., how Madison defines faction in Federalist No. 10).

LAFS.1112.RH.3.7: Integrate and evaluate multiple sources of information presented in diverse formats and media (e.g., visually, quantitatively, as well as in words) in order to address a question or solve a problem.

Continued on page 22

IT MATTERS BECAUSE
Soon after the American Revolution, political problems prompted Congress to seek revisions to the Articles of Confederation. In response, the Constitution was drafted and the emergence of a new federal government—and political parties—began.

Establishing the American Republic

GUIDING QUESTION *How did the constitutions created during the Revolutionary War attempt to limit the power of government and protect the rights of citizens?*

The leaders who created the United States of America knew that they were creating something new. They made a deliberate choice to replace royal rule with a republic. In a republic, power is held by citizens who are entitled to vote. Elected officials are responsible to the citizens and must govern according to laws or a constitution.

Political Ideas of the New Nation
In an ideal republic, all citizens are equal under the law, regardless of their wealth or social class. These ideas contradicted traditional practices that restricted the rights of many people on the basis of their race, class, or gender. Even though America would long struggle with equality, these republican ideas began to change American society. By the end of the Revolution, each state had drawn up its own written constitution. Many, based on the models of Massachusetts and Virginia, called for separate branches of government, two-house legislatures, and a list of rights guaranteed to citizens.

The Articles of Confederation
Initially adopted in 1777 during the Revolution, the Articles of Confederation were ratified in 1781, formally establishing the **framework** for a central national government. The Articles loosely unified the states under a single governing body, the Congress. There were no separate branches of government, and Congress had only limited powers. After fighting to free themselves from British rule, the states did not want a new government that might become tyrannical. Under the Articles, each state had one vote in

Creating a Nation **21**

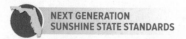
LAFS.1112.WHST.1.2: Write informative/
explanatory texts, including the narration of
historical events, scientific procedures/
experiments, or technical processes.

LAFS.1112.WHST.4.10: Write routinely over
extended time frames (time for reflection and
revision) and shorter time frames (a single
sitting or a day or two) for a range of
discipline-specific tasks, purposes, and
audiences.

SS.912.A.1.4: Analyze how images, symbols,
objects, cartoons, graphs, charts, maps, and
artwork may be used to interpret the
significance of time periods and events from
the past.

SS.912.A.1.6: Use case studies to explore
social, political, legal, and economic
relationships in history.

SS.912.G.4.2: Use geographic terms and tools
to analyze the push/pull factors contributing to
human migration within and among places.

SS.912.G.4.3: Use geographic terms and tools
to analyze the effects of migration both on the
place of origin and destination, including
border areas.

SS.912.H.1.1: Relate works in the arts
(architecture, dance, music, theatre, and visual
arts) of varying styles and genre according to
the periods in which they were created.

SS.912.H.1.5: Examine artistic response to
social issues and new ideas in various cultures.

SS.912.H.3.1: Analyze the effects of
transportation, trade, communication, science,
and technology on the preservation and
diffusion of culture.

framework basic structure

Delegates at the Constitutional
Convention in Philadelphia, 1787

▶ **CRITICAL THINKING**

1 *Making Inferences* Why do
you think Benjamin Franklin
is pictured in the middle of
this painting? SS.912.A.1.4,
SS.912.H.1.3, SS.912.H.1.5

2 *Describing* How does the
artist portray Washington's
role at the convention?
SS.912.A.1.4, SS.912.H.1.3, SS.912.H.1.5

Congress. Congress's power, however, was limited. It could negotiate with other
nations, raise armies, and declare war, but had no authority to regulate trade or
impose taxes. Congress could not raise enough money to pay its debts or expenses.

✓ **READING PROGRESS CHECK**

Describing How did the republic established by the United States differ from Britain's government?

The U.S. Constitution

GUIDING QUESTION *What are the key compromises and provisions incorporated in the
U.S. Constitution?*

The young United States faced several political and economic problems
after the end of the American Revolution. Many American leaders believed
that the new nation would not survive without a strong national
government and that the Articles of Confederation had to be revised.

In May 1787, 55 of the most distinguished leaders in the United States met
in Philadelphia to discuss weaknesses in the Articles of Confederation. They
soon decided that a new form of government was needed. All the delegates
supported a national government with the power to levy taxes and make laws
that would be binding upon the states. The delegates also accepted the idea of
dividing the government into executive, legislative, and judicial branches.

Debate and Compromise

Debate arose about how each state should be represented in the legislative
branch. The larger states insisted that representation be based on population;
smaller states wanted each state to have an equal vote. The convention
appointed a special committee to find a compromise. Benjamin Franklin
warned the delegates that if they failed to agree, they would "become a
reproach and a by-word down to future ages. And what is worse, mankind
may hereafter, from this unfortunate instance, despair of establishing
governments by human wisdom, and leave it to chance, war, and conquest."

Roger Sherman of Connecticut suggested the basis of the committee's
solution. The legislature would be divided into two houses. In the House of
Representatives, the number of a state's representatives would depend on
its population. In the Senate, each state would have equal representation.
Voters in each state would elect the members of the House of Representatives,
but the state legislatures would choose the senators. This proposal came to
be known as the Connecticut Compromise, or the Great Compromise.

The Connecticut Compromise sparked a fresh controversy: whether to
count enslaved people when determining how many representatives each

The Granger Collection, NYC – All rights reserved.

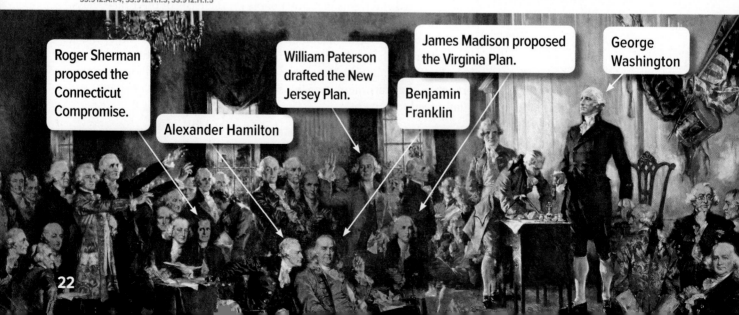

Roger Sherman
proposed the
Connecticut
Compromise.

Alexander Hamilton

William Paterson
drafted the New
Jersey Plan.

Benjamin
Franklin

James Madison proposed
the Virginia Plan.

George
Washington

state would have in the House of Representatives. Southern delegates wanted to count enslaved people. Northern delegates objected, pointing out that enslaved people could not vote. The Three-Fifths Compromise was an imperfect solution. Every five enslaved persons would count as three free persons for determining both representation and taxation. In another compromise, the delegates dealt with the power of Congress to regulate trade, agreeing that the new Congress could not tax exports. They also agreed that it could not ban the slave trade until 1808. This would not be the last time the North and the South debated the presence of slavery.

Framework of Government

Next, the delegates focused on the details of the new government. The government was based on the principle of popular sovereignty, or rule by the people. It created a representative system of government in which elected officials speak for the people they represented. To strengthen the central government but still preserve the rights of the states, the Constitution describes a system known as federalism. Under federalism, power is divided between the national and state governments.

The Constitution also provides for a **separation of powers** by dividing power between three branches of government: the legislative branch, which makes laws; the executive branch, which implements and enforces the laws, among other duties; and the judicial branch, which interprets federal laws and renders judgment in cases involving those laws. A system of checks and balances prevents any one of the three branches from becoming too powerful. Each branch has some ability to limit the power of the other two.

The success of the Constitutional Convention in creating a government that reflected many viewpoints was, in Washington's words, "little short of a miracle." John Adams declared that the convention was "the greatest single effort of national deliberation that the world has ever seen."

Ratification and the Bill of Rights

On September 28, 1787, Congress voted to submit the Constitution to the states. Each state would hold a convention to ratify, or approve, it. Nine states had to vote to approve the Constitution for it to go into effect. As soon as Americans learned about the new Constitution, they began to argue over whether it should be ratified. The debate took place in state legislatures, in mass meetings, in the columns of newspapers, and in everyday conversations.

Supporters of the Constitution called themselves Federalists. They emphasized that the Constitution would create a federal system, with power divided between a central government and state governments. They hoped the name would remind Americans who feared a central government that the states would retain many of their powers.

Opponents to the Constitution were called Anti-Federalists, a somewhat misleading name, as they were not truly against federalism. They accepted the need for a national government. The real issue, as far as they were concerned, was whether the national government or the state governments would be supreme.

The Federalists' arguments for ratification were summarized in *The Federalist*—a collection of 85 essays written by James Madison, Alexander Hamilton, and John Jay. The three men published most of the essays in New York newspapers in late 1787 and early 1788. To this day, *The Federalist* remains a valuable resource for understanding how the Constitution was supposed to work and what the Framers wanted to achieve.

The Federalists knew, however, that the most important votes still lay ahead. The large states of Massachusetts, Virginia, and New York might vote either way. In Massachusetts, opponents of the Constitution included

Library of Congress, Prints & Photographs Division [LC-USZC4-4097]

BIOGRAPHY

James Madison (1751–1836)

Although many individuals contributed to the framing of the U.S. Constitution, James Madison proposed the Virginia Plan, which defined a separation of powers between the legislative, executive, and judicial branches. He was a leader in the First United States Congress and was responsible for the first 10 amendments of the Constitution, known as the Bill of Rights. In 1808, he was elected the fourth president of the United States.

▶ **CRITICAL THINKING**
Drawing Conclusions Why do you think it is important to have a separation of powers?
LAFS.1112.RH.2.4, LAFS.1112.RH.3.7

separation of powers
government principle in which power is divided among different branches

Jefferson believed that an economy based on agriculture and widespread land ownership would cultivate an independent and virtuous citizenry.

▶ CRITICAL THINKING

Identifying Central Ideas How did the Federalists and the Republicans differ in their views of the strength of the United States?

Massachusetts Governor John Hancock and Samuel Adams. Adams refused to support the new constitution unless Federalists gave him a guarantee "that the said Constitution be never construed to authorize Congress to infringe the just liberty of the press, or the rights of conscience; or to prevent the people of the United States . . . from keeping their own arms; . . . or to subject the people to unreasonable searches and seizures of their persons, papers or possessions."

The Federalists moved quickly to meet these objections. They promised to attach a bill of rights to the Constitution once it was ratified. They also agreed to support an amendment that would reserve for the states all powers not given to the federal government. In the end, the promise to add a bill of rights won the vote for ratification in both Massachusetts and Virginia. In New York, Alexander Hamilton and John Jay worked hard to build support. When it became clear the Constitution would go into effect, New York voted by a narrow margin to ratify it as well. Elections for Congress and the new office of president were held in 1788, and the new United States Senate and House of Representatives met for the very first time in March 1789. George Washington was elected the first president under the new Constitution.

With the new government in effect, one of the very first tasks of the new Congress was to pass the Bill of Rights as promised. James Madison, one of the leaders in Congress, made the Bill of Rights a top priority. He hoped it would demonstrate the good faith of federal leaders and build support for the new government.

In drafting the Bill of Rights, Madison relied heavily on the Virginia Declaration of Rights issued in 1776 and the Virginia Statute for Religious Freedom that Thomas Jefferson had written in 1786. In late September 1789, Congress agreed on 12 constitutional amendments. They were then sent to the states for ratification, but only 10 were approved. These 10 went into effect and are generally referred to as the Bill of Rights. The first eight protect the rights of individuals against actions of the federal government. The last two set limits on the powers of the new national government. The Ninth Amendment states that the people have other rights not listed. The Tenth Amendment states that any powers not specifically given to the federal government are reserved for the states.

✓ READING PROGRESS CHECK

Explaining Why did the Anti-Federalists oppose the ratification of the Constitution?

The Rise of Political Parties

GUIDING QUESTION *Why did political parties emerge in the new republic, and what were the consequences?*

George Washington served as the first president under the new Constitution. Congress created three executive departments and organized the judicial branch. Washington appointed the heads of the executive departments, including Thomas Jefferson as secretary of state and Alexander Hamilton as secretary of the treasury.

Jefferson and Hamilton

One of the new government's most pressing concerns involved the national debt. Hamilton proposed a plan to pay off the debt and to create a national bank to manage the country's finances. Jefferson, James Madison, and others

Library of Congress, Prints & Photographs Division [LC-DIG-pga-03624]

opposed the plan, arguing that Congress could not establish a bank because it was not among the federal government's **enumerated powers** specifically listed in the Constitution. Hamilton disagreed, stating that the bank was among the **implied powers**—not explicitly listed in the Constitution but necessary for the government to do its job. Hamilton eventually won approval for his program, and the Bank of the United States was established in 1791.

That same year, Congress enacted a tax on whiskey, to bring in much-needed **revenue.** The tax infuriated many. Some western Pennsylvania farmers resisted tax collectors and destroyed the whiskey stills of those who paid the tax. In August 1794, Washington sent nearly 13,000 troops to put down what was called the Whiskey Rebellion.

The debate over Hamilton's financial program divided Congress into rival political parties. The Federalists supported Hamilton's plans and a strong national government. The Democratic-Republicans, led by Jefferson and Madison, favored a limited federal government and more power for the states.

The Election of 1800

Washington's successor was fellow Federalist John Adams. A series of unpopular taxes and laws passed during his first term gave Adams a disadvantage in seeking reelection in 1800. The Democratic-Republican nominees were Jefferson for president and Aaron Burr for vice president.

Under the Constitution, each state chooses electors—the same number as it has representatives and senators. This group, the Electoral College, then votes for the president. In 1800, each elector was to vote for two people of their choice for president, even if one were nominated for vice president. When the votes were counted, the Federalist candidates had lost and Jefferson and Burr were tied at 73 votes each. Since neither had a majority, the House of Representatives had to choose a president and chose Jefferson.

☑ **READING PROGRESS CHECK**

Explaining Why did Jefferson and others oppose Hamilton's financial program?

enumerated powers
powers listed in the Constitution as belonging to the federal government

implied powers powers not specifically listed in the Constitution but claimed by the federal government

revenue the total income produced by a given source

GEOGRAPHY CONNECTION

The election of 1800 was a major turning point in American political history because it was the first transfer of power between political parties under the federal Constitution.

1 THE WORLD IN SPATIAL TERMS *Which states were split in their choice for president?*
SS.912.A.1.4

2 PLACES AND REGIONS *What region of the country primarily supported Jefferson?*
SS.912.A.1.4

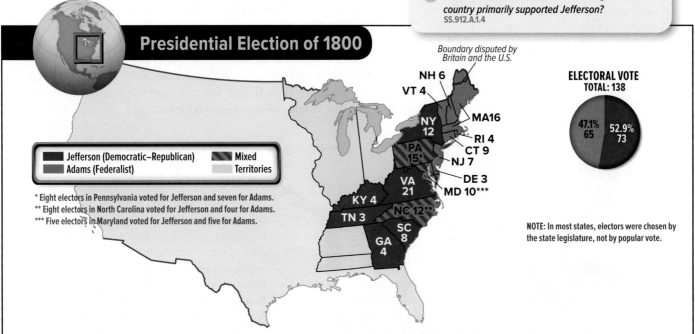

Presidential Election of 1800

Boundary disputed by Britain and the U.S.

- NH 6
- VT 4
- MA 16
- NY 12
- RI 4
- CT 9
- PA 15*
- NJ 7
- DE 3
- MD 10***
- VA 21
- KY 4
- NC 12**
- TN 3
- SC 8
- GA 4

■ Jefferson (Democratic–Republican) ▨ Mixed
■ Adams (Federalist) ☐ Territories

* Eight electors in Pennsylvania voted for Jefferson and seven for Adams.
** Eight electors in North Carolina voted for Jefferson and four for Adams.
*** Five electors in Maryland voted for Jefferson and five for Adams.

ELECTORAL VOTE
TOTAL: 138

47.1% 65
52.9% 73

NOTE: In most states, electors were chosen by the state legislature, not by popular vote.

William Marbury based his request for a court order on the Judiciary Act of 1789, which said that requests for federal court orders go directly to the Supreme Court. In the 1803 case *Marbury* v. *Madison*, the Supreme Court decided that part of the Judiciary Act was unconstitutional and thus invalid. The Constitution specifies which cases can go directly to the Supreme Court, and court orders are not mentioned. In the Court's opinion, Marshall wrote: "So if a law be in opposition to the constitution; if both the law and the constitution apply to a particular case . . . the court must determine which of these conflicting rules governs the case. This is of the very essence of judicial duty."

▶ CRITICAL THINKING
Drawing Conclusions What principle did the ruling in *Marbury* v. *Madison* establish? SS.912.A.1.6

With the help of their Native American guide and interpreter, Sacagawea, Meriwether Lewis and William Clark explored the territory acquired by the Louisiana Purchase.

▶ CRITICAL THINKING
Predicting Consequences Why was the Louisiana Purchase a significant event for the young United States? LAFS.1112.RH.3.7

The Nineteenth Century Begins

GUIDING QUESTION *How did the United States assert itself as an independent nation?*

President Jefferson attempted to limit federal powers and helped expand the size of the country. Later, the United States faced war with Britain.

Jefferson in Office

Thomas Jefferson took office committed to limiting government. He began paying off federal debt, cut government spending, eliminated the hated whiskey tax, and planned to rely on local militia instead of a standing army.

Weakening the Federalists' control of the judiciary was another aim of the new administration. On his last day in office, President Adams had appointed dozens of new Federalist judges and court officers. Jefferson asked the incoming Democratic-Republican Congress to abolish some of the new positions and to withhold the paperwork confirming other appointments. One of those who did not receive his documents, William Marbury, took the matter to the Supreme Court. The Court sympathized with Marbury but ruled in 1803 that it could not issue an enforcement order. According to Chief Justice John Marshall and his colleagues, the law that authorized the Court to write such orders actually was unconstitutional and invalid. The decision established the Court's power of judicial review—the power to declare laws unconstitutional and invalid.

Westward Expansion

Under Jefferson, the size of the country increased considerably. The Treaty of Paris of 1783 had already established the Mississippi River as the nation's western border. After the defeat of Native Americans in the Northwest Territory and the Treaty of Greenville in 1795, more settlers poured into the region. During Washington's term, Kentucky and Tennessee had become states, and Ohio followed in 1803.

In 1800, Spain had given Louisiana back to France. To finance his plans for European conquest, the French leader, Napoleon Bonaparte, now offered to sell all of the Louisiana Territory, as well as New Orleans, to the United States. Congress overwhelmingly approved the Louisiana Purchase on April 30, 1803. The United States paid $11.25 million and also agreed to take on French debts of about $3.75 million owed to U.S. citizens. With the purchase, the nation had more than doubled its size.

Even before Louisiana became part of the United States, Jefferson had asked Congress to fund a secret expedition into the Louisiana Territory. After receiving approval from Congress, Jefferson chose Meriwether Lewis and William Clark to lead the expedition. During their explorations, they found a path through the Rocky Mountains and eventually reached the Pacific Ocean.

The War of 1812

In 1809, James Madison succeeded Jefferson as president and a foreign-relations crisis loomed. The British regularly seized American ships at sea and often practiced impressment, a legalized form of kidnapping that forced people into military service. Britain claimed the right to stop American ships to search for British deserters. On several occasions they

The Granger Collection, New York

impressed American citizens into service as well. Americans in the West also blamed Britain for encouraging attacks by Native Americans along the frontier. President Jefferson had tried economic sanctions against Britain with the Embargo Act of 1807, but the actions mostly hurt the American economy.

Like Jefferson, President Madison first responded with economic measures. After several attempts, the measures finally began to have the desired effect. Unfortunately, word of British cooperation came too late—Congress had already declared war against Britain.

At the beginning of the War of 1812, conquering Canada was the primary objective of the United States. U.S. forces were victorious on Lake Erie and Lake Champlain. The British, however, easily entered Washington, D.C. They dispersed the poorly trained militia defending the capital and set fire to the White House and the Capitol. In Baltimore, however, the city militia inflicted heavy casualties on the British. British forces bombarded Fort McHenry throughout the night of September 13, 1814, and then abandoned their attack. The sight of the U.S. flag still flying over the fort at dawn inspired Francis Scott Key to write "The Star-Spangled Banner," which became the national anthem.

As battles raged, peace talks began in the Belgian city of Ghent. The Treaty of Ghent, signed on December 24, 1814, ended the war and restored prewar boundaries but did not mention impressment. At about the same time, British and U.S. forces faced each other in New Orleans. Unaware that a treaty had been signed, U.S. general Andrew Jackson led his troops to a decisive victory over the British in the Battle of New Orleans in January 1815. Jackson became a national hero.

The War of 1812 increased the prestige of the United States overseas and generated a new spirit of patriotism and national unity. The American victory also weakened the Federalist Party, which had strongly opposed war with Britain.

This engraving depicts the triumph of Andrew Jackson (on horseback at right) over the British at the Battle of New Orleans.

▶ **CRITICAL THINKING**
Drawing Conclusions How could the victory in the Battle of New Orleans have helped Jackson's political ambitions? LAFS.1112.RH.3.7, SS.912.A.1.4

 READING PROGRESS CHECK

Identifying What actions by Britain caused the United States to impose economic sanctions against them?

Anne S.K. Brown, Brown Military Collection/Brown University Library

---

LESSON 2 REVIEW

Reviewing Vocabulary
1. ***Explaining*** Explain the difference between enumerated powers and implied powers. LAFS.1112.RH.2.4

Using Your Notes
2. ***Comparing and Contrasting*** Use the notes you completed during the lesson to compare and contrast the Articles of Confederation and the Constitution. LAFS.1112.RH.3.7

Answering the Guiding Questions
3. ***Identifying*** How did the constitutions created during the Revolutionary War attempt to limit the power of government and protect the rights of citizens?

4. ***Describing*** What are the key compromises and provisions incorporated in the U.S. Constitution?

5. ***Explaining*** Why did political parties emerge in the new republic, and what were the consequences?

6. ***Identifying*** How did the United States assert itself as an independent nation?

Writing Activity
7. **NARRATIVE** Suppose you are a delegate at the Constitutional Convention. Write a journal entry describing the arguments from each side of the debate that led to the Connecticut Compromise. LAFS.1112.WHST.1.2, LAFS.1112.WHST.4.10

The
CONSTITUTION
HANDBOOK

READING HELPDESK

Academic Vocabulary

- grant
- responsive

Content Vocabulary

- popular sovereignty
- federalism
- enumerated powers
- reserved powers
- concurrent powers
- impeach
- bill
- cabinet
- judicial review
- due process

TAKING NOTES

Key Ideas and Details

Outlining As you read about the Constitution, use the major headings of the handbook to fill in an outline like the one below. LAFS.1112.RH.3.7

I. Major Principles
  A.
  B.
  C.
  D.
  E.
  F.

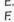
NEXT GENERATION SUNSHINE STATE STANDARDS

ELD.K12.ELL.SI.1: English language learners communicate for social and instructional purposes within the school setting.

Continued on page 30

IT MATTERS BECAUSE

The Constitution is the most important document of the United States. It serves as the framework of national government and the source of American citizens' basic rights. To preserve self-government, all citizens need to understand their rights and responsibilities.

Major Principles

GUIDING QUESTION *How does the Constitution lay the framework for individual rights and a balanced representative government?*

The principles outlined in the Constitution were the Framers' solution to the complex problems of a representative government. The Constitution rests on seven major principles of government: (1) **popular sovereignty,** (2) republicanism, (3) limited government, (4) **federalism,** (5) separation of powers, (6) checks and balances, and (7) individual rights.

Popular Sovereignty and Republicanism

The opening words of the Constitution, "We the people," reinforce the idea of popular sovereignty, or "authority of the people." In the Constitution, the people consent to be governed and specify the powers and rules by which they shall be governed.

The Articles of Confederation's government had few powers, and it was unable to cope with the many challenges facing the nation. The new federal government had greater powers, but it also had specific limitations. A system of interlocking responsibilities kept any one branch of government from becoming too powerful.

Voters are sovereign; that is, they have ultimate authority in a republican system. They elect representatives and give them the responsibility to make laws and run the government. For most Americans today, the terms *republic* and *representative democracy* mean the same thing: a system of limited government in which the people are the final source of authority.

©John Aikins/Corbis

28

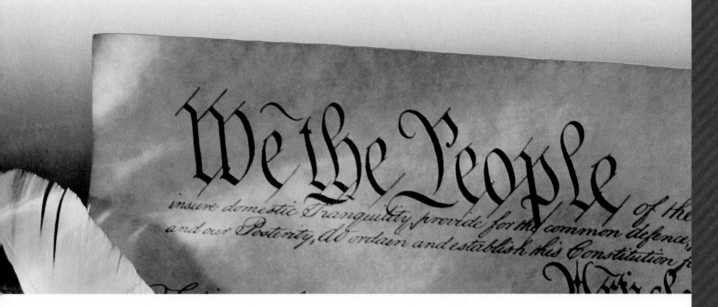

Comstock/PunchStock

A replica of the U.S. Constitution

▶ **CRITICAL THINKING**
Drawing Conclusions Why do you think the first three words of the Constitution were written in such a large size? LAFS.1112.RH.2.5, SS.912.A.1.4

popular sovereignty
authority of the people

federalism political system in which power is divided between the national and state governments

Limited Government

Although the Framers agreed that the nation needed a stronger central authority, they feared misuse of power. They wanted to prevent the government from using its power to give one group special advantages or to deprive another group of its rights. By creating a limited government, they restricted the government's authority to specific powers **granted** by the people.

The delegates to the Constitutional Convention were very specific about the powers granted to the new government. Their decision to provide a written outline of the government's structure also served to show what they intended. Articles I, II and III of the Constitution describe the powers of the federal government and the limits on those powers. Other limits are set forth in the Bill of Rights, which guarantees certain rights to the people.

Federalism

In establishing a strong central government, the Framers did not deprive states of all authority. The states gave up some powers to the national government but retained others. This principle of shared power is called federalism. The federal system allows the people of each state to deal with their needs in their own way, but at the same time it lets the states act together to deal with matters that affect all Americans.

grant to award or give as law

enumerated powers
powers listed in the Constitution as belonging to the federal government

The Constitution defines three types of government powers. Certain powers belong only to the federal government. These **enumerated powers** include the power to coin money, regulate interstate and foreign trade, maintain the armed forces, and create federal courts (Article I, Section 8).

The second kind of powers are those retained by the states, known as **reserved powers,** including the power to establish schools, set marriage and divorce laws, and regulate trade within the state. Although reserved powers are not specifically listed in the Constitution, the Tenth Amendment says that all powers not granted to the federal government "are reserved to the States."

reserved powers powers retained by the states

The third set of powers defined by the Constitution is **concurrent powers**—powers the state and federal governments share. They include the right to raise taxes, borrow money, provide for public welfare, and administer criminal justice. Conflicts between state law and federal law must be settled in a federal court. The Constitution declares that it is "the supreme Law of the Land."

concurrent powers powers shared by the state and federal governments

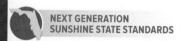
Continued from page 28

ELD.K12.ELL.SS.1: English language learners communicate information, ideas and concepts necessary for academic success in the content area of Social Studies.

LAFS.1112.RH.2.4: Determine the meaning of words and phrases as they are used in a text, including analyzing how an author uses and refines the meaning of a key term over the course of a text (e.g., how Madison defines faction in Federalist No. 10).

LAFS.1112.RH.2.5: Analyze in detail how a complex primary source is structured, including how key sentences, paragraphs, and larger portions of the text contribute to the whole.

Continued on page 31

CHARTS/GRAPHS

The Framers deliberately created a system of checks and balances to limit the power of each branch of government.

▶ **CRITICAL THINKING**

1 *Analyzing Information* How can the president help control the judiciary? **SS.912.A.1.4**

2 *Drawing Conclusions* Why is it important that the legislative branch can override a presidential veto? **SS.912.A.1.4**

Separation of Powers

To prevent any single group or institution in government from gaining too much authority, the Framers divided the federal government into three branches: legislative, executive, and judicial. Each branch has its own functions and powers. The legislative branch, Congress, makes the laws. The executive branch, headed by the president, carries out the laws. The judicial branch, consisting of the Supreme Court and other federal courts, interprets and applies the laws.

In addition to giving separate responsibility to separate branches, the membership of each branch is chosen in different ways. The president nominates federal judges, and the Senate confirms the appointments. People vote for members of Congress. Voters cast ballots for president, but the method of election is indirect. On Election Day, the votes in each state are counted. The candidate who receives the majority receives that state's electoral votes, which total the number of senators and representatives the state has in Congress. Electors from all states meet to formally elect a president. A candidate must win a majority of votes in the Electoral College to win.

Checks and Balances

The Framers who wrote the Constitution deliberately created a system of checks and balances in which each branch of government can check, or limit, the power of the other branches. This system helps balance the power of the three branches and prevents any one branch from becoming too powerful. For example, imagine that Congress passes a law. The president can reject the law by vetoing it. Congress, however, can override, or reverse, the president's veto if two-thirds of the members of both the Senate and the House of Representatives vote again to approve the law.

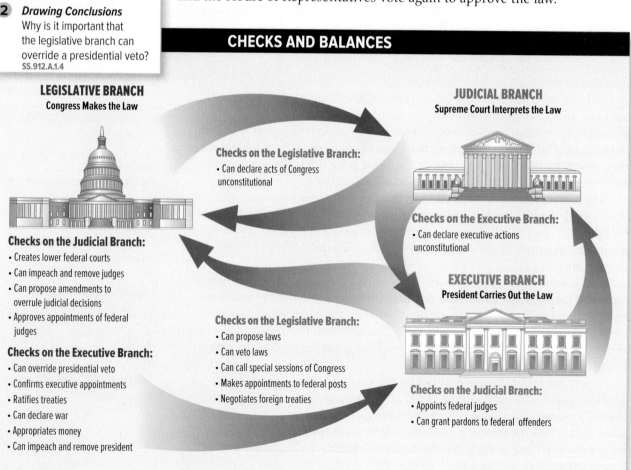

CHECKS AND BALANCES

LEGISLATIVE BRANCH
Congress Makes the Law

JUDICIAL BRANCH
Supreme Court Interprets the Law

Checks on the Legislative Branch:
• Can declare acts of Congress unconstitutional

Checks on the Executive Branch:
• Can declare executive actions unconstitutional

EXECUTIVE BRANCH
President Carries Out the Law

Checks on the Judicial Branch:
• Creates lower federal courts
• Can impeach and remove judges
• Can propose amendments to overrule judicial decisions
• Approves appointments of federal judges

Checks on the Executive Branch:
• Can override presidential veto
• Confirms executive appointments
• Ratifies treaties
• Can declare war
• Appropriates money
• Can impeach and remove president

Checks on the Legislative Branch:
• Can propose laws
• Can veto laws
• Can call special sessions of Congress
• Makes appointments to federal posts
• Negotiates foreign treaties

Checks on the Judicial Branch:
• Appoints federal judges
• Can grant pardons to federal offenders

Individual Rights

In 1791, the states ratified 10 amendments to the Constitution to protect certain basic rights, including freedom of speech, religion, and the right to a trial by jury. Congress approved these 10 amendments and referred to them as the Bill of Rights. Over the years, 17 more amendments have been added to the Constitution. Some give additional rights to American citizens and some modify how the government works. Included among them are amendments that abolish slavery, guarantee voting rights, authorize an income tax, and set a two-term limit on the presidency.

✓ READING PROGRESS CHECK

Explaining Describe some of the principles outlined in the Constitution that help ensure individual rights and a balanced representative government.

The Legislative Branch

GUIDING QUESTION *How is the legislative branch organized, and what are its functions?*

The legislative branch includes the two houses of Congress: the Senate and the House of Representatives. Congress has two primary roles: to make the nation's laws and to decide how to spend federal funds.

The government cannot spend any money unless Congress appropriates, or sets aside, funds. All tax and spending bills must originate in the House of Representatives and be approved in both the House and the Senate before moving to the president to be signed.

Congress also monitors the executive branch and investigates possible abuses of power. The House of Representatives can **impeach,** or bring formal charges against, any federal official it suspects of wrongdoing or misconduct. If an official is impeached, the Senate acts as a court and tries the accused official. Officials who are found guilty may be removed from office.

The Senate has certain additional powers. Two-thirds of the Senate must ratify treaties made by the president. The Senate must also confirm presidential appointments of federal officials such as department heads, ambassadors, and federal judges.

All members of Congress have the responsibility to represent their constituents, the people of their home states and districts. As a constituent, you can expect your senators and representative to promote national and state interests. Congress members introduce thousands of **bills**—proposed laws—every year. Because individual members of Congress cannot possibly study all these bills carefully, both houses form committees of selected members to evaluate proposed legislation.

Standing committees are permanent committees in both the House and the Senate that specialize in a particular topic, such as agriculture, commerce, or veterans' affairs. These committees are usually divided into subcommittees that focus on a particular aspect of an issue. The House and the Senate also form temporary select committees to deal with issues requiring special attention. These committees meet only until they complete their task.

Occasionally the House and the Senate form joint committees with members from both houses. These committees meet to consider specific issues. One type

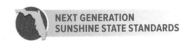

NEXT GENERATION SUNSHINE STATE STANDARDS

Continued from page 30

LAFS.1112.RH.3.7: Integrate and evaluate multiple sources of information presented in diverse formats and media (e.g., visually, quantitatively, as well as in words) in order to address a question or solve a problem.

LAFS.1112.WHST.1.1: Write arguments focused on discipline-specific content.

LAFS.1112.WHST.4.10: Write routinely over extended time frames (time for reflection and revision) and shorter time frames (a single sitting or a day or two) for a range of discipline-specific tasks, purposes, and audiences.

SS.912.A.1.4: Analyze how images, symbols, objects, cartoons, graphs, charts, maps, and artwork may be used to interpret the significance of time periods and events from the past.

impeach to bring formal charges against a federal official

bill a proposed law

In 2010, John Boehner of Ohio became the 61st Speaker of the House. All members of Congress have the responsibility to represent their constituents.

▶ **CRITICAL THINKING**

Identifying Central Ideas Why is it important that members of Congress represent their constituents? LAFS.1112.RH.3.7

Mark Wilson/Getty Images News/Getty Images

1. A legislator introduces a bill in the House or Senate, where it is referred to a committee for review.

 2. After review, the committee decides whether to shelve it or to send it back to the House or Senate with or without revisions.

 3. The House or Senate then debates the bill, making revisions if desired. If the bill is passed, it is sent to the other house.

 4. If the House and Senate pass different versions of the bill, the houses must meet in a conference committee to decide on a compromise version.

 5. The compromise bill is then sent to both houses.

 6. If both houses pass the bill, it is sent to the president to sign.

 7. If the president signs the bill, it becomes law.

 8. The president may veto the bill, but if two-thirds of the House and Senate vote to approve it, it becomes law without the president's approval.

CHARTS/GRAPHS

The legislative process is complex. It begins when a member of Congress introduces a bill. That bill then works its way to the president who either signs the bill into law or vetoes it.

▶ **CRITICAL THINKING**

1 *Analyzing Information*
What is the role of a conference committee? SS.912.A.1.4

2 *Identifying Central Issues*
How can a bill become law without the approval of the president? SS.912.A.1.4

of joint committee, a conference committee, has a special function. If the House and the Senate pass different versions of the same bill, a conference committee meets to work out a compromise bill acceptable to both houses.

Once a committee in either house of Congress approves a bill, it is sent to the full Senate or House for debate. After debate the bill may be passed, rejected, or returned to the committee for further changes. When both houses pass a bill, it goes to the president. If the president approves the bill and signs it, the bill becomes law. If the president vetoes the bill, it does not become law unless Congress takes it up again and votes to override the veto.

☑ READING PROGRESS CHECK

Describing Describe the organization and functions of the legislative branch.

The Executive Branch

GUIDING QUESTION *How does the president carry out laws that Congress passes?*

The executive branch of government includes the president, the vice president, and various executive offices, departments, and agencies. The executive branch executes, or carries out, the laws that Congress passes.

The President's Roles

The president plays a number of different roles in government. These roles include serving as the nation's chief executive, chief diplomat, commander in chief of the military, chief of state, and legislative leader.

Chief Executive As chief executive, the president is responsible for carrying out the nation's laws.

Chief Diplomat As chief diplomat, the president directs foreign policy, appoints ambassadors, and negotiates treaties with other nations.

Commander in Chief As commander in chief of the armed forces, the president can give orders to the military and direct its operations. The president cannot declare war; only Congress holds this power. The president can send troops to other parts of the world for up to 60 days but must notify Congress when doing so. The troops may remain longer only if Congress gives its approval or declares war.

Chief of State As chief of state, the president is symbolically the representative of all Americans. The president fulfills this role when receiving foreign ambassadors or heads of state, visiting foreign nations, or honoring Americans.

Legislative Leader The president serves as a legislative leader by proposing laws to Congress and working to see that they are passed. In the annual State of the Union address to the American people, the president presents his goals for legislation in the upcoming year.

The Executive at Work

Many executive offices, departments, and independent agencies help the president carry out and enforce the nation's laws. The Executive Office of the President (EOP) is made up of individuals and agencies that directly assist the president. Presidents rely on the EOP for advice and for gathering information needed for decision making.

The executive branch has 15 executive departments, each responsible for a different area of government. For example, the Department of State carries out foreign policy, and the Department of the Treasury manages the nation's finances. The department heads have the title of secretary, and are members of the president's **cabinet.** The cabinet helps the president set policies and make decisions.

The Qualities of an Effective Leader

The multiple roles imposed on the president makes his ability to lead the nation very challenging. Throughout American history various presidents have been both praised and criticized for their leadership. Being an effective leader in a federal constitutional republic requires a number of important qualities.

As chief of state and chief diplomat, the president represents the nation to the American people and to the world. To be effective, a president must demonstrate principles and conviction, yet be optimistic and friendly, open to others, and able to communicate clearly and effectively. Great leaders can inspire their people to greatness with their words, their confidence, and their determination.

President Barack Obama signs a bill into law. As chief executive, the president is responsible for carrying out the laws of the nation.

▶ CRITICAL THINKING

Making Generalizations Why is it important that the president carries out the laws of the nation?
LAFS.1112.RH.3.7, SS.912.A.1.4

cabinet a group of advisers to the president

Alex Wong/Getty Images News/Getty Images

As a legislative leader, the president must be able to compromise, to understand different points of view, and to work with many different personalities in Congress, while at the same time understanding clearly what principles and goals should be upheld. A president that bows to political pressures too often will be seen as weak or vacillating, but a president who refuses to negotiate and compromise with Congress will be seen as stubborn, aloof, or ineffective.

As commander-in-chief, the president has to be decisive and willing to make difficult decisions. At the same time, presidents must be willing to listen to advice and the expertise of those serving under them. The president is the final decision maker when the nation is at war, and his or her decisions can impact the lives of hundreds of millions of people. A president who refuses to act when necessary will be seen as timid and indecisive, which can embolden the nation's enemies. But if the president moves too quickly, it will be seen as reckless or dangerous.

As the head of an enormous and complex bureaucracy, the president must resist the temptation to go into too much detail on every little issue. There is not enough time to do so. Instead, an effective chief executive must have the ability to choose good people who can be trusted to implement the president's goals within the executive departments. The president must support the team he or she has chosen and be loyal to them. An effective president will set high expectations, clear goals, and will lead by example. At the same time, presidents have to hold their people and themselves accountable for any failures, and be willing to learn from mistakes.

As the chief executive responsible for carrying out the nation's laws and upholding the Constitution, the president, above all, needs integrity.

CHARTS/GRAPHS

The judicial branch consists of a system of federal courts that reviews and evaluates laws and interprets the Constitution.

1. **Analyzing Information** How many routes to the U.S. Supreme Court are shown in the chart? SS.912.A.1.4

2. **Drawing Conclusions** Why might the Supreme Court review only decisions made by a small number of lower courts? LAFS.1112.RH.3.7, SS.912.A.1.4

THE FEDERAL COURT SYSTEM

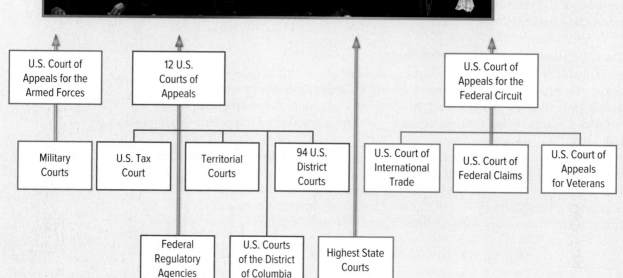

U.S. Supreme Court

Front row, left to right, Justices Clarence Thomas, Antonin Scalia, Chief Justice John Roberts, Anthony Kennedy, and Ruth Bader Ginsburg; back row, left to right, Justices Sonia Sotomayor, Stephen Breyer, Samuel Alito, Elena Kagan

Chip Somodevilla/Getty Images News/Getty Images

U.S. Court of Appeals for the Armed Forces

12 U.S. Courts of Appeals

U.S. Court of Appeals for the Federal Circuit

Military Courts

U.S. Tax Court

Territorial Courts

94 U.S. District Courts

U.S. Court of International Trade

U.S. Court of Federal Claims

U.S. Court of Appeals for Veterans

Federal Regulatory Agencies

U.S. Courts of the District of Columbia

Highest State Courts

Presidents have to implement laws they disagree with; they cannot allow personal feelings to interfere with their decisions or distort their judgment. They cannot give in to corruption and use their office for personal gain. Nor should they make decisions purely on the basis of what will get them re-elected. The president, as the leader of a democratic republic, should listen to the people. But presidents must also reconcile competing demands and goals, and lead the nation in a way that upholds the Constitution and the nation's founding ideals and principles.

✓ READING PROGRESS CHECK

Explaining What functions does the president fulfill as Legislative Leader?

The Judicial Branch

GUIDING QUESTION *How does the judicial branch function to review and evaluate laws and interpret the Constitution?*

Article III of the Constitution calls for the creation of a Supreme Court and "such inferior [lower] courts as Congress may from time to time ordain and establish." The federal courts of the judicial branch review and evaluate laws and interpret the Constitution in making their decisions.

District and Appellate Courts

United States district courts are the lowest level of the federal court system. These courts consider criminal and civil cases that come under federal authority, such as kidnapping, federal tax evasion, claims against the federal government, and cases involving constitutional rights, such as free speech. There are 94 district courts, with at least one in every state.

The appellate courts, or courts of appeal, consider district court decisions in which the losing side has asked for a review of the verdict. If an appeals court disagrees with the lower court's decision, it can overturn the verdict or order a retrial. There are 14 appeals courts: one for each of 12 federal districts, one military appeals court, and an appellate court for the federal circuit.

The Supreme Court

The Supreme Court is the final authority in the federal court system. It consists of a chief justice and eight associate justices. Most of the Court's cases come from appeals of lower court decisions. Only cases involving foreign diplomats or disputes between states can begin in the Supreme Court.

Supreme Court Independence The president appoints the Court's justices for life, and the Senate confirms the appointments. The public has no input. The Framers hoped that by appointing judges, they would be free to evaluate the law with no concern for pleasing voters.

Judicial Review The role of the judicial branch is not described in detail in the Constitution, but the role of the courts has grown as powers implied in the Constitution have been put into practice. In 1803, Chief Justice John Marshall expanded the power of the Supreme Court by striking down an act of Congress in the case of *Marbury* v. *Madison*. Although not mentioned in the Constitution, judicial review has become a major power of the judicial branch. **Judicial review** gives the Supreme Court the ultimate authority to interpret the meaning of the Constitution.

✓ READING PROGRESS CHECK

Analyzing How does the judicial branch evaluate laws and interpret the Constitution?

Jim West/Alamy

Connections to TODAY

Sonia Sotomayor

The daughter of parents who moved from Puerto Rico to New York, Sonia Sotomayor became the first Latino justice of the U.S. Supreme Court. Nominated by President Barack Obama to replace departing Justice David Souter, Sotomayor was confirmed by the Senate in August 2009. She became just the third woman to serve on the Supreme Court.

judicial review the process by which the Supreme Court has the final authority to interpret the Constitution

The First Amendment of the Constitution guarantees basic freedoms, such as the freedom of assembly.

▶ CRITICAL THINKING

Making Inferences Why do you think basic freedoms are just as important today as they were when the Framers wrote the Constitution? LAFS.1112.RH.3.7, SS.912.A.1.4

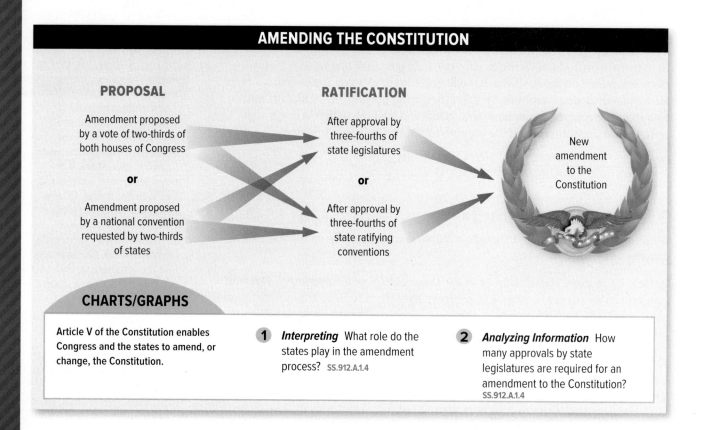

AMENDING THE CONSTITUTION

PROPOSAL

Amendment proposed by a vote of two-thirds of both houses of Congress

or

Amendment proposed by a national convention requested by two-thirds of states

RATIFICATION

After approval by three-fourths of state legislatures

or

After approval by three-fourths of state ratifying conventions

New amendment to the Constitution

CHARTS/GRAPHS

Article V of the Constitution enables Congress and the states to amend, or change, the Constitution.

1 *Interpreting* What role do the states play in the amendment process? SS.912.A.1.4

2 *Analyzing Information* How many approvals by state legislatures are required for an amendment to the Constitution? SS.912.A.1.4

SKILLS PRACTICE

Before you read the text selection about the rights and responsibilities of citizens, make a graphic organizer with three columns. In the first column, record what you know about your rights and responsibilities as a citizen. In the second, write what you would like to learn. Use the third column to record what you learn as you read.
ELD.K12.ELL.SI.1, ELD.K12.ELL.SS.1, SS.912.A.1.4

due process the following of procedures established by law

Rights and Responsibilities

GUIDING QUESTION *What are the protections and freedoms the Constitution and the Bill of Rights provide Americans?*

All citizens of the United States have certain basic rights, but they also have specific responsibilities. Living in a system of self-government means ultimately that every citizen is partly responsible for how society is governed and for the actions the government takes on his or her behalf.

The Rights of Americans

The rights of Americans fall into three broad categories: to be protected from unfair actions of the government, to receive equal treatment under the law, and to retain certain basic freedoms.

Protection From Unfair Actions Parts of the Constitution and the Bill of Rights protect all Americans from unfair treatment by the government or the law. Among these rights are the right to a lawyer when accused of a crime and the right to a trial by jury when charged with a crime. In addition, the Fourth Amendment protects us from unreasonable searches and seizures. This provision requires police to have a court order before searching a person's home for criminal evidence. To obtain this, the police must have a very strong reason to suspect someone of a crime.

Equal Treatment All Americans, regardless of race, religion, or political beliefs, have the right to be treated the same under the law. The Fifth Amendment states that no person shall "be deprived of life, liberty, or property, without due process of law." **Due process** means that the government must follow procedures established by law and guaranteed by the Constitution, treating all people equally. The Fourteenth Amendment requires every state to grant its citizens "equal protection of the laws."

Basic Freedoms The First Amendment describes our basic freedoms—freedom of speech, freedom of religion, freedom of the press, freedom of assembly, and the right to petition. In a democracy, power rests in the hands of the people. Therefore, citizens in a democratic society must be able to exchange ideas freely. The First Amendment allows citizens to criticize the government, in speech or in the press, without fear of punishment.

In addition, the Ninth Amendment states that the rights of Americans are not limited to those in the Constitution. Over the years, this has allowed Americans to assert other basic rights that have been upheld in court or assured by amending the Constitution.

Limits on Rights The rights of Americans are not absolute. They are limited based on the principle of respecting everyone's rights equally. For example, many cities and towns require groups to obtain a permit to march on city streets. Such laws do limit free speech, but they also protect the community by ensuring that the march will not endanger other people.

In this and other cases, the government balances an individual's rights, the rights of others, and the community's health and safety. Most Americans are willing to accept some limitations on their rights to gain these protections as long as the restrictions are reasonable and apply equally to all. A law banning all marches would violate the First Amendment rights of free speech and assembly and be unacceptable. Similarly, a law preventing only certain groups from marching would be unfair because it would not apply equally to everyone.

Citizens' Responsibilities

Citizens in a democratic society have both duties and responsibilities. Duties are actions required by law. Responsibilities are voluntary actions. Fulfilling duties and responsibilities ensures good government and protects rights.

Duties One basic duty of all Americans is to obey the law. Laws serve three important functions. They help maintain order; they protect the health, safety, and property of all citizens; and they make it possible for people to live together peacefully. If you believe a law is wrong, you can work through your representatives to change it.

Americans also have a duty to pay taxes. The government uses tax money to defend the nation, to build roads and bridges, and to assist people in need. Americans often benefit from services provided by the government. Another duty of citizens is to defend the nation. All males aged 18 and older must register with the government in case the nation needs to call on them for military service. Military service is not automatic, but a war could make it necessary.

The Constitution guarantees all Americans the right to a trial by a jury of their equals. For this reason, you may be called to jury duty when you reach the age of 18. Having a large group of jurors on hand is necessary to guarantee the right to a fair and speedy trial. You also have a duty to serve as a trial witness if called to do so.

Most states require you to attend school until a certain age. School is where you gain the knowledge and skills needed to be a good citizen.

Registration drives encourage others to exercise their responsibility to vote.

▶ **CRITICAL THINKING**

Making Inferences How might an increase in young voters make an impact on an election? LAFS.1112.RH.3.7

Haraz N. Ghanbari/AP Images

In school you learn to think more clearly, to express your opinions more accurately, and to analyze the ideas of others. These skills will help you make informed choices when you vote.

Responsibilities The responsibilities of citizens are not as clear-cut as their duties, but they are as important because they help maintain the quality of government and society. One important responsibility is to be well informed. Knowing what your government is doing and expressing your thoughts about its actions helps to keep it **responsive** to the wishes of the people. You also need to be informed about your rights and to assert them when necessary. Knowing your rights helps preserve them. Other responsibilities include accepting responsibility for your actions and supporting your family.

To enjoy your rights to the fullest, you must be prepared to respect the rights of others. Respecting the rights of others also means respecting the rights of people with whom you disagree. Respecting and accepting others regardless of race, religion, beliefs, or other differences is essential in a democracy.

Vote, Vote, Vote! Perhaps the most important civic responsibility of American citizens, beginning when they reach the age of 18, is to vote. Voting allows you to participate in the democratic process and to guide its direction. When you vote for people to represent you in government, you will be exercising your right of self-government. If you disapprove of the job your representatives are doing, it will be your responsibility to help elect other people in the next election.

In addition to voting, there are other ways you can participate in the democratic process. You can let your representatives know what you think about issues through email, letters, telephone calls, petitions, and by taking part in public meetings or political rallies. You can join a political party and help campaign for a candidate that you support. Political parties are always looking for volunteers to help. In addition, membership in a party will let you play a role in choosing who runs as candidates for election. And the time may come when you too may want to participate by running for office.

Participating in the democratic process reflects our patriotism. We live in a constitutional democratic republic. The national ethos—the beliefs and ideas Americans all share as a community—includes the belief that the best and most effective government is government of, for, and by the people. The only way to live up to those beliefs is to embrace them by participating in the democratic process.

The Constitution's preamble states that the goal of the people of the United States is "to form a more perfect union." Because the United States is a government of the people and a democratic republic, it becomes "more perfect" and moves closer to its goals when all of its people, in all of their variation and diversity, participate. If someone does not participate, the union does not have their input and is less likely to reflect a balance of all of the needs, concerns, and goals of the people. This make it harder to achieve justice, peace, security, liberty, or to promote the general welfare.

If we truly love the country then we want it to succeed, and if there are aspects to it that you do not like, the best way to change them is by getting involved in politics and working to bring about the changes you think are needed. Patriotism is not standing by while others act; patriots take action to help make their country better.

The United States is made up of a multitude of people. Many have come from all over the world, sometimes to escape violence or poverty or oppression, and sometimes seeking employment, education, and more opportunity. Whatever

responsive open and quick to take action

38

their reasons, each immigrant who becomes a citizen promises in their oath of allegiance that "I support and defend the Constitution and laws of the United States of America against all enemies, foreign and domestic; that I will bear true faith and allegiance to the same . . ." As citizens of a self-governing democratic republic, all American citizens share a common bond in that they stand for certain self-evident truths: "that all men are created equal, that they are endowed by their Creator with certain unalienable rights, that among these are life, liberty, and the pursuit of happiness."

☑ READING PROGRESS CHECK

Describing What are the rights and responsibilities of an American citizen?

Understanding Symbols and Mottos

GUIDING QUESTION *How do the symbols and mottos of the United States help to define American society?*

All nations make use of symbols. A symbol is something that stands for something else. It is a short-hand way of remembering all the qualities and ideas embodied in something. Nations use symbols to remind people what the nation represents. They are also a statement of sovereignty. When a nation's flag is flown over something, it symbolizes that something belongs to the nation. Similarly, when a national seal is put on a document, it is saying that the document is an official statement of the nation. Symbols remind people of their nation's history, values, and goals. They evoke patriotism and pride. Perhaps most importantly, they remind people that, despite their differences, they are all united in one national community.

The American Flag

The best known and most visible symbol of the United States is the flag, sometimes nicknamed the Stars and Stripes, the Star-Spangled Banner, the Red, White, and Blue, or Old Glory. The Continental Congress approved the design of the flag in June 1777. The 13 alternating stripes on the flag represent the original 13 colonies that founded the United States. Each star in the blue field represents one state.

The stars were a metaphor for the new nation. Stars in the night sky are grouped into constellations, or patterns. The stars on the flag represent that the United States is a new constellation, a new arrangement in the world. The colors used on the flag have been said to have at least two meanings. They are the same colors as used on the British flag, and so remind the United States of its origins as British colonies. They are also the same colors used on the Great Seal of the United States, which was designed before the flag and have specific meanings: red for strength and courage; white for purity and innocence; and blue for perseverance, vigilance, and justice.

E Pluribus Unum

On July 4, 1776, nearly a year before the Continental Congress decided on the design for a flag, it began work on the Great Seal of the United States. A seal is a type of signature. Most nations have an official symbol that they use to "seal," or sign, official documents and treaties with other nations. Seals date to the days when letters and documents would be signed and sealed by melting wax onto them and then pressing a symbol into the wax, "sealing" the envelope closed. They are also commonly put on coins and currency to show that the money has been officially issued by a particular country.

The Great Seal has two sides. On the one side is an eagle holding a banner with the Latin motto "E Pluribus Unum," which means "Out of

Many, One." This motto refers to the creation of a nation from 13 separate colonies. Today, it also is used to describe the United States as a country of many peoples from many different cultures, races, and backgrounds united into one nation. The motto was never made the official motto of the United States, but it has been used on American coins since the late 1700s.

On the same side of the seal, the eagle also clutches an olive branch with 13 leaves in one claw and 13 arrows in the other claw, symbolizing the nation's power in war and peace. The Eagle also carries a shield with red and white stripes and a blue field. Thirteen stars, symbolizing the original 13 colonies, fly above the eagle.

On the opposite side of the seal are symbols that often puzzle people. There is an unfinished pyramid with 13 levels and the date 1776 in Roman numerals at it base. It represents the 13 colonies and the idea that the United States is a work in progress and not yet finished. A pyramid was chosen because it represents strength and duration, like the pyramids of Egypt that have lasted for thousands of years. Hovering over the pyramid is an eye in a triangle. The triangle looks like the capstone, or top of the pyramid, and the eye is intended to represent God watching over the nation. Above the eye are the Latin words "Annuit Coeptis", which mean "He approves the undertaking," indicating God approves of the new nation. Below the pyramid are the Latin words "Novus Ordo Seclorum," meaning "new order of the ages," referring to the idea that the United States, as a democratic republic, was a new way of organizing society in the world.

Star Spangled Banner

The Star Spangled Banner is the national anthem of the United States. Its lyrics were first written down as a poem in 1814 by Francis Scott Key after he watched the British attack Fort McHenry during the War of 1812. The poem describes Key watching anxiously in the early morning dawn to see if

The American flag is one of the most easily recognizable symbols of the United States.

▶ CRITICAL THINKING

Drawing Conclusions How would the flag need to change if more states were added to the Union? SS.912.A.1.4

©iStockphoto/carterdayne

the flag is again raised over the "the land of the free and home of the brave." The song became popular in the 1800s, and was played regularly on July 4th. In 1889, Secretary of the Navy Benjamin Tracy ordered that it be played whenever the Navy raised the American flag, but the song was not made the official national anthem of the United States until 1931.

In God We Trust

The official motto of the United States is "In God We Trust." The origin of the phrase probably dates to the national anthem. In the fourth verse of the Star Spangled Banner is the phrase: "And this be our motto: 'In God is our Trust.'" But the motto was not approved by Congress at the time, and for much of its history, the United States did not have an official motto.

The phrase was used as a battle cry by some units in the Union army, and after the Civil War in the late 1800s, Congress approved the phrase "In God We Trust" for use on American coins. Since 1938, all United States coins have had this phrase inscribed on them. In 1956, with the United States in the midst of the Cold War with the Soviet Union, Congress declared the national motto to be "In God We Trust." The motto was meant to assert the general American belief in God, and to contrast it with the communist belief in atheism. In 1957, the phrase began to be used on American paper currency as well.

In recent years, the motto has become controversial. Some people argue that it violates the First Amendment's ban on government establishing a religion. Lower courts, as well as the Supreme Court, have repeatedly ruled that the motto and its use on coins and currency is not a violation of the First Amendment because it serves a ceremonial, not a religious, purpose and does not constitute the creation of a state church.

The motto of the United States can be found on its currency.

 READING PROGRESS CHECK

Explaining Why was the Great Seal of the United States the first symbol created by Congress?

CONSTITUTION HANDBOOK REVIEW

Reviewing Vocabulary
1. *Analyzing* Explain the significance of popular sovereignty to the Constitution. LAFS.1112.RH.2.4

Using Your Notes
2. *Identifying* Use the notes you completed during the lesson to identify the major principles of the Constitution. LAFS.1112.RH.3.7

Answering the Guiding Questions
3. *Summarizing* How does the Constitution lay the framework for individual rights and a balanced representative government?

4. *Explaining* How is the legislative branch organized, and what are its functions?

5. *Listing* How does the president carry out laws that Congress passes?

6. *Defining* How does the judicial branch function to review and evaluate laws and interpret the Constitution?

7. *Describing* What are the protections and freedoms the Constitution and the Bill of Rights provide Americans?

Writing Activity
8. ARGUMENT Write a short paragraph taking a pro or con position on the following question: Should communities permit rallies by unpopular groups, even though such rallies may upset some members of the community or could possibly incite violence? LAFS.1112.WHST.1.1, LAFS.1112.WHST.4.10

McGraw-Hill Education

THE CONSTITUTION
of the UNITED STATES

The Constitution of the United States is a truly remarkable document. It was one of the first written constitutions in modern history. The entire text of the Constitution and its amendments follow. For easier study, those passages that have been set aside or changed by the adoption of amendments are printed in blue. Also included are explanatory notes that will help clarify the meaning of important ideas presented in the Constitution.

Preamble

We the People of the United States, in Order to form a more perfect Union, establish Justice, insure domestic Tranquility, provide for the common defence, promote the general Welfare, and secure the Blessings of Liberty to ourselves and our Posterity, do ordain and establish this **Constitution** for the United States of America.

Article I

Section 1

All legislative Powers herein granted shall be vested in a Congress of the United States, which shall consist of a Senate and House of Representatives.

Section 2

[1.] The House of Representatives shall be composed of Members chosen every second Year by the People of the several States, and the Electors in each State shall have the Qualifications requisite for Electors of the most numerous Branch of the State Legislature.

[2.] No person shall be a Representative who shall not have attained the Age of twenty five Years, and been seven Years a Citizen of the United States, and who shall not, when elected, be an Inhabitant of that State in which he shall be chosen.

[3.] Representatives and direct Taxes shall be apportioned among the several States which may be included within this Union, according to their respective Numbers, which shall be determined by adding to the whole Number of free Persons, including those bound to Service for a Term of Years, and excluding Indians not taxed, three fifths of all other Persons. The actual **Enumeration** shall be made within three Years after the first Meeting of the Congress of the United States, and within every subsequent Term of ten Years, in such Manner as they shall by Law direct. The Number of Representatives shall not exceed one for every thirty Thousand, but each State shall have at Least one Representative; and until such enumeration shall be made, the State of New Hampshire shall be entitled to chuse three; Massachusetts eight, Rhode-Island and Providence Plantations one, Connecticut five, New-York six, New Jersey four, Pennsylvania eight, Delaware one, Maryland six, Virginia ten, North Carolina five, South Carolina five, and Georgia three.

[4.] When vacancies happen in the Representation from any State, the Executive Authority thereof shall issue Writs of Election to fill such Vacancies.

[5.] The House of Representatives shall chuse their Speaker and other Officers; and shall have the sole Power of **Impeachment**.

The Preamble introduces the Constitution and sets forth the general purposes for which the government was established. The Preamble also declares that the power of the government comes from the people.

The printed text of the document shows the spelling and punctuation of the parchment original.

Article I.
The Legislative Branch

The Constitution contains seven divisions called articles. Each article covers a general topic. For example, Articles I, II, and III create the three branches of the national government—the legislative, executive, and judicial branches. Most of the articles are divided into sections.

Section 1. Congress

Lawmaking The power to make laws is given to a Congress made up of two chambers to represent different interests: the Senate to represent the states and the House to be more responsive to the people's will.

Section 2. House of Representatives

Division of Representatives Among the States The number of representatives from each state is based on the size of the state's population. Each state is entitled to at least one representative. The Constitution states that each state may specify who can vote, but the Fifteenth, Nineteenth, Twenty-fourth, and Twenty-sixth Amendments have established guidelines that all states must follow regarding the right to vote. *What are the qualifications for members of the House of Representatives?*

Vocabulary

preamble: *introduction*
constitution: *principles and laws of a nation*
enumeration: *census or population count*
impeachment: *bringing charges against an official*

Section 3. The Senate

Voting Procedure Originally, senators were chosen by the legislators of their own states. The Seventeenth Amendment changed this, so that senators are now elected by their state's people. There are 100 senators, 2 from each state.

What Might Have Been

Electing Senators South Carolina delegate Charles Pinckney suggested during the Convention that the members of the Senate come from four equally proportioned districts within the United States and that the legislature elect the executive every seven years.

Section 3. The Senate

Trial of Impeachments One of Congress's powers is the power to impeach—to accuse government officials of wrongdoing, put them on trial, and, if necessary, remove them from office. The House decides if the offense is impeachable. The Senate acts as a jury, and when the president is impeached, the Chief Justice of the United States serves as the judge. A two-thirds vote of the members present is needed to convict impeached officials. *What punishment can the Senate give if an impeached official is convicted?*

Vocabulary

president pro tempore: *presiding officer of the Senate who serves when the vice president is absent*

Section 3

[1.] The Senate of the United States shall be composed of two Senators from each State, chosen by the Legislature thereof, for six Years; and each Senator shall have one Vote.

[2.] Immediately after they shall be assembled in Consequence of the first Election, they shall be divided as equally as may be into three Classes. The Seats of the Senators of the first Class shall be vacated at the Expiration of the second Year, of the second Class at the Expiration of the fourth Year, and of the third Class at the Expiration of the sixth Year, so that one third may be chosen every second Year; and if Vacancies happen by Resignation, or otherwise, during the Recess of the Legislature of any State, the Executive thereof may make temporary Appointments until the next Meeting of the Legislature, which shall then fill such Vacancies.

[3.] No Person shall be a Senator who shall not have attained to the Age of thirty Years, and been nine Years a Citizen of the United States, and who shall not, when elected, be an Inhabitant of that State for which he shall be chosen.

[4.] The Vice President of the United States shall be President of the Senate, but shall have no Vote, unless they be equally divided.

[5.] The Senate shall chuse their other Officers, and also a **President pro tempore**, in the Absence of the Vice President, or when he shall exercise the Office of the President of the United States.

[6.] The Senate shall have the sole Power to try all Impeachments. When sitting for that Purpose, they shall be on Oath or Affirmation. When the President of the United States is tried, the Chief Justice shall preside: And no Person shall be convicted without the Concurrence of two thirds of the Members present.

[7.] Judgment in Cases of Impeachment shall not extend further than to removal from Office, and disqualification to hold and enjoy any Office of honor, Trust or Profit under the United States: but the Party convicted shall nevertheless be liable and subject to Indictment, Trial, Judgment and Punishment, according to Law.

Section 4

[1.] The Times, Places and Manner of holding Elections for Senators and Representatives, shall be prescribed in each State by the Legislature thereof; but the Congress may at any time by Law make or alter such Regulations, except as to the Places of chusing Senators.

[2.] The Congress shall assemble at least once in every Year, and such Meeting shall be on the first Monday in December, unless they shall by Law appoint a different Day.

Section 5

[1.] Each House shall be the Judge of the Elections, Returns and Qualifications of its own Members, and a Majority of each shall constitute a **Quorum** to do Business; but a smaller Number may **adjourn** from day to day, and may be authorized to compel the Attendance of absent Members, in such Manner, and under such Penalties as each House may provide.

[2.] Each House may determine the Rules of its Proceedings, punish its Members for disorderly Behaviour, and, with the **Concurrence** of two thirds, expel a Member.

[3.] Each House shall keep a Journal of its Proceedings, and from time to time publish the same, excepting such Parts as may in their Judgment require Secrecy; and the Yeas and Nays of the Members of either House on any question shall, at the Desire of one fifth of those Present, be entered on the Journal.

[4.] Neither House, during the Session of Congress, shall, without the Consent of the other, adjourn for more than three days, nor to any other Place than that in which the two Houses shall be sitting.

Section 6

[1.] The Senators and Representatives shall receive a Compensation for their Services, to be ascertained by Law, and paid out of the Treasury of the United States. They shall in all Cases, except Treason, Felony and Breach of the Peace, be privileged from Arrest during their Attendance at the Session of their respective Houses, and in going to and returning from the same; and for any Speech or Debate in either House, they shall not be questioned in any other Place.

[2.] No Senator or Representative shall, during the Time for which he was elected, be appointed to any civil Office under the Authority of the United States, which shall have been created, or the **Emoluments** whereof shall have been encreased during such time; and no Person holding any Office under the United States, shall be a Member of either House during his Continuance in Office.

Section 7

[1.] All Bills for raising **Revenue** shall originate in the House of Representatives; but the Senate may propose or concur with Amendments as on other **Bills**.

[2.] Every Bill which shall have passed the House of Representatives and the Senate, shall, before it become a Law, be presented to the President of the United States; If he approve he shall sign it, but if not he shall return it, with his Objections to that House in which it shall have originated, who shall enter the Objections at large on their Journal, and proceed to reconsider it. If after such Reconsideration two thirds of that House shall agree to pass the Bill, it shall be sent,

Vocabulary

quorum: *minimum number of members that must be present to conduct sessions*

adjourn: *to suspend a session*

concurrence: *agreement*

emoluments: *salaries*

revenue: *income raised by government*

bill: *draft of a proposed law*

Section 6. Privileges and Restrictions

Pay and Privileges To strengthen the federal government, the Founders set congressional salaries to be paid by the United States Treasury rather than by members' respective states. Originally, members were paid $6 per day. In 2015, all members of Congress received a base salary of $174,000.

Section 7. Passing Laws

Revenue Bill All tax laws must originate in the House of Representatives. This ensures that the branch of Congress that is elected by the people every two years has the major role in determining taxes.

Section 7. Passing Laws

How Bills Become Laws A bill may become a law only by passing both houses of Congress and being signed by the president. The president can check Congress by rejecting—vetoing—its legislation. *How can Congress override the president's veto?*

Section 8. Powers Granted to Congress

Powers of Congress Expressed powers are those powers directly stated in the Constitution. Most of the expressed powers of Congress are listed in Article I, Section 8. These powers are also called enumerated powers because they are numbered 1–18. *Which clause gives Congress the power to declare war?*

Vocabulary

resolution: *legislature's formal expression of opinion*

naturalization: *procedure by which a citizen of a foreign nation becomes a citizen of the United States*

together with the Objections, to the other House, by which it shall likewise be reconsidered, and if approved by two thirds of that House, it shall become a Law. But in all such Cases the Votes of both Houses shall be determined by yeas and Nays, and the Names of the Persons voting for and against the Bill shall be entered on the Journal of each House respectively. If any Bill shall not be returned by the President within ten Days (Sundays excepted) after it shall have been presented to him, the Same shall be a Law, in like Manner as if he had signed it, unless the Congress by their Adjournment prevent its Return, in which Case it shall not be a Law.

[3.] Every Order, **Resolution**, or Vote to which the Concurrence of the Senate and House of Representatives may be necessary (except on a question of Adjournment) shall be presented to the President of the United States; and before the Same shall take Effect, shall be approved by him, or being disapproved by him, shall be repassed by two thirds of the Senate and House of Representatives, according to the Rules and Limitations prescribed in the Case of a Bill.

Section 8

[1.] The Congress shall have the Power to lay and collect Taxes, Duties, Imposts and Excises, to pay the Debts and provide for the common Defence and general Welfare of the United States; but all Duties, Imposts and Excises shall be uniform throughout the United States;

[2.] To borrow Money on the credit of the United States;

[3.] To regulate Commerce with foreign Nations, and among the several States, and with the Indian Tribes;

[4.] To establish an uniform Rule of **Naturalization**, and uniform Laws on the subject of Bankruptcies throughout the United States;

[5.] To coin Money, regulate the Value thereof, and of foreign Coin, and fix the Standard of Weights and Measures;

[6.] To provide for the Punishment of counterfeiting the Securities and current Coin of the United States;

[7.] To establish Post Offices and post Roads;

[8.] To promote the Progress of Science and useful Arts, by securing for limited Times to Authors and Inventors the exclusive Right to their respective Writings and Discoveries;

[9.] To constitute Tribunals inferior to the supreme Court;

[10.] To define and punish Piracies and Felonies committed on the high Seas, and Offences against the Law of Nations;

[11.] To declare War, grant Letters of Marque and Reprisal, and make Rules concerning Captures on Land and Water;

[12.] To raise and support Armies, but no Appropriation of Money to that Use shall be for a longer Term than two Years;

[13.] To provide and maintain a Navy;

[14.] To make Rules for the Government and Regulation of the land and naval Forces;

[15.] To provide for calling forth the Militia to execute the Laws of the Union, suppress Insurrections and repel Invasions;

[16.] To provide for organizing, arming, and disciplining, the Militia, and for governing such Part of them as may be employed in the Service of the United States, reserving to the States respectively, the Appointment of the Officers, and the Authority of training the Militia according to the discipline prescribed by Congress;

[17.] To exercise exclusive Legislation in all Cases whatsoever, over such District (not exceeding ten Miles square) as may, by Cession of particular States, and the Acceptance of Congress, become the Seat of Government of the United States, and to exercise like Authority over all Places purchased by the Consent of the Legislature of the State in which the Same shall be, for the Erection of Forts, Magazines, Arsenals, dock-Yards, and other needful Buildings; And

[18.] To make all Laws which shall be necessary and proper for carrying into Execution the foregoing Powers, and all other Powers vested by this Constitution in the Government of the United States, or in any Department or Officer thereof.

Section 9

[1.] The Migration or Importation of such Persons as any of the States now existing shall think proper to admit, shall not be prohibited by the Congress prior to the Year one thousand eight hundred and eight, but a Tax or duty may be imposed on such Importation, not exceeding ten dollars for each Person.

[2.] The Privilege of the Writ of Habeas Corpus shall not be suspended, unless when in Cases of Rebellion or Invasion the public Safety may require it.

[3.] No Bill of Attainder or ex post facto Law shall be passed.

[4.] No Capitation, or other direct, Tax shall be laid, unless in Proportion to the Census or Enumeration herein before directed to be taken.

[5.] No Tax or Duty shall be laid on Articles exported from any State.

[6.] No Preference shall be given by any Regulation of Commerce or Revenue to the Ports of one State over those of another: nor shall Vessels bound to, or from, one State, be obliged to enter, clear, or pay Duties in another.

[7.] No Money shall be drawn from the Treasury, but in Consequence of Appropriations made by Law; and a regular Statement and Account of the Receipts and Expenditures of all public Money shall be published from time to time.

[8.] No Title of Nobility shall be granted by the United States: And no Person holding any Office of Profit or Trust under them, shall, without the Consent of the Congress, accept of any present, Emolument, Office, or Title, of any kind whatever, from any King, Prince, or foreign State.

Section 8. Powers Granted to Congress

Elastic Clause The final enumerated power is often called the "elastic clause." This clause gives Congress the right to make all laws "necessary and proper" to carry out the powers expressed in the other clauses of Article I. It is called the elastic clause because it lets Congress "stretch" its powers to meet situations the Founders could never have anticipated.

Almost from the beginning, this phrase was a subject of dispute. The issue was whether a strict or a broad interpretation of the Constitution should be applied. The dispute was first addressed in 1819, in the case of *McCulloch* v. *Maryland*, when the Supreme Court ruled in favor of a broad interpretation. The Court stated that the elastic clause allowed Congress to use its powers in any way that was not specifically prohibited by the Constitution. ***What does the phrase "necessary and proper" in the elastic clause mean?***

Section 9. Powers Denied to the Federal Government

Original Rights A writ of habeas corpus issued by a judge requires a law official to bring a prisoner to court and show cause for holding the prisoner. A bill of attainder is a bill that punishes a person without a jury trial. An "ex post facto" law is one that makes an act a crime after the act has been committed. ***What does the Constitution say about bills of attainder?***

Article II. The Executive Branch

Article II creates an executive branch to carry out laws passed by Congress. Article II lists the powers and duties of the president, describes qualifications for office and procedures for electing the president, and provides for a vice president.

What Might Have Been

Term of Office Alexander Hamilton also provided his own governmental outline at the Constitutional Convention. Some of its most distinctive elements were that both the executive and the members of the Senate were "elected to serve during good behaviour," meaning there was no specified limit on their time in office.

Section 1. President and Vice President

Former Method of Election In the election of 1800, the top two candidates received the same number of electoral votes, making it necessary for the House of Representatives to decide the election. To eliminate this problem, the Twelfth Amendment, added in 1804, changed the method of electing the president stated in Article II, Section 3. The Twelfth Amendment requires that the electors cast separate ballots for president and vice president.

Section 10

[1.] No State shall enter into any Treaty, Alliance, or Confederation; grant Letters of Marque and Reprisal; coin Money; emit Bills of Credit; make any Thing but gold and silver Coin a Tender in Payment of Debts; pass any Bill of Attainder, ex post facto Law, or Law impairing the Obligation of Contracts, or grant any Title of Nobility.

[2.] No State shall, without the Consent of the Congress, lay any Imposts or Duties on Imports or Exports, except what may be absolutely necessary for executing its inspection Laws: and the net Produce of all Duties and Imposts, laid by any State on Imports and Exports, shall be for the Use of the Treasury of the United States; and all such Laws shall be subject to the Revision and Controul of the Congress.

[3.] No State shall, without the Consent of Congress, lay any Duty of Tonnage, keep Troops, or Ships of War in time of Peace, enter into any Agreement or Compact with another State, or with a foreign Power, or engage in War, unless actually invaded, or in such imminent Danger as will not admit of delay.

Article II

Section 1

[1.] The executive Power shall be vested in a President of the United States of America. He shall hold his Office during the Term of four Years, and, together with the Vice President, chosen for the same Term, be elected, as follows.

[2.] Each State shall appoint, in such Manner as the Legislature thereof may direct, a Number of Electors, equal to the whole Number of Senators and Representatives to which the State may be entitled in the Congress: but no Senator or Representative, or Person holding an Office of Trust or Profit under the United States, shall be appointed an Elector.

[3.] The Electors shall meet in their respective States, and vote by Ballot for two Persons, of whom one at least shall not be an Inhabitant of the same State with themselves. And they shall make a List of all the Persons voted for, and of the Number of Votes for each; which List they shall sign and certify, and transmit sealed to the Seat of the Government of the United States, directed to the President of the Senate. The President of the Senate shall, in the Presence of the Senate and House of Representatives, open all the Certificates, and the Votes shall then be counted. The Person having the greatest Number of Votes shall be the President, if such Number be a Majority of the whole Number of Electors appointed; and if there be more than one who have such Majority, and have an equal Number of Votes, then the House of Representatives shall immediately chuse by Ballot one of them for President; and if no person have a Majority, then from the five highest on the List the said House shall in like Manner chuse the

President. But in chusing the President, the Votes shall be taken by States, the Representation from each State having one Vote; A quorum for this Purpose shall consist of a Member or Members from two thirds of the States, and a Majority of all the States shall be necessary to a Choice. In every Case, after the Choice of the President, the Person having the greatest Number of Votes of the Electors shall be the Vice President. But if there should remain two or more who have equal Votes, the Senate shall chuse from them by Ballot the Vice President.

[4.] The Congress may determine the Time of chusing the Electors, and the Day on which they shall give their Votes; which Day shall be the same throughout the United States.

[5.] No Person except a natural born Citizen, or a Citizen of the United States, at the time of the Adoption of this Constitution, shall be eligible to the Office of President; neither shall any Person be eligible to that Office who shall not have attained to the Age of thirty five Years, and been fourteen Years a Resident within the United States.

[6.] In Case of the Removal of the President from Office, or of his Death, Resignation, or Inability to discharge the Powers and Duties of the said Office, the Same shall devolve on the Vice President, and the Congress may by Law provide for the Case of Removal, Death, Resignation or Inability, both of the President and Vice President, declaring what Officer shall then act as President, and such Officer shall act accordingly, until the Disability be removed, or a President shall be elected.

[7.] The President shall, at stated Times, receive for his Services, a Compensation, which shall neither be encreased nor diminished during the Period for which he shall have been elected, and he shall not receive within that Period any other Emolument from the United States, or any of them.

[8.] Before he enter on the Execution of his Office, he shall take the following Oath or Affirmation:—"I do solemnly swear (or affirm) that I will faithfully execute the Office of President of the United States, and will to the best of my Ability, preserve, protect and defend the Constitution of the United States."

Section 2

[1.] The President shall be Commander in Chief of the Army and Navy of the United States, and of the Militia of the several States, when called into the actual Service of the United States; he may require the Opinion, in writing, of the principal Officer in each of the executive Departments, upon any Subject relating to the Duties of their respective Offices, and he shall have Power to grant Reprieves and Pardons for Offences against the United States, except in Cases of Impeachment.

What Might Have Been

Qualifications At the Constitutional Convention, the New Jersey Amendments, sponsored by the smaller states, raised the possibility of making the executive a committee of people rather than a single individual. Also, executives were not allowed to run for a second term of office under this plan.

Section 1. President and Vice President

Qualifications The president must be a citizen of the United States by birth, at least 35 years of age, and a resident of the United States for 14 years.

Section 1. President and Vice President

Vacancies If the president dies, resigns, is removed from office by impeachment, or is unable to carry out the duties of the office, the vice president becomes president. (see Amendment XXV)

Section 1. President and Vice President

Salary Originally, the president's salary was $25,000 per year. The president's current salary is $400,000 plus a $50,000 nontaxable expense account per year. The president also receives living accommodations in two residences—the White House and Camp David.

Section 2. Powers of the President

Cabinet Mention of "the principal officer in each of the executive departments" is the only suggestion of the president's cabinet to be found in the Constitution. The cabinet is an advisory body, and its power depends on the president. Section 2, Clause 1 also makes the president the head of the armed forces. This established the principle of civilian control of the military.

Section 2. Powers of the President

Treaties The president is responsible for the conduct of relations with foreign countries. ***What role does the Senate have in approving treaties?***

Section 3. Powers of the President

Executive Orders An important presidential power is the ability to issue executive orders. An executive order is a rule or command the president issues that has the force of law. Only Congress can make laws under the Constitution, but executive orders are considered part of the president's duty to "take care that the laws be faithfully executed." This power is often used during emergencies. Over time, the scope of executive orders has expanded. Decisions by federal agencies and departments are also considered to be executive orders.

Section 4. Impeachment

Reasons for Removal From Office This section states the reasons for which the president and vice president may be impeached and removed from office. Only Andrew Johnson and Bill Clinton have been impeached by the House. Richard Nixon resigned before the House could vote on possible impeachment.

Article III. The Judicial Branch

The term *judicial* refers to courts. The Constitution set up only the Supreme Court but provided for the establishment of other federal courts. The judiciary of the United States has two different systems of courts. One system consists of the federal courts, whose powers derive from the Constitution and federal laws. The other includes the courts of each of the 50 states, whose powers derive from state constitutions and laws.

[2.] He shall have Power, by and with the Advice and Consent of the Senate, to make Treaties, provided two thirds of the Senators present concur; and he shall nominate, and by and with the Advice and Consent of the Senate, shall appoint Ambassadors, other public Ministers and Consuls, Judges of the supreme Court, and all other Officers of the United States, whose Appointments are not herein otherwise provided for, and which shall be established by Law: but the Congress may by Law vest the Appointment of such inferior Officers, as they think proper, in the President alone, in the Courts of Law, or in the Heads of Departments.

[3.] The President shall have Power to fill up all Vacancies that may happen during the Recess of the Senate, by granting Commissions which shall expire at the End of their next Session.

Section 3

He shall from time to time give to the Congress Information of the State of the Union, and recommend to their Consideration such Measures as he shall judge necessary and expedient; he may, on extraordinary Occasions, convene both Houses, or either of them, and in Case of Disagreement between them, with Respect to the Time of Adjournment, he may adjourn them to such Time as he shall think proper; he shall receive Ambassadors and other public Ministers; he shall take Care that the Laws be faithfully executed, and shall Commission all the Officers of the United States.

Section 4

The President, Vice President and all civil Officers of the United States, shall be removed from Office on Impeachment for, and Conviction of, Treason, Bribery, or other high Crimes and Misdemeanors.

Article III

Section 1

The judicial Power of the United States, shall be vested in one supreme Court, and in such inferior Courts as the Congress may from time to time ordain and establish. The Judges, both of the supreme and inferior Courts, shall hold their Offices during good Behaviour, and shall, at stated Times, receive for their Services, a Compensation, which shall not be diminished during their Continuance in Office.

Section 2

[1.] The judicial Power shall extend to all Cases, in Law and Equity, arising under this Constitution, the Laws of the United States, and Treaties made, or which shall be made, under their Authority;—to all Cases affecting Ambassadors, other public Ministers and Consuls;—to all Cases of admiralty and maritime Jurisdiction;—to Controversies to which the United States shall be a Party;—to Controversies between two or more States;—between a State and Citizens of another State;—between Citizens of different States,—between Citizens of the same State claiming Lands under Grants of different States, and between a State, or the Citizens thereof, and foreign States, Citizens or Subjects.

[2.] In all Cases affecting Ambassadors, other public Ministers and Consuls, and those in which a State shall be Party, the supreme Court shall have **original Jurisdiction**. In all the other Cases before mentioned, the supreme Court shall have **appellate Jurisdiction**, both as to Law and Fact, with such Exceptions, and under such Regulations as the Congress shall make.

[3.] The Trial of all Crimes, except in Cases of Impeachment, shall be by Jury; and such Trial shall be held in the State where the said Crimes shall have been committed; but when not committed within any State, the Trial shall be at such Place or Places as the Congress may by Law have directed.

Section 3

[1.] Treason against the United States, shall consist only in levying War against them, or in adhering to their Enemies, giving them Aid and Comfort. No Person shall be convicted of Treason unless on the Testimony of two Witnesses to the same overt Act, or on Confession in open Court.

[2.] The Congress shall have Power to declare the Punishment of Treason, but no Attainder of Treason shall work Corruption of Blood, or Forfeiture except during the Life of the Person attainted.

Article IV

Section 1

Full Faith and Credit shall be given in each State to the public Acts, Records, and judicial Proceedings of every other State. And the Congress may by general Laws prescribe the Manner in which such Acts, Records and Proceedings shall be proved, and the Effect thereof.

Section 2

[1.] The Citizens of each State shall be entitled to all Privileges and Immunities of Citizens in the several States.

[2.] A Person charged in any State with **Treason**, Felony, or other Crime, who shall flee from Justice, and be found in another State, shall on Demand of the executive Authority of the State from which he fled, be delivered up, to be removed to the State having Jurisdiction of the Crime.

[3.] No Person held to Service of Labour in one State, under the Laws thereof, escaping into another, shall, in Consequence of any Law or Regulation therein, be discharged from such Service or Labour, but shall be delivered up on Claim of the Party to whom such Service or Labour may be due.

Section 2. Jurisdiction

General Jurisdiction Federal courts deal mostly with "statute law," or laws passed by Congress, treaties, and cases involving the Constitution itself.

Section 2. Jurisdiction

The Supreme Court A court with "original jurisdiction" has the authority to be the first court to hear a case. The Supreme Court generally has "appellate jurisdiction" in that it mostly hears cases appealed from lower courts.

Section 2. Jurisdiction

Jury Trial Except in cases of impeachment, anyone accused of a crime has the right to a trial by jury. The trial must be held in the state where the crime was committed. Jury trial guarantees were strengthened in the Sixth, Seventh, Eighth, and Ninth Amendments.

Vocabulary

original jurisdiction: *authority to be the first court to hear a case*

appellate jurisdiction: *authority to hear cases appealed from lower courts*

treason: *violation of the allegiance owed by a person to his or her own country, for example, by aiding an enemy*

Article IV. Relations Among the States

Article IV explains the relationship of the states to one another and to the national government. This article requires each state to give citizens of other states the same rights as its own citizens, addresses the admission of new states, and guarantees that the national government will protect the states.

Section 1. Official Acts

Recognition by States This provision ensures that each state recognizes the laws, court decisions, and records of all other states. For example, a marriage license issued by one state must be accepted by all states.

New States Congress has the power to admit new states. It also determines the basic guidelines for applying for statehood. Two states, Maine and West Virginia, were created within the boundaries of another state. In the case of West Virginia, President Lincoln recognized the West Virginia government as the legal government of Virginia during the Civil War. This allowed West Virginia to secede from Virginia without obtaining approval from the Virginia legislature.

Article V.
The Amendment Process

Article V explains how the Constitution can be amended, or changed. All of the 27 amendments were proposed by a two-thirds vote of both houses of Congress. Only the Twenty-first Amendment was ratified by constitutional conventions of the states. All other amendments have been ratified by state legislatures.
What is an amendment?

Vocabulary

amendment: *a change to the Constitution*
ratification: *process by which an amendment is approved*

Article VI.
Constitutional Supremacy

Article VI contains the "supremacy clause." This clause establishes that the Constitution, laws passed by Congress, and treaties of the United States "shall be the supreme Law of the Land." The "supremacy clause" recognizes the Constitution and federal laws as supreme when in conflict with those of the states.

Section 3

[1.] New States may be admitted by the Congress into this Union; but no new State shall be formed or erected within the Jurisdiction of any other State; nor any State be formed by the Junction of two or more States, or Parts of States, without the Consent of the Legislatures of the States concerned as well as of the Congress.

[2.] The Congress shall have Power to dispose of and make all needful Rules and Regulations respecting the Territory or other Property belonging to the United States; and nothing in this Constitution shall be so construed as to Prejudice any Claims of the United States, or of any particular State.

Section 4

The United States shall guarantee to every State in this Union a Republican Form of Government, and shall protect each of them against Invasion; and on Application of the Legislature, or of the Executive (when the Legislature cannot be convened) against domestic Violence.

Article V

The Congress, whenever two thirds of both Houses shall deem it necessary, shall propose **Amendments** to this Constitution, or, on the Application of the Legislatures of two thirds of the several States, shall call a Convention for proposing Amendments, which, in either Case, shall be valid to all Intents and Purposes, as Part of this Constitution, when ratified by the Legislatures of three fourths of the several States, or by Conventions in three fourths thereof, as the one or the other Mode of **Ratification** may be proposed by the Congress; Provided that no Amendment which may be made prior to the Year One thousand eight hundred and eight shall in any Manner affect the first and fourth Clauses in the Ninth Section of the first Article; and that no State, without its Consent, shall be deprived of its equal Suffrage in the Senate.

Article VI

[1.] All Debts contracted and Engagements entered into, before the Adoption of this Constitution, shall be as valid against the United States under this Constitution, as under the Confederation.

[2.] This Constitution, and the Laws of the United States which shall be made in Pursuance thereof; and all Treaties made, or which shall be made, under the Authority of the United States, shall be the supreme Law of the Land; and the Judges in every State shall be bound thereby, any Thing in the Constitution or Laws of any State to the Contrary notwithstanding.

[3.] The Senators and Representatives before mentioned, and the Members of the several State Legislatures, and all executive and judicial Officers, both of the United States and of the several States, shall be bound by Oath or Affirmation, to support this Constitution; but no religious Test shall ever be required as a Qualification to any Office or public Trust under the United States.

Article VII

The Ratification of the Conventions of nine States, shall be sufficient for the Establishment of this Constitution between the States so ratifying the Same.

Done in Convention by the Unanimous Consent of the States present the Seventeenth Day of September in the Year of our Lord one thousand seven hundred and Eighty seven and of the Independence of the United States of America the Twelfth. In witness whereof We have hereunto subscribed our Names,

Article VII. Ratification

Article VII addresses ratification and states that, unlike the Articles of Confederation, which required approval of all thirteen states for adoption, the Constitution would take effect after it was ratified by nine states.

Signers

George Washington,
President and Deputy from Virginia

New Hampshire
John Langdon
Nicholas Gilman

Massachusetts
Nathaniel Gorham
Rufus King

Connecticut
William Samuel Johnson
Roger Sherman

New York
Alexander Hamilton

New Jersey
William Livingston
David Brearley
William Paterson
Jonathan Dayton

Pennsylvania
Benjamin Franklin
Thomas Mifflin
Robert Morris
George Clymer
Thomas FitzSimons
Jared Ingersoll
James Wilson
Gouverneur Morris

Delaware
George Read
Gunning Bedford, Jr.
John Dickinson
Richard Bassett
Jacob Broom

Maryland
James McHenry
Daniel of St. Thomas Jenifer
Daniel Carroll

Virginia
John Blair
James Madison, Jr.

North Carolina
William Blount
Richard Dobbs Spaight
Hugh Williamson

South Carolina
John Rutledge
Charles Cotesworth Pinckney
Charles Pinckney
Pierce Butler

Georgia
William Few
Abraham Baldwin

Attest: William Jackson, Secretary

Amendment I

Congress shall make no law respecting an establishment of religion, or prohibiting the free exercise thereof; or abridging the freedom of speech, or of the press; or the right of the people peaceably to assemble, and to petition the Government for a redress of grievances.

The Amendments

This part of the Constitution consists of changes and additions. The Constitution has been amended 27 times throughout the nation's history.

The first 10 amendments are known as the Bill of Rights (1791). These amendments limit the powers of the federal government. The First Amendment protects the civil liberties of individuals in the United States. Yet, the amendment's freedoms are not absolute. They are limited by the rights of other individuals. *What freedoms does the First Amendment protect?*

Vocabulary

quarter: *to provide living accommodations*
warrant: *document that gives police particular rights or powers*

Amendment 5

Rights of the Accused This amendment contains protections for people accused of crimes. One of the protections is that government may not deprive any person of life, liberty, or property without due process of law. This means that the government must follow proper constitutional procedures in trials and in other actions it takes against individuals. *According to Amendment V, what is the function of a grand jury?*

Amendment 6

Right to Speedy and Fair Trial
A basic protection is the right to a speedy, public trial. The jury must hear witnesses and evidence on both sides before deciding the guilt or innocence of a person charged with a crime. This amendment also provides that legal counsel must be provided to a defendant. In 1963, in *Gideon* v. *Wainwright*, the Supreme Court ruled that if a defendant cannot afford a lawyer, the government must provide one to defend him or her. *Why is the right to a "speedy" trial important?*

Vocabulary

common law: *law established by previous court decisions*

Amendment II

A well regulated Militia, being necessary to the security of a free State, the right of the people to keep and bear Arms, shall not be infringed.

Amendment III

No Soldier shall, in time of peace be **quartered** in any house, without the consent of the Owner, nor in time of war, but in a manner to be prescribed by law.

Amendment IV

The right of the people to be secure in their persons, houses, papers, and effects, against unreasonable searches and seizures, shall not be violated, and no **Warrants** shall issue, but upon probable cause, supported by Oath or affirmation, and particularly describing the place, to be searched, and the persons or things to be seized.

Amendment V

No person shall be held to answer for a capital, or otherwise infamous crime, unless on a presentment or indictment of a Grand Jury, except in cases arising in the land or naval forces, or in the Militia, when in actual service in time of War or public danger; nor shall any person be subject for the same offence to be twice put in jeopardy of life or limb; nor shall be compelled in any criminal case to be a witness against himself, nor be deprived of life, liberty, or property, without due process of law; nor shall private property be taken for public use without just compensation.

Amendment VI

In all criminal prosecutions, the accused shall enjoy the right to a speedy and public trial, by an impartial jury of the State and district wherein the crime shall have been committed, which district shall have been previously ascertained by law, and to be informed of the nature and cause of the accusation; to be confronted with the witnesses against him; to have compulsory process for obtaining Witnesses in his favor, and to have the assistance of counsel for his defence.

Amendment VII

In Suits at common law, where the value in controversy shall exceed twenty dollars, the right of trial by jury shall be preserved, and no fact tried by a jury, shall be otherwise reexamined in any Court of the United States, than according to the rules of **common law**.

Amendment VIII

Excessive **bail** shall not be required, nor excessive fines imposed, nor cruel and unusual punishments inflicted.

Amendment IX

The enumeration in the Constitution, of certain rights, shall not be construed to deny or disparage others retained by the people.

Amendment X

The powers not delegated to the United States by the Constitution, nor prohibited by it to the States, are reserved to the States respectively, or to the people.

Amendment XI

The Judicial power of the United States shall not be construed to extend to any suit in law or equity, commenced or prosecuted against one of the United States by Citizens of another State, or by Citizens or Subjects of any Foreign State.

Amendment XII

The electors shall meet in their respective states and vote by ballot for President and Vice-President, one of whom, at least, shall not be an inhabitant of the same state with themselves; they shall name in their ballots the person voted for as President, and in distinct ballots the person voted for as Vice-President, and they shall make distinct lists of all persons voted for as President, and of all persons voted for as Vice-President, and of the number of votes for each, which lists they shall sign and certify, and transmit sealed to the seat of the government of the United States, directed to the President of the Senate;—The President of the Senate shall, in the presence of the Senate and House of Representatives, open all the certificates and the votes shall then be counted;—The person having the greatest number of votes for President, shall be the President, if such number be a **majority** of the whole number of Electors appointed; and if no person have such majority, then from the persons having the highest numbers not exceeding three on the list of those voted for as President, the House of Representatives shall choose immediately, by ballot, the President. But in choosing the President, the votes shall be taken by states, the representation from each state having one vote; a quorum for this purpose shall consist of a member or members from two-thirds of the states, and a majority of all the states shall be necessary to a choice. And if the House of Representatives shall not choose a President whenever the right of choice shall devolve upon them, before the fourth day of March next following, then the Vice-President shall act as President, as in the case of the death or other constitutional disability of the President. The person having the greatest number of votes as Vice-President, shall be the Vice-President, if such number be a majority of the whole number of Electors appointed, and if no person have a majority, then from the

Amendment 9
Powers Reserved to the People
This amendment prevents government from claiming that the only rights people have are those listed in the Bill of Rights.

Amendment 10
Powers Reserved to the States
This amendment protects the states and the people from the federal government. It establishes that powers not given to the national government and not denied to the states by the Constitution belong to the states or to the people. These are checks on the "necessary and proper" power of the federal government, which is provided for in Article I, Section 8, Clause 18.

Vocabulary

bail: *money that an accused person provides to the court as a guarantee that he or she will be present for a trial*
majority: *more than half*

Amendment XIII

Section 1

Neither slavery nor involuntary servitude, except as a punishment for crime whereof the party shall have been duly convicted, shall exist within the United States, or any place subject to their jurisdiction.

Section 2

Congress shall have power to enforce this article by appropriate legislation.

Amendment XIV

Section 1

All persons born or naturalized in the United States, and subject to the jurisdiction thereof, are citizens of the United States and of the State wherein they reside. No State shall make or enforce any law which shall **abridge** the privileges or immunities of citizens of the United States; nor shall any State deprive any person of life, liberty, or property, without due process of law; nor deny to any person within its jurisdiction the equal protection of the laws.

Section 2

Representatives shall be apportioned among the several States according to their respective numbers, counting the whole number of persons in each State, excluding Indians not taxed. But when the right to vote at any election for the choice of electors for President and Vice President of the United States, Representatives in Congress, the Executive and Judicial officers of a State, or the members of the Legislature thereof, is denied to any of the male inhabitants of such State, being twenty-one years of age, and citizens of the United States, or in any way abridged, except for participation in rebellion, or other crime, the basis of representation therein shall be reduced in the proportion which the number of such male citizens shall bear to the whole number of male citizens twenty-one years of age in such State.

Section 3

No person shall be a Senator or Representative in Congress, or elector of President and Vice President, or hold any office, civil or military, under the United States, or under any State, who, having previously taken an oath, as a member of Congress, or as an officer of the United States, or as a member of any State legislature, or as an executive or judicial officer of any State, to support the Constitution of the United States, shall have engaged in insurrection or rebellion against the

Amendment 13

Abolition of Slavery Amendments Thirteen (1865), Fourteen, and Fifteen often are called the Civil War or Reconstruction amendments. The Thirteenth Amendment outlaws slavery.

Amendment 14

Rights of Citizens The Fourteenth Amendment (1868) originally was intended to protect the legal rights of the freed slaves, although there have been periods when it was not enforced. Its interpretation has been extended to protect the rights of citizenship in general by prohibiting a state from depriving any person of life, liberty, or property without "due process of law." In addition, it states that all citizens have the right to equal protection of the laws in all states.

Vocabulary

abridge: *to reduce*

Amendment 14. Section 2

Representation in Congress This section reduced the number of members a state had in the House of Representatives if it denied its citizens the right to vote. Later civil rights laws and the Twenty-fourth Amendment guaranteed the vote to African Americans.

Amendment 14. Section 3

Penalty for Engaging in Insurrection The leaders of the Confederacy were barred from state or federal offices unless Congress agreed to remove this ban. By the end of Reconstruction, all but a few Confederate leaders were allowed to return to public service.

same, or given aid or comfort to the enemies thereof. But Congress may by a vote of two-thirds of each House, remove such disability.

Section 4

The validity of the public debt of the United States, authorized by law, including debts incurred for payment of pensions and bounties for service in suppressing **insurrection** or rebellion, shall not be questioned. But neither the United States nor any State shall assume or pay any debt or obligation incurred in aid of insurrection or rebellion against the United States, or any claim for the loss or emancipation of any slave; but all such debts, obligations and claims shall be held illegal and void.

Section 5

The Congress shall have power to enforce, by appropriate legislation, the provisions of this article.

Amendment XV

Section 1

The right of citizens of the United States to vote shall not be denied or abridged by the United States or by any State on account of race, color, or previous condition of servitude.

Section 2

The Congress shall have power to enforce this article by appropriate legislation.

Amendment XVI

The Congress shall have power to lay and collect taxes on incomes, from whatever source derived, without **apportionment** among the several States and without regard to any census or enumeration.

Amendment XVII

Section 1

The Senate of the United States shall be composed of two Senators from each State, elected by the people thereof, for six years; and each Senator shall have one vote. The electors in each State shall have the qualifications requisite for electors of the most numerous branch of the State legislatures.

Section 2

When **vacancies** happen in the representation of any State in the Senate, the executive authority of such State shall issue writs of election to fill such vacancies: *Provided,* That the legislature of any State may empower the executive thereof to make temporary appointments until the people fill the vacancies by election as the legislature may direct.

Section 3

This amendment shall not be so construed as to affect the election or term of any Senator chosen before it becomes valid as part of the Constitution.

Amendment 14. Section 4

Public Debt The public debt acquired by the federal government during the Civil War was valid and could not be questioned by the South. The debts of the Confederacy, however, were declared to be illegal. *Could former slaveholders collect payment for the loss of enslaved labor?*

Amendment 15

Voting Rights The Fifteenth Amendment (1870) prohibits the government from denying a person's right to vote on the basis of race. Despite the law, many states denied African Americans the right to vote by such means as poll taxes, literacy tests, and white primaries.

Amendment 16

Income Tax The origins of the Sixteenth Amendment (1913) date back to 1895, when the Supreme Court declared a federal income tax unconstitutional. To overturn this decision, this amendment authorizes an income tax that is levied on a direct basis.

Vocabulary

insurrection: *rebellion against the government*

apportionment: *distribution of seats in House based on population*

vacancy: *an office or position that is unfilled or unoccupied*

Amendment 17

Direct Election of Senators The Seventeenth Amendment (1913) states that the people, instead of state legislatures, elect United States senators. *How many years are in a Senate term?*

Amendment 18

Prohibition The Eighteenth Amendment (1919) prohibited the production, sale, or transportation of alcoholic beverages in the United States. Prohibition proved to be difficult to enforce. This amendment was later repealed by the Twenty-first Amendment.

Amendment 19

Woman Suffrage The Nineteenth Amendment (1920) guaranteed women the right to vote. By then women had already won the right to vote in many state elections, but the amendment made their right to vote in all state and national elections constitutional.

Amendment 20

"Lame-Duck" The Twentieth Amendment (1933) sets new dates for Congress to begin its term and for the inauguration of the president and vice president. Under the original Constitution, elected officials who retired or who had been defeated remained in office for several months. For the outgoing president, this period ran from November until March. Such outgoing officials, referred to as "lame ducks," could accomplish little. *What date was chosen as Inauguration Day?*

Vocabulary

president elect: *individual who is elected president but has not yet begun serving his or her term*

Amendment XVIII

Section 1

After one year from ratification of this article, the manufacture, sale, or transportation of intoxicating liquors within, the importation thereof into, or the exportation thereof from the United States and all territory subject to the jurisdiction thereof for beverage purposes is hereby prohibited.

Section 2

The Congress and the several States shall have concurrent power to enforce this article by appropriate legislation.

Section 3

This article shall be inoperative unless it shall have been ratified as an amendment to the Constitution by the legislatures of the several States, as provided in the Constitution, within seven years from the date of the submission hereof to the States by the Congress.

Amendment XIX

Section 1

The right of citizens of the United States to vote shall not be denied or abridged by the United States or by any State on account of sex.

Section 2

Congress shall have power by appropriate legislation to enforce the provisions of this article.

Amendment XX

Section 1

The terms of the President and Vice President shall end at noon on the 20th day of January, and the terms of the Senators and Representatives at noon on the 3d day of January, of the years in which such terms would have ended if this article had not been ratified; and the terms of their successors shall then begin.

Section 2

The Congress shall assemble at least once in every year, and such meeting shall begin at noon on the 3rd day of January, unless they shall by law appoint a different day.

Section 3

If, at the time fixed for the beginning of the term of the President, the **President elect** shall have died, the Vice President elect shall become President. If a President shall not have been chosen before the time fixed for the beginning of his term, or if the President elect shall have failed to qualify, then the Vice President elect shall act as President until a President shall have qualified; and the Congress may by law provide for the case wherein neither a President elect nor a Vice President elect shall have qualified, declaring who shall then act as President, or the manner in which one who is to act shall be selected, and such person shall act accordingly until a President or Vice President shall have qualified.

Section 4

The Congress may by law provide for the case of the death of any of the persons from whom the House of Representatives may choose a President whenever the right of choice shall have devolved upon them, and for the case of the death of any of the persons from whom the Senate may choose a Vice President whenever the right of choice shall have devolved upon them.

Section 5

Section 1 and 2 shall take effect on the 15th day of October following the ratification of this article.

Section 6

This article shall be inoperative unless it shall have been ratified as an amendment to the Constitution by the legislatures of three-fourths of the several States within seven years from the date of its submission.

Amendment XXI

Section 1

The eighteenth article of amendment to the Constitution of the United States is hereby repealed.

Section 2

The transportation or importation into any State, Territory, or possession of the United States for delivery or use therein of intoxicating liquors, in violation of the laws thereof, is hereby prohibited.

Section 3

This article shall be inoperative unless it shall have been ratified as an amendment to the Constitution by conventions in the several States, as provided in the Constitution, within seven years from the date of the submission hereof to the States by the Congress.

Amendment XXII

Section 1

No person shall be elected to the office of the President more than twice, and no person who had held the office of President, or acted as President, for more than two years of a term to which some other person was elected President shall be elected to the office of the President more than once. But this Article shall not apply to any person holding the office of President when this Article was proposed by the Congress, and shall not prevent any person who may be holding the office of President, or acting as President, during the term within which this Article becomes operative from holding the

Amendment 20. Section 3

Succession of President and Vice President This section provides that if the president elect dies before taking office, the vice president elect becomes president.

Amendment 21

Repeal of Prohibition The Twenty-first Amendment (1933) repeals the Eighteenth Amendment. It is the only amendment ever passed to overturn an earlier amendment. It is also the only amendment ratified by special state conventions instead of state legislatures.

Amendment 22

Presidential Term Limit The Twenty-second Amendment (1951) limits presidents to a maximum of two elected terms. The amendment wrote into the Constitution a custom started by George Washington. It was passed largely as a reaction to Franklin D. Roosevelt's election to four terms between 1933 and 1945. It also provides that anyone who succeeds to the presidency and serves for more than two years of the term may not be elected more than one more time.

office of President or acting as President during the remainder of such term.

Section 2

This article shall be inoperative unless it shall have been ratified as an amendment to the Constitution by the legislatures of three-fourths of the several States within seven years from the date of its submission to the States by the Congress.

Amendment XXIII

Section 1

The District constituting the seat of Government of the United States shall appoint in such manner as the Congress may direct:

A number of electors of President and Vice President equal to the whole number of Senators and Representatives in Congress to which the District would be entitled if it were a State, but in no event more than the least populous State; they shall be in addition to those appointed by the States, but they shall be considered, for the purposes of the election of President and Vice President, to be electors appointed by a State; and they shall meet in the District and perform such duties as provided by the twelfth article of amendment.

Section 2

The Congress shall have power to enforce this article by appropriate legislation.

Amendment XXIV

Section 1

The right of citizens of the United States to vote in any primary or other election for President or Vice President, for electors for President or Vice President, or for Senator or Representative in Congress, shall not be denied or abridged by the United States or any State by reason of failure to pay any poll tax or other tax.

Section 2

The Congress shall have power to enforce this article by appropriate legislation.

Amendment XXV

Section 1

In case of the removal of the President from Office or his death or resignation, the Vice President shall become President.

Section 2

Whenever there is a vacancy in the office of the Vice President, the President shall nominate a Vice President who shall take the office upon confirmation by a majority vote of both Houses of Congress.

Amendment 23

D.C. Electors The Twenty-third Amendment (1961) allows citizens living in Washington, D.C., to vote for president and vice president, a right previously denied residents of the nation's capital. The District of Columbia now has three presidential electors, the number to which it would be entitled if it were a state.

Amendment 24

Abolition of the Poll Tax
The Twenty-fourth Amendment (1964) prohibits poll taxes in federal elections. Prior to the passage of this amendment, some states had used such taxes to keep low-income African Americans from voting. In 1966, the Supreme Court banned poll taxes in state elections as well.

Section 3

Whenever the President transmits to the President pro tempore of the Senate and the Speaker of the House of Representatives his written declaration that he is unable to discharge the powers and duties of his office, and until he transmits to them a written declaration to the contrary, such powers and duties shall be discharged by the Vice President as Acting President.

Section 4

Whenever the Vice President and a majority of either the principal officers of the executive departments or of such other body as Congress may by law provide, transmit to the President pro tempore of the Senate and the Speaker of the House of Representatives their written declaration that the President is unable to discharge the powers and duties of his office, the Vice President shall immediately assume the power and duties of the office of Acting President.

Thereafter, when the President transmits to the President pro tempore of the Senate and the Speaker of the House of Representatives his written declaration that no inability exists, he shall resume the powers and duties of his office unless the Vice President and a majority of either the principal officers of the executive department or of such other body as Congress may by law provide, transmit within four days to the President pro tempore of the Senate and the Speaker of the House of Representatives their written declaration that the President is unable to discharge the powers and duties of his office. Thereupon Congress shall decide the issue, assembling within forty-eight hours for that purpose if not in session. If the Congress, within twenty-one days after receipt of the latter written declaration, or, if Congress is not in session, within twenty-one days after Congress is required to assemble, determines by two-thirds vote of both Houses that the President is unable to discharge the powers and duties of his office, the Vice President shall continue to discharge the same as Acting President; otherwise, the President shall resume the power and duties of his office.

Amendment XXVI

Section 1

The right of citizens of the United States, who are eighteen years of age or older, to vote shall not be denied or abridged by the United States or by any State on account of age.

Section 2

The Congress shall have power to enforce this article by appropriate legislation.

Amendment XXVII

No law, varying the compensation for the services of Senators and Representatives, shall take effect, until an election of representatives shall have intervened.

Amendment 25

Presidential Disability and Succession The Twenty-fifth Amendment (1967) established a process for the vice president to take over leadership of the nation when a president is disabled. It also set procedures for filling a vacancy in the office of vice president.

This amendment was used in 1973, when Vice President Spiro Agnew resigned from office after being charged with accepting bribes. President Richard Nixon then appointed Gerald R. Ford as vice president in accordance with the provisions of the Twenty-fifth Amendment. A year later, President Nixon resigned during the Watergate scandal, and Ford became president. President Ford then had to fill the vice presidency, which he had left vacant upon assuming the presidency. He named Nelson A. Rockefeller as vice president. Thus, individuals who had not been elected held both the presidency and the vice presidency. *Whom does the president inform if he or she cannot carry out the duties of the office?*

Amendment 26

Voting Age of 18 The Twenty-sixth Amendment (1971) lowered the voting age in both federal and state elections to 18.

Amendment 27

Congressional Salary Restraints The Twenty-seventh Amendment (1992) makes congressional pay raises effective during the term following their passage. James Madison offered the amendment in 1789, but it was never adopted. In 1982, Gregory Watson, then a student at the University of Texas, discovered the forgotten amendment while doing research for a school paper. Watson made the amendment's passage his crusade.

LESSON 3

Antebellum America

ESSENTIAL QUESTIONS

• What characteristics define a society?
• Why do people form governments?
• How should societies settle disputes?

READING HELPDESK

Academic Vocabulary

• controversy
• predominantly

Content Vocabulary

• revenue tariff
• protective tariff
• spoils system
• temperance
• emancipate

TAKING NOTES

Key Ideas and Details

Organizing As you read about antebellum America, use a graphic organizer like the one below to take notes on how the North and the South developed in terms of industry, agriculture, and products. LAFS.1112.RH.3.7

North	South

NEXT GENERATION SUNSHINE STATE STANDARDS

LAFS.1112.RH.1.2: Determine the central ideas or information of a primary or secondary source; provide an accurate summary that makes clear the relationships among the key details and ideas.

LAFS.1112.RH.2.4: Determine the meaning of words and phrases as they are used in a text, including analyzing how an author uses and refines the meaning of a key term over the course of a text (e.g., how Madison defines faction in Federalist No. 10).

Continued on page 63

IT MATTERS BECAUSE

The people of the United States established a constitution and survived a second war with Britain. In antebellum America—the period before the Civil War—Americans faced a new question: Could they work together to create a strong and prosperous nation?

The Nation Matures

GUIDING QUESTION *How did the United States develop politically and economically in the early 1800s?*

After the War of 1812, the United States entered an "Era of Good Feelings." A sense of nationalism swept the country. Riding this wave of nationalism was Democratic-Republican James Monroe, the nation's fifth president.

The Missouri Compromise

The Era of Good Feelings could not ward off the nation's growing sectional disputes. Missouri's application for statehood as a slave state stirred up the divisive issue of whether slavery should expand westward. In 1819, the Union consisted of 11 free and 11 slave states. Admitting any new state would upset the balance in the Senate and touch off a bitter struggle over political power. Many Northerners opposed extending slavery into the West, believing it to be morally wrong. The South feared that if slavery could not expand, then new free states would give the North enough votes in the Senate to outlaw slaveholding.

A solution emerged when Maine, which for decades had been part of Massachusetts, requested admission to the Union as a separate state. The Senate voted to admit Maine as a free state and Missouri as a slave state. This solution to the **controversy** kept the balance in the Senate. Senator Jesse Thomas of Illinois then proposed an amendment that would prohibit slavery in the Louisiana Purchase territory north of Missouri's southern border. Slavery could expand into Arkansas Territory south of Missouri, but not into the rest of the

Louisiana Purchase. By a very close vote, carefully managed by Henry Clay of Kentucky, the House of Representatives voted to accept the Missouri Compromise. However, this merely postponed a debate over the future of slavery.

American Nationalism

Following the War of 1812, the Federalist Party rapidly lost political influence. Partisan infighting had largely ended because only one major political party—the Democratic-Republicans—remained. As Monroe's presidency began, focus shifted from world affairs to national growth. In 1823—while many of Spain's colonies were fighting for independence—President Monroe proclaimed what became known as the Monroe Doctrine. It declared the United States's opposition to European interference in the Americas.

The charter of the First Bank of the United States had expired in 1811. In 1816, Representative John C. Calhoun of South Carolina introduced a bill proposing the Second Bank of the United States. The bill passed, giving the bank power to issue national currency and to control state banks.

Inexpensive British goods threatened to put American manufacturers out of business. Congress responded with the Tariff of 1816. Unlike earlier **revenue tariffs,** which provided income for the federal government, this tariff was a **protective tariff** that worked to raise the prices of imports.

Under Chief Justice John Marshall, the Supreme Court issued decisions that helped strengthen the national government. Between 1816 and 1824, Marshall interpreted the Constitution broadly to support federal power. In the 1819 case *McCulloch* v. *Maryland*, the Court decided that Congress had the authority to establish the Second Bank of the United States. It ruled that the federal government could use any method that was necessary and proper for carrying out its powers as long as the method was not expressly forbidden by the Constitution. The ruling meant that a state could not interfere with a federal agency working within that state's borders.

Industrialization and the Transportation Revolution

The Industrial Revolution, which had begun in Europe, spread to the United States during this time. Businesses began large-scale manufacturing using complex machines and organized workforces in factories. As transportation expanded, manufacturers sold their wares nationwide or abroad instead of just locally.

In 1806, Congress funded a major east-west highway called the National Road. Private businesses and state and local governments also built roads and canals. The invention of the steamboat transformed river transportation. By 1835, more than 700 steamboats, called riverboats, traveled on the nation's waterways. Railroads also appeared in the early 1800s. Industrialist Peter Cooper built the *Tom Thumb,* a tiny but powerful locomotive. The new trains helped settle the West and expand trade across the country.

☑ READING PROGRESS CHECK

Explaining What controversy led to the Missouri Compromise?

Life in the North

GUIDING QUESTION *How did life in the North change in the early 1800s?*

Between 1815 and 1860, more than 5 million immigrants came to America. While thousands became farmers in the rural West, many others settled in cities, providing a steady source of cheap labor. In 1845, more than 44,000 Irish arrived after a widespread famine in their homeland.

Analyzing
PRIMARY SOURCES

The Monroe Doctrine

❝ [T]he occasion has been judged proper for asserting . . . that the American continents . . . are henceforth not to be considered as subjects for future colonization by any European powers. . . . With the movements in this hemisphere we are of necessity more immediately connected. . . . With the existing colonies or dependencies of any European power we have not interfered and shall not interfere. But with the Governments who have declared their independence and maintained it . . . we could not view any interposition for the purpose of oppressing them, or controlling in any other manner their destiny, by any European power in any other light than as the manifestation of an unfriendly disposition toward the United States. ❞

—President Monroe, from a message to Congress, December 2, 1823

DBQ **IDENTIFYING CENTRAL IDEAS** What does the Monroe Doctrine prohibit? LAFS.1112.RH.1.2, SS.912.A.1.2

controversy a prolonged public dispute

revenue tariff a tax on imports for the purpose of raising money

protective tariff a tax on imports designed to protect American manufacturers

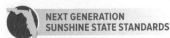

NEXT GENERATION SUNSHINE STATE STANDARDS

Continued from page 62
LAFS.1112.RH.3.7: Integrate and evaluate multiple sources of information presented in diverse formats and media (e.g., visually, quantitatively, as well as in words) in order to address a question or solve a problem.
LAFS.1112.WHST.1.2: Write informative/explanatory texts, including the narration of historical events, scientific procedures/experiments, or technical processes.

Continued on page 64

predominantly most
frequent or common

**NEXT GENERATION
SUNSHINE STATE STANDARDS**

Continued from page 63

LAFS.1112.WHST.4.10: Write routinely over
extended time frames (time for reflection and
revision) and shorter time frames (a single
sitting or a day or two) for a range of
discipline-specific tasks, purposes, and
audiences.

MAFS.912.S-IC.2: Make inferences and justify
conclusions from sample surveys,
experiments, and observational studies.

MAFS.912.S-ID.1: Summarize, represent and
interpret data on a single count or
measurement variable.

SS.912.A.1.2: Utilize a variety of primary and
secondary sources to identify author, historical
significance, audience, and authenticity to
understand a historical period.

SS.912.A.1.4: Analyze how images, symbols,
objects, cartoons, graphs, charts, maps, and
artwork may be used to interpret the
significance of time periods and events from
the past.

SS.912.A.2.1: Review causes and
consequences of the Civil War.

SS.912.A.2.2: Assess the influence of
significant people or groups on Reconstruction.

SS.912.A.2.7: Review the Native American
experience.

SS.912.A.3.13: Examine key events and
peoples in Florida history as they relate to
United States history.

In 1793, Eli Whitney invented the
cotton gin, a device that removed
the seeds from cotton.

▶ **CRITICAL THINKING**

Making Inferences How did the
cotton gin affect cotton production?
LAFS.1112.RH.3.7, SS.912.A.1.4

Not all Americans welcomed the new immigrants. In the 1800s, many
Americans were anti-Catholic, and the arrival of **predominantly** Catholic
Irish and German immigrants led to the rise of nativist groups and a push
for laws banning immigrants from holding public office. In 1854, delegates
from some of these groups formed the American Party, which came to be
called the Know-Nothings.

Owners of the early factory mills expressed a paternalistic concern for
their workers. The relationship between management and labor, however,
became more strained whenever prices slumped and wages dropped. By
1860, factory workers numbered roughly 1.3 million. Men, women, and
children alike typically toiled for 12 or more hours a day. Hoping to gain
higher wages or shorter workdays, some workers began to organize in
labor unions. During the late 1820s and early 1830s, about 300,000 men and
women belonged to some form of union. Most employers refused to
bargain with them, and the courts often saw them as unlawful conspiracies
that limited free enterprise.

Despite the trend toward urban and industrial growth, agriculture
remained the country's leading economic activity. Until the late 1800s,
farming employed more people and produced more wealth than any other
kind of work. Northern farmers produced enough to sell their surplus in
the growing Eastern cities and towns. As one Ohio newspaper reporter
wrote in 1851: "As far as the eye can stretch in the distance nothing but
corn and wheat fields are to be seen; and on some points in the Scioto
Valley as high as a thousand acres of corn may be seen in adjoining fields,
belonging to some eight or ten different proprietors."

☑ **READING PROGRESS CHECK**

Explaining How did the millions of new immigrants make a living in the United States?

The Land of Cotton

GUIDING QUESTION *How did the emergence of "King Cotton" affect the South and its
inhabitants?*

Farming was even more important in the South, which lagged behind the
North in industrialization. The South had few big cities and less industry.
Compared with the many textile mills and factories in the North, the South
had only scattered iron works, textile mills, and coal, iron, salt, and copper
mines. Together, these accounted for only 16 percent of the nation's total
manufacturing. The South thrived on the production of several major cash
crops, including cotton, tobacco, rice, and sugarcane. No crop would play a
greater role in the South's fortunes during this period than cotton. At first,
however, profits from cotton were small, owing to the great amount of
labor needed to produce it.

Cotton Becomes King

Removing cotton seeds by hand from the fluffy bolls, or cotton pods,
was so tedious that it took someone, most often an enslaved person,
an entire day to separate a pound of cotton lint. In 1793, Eli Whitney
invented the cotton gin—*gin* being short for *engine*—a machine that
quickly removed cotton seeds from the bolls. Cotton production
soared, and by 1860, Southern cotton accounted for nearly two-thirds
of the total export trade of the United States. Southerners began
saying, rightly, "Cotton is King."

Cotton was grown in a wide belt stretching from inland South
Carolina west into Texas. The spread of cotton plantations boosted the
Southern economy, and this greatly increased the demand for

National Museum of American History, Smithsonian Institution

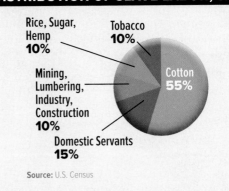

DISTRIBUTION OF SLAVE LABOR, c. 1850 — CHARTS/GRAPHS

Rice, Sugar, Hemp **10%**
Tobacco **10%**
Mining, Lumbering, Industry, Construction **10%**
Domestic Servants **15%**
Cotton **55%**

Source: U.S. Census

Between 1820 and 1850, the number of enslaved persons in the South rose from about 1.5 million to nearly 3.2 million.

1 *Categorizing* How would you categorize 75 percent of the work that enslaved people did?
MAFS.912.S-ID.1, SS.912.A.1.4

2 *Drawing Conclusions* Why did cotton occupy such a large percentage of slave labor?
MAFS.912.S-IC.2, SS.912.A.1.4

Florida CONNECTION

Building History

It is difficult to be an entrepreneur, someone who creates a business and assumes the financial risk for that business. Imagine, then, how much harder it was to be a free African American entrepreneur in the pre-Civil War South. George Proctor was such a man. He first lived in St. Augustine, Florida, where he worked as a carpenter's apprentice. After he moved to Tallahassee, Proctor built some of the most historic houses in that city. One of these, the Knott House, served as the headquarters of the Union Army, and on May 20, 1865, the Emancipation Proclamation was read from its front steps, freeing the enslaved people under Union Protection. This historic moment is recreated at the Knott House each year. SS.912.A.3.13

enslaved labor. Congress had outlawed the foreign slave trade in 1808. However, a high birthrate among enslaved women—encouraged by slaveholders—kept the population growing.

Slavery

The overwhelming majority of enslaved African Americans toiled in the fields on small farms. Some became house servants, while others worked in trades. All enslaved persons suffered indignities. State slave codes forbade enslaved men and women from owning property, leaving a slaveholder's premises without permission, or testifying in court against a white person. Laws even banned them from learning to read and write.

Many enslaved men and women found ways to actively resist the dreadful lifestyle forced on them. Some quietly staged work slowdowns. Others broke tools or set fire to houses and barns. Still others risked beatings or mutilations by running away. Some enslaved persons turned to violence, killing their owners or plotting revolts.

Free African Americans occupied an ambiguous position in Southern society. In cities like Charleston and New Orleans, some were successful enough to become slaveholders themselves. Almost 200,000 free African Americans lived in the North where slavery had been outlawed, but they still faced discrimination. Nonetheless, free African Americans in the North could organize their own churches and voluntary associations. They also were able to earn money from the jobs they held.

✔ **READING PROGRESS CHECK**

Determining Central Ideas Why was cotton called "king"?

The Age of Jackson

GUIDING QUESTION *How would you evaluate the "Age of Jackson"?*

Andrew Jackson was elected president in the election of 1828, supported by rural and small-town voters. As president, Jackson actively tried to make the government more inclusive. He wanted ordinary citizens to play a role in government, and he supported the **spoils system**—the practice of giving people government jobs on the basis of party loyalty. Jackson had not been in office long before he had to focus on a national crisis that highlighted the growing rift between the North and the South.

South Carolina bought many needed goods from England and as a result, had to pay the high tariffs levied on those goods. When another tariff law was passed in 1832, South Carolina adopted an ordinance of nullification declaring the tariffs to be unconstitutional. Jackson regarded

spoils system the practice of handing out government jobs to supporters of the winning candidate

Effects of the Indian Removal Act 1831–1842

In 1832 Sauk and Fox warriors led by Chief Black Hawk fought to reclaim territory east of the Mississippi River but were defeated.

The Cherokee took their refusal to move to the Supreme Court—and won. Federal troops forced them to leave in 1838.

Chief Osceola led the Seminole in rebellion.

Multi-group removal route
Trail of Tears
Fort
1840 border

GEOGRAPHY CONNECTION

In Andrew Jackson's Inaugural Address, he declared his intention to move all Native Americans to the Great Plains.

1 THE WORLD IN SPATIAL TERMS *Where did the Trail of Tears end?* SS.912.A.1.4, SS.912.A.2.7

2 HUMAN SYSTEMS *Name two Native American groups in the northern half of the United States that were forced to relocate.* SS.912.A.1.4, SS.912.A.2.7

nullification as treason and sent a warship to Charleston. When Congress passed a bill that lowered tariffs gradually, South Carolina repealed its nullification of the tariff law.

Along with the nullification crisis, Jackson dismantled the Second Bank of the United States. Like most Westerners, and many working people in the East, he regarded the Bank as a monopoly that benefited the wealthy elite. He vetoed a bill that would have extended its charter and then withdrew all the government's deposits, severely weakening the bank.

In his Inaugural Address, Jackson had declared his intention to move all Native Americans to the Great Plains. In 1830, Jackson signed the Indian Removal Act. The Cherokee in Georgia appealed to the Supreme Court, hoping to gain legal recognition of their territorial rights. Chief Justice Marshall supported this right in two decisions, both of which Jackson refused to carry out. In 1838, Martin Van Buren, Jackson's successor, sent in the army to forcibly move the Cherokee. Roughly 2,000 Cherokee died in camps while waiting for the westward march. On the journey, which became known as the Trail of Tears, about 2,000 others died of starvation, disease, and exposure.

✓ READING PROGRESS CHECK

Identifying What were three key events of Jackson's presidency?

A Reforming Society

GUIDING QUESTION *What common characteristics did reform movements of this era share?*

During the mid-1800s, a number of reformers argued that no social vice caused more crime, poverty, or family hardship than the excessive consumption of alcohol. They advocated **temperance,** or moderation in the consumption of alcohol. Temperance groups formed across the country, preaching the evils of alcohol and urging people to give up liquor. In 1833, a number of groups formed a national organization, the American Temperance Union. In 1851, Maine passed the first state prohibition law, an example 12 other states followed by 1855. Other states passed "local option" laws, which allowed towns and villages to ban liquor sales.

temperance moderation in or abstinence from consuming alcohol

emancipate to set free or grant freedom to

Prisons, Asylums, and School Reform

Some reformers focused on providing better facilities for prisoners and the insane. Many states replaced their overcrowded prisons with penitentiaries so prisoners would be rehabilitated, and by the beginning of the Civil War, most states had established public mental institutions to keep the mentally ill out of the prison system.

Many reformers sought to establish a system of public education. They focused on establishing elementary schools to teach all children the basics of reading, writing, and arithmetic, and to instill a work ethic.

Women's Rights

By the mid-1800s, the development of factories separated the home from the workplace. Men often left home to go to work, while women tended the home. As the reform movements of the 1830s grew, some women set out to create more educational opportunities and began promoting new ideas about their role in society. In 1848, activists Lucretia Mott and Elizabeth Cady Stanton organized the Seneca Falls Convention in New York. The convention issued the Declaration of Sentiments and Resolutions, better known as the Seneca Falls Declaration. It began with words expanding on the Declaration of Independence: "We hold these truths to be self-evident: that all men and women are created equal. . . ." Stanton proposed that they focus on suffrage, or the right to vote, and the convention narrowly passed her proposal.

Abolitionism

Of all the reform movements that began in the early 1800s, the most divisive was the one calling for abolition, or the immediate end to slavery. It polarized the nation and helped bring about the Civil War. Many of the nation's founders knew that the United States would have difficulty remaining true to its ideals of liberty and equality if it did not **emancipate,** or free, all enslaved people. Some religious groups argued that slavery was a sin.

Free African Americans took a prominent role in the movement. One of the most famous was Frederick Douglass, who had escaped from slavery in Maryland. Another key abolitionist was Sojourner Truth. She gained her freedom in 1827 when New York freed all enslaved persons in the state. Her eloquent and deeply religious antislavery speeches attracted huge crowds.

✓ READING PROGRESS CHECK

Specifying What did each of the major reform movements stand for?

©Bettmann/Corbis

BIOGRAPHY

Frederick Douglass (1818–1895)

Born into slavery, Frederick Douglass worked as a field hand and a house servant. In Baltimore, he learned to read. Seeking freedom, he fled and changed his name to elude slave hunters. Douglass then became an eloquent spokesperson for abolition. His autobiography, which described his experiences as an enslaved person, became a classic of American literature. Douglass later founded and edited an antislavery newspaper. He also served as U.S. minister to Haiti, becoming the first African American to gain such a high position in the federal government.

▶ CRITICAL THINKING

Making Inferences How was education important to Douglass's life? LAFS.1112.RH.3.7, SS.912.A.2.2

LESSON 3 REVIEW

Reviewing Vocabulary

1. *Stating* What was the key characteristic that determined who received government jobs under the spoils system? LAFS.1112.RH.2.4

Using Your Notes

2. *Summarizing* Use the notes you completed during the lesson to summarize the differences between the North and the South in the 1800s. LAFS.1112.RH.3.7

Answering the Guiding Questions

3. *Identifying* How did the United States develop politically and economically in the early 1800s?

4. *Explaining* How did life in the North change in the early 1800s?

5. *Describing* How did the emergence of "King Cotton" affect the South and its inhabitants? SS.912.A.2.1

6. *Evaluating* How would you evaluate the "Age of Jackson"?

7. *Identifying* What common characteristics did reform movements of this era share?

Writing Activity

8. NARRATIVE Suppose that you lived in the North during the early 1800s. Write a letter to a cousin in Europe telling about the changes in transportation and daily life that were taking place at the time. LAFS.1112.WHST.1.2, LAFS.1112.WHST.4.10

LAFS.1112.RH.1.1, LAFS.1112.RH.1.2, LAFS.1112.RH.1.3, LAFS.1112.RH.2.4, LAFS.1112.RH.2.5, LAFS.1112.RH.3.8, LAFS.1112.RH.4.10

Tocqueville's Democracy in America

In 1831, Alexis de Tocqueville, a French lawyer, was commissioned by the French government to study American prisons. While in America, Tocqueville traveled to the Michigan frontier and as far south as New Orleans, but spent most of his time in New England. He became convinced that there was something exceptional about American society. Between 1835 and 1839, he published a two volume book, Democracy in America. The book is regarded as one of the great works of political thought because of its discussions of liberty, **egalitarianism,** *individualism,* **populism,** *and laissez-faire economics. Tocqueville argued that these five attributes made America exceptional in the world. America's social and economic equality enabled the United States to have a remarkable amount of political liberty.*

Tocqueville believed the political liberty found on the American frontier helped keep people equal and led to individualism and free economic exchange, both of which benefited America because they were constrained by democratic institutions.

DEMOCRACY AND EQUALITY

Among the novel objects that attracted my attention during my stay in the United States, nothing struck me more forcibly than the general equality of condition among the people. I readily discovered the **prodigious** influence that this primary fact exercises on the whole course of society; it gives a peculiar direction to public opinion and a peculiar tenor to the laws; it imparts new maxims to the governing authorities and peculiar habits to the governed.

I soon perceived that the influence of this fact extends far beyond the political character and the laws of the country, and that it has no less effect on civil society than on the government; it creates opinions, gives birth to

VOCABULARY

egalitarianism
idea that people should be treated as equals

populism
belief in the rights and values of regular people as opposed to the elite

prodigious
remarkable, impressive in size

eminently
highly, greatly, exceptionally

asunder
divided, apart

new sentiments, founds novel customs, and modifies whatever it does not produce.

The emigrants who colonized the shores of America in the beginning of the seventeenth century somehow separated the democratic principle from all the principles that it had to contend with in the old communities of Europe, and transplanted it alone to the New World. It has there been able to spread in perfect freedom and peaceably. . . .

EQUALITY AND THE FRONTIER

Tocqueville believed social equality in the United States prevented the growth of an aristocracy and ensured popular democracy. In the excerpt below, he outlines how this equality combined with the open American frontier made the United States unique among nations and led to the development of capitalism.

The social condition of the Americans is **eminently** democratic; this was its character at the foundation of the Colonies, and is still more strongly marked at the present day. I have stated . . . that great equality existed among the emigrants who settled on the shores of New England. The germ of aristocracy was never planted in that part of the Union.

I do not mean that there is any deficiency of wealthy individuals in the United States; I know of no country, indeed, where the love of money has taken stronger hold on the affections of men, and where the profounder contempt is expressed for the theory of the permanent equality of property. But wealth circulates with inconceivable rapidity, and experience shows that it is rare to find two succeeding generations in the full enjoyment of it.

This picture . . . still gives a very imperfect idea of what is taking place in the new States of the West and South-west. At the end of the last century a few bold adventurers began to penetrate into the valleys of the Mississippi, and the mass of the population very soon began to move in that direction: communities unheard of till then were seen to emerge from the wilds. . . . and in the Western settlements we may behold democracy arrived at its utmost extreme. . . .

PUBLIC GOOD FROM INDIVIDUALISM

Individualism was a new concept in the 1800s, and Tocqueville worried that it would cause people to pursue their self-interest at the expense of others. Tocqueville believed Americans had found ways to combine individual economic activity with democratic institutions so as to benefit rich and poor.

Individualism is a novel expression, to which a novel idea has given birth. Our fathers were only acquainted with egotism. Egotism is a passionate and exaggerated love of self. . . .

Individualism is a mature and calm feeling, which disposes each member of the community to sever himself from the mass of his fellow-creatures; and to draw apart with his family and his friends; so that, after he has thus formed a little circle of his own, he willingly leaves society at large to itself. . . .

The great advantage of the Americans is that they have arrived at a state of democracy without having to endure a democratic revolution; and that they are born equal, instead of becoming so. . . . The Americans have combated by free institutions the tendency of equality to keep men asunder, and they have subdued it. . . .

In the United States the more opulent citizens take great care not to stand aloof from the people; on the contrary, they constantly keep on easy terms with the lower classes: they listen to them, they speak to them every day. They know that the rich in democracies always stand in need of the poor. . . .

It would seem as if every imagination in the United States were upon the stretch to invent means of increasing the wealth and satisfying the wants of the public. The best-informed inhabitants of each district constantly use their information to discover new truths which may augment the general prosperity; and if they have made any such discoveries, they eagerly surrender them to the mass of the people.

DBQ Analyzing Historical Documents

1. What aspect of American society is most striking to Tocqueville? Why does this aspect stand out to him?

2. Tocqueville wrote, "in America I saw more than America." What did he mean by this?

3. How are equality of social and economic conditions and economic opportunities connected in Tocqueville's text?

4. According to Tocqueville, why did an elite aristocracy never take root in the United States?

5. How does the American system encourage both individualism and the general prosperity of everyone?

6. What are some of the problems with American democracy that troubled Tocqueville the most? What are some problems that Tocqueville missed?

LESSON 4
The Sectional Crisis

ESSENTIAL QUESTIONS
- What characteristics define a society?
- Why do people form governments?
- How should societies settle disputes?

READING HELPDESK

Academic Vocabulary

- resolution
- perception

Content Vocabulary

- *empresario*
- popular sovereignty

TAKING NOTES

Key Ideas and Details

Outlining As you read, use the following graphic organizer to record the main ideas about westward expansion and the rise of sectionalism. LAFS.1112.RH.3.7, SS.912.A.2.1

> The Sectional Crisis
> I. Manifest Destiny
>   A.
>   B.
>   C.

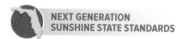

NEXT GENERATION SUNSHINE STATE STANDARDS

LAFS.1112.RH.2.4: Determine the meaning of words and phrases as they are used in a text, including analyzing how an author uses and refines the meaning of a key term over the course of a text (e.g., how Madison defines faction in Federalist No. 10).

LAFS.1112.RH.3.7: Integrate and evaluate multiple sources of information presented in diverse formats and media (e.g., visually, quantitatively, as well as in words) in order to address a question or solve a problem.

LAFS.1112.WHST.1.2: Write informative/explanatory texts, including the narration of historical events, scientific procedures/experiments, or technical processes.

Continued on page 71

IT MATTERS BECAUSE

Sectionalism and disagreements over slavery in the new territories intensified as the United States continued to expand west. The friction led to the collapse of old political parties and the formation of new ones.

Manifest Destiny

GUIDING QUESTION *Why did Americans want to expand westward, and why were they willing to go to war to secure the West?*

After the Louisiana Purchase, thousands of people pushed west, journeying all the way to the Mexican frontier of California and the Oregon Territory, which was jointly controlled by the United States and Britain. Between the late 1830s and early 1860s, more than 250,000 Americans braved great obstacles on overland trails.

Western Pioneers

New opportunities lured farmers, adventurers, and merchants alike to the West. Most believed in Manifest Destiny, the idea that God had bestowed the entire continent to the Americans. By the 1840s, several east-west routes existed. The movement of white settlers along these trails provoked Native Americans' hostility over the threat it posed to their way of life.

Oregon and Texas

At first, **empresarios,** or colonization agents, had encouraged Americans to settle the Mexican region of Texas. Tensions developed, however, and the settlers decided to separate and create their own government. The people of Texas fought for their independence from Mexico. Losses at the Alamo and Goliad galvanized the Texans. They defeated the Mexican army at the Battle of San Jacinto in April 1836.

The citizens of Texas voted in favor of joining the United States. However, Texas wished to be admitted to the Union as a slave state, which antislavery leaders in Congress opposed. The annexation of Texas became a key issue in the presidential race of 1844. Democratic candidate James K. Polk promised to annex Texas. He and the Democrats also demanded the right to all of the Oregon Country, which was then jointly controlled by the United States and Britain.

Polk won the election. In February 1845, Congress passed a joint **resolution** to annex Texas. Britain and the United States agreed to divide Oregon along the 49th parallel the following year. Americans received the land that later became the states of Oregon, Washington, and Idaho.

War With Mexico

Texas's entry into the Union outraged Mexico. Polk's plans to acquire California added to the conflict. In November 1845, the president tried to buy California, but Mexico's president refused to meet with the U.S. envoy.

In January 1846, Polk ordered General Zachary Taylor to lead troops across the Nueces River into territory claimed by both the United States and Mexico. He wanted Mexican troops to fire the first shot, because then he could more easily win support for a war. On May 9, news arrived that a Mexican force had attacked Taylor's men. Four days later, the Senate and House both overwhelmingly voted in favor of the war.

Even before war with Mexico was officially declared, settlers in northern California had begun an uprising. The settlers had little trouble overcoming the weak official Mexican presence in the territory. On June 14, 1846, they declared independence and proclaimed California the Bear Flag Republic. Despite the loss of California and defeat in several battles, Mexico refused to surrender. Then Polk sent General Winfield Scott to seize Mexico City. After a six-month campaign beginning in the Gulf Coast city of Veracruz, Scott's forces captured Mexico's capital in September 1847.

A few months later, the war was over. On February 2, 1848, Mexico's leaders signed the Treaty of Guadalupe Hidalgo. Mexico gave the United States more than 500,000 square miles (1,295,000 sq. km) of territory, which is now the states of California, Nevada, and Utah, as well as most of Arizona and parts of New Mexico, Colorado, and Wyoming. Mexico accepted the Rio Grande as the southern border of Texas. In return, the United States paid Mexico $15 million and took over $3.25 million in debts the Mexican government owed to U.S. citizens.

✓ READING PROGRESS CHECK

Explaining How did the results of the war with Mexico help fulfill what many Americans saw as their country's Manifest Destiny?

empresario a person who arranged for the settlement of Texas in the early 1800s

resolution a formal expression of opinion, will, or intent voted by an official body or assembly

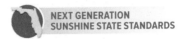

NEXT GENERATION SUNSHINE STATE STANDARDS

Continued from page 70

LAFS.1112.WHST.4.10: Write routinely over extended time frames (time for reflection and revision) and shorter time frames (a single sitting or a day or two) for a range of discipline-specific tasks, purposes, and audiences.

Continued on page 72

GEOGRAPHY CONNECTION

The war between the United States and Mexico ended with the Treaty of Guadalupe Hidalgo, which greatly expanded the territory of the United States.

1 **THE WORLD IN SPATIAL TERMS** *In what regions was the war between the United States and Mexico mostly fought?* SS.912.A.1.4

2 **THE WORLD IN SPATIAL TERMS** *At what city did Scott's troops land to begin their march to capture Mexico City?* SS.912.A.1.4

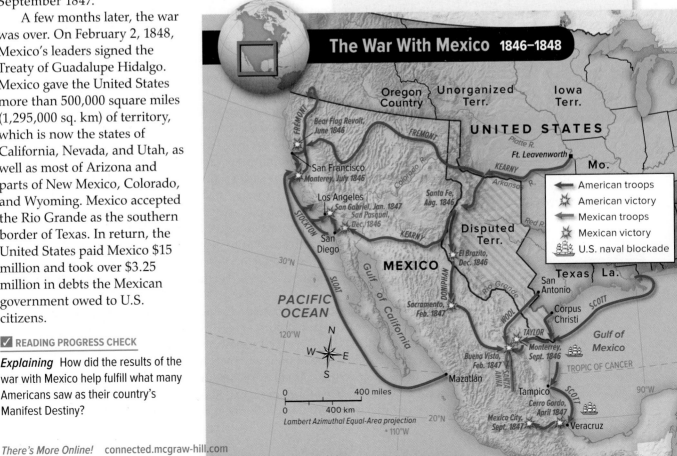

The War With Mexico 1846–1848

- Oregon Country
- Unorganized Terr.
- Iowa Terr.
- UNITED STATES
- FREMONT
- Bear Flag Revolt, June 1846
- FREMONT
- Platte R.
- Ft. Leavenworth
- Mo.
- San Francisco
- Monterey, July 1846
- KEARNY
- Colorado R.
- Arkansas R.
- Los Angeles
- San Gabriel, Jan. 1847
- San Pasqual, Dec. 1846
- Santa Fe, Aug. 1846
- STOCKTON
- KEARNY
- San Diego
- 30°N
- MEXICO
- Disputed Terr.
- El Brazito, Dec. 1846
- Red R.
- Texas
- La.
- San Antonio
- DONIPHAN
- Rio Grande
- Corpus Christi
- SCOTT
- PACIFIC OCEAN
- 120°W
- SLOAT
- Gulf of California
- Sacramento, Feb. 1847
- WOOL
- TAYLOR
- Monterrey, Sept. 1846
- Gulf of Mexico
- Buena Vista, Feb. 1847
- SANTA ANNA
- TROPIC OF CANCER
- Mazatlán
- Tampico
- Cerro Gordo, April 1847
- Mexico City, Sept. 1847
- Veracruz
- SCOTT
- 90°W
- 20°N
- 110°W

Legend:
- ← American troops
- ✦ American victory
- ← Mexican troops
- ✦ Mexican victory
- ⛵ U.S. naval blockade

- 0 | 400 miles
- 0 | 400 km
- Lambert Azimuthal Equal-Area projection

BIOGRAPHY

Harriet Tubman (c. 1820–1913)

Born into slavery in Maryland, Harriet Tubman struggled early against the system's brutality. She escaped to freedom in 1849. About crossing into Pennsylvania, she later wrote: "I looked at my hands to see if I was the same person. There was such a glory over every thing; the sun came like gold through the trees, and over the fields, and I felt like I was in Heaven." After Congress passed the Fugitive Slave Act, Tubman returned to the South 19 times to guide enslaved people along the Underground Railroad to freedom. Slaveholders offered a bounty of $40,000 for her capture.

▶ CRITICAL THINKING
Analyzing Primary Sources
What do you think Tubman meant when she wrote: "I looked at my hands to see if I was the same person"? LAFS.1112.RH.2.4, LAFS.1112.RH.3.7

popular sovereignty
before the Civil War, the idea that people living in a territory had the right to decide by voting if slavery would be allowed there

NEXT GENERATION SUNSHINE STATE STANDARDS

Continued from page 71

SS.912.A.1.2: Utilize a variety of primary and secondary sources to identify author, historical significance, audience, and authenticity to understand a historical period.

SS.912.A.1.4: Analyze how images, symbols, objects, cartoons, graphs, charts, maps, and artwork may be used to interpret the significance of time periods and events from the past.

Continued on page 74

Slavery and Westward Expansion

GUIDING QUESTION *How did the political system attempt to resolve the issues of sectionalism and slavery?*

When California applied for statehood, attempts by Congress to find a compromise on slavery further heightened opposing viewpoints. Senator Lewis Cass of Michigan suggested that the citizens of each new territory should be allowed to decide for themselves if they wanted to permit slavery. This idea came to be called **popular sovereignty.**

As the 1848 presidential election approached, both major candidates—Democrat Lewis Cass and Whig General Zachary Taylor—remained vague on the issues. On Election Day, Taylor won a narrow popular victory, but won more than half of the electoral vote.

Compromise of 1850 and the Fugitive Slave Act

In January 1848, gold was found in the Sierra Nevada in California. News of the find swept the nation, and the California Gold Rush was on. To maintain order, Californians decided to seek statehood and applied to enter the Union as a free state in December 1849. At the time, the Union consisted of 15 free states and 15 slave states. If California tipped the balance, the slaveholding states would become a minority in the Senate.

A few Southern politicians began to talk of secession. In early 1850, Senator Henry Clay of Kentucky proposed allowing a compromise measure:

PRIMARY SOURCE

❝ California, with suitable boundaries, ought, upon her application, to be admitted as one of the States of this Union, without the imposition by Congress of any restriction in respect to the exclusion or introduction of slavery within those boundaries. ❞

—from a speech to Congress, January 29, 1850

Clay further proposed that the rest of the newly acquired land from Mexico be organized without restrictions on slavery. He also called for Congress to be prohibited from interfering with the domestic slave trade and to pass a stronger law to help Southerners recover enslaved African Americans who had fled to the North.

At first, Congress did not pass Clay's bill, in part because President Taylor opposed it. Then, Taylor died unexpectedly in July. Vice President Millard Fillmore succeeded him and quickly threw his support behind the measure, which had been divided into several smaller bills. By September, Congress had passed all parts of the Compromise of 1850.

Henry Clay had conceived the Fugitive Slave Act as a measure to benefit slaveholders. The law, however, actually hurt the Southern cause by creating active hostility toward slavery among many Northerners. Under this law, a slaveholder or slave catcher had only to point out alleged runaways to have them taken into custody. The accused then would be brought before a federal commissioner. With no right to testify on their own behalf, African Americans had no way to prove their cases. An affidavit asserting that the captive had escaped from a slaveholder, or testimony by white witnesses, was all a court needed to order the person sent to the South.

The Underground Railroad helped many African Americans escape from the South. This informal network helped thousands of enslaved persons flee north. "Conductors" transported runaways in secret. The most famous conductor was Harriet Tubman, who was herself a runaway.

A major stop on the railroad was Cincinnati, Ohio, where author Harriet Beecher Stowe had lived for many years. She was inspired to "write something that would make this whole nation feel what an accursed thing slavery is."

©Syracuse Newspapers/Dick Blume/The Image Works

Her book, *Uncle Tom's Cabin,* was first published in 1852. Stowe's powerful depiction changed Northern **perceptions** of slavery.

The Crisis Over Kansas

The opening of the Oregon Territory and the admission of California to the Union convinced many people of the need for a transcontinental railroad. The location of the railroad's eastern starting point was debated. Many Southerners favored the southern route, from New Orleans to San Diego. Democratic senator Stephen A. Douglas of Illinois wanted the eastern starting point to be in Chicago. Knowing a northern route would run through the unsettled lands west of Missouri and Iowa, he prepared a bill to organize the region into a new territory to be called Nebraska. Key Southern committee leaders prevented this bill from coming to a vote in the Senate. They made it clear that before Nebraska could be organized, Congress had to repeal part of the Missouri Compromise and allow slavery in the new territory.

Douglas finally agreed to repeal the antislavery provision of the Missouri Compromise and to divide the region into two territories. Nebraska would be to the north, adjacent to the free state of Iowa; Kansas would be to the south, west of the slave state of Missouri. Under the Missouri Compromise, Nebraska was intended to be free territory, while Kansas was intended for slavery. Warned that the South might secede without such concessions, President Franklin Pierce finally gave his support to the bill. Congress passed the Kansas-Nebraska Act in May 1854.

Hordes of Northerners hurried into Kansas to create an antislavery majority. Before the March elections of 1855, however, thousands of armed Missourians—called "border ruffians" in the press—crossed the border to vote illegally, helping to elect a pro-slavery legislature. Furious antislavery settlers countered by drafting their own constitution that banned slavery. By January 1856, Kansas had two territorial governments, one opposed to slavery and the other supporting it. As more Northern settlers arrived, border ruffians began attacks. "Bleeding Kansas," as newspapers dubbed the territory, had become the scene of a territorial civil war.

Politics and Sectional Divisions

The repeal of the Missouri Compromise had a dramatic effect on the political system. Pro-slavery Southern Whigs and antislavery Northern Whigs began to

BIOGRAPHY

Harriet Beecher Stowe (1811–1896)

In 1832, Harriet Beecher Stowe moved to Cincinnati, Ohio, right across the river from the slave state of Kentucky. She met fugitive slaves, employed a formerly enslaved woman, and learned about slavery from Southern friends. After moving to Maine, she began writing *Uncle Tom's Cabin*, based on her experiences in Ohio and antislavery readings. The novel, which humanized the plight of the enslaved, was an instant sensation and further hardened the positions of both abolitionists and slaveholders.

▶ **CRITICAL THINKING**
Determining Cause and Effect What was the effect of *Uncle Tom's Cabin* on the slavery debate? SS.912.A.1.7, SS.912.A.2.1

THE CANING OF CHARLES SUMNER

POLITICAL CARTOONS

SOUTHERN CHIVALRY — ARGUMENT versus CLUB'S.

During negotiations over the Kansas-Nebraska Act, Representative Preston Brooks beat Senator Charles Sumner with his cane for criticizing Brooks's cousin, Senator Andrew Butler. While many Northerners were outraged by the incident, Southerners voiced their approval by sending Brooks canes.

1 *Analyzing Primary Sources* Which side do you think the cartoonist favored—the North or the South? Explain. SS.912.A.1.4, SS.912.H.1.5

2 *Drawing Conclusions* How might reactions to this incident be different in the North and in the South? LAFS.1112.RH.3.7

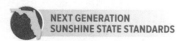
Continued from page 72

SS.912.A.1.6: Use case studies to explore social, political, legal, and economic relationships in history.

SS.912.A.1.7: Describe various socio-cultural aspects of American life including arts, artifacts, literature, education, and publications.

SS.912.A.2.1: Review causes and consequences of the Civil War.

SS.912.G.4.2: Use geographic terms and tools to analyze the push/pull factors contributing to human migration within and among places.

SS.912.G.4.3: Use geographic terms and tools to analyze the effects of migration both on the place of origin and destination, including border areas.

SS.912.H.1.5: Examine artistic response to social issues and new ideas in various cultures.

perception comprehension or understanding influenced by observation, interpretation, and attitude

split the party. During the congressional elections of 1854, many former Northern Whigs joined forces with a few antislavery Democrats and the Free-Soil Party. This coalition was officially organized as the Republican Party in 1856. The party was determined to prevent Southern planters from gaining control of the federal government. Republicans did not agree on abolishing slavery, but they did agree that it had to be kept out of the territories.

At the same time, the American Party, also known as the Know-Nothings, was making gains. This anti-Catholic, nativist party opposed immigration. The party began to come apart, however, when members from the Upper South and the North split over the Kansas-Nebraska Act. Most Northern Know-Nothings were absorbed into the Republican Party.

In the 1856 presidential election, three candidates mounted a serious challenge. Democrat James Buchanan of Pennsylvania, who had campaigned on the idea that only he could save the Union, won the election. Just two days after Buchanan's inauguration, the Supreme Court ruled in a landmark case involving slavery, *Dred Scott* v. *Sandford*.

Dred Scott was an enslaved Missouri man who had been taken north to work in free territory for several years. After he returned with his slaveholder to Missouri, Scott sued for his freedom, arguing that living in free territory had made him a free man. Dred Scott's case went all the way to the Supreme Court, which found against him. While Southerners cheered the Dred Scott decision, Republicans called it a "willful perversion" of the Constitution. After the Dred Scott decision, the conflict in "Bleeding Kansas" intensified.

✓ **READING PROGRESS CHECK**

Explaining How did the Kansas-Nebraska Act affect the national political party system?

🏛 ANALYZING SUPREME COURT CASES

DRED SCOTT v. *SANDFORD*, 1857

Background to the Case

Between 1833 and 1843, enslaved African American Dred Scott and his wife Harriet had lived in the free state of Illinois and in the part of the Louisiana Territory that was considered free under the Missouri Compromise. When he was returned to Missouri, Scott sued his slaveholder, based on the idea that he was free because he had lived in free areas, and won. That decision was reversed by the Missouri Supreme Court, and Scott's case went to the U.S. Supreme Court.

How the Court Ruled

The 7-2 decision enraged many Northerners, and delighted many in the South. In his lengthy opinion for the Court, Chief Justice Taney ruled that African Americans—enslaved or free—were not citizens of the United States. Thus, Scott had no rights under the Constitution and no right to sue in federal court. Further, Taney decreed that Congress did not have the authority to ban slavery in the territories. This made the Missouri Compromise unconstitutional.

Chief Justice Roger B. Taney delivered the Supreme Court's ruling in the **Dred Scott** *case. The decision made Scott and his family a topic for the nation's press.*

❶ *Identifying Central Ideas* Why was the Missouri Compromise declared unconstitutional?
LAFS.1112.RH.3.7, SS.912.A.1.6, SS.912.A.2.1

❷ *Interpreting Significance* Why was the decision in *Dred Scott* v. *Sandford* so significant?
LAFS.1112.RH.3.7, SS.912.A.1.6, SS.912.A.2.1

Library of Congress, Prints & Photographs Division [Lc-Usz62-79305]

The Union Dissolves

GUIDING QUESTION *What events led to the secession of the Southern states?*

In 1859, abolitionist John Brown seized an arsenal in Harpers Ferry, Virginia, in an attempt to begin an insurrection, or rebellion, against slaveholders. His arrest and execution caused him to be viewed as a martyr in a noble cause by some, while others viewed it as a sign of Northern aggression.

The Election of 1860

John Brown's raid on Harpers Ferry became a turning point for the South. In April 1860, Democrats from across the nation gathered in Charleston, South Carolina, to choose their nominee for president. When Northerners rebuffed the idea of a federal slave code in the territories, 50 Southern delegates stormed out of the convention. In June 1860, the Democrats reconvened in Baltimore. Again, Southern delegates walked out. The remaining Democrats then chose Stephen Douglas as their candidate. The Southern Democrats nominated their own candidate.

Republicans, realizing they stood no chance in the South, needed a candidate who could sweep most of the North. They nominated Abraham Lincoln, who had gained a national reputation through a series of debates with Douglas in 1858. Although not an abolitionist, Lincoln believed that slavery was morally wrong, and he opposed its spread into the Western territories. With the Democrats divided, Lincoln won the election.

The South Secedes

Many Southerners viewed Lincoln's election as a threat to their society and culture, and saw no choice but to secede. Shortly after Lincoln's election, the South Carolina legislature called for a convention. On December 20, 1860, amid marching bands, fireworks, and militia drills, the convention voted unanimously to repeal the state's ratification of the Constitution and dissolve its ties to the Union. By February 1, 1861, Mississippi, Florida, Alabama, Georgia, Louisiana, and Texas had also voted to secede and declared themselves to be a new nation: the Confederate States of America, or the Confederacy. Arkansas, Tennessee, North Carolina, and Virginia seceded in April 1861. A minority in these states did not want to leave the Union, but the majority of Southerners viewed secession as similar to the Revolution—a necessary course of action to uphold people's rights.

☑ READING PROGRESS CHECK

Explaining Why did Lincoln's election trigger the secession of the Southern states?

Analyzing PRIMARY SOURCES

Lincoln on Popular Sovereignty

❝What is Popular Sovereignty? Is it the right of the people to have Slavery or not have it, as they see fit, in the territories? . . . [M]y understanding is that Popular Sovereignty, as now applied to the question of Slavery, does allow the people of a Territory to have Slavery if they want to, but does *not* allow them not to have it if they *do not* want it. . . . [A]s I understand the Dred Scott decision, if any one man wants slaves, all the rest have no way of keeping that one man from holding them.❞

—Abraham Lincoln, in a debate with Stephen Douglas, August 21, 1858

DBQ READING CLOSELY

According to Abraham Lincoln, why could people in a territory not ban slavery through popular sovereignty? SS.912.A.1.2, SS.912.A.2.1

LESSON 4 REVIEW

Reviewing Vocabulary

1. *Explaining* Explain how the idea of popular sovereignty relieved some of the tension created by the debate over slavery in the territories. LAFS.1112.RH.2.4, SS.912.A.2.1

Using Your Notes

2. *Explaining* Use the notes you completed during the lesson to write a short paragraph explaining ways that sectional tensions increased during this era. LAFS.1112.RH.3.7, SS.912.A.2.1

Answering the Guiding Questions

3. *Summarizing* Why did Americans want to expand westward, and why were they willing to go to war to secure the West?

4. *Describing* How did the political system attempt to resolve the issues of sectionalism and slavery? SS.912.A.2.1

5. *Making Connections* What events led to the secession of the Southern states? SS.912.A.2.1

Writing Activity

6. NARRATIVE Suppose that you have decided to move from the East to the Western frontier. Write a journal entry telling where you are going, why you are going there, and what you are hoping to achieve. LAFS.1112.WHST.1.2, LAFS.1112.WHST.4.10

PRIMARY SOURCES

LAFS.1112.RH.1.1, LAFS.1112.RH.1.2, LAFS.1112.RH.1.3, LAFS.1112.RH.2.4,
LAFS.1112.RH.2.5, LAFS.1112.RH.3.8, LAFS.1112.RH.4.10, LAFS.1112.SL.1.3

Living Under Slavery

Enslaved persons were not free. That fundamental fact meant they could be sold and separated from their families. They could not legally marry or leave their slaveholder's property without permission. Slaveholders held such power that they controlled access to basic life necessities and could physically punish, even kill, the people they held in slavery without breaking the law.

AUTOBIOGRAPHY, 1845

Colonel Lloyd kept from three to four hundred slaves on his home plantation, and owned a large number more on the neighboring farms belonging to him. . . . The overseers of these, and all the rest of the farms, numbering over twenty, received advice and direction from the managers of the home plantation. This was the great business place. It was the seat of government for the whole twenty farms. . . . If a slave was convicted of any high misdemeanor, became unmanageable, or evinced a determination to run away, he was brought immediately here, severely whipped, put on board the sloop, carried to Baltimore, and sold to Austin Woolfolk, or some other slave-trader, as a warning to the slaves remaining. . . .

The men and women slaves received, as their monthly **allowance** of food, eight pounds of pork, or its equivalent in fish, and one bushel of corn meal. Their yearly clothing consisted of two course linen shirts, one pair of linen trousers, like the shirts, one jacket, one pair of trousers for winter, made of **coarse** negro cloth, one pair of stockings, and one pair of shoes; the whole of which could not cost more than seven dollars. The allowance of the slave children was given to their mothers, or the old women having the care of them. The children unable to work in the field had neither shoes, stockings, jackets, nor trousers, given to them; their clothing consisted of two coarse linen shirts per year. When these failed them, they went naked until the next allowance-day. Children from seven to ten years old, of both sexes, almost naked, might be seen at all seasons of the year.

VOCABULARY

inevitable
impossible to avoid

overarched
forming an arch overhead or above

persecuted
to treat continually in a way meant to be cruel or harmful

allowance
a sum given

coarse
being harsh or rough

privation
lacking the basic necessities or comforts of life

There were no beds given the slaves, unless one coarse blanket be considered such, and none but the men and women had these. This, however, is not considered a very great privation. They find less difficulty from the want of beds, than from the want of time to sleep; for when their day's work in the field is done, the most of them having their washing, mending, and cooking to do, and having few or none of the ordinary facilities for doing either of these, very many of their sleeping hours were consumed in preparing for the field the coming day; and when this is done, old and young, male and female, married and single, drop down side by side, on one common bed,—the cold, damp floor,—each covering himself or herself with their miserable blankets; and here they sleep till they are summoned to the field by the driver's horn. . . . [W]oe betides them who hear not this morning summons to the field. . . . Mr. Severe, the overseer, used to stand by the door of the quarter, armed with a large hickory stick and heavy cowskin, ready to whip any one who was so unfortunate as not to hear, or, from any other cause, was prevented from being ready to start. . . .

—from *Narrative of the Life of Frederick Douglass, an American Slave,* by Frederick Douglass

Reader, it is not to awaken sympathy for myself that I am telling you truthfully what I suffered in slavery. I do it to kindle a flame of compassion in your hearts for my sisters who are still in bondage, suffering as I once suffered.

I once saw two beautiful children playing together. One was a fair white child; the other was her slave, and also her sister. When I saw them embracing each other, and heard their joyous laughter, I turned sadly away from the lovely sight. I foresaw the inevitable blight that would fall on the little slave's heart. I knew how soon her laughter would be changed to sighs. The fair child grew up to be a still fairer woman. From childhood to womanhood her pathway was blooming with flowers, and overarched by a sunny sky. Scarcely one day of her life had been clouded when the sun rose on her happy bridal morning.

How had those years dealt with her slave sister, the little playmate of her childhood? She, also, was very beautiful; but the flowers and sunshine of love were not for her. She drank the cup of sin, and shame, and misery, whereof her persecuted race are compelled to drink.

In view of these things, why are ye silent, ye free men and women of the north? Why do your tongues falter in maintenance of the right? Would that I had more ability! But my heart is so full, and my pen is so weak! There are noble men and women who plead for us, striving to help those who cannot help themselves. God bless them! God give them strength and courage to go on! God bless those, every where who are laboring to advance the cause of humanity!

—from *Incidents in the Life of a Slave Girl,*
by Harriet Ann Jacobs

▲ *Frederick Douglass was one of the leaders of the abolitionist movement.*

FPC/Taxi/Getty Images

DBQ Analyzing Historical Documents

1. **Making Comparisons** According to the narrative, did slaveholders treat the children of slaves better than they treated their parents? Explain your answer.

2. **Paraphrasing** Using your own words, explain what Douglass meant by "They find less difficulty from the want of beds, than from the want of time to sleep."

3. **Judging Reliability** Consider the tone of the excerpt. Does the tone make you more or less likely to believe Douglass's claims? Why or why not?

4. **Interpreting** What does the narrator mean when she says "the other was her slave, and also her sister" in the first paragraph?

5. **Contrasting** How does the narrator use references to flowers to contrast the direction the young girls' lives will take?

LESSON 5

The Civil War and Reconstruction

- What characteristics define a society?
- Why do people form governments?
- How should societies settle disputes?

READING HELPDESK

Academic Vocabulary

- outcome
- requirement

Content Vocabulary

- siege
- pillage
- carpetbaggers
- scalawags

TAKING NOTES

Key Ideas and Details

Sequencing As you read the lesson, complete a time line like the one below to sequence events of the Civil War and Reconstruction. LAFS.1112.RH.3.7, SS.912.A.2.1

NEXT GENERATION SUNSHINE STATE STANDARDS

LAFS.1112.RH.2.4: Determine the meaning of words and phrases as they are used in a text, including analyzing how an author uses and refines the meaning of a key term over the course of a text (e.g., how Madison defines faction in Federalist No. 10).

LAFS.1112.RH.3.7: Integrate and evaluate multiple sources of information presented in diverse formats and media (e.g., visually, quantitatively, as well as in words) in order to address a question or solve a problem.

LAFS.1112.WHST.1.2: Write informative/explanatory texts, including the narration of historical events, scientific procedures/experiments, or technical processes.

LAFS.1112.WHST.4.10: Write routinely over extended time frames (time for reflection and revision) and shorter time frames (a single sitting or a day or two) for a range of discipline-specific tasks, purposes, and audiences.

Continued on page 79

IT MATTERS BECAUSE

In the end, all attempts at compromise between the North and the South over slavery failed. The outcome of the 1860 election triggered the first shots of the long, bloody Civil War.

The Opposing Sides

GUIDING QUESTION *What were the advantages and disadvantages for the North and the South at the start of the war?*

Although the South had many experienced officers to lead its troops in battle, the North had several economic advantages. In 1860 the population of the North was about 22 million, while the South had about 9 million people, more than one-third of whom were enslaved. In 1860 almost 90 percent of the nation's factories were located in the Northern states, which could provide troops with ammunition and other supplies more easily. The South had only half as many miles of railroad track as the North. Northern troops could more easily disrupt the Southern rail system and prevent the movement of supplies and troops.

The Union also controlled the national treasury and could expect continued revenue from tariffs. Many Northern banks held large reserves of cash, which they lent the government by purchasing bonds. In contrast to the Union, the Confederacy's financial situation was poor, and it became worse over time. Most Southern planters were in debt and unable to buy bonds. Southern banks were small and had few cash reserves, so they could not buy many bonds, either. The best hope for the South to raise money was by taxing trade. But the Union navy quickly blockaded Southern ports, reducing trade. The Confederacy enacted direct taxation of its people, but many Southerners refused to pay. The Confederacy was forced to print paper money, causing rapid inflation in the South.

The Civil War was, in many respects, the first modern war. It was fought with a large, civilian army and required vast amounts of supplies. Cone-shaped bullets allowed accuracy at much greater distances. Instead of standing in a line, troops defending positions

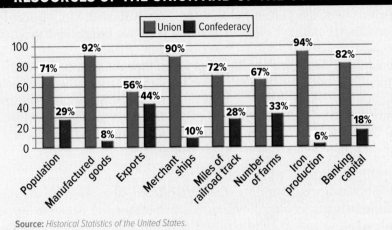

Source: *Historical Statistics of the United States.*

The Union's wealth of resources gave it an advantage over the Confederacy.

 Analyzing Information Based on the graph, what were the North's greatest advantages over the South? MAFS.912.S-IC.2, SS.912.A.1.4, SS.912.A.2.1

2 **Drawing Conclusions** Which of the North's advantages do you think were most important in winning the war? SS.912.A.1.4, SS.912.A.2.1

began to use trenches and barricades for protection. Attrition—the wearing down of one side through exhaustion of soldiers and resources—also played a critical role.

✓ **READING PROGRESS CHECK**

Identifying What advantages did factories and railroads give the North in the Civil War?

The Early Stages

GUIDING QUESTION *When did the war change from a battle over preserving the Union to a war to end slavery? What caused this change?*

The Civil War began in April 1861, when Confederate forces fired upon federal troops in Fort Sumter in Charleston Harbor. Confederate president Jefferson Davis claimed that the seceding states were fighting for the same "sacred right of self-government" that had inspired the American Revolution and that the Confederacy would "seek no conquest . . . all we ask is to be let alone."

First Battle of Bull Run

Soon after the war began, Lincoln approved an assault on Confederate troops gathered near Manassas Junction, Virginia. The First Battle of Bull Run started well for the Union, but the tide turned when reinforcements helped the Confederates defeat the Union forces. The **outcome** made it clear that the North would need a large, well-trained army to prevail against the South.

The War in the West

The Union blockaded Southern ports along the Atlantic, but the South used small, fast ships to smuggle goods past the blockades. In April 1862, Union forces seized New Orleans, the South's largest city, and gained control of the lower Mississippi River.

In early 1862, Union general Ulysses S. Grant began a campaign on the Cumberland and Tennessee Rivers. Control of these rivers would split Tennessee and provide the Union with a route into Confederate territory. All of Kentucky and most of western Tennessee eventually fell.

The War in the East

While Grant fought in the West, Union general George B. McClellan's forces set out to capture Richmond, Virginia, the Confederate capital. In late June 1862, Confederate general Robert E. Lee began a series of attacks on McClellan's forces. Together the two sides suffered more than 30,000 casualties.

NEXT GENERATION SUNSHINE STATE STANDARDS

Continued from page 78

MAFS.912.S-IC.2: Make inferences and justify conclusions from sample surveys, experiments, and observational studies.

SS.912.A.1.2: Utilize a variety of primary and secondary sources to identify author, historical significance, audience, and authenticity to understand a historical period.

SS.912.A.1.3: Utilize timelines to identify the time sequence of historical data.

SS.912.A.1.4: Analyze how images, symbols, objects, cartoons, graphs, charts, maps, and artwork may be used to interpret the significance of time periods and events from the past.

SS.912.A.2.1: Review causes and consequences of the Civil War.

SS.912.A.2.2: Assess the influence of significant people or groups on Reconstruction.

SS.912.A.2.3: Describe the issues that divided Republicans during the early Reconstruction era.

SS.912.A.2.4: Distinguish the freedoms guaranteed to African Americans and other groups with the 13th, 14th, and 15th Amendments to the Constitution.

SS.912.A.2.6: Compare the effects of the Black Codes and the Nadir on freed people, and analyze the sharecropping system and debt peonage as practiced in the United States.

SS.912.A.3.13: Examine key events and peoples in Florida history as they relate to United States history.

SS.912.G.2.1: Identify the physical characteristics and the human characteristics that define and differentiate regions.

SS.912.H.1.5: Examine artistic response to social issues and new ideas in various cultures.

outcome something that follows as a result or consequence

On September 17, 1862, Lee's forces met McClellan's at Antietam (an·TEE·tuhm) Creek. The fight was the bloodiest one-day battle in American history, ending with nearly 6,000 soldiers killed and another 17,000 wounded. McClellan did not break Lee's lines, but he inflicted so many casualties that Lee decided to retreat to Virginia.

The Battle of Antietam was a crucial victory for the Union. The British government had been ready to intervene in the war as a mediator if Lee's invasion had succeeded. Now the British decided to wait and see how the war progressed. The South's defeat at Antietam had an even more important political impact in the United States. It convinced President Lincoln that the time had come to end slavery in the South.

The Emancipation Proclamation

Most Democrats opposed ending slavery, while Republicans were divided. With Union casualties rising, however, many Northerners began to agree that slavery had to end, both to punish the South and to make the soldiers' sacrifices worthwhile. On September 22, 1862, Lincoln publicly announced that he would issue the Emancipation Proclamation—a decree freeing all enslaved persons in states still in rebellion after January 1, 1863. Because the Proclamation freed enslaved African Americans only in states at war with the Union, it did not address slavery in the border states. By its very existence, however, the Proclamation transformed the conflict over preserving the Union into a war of liberation.

☑ READING PROGRESS CHECK

Explaining Why was the Battle of Antietam significant?

GEOGRAPHY CONNECTION

As the Civil War progressed, two separate campaigns emerged.

1 **THE WORLD IN SPATIAL TERMS** *Which of the battles is farthest west?* SS.912.A.1.4, SS.912.A.2.1

2 **HUMAN SYSTEMS** *What purpose did the North have in fighting so many battles along the coasts?* SS.912.A.1.4, SS.912.A.2.1, SS.912.G.2.1

The Turning Points and Final Battles

GUIDING QUESTION *Why were Vicksburg and Gettysburg turning points in the war?*

As 1863 began, there was no end to the war in sight. More than two years of battle lay ahead for Americans, and the casualties would continue to rise steeply. The new military technology produced a huge number of casualties, and doctors struggled to tend to the wounded, having little understanding of infection and germs. Disease was one of the greatest threats facing Civil War soldiers. In many cases, regiments lost half their men to illness. Smallpox, dysentery, typhoid, and pneumonia killed thousands of soldiers. Battlefield physicians often had

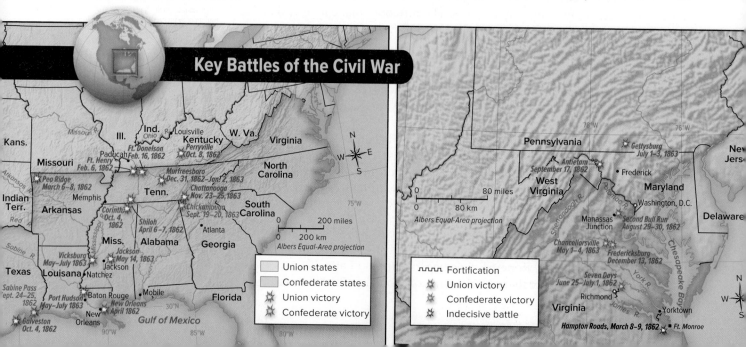

Key Battles of the Civil War

Union states
Confederate states
⚒ Union victory
⚒ Confederate victory

ㅛㅛㅛ Fortification
⚒ Union victory
⚒ Confederate victory
⚒ Indecisive battle

Hampton Roads, March 8–9, 1862

to amputate arms and legs to prevent gangrene and other infections from spreading. General Carl Schurz described one field hospital:

PRIMARY SOURCE

"As a wounded man was lifted on the table . . . the surgeon quickly examined the wound and resolved upon cutting off the wounded limb. Some ether was administered. . . . The surgeon snatched the knife from between his teeth, where it had been while his hands were busy, wiped it rapidly . . . across his blood-stained apron, and the cutting began. The operation accomplished, the surgeon would look around with a deep sigh, and then—'Next!'**"**

—quoted in *The Civil War: An Illustrated History*, 1990

It was in this field of battlefield medicine that the only woman ever to win the Medal of Honor made her contribution. Mary Edwards Walker was one of the few women before the Civil War to earn a medical degree. When the Civil War erupted, she volunteered to help the Union Army and worked as a surgeon near the front lines. She frequently crossed enemy lines to treat civilians, and on one such mission in 1864, she was arrested as a spy and imprisoned for four months. For her contributions to the war effort, she was awarded the Medal of Honor in 1865.

Vicksburg

Gaining control of the Mississippi River was a vital element of the Union strategy for winning the Civil War. If the Union could capture Vicksburg, Mississippi, the last major Confederate stronghold on the river, then the North could cut the South in two. In May 1863, Grant launched two assaults on Vicksburg, but the city's defenders repulsed both attacks and inflicted high casualties. Grant decided to put the city under **siege** by cutting off its food and supplies and bombarding it until its defenders gave up. On July 4, 1863, with his troops starving, the Confederate commander at Vicksburg surrendered.

Gettysburg

Meanwhile, in Virginia, Lee had been able to defeat Union forces at Fredericksburg and Chancellorsville. Emboldened by these victories, Lee decided in June 1863 to launch another invasion of the North. At the end of June, as Lee's army foraged in the Pennsylvania countryside, some of his troops headed into Gettysburg, hoping to seize a supply of shoes.

When they arrived near the town, they discovered two brigades of Union cavalry. On July 1, 1863, as Confederates pushed the Union troops out of the town, the main forces of both armies hurried to the scene of the fighting. On July 2, Lee attacked, but the Union troops held their ground. The following day, Lee ordered nearly 15,000 men under the command of General George E. Pickett and General A. P. Hill to make a massive assault. The attack, known as Pickett's Charge, caused 7,000 casualties in less than half an hour, but failed to break the Union lines. ". . . [A]ll this has been my fault," said Lee. "It is I that have lost this fight."

Lee's troops retreated to Virginia. At Gettysburg, the Union suffered 23,000 casualties, the South an estimated 28,000, more than one-third of Lee's entire force. The disaster at Gettysburg proved to be the turning point of the war in the East. The Union's victory strengthened the Republicans politically and ensured once again that the British would not recognize the Confederacy. For the remainder of the war, Lee's forces remained on the defensive, slowly giving ground to the advancing Union army.

The Thirteenth Amendment

More Union successes followed. General Grant succeeded in securing control of the Mississippi River. Lincoln rewarded him by appointing him general

Analyzing
PRIMARY SOURCES

The Gettysburg Address

"Four score and seven years ago our fathers brought forth on this continent, a new nation, conceived in Liberty, and dedicated to the proposition that all men are created equal.

Now we are engaged in a great civil war, testing whether that nation, or any nation so conceived and so dedicated, can long endure. . . .

. . . It is rather for us to be here dedicated to the great task remaining before us—that from these honored dead we take increased devotion to that cause for which they gave the last full measure of devotion—that we here highly resolve that these dead shall not have died in vain—that this nation, under God, shall have a new birth of freedom—and that government of the people, by the people, for the people, shall not perish from the earth.**"**

—President Lincoln, from the Gettysburg Address, November 19, 1863

DBQ **READING CLOSELY**

What does Lincoln say is the main purpose of the Civil War and the reason for the sacrifices at Gettysburg? SS.912.A.1.2, SS.912.A.2.1

siege a military blockade of a city or fortified place to force it to surrender

The war devastated the South. Hundreds of thousands of people died, and several major cities, including Richmond (shown above), lay in ruins.

▶ CRITICAL THINKING

Predicting Consequences What consequences do you think the damage caused by the Civil War had on the South in years to come? SS.912.A.1.4, SS.912.A.2.1

pillage to loot or plunder

Florida CONNECTION

Buffalo Soldiers

African American soldiers fought in the Civil War on the Union side, making up about 9 percent of the army and 12 percent of the navy. These veterans of the Civil War later fought in the Indian wars on the Plains. The Native Americans called them "buffalo soldiers" as a sign of respect for their toughness in a fight. The buffalo soldiers of the Ninth and Tenth Cavalry later gathered in Tampa for training before disembarking for Cuba to fight alongside Theodore Roosevelt in the Spanish-American War. While in Florida, these soldiers did not take kindly to the racial harassment they encountered. SS.912.A.2.2

in chief of the Union forces. Grant then began a relentless series of attacks against Lee's forces, slowly pushing deeper into Virginia. In June 1864, Grant forces reached the fortifications outside the city of Petersburg. Instead of attacking, he put the city under siege. As the siege dragged on, support for the war declined, and Lincoln expected to lose the 1864 presidential election. In September 1864, however, General William Tecumseh Sherman captured Atlanta and then began a march to sea, **pillaging** and destroying railroads, warehouses, mills and factories. Sherman's success revitalized northern support for the war, and Lincoln won in a landslide.

The president interpreted his reelection as a mandate from the voters to end slavery permanently by amending the Constitution. The Senate had passed an amendment the previous spring, but Lincoln and Congressional Republicans had to build a coalition of anti-slavery Democrats to get the amendment passed in the House of Representatives.

On January 31, 1865, the Thirteenth Amendment to the Constitution, banning slavery in the United States, narrowly passed the House of Representatives and went to the states for ratification. It took the remainder of the year, but by December 1865, enough states had ratified the amendment for it to go into effect. The Thirteenth Amendment marked a culmination of the abolition movement that had begun in the years after the American Revolution. It also finally applied the founding principles of the Declaration of Independence, the self-evident truths, as the Declaration put it, "that all men are created equal" and had an unalienable right to liberty.

The War Ends

By the spring of 1865, Lee knew that time was running out. On April 1, 1865, Union troops cut the last rail line into Petersburg, Virginia. Lee's troops attempted to escape Grant's forces in the area, but Union cavalry blocked the road. With his battered troops surrounded and outnumbered, Lee surrendered to Grant at Appomattox Court House on April 9, 1865. Grant's generous terms of surrender guaranteed that the Union would not prosecute Confederate soldiers for treason. When Grant agreed to let Confederates take their horses home "to put in a crop to carry themselves and their families through the next winter," Lee thanked him, saying the kindness would "do much toward conciliating our people."

With the war over, Lincoln delivered a speech describing his plan to restore the Southern states to the Union. In the speech, he mentioned including African Americans in Southern state governments. One listener, actor John Wilkes Booth, sneered to a friend, "That is the last speech he will ever make." Although his advisers had repeatedly warned him not to appear unescorted in public, Lincoln went to Ford's Theatre with his wife to see a play on the evening of April 14, 1865. During the third act, Booth slipped quietly behind the president and shot him in the back of the head. Lincoln died the next morning.

The North's victory in the Civil War saved the Union and strengthened the power of the federal government over the states. It transformed American society by ending slavery, but it also left the South socially and economically devastated, and many questions unresolved. Americans from the North and the South tried to answer these questions in the years following the Civil War—an era known as Reconstruction.

☑ READING PROGRESS CHECK

Drawing Conclusions What differences did the South experienced before and after the Battle of Gettysburg?

©Bettmann/Corbis

This sketch from the 1870s shows South Carolina's legislature—the only state legislature with an African American majority during Reconstruction.

▶ CRITICAL THINKING
Identifying Central Ideas
Why do you think African Americans were so enthusiastic about participating in politics? SS.912.A.1.4, SS.912.A.2.1, SS.912.A.2.2, SS.912.H.1.5

Reconstruction

GUIDING QUESTION *What important decisions had to be made concerning the fate of the seceded states and the rights of those freed from slavery?*

At the end of the Civil War, the South was a defeated region with a devastated economy. While some Southerners were bitter over the loss, for many, rebuilding their land and their lives was more important. The president and Congress grappled with the difficult task of Reconstruction.

Opposing Plans for Reconstruction

In December 1863, President Lincoln offered a general amnesty, or pardon, to Southerners who took an oath of loyalty to the United States and accepted the Union's **requirements** concerning slavery. However, certain Confederate officials and military officers were not included in the offer. In his Second Inaugural Address in March 1865, Lincoln spoke of ending the war "with malice toward none, with charity for all."

Resistance to Lincoln's plan surfaced among a group of Republicans in Congress known as Radical Republicans. They wanted to prevent the leaders of the Confederacy from returning to power. They also wanted the federal government to guarantee African Americans their right to vote.

Vice President Andrew Johnson, a Democrat from Tennessee, assumed the presidency after Lincoln's death. His 1865 plan for Reconstruction closely resembled Lincoln's, and offered amnesty to all former citizens of the Confederacy except for former Confederate officials and wealthy planters. Many congressional Republicans were angered when Southerners elected many former Confederate officials to Congress. They were further outraged when Southern state legislatures passed a series of laws known as black codes that limited African Americans' rights.

requirement something essential to the existence or occurrence of something else

The Fourteenth Amendment

In June 1866, in order to permanently block states from imposing black codes or other restrictions on African American rights, Congress passed the Fourteenth Amendment to the Constitution. This amendment granted citizenship to all persons born or naturalized in the United States and declared that no state could deprive any person of life, liberty, or property "without due process of law." It also declared that no state could deny any person "equal protection of the laws."

The Granger Collection, NYC – All rights reserved.

There's More Online! connected.mcgraw-hill.com

Connections to
TODAY

Historically Black Colleges

Ending the Civil War was about more than bringing the former Confederate states back into the Union. It was also about helping freed African Americans transition from enslavement to freedom. Increased education was key in this effort. Florida A& M University traces its origins back to 1887. Originally named the State Normal College for Colored Students, the school's first president was Thomas DeSaille Tucker, an attorney. Tucker was only the second teacher at the school and presided over its first fourteen years. The school became Florida's land-grant college for African Americans and received financial aid from the Morrill Land Grant Act. Today, Florida A & M continues the tradition of educating African Americans as one of the premier historically black institutions of higher education in the United States. **SS.912.A.2.1, SS.912.3.13**

EXTREMIST ORGANIZATIONS

POLITICAL CARTOON

During Reconstruction, secret societies such as the White League and the Pale Faces formed to prevent African Americans from exercising their rights. The largest of these groups, the Ku Klux Klan, used violence to drive out carpetbaggers and intimidate African Americans. Other white extremist organizations included the Red Shirts and the Knights of the White Camellia. The Red Shirts originated in Mississippi and the Knights of the White Camellia first formed in New Orleans.

Defending Do you think the cartoon text is correct in its assertion that these groups were "worse than slavery"? Explain.
LAFS.1112.RH.2.4, SS.912.A.1.4, SS.912.A.2.2, SS.912.H.1.5

In March 1867, Congressional Republicans passed the Military Reconstruction Act dividing the former Confederacy, except for Tennessee which had ratified the Fourteenth Amendment in 1866, into five military districts. In order for the former Confederate states to regain control of their state government and be allowed to elect members to Congress, they had to give the right to vote to all adult male citizens, regardless of race, and ratify the Fourteenth Amendment.

The Fourteenth Amendment was a turning point in American political and legal history. Since its ratification in 1868, it has been used to expand federal power over the states, and to extend civil rights through its equal protection clause. It also led to the doctrine of incorporation, the idea that the Bill of Rights applies to state governments, not just the federal government. Although it did not prevent Southern states from imposing restrictions on African Americans in the late 19th century, the Fourteenth Amendment would empower the African American civil rights movement and help ensure its success in the 1950s and 1960s.

The Fifteenth Amendment

In the meantime, tensions between Radical Republicans and Johnson increased and eventually the House of Representatives voted to impeach the president. The impeachment trial in the Senate ended one vote short of convicting Johnson. Although Johnson remained in office, he did not run for re-election in 1868. That year the Republicans nominated General Grant for president. Grant won easily, and Republicans kept control of Congress.

Republicans moved rapidly to expand their Reconstruction program. Recognizing the importance of African American suffrage, Congress passed the Fifteenth Amendment to the Constitution. This amendment declared that the right to vote "shall not be denied...on account of race, color, or previous condition of servitude." By March 1870, enough states

The Granger Collection, New York

had ratified the amendment to make it part of the Constitution. Radical Reconstruction had a dramatic impact on the South, particularly in the short term. It changed Southern politics by bringing hundreds of thousands of African Americans into the political process for the first time. It also began to change Southern society. As it did so, it angered many white Southerners, who began to fight back against the federal government's policies.

The South During Reconstruction

By the autumn of 1870, all former Confederate states had rejoined the Union. The Freedmen's Bureau worked to feed and clothe war refugees and help formerly enslaved people. A large number of Northerners traveled to the South, where many were elected or appointed to positions in the new state governments. Southerners called these newcomers **carpetbaggers** because some arrived with their belongings in suitcases made of carpet fabric. Local residents saw them as intruders seeking to exploit the South. Some white Southerners did work with the Republicans and supported Reconstruction. Other Southerners called such supporters **scalawags**—an old Scots-Irish term for weak, underfed, worthless animals.

Having gained the right to vote, African American men entered into politics with great enthusiasm. They served as legislators and administrators for nearly all levels of government. Republicans built a coalition of poor Southern-born white farmers, African Americans, and Northern carpetbaggers to elect Republican candidates.

carpetbagger name given to many Northerners who moved to the South after the Civil War and supported the Republicans

scalawag name given to Southerners who supported Republicans and Reconstruction of the South

Compromise of 1877

After Ulysses S. Grant became president in 1869, scandals and economic pressures damaged his administration. In the 1870s, Democrats began to regain power in the South. The 1876 presidential election pitted Republican Rutherford B. Hayes against Democrat Samuel Tilden. On Election Day, 20 electoral votes were disputed, including 19 in the three Southern states controlled by Republicans. The Compromise of 1877 emerged. Historians are not sure if a deal really took place, but the compromise reportedly included a promise to pull federal troops out of the South in return for a Republican victory. This did in fact happen within a month of Hayes taking office; however, it is also true that the nation and Republican leaders were ready to end Reconstruction.

☑ READING PROGRESS CHECK

Identifying What steps were taken during Reconstruction to rebuild the South and preserve the rights of African Americans?

LESSON 5 REVIEW

Reviewing Vocabulary

1. *Explaining* Who were the scalawags? LAFS.1112.RH.2.4

Using Your Notes

2. *Sequencing* Use the notes you completed during the lesson to sequence the main events of the Civil War and Reconstruction. LAFS.1112.RH.3.7, SS.912.A.2.1

Answering the Guiding Questions

3. *Assessing* What were the advantages and disadvantages for the North and the South at the start of the war? SS.912.A.2.1

4. *Analyzing Cause and Effect* When did the war change from a battle over preserving the Union to a war to end slavery? What caused this change? SS.912.A.2.1

5. *Understanding Historical Interpretation* Why were Vicksburg and Gettysburg turning points in the war? SS.912.A.2.1

6. *Making Connections* What important decisions had to be made concerning the fate of the seceded states and the rights of those freed from slavery? SS.912.A.2.1, SS.912.A.2.3

Writing Activity

7. INFORMATIVE/EXPLANATORY Write a short essay explaining the effects of the three Reconstruction Amendments and how they continue to shape the United States today. LAFS.1112.WHST.1.2, LAFS.1112.WHST.4.10, SS.912.A.2.1, SS.912.A.2.4

PRIMARY SOURCES

LAFS.1112.RH.1.1, LAFS.1112.RH.1.2, LAFS.1112.RH.1.3, LAFS.1112.RH.2.4, LAFS.1112.RH.2.5, LAFS.1112.RH.3.8, LAFS.1112.RH.4.10

The Emancipation Proclamation

The secession of the Southern states was prompted by fear that the institution of slavery was under attack. The Civil War, however, began as a battle over the question of the right of the Southern states to secede. When Abraham Lincoln decided to issue the Emancipation Proclamation, he put ending slavery at the heart of the Union effort. In doing so, he changed the meaning of the war. The proclamation was the first bold step in the abolition of slavery throughout the nation.

VOCABULARY

subordination
in a state yielding to or being controlled by authority

canker
a sore that spreads

deference
respect for someone else's wishes or desires

paramount
superior to all others

hostilities
acts of warfare

POLITICAL SPEECH, 1861

[The Confederate States of America's] constitution has put at rest, forever, all the agitating questions relating to our peculiar institution—African slavery as it exists among us—the proper status of the negro in our form of civilization. . . . The prevailing ideas entertained by . . . most of the leading statesmen at the time of the formation of the old constitution, were that the enslavement of the African was in violation of the laws of nature; that it was wrong in principle, socially, morally, and politically. . . .

Our new government is founded upon exactly the opposite idea; its foundations are laid, its cornerstone rests, upon the great truth that the negro is not equal to the white man; that slavery—**subordination** to the superior race—is his natural and normal condition.

—Alexander H. Stephens, vice president of the Confederate States of America, March 21, 1861

POLITICAL SPEECH, 1862

Mr. Speaker . . . the people of the loyal States . . . know that slavery lies at the bottom of all our troubles. They know that but for this curse this horrid revolt against liberty and law would not have occurred. They know that all the unutterable agonies of our many battlefields, all the terrible sorrows which rend so many thousands of loving hearts, all the ravages and desolation of this stupendous conflict, are to be charged to slavery. They know that its barbarism has molded the leaders of this rebellion into the most atrocious scoundrels of the nineteenth century. . . . What I said on this floor in January last, I repeat now, that the mere suppression of this rebellion will be an empty mockery of our sufferings and sacrifices, if slavery shall be spared to **canker** the heart of the nation anew, and repeat its diabolical deeds.

—Representative George W. Julian of Indiana in the U.S. House of Representatives, May 23, 1862

LETTER, 1863

My dear Sir—

. . . After the commencement of **hostilities** I struggled nearly a year and a half to get along without touching the 'institution' [of slavery]; and when finally I conditionally determined to touch it, I gave a hundred days fair notice of my purpose, to all the States and people, within which time they could have turned it wholly aside, by simply again becoming good citizens of the United States. They chose to disregard it, and I made the peremptory proclamation on what appeared to me to be a military necessity. And being made, it must stand. As to the States not included in it, of course they can have their rights in the Union as of old. Even the people of the states included, if they choose, need not to be hurt by it. Let them adopt systems of apprenticeship . . . conforming substantially to the most approved plans of gradual emancipation; and, with the aid they can have from the general government, they may be nearly as well off, in this respect, as if the present trouble had not occurred, and much better off than they can possibly be if the contest continues persistently.

—Abraham Lincoln, letter to Major General John A. McClernand, January 8, 1863

LETTERS, 1862

To Abraham Lincoln, president of the United States:

. . . On the face of this wide earth, Mr. President, there is not one disinterested,

▲ Horace Greeley, editor of the weekly "New Yorker" and founder of the New York Tribune.

▲ President Abraham Lincoln

determined, intelligent champion of the Union cause who does not feel that all attempts to put down the Rebellion, and at the same time uphold its inciting cause, are preposterous and futile—that the Rebellion, if crushed out tomorrow, would be renewed within a year if Slavery were left in full vigor—that Army officers who remain to this day devoted to Slavery can at best be but halfway loyal to the Union—and that every hour of **deference** to Slavery is an hour of added and deepened peril to the Union.

—Horace Greeley, editor of the *New York Tribune*, August 19, 1862

Dear Sir—

. . . If there be those who would not save the Union unless they could at the same time save slavery, I do not agree with them—if there be those who would not save the Union unless they could at the same time destroy slavery, I do not agree with them.

My **paramount** object in this struggle is to save the Union, and is not either to save or destroy slavery—if I could save the Union without freeing any slave, I would do it; and if I could save it by freeing all the slaves, I would do it; and if I could do it by freeing some and leaving others alone, I would also do that.

—Abraham Lincoln's response, August 22, 1862

DBQ Analyzing Historical Documents

1. **Comparing** How do Stephens and Julian differ on their opinions of slavery? Cite evidence from their speeches to support your answer.

2. **Explaining** Does Alexander Stephens support slavery as a matter of states' rights or does he approve of the practice for other reasons? Provide evidence to support your answer.

3. **Stating** Representative Julian's speech is very critical of the rebellion. What do you think he means when he laments about "unutterable agonies" and the "terrible sorrows?"

4. **Citing Text Evidence** What is Horace Greeley's prediction for Lincoln's efforts to "put down the Rebellion, and at the same time uphold its inciting cause?" What argument does Greeley use to support his prediction?

5. **Specifying** President Lincoln's response to Greeley is neither pro nor anti slavery. What does President Lincoln state is his primary goal?

6. **Paraphrasing** Using your own words, explain President Lincoln's letter to Union Major General John A. McClernand.

7. **Identifying Alternatives** What alternative to slavery does President Lincoln suggest in his letter to McClernand?

(l)Hulton Archive/Getty Images; (r)Time Life Pictures/Getty Images

Understanding Historical Eras

Why Learn This Skill?

Have you ever heard someone refer to music from "the 60s" or art from the Renaissance? Has your history teacher ever referred to the Middle Ages, or to the Gilded Age, or to the Cold War era? In each case, they are referring to an historical era. An era is a period of time in history that has distinct characteristics. Historians divide history into eras as a form of shorthand. Instead of having to refer to "the time when many people were out of work; the Great Plains were suffering dust storms, and the government was creating programs to help people," historians can simply refer to "The Great Depression." Understanding historical eras makes learning history easier. By breaking history into chunks, it is easier to remember what was happening and why.

Learning the Skill

To be an historical era, a period of time has to have a common set of major characteristics. These characteristics are based on a combination of the unique politics, economics, technology, social issues, culture, and major events that were shaping people's lives at the time. It is not always clear when an era begins or ends. Some of the things common in one era may continue into the next era, but usually several major things change, leading historians to identify it as a new era.

Historians often use a major event to mark the break or turning point that leads to a new era. Historians also break up history differently depending on what they are studying. An historian looking at international events regards the 1920s and 1930s as the "Interwar Era" between World War I and World War II. But an historian looking at economics sees the booming 1920s as very different from the depression of the 1930s.

Because the history of the United States is so short, the historical eras people use tend to be only a few decades long at most. Modern American history is usually said to begin in 1877.

The reason 1877 is chosen as the start is because it marks the last year when political debates still involved the issues of the Civil War and Reconstruction. After 1877, historians generally agree that the United States began to change and deal with issues unrelated to the Civil War era.

These are the major eras of American history since 1877 that most historians reference:

- The Industrial Era, or Gilded Age, 1877–1900
- The Progressive Era & World War I, 1900–1920
- The Roaring 20s, or The New Era, 1920–1929
- The Great Depression, or New Deal, 1929–1939
- World War II, 1939–1945
- Post War America, 1945 to the present

Some eras, like the Industrial Era, become known for the rapid growth of urban areas.

Library of Congress, Prints & Photographs Division [LC-DIG-nclc-01366]

The decades since the end of World War II have been a time of great change, and historians disagree over how best to divide it into historical eras. Many historians see 1945 to 1991 as an historical era, because 1945 marks the start of the Cold War and 1991 marks the end of the Soviet Union. Others focus on events within the United States. Some like to divide the post-war era into decades, "the 50s," "the 60s," "the 70s" etc., because they see dramatic cultural changes in each decade. Others prefer to divide the post-war years into eras based on major political, economic, or technological changes, including the following:

Certain individuals often represent eras in iconic ways. Martin Luther King, for instance, has become an icon of the Civil Rights Era.

- Post-War America, 1945–1953
- Civil Rights Era, 1954–1968
- Vietnam Era, 1965–1975
- The Conservative Resurgence, 1976–1992
- End of the Century, 1980–2000
- The Technology Revolution, 1981–present
- The Post-9/11 Era, 2001–present
- The Great Recession, 2007–present

Whatever era is used, the best way to understand it is to focus on the major characteristics that make it different from other times in history. Learning those characteristics will help you remember American history, and you will be able to make connections and generalizations about history more easily.

1. What made the era from 1877 to 1900 different from previous eras?
2. What issues and concerns seem to characterize the Progressive Era?
3. Why do you think World War I is included as part of the Progressive Era?
4. What makes the 1920s a unique era according to some historians?
5. Why might some historians combine the 1930s and World War II into one era?
6. What other ways could you divide up the time period from 1877 to 1929? Identify alternative eras and make a brief list of the characteristics that define them.

Practicing this Skill

Open up your textbook or the online student edition website. Look through the different chapters and lessons, paying attention to the headings and topics to get a sense of the major characteristics of each era. Then answer the following questions:

Applying the Skill

Look through the different chapters and lessons from 1945 to the present. Examine the headings and topics. Think about what you already know about recent events in American history. Create a timeline illustrating the major historical eras you would use to understand 1945 to the present. Identify the dates for each era and list a few bullet points for each era describing its characteristics.

PHOTO: Francis Miller/Time & Life Pictures/Getty Images; TEXT: Martin Luther King Jr., "I Have a Dream," August 28, 1963. Reprinted by arrangement with The Heirs to the Estate of Martin Luther King Jr., c/o Writers House as agent for the proprietor New York, NY. Copyright 1963 Dr. Martin Luther King Jr.; copyright renewed 1991 Coretta Scott King.

STUDY GUIDE

ORIGINS OF THE AMERICAN NATION
LESSON 1

SPANISH COLONIES
- Searching for gold, to convert native population
- Located in the Caribbean & streched from California along southern border to Florida
- Agriculture and herding economy

FRENCH COLONIES
- Looking for new business opportunities for fur trading
- Located in Canada and down Mississippi River to New Orleans & coastal Alabama
- Fur trapping economy

ENGLISH COLONIES
- Establishing colonies for religious freedom and for economic profit
- Located north and south along the Atlantic Ocean coastline
- Diverse economy of farming & small manufacturing

THE YOUNG REPUBLIC
Lesson 2

ARTICLES OF CONFEDERATION
- Single governing body
- Weak central government; could not regulate trade or impose taxes

U.S. CONSTITUTION
- Three cooperating branches of government
- Strong central government, checked by separation of powers

POLITICAL PARTIES
- Federalists: supportive of the new constitutional government
- Democratic-Republicans: supported independent farmers, states rights

NATIONAL GROWTH
- Louisiana Purchase expands nation's geography
- Lewis and Clark expedition
- War of 1812 solidifies young nation and increases patriotic pride

ANTEBELLUM AMERICA
Lesson 3

IN THE NORTH
- Large numbers of immigrants settled in cities, providing a source of cheap labor
- Over a million factory workers; workers labored 12 or more hours a day
- Despite urban and industrial growth, Northern farms produced enough surplus to sell to Eastern cities

IN THE SOUTH
- Lagged behind the North in Industrialization, but had some scattered factories and milles
- Tobacco, rice, sugarcane farms; but dominated by growing emphasis on cotton
- Enslaved labor the key to large scale agricultural profit

THE CIVIL WAR AND RECONSTRUCTION
Lesson 5

THE SECTIONAL CRISIS
Lesson 4

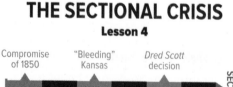

Compromise of 1850 — "Bleeding" Kansas — *Dred Scott* decision — THE SOUTH SECEDES

Fugitive Slave Act — Free Soil Party & Know Nothings — Abraham Lincoln is elected

RESOURCES OF THE UNION AND OF THE CONFEDERACY

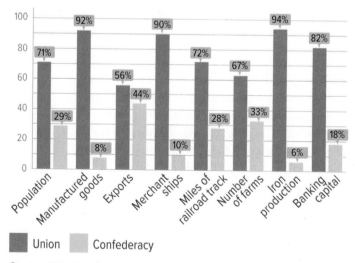

- Population: 71% / 29%
- Manufactured goods: 92% / 8%
- Exports: 56% / 44%
- Merchant ships: 90% / 10%
- Miles of railroad track: 72% / 28%
- Number of farms: 67% / 33%
- Iron production: 94% / 6%
- Banking capital: 82% / 18%

■ Union ■ Confederacy

Source: Historical Statistics of the United States

Directions: On a separate sheet of paper, answer the questions below. Make sure you read carefully and answer all parts to the question.

Lesson Review

Lesson 1

1 **Identifying Cause and Effect** What factors caused European nations to explore the Western Hemisphere and establish colonies?
SS.912.G.4.2, SS.912.G.4.3, SS.912.H.3.1

2 **Describing** Colonies took on unique characteristics based on charters and colony formation. Explain how certain colonies offered freedom from religious persecution for colonists.
SS.912.G.2.1

3 **Explaining Continuity and Change** How was the idea of "No taxation without representation" an important factor leading to the American Revolution?
LAFS.1112.RH.2.4

Lesson 2

4 **Contrasting** What was a key difference between the Federalists and the Democratic-Republicans?
LAFS.1112.RH.3.7

5 **Analyzing and Evaluating** What is the intent of the Bill of Rights? The Constitutional Convention did not think the Constitution needed a Bill of Rights. Why did the Framers agree to add it later? Do you think it was necessary? Explain your answer.
LAFS.1112.RH.3.8

6 **Understanding Relationships Among Events** How do the ideas of the Connecticut Compromise affect the structure of our federal government today?

Constitution Handbook

7 **Analyzing and Evaluating** Why are the Constitution and the Bill of Rights important? What purpose do they serve and have they been effective?

8 **Explaining** What is the meaning and historical significance of the motto "E Pluribus Unum"?
LAFS.1112.RH.2.4, LAFS.1112.RH.3.7

Lesson 3

9 **Identifying Central Issues** How did opposing views on slavery lead to the Missouri Compromise?
SS.912.A.2.1

10 **Comparing and Contrasting** Compare the economies in the North and South. What type of industry or agriculture existed and who performed the labor? SS.912.A.2.1

Lesson 4

11 **Making Connections** How was the addition of Oregon to the United States an example of the idea of Manifest Destiny?

12 **Explaining** What was the Fugitive Slave Act?
SS.912.A.2.1

13 **Identifying Cause and Effect** Why was there so much violence in Kansas in 1855 and 1856?
SS.912.A.2.1

14 **Explaining** Why did the South secede from the Union? SS.912.A.2.1

Lesson 5

15 **Identifying** What were the South's financial disadvantages at the start of the Civil War?
SS.912.A.2.1

16 **Explaining** Why did President Lincoln feel that the Emancipation Proclamation was necessary? How did this show effective leadership? SS.912.A.2.1

17 **Analyzing** What method was used to expand the right of African Americans to participate in the democratic process after the Civil War? What changes resulted? SS.912.A.2.1, SS.912.A.2.4

Exploring the Essential Questions

18 **Analyzing** Write a short essay explaining why participating in the democratic process reflects the national ethos, or ideals, of patriotism and civic responsibility. Use the example of voting to give specific evidence for your answer. Your essay should have an introduction, at least three paragraphs, and a conclusion. LAFS.1112.RH.1.1, LAFS.1112.WHST.1.1, LAFS.1112.WHST.2.4, LAFS.1112.WHST.3.9, LAFS.1112.WHST.4.10

Critical Thinking

19 **Analyzing Text** What are the four major sections of the Declaration of Independence? Evaluate the purpose of each section. LAFS.1112.RH.2.5, SS.912.A.1.2

Need Extra Help?

If You've Missed Question	1	2	3	4	5	6	7	8	9	10	11	12	13	14	15	16	17	18	19
Go to Lesson	1	1	1	2	2	2	CHB	CHB	3	3	4	4	4	4	5	5	5	CHB	1

20 *Summarizing* Analyze the text of the Bill of Rights and write a summary evaluating what each amendment means and what rights are protected. Explain how the Tenth Amendment is different from the others. Which rights do you think are the most important? LAFS.1112.RH.1.2, LAFS.1112.RH.2.5

21st Century Skills

21 *Applying Absolute and Relative Chronology* Create a time line illustrating the major historical eras of the United States from 1877 to the present. On the time line, identify the approximate start and end date for each era, and use captions to briefly describe the era's characteristics. SS.912.A.1.3

22 *Sequencing Historical Events* In what way was the Thirteenth Amendment the culmination of the abolitionist movement? Why might the abolitionist movement be considered the first civil rights movement of the nineteenth century? How did abolitionism represent an application of the founding principles of the United States? SS.912.A.1.3, SS.912.A.2.1

23 *Explaining Continuity and Change* What rights did the Fourteenth and Fifteenth Amendments confer, and how did they set the stage for a new civil rights movement for African Americans? SS.912.A.2.4

DBQ Analyzing Primary Sources

Read the following excerpt, and then answer the questions that follow.

PRIMARY SOURCE

❝When in the Course of human events, it becomes necessary for one people to dissolve the political bands which have connected them with another, and to assume among the Powers of the earth, the separate and equal station to which the Laws of Nature and of Nature's God entitle them, a decent respect to the opinions of mankind requires that they should declare the causes which impel them to the separation.

We hold these truths to be self-evident, that all men are created equal, that they are endowed by their Creator with certain unalienable Rights, that among these are Life, Liberty, and the pursuit of Happiness.

That to secure these rights, Governments are instituted among Men, deriving their just powers from the consent of the governed.❞

24 *Identifying* The three paragraphs come from what document? What date was this document issued? LAFS.1112.RH.4.10

25 *Analyzing and Evaluating* What organization issued the document, and what was the intent of the document? Did the document achieve what it was intended to do? LAFS.1112.RH.4.10

26 *Analyzing and Evaluating Meaning* What does the document mean when it says that "We hold these truths to be self-evident?" To what truths is it referring? According to the document, why do people create governments? LAFS.1112.RH.2.4, LAFS.1112.RH.4.10

27 *Analyzing and Evaluating Significance* Why is the document important? What has been its significance to both American history and world history? LAFS.1112.RH.4.10

Analyzing Visuals

Use the drawing to answer the following question.

28 *Analyzing Visuals* What message does this cartoon convey about the fate of the colonies as they faced challenges leading up to the American Revolution? SS.912.A.1.4, SS.912.H.1.5

Extended Response Questions

29 *Analyzing* Write an essay that analyzes and evaluates the text of the U.S. Constitution and the intent of the document. What kind of structure does it impose on the U.S. government? What is the intent of the U.S. Constitution? How does it structure the government to achieve its purpose? Cite text from the document to support your evaluation and analysis. LAFS.1112.RH.1.1, LAFS.1112.WHST.2.4, LAFS.1112.WHST.4.10

Library of Congress, Prints & Photographs Division [LC-USZC4-5315]

Need Extra Help?

If You've Missed Question	**20**	**21**	**22**	**23**	**24**	**25**	**26**	**27**	**28**	**29**
Go to Lesson	3	1, 2, 3, 4, 5	4, 5	5	2	2	2	2	2	3

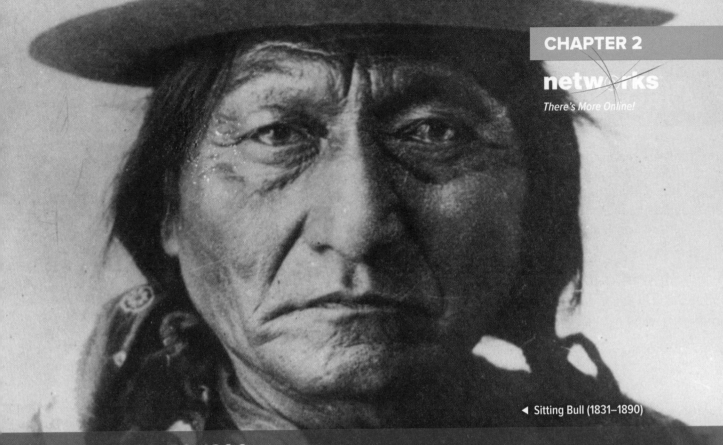

◀ Sitting Bull (1831–1890)

FROM 1865 TO 1890

Settling the West

The Granger Collection, New York

THE STORY MATTERS ...

After the Civil War, Americans continued migrating to the western frontier. Their lives were filled with hardships. But this movement west created more hardships for the Native Americans, which dramatically altered their way of life.

Sitting Bull, a leader of the Sioux, steadfastly defended his people against forces trying to strip them of their homes, their culture, and their very existence.

ESSENTIAL QUESTION

- Why would people take on the challenges of life in the West?

Place & Time: United States 1860–1900

Miners, ranchers, and farmers led the way to the expansion of the western territories. Homesteading allowed settlers to claim acres of land to cultivate and build new lives. With the building of railroads to connect the western states to the East, the population quickly grew. For centuries this land was home to many groups of Native Americans. The settling of the West altered their way of life forever.

Step Into the Place

Read the quotes and look at the information presented on the map.

DBQ **Analyzing Historical Documents** How does the first quote compare to the information and feelings expressed in the second quote from the document?

PRIMARY SOURCE

❝ My heart is full of sorrow that so many were killed on each side, but when they compel us to fight, we must fight. . . . Tonight we shall mourn for our dead, and for those brave white men lying up yonder on the hillside. ❞

—Sitting Bull, after the Battle of the Little Bighorn, 1876

PRIMARY SOURCE

❝ The Seventh [Infantry] can handle anything it meets. ❞

—General George A. Custer while declining reinforcements for the Battle of the Little Bighorn

❝ . . . It is the opinion at headquarters among those who are most familiar with the situation, that Custer struck Sitting Bull's main camp. . . . Custer dropped squarely into the midst of no less than ten thousand red devils and was literally torn to pieces. The movement made by Custer is censured to some extent at military headquarters in this city. . . . ❞

—as reported in the *New York Times*, July 7, 1876

left page (t)©Historical/Corbis, (tr)The Granger Collection, NYC– All rights reserved. (bl br)detail/White House Collection/The White House Historical Association; **right page** detail/White House Collection/The White House Historical Association

Step Into the Time

MAKING CONNECTIONS Research a president listed on the time line. Write a paragraph explaining how this president might have influenced westward expansion.

1862 Homestead Act makes cheap land available to settlers

1864 Sand Creek Massacre takes place

A. Johnson 1865–1869

1867 Chisholm Trail cattle drive begins

1868 Sioux move to Black Hills reservation

Grant 1869–1877

U.S. PRESIDENTS

UNITED STATES

WORLD

1860

1870

1866 French explore the Mekong River

1873 British raise their flag at Port Moresby in New Guinea

1876 Belgium founds Internati Association for the Exploration a Civilization of Africa

NEXT GENERATION SUNSHINE STATE STANDARDS
Students will understand the following benchmarks from the Florida NGSSS

LAFS.1112.RH.3.7: Integrate and evaluate multiple sources of information presented in diverse formats and media (e.g., visually, quantitatively, as well as in words) in order to address a question or solve a problem.

LAFS.1112.RH.3.9: Integrate information from diverse sources, both primary and secondary, into a coherent understanding of an idea or event, noting discrepancies among sources.

LAFS.1112.RH.4.10: By the end of grade 12, read and comprehend history/social studies texts in the grades 11–CCR text complexity band independently and proficiently.

SS.912.A.1.2: Utilize a variety of primary and secondary sources to identify author, historical significance, audience, and authenticity to understand a historical period.

SS.912.A.1.3: Utilize timelines to identify the time sequence of historical data.

SS.912.A.1.4: Analyze how images, symbols, objects, cartoons, graphs, charts, maps, and artwork may be used to interpret the significance of time periods and events from the past.

SS.912.A.2.7: Review the Native American experience.

SS.912.A.3.1: Analyze the economic challenges to American farmers and farmers' responses to these challenges in the mid to late 1800s.

The Battle of the Little Bighorn, 1876

Legend:
- → U.S. Movements – known
- → U.S. Movements – conjectured
- → Native American Movements – known
- → Native American Movements – conjectured
- ✳ Battle
- ■ Point of Interest
- ☐ Native American Encampment

The Last Stand
Calhoun Hill
Native American Movements After Custer's Defeat
Custer's Route
Little Bighorn River
Weir's Attempt to Aid Custer
Sioux/Cheyenne Encampment
Retreat Crossing
Reno's 2nd Position
Reno's Retreat
Entrenchment
Custer's Advance
Reno's 1st Position
Little Bighorn River
Benteen's Advance
Reno's Advance
Reno Creek
Reno Ford

0 — 1 mile
0 — 1 km
GCS WGS 1984 projection

Hayes 1877–1881
Garfield 1881
Arthur 1881–1885
Cleveland 1885–1889
1887 Dawes Act passed
1889 Oklahoma Land Rush takes place
B. Harrison 1889–1893
Cleveland 1893–1897
McKinley 1897–1901

1880 — 1890 — 1900

1884 Fifteen nations meet at Berlin West Africa Conference to set rules for the colonization of Central Africa

1886 Gold is discovered in South Africa

1889 Boer War begins between Afrikaners and British in southern Africa

1891 Russia begins Trans-Siberian railway

LESSON 1
Miners and Ranchers

ESSENTIAL QUESTION

• Why would people take on the challenges of life in the West?

READING HELPDESK

Academic Vocabulary

- extract
- adapt
- prior

Content Vocabulary

- vigilance committee
- hydraulic mining
- open range
- hacienda
- barrios

TAKING NOTES

Key Ideas and Details

Organizing As you read, complete a graphic organizer like the one below listing the locations of mining booms and the discoveries made there.
LAFS.1112.RH.3.7, SS.912.A.3.4

Mining Booms & Discoveries

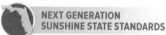

**NEXT GENERATION
SUNSHINE STATE STANDARDS**

LAFS.1112.RH.2.4: Determine the meaning of words and phrases as they are used in a text, including analyzing how an author uses and refines the meaning of a key term over the course of a text (e.g., how Madison defines faction in Federalist No. 10).

LAFS.1112.RH.3.7: Integrate and evaluate multiple sources of information presented in diverse formats and media (e.g., visually, quantitatively, as well as in words) in order to address a question or solve a problem.

LAFS.1112.WHST.1.1: Write arguments focused on discipline-specific content.

Continued on page 97

IT MATTERS BECAUSE
The migration of miners and ranchers to western territories resulted in populations large enough to qualify for statehood. People mined for gold, silver, and lead or shipped longhorn cattle to the East.

Growth of the Mining Industry

GUIDING QUESTION *How did mineral discoveries shape the settlement of the West?*

Mining played an important role in the settling of the American West. Demand for minerals rose dramatically after the Civil War as the United States changed from a farming nation to an industrial nation. Mining also led to the building of railroads to connect the mines to factories back east.

Boomtowns

In 1859, a prospector named Henry Comstock staked a claim near Virginia City, Nevada. When others found a rich source nearby, Comstock claimed he owned the land and quickly struck a deal to share the fortune. He later sold his claim for thousands of dollars, not realizing that the sticky, blue-gray clay that made mining in the area difficult was nearly pure silver ore worth millions.

News of the Comstock Lode, as the strike came to be called, brought a flood of prospectors to Virginia City. So many people arrived that, in 1864, Nevada was admitted as the thirty-sixth state in the Union. This occurred many times in the American West. News of a mineral strike would start a stampede of prospectors. Almost overnight, tiny frontier towns were transformed into small cities. Virginia City, for example, grew from a town of a few hundred people to nearly 30,000 in just a few months. It had an opera house, shops with furniture and fashions from Europe, several newspapers, and a six-story hotel.

These quickly growing towns were called boomtowns. The term *boom* refers to a time of rapid economic growth. Boomtowns were rowdy places. Prospectors fought over claims, and thieves haunted the streets and trails. Often, "law and order" was enforced by **vigilance committees**—self-appointed volunteers who would track down and punish wrongdoers. In some cases, they responded with their own form of justice, but most people respected the law and tried to deal firmly but fairly with the accused.

Eventually, the mines that supported the boomtown economy were used up. A few boomtowns were able to survive when the mines closed, but many of them did not. Instead, these boomtowns went "bust"—a term borrowed from card games in which players lost all of their money. In Virginia City, for example, the silver mines were exhausted by the 1880s, and most residents moved on; only about 500 people remained by 1930. Other towns were completely abandoned and became ghost towns.

Mining Leads to Statehood

After gold was discovered in 1858 in Colorado near Pikes Peak, miners rushed to the area, declaring "Pikes Peak or Bust." Many panned for gold without success and headed home, complaining of a "Pikes Peak hoax." In truth, the Colorado mountains contained plenty of gold and silver, although much of it was hidden beneath the surface and hard to **extract.** Deep deposits of lead mixed with silver were found at Leadville in the 1870s. News of the strike attracted as many as 1,000 newcomers a week, making Leadville one of the West's most famous boomtowns. This bonanza spurred the building of railroads through the Rocky Mountains and transformed Denver, the supply point for the mining areas, into the second-largest city in the West, after San Francisco.

vigilance committee
group of ordinary citizens who organize to find criminals and bring them to justice

extract to remove by force

NEXT GENERATION SUNSHINE STATE STANDARDS

Continued from page 96

LAFS.1112.WHST.4.10: Write routinely over extended time frames (time for reflection and revision) and shorter time frames (a single sitting or a day or two) for a range of discipline-specific tasks, purposes, and audiences.

SS.912.A.1.4: Analyze how images, symbols, objects, cartoons, graphs, charts, maps, and artwork may be used to interpret the significance of time periods and events from the past.

SS.912.A.3.1: Analyze the economic challenges to American farmers and farmers' responses to these challenges in the mid to late 1800s.

SS.912.A.3.4: Determine how the development of steel, oil, transportation, communication, and business practices affected the United States economy.

SS.912.A.3.13: Examine key events and peoples in Florida history as they relate to United States history.

Continued on page 98

Mining Helps Build a Nation 1848–1890

GEOGRAPHY CONNECTION

The discovery of gold and silver led to the growth of western territories.

1 **THE WORLD IN SPATIAL TERMS** *What is a likely reason Nevada and California were two of the first western territories to become states?* SS.912.A.1.4

2 **PLACES AND REGIONS** *Which territories were the last to enter as states? Why might this have been the case?* SS.912.A.1.4, SS.912.G.4.9

Legend:
- States where mining contributed to growth
- Gold
- Silver
- 1890 border

Lambert Azimuthal Equal-Area projection

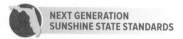

NEXT GENERATION SUNSHINE STATE STANDARDS

Continued from page 97

SS.912.G.1.2: Use spatial perspective and appropriate geographic terms and tools, including the Six Essential Elements, as organizational schema to describe any given place.

SS.912.G.2.1: Identify the physical characteristics and the human characteristics that define and differentiate regions.

SS.912.G.4.3: Use geographic terms and tools to analyze the effects of migration both on the place of origin and destination, including border areas.

SS.912.G.4.9: Use political maps to describe the change in boundaries and governments within continents over time.

hydraulic mining method of mining by which water is sprayed at a very high pressure against a hill or mountain, washing away large quantities of dirt, gravel, and rock and exposing the minerals beneath the surface

Miners used high-pressure water to wash loose earth into ditches. The ditches carried the water and earth into riffle boxes that agitated the water, causing the silver or gold to settle out. The leftover debris, called tailings or "slickens," was then washed into a nearby stream.

▶ **CRITICAL THINKING**
Determining Cause and Effect How might this mining practice have helped miners in their search for minerals?
SS.912.A.1.4

The discovery of gold in the Black Hills of the Dakota Territory and copper in Montana drew miners to the region in the 1870s. When the railroads were completed, many farmers and ranchers settled the area. In 1889, Congress admitted three new states: North Dakota, South Dakota, and Montana.

In the Southwest, the Arizona Territory followed a similar pattern. Miners had already begun moving to Arizona in the 1860s and 1870s to work one of the nation's largest copper deposits. When silver was found at the town of Tombstone in 1877, it set off a boom that attracted a huge wave of prospectors to the territory.

The boom lasted about 30 years, and during that time Tombstone became famous for its lawlessness. Marshal Wyatt Earp and his brothers gained their reputations there during the famous gunfight at the O.K. Corral in 1881. Although Arizona did not grow as quickly as Colorado, Nevada, or Montana, by 1912 it had enough people to apply for statehood, as did the neighboring territory of New Mexico.

Mining Technology

Extracting minerals from the rugged mountains of the American West required ingenuity and patience. Early prospectors extracted shallow deposits of ore in a process called placer mining, using simple tools like picks, shovels, and pans.

Other prospectors used sluice mining to search riverbeds more quickly than the panning method. A sluice diverted the current of a river into trenches. The water was directed to a box with metal "riffle" bars that caused heavier minerals to settle to the bottom of the box. A screen at the end kept the minerals from escaping with the water and sediment.

When deposits near the surface ran out, miners began **hydraulic mining** to remove large quantities of earth and process it for minerals. Miners sprayed water at very high pressure against the hill or mountain they were mining. The water pressure washed away the dirt, gravel, and rock and exposed the minerals beneath the surface.

Changes to the Land

Hydraulic mining began in the Sierra Nevada mountains in California. It effectively removed large quantities of minerals and generated millions of dollars in gold. Unfortunately, it also had a devastating effect on the local environment. Millions of tons of silt, sand, and gravel were washed into local rivers. This sediment raised the riverbed. As a result, the rivers began overflowing their banks, causing major floods that wrecked fences, destroyed orchards, and deposited rocks and gravel on what had been good farm soil, destroying thousands of acres of rich farmland. In the 1880s, farmers fought back by suing the mining companies. In 1884, federal judge Lorenzo Sawyer ruled in favor of the farmers. He declared hydraulic mining a "public and private nuisance" and issued an injunction stopping the practice.

Congress eventually passed a law in 1893 allowing hydraulic mining if the mining company created a place to store the sediment. By then, most mining companies had moved to quartz mining—the kind of mining familiar to people today—in which deep mine shafts are dug, and miners go underground to extract the minerals.

☑ **READING PROGRESS CHECK**

Explaining What role did mining play in the development of the American West?

Library of Congress Prints and Photographs Division [LC-USZ62-9889]

Ranching and Cattle Drives

GUIDING QUESTION *Why was cattle ranching an important business for the Great Plains?*

The lure of the Great Plains brought other Americans west to herd cattle. The Texas longhorn, a cattle breed descended from Spanish cattle introduced two centuries earlier, was well **adapted** to this region and flourished on scarce water and tough prairie grasses. By 1865, some 5 million roamed the Texas grasslands. Another boon to cattle ranching was the **open range,** a vast area of grassland that the federal government owned. Here, ranchers could graze their herds free of charge and unrestricted by private property.

The Long Drive Begins

Prior to the Civil War, ranchers had little incentive to round up the longhorns and move them to market. Beef prices were low, and moving cattle to eastern markets was not practical. But during the war, eastern cattle had been slaughtered in huge numbers to feed the armies of the Union and the Confederacy. After the war, beef prices soared. Also, by this time, railroads had reached the Great Plains, heading to towns in Kansas and Missouri. Ranchers and livestock dealers realized that if they could move their cattle to the railroad, the longhorns could be sold for a huge profit and shipped east to market.

In 1866 ranchers rounded up about 260,000 longhorns and drove them to Sedalia, Missouri—the first "long drive." Other cattle trails soon opened, including the route to Abilene, Kansas, as the railroads expanded in the West. Cowboys from major ranches went north with the herds, which could number anywhere from 2,000 to 5,000 cattle.

The End of the Open Range

Before long, sheep herders moved their flocks onto the range and farmers came in, breaking up the land for their crops. Eventually, hundreds of square miles of fields were fenced cheaply and easily with a new invention—barbed wire. The fences blocked the cattle trails. The cattle industry faced other struggles. Prices plunged in the mid-1880s, and many ranchers went bankrupt. The harsh winter of 1886–1887 buried the Plains in deep snow. Many cattle froze or starved to death.

Although it survived these terrible blows, the cattle industry was changed forever. The era of the open range ended, and cowboys became ranch hands. From then on, herds were raised on fenced-in ranches.

✔ READING PROGRESS CHECK

Analyzing Describe the reasons for the growth of the cattle industry on the Great Plains.

New Settlers Arrive in the Southwest

GUIDING QUESTION *What was the relationship like between Hispanics in the Southwest and new settlers?*

For centuries, much of what is today the American Southwest belonged to Spain's empire. After Mexico won its independence, the region became the northern territories of the Republic of Mexico. When the United States defeated Mexico in 1848, it acquired this vast region. According to the Treaty of Guadalupe Hidalgo, which ended the war, the region's residents retained their property rights and could become American citizens.

Cowboys drove millions of cattle north from Texas to the railroads in Kansas and points beyond.

▶ CRITICAL THINKING
Making Generalizations What effect did the increased ability to move cattle to different parts of the country have on the cattle industry? LAFS.1112.RH.3.7, SS.912.A.1.4

 Florida
CONNECTION

Florida's Cattle Industry

When people think of cattle drives, they usually think of the Wild West on the Great Plains. Florida has its own rich history of cattle raising adapted to its geography and climate. The Spanish originally brought the cow to Florida in the 15th century. Florida cattle men such as Jacob Summerlin (1820-1893), the "King of the Crackers" (as Florida cattlemen were sometimes called), first grew wealthy by selling beef to Confederate Rebels during the Civil War. When Cuban revolutionaries were trying to gain independence from Spain in the 1880s and 1890s, Summerlin shipped cattle to Cuba from the ports near Fort Myers and Punta Rassa. SS.912.A.3.13

The Granger Collection, New York

adapt to change in order to meet the demands of a certain environment or circumstance

open range vast areas of grassland owned by the federal government

prior before or previous

hacienda a huge ranch

In the mid-19th century, most Hispanics in the Southwest lived on large haciendas where they worked in the fields or helped tend cattle.

▶ CRITICAL THINKING
Identifying Central Ideas How might the change from being the majority to becoming the minority have affected Hispanics in the Southwest? LAFS.1112.RH.3.7, SS.912.A.1.4

Changing Demographics in the Southwest

In California, the Spanish mission system had collapsed by the early 1800s. In its place, a society dominated by a landholding elite had emerged. These landowners owned vast **haciendas**—ranches that covered thousands of acres. The heavy influx of "Forty-Niners" during the California gold rush of 1849, however, changed this society dramatically. California's population grew from about from 14,000 to around 100,000 in less than two years and its demographic pattern changed dramatically. Suddenly, Hispanic Californians were vastly outnumbered.

Some Hispanic Californians welcomed the newcomers and the economic growth that resulted. Others distrusted the English-speaking prospectors, who tried to exclude them from the mines. When California achieved statehood in 1850, Hispanics served in many state and local offices. Increasingly, however, the original Hispanic population found its status diminished, and Hispanics were often relegated to lower-paying and less desirable jobs.

As they had done with Native Americans, settlers from the East clashed with Mexican Americans over land. Across the region, many Hispanics lost their land to the new settlers. Mexican American claims to the land often dated back to Spanish land grants. These grants were hundreds of years old and defined the boundaries of property in vague terms. When more than one person claimed ownership of a property, American courts frequently held that the old land grants were insufficient proof of ownership. This allowed others to stake claim to the property. In some instances, outright fraud was used to take land illegally from Mexican Americans.

The cattle boom of the 1870s and 1880s had a tremendous impact on Hispanics in the Southwest, where many had long worked as vaqueros (the Spanish word for "cowboys"). Spanish vaqueros had a long history of sharing their techniques for managing cattle. They shared methods of branding with Florida cattlemen as far back in history as when Florida was a Spanish colony. This interaction with American cowboys enriched the English language with such Spanish words as *lariat, lasso,* and *stampede.*

American Stock Archive/Archive Photos/Getty Images

Clashes and Compromises in the Southwest

With the increasing demand for beef in the eastern United States, English-speaking ranchers wanted to expand their herds and claimed large tracts of land of Mexican origin. In some cases, the Hispanic population fought back. In New Mexico, residents of the town of Las Vegas were outraged when English-speaking ranchers tried to fence in land that had long been used by the community to graze livestock. In 1889, a group of Hispanic New Mexicans calling themselves *Las Gorras Blancas* ("The White Caps") raided ranches owned by English speakers, tore down their fences, and burned their barns and houses. Attempts were made to call in federal troops to stop the raids, but the president refused to send them. The raids finally ended in 1891.

Despite the influx of English-speaking settlers, Hispanics in New Mexico remained more influential in public affairs than did their counterparts in California and Texas. Hispanics remained the majority, both in population and in the territorial legislature. In addition, Hispanics frequently served as New Mexico's territorial delegates to Congress.

As more railroads were built in the 1880s and 1890s, the population of the Southwest continued to swell. The region attracted not only Americans and European immigrants from the East but also immigrants from Mexico. Mexican immigrants worked mainly in agriculture and on the railroads. In the growing cities of the Southwest—such as El Paso, Albuquerque, and Los Angeles—Hispanics settled in neighborhoods called **barrios.** These neighborhoods had Spanish-speaking businesses and Spanish-language newspapers, and they helped keep Hispanic cultural and religious traditions alive. As native Californian Mariano Guadalupe Vallejo explained in 1890:

A fancily dressed vaquero, known as a *charro*, poses for a photo in 1890.

▶ **CRITICAL THINKING**
Making Generalizations Based on the appearance of the vaquero, what generalizations can be made about the man?
LAFS.1112.RH.3.7, SS.912.A.1.4

barrios Spanish-speaking neighborhoods in a town or city

PRIMARY SOURCE

❝No class of American citizens is more loyal than the Spanish Californians, but we shall always be especially proud . . . to honor the founders of our ancient families, and the saints and heroes of our history since the days when Father Junipero planted the cross at Monterey.❞

—quoted in *Foreigners in Their Native Land*

☑ **READING PROGRESS CHECK**

Describing How did vaqueros contribute to the cattle industry in the West?

LESSON 1 REVIEW

Reviewing Vocabulary
1. ***Analyzing*** What was the significance of barrios to Hispanic culture in the West? LAFS.1112.RH.2.4

Using Your Notes
2. ***Listing*** Review the notes that you completed throughout the lesson and list the discoveries that attracted prospectors and settlers to the boomtowns of the American West.

Answering the Guiding Questions
3. ***Determining Cause and Effect*** How did mineral discoveries shape the settlement of the West?

4. ***Summarizing*** Why was cattle ranching an important business for the Great Plains?

5. ***Analyzing*** What was the relationship like between Hispanics in the Southwest and new settlers? SS.912.G.4.3

Writing Activity
6. **ARGUMENT** Suppose that you are a farmer near Nevada City, California, in the 1880s. Write a letter explaining why hydraulic mining endangers your livelihood and therefore should be banned. LAFS.1112.WHST.1.1, LAFS.1112.WHST.4.10

The Art Archive/Bill Manns

Reading and Creating a Thematic Map

Why Learn This Skill?

You will often encounter thematic maps when studying history. Knowing how to read and create a thematic map will help you understand the information this type of map presents.

Learning the Skill

A thematic map takes data about a region and puts it on a map using colors and symbols that show how the data connects to geographical features. Thematic maps can help you identify the physical and human systems of a geographic area. These maps can portray the politics, economy, society, culture, climate, or history of that area, or any combination of those characteristics.

A land use map is an example of a thematic map. It uses colors and symbols to show things such as where crops are grown, where mines are located, or the population density. Another example is a historical map that uses symbols, arrows, and colors to show the routes followed by explorers or how borders change over time.

When reading a thematic map:

- **Read the title:** This will help you understand the map's theme, location, time period, and type of data being shown.
- **Read the map key:** Thematic maps use symbols and colors to convey information. Sometimes the symbols change size to indicate if more or less of something exists at that point on the map.
- **Study the map and draw conclusions:** Look for patterns on the map. They reveal how the data presented by the thematic symbols and colors relates to the geographic features.

When creating a thematic map:

- **Identify the data you want to present.**
- **Decide what kind of map you need.** What region do you want to show? What geographic features have to be included? This decision is usually based on the patterns you want to show.

- **Decide on what scale and units of measurement you will use.** Make sure your map is large enough to show the area you are concerned with, but small enough that your data is readable. Make sure you use the right units of measurement, and that you include a map scale.
- **Decide what symbols and colors best present the data.** Should the symbols change size or color for different sets of data? Does the map need to show things changing over time?
- **Prepare your map key carefully.**

Practicing this Skill

Analyze thematic map *"Mining Helps Build a Nation,"* then answer the following questions:

1. What part of the United States does the map show?
2. What symbols are used to depict mining activities?
3. What other information does the map provide?
4. Use the patterns on the map to list the states in order of their gold and silver discoveries. Explain why you put them in the order you did.

Applying the Skill

Create your own thematic map. Research where different types of crops were grown in the American West from 1870 to 1900. Use the thematic map to show key events and the geographic patterns that resulted from farming and ranching in the West.

LESSON 2
Farming the Plains

ESSENTIAL QUESTION

• Why would people take on the challenges of life in the West?

READING HELPDESK

Academic Vocabulary

• prospective • innovation

Content Vocabulary

• homestead
• dry farming
• sodbuster
• bonanza farm

TAKING NOTES:

Key Ideas and Details

Organizing As you read about the settlement of the Great Plains, complete a graphic organizer similar to the one below by listing the ways the government encouraged settlement. LAFS.1112.RH.3.7

Assistance in Settling Great Plains

NEXT GENERATION SUNSHINE STATE STANDARDS

LAFS.1112.RH.2.4: Determine the meaning of words and phrases as they are used in a text, including analyzing how an author uses and refines the meaning of a key term over the course of a text (e.g., how Madison defines faction in Federalist No. 10).

LAFS.1112.RH.3.7: Integrate and evaluate multiple sources of information presented in diverse formats and media (e.g., visually, quantitatively, as well as in words) in order to address a question or solve a problem.

LAFS.1112.WHST.1.1: Write arguments focused on discipline-specific content.

Continued on page 104

IT MATTERS BECAUSE
The Homestead Act encouraged settlers to move to the Great Plains. Although life was difficult, settlers discovered that they could grow wheat using new technologies. By 1890, the land had been settled and cultivated, and there was no longer a true frontier in the United States.

Beginnings of American Settlement

GUIDING QUESTION *What encouraged settlers to move west to the Great Plains?*

The Great Plains is a vast region of prairie roughly west of the Mississippi River and east of the Rocky Mountains in the United States and Canada. Although the population of the Great Plains grew steadily after the Civil War, the settlers faced many challenges. Summer temperatures could top 100°F. Prairie fires were a frequent danger. Sometimes swarms of grasshoppers destroyed crops. Winter brought terrible blizzards and extreme cold. A settler who experienced the fierce winters wrote in her diary on March 12, 1884:

PRIMARY SOURCE

"Nobody can describe a blizzard. There is one kind in which the snow sticks all over everything, and another that is colder, in which the snow drives with terrible force, the sun shining above it. This is the Dakota boomer's exhilarating weather!"

—from *The Checked Years: A Bonanza Farm Diary, 1884–1888*

In this dry grassland, trees grew naturally only along rivers and streams. Without trees to use as timber, many settlers cut chunks of sod, densely packed soil held together by grass roots, to build their homes. To obtain water, they had to drill wells more than 100 feet deep and operate the pump by hand. Land once thought to be worthless was eventually transformed into America's wheat belt. Major Stephen Long, who explored the region with an army expedition in 1819, called it the "Great American Desert":

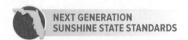

**NEXT GENERATION
SUNSHINE STATE STANDARDS**

Continued from page 103

LAFS.1112.WHST.4.10: Write routinely over extended time frames (time for reflection and revision) and shorter time frames (a single sitting or a day or two) for a range of discipline-specific tasks, purposes, and audiences.

SS.912.A.1.4: Analyze how images, symbols, objects, cartoons, graphs, charts, maps, and artwork may be used to interpret the significance of time periods and events from the past.

SS.912.A.3.1: Analyze the economic challenges to American farmers and farmers' responses to these challenges in the mid to late 1800s.

SS.912.A.3.4: Determine how the development of steel, oil, transportation, communication, and business practices affected the United States economy.

SS.912.A.3.13: Examine key events and peoples in Florida history as they relate to United States history.

prospective to be likely to, or have intentions to, perform an act

homestead a piece of U.S. public land acquired by living on it and cultivating it

dry farming a way of farming dry land in which seeds are planted deep in the ground where there is some moisture

sodbuster a name given to Great Plains farmers

innovation a new idea or method

bonanza farm a large, highly profitable wheat farm

PRIMARY SOURCE

❝[I]t is almost wholly unfit for cultivation, and of course uninhabitable by a people depending upon agriculture for their subsistence. . . . [T]he scarcity of wood and water, almost uniformly prevalent, will prove an insuperable obstacle in the way of settling the country.❞

—quoted in *An Account of an Expedition from Pittsburgh to the Rocky Mountains, Performed in the Years 1819, 1820*

During the late 1800s, the construction and development of the railroads stimulated growth. Railroad companies sold land along the rail lines at low prices and provided credit to **prospective** settlers. Pamphlets and posters spread the news across Europe and America that cheap land could be claimed by anyone willing to move.

In 1862, the government encouraged settlement on the Great Plains by passing the Homestead Act. For a small registration fee, an individual could file for a **homestead**—a tract of public land available for settlement. A homesteader could claim up to 160 acres of land and receive title to it after living there for five years. The Homestead Act provided a legal method for settlers to acquire a clear title to property on the frontier. With their property rights assured and the railroads providing lumber and supplies, settlers began moving to the Plains in large numbers.

☑ **READING PROGRESS CHECK**

Analyzing What developments of the late 1800s attracted settlers to endure the hardships of the Great Plains?

Technology and the Wheat Belt

GUIDING QUESTION *What new methods and technologies revolutionized agriculture and made it practical to cultivate the Plains?*

The harsh, dry climate and densely packed soil of the Great Plains required new farming methods and technological innovations in order for settlement to begin. One new farming method, called **dry farming,** was to plant seeds deep in the ground, where there was enough moisture for them to grow. By the 1860s, Plains farmers were using steel plows, threshing machines, seed drills, and reapers. These new machines made dry farming possible. Still, soil on the Plains could blow away during a dry season. As the population grew, the impact of the **sodbusters,** as those who plowed the Plains were called, helped change the environment. Many farmers eventually lost their homesteads through the combined effects of drought, wind erosion of the soil they had loosened, and overuse of the land.

Large landholders could buy mechanical reapers and steam tractors that made it easier to harvest a large crop. Threshing machines knocked kernels loose from the stalks. Mechanical binders tied the stalks into bundles for collection. These **innovations** were well suited for harvesting wheat, a crop that could endure the dry conditions of the Plains.

During the 1880s, many farmers from the states of the old Northwest Territory moved to the Great Plains to take advantage of the inexpensive land and new technology. The Wheat Belt began at the eastern edge of the Great Plains and covered much of the Dakotas and parts of Nebraska and Kansas. The new machines allowed a family to bring in a substantial harvest on a wheat farm of several hundred acres. Some wheat farms covered up to 65,000 acres. These were called **bonanza farms** because they yielded big profits. Like mine owners, bonanza farmers formed companies, invested in property and equipment, and hired laborers as needed.

Farmers Fall on Hard Times

The bountiful harvests in the Wheat Belt helped the United States become the world's leading exporter of wheat by the 1880s. Then things began to go wrong. A severe drought struck the Plains in the late 1880s, destroying crops and ruining the soil. In addition, competition from other wheat-producing nations increased. By the 1890s, a glut of wheat on the world market caused prices to drop.

Some farmers tried to make it through these difficult times by mortgaging their land—that is, they borrowed money from a bank based on the value of their land. If they failed to meet their mortgage payments, they forfeited the land to the bank. Some who lost their land continued to work it as tenant farmers, renting the land from its new owners. By 1900, tenants cultivated about one-third of the farms on the Plains.

Closing the Frontier

On April 22, 1889, the government opened one of the last large territories for settlement. Within hours, thousands of people raced to stake claims in an event known as the Oklahoma Land Rush. The next year, the Census Bureau reported that there was no longer a true frontier left in America. In reality, there was still a lot of unoccupied land, and the Homestead Act continued to encourage new settlement into the 1900s, but the "closing of the frontier" marked the end of an era. It worried many people, including historian Frederick Jackson Turner. Turner believed that the frontier had provided a "safety-valve of social discontent." It was a place where Americans could always make a fresh start.

Most settlers did indeed make a fresh start, adapting to the difficult environment of the Plains. Water from their deep wells enabled them to plant trees and gardens. Railroads brought lumber and brick to replace sod as a building material, coal for fuel, and manufactured goods from the East, such as clothes and household goods. Small-scale farmers rarely became wealthy, but they could be self-sufficient. Typical homesteaders raised cattle, chickens, and a few crops. The real story of the West was about ordinary people who settled down and built homes and communities through great effort.

✔ **READING PROGRESS CHECK**

Identifying How did new technologies help improve settlers' ability to cultivate larger, more profitable farms?

Technology helped make it possible to farm the vast open grasslands of America. Here, horse-drawn farm equipment is used to gather hay in the 1880s.

▶ CRITICAL THINKING
Determining Cause and Effect
How did technology help facilitate the settlement of the Great Plains?
LAFS.1112.RH.3.7, SS.912.A.1.4

 Florida
CONNECTION

Funding for Agricultural Colleges

The Morrill Land Grant College Acts of 1862 and 1890 granted land and funding, respectively, to state colleges that had a focused curriculum on agriculture, agricultural sciences, and scientific research, as well as general courses of study. Seventeen states established land-grant colleges. Florida Agricultural College was established in 1884 after the sale of the land appropriated by the first land-grant act. Today, it is the Institute of Food and Agricultural Sciences at the University of Florida.
SS.912.A.3.1, SS.912.A.3.13

LESSON 2 REVIEW

Reviewing Vocabulary

1. ***Explaining*** Why were some settlers on the Great Plains called homesteaders? LAFS.1112.RH.2.4

2. ***Explaining*** How did new machinery make dry farming easier for farmers? LAFS.1112.RH.2.4

Using Your Notes

3. ***Drawing Conclusions*** Use your notes to explain why you think the government and the railroads used special policies to attract settlement in the Great Plains.

Answering the Guiding Questions

4. ***Identifying Cause and Effect*** What encouraged settlers to move west to the Great Plains? SS.912.A.3.1

5. ***Summarizing*** What new methods and technologies revolutionized agriculture and made it practical to cultivate the Plains? SS.912.A.3.1

Writing About History

6. **ARGUMENT** Write an essay expressing your opinion about whether the "closing of the frontier" described by historian Frederick Jackson Turner was good or bad for the country.
LAFS.1112.WHST.1.1, LAFS.1112.WHST.4.10

LAFS.1112.WHST.3.9, MAFS.912.S-IC.2, MAFS.K12.MP.1.1, MAFS.K12.MP.5.1, SS.912.G.2.1

Interpreting Statistics

Why Learn This Skill?

Statistics are collections of data. They are often presented in charts and graphs and play an important role in inductive reasoning. **Inductive reasoning** is when we use evidence to make broad generalizations. Inductive reasoning does not prove something is true. Instead, when you reach a conclusion through inductive reasoning, you decide how probable, or likely, it is to be true. Inductive arguments can be strong or weak, not right or wrong. They help us make predictions and form hypotheses that we can test to see if they are true. Learning to interpret statistics improves inductive reasoning and helps us make better predictions.

Learning the Skill

Use the following steps to help you interpret statistical information:

- **Scan** the chart or graph, reading the titles and labels to get an idea of what is being shown.
- **Examine** the statistics shown, looking for increases and decreases, similarities and differences.
- **Look** for a correlation. When two pieces of data appear to be related, we say there is a correlation between them. In a positive correlation, as one number rises, the other number rises. In a negative correlation, as one number rises, the other number falls. For example, the percentage of overweight people has increased since 1970. At the same time the percentage of people living in the suburbs has also increased since 1970. There is a positive correlation between these two numbers.
- **Determine** the conclusions you can draw. A correlation does not imply causation. Just because two numbers appear to have a relationship does not mean the one set of data causes the other. Using the example above, you might think being overweight makes you live in the suburbs. But you have to ask whether that is probable. In this case, it seems more likely there are independent reasons causing both numbers to rise. On the other hand, using inductive reasoning,

we can create a hypothesis to explain the relationship. For example, living in the suburbs might mean people exercise less because they don't walk to work. As a result, they gain weight. Having used the statistics to create a hypothesis, we can now use other means to check if it is true.

Geographic Distribution of Population in the United States, 1870–1890						
Year	Born in the West			Born Somewhere Else		
	Living in the West	Living in the East		Living in the East	Living in the West	
	Number	Number	Percent	Number	Number	Percent
1890	9,416,035	282,359	2.9	38,906,809	4,360,516	10.1
1880	6,069,112	210,359	3.3	33,685,290	3,510,737	9.4
1870	3,324,048	135,769	3.9	27,084,122	2,434,721	8.2

Practicing this Skill

Analyze the geographic distribution and geographic patterns in the chart and answer the following questions.

1. *Analyzing Geographic Distributions* What data does the chart show?
2. *Analyzing Geographic Patterns* Which figures in the chart are rising? Which are falling?
3. *Analyzing Geographic Patterns* Is there a positive or negative correlation in the data?
4. *Analyzing Geographic Distributions* What hypothesis or prediction can you conclude from these statistics?

Applying the Skill

Posing Questions Reexamine the chart. Pose additional questions that call into question the conclusions you reached. What other questions about the geographic distribution and geographic patterns do you need answered to test your conclusions? Convey your information visually by presenting the statistical information as a bar graph or circle graph. If available, use spreadsheet software to create the graph.

LESSON 3
Native Americans

ESSENTIAL QUESTION
• Why would people take on the challenges of life in the West?

READING HELPDESK

Academic Vocabulary
- relocate
- ensure
- approximately

Content Vocabulary
- nomad
- assimilate
- annuity
- allotment

TAKING NOTES:

Key Ideas and Details

Sequencing As you read about Native Americans during the late 1800s, complete a time line like the one below to record the clashes between Native Americans and the U.S. government and the results of each.
LAFS.1112.RH.3.7, SS.912.A.1.3, SS.912.A.2.7

NEXT GENERATION SUNSHINE STATE STANDARDS

ELD.K12.ELL.SI.1: English language learners communicate for social and instructional purposes within the school setting.

ELD.K12.ELL.SS.1: English language learners communicate information, ideas and concepts necessary for academic success in the content area of Social Studies.

LAFS.1112.RH.2.4: Determine the meaning of words and phrases as they are used in a text, including analyzing how an author uses and refines the meaning of a key term over the course of a text (e.g., how Madison defines faction in Federalist No. 10).

Continued on page 108

IT MATTERS BECAUSE
As miners, ranchers, and farmers entered Native American lands on the Great Plains, clashes grew more common. Conflicts continued as the government tried to force Native Americans onto reservations and pressured them to assimilate into the culture of the United States.

The Struggle on the Plains

GUIDING QUESTION *How did westward migration change the Plains Indians' way of life?*

For centuries the Great Plains were home to many groups of Native Americans. Some lived in farming and hunting communities, but many were **nomads** who roamed the land following their main source of food—the buffalo. The Plains Indian nations were divided into bands, ranging from a few dozen to several hundred people, who lived in extended family groups and respected nature.

The settlers who migrated to the Plains deprived these Native Americans of their hunting grounds, broke treaties that guaranteed them land, and often forced them to **relocate.** Native Americans resisted by attacking settlers' property and occasionally going to war with them.

The Dakota Sioux Uprising
In 1862, the Dakota people (part of the Sioux) had a conflict with the settlers in Minnesota. The Sioux had agreed to live on a reservation in exchange for **annuities** that frequently never reached them. At the time, many Dakota lived in poverty and faced starvation. When local traders refused to provide food on credit, the Dakota protested by launching a rebellion that killed hundreds of settlers.

A military tribunal sentenced more than 300 Dakota to death after the uprising. After reviewing the evidence, however, President Lincoln reduced the number condemned to death to 38. Others fled the reservation when federal troops arrived and became exiles in a region that bore their name—the Dakota Territory.

Native Americans are attacked by U.S. troops at Sand Creek.

▶ CRITICAL THINKING

Making Inferences Why do you think obtaining peace between Native Americans and settlers was so difficult?
LAFS.1112.RH.3.7, SS.912.A.1.4, SS.912.A.2.7

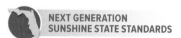

NEXT GENERATION SUNSHINE STATE STANDARDS

Continued from page 107

LAFS.1112.RH.3.7: Integrate and evaluate multiple sources of information presented in diverse formats and media (e.g., visually, quantitatively, as well as in words) in order to address a question or solve a problem.

LAFS.1112.WHST.1.1: Write arguments focused on discipline-specific content.

LAFS.1112.WHST.4.10: Write routinely over extended time frames (time for reflection and revision) and shorter time frames (a single sitting or a day or two) for a range of discipline-specific tasks, purposes, and audiences.

SS.912.A.1.4: Analyze how images, symbols, objects, cartoons, graphs, charts, maps, and artwork may be used to interpret the significance of time periods and events from the past.

SS.912.A.2.7: Review the Native American experience.

SS.912.G.1.2: Use spatial perspective and appropriate geographic terms and tools, including the Six Essential Elements, as organizational schema to describe any given place.

SS.912.G.2.1: Identify the physical characteristics and the human characteristics that define and differentiate regions.

SS.912.G.4.3: Use geographic terms and tools to analyze the effects of migration both on the place of origin and destination, including border areas.

nomad a person who continually moves from place to place, usually in search of food

relocate to move to a new place

annuity money paid by contract at regular intervals

ensure to guarantee or make certain

Red Cloud's War

The Dakota Territory was home to another group of Sioux, the Lakota, nomads who had won control of their hunting grounds from other Native Americans. Their chiefs were Red Cloud, Crazy Horse, and Sitting Bull. In December 1866, the U.S. Army was building forts along the Bozeman Trail, the path to the Montana gold mines. Crazy Horse tricked the fort's commander into sending Captain William Fetterman and about 80 soldiers out to pursue what they thought was a small raiding party.

Hundreds of waiting warriors wiped out the unit, an event that became known as Fetterman's Massacre, marking the start of "Red Cloud's War." The Sioux continued to resist any military presence in the region, and in 1868 the army abandoned its posts along the trail.

Sand Creek Massacre

In Colorado, tensions began to rise in the 1860s between miners entering the territory in search of silver and gold and the Cheyenne and Arapaho who already lived there. As the number of settlers increased, bands of Native Americans began raiding wagon trains and ranches. By the summer of 1864, dozens of homes had been burned and an estimated 200 settlers killed. The governor persuaded the Native Americans to surrender at Fort Lyon, where he promised food and protection. Those who failed to report would be subject to attack.

Although a number of Native Americans surrendered, many others did not. In November 1864, Chief Black Kettle brought several hundred Cheyenne to the fort to negotiate a peace deal. Fort Lyon's commander, Major Scott Anthony, allowed the chief to make camp at nearby Sand Creek while he awaited orders. Shortly afterward, Colonel John Chivington of the Colorado Volunteers attacked Black Kettle's camp, even though the Cheyenne were there to negotiate.

Some witnesses claim that because of the Cheyenne's goal to negotiate, there was a white flag of truce flying at Black Kettle's camp. Those witnesses say that Chivington ignored the flag and began an attack on the unsuspecting Native Americans. Some reports of the attack at Sand Creek described it as a brutal two-day battle. Fourteen U.S. soldiers died during the struggle, and estimates of the number of Native American warriors, women, and children killed vary from 69 to 600.

A Doomed Plan for Peace

As conflicts escalated with Native Americans, Congress took action. In 1867, Congress formed an Indian Peace Commission, which proposed creating two large reservations on the Plains, one for the Sioux and another for Native Americans of the southern Plains. Federal agents would run the reservations, and the army would deal with any groups that refused to report or remain there.

The Indian Peace Commission's plan was doomed to failure. Although negotiators pressured Native American leaders into signing treaties, they could not **ensure** that those leaders or their followers would abide by them. Nor could anyone prevent settlers from violating their terms. The Native Americans who did move to reservations faced many of the same conditions that drove the Dakota Sioux to violence—poverty, despair, and the corrupt practices of American traders.

✅ READING PROGRESS CHECK

Explaining How did the arrival of new settlers affect the Plains Indians?

North Wind Picture Archives/Alamy

The Last Native American Wars

GUIDING QUESTION *Were Native Americans justified in leaving the reservations and refusing further relocation by the government?*

By the 1870s, many Native Americans had left the reservations in disgust. They preferred hunting buffalo on the open plains. The buffalo were rapidly disappearing, however, as professional buffalo hunters sought hides for markets in the East and other hunters killed for sport. When buffalo blocked rail traffic, the railroads killed them and fed the meat to workers. The army, determined to force Native Americans onto reservations, encouraged buffalo killing. By 1889, very few buffalo remained.

Battle of the Little Bighorn

In 1876, prospectors overran the Lakota Sioux reservation in the Dakota Territory to mine gold in the Black Hills. The Lakota saw no reason to abide by a treaty that settlers were violating, so many left the reservation to hunt near the Bighorn Mountains in Montana. The government responded by sending an expedition accompanied by Lieutenant Colonel George A. Custer and the Seventh Cavalry. Custer underestimated the fighting capabilities of the Lakota and the Cheyenne. On June 25, 1876, he launched an attack on one of the largest groups of Native American warriors ever assembled on the Great Plains. The Native American forces rapidly defeated Custer and his more than 200 soldiers, killing them all. Newspaper accounts portraying Custer as a victim of a massacre produced a public outcry in the East, and the army stepped up its campaign on the Plains.

GEOGRAPHY CONNECTION

Native Americans fought hard to maintain their land and way of life, but following a series of defeats by the U.S. Army, they agreed to move to reservations in different areas of the country to save their people.

1 **PLACES AND REGIONS** *In what region of the United States did a majority of battles occur between the settlers and the Native Americans during this time period?*
SS.912.A.1.4, SS.912.A.2.7, SS.912.G.1.2

2 **HUMAN SYSTEMS** *From what state to what state did the Nez Perce travel in 1877? Through what other states did they pass?*
SS.912.A.1.4, SS.912.A.2.7, SS.912.G.1.2

Native American Battles and Reservations 1860–1890

Fort Laramie Treaties:
1851: Native Americans agreed to the construction of roads and forts on their lands.
1868: The Sioux agreed to move to a reservation in the Black Hills.

Treaty of Medicine Lodge, 1867: Southern Plains Indians agreed to move to Indian Territory.

Skeleton Canyon, 1886: Apache leader Geronimo surrendered.

Legend:
- Reservation in 1890
- Route of Chief Joseph and the Nez Perce, 1877
- Battle
- Fort
- Treaty Site
- 1890 border

0 — 200 miles
0 — 200 km
Lambert Azimuthal Equal-Area projection

**George Custer
(1839–1876)**

George Custer graduated at the bottom of his West Point class, but through heroism during the Civil War, he became a general at age 23. The Cheyenne called him "Yellow Hair" because he wore his curly blond hair to his shoulders. President Grant removed Custer from his post for testifying about corruption in the Bureau of Indian Affairs, but he was soon reinstated—a decision that cost him his life and those of his troops.

▶ **CRITICAL THINKING**
Drawing Conclusions Why do you think Custer was removed from his command for testifying against the Bureau of Indian Affairs?
LAFS.1112.RH.3.7

Sitting Bull and his followers fled to Canada, but the other Lakota were forced to return to the reservation and give up the Black Hills.

Flight of the Nez Perce

Farther west, the Nez Perce people, led by Chief Joseph, refused to be moved to a smaller reservation in Idaho in 1877. When the army came to relocate them, they fled their homes and embarked on a journey of more than 1,300 miles. Finally, in October 1877, Chief Joseph acknowledged that the struggle was over. He and his followers were then exiled to Oklahoma.

Tragedy at Wounded Knee

Native American resistance came to a final, tragic end on the Lakota Sioux reservation in 1890. Defying government orders, the Lakota continued to perform the Ghost Dance, a ritual that celebrated a hoped-for day of reckoning when settlers would disappear, the buffalo would return, and Native Americans would be reunited with their dead ancestors.

Federal authorities had banned the ceremony, fearing it would lead to violence. They blamed the latest defiance on Sitting Bull, who had returned from Canada, and sent police to arrest the chief. Sitting Bull's supporters tried to stop the arrest. In the exchange of gunfire that followed, Sitting Bull was killed and a group of Ghost Dancers fled the reservation. On December 29, 1890, a battle ensued at Wounded Knee Creek in South Dakota, taking the lives of 25 U.S. soldiers and **approximately** 200 Lakota men, women, and children.

Americanization and the Dawes Act

Some Americans had long opposed the mistreatment of Native Americans. In her 1881 book *A Century of Dishonor,* Helen Hunt Jackson detailed the years of broken promises and injustices. Her descriptions of events such as the Sand Creek Massacre sparked new debate on the issue. Some Americans believed the solution was Americanization. They thought that Native Americans should be encouraged to abandon their traditional tribal culture and **assimilate** into American society by learning English, adopting American culture and values, and eventually becoming American citizens. Beginning in the 1880s, the Bureau of Indian Affairs sponsored the creation of Indian boarding schools separate from reservations. By 1902, some 25 schools had been set up. Officials then pressured parents to send children to

---

POLITICAL CARTOONS

CARL SCHURZ INVESTIGATING THE BUREAU OF INDIAN AFFAIRS

This cartoon from 1878 shows Secretary of the Interior Carl Schurz investigating the Indian "bureau."

1 ***Analyzing*** According to the cartoon, why was the Bureau of Indian Affairs unable to help Native Americans? SS.912.A.1.4

2 ***Making Inferences*** Why do you think Schurz did not want the War Department to regain control of Indian affairs? SS.912.A.1.4

Due to a cumbersome system of handling the administration of Indian laws, the agents of the Bureau of Indian Affairs (BIA) had many opportunities for personal enrichment and an invitation for large-scale corruption. Secretary of the Interior Carl Schurz attempted to cleanse the BIA of corruption and prevent the War Department from regaining management of Indian affairs.

(t)©Historical/Corbis; (b)MPI/Archive Photos/Getty Images

these schools. There they were required to speak English, choose an English name, dress in American-style clothes, cut their hair to match American styles, attend church, and learn vocational skills. Over time the schools became controversial. They were often underfunded and poorly maintained, and discipline was strict. Some students found the schools repressive, and many cases of abuse were reported.

A second Americanization strategy was to encourage Native Americans to abandon the reservation system and become independent landowners. In 1887, Congress passed the Dawes Act, which altered the reservation system by dividing reservation land into **allotments** for farming or ranching. Under the act, 160 acres were allotted to each head of household, 80 acres to each single adult, and 40 acres to each child. Any land remaining after allotments would be sold to American settlers, with the proceeds going into a trust for Native Americans. Citizenship would be granted to Native Americans who stayed on their allotments for 25 years.

While some Native Americans succeeded as farmers or ranchers, many had little training or enthusiasm for either pursuit. They often found their allotments too small to be profitable, so they leased them. In addition, some Native American groups had grown attached to their reservations and hated to see them divided into homesteads. Few stayed long enough to qualify for citizenship.

In the end, the assimilation policy proved a dismal failure. Native American culture on the Plains was doomed because it depended on buffalo for food, clothing, fuel, and shelter. When the herds were wiped out, there was no way to sustain the traditional way of life. Although the Dawes Act failed in its goals, American reformers continued to advocate for assimilation. In the early 1900s, reform groups such as the Friends of the Indians and the Indian Rights Association began to push for citizenship for all Native Americans, believing it would encourage greater assimilation. Finally, in 1924 Congress passed the Citizenship Act, granting all Native Americans citizenship. In 1934, the Indian Reorganization Act reversed the Dawes Act's policy of assimilation. It restored some reservation lands, gave Native Americans control over those lands, and permitted them to elect their own governments.

☑ **READING PROGRESS CHECK**

Cause and Effect What effect did Helen Hunt Jackson's book *A Century of Dishonor* have?

approximately an estimate of a figure that is close to the actual figure

assimilate to absorb a group into the culture of another population

allotment a plot of land assigned to an individual or a family for a specified use

SKILLS PRACTICE

Ask for help when you hear something you do not understand in class discussion. Raise your hand or use some other signal. This may seem basic, but sometimes people feel embarrassed or unsure and don't want others to know they don't understand something. Successful learning requires practice asking questions. So, raise your hand! ELD.K12.ELL.SI.1, ELD.K12.ELL.SS.1

LESSON 3 REVIEW

Reviewing Vocabulary
1. *Making Connections* What is an annuity? What was the connection between annuities and the Dakota Sioux Uprising of 1862? LAFS.1112.RH.2.4

2. *Summarizing* How did settlers think they would get Native Americans to assimilate into their culture? LAFS.1112.RH.2.4

Using Your Notes
3. *Making Generalizations* Review the notes that you completed throughout the lesson to write a generalization about the result of the battles between Native Americans and the United States government. SS.912.A.2.7

Answering the Guiding Questions
4. *Summarizing* How did westward migration change the Plains Indians' way of life? SS.912.A.2.7

5. *Defending* Were Native Americans justified in leaving the reservations and refusing further relocation by the government? SS.912.A.2.7

Writing About History
6. NARRATIVE Imagine you are a journalist interviewing a Native American who has been granted an allotment under the Dawes Act. Write an article describing how it affected their life. LAFS.1112.WHST.4.10

STUDY GUIDE

MINERS AND RANCHERS
LESSON 1

Discovery of gold, silver, and copper attracted settlers to Colorado, the Dakota Territory, Nevada, and Montana, creating boomtowns

Growth of cattle and sheep ranching attracted settlers to Texas, Montana, Wyoming, and other western areas

ECONOMIC GROWTH INCREASES POPULATION

American settlers began moving into the Southwest, which had previously been held and settled by Mexico

FARMING THE PLAINS
LESSON 2

NEW SETTLERS & NEW TECHNOLOGY

Cheap land of Homestead Act encouraged settlement in the Great Plains

Farming technology made the Great Plains into the Wheat Belt

However, many farmers lost their homesteads due to drought, erosion, and overuse of the land

NATIVE AMERICANS
LESSON 3

PRESSURES ON NATIVE AMERICANS

Conflicts between Native Americans and settlers

Federal government forced Plains Indians off their lands with promise of new land, allowing white settlers to move in

Slaughter of buffalo removed a major part of Native American way of life

Directions: On a separate sheet of paper, answer the questions below. Make sure you read carefully and answer all parts to the question.

Lesson Review

Lesson 1

1 *Comparing* How did the cattle industry boom affect the economy of the West?
SS.912.A.3.13

2 *Explaining* Identify and explain the reasons western political boundaries changed between 1870 and 1900. SS.912.A.3.4, SS.912.G.4.9

Lesson 2

3 *Analyzing* How did railroad companies help to encourage settlement of the Great Plains? What other human geographic factors affected settlement of the Great Plains? SS.912.A.3.4, SS.912.G.1.2, SS.912.G.2.1, SS.912.G.4.7

4 *Evaluating* How did the economic impact of the Homestead Act contribute to the close of the frontier in the late 19th century? SS.912.A.3.1

Lesson 3

5 *Analyzing* How did the Indian policies of the United States government affect the relationship between settlers in the West and Native Americans? SS.912.A.2.7

6 *Explaining* What actions did Congress take to expand political rights for Native Americans? What influenced the legislation they passed? SS.912.A.2.7

Exploring the Essential Question

7 *Discussing* Write an essay in which you describe the hardships of and advantages to emigrating west during the 19th century. LAFS.1112.WHST.2.4

Critical Thinking

8 *Analyzing* How did the physical geography of the Great Plains impact the farmers who settled there, and how did the population growth affect the environment? SS.912.A.3.1, SS.912.G.1.2

9 *Explaining* What specific needs facing settlers on the Great Plains led to new scientific discoveries and technological innovations in agriculture? How did these innovations contribute to the formation of the Wheat Belt? SS.912.A.3.1, SS.912.A.3.4

21st Century Skills

10 *Identifying Cause and Effect* How did societal changes brought about by the gold rush impact Hispanics in California? SS.912.G.4.7

11 *Synthesizing* What territory did the Wheat Belt encompass? Use correct social studies terminology to explain the territories involved. SS.912.G.1.2

12 *Problem-Solving* What problems did sodbusters encounter when farming the Great Plains? How did some sodbusters overcome these problems?
SS.912.A.3.1

13 *Research Skills* Use Internet or print resources to research the major characteristics that defined the historical era of the 1860s to 1900. Write a short summary of the era and how each characteristic of the era was important to the history of the country. LAFS.1112.WHST.3.7, LAFS.1112.WHST.3.8, LAFS.1112.WHST.4.10

14 *Identifying Perspectives and Differing Interpretations* Conduct research to find statistics about the wages, land prices, and employment opportunities on the Great Plains. Create a video or print advertisement that uses those statistics to promote life in the West. The advertisement should try to persuade people from different countries to move to the West and take advantages of its rich resources, and economy. LAFS.1112.RH.3.7, LAFS.1112.RH.3.9, LAFS.1112.SL.2.5, LAFS.1112.WHST.2.4, LAFS.1112.WHST.3.8

15 *Geography Skills* Create a thematic map of the major cattle trails in the United States during the late 1800s. Compare the map with a classmate and then display the map in the classroom. SS.912.G.1.2

Need Extra Help?

If You've Missed Question	**1**	**2**	**3**	**4**	**5**	**6**	**7**	**8**	**9**	**10**	**11**	**12**	**13**	**14**	**15**
Go to Lesson	1	1	2	2	3	3	1	1, 2	2	1	2	2	3	1	1

16 *Problem Solving* Suppose you lived in the 1800s and received a letter from a relative who was struggling to make a living farming on the frontier. Write a letter to the relative in return to suggest a solution for the problem and a suggestion as to how the solution can be implemented. LAFS.WHST.2.4, SS.912.A.3.1

Examine the chart and answer the following question.

Native American Population		
Year	Total	On Reservations
1870	313,712	288,646
1880	306,543	256,127
1890	248,253	243,534

Source: *Nations Within a Nation;* U.S. Census.

17 *Geographic Distributions and Patterns* What geographic patterns do you see in the chart? Is there a positive or negative correlation in the geographic distribution? What is different about the distribution in 1880 compared to the other two years? What might have caused this difference? What questions would you need answered in order to be sure your explanation of why 1880 is different from the other two years is correct? MAFS.912.S-ID.1, SS.912.G.2.1

DBQ Analyzing Primary Sources

Read the excerpt from Chief Joseph, leader of the Nez Perce, and answer the questions that follow.

PRIMARY SOURCE

❝Our chiefs are killed. . . . The little children are freezing to death. My people . . . have no blankets, no food. . . . Hear me, my chiefs; I am tired; my heart is sick and sad. From where the sun now stands I will fight no more forever. ❞

—from his speech of surrender to the U.S. Army, 1877

18 *Analyzing Primary Sources* What does the quotation say about the government effort to Americanize Native Americans? LAFS.1112.RH.3.8, LAFS.1112.RH.4.10, SS.912.A.2.7

19 *Constructing Arguments* What argument could you have made to the U.S. Army to help Chief Joseph and the Nez Perce instead of accepting their surrender? LAFS.1112.RH.3.7, LAFS.1112.RH.3.8, LAFS.1112.RH.4.10, SS.912.A.2.7

Analyzing Visuals

Use the image to answer the following question.

20 *Interpreting* What is the significance of the title of this engraving, *The Rush for the Promised Land: Over the Border to Oklahoma*? What impression does this image give about the settlers who are rushing to the "Promised Land"? SS.912.A.1.4, SS.912.G.4.2, SS.912.H.1.3

THE RUSH FOR THE PROMISED LAND

Extended Response Question

21 *Expository* Write an essay comparing two different perspectives of the settlement of the West. Analyze how the views of Native Americans and white settlers differed on settling the Great Plains. How did each group view the government's involvement and the environment? The essay should include an introduction, at least three paragraphs, and a conclusion that supports your opinion. Use information gathered from primary and secondary sources to provide examples to support your answer. Edit and revise your writing for clarity. LAFS.1112.WHST.2.4, LAFS.1112.WHST.2.5, LAFS.1112.WHST.4.10, SS.912.A.2.7

Library of Congress, Prints & Photographs Division [LC-US262-77823]

Need Extra Help?

If You've Missed Question	**16**	**17**	**18**	**19**	**20**	**21**
Go to Lesson	1	3	3	3	2	2

Andrew Carnegie devoted his full attention to the steel industry in the 1870s.

The Granger Collection, New York

FROM 1865 TO 1901

Industrialization

THE STORY MATTERS ...

Andrew Carnegie founded Carnegie Steel, one of the new businesses that fueled the Industrial Revolution in the United States. He became a multimillionaire, his company employed tens of thousands of workers, and his steel built the skyscrapers, bridges, and railroads that made the United States the world's leading industrial nation. Carnegie and other big-business leaders provided the leadership for an industrial society.

ESSENTIAL QUESTION

- How did the United States become an industrialized society after the Civil War?

Place & Time: United States 1865–1901

American business and industry grew rapidly after the Civil War ended. Natural resources and a large labor force contributed to industry's growth. Inventions, such as the telephone and the lightbulb, spurred economic development. Railroads accelerated the nation's industrialization and linked the country together. Corporations could produce goods more efficiently. With industrialization came the benefits of new products versus the struggles of low wages, long hours, and difficult working conditions. All of these things changed the way people lived and worked.

Step Into the Place

Look at the information presented on the map to identify the regions affected by the building of the transcontinental railroad.

DBQ **Analyzing Historical Documents** How could an increase in the number of railroad lines across the West contribute to the economic growth of the United States?

left page: (l to r)detail/White House Collection/The White House Historical Association;
right page: (l to r)detail/White House Collection/The White House Historical Association

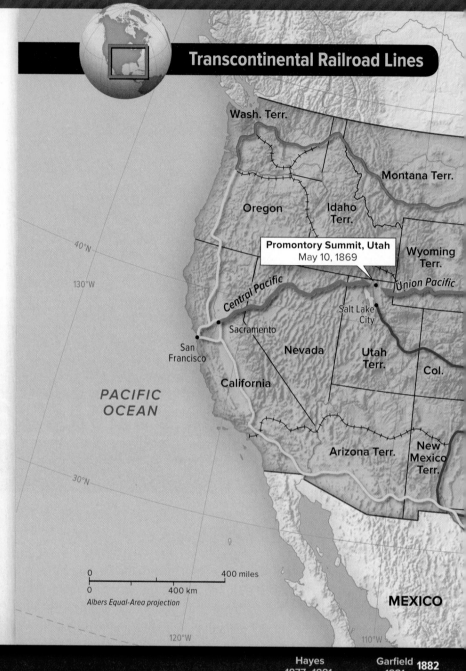

Transcontinental Railroad Lines

Wash. Terr.

Montana Terr.

Oregon

Idaho Terr.

40°N

130°W

Promontory Summit, Utah
May 10, 1869

Wyoming Terr.

Union Pacific

Central Pacific

Salt Lake City

Sacramento

San Francisco

Nevada

Utah Terr.

Col.

California

PACIFIC OCEAN

30°N

Arizona Terr.

New Mexico Terr.

0 400 miles
0 400 km
Albers Equal-Area projection

MEXICO

120°W   110°W

Step Into the Time

MAKING GENERALIZATIONS Choose an event from the time line and write a paragraph reflecting on how that event is representative of the changing times during the late 1800s.

1876 Alexander Graham Bell invents telephone

Hayes 1877–1881

Garfield 1881

1882 Standard Oil forms trust

U.S. PRESIDENTS

UNITED STATES

WORLD

1865   1875   1880

1869 Dmitry Mendeleyev creates periodic table of elements

1873 Jules Verne's *Around the World in 80 Days* is published

1876 Nikolaus Otto builds first practical gasoline engine

1880 John Milne develops seismograph

NEXT GENERATION SUNSHINE STATE STANDARDS
Students will understand the following benchmarks from the Florida NGSSS

LAFS.1112.RH.3.7: Integrate and evaluate multiple sources of information presented in diverse formats and media (e.g., visually, quantitatively, as well as in words) in order to address a question or solve a problem.

LAFS.1112.RH.3.9: Integrate information from diverse sources, both primary and secondary, into a coherent understanding of an idea or event, noting discrepancies among sources.

SS.912.A.1.2: Utilize a variety of primary and secondary sources to identify author, historical significance, audience, and authenticity to understand a historical period.

SS.912.A.1.3: Utilize timelines to identify the time sequence of historical data.

SS.912.A.1.4: Analyze how images, symbols, objects, cartoons, graphs, charts, maps, and artwork may be used to interpret the significance of time periods and events from the past.

SS.912.A.3.2: Examine the social, political, and economic causes, course, and consequences of the second Industrial Revolution that began in the late 19th century.

SS.912.A.3.4: Determine how the development of steel, oil, transportation, communication, and business practices affected the United States economy.

SS.912.A.3.5: Identify significant inventors of the Industrial Revolution including African Americans and women.

Legend:
- Transcontinental Railroad
- Southern Pacific Railroad (and connector lines)
- Denver & Rio Grande/Atchison & Topeka Railroad
- Northern Pacific Railroad
- Texas & Pacific Railroad (and connector lines)

Arthur 1881–1885
Cleveland 1885–1889
1886 Haymarket riot occurs
B. Harrison 1889–1893
1892 Homestead strike occurs
Cleveland 1893–1897
McKinley 1897–1901
1901 J. P. Morgan forms U.S. Steel

1885 — 1890 — 1895 — 1900

1885 Canada's transcontinental railroad is completed

1892 Rudolf Diesel patents diesel engine

1895 Louis and Auguste Lumière introduce motion pictures

LESSON 1
The Rise of Industry

ESSENTIAL QUESTION

• How did the United States become an industrialized society after the Civil War?

READING HELPDESK

Academic Vocabulary

• resource   • practice

Content Vocabulary

• gross national product
• laissez-faire
• entrepreneur

TAKING NOTES

Key Ideas and Details

Organizing As you read about the changes industrialization brought to the United States, complete the graphic organizer shown below with the causes of industrialization. **LAFS.1112.RH.3.7**

Causes

United States Becomes an Industrial Nation

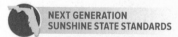

NEXT GENERATION SUNSHINE STATE STANDARDS

ELD.K12.ELL.SI.1: English language learners communicate for social and instructional purposes within the school setting.

ELD.K12.ELL.SS.1: English language learners communicate information, ideas and concepts necessary for academic success in the content area of Social Studies.

LAFS.1112.RH.2.4: Determine the meaning of words and phrases as they are used in a text, including analyzing how an author uses and refines the meaning of a key term over the course of a text (e.g., how Madison defines faction in Federalist No. 10).

Continued on page 119

IT MATTERS BECAUSE
American business and industry grew rapidly after the end of the Civil War. Industrialization changed the way people lived and worked.

The United States Industrializes

GUIDING QUESTION *Why was the United States successful at industrialization?*

Although the First Industrial Revolution reached the United States in the early 1800s, most Americans still lived on farms when the Civil War began. After the war, industry rapidly expanded in a Second Industrial Revolution. Millions of Americans left their farms to work in mines and factories. The Second Industrial Revolution was characterized by an increase in technology due to advances in electricity after 1890. By the early 1900s, the United States was the leading industrial nation. Its **gross national product** (GNP)—the total value of all goods and services a country produces during a year—was roughly three times what it had been in the late 1860s.

Natural Resources

Abundant raw materials aided the nation's industrial success. The United States had vast natural **resources,** including timber, coal, iron, and copper. This allowed American companies to obtain resources cheaply without importing them from other countries. Many of these resources were located in the American West. Western settlement helped accelerate industrialization, as did the transcontinental railroad. Railroads took settlers and miners to the West and carried resources back to the East.

At the same time, people began using a new resource: petroleum. Even before the automotive age, petroleum was in high demand because it could be turned into kerosene. The American oil industry was built on the demand for kerosene, a fuel used in lanterns and stoves. The industry began in western Pennsylvania, where residents had long noticed oil bubbling to the surface of area springs and streams. In 1859, Edwin Drake drilled the first oil well near Titusville, Pennsylvania, and by 1900, oil fields had been drilled from Pennsylvania to Texas. As oil production rose, it fueled economic expansion.

A Large Workforce

The human resources available to American industry were as important as natural resources in enabling the nation to industrialize rapidly. Between 1860 and 1910, the population of the United States nearly tripled. This population growth provided industry with a large workforce and created greater demand for consumer goods.

Population growth stemmed from two sources—large families and a flood of immigrants. Because of better living conditions, more children survived and grew to adulthood. At the same time, social and economic conditions in parts of Europe and China convinced many people to immigrate to the United States in search of a better life. Between 1870 and 1910, more than 17 million immigrants arrived in the United States.

✓ READING PROGRESS CHECK

Summarizing What were two significant factors in the growth of U.S. industry?

New Inventions

GUIDING QUESTION *What invention from this period has had the most impact on your daily life?*

New inventions and technology were also important to industrialization. New technology increased the nation's productivity and improved transportation and communication. New inventions also resulted in new industries, which in turn produced more wealth and jobs.

Electric Power

Perhaps the leading pioneer in new technology was Thomas Alva Edison. A great innovator, Edison and his company worked tirelessly

gross national product the total value of goods and services produced by a country during a year

resources materials used in the production process, such as money, people, land, wood, or steel

NEXT GENERATION SUNSHINE STATE STANDARDS

Continued from page 118

LAFS.1112.RH.3.7: Integrate and evaluate multiple sources of information presented in diverse formats and media (e.g., visually, quantitatively, as well as in words) in order to address a question or solve a problem.

LAFS.1112.RH.4.10: By the end of grade 12, read and comprehend history/social studies texts in the grades 11–CCR text complexity band independently and proficiently.

LAFS.1112.WHST.1.1: Write arguments focused on discipline-specific content.

LAFS.1112.WHST.4.10: Write routinely over extended time frames (time for reflection and revision) and shorter time frames (a single sitting or a day or two) for a range of discipline-specific tasks, purposes, and audiences.

Continued on page 121

GEOGRAPHY CONNECTION

A wealth of natural resources helped fuel U.S. industrialization.

1 **PLACES AND REGIONS** *What natural resource in the states of West Virginia, Ohio, and Pennsylvania attracted high demand?* SS.912.A.1.4

2 **HUMAN SYSTEMS** *Why might the first steel factories have been built in Pennsylvania?* SS.912.A.1.4

Natural Resource Sites of the United States

Coal
Copper
Iron
Limestone
Petroleum
Softwood timber
Other timber

0 400 miles
0 400 km
Lambert Azimuthal Equal-Area projection

The Birth of the Telephone

"He then sketched for me an instrument that he thought would [transmit speech], and we discussed the possibility of constructing one. I did not make it; it was altogether too costly and the chances of its working too uncertain, to impress his financial backers . . . who were insisting that the wisest thing for Bell to do was to perfect the harmonic telegraph; then he would have money and leisure enough to build air castles like the telephone."

—Thomas A. Watson, from "Recollections of the Birth and Babyhood of the Telephone," 1913

DBQ **MAKING INFERENCES**
What can you infer about the difficulties that inventors faced during the late 1800s?
LAFS.1112.RH.4.10, SS.912.A.1.2, SS.912.A.3.5

to invent new products and to improve products invented by others. He first achieved international fame in 1877 with the invention of the phonograph. Two years later he perfected the electric generator and the lightbulb. His laboratory then went on to invent or improve several other devices, including the battery and the motion picture. In 1882, Lewis Latimer, who worked for Edison, invented a process for making cheap long-lasting carbon filaments for lightbulbs. With this invention, electric lighting became increasingly affordable. In 1889, several Edison companies merged to form the Edison General Electric Company (today known as GE).

The revolution in electricity took another step forward when engineer George Westinghouse developed an alternating current (AC) system to distribute electricity over long distances using transformers and generators. With this innovation, electricity began to improve living standards rapidly. City streets became safer as streetlights were installed. Electric trolley cars improved commute times to work, and new electric devices in the home made domestic chores easier and less time consuming. AC current and transformers are still used today to distribute electricity.

Cyrus Field laid a telegraph cable across the Atlantic Ocean in 1866, enabling faster communication between the United States and Europe. In 1874, Alexander Graham Bell began experimenting with ways to transmit sound via an electric current. In 1876, he succeeded. In 1877, Bell founded the Bell Telephone Company, which eventually became the American Telephone and Telegraph Company (AT&T). Bell's telephone transformed communications and helped improve the nation's standard of living. Businesses could place orders much more quickly and news of events that might shape business choices could be obtained in time for better decision making.

Innovation Improves the Standard of Living

In ways big and small, technology improved the standard of living. Shortly after the Civil War, Thaddeus Lowe invented an ice-making machine—enabling people to obtain low-cost ice year round for ice boxes that kept

POLITICAL CARTOONS

GOVERNMENT AND THE ECONOMY

These two political cartoons address tariffs and protectionism in the United States in the late 1800s.

The cartoon on the left depicts a flood of European goods damaging the demand for products made at American factories. The cartoon on the right shows a shopper being pulled between paying extra money to trusts (monopolies) to buy domestic goods and extra money (duties) to buy foreign goods.

1. **Interpreting** What event is shown as leading to the destruction of American factories? SS.912.A.1.4

2. **Analyzing** What argument does the cartoon on the right make about free trade? SS.912.A.1.4, SS.912.A.3.6

The gate is labeled "Protection." The flood is labeled "European Pauper Manufactures."

This cartoon is entitled "The Consumer Consumed."

(l)Library of Congress, Prints & Photographs Division [LC-USZ62-99407]; (r)Library of Congress, Prints & Photographs Division [LC-USZ62-99122] food fresh. A few years later, in the early 1870s, Gustavus Swift hired an engineer to develop a refrigerated railroad car. Swift shipped the first refrigerated load of fresh meat in 1877. The widespread use of refrigerated shipping containers enabled fresh food, especially meat, to be shipped long distances. As a result, the price of food began to drop and the quality of food people could obtain year round rose dramatically.

The pace of innovation continued rapidly throughout the late 1800s. In 1873, Christopher Scholes invented the typewriter. In 1886, Josephine Cochrane developed the automatic dishwasher. In 1888, George Eastman patented the first handheld camera—the Kodak camera. In 1893, Frank and Charles Duryea built the first gasoline-powered carriage. Power-driven sewing machines and cloth cutters rapidly moved the clothing business from small tailor shops to large factories. Similar changes took place in shoemaking. Large factories began using new processes and inventions to mass-produce shoes efficiently and inexpensively and could pass those savings on to their customers in the form of lower prices. By the early 1900s, tailors and cobblers had nearly disappeared. Prices of many other products also dropped as the United States industrialized.

☑ READING PROGRESS CHECK

Evaluating Which invention do you think has had the most lasting influence?

Free Enterprise

GUIDING QUESTION *How did laissez-faire economics promote industrialization?*

Another important reason the United States industrialized rapidly was the nation's free enterprise system. In the late 1800s, the profit motive attracted many people of high ability and ambition into business. **Entrepreneurs**—people who risk their capital in organizing and running a business—believed they could make money in manufacturing and transportation. Many of the new inventions that transformed society would not have been possible without entrepreneurs willing to risk their money to help develop and implement their inventions. Many entrepreneurs from New England, who had accumulated money by investing in trade, fishing, and textile mills, invested their money in factories and railroads. An equally important source of private capital was Europe, especially Great Britain. Foreign investors saw great opportunities for profit in the United States.

The Benefits of Laissez-Faire

Part of what attracted entrepreneurs to invest in American businesses was society's and government's support in principle for the idea of **laissez-faire** (leh•say•FAYR), a French phrase meaning "let people do as they choose." Supporters of laissez-faire believe that the government should not interfere in the economy other than to protect private property rights and maintain peace. They argue that if the government regulates the economy, it increases costs and eventually hurts society more than it helps.

Laissez-faire relies on supply and demand rather than the government to regulate wages and prices. Supporters believe a free market with competing companies leads to greater efficiency and creates more wealth for everyone. Laissez-faire advocates also support low taxes and limited government debt to ensure that private individuals, not the government, will make most of the decisions about how the nation's wealth is spent.

NEXT GENERATION SUNSHINE STATE STANDARDS

Continued from page 119

SS.912.A.1.2: Utilize a variety of primary and secondary sources to identify author, historical significance, audience, and authenticity to understand a historical period.

SS.912.A.1.4: Analyze how images, symbols, objects, cartoons, graphs, charts, maps, and artwork may be used to interpret the significance of time periods and events from the past.

SS.912.A.3.2: Examine the social, political, and economic causes, course, and consequences of the second Industrial Revolution that began in the late 19th century.

SS.912.A.3.3: Compare the first and second Industrial Revolutions in the United States.

SS.912.A.3.4: Determine how the development of steel, oil, transportation, communication, and business practices affected the United States economy.

SS.912.A.3.5: Identify significant inventors of the Industrial Revolution including African Americans and women.

SS.912.A.3.6: Analyze changes that occurred as the United States shifted from agrarian to an industrial society.

SS.912.A.3.10: Review different economic and philosophic ideologies.

SS.912.A.3.13: Examine key events and peoples in Florida history as they relate to United States history.

SS.912.G.1.2: Use spatial perspective and appropriate geographic terms and tools, including the Six Essential Elements, as organizational schema to describe any given place.

entrepreneur one who organizes, manages, and assumes the risks of a business or enterprise

laissez-faire a policy that government should interfere as little as possible in the nation's economy

practice to do something repeatedly so it becomes the standard

SKILLS PRACTICE

Use a concept map to help you understand new vocabulary in this lesson. Write the word "laissez-faire" in the center circle, and write details and ideas about the word in the surrounding circles. Do the same with the term "entrepreneur."

ELD.K12.ELL.SI.1, ELD.K12.ELL.SS.1

The Government's Relationship to Business

In many ways, the United States **practiced** laissez-faire economics in the late 1800s. State and federal governments kept taxes and spending low. They did not impose costly regulations on industry or try to control wages and prices. In the late 1800s, the United States was also one of the largest free trade areas in the world. Unlike Europe, which was divided into dozens of countries, each with tariffs, the entire United States was open to trade. The Constitution bans states from imposing tariffs, and there were few regulations on commerce or immigration. Supporters of laissez-faire say these factors played a major role in the country's rapid economic growth.

In other ways, however, the government went beyond laissez-faire and introduced policies intended to promote business. Since the early 1800s, leaders in the North and the South had different ideas about the proper role of the government in the economy. Northern leaders wanted high tariffs to protect manufacturers from foreign competition and supported federal subsidies for companies building roads, canals, and railroads. Southern leaders opposed subsidies and favored low tariffs to promote trade and to keep the cost of imported goods low.

The Civil War ended the debate. After the southern states seceded, the Republican-controlled Congress passed the Morrill Tariff, greatly increasing tariff rates. By 1865, tariffs had nearly tripled. Congress also gave vast tracts of western land and nearly $65 million in loans to western railroads and sold public lands with mineral resources for much less than their market value. Historians still debate whether these policies helped the economy grow.

High tariffs, however, contradicted laissez-faire ideas. When the nation raised tariffs on foreign goods, other countries raised their tariffs on American goods. This hurt American companies trying to sell goods abroad, particularly farmers who sold their products overseas. Despite these problems, many business leaders and members of Congress believed tariffs were necessary. Few believed that new American industries could compete with established European factories without tariffs to protect them. Later, in the early 1900s, after American companies had become large and efficient, business leaders began to push for free trade. They believed they could now compete internationally and win sales in foreign markets.

☑ READING PROGRESS CHECK

Assessing How did laissez-faire economics encourage businesses to industrialize?

LESSON 1 REVIEW

Reviewing Vocabulary

1. *Defining* What does gross national product measure? Create a line graph of the nation's Gross National Product over the last five years. LAFS.1112.RH.2.4

Using Your Notes

2. *Defending* Use your notes to identify what you think was the most important cause of American industrialization. Then write a sentence or two identifying your choice and defending its importance. LAFS.1112.WHST.4.10, SS.912.A.3.2

Answering the Guiding Questions

3. *Evaluating* Why was the United States successful at industrialization? SS.912.A.3.2, SS.912.A.3.4

4. *Making Connections* What invention from this period has had the most impact on your daily life? SS.912.A.3.5

5. *Analyzing Cause and Effect* How did laissez-faire economics promote industrialization? SS.912.A.3.10

Writing Activity

6. ARGUMENT Industrialization changed nearly every aspect of American life. Consider whether these changes have been generally positive or generally negative. Write a paragraph in which you express your thoughts and feelings about the pros and cons of widespread industrialization. LAFS.1112.WHST.1.1, LAFS.1112.WHST.4.10

LESSON 2

The Railroads

ESSENTIAL QUESTION

- How did the United States become an industrialized society after the Civil War?

READING HELPDESK

Academic Vocabulary

- integrate • investor

Content Vocabulary

- land grant

TAKING NOTES

Key Ideas and Details

Organizing As you read about the development of a nationwide rail network, complete a graphic organizer similar to the one below to list the effects of this network on the nation. LAFS.1112.RH.3.7

Effects

Nationwide Rail Network

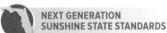

NEXT GENERATION SUNSHINE STATE STANDARDS

LAFS.1112.RH.2.4: Determine the meaning of words and phrases as they are used in a text, including analyzing how an author uses and refines the meaning of a key term over the course of a text (e.g., how Madison defines faction in Federalist No. 10).

LAFS.1112.RH.3.7: Integrate and evaluate multiple sources of information presented in diverse formats and media (e.g., visually, quantitatively, as well as in words) in order to address a question or solve a problem.

LAFS.1112.WHST.1.1: Write arguments focused on discipline-specific content.

Continued on page 124

IT MATTERS BECAUSE

Major railroads, including the transcontinental railroad, were constructed rapidly after the Civil War ended. Railroads required major capital investment and government land grants. The potential profits led to some corruption as well.

Linking the Nation

GUIDING QUESTION *How did the transcontinental railroad transform the West?*

In 1865, the United States had about 35,000 miles of railroad track, almost all of it east of the Mississippi River. After the Civil War, railroad construction expanded dramatically. By 1900, the United States had more than 200,000 miles of track.

The Transcontinental Railroad

The railroad boom began in 1862 with the Pacific Railway Act. This act gave two corporations—the Union Pacific and the Central Pacific—permission to build a transcontinental railroad. It also offered each company land along its right-of-way.

Under the direction of engineer Grenville Dodge, a former Union general, the Union Pacific Railroad began pushing westward from Omaha, Nebraska, in 1865. The railroad workers of the Union Pacific included Civil War veterans, newly recruited Irish immigrants, frustrated miners and farmers, cooks, adventurers, and ex-convicts. At the height of the project, the Union Pacific employed about 10,000 workers.

The Central Pacific Railroad began as the dream of engineer Theodore Judah. He sold stock in his fledgling Central Pacific Railroad Company to four Sacramento merchants: Leland Stanford, Charley Crocker, Mark Hopkins, and Collis P. Huntington. These "Big Four" eventually made huge fortunes. Stanford became governor of California, served as a U.S. senator, and founded Stanford University. Because of a shortage of labor in California, the Central Pacific Railroad hired about 10,000 workers from China. It paid them

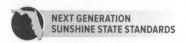
Continued from page 123

LAFS.1112.WHST.4.10: Write routinely over extended time frames (time for reflection and revision) and shorter time frames (a single sitting or a day or two) for a range of discipline-specific tasks, purposes, and audiences.

SS.912.A.1.2: Utilize a variety of primary and secondary sources to identify author, historical significance, audience, and authenticity to understand a historical period.

SS.912.A.1.4: Analyze how images, symbols, objects, cartoons, graphs, charts, maps, and artwork may be used to interpret the significance of time periods and events from the past.

SS.912.A.3.2: Examine the social, political, and economic causes, course, and consequences of the second Industrial Revolution that began in the late 19th century.

SS.912.A.3.4: Determine how the development of steel, oil, transportation, communication, and business practices affected the United States economy.

SS.912.A.3.13: Examine key events and peoples in Florida history as they relate to United States history.

SS.912.G.1.2: Use spatial perspective and appropriate geographic terms and tools, including the Six Essential Elements, as organizational schema to describe any given place.

SS.912.G.2.1: Identify the physical characteristics and the human characteristics that define and differentiate regions.

SS.912.G.4.7: Use geographic terms and tools to explain cultural diffusion throughout places, regions, and the world.

integrate to combine two previously separate things

investor one who puts money into a company in order to gain a future financial reward

land grant a grant of land by the federal government, especially for roads, railroads, or agricultural colleges

about $1 a day. All the equipment—rails, cars, locomotives, and machinery—was sent by ship from the eastern United States to San Francisco.

Workers completed the transcontinental railroad in only four years, despite the physical challenges. Each mile of track required 400 rails, and each rail took 10 spikes. The Central Pacific, starting from the west, laid a total of 688 miles of track. The Union Pacific laid 1,086 miles. On May 10, 1869, hundreds of spectators gathered at Promontory Summit, Utah. They watched dignitaries hammer five gold and silver spikes into the final rails that would join the Union Pacific and Central Pacific. Engineer Grenville Dodge was at the ceremony:

PRIMARY SOURCE

"The two trains pulled up facing each other, each crowded with workmen. . . . The officers and invited guests formed on each side of the track. . . . Prayer was offered; a number of spikes were driven in the two adjoining rails . . . and thus the two roads were wedded into one great trunk line from the Atlantic to the Pacific."

— from *How We Built the Union Pacific Railway*, 1910

Railroads Spur Growth

The transcontinental railroad was the first of many lines that began crisscrossing the nation after the Civil War. By linking the nation, railroads increased the markets for many products, spurring industrial growth. Railroad companies also stimulated the economy by spending huge amounts of money on steel, coal, timber, and other materials.

Large rail companies consolidated hundreds of small, unconnected railroads to create large, **integrated** railroad systems. Meanwhile, new locomotive technology and the invention of air brakes enabled railroads to put longer and heavier trains on their lines. When combined with the new integrated rail systems, operations became so efficient that the average rate per mile for a ton of freight dropped from two cents in 1860 to three-quarters of a cent in 1900.

Railroads Help Close the Frontier

Building railroad lines often required more money than most private **investors** could raise on their own. To encourage railroad construction across the Great Plains, the federal government gave **land grants** to many railroad companies. The railroads then sold the land to settlers, real estate companies, and other businesses to raise money to build the railroad. During the 1850s and 1860s, the federal land grant system gave railroads more than 120 million acres of public land, an area larger than New England, New York, and Pennsylvania combined. Several railroads,

The Union Pacific and Central Pacific lines met in Utah. Ceremonial gold and silver spikes were driven into the track, joining the two lines.

▶ **CRITICAL THINKING**

Predicting Consequences How might the completion of the transcontinental railroad change American life? SS.912.A.3.4, SS.912.G.4.7

©Philip Gendreau/Bettmann/Corbis

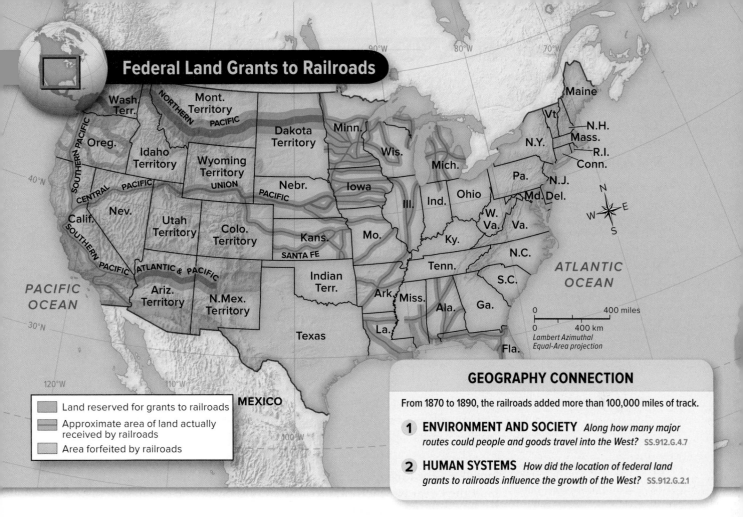

Federal Land Grants to Railroads

GEOGRAPHY CONNECTION

From 1870 to 1890, the railroads added more than 100,000 miles of track.

1 **ENVIRONMENT AND SOCIETY** *Along how many major routes could people and goods travel into the West?* SS.912.G.4.7

2 **HUMAN SYSTEMS** *How did the location of federal land grants to railroads influence the growth of the West?* SS.912.G.2.1

Map Legend:
- Land reserved for grants to railroads
- Approximate area of land actually received by railroads
- Area forfeited by railroads

including the Union Pacific and Central Pacific, received enough land to cover most of the cost of building their lines.

The land was only valuable, however, if the railroads could sell it. To convince people to move west, railroads and real estate companies offered the land at low prices and provided credit to settlers. Pamphlets, posters, and newspaper advertisements enticed people to move west. The building of the railroads themselves offered further encouragement, as settlers no longer had to migrate the entire distance on their own. They could take the train to a location near the land they bought. In all of these ways, the railroads helped move settlers onto the Great Plains and thereby close the American frontier.

☑ **READING PROGRESS CHECK**

Explaining How did the transcontinental railroad help unite the nation?

Robber Barons

GUIDING QUESTION *How did government grants to build railroads result in large-scale corruption?*

The great wealth many railroad entrepreneurs acquired in the late 1800s led to accusations that they had built their fortunes by swindling investors and taxpayers, bribing officials, and cheating on their contracts and debts. Perhaps the most notoriously corrupt railroad owner was Jay Gould, who practiced "insider trading" and manipulated stock prices. Bribery occurred frequently, partly because government was so deeply entangled in funding the railroads. Railroad investors discovered they could make more money by selling free government land grants than by operating a railroad, and some bribed political representatives to vote for more grants.

Florida CONNECTION

Investment, Tourism, and the Railroads

Northern businessmen invested heavily in the South after the Civil War. Henry Flagler built bridges to the Florida Keys and rail lines to St. Augustine. He built a luxury hotel which attracted wealthy guests from the East Coast. Henry Platt coordinated several rail line connections that ended in Tampa. He also built an opulent hotel there that was a favorite of Theodore Roosevelt. William Chipley built railroads across the Florida Panhandle, connecting it to the Atlantic coast for the first time. As a result of these improvements, by 1890 Florida's miles of track had increased over 400 percent. SS.912.A.3.13

POLITICAL CARTOONS — JAY GOULD: ROBBER BARON

Jay Gould bowls on Wall Street with balls labeled "Trickery" and "False Reports." The pins are labeled "Banker," "Inexperienced Investor," "Small Operator," and "Stock Broker."

1 *Analyzing Primary Sources*
What does this political cartoon suggest about attitudes toward Jay Gould? LAFS.1112.RH.3.7, SS.912.A.1.4, SS.912.A.3.4

2 *Predicting Consequences*
What is a likely outcome of the actions of robber barons on the people represented by the bowling pins? LAFS.1112.RH.3.7, SS.912.A.1.4, SS.912.A.3.4

Railroad owners became condemned as robber barons as the American public increasingly began to suspect them of bribery, cheating, and swindling.

The Crédit Mobilier Scandal

Corruption in the railroad industry became public in 1872 with the Crédit Mobilier scandal. Crédit Mobilier was a construction company set up by several stockholders of the Union Pacific Railroad, including Oakes Ames, a member of Congress. To convince Congress to give the railroad more grants, Ames sold other members of Congress shares at a price well below their market value.

During the election campaign of 1872, a letter appeared in the *New York Sun* listing members of Congress who had bought shares. The Crédit Mobilier scandal produced widespread anger and led to the impression that railroad entrepreneurs were "robber barons"—people who loot an industry and become rich unethically.

The Great Northern Railroad

Not all railroad men were robber barons. James J. Hill was clearly not. Hill built the Great Northern Railroad from Wisconsin and Minnesota to Washington state without any federal land grants or subsidies. He planned the railroad's route to pass by existing towns in the region and offered low fares to settlers who homesteaded along his route. He also identified products that were in demand in China, including cotton, textiles, and flour, and hauled those goods to Washington to ship to Asia. This way, his railroad efficiently hauled goods both east and west, instead of simply sending goods east and coming back empty like other railroads. The Great Northern became the most successful transcontinental railroad and one of the few railroads of the time that was not eventually forced into bankruptcy.

✔ READING PROGRESS CHECK

Explaining Why did robber barons bribe people in Congress?

©Bettmann/Corbis

LESSON 2 REVIEW

Reviewing Vocabulary

1. *Explaining* Why did the government give land grants to railroad companies? LAFS.1112.RH.2.4

2. *Describing* What were the advantages of integrating railroads into one interconnected network? LAFS.1112.RH.2.4

Using Your Notes

3. *Identifying Cause and Effect* Review your notes and write a brief explanation of how the growth of railroads helped American businesses expand.

Answering the Guiding Questions

4. *Analyzing Information* How did the transcontinental railroad transform the West? SS.912.A.3.4

5. *Drawing Conclusions* How did government grants to build railroads result in large-scale corruption? SS.912.A.3.4

Writing Activity

6. INFORMATIVE/EXPLANATORY Between 1860 and 1890, the amount of railroad track in the United States increased dramatically. How would you expect the growth of the railroad to influence settlement patterns? LAFS.1112.WHST.1.2, LAFS.1112.WHST.4.10

LESSON 3
Big Business

ESSENTIAL QUESTION

• How did the United States become an industrialized society after the Civil War?

READING HELPDESK

Academic Vocabulary

• distribution
• consumer

Content Vocabulary

• corporation
• economies of scale
• monopoly
• holding company
• trust

TAKING NOTES

Key Ideas and Details

Organizing As you read about the rise of corporations in the United States, use the following graphic organizer to identify the steps big businesses took to weaken or eliminate competition. **LAFS.1112.RH.3.7**

Slashed prices temporarily

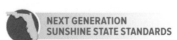
NEXT GENERATION SUNSHINE STATE STANDARDS

ELD.K12.ELL.SI.1: English language learners communicate for social and instructional purposes within the school setting.

ELD.K12.ELL.SS.1: English language learners communicate information, ideas and concepts necessary for academic success in the content area of Social Studies.

LAFS.1112.RH.2.4: Determine the meaning of words and phrases as they are used in a text, including analyzing how an author uses and refines the meaning of a key term over the course of a text (e.g., how Madison defines faction in Federalist No. 10).

Continued on page 128

IT MATTERS BECAUSE

Following the Civil War, large corporations developed that could consolidate business functions and produce goods more efficiently. Retailers began using new techniques to attract consumers.

The Rise of Big Business

GUIDING QUESTION *What advantages do large corporations have over small businesses?*

By 1900, big business dominated the economy, operating vast complexes of factories and **distribution** facilities. The **corporation**, an organization owned by many people but treated by law as though it were a person, made big business possible. Stockholders own corporations through shares of ownership called stock. Selling stock allows a corporation to raise money while spreading out the financial risk. Before the 1830s, few corporations existed because entrepreneurs had to convince state legislatures to issue them charters. In the 1830s, however, states began allowing companies to become corporations and issue stock without a charter from the legislature.

The freedom to form a corporation was one of the great benefits of the laissez-faire approach to economics in the later half of the 1800s. With the money raised from selling stock, corporations could invest in new technologies, hire large workforces, and purchase machines. This greatly increased their efficiency. They achieved **economies of scale**, in which the cost of manufacturing is decreased by producing goods quickly in large quantities.

All businesses have fixed costs and operating costs. *Fixed costs* are costs a company pays even if it is not operating (loans, mortgages, and taxes). *Operating costs* are incurred when running a company (wages, shipping costs, buying raw materials). Small manufacturers usually had low fixed costs but high operating costs. If sales dropped, it was cheaper to shut down temporarily. Big manufacturers, however, had the high fixed costs of building and maintaining a factory, while operating costs were low. Operating

distribution the act or process of being given out or disbursed to clients, consumers, or members of a group

corporation an organization that is authorized by law to carry on an activity but treated as though it were a single person

economies of scale the reduction in the cost of a good brought about especially by increased production at a given facility

consumer a person who buys what is produced by an economy

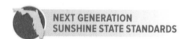
NEXT GENERATION SUNSHINE STATE STANDARDS

Continued from page 127

LAFS.1112.RH.3.7: Integrate and evaluate multiple sources of information presented in diverse formats and media (e.g., visually, quantitatively, as well as in words) in order to address a question or solve a problem.
LAFS.1112.WHST.1.1: Write arguments focused on discipline-specific content.
LAFS.1112.WHST.4.10: Write routinely over extended time frames (time for reflection and revision) and shorter time frames (a single sitting or a day or two) for a range of discipline-specific tasks, purposes, and audiences.

Continued on page 129

costs, such as wages, were such a small part of total costs that it made sense to continue operating, even in a recession.

In these circumstances, big corporations had several advantages. They could produce more goods at a lower cost and could stay open in bad economic times by cutting prices to increase sales. Rebates from the railroads further lowered their operating costs. Of course, this also led eventually to one of the major costs of laissez-faire economics: small businesses, many family owned, that could not compete with large corporations were forced out of business.

☑ READING PROGRESS CHECK

Explaining How do economies of scale affect corporations?

Consolidating Industry

GUIDING QUESTION *What new business strategies allowed businesses to weaken or eliminate competition?*

Although a laissez-faire economy benefited **consumers** because the intense competition led to falling prices, business leaders did not like the intense competition that had been forced on them. Cutting prices to beat the competition also cut into profits. This situation demonstrated one of the potential costs of laissez-faire. With no regulations governing their competition, companies were also free to make deals with each other to fix prices by organizing pools, or agreements to keep prices at a certain level. Another term for a pool that is used today is cartel.

American courts and legislatures, however, were suspicious of pools because they interfered with competition and property rights. As a result, even though the laissez-faire economy meant that companies could try to fix prices, companies that formed pools found that it also meant they had no legal protection and could not enforce their pool agreements in court. As a result pools generally broke apart whenever one member cut prices to

CHARTS/GRAPHS	TYPES OF BUSINESS ORGANIZATIONS		
	Sole Proprietorship	**Partnership**	**Corporation**
Who owns the business?	One owner who often manages the business	Two or more owners who usually manage the business	Shareholders, whether private or public Managers are hired
How is money raised?	Uses savings of owner Borrows from creditors	Invests savings from limited partners Borrows from creditors	Sells stock Borrows from creditors
Advantages	Ease of setup Nominal cost	Shared responsibility by each partner	Exists as a separate entity Limited liability
Disadvantages	Owner is personally liable for all debts Commingling of personal and business property and funds Cannot raise capital by selling an interest in the business	Owners are personally liable for obligations and debts Requires more legal and accounting services Partners may disagree on the management of the company	Must adhere to the principles that govern a corporation

1 *Making Inferences* Comparing proprietorships and corporations, why do you think both still exist today?
LAFS.1112.RH.3.7, SS.912.A.3.4

2 *Making Generalizations* Based on the chart, what generalizations can you make about why a corporation might have a competitive advantage over a sole proprietorship?
LAFS.1112.RH.3.7, SS.912.A.3.4

Vertical Integration

Integrated steel company

Steel mill

Shipping facilities

Iron mine   Limestone quarry   Coal mine

Vertical integration occurs when a company owns all parts of the industrial process.

Horizontal Integration

Integrated steel company   Independent steel mills

Horizontal integration occurs when a company grows by buying its competitors.

Vertical integration and horizontal integration helped consolidate industry.

1 *Analyzing Information*
How does a large company benefit when it buys its competitors?
LAFS.1112.RH.3.7, SS.912.A.3.4

2 *Identifying Central Ideas*
Why did business owners want to vertically integrate their companies?
LAFS.1112.RH.3.7, SS.912.A.3.4

3 *Creating a Written Presentation*
Using correct social studies terminology, write a report explaining the main reasons the American economy changed so dramatically in the years after the Civil War. As part of your report be sure to explain key historical concepts including industrialization, entrepreneurialism, laissez-faire economics, economies of scale, and corporations. LAFS.1112.RH.3.7, LAFS.1112.SL.2.6, SS.912.A.3.4

steal market share from another. As a result, by the late 1870s, competition had reduced many industries to a few large highly efficient corporations.

Andrew Carnegie and Steel

The remarkable life of Andrew Carnegie illustrates the rise of big business in the United States. A Scottish immigrant, Carnegie went to work at age 12 in a textile factory. He worked his way up to become secretary to Thomas Scott, a superintendent of the Pennsylvania Railroad. When Scott was promoted, Carnegie became the new superintendent.

Carnegie bought shares in iron mills and factories that made sleeping cars and railroad locomotives, as well as a company that built railroad bridges. By his early 30s, he quit his job to concentrate on his investments. As part of his business activities, Carnegie often traveled to Europe. On one trip, he met Sir Henry Bessemer, who had invented a new process for making high quality steel efficiently and cheaply. After meeting Bessemer, Carnegie opened a steel mill in Pittsburgh in 1875 and began using the Bessemer process. He boasted about how cheaply he could produce steel:

PRIMARY SOURCE

❝Two pounds of ironstone . . . one pound and a half of coal, mined, manufactured into coke . . . one-half pound of lime, . . . [and] a small amount of manganese ore, . . . these four pounds of materials manufactured into one pound of steel, for which the consumer pays one cent.❞

—from *Triumphant Democracy*, 1893

To make his company more efficient, Carnegie began the vertical integration of the steel industry. A vertically integrated company owns all of the different businesses on which it depends for its operation. Instead of paying companies for coal, lime, and iron, Carnegie's steel company bought coal mines, limestone quarries, and iron ore fields. Vertical integration saved money and enabled many companies to expand.

Rockefeller and Standard Oil

Successful business leaders also pushed for horizontal integration, or combining many firms engaged in the same type of business into one large

NEXT GENERATION SUNSHINE STATE STANDARDS

Continued from page 128

SS.912.A.1.4: Analyze how images, symbols, objects, cartoons, graphs, charts, maps, and artwork may be used to interpret the significance of time periods and events from the past.

SS.912.A.3.2: Examine the social, political, and economic causes, course, and consequences of the second Industrial Revolution that began in the late 19th century.

SS.912.A.3.4: Determine how the development of steel, oil, transportation, communication, and business practices affected the United States economy.

SS.912.A.3.6: Analyze changes that occurred as the United States shifted from agrarian to an industrial society.

SS.912.A.3.10: Review different economic and philosophic ideologies.

corporation. Horizontal integration took place frequently as companies competed. When a company began to lose market share, it would often sell out to competitors to create a larger organization.

Perhaps the most famous example of an industrialist who achieved almost complete horizontal integration of his industry is John D. Rockefeller. Through a series of buyouts, Rockefeller's Standard Oil began to horizontally integrate the oil industry. By 1880, the company controlled about 90 percent of the oil refining industry in the United States. When a single company achieves control of an entire market, it becomes a **monopoly**.

monopoly total control of a type of industry by one person or one company

New Business Organizations

Many Americans feared monopolies because they believed that a monopoly could charge whatever it wanted for its products. They argued that one of the costs of laissez-faire economics was that it created large powerful corporations that could control prices, and manipulate politicians and laws to ensure that they did not face any new competition.

Supporters of laissez-faire disagreed. They asserted that monopolies had to keep prices low because raising prices would allow competitors to reappear and offer products at a lower price. In some industries, even though a company had a near monopoly in the United States, it was not really a monopoly because it was competing on a global scale. Standard Oil, for example, came very close to having a monopoly in the United States, but it was competing against European oil companies and the competition forced the company to keep its prices low in the late 1800s and early 1900s.

Trusts In the late 1800s, in an effort to stop horizontal integration and the rise of monopolies, many states made it illegal for one company to own stock in another company. It did not take long, however, for companies to find ways around the laws. In 1882, Standard Oil formed the first trust, a new way of merging businesses that did not violate the law. A **trust** is a legal arrangement that allows one person to manage another person's property. The person who manages that property is called a trustee.

trust a combination of firms or corporations formed by a legal agreement, especially to reduce competition

Instead of buying a company outright, Standard Oil had stockholders give their stocks to a group of Standard Oil trustees. In exchange, the stockholders received shares in the trust, which entitled them to a portion of the trust's profits. Since the trustees did not own the stock but were merely managing it, they were not violating any laws. The trustees could control a group of companies as if they were one large merged company.

Holding Companies In 1889, the state of New Jersey further accelerated the rise of big business with a new incorporation law. This law allowed corporations set up in New Jersey to own stock in other businesses. Many companies immediately used the law to create holding companies. A **holding company** does not produce anything. Instead, it owns the stock of companies that do produce goods. The holding company manages the companies it owns, effectively merging them into one large enterprise.

holding company
a company whose primary business is owning a controlling share of stock in other companies

Investment Banking Another increase in the size of corporations began in the 1890s, when investment bankers began helping to create holding companies. Investment bankers specialized in helping companies issue stock. Companies would sell large blocks of stock to investment bankers at a discount. The bankers would then find the investors and sell the stock for a profit. Perhaps the most successful investment banker was J. P. Morgan.

In the mid-1890s, investment bankers began merging many of America's large corporations into holding companies and then selling their stock. In 1901, J.P. Morgan bought out Andrew Carnegie. He then merged Carnegie Steel with other large steel companies into an enormous holding company called the United States Steel Company. U.S. Steel was worth $1.4 billion, the first billion-dollar company in American history.

Selling the Product

The creation of giant manufacturing companies in the United States pushed retailers to expand in size as well. The vast array of products that American industries produced led retailers to look for new ways to attract consumers. N. W. Ayer and Son, the first advertising company, began creating large illustrated ads instead of relying on the old small print line ads previously used in newspapers. By 1900, retailers were spending over $90 million a year on advertising in newspapers and magazines.

Advertising attracted readers to the newest retail business: the department store. In 1877, advertisements billed John Wanamaker's new Philadelphia department store, the Grand Depot, as the "largest space in the world devoted to retail selling on a single floor." When it opened, only a handful of department stores existed in the United States. Soon hundreds sprang up, providing a huge selection of products in one large building.

Chain stores, a group of retail outlets owned by the same company, first appeared in the mid-1800s. In contrast to department stores, chain stores such as Woolworth's focused on offering low prices.

To reach the millions of people who lived in rural areas, retailers began issuing mail-order catalogs. Two of the largest mail-order retailers were Montgomery Ward and Sears, Roebuck and Co. Their huge catalogs were widely distributed through the mail. They used attractive illustrations and appealing descriptions to advertise thousands of items for sale.

 READING PROGRESS CHECK

Summarizing Why did some people think monopolies were disadvantageous for the consumer?

▲ J. P. Morgan created one of the largest holding companies, United States Steel Company.

SKILLS PRACTICE

Work with a partner. Take turns using the following vocabulary words in sentences: corporation, consumer, monopoly, trust.
ELD.K12.ELL.SI.1, ELD.K12.ELL.SS.1

LESSON 3 REVIEW

Reviewing Vocabulary

1. *Summarizing* Describe vertical and horizontal integration and explain how it contributed to the economic development of the United States. LAFS.1112.RH.2.4

2. *Explaining* How did trusts and holding companies create unofficial monopolies? LAFS.1112.RH.2.4

Using Your Notes

3. *Making Connections* Review the notes you completed throughout the lesson to identify a way that a corporation today could use similar tactics to weaken its competition.

Answering the Guiding Questions

4. *Evaluating* What advantages do large corporations have over small businesses? SS.912.A.3.4

5. *Synthesizing* What new business strategies allowed businesses to weaken or eliminate competition? SS.912.A.3.4

Writing Activity

6. INFORMATIVE/EXPLANATORY Industrialization introduced many new ideas about how businesses could be formed and operated. Write a one-page essay explaining how these new ways of organizing businesses helped to improve the standard of living in the United States. LAFS.1112.WHST.1.2, LAFS.1112.WHST.4.10

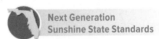

LESSON 4
Unions

ESSENTIAL QUESTION

• How did the United States become an industrialized society after the Civil War?

READING HELPDESK

Academic Vocabulary

• restraint   • constitute

Content Vocabulary

• deflation
• industrial union
• lockout
• arbitration
• injunction
• closed shop

TAKING NOTES

Key Ideas and Details

Sequencing As you read about the increase of labor unions in the late 1800s, complete a time line similar to the one below by filling in the year of each incident of labor unrest discussed and the results of each incident. LAFS.1112.RH.3.7

1877 ☐—☐—☐

Next Generation Sunshine State Standards

LAFS.1112.RH.2.4: Determine the meaning of words and phrases as they are used in a text, including analyzing how an author uses and refines the meaning of a key term over the course of a text (e.g., how Madison defines faction in Federalist No. 10).

LAFS.1112.RH.3.7: Integrate and evaluate multiple sources of information presented in diverse formats and media (e.g., visually, quantitatively, as well as in words) in order to address a question or solve a problem.

LAFS.1112.WHST.1.1: Write arguments focused on discipline-specific content.

Continued on page 134

IT MATTERS BECAUSE

Workers tried to form unions in the 1800s, hoping to improve wages, hours, and working conditions. Business leaders worked with some trade unions but generally opposed industrial unions. Strikes during this era sometimes led to violence, which hurt the unions' image and slowed their growth.

Working in the United States

GUIDING QUESTION *Why did workers try to form unions in the late 1800s?*

There were many benefits of laissez-faire economics in the late 1800s--including rapid industrialization, dramatic innovation, and an improving standard of living--but the laissez-faire idea that governments should avoid regulating the economy had costs as well. Working conditions in factories and mines were difficult and often dangerous. Many workers performed dull, repetitive tasks in dangerous, unhealthy working conditions. Workers breathed in lint, dust, and toxic fumes. Heavy machines lacking safety devices led to injuries. With no regulations governing workplace safety or training requirements, workers had no recourse when they were poorly treated other than to quit and look for a new job.

Despite these conditions, industrialism led to a dramatic rise in the standard of living. The average worker's wages rose by 50 percent between 1860 and 1890. Nevertheless, the uneven division of income between the wealthy and the working class caused resentment among workers. In 1900, the average industrial worker made 22¢ per hour and worked 59 hours per week.

Deflation, or a rise in the value of money, added to tensions. Between 1865 and 1897, deflation caused prices to fall, which increased the buying power of workers' wages. Although companies cut wages regularly in the late 1800s, prices fell even faster, so that wages were actually still going up in buying power. Workers, however, resented getting less money. Eventually, many concluded that they needed a union to bargain for higher wages and better working conditions.

Early Unions

There were two basic types of industrial workers in the United States in the 1800s—craft workers and common laborers. Craft workers, such as machinists, iron molders, stonecutters, shoemakers, and printers, had special skills and training. They received higher wages and had more control over their time. Common laborers had few skills and received lower wages.

In the 1830s, as industrialization began to spread, craft workers began to form trade unions. By 1873, there were 30 national trade unions in the United States. Among the largest and most successful were the Iron Molders' International Union, the International Typographical Union, and the Knights of St. Crispin—the shoemakers' union.

Opposition to Unions

Employers often had to negotiate with trade unions because the unions represented workers whose skills they needed. Employers, however, generally viewed unions as conspiracies that interfered with property rights. Business leaders particularly opposed **industrial unions,** which united all the workers in a particular industry.

Companies used several techniques to stop workers from forming unions. They required workers to take oaths or sign contracts promising not to join a union. They hired detectives to identify union organizers. Workers who tried to organize a union or strike were fired and placed on a blacklist—a list of "troublemakers"—so that no company would hire them. Companies used **"lockouts"** to break up existing unions. They locked workers out of the property and refused to pay them. If the union called a strike, employers would hire replacements, or strikebreakers.

Efforts to break unions often succeeded because there were no laws giving workers the right to form unions or requiring owners to negotiate with them. Government policies toward unions did not really reflect a commitment to laissez-faire economics. Instead of staying out of economic disputes, and allowing workers to confront owners and work out their disagreements on their own, the government's relationship toward business shifted toward policies that supported business owners and impeded the development of unions. Courts frequently ruled that strikes were "conspiracies in **restraint** of trade," and labor leaders were often fined or jailed. Eventually even state militias and federal troops would be used to break up strikes.

deflation a decline in the volume of available money or credit that results in lower prices, and therefore increases the buying power of money

industrial union
an organization of common laborers and craft workers in a particular industry

lockout a company tool to fight union demands by refusing to allow employees to enter its facilities to work

restraint the act of limiting, restricting, or keeping under control

---

ANNUAL NONFARM EARNINGS

Earnings (dollars) vs. Year (1865–1900)

— Real wages
— Not adjusted for inflation

Source: *Historical Statistics of the United States: Colonial Times to 1970*

CHARTS/GRAPHS

In the late 1800s, industrial workers toiled in dangerous, unhealthy conditions. Bad working conditions eventually led workers to seek to organize unions, hoping to improve their situations.

1 *Comparing and Contrasting* How did changes in real wages and wages that were not adjusted for deflation differ? MAFS.912.S-ID.1

2 *Drawing Conclusions* Why do you think workers wanted to organize? SS.912.A.3.9

©Historical/Corbis

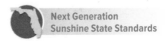

Next Generation Sunshine State Standards

Continued from page 132

LAFS.1112.WHST.4.10: Write routinely over extended time frames (time for reflection and revision) and shorter time frames (a single sitting or a day or two) for a range of discipline-specific tasks, purposes, and audiences.

SS.912.A.1.4: Analyze how images, symbols, objects, cartoons, graphs, charts, maps, and artwork may be used to interpret the significance of time periods and events from the past.

SS.912.A.3.2: Examine the social, political, and economic causes, course, and consequences of the second Industrial Revolution that began in the late 19th century.

SS.912.A.3.9: Examine causes, course, and consequences of the labor movement in the late 19th and early 20th centuries.

SS.912.A.3.10: Review different economic and philosophic ideologies.

SS.912.A.3.12: Compare how different nongovernmental organizations and progressives worked to shape public policy, restore economic opportunities, and correct injustices in American life.

Part of the reason for the government's objection to unions and collective action by workers was the perception that unions were un-American. In the 1800s, the ideas of Karl Marx, called Marxism, became very influential in Europe. Marx argued that the basic force shaping capitalist society was the class struggle between workers and owners. He believed that workers would eventually revolt, seize control of the factories, and overthrow the government. Eventually, Marx thought, the state would disappear, leaving a communist society in which classes did not exist.

While many labor supporters agreed with Marx, a few supported anarchism. Anarchists believe that society does not need any government. In the late 1800s, anarchists assassinated government officials and set off bombs across Europe, hoping to begin a revolution.

During the same period, tens of thousands of European immigrants headed to America. Anti-immigrant feelings were already strong in the United States and, as people began to associate immigrant workers with radical ideas, they became suspicious of unions. These fears, and concerns for law and order, often led officials to use the courts, the police, and even the army to crush strikes and break up unions.

✓ **READING PROGRESS CHECK**

Determining Cause and Effect How did working conditions encourage workers to form unions in the late 1800s?

GEOGRAPHY CONNECTION

Strikes and labor unrest were felt in all regions of the United States.

1 PLACES AND REGIONS *What region of the country seems to have had the most strikes? Why do you think this was so?* SS.912.G.2.1

2 PLACES AND REGIONS *What region of the country seems to have had the fewest strikes? Why do you think this was so?* SS.912.A.3.9, SS.912.G.2.1

Strikes and Labor Unrest 1870–1900

Haymarket Riot, 1886

Pullman Railroad Strike, 1894

Homestead Steel Strike, 1892

Great Railroad Strike begins in Martinsburg, West Virginia, 1877

County with strike activity, 1881–1894

No strikes reported

0   400 miles
0   400 km
Lambert Azimuthal Equal-Area projection

PACIFIC OCEAN

ATLANTIC OCEAN

MEXICO

Gulf of Mexico

Struggling to Organize

GUIDING QUESTION *What made it difficult for union workers to create large industrial unions?*

Although workers attempted on many occasions to create large industrial unions, they rarely succeeded. In many cases, the confrontations with owners and the government led to violence and bloodshed.

The Great Railroad Strike

The Panic of 1873 was a severe recession that struck the American economy and forced many companies to cut wages. The economy had still not recovered when, in July 1877, the Baltimore and Ohio Railroad announced it was cutting wages for the third time. In Martinsburg, West Virginia, workers walked off the job and blocked the tracks.

As word spread, railroad workers across the country walked off the job. The strike eventually involved some 80,000 railroad workers and affected two-thirds of the nation's railways. Angry strikers smashed equipment, tore up tracks, and blocked rail service in New York City, Baltimore, Pittsburgh, St. Louis, and Chicago. The governors of several states called out their militias. In many places, gun battles erupted between the militia and the strikers.

Declaring a state of "insurrection," President Rutherford B. Hayes sent federal troops to Martinsburg, Baltimore, Pittsburgh, and elsewhere. It took 12 bloody days for police, state militias, and federal troops to restore order. By the time the strike collapsed, more than 100 people lay dead, and over $10 million in railroad property had been destroyed. The violence of this strike alarmed many Americans and only further contributed to the idea that allowing workers to organize was dangerous to society.

The Knights of Labor

The Knights of Labor, founded in 1869, took a different approach to labor issues. Its leader, Terence Powderly, opposed strikes in favor of boycotts and **arbitration,** in which a third party helps workers and employers reach an agreement. Unlike other unions, the Knights welcomed women and African Americans. They called for an eight-hour workday, equal pay for women, no child labor, and worker-owned factories.

The Haymarket Riot In 1886, supporters of the eight-hour workday called for a nationwide strike on May 1. On May 3, Chicago police intervening in a fight on a picket line opened fire on the strikers, killing four. The next day, about 3,000 people gathered to protest the shootings in Chicago's Haymarket Square. Someone threw a bomb, police opened fire, and workers shot back, injuring about 170 people and killing 10 policemen. Eight men were arrested for the bombing. Though evidence against them was weak, public anger resulted in eight convictions. Four were executed.

Union critics used the Haymarket riot to claim that dangerous radicals dominated the unions. One of the men arrested was a member of the Knights of Labor. The blow to the Knights' reputation along with lost strikes led to a decline in their membership and influence.

The Homestead and Pullman Strikes

In the summer of 1892, another labor dispute led to bloodshed. A steel mill owned by Andrew Carnegie in Homestead, Pennsylvania, was managed by Henry Clay Frick, an anti-union business partner. Frick proposed cutting wages by 20 percent. He then locked out employees (who were members of the Amalgamated Association of Iron, Steel, and Tin Workers) and had the Pinkerton Detective Agency bring in replacements. When the Pinkertons and strikebreakers approached the plant, the strikers resisted. Over the

In 1894 a former quarry foreman named Jacob Coxey organized unemployed workers and began a march on Washington to demand jobs on public works projects. The marchers were known as "Coxey's Army."

▶ CRITICAL THINKING
Analyzing Primary Sources What does this photograph indicate about workers' interest in organizing to achieve their goals?
LAFS.1112.RH.3.7, SS.912.A.1.4, SS.912.A.3.9

arbitration settling a dispute by agreeing to accept the decision of an impartial outsider

©Historical/Corbis

next 14 hours, Pinkertons and strikers clashed, leaving several dead and dozens injured. The governor of Pennsylvania sent in the militia to protect the strikebreakers, and four months later, the strike collapsed.

In 1894, the Pullman Palace Car Company slashed workers' wages without lowering rents and prices in the company town. American Railway Union (ARU) workers refused to handle Pullman cars, and railroads ground to a near halt. Railroad managers arranged to have U.S. mail cars attached to the Pullman cars, and President Cleveland sent in federal troops to keep the mail running. A federal court then issued an **injunction,** or formal order, to halt the boycott. Both the strike and the ARU collapsed. The Supreme Court later upheld the right to issue such an injunction. This gave business a powerful tool for dealing with labor unrest.

✓ READING PROGRESS CHECK

Identifying Central Ideas How did major strikes prevent large industrial unions from maintaining power and influence?

New Unions Emerge

GUIDING QUESTION *How were the new industrial unions different from the older trade unions?*

Although workers often shared the same complaints about wages and working hours, unions took different approaches to how they tried to improve workers' lives. Trade unions remained the most common type of labor organization, but unskilled workers were not represented by trade unions. New types of unions emerged to support these workers.

The Rise of the AFL

The American Federation of Labor (AFL) was the dominant labor organization of the late 1800s. In 1886, leaders of several national trade unions created the AFL. It focused on promoting the interests of skilled workers.

Samuel Gompers was the first president of the AFL, a position he held almost continuously until 1924. While other unions became involved in politics, Gompers tried to concentrate on "pure and simple" unionism, focusing on wages, working hours, and working conditions. He was willing to use strikes to create change but preferred to negotiate.

The AFL had three main goals. First, it tried to convince companies to recognize unions and agree to collective bargaining. Second, it pushed for **closed shops,** meaning that companies could hire only union members. Third, it promoted an eight-hour workday. By 1900, the AFL was the biggest union in the country with more than 500,000 members. Still, at that time, the AFL represented less than 15 percent of all nonfarm workers. Most AFL members were white men, because the unions discriminated against African Americans, and only a few would admit women.

The IWW

In 1905, a group of labor radicals, many of them socialists, created the Industrial Workers of the World (IWW). Nicknamed "the Wobblies," the IWW wanted to organize all workers according to industry, without making distinctions between skilled and unskilled workers. The IWW endorsed using strikes and declared: "The working class and the employing class have nothing in common." The IWW believed all workers should be organized into "One Big Union." In particular, the IWW tried to organize the unskilled workers who were ignored by most unions.

In 1912, the IWW led a successful strike of 25,000 textile workers in Lawrence, Massachusetts, to protest wage cuts. The companies reversed the

injunction a court order whereby one is required to do or to refrain from doing a specified act

closed shop an agreement in which a company agrees to hire only union members

Samuel Gompers concentrated his efforts on improving working conditions and believed that a just society was built on a fair labor policy.

▶ CRITICAL THINKING
Drawing Conclusions How do you think Gompers would view a society that did not allow labor unions? SS.912.A.3.9

Library of Congress, Prints & Photographs Division [LC-US262-88511]

wage cuts after 10 weeks. The Lawrence strike was the Wobblies' greatest victory. Most IWW strikes failed. The IWW never gained a large membership, in part because its radical philosophy and controversial strikes led many to condemn the organization.

Women and Organized Labor

After the Civil War, the number of female wage earners began to increase. By 1900, women made up more than 18 percent of the labor force. The types of jobs women did outside the home reflected society's ideas about what **constituted** "women's work." About one-third of women wage earners worked as domestic servants. Another third worked as teachers, nurses, sales clerks. and office clerical workers. The remaining third were industrial workers, often in the garment industry or food-processing plants.

Women were paid less than men even when they performed the same jobs. It was assumed that a woman had a man helping to support her, and that a man needed higher wages in order to support a family. Most unions excluded women.

One of the most famous labor leaders of the era was Mary Harris Jones, also known as "Mother Jones." Jones worked as a labor organizer for the Knights of Labor before helping organize mine workers. Her public speaking abilities made her a very successful organizer, leading John D. Rockefeller to dub her "the most dangerous woman in America."

In 1900, Jewish and Italian immigrants who worked in the clothing business in New York City founded the International Ladies' Garment Workers Union (ILGWU), which represented female and male workers in the women's clothing industry. Membership expanded rapidly, and in 1909, a strike of some 30,000 garment workers won the ILGWU recognition in the industry, better wages, and benefits for employees.

In 1903, Mary Kenney O'Sullivan and Leonora O'Reilly decided to establish a separate union for women. With the help of Jane Addams and Lillian Wald, they established the Women's Trade Union League (WTUL), which pushed for an eight-hour workday, a minimum wage, an end to evening work for women, and the abolition of child labor.

The Granger Collection, New York

 READING PROGRESS CHECK

Explaining Why did women need to form their own trade unions?

By the beginning of the twentieth century, many women had entered the workforce. Some were industrial workers in clothing or food-processing factories.

▶ **CRITICAL THINKING**
Formulating Questions What is one question that you could ask to begin researching women in the industrial workforce?
LAFS.1112.RH.3.7, SS.912.A.1.4

constitute to compose, make up, or form

LESSON 4 REVIEW

Reviewing Vocabulary
1. *Contrasting* What is the difference between a closed shop and a lockout? LAFS.1112.RH.2.4

2. *Paraphrasing* What is another word or phrase for an injunction? LAFS.1112.RH.2.4

Using Your Notes
3. *Comparing* Use your notes from the lesson to identify some common features of incidents of labor unrest.

Answering the Guiding Questions
4. *Drawing Conclusions* Why did workers try to form unions in the late 1800s? SS.912.A.3.9

5. *Making Generalizations* What social issues led to the rise of the effort to form labor unions for women? SS.912.A.3.9

6. *Contrasting* How were the new industrial unions different from the older trade unions? SS.912.A.3.6, SS.912.A.3.9

Writing Activity
7. **NARRATIVE** Suppose that you are a union leader. Write a letter to a factory owner in which you try to persuade him or her to make changes in wages or other work policies on behalf of the factory's workers. Be sure to be specific about your requests and the reasons why they are necessary.
LAFS.1112.WHST.1.2, LAFS.1112.WHST.4.10

STUDY GUIDE

THE RISE OF INDUSTRY
LESSON 1

Natural Resources
- timber and minerals
- fossil fuels
- petroleum

+

Railroads
- move in settlers and minerals
- move out raw materials

+

New Inventions
- electric power
- advances in communication and increased standard of living

+

Large Workforce
- large families
- new immigrants

=

Industrial Economy

THE RAILROADS
LESSON 2

Effects of the Railroads

Spurred industrial growth and stimulated the economy with the demand for steel, coal, timber, and other materials

Increased markets for many products and lowered the cost to transport goods

Railroads encouraged westeward migration and helped close the American frontier

Railroad entreprenuers acquired great wealth; many were corrupt robber barons

BIG BUSINESS
LESSON 3

Laissez Faire

+ Advantages
- ease of forming a corporation, which made big business possible
- initial intense competition led to lower prices for consumers
- large corporations could consolidate and produce goods more efficiently

– Disadvantages
- small businesses could not compete with large corporations and were forced out of business
- lack of regulations meant the companies could collude to fix prices
- mergers, trusts, and holding companies created large, powerful companies that could control prices and manipulate politicians

UNIONS
LESSON 4

- July 1877
- Baltimore and Ohio Railroad announce wage cuts for a third time
- President Hayes violently ends protest

- Summer 1892
- striking employees are locked out and strikebreakers brought in; violence erupts
- Unrest lasts four months

Great Railroad Strike **Haymarket Riot** **Homestead Strike** **Pullman Strike**

- May 1886
- call for a nationwide strike to support an eight-hour workday
- cast unions as radical organizations

- 1894
- Pullman Car Company cuts workers' wages without lowering rents and prices in company town
- President Cleveland uses federal injunction to halt boycott

Directions: On a separate sheet of paper, answer the questions below. Make sure you read carefully and answer all parts to the question.

Lesson Review

Lesson 1

1 **Analyzing Cause and Effect** What role did entrepreneurs play in the industrialization of the United States and why were they willing to invest their money in American companies? SS.912.A.3.2, SS.912.A.3.4

2 **Explaining** How did the development of technological innovations using electric power contribute to the economic development of the United States in the Second Industrial Revolution? SS.912.A.3.3, SS.912.A.3.4

3 **Analyzing** How did innovation in communication improve the standard of living in the United States? SS.912.A.3.4

Lesson 2

4 **Analyzing** Why did railroad construction expand so rapidly after the Civil War? SS.912.A.3.2, SS.912.A.3.3

5 **Identifying Central Issues** What kinds of business practices caused some railroad owners to be accused of being "robber barons"? SS.912.A.3.2

6 **Describing** How did the completion of the Transcontinental Railroad contribute to the closing of the frontier? SS.912.A.3.4

Lesson 3

7 **Evaluating** How do big businesses benefit from economies of scale? SS.912.A.3.2

8 **Describing** What technological innovation did Andrew Carnegie bring to the steel industry and how did it affect economic development in the United States? SS.912.A.3.4

9 **Describing** In what ways did the laissez-faire economic policy change the structure of American business and how did these changes affect the government's relationship with business? SS.912.A.3.6, SS.912.A.3.10

Lesson 4

10 **Describing** What were some of the costs of the laissez-faire approach to economics for American workers? SS.912.A.3.2, SS.912.A.3.6

11 **Explaining** What actions did union leaders take to expand economic opportunities for women in the late 1800s? SS.912.A.3.9, SS.912.A.3.12

12 **Identifying** What contribution did Jane Addams make to help women workers? SS.912.A.3.12

Exploring the Essential Question

13 **Analyzing** Write an oral presentation explaining the factors that contributed to the United States becoming an industrialized society after the Civil War. Revise your presentation as needed to make sure the content is clear to your audience. LAFS.1112.SL.2.4, LAFS.1112.WHST.2.4, LAFS.1112.WHST.2.5, SS.912.A.3.2, SS.912.A.3.4

Critical Thinking

14 **Analyzing** Write a short essay explaining how industrialism changed the American economy. Be sure to include in your discussion the impact of the railroads, the rise of entrepreneurship and attempts to form labor unions, and the pros and cons of big business. Before you write your essay, plan out the points you want to cover. LAFS.1112.WHST.2.5, LAFS.1112.WHST.4.10, SS.912.A.3.2, SS.912.A.3.4

15 **Analyzing Issues** Define the term *laissez-faire* and describe the costs and benefits of the laissez-faire approach to economic policy in the late 1800s. As part of your answer, outline how the relationship between the federal government and private business changed during the late 1800s and explain whether government policy was shaped solely by laissez-faire ideas. LAFS.1112.RH.2.4, SS.912.A.3.2, SS.912.A.3.4, SS.912.A.3.6, SS.912.A.3.10

21st Century Skills

16 **Time, Chronology, and Sequencing** Using a time line, describe what led to the formation of the first women's unions. SS.912.A.1.3, SS.912.A.3.9

Need Extra Help?

If You've Missed Question	1	2	3	4	5	6	7	8	9	10	11	12	13	14	15	16
Go to Lesson	1	1	1	2	2	2	3	3	3	4	4	4	1	1	1	4

DBQ Analyzing Primary Sources

Read the following two excerpts and answer the questions that follow. The first is from a letter to Karl Marx, written by William Sylvis, president of the National Labor Union in 1869. The second is from a book written by Terence Powderly, leader of the Knights of Labor, published in 1889.

PRIMARY SOURCE

"[M]onied power is fast eating up the substance of the people. We have made war upon it, and we mean to win it. If we can we will win through the ballot box; if not, we will resort to sterner means. A little blood-letting is sometimes necessary in desperate cases. "

—*History of Labour in the United States,* 1921

PRIMARY SOURCE

"Co-operation for a common end was necessary. That common end was to forever stop the suicidal policy that debarred workingmen from entry to the workshop because of a difference of opinion which should have been submitted to a tribunal where the interests, not alone of the employer and his workmen would be considered, but a tribunal which would carefully investigate the cause of the strike and the effect of the stoppage of work by one branch of industry upon all others. "

—Terence Powderly, *Thirty Years of Labor, 1859-1889*

17 *Interpreting* What is the "suicidal policy" of employers that Powderly wants to end? What technique to resolving labor disputes is he advocating? LAFS.1112.RH.2.4, LAFS.1112.RH.3.8, LAFS.1112.RH.4.10, SS.912.A.3.9, SS.912.A.3.10

18 *Detecting Bias* What bias do you see in the quotes above? Which of the two men do you think was most biased against business owners? Explain your conclusion, citing details from the sources. LAFS.1112.RH.1.1, LAFS.1112.RH.2.6, LAFS.1112.RH.3.8, LAFS.1112.RH.4.10, LAFS.1112.RH.3.9, SS.912.A.3.9, SS.912.A.3.10

Analyzing Visuals

Use the map Natural Resource Sites of the United States *to answer the following questions.*

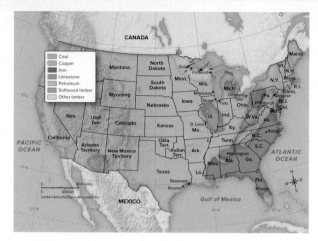

19 *Extrapolating* Given that most of the nation's first steel mills were set up near Pittsburgh, what resources do you think were most important to making steel? SS.912.A.1.4, SS.912.A.3.4, SS.912.G.2.1

20 *Analyzing Maps* Why do you think the iron mines in Minnesota and Wisconsin became major suppliers to the steel mills in Ohio and Pennsylvania? SS.912.A.1.4, SS.912.A.3.4

21 *Posing Questions About Maps* Based on the location of softwood timber, what questions would you ask about the construction of railroads in the United States? SS.912.A.1.4, SS.912.A.3.4

Extended Response Questions

22 *Presenting Information* Write an expository essay explaining three ways retailers—companies that sell products directly to consumers— responded to growing industrialization. Revise your essay as necessary, and then read your essay to the class. Make sure to consider your purpose and audience when revising. LAFS.1112.SL.2.4, LAFS.1112.WHST.1.2, LAFS.1112.WHST.2.4, LAFS.1112.WHST.2.5, SS.912.A.3.2

23 *Writing Presentations* Research the work of Thomas Edison, Alexander Graham Bell, or another inventor in the field of communications during the Industrial Revolution. Write a script for a short play about their impact on America. Before writing the play, make sure that you plan out the details you want to cover, and revise as necessary to communicate clearly. LAFS.1112.SL.2.4, LAFS.1112.WHST.1.2, LAFS.1112.WHST.2.4, LAFS.1112.WHST.2.5, LAFS.1112.WHST.3.8, LAFS.1112.WHST.4.10, SS.912.A.3.2, SS.912.A.3.5

Need Extra Help?

If You've Missed Question	**17**	**18**	**19**	**20**	**21**	**22**	**23**
Go to Lesson	4	4	1	1	1	4	1

◀ For many European immigrants, the Statue of Liberty was their first glimpse of America. The Statue of Liberty often represented the hopes and dreams of people looking for a better life.

FROM 1865 TO 1896

Urban America

THE STORY MATTERS ...

European and Asian immigrants arrived in the United States in great numbers during the late 1800s. Providing cheap labor, they made rapid industrial growth possible. They also helped populate the growing cities. As jobs in urban areas became more plentiful, many Americans moved from farms and small towns to cities. Read the chapter to learn how the events of the late nineteenth century shaped the United States as it is today.

ESSENTIAL QUESTIONS

- Why do people migrate?
- How is urban life different from rural life?

PhotoLink/Photodisc/Getty Images

Place & Time: United States 1865–1896

Drawn to cities by jobs available in America's growing industries, the urban population of the United States grew from around 10 million in 1870 to more than 30 million by the turn of the century. Immigrants from Europe, Africa, Asia, Canada, Mexico, and South America began looking for better work and a higher standard of living. Rural Americans also began moving to the cities. Industrialization led to urbanization, new political parties, new art and literature, and different ideas about government's role in society. Industrialization brought changes to society, including new social classes and increased segregation for African Americans. New philosophies and movements sprang up to respond to all of these changes.

Step Into the Place

Look at the information presented on the map.

DBQ **Analyzing Historical Documents** Why might the levels of immigration between "old" and "new" immigrants from Europe be roughly equal?

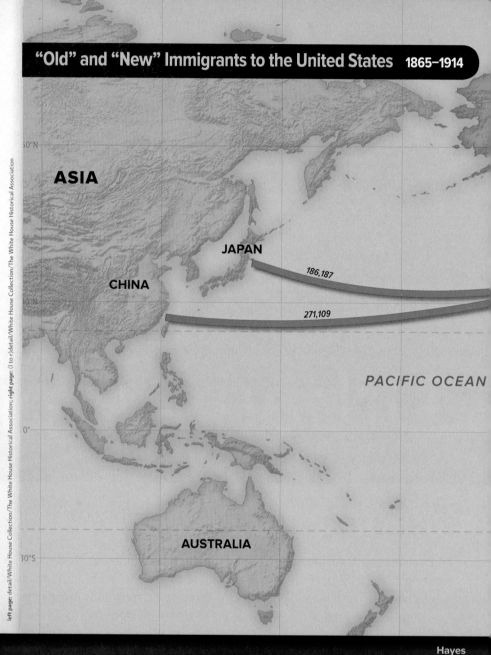

left page: detail/White House Collection/The White House Historical Association; right page: (l to r)detail/White House Collection/The White House Historical Association

"Old" and "New" Immigrants to the United States 1865–1914

ASIA

JAPAN

CHINA

186,187

271,109

PACIFIC OCEAN

AUSTRALIA

60°N

0°

30°S

Step Into the Time

MAKING CONNECTIONS Choose an event from the time line and write a paragraph about how that event might have affected the movement of people to the United States during the late 1800s.

U.S. PRESIDENTS

UNITED STATES

WORLD

1860s First Japanese immigrants arrive in California

1870 Fifteenth Amendment ratified

1874 Farmers' Alliance founded

Hayes 1877–1881

1870

1875

1871 Britain legalizes labor unions

1872 Ballot Act makes voting secret in Britain

1875 Work begins in France on Statue of Liberty

NEXT GENERATION SUNSHINE STATE STANDARDS
Students will understand the following benchmarks from the Florida NGSSS

LAFS.1112.RH.3.7: Integrate and evaluate multiple sources of information presented in diverse formats and media (e.g., visually, quantitatively, as well as in words) in order to address a question or solve a problem.

SS.912.A.1.2: Utilize a variety of primary and secondary sources to identify author, historical significance, audience, and authenticity to understand a historical period.

SS.912.A.1.3: Utilize timelines to identify the time sequence of historical data.

SS.912.A.1.4: Analyze how images, symbols, objects, cartoons, graphs, charts, maps, and artwork may be used to interpret the significance of time periods and events from the past.

SS.912.A.3.7: Compare the experience of European immigrants in the east to that of Asian immigrants in the west (the Chinese Exclusion Act, Gentlemen's Agreement with Japan).

SS.912.G.4.2: Use geographic terms and tools to analyze the push/pull factors contributing to human migration within and among places.

CANADA
Canadian immigrants 1,373,676

"Old" Immigrants Northern & Western Europe

EUROPE

11,637,533

Ellis Island

Angel Island

UNITED STATES

12,216,039

23,853,574 European immigrants

Asian immigrants 457,296

"New" Immigrants Southern & Eastern Europe

MEXICO

TROPIC OF CANCER

2,500 African immigrants

Latin American immigrants 426,002

ATLANTIC OCEAN

AFRICA

EQUATOR

SOUTH AMERICA

TROPIC OF CAPRICORN

0   2,000 miles
0   2,000 km

Miller projection

N W E S

Garfield 1881

Arthur 1881–1885

1882 Chinese Exclusion Act passed

Cleveland 1885–1889

1886 Statue of Liberty dedicated in New York Harbor

B. Harrison 1889–1893

1890 Sherman Antitrust Act passed

Cleveland 1893–1897

1896 Plessy v. Ferguson legalizes "separate but equal" doctrine

1880

1885

1890

1895

1881 Anti-Jewish pogroms erupt in Russia

1888 Brazil ends slavery

1894 Karl Marx's Das Kapital, Vol. 3 published, continuing his ideas on socialist theories

LESSON 1
Immigration

ESSENTIAL QUESTIONS

• Why do people migrate?
• How is urban life different from rural life?

READING HELPDESK

Academic Vocabulary

• ethnic

Content Vocabulary

• immigrant
• nativism

TAKING NOTES

Key Ideas and Details

Categorizing As you read, fill out a graphic organizer similar to the one below with the reasons people left their homelands to immigrate to the United States. LAFS.1112.RH.3.7, SS.912.G.4.2

Reasons for Immigrating to U.S.	
Push Factors	Pull Factors

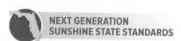
**NEXT GENERATION
SUNSHINE STATE STANDARDS**

LAFS.1112.RH.2.4: Determine the meaning of words and phrases as they are used in a text, including analyzing how an author uses and refines the meaning of a key term over the course of a text (e.g., how Madison defines faction in Federalist No. 10).

LAFS.1112.WHST.1.2: Write informative/ explanatory texts, including the narration of historical events, scientific procedures/ experiments, or technical processes.

Continued page on 146

IT MATTERS BECAUSE

In the late nineteenth century, a major wave of immigration began. Most immigrants settled in cities, where distinctive ethnic neighborhoods emerged. Some Americans, however, feared that the new immigrants would not adapt to American culture or might be harmful to American society.

Immigrants Flood Into America

GUIDING QUESTION *How did immigrants of the late 1800s change American society?*

Between 1865, the year the Civil War ended, and 1914, the year World War I began, nearly 25 million people immigrated to the United States. Most, nearly 24 million, came from Europe, but more than 1.3 million Canadians moved south of the border, over 425,000 Latin Americans came north, and more than 450,000 Asians arrived as well during those years.

European Immigration

Europeans immigrated to the United States for many reasons. Many came because they were poor and American industries had plenty of jobs available, or because they had special skills. Europe's industrial cities, however, also offered plenty of jobs, so economic factors do not entirely explain why people migrated. Many **immigrants** came to the United States not just to find work, but to escape the restrictions of social class in Europe that kept them trapped at the bottom of society. In some cases, as in Italy, high rents and a cholera epidemic encouraged people to leave. In Poland and Russia, land shortages, unemployment, high taxes, and a long military draft caused emigration. Others, especially Jews living in Russia and the Austro-Hungarian Empire, fled to escape religious persecution.

Ellis Island

Most immigrants passed through Ellis Island, a tiny island in New York Harbor. There, a huge, three-story building served as the processing center for many of the immigrants arriving from Europe after 1892. In Ellis Island's enormous hall, crowds of immigrants filed past doctors for an inspection. Those who failed inspection might be separated from their families and returned to Europe. A medical examiner who worked there later described how "hour after hour, ship load after ship load . . . the stream of human beings with its kaleidoscopic variations was . . . hurried through Ellis Island by the equivalent of 'step lively' in every language of the earth." About 12 million immigrants passed through Ellis Island between 1892 and 1954.

Changing Demographics and Culture

By the late 1890s, more than half of all immigrants entering the United States were from eastern and southern Europe, including Italy, Greece, Austria-Hungary, Russia, and Serbia. This period of immigration is known as "new" immigration. The "old" immigration, which occurred before 1890, had been primarily of people from northern and western Europe.

This wave of immigrants changed the culture of America's cities and the demographics of its workforce. Although every immigrant group had some of its members working in every type of job and profession available, certain patterns emerged. Skilled Italian bricklayers and stonemasons contributed to the construction of many homes, churches and buildings in American cities. Polish immigrants often became coal miners, meatpackers and steel workers. Jewish immigrants often worked in the garment industry or as common laborers, although many became merchants as well. Irish immigrants, often among the poorest to arrive in America, frequently ended up as railroad workers, miners, dockworkers, ditch-diggers, and factory workers. And members of all **ethnic** groups also headed west to settle the Great Plains as farmers and ranchers.

By the 1890s, immigrants made up a large percentage of the population of major cities, including New York, Chicago, Milwaukee, and Detroit. Immigrants lived in neighborhoods that were often separated into ethnic groups, such as "Little Italy" or the Jewish "Lower East Side" in New York City. There they spoke their native languages and re-created the churches,

Immigrants migrated to the United States from all across Europe seeking an opportunity to better their lives.

▶ CRITICAL THINKING
Drawing Conclusions Why do you think most immigrants came to the cities? LAFS.1112.RH.3.7, SS.912.A.1.4, SS.912.A.3.7

immigrant one who enters and becomes established in a country other than that of his or her original nationality

ethnic relating to large groups of people classed according to common racial, national, tribal, religious, linguistic, or cultural origin or background

---

WHY DID PEOPLE EMIGRATE?

Immigrants (thousands) (y-axis: 0, 200, 400, 600, 800, 1,000)

Legend:
- From northern and western Europe
- From southern and eastern Europe
- From the Americas
- From Asia

Year (x-axis: 1865 1870, 1880, 1890, 1900, 1910 1914)

Source: *Historical Statistics of the United States.*

Push Factors
- Farm poverty and worker uncertainty
- Wars and compulsory military service
- Political tyranny
- Religious oppression
- Population pressure

Pull Factors
- Plenty of land and plenty of work
- Higher standard of living
- Democratic political system
- Opportunity for social advancement

CHARTS/GRAPHS

Push factors and pull factors impacted U. S. immigration.

1 Look at the geographic distribution on the graph. Which two regions had the lowest immigration rates to the United States between 1865 and 1914? LAFS.1112.RH.3.7, SS.912.A.1.4, SS.912.G.4.2

2 Compare European immigration before and after the mid-1890s. What geographic pattern do you see on the graph? LAFS.1112.RH.3.7, SS.912.A.1.4, SS.912.G.4.2

©Michael Maslan Historic Photographs/Historical/Corbis

Many Chinese came to America to escape poverty and civil war. Some helped build railroads. Others set up small businesses. These children were photographed in San Francisco's Chinatown around 1900.

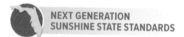

NEXT GENERATION SUNSHINE STATE STANDARDS

Continued from page 144

LAFS.1112.WHST.2.4: Produce clear and coherent writing in which the development, organization, and style are appropriate to task, purpose, and audience.

LAFS.1112.WHST.3.9: Draw evidence from informational texts to support analysis, reflection, and research.

LAFS.1112.WHST.4.10: Write routinely over extended time frames (time for reflection and revision) and shorter time frames (a single sitting or a day or two) for a range of discipline-specific tasks, purposes, and audiences.

MAFS.912.S-IC.2: Make inferences and justify conclusions from sample surveys, experiments, and observational studies.

MAFS.912.S-ID.1: Summarize, represent and interpret data on a single count or measurement variable.

SS.912.A.1.4: Analyze how images, symbols, objects, cartoons, graphs, charts, maps, and artwork may be used to interpret the significance of time periods and events from the past.

SS.912.A.3.2: Examine the social, political, and economic causes, course, and consequences of the second Industrial Revolution that began in the late 19th century.

SS.912.A.3.6: Analyze changes that occurred as the United States shifted from agrarian to an industrial society.

SS.912.A.3.7: Compare the experience of European immigrants in the east to that of Asian immigrants in the west (the Chinese Exclusion Act, Gentlemen's Agreement with Japan).

SS.912.G.4.2: Use geographic terms and tools to analyze the push/pull factors contributing to human migration within and among places.

SS.912.H.3.1: Analyze the effects of transportation, trade, communication, science, and technology on the preservation and diffusion of culture.

synagogues, clubs, and newspapers of their homelands. Because immigrants tended to settle near others from their homeland, regional demographic patterns also emerged. For example: although there were large numbers of every ethnic group in New York City, Italians, Russians, and Jews were more likely to remain there, while large numbers of Germans, Swedes, and Poles moved to Midwestern cities such as Milwaukee, Pittsburgh and Chicago. Many Germans also moved to Texas to become farmers. Large numbers of Irish settled in the northeast and upper Midwest, and they were the largest ethnic group in Boston.

The wave of immigration in the late 1800s also brought about a cultural shift in American religion. In 1850, Catholics were only five percent of the population. By the early 1900s, they made up 17 percent of the total, and had become the single largest religious denomination in the country. While there had been Catholics in America from the earliest days when Lord Baltimore founded Maryland colony as a refuge for English Catholics, American culture had been overwhelmingly Protestant in its outlook and religious perspective. That began to change in the late 1800s as the United States became more culturally diverse.

Catholics were not the only contributors to a new religious diversity in American culture. The large number of Greeks and Russians arriving in the nation meant that the number of Orthodox Christians began to increase as well. And as persecution mounted in Russia, Poland, and Romania in the 1880s, a mass migration of East European Jews began. Most settled in New York City and elsewhere on the east coast, but Jewish communities appeared all across the United States. By the early 1920s, nearly 2 million Jews had settled in America.

Asian Immigration

The first large wave of Asian immigration to the United States began in the years following the Civil War. In the mid-1800s, China was suffering from severe unemployment, poverty, famine, and a civil war, known as the Taiping Rebellion. These problems convinced tens of thousands of Chinese to head to the United States, as did news of the California Gold Rush. Almost all were young men in their teens or twenties seeking work, or hoping to strike it rich in the gold fields. Japanese immigrants also came to the United States. Until 1910, however, their numbers remained small. Between 1900 and 1908, large numbers of Japanese migrated to the United States as Japan began building both an industrial economy and an empire. These developments disrupted Japan's economy and caused hardships for its people, thus stimulating emigration.

Chinese immigrants settled mainly in west coast cities, especially San Francisco. Although many headed to the gold fields, most failed to make much money and took jobs as laborers and servants. Some became merchants or skilled at a trade. Many helped build the Central Pacific Railroad. Initially, Asian immigrants arriving in San Francisco were inspected at a two-story shed on the wharf. In 1910, California opened a barracks on Angel Island for Asian immigrants. Most of the immigrants were young males in their teens or twenties, who nervously awaited the results of their immigration hearings in dormitories packed with double or triple tiers of bunks. This unpleasant delay could last for months. On the walls of the detention barracks, the immigrants wrote anonymous poems in pencil or ink. Some even carved their verses into the wood.

☑ READING PROGRESS CHECK

Making Generalizations How did the experiences of immigrating to the United States compare for Chinese and Europeans?

Library of congress, Prints & photographs division [LC-USZC4-5265]

IMMIGRATION SETTLEMENT PATTERNS, LATE NINETEENTH CENTURY

Legend:
- China
- Germany
- Ireland
- Italy
- Japan
- Mexico
- Poland
- Russia
- Scandinavia

Settlement figures in thousands

California: 72 44 40 10 8
Wisconsin: 242 61 30 23
Texas: 72 48
Illinois: 332 129 114 64 28 23
Ohio: 204 55
Pennsylvania: 212 205 72 66 50
Massachusetts: 249 32 28 26
New York: 480 425 182 165 66 42 7

Nativism Resurges

GUIDING QUESTION *Why did nativists oppose immigration?*

Eventually, the wave of immigration led to increased feelings of **nativism** for many Americans. Nativism is an extreme dislike of immigrants by native-born people. It had surfaced during the heavy wave of Irish immigration in the 1840s and 1850s. By the late 1800s, it was focused mainly on Asians, Jews, and eastern Europeans.

Nativists opposed immigration for many reasons. Some feared that the influx of Catholics from countries such as Ireland, Italy, and Poland would swamp the mostly Protestant United States. Many labor unions argued that immigrants undermined American workers because they would work for low wages and accept jobs as strikebreakers.

Nativists Organize

Increased feelings of nativism led to the founding of two major anti-immigrant organizations. The American Protective Association, founded by Henry Bowers in Iowa, in 1887, was an anti-Catholic organization. Its members vowed not to hire or vote for Catholics and the organization lobbied for restrictions of Catholic immigration to the United States. The APA built a large following in the Midwest and Northeast of the United States. On the West Coast, where sentiment against the Chinese was very strong, widespread racial violence erupted. Denis Kearney, an Irish immigrant, formed the Workingman's Party of California to fight Chinese immigration. The party won seats in the California legislature and made opposition to Chinese immigration a national issue.

Congress Passes New Immigration Laws

Opposition to immigration led Congress to pass several laws designed to limit the massive number of immigrants arriving in the United States. Most of these were vetoed by the presidents of the era. In 1882, however, President Chester Arthur signed two bills—the Chinese Exclusion Act of 1882, and the Immigration Act of 1882. The Chinese Exclusion Act barred

CHARTS/GRAPHS

This graph shows where different immigrant groups settled in the United States.

1 Which two states had the highest number of Irish immigrants? LAFS.1112.RH.3.7, MAFS.912.S-ID.1, SS.912.A.1.4

2 *Analyzing Information* How would you contrast the immigration settlement patterns in Texas and Ohio? LAFS.1112.RH.3.7, LAFS.1112.WHST.3.9, MAFS.912.S-IC.2, SS.912.A.1.4

nativism hostility toward immigrants by native-born people

Chinese immigration for 10 years, and prevented Chinese already in the United States from becoming citizens. The Chinese in the United States organized a letter-writing campaign, petitioned Arthur, and filed suit in federal court, all to no avail. The ban on Chinese immigration was renewed in 1892, and then made permanent in 1902. It was not repealed until 1943.

The Immigration Act of 1882 imposed a head tax of 50 cents on each immigrant who arrived by ship at a United States port. The law also gave immigration officials the authority to reject immigrants who had a criminal record, were mentally disabled, or who were unable to take care of themselves "without becoming a public charge."

For most of American history, the borders had been open, and virtually anyone who could get to the United States could settle there. State and local governments controlled the ports and border crossings. The Immigration Act of 1882 began federal oversight of immigration and gave responsibility to the Treasury Department to issue regulations, hire immigration agents, and build inspection stations. One of the purposes of the head tax was to pay for the cost of the agents and offices needed to inspect immigrants. The law triggered a debate in American politics over the correct policies and regulations to adopt toward immigrants. The debate has continued to the present day.

Immigrant Optimism

Despite the difficulties of the journey, the challenges of finding work, and the anger of nativists, many immigrants to the United States remained optimistic—in part because of what they were fleeing from, and in part because of what they discovered upon arriving. Although many Americans were poor and faced very difficult lives, there was no widespread famine, war, or rebellion, unlike parts of China and Europe. There was no rigid class system. Immigrants understood that even though they were poor, they could attempt to improve their position in life and were not permanently trapped because of the class into which they were born. In addition, wages were high compared to much of the world; jobs were plentiful, even if difficult and sometimes demeaning, and there remained a lot of cheap land on the Great Plains for those wishing to strike out on their own. In short, there was an opportunity to be free that many immigrants had never experienced before, and it created both optimism and a sense of possibility.

✓ READING PROGRESS CHECK

Explaining How did nativism affect Chinese immigrants on the West Coast?

LESSON 1 REVIEW

Reviewing Vocabulary

1. *Explaining* What is nativism, and why did some Americans dislike immigrants? LAFS.1112.RH.2.4

Using Your Notes

2. *Categorizing* Use your notes on the reasons for immigrating to explain the push and pull factors for one of the immigrant groups discussed in the lesson. SS.912.G.4.2

Answering the Guiding Questions

3. *Interpreting* How did European immigrants of the late 1800s change American society? SS.912.A.3.7

4. *Comparing and Contrasting* How were the experiences of Asian immigrants different from those of European immigrants? SS.912.A.3.7

5. *Analyzing* How did the arrival of East European immigrants change American culture? LAFS.1112.WHST.3.9, SS.912.H.3.1

Writing Activity

6. NARRATIVE Suppose that you are an immigrant who has arrived in the United States in the 1800s. Choose a country to be from and write a letter to a relative in your home country describing why you decided to move to America, and what you found when you arrived. LAFS.1112.WHST.1.2, LAFS.1112.WHST.2.4, LAFS.1112.WHST.4.10

SKILLBUILDER

LAFS.1112.RH.1.1, LAFS.1112.RH.1.2, LAFS.1112.RH.2.4, LAFS.1112.RH.2.6, LAFS.1112.RH.3.8, LAFS.1112.RH.4.10, LAFS.1112.SL.1.2, LAFS.1112.SL.1.3, SS.912.A.1.1, SS.912.A.1.2, SS.912.A.1.4, SS.912.A.5.8, SS.912.H.1.5

Identifying Bias and Points of View

Why Learn This Skill?

Everyday social media, talk shows, blog posts, text messages, and email flood us with opinions and commentary. In order to understand and assess what we see, hear, and read, and then make good decisions and choices, we need to be able to detect bias and a source's point of view, so as to evaluate the information we are receiving. Understanding bias and point of view are especially useful when using primary sources to understand a historical era and interpret events.

Learning the Skill

Everyone has bias—or tendency to look at information based on their own experiences, knowledge, prejudices, and emotional reactions. People's biases and points of view are based on many factors including age, gender, race, ethnic background, economic class, religion, education, location, occupation, relationships, and personal experiences. All of these things need to be taken into account when looking for bias in a point of view.

To determine a point of view and detect bias in written, oral, or visual materials, follow these steps:

1. **What argument is being made?** What are you being asked to think, do, feel, or believe? This is the point of view.
2. **Gather information about the author.** Is there anything that would cause the author to have a particular bias?
3. **Assess motivation.** Will the author benefit from people adopting their point of view? Who will benefit?
4. **Determine the context.** What was going on when the argument was made?

5. **Examine the language or visual imagery being used.** Is it emotional? Do the words or pictures have positive or negative overtones? Are facts included that can be verified? Does the author use a lot of metaphors or analogies? Are there terms that the author uses that may have a different connotation because of when they wrote them or where they were from?
6. **Apply prior knowledge about the subject.** Does the point of view match other sources? If necessary, research other sources on the subject and compare them to the author's viewpoint. How might the author's bias affect how they interpret events, and how might others, with different biases, interpret the same events differently?

Practicing this Skill

Detecting Bias in Visuals Examine the cartoon by Thomas Nast published in 1871. It was drawn soon after New York City decided to fund Catholic schools.

1. How would you describe the image's emotional content?
2. Thomas Nast was an immigrant who had converted to Protestantism from Catholicism. At the time, he also supported the Republican Party. What might that suggest about his point of view?
3. Based on your knowledge of the late 1800s, what bias and point of view is being depicted in this cartoon?

THE AMERICAN RIVER GANGES.

The Granger Collection, New York

Applying the Skill

Detecting Bias in Oral Material Go to the last page of the lesson "The Rise of Segregation." Read the quote from a speech by Booker T. Washington. What point of view does the speech reveal? What bias do you detect? Research Booker T. Washington and write a paragraph explaining his point of view.

LAFS.1112.RH.1.1, LAFS.1112.RH.1.2, LAFS.1112.RH.1.3, LAFS.1112.RH.2.5, LAFS.1112.RH.3.7, LAFS.1112.RH.3.9, LAFS.1112.RH.4.10, SS.912.A.1.4, SS.912.A.1.6, SS.912.A.3.7

The Immigrant Experience

Ellis Island operated as a federal immigration station from 1892 to 1954. More than 20 million people passed through on their way to a new life in the United States. After a long journey across the Atlantic, immigrants would be subject to long lines for medical and legal inspections, which would determine if they were permitted entry into the United States. For more than 80 percent of immigrants, the process took only a matter of hours. For the less fortunate, it took days or weeks. These excerpts provide first-hand accounts of two different immigrant experiences—one of a Chinese boy entering the United States from San Francisco, and the other of a Slovenian immigrant's experience at Ellis Island.

VOCABULARY

imitate
to follow as an example

consisted
to be made up or composed of something

custom
the usual practice of a person or group

dumbfounded
to become speechless with astonishment

MEMOIR, *Arriving on Ellis Island, 1906*

"A group of Slovenian immigrants, of which this writer was one, arrived in New York from . . . Austria. . . . It was a beautiful morning in May 1906. After leaving the French ship LA TOURAINE, we were transported to Ellis Island for landing and inspection. There we were 'sorted out' as to the country we came from and placed in a 'stall' with the letter 'A' above us. ('A' was for Austria).

There were at least a hundred Slovenian immigrants. We separated ourselves, as was the **custom** at home—men on the right and women and children on the left. All of us were waiting to leave for all parts of the United States.

The day was warm and we were very thirsty. An English speaking immigrant asked the near-by guard where we could get a drink of water. The guard withdrew and returned shortly with a pail of water, which he set before the group of women. Some men stepped forward quickly to have a drink, but the guard pushed them back saying: 'Ladies first!' When the women learned what the guard had said, they were **dumbfounded**, for in Slovenia . . . women always were second to men. . . . Happy at the sudden turn of events, one elderly lady stepped forward, holding a dipper of water, and proposed this toast:

'Živijo Amerika, kjer so ženske prve!'

(Long live America, where women are first!)"

—Marie Priesland, recalling her arrival in the United States

PHOTOGRAPH, *Ellis Island Health Inspection, 1905*

Immigrants entering the United States were inspected for health problems before being allowed entry into the country.

PHOTO: Library of Congress, Prints & Photographs Division [LC-USZ62-7386]; TEXT: Copyright © 1968 Marie Priesland.

US IMMIGRATION SERVICE

1	Calling or Occupation?	**Farmer**
2	Able to Read?	**Yes**
3	Able to Write?	**Yes**
4	Nationality?	**Germany**
5	Whether having a ticket to final destination?	**Yes**
6	By whom was passage paid?	**Father**
7	Whether in possession of $50, and if less, how much?	**$20**
8	Whether going to join a relative or friend?	**Friend**
9	Ever in prison or almshouse or institution for care or treatment of the insane or supported by charity	**No**

MAGAZINE ARTICLE, *Starting Out in America*, 1903

"My father gave me $100, and I went to Hong Kong with five other boys from our place and we got steerage passage on a steamer, paying $50 each. Everything was new to me. All my life I had been used to sleeping on a bord bed with a wooden pillow, and I found the steamer's bunk very uncomfortable, because it was so soft. The food was different from that which I had been used to, and I did not like it at all. I was afraid of the stews, for the thought of what they might be made of by the wicked wizards of the ship made me ill. Of the great power of these people I saw many signs. The engines that moved the ship were wonderful monsters, strong enough to lift mountains. When I got to San Francisco . . . I was half starved because I was afraid to eat the provisions of the barbarians, but a few days' living in the Chinese quarter made me happy again. A man got me work as a house servant in an American family, and my start was the same as that of almost all the Chinese in this country.

The Chinese laundryman does not learn his trade in China; there are no laundries in China. The women there do the washing in tubs and have no washboards or flat irons. All the Chinese laundrymen here were taught in the first place by American women just as I was taught.

When I went to work for that American family I could not speak a word of English, and I did not know anything about housework. The family **consisted** of husband, wife and two children. They were very good to me and paid me $3.50 a week, of which I could save $3.

I did not understand what the lady said to me, but she showed me how to cook, wash, iron, sweep, dust, make beds, wash dishes, clean windows, paint and brass, polish the knives and forks, etc., by doing the things herself and then overseeing my efforts to **imitate** her. She would take my hands and show them how to do things. She and her husband and children laughed at me a great deal, but it was all good natured. . . . In six months I had learned how to do the work of our house quite well, and . . . I had also learned English. . . . I worked for two years as a servant . . . and I was now ready to start in business."

—Chinese immigrant Lee Chew, reflecting on his first years in America

DBQ Analyzing Historical Documents

1. **Evaluating** According to Lee Chew, what were some of the factors that helped him adapt as an immigrant and become a small business owner?

2. **Summarizing** Based on the questions from this 1907 immigration questionnaire, what would you determine to be the main concerns of immigration officials regarding potential immigrants?

3. **Integrating Visual Information** Based on the questionnaire questions and this photograph from Ellis Island in the 1920s, how would you describe the overall process of immigration? What potential problems would you expect that are not documented in either source?

4. **Making Inferences** What question is omitted from the questionnaire that you think would have been very important to immigration officials?

5. **Explaining** Why were immigrants taken to Ellis Island for "processing"?

6. **Differentiating** In Marie Priesland's memoir, why did the American guards yell "Ladies first!" and push the men away from the water pail? Why were the women dumbfounded by the guard's actions?

The Biography of a Chinaman: Lee Chew, Published February 19, 1903. Copyright ©1903 by The Independent.

LESSON 2
Urbanization

ESSENTIAL QUESTIONS

• Why do people migrate?
• How is urban life different from rural life?

READING HELPDESK

Academic Vocabulary

• incentive • trigger

Content Vocabulary

• skyscraper
• tenement
• political machine
• party boss
• graft

TAKING NOTES

Key Ideas and Details

Organizing As you read, use the following graphic organizer to identify the problems the nation's cities faced. LAFS.1112.RH.3.7, SS.912.A.3.6, SS.912.A.3.8

Urban Problems

NEXT GENERATION SUNSHINE STATE STANDARDS

LAFS.1112.RH.2.4: Determine the meaning of words and phrases as they are used in a text, including analyzing how an author uses and refines the meaning of a key term over the course of a text (e.g., how Madison defines faction in Federalist No. 10).

LAFS.1112.RH.3.7: Integrate and evaluate multiple sources of information presented in diverse formats and media (e.g., visually, quantitatively, as well as in words) in order to address a question or solve a problem.

LAFS.1112.WHST.1.1: Write arguments focused on discipline-specific content.

Continued on page 154

IT MATTERS BECAUSE

Native-born Americans and immigrants were drawn to cities by the jobs available in America's growing industries. The new, modern cities developed skyscrapers, public transportation systems, and neighborhoods divided by social class. In many cities, political machines controlled city government.

Americans Migrate to the Cities

GUIDING QUESTION *How do you think life in big cities was different from life on farms and in small towns?*

Most of the immigrants who arrived in the United States in the late 1800s lacked both the money to buy farms and the education to obtain higher-paying jobs. Thus, they settled in the nation's growing cities and took jobs in the rapidly expanding factories of the United States. At the same time, rural Americans also began moving to the cities. Farmers moved to cities because urban areas offered better-paying jobs than did rural areas. Many young men and women growing up on farms in the east, where cheap land was no longer available, preferred to build a life in the cities instead of becoming settlers on the distant Plains. Cities had much to offer, too—electric lights, running water, modern plumbing, plus attractions such as museums, libraries, and theaters.

As a result, after the Civil War, the United States steadily changed from a rural nation to an urban one. New York City, which had more than 800,000 inhabitants in 1860, grew to almost 3.5 million by 1900. During the same period, Chicago swelled from some 109,000 residents to more than 1.6 million. The United States had only 131 cities with populations of 2,500 or more residents in 1840; by 1900, there were more than 1,700 such urban areas. By 1920, more Americans lived in urban areas than rural areas.

As city populations grew, the rising value of land provided an **incentive** to try new strategies of urban development. Some businessmen built upward rather than outward. Tall, steel frame buildings called **skyscrapers** began to appear. To move people around cities quickly, various kinds of mass transit developed. At first, almost all cities relied on the horsecar, a railroad car pulled by horses. In 1890, horsecars moved about 70 percent of urban traffic in the United States. More than 20 cities, beginning with San Francisco in 1873, installed cable cars, which were pulled along tracks by underground cables. Then, in 1887, engineer Frank J. Sprague developed the electric trolley car. The country's first electric trolley line opened the following year in Richmond, Virginia.

In the largest cities, congestion became a severe problem. Chicago responded by building an elevated railroad, while Boston, followed by New York, built the first subway systems.

✔ READING PROGRESS CHECK

Summarizing What attracted people to cities in the 1800s?

Separation by Class

GUIDING QUESTION *How did the living conditions of the urban working class differ from those of other social classes?*

In the growing cities, the upper, middle, and working classes lived in separate and distinct parts of town. The boundaries between neighborhoods can still be seen in many American cities today.

During the last half of the 1800s, the wealthiest families established fashionable districts in the heart of a city. As their homes grew larger, wealthy women increasingly relied on more servants, such as cooks, maids, butlers, nannies, and chauffeurs, and spent a great deal of money on social activities. In an age in which many New Yorkers lived on $500 a year, socialite Cornelia Sherman Martin spent $360,000 on a dance.

American industrialization expanded the middle class, which included doctors, lawyers, engineers, managers, social workers, architects, and teachers. Many middle-class people moved away from the central city to escape the crime and pollution and to be able to afford larger homes. Some used new commuter rail lines to move to "streetcar suburbs."

In the late 1800s, wealthier families had at least one live-in servant. This gave the woman of the house more time to pursue activities outside the home, including "women's clubs." At first these clubs focused on social and educational activities, but over time "club women" became active in charitable and reform activities. In Chicago, for example, the Women's Club helped establish juvenile courts and exposed the terrible conditions at the Cook County Insane Asylum.

Few families in the urban working class could hope to own a home. Most spent their lives in crowded **tenements,** or multifamily apartment buildings. The first tenement in the United States was built in 1839.

Before the mid-1800s, few buildings exceeded four or five stories. To make wooden and stone buildings taller required thick lower walls. This changed when steel companies began mass-producing cheap steel girders and steel cable.

▶ CRITICAL THINKING
Predicting Consequences What long-term effects do you think new building technologies had on cities? LAFS.1112.RH.3.7, SS.912.A.3.6, SS.912.A.3.8

incentive something that motivates a person into action

skyscraper a very tall building

tenement multifamily apartments, usually dark, crowded, and barely meeting minimum living standards

In the late 1800s, large numbers of people from farms and small towns, as well as immigrants, settled in cities.

▶ CRITICAL THINKING
Identifying Central Ideas Why were so many people drawn to cities during this era? LAFS.1112.RH.3.7, SS.912.A.3.8

(t)©Museum of the City of New York/Corbis Museum/Corbis; (b)©Robert L. Bracklow/Photo Collection Alexander Alland, Sr./Corbis

Most working-class families lived in apartments, often only a single room in size. They had no servants, and typically husbands and wives both had to work.

▶ CRITICAL THINKING
Drawing Conclusions How effective was urban society at meeting the needs of the working class? LAFS.1112.RH.3.7, SS.912.A.3.8

NEXT GENERATION
SUNSHINE STATE STANDARDS

Continued from page 152

LAFS.1112.WHST.2.4: Produce clear and coherent writing in which the development, organization, and style are appropriate to task, purpose, and audience.

LAFS.1112.WHST.3.9: Draw evidence from informational texts to support analysis, reflection, and research.

LAFS.1112.WHST.4.10: Write routinely over extended time frames (time for reflection and revision) and shorter time frames (a single sitting or a day or two) for a range of discipline-specific tasks, purposes, and audiences.

SS.912.A.1.4: Analyze how images, symbols, objects, cartoons, graphs, charts, maps, and artwork may be used to interpret the significance of time periods and events from the past.

SS.912.A.3.2: Examine the social, political, and economic causes, course, and consequences of the second Industrial Revolution that began in the late 19th century.

SS.912.A.3.6: Analyze changes that occurred as the United States shifted from agrarian to an industrial society.

Continued page on 155

trigger to cause an action that causes a greater reaction

political machine an organization linked to a political party that often controlled local government

party boss the person in control of a political machine

In New York City, three out of four residents squeezed into dark and crowded tenements. To supplement the average industrial worker's annual income of $445, many families rented precious space to a boarder. Zalmen Yoffeh, a Jewish immigrant journalist, lived in a New York tenement as a child. He recalled his family's everyday struggle:

PRIMARY SOURCE

❝ With . . . one dollar a day [our mother] fed and clothed an ever-growing family. She took in boarders. Sometimes this helped; at other times it added to the burden of living. Boarders were often out of work and penniless; how could one turn a hungry man out? She made all our clothes. She walked blocks to reach a place where meat was a penny cheaper, where bread was a half cent less. She collected boxes and old wood to burn in the stove. ❞
—from "The Passing of the East Side," *Menorah Journal*, 1929

Within the working class, some people were better off than others. For example, white native-born men earned higher wages than African American men, immigrants, and women. One economist estimated that 64 percent of working-class families began to rely on more than one wage earner. In some cases, the whole family worked, including the children. The dangerous working conditions faced by child workers, and the fact that they were not in school, alarmed many reformers.

A growing number of women took jobs outside the home. White native-born women were better educated than other women. Thus, many found jobs as teachers, clerks, or secretaries. Many women, however, were domestic servants, with immigrant women filling these jobs in the North and African American women doing such work in the South. Domestic servants endured long hours, low wages, and social isolation.

✓ READING PROGRESS CHECK

Explaining What was working life like for working-class families?

Urban Problems

GUIDING QUESTION *What types of problems developed due to the rapid growth of urban areas?*

City living posed the risks of crime, violence, fire, disease, and pollution. The rapid growth of cities made these problems worse and complicated the ability of urban governments to respond to these problems.

Crime was a growing problem in American cities. Minor criminals, such as pickpockets, swindlers, and thieves, thrived in crowded urban living conditions. Major crimes multiplied as well. From 1880 to 1900, the murder rate jumped sharply from 25 per million people to more than 100 per million people.

Disease and pollution posed even bigger threats. Improper sewage disposal contaminated city drinking water and **triggered** epidemics of typhoid fever and cholera. Though sewer systems existed in the 1870s, pollution remained a severe problem. Horse manure was left in the streets, chimney's belched smoke, and soot and built up from coal or wood fires.

The **political machine,** an informal political group designed to gain and keep power, came about partly because cities had grown much faster than their governments. New city dwellers needed jobs, housing, food, heat, and police protection. In exchange for votes, political machines and the **party bosses** who ran them eagerly provided these necessities. George Plunkitt, one of New York's most powerful bosses, explained the benefit of political machines: "I can always get a job for a deservin' man. . . . I know

©Lewis Wickes Hine/Historical/Corbis

The Granger Collection, New York

Critics of political machines said that they took bribes and gave contracts to friends, robbing cities of resources. In this image, workers in New York find the city treasury empty, while behind the scenes, Boss Tweed and other city politicians enjoy a sumptuous feast.

1 *Making Inferences* What point is the artist trying to make? LAFS.1112.RH.3.7, SS.912.A.1.4, SS.912.A.3.11, SS.912.H.1.5

2 *Making Consequences* What problems could develop in cities as a result of the fraud of political machines? LAFS.1112.RH.3.7, SS.912.A.1.4, SS.912.A.3.11

every big employer in the district and in the whole city, for that matter, and they ain't in the habit of sayin' no to me when I ask them for a job."

The party bosses also controlled the city's finances. Many machine politicians grew rich as the result of fraud or **graft,** gaining money or power illegally. Outright fraud occurred when party bosses accepted bribes from contractors who were supposed to compete fairly to win contracts to build streets, sewers, and buildings. Corrupt bosses also sold permits to their friends to operate public utilities, such as railroads, waterworks, and power systems. Tammany Hall, the New York City Democratic political machine, was the most infamous example. William "Boss" Tweed was its leader during the 1860s and 1870s. Tweed's corruptness led to a prison sentence in 1874.

City machines often controlled all the city services, including the police department. In St. Louis, the "boss" never feared arrest when he called out to his supporters at the police-supervised voting booth, "Are there any more repeaters out here that want to vote again?"

Opponents of political machines, such as cartoonist Thomas Nast, blasted corrupt bosses. Defenders argued that political machines provided necessary services and helped assimilate new city dwellers.

graft the acquisition of money in dishonest ways, as in bribing a politician

NEXT GENERATION SUNSHINE STATE STANDARDS

Continued from page 154

SS.912.A.3.8: Examine the importance of social change and reform in the late 19th and early 20th centuries (class system, migration from farms to cities, Social Gospel movement, role of settlement houses and churches in providing services to the poor).

SS.912.A.3.11: Analyze the impact of political machines in United States cities in the late 19th and early 20th centuries.

SS.912.A.3.12: Compare how different nongovernmental organizations and progressives worked to shape public policy, restore economic opportunities, and correct injustices in American life.

SS.912.H.1.5: Examine artistic response to social issues and new ideas in various cultures.

☑ **READING PROGRESS CHECK**

Identifying Why were political machines so influential in cities?

LESSON 2 REVIEW

Reviewing Vocabulary
1. *Explaining* Explain why tenements were a difficult place to live for the urban working class. LAFS.1112.RH.2.4, SS.912.A.3.2

Using Your Notes
2. *Summarizing* Use your notes on urban problems to explain why life in cities could be so difficult.

Answering the Guiding Questions
3. *Interpreting* How do you think life in big cities was different from life on farms and in small towns? SS.912.A.3.6, SS.912.A.3.8

4. *Analyzing* Why did "political machines" develop in cities? LAFS.1112.WHST.3.9, SS.912.A.3.11

5. *Making Connections* What types of problems developed due to the rapid growth of urban areas? SS.912.A.3.8

Writing Activity
6. ARGUMENT Take on the role of an urban planner in a major city in the late 1800s. Write a letter to members of the city government listing specific reasons for the importance of setting aside city land for parks and recreational areas. LAFS.1112.WHST.1.1, LAFS.1112.WHST.2.4, LAFS.1112.WHST.4.10, SS.912.A.3.8

LESSON 3

Social Darwinism and Social Reform

ESSENTIAL QUESTIONS

• Why do people migrate?
• How is urban life different from rural life?

READING HELPDESK

Academic Vocabulary

• evolution • publish

Content Vocabulary

• individualism
• Social Darwinism
• philanthropy
• settlement house
• Americanization

TAKING NOTES

Key Ideas and Details

Categorizing As you read, complete a graphic organizer similar to the one below by filling in the main idea of each of the theories and movements listed.
LAFS.1112.RH.3.7, SS.912.A.3.8

Theory or Movement	Main Idea
Social Darwinism	
Laissez-Faire	
Gospel of Wealth	
Realism	

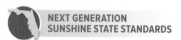

NEXT GENERATION SUNSHINE STATE STANDARDS

ELD.K12.ELL.SI.1: English language learners communicate for social and instructional purposes within the school setting.

ELD.K12.ELL.SS.1: English language learners communicate information, ideas and concepts necessary for academic success in the content area of Social Studies.

Continued on page 158

IT MATTERS BECAUSE

The industrialization of the United States led to new art and literature and new ideas about government's role in society. Social Darwinists believed society developed through "survival of the fittest." Other Americans thought steps needed to be taken to help the less fortunate.

Gilded Age Ideas

GUIDING QUESTION *What was the main idea of Social Darwinism, and how did it compare with the idea of individualism?*

In 1873, Mark Twain and Charles Warner wrote a novel entitled *The Gilded Age: A Tale of Today*. Historians later adopted the term and applied it to the era in American history that began about 1870 and ended around 1900. The era was in many ways a time of marvels. Amazing new inventions led to rapid industrial growth. Cities grew in size and people thronged the crowded streets. Wealthy entrepreneurs built spectacular mansions. Skyscrapers reached to the sky, and electric lights banished the darkness.

By calling this era the Gilded Age, Twain and Warner were sounding an alarm. Something is gilded if it is covered with gold on the outside but made of cheaper material inside. A gilded age might appear to sparkle, but critics pointed to corruption, poverty, crime, and great disparities in wealth between the rich and the poor.

Whether the era was golden or merely gilded, it was certainly a time of great cultural activity. Industrialism and urbanization altered the way Americans looked at themselves and their society, and these changes gave rise to new values, new art, and new entertainment.

The Idea of Individualism

One of the strongest beliefs of the era—and one that remains strong today—was the idea of **individualism**. Many Americans firmly believed that no matter how humble their origins, Americans could rise in society and go as far as their talents and commitment would take them. No one expressed the idea of individualism better than

Horatio Alger, who wrote more than 100 "rags-to-riches" novels. In his books, a poor person goes to the big city and, through a combination of hard work and luck, becomes successful. Even though such dramatic jumps upward in social standing were not commonplace, Alger's popular books convinced many young people that no matter how many obstacles they faced, success was possible.

Social Darwinism

Another powerful idea of the era was **Social Darwinism.** This philosophy, loosely derived from Charles Darwin's theories, strongly reinforced the idea of individualism.

Herbert Spencer British philosopher Herbert Spencer applied Darwin's theory of **evolution** and natural selection to human society. In his 1859 book *On the Origin of Species by Means of Natural Selection,* Darwin argued that plant and animal life had evolved over millions of years by a process he called natural selection. In this process, those species that cannot adapt to the environment in which they live gradually die out, while those that do adapt, thrive, and live on.

Spencer used this theory to argue that human society also evolved through competition and natural selection. He said that society became better because only the fittest people survived. Spencer and others, such as American scholar William Graham Sumner, became known as Social Darwinists and their ideas as Social Darwinism. "Survival of the fittest" became the catchphrase of their philosophy. Some industrial leaders used Social Darwinism to justify their support of laissez-faire capitalism. This economic doctrine opposed any government programs that interfered with business.

Darwinism and the Church Many devout Christians found Darwin's conclusions offensive. They rejected the theory of evolution because they believed it contradicted the Bible's account of creation. Some clergy, however, concluded that evolution might have been God's way of creating the world. One of the most famous ministers of the era, Henry Ward Beecher, called himself a "Christian evolutionist."

Carnegie's Gospel of Wealth Andrew Carnegie advocated a gentler version of Social Darwinism that he called the Gospel of Wealth. This philosophy held that wealthy Americans should engage in **philanthropy,** using their fortunes to create the conditions that would help people help themselves. Building schools and hospitals, for example, was better than giving handouts to the poor. Carnegie funded the creation of public libraries in cities across the nation because libraries provide the information people needed to get ahead in life.

> **PRIMARY SOURCE**
>
> ❝In bestowing charity, the main consideration should be to help those who will help themselves; to provide part of the means by which those who desire to improve may do so; to give those who desire to rise the aids by which they may rise; to assist, but rarely or never to do all. Neither the individual nor the race is improved by almsgiving. Those worthy of assistance, except in rare cases, seldom require assistance. The really valuable men of the race never do, except in cases of accident or sudden change. . . . He is the only true reformer who is as careful and as anxious not to aid the unworthy as he is to aid the worthy, and, perhaps, even more so, for in almsgiving more injury is probably done by rewarding vice than by relieving virtue. . . .❞
>
> —Andrew Carnegie, from *The Gospel of Wealth and Other Timely Essays,* 1886

Carnegie's ideas were widely embraced by the nation's wealthy. The late 1800s was a time when many people made a great deal of money. But it was

©Hulton-Deutsch Collection/Historical/Corbis

BIOGRAPHY

Herbert Spencer (1820–1903)

Herbert Spencer was a philosopher who wrote about "survival of the fittest" several years before Darwin's *Origin of Species* was published. In his major series, *Synthetic Philosophy,* Spencer tried to apply his beliefs about evolution to a variety of social sciences. He believed that both philosophy and science created an ordered system that supported human progress.

▶ **CRITICAL THINKING**
Drawing Conclusions Why might Spencer's ideas have seemed controversial at the time they were written?
LAFS.1112.RH.3.7, SS.912.A.3.6

individualism the belief that no matter what a person's background is, he or she can still become successful through effort

Social Darwinism a philosophy based on Charles Darwin's theories of evolution and natural selection, asserting that humans have developed through competition and natural selection with only the strongest surviving

evolution the scientific theory that humans and other forms of life have evolved over time

philanthropy providing money to support humanitarian or social goals

NEXT GENERATION SUNSHINE STATE STANDARDS

Continued from page 156

LAFS.1112.RH.2.4: Determine the meaning of words and phrases as they are used in a text, including analyzing how an author uses and refines the meaning of a key term over the course of a text (e.g., how Madison defines faction in Federalist No. 10).

LAFS.1112.RH.3.7: Integrate and evaluate multiple sources of information presented in diverse formats and media (e.g., visually, quantitatively, as well as in words) in order to address a question or solve a problem.

LAFS.1112.WHST.1.1: Write arguments focused on discipline-specific content.

LAFS.1112.WHST.4.10: Write routinely over extended time frames (time for reflection and revision) and shorter time frames (a single sitting or a day or two) for a range of discipline-specific tasks, purposes, and audiences.

SS.912.A.1.4: Analyze how images, symbols, objects, cartoons, graphs, charts, maps, and artwork may be used to interpret the significance of time periods and events from the past.

SS.912.A.1.7: Describe various socio-cultural aspects of American life including arts, artifacts, literature, education, and publications.

SS.912.A.3.2: Examine the social, political, and economic causes, course, and consequences of the second Industrial Revolution that began in the late 19th century.

SS.912.A.3.6: Analyze changes that occurred as the United States shifted from agrarian to an industrial society.

SS.912.A.3.8: Examine the importance of social change and reform in the late 19th and early 20th centuries (class system, migration from farms to cities, Social Gospel movement, role of settlement houses and churches in providing services to the poor).

SS.912.A.3.12: Compare how different nongovernmental organizations and progressives worked to shape public policy, restore economic opportunities, and correct injustices in American life.

SS.912.H.1.3: Relate works in the arts to various cultures.

SS.912.H.1.5: Examine artistic response to social issues and new ideas in various cultures.

A young newsboy sells papers on a street corner in 1910.

also an era of philanthropy when the wealthy gave away a great deal of money to improve American society and build up American culture. John D. Rockefeller founded the University of Chicago, and many universities, including Stanford, Vanderbilt, and Johns Hopkins were named for the wealthy businessmen who helped found them. All across the nation, museums of art, symphonies, and operas were funded by wealthy patrons.

✅ **READING PROGRESS CHECK**

Summarizing How did Horatio Alger's books demonstrate the idea of individualism?

The Rebirth of Reform

GUIDING QUESTION *What methods and philosophies were developed for helping the urban poor?*

The tremendous changes that industrialism and urbanization brought triggered a debate over how best to address society's problems. Some Americans embraced the ideas of individualism and Social Darwinism. Others disagreed, arguing that society's problems could be fixed only if Americans and their government began to take a more active role in regulating the economy and helping those in need.

Challenging Social Darwinism

In 1880, journalist Henry George published *Progress and Poverty*, a discussion of the American economy that quickly became a national best seller. George observed, "The present century has been marked by a prodigious increase in wealth-producing power." This should, he asserted, have made poverty "a thing of the past." Instead, he claimed, the "gulf between the employed and the employer is growing wider; social contrasts are becoming sharper." In other words, laissez-faire economics was making society worse—not better.

Most economists now argue that George's analysis was flawed. Industrialism did make some Americans very wealthy, but it also improved the standard of living for most others as well. At the time, however, Americans in the midst of poverty did not see improvement. George's ideas spurred reformers to challenge Social Darwinism.

Lester Frank Ward In 1883, Lester Frank Ward published *Dynamic Sociology*, in which he argued that humans were different from animals because they had the ability to make plans to produce the future outcomes they desired. Ward's ideas came to be known as Reform Darwinism. People, he insisted, had succeeded in the world because of their ability to cooperate. Government, he argued, could regulate the economy, cure poverty, and promote education more efficiently than competition in the marketplace could.

Looking Backward Writer Edward Bellamy promoted another alternative to Social Darwinism and laissez-faire economics. In 1888, he published Looking Backward, a novel about a man who falls asleep in 1887 and awakens in the year 2000 to find that the nation has become a perfect society with no crime, poverty, or politics. In this fictional society, the government owns all industry and shares the wealth equally with all Americans. Bellamy's ideas were essentially a form of socialism.

Naturalism in Literature Criticism of industrial society also appeared in literature in a new style of writing known as naturalism. Naturalists challenged the idea of Social Darwinism by suggesting that some people failed in life simply because they were caught up in circumstances they could not control.

The Granger Collection, New York

Among the most prominent naturalist writers were Stephen Crane, Jack London, and Theodore Dreiser. Stephen Crane's novel *Maggie, A Girl of the Streets* (1893) told the story of a girl's descent into prostitution and death. Jack London's tales of the Alaskan wilderness demonstrated the power of nature over civilization. Theodore Dreiser's novels, such as *Sister Carrie* (1900), painted a world where people sinned without punishment and where the pursuit of wealth and power often destroyed their character.

Naturalist literature drew people's attention to the issues and problems facing American society as a result of rapid industrialization and urbanization—issues such as poverty, violence, safety, disease, and isolation. The literature had a positive impact in that it encouraged readers to look at social problems. It encouraged some people to become reformers, and to try to help the less fortunate. But the literature also had a negative impact. By downplaying heroism and the ability of people to make a difference in their life, it discouraged people from taking action, and encouraged envy and resentment toward people of different social classes.

Naturalism also implicitly asked readers to consider whether individualism and laissez-faire was leading to the best possible society. So it was not surprising that readers of naturalist literature might conclude that the way to make things better was by government intervention. Whether that was a positive or negative impact of the literature depended on whether a person thought an increased government role in society and the economy was a good idea.

Helping the Urban Poor

The plight of the urban poor prompted some reformers to find new ways to help. The Social Gospel movement worked to better conditions in cities according to the biblical ideals of charity and justice. Washington Gladden, a minister, was an early advocate who popularized the movement in writings such as *Applied Christianity* (1887). Walter Rauschenbusch, a Baptist minister from New York, became the leading voice in the Social Gospel movement. The Church, he argued, must "demand protection for the moral safety of the people." The Social Gospel movement inspired many churches to build gyms, provide social programs and child care, and help the poor.

The Salvation Army and the Young Men's Christian Association (YMCA) also combined faith and an interest in reform. The Salvation Army offered practical aid and religious counseling to the urban poor. The YMCA tried to help industrial workers and the urban poor by organizing Bible studies, citizenship training, and group activities. The YMCA also provided low-cost boarding houses for young men. The head of the Chicago YMCA, Dwight L. Moody, was a gifted preacher whose revival meetings drew thousands of people. Moody rejected both the Social Gospel movement and Social Darwinism. He believed the way to help the poor was not by providing them with services but by redeeming their souls and reforming their character.

The **settlement house** movement began as an offshoot of the Social Gospel movement. In the late 1800s, idealistic reformers—including many college-educated women—established settlement houses in poor, often heavily immigrant neighborhoods. The reformers lived in these settlement houses, which were community centers offering everything from medical care and English classes to kindergartens and recreational programs. Jane Addams opened Hull House in Chicago in 1889. Jewish reformer Lillian Wald founded the Henry Street Settlement in New York City. Both women were a powerful force in social work and the settlement house movement.

settlement house an institution located in a poor neighborhood that provided numerous community services such as medical care, child care, libraries, and classes in English

After visiting a settlement house in London, England, Jane Addams decided to open Hull House in 1889 to assist poor immigrants in Chicago. Addams wrote books about her experience at Hull House, giving an example to others throughout the nation.

▶ CRITICAL THINKING
Drawing Conclusions Based on her involvement with Hull House, how would you describe Jane Addams as a person? LAFS.1112.RH.3.7, SS.912.A.1.4, SS.912.A.3.12

Americanization the process of acquiring or causing a person to acquire American traits and characteristics

Library of Congress, Prints & Photographs Division [LC-USZ61-144]

Public Education

As the United States became increasingly industrialized and urbanized, it needed more trained and educated workers. The number of public schools increased dramatically after the Civil War. The number of children attending school rose from 7,562,000 in 1870 to 15,503,000 in 1900. Public schools were often crucial to the success of immigrant children. At school they were taught English and learned about American history and culture, a process known as **Americanization.**

Schools also tried to instill discipline. Grammar schools divided students into grades and drilled them in punctuality, neatness, and efficiency—necessary habits for the workplace. Vocational education in high schools taught skills required in specific trades. However, children in cities had greater access to education than those in rural areas. Many African Americans also faced education inequalities. Some started their own schools, following the example of Booker T. Washington, who founded the Tuskegee Institute in 1881.

☑ READING PROGRESS CHECK

Explaining Why were public schools important to the success of immigrant children?

SKILLS PRACTICE

There are many words that may be new to you in this lesson such as evolution, individualism, philanthropy, and Americanization. When you see a new word, think about it. Do you already know something about it? Use what you know to help you understand the new word.
ELD.K12.ELL.SI.1, ELD.K12.ELL.SS.1

A Changing Culture

GUIDING QUESTION *Why do you think artists and writers started portraying America more realistically?*

The late 1800s was a period of great cultural change for writers and artists. It was also a time when many urban Americans took advantage of new forms of entertainment.

Realism in Art & Literature

A new movement in art and literature called realism began in the 1800s. Just as Darwin tried to explain the natural world scientifically, artists and writers tried to portray the world realistically. Realist artists did not generally choose heroic or historical topics. Nor did they try to idealize people as romantic artists had done. Instead they painted ordinary people doing ordinary things. Among the best known of the realist painters are John Singer Sargent and Thomas Eakins. Much of the work they did was portraiture—formal paintings in realistic detail of people posing for the artist. Eakins, however, was also known for paintings that depicted people in action. He painted men rowing, athletes playing baseball, a family out for a carriage ride, doctors performing surgery, and scientists in action in their laboratories. The realist style captured many of the characteristics of the era such as clothing styles, social relationships, the differences between the social classes, and the way people looked doing ordinary things in life.

Writers also attempted to capture the world as they saw it. In several novels, William Dean Howells presented realistic descriptions of American life. For example, his novel *The Rise of Silas Lapham* (1885) described the attempts of a self-made man to enter Boston society. Also an influential literary critic, Howells was the first to declare Mark Twain an incomparable American genius. Twain, whose real name was Samuel Clemens, **published** his masterpiece, *Adventures of Huckleberry Finn,* in 1884. In this novel, the title character and his friend Jim, who has escaped from slavery, float down the Mississippi River on a raft. Twain wrote in local dialect with a lively sense of humor. Through the innocent eyes of his characters who question right and wrong in American society as they encounter it, Twain gave readers a humorous yet critical account of racism, violence, and poverty in the nation.

Popular Culture

Popular culture changed considerably in the late 1800s. Industrialization improved the standard of living for many people, enabling them to spend money on entertainment and recreation. Increasingly, urban Americans divided their lives into separate units—that of work and that of home. People began "going out" to public entertainment.

In cities, saloons often outnumbered groceries. As a place for social gathering, saloons played a major role in the lives of male workers. Saloons offered drinks, free toilets, water for horses, and free newspapers for customers. They even offered the first "free lunch": salty food that made patrons thirsty and eager to drink more. Saloons also served as political centers, and saloonkeepers were often key figures in political machines.

Working-class families and single adults could find entertainment at new amusement parks such as New York City's Coney Island. Amusements such as water slides and railroad rides cost only a nickel or dime. People also began watching professional sports. Formed in 1869, the first professional baseball team was the Cincinnati Red Stockings. In 1903, the first official World Series was played between the Boston Americans and the Pittsburgh Pirates. Football gained in popularity, and by the late 1800s had spread to public colleges.

As work became less strenuous, many people looked for activities involving physical exercise. Tennis, golf, and croquet became popular. In 1891, James Naismith, athletic director for a college in Massachusetts, invented a new indoor game called basketball.

Tin Pan Alley

People also enjoyed comic theater and music. Adapted from French theater, vaudeville took on an American flavor in the early 1880s with its hodgepodge of animal acts, singers, comedians, acrobats, and dancers. Like

With his book *Adventures of Huckleberry Finn*, Mark Twain had written a true American novel. The setting, subject, characters, and style were clearly American.

▶ **CRITICAL THINKING**
Making Inferences Why did Mark Twain write *Adventures of Huckleberry Finn* using local dialect? LAFS.1112.RH.3.7, SS.912.A.1.7, SS.912.H.1.2, SS.912.H.1.3, SS.912.H.1.5

publish to make a document available to the general public

Library of Congress, Prints & Photographs Division [LC-USZ62-5513]

vaudeville, ragtime music echoed the hectic pace of city life. Its syncopated rhythms grew out of the music of riverside honky-tonks, saloon pianists, and banjo players, using the patterns of African American music. Scott Joplin, one of the most important African American ragtime composers, became known as the King of Ragtime. He wrote his most famous piece, "The Maple Leaf Rag," in 1899.

From the early 1880s to the late 1930s, the music industry in America was centered in New York City. The part of the city where many music publishers and songwriters were located became known as Tin Pan Alley. The name is thought to have come from a sarcastic description of the sound of many pianos playing different ragtime songs all at once—that it sounded like tin pans banging together. Tin Pan Alley musicians and publishers made most of their money by selling sheet music. Very few people owned phonographs in the 1880s and 1890s, but many homes had pianos, banjos and other instruments, and people would play popular songs for themselves and their families. Musicians, known as pluggers, put on performances to advertise songs and get people to buy the sheet music.

The negative impact of Tin Pan Alley, especially in its early years, was that it also continued to promote racial stereotypes. Much of Tin Pan Alley's style and sound derived from African American songs and music but with themes and content that appealed to white Americans. A portion of the music published, especially in the 1880s and 1890s, included racial jokes and ideas that probably played a role in sustaining the racism of the era and the social separation of whites and African Americans.

Despite this, Tin Pan Alley's positive impact on America was much greater than its negative impact. It was largely responsible for the birth of the modern music industry and made possible the careers of such famous songwriters as Irving Berlin, George Cohan, Ira Gershwin, Cole Porter, Scott Joplin and many others. Some of the most popular songs of the era are still known today, including "Hello! Ma Baby (Hello Ma Ragtime Gal)," "Give My Regards to Broadway," and "Take Me Out to the Ball Game." Tin Pan Alley also played an important role in World War I, deliberately publishing music to help the morale of soldiers and people at home. "Perhaps the best known song from World War I is "Over There."

✓ READING PROGRESS CHECK

Analyzing Why was it possible to pursue more leisure activities and popular entertainment during this time period?

LESSON 3 REVIEW

Reviewing Vocabulary
1. *Explaining* Explain the significance of philanthropy, and identify the reason for its growth during the late 1800s.
LAFS.1112.RH.2.4, SS.912.A.3.8

Using Your Notes
2. *Defining* Use your notes on the theories and movements of the Gilded Age to explain its defining characteristics.
SS.912.A.1.7, SS.912.A.3.8, SS.912.H.1.4

Answering the Guiding Questions
3. *Comparing* What was the main idea of Social Darwinism, and how did it compare with the idea of individualism?
SS.912.A.3.8

4. *Summarizing* What methods and philosophies were developed for helping immigrants and the urban poor?
SS.912.A.3.8

5. *Making Connections* Why do you think artists and writers started portraying America more realistically?
SS.912.A.1.7, SS.912.H.1.3, SS.912.H.1.5, SS.912.H.2.5, SS.912.H.3.2

Writing Activity
6. ARGUMENT Suppose that you are a newspaper editor in the late 1800s. Write an editorial in which you support or oppose government involvement in the economy.
LAFS.1112.WHST.1.1, LAFS.1112.WHST.4.10, SS.912.A.3.8

LESSON 4
Politics of the Gilded Age

ESSENTIAL QUESTIONS
• Why do people migrate?
• How is urban life different from rural life?

READING HELPDESK

Academic Vocabulary
• currency   • bond
• strategy

Content Vocabulary
• populism
• greenbacks
• inflation
• graduated income tax
• deflation
• cooperatives

TAKING NOTES

Key Ideas and Details

Organizing As you read about the emergence of populism in the 1890s, use the major headings of the lesson to create an outline similar to the one below. LAFS.1112.RH.3.7, S.912.A.3.8

> *Politics of the Gilded Age*
> I. Politics in Washington
>   A.
>   B.

**NEXT GENERATION
SUNSHINE STATE STANDARDS**

LAFS.1112.RH.2.4: Determine the meaning of words and phrases as they are used in a text, including analyzing how an author uses and refines the meaning of a key term over the course of a text (e.g., how Madison defines faction in Federalist No. 10).

Continued on page 164

IT MATTERS BECAUSE
In the late 1800s, the two major political parties were closely competitive, and issues such as tariffs and business regulations were hotly debated. Meanwhile, farmers facing falling crop prices and deflation tried to overcome their problems by forming organizations. In the 1890s, many farmers joined the Populist Party.

Politics in Washington

GUIDING QUESTION *Why was civil service reform needed?*

Up until the 1880s, most jobs in the federal government were subject to the spoils system. After candidates won election and took office, they fired all of the people who worked for the government, and gave the jobs to people who had supported their election. This practice of rewarding political supporters with government jobs is known as patronage. Supporters of patronage claimed it was necessary to ensure that government workers stayed loyal to the elected representatives of the people. But after the Civil War, many Americans came to believe patronage made the government inefficient and corrupt.

Civil Service Reforms

When Rutherford B. Hayes became president in 1877, he tried to end patronage by firing officials who had been given jobs because of their support of the party and replacing them with reformers. His actions split the Republican Party between "Stalwarts" (who supported patronage), "Halfbreeds" (who backed some reform), and reformers. No reforms were passed. In 1880, the Republicans nominated James Garfield, a "Halfbreed," for president and Chester A. Arthur, a "Stalwart," for vice president. Despite the feud over patronage, the Republicans managed to win the election. A few months later, President Garfield was assassinated by a man angry that he had not been given a government job.

Garfield's assassination turned public opinion against the spoils system. In 1883, Congress passed the Pendleton Act, requiring that

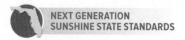

NEXT GENERATION
SUNSHINE STATE STANDARDS

Continued from page 163

LAFS.1112.RH.3.7: Integrate and evaluate multiple sources of information presented in diverse formats and media (e.g., visually, quantitatively, as well as in words) in order to address a question or solve a problem.

LAFS.1112.WHST.4.10: Write routinely over extended time frames (time for reflection and revision) and shorter time frames (a single sitting or a day or two) for a range of discipline-specific tasks, purposes, and audiences.

SS.912.A.1.4: Analyze how images, symbols, objects, cartoons, graphs, charts, maps, and artwork may be used to interpret the significance of time periods and events from the past.

SS.912.A.3.1: Analyze the economic challenges to American farmers and farmers' responses to these challenges in the mid to late 1800s.

Continued on page 165

some jobs be filled by competitive written exams, rather than by patronage. This marked the beginning of professional civil service—a system where most government workers are given jobs based on qualifications rather than on political affiliation. Only about 10 percent of federal jobs were made civil service positions in 1883, but the percentage increased over time.

In 1884, the Democrats nominated Grover Cleveland, the governor of New York, for president. Cleveland was a reformer with a reputation for honesty. The Republicans nominated James G. Blaine, a former Speaker of the House rumored to have accepted bribes. Some Republicans were so unhappy with Blaine that they supported Cleveland.

Cleveland narrowly won the election, and then he faced supporters who expected him to reward them with jobs. Reformers, on the other hand, expected him to increase the number of jobs under the civil service system. Cleveland chose a middle course and angered both sides. Soon, however, economic issues replaced the patronage reform debate.

Debating Economic Policy

By the 1880s, the American people had become increasingly concerned about the power of large corporations, fearful they were controlling prices and wages and corrupting the government. Small businesses and farmers had become particularly angry at the railroads. While large corporations could negotiate rebates and lower rates because of the volume of goods they shipped, others were forced to pay much higher rates. Eventually many states passed laws regulating railroad rates. In 1886, the Supreme Court ruled in the case of *Wabash, St. Louis, and Pacific Railway* v. *Illinois* that only the federal government could regulate interstate commerce. Public pressure forced Congress to act, and in 1887 Cleveland signed the Interstate Commerce Act. This was the first federal law to regulate interstate commerce.

The law limited railroad rates to what was "reasonable and just," outlawed rebates, and made it illegal to charge higher rates for shorter hauls where the short haul was part of a longer haul. The law also created the Interstate Commerce Commission (ICC); the nation's first independent regulatory agency. The ICC was not very effective in regulating the industry because it had to take railroads to court, prove they were violating the law, then ask the court to enforce the ICC's rulings.

Despite its weaknesses, the creation of the ICC had some benefits. By banning rebates and higher rates for short hauls, it reduced some of the pressure on farmers and small businesses who were struggling to compete with large companies. On the other hand, it imposed costs on consumers. Eliminating rebates and different rates for short and long hauls meant the costs of shipping goods increased for large companies. They in turn passed those costs along in the form of higher prices to consumers. In 1893, Congress gave the ICC the power to regulate railroad safety as well, a decision that brought its own costs and benefits. Safer railroads benefited both passengers and railroad workers. But at the same time, the costs of implementing safety regulations increased railroad costs which in turn meant they charged high fees for shipping and passenger tickets.

Tariffs were another economic issue. Many Democrats thought that Congress should cut tariffs because they raised the price of imported goods.

POLITICAL DEBATES OF THE GILDED AGE

POLITICAL CARTOONS

Senator George H. Pendleton is congratulated for his civil service bill. An overflowing trash bin suggests that reform is impossible.

1 Did the artist who drew the cartoon favor civil service reform? How does he indicate his opinion? LAFS.1112.RH.3.7, SS.912.A.1.4, SS.912.A.3.1, SS.912.H.1.5

2 How might the passage of civil service reform change how government works? LAFS.1112.RH.3.7, SS.912.A.3.1, SS.912.A.3.8

The Granger Collection, New York

High tariffs also forced other nations to respond in kind, making it difficult for farmers to export surpluses. In December 1887, President Cleveland proposed lowering tariffs. The Democratic House passed moderate tariff reductions, but the Republican Senate rejected the bill.

In 1888, the Republicans and their presidential candidate, Benjamin Harrison, received large campaign contributions from industrialists who benefited from high tariffs. Cleveland and the Democrats campaigned against high tariff rates. In one of the closest presidential elections in American history, Harrison lost the popular vote but won the electoral vote, giving Republicans control of the White House.

In 1890, Representative William McKinley pushed through a bill that cut some taxes and tariff rates but increased rates on other goods. The McKinley Tariff, intended to protect American industry from foreign competition, instead helped trigger a steep rise in the price of all goods. In 1890, Congress also passed the Sherman Antitrust Act to curb the power of the large business combinations known as trusts. The act prohibited any "combination . . . or conspiracy, in restraint of trade or commerce among the several States."

✓ **READING PROGRESS CHECK**

Summarizing What actions did Congress take to reform the civil service? Why were these steps necessary?

Unrest in Rural America

GUIDING QUESTION *What kinds of problems did farmers face?*

Populism was a movement to increase farmers' political power and work for legislation in their interest. An economic crisis following the Civil War led farmers to join the Populist movement. New technology enabled farmers to produce more crops, but increased supply caused prices to fall. High tariffs also made it hard for farmers to sell their goods overseas. In addition, mortgages with large banks and rail shipping costs that continued to increase made the farmers' difficulties worse.

The Money Supply

Some farmers thought adjusting the money supply would solve their problems. During the Civil War, the government had expanded the money supply by issuing millions of dollars in **greenbacks,** paper **currency** that could not be exchanged for gold or silver coins. When currency is issued that cannot be exchanged for a commodity, like gold or silver, it is called fiat currency. It holds value only because the government says it does. The increased money supply without an increase in goods for sale caused **inflation,** or a decline in the value of money. As the paper money lost value, the prices of goods soared.

After the Civil War ended, the United States had three types of currency in circulation—greenbacks, gold and silver coins, and national banknotes backed by government **bonds.** To get inflation under control, the federal government stopped printing greenbacks and began paying off its bonds. In 1873, Congress also decided to stop making silver into coins. These decisions meant that the money supply was insufficient for the country's growing economy. As the economy expanded, **deflation**—an increase in the value of money and a decrease in prices—began.

Deflation hit farmers especially hard. Falling prices meant that they sold their crops for less and then had to borrow money for seed and other

Image provided courtesy of Paul A. Hubanks

Continued from page 164

S.912.A.3.8: Examine the importance of social change and reform in the late 19th and early 20th centuries (class system, migration from farms to cities, Social Gospel movement, role of settlement houses and churches in providing services to the poor).

SS.912.A.3.12: Compare how different nongovernmental organizations and progressives worked to shape public policy, restore economic opportunities, and correct injustices in American life.

SS.912.H.1.5: Examine artistic response to social issues and new ideas in various cultures.

populism a political movement founded in the 1890s representing mainly farmers that favored free coinage of silver and government control of railroads and other large industries

greenback a unit of paper currency first issued by the federal government during the Civil War

currency paper money used as a medium of exchange

inflation an ongoing increase in prices and decrease in the value of money

bond a note issued by the government that promises to pay off a loan with interest

This Civil War–era banknote from 1862 was part of the expanded money supply that caused a rise in inflation.

▶ CRITICAL THINKING
Making Inferences Why would an increase in the amount of paper currency cause it to lose value? LAFS.1112.RH.3.7

deflation an ongoing decrease in prices and an increase in the value of money

supplies to plant their next crops. With money in short supply, interest rates began to rise, increasing the amount farmers owed. Rising interest rates also made mortgages more expensive, and despite their lower income, farmers had to make the same mortgage payments to the banks. Farmers knew their problems were partly due to a shortage of currency. Some wanted the government to print more greenbacks. Others, especially those in the West where new silver mines had been found, wanted silver coins to be issued again. Increasingly, farmers realized that if they wanted the government to meet their demands, they had to organize.

The Grange Takes Action

In 1866, the Department of Agriculture sent Oliver H. Kelley to tour the rural South and report on farmers' conditions. Realizing that farmers were isolated, Kelley founded the first national farm organization, the Patrons of Husbandry, in 1867. It became known as the Grange.

In 1873, the nation plunged into a severe recession, and farm income fell sharply. Grangers responded by pressuring states to regulate railroad and warehouse rates. To reduce harmful competition among farmers, the Grangers also tried creating organizations called **cooperatives** in which member farmers worked together to increase prices and lower costs. None of the **strategies** improved farmers' economic conditions.

cooperative a store where farmers buy products from each other; an enterprise owned and operated by those who use its services

strategy a plan or method for achieving a goal

The Farmers' Alliance

As the Grange began to fall apart, a new organization, known as the Farmers' Alliance, began to form. By 1890, the Alliance had between 1.5 and 3 million members. When Charles W. Macune became the leader of the Alliance, he announced a plan to organize very large cooperatives, which he called exchanges. The exchanges failed because they overextended themselves, or because wholesalers, railroad owners, and bankers made it difficult for them to stay in business. They also failed because they were still too small to affect world prices for farm products.

POLITICAL CARTOONS | **FORMATION OF THE PEOPLE'S PARTY**

The People's Party, also known as the Populist Party, is shown as a patchwork of assorted movements and philosophies supporting a "Platform of Lunacy."

1 Why do you think the People's Party platform is portrayed as one of lunacy?
LAFS.1112.RH.3.7, SS.912.A.1.4, SS.912.A.3.1

2 How does the patchwork balloon represent the artist's point of view?
LAFS.1112.RH.3.7, SS.912.A.1.4, SS.912.A.3.1, SS.912.H.1.5

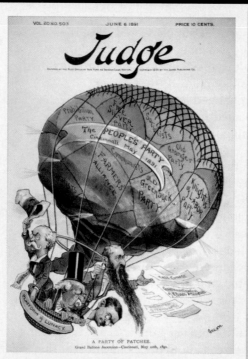

A PARTY OF PATCHES.
Grand Balloon Ascension—Cincinnati, May 20th, 1891.

The Granger Collection, New York

✔ **READING PROGRESS CHECK**

Explaining What measures did the nation take after the Civil War to improve its economic situation? What was the result?

The Rise of Populism

GUIDING QUESTION *What were the goals of the Populist Party?*

By 1890, many people in the Alliance were dissatisfied. They felt that only through politics could they achieve their goals. However, many Alliance members had become distrustful of both the Republican and Democratic Parties. They believed that both parties favored industry and banks over farmers. In July 1892, more than 1,000 delegates met in Omaha, Nebraska, to form the People's Party. The party held its first national convention and nominated James B. Weaver to run for president. The Omaha convention's platform called for a return to unlimited coinage of silver. It also called for federal ownership of railroads and a **graduated income tax.**

Populists also adopted proposals that were designed to appeal to organized labor. Ideas such as an eight-hour workday and immigration restrictions were put forth as appealing options. In the end, however, populism held little appeal to urban voters, who continued their traditional party allegiances. Many workers continued to vote for the Democrats, whose candidate, Grover Cleveland, won the election.

✔ **READING PROGRESS CHECK**

Summarizing Why did Southern Alliance groups resist the idea of a national People's Party?

graduated income tax
a tax based on the net income of an individual or business and which taxes different income levels at different rates

The Election of 1896

GUIDING QUESTION *Why did the Populists support the Democratic candidate—William Jennings Bryan—in 1896?*

As the election of 1896 approached, leaders of the People's Party decided to make the free coinage of silver the focus of their campaign and to hold their convention after the Republican and Democratic conventions. They believed, correctly, that the Republicans would endorse a gold standard. They also expected the Democrats to nominate Grover Cleveland, even though Cleveland favored a gold standard. The People's Party hoped that when it endorsed silver, pro-silver Democrats would choose the Populists.

Unfortunately, their strategy failed. William Jennings Bryan made an impassioned pro-silver speech at the convention and won the Democratic nomination.

PRIMARY SOURCE

❝Having behind us the producing masses of this nation and the world supported by the commercial interests, the laboring interests and the toilers everywhere, we will answer their demand for a gold standard by saying to them: You shall not press down upon the brow of labor this crown of thorns; you shall not crucify mankind upon a cross of gold.❞

—from Bryan's speech at the Democratic National Convention, 1896

The Populists faced a difficult choice: endorse Bryan and risk undermining their identity as a party, or nominate their own candidate and risk splitting the silver vote. They chose to support Bryan.

The Republicans appealed to workers with the promise that McKinley would provide a "full dinner pail." Also most business leaders supported the Republicans, convinced that unlimited silver coinage would ruin the country. Many employers warned workers that if Bryan won, businesses would fail and unemployment would rise further. McKinley's reputation as a moderate on labor issues and as tolerant toward ethnic groups helped improve the Republican Party's image with urban workers and immigrants. When the votes were counted, McKinley had won with a decisive victory.

Evaluating Populism's Impact

Discouraged by defeat, the People's Party declined after 1896. The Populist goal of using the federal government to ease the economic hardships of farmers and regulate big business failed, primarily because of the party's inability to appeal successfully to urban workers in the northeast. Populist ideas, however, were not forgotten and continued to influence the political debate. In the years ahead, many items on the Populist program would be realized, including the eight hour workday, restrictions on immigration, and a graduated income tax. Ironically, the key Populist goal of increasing the money supply came about almost immediately following the election, as gold from the Klondike and new gold mines in South Africa flooded into the world's economy.

The Klondike Gold Rush

In August 1896, an American prospector discovered gold near the Klondike River in the Yukon territory of northern Canada. When the news reached San Francisco and Seattle the following year the last great gold rush in American history began. Within months, an estimated 100,000 people set out for the Klondike determined to strike it rich.

Physical geographic factors made getting to the Klondike very difficult. The region was extremely remote. The most direct route was to book passage to the ports of Dyea or Skagway, then hike approximately 30 miles over the mountains before sailing the final 500 miles down the Yukon River to Dawson City, the nearest settlement to the gold fields. Prospectors were required to bring a year's worth of supplies so as to ensure no one starved to death in the remote region. To do that, each person had to bring in nearly a ton of material. Boomtowns full of hotels, storehouses, saloons, and general stores popped up. Prices soared as merchants sought to supply tools, food, shelter, transportation and entertainment to the prospectors pouring into the region. Hundreds died; some from the cold, some from starvation, others from avalanches, accidents while climbing mountains or crossing frozen lakes, or from outbreaks of dysentery and typhoid fever.

By 1899, the gold rush was over, although companies using heavy equipment continued to expand gold production into the early 1900s. Fewer than 40,000 people made it to the gold fields and only about 4,000 found gold. Of those, only a few hundred became wealthy. The gold rush helped develop lower Alaska. It also poured millions of dollars into the nation's money supply without requiring a return to silver coins or paper currency. Mild inflation set in; credit became easier to obtain, and farmers and workers were less distressed. In 1900, the United States officially adopted a gold-based currency with the passage of the Gold Standard Act.

✔ READING PROGRESS CHECK

Evaluating Why did the Republicans win the election of 1896?

LESSON 4 REVIEW

Reviewing Vocabulary

1. *Explaining* Explain the significance of: populism, greenbacks, inflation, deflation. LAFS.1112.RH.2.4

Using Your Notes

2. *Comparing and Contrasting* Use your notes to explain how the Farmers' Alliance contributed to the rise of a new political party. SS.912.A.3.1

Answering the Guiding Questions

3. *Cause and Effect* Why was civil service reform needed? SS.912.A.3.1

4. *Describing* What kinds of problems did farmers face? SS.912.A.3.1

5. *Summarizing* What were the goals of the People's Party? SS.912.A.3.1

6. *Making Connections* Why did the Populists support the Democratic candidate—William Jennings Bryan—in 1896? SS.912.A.3.1

Writing Activity

7. NARRATIVE Imagine you are a prospector just returned from the Klondike. Write a short narrative describing your adventures, your struggle with the environment, and life in the boomtowns. LAFS.1112.WHST.1.2, LAFS.1112.WHST.2.4, LAFS.1112.WHST.4.10

LESSON 5
The Rise of Segregation

ESSENTIAL QUESTIONS

• Why do people migrate?
• How is urban life different from rural life?

READING HELPDESK

Academic Vocabulary

• discrimination

Content Vocabulary

• poll tax
• segregation
• Jim Crow laws
• lynch

TAKING NOTES

Key Ideas and Details

Organizing Use a graphic organizer similar to the following to list the ways that states disenfranchised African Americans and legalized discrimination.
LAFS.1112.RH.3.7, SS.912.A.2.5, SS.912.A.2.6

Forms of Discrimination

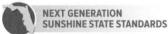
NEXT GENERATION SUNSHINE STATE STANDARDS

LAFS.1112.RH.2.4: Determine the meaning of words and phrases as they are used in a text, including analyzing how an author uses and refines the meaning of a key term over the course of a text (e.g., how Madison defines faction in Federalist No. 10).

LAFS.1112.RH.3.7: Integrate and evaluate multiple sources of information presented in diverse formats and media (e.g., visually, quantitatively, as well as in words) in order to address a question or solve a problem.

Continued on page 170

IT MATTERS BECAUSE

After Reconstruction ended, Southern states began passing laws that weakened the rights of African Americans by introducing segregation and denying voting rights. African American leaders struggled to protect civil rights and improve their quality of life.

Resistance and Repression

GUIDING QUESTION *How did African Americans resist racism and try to improve their way of life following Reconstruction?*

After Reconstruction, many African Americans in the rural South lived in poverty. Most were sharecroppers, landless farmers who gave their landlords a large portion of their crops as rent. Sharecropping usually left farmers in chronic debt. Many eventually left farming and sought jobs in Southern towns, or headed west to claim homesteads.

In the mid-1870s, Benjamin "Pap" Singleton became convinced that African Americans would never be given a chance to get ahead in the South. He began urging African Americans to move west, specifically to Kansas, and form their own independent communities. His ideas soon set in motion a mass migration. In less than two months, approximately 6,000 African Americans left their homes in the rural South and headed to Kansas. The newspapers called it "an Exodus," like the ancient Jews' escape from Egyptian bondage referred to in the Bible. The migrants themselves came to be known as "Exodusters." The first Exodusters, many possessing little more than hope and the clothes on their backs, arrived in Kansas in the spring of 1879.

While some African Americans fled the South, others joined poor white farmers who had created the Farmers' Alliance. Alliance leaders urged African Americans to form a similar organization. In 1886, African American farmers established the Colored Farmers' National Alliance, which numbered about 1.2 million members by 1890.

In 1879 an estimated 6,000 to 15,000 African Americans known as Exodusters left the rural South and headed to Kansas.

▶ **CRITICAL THINKING**
Examining Why did the Exodusters migrate to Kansas?
LAFS.1112.RH.3.7, SS.912.A.3.1

poll tax a tax of a fixed amount per person that had to be paid before the person could vote

NEXT GENERATION SUNSHINE STATE STANDARDS

Continued from page 169

LAFS.1112.WHST.1.2: Write informative/explanatory texts, including the narration of historical events, scientific procedures/experiments, or technical processes.

LAFS.1112.WHST.2.4: Produce clear and coherent writing in which the development, organization, and style are appropriate to task, purpose, and audience.

LAFS.1112.WHST.4.10: Write routinely over extended time frames (time for reflection and revision) and shorter time frames (a single sitting or a day or two) for a range of discipline-specific tasks, purposes, and audiences.

SS.912.A.1.4: Analyze how images, symbols, objects, cartoons, graphs, charts, maps, and artwork may be used to interpret the significance of time periods and events from the past.

SS.912.A.1.6: Use case studies to explore social, political, legal, and economic relationships in history.

SS.912.A.2.4: Distinguish the freedoms guaranteed to African Americans and other groups with the 13th, 14th, and 15th Amendments to the Constitution.

SS.912.A.2.5: Assess how Jim Crow Laws influenced life for African Americans and other racial/ethnic minority groups.

Continued on page 171

When the Populist Party formed in 1891, many African American farmers joined the new organization. This posed a major challenge to the Democratic Party in the South. If poor whites joined African Americans in voting for the Populists, the coalition might be unbeatable. To win back the poor white vote, Democratic leaders began appealing to racism. In addition, election officials began using various methods to make it harder and harder for African Americans to vote. As one Democratic leader in the South told a reporter, "Some of our people, some editors especially, deny that [African Americans] are hindered from voting; but what is the good of lying? They are interfered with, and we are obliged to do it, and we may as well tell the truth."

✔ **READING PROGRESS CHECK**

Summarizing What did the Democratic Party do to prevent the Populists from gaining too much power?

Imposing Segregation

GUIDING QUESTION *What laws did Southern states pass to impose segregation and deny African Americans their voting rights?*

After Reconstruction ended in 1877, the rights of African Americans were gradually undermined. Attempts to unify whites and African Americans failed. Instead, a movement to diminish the civil rights of African Americans gained momentum as the century ended.

Taking Away the Vote

The Fifteenth Amendment prohibits states from denying citizens the right to vote on the basis of "race, color, or previous condition of servitude." However, it does not bar states from denying the right to vote on other grounds. In the late 1800s, Southern states began imposing restrictions. Though they did not mention race, they were meant to make it hard or impossible for African Americans to vote.

In 1890, Mississippi began requiring all citizens registering to vote to pay a **poll tax** of $2, a sum beyond the means of most poor African Americans or poor whites. Mississippi also instituted a literacy test, requiring voters to read and understand the state constitution. Few African Americans born after the Civil War had been able to attend school, and those who had grown up under slavery were largely illiterate. Even those who knew how to read often failed the test because officials deliberately picked passages that few people could understand. Other Southern states adopted similar restrictions. The number of African Americans registered to vote in Southern states fell drastically between 1890 and 1900.

Election officials were far less strict in applying the poll tax and literacy requirements to whites, but the number of white voters also fell significantly. To let more whites vote, Louisiana introduced the

Library of Congress

"grandfather clause." This allowed any man to vote if he had an ancestor who could vote in 1867. This provision, adopted in several Southern states, exempted most whites from voting restrictions.

Legalizing Segregation

African Americans in the North were often discriminated against, but **segregation,** or the separation of the races, was different in the South. Southern states passed laws that rigidly enforced **discrimination.** These laws became known as **Jim Crow laws.**

In 1883 the Supreme Court set the stage for legalized segregation when it overturned the Civil Rights Act of 1875. That law had prohibited keeping people out of public places on the basis of race and barred racial discrimination in selecting jurors. The Supreme Court, however, ruled that the Fourteenth Amendment provided only that "no state" could deny citizens equal protection under the law. Private organizations, such as hotels, theaters, and railroads, were free to practice segregation.

Encouraged by the Supreme Court's ruling and by the decline of congressional support for civil rights, Southern states passed a series of laws establishing racial segregation in virtually all public places. Southern whites and African Americans could no longer ride together in the same railroad cars or even drink from the same water fountains.

In 1892, an African American named Homer Plessy challenged a Louisiana law after he was arrested for riding in a "whites-only" car. In

segregation the separation or isolation of a race, class, or group

discrimination different treatment or preference on a basis other than individual merit

Jim Crow laws statutes enacted to enforce segregation

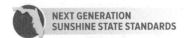

NEXT GENERATION SUNSHINE STATE STANDARDS

Continued from page 170

SS.912.A.2.6: Compare the effects of the Black Codes and the Nadir on freed people, and analyze the sharecropping system and debt peonage as practiced in the United States.

SS.912.A.3.1: Analyze the economic challenges to American farmers and farmers' responses to these challenges in the mid to late 1800s.

SS.912.A.3.12: Compare how different nongovernmental organizations and progressives worked to shape public policy, restore economic opportunities, and correct injustices in American life.

SS.912.A.7.8: Analyze significant Supreme Court decisions relating to integration, busing, affirmative action, the rights of the accused, and reproductive rights.

𝕀𝕀𝕀𝕀 ANALYZING SUPREME COURT CASES

PLESSY v. *FERGUSON*, 1896

Background to the Case

When Homer Adolph Plessy, a light-skinned man who was one-eighth African American, took a seat in the whites-only section of an East Louisiana Railway train and refused to move, he was arrested. Convicted of breaking a Louisiana law enacted in 1890, Plessy appealed his case to the Louisiana Supreme Court, then to the United States Supreme Court. The incident was planned in advance to test the statute to emphasize the folly of the law.

A conductor orders an African American off a whites-only train car in Philadelphia, Pennsylvania.

How the Court Ruled

The Court upheld the right of states to make laws that sustained segregation. The majority of justices wanted to distinguish between political rights guaranteed by the Fourteenth and Fifteenth Amendments and social rights. Although the words *separate but equal* do not appear in the Court's responses, the ruling of the Court allowed for the separation of the races in public facilities. This phrase came to describe a condition that persisted until 1954.

❶ **Identifying Central Ideas** Why did the words separate but equal become associated with the Supreme Court ruling against Homer Plessy? LAFS.1112.RH.3.7, SS.912.A.1.6, SS.912.A.7.8

❷ **Making Generalizations** How do you interpret the fact that it took the Supreme Court until 1954 to change the *Plessy* v. *Ferguson* ruling? LAFS.1112.RH.3.7, SS.912.A.1.6, SS.912.A.7.8

Snark/Art Resource, NY

BIOGRAPHY

Ida B. Wells (1862–1931)

Born in Holly Springs, Mississippi, Ida B. Wells is best known for her strong criticism of lynching, which she called "our country's national crime." Wells's political and reform activities included other issues such as segregation and women's suffrage. In 1913, she marched with an integrated group of suffragists in Washington, D.C. Wells married Chicago lawyer and editor Ferdinand L. Barnett in 1895. In 1910, she formed the Negro Fellowship League. She and her husband moved to an all-white Chicago neighborhood to challenge restrictive housing agreements.

▶ **CRITICAL THINKING**
Describing How did Ida B. Wells try to stop the practice of lynching? LAFS.1112.RH.3.7, SS.912.A.3.12

lynch to execute, by hanging, without lawful approval

1896, the Supreme Court, in *Plessy* v. *Ferguson*, upheld the Louisiana law and the doctrine of "separate but equal" facilities for African Americans. The ruling established the legal basis for discrimination in the South for more than 50 years. While public facilities for African Americans in the South were always separate, they were far from equal.

✓ READING PROGRESS CHECK

Summarizing What was the purpose of the "grandfather clause"?

The African American Response

GUIDING QUESTION *How did African American community leaders respond to legalized segregation?*

Historian Rayford Logan characterized the last decade of the nineteenth century and the opening of the twentieth century as the nadir, or low point, of African American status in American society. The African American community responded to violence and discrimination in several ways. Ida B. Wells, Mary Church Terrell, Booker T. Washington, and W.E.B. Du Bois each used different approaches to address these issues.

Ida B. Wells

In the late 1800s, mob violence increased in the United States, particularly in the South. Between 1890 and 1899, there was an average of 154 people **lynched**—executed, by hanging, without a legal trial—each year.

In 1892, Ida B. Wells, a fiery young African American woman from Tennessee, launched a fearless crusade against lynching. After a mob drove Wells out of town, she settled in Chicago and continued her campaign. In 1895, she published a book denouncing mob violence and demanding "a fair trial by law for those accused of crime, and punishment by law after honest conviction." Although Congress rejected an antilynching bill, the number of lynchings decreased significantly in the 1900s, due in part to the efforts of activists such as Wells.

Mary Church Terrell

One lynching victim had been a close friend of Mary Church Terrell, a college-educated woman who had been born during the Civil War. This death, and President Benjamin Harrison's refusal to publicly condemn lynching, started Terrell on her lifelong battle against lynching, racism, and sexism. Terrell worked with woman suffrage workers such as Jane Addams and Susan B. Anthony. She helped found the National Association for the Advancement of Colored People. She also formed the Women Wage Earner's Association, which assisted African American nurses, waitresses, and domestic workers.

Terrell led a boycott against department stores in Washington, D.C. that refused to serve African Americans. In an address to the National American Woman Suffrage Association, Terrell said, "With courage, born of success achieved in the past, with a keen sense of the responsibility which we shall continue to assume, we look forward to a future large with promise and hope. Seeking no favors because of our color, nor patronage because of our needs, we knock at the bar of justice, asking an equal chance."

Calls for Compromise

One of the most famous African Americans of the late nineteenth century was the influential educator Booker T. Washington. He proposed that African Americans concentrate on achieving economic goals rather than political ones. In 1895, Washington summed up his views in a speech before a mostly white audience in Atlanta. Known as the Atlanta Compromise,

©Bettmann//Corbis

the speech urged African Americans to postpone the fight for civil rights and instead concentrate on preparing themselves educationally and vocationally for full equality.

©Frances Benjamin Johnston/Historical/Corbis

PRIMARY SOURCE

❝The wisest among my race understand that the agitation of questions of social equality is the extremest folly, and that progress in the enjoyment of all the privileges that will come to us must be the result of severe and constant struggle rather than of artificial forcing. . . . It is important and right that all privileges of the law be ours, but it is vastly more important that we be prepared for the exercises of these privileges. The opportunity to earn a dollar in a factory just now is worth infinitely more than the opportunity to spend a dollar in an opera-house.❞

—Booker T. Washington, from *Up From Slavery*, 1901

With the help of Booker T. Washington, Tuskegee Institute was founded in 1881 to teach African Americans trades and agricultural skills. In this image, students are working in the Tuskegee Institute print shop.

▶ CRITICAL THINKING

Drawing Conclusions What do you think was Booker T. Washington's economic goal for establishing the Tuskegee Institute? LAFS.1112.RH.3.7, SS.912.A.1.4, SS.912.A.3.12

Du Bois Rejects Compromise

The Atlanta Compromise speech provoked a strong challenge from W.E.B. Du Bois, the leader of a new generation of African American activists. In his 1903 book *The Souls of Black Folk,* Du Bois explained why he saw no advantage in giving up civil rights, even temporarily. He was particularly concerned with protecting and exercising voting rights. "Negroes must insist continually, in season and out of season," he wrote, "that voting is necessary to proper manhood, that color discrimination is barbarism." In the years that followed, many African Americans worked to win the vote and end discrimination. The struggle, however, would prove to be a long one.

☑ READING PROGRESS CHECK

Describing What was the nature of the compromise urged by Booker T. Washington in the Atlanta Compromise speech?

LESSON 5 REVIEW

Reviewing Vocabulary
1. *Explaining* Explain the importance of Jim Crow laws and how these laws contributed to segregation. LAFS.1112.RH.2.4, SS.912.A.2.5

Using Your Notes
2. *Describing* Use your notes on the forms of discrimination to describe the conditions in which many African Americans in the South lived after Reconstruction.

Answering the Guiding Questions
3. *Identifying Cause and Effect* How did African Americans resist racism and try to improve their way of life following Reconstruction? SS.912.A.2.5, SS.912.A.2.6, SS.912.A.3.12

4. *Identifying* What laws did Southern states pass to impose segregation and deny African Americans their voting rights? SS.912.A.2.5
5. *Differentiating* What are the different ways African American community leaders responded to legalized segregation? SS.912.A.3.12

Writing Activity
6. INFORMATIVE/EXPLANATORY Imagine that you are living in the 1890s. Write a letter to the editor of the local newspaper explaining the Supreme Court ruling in *Plessy* v. *Ferguson* and its effects. LAFS.1112.WHST.1.2, LAFS.1112.WHST.2.4, LAFS.1112.WHST.4.10, SS.912.A.1.6, SS.912.A.7.8

STUDY GUIDE

IMMIGRATION
LESSON 1

PULL FACTORS
- Plenty of land and work
- Higher standards of living
- Wages were comparatively high
- Democratic political system
- Opportunity for social advancement

PUSH FACTORS
- Economic issues and disease
- Farm poverty and worker uncertainty
- Wars and compulsory military service
- Political tyranny and oppressive class structure
- Religious oppression and population pressure

URBANIZATION
LESSON 2

MIGRATION TO GROWING URBAN AREAS
- Expanding number of factory jobs draw immigrants and American citizens to cities
- Cheap land no longer available
- Cities offered modern conviences

URBAN PROBLEMS
- Congestion
- Crime and violence
- Disease
- Pollution
- Overwhelmed local government

SOCIAL DARWINISM AND SOCIAL REFORM
LESSON 3

NATURALISM
Some people fail in life because circumstances are beyond their control

INDIVIDUALISM
No matter what, a person can become successful

IDEAS OF THE GILDED AGE

PHILANTHROPY
The wealthy should use their wealth to help the less fortunate help themselves

SOCIAL DARWINISM
Survival of the fittest; used to support laissez-faire capitalism

REFORM
Society's problems can be fixed by taking a more active role

POLITICS OF THE GILDED AGE
LESSON 4

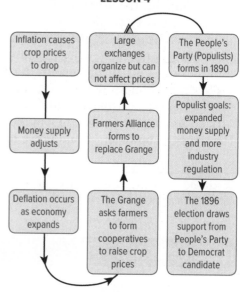

- Inflation causes crop prices to drop
- Money supply adjusts
- Deflation occurs as economy expands
- Large exchanges organize but can not affect prices
- Farmers Alliance forms to replace Grange
- The Grange asks farmers to form cooperatives to raise crop prices
- The People's Party (Populists) forms in 1890
- Populist goals: expanded money supply and more industry regulation
- The 1896 election draws support from People's Party to Democrat candidate

THE RISE OF SEGREGATION
LESSON 5

SEGREGATION
- Denying the vote
  - poll tax and literacy tax
  - grandfather clause
- Jim Crow laws enforced racial discrimination.
- *Plessy* v. *Ferguson* upheld "separate but equal".

AFRICAN AMERICAN RESPONSE

RESISTANCE:
- Ida B. Wells crusaded against lynching.
- Mary Church Terrell helped found the NAACP.
- W.E.B. DuBois argued strongly for civil rights and rejected compromise.

COMPROMISE:
- Booker T. Washington fought for economic rather than political gains

Directions: On a separate sheet of paper, answer the questions below. Make sure you read carefully and answer all parts to the question.

Lesson Review

Lesson 1

1 ***Explaining*** How did the ethnic and religious groups from Eastern Europe contribute to shaping American culture in the late 1800s? SS.912.G.2.1

2 ***Identifying Cause and Effect*** What economic and cultural issues led to protests against the Chinese immigrants in California, and what foreign policy did the U.S. government adopt in response? SS.912.A.3.6, SS.912.A.3.7, SS.912.G.4.3

Lesson 2

3 ***Analyzing*** Describe the social issues and problems that resulted from rapid urbanization, and what some social movements did to address these issues. SS.912.A.3.2, SS.912.A.3.6, SS.912.A.3.8, SS.912.A.3.12

4 ***Synthesizing*** Explain how the free enterprise system improved the standard of living in the United States by applying innovations in transportation to urban America. SS.912.A.3.2, SS.912.A.3.4, SS.912.A.3.8, SS.912.A.3.10

Lesson 3

5 ***Explaining*** How did the Americanization movement seek to assimilate American immigrants into U.S. culture? SS.912.A.3.8, SS.912.G.4.3

6 ***Describing*** How did naturalism reflect the issues facing the United States in the late 1800s? Explain the positive and negative impact of naturalism in literature. SS.912.A.1.7, SS.912.A.3.2, SS.912.A.3.6, SS.912.H.1.5

Lesson 4

7 ***Explaining*** Define patronage and explain the spoils system. Then explain why many Americans believed that civil service reform was needed. SS.912.A.3.11, LAFS.1112.RH.2.4

8 ***Analyzing*** How did physical and human geographic factors impact the Klondike Gold Rush? SS.912.G.2.1, SS.912.G.4.3

Lesson 5

9 ***Summarizing*** What social issues faced African Americans in the rural South in the years after the Civil War? How did they respond? SS.912.A.2.5, SS.912.A.2.6, SS.912.A.3.12

10 ***Explaining*** What actions did Ida B. Wells, Mary Church Terrell, Booker T. Washington, and W.E.B Du Bois take to expand political rights for African Americans? Were they successful? Explain and evaluate their impact. SS.912.A.3.12

Exploring the Essential Questions

11 ***Exploring Issues*** Analyze the push-pull factors affecting immigration in the late 1800s. Draw a map and use it to illustrate the push factors (the reasons people were being pushed out of their countries), and the pull factors (the reasons the United States was pulling people to it) using detailed caption boxes. SS.912.A.3.6, SS.912.A.3.7, SS.912.G.2.1, SS.912.G.4.2

Critical Thinking

12 ***Analyzing Cause and Effect*** What caused Europeans and Chinese to migrate to America in the late 1800s? What effects did this migration have on the demographic patterns of America? SS.912.A.3.7, SS.912.G.2.1

21st Century Skills

13 ***Identifying Cause and Effect Relationships*** Analyze the problems and issues facing farmers in the late 1800s, and explain what caused the Populist movement to begin. SS.912.A.3.1

DBQ Analyzing Primary Sources

Read the excerpt from industrialist Andrew Carnegie's article and answer the questions that follow.

PRIMARY SOURCE

❝We assemble thousands of operatives in the factory, in the mine, and in the counting-house, of whom the employer can know little or nothing, and to whom the employer is little better than a myth. Rigid castes are formed, and, as usual, mutual ignorance breeds mutual distrust. The price which society pays for the law of competition, like the price it pays for cheap comforts and luxuries, is great; but the advantages of this law are also greater still than its cost—

Need Extra Help?

If You've Missed Question	**1**	**2**	**3**	**4**	**5**	**6**	**7**	**8**	**9**	**10**	**11**	**12**	**13**
Go to Lesson	1	1	2, 3	2	3	3	4	4	5	5	1	1	4

for it is to this law that we owe our wonderful material development, which brings improved conditions in its train. But, whether the law be benign or not, we must say of it: It is here; we cannot evade it; no substitutes for it have been found; and while the law may be sometimes hard for the individual, it is best for the race, because it ensures the survival of the fittest in every department. "

—Andrew Carnegie, from "The Gospel of Wealth," 1901

14 *Identifying Bias in Written Material* What ideas and words from Carnegie's article show his biases about the business world? LAFS.1112.RH.1.1, LAFS.1112.RH.4.10, LAFS.1112.SL.1.3

15 *Identifying Points of View* By the late 1800s, a major issue in American politics was whether laissez-faire and Social Darwinism were the best policies for the nation. Based on the text excerpt above, summarize Carnegie's point of view of this question. LAFS.1112.RH.4.10, SS.912.A.3.8, SS.912.A.3.10

Analyzing Visuals

Use the graph Why Did People Emigrate? *to answer the following questions.*

Source: *Historical Statistics of the United States.*

16 *Analyzing Geographic Patterns on Graphs* What pattern on the map helps to explain why Congress passed the Chinese Exclusion Act when it did? MAFS.912.S-ID.1, SS.912.A.3.7, SS.912.G.2.1

17 *Analyzing Geographic Distributions on Graphs* If the trend that is developing on the graph from 1900–1914 continues, make a prediction about how the distribution of immigrants in the United States will change in the following decades. MAFS.912.S-IC.2, MAFS.912.S-ID.1, SS.912.A.3.7, SS.912.G.2.1

Extended Response Questions

18 *Drawing Conclusions* Analyze the changes in the United States in the late 1800s. Write an essay that explains and draws conclusions about why the political and economic issues of the time led to the growth of political machines, a demand for civil service reform, problems for farmers, and the beginnings of the Populist movement. Select the most relevant details to support your conclusions, and revise and rewrite as necessary to ensure clarity in your writing. LAFS.1112.WHST.1.2, LAFS.1112.WHST.2.4, LAFS.1112.WHST.2.5, LAFS.1112.WHST.4.10, SS.912.A.3.1, SS.912.A.3.2, SS.912.A.3.11

19 *Discussing* Prepare for a class discussion on the debate over the money supply by reviewing your notes, the lesson materials, and conducting further research as needed. Then, as a class, divide into two groups, one representing big companies and banks, the other representing the government. Discuss why the big companies and banks wanted to have a gold standard while the government might prefer to switch to fiat currency. When participating, make sure to ask questions to respond thoughtfully to your classmates' remarks. LAFS.1112.RH.3.9, LAFS.1112.SL.1.1, LAFS.1112.SL.2.6, SS.912.A.3.10

Need Extra Help?

If You've Missed Question	**14**	**15**	**16**	**17**	**18**	**19**
Go to Lesson	3	3	1	1	4	4

◀ Matthew Calbraith Perry, commodore of the U.S. Navy, negotiated the opening of Japan to the West with the Treaty of Kanagawa in 1854.

FROM 1872 TO 1917

Becoming a World Power

The Granger Collection, New York

THE STORY MATTERS ...

International economic and military competition convinced the United States that it must become a world power, on par with Britain and Spain. By acquiring new lands before and after the Spanish-American War, the United States became more prominent, but it also took on new responsibilities. In the late 1800s, the United States increased its trade and military presence in East Asia and Latin America. By the early 1900s, it had created an American empire.

ESSENTIAL QUESTION

- How are empires built?

Place & Time: United States 1872–1917

U.S. economists, politicians, and other leaders recognized that economic growth could only come through expansion into foreign markets. With that in mind, the United States embarked on a path toward imperialism that included colonization and the acquisition of new territory. One strategic acquisition was the Panama Canal. After agreeing to pay for the rights to the project and the land around it, President Roosevelt pushed for the canal's completion. William Gorgas, a U.S. Army surgeon, helped control a major obstacle facing the construction of the Panama Canal: disease.

Step Into the Place

Read the quotes and look at the information presented on the map.

 Analyzing Historical Documents Did Roosevelt and Gorgas agree on the challenges the construction of the Panama Canal posed?

PRIMARY SOURCE

"No single great material work which remains to be undertaken on this continent is as of such consequence to the American people as the building of a canal across the isthmus connecting North and South America."

—Theodore Roosevelt, from a speech to Congress, 1901

PRIMARY SOURCE

"The route of the Panama Canal lay through a low, swampy country . . . where . . . yellow fever and malaria prevailed to an alarming extent. . . .

We appreciated that, if the Americans were subject to this disease to any considerable extent, we should have great difficulty in keeping them at Panama . . . and if we could afford to pay sufficiently high wages to induce them to stay, Congress, in all probability, would not sanction the continuance of the work, if we lost from yellow fever fifteen or sixteen hundred Americans every year."

—William C. Gorgas, from *Sanitation in Panama*, 1915

left page (t)Library of Congress, Prints & Photographs Division [LC-DIG-hec-03937], (tr)Library of Congress, Prints & Photographs Division [LC-USZC2-6273]; (bl to br)detail/White House Collection/The White House Historical Association; right page (bl to br)detail/White House Collection/The White House Historical Association

Step Into the Time

MAKING CONNECTIONS
Determine which president had the greatest influence on U.S. expansionism. Write a paragraph explaining how this leader pushed for expansion.

Grant 1869–1877

1878 U.S. signs treaty with Samoa to use the harbor of Pago Pago

Hayes 1877–1881

Garfield 1881

Arthur 1881–1885

Cleveland 1885–1889

U.S. PRESIDENTS

UNITED STATES

WORLD

1872   1877   1882   1887

1874 Britain annexes Fiji Islands

1882 Germany, Austria, and Italy form Triple Alliance

1889 First Pan-American conference is held

NEXT GENERATION SUNSHINE STATE STANDARDS
Students will understand the following benchmarks from the Florida NGSSS

LAFS.1112.RH.3.7: Integrate and evaluate multiple sources of information presented in diverse formats and media (e.g., visually, quantitatively, as well as in words) in order to address a question or solve a problem.

LAFS.1112.RH.3.9: Integrate information from diverse sources, both primary and secondary, into a coherent understanding of an idea or event, noting discrepancies among sources.

LAFS.1112.RH.4.10: By the end of grade 12, read and comprehend history/social studies texts in the grades 11–CCR text complexity band independently and proficiently.

SS.912.A.1.2: Utilize a variety of primary and secondary sources to identify author, historical significance, audience, and authenticity to understand a historical period.

SS.912.A.1.3: Utilize timelines to identify the time sequence of historical data.

SS.912.A.1.4: Analyze how images, symbols, objects, cartoons, graphs, charts, maps, and artwork may be used to interpret the significance of time periods and events from the past.

SS.912.A.4.1: Analyze the major factors that drove United States imperialism.

SS.912.A.4.4: Analyze the economic, military, and security motivations of the United States to complete the Panama Canal as well as major obstacles involved in its construction.

The Panama Canal

Legend:
- Canal Zone
- Canal route
-) (Locks

Timeline:

B. Harrison 1889–1893

1893 Americans overthrow Queen Liliuokalani of Hawaii

Cleveland 1893–1897

1898 USS *Maine* explodes in Havana Harbor

McKinley 1897–1901

T. Roosevelt 1901–1909

1904 Senate approves treaty leasing the Panama Canal

Taft 1909–1913

1892 — 1897 — 1902 — 1907 — 1912 — 1917

1894 Sino-Japanese War breaks out

1899 John Hay sends Open Door notes

1900 Boxer Rebellion begins in China

1904 Russo-Japanese War begins

LESSON 1
The Imperialist Vision

ESSENTIAL QUESTION

• How are empires built?

READING HELPDESK

Academic Vocabulary

• expansion • conference

Content Vocabulary

• imperialism
• protectorate

TAKING NOTES

Key Ideas and Details

Organizing As you read about the development of the United States as a world power, use the major headings of the lesson to create an outline for the lesson similar to the one below.
LAFS.1112.3.7, SS.912.A.4.1

> The Imperialist Vision
> I. Building Support for Imperialism
>   A.
>   B.
>   C.

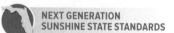

**NEXT GENERATION
SUNSHINE STATE STANDARDS**

LAFS.1112.RH.2.4: Determine the meaning of words and phrases as they are used in a text, including analyzing how an author uses and refines the meaning of a key term over the course of a text (e.g., how Madison defines faction in Federalist No. 10).

LAFS.1112.RH.3.7: Integrate and evaluate multiple sources of information presented in diverse formats and media (e.g., visually, quantitatively, as well as in words) in order to address a question or solve a problem.

LAFS.1112.RH.3.8: Evaluate an author's premises, claims, and evidence by corroborating or challenging them with other information.

IT MATTERS BECAUSE
During the late 1800s, the desire to find new markets, increase trade, and build a powerful navy caused the United States to become more involved in international affairs.

Building Support for Imperialism
GUIDING QUESTION *Why did the United States assert itself as a world power?*

Following the Civil War, most Americans showed little interest in expanding their nation's territory outside the United States. Instead, they focused on reconstructing the South, settling the West, and building up industry. In the 1880s, economic and military competition from Europe and a growing feeling of cultural superiority convinced many Americans that the United States should become a world power.

A Desire for New Markets
Many European nations were expanding overseas, a development called the New Imperialism. **Imperialism** is the economic and political domination of a strong nation over weaker ones. European nations expanded their power overseas for many reasons. They needed to import raw materials for manufacturing. High tariffs in industrialized nations—intended to protect domestic industries—reduced trade, forcing companies to look for new markets overseas. Investment opportunities had also slowed in Western Europe, so Europeans began looking overseas for places to invest their capital.

To protect their investments, European nations began exerting control over territories, making some into colonies and others into **protectorates.** In a protectorate, the imperial power protected local rulers against rebellions and invasion. In return, rulers usually had to accept Europeans' advice on how to govern their countries.

As the United States industrialized, many Americans noticed the **expansion** of European power overseas and took an interest in the new imperialism. Many concluded that the nation needed new overseas markets to keep its economy strong.

Continued on page 181

A Feeling of Superiority

Certain key ideas encouraged Americans to support the nation's expansion overseas. Historian John Fiske argued that English-speaking nations had superior character, ideas, and systems of government. Many Americans linked his ideas, known as Anglo-Saxonism, with the idea of Manifest Destiny. These Americans believed the nation was destined to expand overseas to spread its civilization to others.

PRIMARY SOURCE

"The work which the English race began when it colonized North America is destined to go on until every land . . . that is not already the seat of an old civilization shall become English in its language, in its religion, in political habits and traditions, and to a predominant extent in the blood of its people."

—John Fiske, from "Manifest Destiny," *Harper's Magazine*, 1885

Another influential advocate of Anglo-Saxonism was Josiah Strong, a popular American minister in the late 1800s. Strong linked Anglo-Saxonism to Christian missionary ideas. His ideas influenced many Americans. "The Anglo-Saxon," Strong declared, "[is] divinely commissioned to be, in a peculiar sense, his brother's keeper." By linking missionary work to Anglo-Saxonism, Strong convinced many Americans to support an expansion of American power overseas.

Building a Modern Navy

As these ideas gained support, the United States became more assertive in foreign affairs. In 1888, the country risked war to prevent Germany from taking control of Samoa. The crisis ended peacefully. However, it led some Americans to believe that the United States would be shut out of foreign markets if it did not build up its navy and acquire bases overseas.

imperialism the actions used by one nation to exercise political or economic control over a smaller or weaker nation

protectorate a country that is technically independent but is actually under the control of another country

expansion the act or process of increasing or enlarging the extent, number, volume, or scope

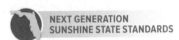

NEXT GENERATION SUNSHINE STATE STANDARDS

Continued from page 180

LAFS.1112.RH.4.10: By the end of grade 12, read and comprehend history/social studies texts in the grades 11–CCR text complexity band independently and proficiently.

LAFS.1112.WHST.1.1: Write arguments focused on discipline-specific content.

LAFS.1112.WHST.2.4: Produce clear and coherent writing in which the development, organization, and style are appropriate to task, purpose, and audience.

LAFS.1112.WHST.2.5: Develop and strengthen writing as needed by planning, revising, editing, rewriting, or trying a new approach, focusing on addressing what is most significant for a specific purpose and audience.

Continued on page 183

Major Imperial Powers 1900

ARCTIC OCEAN

BELGIUM
NETH.
GREAT BRITAIN
GERMANY
FRANCE
RUSSIA
UNITED STATES
ATLANTIC OCEAN
OTTOMAN EMPIRE
CHINA
PACIFIC OCEAN
EQUATOR
INDIAN OCEAN
TROPIC OF CANCER
TROPIC OF CAPRICORN
40°N
0°
40°S
140°W
100°W
140°E
180°

0   2000 miles
0   2000 km
Miller projection

GEOGRAPHY CONNECTION

A desire for new markets led many nations to expand overseas.

1 **GEOGRAPHIC PATTERNS** *Which two regions were most affected by European imperialism?*
LAFS.1112.RH.3.7, SS.912.G.1.2, SS.912.G.2.3

2 **GEOGRAPHIC DISTRIBUTIONS** *Which imperial power had the most widely disbursed territories?*
LAFS.1112.RH.3.7, SS.912.A.4.1, SS.912.G.1.2, SS.912.G.2.3

Empires
- British
- Chinese
- Belgian
- United States
- Dutch
- French
- German
- Ottoman
- Russian

In the wedding depicted in this cartoon, President McKinley is Uncle Sam's best man and Sanford B. Dole gives away the bride, who represents Hawaii.

1 *Interpreting Political Cartoons* Do you think the artist believes the American people want to annex Hawaii? Explain. LAFS.1112.RH.3.7, SS.912.A.1.4, SS.912.A.4.2, SS.912.H.1.5, SS.912.H.3.1

2 *Analyzing Political Cartoons* Use your knowledge of social issues in America in the late 1800s. How is the cartoon using the emotions of some Americans to sway their opinion about annexation? LAFS.1112.RH.3.7, LAFS.1112.RH.3.8, SS.912.A.1.4, SS.912.A.4.2, SS.912.H.1.5, SS.912.H.3.1

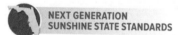

NEXT GENERATION SUNSHINE STATE STANDARDS

Continued from page 181

LAFS.1112.WHST.4.10: Write routinely over extended time frames (time for reflection and revision) and shorter time frames (a single sitting or a day or two) for a range of discipline-specific tasks, purposes, and audiences.

SS.912.A.1.2: Utilize a variety of primary and secondary sources to identify author, historical significance, audience, and authenticity to understand a historical period.

SS.912.A.1.4: Analyze how images, symbols, objects, cartoons, graphs, charts, maps, and artwork may be used to interpret the significance of time periods and events from the past.

Continued on page 183

Analyzing
PRIMARY SOURCES

Mahan on Military Bases

❝ To provide resting places for them [warships], where they can coal and repair, would be one of the first duties of a government proposing to itself the development of the power of the nation at sea. ❞

—Alfred Thayer Mahan, from *The Influence of Sea Power Upon History*, 1890

DBQ *IDENTIFYING CENTRAL IDEAS* Why do you think establishing "resting places" is a key issue for developing naval power? LAFS.1112.RH.3.7, LAFS.1112.RH.4.10, SS.912.A.1.2, SS.912.A.4.1

U.S. naval officer Captain Alfred T. Mahan helped build public support for a navy when he published *The Influence of Sea Power Upon History* in 1890. Mahan pointed out that many prosperous nations had a large fleet of merchant ships to trade with the world and a large navy to defend the nation's trade. Mahan's book helped build public support for a big navy. Two powerful senators, Henry Cabot Lodge and Albert J. Beveridge, used their position to convince Congress to support a new navy. In the executive branch, Benjamin Tracy, secretary of the navy under President Harrison, John D. Long, secretary of the navy under President McKinley, and his assistant secretary Theodore Roosevelt, all supported Mahan's ideas.

By the 1890s, several different ideas had come together. Business leaders wanted new markets overseas. Anglo-Saxonism had convinced many Americans they were destined to expand into the world, while growing European imperialism threatened U.S. security. These ideas, along with Mahan's book, convinced Congress to authorize a large modern navy.

☑ **READING PROGRESS CHECK**

Summarizing Why did Americans' attitudes toward overseas expansion change?

American Expansion in the Pacific

GUIDING QUESTION *Why did the United States look to the Pacific for new markets?*

From the earliest days of the Republic, Americans had expanded their nation by moving westward. When looking overseas for new markets, the United States naturally looked to the Pacific.

Perry Opens Japan

In 1852, President Millard Fillmore ordered Commodore Matthew C. Perry to negotiate a trade treaty with Japan. In 1853, warships under Perry's command entered Edo Bay (now Tokyo Bay). Japan's rulers, fearing the influence of Western ideas, had limited contact with the West. After seeing the warships, however, the Japanese realized they were not powerful

The Granger Collection, New York

enough to resist modern weapons. In 1854, Japan signed the Treaty of Kanagawa, giving the United States trading rights at two Japanese ports.

Annexing Samoa and Hawaii

As trade with Asia grew, the United States needed ports for its ships to refuel and resupply as they crossed the Pacific. Pago Pago, in the Samoan Islands, had one of the finest harbors in the South Pacific. In 1878, the United States negotiated permission to open a base there. An 1899 agreement divided Samoa between Germany and the United States.

More important was Hawaii. Americans found that sugarcane grew well in Hawaii, and planters established sugar plantations there. In 1875, the United States signed a treaty exempting Hawaiian sugar from tariffs. This action was taken to aid Hawaii during an economic recession and to prevent Hawaii from turning to Britain or France for help. When the treaty was up for renewal, the United States insisted Hawaii grant it exclusive rights to a naval base at Pearl Harbor.

In 1887, wealthy sugar planters led by Sanford Dole forced the Hawaiian king to accept a new constitution that limited the king's authority. The planters eventually wanted to make Hawaii part of the United States. Tensions grew worse when Congress passed a new tariff in 1890. The tariff gave subsidies to American sugar producers, making Hawaiian sugar more expensive. The planters knew that if Hawaii joined the United States, they too would get the subsidies. The next year, Queen Liliuokalani ascended the Hawaiian throne and tried to restore the monarchy's authority.

In response, the planters overthrew the queen. Backed by the American ambassador and U.S. Marines, the planters forced Liliuokalani to give up power, and asked Dole to serve as president of the new Hawaiian Republic. Dole then requested the United States annex Hawaii. President Cleveland, who opposed imperialism, tried instead to restore the queen to power, but Hawaii's new leaders refused. Instead, they decided to wait until a new president took office. In 1898, under President McKinley, the United States annexed Hawaii and McKinley chose Dole to be Hawaii's first governor.

✔ **READING PROGRESS CHECK**

Explaining How did the search for new overseas markets push the United States to become a world power?

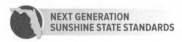

NEXT GENERATION SUNSHINE STATE STANDARDS

Continued from page 182

SS.912.A.4.1: Analyze the major factors that drove United States imperialism.

SS.912.A.4.2: Explain the motives of the United States acquisition of the territories.

SS.912.G.1.2: Use spatial perspective and appropriate geographic terms and tools, including the Six Essential Elements, as organizational schema to describe any given place.

SS.912.G.2.3: Use geographic terms and tools to analyze case studies of regional issues in different parts of the world that have critical economic, physical, or political ramifications.

SS.912.H.1.1: Relate works in the arts (architecture, dance, music, theatre, and visual arts) of varying styles and genre according to the periods in which they were created.

SS.912.H.1.5: Examine artistic response to social issues and new ideas in various cultures.

LESSON 1 REVIEW

Reviewing Vocabulary

1. *Explaining* How did Anglo-Saxonism help foster American imperialism? LAFS.1112.RH.2.4, SS.912.A.4.1

Using Your Notes

2. *Listing* Review the notes you completed during the lesson to list the factors that led the United States to realize an imperialist vision in the 1890s. SS.912.A.4.1, SS.912.A.4.2

Answering the Guiding Questions

3. *Analyzing* Why did the United States assert itself as a world power? SS.912.A.4.1, SS.912.G.2.3

4. *Summarizing* Why did the United States look to the Pacific for new markets? SS.912.A.4.2, SS.912.G.2.3

5. *Describing* What role did Sanford Dole play in Hawaii's annexation to the United States? SS.912.A.4.1, SS.912.A.4.2

Writing Activity

6. ARGUMENT Suppose that you are living in the United States in the 1890s. Write a letter to the president persuading him to support or oppose an imperialist policy for the United States. When writing your letter, focus on the details that would be most effective at persuading your audience. LAFS.1112.WHST.1.1, LAFS.1112.WHST.2.4, LAFS.1112.WHST.4.10, SS.912.A.4.1

LESSON 2
The Spanish-American War

ESSENTIAL QUESTION

• How are empires built?

READING HELPDESK

Academic Vocabulary

• intervene • volunteer

Content Vocabulary

• yellow journalism
• autonomy
• jingoism

TAKING NOTES

Key Ideas and Details

Organizing As you read about the Spanish-American War, complete a graphic organizer like the one below by listing the circumstances that contributed to war with Spain.
LAFS.1112.RH.3.7, SS.912.A.4.3

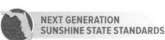

NEXT GENERATION SUNSHINE STATE STANDARDS

ELD.K12.ELL.SI.1: English language learners communicate for social and instructional purposes within the school setting.

ELD.K12.ELL.SS.1: English language learners communicate information, ideas and concepts necessary for academic success in the content area of Social Studies.

LAFS.1112.RH.1.1: Cite specific textual evidence to support analysis of primary and secondary sources, connecting insights gained from specific details to an understanding of the text as a whole.

Continued on page 187

IT MATTERS BECAUSE

During the Spanish-American War, the United States defeated Spanish troops in Cuba and the Philippines. Afterward, the United States annexed the Philippines and became an imperial power.

The Coming of War

GUIDING QUESTION *Why was the United States willing to go to war with Spain over Cuba?*

Cuba was one of Spain's oldest colonies in the Americas. Its sugarcane plantations generated considerable wealth for Spain and produced nearly one-third of the world's sugar in the mid-1800s. Until Spain abolished slavery in 1886, about one-third of the Cuban population was enslaved and forced to work for wealthy landowners on the plantations.

In 1868, Cuban rebels declared independence and launched a guerrilla war against Spanish authorities. Lacking internal support, the rebellion collapsed a decade later. Many Cuban rebels then fled to the United States, including their leader, José Martí.

By the early 1890s, the United States and Cuba had become closely linked economically. Cuba exported much of its sugar to the United States, and Americans had invested approximately $50 million in Cuba's sugar plantations, mines, and railroads. These economic ties created a crisis in 1894, when the United States imposed a new tariff on sugar that devastated Cuba's economy. With Cuba in financial distress, the Cuban rebels launched a new rebellion in February 1895. Martí died during the fighting, but the rebels seized control of eastern Cuba, declared independence, and formally established the Republic of Cuba in September 1895.

America Supports Cuba

When the uprising began, President Cleveland declared the United States neutral. However, stories of Spanish atrocities in two major newspapers, the *New York Journal* and the *New York World,* swayed many Americans in the rebels' favor. The news reports, in which writers exaggerated or made up stories to attract readers, became known as **yellow journalism.** Although some stories were invented, Cubans indeed suffered horribly.

The Spanish sent nearly 200,000 troops to put down the rebellion. The rebels destroyed a considerable amount of property, some belonging to Americans, hoping to provoke American intervention in the war. To prevent villagers from helping the rebels, the Spanish herded hundreds of thousands of rural men, women, and children into "reconcentration camps," where tens of thousands died of starvation and disease.

Calls for War

In 1897, William McKinley became president of the United States. In September 1897, he asked Spain whether the United States could help negotiate an end to the conflict, so that the United States would not have to **intervene** in the war. Spain removed Weyler from office and offered the Cubans **autonomy,** but only if Cuba remained part of the Spanish Empire. The rebels refused to negotiate.

Spain's concessions enraged many Spanish loyalists in Cuba. In January 1898, the loyalists rioted in Havana. McKinley sent the battleship USS *Maine* to Havana to protect Americans living there. Then, on February 15, 1898, the *Maine* exploded in Havana Harbor. To this day, no one is sure why the *Maine* exploded. Many Americans believed the Spanish did it. "Remember the *Maine*!" became the rallying cry for war against Spain.

McKinley faced tremendous pressure to go to war. Within the Republican Party, **jingoism**—aggressive nationalism—was very strong. On April 11, 1898, McKinley asked Congress to authorize the use of force. On April 19, Congress proclaimed Cuba independent, demanded that Spain withdraw from the island, and authorized the president to use armed force. On April 24, Spain declared war on the United States.

✓ **READING PROGRESS CHECK**

Examining What events led to the war with Spain in 1898?

A War on Two Fronts

GUIDING QUESTION *How was the Spanish-American War different from earlier U.S. wars?*

The U.S. Navy was ready for war with Spain. The navy blockaded Cuba, and Commodore George Dewey, commander of the American naval squadron based in Hong Kong, was ordered to attack the Spanish fleet based in the Philippines, then a Spanish colony. American naval planners wanted to prevent the Spanish fleet from sailing east to attack the United States.

---

yellow journalism type of sensational, biased, and often false reporting for the sake of attracting readers

intervene to get involved in the affairs of another

autonomy the quality of or state of being self-governing

jingoism extreme nationalism marked by aggressive foreign policy

Florida CONNECTION

José Martí

José Martí was a leader in the Cuban rebellion. Exiled from Cuba, he lived in New York City most of his life. Martí brought together other Cuban exiles in the United States. Together they raised funds, purchased weapons, and prepared troops for a hoped for invasion of Cuba.

In 1894 José Martí met with leaders of the Cuba Libre ("Free Cuba") movement in Ybor City, Florida—now part of Tampa. Ybor City was known as the Cigar Capital of the World, and many of its residents were immigrants from Cuba who worked in the cigar industry. SS.912.A.4.11

President McKinley sent the battleship *Maine* to Cuba to help Americans evacuate. When the ship exploded, an enraged nation blamed Spain, although the explosion may have originated within the ship. "Remember the *Maine*!" became the battle cry for war.

▶ **CRITICAL THINKING**
Analyzing What do you think contributed to American sympathy with the Cubans?
LAFS.1112.RH.3.7, SS.912.A.4.3

The Granger Collection, New York

SKILLS PRACTICE

When trying to learn a lot of new ideas, names, and events, use the words *who*, *what*, *when*, and *where* to ask questions. As you read about the war between Spain and the United States, use words you know in the questions.
ELD.K12.ELL.SI.1, ELD.K12.ELL.SS.1

volunteer person who joins the military by choice

Rough Rider and future president Theodore Roosevelt

The Battle of Manila Bay

On May 1, 1898, the American ships in Dewey's squadron entered Manila Bay in the Philippines. They quickly destroyed the Spanish fleet. Dewey's quick victory surprised McKinley. Hastily, the army assembled 20,000 troops to sail from San Francisco to the Philippines. On the way, the Americans also seized the island of Guam, another Spanish possession.

While waiting for the American troops to arrive, Dewey contacted Emilio Aguinaldo, a Filipino revolutionary leader who had staged an unsuccessful uprising against the Spanish in 1896. Now, while Aguinaldo and his rebels took control of most of the islands, American troops seized the Philippine capital of Manila.

American Forces in Cuba

The Spanish in Cuba were not prepared for war. Their soldiers were weak and sick, and their warships were old with untrained crews. If the United States could defeat the Spanish fleet, Spain would not be able to supply its troops in Cuba. Eventually, Spain would have to surrender.

The U.S. Army was not prepared for war, either. The army had recruited **volunteers** but lacked proper resources to train and equip them. One volunteer cavalry unit was a rough mix of cowboys, miners, and law officers known as the "Rough Riders." Theodore Roosevelt was second in command.

Between June 22 and 24, some 17,000 U.S. troops had landed east of Santiago, Cuba. The Spanish fleet, well protected by powerful shore-based guns, occupied Santiago Harbor. Americans wanted to capture those guns to drive the Spanish fleet out of the harbor and into battle with the American fleet waiting nearby.

On July 1, American troops attacked Spanish positions near Santiago and the San Juan Heights. The Rough Riders and the all African American 9th and 10th Cavalry Regiments attacked and held Kettle Hill, then assisted in the capture of San Juan Hill. In Santiago the Spanish commander ordered the Spanish fleet to flee the harbor. On July 3, American warships attacked them, destroying every Spanish vessel. Later, the Spanish in Santiago surrendered, leaving American troops to occupy nearby Puerto Rico.

✓ READING PROGRESS CHECK

Summarizing On what two fronts was the Spanish-American War fought?

An American Empire

GUIDING QUESTION *How did the United States develop an overseas empire?*

As American and Spanish leaders met to discuss the terms for a peace treaty, Americans debated what to do about their newly acquired lands. Cuba would receive its independence as promised, and Spain had agreed to the U.S. annexation of Guam and Puerto Rico. The big question was what to do with the Philippines. The United States faced a difficult choice—remain true to its republican ideals or become an imperial power that ruled a foreign country without the consent of its people. The issue sparked an intense political debate.

The Debate Over Annexation

Many people emphasized the economic and military benefits of taking the Philippines. It would provide another Pacific naval base, a stopover on the way to China, and a large market for American goods. Others believed America had a duty to help "less civilized" peoples. "Surely this Spanish

©Bettmann/Corbis

war has not been a grab for the empire," commented one minister, "but a heroic effort [to] free the oppressed and to teach millions of ignorant, debased human beings thus freed how to live."

Not all Americans supported annexation. An anti-imperialist movement quickly formed and many prominent Americans voiced their opposition to the United States becoming an imperial power. Andrew Carnegie argued that the cost of empire far outweighed the economic benefits. Samuel Gompers, the head of the American Federation of Labor, worried that competition from cheap Filipino labor would drive down American wages. The social worker and reformer Jane Addams and the writer Samuel Clemens both believed imperialism violated American principles and traditions. Many people argued that it was inconsistent for a democratic-republic founded on the idea of self-government to rule over others who would have no say in who was appointed to rule them.

Despite the objections of anti-imperialists, President McKinley ultimately decided to annex the islands. He later explained his reasoning as follows:

PRIMARY SOURCE

"When I next realized that the Philippines had dropped into our laps I confess I did not know what to do with them. I sought counsel from all sides—Democrats as well as Republicans—but got little help. . . . And one night late it came to me this way—I don't know how it was, but it came: (1) That we could not give them back to Spain—that would be cowardly and dishonorable; (2) that we could not turn them over to France and Germany—our commercial rivals in the Orient—that would be bad business and discreditable; (3) that we could not leave them to themselves—they were unfit for self-government—and they would soon have anarchy and misrule over there worse than Spain's was; and (4) that there was nothing left for us to do but to take them all, and to educate the Filipinos, and uplift and civilize and Christianize them, and by God's grace do the very best we could by them, as our fellow-men for whom Christ also died."

—James Rusling, "Interview with President William McKinley," *The Christian Advocate*, January 1903

McKinley's thinking blended the ideas of many military and business leaders with the ideas of Anglo-Saxonism. On December 10, 1898, the United States and Spain signed the Treaty of Paris, under which Cuba became independent. Also, the United States acquired Puerto Rico and Guam and paid Spain $20 million for the Philippines. After an intense debate, the Senate approved the treaty in February 1899.

1898: A Turning Point

The year 1898 was a major turning point in American history. In just a few short months, the United States had defeated a European nation, demonstrated that its navy was one of the most powerful in the world, and had acquired its own empire. The reputation of the United States for being a nation that did not involve itself in global affairs was shattered. Increasingly the world's other great powers had to take American perspectives and policies into account, and in the years ahead the United States would find itself drawn into issues and events thousands of miles from its own shores. After 1898, the United States had become a world power.

The Platt Amendment

Although the United States had promised to grant Cuba its independence, conditions were attached to the new Cuban constitution. The Platt Amendment, submitted by Senator Orville Platt, specified the following: (1) Cuba could not make any treaty with another nation that would weaken its independence; (2) Cuba had to allow the United States to buy or lease

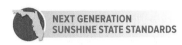

NEXT GENERATION SUNSHINE STATE STANDARDS

Continued from page 184

LAFS.1112.RH.2.4: Determine the meaning of words and phrases as they are used in a text, including analyzing how an author uses and refines the meaning of a key term over the course of a text (e.g., how Madison defines faction in Federalist No. 10).

LAFS.1112.RH.2.6: Evaluate authors' differing points of view on the same historical event or issue by assessing the authors' claims, reasoning, and evidence.

LAFS.1112.RH.3.7: Integrate and evaluate multiple sources of information presented in diverse formats and media (e.g., visually, quantitatively, as well as in words) in order to address a question or solve a problem.

LAFS.1112.RH.3.9: Integrate information from diverse sources, both primary and secondary, into a coherent understanding of an idea or event, noting discrepancies among sources.

LAFS.1112.RH.4.10: By the end of grade 12, read and comprehend history/social studies texts in the grades 11–CCR text complexity band independently and proficiently.

LAFS.1112.SL.1.3: Evaluate a speaker's point of view, reasoning, and use of evidence and rhetoric, assessing the stance, premises, links among ideas, word choice, points of emphasis, and tone used.

LAFS.1112.WHST.1.2: Write informative/ explanatory texts, including the narration of historical events, scientific procedures/ experiments, or technical processes.

LAFS.1112.WHST.2.4: Produce clear and coherent writing in which the development, organization, and style are appropriate to task, purpose, and audience.

LAFS.1112.WHST.3.7: Conduct short as well as more sustained research projects to answer a question (including a self-generat-ed question) or solve a problem; narrow or broaden the inquiry when appropriate; synthesize multiple sources on the subject, demonstrating understanding of the subject under investigation.

LAFS.1112.WHST.4.10: Write routinely over extended time frames (time for reflection and revision) and shorter time frames (a single sitting or a day or two) for a range of discipline-specific tasks, purposes, and audiences.

SS.912.A.1.2: Utilize a variety of primary and secondary sources to identify author, historical significance, audience, and authenticity to understand a historical period.

SS.912.A.1.4: Analyze how images, symbols, objects, cartoons, graphs, charts, maps, and artwork may be used to interpret the significance of time periods and events from the past.

Continued on page 188

NEXT GENERATION SUNSHINE STATE STANDARDS

Continued from page 187

SS.912.A.1.6: Use case studies to explore social, political, legal, and economic relationships in history.

SS.912.A.4.1: Analyze the major factors that drove United States imperialism.

SS.912.A.4.2: Explain the motives of the United States acquisition of the territories.

SS.912.A.4.3: Examine causes, course, and consequences of the Spanish American War.

SS.912.A.4.11: Examine key events and peoples in Florida history as they relate to United States history.

naval stations in Cuba; (3) Cuba's debts had to be kept low to prevent foreign countries from landing troops to enforce payment; and (4) the United States would have the right to intervene to protect Cuban independence and keep order. The Platt Amendment, which effectively made Cuba an American protectorate, remained in effect until its repeal in 1934.

Governing Puerto Rico

In 1900, Congress passed the Foraker Act, establishing a civil government for Puerto Rico. The law provided for an elected legislature, and a governor and executive council that were appointed by the U.S. president. Congress gradually allowed Puerto Ricans greater self-government. In 1917, it granted Puerto Ricans U.S. citizenship. Thirty years later, Puerto Ricans were allowed to elect their own governor. A debate eventually began over whether Puerto Rico should become a state, become independent, or continue as a self-governing commonwealth of the United States. The debate over Puerto Rico's status continues today.

Rebellion in the Philippines

In 1899, Emilio Aguinaldo ordered his troops to attack the American soldiers who had been sent there. Aguinaldo wanted the Philippines to be independent. To fight the Filipino guerrillas, the U.S. military established reconcentration camps to separate Filipino guerrillas from civilians. Thousands died from disease and starvation. Many U.S. soldiers died fighting the guerrillas.

While American troops fought the guerrillas, the first U.S. civilian governor of the islands, William Howard Taft, tried to win over the

(l)Library of Congress, Prints & Photographs Division [LC-DIG-ggbain-04826]; (r)Hulton Archive/Archive Photos/Getty Images

ANALYZING PRIMARY SOURCES

The Annexation Debate

Americans were divided over whether the United States should give the Filipinos their independence or become an imperial power by annexing the Philippines.

PRIMARY SOURCE

❝The Opposition tells us that we ought not to govern a people without their consent. I answer, The rule of liberty that all just government derives its authority from the consent of the governed, applies only to those who are capable of self-government. We govern the Indians without their consent, we govern our territories without their consent, we govern our children without their consent.... Would not the people of the Philippines prefer the just, humane, civilizing government of this Republic to the savage, bloody rule of pillage and extortion from which we have rescued them?❞

—from *The Meaning of the Times*

Albert J. Beveridge
United States Senator

PRIMARY SOURCE

❝A harbor and coaling station in the Philippines would answer every trade and military necessity and such a concession could have been secured at any time without difficulty. It is not necessary to own people in order to trade with them. We carry on trade today with every part of the world, and our commerce has expanded more rapidly than the commerce of any European empire.

... Imperialism finds no warrant in the Bible. The command 'Go ye into all the world and preach the gospel to every creature' has no Gatling gun attachment. ...❞

—from *Speeches of William Jennings Bryan*

William Jennings Bryan
Presidential Candidate

DBQ Analyzing Historical Documents

1. **Making Inferences** According to Albert Beveridge, why is annexation of the Philippines an honorable course of action? What bias does the language he uses reveal? LAFS.1112.RH.1.1, LAFS.1112.RH.2.6, LAFS.1112.RH.3.9, LAFS.1112.RH.4.10, LAFS.1112.SL.1.3, LAFS.1112.WHST.3.9, SS.912.A.1.2, SS.912.A.1.6, SS.912.A.4.2

2. **Analyzing** What are William Jennings Bryan's two main criticisms of imperialism? LAFS.1112.RH.2.6, LAFS.1112.RH.3.9, LAFS.1112.RH.4.10, SS.912.A.1.2, SS.912.A.1.6

Filipinos by improving education, transportation, and health care. These reforms slowly reduced Filipino hostility. In March 1901, American troops captured Aguinaldo. On July 4, 1902, the United States declared the war over. Gradually the Filipinos gained more control over their government. By the mid-1930s, they elected their own congress and president. In 1946, they gained full independence from the United States.

The Economic Effects of the War

In 1897, the year before the war, Americans had invested roughly $700 million in business ventures overseas. By 1904, they had invested over $2.5 billion. The war made Cuba safe again, and American investment in sugar plantations and mining surged. Hawaii was now an American territory and companies there no longer had to pay tariffs to ship goods to the United States, making it attractive to investors. Puerto Rico was in a similar position. American investors revived the island's sugar industry and expanded its tobacco industry. American investments in the Philippines helped build railroads and open mines, and expanded its sugar industry as well.

All of these developments came at a cost. Together, the war with Spain and the battle against the Filipino guerrillas had cost some $400 million. Over 5,400 men had died in the war with Spain, and another 4,200 died fighting Filipino guerrillas. The war also led to a steady increase in naval spending, from $64 million in 1899 to $135 million in 1912. The spending helped stimulate parts of the economy related to shipbuilding, though it also diverted money from investment in other areas. But as a new world power with far-flung bases and territories, the United States now needed a larger naval force to project its power and safeguard its interests.

✓ READING PROGRESS CHECK

Explaining What did the United States do to expand its territorial interests?

Library of Congress, Prints & Photographs Division [LC-USZC4-5392]

POLITICAL CARTOONS — THE DEBATE OVER EMPIRE

Many people debated the decision to annex the Philippines, arguing over costs and benefits of the new empire.

President McKinley raises the American flag over the Philippines while William Jennings Bryan tries to chop it down.

1 *Identifying Central Ideas* Based on the cartoon, what do you think McKinley is trying to accomplish? LAFS.1112.RH.3.7, SS.912.A.1.4

2 *Drawing Conclusions* How do the actions of McKinley in the cartoon represent his feelings about U.S. imperialism? LAFS.1112.RH.3.7, SS.912.A.1.4, SS.912.H.1.5

LESSON 2 REVIEW

Reviewing Vocabulary

1. *Describing* Describe the level of autonomy that Cuba obtained after the Spanish-American War. LAFS.1112.RH.2.4

2. *Identifying Central Ideas* Identify two results of the United States's intervening in the revolution in Cuba. LAFS.1112.RH.2.4

Using Your Notes

3. *Finding the Main Idea* Review the notes that you completed during the lesson to identify how the Spanish-American War altered America's foreign policy. SS.912.A.4.1, SS.912.A.4.2, SS.912.A.4.3

Answering the Guiding Questions

4. *Explaining* Why was the United States willing to go to war with Spain over Cuba? SS.912.A.4.3

5. *Contrasting* How was the Spanish-American War different from earlier U.S. wars? SS.912.A.4.3

6. *Analyzing* How did the United States develop an overseas empire? SS.912.A.4.1, SS.912.A.4.2

Writing Activity

7. **NARRATIVE** Suppose that you are a Filipino living during the time of the U.S. annexation of the Philippine Islands. Write a journal entry in which you describe your feelings about American control of the islands. Conduct additional research to help you construct an effective narrative. LAFS.1112.WHST.1.2, LAFS.1112.WHST.2.4, LAFS.1112.WHST.3.7, LAFS.1112.WHST.3.9, LAFS.1112.WHST.4.10, SS.912.A.4.1, SS.912.A.4.2

LESSON 3
New American Diplomacy

ESSENTIAL QUESTION
• How are empires built?

READING HELPDESK

Academic Vocabulary

• access   • tension

Content Vocabulary

• sphere of influence
• Open Door policy
• dollar diplomacy
• guerrilla

TAKING NOTES

Key Ideas and Details

Organizing Complete a graphic organizer similar to the one below to list reasons the United States wanted a canal through Central America.
LAFS.1112.RH.3.7, SS.912.A.4.4

Reasons to Build Canal

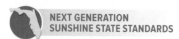

NEXT GENERATION SUNSHINE STATE STANDARDS

LAFS.1112.RH.2.4: Determine the meaning of words and phrases as they are used in a text, including analyzing how an author uses and refines the meaning of a key term over the course of a text (e.g., how Madison defines faction in Federalist No. 10).

LAFS.1112.RH.4.10: By the end of grade 12, read and comprehend history/social studies texts in the grades 11–CCR text complexity band independently and proficiently.

Continued on page 194

IT MATTERS BECAUSE

The United States's influence continued to expand into foreign countries. President Theodore Roosevelt mediated disputes in Asia and Latin America and acquired the Panama Canal Zone. Presidents Taft and Wilson increased U.S. trade and influence in Latin America.

American Diplomacy in Asia

GUIDING QUESTION *Why did the United States want to eliminate spheres of influence in China?*

In 1899, the United States was a major power in Asia, with naval bases all across the Pacific. Operating from those bases, the United States Navy—by then the world's third-largest navy—could exert American power anywhere in East Asia. The nation's main interest in Asia, however, was not conquest but commerce. Between 1895 and 1900, U.S. exports to China quadrupled. Although China bought only about two percent of U.S. exports, the vast Chinese markets excited American business leaders, especially those in the textile, oil, and steel industries.

The Open Door Policy

In 1894, war erupted between China and Japan over Korea, which was a client state dependent upon China. Western observers were astonished when Japan easily defeated China's massive military. The war showed that Japan had mastered Western technology and that China was weaker than anyone had thought. In the peace treaty, China recognized Korea's independence and gave Japan territory in Manchuria.

The Russians were concerned about Japan's rising power. They did not want Japan to acquire the territory in Manchuria because it bordered Russia. Backed by France and Germany, Russia forced Japan to return the Manchurian territory it had acquired. Then, in 1898, Russia demanded China lease the territory to Russia instead.

Leasing meant the territory would still belong to China, even though a foreign government would maintain overall control. Soon Germany, France, and Britain also demanded "leaseholds" in China.

Each leasehold became the center of a country's **sphere of influence,** an area where a foreign nation controlled economic development.

U.S. politicians and businessmen worried that China would be divided among the Europeans and Americans would not be allowed to do business there. President McKinley and Secretary of State John Hay both supported what they called an **Open Door policy,** which would allow all countries to trade with China.

In 1899, Hay asked countries with leaseholds in China not to discriminate against other nations wanting to do business in their sphere of influence. Each nation responded by saying it accepted the Open Door policy but would not follow it unless all the others agreed. Once Hay had received assurances from all of the nations with leaseholds, he declared that the United States expected the other powers to uphold the policy. The policy helped the U.S. economy by ensuring that American companies could continue to trade with China.

The Boxer Rebellion

While foreign countries debated **access** to China's market, secret Chinese societies organized to fight foreign control and influence. One group, the Society of Righteous and Harmonious Fists, was known to Westerners as the Boxers. In 1900, this group decided to destroy both the "foreign devils" and their Chinese Christian converts, whom they believed were corrupting Chinese society.

In what came to be called the Boxer Rebellion, the Boxers and some Chinese troops attacked foreign embassies in Peking (now Beijing) and Tientsin (now Tianjin), killing more than 200 foreigners, including many Christian missionaries. After the German ambassador to China was killed, eight nations—Germany, Austria-Hungary, Britain, France, Italy, Japan, Russia, and the United States—intervened. A large multinational force rescued the foreigners and ended the rebellion.

During the crisis, Secretary of State John Hay worked with British diplomats to persuade the other powers not to partition China. In a second set of Open Door notes, Hay convinced the participating powers to accept compensation from China for damages caused by the rebellion. After some discussion, the powers agreed not to break up China into European-controlled colonies. The United States retained access to China's lucrative trade in tea, spices, and silk and gained a larger market for its own goods.

☑ **READING PROGRESS CHECK**

Making Inferences What was the importance of the Open Door policy to the United States?

sphere of influence
section of a country where a foreign nation enjoys special rights and powers

Open Door policy a policy that allowed each foreign nation in China to trade freely in the other nations' spheres of influence

access freedom or ability to obtain or make use of

International soldiers pose in Tientsin (now Tianjin) after rescuing their besieged delegations during the Boxer Rebellion. The American is second from the left.

▶ **CRITICAL THINKING**
Drawing Conclusions Why were the Boxers and other secret Chinese societies organized? LAFS.1112.RH.3.7

ullstein bild/The Granger Collection, New York

Roosevelt and Taft's Diplomacy

GUIDING QUESTION *Was President Roosevelt correct in his belief that a strong military presence promoted global peace?*

President McKinley was reelected in 1900, but his second term was cut short by an assassin's bullet. After McKinley's death in September 1901, Vice President Theodore Roosevelt assumed the presidency. Roosevelt favored increasing U.S. power and believed that the United States had a duty to shape the "less civilized" corners of the Earth.

Balancing Power in East Asia

President Roosevelt supported the Open Door policy in China and worked to prevent any nation from controlling trade there. To that end, he helped negotiate a resolution to a war between Japan and Russia that had begun in 1904. At a 1905 peace conference, Roosevelt convinced Russia to recognize Japan's territorial gains and persuaded Japan to end the conflict and seek no further territory. In the years after the treaty, as the United States and Japan continued to compete for greater influence in Asia, they pledged to respect each other's territorial possessions, uphold the Open Door policy, and support China's independence.

The Panama Canal

Roosevelt believed that displaying U.S. power to the world would deter nations from fighting. He expressed this belief with a West African saying, "Speak softly and carry a big stick." His "big stick" policy was evident in the U.S. acquisition and construction of the Panama Canal. He and others believed that having a canal through Central America was vital to U.S. power in the world and would save time and money for commercial and military shipping. In 1889, a French company abandoned its efforts to build a canal in Panama. In 1902, Congress authorized the U.S. purchase of the French company's assets and the construction of a canal.

Panama was a province of Colombia at that time. In 1903, the United States offered Colombia a large sum of money and yearly rent for the right to build the canal and to control a narrow strip of land on either side of it. When Colombia refused, **tension** increased between Colombia and Panamanians who opposed Colombian rule. Worried that the United States might back out of its offer, the French company met with Panamanian officials and together they decided to make a deal with the United States. In November 1903, with U.S. warships looming offshore, Panama revolted against Colombia. Within days, the United States recognized Panama's independence, and the two nations signed a treaty allowing the canal to be built.

©Bettmann/Corbis

Connections to
TODAY

Panama Canal

Grain, petroleum products, and coal are just a few of the goods that passed through the Panama Canal in 2009 on their way to or from the United States. Recognized as a remarkable feat of civil engineering, the Panama Canal remains a vital link in international trade almost a century after it was completed. A $5.25 billion expansion project, expected to be finished in 2014, will allow today's larger vessels to use the canal, thus increasing the amount of goods that can be shipped through the canal each year. SS.912.A.4.4

tension friction or opposition between groups

In 1907 President Roosevelt sent 16 new battleships on a tour around the world to showcase the nation's power. Painted white, these ships became known as "The Great White Fleet."

▶ **CRITICAL THINKING**
Making Inferences Do you think the display of a large navy is a powerful tool in diplomacy? LAFS.1112.RH.3.7, SS.912.A.4.1

The Roosevelt Corollary and Dollar Diplomacy 1903–1934

UNITED STATES

ATLANTIC OCEAN

1916: U.S. forces entered Mexico to capture Pancho Villa and end raids on U.S. towns

1915–1934: Marines deployed to put down revolt and limit French and German influence

1906–1922: U.S. repeatedly intervened in Cuba to prevent revolution and protect U.S. interests

1905: Marines landed to enforce tariff collections and debt payments

MEXICO

Gulf of Mexico

Bahamas Br.

1914: U.S. troops occupied Veracruz to force Huerta from power

Havana

CUBA

Guantanamo

HAITI DOM. REP.

1916–1924: U.S. troops occupied the country to maintain order

Mexico City

Veracruz

1903: U.S. leased base at Guantanamo, Cuba

Puerto Rico *Virgin Is.* *Antigua* Br.

British Honduras

Guadeloupe Fr.
Dominica Br.

PACIFIC OCEAN

GUATEMALA HONDURAS

Caribbean Sea

Martinique Fr. *St. Lucia* Br.

EL SALVADOR

NICARAGUA

Barbados Br.

1909: U.S. troops supported rebels and forced regime change

Grenada Br.

COSTA RICA

PANAMA

1903-1904: U.S. supported Panama's independence; negotiated rights to Panama Canal Zone

Trinidad Br.

1912–1933: U.S. troops put down revolts and enforced tariff collection

0   400 miles

0   400 km

Miller projection

GEOGRAPHY CONNECTION

The United States became increasingly involved in the affairs of Latin America.

1 **GEOGRAPHIC DISTRIBUTIONS** *What questions would you need to ask to explain whether U.S. interventions in Latin America were caused by economic concerns or by security concerns?* LAFS.1112.RH.3.7, SS.912.A.1.4, SS.912.A.4.4, SS.912.G.1.2, SS.912.G.4.9

2 **GEOGRAPHIC PATTERNS** *What questions would you need to ask to be able to explain where the United States invested the most money in Latin America and why?* LAFS.1112.RH.3.7, SS.912.A.1.4, SS.912.A.4.4, SS.912.G.1.2, SS.912.G.2.1, SS.912.G.4.9

Geography and the Canal

Before the Panama Canal opened, ships sailing from New York to San Francisco traveled over 12,000 miles around the treacherous tip of South America. After the canal opened, the trip was only 4900 miles, and could be completed in half the time. Panama's geography made building the canal a challenge because the center of the country is much higher than sea level. Engineers built a series of lakes and concrete locks to raise and lower ships as they traveled the 51-mile canal. The also built a dam to create an artificial lake, Lake Gatún, in the center of Panama.

During the construction, malaria and yellow fever, transmitted by mosquitoes, sickened workers and slowed their progress. By inspecting and controlling all potential breeding places, Surgeon General of the U.S. Army William Crawford Gorgas helped minimize disease and allowed workers to continue the building of the canal. The canal was completed in 1914.

The Roosevelt Corollary

By the early 1900s, American officials had become concerned about large debts that Latin American nations owed European banks. In 1902, after Venezuela defaulted on its debts, Britain, Germany, and Italy blockaded Venezuelan ports. The crisis was resolved peacefully after the United States pressed both sides to reach an agreement. Roosevelt then gave an address

Analyzing
PRIMARY SOURCES

Roosevelt Corollary

❝ Chronic wrongdoing . . . may, in America, as elsewhere, ultimately require intervention by some civilized nation, and in the Western Hemisphere the adherence of the United States to the Monroe Doctrine may force the United States, however reluctantly, in flagrant cases of such wrongdoing or impotence, to the exercise of an international police power. ❞

—Theodore Roosevelt, from his Fourth Annual Message to Congress, December 6, 1904

DBQ **PREDICTING CONSEQUENCES** How would the Roosevelt Corollary extend the original intention of the Monroe Doctrine? LAFS.1112.RH.4.10, SS.912.A.1.2

dollar diplomacy a policy of joining the business interests of a country with its diplomatic interests abroad

NEXT GENERATION SUNSHINE STATE STANDARDS

Continued from page 190

LAFS.1112.WHST.1.2: Write informative/ explanatory texts, including the narration of historical events, scientific procedures/ experiments, or technical processes.

LAFS.1112.WHST.2.4: Produce clear and coherent writing in which the development, organization, and style are appropriate to task, purpose, and audience.

LAFS.1112.WHST.2.5: Develop and strengthen writing as needed by planning, revising, editing, rewriting, or trying a new approach, focusing on addressing what is most significant for a specific purpose and audience.

LAFS.1112.WHST.3.9: Draw evidence from informational texts to support analysis, reflection, and research.

LAFS.1112.WHST.4.10: Write routinely over extended time frames (time for reflection and revision) and shorter time frames (a single sitting or a day or two) for a range of discipline-specific tasks, purposes, and audiences.

SS.912.A.1.2: Utilize a variety of primary and secondary sources to identify author, historical significance, audience, and authenticity to understand a historical period.

SS.912.A.1.4: Analyze how images, symbols, objects, cartoons, graphs, charts, maps, and artwork may be used to interpret the significance of time periods and events from the past.

SS.912.A.4.1: Analyze the major factors that drove United States imperialism.

SS.912.A.4.4: Analyze the economic, military, and security motivations of the United States to complete the Panama Canal as well as major obstacles involved in its construction.

SS.912.G.1.2: Use spatial perspective and appropriate geographic terms and tools, including the Six Essential Elements, as organizational schema to describe any given place.

SS.912.G.2.1: Identify the physical characteristics and the human characteristics that define and differentiate regions.

SS.912.G.4.9: Use political maps to describe the change in boundaries and governments within continents over time.

to Congress in which he stated what came to be known as the Roosevelt Corollary to the Monroe Doctrine. It stated that the United States would intervene in Latin American affairs when necessary to maintain economic and political stability in the Western Hemisphere.

The goal of the Roosevelt Corollary was to prevent European powers from using the debt problems of Latin America to justify intervening in the region. The United States first applied the Roosevelt Corollary in the Dominican Republic, which had fallen behind on its debt payments to European nations. In 1905, the United States began collecting customs tariffs in the Dominican Republic, using the Marine Corps as its agent.

Dollar Diplomacy

Roosevelt's successor, William Howard Taft, placed less emphasis on military force and more on economic development. Taft believed that supporting Latin American industry would increase trade and profits for American businesses and lift Latin America countries out of poverty and social disorder. His policy came to be called **dollar diplomacy.**

To give Europeans less reason to intervene in Latin American affairs, Taft's administration worked to replace European loans with loans from American banks. In 1911, American bankers began making loans to Nicaragua to support its shaky government. The next year, civil unrest forced Nicaragua's president to ask for greater assistance. U.S. marines entered Nicaragua, replaced the customs collector with an American agent, and formed a committee to control the customs commissions. U.S. troops supported the government and customs until 1933.

☑ READING PROGRESS CHECK

Explaining Why was it important for the United States to influence Latin American nations?

Woodrow Wilson's Diplomacy in Mexico

GUIDING QUESTION *How did "moral diplomacy" shape President Wilson's foreign policy?*

"It would be the irony of fate," said Woodrow Wilson just before he was inaugurated in 1913, "if my administration had to deal chiefly with foreign affairs." Wilson's experience and interest were in domestic policy. He was a university professor before entering politics and was a committed progressive. Foreign affairs, however, absorbed much of Wilson's time and energy as president.

Wilson opposed imperialism. He believed that democracy was essential to a nation's stability and prosperity. He wanted the United States to promote democracy to create a world free of revolution and war. He hoped the United States would lead by moral example, but his first international crisis thwarted that hope.

The Mexican Revolution

For more than 30 years, Porfirio Díaz ruled Mexico as a dictator. During Díaz's reign, Mexico became much more industrialized, but foreign investors owned the new railroads and factories that were built. Most Mexican citizens remained poor and landless. In 1910, discontent erupted into revolution. Francisco Madero, a reformer who seemed to support democracy, constitutional government, and land reform, led the revolution. Madero, however, was an unskilled administrator. Worried about Madero's plans for land reform, landowners plotted against him. In 1913, General Victoriano Huerta seized power, and Madero was murdered.

Huerta's brutality repulsed Wilson, who refused to recognize the new government. Instead, Wilson announced a new policy. To win U.S. recognition, groups that seized power in Latin America would have to establish a government based on law, not on force. Wilson believed that, without U.S. support, Huerta soon would be overthrown. Meanwhile, Wilson ordered the navy to intercept arms shipments to Huerta's government. He also permitted Americans to arm Huerta's opponents.

Wilson Sends Troops Into Mexico

In April 1914, American sailors visiting the Mexican city of Tampico were arrested after entering a restricted area. After their release, their commander demanded an apology. The Mexicans refused. Wilson saw the refusal as an opportunity to overthrow Huerta. Soon after Congress authorized the use of force, Wilson learned that a German ship was unloading weapons at the Mexican port of Veracruz. Wilson immediately ordered American warships to Veracruz, where U.S. Marines forcibly seized the city.

Although the president expected the Mexican people to welcome his action, anti-American riots broke out. Wilson then accepted international mediation to settle the dispute. Venustiano Carranza, whose forces had acquired arms from the United States, became Mexico's president.

Mexican forces opposed to Carranza conducted raids into the United States, hoping to force Wilson to intervene. In March 1916, Pancho Villa (VEE•yuh) and a group of **guerrillas**—armed fighters who carry out surprise attacks—burned the town of Columbus, New Mexico, killing 17 Americans. Wilson responded by sending about 5,800 troops under General John J. Pershing across the border to find and capture Villa. The expedition ended without success.

Wilson's Mexican policy damaged U.S. foreign relations. The British ridiculed the president's attempt to "shoot" the Mexicans into self-government. Latin Americans regarded his "moral imperialism" as no improvement over Theodore Roosevelt's "big stick" diplomacy. In fact, Wilson followed Roosevelt's example in the Caribbean. In 1914, he negotiated exclusive rights for naval bases and a canal with Nicaragua. In 1915, he sent marines into Haiti to put down a rebellion. In 1916, he sent troops into the Dominican Republic to set up a government he hoped would be more stable and democratic than the current regime.

✓ READING PROGRESS CHECK

Examining Why did President Wilson's "moral diplomacy" not accomplish its intended purpose?

Library of Congress, Prints & Photographs Division [LC-H823-1534]

BIOGRAPHY

General John J. Pershing 1860–1948

During the Spanish-American War, General John J. Pershing earned the praise of his superior officers, one of whom said that Pershing was "the coolest and bravest man I ever saw under fire." Pershing was made commander of the expedition into Mexico to capture Pancho Villa. Though the mission failed, it made Pershing a respected public figure.

▶ CRITICAL THINKING
Predicting
Consequences After the failed expedition to capture Villa, what was the next military conflict in which General Pershing commanded troops? LAFS.1112.RH.3.7

guerrillas armed fighters who carry out surprise attacks

LESSON 3 REVIEW

Reviewing Vocabulary

1. *Explaining* How did the Open Door policy help prevent any one nation from monopolizing trade with China? LAFS.1112.RH.2.4

Using Your Notes

2. *Identifying* Use your notes to identify major reasons that the United States wanted to build a canal through Central America.

Answering the Guiding Questions

3. *Analyzing* Why did the United States want to eliminate spheres of influence in China? LAFS.1112.WHST.3.9, SS.912.A.4.1

4. *Evaluating* Was President Roosevelt correct in his belief that a strong military presence promoted global peace? SS.912.A.4.1

5. *Comparing and Contrasting* How did "moral diplomacy" shape President Wilson's foreign policy? SS.912.A.4.1

Writing Activity

6. **NARRATIVE** Suppose that you are a Mexican citizen during Wilson's presidency. Write a radio news broadcast expressing your feelings about American actions in Mexico. Consider how best to communicate your message with your audience. LAFS.1112.WHST.1.2, LAFS.1112.WHST.2.4, LAFS.1112.WHST.2.5, LAFS.1112.WHST.1.2

STUDY GUIDE

THE IMPERIALIST VISION
LESSON 1

American Imperialism

A desire for new markets for industrial products

A belief in manifest destiny to spread American culture and democracy around the world

Emphasis on powerful navy and controlling trade as key to global power

THE SPANISH-AMERICAN WAR
LESSON 2

Aggressive nationalism by the Republican Party helped push the U.S. into the Spanish-American war.

Following victory, the United States acquired Puerto Rico, Guam, and the Philippines.

Cuba became an independent nation, but with very strong U.S. influence.

NEW AMERICAN DIPLOMACY
LESSON 3

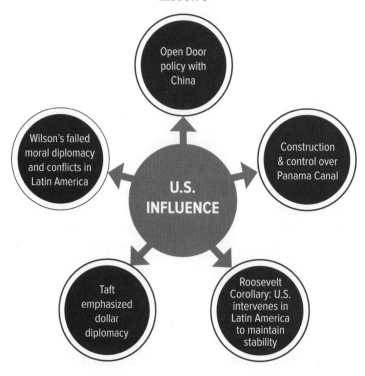

Open Door policy with China

Construction & control over Panama Canal

Wilson's failed moral diplomacy and conflicts in Latin America

U.S. INFLUENCE

Taft emphasized dollar diplomacy

Roosevelt Corollary: U.S. intervenes in Latin America to maintain stability

Directions: On a separate sheet of paper, answer the questions below. Make sure you read carefully and answer all parts to the question.

Lesson Review

Lesson 1

1 *Describing* How did Josiah Strong's ideas help propel the United States to build an empire? SS.912.A.4.1

2 *Explaining* Why did Sanford Dole and other Hawaiian sugar planters want Hawaii to join the United States? SS.912.A.4.1

Lesson 2

3 *Summarizing* What were the main results of the United States's victory in the Spanish-American War? SS.912.A.4.1, SS.912.A.4.2, SS.912.A.4.3

4 *Evaluating* How did Filipinos feel about the U.S. government after the Spanish-American War? SS.912.A.4.2, SS.912.A.4.3

Lesson 3

5 *Analyzing* What were the human geographic factors that led the United States to build a canal through Panama? SS.912.A.4.4, SS.912.G.1.2

6 *Explaining* How did the Open Door Policy and dollar diplomacy affect the economy in the United States? SS.912.A.4.1

Exploring the Essential Question

7 *Determining Cause and Effect* Create a cause-and-effect diagram that identifies the causes of American imperialism and the effects of the United States's decision to build an empire in the late 1800s and early 1900s. SS.912.A.4.1, SS.912.A.4.2

Critical Thinking

8 *Explaining* What was the significance of 1898, and why might it be considered a turning point in U.S. history? SS.912.A.4.1, SS.912.A.4.3

21st Century Skills

9 *Evaluating the Validity of a Source* Use the library or Internet to find writings by people in support of and against the annexation of the Philippines. Evaluate their points of view based on their language and logic they use, and cite specific examples to support your analysis. Then evaluate each writer's background and experience to determine if they are reliable or objective sources. Consider each person's historical context and what shaped their thinking; also, consider the validity of sources you use to find this information. Examples of people you may wish to research include Alfred Mahan, Albert Beveridge, Henry Cabot Lodge, Theodore Roosevelt, William McKinley, Jane Addams, Samuel Clemens, Andrew Carnegie, Samuel Gompers, Carl Schurz. LAFS.1112.RH.1.1, LAFS.1112.RH.1.3, LAFS.1112.RH.3.8, LAFS.1112.RH.3.9, LAFS.1112.SL.1.2, LAFS.1112.WHST.2.6, LAFS.1112.WHST.3.7, LAFS.1112.WHST.3.8, SS.912.A.1.5, SS.912.A.4.1, SS.912.A.4.2, SS.912.A.3

DBQ Analyzing Primary Sources

Read the following excerpts, one from Alfred Mahan's book The Influence of Sea Power Upon History *and the other from a speech by Republican Carl Schurz, a leading opponent of imperialism, and then answer the questions.*

PRIMARY SOURCE

" The protection of [naval] stations must depend either upon direct military force, as do Gibraltar and Malta, or upon a surrounding friendly population, such as the American colonists once were to England, and, it may be presumed, the Australian colonists now are. Such friendly surroundings and backing, joined to a reasonable military provision, are the best of defenses.... Colonies attached to the mother-country afford, therefore, the surest means of supporting abroad the sea power of a country. In peace, the influence of the government should be felt in promoting by all means a warmth of attachment and a unity of interest which will make the welfare of one the welfare of all, and the quarrel of one the quarrel of all; and in war, or rather for war, by inducing such measures of organization and defense as shall be felt by all to be a fair distribution of a burden of which each reaps the benefit. "

—Alfred Thayer Mahan, from
The Influence of Sea Power Upon History, 1890

Need Extra Help?

If You've Missed Question	**1**	**2**	**3**	**4**	**5**	**6**	**7**	**8**	**9**
Go to Lesson	1	1	2	2	3	3	1	2	2

Library of Congress, Prints & Photographs Division [LC-USZC4-5392]

PRIMARY SOURCE

❝Many imperialists admit that our trade with the Philippines themselves will not nearly be worth its cost; but they say that we must have the Philippines as a foothold, a sort of power station, for the expansion of our trade on the Asiatic continent, especially in China. Admitting this, for argument's sake, I ask what kind of a foothold we should really need. Coaling-stations and docks for our fleet, and facilities for the establishment of commercial houses and depots. That is all. And now I ask further, whether we could not easily have had these things if we had, instead of making war upon the Filipinos, favored the independence of the islands. Everybody knows that we could. We might have those things now for the mere asking, if we stopped the war and came to a friendly understanding with the Filipinos to-morrow.❞

—Carl Schurz, "The Policy of Imperialism," Address to the Anti-Imperialist Conference, 1899

10 *Interpreting Speeches* What policies does Schurz suggest the United States could have followed instead of annexing the Philippines and going to war with the Filipino guerrillas? LAFS.1112.RH.3.8, LAFS.1112.RH.4.10, SS.912.A.1.2, SS.912.A.4.1, SS.912.A.4.2, SS.912.A.4.3

11 *Analyzing* Why does Mahan think colonies are the best way to support a nation's navy? Cite specific language to support your answer. LAFS.1112.RH.1.1, LAFS.1112.RH.3.8, LAFS.1112.RH.4.10, SS.912.A.1.2, SS.912.A.4.1, SS.912.A.4.2, SS.912.A.4.3

12 *Comparing and Contrasting Primary Sources* In what ways do Schurz and Mahan agree? What is the main point on which they disagree? Which argument do you find more persuasive, and why? LAFS.1112.RH.1.1, LAFS.1112.RH.1.2, LAFS.1112.RH.2.6, LAFS.1112.RH.3.8, LAFS.1112.RH.3.9, LAFS.1112.RH.4.10, SS.912.A.1.2, SS.912.A.4.1, SS.912.A.4.2, SS.912.A.4.3

Analyzing Visuals

Use the political cartoon to answer the following questions.

13 *Interpreting Political Cartoons* Using your skills in detecting bias and points of view, which side of the debate over imperialism do you think the cartoonist supports? Explain why and also explain what he thinks the debate over imperialism is doing to the United States. LAFS.1112.RH.1.1, LAFS.1112.RH.3.8, SS.912.A.1.4, SS.912.A.1.7, SS.912.A.4.1, SS.912.H.1.5

14 *Analyzing Political Cartoons* Using your knowledge of why many American leaders wanted to expand overseas, who do you think the man in the suit beside Uncle Sam represents? LAFS.1112.RH.1.1, LAFS.1112.RH.3.7, SS.912.A.1.4, SS.912.A.1.7, SS.912.A.4.1, SS.912.H.1.5

Extended-Response Question

15 *Evaluating* Think about American expansionism and the nation's acquisition of Guam, Hawaii, the Philippines and Puerto Rico. Imagine you are a U.S. senator about to vote on the decision to annex the Philippines. Taking into account the nation's values and traditions, as well as its economic needs, and the world's military and political situation in the 1800s, write a speech evaluating whether American foreign policy was correct or not, and explaining how you are going to vote. Be sure to focus on the details that would be most significant to your audience—your constituents and fellow senators. LAFS.1112.WHST.1.2, LAFS.1112.WHST.2.4, LAFS.1112.WHST.2.5, LAFS.1112.WHST.4.10, LAFS.1112.SL.2.4, SS.912.A.4.1, SS.912.A.4.2, SS.912.A.4.3, SS.912.H.3.1

Need Extra Help?

If You've Missed Question	❿	⓫	⓬	⓭	⓮	⓯
Go to Lesson	2	1	1	2	2	2

◀ Alice Paul, a Quaker social worker, fought militantly for woman suffrage, enduring several incarcerations for her efforts to win women the right to vote.

FROM 1890 TO 1920

The Progressive Movement

THE STORY MATTERS ...

Today we assume that our foods and medicines are safe, but in the 1800s, that was not so. Through the efforts of the progressives, who wanted to improve life for all Americans, changes were made that not only safeguarded food and medicine, but also gave women the right to vote, improved working conditions, and conserved the nation's natural places.

ESSENTIAL QUESTION

• Can politics fix social problems?

The Granger Collection, New York

Place & Time: United States 1890–1920

Industrialization changed American society. Cities were crowded, working conditions were often poor, and the political system was unresponsive. These conditions gave rise to the Progressive movement. Led by journalists, clergy, social workers, and other concerned citizens, the Progressive movement campaigned for both political and social reforms.

Step Into the Place

Read the quotes and look at the information presented on the map.

DBQ **Analyzing Historical Documents** As the United States became an industrialized nation, how did the government address the rapid exploitation of public lands and natural resources? Based on the quotes, did Roosevelt and Pinchot agree or disagree on this issue?

PRIMARY SOURCE

"We have become great because of the lavish use of our resources and we have just reason to be proud of our growth. But the time has come to inquire seriously what will happen when our forests are gone, when the coal, the iron, the oil and the gas are exhausted, when the soils shall have been still further impoverished and washed into the streams, polluting the rivers, denuding the fields and obstructing navigation."

—President Theodore Roosevelt, from a speech delivered at the Conference on the Conservation of the Nation's Resources, 1908

PRIMARY SOURCE

"The first principle of conservation is development, the use of the natural resources now existing on this continent for the benefit of the people who live here now. There may be just as much waste in neglecting the development and use of certain natural resources as there is in their destruction. . . .

Conservation stands emphatically for the development and use of water-power now, without delay. It stands for the immediate construction of navigable waterways . . . as assistants to the railroads. . . .

In addition . . . natural resources must be developed and preserved for the benefit of the many, and not merely for the profit of the few."

— Gifford Pinchot, Chief of U.S. Forest Service, from *The Fight for Conservation*, 1910

left page: (tl)The Granger Collection, New York; (tr)Library of Congress, Prints & Photographs Division [LC-USZC4-11548]; (bl to br)detail/White House Collection/The White House Historical Association; right page (l & r)detail/White House Collection/The White House Historical Association

Step Into the Time

DRAWING CONCLUSIONS Research a piece of legislation from the time line. Write a paragraph that suggests how this legislation might have impacted social reform.

1889 Jane Addams opens Hull House in Chicago

B. Harrison 1889–1893

Cleveland 1893–1897

McKinley 1897–1901

T. Roosevelt 1901–1909

U.S. PRESIDENTS

UNITED STATES

WORLD

1890

1895

1900

1884 Toynbee Hall, the first settlement house, is established in London

1891 Australian Woman Suffrage League founded in Sydney

1893 New Zealand becomes the first nation to grant suffrage to women

NEXT GENERATION SUNSHINE STATE STANDARDS
Students will understand the following benchmarks from the Florida NGSSS

LAFS.1112.RH.3.7: Integrate and evaluate multiple sources of information presented in diverse formats and media (e.g., visually, quantitatively, as well as in words) in order to address a question or solve a problem.

LAFS.1112.RH.3.9: Integrate information from diverse sources, both primary and secondary, into a coherent understanding of an idea or event, noting discrepancies among sources.

SS.912.A.1.2: Utilize a variety of primary and secondary sources to identify author, historical significance, audience, and authenticity to understand a historical period.

SS.912.A.1.3: Utilize timelines to identify the time sequence of historical data.

SS.912.A.1.4: Analyze how images, symbols, objects, cartoons, graphs, charts, maps, and

artwork may be used to interpret the significance of time periods and events from the past.

SS.912.A.2.5: Use geographic terms and tools to analyze case studies of debates over how human actions modify a selected region.

SS.912.A.3.12: Compare how different nongovernmental organizations and progressives worked to shape public policy, restore economic opportunities, and correct injustices in American life.

National Parks of the Western United States 1872–1920

CANADA

■ National Park

Washington
■ Mt. Rainier (1899)

Glacier (1910)

Montana

North Dakota

Minnesota

Wisc.

Columbia R.

Oregon

Crater Lake (1902)

Idaho

Snake R.

Yellowstone (1872)

Yellowstone is the home to Old Faithful, the most famous geyser in North America. Old Faithful erupts every 33 to 120 minutes, spouting over 200-degree water up to nearly 150 feet.

Wyoming

South Dakota

Wind Cave (1903)

Mississippi R.

Lassen Volcanic (1916)

California

Nebraska

Iowa

Platte R.

Missouri R.

Ill.

PACIFIC OCEAN

In 1940 General Grant National Park was incorporated into Kings Canyon National Park

Yosemite (1890)

General Grant (1890)

Nevada

Utah

Zion (1919)

Colorado R.

Rocky Mountain (1915)

Colorado

Mesa Verde (1906)

Kansas

Missouri

Sequoia (1890)

Sequoia National Park was established in 1890 in an effort to protect Giant Sequoia trees. The largest of the Giant Sequoias, General Sherman, is thought to be 2,300 to 2,700 years old and is the largest living thing on earth.

Grand Canyon (1919)

Arkansas R.

Arkansas

Oklahoma

Arizona

New Mexico

Red R.

0 — 400 miles
0 — 400 km

Gulf of California

Texas

La.

MEXICO

Lambert Azimuthal Equal-Area projection

120°W   110°W   100°W

1902 Maryland passes first U.S. workers' compensation laws

1906 Pure Food and Drug Act passed

Taft 1909–1913

1910 Mann-Elkins Act passed

Wilson 1913–1921

1914 Clayton Antitrust Act is enacted

1916 National Park Service is created

1919 Eighteenth Amendment, establishing Prohibition, is ratified

1920 Nineteenth Amendment gives women voting rights

1905   1910   1915   1920

4 International Council of [Wo]men meets to create International [Wom]an Suffrage Alliance

1906 Britain enacts workers' compensation law

1907 Austria establishes universal suffrage

1908 Germany limits working hours for children and women

1911 Britain establishes a national health-insurance program

1913 Canada's government creates Quetico Provincial Park in Ontario

The Progressive Movement **201**

LESSON 1

The Roots of Progressivism

ESSENTIAL QUESTION

• Can politics fix social problems?

READING HELPDESK

Academic Vocabulary

• legislation   • advocate
• lobbying

Content Vocabulary

• muckraker
• direct primary
• initiative
• referendum
• recall
• suffrage
• prohibition

TAKING NOTES

Key Ideas and Details

Organizing As you read about progressivism, complete a graphic organizer similar to the one below by filling in the beliefs of progressives.
LAFS.1112.RH.3.7, SS.912.A.3.8, SS.912.A.3.12

Progressive Beliefs

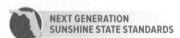

NEXT GENERATION SUNSHINE STATE STANDARDS

ELD.K12.ELL.SI.1: English language learners communicate for social and instructional purposes within the school setting.

ELD.K12.ELL.SS.1: English language learners communicate information, ideas and concepts necessary for academic success in the content area of Social Studies.

Continued on page 203

IT MATTERS BECAUSE

The Progressive Era was a time when many Americans tried to improve their society. They tried to make government honest, efficient, and more democratic. The movement for woman suffrage gained more support, as did efforts to limit child labor and reduce alcohol abuse.

The Rise of Progressivism

GUIDING QUESTION *Who were progressives, and what did they believe caused social problems?*

Progressivism was a collection of different ideas and activities, not a tightly organized political movement with a specific set of goals. Rather, it was a series of responses to problems in American society that had emerged from the growth of industry. Progressives had many different ideas about how to fix the problems they saw in American society.

Who Were the Progressives?

Progressivism was partly a reaction against laissez-faire economics and its emphasis on an unregulated market. Progressives generally believed that industrialization and urbanization had created many social problems. After seeing the poverty of the working class and the filth and crime of urban society, reformers began doubting the free market's ability to address those problems.

Progressives belonged to both major political parties. Most were urban, educated, middle-class Americans. Among their leaders were journalists, social workers, educators, politicians, and members of the clergy. Most agreed that government should take a more active role in solving society's problems. At the same time, they doubted that the government in its present form could fix those problems. They concluded that government had to be fixed before it could be used to fix other problems.

One reason progressives thought they could improve society was their strong faith in science and technology. The application of scientific knowledge had produced the lightbulb, the telephone,

202

and the automobile. It had built skyscrapers and railroads. Science and technology had benefited people; thus, progressives believed using scientific principles could also produce solutions for society.

The Muckrakers

Among the first people to articulate progressive ideas was a group of crusading journalists who investigated social conditions and political corruption. President Theodore Roosevelt nicknamed these writers **"muckrakers"** because of what he perceived as their obsession with scandal and corruption. Widely circulated, cheap newspapers and magazines helped spread the muckrakers' ideas.

Muckrakers uncovered corruption in many areas. Some, such as Ida Tarbell and Charles Edward Russell, concentrated on exposing the unfair practices of large corporations. Other muckrakers targeted government and social problems. Lincoln Steffens reported on vote stealing and other corrupt political practices of political machines.

Still other muckrakers concentrated on social problems. In his influential book *How the Other Half Lives* (1890), Jacob Riis published photographs and descriptions of the poverty, disease, and crime that afflicted many immigrant neighborhoods in New York City. By raising awareness of these problems, the muckrakers stimulated calls for reform.

✅ **READING PROGRESS CHECK**

Stating What groups of people made up the Progressive movement?

Reforming Government

GUIDING QUESTION *How did progressives hope to make government more efficient and responsive to citizens?*

Progressivism included a wide range of reform activities. Different issues led to different approaches, and some progressives even took opposing positions on how to address some problems. They condemned government corruption but did not always agree on the best way to fix the problem.

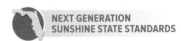

NEXT GENERATION SUNSHINE STATE STANDARDS

Continued from page 202

HE.912.C.2.4: Evaluate how public health policies and government regulations can influence health promotion and disease prevention.

LAFS.1112.RH.2.4: Determine the meaning of words and phrases as they are used in a text, including analyzing how an author uses and refines the meaning of a key term over the course of a text (e.g., how Madison defines faction in Federalist No. 10).

LAFS.1112.RH.3.7: Integrate and evaluate multiple sources of information presented in diverse formats and media (e.g., visually, quantitatively, as well as in words) in order to address a question or solve a problem.

LAFS.1112.WHST.1.1: Write arguments focused on discipline-specific content.

LAFS.1112.WHST.4.10: Write routinely over extended time frames (time for reflection and revision) and shorter time frames (a single sitting or a day or two) for a range of discipline-specific tasks, purposes, and audiences.

Continued on page 204

muckraker a journalist who uncovers abuses and corruption in a society

Progressive photographer Jacob Riis captured the poverty, disease, and crime common in many of New York City's immigrant neighborhoods.

▶ **CRITICAL THINKING**
Determining Cause and Effect What did progressives believe caused the social problems that Riis photographed?
LAFS.1112.RH.3.7, SS.912.A.1.4, SS.912.A.3.12

direct primary a vote held by all members of a political party to decide their candidate for public office

initiative the right of citizens to place a measure or issue before the voters or the legislature for approval

legislation a proposed law to be voted on by a governing body

referendum the practice of letting voters accept or reject measures proposed by the legislature

recall the right that enables voters to remove unsatisfactory elected officials from office

NEXT GENERATION SUNSHINE STATE STANDARDS

Continued from page 203

SS.912.A.1.2: Utilize a variety of primary and secondary sources to identify author, historical significance, audience, and authenticity to understand a historical period.

SS.912.A.1.4: Analyze how images, symbols, objects, cartoons, graphs, charts, maps, and artwork may be used to interpret the significance of time periods and events from the past.

SS.912.A.3.8: Examine the importance of social change and reform in the late 19th and early 20th centuries (class system, migration from farms to cities, Social Gospel movement, role of settlement houses and churches in providing services to the poor).

Continued on page 205

In 1900 the political machine running Galveston, Texas, failed to help the city recover from a devastating hurricane, so local business leaders convinced the state to allow them to take control.

Making Government Efficient

One group of progressives drew its ideas for increasing government efficiency from business. Theories of business efficiency first became popular in the 1890s. Books such as Frederick W. Taylor's *The Principles of Scientific Management* (1911) described how a company could increase efficiency by managing time, breaking tasks down into small parts, and using standardized tools—a scientific approach to business that some progressives wanted to extend to government.

Progressives saw corruption and inefficiency in city government. Many municipal leaders traditionally chose political supporters and friends to run city departments, even though these people often knew little about managing city services.

Progressives supported proposals to reform city government. One, a commission plan, divided city government into several departments, with each one under an expert commissioner's control. A second, a council-manager system, employed a city manager who was hired by the city council. In both systems, experts play a major role in managing the city. Galveston, Texas, adopted the commission system in 1901. In other cities, political machines were weakened by having officials elected city-wide instead of by neighborhoods.

Democratic Reforms

Another group of progressives focused on making government more democratic and more responsive to citizens. Many believed that the key to improving government was to make elected officials more responsive and accountable to voters.

Wisconsin became a "laboratory of democracy" under the leadership of its governor, Robert M. La Follette, who attacked the way political parties ran their conventions. Party bosses controlled the selection of convention delegates and the nomination of candidates. La Follette pressured the state legislature to pass a law requiring parties to hold a **direct primary,** in which all party members could vote for a candidate to run in the general election.

The direct primary soon spread to other states. Other progressives also pushed for additional reforms: the initiative, the referendum, and the recall. The **initiative** permits citizens to introduce **legislation** and requires the legislature to vote on it. Typically, citizens have to gather a certain number of signatures on a petition to make the initiative legally binding. In an indirect initiative, the proposed law goes to the legislature first. If the legislature refuses to act on it, it goes on the ballot for the public to vote on it. A direct initiative goes directly to the public for a vote.

A **referendum** allows citizens to vote on proposed laws directly. In some states, if the legislature passes certain laws, such as a change to taxes, the new law has to be approved by the public in a referendum. Referendums are also used to repeal existing laws. Both the referendum and the initiative gave reformers the power to bypass or overrule the legislature if it refused to support something the people wanted. The idea of the initiative and the referendum was more popular in the West and Midwest. Today, 26 states allow some form of initiative and/or referendum. Since 1904, more than 2000 statewide referendums have been initiated by citizens.

The **recall** provided voters an option to demand a special election to remove an elected official from office before his or her term had expired.

Library of Congress, Prints & Photographs Division LC-USZ62-123884

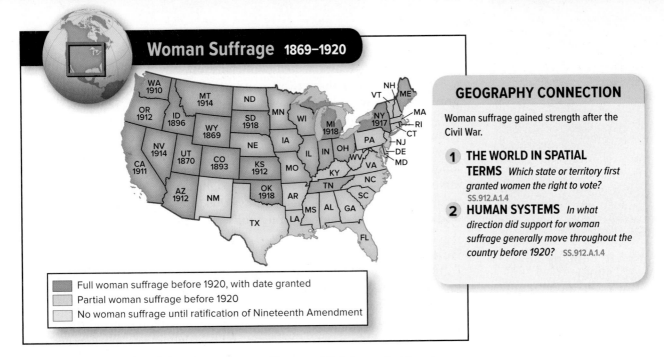

Woman Suffrage 1869–1920

GEOGRAPHY CONNECTION

Woman suffrage gained strength after the Civil War.

1. **THE WORLD IN SPATIAL TERMS** *Which state or territory first granted women the right to vote?* SS.912.A.1.4

2. **HUMAN SYSTEMS** *In what direction did support for woman suffrage generally move throughout the country before 1920?* SS.912.A.1.4

Full woman suffrage before 1920, with date granted
Partial woman suffrage before 1920
No woman suffrage until ratification of Nineteenth Amendment

Today, nineteen states allow citizens to recall state officials, and at least 29 states allow recalls of local officials. Recalls are frequent for local officials. Hundreds of city council members, school board members, and mayors have been recalled over the years but, as of 2013, only 20 state legislators have been recalled and only two governors.

Progressives also targeted the U.S. Senate. The U.S. Constitution originally directed each state legislature to elect two senators. Political machines and business interests often influenced these elections. Some senators, once elected, repaid their supporters with federal contracts and jobs. To counter corruption in the Senate, reformers called for the direct election of senators by voters. In 1912 Congress passed a direct-election amendment. In 1913 the amendment was ratified and became the Seventeenth Amendment to the Constitution. Although direct election was meant to end corruption, it also removed one of the state legislatures' checks on federal power.

✓ READING PROGRESS CHECK

Summarizing How did progressives hope to solve problems through political reform?

Woman Suffrage

GUIDING QUESTION *Why did the progressives support the woman suffrage movement?*

At the first women's rights convention in Seneca Falls, New York, in 1848, Elizabeth Cady Stanton convinced the delegates that winning **suffrage**—the right to vote—should be a priority. Decades later, this right still had not been gained. It became a major goal for female progressives.

Early Challenges

The woman suffrage movement started slowly. Suffragists were threatened and called unfeminine and immoral. Many of the movement's supporters were abolitionists as well, and in the years before the Civil War, ending slavery took priority over women's voting rights.

After the Civil War, Congress introduced the Fourteenth and Fifteenth Amendments to grant citizenship to African Americans and voting rights to African American men. Leaders of the woman suffrage movement wanted

NEXT GENERATION SUNSHINE STATE STANDARDS

Continued from page 204

SS.912.A.3.9: Examine causes, course, and consequences of the labor movement in the late 19th and early 20th centuries.

SS.912.A.3.10: Review different economic and philosophic ideologies.

SS.912.A.3.12: Compare how different nongovernmental organizations and progressives worked to shape public policy, restore economic opportunities, and correct injustices in American life.

SS.912.G.1.2: Use spatial perspective and appropriate geographic terms and tools, including the Six Essential Elements, as organizational schema to describe any given place.

suffrage the right to vote

(t)Library of Congress, Prints & Photographs Division [LC-US262-46713]; (b)Library of Congress, Prints & Photographs Division [LC-DIG-nclc-02949]

Susan B. Anthony (1820–1906)

Susan B. Anthony left teaching to join the temperance and antislavery movements in the early 1850s. She found that the male leaders of both movements discriminated against women so she turned to the women's rights movement.

She was the president of the National American Woman Suffrage Association, from 1892 to 1900. She lectured constantly on the right of women to vote, often to hostile audiences, and traveled extensively, lobbying state legislators to pass suffrage laws. Her ultimate goal was an amendment to the United States Constitution that would recognize a woman's right to vote in every state. On her 86th birthday in 1906, she attended a dinner in her honor and spoke briefly, concluding her remarks with these words: "Failure is impossible!" She was right but did not live to see the Nineteenth Amendment, which gave women the right to vote, ratified in 1920.

lobbying the act of contacting a political leader to explain a concern in order to convince them to vote for a cause

Many progressives focused on fixing social-welfare problems, such as child labor.

▶ **CRITICAL THINKING**
Drawing Conclusions Why do you think progressives made their fight against child labor a key issue? SS.912.A.3.12

these amendments to give women the right to vote as well. They were disappointed when established politicians refused.

The debate over these two amendments split the movement into two groups: the New York City–based National Woman Suffrage Association, founded by Stanton and Susan B. Anthony in 1869, and the Boston-based American Woman Suffrage Association, led by Lucy Stone and Julia Ward Howe. The first group wanted to focus on passing a constitutional amendment. The second believed that the best strategy was convincing state governments to grant women the right to vote first. This split weakened the suffrage movement. By 1900, only Wyoming, Idaho, Utah, and Colorado had granted women full voting rights.

Building Support

In 1890, the two groups united to form the National American Woman Suffrage Association (NAWSA). The movement still faced the challenge of convincing women to become politically active. As the Progressive movement gained momentum, however, many women realized that they needed the vote to promote reforms and pass labor laws. Women began organizing events, handing out pamphlets, and delivering speeches. Many leaders of the suffrage movement were also able to lobby state and federal legislators directly. **Lobbying** is when you contact a political leader personally, explain your concern, and try to convince them to vote for a legislation that supports your causes. Often lobbyists promise to support the legislator financially when they run for reelection in return for their support. To gain influence with legislators and make their lobbying more effective, suffrage leaders raised funds for legislators who supported suffrage and campaigned for their election even though they could not actually vote for them. They also worked to defeat legislators who opposed women's suffrage.

Quaker social worker and former NAWSA member Alice Paul founded the National Woman's Party (NWP). The NWP emphasized non-violent protest to promote women's right to participate in the democratic process. Its members picketed, blocked sidewalks, chained themselves to lampposts, and went on hunger strikes if arrested. Suffragist Rose Winslow and several other women, including Alice Paul, were arrested for picketing the White House. After being sentenced to seven months in jail, Winslow and other women prisoners went on a hunger strike.

❝We have been in solitary for five weeks. . . . I have felt quite feeble the last few days—faint, so that I could hardly get my hair brushed, my arms ached so. But today I am well again. . . . [Alice Paul] dreaded forcible feeding frightfully, and I hate to think how she must be feeling. . . . I am really all right. If this continues very long perhaps I won't be. All the officers here know we are making this hunger strike [so] that women fighting for liberty may be considered political prisoners. . . . [W]e don't want women ever to have to do this over again.❞

—Rose Winslow, quoted in *Jailed for Freedom*, 1920

The hunger strikers were force fed in prison, and the story gathered a lot of attention in the press, creating a national scandal. Equally disturbing was a police attack on a group of woman protestors that left several women with concussions and broken ribs.

The United States had entered World War I a few months before, and President Wilson was trying to portray the United States as fighting for freedom and democracy. As a result the NWP's protests may have helped convince Wilson to publicly ask Congress to pass an amendment giving women the right to vote. Wilson may also have been influenced by the public support that NAWSA had given him.

While the NWP had focused on non-violent protest, the leader of NAWSA, Carrie Chapman Catt, had organized the suffrage movement for one final nationwide push for suffrage. She used the organization's funds to support politicians who backed suffrage. She convinced the organization to support President Wilson's re-election in 1916 and then supported the president when he took the country into war in 1917. As more states granted women the right to vote, Congress began to favor a constitutional amendment. In 1918 the House of Representatives passed a woman suffrage amendment. In the Senate, however, the amendment failed by two votes.

During the midterm elections of 1918, Catt used NAWSA's resources to defeat two antisuffrage senators. In 1919 the Senate passed the amendment by slightly more than the two-thirds vote needed. On August 26, 1920, after three-fourths of the states had ratified it, the Nineteenth Amendment guaranteeing women the right to vote went into effect.

✓ READING PROGRESS CHECK

Determining Cause and Effect What progressive goals did suffragists believe they could achieve if women had the right to vote?

Reforming Society

GUIDING QUESTION *What problems did social-welfare progressives attempt to reform?*

While many progressives focused on reforming the political system, others focused on social problems, such as crime, illiteracy, alcohol abuse, child labor, and the health and safety of Americans. These social-welfare progressives created charities to help the poor and disadvantaged. They also pushed for new laws they hoped would fix social problems.

Women were prominent leaders of the social-welfare progressives. Most women in the progressive movement came from the middle or upper class, and felt a responsibility toward working class women. The main issues that working class women faced were poverty, safety, and abuse. Because the culture of the time generally expected fathers and husbands to work and provide for their families, women and children who lost their husbands and fathers were seen as exceptionally vulnerable and likely to be forced into

BIOGRAPHY

Florence Kelley
(1859–1932)

Progressive Florence Kelley dedicated her life to campaigning for reforms. While working at Chicago's Hull House in the 1890s, she conducted research that encouraged the passage of the first law banning children younger than 14 from factory work. Later, she contributed to the foundation of the United States Children's Bureau to protect children. Her research on the effects of long workdays on women's health contributed to the Supreme Court's decision in *Muller* v. *Oregon*.

▶ CRITICAL THINKING
Making Generalizations In what areas did Florence Kelley's actions contribute to significant reform? SS.912.A.3.12

Library of Congress, Prints & Photographs Division, [LC-US262-137950]

Jane Addams on Unsafe Working Conditions for Children

"When the injury of one of the boys resulted in his death, we felt quite sure that the owners of the factory would share our horror and remorse, and that they would do everything possible to prevent the recurrence of such a tragedy. To our surprise they did nothing whatever, and I made my first acquaintance then with those pathetic documents signed by the parents of working children, that they will make no claim for damages resulting from 'carelessness.'"

—from *Twenty Years at Hull House, 1910*

DBQ *DRAWING CONCLUSIONS*

Based on this excerpt, what insight does Addams's description offer about the progressives' view of child labor and the conditions in factories? SS.912.A.1.2, SS.912.A.3.12

poverty. Society also believed that women were more physically vulnerable than men, and for progressives the idea that poor women and their children might be forced into difficult and dangerous working conditions was an important women's issue.

Child Labor

Probably the most emotional progressive issue was the campaign against child labor. Children had always worked on family farms, but mines and factories presented more dangerous and unhealthy working conditions. Muckraker John Spargo's 1906 book, *The Bitter Cry of the Children,* presented detailed evidence of child labor conditions. It told of coal mines that hired thousands of 9- or 10-year-old "breaker boys" to pick slag out of coal, paying them 60 cents for a 10-hour day. It described how the work bent their backs permanently and often crippled their hands. Reports like these convinced states to pass laws that set a minimum age for employment and established other limits on child labor, such as maximum hours children could work. At the same time, many states began passing compulsory education laws, requiring young children to be in school instead of at work.

Health and Safety Codes

Many adult workers also labored in difficult conditions. Factories, coal mines, and railroads were particularly dangerous. When workers were injured or killed on the job, they and their families received little or no compensation. Progressives joined union leaders to pressure states for workers' compensation laws. These laws established insurance funds that employers financed. Workers injured in accidents received payments from the funds.

In two cases, *Lochner* v. *New York* (1905) and *Muller* v. *Oregon* (1908), the U.S. Supreme Court addressed government's authority to regulate business to protect workers. In the *Lochner* case, the Court ruled that a New York law forbidding bakers to work more than 10 hours a day was unconstitutional, saying the state did not have the right to interfere with the liberty of employers and employees. In the *Muller* case, which involved women working in laundries in Oregon, however, the Court upheld the state's right to limit hours.

The different judgments were based on gender differences. The Court stated that healthy mothers were the state's concern and, therefore, the limits on women's working hours did not violate their Fourteenth Amendment rights. In the *Lochner* case, the Court had adhered to a strict construction of the Constitution and decided that government did not have the power to interfere in the right of an employer and employee to make a contract. In the *Muller* case, the Court had been more activist. It interpreted the Constitution so as to give government the power to regulate the workplace because of perceived public need to keep women safe by treating them differently from men.

On March 25, 1911, a tragedy occurred in New York City that led to new reforms. A fire on the top floors of the Triangle Shirtwaist Company caused nearly 150 of the factory's 500 workers to lose their lives. The disaster illustrated that fire precautions and inspections were inadequate. In response, New York created a Factory Investigating Commission and soon passed new laws that reformed the labor code.

Some progressives also favored zoning laws as a method of protecting the public. These laws divided a town or city into zones for commercial, residential, or other development, thereby regulating how land and buildings could be used. Building codes set minimum standards for light, air, room size, and sanitation and required buildings to have fire escapes. Health codes required restaurants and other facilities to maintain clean environments for their patrons.

Zoning laws created a constitutional question. The Fifth Amendment of the Constitution says that no one shall be "deprived of life, liberty, or property, without due process of law; nor shall private property be taken for public use, without just compensation." If the government takes something of value from someone, it is supposed to pay for it. As governments began to impose zoning laws on communities to improve sanitation, safety, and the quality of life, individuals and businesses began to complain that they were losing the use of their property. They argued that the government should compensate them for the loss.

In *Hadacheck* v. *Sebastian* (1915), a brick-maker argued that he needed clay on his land to make bricks and that zoning laws forcing him to move his kiln deprived him of his Fifth Amendment rights. The Court disagreed finding that the zoning laws were a constitutional use of a government's police power to protect public health. In 1922, in *Pennsylvania Coal* v. *Mahon*, however, the court narrowed its interpretation. A coal company owned the rights to mine under a piece of land but a law prohibited mining below land that supported buildings on the surface. The Court agreed that the law had gone too far. Under its Fifth Amendment rights, the coal company had been deprived of its property and was owed compensation. The case established that the government does not have an unlimited right to regulate property use. At some point government regulation of property, even when done in the public interest, does require compensation.

The Prohibition Movement

Many progressives blamed alcohol for many of society's problems. Society at the time tended to view drinking alcohol as acceptable for men, not women, and men consumed the vast majority of all the alcohol produced. As a result social-welfare progressives focused on the problems that alcohol abuse created for women. Settlement-house workers knew that wages were often spent on alcohol instead of the family, and that drunkenness often led to physical abuse, illness, poverty, and abandonment. From these concerns emerged one of the major women's issues of the era, the temperance movement, which **advocated** that people stop, or at least moderate, their alcohol consumption.

Women were important leaders of the temperance movement. In 1874 a group of women formed the Woman's Christian Temperance Union (WCTU). In 1879, Frances Willard became president of the WCTU and held the post for nearly 20 years. Under her leadership, the temperance movement grew to a national movement with significant political influence. In addition to temperance, Willard convinced the WCTU to support women's suffrage and champion many social welfare causes, including prison reform, equal pay for women, protections for children, and the eight hour day. By 1911, the

Library of Congress, Prints & Photographs Division [LC-US262-90543]

The temperance movement gained a key victory in 1917 when Congress passed the Eighteenth Amendment. Prohibition went into effect in 1920, after the amendment was ratified.

▶ CRITICAL THINKING

Summarizing Why did the temperance movement push for the prohibition of alcoholic beverages? HE.912.C.2.7, LAFS.1112.RH.3.7, SS.912.A.1.4, SS.912.A.3.12

advocate to propose a certain position or viewpoint

prohibition laws
banning the manufacture,
transportation, and sale of
alcoholic beverages

WCTU had nearly a quarter of million members. In 1893 evangelical Protestant ministers formed another group, the Anti-Saloon League. When the temperance movement began, it concentrated on reducing alcohol consumption. Later it pressed for **prohibition**—laws banning the manufacture, transportation, and sale of alcoholic beverages.

Despite significant opposition, especially from working-class voters, support for prohibition grew steadily. By 1916, nineteen states had introduced some form of prohibition on alcohol, and leaders of the prohibition movement began to push for a constitutional amendment banning the manufacture, transportation, or sale of alcohol in all of the United States. In 1919, the amendment was ratified. It went into effect in January 1920.

SKILLS PRACTICE

There are many new words in this lesson, including *initiative, referendum, primary, suffrage, prohibition, lobbying* and others. Discuss the new words with a partner. If a word reminds you of any past experience, tell your partner about the experience.
ELD.K12.ELL.SI.1, ELD.K12.ELL.SS.1

Progressives Versus Big Business

Some of the most visible and long-lasting efforts to regulate business during the Progressive Era were focused at the national level. Congress passed a number of proposals to regulate the economy under the presidential administrations of Theodore Roosevelt, William Howard Taft, and Woodrow Wilson. Many progressives agreed that big business needed regulation. Some believed the government should break up big companies to restore competition. This led to the passage of the Sherman Antitrust Act in 1890. Others argued that big business was the most efficient way to organize the economy. They pushed for government to regulate big companies and prevent them from abusing their power. The Interstate Commerce Commission (ICC), created in 1887 to regulate the railroads, was an early example of this kind of thinking.

Some activists even went so far as to advocate socialism—the idea that the government should own and operate industry for the community. They wanted the government to buy up large companies, especially industries that affected everyone, such as railroads and utilities. At its peak, socialism had some national support. Eugene V. Debs, the former leader of the American Railway Union, won nearly a million votes as the American Socialist Party candidate for president in 1912. Most progressives and most Americans, however, believed in the superiority of the American system of free enterprise.

✓ READING PROGRESS CHECK

Explaining How did progressives seek to improve working conditions?

LESSON 1 REVIEW

Reviewing Vocabulary
1. *Drawing Conclusions* What was the primary goal of Progressive Era muckrakers? LAFS.1112.RH.2.4
2. *Determining Cause and Effect* Why did women's organizations work for the passage of prohibition?
HE.912.C.2.7, LAFS.1112.RH.2.4

Using Your Notes
3. *Organizing* Use your notes to write a statement summarizing progressive beliefs. SS.912.A.3.12

Answering the Guiding Questions
4. *Identifying Central Ideas* Who were progressives, and what did they believe caused social problems? SS.912.A.3.12

5. *Summarizing* How did progressives hope to make government more efficient and responsive to citizens?
SS.912.A.3.12
6. *Monitoring* Why did the progressives support the woman suffrage movement? SS.912.A.3.12

7. *Identifying* What problems did social-welfare progressives attempt to reform? SS.912.A.3.12

Writing Activity
8. ARGUMENT Suppose that you are one of the progressives who wanted to bring about change to municipal government. Prepare a persuasive speech that you could deliver to convince people to support your call for reform.
LAFS.1112.WHST.1.1, LAFS.1112.WHST.4.10

Making Generalizations

Why Learn This Skill?

Have you heard statements such as "Only tall people play basketball well," or "Dogs make better pets than cats"? Do you accept these statements at face value, or do you stop and consider whether or not they are valid?

Learning the Skill

The statements listed above are called generalizations. A generalization is a broad statement about a topic. A generalization takes facts from specific cases and then makes an inference that certain general conclusions can be derived from those facts. At a minimum, to be valid, a generalization must be based on accurate information.

Let's examine the generalization, "Only tall people play basketball well." We can find many examples of tall basketball players, but there are also many shorter players who excel at this sport. In other words we can find facts that disprove the generalization.

Suppose that you want to make a generalization about the relative danger of airplane travel compared to automobile travel. First, you would collect accident statistics involving airplanes and cars. Your next step would be to classify the information into categories. Then you would look for relationships between these categories. For example, you might put the airplane and automobile statistics in separate categories. You might also categorize the number of accidents and the number of fatalities. Finally, you should make a generalization that is consistent with most of the facts you gathered.

To make and test generalizations, follow these steps:

- To make a valid generalization, first collect information about a topic. This information must consist of accurate facts, not opinions.
- Compare and contrast what those facts are telling you.

- Look for a conclusion or common element that fits all the facts. Make a generalization from these common elements.
- Test your generalization to see if you can falsify it. Look for facts to support or disprove it.

Practicing this Skill

Reread the lesson "The Roots of Progressivism" and examine the above photo of immigrants in New York in the early 1900s. Then answer these questions:

1. What categories of progressives were there?
2. A progressive muckraker, Jacob Riis, took the photo above. What kinds of issues is he trying to show in the photo?
3. What are the problems that progressives tried to solve?
4. What methods did progressives favor when trying to resolve problems?
5. What generalizations can you make about progressive reformers and the types of reforms they wanted?

Applying the Skill

Making Generalizations Read the lesson "Roosevelt and Taft." Write a generalization about each president that describes their progressivism.

©Bettmann/Corbis

LESSON 2

Roosevelt and Taft

• Can politics fix social problems?

READING HELPDESK

Academic Vocabulary

• regulate
• environmental

Content Vocabulary

• Social Darwinism
• arbitration
• insubordination

TAKING NOTES

Key Ideas and Details

Outlining As you read about the Roosevelt and Taft administrations, use the headings from the lesson to create an Outline similar to the one below.
LAFS.1112.RH.3.7

Roosevelt and Taft
I. Roosevelt Revives the Presidency
  A.
  B.
  C.
II.

**NEXT GENERATION
SUNSHINE STATE STANDARDS**

ELD.K12.ELL.SI.1: English language learners communicate for social and instructional purposes within the school setting.

ELD.K12.ELL.SS.1: English language learners communicate information, ideas and concepts necessary for academic success in the content area of Social Studies.

HE.912.C.2.4: Evaluate how public health policies and government regulations can influence health promotion and disease prevention.

Continued on page 213

IT MATTERS BECAUSE

Energetic and strong-willed, Theodore Roosevelt extended the federal government's ability to conserve natural resources and to curb the power of big business. His successor, William Howard Taft, was less popular with progressives.

Roosevelt Revives the Presidency

GUIDING QUESTION *How much do you think a president's personal beliefs should shape national policy?*

Theodore Roosevelt became president at age 42—the youngest person ever to take the office. In international affairs, he believed in **Social Darwinism,** which held that nations were in competition and only the strongest would survive. Domestically, however, he was a committed progressive. He believed that government should balance the needs of competing groups in American society on behalf of the public interest. His reform programs soon became known as the Square Deal.

Roosevelt Takes on the Trusts

Roosevelt thought that trusts and other large business organizations were efficient and part of the reason for the prosperity of the United States. Yet he also felt that the monopoly power of some trusts hurt the public interest. He wanted to ensure that trusts did not abuse their power.

His first target was J. P. Morgan's railroad holding company, Northern Securities. The company planned an exchange of stock that would merge existing railroad systems, creating a monopoly on railroad traffic in the Northwest. Farmers and business owners feared that without railroad competition, shipping rates would rise and reduce their profits. In 1902, Roosevelt ordered the attorney general to sue Northern Securities under the Sherman Antitrust Act. The suit charged Northern Securities with restraint of trade.

Wealthy, powerful businessmen, including John D. Rockefeller (top right) and J. P. Morgan (right), tower over Theodore Roosevelt, who stands on Wall Street, carrying a sword labeled "Public Service."

1 **Analyzing** What do the giants in the political cartoon represent? LAFS.1112.RH.3.7, SS.912.A.1.4

2 **Making Inferences** What point does the cartoon make by picturing Roosevelt as tiny in relation to the giants? LAFS.1112.RH.3.7, SS.912.A.1.4

Social Darwinism
a philosophy, based on Charles Darwin's theories of evolution and natural selection, stating that humans have developed through competition and natural selection with only the strongest surviving

NEXT GENERATION SUNSHINE STATE STANDARDS

Continued from page 212

LAFS.1112.RH.2.4: Determine the meaning of words and phrases as they are used in a text, including analyzing how an author uses and refines the meaning of a key term over the course of a text (e.g., how Madison defines faction in Federalist No. 10).

LAFS.1112.RH.3.7: Integrate and evaluate multiple sources of information presented in diverse formats and media (e.g., visually, quantitatively, as well as in words) in order to address a question or solve a problem.

LAFS.1112.WHST.1.1: Write arguments focused on discipline-specific content.

LAFS.1112.WHST.4.10: Write routinely over extended time frames (time for reflection and revision) and shorter time frames (a single sitting or a day or two) for a range of discipline-specific tasks, purposes, and audiences.

SS.912.A.1.2: Utilize a variety of primary and secondary sources to identify author, historical significance, audience, and authenticity to understand a historical period.

SS.912.A.1.4: Analyze how images, symbols, objects, cartoons, graphs, charts, maps, and artwork may be used to interpret the significance of time periods and events from the past.

SS.912.A.3.6: Analyze changes that occurred as the United States shifted from agrarian to an industrial society.

SS.912.A.3.12: Compare how different nongovernmental organizations and progressives worked to shape public policy, restore economic opportunities, and correct injustices in American life.

The suit puzzled J. P. Morgan, who asked what could be done to fix the problem. Unmoved, Roosevelt proceeded with the case. In 1904, in *Northern Securities* v. *United States*, the Supreme Court ruled that Morgan's firm had violated the Sherman Antitrust Act. Roosevelt was hailed as a "trustbuster," and his popularity with the public grew.

Northern Securities and the Commerce Clause

The Supreme Court's decision in the *Northern Securities* case marked yet another shift in the relationship between the federal government and private business. Article I, Section 8, of the Constitution states that "The Congress shall have Power . . . To regulate Commerce with foreign Nations, and among the several States. . . ." It was agreed that the Constitution gives the federal government the power to regulate commerce between the states, not within a state. But the definition of what actually constituted "interstate commerce" was open to interpretation.

In the late 1800s, the Court had applied a very strict interpretation of the commerce power. For example, when a sugar company gained control of 98 percent of the sugar industry, the Court ruled in *U.S.* v. *E.C. Knight* (1894), that the Sherman Anti-Trust Act could not be applied because the sugar was manufactured within a state. Manufacturing, the Court said, did not involve interstate commerce, even though the sugar was sold across state lines.

In the *Northern Securities* case, the Court began broadening its interpretation. Northern Securities was based in one state and was simply buying stock in other companies, but the Court, in a narrow 5-4 decision, decided the Antitrust Act could still be applied. In dissent, Justice Oliver Wendell Holmes warned that the decision created a slippery slope: "If the act before us is to be carried out according to what seems to me the logic of the argument . . . I can see no part of the conduct of life with which, on similar principles, Congress might not interfere." Over time, his comment has proved accurate. It would take many decades and several Supreme Court decisions, but the interpretation of the commerce clause of the Constitution has been gradually expanded allowing the federal government more and more power to regulate private business.

SKILLS PRACTICE

Before you read text about changes in how the federal government regulated business, build background by discussing the topic with a partner. Tell your partner what you know, listen to what your partner knows, and combine your background knowledge. ELD.K12.ELL.SI.1, ELD.K12.ELL.SS.1

Library of Congress, Prints & Photographs Division [LC-USZC4-434]

The Coal Strike of 1902

As president, Roosevelt believed that it was his job to keep society operating efficiently by helping settle conflicts between different groups and their interests. In the fall of 1902, he put this belief into practice. He worked to help resolve a coal strike between mine owners and nearly 150,000 members of the United Mine Workers (UMW). The UMW wanted increased pay, reduced hours, and union recognition. If the strike had dragged on, the nation would have faced a coal shortage that could have shut down factories and left many homes unheated.

Roosevelt urged the UMW and the mine owners to accept **arbitration**—a settlement negotiated by an outside party. The union agreed to arbitration. The mine owners refused, however, until Roosevelt threatened to order the army to run the mines. By intervening in the dispute, he took the first step toward establishing the federal government as an honest broker between powerful groups in society.

arbitration settling a dispute by agreeing to accept the decision of an impartial outsider

Regulating Big Business

Despite his lawsuit against Northern Securities and his role in the coal strike, Roosevelt believed that most trusts were good for the economy and that the costs of antitrust action outweighed its benefits. He agreed with the opponents of trust-busting who argued that companies generally formed trusts because it was the most efficient way to do business. Breaking up a trust would make an industry less efficient and drive up costs for the public. Furthermore, by taking a company to court, the government created uncertainty in the industry until the case was resolved. Business leaders would not know how to plan or what to expect, and that too would distort the economy and make it less efficient.

Roosevelt generally accepted these arguments against antitrust action, and he was also keenly aware that America's biggest companies were now competing globally against foreign companies. U.S. Steel had formed a trust in the United States, but it was competing against huge European steel companies in Britain, France, and Germany. Standard Oil had formed a trust in the United States, but it was competing globally against Burmah Oil in Britain (today known as BP), Royal Dutch Petroleum (today known as Shell Oil), and many other companies. Antitrust action against an American company might cripple its ability to compete internationally.

As a progressive, Roosevelt valued efficiency, and he believed that the United States had to be a world power, militarily and economically, in order to prosper. But as a progressive, he also distrusted large concentrations of power and the potential for corruption and harm to the public good. So instead of aggressively seeking to break up trusts, he proposed to create a federal agency to investigate corporations and publicize the findings. He believed the most effective way to prevent big business from abusing its power was to keep the public informed.

In 1903, Roosevelt convinced Congress to create the Department of Commerce and Labor. The following year, this department began investigating U.S. Steel, a gigantic holding company that had been created in 1901. Worried about a possible antitrust lawsuit, the company's leaders met privately with Roosevelt. They offered to open their files for examination. In exchange, the Department of Commerce and Labor would privately tell the company about any problems and allow them to fix the problems quietly. Roosevelt accepted this "gentlemen's agreement," as he called it, and soon made similar deals with other companies. These deals gave him the ability to **regulate** big business without having to sacrifice economic efficiency by breaking up the trusts.

In keeping with his belief in regulation, Roosevelt pushed the Hepburn Act through Congress in 1906. The act was intended to strengthen the Interstate Commerce Commission (ICC) by giving it the power to set railroad rates. At first, railroad companies were suspicious of the ICC. However, the railroads eventually realized they could work with the commission to set rates and regulations that limited competition and prevented new competitors from entering the industry. By 1920, the ICC had begun setting rates at levels intended to ensure the industry's profits.

By 1905, consumer protection had become a national issue. As Americans read news stories by muckrakers and listened to the concerns of progressive reformers, they increasingly felt that the costs of a laissez-faire approach to the economy outweighed the benefits. That year, a muckraker journalist named Samuel Hopkins Adams published several articles in Collier's magazine describing the patent medicine business. Many companies patented and marketed potions they claimed would cure a variety of ills. Many of these medicines were little more than alcohol, colored water, and sugar. Others contained caffeine, opium, cocaine, and other dangerous compounds. Consumers had no way to know what they were taking, nor did they know whether the medicines worked as claimed. Many Americans were equally concerned about the food they ate. Dr. W. H. Wiley, chief chemist at the United States Department of Agriculture, had issued reports documenting dangerous preservatives, including formaldehyde and borax, being used in what he called "embalmed meat."

For similar reasons, food preparation businesses came under scrutiny. In 1906 Upton Sinclair published a novel, *The Jungle*, based on his close observations of the slaughterhouses of Chicago. The appalling conditions in the meatpacking industry, as described by Sinclair, enraged consumers.

Roosevelt and Congress responded with the Meat Inspection Act, passed in 1906. It required federal inspection of meat sold through interstate commerce and required the Agriculture Department to set standards of cleanliness in meatpacking plants. The Pure Food and Drug Act, passed on the same day in 1906, prohibited the manufacture, sale, or shipment of impure or falsely labeled food and drugs.

These two acts marked yet another change in the relationship between government and business. In both cases, the U.S. Department of Agriculture (USDA) was given authority to inspect business operations and ensure that products were safe before they could be sold to the public. Initially, the Bureau of Chemistry at the U.S. Department of Agriculture was in charge of enforcing the Pure Food and Drug Act. The Bureau later became the Food and Drug Administration, or FDA, that continues to regulate food and drugs today. The benefits of the new laws were obvious. Consumers were less likely to become sick and could expect that products actually contained the ingredients on their labels. The costs of the law, as with other regulations of the economy, meant that companies had to charge more for their products. Putting labels on products cost money, and companies passed that on to consumers. Given what Wiley had found in people's food prior to the law, many Americans and government leaders thought the costs were worth it.

☑ READING PROGRESS CHECK

Analyzing What were Theodore Roosevelt's beliefs about big business, and how did he act on those beliefs during the early 1900s?

There's More Online! connected.mcgraw-hill.com

Analyzing
PRIMARY SOURCES

Upton Sinclair on the Meatpacking Industry

❝[T]here would come all the way back from Europe old sausage that had been rejected, and that was [moldy] and white—it would be dosed with borax and glycerine, and dumped into the hoppers, and made over again for home consumption. . . . There would be meat stored in great piles in rooms; and the water from leaky roofs would drip over it, and thousands of rats would race about [upon] it.❞

—from *The Jungle*, 1906

DBQ ***DRAWING CONCLUSIONS***

Based on this excerpt, how would you describe the attitude of slaughterhouse owners in Sinclair's time? SS.912.A.1.2

regulate to control or direct with rules

environmental relating to the environment; the complex system of plants, animals, water, and soil

Gifford Pinchot (1865–1946)

Connecticut native Gifford Pinchot studied forestry at schools in Europe before becoming head of the U.S. Forest Service. As head, he helped develop the forest service system and was influential in the conservation movement, which he enthusiastically supported. He advocated wise use of natural resources and their stewardship by the federal government, believing that business would not sufficiently protect America's natural resources.

▶ **CRITICAL THINKING**

Making Generalizations How might Pinchot's study of forestry have helped him in his work with the U.S. Forest Service?
SS.912.A.3.12

American naturalist John Muir looks out over Yosemite. Muir believed in preserving wilderness areas and successfully lobbied for the creation of Yosemite National Park.

Conservation

GUIDING QUESTION *Why did President Roosevelt support conservation?*

Of all his progressive actions, Roosevelt may be best remembered for his efforts in the area of **environmental** conservation. Roosevelt realized that the nation's bountiful natural resources were being used up at an alarming rate. He urged Americans to conserve those resources.

Roosevelt was an enthusiastic outdoorsman, and he valued the country's minerals, animals, and rugged terrain. He cautioned against unregulated use of public lands and argued that conservation should be the guiding principle in managing the United States's natural resources.

In his 1907 annual message to Congress, Roosevelt said: "[T]o waste, to destroy our natural resources, to skin and exhaust the land instead of using it so as to increase its usefulness, will result in undermining in the days of our children the very prosperity which we ought by right to hand down to them amplified and developed."

Western Land Development

Roosevelt quickly applied his philosophy in the dry Western states, where farmers and city dwellers competed for scarce water. In 1902, Roosevelt supported passage of the Newlands Reclamation Act. This act authorized the use of federal funds from public land sales to pay for irrigation and land development projects. The federal government thus began transforming the West's landscape and economy on a large scale.

Roosevelt also backed efforts to save the nation's forests. He supported careful management of the timber resources of the West. He appointed his close friend Gifford Pinchot to head the United States Forest Service, established in 1905.

As progressives, Roosevelt and Pinchot both believed that trained experts in forestry and resource management should manage the nation's forests. These professional managers would apply the same scientific standards to the landscape that others were applying to managing cities and industry. With the president's support, Pinchot's department drew up regulations to control lumbering on federal lands. Roosevelt also added more than 100 million acres to the protected national forests and established five new national parks and 51 federal wildlife reservations.

Roosevelt's Legacy

President Theodore Roosevelt changed the role of the federal government. He used his power in the White House to present his views, calling it his "bully pulpit." Increasingly, Americans began looking to the federal government to solve the nation's economic and social problems.

Under Roosevelt, the power of the executive branch of government had dramatically increased. The Interstate Commerce Commission, through the Hepburn Act, could set rates. The Department of Commerce and Labor could monitor business. And the attorney general could rapidly bring antitrust lawsuits under the Expedition Act. In addition, Roosevelt's concern for the environment and for protection of the wild areas of the United States helped develop a national parks system that preceded the establishment of the National Park Service in 1916.

☑ **READING PROGRESS CHECK**

Examining What were President Roosevelt's views on conservation, and how did he act on those views?

(t)The Granger Collection, New York; (b)Library of Congress, Prints & Photographs Division [LC-DIG-ggbain-06861]

Taft's Reforms

GUIDING QUESTION *How did President Taft's beliefs differ from the progressives' beliefs?*

Roosevelt believed William Howard Taft, his secretary of war, was the ideal person to continue his policies. Taft easily secured the Republican nomination and won the election of 1908. The Democratic candidate, William Jennings Bryan, lost for a third time.

Taft Angers Progressives

Like many progressives, Taft believed high tariffs limited competition, hurt consumers, and protected trusts. Roosevelt had warned him to stay away from tariff reform because it would divide the Republican Party. Nevertheless, Taft called Congress into special session to lower tariff rates. The tariff debate did, indeed, divide the Republican Party into two groups: the progressives, who favored tariff reduction, and conservative Republicans, who wanted to maintain high tariffs. As negotiations dragged on, Taft's support for tariff reductions waned. Finally, he signed into law the Payne-Aldrich Tariff, which hardly cut tariffs at all and actually raised them on some goods. Progressives felt outraged by Taft's decision.

In 1909, Taft further angered progressives by replacing Roosevelt's secretary of the interior, James R. Garfield, with Richard A. Ballinger. Garfield was an aggressive conservationist; Ballinger was a conservative corporate lawyer. Once in office, Ballinger tried to open nearly a million acres of public lands to private development. Gifford Pinchot accused Ballinger of planning to give valuable public lands in Alaska to a private business group for his own profit. Taft's attorney general investigated the charges and decided they were unfounded. Not satisfied, Pinchot went to the press and asked Congress to investigate. Taft fired Pinchot for **insubordination,** or disobedience to authority. The congressional investigation cleared Ballinger.

By the second half of Taft's term of office, many Americans had become so frustrated with him that the congressional elections of 1910 resulted in a sweeping Democratic victory. Democrats took the majority in the House, and Democrats and progressive Republicans gained control of the Senate from conservative Republicans.

(t)©Corbis; (b)Picture Research Consultants & Archives

At a Georgia cotton mill in 1909, two boys keep a spinning machine running by repairing broken thread and replacing bobbins as they are filled.

▶ CRITICAL THINKING

Predicting Consequences What might happen if one of these boys slips? LAFS.1112.RH.3.7, SS.912.A.1.4

This page from the *Los Angeles Times*, January 9, 1910, highlights the controversy between progressive Gifford Pinchot and Taft's secretary of the interior, Richard Ballinger. Pinchot leaked a story to the press alleging that Ballinger turned over public lands for personal profit.

▶ CRITICAL THINKING

Determining Cause and Effect Why do you think Pinchot made accusations against Ballinger? LAFS.1112.RH.3.7, SS.912.A.1.4

n Nine Parts, Complete—150 Pages   Part 1—Telegraph Sheet—12 Pages

The Los Angeles Times

enty-Ninth Year.   MINIMUM TEMPERATURES: LOS ANGELES, 45; Boston, 20; New York, 18; Washington to; Pittsburgh, 8; Cincinnati, 6; Chicago, 14; Kansas City, 26; St. Paul, —4; Jacksonville, 30.

ER ANNUM, $9.00 { Per Month, 75 Cents, Or 2½ Cents a Copr.   SUNDAY MORNING, JANUARY 9, 1910.   On All News Stands, Trains and Streets, }5 CENTS.

THE WEATHER.
BRIEF REPORT.

FORECAST—For Los Angeles and nity: Cloudy; light northeast wind, anging to south. For San Francisco d vicinity: Cloudy, with rain by ht; fresh southeast wind. unrise, 6:59; sunset, 5:01; moon es 6:51 a.m. Monday.
YESTERDAY: Maximum tempera-e, 64 deg.; minimum, 45 deg. Wind ..m., northeast; velocity, 14 miles. At p.m., west; velocity 9 miles. At night the temperature was 46 deg.; ar.
TODAY—A 2 a.m. the temperature s 47 deg.; partly cloudy. The complete weather report to-y comparative temperatures, l be found on page 23, Part V.)

The Times

tion Yesterday..............64,750

INDEX TO PARTS AND PAGES.

rt 1.
Political Excitement in England.
Developments in Pinchot Case.
Violet Asquith Going Insane.
All the Latest Foreign News.
News of the Pacific Slope.
ding Comparisons at National Capital.
Life's Seamy Side Exposed.

TRAITOR

BETRAYER CAUGHT.

Federal Official Is in Tombs.

Theft of Attorney-General's Letter Is Traced to Trusted Man.

Sugar Frauds Case Missive Is Published in a Magazine.

Other Communications Have Been Stolen and Copied

BELLIGERENT.

PINCHOT DEFIANT.

Urges Friends to Fight.

Tells Former Subordinates That Battle Has Just Begun.

*"You Serve Greater Master Than Administration."
He Says.*

Washington Excited Over Possible Results of For-

THE MAN WHO STARTED ALL THE RUMPUS.

BRITAIN BOILING.

PRESS IS ABLAZE.

British Election Hottest in History.

Despite Invective Margin Between Victory and Defeat Is Narrow.

Curzon Calls Old-Age Pension Canard "Calculated and Frigid Lie."

Orators Refight Boer War and Resurrect Statesmen to

insubordination
disobedience to authority

Taft disappointed Roosevelt, who attempted to unseat him in the 1912 Republican nomination.

Taft's Achievements

Despite his political problems, Taft also had several successes. Although Roosevelt was nicknamed the "trustbuster," Taft actually brought twice as many antitrust cases in four years as his predecessor had in seven. In other areas, Taft also pursued progressive policies. In 1912, he established the Children's Bureau. This agency investigated and publicized the problems of child labor.

The Ballinger-Pinchot controversy aside, Taft was also a dedicated conservationist. In 1910, Taft set up the Bureau of Mines to monitor the activities of mining companies, expand national forests, and protect waterpower sites from private development. The bureau helped make possible many new technologies in the field of mining.

Although disturbed by stories of Taft's "betrayal" of his progressivism, Roosevelt refused to criticize the president. He soon became impatient. In 1907, while president, Roosevelt had approved the purchase of the Tennessee Coal and Iron Company by U.S. Steel. In October 1911, Taft declared that the deal violated the Sherman Antitrust Act. Roosevelt believed Taft's focus on breaking up trusts was destroying the system of cooperation and regulation that he had set up with big business. In November 1911, Roosevelt publicly criticized Taft for this decision.

After Roosevelt broke with Taft, it was only a matter of time before progressives convinced Roosevelt to reenter politics. In late February 1912, Roosevelt announced he would enter the presidential campaign of 1912 and attempt to replace Taft as the Republican nominee for president.

☑ READING PROGRESS CHECK

Evaluating Which of Taft's actions most harmed his standing among progressives?

Library of Congress, Prints and Photographs Division [LC-USZ62-13027]

LESSON 2 REVIEW

Reviewing Vocabulary
1. *Explaining* Why did President Taft fire Gifford Pinchot for insubordination? LAFS.1112.RH.2.4

Using Your Notes
2. *Identifying* Use your notes to identify ways in which Taft helped conservation efforts and child labor problems. SS.912.A.3.12

Answering the Guiding Questions
3. *Evaluating* What approach did Roosevelt take toward regulating big business? LAFS.1112.RH.3.7, SS.912.A.3.12

4. *Analyzing* Why did President Roosevelt support conservation? LAFS.1112.RH.3.7, SS.912.A.3.12

5. *Examining* How did President Taft's beliefs differ from the progressives' beliefs? LAFS.1112.RH.3.7, SS.912.A.3.12

Writing Activity
6. ARGUMENT Who did more to support the conservation of natural resources: President Roosevelt or President Taft? Write an essay in which you express your opinion and support it with specific examples. LAFS.1112.WHST.1.1, LAFS.1112.WHST.4.10

Drawing Inferences

Why Learn This Skill?

Just as you are about to leave home to catch your school bus, you hear a radio report. There is a traffic jam near the bus garage. Your bus is late. Although no one told you, you conclude that the traffic jam probably made the bus late, and you use your phone to call a friend for a ride home. You have made an inference. From the limited facts available, you formed a conclusion. By combining facts and general knowledge, you made an inference about the reasons the bus was late. Making inferences is an important skill because we live in a world of imperfect knowledge. We cannot always have all the facts, but we have to make decisions based on what we do know. Many times, having only some of the facts is enough to reach a conclusion that lets you make a decision, if you have been careful about the inferences you have made.

Learning the Skill

Learning how to make inferences will help you draw conclusions about particular situations. To make accurate inferences, follow these steps:

- Read or listen carefully for stated facts and ideas.
- Review what you already know about the topic or situation.
- Think about similar experiences you have had in the past to help understand the current situation.
- Use logic and common sense to form a conclusion about the topic or situation.
- If possible, find information that confirms or disproves your inference.
- Recognize that you don't have all the information you need, and you might be wrong.
- Decide whether to act on your inference.

Practicing this Skill

On December 8, 1903, Samuel Langley was ready for his second attempt at flying a manned, self-propelled aircraft. This had never been done before. Langley used a $50,000 U.S. government grant to build a plane based on unmanned aircraft designs, adding a very powerful engine. The plane broke apart on takeoff and crashed into the Potomac River.

In contrast, Wilbur and Orville Wright used a little more than $1,000 of their personal savings to build an aircraft. The brothers carefully studied the problems with previous planes and designed one with better wings, a more efficient propeller, and a strong but light engine. On December 17, 1903, these intrepid Americans made the first manned, powered flight in history on the sand dunes of Kitty Hawk, North Carolina.

1. What are the facts regarding Langley's attempt?
2. What are the facts regarding the Wright brothers' attempt?
3. What inferences might you draw based on the success of the Wright brothers and failure of Langley?
4. What experience and prior knowledge helped you make your inference?
5. How could you prove or disprove your inference?

Applying the Skill

Drawing Inferences Both President Roosevelt and President Wilson created several agencies to regulate business. Read the lessons describing their presidencies and then answer these questions. What inferences can you make about their beliefs concerning government agencies and the economy? Based on what you know about government agencies today, what inferences can you make about the progressive emphasis on creating government agencies?

U.S. Air Force photo

LESSON 3
The Wilson Years

ESSENTIAL QUESTION

• Can politics fix social problems?

READING HELPDESK

Academic Vocabulary

- academic
- unconstitutional

Content Vocabulary

- direct tax
- indirect tax
- income tax
- unfair trade practices

TAKING NOTES

Key Ideas and Details

Outlining As you read about progressivism during the Wilson administration, complete a chart similar to the one below by listing Wilson's progressive economic and social reforms. LAFS.1112.RH.3.7, SS.912.A.3.12

Economic Reforms	Social Reforms

NEXT GENERATION SUNSHINE STATE STANDARDS

LAFS.1112.RH.2.4: Determine the meaning of words and phrases as they are used in a text, including analyzing how an author uses and refines the meaning of a key term over the course of a text (e.g., how Madison defines faction in Federalist No. 10).

Continued on page 221

IT MATTERS BECAUSE
Woodrow Wilson, a progressive Democrat, won the election of 1912. While in office, he supported lower tariffs, more regulation of business, and the creation of the Federal Reserve System.

The Election of 1912

GUIDING QUESTION *How was the election of 1912 different from previous presidential elections?*

The 1912 presidential campaign featured a current president, a former president, and an **academic** who had entered politics only two years earlier. The election's outcome determined the path of the Progressive movement.

Picking the Candidates

Believing that President William Howard Taft had failed to live up to progressive ideals, Theodore Roosevelt informed seven state governors that he was willing to accept the Republican nomination. "My hat is in the ring!" he declared. "The fight is on."

The struggle for control of the Republican Party reached its climax at the national convention in Chicago in June 1912. Conservatives rallied behind Taft. Most progressives supported Roosevelt. When it became clear that Taft's delegates controlled the nomination, Roosevelt decided to leave the party and campaign as an independent.

Declaring himself "fit as a bull moose," Roosevelt became the presidential candidate for the newly formed Progressive Party, which quickly became known as the Bull Moose Party. Because Taft had alienated so many groups, the election of 1912 became a contest between two progressives: Roosevelt and the Democratic candidate Woodrow Wilson.

After a university teaching career that culminated in his becoming the president of Princeton University, Woodrow Wilson entered politics as a firm progressive. As the governor of New Jersey, he pushed through many progressive reforms.

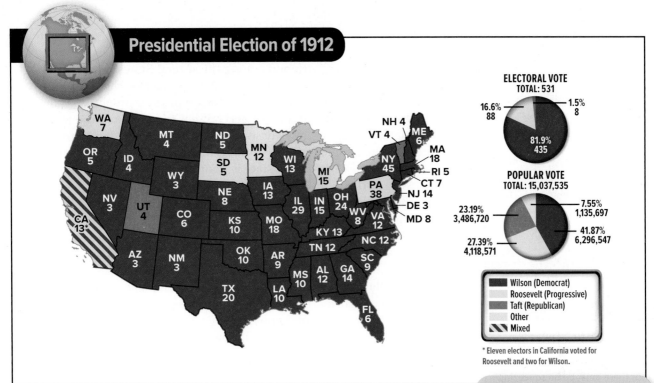

Presidential Election of 1912

ELECTORAL VOTE
TOTAL: 531

16.6%
88

1.5%
8

81.9%
435

POPULAR VOTE
TOTAL: 15,037,535

23.19%
3,486,720

7.55%
1,135,697

41.87%
6,296,547

27.39%
4,118,571

- ■ Wilson (Democrat)
- □ Roosevelt (Progressive)
- ▨ Taft (Republican)
- □ Other
- ▨ Mixed

* Eleven electors in California voted for Roosevelt and two for Wilson.

He introduced the direct primary, established utility regulatory boards, and allowed cities to adopt the commissioner form of government. In less than two years, New Jersey became a model of progressive reform.

Wilson Versus Roosevelt

The election of 1912 was a contest between two progressives with different approaches to reform. Roosevelt accepted large trusts as a fact of life and set out to create proposals to increase regulation. He favored laws to protect women and children in the labor force and supported workers' compensation for those injured on the job. Roosevelt called his program the New Nationalism.

Wilson countered with what he called the New Freedom. He criticized Roosevelt's New Nationalism for supporting "regulated monopoly." Wilson argued that Roosevelt's approach gave the federal government too much power in the economy and did nothing to restore competition. Wilson believed that freedom outweighed efficiency.

As expected, Roosevelt and Taft split the Republican voters. Wilson won the Electoral College with 435 votes. He won the election even though he received less than 42 percent of the popular vote. For the first time since Grover Cleveland's election in 1892, a Democrat was elected president.

✅ **READING PROGRESS CHECK**

Summarizing How did having three nominees running for president make the election of 1912 different from others?

Wilson's Reforms

GUIDING QUESTION *How did Wilson earn the respect of progressives?*

As the new Chief Executive, Wilson lost no time in embarking on his program of progressive reform. During his eight years as president, Wilson demonstrated his executive power as he crafted reforms affecting tariffs, the banking system, trusts, and workers' rights.

GEOGRAPHY CONNECTION

The election of 1912 was the first presidential election in which all of the then 48 states participated.

1 THE WORLD IN SPATIAL TERMS
In which two states did Taft win electoral votes? SS.912.A.1.4

2 PLACES AND REGIONS
In what region did Roosevelt have the most electoral support? SS.912.A.1.4

NEXT GENERATION SUNSHINE STATE STANDARDS

Continued from page 220

LAFS.1112.RH.3.7: Integrate and evaluate multiple sources of information presented in diverse formats and media (e.g., visually, quantitatively, as well as in words) in order to address a question or solve a problem.

LAFS.1112.WHST.1.1: Write arguments focused on discipline-specific content.

LAFS.1112.WHST.4.10: Write routinely over extended time frames (time for reflection and revision) and shorter time frames (a single sitting or a day or two) for a range of discipline-specific tasks, purposes, and audiences.

SS.912.A.1.2: Utilize a variety of primary and secondary sources to identify author, historical significance, audience, and authenticity to understand a historical period.

SS.912.A.1.4 :Analyze how images, symbols, objects, cartoons, graphs, charts, maps, and artwork may be used to interpret the significance of time periods and events from the past.

Continued on page 222

---

academic a person associated
with higher learning at a scholarly
institution

direct tax a tax imposed
directly on a person or their
property

indirect tax a tax that
someone pays, but the tax burden
falls on someone else

Analyzing
PRIMARY SOURCES

Wilson's New Freedom

"I am perfectly willing that
[a business] should beat any
competitor by fair means. . . .
But there must be no squeezing
out the beginner . . . no secret
arrangements against him. All
the fair competition you choose,
but no unfair competition of
any kind . . ."

—from *The New Freedom*, 1918

 DBQ *MAKING INFERENCES*

What can you infer about Wilson's
belief in free enterprise? SS.912.A.1.2

income tax a tax based
on the net income of a person
or business

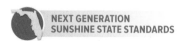

**NEXT GENERATION
SUNSHINE STATE STANDARDS**

Continued from page 221

SS.912.A.1.7: Describe various socio-cultural
aspects of American life including arts, artifacts,
literature, education, and publications.

SS.912.A.3.9: Examine causes, course, and
consequences of the labor movement in the late
19th and early 20th centuries.

SS.912.A.3.12: Compare how different
nongovernmental organizations and
progressives worked to shape public policy,
restore economic opportunities, and correct
injustices in American life.

SS.912.H.1.6: Analyze how current events are
explained by artistic and cultural trends of the
past.

SS.912.H.2.5: Analyze how current events
are explained by artistic and cultural trends of
the past.

Income Taxes and the 16th Amendment

Article 1, section 2 of the Constitution states that "Representatives and
direct Taxes shall be apportioned among the several States which may be
included within this Union, according to their respective Numbers . . ." A
direct tax is a tax imposed directly on a person or their property. If the
federal government wants to tax property, it has to make sure the tax is
proportionate among the states based on their population. If a state has
20 percent of the people in the country, it has to pay 20 percent of the
taxes, regardless of whether the state is poor or wealthy. This requirement
makes it very difficult for Congress to pass direct taxes.

An **indirect tax** is a tax that someone pays, but the tax burden falls on
someone else. For example, if a company pays a tax for each car it makes, it
simply includes that tax in the price of the car. The person who really pays
the tax is the consumer, but they pay it *indirectly.* Sales taxes, excise taxes,
and tariffs are all indirect taxes. An income tax on wages is also an indirect
tax. It is actually an indirect tax on an employer. Employers know workers
have to pay income taxes. So they have to pay high enough wages that
workers will still take the job knowing they will pay income taxes. If there
were no income taxes, employers could pay workers less and still get them
to take the job.

Up until the early 1900s, the federal government had raised most of its
money using sales taxes, excise taxes, and tariffs. As the progressive movement
began, many progressives began to argue that **income taxes** were the best way
to fund the federal government. An income tax could be graduated. You could
tax wealthy people at a higher percentage than poor people. A graduated
income tax is sometimes called a progressive tax.

In 1894, Congress imposed income taxes on wealthy Americans. The
following year, the Supreme Court struck down the income tax law because it
was not just a tax on wages, but a tax on all types of income. If a person earned
income because they rented property, or because they owned stocks that paid
dividends, they still had to pay the income tax. The Supreme Court declared
that an income tax that included income from property was a direct tax, not an
indirect tax, and since it had not been divided proportionately among the
states, it was unconstitutional.

The Court's decision frustrated progressives. It meant that income
taxes could be put on wages, and fall on working class Americans, but that
rich people who earned most of their income from property could not be
taxed on that income. Soon afterward, progressives began pressing for a
Constitutional amendment that would allow the federal government to tax
income, no matter its source, and without having to divide it
proportionately among the states. Both President Roosevelt and President
Taft supported the amendment as did many political leaders in both parties.
In February 1913, the 16th amendment allowing for taxes on incomes was
ratified by the states.

A little over two months later, and only five weeks after taking office,
President Wilson appeared before Congress, the first president to do so
since John Adams. He had come to present his bill to reduce tariffs and
introduce a federal income tax. Wilson personally lobbied members of
Congress to support the tariff reduction bill. Not even Roosevelt had taken
such an active role in promoting legislation. In 1913 Congress passed the
Revenue Act of 1913, also known as the Underwood-Simmons Act, and
Wilson signed it into law. This law reduced the average tariff on imported
goods to about 30 percent of the value of the goods and provided for levying

a federal graduated income tax. The income tax was intended to replace the revenue lost by the tariff reductions.

Reforming the Banks

The United States had not had a central bank since the 1830s. Periodic economic depressions that had occurred after that time had destroyed numerous small banks, wiping out many of their customers' life savings.

To restore public confidence in the banking system, Wilson supported a federal reserve system. Banks would have to keep part of their deposits in one of 12 reserve banks, providing a cushion against unexpected financial losses. The Federal Reserve Act of 1913 created the regional reserve banks, supervised by a Board of Governors appointed by the president. The Board could set the interest rates the reserve banks charged other banks, thereby indirectly controlling the nation's interest rates and the amount of money in circulation.

The Federal Reserve Act became one of the most significant pieces of legislation in American history. It created an independent agency that began to use monetary policy to manage the nation's economy. Monetary policy refers to policies that adjust a nation's money supply in order to regulate the economy. If the Federal Reserve sets interest rates low, businesses and individuals will generally borrow more money. This increases the amount of money in circulation and causes the economy to grow. If interest rates are raised, people borrow less, which slows the economy, but also reduces inflation. Generally speaking, the goal of monetary policy is to contract the money supply if inflation is too high, and expand the money supply if the economy is in a recession and unemployment is too high.

Antitrust Action

During his campaign, Wilson had promised to restore competition to the economy by breaking up monopolies. After the election, he realized that Roosevelt had been right: big businesses were more efficient and unlikely to be replaced by smaller, more competitive firms. Wilson decided against pursuing the monopolies. Progressives in Congress, however, continued to demand action against big business. In 1914, at Wilson's request, Congress created the Federal Trade Commission (FTC) to monitor American business. The FTC had the power to investigate companies and issue "cease and desist" orders against those it found to be engaging in **unfair trade practices,** or practices that hurt competition. If a business disagreed with its rulings, it could take the FTC to court.

unfair trade practices
trading practices that derive a gain at the expense of competition

Wilson did not want the FTC to break up big business. Instead, it was to work toward limiting unfair trade practices. He deliberately appointed conservative business leaders as the FTC's first commissioners. Unsatisfied by Wilson's approach, progressives in Congress responded by passing the Clayton Antitrust Act in 1914. The act outlawed certain practices that restricted competition such as price discrimination, or charging different customers different prices. The passing of the Clayton Antitrust Act corrected deficiencies in the Sherman Antitrust Act of 1890.

Before the law passed, labor unions lobbied Congress to exempt unions. As a result, the Clayton Antitrust Act stated that its provisions did not apply to labor organizations or agricultural organizations. When the bill became law, Samuel Gompers, the head of the American Federation of Labor, called the act the workers' "Magna Carta" because it gave unions the right to exist.

Regulating Big Business

In 1916 Wilson signed the first federal law regulating child labor. The Keating-Owen Child Labor Act prohibited the employment of children unconstitutional not in accordance with or authorized by the constitution of a state or society

under the age of 14 in factories producing goods for interstate commerce. Although the Supreme Court declared the law **unconstitutional** in 1918, Wilson's effort helped his reputation among progressives. He also supported the Adamson Act, which established the eight-hour workday for railroad workers, and the Federal Farm Loan Act, which helped provide low-interest loans to farmers.

☑ READING PROGRESS CHECK

Drawing Conclusions Why was the Federal Reserve Act so important?

Progressivism's Legacies and Limits

GUIDING QUESTION *What do you believe were progressivism's most important success and biggest failure?*

During his presidency, Wilson built upon Roosevelt's foundation. He expanded both the federal government and the power of the president.

New Roles for Government
Progressivism made important changes in the political life of the United States. Before this era, most Americans did not expect the government to pass laws protecting workers or regulating big business. In fact, many courts had previously ruled the passage of such laws unconstitutional. By the end of the Progressive Era, however, both legal and public opinion had shifted. Increasingly, Americans expected the government, particularly the federal government, to play a more active role in regulating the economy and solving social problems.

The Limits of Progressivism
The most conspicuous limit to progressivism was its failure to address racial and religious discrimination. African Americans themselves, however, were absorbing the reform spirit, which fueled their long-standing desire for advancement. In 1905 W.E.B. Du Bois and 28 other African American leaders met at Niagara Falls to demand full rights for African Americans. There they launched what became known as the Niagara Movement.

African American leaders such as W.E.B. Du Bois worked to end racial discrimination, communicating through publications including the NAACP's journal, *The Crisis.*

▶ CRITICAL THINKING
Making Connections What are ways that people today work to reduce discrimination? SS.912.A.1.4, SS.912.H.1.6

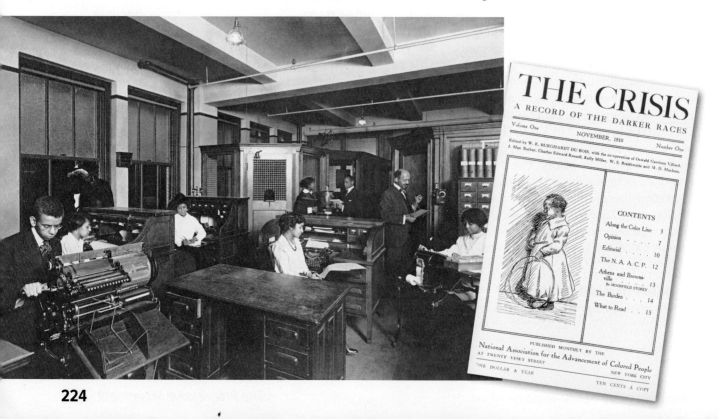

Du Bois and other African American leaders believed that voting rights were essential to end lynching and racial discrimination. "The power of the ballot we need in sheer self-defense," Du Bois said, "else what shall save us from a second slavery? Freedom too, the long-sought we still seek,—the freedom of life and limb, the freedom to work and think, the freedom to love and aspire. Work, culture, liberty,—all these we need, not singly, but together."

In 1908 race riots in Springfield, Illinois, shocked many people, including Mary White Ovington, a settlement house worker. She had been studying the living conditions of African Americans in New York, determined to do something to improve their situation. Other progressives, including Jane Addams of Hull House and muckrakers Ida Wells-Barnett and Lincoln Steffens, joined Ovington in calling for change. Capitalizing on Springfield as Abraham Lincoln's hometown and on the centennial of his birthday on February 12, 1909, they organized a national conference in Springfield to take stock of the progress in emancipation. At a second conference the following year, the National Association for the Advancement of Colored People (NAACP) was born. Through Du Bois, the members learned of the Niagara Movement, and the two groups eventually merged.

African Americans were not the only minority group facing discrimination. Jewish people also lived in fear of mob violence. In 1913 Leo Frank, a Jew being tried in Atlanta for a murder that the facts proved he did not commit, was sentenced to death. Although his sentence was changed to life imprisonment, a mob lynched him two years later.

In this context, lawyer Sigmund Livingston started the Anti-Defamation League (ADL) to combat stereotypes and discrimination. According to its 1913 charter, the ADL's "ultimate purpose [was] to secure justice and fair treatment to all citizens alike and to put an end forever to unjust and unfair discrimination against and ridicule of any sect or body of citizens." The ADL worked to remove negative portrayals of Jews in movies, in print, and on stage. For example, the League protested a World War I army manual that claimed Jews were likely to pretend to be sick to escape work or battle. When the ADL complained, President Wilson had the manual recalled.

✓ **READING PROGRESS CHECK**

Identifying What do you think were progressivism's most important success and biggest failure?

LESSON 3 REVIEW

Reviewing Vocabulary
1. *Defining* The Federal Trade Commission had the power to investigate companies engaging in what actions that unfairly limited competition? LAFS.1112.RH.2.4

Using Your Notes
2. *Comparing and Contrasting* Review the notes that you completed during the lesson to write a statement comparing and contrasting Wilson's economic and social reforms.

Answering the Guiding Questions
3. *Contrasting* How was the election of 1912 different from previous presidential elections?

4. *Monitoring* How did Wilson earn the respect of progressives? SS.912.A.3.12

5. *Evaluating* What do you believe were progressivism's most important success and biggest failure? SS.912.A.3.12

Writing Activity
6. INFORMATIVE/EXPLANATORY During the Progressive Era, nongovernmental organizations such as the NAACP and the ADL worked to gain rights and end discrimination for minority groups. Explain what steps these groups took to correct injustices in American life. LAFS.1112.WHST.1.2, LAFS.1112.WHST.4.10

STUDY GUIDE

THE ROOTS OF PROGRESSIVISM
LESSON 1

PROGRESSIVES WERE . . .
- Reformers
- Idealists

GOVERNMENT REFORMS . . .
- Improved efficiency
- Increased democracy

SOCIAL CHANGES INCLUDED . . .
- Woman suffrage
- Health & safety codes
- Prohibition

ROOSEVELT AND TAFT
LESSON 2

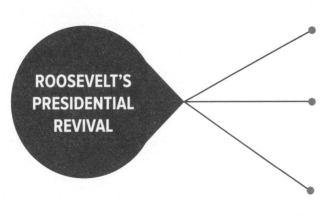

ROOSEVELT'S PRESIDENTIAL REVIVAL

TRUSTBUSTING
- *Northern Securities* v. *United States*
- Coal Strike of 1902

REGULATING BIG BUSINESS
- Created Department of Commerce and Labor
- Food and Drug Administration
- Meat Inspection Act
- Children's Bureau

CONSERVATION
- Newlands Reclamation Act
- United States Forest Service
- System of National Parks
- Bureau of Mines

THE WILSON YEARS
LESSON 3

PROGRESSIVISM'S LEGACIES
- Sixteenth Amendment: progressive income taxes
- Revenue Act of 1913: reduced tariffs
- Federal Reserve Act: created a federal reserve system and restored public confidence
- Federal Trade Commission: monitored American business and investigated unfair trade practices
- Keating-Owens Child Labor Act: regulated child labor

LIMITS OF PROGRESSIVISM
- Progressives did not adequately address racial and religious discrimination

Directions: On a separate sheet of paper, answer the questions below. Make sure you read carefully and answer all parts to the question.

Lesson Review

Lesson 1

1 *Evaluating* What progressive issue eventually led to the passage of the Eighteenth Amendment? What was the impact on American society of the campaign for the Eighteenth Amendment and related reforms? SS.912.A.3.8, SS.912.A.3.12

2 *Analyzing* What were the main social issues affecting women and children in the Progressive Era, and what reforms did progressives seek to help them? SS.912.A.3.8, SS.912.A.3.12

3 *Describing* What were the roles of the National American Woman Suffrage Association (NAWSA) and the National Woman's Party in the women's civil rights movement? HE.912.C.2.7, SS.912.A.3.12

Lesson 2

4 *Sequencing* Describe the steps Theodore Roosevelt took to rein in big business and then summarize his approach to regulating business. SS.912.A.3.12

5 *Comparing and Contrasting* Compare President Taft's record as a progressive to President Roosevelt's achievements. How were the two men similar? Where did they differ?

Lesson 3

6 *Evaluating* What was the impact of the Progressive Party on the 1912 election? SS.912.A.3.12

7 *Explaining* What actions did W.E.B. Du Bois take to expand political rights and economic opportunities for African Americans during the Progressive Era? SS.912.A.3.12

8 *Identifying Cause and Effect* Explain the actions that lawyer Sigmund Livingston took to help the Jewish religious minority expand its political rights and economic opportunities in American society. SS.912.A.3.12

Exploring the Essential Questions

9 *Identifying Central Issues* Make an informative poster that identifies how progressives tried to fix society's problems and documents their success. Your poster should include charts, illustrations, graphs, or lists to support your information. SS.912.A.3.8, SS.912.A.3.12

Critical Thinking

10 *Describing Change and Continuity* How did the Pure Food and Drug Act change the relationship between the federal government and business? What were the costs and benefits of the act? HE.912.C.2.4, HE.912.C.2.7, SS.912.A.3.9

11 *Comparing and Contrasting* Evaluate the Supreme Court decisions in *Lochner* v. *New York* (1905), and *Northern Securities* v. *United States* (1904). In which case does the Court take a more strict construction approach? Explain why and evaluate which case had more of a long-term effect on the federal government's relationship to business. HE.912.C.2.4, SS.912.A.1.6, SS.912.A.3.9

21st Century Skills

12 *Transferring Information* Do additional research using print and/or online sources into the life and achievements of Frances Willard. Make sure to pick reliable and authoritative sources to use in your research. Then write a short report based on the research describing her social, political and economic contributions. Turn the report into a digital visual presentation using computer software, revising and rewriting the content of your short report as needed to suit the new medium. LAFS.1112.RH.3.9, LAFS.1112.SL.1.2, LAFS.1112.SL.2.5, LAFS.1112.WHST.1.2, LAFS.1112.WHST.2.4, LAFS.1112.WHST.2.5, LAFS.1112.WHST.2.6, LAFS.1112.WHST.3.7, LAFS.1112.WHST.3.9, LAFS.1112.WHST.4.10

Need Extra Help?

If You've Missed Question	1	2	3	4	5	6	7	8	9	10	11	12
Go to lesson	1	1	2	2	3	1	3	3	1	2	1	1

DBQ Analyzing Primary Sources

Read the excerpt and answer the questions that follow.

PRIMARY SOURCE

"I am perfectly willing that [a business] should beat any competitor by fair means . . . but there must be no squeezing out the beginner . . . no secret arrangements against him. All the fair competition you choose, but no unfair competition of any kind . . . . A trust is an arrangement to get rid of competition. . . . A trust does not bring efficiency . . . it buys efficiency out of business. I am for big business, and I am against the trusts . . . any man who can put others out of business by making a thing cheaper for the consumer . . . I take off my hat to . . . "

—quoted in *The New Freedom*

13 *Analyzing Primary Sources* Which of the presidential contenders in the 1912 election do you think said the above quote? Explain your choice. What policies were enacted during his administration that reflected the beliefs expressed above? LAFS.1112.RH.3.7, LAFS.1112.RH.3.8, LAFS.1112.RH.4.10, SS.912.A.1.2

Analyzing Visuals

Use the image to answer the following questions.

FRANK LESLIE'S ILLUSTRATED NEWSPAPER.

14 *Drawing Inferences* What does the image tell you about who supported the prohibition of alcohol? Why do you think the consumption of alcohol was such an important issue for this group of Americans? What impression does the image give of the protesters as compared to the people in the saloon? HE.912.C.2.7, LAFS.1112.RH.1.1, LAFS.1112.RH.3.7, SS.912.A.1.2, SS.912.A.1.4, SS.912.H.1.5

Use the map Woman Suffrage 1869–1920 *to answer the following questions.*

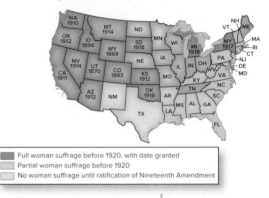

Full woman suffrage before 1920, with date granted
Partial woman suffrage before 1920
No woman suffrage until ratification of Nineteenth Amendment

15 *Analyzing Geographic Patterns* Describe the geographic pattern that developed among states as they granted woman suffrage. SS.912.G.1.2

16 *Analyzing Geographic Distributions* Why was the fact that so many states granted full or partial suffrage before 1920 important to the success of the effort to amend the Constitution? SS.912.G.1.2

Extended-Response Question

17 *Analyzing* Write an essay tracing the historical development of the suffrage movement culminating in the Nineteenth Amendment. Identify the major leaders of the movement and explain the different strategies they wanted to use to expand political rights for women and the resulting split of the movement into two groups. Then identify the different methods suffragists used to convince political leaders to expand women's participation in the democratic process and evaluate their effectiveness. Which methods appear to have been most effective in helping suffragists reach their goals? Your essay should include an introduction, at least three supporting paragraphs, and a conclusion. LAFS.1112.RH.3.7, LAFS.1112.WHST.2.4, LAFS.1112.WHST.4.10

Library of Congress, Prints & Photographs Division [LC-USZ62-90543]

Need Extra Help?

If You've Missed Question	**13**	**14**	**15**	**16**	**17**
Go to lesson	3	1	1	1	1

◀ General John J. Pershing commanded the American Expeditionary Force in several successful battles against the Central Powers during World War I.

FROM 1914 TO 1920

World War I and Its Aftermath

THE STORY MATTERS ...

When war began between European nations in 1914, the United States tried to remain neutral, but attacks on U.S. ships eventually caused the United States to enter the war.

To successfully fight the war, the U.S. government used progressive ideas to manage the economy, build a large military, and shape public opinion. America's involvement in the war effort had a profound impact on American society for years to come.

ESSENTIAL QUESTION

- Why do nations go to war?

©Underwood & Underwood/Bettmann/Corbis

Place & Time: United States 1914–1920

Political conflicts in Europe sparked the beginning of World War I. The United States attempted to keep its long-standing policy to remain neutral in Europe's wars until events eroded U.S. neutrality and finally led to the nation's involvement. World War I was the first time in U.S. history that the United States sent troops to fight in Europe. After the war, the United States suffered economic uncertainty and social tensions as many Americans became anti-immigrant, anticommunist, and antiunion.

Step Into the Place

Read the quotes and look at the information presented on the map.

 Analyzing Historical Documents How do the concerns addressed in the quotes reflect conflicting opinions about the United States becoming involved in World War I?

PRIMARY SOURCE

"We have been neutral not only because it was the fixed and traditional policy of the United States to stand aloof from the politics of Europe and because we had had no part either of action or of policy in the influences which brought on the present war, but also because it was manifestly our duty to prevent, if it were possible, the indefinite extension of the fires of hate and desolation kindled by that terrible conflict and seek to serve mankind by reserving our strength and our resources for the anxious and difficult days of restoration and healing which must follow. . . ."

—President Woodrow Wilson, *Wilson Accepts His Renomination,* speech delivered at Long Branch, New Jersey, September 2, 1916

PRIMARY SOURCE

"It is to be expected that nations will continue to arm in defense of their respective interests, as they are conceived, and nothing will avail to diminish this burden save some practical guaranty of international order. We, in this country, can, and should, maintain our fortunate freedom from entanglements with interests and policies, which do not concern us. But there is no national isolation in the world of the twentieth century."

—Charles Evans Hughes, quoted in *The Official Report of the Proceedings of the Sixteenth Republican National Convention,* June 1916

(tl)Library of Congress, Prints & Photographs Division [LC-USZ62-91089]; (tr)Library of Congress, Prints & Photographs Division [LC-USZC2-6247]; (b)detail/White House Collection/The White House Historical Association

Step Into the Time

MAKING CONNECTIONS
Choose an event from the time line and write a paragraph describing the general social, political, or economic effect the event might have for World War I and its aftermath.

Wilson
1913–1921

U.S. PRESIDENTS

UNITED STATES

WORLD

1914

1915

1916

May 7, 1915 German submarine sinks the *Lusitania*

June 28, 1914 Franz Ferdinand assassinated

February 21, 1916 Battle of Verdun

July 1, 1916 Battle of the Somme begins

NEXT GENERATION SUNSHINE STATE STANDARDS
Students will understand the following benchmarks from the Florida NGSSS

LAFS.1112.RH.3.7: Integrate and evaluate multiple sources of information presented in diverse formats and media (e.g., visually, quantitatively, as well as in words) in order to address a question or solve a problem.

LAFS.1112.RH.3.9: Integrate information from diverse sources, both primary and secondary,

into a coherent understanding of an idea or event, noting discrepancies among sources.

SS.912.A.1.2: Utilize a variety of primary and secondary sources to identify author, historical significance, audience, and authenticity to understand a historical period.

SS.912.A.1.3: Utilize timelines to identify the time sequence of historical data.

SS.912.A.1.4: Analyze how images, symbols, objects, cartoons, graphs, charts, maps, and artwork may be used to interpret the significance of time periods and events from the past.

SS.912.A.4.5: Examine causes, course, and consequences of United States involvement in World War I.

Militarism and Alliances in Europe 1914

In 1839 Britain guaranteed that it would help protect Belgium's neutrality.

Legend:
- Triple Entente
- Triple Alliance
- Other European states

Germany took Alsace-Lorraine from France in 1870. The French were determined to recover the territory.

Russia and Serbia were both Slavic countries. Russia did not have an alliance with Serbia but was determined to help Serbia against Austria-Hungary.

Balkan Nationalism
Southeastern Europe is known as the Balkans. In the 1800s the Austro-Hungarian Empire and the Ottoman Empire controlled this region. As the idea of nationalism spread across Europe, the people in the region fought a series of wars to gain their independence. By 1914 most of the Balkan people were free, except for the Slavs living in Bosnia.

0   400 mi.
0   400 km
Lambert Azimuthal Equal Area projection

Timeline:

April 6, 1917 United States declares war

April 28, 1917 Congress passes Selective Service Act

May 16, 1918 Sedition Act enacted

November 11, 1918 Armistice ends fighting

1919 Race riots and strikes take place in Northern cities

1920 Red Scare and Palmer Raids occur

1917   1918   1919   1920

October 1917 Bolshevik Revolution begins

March 3, 1918 Treaty of Brest-Litovsk ends Russian-German war

1919 Versailles Peace Conference begins

LESSON 1

The United States Enters World War I

ESSENTIAL QUESTION
• Why do nations go to war?

READING HELPDESK

Academic Vocabulary
• emphasis   • erode

Content Vocabulary
• militarism
• nationalism
• propaganda
• contraband

TAKING NOTES

Key Ideas and Details

Organizing As you read, identify the factors that contributed to World War I by completing a graphic organizer similar to the one below. LAFS.1112.RH.3.7, SS.912.A.4.5

Factors Contributing to World War I

NEXT GENERATION SUNSHINE STATE STANDARDS

LAFS.1112.RH.2.4: Determine the meaning of words and phrases as they are used in a text, including analyzing how an author uses and refines the meaning of a key term over the course of a text (e.g., how Madison defines faction in Federalist No. 10).

LAFS.1112.RH.3.7: Integrate and evaluate multiple sources of information presented in diverse formats and media (e.g., visually, quantitatively, as well as in words) in order to address a question or solve a problem.

LAFS.1112.WHST.1.1: Write arguments focused on discipline-specific content.

Continued on page 233

IT MATTERS BECAUSE

Through the late 1800s and early 1900s, imperialism, shifting national boundaries, old alliances, and nationalist sentiments among European nations set the stage for World War I. Attacks on U.S. ships and American support for the Allies eventually caused the United States to enter the war.

The Causes of World War I

GUIDING QUESTION *What political circumstances in Europe led to World War I?*

In 1914, tensions were building among European nations, stemming from events that dated to the 1860s. In 1864, while Americans fought the Civil War, the German kingdom of Prussia launched the first of a series of wars to unite the various German states into one nation. By 1871, Prussia had united Germany and established the German Empire, which became one of the most powerful nations in the world, transforming European politics.

Militarism and Alliances

In 1870, as part of its plan to unify Germany, Prussia forced France to give up territory along the German border. As a result, France and Germany became enemies. To protect itself, Germany signed alliances with Italy and with the huge empire of Austria-Hungary, which controlled much of southeastern Europe. This became known as the Triple Alliance.

The new alliance alarmed Russian leaders, who feared that Germany intended to expand eastward. In addition, Russia and Austria-Hungary were competing for influence in southeastern Europe. A common interest in opposing Germany and Austria-Hungary led Russia and France to sign the Franco-Russian Alliance in 1894. Under the alliance, the two nations promised to come to each other's aid in a war against the Triple Alliance.

Such alliances fostered **militarism**—the strong buildup of armed forces to intimidate and threaten other nations. Over time, German militarism led Britain to become involved in the alliance system. Britain's policy was to try to prevent one nation from controlling all of Europe. By the late 1800s, Germany had clearly become Europe's strongest nation.

In 1898, Germany began building a large modern navy. The buildup threatened the British, who rushed to build warships. By the early 1900s, Britain and Germany were engaged in an arms race. The race convinced Britain to build closer ties with France and Russia. The British refused to sign a formal alliance, so the relationship became known as an *entente cordiale,* or friendly understanding. Britain, France, and Russia became known as the Triple Entente.

Imperialism and Nationalism

By the late 1800s, **nationalism,** or a feeling of intense pride in one's homeland, had become a powerful idea in Europe. Nationalists place primary **emphasis** on promoting their homeland's culture and interests. They believe in the right of self-determination—the idea that those who share a national identity should have their own country and government. In the 1800s, nationalism led to a crisis in the Balkan region of southeastern Europe.

In the 1700s and 1800s, imperialism—the ruling or controlling of other peoples or nations through annexation, military conquest, or economic domination—was how European powers built empires. For years the Ottoman Empire and the Austro-Hungarian Empire had ruled the Balkans. But as nationalism spread in the late 1800s and early 1900s, national groups such as the South Slavs—Serbs, Bosnians, Croats, and Slovenes—began to press for independence. The Serbs, who were the first to gain independence, formed a nation called Serbia between the two empires. Serbia believed that its mission was to unite the South Slavs.

Russia supported the Serbs, but Austria-Hungary worked to limit Serbia's growth. In 1908, Austria-Hungary annexed Bosnia, which had belonged to the Ottoman Empire, outraging the Serbs. The annexation demonstrated that Austria-Hungary had no intention of letting the Slavic people in its empire become independent.

An Assassination Brings War

In June 1914, Archduke Franz Ferdinand, heir to the Austro-Hungarian throne, visited the Bosnian capital of Sarajevo. As he and his wife rode through the city, Bosnian revolutionary Gavrilo Princip rushed their car and shot them dead. The assassination occurred with the knowledge of Serbian officials who hoped to start a war that would damage Austria-Hungary.

Austria-Hungary decided the time had come to crush Serbia in order to prevent Slavic nationalism from undermining its empire. Knowing an attack on Serbia might trigger a war with Russia, the Austrians asked their German allies for support. Austria-Hungary then issued an ultimatum to the Serbian government. The Serbs counted on Russia to back them up, and the Russians, in turn, counted on France.

On July 28, Austria-Hungary declared war on Serbia. Russia immediately mobilized its army, including troops stationed on the German border. Within days, Germany declared war on Russia and France. World War I had begun.

Germany immediately launched a massive invasion of France, hoping to knock the French out of the war, so it could turn its attention east to Russia. But the German plan required their forces to advance through Belgium, and

NEXT GENERATION SUNSHINE STATE STANDARDS

Continued from page 232

LAFS.1112.WHST.4.10: Write routinely over extended time frames (time for reflection and revision) and shorter time frames (a single sitting or a day or two) for a range of discipline-specific tasks, purposes, and audiences.

SS.912.A.1.2: Utilize a variety of primary and secondary sources to identify author, historical significance, audience, and authenticity to understand a historical period.

SS.912.A.1.4: Analyze how images, symbols, objects, cartoons, graphs, charts, maps, and artwork may be used to interpret the significance of time periods and events from the past.

SS.912.A.4.5: Examine causes, course, and consequences of United States involvement in World War I.

militarism a policy of aggressive military preparedness

nationalism loyalty and devotion to a nation

emphasis a special importance given to an object or idea

The assassination of Archduke Franz Ferdinand in late June 1914 spurred Austria-Hungary to declare war on Serbia, beginning World War I.

▶ **CRITICAL THINKING**
Identifying Central Ideas How did the conflict between the policy of imperialism and the principle of nationalism lead to war between Austria-Hungary and Serbia? LAFS.1112.RH.3.7, SS.912.A.1.4, SS.912.A.4.5

©Bettmann/Corbis

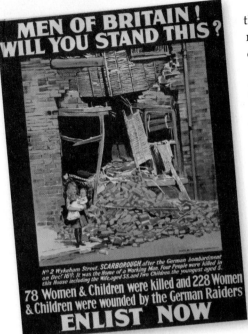

MEN OF BRITAIN!
WILL YOU STAND THIS?

Nº 2 Wykeham Street, SCARBOROUGH after the German bombardment on Dec! 16th. It was the Home of a Working Man. Four People were killed in this House including the Wife, aged 33, and Two Children, the youngest aged 5.

78 Women & Children were killed and 228 Women & Children were wounded by the German Raiders

ENLIST NOW

During World War I, both Britain and Germany produced propaganda posters. German propaganda was mostly anti-Russian and did not appeal to Americans, however, while British propaganda did.

► CRITICAL THINKING
Analyzing Primary Sources What message does this poster want to convince the viewer to believe?
LAFS.1112.RH.3.7, SS.912.A.1.4

propaganda the spreading of ideas about an institution or individual for the purpose of influencing opinion

— *Thinking Like a* —
HISTORIAN

Determining Cause and Effect

Propaganda is a powerful force to influence opinion.
In wartime, propaganda can be used to convince people to take sides or participate for a particular cause or reason.
As a historian, how much do you think the British propaganda swayed the United States to support the Allies in World War I, or were other reasons, such as business, more of a deciding factor?
SS.912.A.1.1

the British had signed a treaty with Belgium guaranteeing the country's neutrality. When German forces crossed into Belgium, Britain declared war.

Those fighting for the Triple Entente were called the Allies. Italy joined them in 1915 after being promised part of Austro-Hungarian territory after the war. Germany and Austria-Hungary joined with the Ottoman Empire and Bulgaria to form the Central Powers. Germany's plan to defeat France before Russia could mobilize failed. When Russia invaded Germany, the Germans were forced to move some troops eastward to thwart the attack. The Western Front became a bloody stalemate along hundreds of miles of trenches, with British and French forces on one side and German forces on the other.

☑ READING PROGRESS CHECK

Evaluating How did the complex web of European alliances contribute to the outbreak of World War I?

The United States Enters the War

GUIDING QUESTION *What events motivated the United States to join the war?*

When World War I began, President Wilson was determined to keep the United States out of a European conflict. He immediately declared the United States to be neutral and asked all Americans "to be impartial in thought as well as in action." Despite Wilson's hopes for neutrality, events gradually drew the United States into the war on the side of the Allies.

The Neutrality Debate

Despite the president's plea, most Americans supported one side or the other. Many German Americans supported their homeland, and many Irish Americans harbored hostility toward Britain, but in general public opinion favored the Allies. Many Americans valued the heritage, language, and political ideals they shared with Britain. Others treasured America's links with France, a great friend to America during the Revolutionary War.

For more than two years, the United States remained neutral. During this time, a great debate began over whether the country should prepare for war. Supporters of the "preparedness" movement believed that preparing was the best way to make sure the United States was not forced into the conflict. Others disagreed. In 1915, Carrie Chapman Catt and Jane Addams—leaders of the women's suffrage movement—founded the Women's Peace Party. This organization, along with others such as the League to Limit Armament, worked to keep America out of the war.

One select group of Americans was decidedly pro British: President Wilson's cabinet. Only Secretary of State William Jennings Bryan favored neutrality. The other cabinet members argued forcefully on behalf of Britain. Many U.S. military leaders also backed Britain, believing an Allied victory was the only way to preserve the world's balance of power.

British officials worked diligently to win American support. One method they used was **propaganda,** or information designed to influence opinion. The British cut the transatlantic telegraph cable from Europe to the United States so most war news would be based on British reports. The American ambassador to Britain endorsed many of these reports, and American public opinion swayed in favor of the Allies.

Companies in the United States also had strong ties to the Allies, and many American banks invested heavily in an Allied victory. By 1917,

Library of Congress, Prints & Photographs Division [LC-USZC4-11297]

American loans to the Allies totaled over $2 billion. Although other banks, particularly in the Midwest where pro-German feelings were strongest, lent some $27 million to Germany, the country's prosperity was intertwined with the Allies. If the Allies won, the investments would be paid back; if not, the money might never be repaid.

Moving Toward War

A series of events gradually **eroded** American neutrality and drew the United States into the war. Shortly after the war began, the British blockaded German ports. They forced neutral merchant ships sailing to Europe to land at British ports to be inspected for **contraband,** or goods prohibited from shipment to Germany and its allies. Although the U.S. government protested Britain's decision, the German response angered Americans even more. In February 1915, the Germans announced that they would use submarines called U-boats to sink without warning any ship they found in the waters around Britain. This decision violated an international treaty signed by Germany that banned attacks on civilian ships without warning.

erode to wear away at something until it disappears

contraband goods whose importation, exportation, or possession is illegal

ANALYZING PRIMARY SOURCES

Should the United States Stay Neutral in World War I?

Many Americans were divided about whether the United States should remain neutral. Voices spoke out loudly on both sides.

——— YES ———

" Germany is not moving against this country. She has not been guilty of any aggression against us. She has taken the lives of a few of our citizens, because they got in the way when she was prosecuting a war against another nation and fighting to preserve her existence. If the German Government should make aggressive warfare against the United States you would not need any exhortation in the Senate of the United States to arouse the patriotism of the American people. You would not be holding open your enlisting stations without getting any soldiers. "

—from the *Congressional Record,* March 4, 1917

John Works, Civil War veteran and U.S. senator

——— NO ———

" I have come to the conclusion that the German Government is utterly hostile to all nations with democratic institutions because those who compose it see in democracy a menace to absolutism and the defeat of the German ambition for world domination. . . .

. . . Germany must not be permitted to win this war and to break even, though to prevent it this country is forced to take an active part. This ultimate necessity must be constantly in our minds in all our controversies with the belligerents. American public opinion must be prepared for the time, which may come, when we will have to cast aside our neutrality and become one of the champions of democracy. "

—from *War Memoirs of Robert Lansing,* July 11, 1915

Robert Lansing, Secretary of State

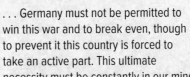
DBQ Analyzing Historical Documents

1 *Summarizing* When does Senator Works believe war against Germany would be justified? LAFS.1112.RH.3.7, SS.912.A.1.1, SS.912.A.1.2, SS.912.A.4.5

2 *Supporting A Point of View* Which side of the neutrality issue do you think was correct? Use historical evidence to explain your point of view. LAFS.1112.RH.3.7, SS.912.A.1.1, SS.912.A.1.2, SS.912.A.4.5

3 *Creating an Oral Presentation* Using correct social studies terminology, prepare a lecture for your class explaining the causes of World War I and the reasons America did not stay neutral. Be sure to explain key historical concepts including nationalism, imperialism, and militarism. LAFS.1112.WHST.1.1, SS.912.A.1.1, SS.912.A.4.5

(l)Library of Congress, Prints & Photographs Division [LC-DIG-ggbain-05650]; (r)©Historical/Corbis

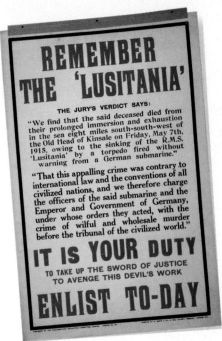

REMEMBER THE 'LUSITANIA'

THE JURY'S VERDICT SAYS:

"We find that the said deceased died from their prolonged immersion and exhaustion in the sea eight miles south-south-west of the Old Head of Kinsale on Friday, May 7th, 1915, owing to the sinking of the R.M.S. 'Lusitania' by a torpedo fired without warning from a German submarine."

"That this appalling crime was contrary to international law and the conventions of all civilized nations, and we therefore charge the officers of the said submarine and the Emperor and Government of Germany, under whose orders they acted, with the crime of wilful and wholesale murder before the tribunal of the civilized world."

IT IS YOUR DUTY

TO TAKE UP THE SWORD OF JUSTICE TO AVENGE THIS DEVIL'S WORK

ENLIST TO-DAY

The sinking of the *Lusitania* angered many Americans and proved to be a turning point in the war.

▶ **CRITICAL THINKING**
Determining Cause and Effect What were two long-term effects of the sinking of the *Lusitania*?
LAFS.1112.RH.3.7, SS.912.A.1.4, SS.912.A.4.5

On May 7, 1915, a U-boat sank the British passenger ship *Lusitania*, killing over 1,000 passengers—including 128 Americans. The attack gave credibility to British propaganda and changed American attitudes about the war. Wilson sent an official protest to Germany, but in March 1916, a U-boat torpedoed a French passenger ship. Wilson then decided to issue one last warning demanding that the German government abandon its methods or risk war with the United States.

Germany did not want to strengthen the Allies by drawing the United States into the war. It promised with certain conditions to stop sinking merchant ships without warning. President Wilson's success played an important part in his reelection bid in 1916. His campaign slogan, "He kept us out of war," helped him win a narrow victory.

The United States Declares War

In January 1917, German official Arthur Zimmermann sent a telegram to the German ambassador in Mexico promising Mexico the return of its "lost territory in Texas, New Mexico, and Arizona" if it allied with Germany. British intelligence intercepted the Zimmermann telegram, and it ran in American newspapers. Furious, many Americans concluded that war with Germany was necessary.

Then, on February 1, 1917, Germany resumed unrestricted submarine warfare. German military leaders believed that they could starve Britain into submission if U-boats began sinking all ships on sight. They did not believe that the United States could raise an army and transport it to Europe in time if it decided to enter the war. Between February 3 and March 21, U-boats sank six American ships. Roused to action, President Wilson asked Congress to declare war on Germany on April 2, 1917:

PRIMARY SOURCE

❝It is a fearful thing to lead this great peaceful people into war. . . . But the right is more precious than peace, and we shall fight for the things which we have always carried nearest to our hearts—for democracy, for the right of those who submit to authority to have a voice in their own governments, for the rights and liberties of small nations. . . .❞

—quoted in the *Congressional Record*, 1917

Within days, the Senate and the House had voted for the resolution, and Wilson signed it. The United States was at war.

☑ **READING PROGRESS CHECK**

Summarizing How did Germany's use of unrestricted submarine warfare bring the United States into World War I?

Library of Congress, Prints & Photographs Division [LC-USZC4-10930]

LESSON 1 REVIEW

Reviewing Vocabulary

1. ***Explaining*** Explain how militarism contributed to the beginning of World War I. LAFS.1112.RH.2.4

2. ***Monitoring*** How did British propaganda influence American public opinion? LAFS.1112.RH.2.4

Using Your Notes

3. ***Comparing and Contrasting*** Use your notes to write a short essay comparing and contrasting the factors that caused European nations and the United States to become involved in World War I. LAFS.1112.WHST.1.1

Answering the Guiding Questions

4. ***Identifying Cause and Effect*** What political circumstances in Europe led to World War I? SS.912.A.4.5

5. ***Summarizing*** What events motivated the United States to join the war? SS.912.A.4.5

Writing Activity

6. **ARGUMENT** Suppose you are an American survivor of the sinking of the *Lusitania*. Write a letter to President Wilson about what you think he should do. LAFS.1112.WHST.1.1, LAFS.1112.WHST.4.10

networks
There's More Online!

LESSON 2
The Home Front

ESSENTIAL QUESTION
• Why do nations go to war?

READING HELPDESK

Academic Vocabulary
• migrate   • draft

Content Vocabulary
• victory garden
• espionage

TAKING NOTES

Key Ideas and Details

Organizing As you read, use the major headings of this lesson to create an outline similar to the one below. LAFS.1112.RH.3.7

> The Home Front
> I. Organizing the Economy
>   A.
>   B.
>   C.

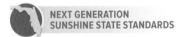
**NEXT GENERATION
SUNSHINE STATE STANDARDS**

LAFS.1112.RH.2.4: Determine the meaning of words and phrases as they are used in a text, including analyzing how an author uses and refines the meaning of a key term over the course of a text (e.g., how Madison defines faction in Federalist No. 10).

LAFS.1112.RH.3.7: Integrate and evaluate multiple sources of information presented in diverse formats and media (e.g., visually, quantitatively, as well as in words) in order to address a question or solve a problem.

LAFS.1112.WHST.1.1: Write arguments focused on discipline-specific content.

Continued on page 238

IT MATTERS BECAUSE

To fight World War I, the U.S. government used progressive ideas and new government agencies to mobilize the population and organize the economy.

Organizing the Economy

GUIDING QUESTION *What did Congress do to prepare the economy for war?*

When the United States entered the war in April 1917, progressives controlled the federal government. Their ideas about planning and management shaped how the government organized the war effort.

Wartime Agencies

As part of the war effort, Congress created new agencies staffed by business executives, managers, and government officials to coordinate mobilization and ensure the efficient use of national resources. These agencies emphasized cooperation between big business and government.

The War Industries Board (WIB) coordinated the production of war materials. Early problems convinced President Wilson to expand the Board's powers. The WIB told manufacturers what they could produce, allocated raw materials, ordered new factory construction, and sometimes set prices.

The Food Administration, run by Herbert Hoover, was responsible for increasing food production while reducing civilian consumption. The agency encouraged families to conserve food and grow their own vegetables in **victory gardens.** "Eat more corn, oats and rye products—fish and poultry—fruits, vegetables and potatoes, baked, boiled and broiled foods. . . . Eat less wheat, meat, sugar and fats to save for the army and our allies," urged Food Administration posters.

The Fuel Administration managed use of coal and oil. To conserve energy, it introduced the first usage of daylight saving time, shortened workweeks for civilian goods factories, and encouraged Heatless Mondays.

NEXT GENERATION SUNSHINE STATE STANDARDS

Continued from page 237

LAFS.1112.WHST.4.10: Write routinely over extended time frames (time for reflection and revision) and shorter time frames (a single sitting or a day or two) for a range of discipline-specific tasks, purposes, and audiences.

SS.912.A.1.2: Utilize a variety of primary and secondary sources to identify author, historical significance, audience, and authenticity to understand a historical period.

SS.912.A.1.4: Analyze how images, symbols, objects, cartoons, graphs, charts, maps, and artwork may be used to interpret the significance of time periods and events from the past.

SS.912.A.4.5: Examine causes, course, and consequences of United States involvement in World War I.

SS.912.A.4.6: Examine how the United States government prepared the nation for war with war measures (Selective Service Act, War Industries Board, war bonds, Espionage Act, Sedition Act, Committee of Public Information).

Continued on page 239

victory garden a garden planted by civilians during war to raise vegetables for home use, leaving more of other foods for the troops

migrate to move from one location to another

By the end of the war, the United States had spent about $32 billion. To fund the war effort, Congress raised income tax rates, placed new taxes on corporate profits, imposed an extra tax on the profits of arms factories, and borrowed over $20 billion through the sale of Liberty Bonds and Victory Bonds. Americans who bought bonds were lending money to the government to be repaid with interest in a specified number of years.

Mobilizing the Workforce

The war effort also required the cooperation of workers. To prevent strikes from disrupting the war effort, the government established the National War Labor Board (NWLB) in April 1918. The NWLB often pressured industry to improve wages, adopt an eight-hour workday, and allow unions the right to organize and bargain collectively. In exchange, labor leaders agreed not to disrupt war production. As a result, membership in unions increased by over one million between 1917 and 1919.

With so many men in the military, employers were willing to hire women for jobs traditionally held by men. Some 1 million women joined the workforce for the first time, and another 8 million switched to better industrial jobs. Women worked in factories, shipyards, and railroad yards, and served as police officers, mail carriers, and train engineers. When the war ended, however, most women returned to their previous jobs or stopped working. Yet the changes demonstrated that women were capable of holding jobs that many had believed only men could do.

Desperate for workers, Henry Ford sent agents to the South to recruit African Americans. Other companies quickly followed suit. Promises of high wages and plentiful work convinced between 300,000 and 500,000 African Americans to move north. This massive population movement became known as the Great Migration. The racial makeup of such cities as Chicago, New York, Cleveland, and Detroit changed greatly. Eventually, so did politics in the Northern cities, where African Americans were able to vote.

The war also encouraged other groups to **migrate.** Between 1917 and 1920, more than 100,000 Mexicans migrated into the Southwest, providing labor for farmers and ranchers. Mexican Americans also found new

---

| CHARTS/GRAPHS | PAYING FOR WORLD WAR I |

To pay for the war, the U.S. government raised taxes and issued bonds. The government printed posters, organized parades, and asked movie stars to help promote war bonds. Here, actor Douglas Fairbanks urges Americans to buy Liberty Bonds at a rally in New York City in 1918.

1. **Making Inferences** What can you infer about government finances by the disparity between the amount of revenue raised through loans versus taxation? LAFS.1112.RH.3.7, MAFS.912.S-ID.1, SS.912.A.1.4

2. **Predicting Consequences** What consequence might result from the way the war was paid for? LAFS.1112.RH.3.7, MAFS.912.S-ID.1, SS.912.A.1.4

©Bettmann/Corbis

opportunities in factory jobs in many American cities. Like other immigrant groups before them, they faced hostility and discrimination. Mexican Americans tended to settle in separate neighborhoods, called *barrios*, where they could support one another.

Shaping Public Opinion

Progressives did not think that organizing the economy was enough to ensure the success of the war effort. They also believed the government needed to shape public opinion. Soon after Congress declared war, Wilson created the Committee on Public Information (CPI) to "sell" the war to the American people. Headed by journalist George Creel, the CPI recruited advertising executives, artists, authors, songwriters, entertainers, public speakers, and motion picture companies to help sway public opinion in favor of the war.

The CPI distributed pamphlets and arranged for thousands of "four-minute speeches" to be delivered at movie theaters and other public places. Some 75,000 speakers, known as Four-Minute Men, urged audiences to support the war in various ways, from buying war bonds to reporting draft dodgers to the authorities. Nongovernmental groups also helped raise awareness and funds for the war. For example, the American Jewish Joint Distribution Committee raised $63 million in relief funds. The Jewish Welfare Board set up centers at home and abroad for Jewish servicemen.

Eugene V. Debs, leader of the American Socialist Party, was arrested and sentenced to 10 years in prison under the Espionage Act for giving an antiwar speech in Canton, Ohio.

▶ CRITICAL THINKING
Interpreting What did the sentencing of Debs and others show about wartime freedom?
LAFS.1112.RH.3.7, SS.912.A.1.4, SS.912.A.4.6

The Supreme Court Limits Free Speech

In addition to using propaganda, the government passed legislation to limit opposition to the war and to fight **espionage,** or spying to acquire government information. The Espionage Act of 1917 made it illegal to aid the enemy, give false reports, or interfere with the war effort. The Sedition Act of 1918 made it illegal to speak against the war publicly. In practice, it allowed officials to prosecute anyone who criticized the government. These two laws led to more than 2,000 convictions.

espionage spying, especially to gain government secrets

Despite protests, the Espionage and Sedition Acts were upheld by the Supreme Court. Although the First Amendment states that "Congress shall make no law . . . abridging the freedom of speech, or of the press," the Supreme Court departed from a strict interpretation of the Constitution. In *Schenck* v. *United States* (1919), Justice Oliver Wendell Holmes wrote the unanimous opinion. The Court ruled that the government could restrict speech when the speech constituted a "clear and present danger."

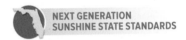

NEXT GENERATION
SUNSHINE STATE STANDARDS

Continued from page 238

SS.912.A.4.8: Compare the experiences Americans (African Americans, Hispanics, Asians, women, conscientious objectors) had while serving in Europe.

SS.912.A.4.9: Compare how the war impacted German Americans, Asian Americans, African Americans, Hispanic Americans, Jewish Americans, Native Americans, women and dissenters in the United States.

SS.912.A.4.11: Examine key events and peoples in Florida history as they relate to United States history.

PRIMARY SOURCE

❝The most stringent protection of free speech would not protect a man in falsely shouting fire in a theatre and causing a panic. . . . The question in every case is whether the words used are used in such circumstances and are of such a nature as to create a clear and present danger that they will bring about the substantive evils that Congress has a right to prevent. It is a question of proximity and degree. When a nation is at war, many things that might be said in time of peace are such a hindrance to its effort that their utterance will not be endured so long as men fight, and that no Court could regard them as protected by any constitutional right. ❞
—from *United States Supreme Court Reports*, 1920.

✔ READING PROGRESS CHECK

Explaining What were some new agencies that Congress established to help manage the wartime economy?

©Bettmann/Corbis

Building the Military

GUIDING QUESTION *How were progressive ideals used in preparing the military for war?*

Progressives did not abandon their ideas when it came to building up the military. Instead, they applied those ideas to develop a new system for recruiting a large army.

Volunteers and Conscripts

When the United States entered the war in 1917, the army and the National Guard together had slightly more than 200,000 troops. Many men quickly volunteered, but many more were still needed.

Many progressives believed that forced military service was a violation of democratic and republican principles. Believing a **draft** was necessary, however, Congress, with Wilson's support, created a new system called selective service.

Instead of having the military run the draft from Washington, D.C., the Selective Service Act of 1917 required all men between 21 and 30 to register for the draft. A lottery randomly determined the order in which they were called before a local draft board in charge of selecting or exempting people from military service. The thousands of local boards were the heart of the system. The members of the draft boards were civilians from local communities. Progressives believed local people, understanding community needs, would know which men to draft and would do a far better job than a centralized government bureaucracy. Eventually, about 2.8 million Americans were drafted.

Not all American soldiers were drafted. Approximately 2 million men volunteered for military service. Some had heard stories of German atrocities and wanted to fight back. Others believed democracy was at stake. Many believed they had a duty to respond to their nation's call.

Although the horrors of war soon became apparent to the American troops, their morale remained high, helping to ensure victory. More than 50,000 Americans died in combat, and over 200,000 were wounded. Another 60,000 soldiers died from disease, mostly from the influenza epidemic of 1918 and 1919. The flu epidemic was not limited to the battlefield. It spread around the world and made more than a quarter of all Americans sick. The disease killed an estimated 25 to 50 million people worldwide, including more than 500,000 Americans.

draft to select a person at random for mandatory military service

Florida CONNECTION

Florida's Service Members

More than 42,000 Floridians served in the Great War. Over 13,000 were African Americans in the U.S. Army. Thousands of Florida women served in office and other noncombat positions in the Navy and the Marine Corps. Other citizens who belonged to historically pacifist religious groups chose noncombat service as conscientious objectors under the Selective Service Act. SS.912.A.4.8, SS.912.A.4.11

The U.S. Army kept many African American soldiers from combat, assigning them to work as cooks, laborers, and laundrymen. The 369th Regiment, however, was assigned to the French Army and spent 191 days in the frontline trenches. The entire regiment was awarded the French Croix de Guerre for gallantry in combat.

▶ **CRITICAL THINKING**

Comparing and Contrasting Why do you think the experiences of the 369th Regiment differed from those of other African American soldiers during World War I? LAFS.1112.RH.3.7, SS.912.A.1.4, SS.912.A.4.8, SS.912.A.4.9

Library of Congress, Prints & Photographs Division [LC-US262-116442]

Of the nearly 400,000 African Americans who were drafted, about 42,000 served overseas as combat troops. African American soldiers encountered discrimination and prejudice in the army, where they served in racially segregated units, almost always under the supervision of white officers. Despite these challenges, many African American soldiers fought with distinction. For example, the African American 92nd and 93rd Infantry Divisions fought in bitter battles along the Western Front. Many of the soldiers in those divisions won praise from the French commander, Marshal Philippe Pétain, and the United States commander, General John Pershing.

An estimated 12,000 Native Americans and about 20,000 Puerto Ricans served in the armed forces. Thousands of Mexican Americans also served in the war, volunteering for service more than any other minority group in the United States. Some Asian immigrants fought on the side of the United States even before they were citizens. Though they faced discrimination, many Asians served in the U.S. Army with distinction, being granted citizenship in recognition of their contributions.

Women Join the Military

World War I was the first war in which women officially served in the armed forces, although they served only in noncombat positions. As the military prepared for war in 1917, it faced a severe shortage of clerical workers because so many men were assigned to active duty. Early in 1917, the navy authorized the enlistment of women to meet its clerical needs.

Women serving in the navy wore a standard uniform and were assigned the rank of yeoman. By the end of the war, more than 11,000 women had served in the navy. Although most performed clerical duties, others served as radio operators, electricians, pharmacists, chemists, and photographers. Unlike the navy, the army refused to enlist women. Instead, it began hiring women as temporary employees to fill clerical jobs. The only women to actually serve in the army were in the Army Nurse Corps.

Women had served as nurses in both the army and the navy since the early 1900s, but as auxiliaries. They were not assigned ranks and were not technically enlisted in the army or navy. More than 20,000 nurses served in the Army Nurse Corps during the war, including more than 10,000 overseas.

☑ READING PROGRESS CHECK

Synthesizing How did progressive ideas influence the roles of women during World War I?

Connections to
TODAY

Women in the Military

Although women's roles in the military during World War I were limited, their entry into service paved the way for many advances. Today, about 5 percent of general officers in the U.S. Army, including the Army Reserve and the Army National Guard, are women. In 2008, Ann E. Dunwoody became the first female four-star general in army history.

LESSON 2 REVIEW

Reviewing Vocabulary

1. *Explaining* How did victory gardens help civilians contribute to the war effort? LAFS.1112.RH.2.4

Using Your Notes

2. *Summarizing* Use the notes you completed during the lesson to write a short summary of how World War I affected life on the home front. LAFS.1112.WHST.1.1

Answering the Guiding Questions

3. *Making Generalizations* What did Congress do to prepare the economy for war? SS.912.A.4.6

4. *Synthesizing* How were progressive ideals used in preparing the military for war? SS.912.A.4.6

5. *Explaining* What constitutional issues were raised by federal policies during the war? SS.912.A.4.5, SS.912.A.4.6

Writing Activity

6. NARRATIVE Suppose that you are a woman entering the workforce for the first time during World War I. Write a letter to a friend in which you explain why you have decided to go to work and what type of job you are doing. Share your feelings about your new job. LAFS.1112.WHST.1.2, LAFS.1112.WHST.4.10

LAFS.1112.RH.1.1, LAFS.1112.RH.1.2, LAFS.1112.RH.1.3, LAFS.1112.RH.2.5, LAFS.1112.RH.4.10, SS.912.A.1.2, SS.912.A.1.6, SS.912.A.4.6, SS.912.H.1.2

All of the warring nations in World War I used propaganda to boost support for their side. Many Americans believed the propaganda coming from Europe, particularly from the British government and press. When the United States entered the war, the American government also began using propaganda in an attempt to unite Americans behind the war effort.

For Home and Country

This 1918 poster is one of many used to drum up support for America's involvement in World War I.

VOCABULARY

ethical
conforming to accepted standards of conduct, good behavior

prestige
admiration and respect because something is successful or important

DBQ Analyzing Historical Documents

1. **Differentiating** What do you think the American soldier meant by the statement "Germans, and a German—so different"?

2. **Contrasting** What words does the American soldier use to describe the German soldier that contrast to the perception of "Germans" on the American home front?

3. **Identifying** What does the U.S. pamphlet claim is an important element to be bred in the population?

4. **Evaluating Validity** Examine the language and point of view of the U.S. Government pamphlet. Do you think its opinion can be trusted? Why or why not?

5. **Detecting Bias** How could this 1918 World War I poster be used to support the claims of the American soldier?

Propaganda in World War I

U.S. GOVERNMENT PAMPHLET, 1918

"Fear, perhaps, is rather an important element to be bred in the civilian population. It is difficult to unite a people by talking only on the highest **ethical** plane. To fight for an ideal, perhaps, must be coupled with thoughts of self preservation. So a truthful appeal to the fear of men, the recognition of the terrible things that would happen if the German Government were permitted to retain its **prestige**, may be necessary in order that all people unite in the support of the needed sacrifices."

—Pamphlet for speakers from the Committee on Public Information, quoted in the *New York Times*, February 4, 1918

AMERICAN SOLDIER'S DIARY, 1918

"Germans, and a German—so different. Fishing through the poor, torn pockets of shabby German body, drooping over wreck of machine gun, to find wellthumbed photograph of woman and little boy and little girl—so like one's own . . . impossible to hate what had been that body. Nothing so revolting as bitter, pitiless cruelty of those who know nothing of reality of it all. Those . . . Germanobaiters at home, so much more cruel than those who have the right—and are not."

—Diary of Lieutenant Howard V. O'Brien, October 6, 1918

MPI/Archive Photos/Getty Images

LESSON 3
A Bloody Conflict

ESSENTIAL QUESTION
• Why do nations go to war?

READING HELPDESK

Academic Vocabulary
• network • resolve
• adequately

Content Vocabulary
• convoy
• armistice
• national self-determination
• reparations

TAKING NOTES

Key Ideas and Details

Organizing As you read, complete a graphic organizer similar to the one below by listing the kinds of warfare and technology used in the fighting.
LAFS.1112.RH.3.7, SS.912.A.4.7

Warfare and Technology Used in World War I

NEXT GENERATION SUNSHINE STATE STANDARDS

LAFS.1112.RH.2.4: Determine the meaning of words and phrases as they are used in a text, including analyzing how an author uses and refines the meaning of a key term over the course of a text (e.g., how Madison defines faction in Federalist No. 10).

LAFS.1112.RH.3.7: Integrate and evaluate multiple sources of information presented in diverse formats and media (e.g., visually, quantitatively, as well as in words) in order to address a question or solve a problem.

Continued on page 245

IT MATTERS BECAUSE
New technology caused both sides to lose millions of lives during World War I. The arrival of American troops helped the Allies win, but the peace treaty set the stage for another war to come.

Combat in World War I

GUIDING QUESTION *How did new technologies increase the number of casualties compared with previous wars?*

By the spring of 1917, World War I had devastated Europe. Old-fashioned strategies and new technologies resulted in terrible destruction. Many Americans believed, however, that their troops would make a difference and quickly bring the war to an end.

Trench Warfare
Early offensives demonstrated that warfare had changed. Powerful artillery guns placed far behind the front lines hurled huge explosive shells onto the battlefield. More people were killed by artillery fire than by any other weapon. As one American noted in his diary:

PRIMARY SOURCE

❝Many dead Germans along the road. One heap on a manure pile. . . . Devastation everywhere. Our barrage has rooted up the entire territory like a plowed field. Dead horses galore, many of them have a hind quarter cut off—the [Germans] need food. Dead men here and there.❞
—quoted in *The American Spirit*, November 3, 1918

To protect themselves from artillery, troops began digging trenches. On the Western Front—where German troops fought French, British, and Belgian forces—the troops dug a **network** of trenches that stretched from the English Channel to the Swiss border. Both sides used barbed wire and a new weapon, the machine gun, to guard against the enemy. Attacks usually began with a massive artillery barrage. Soldiers then raced across the rough landscape toward enemy trenches. Troops used any weapon available to kill the enemy. The new style of fighting, which both sides eventually utilized, resulted in the loss of hundreds of thousands of men and a stalemate on the Western Front. Offensive and defensive moves by the Allies and the Germans failed to be particularly successful.

New Technology

Breaking through enemy lines required new technologies. The Germans first used poison gas in 1915, and the Allies soon followed. Gas caused vomiting, blindness, and suffocation. Both sides developed gas masks to counter fumes. In 1916, the British introduced the armored tank, which could crush barbed wire and cross trenches. But there were still too few of the slow, unreliable machines to revolutionize warfare.

World War I also marked the first use of aircraft in war. Early in the war, the Germans used giant rigid balloons called zeppelins to drop bombs on British warships in the North Sea. At first, airplanes were used to spy on enemy troops and ships. Then the Allies equipped them with machine guns and rockets to attack the German zeppelin fleet. Other aircraft carried small bombs to drop on enemy lines. As technology advanced, airplanes shot down other airplanes in battles known as dogfights. But early military aircraft were difficult to fly and easy to destroy. A combat pilot had an average life expectancy of about two weeks.

To protect against poison gas attacks, troops carried gas masks similar to these masks worn by American soldiers in 1917.

network an interconnected system

✓ READING PROGRESS CHECK

Describing What new technologies were introduced in World War I, and how did they impact the war?

©Bettmann/Corbis

The War in the Trenches

From Ypres on France's coast, down through Somme, Marne, and Verdun, Allied forces held off German advances.

North Sea

Baltic Sea

UNITED KINGDOM

London

NETH.

Tannenberg

Eastern Front

Ypres
Somme

BELG.

GERMANY

Berlin

RUSSIA

Paris
Marne Verdun

Western Front

FRANCE

SWITZ.

Vienna

Budapest

AUSTRIA-HUNGARY

Italian Front

Isonzo Trieste

ROMANIA

Sarajevo

SERBIA

Black Sea

ITALY MONTENEGRO

BULGARIA

Rome

Constantinople

ALBANIA

Gallipoli

GREECE

OTTOMAN EMPIRE

Mediterranean Sea

GEOGRAPHY CONNECTION

Troops on both sides of the conflict dug an extensive network of trenches to protect themselves from artillery fire and enemy attacks.

1 **THE WORLD IN SPATIAL TERMS** *Along which borders did the line of trench warfare stretch?* SS.912.A.1.4, SS.912.G.1.2

2 **PLACES AND REGIONS** *How do you think the Central Powers' war efforts were affected by fighting the war in the west and in the east?* SS.912.A.1.4, SS.912.A.4.5

	Allied Powers
	Central Powers
	Neutral Powers
—	Line of trench warfare, 1914–1916
✸	Allied victory
✸	Central Powers victory

0   400 miles
0   400 km

Lambert Azimuthal Equal-Area projection

20°E

40°E

The Americans Arrive

GUIDING QUESTION *Why was the arrival of U.S. forces so important to the war effort?*

Nearly two million American troops marched into the bloody stalemate in the Western Front. Although the American "doughboys" were inexperienced, they were fresh and eager to fight. As the Americans began to arrive, many in Germany concluded that the war was lost.

Winning the War at Sea

American admiral William S. Sims proposed that merchant ships and troop transports travel in groups called **convoys.** Small, maneuverable warships called destroyers protected convoys across the Atlantic. If a ship was sunk, other ships in the convoy could rescue survivors. Convoys greatly reduced shipping losses and ensured that American troops arrived safely in time to help the Allies on the Western Front.

Russia Leaves the War

In March 1917, riots broke out in Russia. Czar Nicholas II, the leader of the Russian Empire, abdicated his throne, and the Russian Revolution began. A temporary government took command whose leaders wanted Russia to stay in the war. However, the government was unable to deal **adequately** with the problems afflicting the nation, so Vladimir Lenin's Bolshevik Party seized power and established a Communist government in November 1917.

Germany's military fortunes improved with the Bolshevik takeover. Lenin pulled Russia out of the war to concentrate on establishing a Communist state. He explained:

PRIMARY SOURCE

"[I]t is necessary with particular thoroughness, persistence and patience to . . . prove without overthrowing capital it is impossible to end the war by a truly democratic peace.*"*

—from *The April Theses,* 1917

Lenin agreed to the Treaty of Brest-Litovsk with Germany on March 3, 1918. Under this treaty, Russia gave up the Ukraine, its Polish and Baltic territories, and Finland. With the Eastern Front settled, Germany could concentrate its forces in the west.

Americans Enter Combat

At the time World War I began, many Americans believed they owed the French a debt for their help in the American Revolution. General John J. Pershing, commander of the American Expeditionary Force (AEF), arrived in Paris on July 4, 1917. British and French commanders wanted to integrate American troops into their armies. Pershing refused, and eventually only one unit, the 93rd Infantry Division—an African American unit—was transferred to the French.

Germany's Last Offensive On March 21, 1918, the Germans launched a massive gas attack and artillery bombardment along the Western Front. Strengthened by reinforcements from the Russian front, the Germans pushed deep into Allied lines. By early June, they were less than 40 miles (64 km) from Paris. In late May, as the

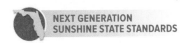

NEXT GENERATION SUNSHINE STATE STANDARDS

Continued from page 243

LAFS.1112.WHST.1.1: Write arguments focused on discipline-specific content.

LAFS.1112.WHST.4.10: Write routinely over extended time frames (time for reflection and revision) and shorter time frames (a single sitting or a day or two) for a range of discipline-specific tasks, purposes, and audiences.

SS.912.A.1.2: Utilize a variety of primary and secondary sources to identify author, historical significance, audience, and authenticity to understand a historical period.

SS.912.A.1.4: Analyze how images, symbols, objects, cartoons, graphs, charts, maps, and artwork may be used to interpret the significance of time periods and events from the past.

SS.912.A.4.5: Examine causes, course, and consequences of United States involvement in World War I.

Continued on page 247

convoy a group that travels with something, such as a ship, to protect it

adequately sufficiently; completed to its minimum requirements

Air battles first occurred during World War I. These early planes, however, were hard to fly and easy to destroy during dogfights.

▶ **CRITICAL THINKING**

Making Generalizations How did the use of aircraft change battle during World War I?
LAFS.1112.RH.3.7, SS.912.A.1.4, SS.912.A.4.7

©Stapleton Collection/Historical Picture Library/Corbis

©Bettmann/Corbis

Alvin York (1887–1964)

Alvin York grew up poor in the mountains of Tennessee. After being drafted, he tried to avoid military service as a conscientious objector due to his pacifist Christian beliefs. York later became convinced that he could fight for a just cause. During the Battle of the Argonne Forest, German machine guns on a fortified hill fired on York's platoon and killed nine men. York took command and charged the machine guns. He went on to kill several Germans, capture the machine guns, and take 132 prisoners. For his actions, he received the Medal of Honor and the French Croix de Guerre.

▶ **CRITICAL THINKING**
Describing How did York contribute to the American victory at the Argonne? LAFS.1112.RH.3.7, SS.912.A.1.4, SS.912.A.4.8

armistice a temporary agreement to end fighting

SKILLS PRACTICE

There are many new words in this section, including *legitimate, disarmament, self-determination, reparations,* and *arbitration.* As you read, list the words you do not know. Then ask for help with the words. ELD.K12.ELL.SI.1, ELD.K12.ELL.SS.1

offensive continued, the Americans launched their first major attack, quickly capturing the village of Cantigny. On June 1, American and French troops blocked the German drive on Paris at the town of Château-Thierry. On July 15, the Germans launched one last massive attack in an attempt to take Paris, but American and French troops held their ground.

The Battle of the Argonne Forest With the German drive stalled, French marshal Ferdinand Foch, supreme commander of the Allied forces, ordered massive counterattacks. In mid-September, American troops drove back German forces at the battle of Saint-Mihiel. On September 26, 1918, the most massive offensive for the American Expeditionary Force was launched in the region between the Meuse River and the Argonne Forest. Although the Germans inflicted heavy casualties, their positions slowly fell to the advancing American troops. By early November, the Americans had opened a hole on the eastern flank of the German lines. All across the Western Front, the Germans began to retreat.

The War Ends

Meanwhile, a revolution had engulfed Austria-Hungary. In October 1918, Poland, Hungary, and Czechoslovakia declared independence. By early November, the governments of the Austro-Hungarian Empire and the Ottoman Empire had surrendered to the Allies.

In late October, sailors in Kiel, the main base of the German fleet, mutinied. Within days, groups of workers and soldiers seized power in other German towns. The German emperor stepped down, and on November 9, Germany became a republic. Two days later, the government signed an **armistice**—an agreement to stop fighting. On November 11, 1918, the fighting stopped.

☑ READING PROGRESS CHECK

Determining Cause and Effect How did the arrival of American troops affect German attitudes about the war?

A Flawed Peace

GUIDING QUESTION *Why did President Wilson's ideas for peace negotiations differ from those of French premier Clemenceau and British prime minister Lloyd George?*

Although the fighting had stopped, World War I was not over. In January 1919, delegates from 27 countries traveled to the peace conference at the Palace of Versailles, near Paris. The treaty with Germany that resulted came to be called the Treaty of Versailles. The conference also negotiated the Treaty of Saint-Germain, ending the war with Austria-Hungary. Negotiations on the Treaty of Versailles lasted five months. The most important participants were the so-called "Big Four": President Wilson of the United States, British prime minister David Lloyd George, French premier Georges Clemenceau, and Italian prime minister Vittorio Orlando. Russian representatives were not invited to the conference because Allied leaders refused to recognize Lenin's government as legitimate.

The Fourteen Points

President Wilson arrived in Paris in 1919 with a peace plan known as the Fourteen Points. It was based on "the principle of justice to all peoples and nationalities." In the first five points, Wilson proposed to eliminate the causes of the war through free trade, freedom of the seas, disarmament, an impartial adjustment of colonial claims, and open diplomacy.

Changes in Europe 1919

Legend:
- Former Austria-Hungary boundary
- Former German boundary
- Former Russian boundary
- Former Serbian boundary
- Former Montenegran boundary
- Former Romanian boundary

GEOGRAPHY CONNECTION

European borders were redrawn as a result of World War I.

1 PLACES AND REGIONS *What was one unusual characteristic of the new state of Poland?* SS.912.A.1.4, SS.912.G.2.1, SS.912.G.4.9

2 PLACES AND REGIONS *How did the regions controlled by Russia change in 1919?* SS.912.A.1.4, SS.912.G.2.1, SS.912.G.4.9

The next eight points addressed the right of **national self-determination,** the idea that the borders of countries should be based on ethnicity and national identity. Supporters of this idea believed that when borders are not based on national identity, nations are more likely to go to war to **resolve** border disputes. This principle also meant that no nation should keep territory taken from another nation. This required the Central Powers to evacuate all invaded countries and Germany to restore the French territory of Alsace-Lorraine, taken in 1871.

The fourteenth point called for the creation of a League of Nations. The League's members would help preserve peace by pledging to respect and protect each other's territory and political independence. Wilson was willing to give up his other goals in exchange for support for the League.

The Treaty of Versailles

Wilson's popularity in Europe put him in a strong negotiating position. The peace conference decided to use the Fourteen Points as the basis for negotiations. But not everyone was impressed by Wilson's ideas. Premier Clemenceau of France and British prime minister Lloyd George wanted to punish the Germans for the suffering they had inflicted on the rest of Europe. Additionally, Britain refused to give up its sizable naval advantage by agreeing to Wilson's call for freedom of the seas.

The Treaty of Versailles, reluctantly signed by Germany on June 28, 1919, included many terms designed to punish and weaken Germany. Germany's armed forces were greatly reduced and its troops were not allowed west of the Rhine River. The treaty also specifically blamed "the aggression of Germany" for the war. This allowed the Allies to demand that Germany pay **reparations**—monetary compensation for all of the war damages it had caused. A commission decided that Germany owed the Allies about $33 billion. This sum far exceeded what Germany could pay all at once and was intended to keep its economy weak for a long time.

Wilson had somewhat better success in promoting national self-determination. The Austro-Hungarian Empire, the Russian Empire, the

national self-determination the free choice by the people of a nation of their own future political status

resolve to come to an agreement

NEXT GENERATION SUNSHINE STATE STANDARDS

Continued from page 245

SS.912.A.4.7: Examine the impact of airplanes, battleships, new weaponry and chemical warfare in creating new war strategies (trench warfare, convoys).

SS.912.A.4.8: Compare the experiences Americans (African Americans, Hispanics, Asians, women, conscientious objectors) had while serving in Europe.

SS.912.A.4.10: Examine the provisions of the Treaty of Versailles and the failure of the United States to support the League of Nations.

SS.912.A.5.5: Describe efforts by the United States and other world powers to avoid future wars.

SS.912.G.1.2: Use spatial perspective and appropriate geographic terms and tools, including the Six Essential Elements, as organizational schema to describe any given place.

SS.912.G.4.3: Use geographic terms and tools to analyze the effects of migration both on the place of origin and destination, including border areas.

reparations payment by the losing country in a war to the winner for the damages caused by the war

The Belgian town of Ypres (shown above) was the site of some of the heaviest fighting of World War I. The war devastated Europe's people and places. The physical scars on the landscape and the millions of casualties affected Europe for years to come.

▶ CRITICAL THINKING

Predicting Consequences How did the damage caused during World War I change Europe in later years? LAFS.1112.RH.3.7, SS.912.A.1.4, SS.912.A.4.5

German Empire, and the Ottoman Empire were dismantled, and new nations created. In general, the majority of people in each new country were from one ethnic group. But both Poland and Czechoslovakia were given territory where the majority of the people were German, and Germany was split in two in order to give Poland access to the Baltic Sea. This arrangement helped set the stage for a new series of crises in the 1930s.

The Treaty of Versailles ignored freedom of the seas, free trade, and Wilson's goal of a fair settlement of colonial claims. No colonial people in Asia or Africa received independence. France and Britain took over colonial areas in Africa and the Middle East, and received mandates from the League of Nations to rule the areas in preparation for independence. France received mandates for Syria and Lebanon, and Britain for Palestine including Transjordan and Iraq. The treaty did, however, call for the creation of a League of Nations. League members promised to reduce armaments, to submit all disputes that endangered the peace to arbitration, and to aid any member who was threatened with aggression.

The U.S. Senate Rejects the Treaty

President Wilson was confident the American people would support the Treaty of Versailles. But he had badly underestimated opposition to the League of Nations in the Senate. All treaties signed by the United States must be ratified by two-thirds of the Senate, and in November 1918, the Democratic Party had lost control of the Senate. Even though he needed Republican support to ratify the treaty, Wilson refused to take any Republican leaders with him to the peace conference. This ensured that Wilson's views prevailed, but it also meant that Republican concerns were not addressed.

Opposition in the Senate focused on the League of Nations. One group of senators, nicknamed "the Irreconcilables," refused to support the treaty under any circumstances. They assailed the League as the kind of "entangling alliance" that George Washington and the other Founders had warned against. They believed that joining an international organization endangered American sovereignty. As a democratic-republic, the American government was supposed to act based on what its own citizens wanted, not what people in other countries wanted.

A larger group of senators, known as the "Reservationists," was led by the powerful chairman of the Foreign Relations committee, Henry Cabot Lodge. The reservationists were willing to support the Treaty of Versailles if amendments were made to the League of Nations. The reservationists pointed out that the Constitution requires Congress to declare war. Yet the League of Nations could require member states to aid any member who was attacked. The reservationists argued that this might force the United States into a war without Congressional approval. They agreed to ratify the treaty if it was amended to say that any military action by the United States

Hulton Archive/Getty Images

required the approval of Congress. Wilson refused, fearing the change would undermine the League's effectiveness.

Wilson decided to take his case directly to the American people. Starting in September 1919, he traveled some 8,000 miles and made more than 30 major speeches in three weeks. Soon afterward he suffered a stroke. Although bedridden, Wilson still refused to compromise on the treaty.

The Senate voted in November 1919 and in March 1920, but both times it refused to give its consent to the treaty. After Wilson left office in 1921, the United States negotiated separate peace treaties with each of the Central Powers. The League of Nations took shape without the United States.

The debate had pointed out the pros and cons of international treaties and international organizations. On the one hand, once the United States joined an international organization and signed an international treaty, it was bound by those agreements which would limit the nation's ability to act independently. Of course, the United States could always withdraw from a treaty, but when a nation does that too often, its credibility is damaged and other nations will no longer trust it to keep its agreements. On the other hand, had the United States joined the League of Nations, it would have been able to use its power and influence to shape League policies and enforce League actions. It could have helped promote international cooperation and peace. In the years ahead, many people would argue that the League of Nations was ineffective because many powerful nations, such as the United States, were not members.

World War I: A Turning Point

World War I marked an important turning point in world history. The war had destroyed the German, Russian, and Austro-Hungarian empires and badly weakened Britain and France. All across the world, Wilson's idea of national self-determination began to take hold as people in Europe's colonies began to work for independence. The war had also triggered a communist revolution in Russia. The rest of the twentieth century would be affected by the slow motion struggle between supporters of democratic institutions and free enterprise and supporters of communism and revolution.

✔ **READING PROGRESS CHECK**

Comparing and Contrasting How did Wilson's perspective on the best outcome of the peace process differ from those of European leaders?

LESSON 3 REVIEW

Reviewing Vocabulary

1. *Contrasting* What is the difference between an armistice and a treaty? LAFS.1112.RH.2.4

2. *Applying* How did ideas of national self-determination influence the Treaty of Versailles? LAFS.1112.RH.2.4

Using Your Notes

3. *Explaining* Review the notes you completed during the lesson and then write a paragraph explaining how new technology changed warfare during World War I. LAFS.1112.WHST.1.1

Answering the Guiding Questions

4. *Identifying Cause and Effect* How did new technologies increase the number of casualties compared with previous wars? SS.912.A.4.7

5. *Drawing Conclusions* Why was the arrival of American forces so important to the war effort? SS.912.A.4.5

6. *Identifying Perspectives* Why did President Wilson's ideas for peace negotiations differ from those of French premier Clemenceau and British prime minister Lloyd George? SS.912.A.4.10

Writing Activity

7. INFORMATIVE/EXPLANATORY Write a brief essay that explains the reasons why the U.S. Senate refused to give its consent to the Treaty of Versailles. LAFS.1112.WHST.1.2, LAFS.1112.WHST.4.10

LESSON 4
The War's Impact

ESSENTIAL QUESTION
• Why do nations go to war?

READING HELPDESK

Academic Vocabulary
• **widespread** • **authorities**

Content Vocabulary
• cost of living
• deport
• general strike

TAKING NOTES

Key Ideas and Details

Organizing As you read, complete a graphic organizer similar to the one below to list the effects of the end of World War I on the U.S. economy.
LAFS.1112.RH.3.7, SS.912.A.4.5

**NEXT GENERATION
SUNSHINE STATE STANDARDS**

LAFS.1112.RH.2.4: Determine the meaning of words and phrases as they are used in a text, including analyzing how an author uses and refines the meaning of a key term over the course of a text (e.g., how Madison defines faction in Federalist No. 10).

LAFS.1112.RH.3.7: Integrate and evaluate multiple sources of information presented in diverse formats and media (e.g., visually, quantitatively, as well as in words) in order to address a question or solve a problem.

LAFS.1112.WHST.1.1: Write arguments focused on discipline-specific content.

Continued on page 252

IT MATTERS BECAUSE
America's victory overseas led to turmoil at home. The end of the wartime economy led to a depression and fears of communism, as strikes, riots, and bombings took place.

An Economy in Turmoil

GUIDING QUESTION *Why did many workers participate in strikes following the war?*

After the war ended, government agencies removed their controls from the economy. People raced to buy goods that had been rationed, while businesses raised prices they had been forced to keep low. The result was rapid inflation that greatly increased the **cost of living**—the cost of food, clothing, shelter, and other essentials. With orders for war materials evaporating, factories laid off workers. Returning soldiers found that jobs were scarce.

Inflation Leads to Strikes
While workers wanted higher wages to keep up with inflation, companies resisted because inflation was also driving up their operating costs. During the war, union membership had increased greatly. Business leaders, however, were determined to break the power of the unions. By the end of 1919, more than 3,600 strikes involving more than four million workers had taken place.

The Seattle General Strike In Seattle, some 35,000 shipyard workers walked off the job demanding higher wages and shorter hours. Other unions in Seattle soon organized a **general strike**—a strike that involves all workers in a community—of more than 60,000 people that paralyzed the city for five days. The strikers returned to work without making any gains, but their actions worried many Americans because the general strike was a common tactic of Communists and some radical groups in Europe.

The Boston Police Strike One of the most famous strikes of 1919 occurred in Boston, where roughly 75 percent of the police force walked off the job. Riots and looting forced Governor Calvin

Coolidge to call in the National Guard. When the strikers tried to return to work, the police commissioner instead fired them. Despite protests, Coolidge agreed that the men should be fired, declaring: "There is no right to strike against the public safety by anybody, anywhere, anytime." Coolidge's response earned him **widespread** public support and convinced the Republicans to make him their vice-presidential candidate in 1920.

The Steel Strike Soon after the police strike, an estimated 350,000 steelworkers went on strike for higher pay, shorter hours, and recognition of their union. U.S. Steel refused to talk to union leaders and set out to break the union. It blamed the strike on foreign radicals and called for loyal Americans to return to work. Meanwhile, the company hired African American and Mexican workers as replacements. Clashes between company guards and strikers were frequent. In Gary, Indiana, a riot left 18 strikers dead. The strike collapsed in 1920, setting back the union cause in the steel industry for more than a decade.

Racial Unrest

Postwar economic turmoil also contributed to widespread racial unrest. Many African Americans had moved north during the war to take factory jobs. As people began to be laid off and returning soldiers found it hard to find work and affordable housing, many blamed African Americans for taking their jobs. Frustration and racism combined to produce violence.

In the summer of 1919, 25 race riots broke out across the nation. The riots began in July, when a mob of angry whites burned shops and homes in an African American neighborhood in Longview, Texas. A week later in Washington, D.C., gangs of African Americans and whites fought each other for four days before troops got the riots under control.

The worst violence occurred in Chicago. On a hot July day, African Americans went to a whites-only beach. Both sides began throwing stones, and an African American teenager drowned as a result. A full-scale riot then erupted. Angry African Americans attacked white neighborhoods while whites attacked African American neighborhoods. The riot lasted for almost two weeks until the government sent in the National Guard to impose order. By the time the rioting ended, 38 people had been killed—15 white and 23 African American—and more than 500 had been injured.

cost of living the cost of purchasing goods and services essential for survival

general strike a strike involving all the workers in a particular geographic location

widespread widely diffused or prevalent

Some strikes became so violent and out of control that the federal government was forced to call in the National Guard to impose order. Here, troops get rioting under control during the Boston Police Strike of 1919.

▶ CRITICAL THINKING
Analyzing Information Why do you think the government reacted against strikes so strongly in 1919? LAFS.1112.RH.3.7, SS.912.A.1.4, SS.912.A.5.1

©Underwood & Underwood/Bettmann/Corbis

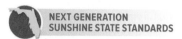
Continued from page 250

LAFS.1112.WHST.4.10: Write routinely over extended time frames (time for reflection and revision) and shorter time frames (a single sitting or a day or two) for a range of discipline-specific tasks, purposes, and audiences.

SS.912.A.1.2: Utilize a variety of primary and secondary sources to identify author, historical significance, audience, and authenticity to understand a historical period.

SS.912.A.1.4: Analyze how images, symbols, objects, cartoons, graphs, charts, maps, and artwork may be used to interpret the significance of time periods and events from the past.

SS.912.A.4.5: Examine causes, course, and consequences of United States involvement in World War I.

SS.912.A.4.9: Compare how the war impacted German Americans, Asian Americans, African Americans, Hispanic Americans, Jewish Americans, Native Americans, women and dissenters in the United States.

SS.912.A.5.1: Discuss the economic outcomes of demobilization.

SS.912.A.5.2: Explain the causes of the public reaction (Sacco and Vanzetti, labor, racial unrest) associated with the Red Scare.

deport to expel an individual from the country

In September 1920, a bomb made of 100 pounds of dynamite and 500 pounds of steel fragments exploded in New York City, killing 38 people and injuring 100 others.

▶ **CRITICAL THINKING**
Analyzing Primary Sources
What effect do you think the event depicted below had on public attitudes toward political radicals? LAFS.1112.RH.3.7, SS.912.A.1.4, SS.912.A.5.2

The race riots of 1919 disillusioned some African Americans who felt their wartime contributions had been for nothing. For others, however, the wartime struggle for democracy encouraged them to fight for their rights at home. For the first time, African Americans organized and fought back. The NAACP experienced a surge in membership after the war, and in 1919 it launched a new campaign for a federal law against lynching.

✅ **READING PROGRESS CHECK**

Determining Cause and Effect Why did the number of strikes increase after the war?

The Red Scare

GUIDING QUESTION *Do you agree or disagree with A. Mitchell Palmer's efforts to prevent a "radical" revolution in the United States?*

Since the late 1800s, many Americans had accused immigrants of importing socialist and communist ideas and had blamed them for labor unrest and violence. Events in Russia seemed to justify fears of a Communist revolution. The strikes of 1919 fueled fears that Communists, or "reds," might seize power, leading to a nationwide panic known as the Red Scare. Many people were particularly concerned about workers using strikes to start a revolution.

The Palmer Raids

In April, the postal service intercepted more than 30 parcels containing homemade bombs addressed to prominent Americans. The next month, a parade in Cleveland to protest the jailing of American Socialist Party leader Eugene Debs turned into a series of riots. Two people were killed and another 40 were injured. In June, eight bombs in eight cities exploded within minutes of one another, suggesting a nationwide conspiracy.

One of these bombs damaged the home of United States attorney general A. Mitchell Palmer. Palmer took action, establishing a special division within the Justice Department, the General Intelligence Division, which eventually became the Federal Bureau of Investigation (FBI). Although evidence pointed to no single group, Palmer's agents targeted the foreign-born. On November 7, 1919, Palmer ordered a series of raids on offices of the Union of Russian Workers in 12 cities. Less than seven weeks later, a transport ship left New York for Russia carrying 249 immigrants who had been **deported,** or expelled from the country.

Brown Brothers

In January 1920, Palmer ordered another series of raids on the headquarters of various radical organizations. Nearly 6,000 people were arrested. Palmer's raids continued until the spring of 1920, and **authorities** detained thousands of suspects. Palmer's agents often ignored the civil liberties of suspects. Officers entered homes and offices without search warrants. Some suspects were jailed indefinitely and were not allowed to talk to their attorneys. Many of the nearly 600 immigrants who were deported never had a court hearing. Palmer defended his actions:

authorities those who have control over determining and enforcing what is right or wrong

PRIMARY SOURCE

❝Like a prairie-fire, the blaze of revolution was sweeping over every American institution of law and order a year ago. It was eating its way into the homes of the American workmen . . . leaping into the belfry of the school bell, crawling into the sacred corners of American homes . . . burning up the foundations of society.❞

—from "The Case Against the 'Reds'," *Forum*, 1920

For a while, Palmer was regarded as a national hero. But his raids failed to turn up any hard evidence of revolutionary conspiracy. The Red Scare, however, greatly influenced people's attitudes during the 1920s. The New York state legislature expelled five members of the Socialist Party in January 1920, and within a few months, nearly 30 states passed sedition laws making it illegal to join groups advocating revolution. Many linked radicalism with immigrants, which led to calls to limit immigration.

The Election of 1920

Economic problems, labor unrest, racial tensions, and the fresh memories of World War I created a general sense of disillusionment in the United States. During the 1920 campaign, Ohio governor James M. Cox and his running mate, Assistant Secretary of the Navy Franklin D. Roosevelt, ran on a platform of progressive ideals. President Wilson tried to convince the Democrats to make the campaign a referendum on the Treaty of Versailles and the League of Nations. The Republican candidate, Warren G. Harding, called for a return to "normalcy," arguing that the country needed to return to the days before the Progressive Era reforms. Harding won the election by a landslide. Many Americans hoped to put racial, labor, and economic troubles behind them and build a more prosperous and stable society.

✔ **READING PROGRESS CHECK**

Theorizing Do you think that the events of 1919 justified Palmer's actions? Why or why not?

Analyzing
PRIMARY SOURCES

Warren G. Harding on a Return to Normalcy

❝[Our] present need is not heroics, but healing; not nostrums, but normalcy; not revolution, but [bold] restoration; not agitation, but adjustment; not surgery, but serenity; not the dramatic, but the dispassionate; . . . not submergence in internationality, but sustainment in triumphant nationality.❞

—from a speech given May 14, 1920

DBQ *MAKING GENERALIZATIONS*
What feelings did Harding hope to promote in this speech? SS.912.A.1.2

LESSON 4 REVIEW

Reviewing Vocabulary

1. *Defining* What types of costs are included in the cost of living? LAFS.1112.RH.2.4

2. *Stating* What happens to a person who is deported? LAFS.1112.RH.2.4

Using Your Notes

3. *Explaining* Use the notes you completed during the lesson to write a paragraph explaining the effects of the end of World War I on the U.S. economy. LAFS.1112.WHST.1.1

Answering the Guiding Questions

4. *Identifying Cause and Effect* Why did many workers participate in strikes following the war? SS.912.A.5.1

5. *Identifying Central Issues* Do you agree or disagree with A. Mitchell Palmer's efforts to prevent a "radical" revolution in the United States? SS.912.A.4.5, SS.912.A.5.2

Writing Activity

6. **ARGUMENT** Radical, labor, and racial unrest increased after World War I, and the federal government responded strongly. The National Guard was sent in to break up strikes and riots, and government agents detained and deported thousands of immigrants and radicals. Do you sympathize with those reacting against society, or with the government? Write a short persuasive speech explaining your position and offering reasons to support it. LAFS.1112.WHST.1.1, LAFS.1112.WHST.4.10

STUDY GUIDE

THE UNITED STATES ENTERS WORLD WAR I
LESSON 1

CAUSES OF AMERICAN ENTRY INTO WORLD WAR I

Anti-German propaganda by Allied nations turn many Americans against Germany	U.S. banks and businesses provide loans and goods to Allied nations	German submarine attacks on neutral supply ships anger United States	Sinking of *Lusitania* and *Sussex* anger American public	Germany's secret attempt to ally with Mexico further angers the American public.	U.S. declares war on Germany in April 1917

THE HOME FRONT
LESSON 2

THE WAR EFFORT

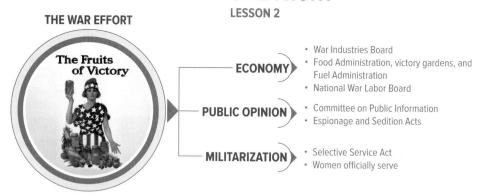

The Fruits of Victory

ECONOMY
- War Industries Board
- Food Administration, victory gardens, and Fuel Administration
- National War Labor Board

PUBLIC OPINION
- Committee on Public Information
- Espionage and Sedition Acts

MILITARIZATION
- Selective Service Act
- Women officially serve

A BLOODY CONFLICT
LESSON 3

THE TREATY OF VERSAILLES

Wilson's Fourteen Points used as a basis for negotiations	League of Nations created; however, due to opposition in Senate, the United States does not join
	Final treaty ignores freedom of the seas, free trade, and fair settlement of colonial claims
Britain and France wanted to punish Germany	Germany has to pay reparations, which far exceeds what it can pay
	German armed forces greatly reduced and not allowed west of the Rhine River
Promoted self-determination	The Austro-Hungarian Empire, the Russian Empire, the German Empire, and the Ottoman Empire are dismantled into smaller nations

THE WAR'S IMPACT
LESSON 4

SOCIAL AND CULTURAL EFFECTS OF WORLD WAR I

African Americans migrate to factory jobs in North; standard of living and political influence improves	Women enter workforce in larger numbers because men are enlisted in the military	Hispanic Americans shift from field work to industrial work; more Mexicans migrate into the U.S.	Postwar economic transition is disrupted by worker strikes and race riots in several cities	Rise in anti-immigrant, anti-communist, and anti-union beliefs following the war

Directions: On a separate sheet of paper, answer the questions below. Make sure you read carefully and answer all parts to the question.

Lesson Review

Lesson 1

1 *Specifying* What were the major empires in Europe prior to World War I, and why did nationalism threaten the stability of Europe? SS.912.A.4.5

2 *Explaining* What event began the chain reaction that led to World War I? SS.912.A.4.5

Lesson 2

3 *Making Generalizations* How were economic opportunities expanded for African Americans, Mexican Americans, and women during World War I? SS.912.A.4.9

4 *Explaining* How did the Food Administration help to ensure troops had enough food overseas? SS.912.A.4.6

5 *Explaining* What constitutional issues were raised by the federal government's efforts to ensure public support during World War I? How did the Court deviate from a strict construction view of the First Amendment? SS.912.A.4.6

Lesson 3

6 *Interpreting Significance* What impact did the arrival of American troops have on the course of the war? SS.912.A.4.5

7 *Specifying* Which countries did Russia give up as a result of pulling out of the war and signing the Treaty of Brest-Litovsk? SS.912.A.4.7

Lesson 4

8 *Identifying Perspectives* What economic and social issues caused the racial unrest in 1919? What effects did the war and the race riots have on African Americans and their struggle for civil rights? SS.912.A.4.9

9 *Analyzing Cause and Effect* Why did many Americans come to fear Communists and other radicals during the Red Scare after World War I? What was the effect of the Red Scare? SS.912.A.5.2

Exploring the Essential Questions

10 *Identifying Cause and Effect* Write a brief essay discussing why each of the following countries took part in World War I: Germany, Austria-Hungary, the Balkan states, France, Russia, Italy, Britain, and the United States. Synthesize these reasons and explain the main causes of World War I. What major themes emerge as to why nations go to war? SS.912.A.4.5

Critical Thinking

11 *Analyzing* Discuss the major issues of the neutrality debate that began in the United States after the start of World War I. What were the major issues being debated? Explain why Americans were divided in their opinions and identify people and groups on different sides of the issue. SS.912.A.4.5, SS.912.A.4.9

12 *Drawing Conclusions* Explain the significance of World War I. Why is it a turning point in history? SS.912.A.4.5

13 *Describing* What were the economic effects of World War I on the United States? Be sure to include the impact on the economy prior to America's entry into the war, the effect of mobilization, and the economic changes that took place after the war ended. SS.912.A.4.5, SS.912.A.4.6, SS.912.A.5.1

21st Century Skills

14 *Preparing an Oral Presentation* Prepare a lecture that describes the contributions of the American Expeditionary Force (AEF) and General John Pershing during World War I. Include an assessment of how important the AEF was to bringing an end to the war. LAFS.1112.RH.3.9, LAFS.1112.SL.2.4, SS.912.A.4.5

Need Extra Help?

If You've Missed Question	**1**	**2**	**3**	**4**	**5**	**6**	**7**	**8**	**9**	**10**	**11**	**12**	**13**	**14**
Go to Lesson	1	1	2	2	2	3	3	4	4	1	1	3	4	3

DBQ Analyzing Primary Sources

Read the following excerpt from President Wilson's Fourteen Points and answer the questions that follow.

PRIMARY SOURCE

❝ I. Open covenants of peace, openly arrived at. . . .

II. Absolute freedom of navigation upon the seas. . . .

III. The removal, so far as possible, of all economic barriers and the establishment of an equality of trade. . . .

IV. . . . that national armaments will be reduced to the lowest point consistent with domestic safety.

V. A free, open-minded, and absolutely impartial adjustment of all colonial claims. . . .

VI. The evacuation of all Russian territory. . . .

VII. Belgium . . . must be evacuated and restored. . . .

VIII. All French territory should be freed. . . .

IX. A readjustment of the frontiers of Italy should be effected along clearly recognizable lines of nationality.

X. The peoples of Austria-Hungary . . . should be accorded the freest opportunity to autonomous development.

XI. Rumania, Serbia, and Montenegro should be evacuated; occupied territories restored; Serbia accorded free and secure access to the sea. . .

XII. The Turkish portion of the present Ottoman Empire should be assured a secure sovereignty, but the other nationalities which are now under Turkish rule should be assured an . . . opportunity of autonomous development. . . .

XIII. An independent Polish state should be erected. . . .

XIV. A general association of nations must be formed under specific covenants for the purpose of affording mutual guarantees of political independence and territorial integrity to great and small states alike.❞

—President Wilson's Fourteen Points, January 1918

⓯ *Analyzing* What were the major issues raised by President Wilson's Fourteen Points? Why did they represent a challenge to the way the major powers had conducted themselves before the war?
LAFS.1112.RH.1.2, LAFS.1112.RH.3.8, LAFS.1112.RH.4.10, SS.912.A.4.5

⓰ *Interpreting Texts* Based on the text of the Fourteen Points, what groups of people did Wilson think should be given their own countries?
LAFS.1112.RH.1.1, LAFS.1112.RH.3.8, LAFS.1112.RH.4.10, SS.912.A.4.5

Need Extra Help?

If You've Missed Question	⓯	⓰	⓱	⓲	⓳
Go to Lesson	3	3	3	1	1

Analyzing Visuals

Use the recruiting poster Men of Britain *to answer the following questions.*

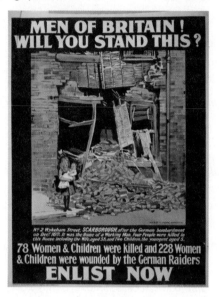

⓱ *Detecting Bias in Visuals* Who is the poster trying to influence? What visual elements and words are used in this poster to create an emotional reaction among viewers? What values is the poster appealing to in order to get people to enlist?
LAFS.1112.RH.1.1, SS.912.A.1.4, SS.912.A.4.6, SS.912.H.1.2

⓲ *Creating a Visual Presentation* Search the Internet to find examples of propaganda posters from World War I. Create a multimedia presentation or a poster board display that shows the different ways nations used words and images to build support for the war and recruit soldiers.
LAFS.1112.RH.3.9, LAFS.1112.SL.2.5, LAFS.1112.WHST.3.7, LAFS.1112.WHST.3.8, SS.912.A.1.4, SS.912.A.4.6, SS.912.H.1.1, SS.912.H.1.3, SS.912.H.1.5

Extended Response Question

⓳ *Expressing a Point of View* After World War I, the United States refused to ratify the Treaty of Versailles despite the efforts of Woodrow Wilson to convince Americans that ratification would help ensure an enduring peace. Write a persuasive essay using historical evidence that analyzes the major issues raised by the Treaty of Versailles and either supports or opposes the ratification of the treaty. Your essay should include an introduction, at least three paragraphs, and a conclusion.
LAFS.1112.RH.3.9, LAFS.1112.WHST.2.4, LAFS.1112.WHST.2.5, SS.912.A.4.10, LAFS.1112.WHST.4.10

◄ The works of legendary jazz singer and trumpet player Louis Armstrong are still widely played in many areas of contemporary culture. His improvised melodies influence jazz and other American music to this day.

FROM 1921 TO 1929

The Jazz Age

THE STORY MATTERS ...

American culture changed in the 1920s, although not everyone approved. Young people adopted new styles of dress, listened to new kinds of music, and had more independence than earlier generations.

African American artists and entertainers of the Harlem Renaissance reached a wide audience, helping overcome racial barriers in American society.

ESSENTIAL QUESTIONS

- How was social and economic life different in the early twentieth century from that of the late nineteenth century?
- How has the cultural identity of the United States changed over time?

Place & Time: United States 1920–1930

After the suffering of World War I, Americans were ready to enjoy life and eager to buy new goods that had not been available during the war. The new technology of the assembly line made the automobile much more affordable and spurred economic growth. The growing African American population in the North sparked new trends in literature, music, and art, and made African Americans a powerful political voice. Yet some people believed traditional society and morality were under attack, causing nativism and racism to increase in the 1920s.

Step Into the Place

Read the quotes and look at the information presented on the map.

 Analyzing Historical Documents How do the following quote and the information in the map show how technology changed life in the 1920s?

PRIMARY SOURCE

"Every piece of work in the shop moves; it may move on hooks on overhead chains going to assembly in the exact order in which the parts are required; it may travel on a moving platform, or it may go by gravity, but the point is that there is no lifting or trucking of anything other than materials. . . . No workman has anything to do with moving or lifting anything."

—Henry Ford describing his assembly line, from *My Life and Work*, 1922

left page: (b)Library of Congress, Prints & Photographs Division [LC-USZ62-111278]; (bl & br)detail/White House Historical Association/The White House Historical Association/The White House Historical Association/The White House Historical Association; right page detail/White House Historical Association

Step Into the Time

DRAWING CONCLUSIONS Research an event from the time line. Write a paragraph explaining how this event helped to shape the identity of the United States.

U.S. PRESIDENTS

Harding 1921–1923

Coolidge 1923–1929

1920 Prohibition begins

1922 Claude McKay's *Harlem Shadows* is published

UNITED STATES
WORLD

1920

1922

1921 Chinese Communist Party founded

1922 James Joyce's *Ulysses* is published

NEXT GENERATION SUNSHINE STATE STANDARDS
Students will understand the following benchmarks from the Florida NGSSS

LAFS.1112.RH.3.7: Integrate and evaluate multiple sources of information presented in diverse formats and media (e.g., visually, quantitatively, as well as in words) in order to address a question or solve a problem.

LAFS.1112.RH.4.10: By the end of grade 12, read and comprehend history/social studies texts in the grades 11–CCR text complexity band independently and proficiently.

SS.912.A.1.2: Utilize a variety of primary and secondary sources to identify author, historical significance, audience, and authenticity to understand a historical period.

SS.912.A.1.3: Utilize timelines to identify the time sequence of historical data.

SS.912.A.1.4: Analyze how images, symbols, objects, cartoons, graphs, charts, maps, and artwork may be used to interpret the significance of time periods and events from the past.

SS.912.A.3.2: Examine the social, political, and economic causes, course, and consequences of the second Industrial Revolution that began in the late 19th century.

SS.912.A.3.5: Identify significant inventors of the Industrial Revolution including African Americans and women.

SS.912.A.5.4: Evaluate how the economic boom during the Roaring Twenties changed consumers, businesses, manufacturing, and marketing practices.

U.S. Industrialization

CANADA

Detroit:
While older industries remained in the region, the economy of Detroit was quickly changed by the automobile industry in the 1920s.

Los Angeles:
Los Angeles rose to lead the nation's entertainment industry in the early 1900s, attracting filmmakers because its sunny climate allowed year-round film production.

Dallas:
The discovery of large oilfields in the early twentieth century, many of them in Texas, touched off "oil crazes." By 1920 the national demand for oil had grown as more people drove cars and used petroleum-based products.

Omaha
Chicago
Detroit
Akron
Pittsburgh
Cincinnati
New York City
Baltimore
San Francisco
Los Angeles
Dallas

PACIFIC OCEAN

ATLANTIC OCEAN

MEXICO

N W E S

0   400 miles
0   200 km
Lambert Azimuthal Equal-Area projection

TROPIC OF CANCER

Legend:
- Principal manufacturing cities
- Slaughtering and meat packing
- Textiles
- Iron and steel work
- Automobiles and parts
- Lumber and timber
- Oil and gas drilling

1924 Membership in the Ku Klux Klan peaks

1925 Scopes trial ignites debate over teaching of evolution

May 21, 1927 Lindbergh completes first solo transatlantic flight

1927 *The Jazz Singer* is first "talking" motion picture

Aug. 27, 1928 Kellogg-Briand Pact renounces war

Hoover 1929–1933

1924   1926   1928   1930

1924 Soviet leader Vladimir Lenin dies

1926 British inventor John Logie Baird demonstrates early version of television

1927 German scientist Werner Heisenberg announces the uncertainty principle

1929 National Revolutionary Party (PRI) founded in Mexico

The Jazz Age **259**

LESSON 1

The Politics of the 1920s

ESSENTIAL QUESTIONS

• How was social and economic life different in the early twentieth century from that of the late nineteenth century?
• How has the cultural identity of the United States changed over time?

READING HELPDESK

Academic Vocabulary
• investigation
• revelation

Content Vocabulary
• supply-side economics
• cooperative individualism
• isolationism

TAKING NOTES

Key Ideas and Details

Organizing As you read about Presidents Harding and Coolidge, create an outline similar to the one below to list features and accomplishments of their administrations. **LAFS.1112.RH.3.7, SS.912.A.5.3**

> The Politics of the 1920s
> I. The Harding Administration
>   A.
>   B.
> II.
> III.
>   A.
>   B.

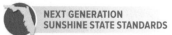
**NEXT GENERATION
SUNSHINE STATE STANDARDS**

LAFS.1112.RH.2.4: Determine the meaning of words and phrases as they are used in a text, including analyzing how an author uses and refines the meaning of a key term over the course of a text (e.g., how Madison defines faction in Federalist No. 10).

LAFS.1112.RH.3.7: Integrate and evaluate multiple sources of information presented in diverse formats and media (e.g., visually, quantitatively, as well as in words) in order to address a question or solve a problem.

Continued on page 261

IT MATTERS BECAUSE

Warren G. Harding's administration suffered from corruption and scandals. This damaged Americans' faith in their government. Harding's successor, Calvin Coolidge, worked to restore confidence, to promote a healthy U.S. economy, and to facilitate peace and restore economic stability abroad.

The Harding Administration

GUIDING QUESTION *How was Harding's effort to return to "normalcy" prevented by political scandals?*

Born in 1865 in Corsica, Ohio, Warren G. Harding began his career in Ohio state politics. In 1898, voters elected Harding to the Ohio General Assembly, where he fit in comfortably with the powerful Ohio Republican political machine. In 1903, he was elected lieutenant governor. He became a U.S. senator in 1914. After serving one term, Harding ran for and won the presidency in 1920.

In his campaign, Harding promised "a return to normalcy" following the war. For Harding and his administration, a "return to normalcy" meant an end to progressive experimentation, an end to high taxes on the wealthy, and an end to government intervention in the economy. In particular, it meant an end to the economic controls imposed during World War I. The Harding administration committed itself to restoring economic growth and prosperity by getting the government out of the economy. His genial manner endeared him to the nation. People applauded the easygoing atmosphere of the Harding administration, replacing the reform and war fervor of President Wilson's last years.

Teapot Dome and Other Scandals

Harding made several notable appointments to the cabinet. These included former Supreme Court justice Charles Evans Hughes as secretary of state, former Food Administrator Herbert Hoover as secretary of commerce, and business tycoon Andrew Mellon as secretary of the treasury. Many of his other appointments, however, were disastrous. He gave cabinet posts and other high-level jobs to friends and political allies from Ohio. Harding felt comfortable among his old friends, known as the Ohio Gang. Alice Roosevelt Longworth, daughter of President Theodore Roosevelt, described a typical evening in Harding's White House study:

PRIMARY SOURCE

❝The air [would be] heavy with tobacco smoke, trays with bottles containing every imaginable brand of whiskey . . . cards and poker chips at hand—a general atmosphere of waistcoat unbuttoned, feet on desk, and spittoons alongside.❞

—from *Crowded Hours*, 1933

Several of these men used their influential posts for their own gain. Colonel Charles R. Forbes, an Ohio acquaintance of Harding's, sold scarce medical supplies from veterans' hospitals and kept the money for himself. He cost the public about $250 million.

The most famous scandal, known as Teapot Dome, began in early 1922. Harding's secretary of the interior, Albert B. Fall, secretly allowed private interests to lease lands containing U.S. Navy oil reserves at Teapot Dome, Wyoming, and Elk Hills, California. In return, Fall received bribes from these private interests totaling more than $300,000. After the *Wall Street Journal* broke the story, the Senate launched an **investigation** that took most of the 1920s to complete. In 1929, Secretary Fall became the first cabinet secretary to go to prison.

Attorney general Harry Daugherty was investigated for accepting bribes from a German agent seeking to buy a German-owned company that had been seized by the U.S. government during World War I. Daugherty refused to open Justice Department files to a congressional committee. He also refused to testify under oath, claiming immunity, or freedom from prosecution, on the grounds that he had had confidential dealings with President Harding. Daugherty was later dismissed by President Coolidge.

The Granger Collection, New York

NEXT GENERATION
SUNSHINE STATE STANDARDS

Continued from page 260

LAFS.1112.WHST.1.1: Write arguments focused on discipline-specific content.

LAFS.1112.WHST.3.9: Draw evidence from informational texts to support analysis, reflection, and research.

LAFS.1112.WHST.4.10: Write routinely over extended time frames (time for reflection and revision) and shorter time frames (a single sitting or a day or two) for a range of discipline-specific tasks, purposes, and audiences.

SS.912.A.1.2: Utilize a variety of primary and secondary sources to identify author, historical significance, audience, and authenticity to understand a historical period.

SS.912.A.1.4: Analyze how images, symbols, objects, cartoons, graphs, charts, maps, and artwork may be used to interpret the significance of time periods and events from the past.

SS.912.A.4.5: Examine causes, course, and consequences of United States involvement in World War I.

SS.912.A.5.3: Examine the impact of United States foreign economic policy during the 1920s.

SS.912.A.5.4: Evaluate how the economic boom during the Roaring Twenties changed consumers, businesses, manufacturing, and marketing practices.

SS.912.A.5.5: Describe efforts by the United States and other world powers to avoid future wars.

SS.912.H.1.2: Describe how historical events, social context, and culture impact forms, techniques, and purposes of works in the arts, including the relationship between a government and its citizens. .

SS.912.H.1.5: Examine artistic response to social issues and new ideas in various cultures.

investigation a systematic examination or official inquiry

CORRUPTION IN GOVERNMENT

POLITICAL CARTOONS

"Bargain Day in Washington" shows the U.S. Capitol, the Washington Monument, the army, the White House, and the navy as having been "sold" to the highest bidder.

1 *Comparing and Contrasting*
What similarity does the cartoon suggest between the White House and the U.S. Capitol? LAFS.1112.RH.3.7, SS.912.A.1.4, SS.912.H.1.5

2 *Analyzing Information*
What does the cartoon imply about corruption in the federal government? LAFS.1112.RH.3.7, SS.912.A.1.4, SS.912.H.1.2, SS.912.H.1.5

Teapot Dome and the other scandals of the Harding administration increased Americans' distrust of the federal government and political leaders. This distrust added to the growing frustration with progressive policies caused by World War I. Many progressive ideas depended on efficient, honest government to be effective. If the government was corrupt, it helped make the case for reducing the role of government in the economy.

In June 1923, while traveling from Alaska to California, Harding became ill with what was probably a heart attack. He died in San Francisco on August 2, shortly before the news of the Forbes scandal broke. Early the next morning, the vice president, Calvin Coolidge, took the oath of office and became president.

"Silent Cal" Takes Over

Calvin Coolidge was very different from Harding. A critic joked that Coolidge could be "silent in five languages." Coolidge quickly distanced himself from the Harding administration. However, he asked the most capable cabinet members—Hughes, Mellon, and Hoover—to remain. Coolidge believed that prosperity rested on business leadership and that government should interfere with business and industry as little as possible.

In the year following Harding's death and the **revelations** of the scandals, Coolidge avoided crises and adopted policies intended to keep the nation prosperous. He easily won the Republican nomination for president in 1924. The Republicans promised the American people that the policies that had brought prosperity would continue. Coolidge won the election easily.

✓ **READING PROGRESS CHECK**

Comparing How did the Coolidge administration differ from the Harding administration?

revelation an act of revealing to view or making known

supply-side economics an economic theory that lower taxes will boost the economy as businesses and individuals invest their money, thereby creating higher tax revenue

cooperative individualism President Hoover's policy of encouraging manufacturers and distributors to form their own organizations and volunteer information to the federal government in an effort to stimulate the economy

Library of Congress, Prints & Photographs Division [LC-DIG-ppmsc-03670]

ANALYZING PRIMARY SOURCES

Coolidge and Prosperity

*"*After all, the chief business of the American people is business. They are profoundly concerned with producing, buying, selling, investing and prospering in the world. . . . In all experience, the accumulation of wealth means the multiplication of schools, the increase of knowledge, the dissemination of intelligence, the encouragement of science, the broadening of outlook, the expansion of liberties, the widening of culture.*"*

—Calvin Coolidge, from a speech to newspaper editors, quoted in the *New York Times,* January 18, 1925

DBQ Document Based Questions

Drawing Conclusions Why did Coolidge think that "the accumulation of wealth" was so important? SS.912.A.1.2

Policies of Prosperity

GUIDING QUESTION *What government policies helped the economy recover from the postwar recession?*

Andrew Mellon, a successful banker and industrialist, was secretary of the treasury under President Harding and the chief architect of economic policy. When Mellon took office, he had three major goals: to balance the budget, to reduce the government's debt, and to cut taxes. Mellon argued that if taxes were lower, businesses and some consumers would spend and invest their extra money. This would cause the economy to grow, and Americans would earn more money. The government then would collect more in taxes. This idea is known today as **supply-side economics.**

At Mellon's urging, Congress dramatically reduced tax rates. By 1928, Congress had reduced the income tax rate most Americans paid to 0.5 percent, down from 4 percent. They cut the rate for the wealthiest Americans to 25 percent, down from 73 percent. The federal budget fell from $6.4 billion to less than $3 billion in seven years.

Secretary of Commerce Herbert Hoover also sought to promote economic growth. He tried to balance government regulation with his philosophy of **cooperative individualism.** This idea involved encouraging businesses to form trade associations that would voluntarily share information with the federal government. Hoover believed this system would reduce costs and promote economic efficiency.

✔ READING PROGRESS CHECK

Summarizing What strategies helped promote economic growth and recovery after World War I?

Trade and Arms Control

GUIDING QUESTION *Do you think it is possible to abolish war?*

Before World War I, the United States was a debtor nation. By the end of the war, wartime allies owed the United States more than $10 billion in war debts. By the 1920s, the United States was the dominant economic power in the world. Under Secretary of State Charles Evans Hughes, the nation tried to use its economic power to promote peace and stability.

The Myth of Isolationism

Most Americans, tired of being entangled in the politics of Europe, favored **isolationism.** This is the idea that the United States will be safer and more prosperous if it stays out of world affairs. To many, it appeared that the United States had become isolationist. It had not ratified the Treaty of Versailles and had not joined the League of Nations. But in fact, the United States was too powerful and too interconnected with other countries economically to be truly isolationist. Instead of relying on armed force and the collective security of the League of Nations, the United States tried to promote peace by using economic policies and arms control agreements.

The Dawes Plan

America's former allies, Britain and France, had difficulty making the payments on their immense war debts. Meanwhile, Germany was trying to make huge cash payments to these nations as punishment for starting the war—payments that were crippling the German economy.

Library of Congres, Prints & Photographs Division [LC-DIG-hec-19933]

BIOGRAPHY

Andrew Mellon (1855–1937)

Secretary of the treasury and renowned art collector, Andrew W. Mellon was responsible for reforming the U.S. tax structure and reviving the national economy following World War I. Born in Pittsburgh, Pennsylvania, in 1855, Mellon went to work at his father's bank when he was still in his teens. Eventually his father made Andrew the bank's owner, and he went on to supply funds for local corporations, building his own empire in the process. He founded several profitable companies, including the Union Trust Company. This company was Mellon's chief source of income and proved so profitable that he was among the richest people in the United States by the 1920s.

In 1921 President Warren G. Harding appointed Mellon secretary of the treasury. In his new role, he worked to reduce the national debt in the wake of World War I by lowering taxes to allow business expansion. Mellon held his position in the treasury through the presidencies of Calvin Coolidge and Herbert Hoover; however, his failure to fend off the Great Depression caused him to resign in 1932. Andrew Mellon next served as U.S. ambassador to Britain, a position he held for a year. He died in 1937.

isolationism a national policy of avoiding involvement in world affairs

To address this problem, in 1924 American diplomat Charles G. Dawes negotiated an agreement with France, Britain, and Germany. American banks would make loans to Germany to help it to make reparations payments. In exchange, Britain and France would accept less in reparations and pay back more on their war debts to the United States.

The Washington Conference

Despite their debts, the major powers were involved in a costly postwar naval arms race. In 1921, the United States invited representatives from eight major countries—Britain, France, Italy, China, Japan, Belgium, the Netherlands, and Portugal—to Washington, D.C., to discuss disarmament. Secretary of State Charles Evans Hughes proposed a 10-year halt on the construction of new warships. This resulted in three agreements. In the Five-Power Naval Limitation Treaty, Britain, France, Italy, Japan, and the United States essentially formalized Hughes's proposal. The Four-Power Treaty between the United States, Japan, France, and Great Britain recognized each country's island possessions in the Pacific. Finally, all the participant countries signed the Nine-Powers Treaty, which guaranteed China's independence. As a long-term effort to prevent war, the conference had some serious shortcomings. It did nothing to limit land forces. It also angered the Japanese because it required Japan to maintain a smaller navy than either the United States or Great Britain. It did, however, give Americans cause to look forward to a period of peace, recovery, and prosperity.

The Kellogg-Briand Pact

The Washington Conference inspired U.S. secretary of state Frank Kellogg and French foreign minister Aristide Briand to propose a treaty to outlaw war altogether. On August 27, 1928, the United States and 14 other nations signed the Kellogg-Briand Pact. All signing nations agreed to abandon war and to settle all disputes by peaceful means.

The London Naval Treaties

From January to April 1930, five nations met in London to extend the Washington Conference. The United States, Britain, France, Italy, and Japan agreed on ratios for war ships, halting the arms race through 1936. In 1934, Japan announced it would not extend the treaty past 1936, so the five nations met again in December 1935. The United States, Britain, and France again signed the treaty. Japan and Italy declined to sign the treaty.

 READING PROGRESS CHECK

Identifying What initiatives did the United States take in the 1920s to help ensure economic stability and peace in Europe?

U.S. secretary of state Frank Kellogg is remembered today for promoting the Kellogg-Briand Pact, a treaty to outlaw war.

▶ CRITICAL THINKING
Predicting Consequences What might happen today if the United States and other nations followed the key idea of the Kellogg-Briand Pact? LAFS.1112.RH.3.7, SS.912.A.5.5

LIBRARY OF CONGRESS, PRINTS & PHOTOGRAPHS DIVISION [LC-US262-99922]

LESSON 1 REVIEW

Reviewing Vocabulary

1. *Specifying* What were some ways in which the United States showed signs of isolationism after World War I? LAFS.1112.RH.2.4, SS.912.A.4.5

Using Your Notes

2. *Comparing* Name one important way in which the Harding and Coolidge administrations were alike in terms of political appointments.

Answering the Guiding Questions

3. *Drawing Conclusions* How was Harding's effort to return to "normalcy" prevented by political scandals?

4. *Cause and Effect* What government policies helped the economy recover from the postwar recession? SS.912.A.5.3

5. *Analyzing* Do you think it is possible to abolish war? LAFS.1112.WHST.1.1, LAFS.1112.WHST.3.9, LAFS.1112.WHST.4.10, SS.912.A.5.5

Writing About History

6. ARGUMENT Suppose that you are a farmer or business owner in the 1920s. Write a letter to your representatives in Congress about why tax cuts are a good or bad idea. LAFS.1112.WHST.1.1, SS.912.A.5.4

LESSON 2
A Growing Economy

ESSENTIAL QUESTIONS

- How was social and economic life different in the early twentieth century from that of the late nineteenth century?
- How has the cultural identity of the United States changed over time?

READING HELPDESK

Academic Vocabulary

- disposable
- credit

Content Vocabulary

- mass production
- assembly line
- Model T

TAKING NOTES:

Key Ideas and Details

Organizing As you read about the booming era of the 1920s, complete a graphic organizer like the one below to analyze the causes of growth and prosperity. LAFS.1112.RH.3.7, SS.912.A.5.4

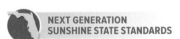

NEXT GENERATION SUNSHINE STATE STANDARDS

ELD.K12.ELL.SI.1: English language learners communicate for social and instructional purposes within the school setting.

ELD.K12.ELL.SS.1: English language learners communicate information, ideas and concepts necessary for academic success in the content area of Social Studies.

LAFS.1112.RH.2.4: Determine the meaning of words and phrases as they are used in a text, including analyzing how an author uses and refines the meaning of a key term over the course of a text (e.g., how Madison defines faction in Federalist No. 10).

Continued on page 266

IT MATTERS BECAUSE

In the 1920s, widespread ownership of automobiles, radios, and other innovations changed how Americans lived. The Coolidge administration tried to promote stability in international affairs and encouraged business growth.

The Rise of New Industries

GUIDING QUESTION *How did new industries change the lives of Americans in the 1920s?*

By the 1920s, the automobile had become part of American life. A 1925 survey conducted in Muncie, Indiana, found that 21 out of 26 families who owned cars did not have bathtubs with running water. As one farm wife explained, "You can't ride to town in a bathtub."

Increased automobile ownership was just one example of Americans' rising standard of living. Real per capita earnings soared 22 percent between 1923 and 1929 even as work hours decreased. In 1923, U.S. Steel cut its daily work shift from 12 hours to 8 hours. In 1926, Henry Ford cut the workweek for his employees from six days to five, and farm machinery company International Harvester instituted an annual two-week paid vacation for employees. **Mass production,** or large-scale manufacturing done with machinery, made these changes possible by increasing supply and reducing costs. Workers made more, and the goods they bought cost less.

Ford, the Assembly Line, and the Model T

The moving **assembly line** divided operations into simple tasks and cut unnecessary motion to a minimum. In 1913, automaker Henry Ford installed the first moving assembly line at a plant in Highland Park, Michigan. By the following year, workers were building an automobile every 93 minutes. By 1925, a Ford car was rolling off the line every 10 seconds.

Ford's assembly line product, the **Model T,** demonstrated the economic concept of elasticity, or how sensitive product demand is to price. In 1908, the Model T's first year, the car sold for $850. In 1914, mass production reduced the price to $490. Ford also increased his workers' wages in 1914 to $5 a day—doubling their pay—and reduced the workday to eight-hour shifts. He took these dramatic steps to win workers' loyalty and to undercut union organizers. By 1924, Model Ts were selling for $295, and Ford sold millions of them.

PRIMARY SOURCE

❝ There is one rule for the industrialist and that is: Make the best quality of goods possible at the lowest cost possible paying the highest wages possible. ❞

—Henry Ford, quoted in *Mass Production, the Stock Market Crash, and the Great Depression*, 1996

Ford's mass-production methods opened the door for new companies to manufacture cars. By the mid-1920s, General Motors and Chrysler competed successfully with Ford. The auto industry also spurred growth in the production of steel, petroleum, rubber, plate glass, nickel, and lead.

Cars revolutionized American life. They eased the isolation of rural families and let more people live farther from work. A new kind of worker, the auto commuter, appeared. Other forms of urban transportation, such as the trolley, became less popular.

Consumer Products

In response to rising **disposable** income, many other new goods came on the market. Americans bought such innovations as electric razors, facial tissues, frozen foods, and home hair color. Mouthwash, deodorants, cosmetics, and perfumes became popular products.

Companies created many new products for the home. As indoor plumbing became more common, Americans' concern for hygiene led to the development of numerous household cleaning products. New appliances advertised as labor-savers—such as electric irons, vacuum cleaners, washing machines, and refrigerators—changed the way people cleaned their homes and clothing and prepared meals.

Birth of the Airline Industry

After the Wright brothers' first successful flight in 1903, the aviation industry began developing. Leading the way was American inventor Glenn Curtiss, who invented ailerons—surfaces attached to wings that could be tilted to steer the plane. Ailerons made it possible to build rigid wings and much larger aircraft. The federal government began to support the airline industry. In 1918, the postmaster general introduced the world's first airmail service.

In 1925, Congress passed the Kelly Act, authorizing postal officials to hire private airplane operators to carry mail. The Air Commerce Act of 1926 provided federal aid to build airports. The transatlantic solo flight of former airmail pilot Charles Lindbergh in 1927 banished doubt about the potential of aircraft. By 1928, 48 airlines were serving 355 American cities.

The Radio Industry

In 1913, American engineer Edwin Armstrong invented a special circuit that made it practical to transmit sound via long-range radio. The radio industry began a few years later. In November 1920, the Westinghouse Company broadcast the news of Harding's landslide election victory from station KDKA in Pittsburgh—one of the first public broadcasts in history. That success persuaded Westinghouse to open other stations.

In 1926, the National Broadcasting Company (NBC) set up a network of stations to broadcast daily radio programs. By 1927, almost 700 stations

---

The popularity of the automobile led to an increase in American industries that produced materials needed to build cars.

▶ **CRITICAL THINKING**
Determining Cause and Effect
How was the rubber industry affected by the invention of the car? SS.912.A.5.4

mass production the production of large quantities of goods using machinery and often an assembly line

assembly line a production system with machines and workers arranged so that each person performs an assigned task again and again as the item passes before him or her

Model T automobile built by the Ford Motor Company from 1908 until 1927

disposable remaining to a person after deduction of taxes and living expenses

NEXT GENERATION SUNSHINE STATE STANDARDS

Continued from page 265

LAFS.1112.RH.3.7: Integrate and evaluate multiple sources of information presented in diverse formats and media (e.g., visually, quantitatively, as well as in words) in order to address a question or solve a problem.

LAFS.1112.WHST.1.1: Write arguments focused on discipline-specific content.

LAFS.1112.WHST.2.4: Produce clear and coherent writing in which the development, organization, and style are appropriate to task, purpose, and audience.

Continued on page 267

Topham/The Image Works

©Bettmann/Corbis

This is an early radio broadcast for the NBC network. Radio networks helped create a national community as people across the country listened to the same political speeches, music, sports, news, and entertainment programs.

▶ **CRITICAL THINKING**
Drawing Conclusions How might the growing nationwide availability of radio programs have affected Americans' sense of their culture? LAFS.1112.RH.3.7, SS.912.A.1.4, SS.912.H.3.1

Florida CONNECTION

Alfred I. du Pont

In 1902 Alfred I. du Pont and his cousins purchased their family's gunpowder manufacturing plant. They transformed E. I. du Pont de Nemours and Company into the largest chemical company in the United States, known for manufacturing products such as nylon, Teflon, and Kevlar. Du Pont later moved to Jacksonville and invested heavily in real estate and banking. Upon his death, Du Pont's fortune was left to a charitable organization aiding children's medical facilities in Florida and Delaware. SS.912.A.5.12

credit an amount or sum of money placed at a person's disposal by a bank on condition that it will be repaid with interest

dotted the country. Sales of radio equipment grew from $10.6 million in 1921 to $411 million in 1929, by which time more than 12 million radios were in use across the country.

In 1928, the Columbia Broadcasting System (CBS) assembled a coast-to-coast network of stations to rival NBC. The two networks sold advertising time and hired musicians, actors, and comedians from vaudeville, movies, and the nightclub circuit to appear on their shows. Americans experienced the first presidential election campaign to use radio in 1928, when the radio networks sold more than $1 million in advertising time to the Republican and Democratic Parties.

✓ **READING PROGRESS CHECK**

Analyzing How did new industries such as the automobile and radio change the way people lived?

The Consumer Society

GUIDING QUESTION *How did attitudes toward credit and consumerism change in the 1920s?*

Higher wages and shorter workdays resulted in a decade-long buying spree that kept the economy booming. Shifting from traditional attitudes of thrift and prudence, Americans in the 1920s enthusiastically accepted their new role as consumers.

Easy Consumer Credit

One notable aspect of the economic boom was the growth of individual borrowing. **Credit** had been available before the 1920s, but most Americans had considered debt shameful. Now attitudes toward debt started changing, as people began believing in their ability to pay their debts over time. Many listened to the sales pitch "Buy now and pay in easy installments," and began to accumulate debt. Americans bought 75 percent of their radios and 60 percent of their automobiles on the installment plan. Some started buying on credit at a rate exceeding their income.

Mass Advertising

When Otto Rohwedder developed a commercial bread slicer in 1928, he faced a problem common to inventions: the invention—sliced bread—was

NEXT GENERATION SUNSHINE STATE STANDARDS

Continued from page 266

LAFS.1112.WHST.2.5: Develop and strengthen writing as needed by planning, revising, editing, rewriting, or trying a new approach, focusing on addressing what is most significant for a specific purpose and audience.

LAFS.1112.WHST.4.10: Write routinely over extended time frames (time for reflection and revision) and shorter time frames (a single sitting or a day or two) for a range of discipline-specific tasks, purposes, and audiences.

SS.912.A.1.4: Analyze how images, symbols, objects, cartoons, graphs, charts, maps, and artwork may be used to interpret the significance of time periods and events from the past.

Continued on page 268

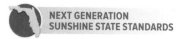

**NEXT GENERATION
SUNSHINE STATE STANDARDS**

Continued from page 267

SS.912.A.3.5: Identify significant inventors of the Industrial Revolution including African Americans and women.

SS.912.A.3.6: Analyze changes that occurred as the United States shifted from agrarian to an industrial society.

SS.912.A.5.1: Discuss the economic outcomes of demobilization.

SS.912.A.5.3: Examine the impact of United States foreign economic policy during the 1920s.

SS.912.A.5.4: Evaluate how the economic boom during the Roaring Twenties changed consumers, businesses, manufacturing, and marketing practices.

SS.912.A.5.12: Examine key events and people in Florida history as they relate to United States history.

SS.912.H.3.1: Analyze the effects of transportation, trade, communication, science, and technology on the preservation and diffusion of culture.

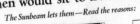

Advertisements in the 1920s enticed buyers with new technology, endorsements, money-back guarantees, and quick credit approval.

▶ **CRITICAL THINKING**

1 *Drawing Conclusions* Why did manufacturers offer money back when paid for at time of purchase? LAFS.1112.RH.3.7, SS.912.A.1.4, SS.912.A.5.4

2 *Predicting Consequences* What was the danger of buying products on credit? SS.912.A.1.4, SS.912.A.5.4

something no one knew they needed. To attract consumers, manufacturers turned to advertising, another booming industry in the 1920s.

Advertisers linked products with qualities associated with the modern era, such as progress, convenience, leisure, success, and style. Advertisers also preyed on consumers' fears and anxieties, such as insecurities about one's status or weight. For example, a 1923 advertisement for face cream read: "These premature lines are only the troubles of a skin allowed to be too dry. . . . The society woman keeps her skin smooth and fresh season in and season out."

The Managerial Revolution

By the early 1920s, many industries had already created modern organizational structures. Companies were split into divisions with functions such as sales, marketing, and accounting. Managers were hired to run these divisions, freeing executives and owners from the day-to-day running of the companies. The large numbers of new managers helped expand the middle class, adding to the nation's prosperity. These new developments in business organization generated more business profit, which improved the nation's standard of living.

> **PRIMARY SOURCE**
>
> ❝[I]t is not only by technical skill that modern civilization is sustained. It depends to a large degree on accumulated and invested capital. . . . Civilization and profits go hand in hand.❞
>
> —Calvin Coolidge, quoted in the *New York Times*, November 28, 1920

In addition to these innovations in management, companies in the 1920s began conducting time and motion studies, applying the ideas in Frederick Taylor's *Principles of Scientific Management*. They systematically broke down manufacturing work into small discrete tasks and then analyzed how best to use workers to do each task as efficiently as possible. Henry Ford's assembly line was an example of this approach. Time-study analysis made workers more productive, but in some ways it made work more difficult. Instead of a variety of changing tasks, workers on an assembly line had to do the same repetitive task over and over again.

Uneven Prosperity

Not all Americans shared in the economic boom. For example, thousands of African Americans who held factory jobs during World War I were replaced by returning servicemen. Native Americans, though granted citizenship in 1924, were often isolated on reservations where there was little productive work. Also, many immigrants had difficulty finding work. Most were farmers and factory workers with pitifully low wages. Many people in the Deep South were also left out of the economic boom as the traditional agricultural economic base there eroded after the war.

☑ **READING PROGRESS CHECK**

Explaining How did changing attitudes about credit affect people's daily lives?

The Farm Crisis

GUIDING QUESTION *Why did farmers miss out on the prosperity of the 1920s?*

American farmers did not share in the prosperity of the 1920s. On average, they earned less than one-third of the income of other American workers. Technological advances in fertilizers, seed varieties, and farm machinery allowed them to produce more, but higher yields without an increase in demand meant that they received lower prices. Between 1920 and 1921,

The Granger Collection, New York

Although many people benefited from the economic boom of the 1920s, several groups did not share in the general prosperity. For many African Americans, such as this family in rural Georgia, the 1920s were a time of poverty.

▶ **CRITICAL THINKING**
Comparing and Contrasting
In the 1920s, how was the life of a factory worker who lived in a big city different from the life of a farmer living in a rural area?
LAFS.1112.RH.3.7, SS.912.A.3.6

corn and wheat prices declined considerably. Costs for improved farming technology, meanwhile, continued to increase.

Many factors contributed to this "quiet depression" in American agriculture. During the war, the government had urged farmers to produce more to meet the great need for food in Europe. Many farmers borrowed heavily to buy new land and new machinery to raise more crops. Sales were strong, prices were high, and farmers prospered. After the war, however, European farm output rose, and the debt-ridden countries of Europe had little money to spend on American farm products. In addition, Congress passed the Fordney-McCumber Act in 1922, making matters worse by raising tariffs dramatically. This dampened the American market for foreign goods and sparked a reaction in foreign markets against buying American agricultural products.

Congress tried to pass legislation to help farmers sell their surpluses, but President Coolidge vetoed the bills. He argued that with money flowing to farmers under the proposed law, they would be encouraged to produce even greater surpluses. Agriculture remained in recession throughout the 1920s.

✓ **READING PROGRESS CHECK**

Synthesizing What factors led to the growing economic crisis in farming?

Hulton Archive/Getty Images

SKILLS PRACTICE

Look back through the lesson at the headings, important words and pictures. Retell the story of the 1920s economy using words you know. ELD.K12.ELL.SI.1, ELD.K12.ELL.SS.1

LESSON 2 REVIEW

Reviewing Vocabulary
1. *Explaining* How did the assembly line help make cars affordable for more Americans? LAFS.1112.RH.2.4, SS.912.A.5.4

Using Your Notes
2. *Hypothesizing* Review your notes on the economic growth of the 1920s. How might the economy of the 1920s have been different without the advertising industry?

Answering the Guiding Questions
3. *Summarizing* How did new industries change the lives of Americans in the 1920s? SS.912.5.4

4. *Synthesizing* How did attitudes toward credit and consumerism change in the 1920s? SS.912.5.4

5. *Identifying Cause and Effect* Why did farmers miss out on the prosperity of the 1920s? SS.912.A.3.6, SS.912.A.5.4

Writing Activity
6. **ARGUMENT** Think about the advantages of buying an automobile for rural families of the 1920s. Then write an advertisement for a Model T aimed at a farm family of the era. LAFS.1112.WHST.1.1, LAFS.1112.WHST.2.4, LAFS.1112.WHST.2.5, LAFS.1112.WHST.4.10, SS.912.A.3.6, SS.912.A.5.4

LESSON 3
A Clash of Values

ESSENTIAL QUESTIONS
• How was social and economic life different in the early twentieth century from that of the late nineteenth century?
• How has the cultural identity of the United States changed over time?

READING HELPDESK

Academic Vocabulary
• source   • deny

Content Vocabulary
• nativism
• creationism
• anarchist
• speakeasy
• evolution

TAKING NOTES

Key Ideas and Details

Organizing As you read about Americans' reactions to immigrants during the 1920s, complete a graphic organizer similar to the one below by filling in the causes and effects of anti-immigrant prejudices. **LAFS.1112.RH.3.7, SS.912.A.5.9**

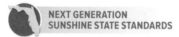
Anti-Immigrant Prejudices

NEXT GENERATION SUNSHINE STATE STANDARDS

MAFS.912.S-ID.1: Summarize, represent and interpret data on a single count or measurement variable.

LAFS.1112.RH.1.1: Cite specific textual evidence to support analysis of primary and secondary sources, connecting insights gained from specific details to an understanding of the text as a whole.

LAFS.1112.RH.2.4: Determine the meaning of words and phrases as they are used in a text, including analyzing how an author uses and refines the meaning of a key term over the course of a text (e.g., how Madison defines faction in Federalist No. 10).

Continued on page 272

IT MATTERS BECAUSE
The 1920s are often called the Roaring Twenties because to many the decade seemed to be one long party. Many urban Americans celebrated the new "modern" culture. However, many rural Americans believed traditional society was under attack. Nativism and racism increased, women sought to break free of traditional roles, and supporters of the new morality clashed with those who supported more traditional values.

Nativism and Immigration Policies

GUIDING QUESTION *Why did nativism strengthen during the 1920s, and how did the government deal with the tensions?*

The 1920s was a time of economic growth, but it was also a time of turmoil. An economic recession, an influx of immigrants, and cultural tensions combined to create an atmosphere of disillusionment and intolerance. The fear and prejudice many felt toward Germans and Communists during and after World War I expanded to include all immigrants. This triggered a general rise in racism and **nativism**—a belief that one's native land needs to be protected against immigrants.

During World War I, immigration to the United States had dropped sharply. By 1921, however, it had returned to prewar levels, with the majority of immigrants coming from southern and eastern Europe. Many Americans blamed the bombings, strikes, and recession of the postwar years on immigrants. Many believed immigrants were taking jobs that would otherwise have gone to soldiers returning home from the war.

The Sacco-Vanzetti Case
The Sacco-Vanzetti case reflected the prejudices and fears of the era. On April 15, 1920, two men robbed and murdered two employees of a shoe factory in Massachusetts. Police subsequently arrested two Italian immigrants, Nicola Sacco and Bartolomeo Vanzetti, for the crime.

EUROPEAN IMMIGRATION, 1900–1924

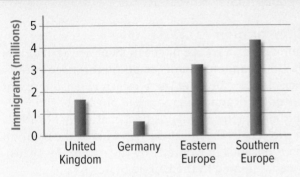

Immigrants (millions)

United Kingdom, Germany, Eastern Europe, Southern Europe

Source: *Historical Statistics of the United States: Millennial Edition*

Nicola Sacco and Bartolomeo Vanzetti were anarchists who were convicted of murdering two men during a 1920 armed robbery.

1 *Making Connections*
From which two regions did the majority of immigrants come? SS.912.A.1.4, MAFS.912.S-ID.1

2 *Drawing Conclusions*
Why might Americans have thought that immigrants from eastern and southern Europe would have trouble fitting in with American society? LAFS.1112.RH.3.7, SS.912.A.5.2

The case created a furor when newspapers revealed that the two men were **anarchists,** or people who oppose all forms of government. They also reported that Sacco owned a gun similar to the murder weapon and that the bullets used in the murders matched those in Sacco's gun. The evidence was questionable, but the fact that the accused men were anarchists and foreigners led many people to assume they were guilty, including the jury. On July 14, 1921, Sacco and Vanzetti were found guilty and sentenced to death. After six years of appeals, Sacco and Vanzetti were executed on August 23, 1927.

nativism hostility toward immigrants

anarchist a person who believes that there should be no government

source the point at which something is provided

PRIMARY SOURCE

❝I might have died, unmarked, unknown, a failure. Now we are not a failure. This is our career and our triumph.❞
—Bartolomeo Vanzetti before his execution, *The Letters of Sacco and Vanzetti,* 2007

Return of the Ku Klux Klan

The group that most wanted to restrict immigration was the Ku Klux Klan, or KKK. The old KKK began in the South after the Civil War and used threats and violence to intimidate newly freed African Americans. The new Klan also targeted Catholics, Jews, immigrants, and other groups said to be "un-American." William J. Simmons founded the new Ku Klux Klan in 1915, with a pledge to preserve America's white, Protestant civilization. With the help of professional promoters to sell Klan memberships, more and more people joined. By 1924, membership was close to 4 million as it spread beyond the South into the North and West.

Klan membership began to decline in the late 1920s, mainly due to scandals and power struggles among its leaders. In addition, new restrictions on immigration deprived the Klan of one of its major issues.

National Origins Act

American immigration policies became more restrictive in response to nativist groups like the KKK. Even some business leaders, who had favored immigration as a **source** of cheap labor, now saw the new immigrants as radicals. In 1921, President Harding signed the Emergency Quota Act, which restricted annual admission to the United States by ethnic group. In 1924, the National Origins Act made immigration restriction a permanent policy. The law set quotas at 2 percent of each national group represented in

Analyzing
PRIMARY SOURCES

Ku Klux Klan Poster

WE ARE ALL LOYAL KLANSMEN

DBQ **MAKING INFERENCES**
In what way can the message in this Klan poster be construed as nativism? LAFS.1112.RH.3.7, SS.912.A.1.2, SS.912.A.1.4, SS.912.A.5.9, SS.912.A.5.10, SS.912.H.1.5

(1) Library of Congress; (b) ©David J. Frent/David J. & Janice L. Frent Collection/Historical/Corbis

**NEXT GENERATION
SUNSHINE STATE STANDARDS**

Continued from page 270

LAFS.1112.RH.3.7: Integrate and evaluate multiple sources of information presented in diverse formats and media (e.g., visually, quantitatively, as well as in words) in order to address a question or solve a problem.

LAFS.1112.WHST.1.1: Write arguments focused on discipline-specific content.

LAFS.1112.WHST.4.10: Write routinely over extended time frames (time for reflection and revision) and shorter time frames (a single sitting or a day or two) for a range of discipline-specific tasks, purposes, and audiences.

SS.912.A.1.2: Utilize a variety of primary and secondary sources to identify author, historical significance, audience, and authenticity to understand a historical period.

SS.912.A.1.4: Analyze how images, symbols, objects, cartoons, graphs, charts, maps, and artwork may be used to interpret the significance of time periods and events from the past.

SS.912.A.5.2: Explain the causes of the public reaction (Sacco and Vanzetti, labor, racial unrest) associated with the Red Scare.

SS.912.A.5.6: Analyze the influence that Hollywood, the Harlem Renaissance, the Fundamentalist movement, and prohibition had in changing American society in the 1920s.

Continued on page 273

During the 1920s, fashions changed for women who wanted the glamorous look of movie stars.

▶ **CRITICAL THINKING**
Analyzing Visuals How do you think these women portray the attitude and "new morality" of the 1920s? LAFS.1112.RH.3.7, SS.912.A.1.4, SS.912.A.5.10

the U.S. Census of 1890—long before the heavy wave of Catholic and Jewish immigration from southern and eastern Europe. As a result, new quotas deliberately favored immigrants from northwestern Europe.

Increasing Mexican Immigration

Employers still needed immigrants, a source of cheap labor, for agriculture, mining, and railroad work. Mexican immigrants could fill this need because the National Origins Act exempted natives of the Western Hemisphere from the quotas. Large numbers of Mexican immigrants had already begun moving to the United States due to the Newlands Reclamation Act of 1902. The act funded irrigation projects in the Southwest and led to the creation of large farms that needed thousands of workers. By the end of the 1920s, nearly 700,000 Mexicans had migrated to the United States.

✓ **READING PROGRESS CHECK**

Contrasting How did the National Origins Act help deal with the tensions created by nativism?

A Clash of Cultures

GUIDING QUESTION *Why do you think some Americans feared the "new morality"?*

Groups that wanted to restrict immigration also wanted to preserve what they considered to be traditional values. They feared that a "new morality" was taking over. This trend glorified youth and personal freedom and brought big changes—particularly to the status of women.

Changes for Women

Having won the right to vote in 1920, many women sought to break free from traditional roles. Women who attended college often found support to pursue careers. Many working-class women took jobs because they needed the wages, but work was also a way to break away from parental authority and establish financial independence. Romance, pleasure, and friendship

©Bettmann/Corbis

became linked to successful marriages. Sigmund Freud's theories also affected people's ideas about relationships, especially his theories about human sexuality. Women's fashions changed during the 1920s: women "bobbed," or shortened, their hair and wore flesh-colored silk stockings. Some women, known as flappers, smoked cigarettes, drank prohibited liquor, and wore makeup and sleeveless dresses with short skirts.

Many professional women made major contributions in science, medicine, law, and literature. In medicine, Florence Sabin's research led to a dramatic drop in death rates from tuberculosis. Public-health nurse Margaret Sanger believed that families could improve their standard of living by limiting the number of children they had. She founded the American Birth Control League in 1921 to promote knowledge about birth control. During the 1920s and 1930s, the use of birth control increased dramatically, particularly in the middle class.

Religious Fundamentalism

While many Americans embraced the new morality of the 1920s, others feared that the country was losing its traditional values. They viewed the consumer culture, relaxed ethics, and changing roles of women as evidence of the nation's moral decline. Many of these people, especially in rural towns, responded by joining a religious movement known as Fundamentalism, a name derived from a series of Christian religious pamphlets titled *The Fundamentals,* published by millionaire Lyman Stewart.

Fundamentalists believed that the Bible was literally true and without error. They defended the Protestant faith against the implication that human beings derived their moral behavior from society and nature, not God. In particular, they rejected Charles Darwin's theory of **evolution,** which said that human beings had developed from lower forms of life over the course of millions of years. Instead, they believed in **creationism**—the belief that God created the world as described in the Bible.

Two popular evangelical preachers, Billy Sunday and Aimee Semple McPherson, stirred supporters by preaching in very nontraditional ways. Sunday, a former professional baseball player, drew huge crowds with his rapid-fire sermons and on-stage showmanship. McPherson conducted her revivals and faith healings in Los Angeles in a flamboyant theatrical style, using stage sets and costumes that expressed the themes of her highly emotional sermons.

In 1925, Tennessee outlawed any teaching that **denied** "the story of the Divine Creation of man as taught in the Bible," or taught that "man descended from a lower order of animals." The American Civil Liberties Union (ACLU) advertised for a teacher willing to be arrested for teaching evolution. John T. Scopes, a biology teacher in Dayton, Tennessee, volunteered. At Scopes's trial, William Jennings Bryan, a three-time presidential candidate, was the prosecutor representing the creationists. Clarence Darrow, one of the country's most celebrated trial lawyers, defended Scopes. Scopes was found guilty and fined $100, although the conviction was later overturned on a technicality. The trial had been broadcast over the radio, and Darrow's blistering cross-examination of Bryan hurt the Fundamentalist cause.

PRIMARY SOURCE

❝You can only protect your liberties in this world by protecting the other man's freedom. You can only be free if I am free.❞

—Clarence Darrow, address to the court in *People v. Lloyd,* 1920

**NEXT GENERATION
SUNSHINE STATE STANDARDS**

Continued from page 272

SS.912.A.5.9: Explain why support for the Ku Klux Klan varied in the 1920s with respect to issues such as anti-immigration, anti-African American, anti-Catholic, anti-Jewish, anti-women, and anti-union ideas.

SS.912.A.5.10: Analyze support for and resistance to civil rights for women, African Americans, Native Americans, and other minorities.

SS.912.H.1.5: Examine artistic response to social issues and new ideas in various cultures.

evolution the scientific theory that humans and other forms of life have evolved over time

creationism the belief that God created the world and everything in it, usually in the way described in the Bible

deny to declare untrue

speakeasy a place where alcoholic beverages are sold illegally

Prohibition

The movement to ban alcohol sales grew stronger in the early 1900s. Many people believed the prohibition of alcohol would help reduce unemployment, domestic violence, and poverty in the country. When the Eighteenth Amendment went into effect in January 1920, the Volstead Act gave the U.S. Treasury Department the power to enforce Prohibition, marking a dramatic increase in federal police powers.

In the 1920s, Treasury Department agents made more than 540,000 arrests, but Americans still ignored the law. People flocked to secret bars called **speakeasies** to purchase alcohol. In New York City alone, an estimated 32,000 such bars sold illegal liquor. Liquor also was readily available in rural areas through bootlegging—the illegal production and distribution of alcohol. Huge profits could be made smuggling liquor from Canada and the Caribbean. Organized crime became big business, and gangsters used their money to corrupt local politicians. Al Capone, one of the most successful and well-known gangsters of the era, had many police officers, judges, and other officials on his payroll.

The battle to repeal Prohibition began almost as soon as the Eighteenth Amendment was ratified. The Twenty-first Amendment, ratified in 1933, repealed the Eighteenth Amendment. Though diseases and some social problems were reduced, Prohibition did not improve society as dramatically as its supporters had hoped.

Prohibition led to the creation of a special federal bureau charged with stopping the sale of illegal alcohol. In this photo, a federal agent cracks open barrels of illegal rum to prevent it from being sold.

▶ CRITICAL THINKING

Analyzing Primary Sources The Volstead Act greatly increased federal police powers. What elements of this photo convey a sense of power? LAFS.1112.RH.1.1, LAFS.1112.RH.3.7, SS.912.A.1.4, SS.912.A.5.6

☑ READING PROGRESS CHECK

Identifying What political, social, and economic contributions did women make to American society in the 1920s?

Library of Congress/Archive Photos/Getty Images

LESSON 3 REVIEW

Reviewing Vocabulary
1. *Explaining* Why were Sacco and Vanzetti considered anarchists, and how did that affect the result of their trial? LAFS.1112.RH.2.4, SS.912.A.5.2

Using Your Notes
2. *Making Connections* Use your notes from this lesson to write a statement that makes a case for the connection between the causes of nativism and the rise of the Ku Klux Klan. SS.912.A.5.9

Answering the Guiding Questions
3. *Identifying Cause and Effect* Why did nativism strengthen during the 1920s, and how did the government deal with the tensions? SS.912.A.5.9

4. *Drawing Conclusions* Why do you think some Americans feared the "new morality"? LAFS.1112.RH.2.4, SS.912.A.5.6

Writing About History
5. ARGUMENT Suppose it is the 1920s. Write a letter to your senator to persuade him to support Prohibition or its repeal. LAFS.1112.WHST.1.1, LAFS.1112.WHST.4.10, SS.912.A.5.6

LESSON 4
Cultural Innovations

ESSENTIAL QUESTIONS
• How was social and economic life different in the early twentieth century from that of the late nineteenth century?
• How has the cultural identity of the United States changed over time?

READING HELPDESK

Academic Vocabulary
• diverse   • unify

Content Vocabulary
• bohemian
• mass media

TAKING NOTES:

Key Ideas and Details

Organizing As you read about the 1920s, complete a graphic organizer like the one below by filling in the main characteristics of art, literature, and popular culture of the era. LAFS.1112.RH.3.7, SS.912.A.5.6, SS.912.H.1.1

Cultural Movement	Main Characteristics
Art	
Literature	
Popular Culture	

NEXT GENERATION SUNSHINE STATE STANDARDS

ELD.K12.ELL.SI.1: English language learners communicate for social and instructional purposes within the school setting.

ELD.K12.ELL.SS.1: English language learners communicate information, ideas and concepts necessary for academic success in the content area of Social Studies.

LAFS.1112.RH.2.4: Determine the meaning of words and phrases as they are used in a text, including analyzing how an author uses and refines the meaning of a key term over the course of a text (e.g., how Madison defines faction in Federalist No. 10).

Continued on page 277

IT MATTERS BECAUSE
The 1920s was an era of great artistic innovation and enormous change in popular culture. Artists and writers experimented with new techniques. Broadcast radio introduced the latest trends in music and entertainment. Motion pictures became a major leisure-time activity, and Americans began to fall in love with sports such as baseball and boxing.

Art and Literature

GUIDING QUESTION *How did many artists and writers of the time describe the 1920s?*

During the 1920s, American artists and writers challenged traditional ideas as they searched for meaning in the modern world. Many artists, writers, and intellectuals flocked to Manhattan's Greenwich Village and Chicago's South Side. The artistic and unconventional, or **bohemian,** lifestyle of these places allowed artists, musicians, and writers greater freedom of expression.

Modern American Art
European art movements greatly influenced the modernists of American art. Perhaps most striking was the **diverse** range of artistic styles, each attempting to express the individual, modern experience. American painter John Marin drew on the urban dynamics of New York City for inspiration:

PRIMARY SOURCE

❝[T]he whole city is alive; buildings, people, all are alive; and the more they move me the more I feel them to be alive.

It is this 'moving of me' that I try to express, so that I may recall the spell I have been under and behold the expression of the different emotions that have been called into being. ❞

—from *Camera Work*, No. 42–43, April–July, 1913

Painter Charles Sheeler applied the influences of photography and the geometric forms of Cubism to urban and rural American landscapes.

Ernest Hemingway (1899–1961)

Ernest Hemingway was one of the most important American authors during the early 1920s. His writings focus on one theme—the search for the meaning of life during a time filled with violence. Hemingway's writing style reflects his purpose. He writes in the simple and direct style that he learned while working as a journalist. His characters are often engaged in war or on a violent adventure like hunting or bullfighting. The main character almost always tries to face his challenges with a strong personal code of courage, professionalism, and skill. His first novel, *The Sun Also Rises,* was published in 1926. His two famous war novels, *A Farewell to Arms* and *For Whom the Bell Tolls,* were very popular when they were published and are still considered great American novels. In the 1950s, Hemingway won the Pulitzer Prize and the Nobel Prize in Literature for *The Old Man and the Sea.*

Willa Cather (1873–1947)

Journalist, poet, and novelist, Willa Cather was among the most important writers of the first half of the twentieth century. Her work was known for its unconventional approach to structure, humanity, beauty, and drama. Having spent much of her childhood on the Nebraska frontier, she often explored the pioneer life in her writing. Her first book of poetry, *April Twilights,* was published in 1903, and a short story collection, *The Troll Garden,* followed in 1905. She then spent six years working for McClure's Magazine until a fellow writer at the magazine encouraged her to return to fiction. Cather immediately went to work on a string of successful books, including *O Pioneers!* (1913), *My Antonia* (1918), and *One of Ours* (1922), for which she won the Pulitzer Prize for fiction.

bohemian unconventional; not bound by the rules of society

diverse being different from one another

Edward Hopper revived the visual accuracy of realism. His paintings conveyed a modern sense of disenchantment and isolation in haunting scenes. Georgia O'Keeffe's landscapes and flowers were admired in many museums throughout her long life and are still admired today.

Much of American modern art in the 1920s focused on trying to portray the inner moods and feelings of people. As a result, much of the art was surreal or expressionist. It did not depict the outer world in a realistic way because it sought to use color and shape and lines to portray the inner world of people's emotions, moods, and relationship to the outer world. This was a positive contribution of the art, because its themes had been generally unexplored by American artists in the past. On the other hand, surrealism and expressionism were often difficult for the general public to appreciate, and could be discouraging in their depiction of society as fragmented and discordant, and individuals as isolated.

Poets and Writers

Writers of the 1920s varied greatly in their styles and subject matter. Illinois poet and writer Carl Sandburg used common speech to glorify the Midwest. So did the novels of Pulitzer Prize winner Willa Cather, such as *The Song of the Lark*. Sinclair Lewis poked fun at small-town life in *Main Street*. Edith Wharton criticized upper-class ignorance and pretensions in her Pulitzer Prize–winning novel *The Age of Innocence*. In Greenwich Village, another Pulitzer Prize winner, Edna St. Vincent Millay, wrote about women's inner lives.

Several poets influenced poetic style and subject matter. Some—such as Amy Lowell, Ezra Pound, and William Carlos Williams—used clear, concise images to express moments in time. Others, such as T. S. Eliot, criticized what they saw as a loss of spirituality in modern life.

SKILLS PRACTICE

Read the lesson on 1920s culture with a partner. Ask your partner questions about the lesson. Have your partner read aloud the sentences in the text that give the answer. Then have your partner ask you questions. Read aloud the sentences in the text that answer the questions.
ELD.K12.ELL.SI.1, ELD.K12.ELL.SS.1

(l)Hulton Archive/Stringer/Archive Photos/Getty Images; (r)Library of Congress, Prints & Photographs Division [LC-USZ62-82912]

Among playwrights, Eugene O'Neill was probably the most innovative. His plays, filled with bold artistry and modern themes, portrayed realistic characters and situations, offering a modern vision of life that often touched on the tragic. *Long Day's Journey Into Night* is a memorable example.

Some American writers, disillusioned by World War I and the emerging consumer society, moved to Paris, a center of artistic activity. American experimental writer Gertrude Stein dubbed them a "Lost Generation." Her Paris apartment became a home away from home for many writers. Among them was Ernest Hemingway, who wrote moving novels about war and its aftermath, such as *A Farewell to Arms.* Another visitor was F. Scott Fitzgerald. He criticized society's superficiality in *The Great Gatsby,* in which colorful characters—some modeled after his wife Zelda, who was a dancer, painter, and novelist—chased futile dreams:

PRIMARY SOURCE

❝They were careless people, Tom and Daisy—they smashed up things and creatures and then retreated back into their money or their vast carelessness, or whatever it was that kept them together, and let other people clean up the mess they had made.**❞**

—from *The Great Gatsby*, 1925

The literature of the 1920s had potentially both positive and negative impacts on American readers. On the one hand, by criticizing class pretensions, consumerism, and the pursuit of material goods, the literature of the era encouraged people to think seriously about how modern life was changing things.

On the other hand, literature also challenged traditional values and beliefs that might have played an important role in sustaining society. Many artists and writers of the 1920s attempted to portray the sense that modern life was meaningless, that moral progress was impossible, and that people were losing their relationships and connections. By saying that life has no meaning and nothing was constant, this type of literature implied that there was little purpose to life and therefore no reason to try to achieve anything.

✓ **READING PROGRESS CHECK**

Describing Why did many artists, poets, playwrights, and novelists move to Paris in the 1920s?

Popular Culture

GUIDING QUESTION *Why did many Americans have more time for entertainment, and how did they spend their time?*

The economic prosperity and new technology of the 1920s provided many Americans with more spending money and leisure time. Millions of Americans eagerly watched sports and enjoyed music, theater, and other forms of popular entertainment.

Movies and Radio Shows

During the era of silent films, theaters hired piano players to provide music during the feature, while subtitles explained the plot. Audiences gathered

Part of what made the 1920s feel new and modern was the rise of mass culture. Movies, which were very popular in the 1920s, brought Americans together in a shared experience.

▶ **CRITICAL THINKING**
Compare and Contrast How does seeing a movie today compare and contrast with what you observe in the photograph of early moviegoers? LAFS.1112.RH.3.7, SS.912.A.1.4, SS.912.A.5.6, SS.912.H.1.1, SS.912.H.2.5

NEXT GENERATION SUNSHINE STATE STANDARDS

Continued from page 275

LAFS.1112.RH.3.7: Integrate and evaluate multiple sources of information presented in diverse formats and media (e.g., visually, quantitatively, as well as in words) in order to address a question or solve a problem.

LAFS.1112.WHST.1.2: Write informative/ explanatory texts, including the narration of historical events, scientific procedures/ experiments, or technical processes.

LAFS.1112.WHST.3.7: Conduct short as well as more sustained research projects to answer a question (including a self-generated question) or solve a problem; narrow or broaden the inquiry when appropriate; synthesize multiple sources on the subject, demonstrating understanding of the subject under investigation.

LAFS.1112.WHST.3.9: Draw evidence from informational texts to support analysis, reflection, and research.

LAFS.1112.WHST.4.10: Write routinely over extended time frames (time for reflection and revision) and shorter time frames (a single sitting or a day or two) for a range of discipline-specific tasks, purposes, and audiences.

SS.912.A.1.4: Analyze how images, symbols, objects, cartoons, graphs, charts, maps, and artwork may be used to interpret the significance of time periods and events from the past.

Continued on page 278

Culver Pictures, Inc./SuperStock

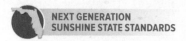

NEXT GENERATION SUNSHINE STATE STANDARDS

Continued from page 277

SS.912.A.5.6: Analyze the influence that Hollywood, the Harlem Renaissance, the Fundamentalist movement, and prohibition had in changing American society in the 1920s.

SS.912.H.1.1: Relate works in the arts (architecture, dance, music, theatre, and visual arts) of varying styles and genre according to the periods in which they were created.

SS.912.H.1.5: Examine artistic response to social issues and new ideas in various cultures.

SS.912.H.2.5: Describe how historical, social, cultural, and physical settings influence an audience's aesthetic response.

SS.912.H.3.1: Analyze the effects of transportation, trade, communication, science, and technology on the preservation and diffusion of culture.

mass media medium of communication (such as television and radio) intended to reach a wide audience

unify to bring together with similar goals or ideas

to see such stars as Mary Pickford, Charlie Chaplin, Douglas Fairbanks, Sr., and Rudolph Valentino. In 1927, the golden age of Hollywood began with the first "talking" picture, *The Jazz Singer*.

Films of the 1920s reflected the issues and characteristics of the era in many ways. Some told stories of World War I and its aftermath, and were often blunt about the cost and impact of the war on people's lives. Many told stories of complicated relationships between men and women and reflected the new morality and changing nature of relationships of the 1920s. Many films focused on Christian themes, dramatizing stories from the Bible and the values and beliefs of Protestant Christianity.

Famous songwriter Irving Berlin worked in New York City's Tin Pan Alley, where composers wrote popular music. Berlin's famous songs include "Puttin' on the Ritz" and "White Christmas." Radio broadcasts offered everything from classical music to comedy. In the popular show *Amos 'n' Andy,* the troubles of two African American characters (portrayed by white actors) captured the nation's attention; however, the show also was criticized for its use of crude racial stereotypes and blackface.

The **mass media**—radio, movies, newspapers, and magazines aimed at a broad audience—did more than just entertain. They also fostered a sense of shared experience that helped **unify** the nation.

Sports

Sports such as baseball and boxing reached new heights of popularity in the 1920s, thanks to motion pictures and radio. Baseball star Babe Ruth became a national hero, famous for hitting hundreds of home runs. Fans also idolized boxer Jack Dempsey, who was world heavyweight champion from 1919 until 1926, when he lost the title to Gene Tunney. When Dempsey attempted to win back the title in 1927, one store sold $90,000 worth of radios in the two weeks before the event.

Newspaper coverage helped build enthusiasm for college football. One of the most famous players of the 1920s was Red Grange of the University of Illinois. He was known as the "Galloping Ghost" because of his speed and ability to evade the opposing team. The triumphs of Bobby Jones, the best golfer of the decade, and tennis players Bill Tilden and Helen Wills also thrilled sports fans. When swimmer Gertrude Ederle shattered records by swimming the English Channel in a little over 14 hours in 1927, Americans were enchanted.

☑ READING PROGRESS CHECK

Explaining Why did new national pastimes emerge during the 1920s, and what were some of the most popular new ways for Americans to spend their leisure time?

LESSON 4 REVIEW

Vocabulary Review

1. *Comparing* How is today's mass media similar to that of the 1920s? LAFS.1112.RH.2.4, SS.912.H.1.1

Using Your Notes

2. *Drawing Conclusions* Review the notes that you completed during the lesson. Why do you think the art and literature of the 1920s had such a diverse range of styles? LAFS.1112.WHST.3.9, SS.912.H.1.1, SS.912.H.1.5

Answering the Guiding Questions

3. *Synthesizing* How did many artists and writers of the time describe the 1920s? SS.912.A.5.6

4. *Summarizing* Why did many Americans have more time for entertainment, and how did they spend their time? SS.912.A.5.6, SS.912.H.2.5

Writing Activity

5. NARRATIVE Imagine that you are a teenager of the 1920s and your parents have just purchased your family's first radio. Write about something you are excited to be able to listen to. Research radio programs that were on during the time to help you construct your narrative. LAFS.1112.WHST.1.2, LAFS.1112.WHST.3.7, LAFS.1112.WHST.4.10, SS.912.H.1.1, SS.912.A.5.6

LESSON 5

African American Culture and Politics

ESSENTIAL QUESTIONS
- How was social and economic life different in the early twentieth century from that of the late nineteenth century?
- How has the cultural identity of the United States changed over time?

READING HELPDESK

Academic Vocabulary
- symbolize
- ongoing
- impact

Content Vocabulary
- jazz
- blues

TAKING NOTES:

Key Ideas and Details

Organizing As you read about the African American experience in the 1920s, complete a graphic organizer similar to the one below by filling in the causes and effects of the Harlem Renaissance. LAFS.1112.RH.3.7, SS.912.A.5.6

Causes   Effects

Harlem Renaissance

NEXT GENERATION SUNSHINE STATE STANDARDS

LAFS.1112.RH.2.4: Determine the meaning of words and phrases as they are used in a text, including analyzing how an author uses and refines the meaning of a key term over the course of a text (e.g., how Madison defines faction in Federalist No. 10).

LAFS.1112.RH.3.7: Integrate and evaluate multiple sources of information presented in diverse formats and media (e.g., visually, quantitatively, as well as in words) in order to address a question or solve a problem.

LAFS.1112.WHST.1.2: Write informative/ explanatory texts, including the narration of historical events, scientific procedures/ experiments, or technical processes.

Continued on page 280

IT MATTERS BECAUSE

The Harlem Renaissance was a creative era for African American artists. It sparked new trends in literature, music, and art. The growing African American population in the North meant an increasing number of African Americans had political power to continue the struggle for civil rights.

The Harlem Renaissance

GUIDING QUESTION *What does the Harlem Renaissance reveal about African American culture in the 1920s?*

During World War I and the 1920s, hundreds of thousands of African Americans joined the Great Migration from the rural South to industrial cities in the North. Populations swelled in large Northern cities. Nightclubs and music filled these cities, particularly the New York City neighborhood of Harlem. Artistic development, racial pride, and political organization combined in a flowering of African American arts. This became known as the Harlem Renaissance.

The Writers

Claude McKay was the first important writer of the Harlem Renaissance. In his 1922 poetry collection, *Harlem Shadows*, McKay expressed a proud defiance and bitter contempt of racism. These were two major characteristics of Harlem Renaissance writing.

PRIMARY SOURCE

❝O kinsmen! we must meet the common foe!

Though far outnumbered let us show us brave,

And for their thousand blows deal one deathblow!

What though before us lies the open grave?

Like men we'll face the murderous, cowardly pack,

Pressed to the wall, dying, but fighting back!❞

—from "If We Must Die," in *African American Literature*

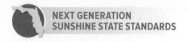
Continued from page 279

LAFS.1112.WHST.4.10: Write routinely over extended time frames (time for reflection and revision) and shorter time frames (a single sitting or a day or two) for a range of discipline-specific tasks, purposes, and audiences.

SS.912.A.1.4: Analyze how images, symbols, objects, cartoons, graphs, charts, maps, and artwork may be used to interpret the significance of time periods and events from the past.

SS.912.A.1.7: Describe various socio-cultural aspects of American life including arts, artifacts, literature, education, and publications.

SS.912.A.5.6: Analyze the influence that Hollywood, the Harlem Renaissance, the Fundamentalist movement, and prohibition had in changing American society in the 1920s.

SS.912.A.5.7: Examine the freedom movements that advocated civil rights for African Americans, Latinos, Asians, and women.

SS.912.A.5.8: Compare the views of Booker T. Washington, W.E.B. DuBois, and Marcus Garvey relating to the African American experience.

SS.912.A.5.12: Examine key events and people in Florida history as they relate to United States history.

Continued on page 281

jazz American style of music that developed from ragtime and blues and that uses syncopated rhythms and improvisation

symbolize to represent, express, or identify by a symbol

blues style of music evolving from African American spirituals and noted for its melancholy sound

Florida
CONNECTION

Artists & Achievers

Zora Neale Hurston grew from a childhood in Eastonville to become one of the most successful African American Writers of her lifetime. James Weldon Johnson's life took him from Jacksonville to Nicaragua as a U.S. consul for President Theodore Roosevelt. Hurston's works, such as *Their Eyes Were Watching God*, spoke with honesty and pride about African American life during the early twentieth century. Johnson created prose, poetry, and wrote the song "Life Every Voice and Sing," which became the NAACP's anthem. SS.912.A.5.12

Langston Hughes was a prolific, original, and versatile writer. He became a leading voice of the African American experience in America. Zora Neale Hurston wrote some of the first major stories featuring African American women as central characters. Other notable writers of the Harlem Renaissance include Countee Cullen, Alain Locke, and Dorothy West.

The literature of the Harlem Renaissance helped to instill a strong sense of pride, defiance, and confidence in African Americans. It encouraged resistance to racism and challenged stereotypes, and it also reminded African Americans of their roots and the difficulties they had already overcome. It helped lay the foundations for the civil rights movement that would begin after World War II.

In helping instill pride and confidence, the literature of the Harlem Renaissance also helped create a distinct and separate African American culture apart from the wider culture of the nation. This, in turn, contributed to the rise of movements advocating that African Americans separate themselves from the rest of society in order to protect themselves, and preserve their own identity.

Jazz, Blues, and the Theater

New Orleans native Louis Armstrong moved to Chicago in 1922. There he introduced an early form of **jazz,** a musical style influenced by Dixieland and ragtime, with syncopated rhythms and improvisational elements. In Chicago, Armstrong broke away from the New Orleans tradition of group playing by performing highly imaginative solos on the cornet and trumpet.

Composer, pianist, and bandleader Edward "Duke" Ellington also had a special sound, a blend of improvisation and orchestration using different combinations of instruments. Like many other African American entertainers, Ellington got his start at the Cotton Club, the most famous nightclub in Harlem (but one that served only white customers). Years later, Ellington reflected on the music of the era by saying, "Everything, and I repeat, everything had to swing. And that was just it, those cats really had it; they had that soul. And you know you can't just play some of this music without soul. Soul is very important."

Bessie Smith seemed to **symbolize** soul. She became known as the Empress of the Blues. Smith sang of unfulfilled love, poverty, and oppression—the classic themes of the **blues,** a soulful style of music that evolved from African American spirituals.

Jazz reflected the characteristics and issues of the 1920s era in many ways. With its emphasis on improvisation, it reflected the feelings of many people that the 1920s was a time of experimentation and a breaking away from old rules and values. It expressed the individualism of the era, and because many of the popular jazz singers were women, it also reflected the new role of women in American society. Blues and soul music also enabled African Americans to give voice to their difficult social and economic position in American society.

Jazz had an enormously positive impact on society. It built a connection between African American culture and the rest of American society, helping to reduce racism by the shared experience of the music. Not everyone, however, appreciated the music at the time. During Prohibition, jazz music became associated with the speakeasies where alcohol was consumed illegally. As a result, many people believed the music contributed to immoral behavior and threatened traditional values.

American jazz music was also one of the first American cultural expressions that had a significant impact on the rest of the world. In part because of America's role in ending World War I, many Europeans, especially in France, became fascinated with American culture. Many

American jazz musicians visited Europe after World War I, and their performances helped develop a European audience for the music. Paris, in particular, became a center for jazz in Europe, just as it became home to many American expatriate writers in the years after the war.

Theater also flourished during the Harlem Renaissance. *Shuffle Along,* the first musical written, produced, and performed by African Americans, made its Broadway debut in 1921. The show's success helped launch a number of careers, including those of Florence Mills and Paul Robeson. Robeson received wide acclaim for his performance in the title role of Eugene O'Neill's *Emperor Jones.* He also gained fame four years later for his work in the musical *Show Boat.* Robeson often appeared at the famous Apollo Theater in Harlem.

✔ READING PROGRESS CHECK

Making Generalizations What does the work of writers and performers of the Harlem Renaissance show about African American culture of the 1920s?

African Americans and 1920s Politics

GUIDING QUESTION *How did African American leaders differ in their approaches to political actions during this decade?*

In 1919, approximately 1,300 African American veterans of World War I marched through Manhattan to Harlem. W.E.B. Du Bois captured their sense of pride and defiance in a speech:

PRIMARY SOURCE

❝We return. We return from fighting. We return fighting. Make way for Democracy! We saved it in France, and by the Great Jehovah, we will save it in the United States of America, or know the reason why.❞

—from *The Crisis,* May 1919

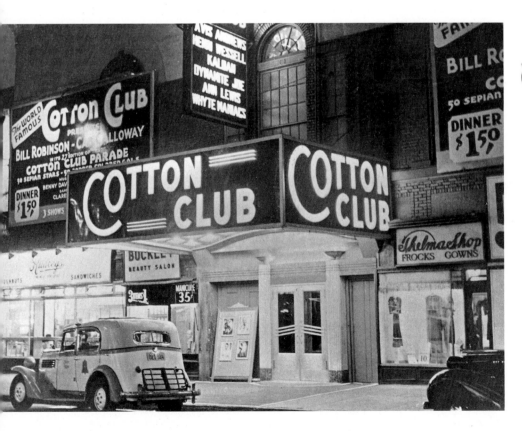

(t)Carl Van Vechten/The Granger Collection, New York/Reprinted with permission of the Van Vechten Trust; (b)Frank Driggs Collection/Archive Photos/Getty Images

BIOGRAPHY

Zora Neale Hurston (1891–1960)

Zora Neale Hurston was one of the major literary voices of the Harlem Renaissance. Hurston presented a unique, insightful, and often quite humorous perspective of the African American experience through her work. She was also an accomplished traveler, anthropologist, and an instructor at North Carolina College for Negroes. She had great success with her novels, such as *Jonah's Gourd Vine* (1934), the perennial classic, *Their Eyes Were Watching God* (1937), and *Moses, Man of the Mountain* (1939). In 1942, she published her autobiography, *Dust Tracks on a Road,* to great acclaim.

 NEXT GENERATION SUNSHINE STATE STANDARDS

Continued from page 280

SS.912.G.4.3: Use geographic terms and tools to analyze the effects of migration both on the place of origin and destination, including border areas.

SS.912.H.1.1: Relate works in the arts (architecture, dance, music, theatre, and visual arts) of varying styles and genre according to the periods in which they were created.

SS.912.H.1.3: Relate works in the arts to various cultures.

SS.912.H.1.5: Examine artistic response to social issues and new ideas in various cultures.

Along with the Apollo Theater, the Cotton Club was one of the famous clubs in Harlem. Many performers launched careers by appearing on its stage.

▶ CRITICAL THINKING

Making Generalizations How did Harlem nightclubs like the Cotton Club help promote African American performing arts?
LAFS.1112.RH.3.7, SS.912.A.1.4, SS.912.A.5.6

The Jazz Age **281**

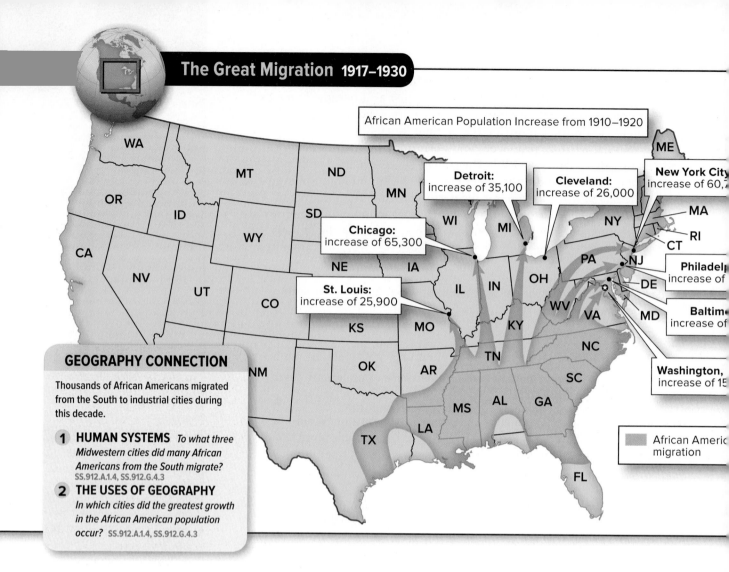

The Great Migration 1917–1930

African American Population Increase from 1910–1920

Detroit: increase of 35,100

Cleveland: increase of 26,000

New York City increase of 60,?

MA

RI

CT

Chicago: increase of 65,300

St. Louis: increase of 25,900

Philadel increase of

Baltim increase of

Washington, increase of 15

African Americ migration

GEOGRAPHY CONNECTION

Thousands of African Americans migrated from the South to industrial cities during this decade.

1 HUMAN SYSTEMS *To what three Midwestern cities did many African Americans from the South migrate?* SS.912.A.1.4, SS.912.G.4.3

2 THE USES OF GEOGRAPHY *In which cities did the greatest growth in the African American population occur?* SS.912.A.1.4, SS.912.G.4.3

---

impact a lasting impression upon an individual or group

ongoing being in process; continuing

Florida CONNECTION

The Rosewood Riot

In January 1923 Rosewood, Florida, was rocked by racial violence. An African American mill worker was accused of assaulting a white woman. Unable to capture the accused, mobs burned homes and at least five residents died. After five days the turmoil ended and the town of less than 200 was abandoned. In 1994 the Florida legislature awarded reparations to over 100 of the former town's survivors. SS.912.A.5.12

Growing Political Power in the North

World War I set the stage for African Americans to reenter American politics. The Great Migration of African Americans to the North had a significant **impact** as well. As their numbers grew in city neighborhoods, African Americans became an influential voting bloc. In 1928, African American voters in Chicago helped elect Oscar DePriest. He was the first African American representative in Congress from a Northern state.

The NAACP Battles Injustice

The National Association for the Advancement of Colored People (NAACP) battled hard against segregation and discrimination against African Americans. Its efforts focused primarily on lobbying public officials and working through the court system. The NAACP's persistent protests against the horrors of lynching led to the passage of antilynching legislation in the House of Representatives in 1922. The Senate defeated the bill, but the NAACP's **ongoing** protests kept the issue in the news. This probably helped reduce the number of lynchings that took place.

In 1930, the NAACP joined with labor unions to launch a highly organized national campaign against the nomination of Judge John J. Parker to the U.S. Supreme Court. Parker's support for African American disenfranchisement and anti-union contracts moved the NAACP and labor leaders to campaign against him. By a narrow margin, the Senate refused to confirm Parker's nomination. This proved that African Americans had become a powerful political force.

Black Nationalism and Marcus Garvey

While the NAACP fought for integration and improvement in the economic and political position of African Americans, other groups began to emphasize black nationalism and black pride. Some began calling for African Americans to separate from white society.

A dynamic leader from Jamaica, Marcus Garvey captured the imagination of millions of African Americans with his "Negro Nationalism." Garvey founded the Universal Negro Improvement Association (UNIA), aimed at promoting black pride and unity. He was inspired by Booker T. Washington's call for self-reliance. The central message of Garvey's Harlem-based movement was that African Americans could gain economic and political power by educating themselves. Garvey also advocated separation and independence from whites. In 1920, he told his followers they would never find justice or freedom in America. He proposed leading them to Africa.

The emerging African American middle class and intellectuals distanced themselves from Garvey and his push for racial separation. The FBI saw UNIA as a dangerous catalyst for African American uprisings. Garvey also alienated key figures in the Harlem Renaissance by calling them "weak-kneed and cringing . . . [flatterers of] the white man." Convicted of mail fraud in 1923, he served time in prison. In 1927, President Coolidge used Garvey's immigrant status to have him deported to Jamaica.

Despite Garvey's failure to keep his movement alive, he instilled millions of African Americans with a sense of pride in their heritage and inspired hope for the future. These feelings reemerged strongly in the 1950s and played a vital role in the civil rights movement of the 1960s.

Marcus Garvey's "back to Africa" movement gave pride and hope to millions of African Americans.

▶ CRITICAL THINKING
Comparing and Contrasting
How did Marcus Garvey's approach to political action differ from that of the NAACP?
LAFS.1112.RH.3.7, SS.912.A.5.7, SS.912.A.5.8

 READING PROGRESS CHECK

Summarizing What differing steps did African Americans take to achieve political goals during the 1920s?

LESSON 5 REVIEW

Reviewing Vocabulary
1. *Drawing Conclusions* Why do you think the blues emerged as a main musical form of the Harlem Renaissance?
LAFS.1112.RH.2.4, SS.912.A.1.7, SS.912.A.5.6, SS.912.H.1.1

Using Your Notes
2. *Synthesizing* Review the notes that you completed during the lesson to determine how the Harlem Renaissance reflected the growing cultural and political power of African Americans. SS.912.A.1.7, SS.912.A.5.7, SS.912.H.1.1

Answering the Guiding Questions
3. *Explaining* What does the Harlem Renaissance reveal about African American culture in the 1920s?
SS.912.A.1.7, SS.912.A.5.6, SS.912.H.1.1, SS.912.H.1.3, SS.912.H.1.5

4. *Contrasting* How did African American leaders differ in their approaches to political actions during this decade?
SS.912.A.5.7, SS.912.A.5.8

Writing Activity
5. INFORMATIVE/EXPLANATORY Suppose that you witnessed African American men back from World War I marching through New York City and heard the beginnings of W.E.B. Du Bois's speech. Write a paragraph describing the event, including the ideas and attitudes the event conveyed.
LAFS.1112.WHST.1.2, LAFS.1112.WHST.4.10, SS.912.A.5.6, SS.912.A.5.7

Hulton Archive/Archive Photos/Getty Images

STUDY GUIDE

THE POLITICS OF THE 1920S
LESSON 1

ANDREW MELLON'S ECONOMIC THEORY

UNITED STATES A DEBTOR NATION AND THE DOMINANT ECONOMIC POWER IN THE WORLD	MANY AMERICANS FAVORED ISOLATIONISM	UNITED STATES TRIED TO PROMOTE PEACE THROUGH ECONOMIC POLICIES AND ARMS CONTROL AGREEMENTS	

MANY AMERICANS FAVORED ISOLATIONISM
- U.S. did not ratify the Treaty of Versailles
- Did not join League of Nations

UNITED STATES TRIED TO PROMOTE PEACE THROUGH ECONOMIC POLICIES AND ARMS CONTROL AGREEMENTS

Dawes Plan	Five-Power Naval Limitation Treaty
Four-Power Treaty	Nine-Powers Treaty
Kellogg-Briand Pact	London Naval Treaties

A GROWING ECONOMY
LESSON 2

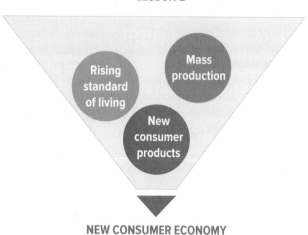

- Rising standard of living
- Mass production
- New consumer products

NEW CONSUMER ECONOMY

A CLASH OF VALUES
LESSON 3

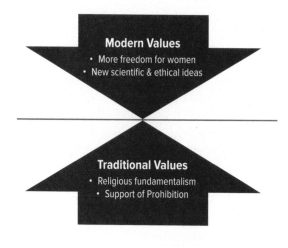

Modern Values
- More freedom for women
- New scientific & ethical ideas

Traditional Values
- Religious fundamentalism
- Support of Prohibition

CULTURAL INNOVATIONS
LESSON 4

ARTISTS & WRITERS
- Edward Hopper
- Georgia O'Keeffe
- Willa Cather
- Sinclair Lewis
- F. Scott Fitzgerald
- Gertrude Stein

MOVIES & RADIO
- Charlie Chaplin
- Douglas Fairbanks
- Mary Pickford
- Irving Berlin

SPORTS
- Babe Ruth
- Jack Dempsey
- Red Grange
- Bobby Jones

AFRICAN AMERICAN CULTURE AND POLITICS
LESSON 5

THE HARLEM RENAISSANCE

Writers: Claude McKay & Langston Hughes

Music: Jazz & Blues

Politics: The Great Migration, the NAACP, Marcus Garvey

Directions: On a separate sheet of paper, answer the questions below. Make sure you read carefully and answer all parts to the question.

Lesson Review

Lesson 1

1 *Analyzing* What did President Warren Harding mean when he promised a "return to normalcy" and what policies did his administration pursue to promote economic growth and prosperity? SS.912.A.4.5

2 *Making Connections* How did the Dawes plan prevent an economic crisis in Europe and help resolve the issues of war debt and reparations? SS.912.A.5.3

Lesson 2

3 *Analyzing* How did technological innovations in the workplace, such as the assembly line and mass production, affect American workers and American businesses? SS.912.A.5.4

4 *Analyzing* Identify four major scientific discoveries or technological innovations that occurred in the 1920s and explain how each improved the standard of living in the United States. SS.912.A.5.4

Lesson 3

5 *Identifying Cause and Effect* Why was there a general rise in nativism in the 1920s? How did Congress respond to nativism? SS.912.A.5.2

6 *Explaining* How did women's roles change during the 1920s? What caused these changes and what were the effects? SS.912.A.5.7

Lesson 4

7 *Making Connections* Why did many members of the "Lost Generation" choose to leave the United States? How does the book *The Great Gatsby* reflect their view of American culture at the time? SS.912.H.1.5

8 *Describing* In what ways did Hollywood films of the 1920s express the issues and characteristics of the time? SS.912.A.5.6, SS.912.H.1.5, SS.912.H.2.5

Lesson 5

9 *Identifying Cause and Effect* What caused the Great Migration and what effect did it have on the political power of African Americans? SS.912.A.5.7, SS.912.G.4.3

10 *Analyzing Significance* What impact did Marcus Garvey have on the African American community and what actions did he and his organization take to expand economic opportunity for African Americans? SS.912.A.5.8

Exploring the Essential Questions

11 *Comparing and Contrasting* How was the economy and society of the United States different in the 1920s from what it had been in the late 1800s? SS.912.A.5.4

Critical Thinking

12 *Analyzing* Evaluate the effects of the passage of the Eighteenth Amendment. How did this reform change American society? SS.912.A.5.6

21st Century Skills

13 *Making Generalizations* Pick one of the following cultural categories: Art, Music, Film, Literature. Research several artists, musicians, writers, or films from the 1920s in the category you have chosen. In your research, make sure you chose authoritative sources and cite those sources accordingly. Identify the common elements and similar themes and ideas they shared. Prepare a presentation, either online, or on a poster board using images, quotes, audio recordings if possible, and written descriptions that illustrate the common themes of 1920s culture. View the presentations of your classmates and then, either in class or on an online forum, discuss common themes that appear throughout this era. LAFS.1112.RH.3.9 , LAFS.1112.RH.4.10 , LAFS.1112.SL.1.1, LAFS.1112.SL.1.3, LAFS.1112.WHST.1.2, LAFS.1112. WHST.2.4, LAFS.1112.WHST.2.6, LAFS.1112.WHST.3.7, LAFS.1112. WHST.3.8, LAFS.1112.WHST.4.10, SS.912.A.1.2, SS.912.A.1.4, SS.912.A.1.7, SS.912.H.1.1, SS.912.H.1.5

Need Extra Help?

If You've Missed Question	❶	❷	❸	❹	❺	❻	❼	❽	❾	❿	⓫	⓬	⓭
Go to Lesson	1	1	2	2	3	3	4	4	5	5	2	3	4

14 *Interpreting the Past* After World War II, it was common for historians to argue that the United States turned isolationist after World War I, and that the isolationism was one of the causes of World War II. Do you agree with that interpretation? Analyze U.S. policies toward other nations in the 1920s, and write a brief report on whether or not the United States was isolationist. Begin with an introduction where you define isolationism, then write two paragraphs and a conclusion giving your interpretation of the past. LAFS.1112.RH.1.3 , LAFS.1112.RH.3.7, LAFS.1112.RH.3.9, LAFS.1112.WHST.4.10, SS.912.A.1.1, SS.912.A.5.3, SS.912.A.5.5

DBQ Analyzing Primary Sources

Read the following excerpts from writings by W.E.B. DuBois and Claude McKay and answer the questions that follow.

PRIMARY SOURCE

"We return. We return from fighting. We return fighting. Make way for Democracy! We saved it in France, and by the Great Jehovah, we will save it in the United States of America, or know the reason why."

—W.E.B. DuBois, *The Crisis,* May 1919

PRIMARY SOURCE

"O kinsmen! we must meet the common foe!
Though far outnumbered let us show us brave,
And for their thousand blows deal one deathblow!
What though before us lies the open grave?
Like men we'll face the murderous, cowardly pack,
Pressed to the wall, dying, but fighting back!"

—Claude McKay, "If We Must Die," 1919

15 *Interpreting* What event is DuBois referencing when he says "We return?" When he says "We saved it in France" and "we will save it in the United States" what is he referring to, and what is he calling on African Americans to do? LAFS.1112.RH.1.1, LAFS.1112.RH.2.4, LAFS.1112.RH.3.8, SS.912.A.5.6, SS.912.A.5.7

16 *Comparing* What emotions are both W.E.B DuBois and Claude McKay trying to instill in African Americans with their writing? LAFS.1112.RH.3.8, LAFS.1112.RH.4.10, LAFS.1112.SL.1.3, SS.912.A.5.6, SS.912.A.5.7

Analyzing Visuals

Use the cartoon to answer the following questions.

17 *Identifying* What incident is depicted in the cartoon? How do you know? LAFS.1112.RH.3.7, SS.912.A.1.4, SS.912.H.1.5

18 *Interpreting* Why do you think the artist named this cartoon the "White House Highway"? LAFS.1112.RH.3.7, SS.912.A.1.4, SS.912.H.1.5

Extended Response Question

19 *Summarizing* The policies of the Harding and Coolidge administrations were intended to promote economic growth and world peace. Write an essay explaining and summarizing the methods they used to create economic growth at home and to promote political and economic stability worldwide. Give your opinion as to whether they were successful or not and explain your reasoning. Your essay should include an introduction, several paragraphs, and a conclusion and should reference historical facts and details to support your conclusion. LAFS.1112.WHST.2.4, LAFS.1112.WHST.4.10, SS.912.A.5.3, SS.912.A.5.5

The Granger Collection, New York

Need Extra Help?

If You've Missed Question	**14**	**15**	**16**	**17**	**18**	**19**
Go to Lesson	1	5	5	1	1	1

◄ A destitute mother and other workers' families were stranded after the pea crop they were to harvest failed. The government sent 20,000 pounds of food to help the stranded workers at the farm in California.

FROM 1929 TO 1932

The Great Depression Begins

THE STORY MATTERS ...

During the prosperous 1920s, optimism drove stock prices to new highs, but risky investment practices set the stage for a crash. Sensing danger, investors sold their holdings, causing the market to lose billions of dollars and the nation's banks to collapse.

Companies went out of business, millions of Americans were unemployed, and families could not buy food. When a terrible drought struck the Great Plains, farmers were unable to grow crops, leading to even more devastation.

ESSENTIAL QUESTIONS
- What causes changes in the economy over time?
- How do depressions affect societies?

Place & Time: United States 1928–1933

When the stock market crashed in October 1929, the extreme optimism of the 1920s turned to the profound despair of the Great Depression. By the early 1930s, more Americans were demanding the government's help. Veterans grew frustrated and began to march to Capitol Hill to demand the immediate payment of a promised bonus. Wearing ragged military uniforms and singing old war songs, this "Bonus Army" traveled the highways and railroads to Washington, D.C., to protest their plight. By July 1932, more than 15,000 unemployed veterans, each asking the government for early payment of cash bonuses due to be paid in 1945, converged on the nation's capital.

Step Into the Place

Read the quotes and look at the information presented on the map.

 Analyzing Historical Documents How do the following quotes reflect the ways people helped one another during the Great Depression?

PRIMARY SOURCE

"The conductor'd want to find out how many guys were in the yard, so he would know how many empty boxcars to put onto the train. Of course, the railroad companies didn't know this, but these conductors, out of their sympathy, would put two or three empty boxcars in the train, so these bonus marchers could crawl into them and ride comfortable into Washington."

—Jim Sheridan, a traveler with the Bonus Army in 1932, quoted in *An American Epic*

PRIMARY SOURCE

"With American flags flying before them, sixteen truckloads of war veterans came to the end of a transcontinental hitch-hike today with the avowed purpose of remaining in Washington until Congress pays their bonus in full.

Weather-beaten, travel-strained and dog-tired, the former soldiers—330 from the Pacific Coast—crossed the District line in trucks supplied by Maryland and found a hot stew, bread, milk and coffee awaiting them."

—from the *New York Times*, May 30, 1932

Step Into the Time

MAKING CONNECTIONS

Choose an event from the time line and write a paragraph describing the general social, political, or economic consequences that event had on the Great Depression.

U.S. PRESIDENTS

UNITED STATES

WORLD

1928

1929

November 1928 Herbert Hoover is elected president

1929 Wall Street crashes on October 24 ("Black Thursday") and October 29 ("Black Tuesday")

Hoover 1929–1933

1928 First Five-Year Plan to industrialize the Soviet Union begins

1929 Young Plan reduces war reparations for Germany

left page (tl)©Historical/Corbis; (tr)©Underwood & Underwood/Historical/Corbis; (bl)detail/White House Collection/The White House Historical Association; right page (b)detail/White House Collection/The White House Historical Association ; TEXT: "Weary Bonus Army Reaches Capital by Truck; Police Demand Congress Care for Hundreds," by The Associated Press. Published May 30, 1932.

NEXT GENERATION SUNSHINE STATE STANDARDS
Students will understand the following benchmarks from the Florida NGSSS

LAFS.1112.RH.3.7: Integrate and evaluate multiple sources of information presented in diverse formats and media (e.g., visually, quantitatively, as well as in words) in order to address a question or solve a problem.

LAFS.1112.RH.3.9: Integrate information from diverse sources, both primary and secondary, into a coherent understanding of an idea or event, noting discrepancies among sources.

SS.912.A.1.2: Utilize a variety of primary and secondary sources to identify author, historical significance, audience, and authenticity to understand a historical period.

SS.912.A.1.3: Utilize timelines to identify the time sequence of historical data.

SS.912.A.1.4: Analyze how images, symbols, objects, cartoons, graphs, charts, maps, and artwork may be used to interpret the significance of time periods and events from the past.

SS.912.A.5.11: Examine causes, course, and consequences of the Great Depression and the New Deal.

Bonus Army March 1932

1. The staging point for the U.S. Army tasked with expelling the Bonus Army from Washington, D.C.

2. Camp Glassford - the site where veterans clashed with police. Veterans William Hushka and Eric Carlson were killed when police opened fire on the crowd. Camp Glassford was the first site forcibly evacuated by the army.

3. The Red Camp - the site of the second evacuation of veterans. Many of the Communists that made up this camp had fled before the army arrived.

4. Camp Marks - the camp of 7,000 veterans and their families was cleared and burned in the late hours of July 28th.

Route of the U.S. Army

0   0.5 mile
0   0.5 km

F. Roosevelt
1933–1945

1930 Hawley-Smoot Tariff is enacted

1931 National Credit Corporation is established to help troubled banks

May 1932 Bonus Army marchers arrive in Washington, D.C.

1930   **1931**   **1932**   **1933**

1930 European countries begin to raise tariff rates and boycott American products

1931 Britain abandons the gold standard

1932 Unemployment in Germany nears 30 percent

The Great Depression Begins **289**

The Causes of the Great Depression

netw✺rks™
There's More Online!

ESSENTIAL QUESTIONS

• What causes changes in the economy over time?
• How do depressions affect societies?

READING HELPDESK

Academic Vocabulary

• collapse   • sum
• invest

Content Vocabulary

• stock market   • margin call
• bull market   • bank run
• speculation   • installment
• margin

TAKING NOTES:

Key Ideas and Details

Organizing As you read the lesson, complete a graphic organizer similar to the one below to list the causes of the Depression. LAFS.1112.RH.3.7, SS.912.A.5.11

Causes

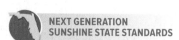

Great Depression

NEXT GENERATION SUNSHINE STATE STANDARDS

ELD.K12.ELL.SI.1: English language learners communicate for social and instructional purposes within the school setting.

ELD.K12.ELL.SS.1: English language learners communicate information, ideas and concepts necessary for academic success in the content area of Social Studies.

LAFS.1112.RH.2.4: Determine the meaning of words and phrases as they are used in a text, including analyzing how an author uses and refines the meaning of a key term over the course of a text (e.g., how Madison defines faction in Federalist No. 10).

Continued on page 291

IT MATTERS BECAUSE

Although the 1920s were prosperous, speculation in the stock market, risky lending policies, overproduction, and uneven income distribution eventually undermined the economy and led to the Great Depression.

The Long Bull Market

GUIDING QUESTION *What economic choices caused the economy to become unstable in the late 1920s?*

The economic **collapse** that began in 1929 seemed unimaginable months before. In the 1928 election, both presidential candidates painted a rosy picture of the future. Republican presidential nominee Herbert Hoover declared, "We are nearer to the final triumph over poverty than ever before in the history of any land."

The Election of 1928

For the presidential election of 1928, the Democrats chose Alfred E. Smith, governor of New York. Smith was the first Roman Catholic to win a major party's presidential nomination. He faced a tough challenger, as Herbert Hoover was secretary of commerce and former head of the Food Administration.

Smith's religious beliefs became a campaign issue. Some Protestants claimed the Catholic Church financed Smith's campaign and would have inappropriate influence on American politics. The attacks embarrassed Hoover, a Quaker, and he tried to quash them, but the charges damaged Smith's candidacy.

The prosperity of the 1920s—for which the Republicans took full credit—was a bigger challenge to Smith's candidacy. Hoover won in a landslide. On March 4, 1929, an estimated 50,000 onlookers stood in the rain to listen to Hoover's Inaugural Address. "I have no fears for the future of our country," proclaimed Hoover. "It is bright with hope."

The Stock Market Soars

The optimism that swept Hoover into office also drove stock prices to new highs. Sometimes the **stock market** has a long period of rising stock prices, or a **bull market.** The bull market of the 1920s convinced many to **invest** in stocks. By 1929, approximately 10 percent of American households owned stocks.

Before the late 1920s, stock prices generally reflected their true values. In the late 1920s, however, many investors failed to consider a company's earnings and profits. Buyers engaged in **speculation,** or betting the market would continue to climb, thus enabling them to sell stock and make money quickly.

Many investors bought stocks on **margin,** making only a small cash down payment (as low as 10 percent of the price). With $1,000, an investor could buy a **sum** of $10,000 worth of stock. The remaining $9,000 came as an interest-bearing loan from the stockbroker. Quick profits were possible if stock prices kept rising, but problems came when prices began to fall. To protect a loan, a broker could issue a **margin call,** demanding the investor repay the loan at once.

✅ **READING PROGRESS CHECK**

Summarizing What investment decisions destabilized the economy during the 1920s?

The Great Crash

GUIDING QUESTION *How did the stock market crash trigger a chain of events that led to the Depression?*

The bull market lasted only as long as investors continued putting new money into it. In September 1929, the market peaked. Prices then began an uneven downward slide. As investors decided the boom was over, they sold more stock, causing prices to decline even further.

The Stock Market Crash

On Monday, October 21, 1929, the comedian Groucho Marx was awakened by a telephone call from his broker. "You'd better get down here with some cash to cover your margin," the broker said. The stock market had plunged. The dazed comedian had to pay back the money he had borrowed to buy stocks, which were now selling for far less than he had paid for them. Other brokers made similar margin calls. Customers put stocks up for sale at a frenzied pace, driving the market into a tailspin.

On October 24, a day that came to be called Black Thursday, the market plummeted further. Marx was wiped out. His earnings from plays and films were

collapse a sudden loss of force, value, or effect

stock market a system for buying and selling stocks in corporations

bull market a long period of rising stock prices

invest to put money into a company in order to gain a future financial reward

speculation act of buying stocks at great risk with the anticipation that the prices will rise

margin buying a stock by paying only a fraction of the stock price and borrowing the rest

sum a specified amount of money

margin call demand by a broker that investors pay back loans made for stocks purchased on margin

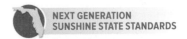 **NEXT GENERATION SUNSHINE STATE STANDARDS**

Continued from page 290

LAFS.1112.RH.3.7: Integrate and evaluate multiple sources of information presented in diverse formats and media (e.g., visually, quantitatively, as well as in words) in order to address a question or solve a problem.

LAFS.1112.WHST.1.1: Write arguments focused on discipline-specific content.

LAFS.1112.WHST.4.10: Write routinely over extended time frames (time for reflection and revision) and shorter time frames (a single sitting or a day or two) for a range of discipline-specific tasks, purposes, and audiences.

Continued on page 293

THE MARKET FALLS

Price per Share (y-axis: $100, $200, $300, $400)

Legend:
— Annual High
— Annual Low

Dow-Jones Industrial Averages (x-axis: 1920, 1921, 1922, 1923, 1924, 1925, 1926, 1927, 1928, 1929, 1930, 1931, 1932)

Source: Standard and Poor's *Security Price Index Record.*

CHARTS/GRAPHS

Until the crash of 1929, investors pumped money into the market, often buying stocks on margin.

1 *Making Inferences* What can you infer about the health of the stock market prior to 1929? LAFS.1112.RH.3.7, MAFS.912.S-ID.1, SS.912.A.1.4

2 *Making Generalizations* What generalization can you make about the variation in highs and lows of the stock market from 1920 to 1932? LAFS.1112.RH.3.7, MAFS.912.S-ID.1, SS.912.A.1.4

There's More Online! connected.mcgraw-hill.com

Mayhem erupted on Wall Street after the stock market crashed.

▶ **CRITICAL THINKING**
Identifying Central Ideas What investment practices most destabilized the stock market?
LAFS.1112.RH.3.7, SS.912.A.1.4, SS.912.A.5.11

gone, and he was deeply in debt. His son recalled his visit to the brokerage firm, as Groucho spotted his broker:

PRIMARY SOURCE

❧ He was sitting in front of the now-stilled ticker-tape machine, with his head buried in his hands. Ticker tape was strewn around him on the floor, and the place . . . looked as if it hadn't been swept out in a week. [Groucho] tapped [him] on the shoulder, [and said] 'Aren't you the fellow who said nothing could go wrong—that we were in a world market?' 'I guess I made a mistake,' said Mr. Green. 'No, I'm the one who made a mistake,' said [Groucho]. 'I listened to you.' ❧

—from *Life with Groucho*, 1954

The following week, on October 29, a day that was later dubbed Black Tuesday, prices took the steepest dive yet. That day, more than 16 million shares of stock were sold, and the value of the industrial index (a measure of the value of leading industrial companies) dropped by 10 percent. By mid-November, the market price of stocks had dropped by more than one-third. Some $30 billion was lost, a sum roughly equal to the total wages Americans earned in 1929. Although the stock market crash was not the major cause of the Depression, it undermined the economy's ability to overcome other weaknesses.

Banks Begin to Close

The market crash weakened the nation's banks in two ways. First, by 1929, banks had lent billions to stock speculators. Second, many banks had invested depositors' money in the stock market, hoping for high returns. When stock values collapsed, banks lost money on their investments, and speculators defaulted on their loans. Having suffered serious losses, many banks cut back drastically on loans. With less credit available, consumers and businesses were not able to borrow as much money, sending the economy into a recession.

Some banks could not absorb the losses they suffered and had to close. The government did not insure bank deposits, so if a bank failed, customers, including even those who did not invest in the stock market, lost their savings. As a growing number of banks closed in 1929 and 1930, a severe crisis of confidence in the banking system further destabilized the economy.

News of bank failures worried Americans. Some depositors made runs on banks, thus causing the banks to fail. A **bank run** takes place when many depositors decide to withdraw their money at the same time, usually out of fear that the bank will collapse. Most banks make a profit by lending money received from depositors and collecting interest on the loans. The bank keeps only a fraction of depositors' money in reserve. Usually, that reserve is enough to meet the bank's needs. If too many people withdraw their money, however, the bank will collapse. By 1932, about one in four banks in the United States had gone out of business.

☑ **READING PROGRESS CHECK**

Determining Cause and Effect How did the failure of the stock market contribute to a larger economic decline?

Florida CONNECTION

The Florida Land Boom

The risks involved in market speculation were shown by the 1920s Florida land boom. The automobile and improved railway lines made southern Florida more accessible. Real estate developers believed people would eagerly move there, attracted by the climate. Prices for land rose rapidly, attracting speculators who hoped to profit from buying and selling land. Then, in 1926, the Great Miami Hurricane struck, devastating the city. Hundreds of people were killed and thousands more were left homeless. The storm brought an end to the Florida land boom. Land prices dropped, speculators were financially ruined, and the state's economy slid into a depression years before the rest of the nation.
SS.912.A.5.12

©Hulton-Deutsch Collection/Historical/Corbis

The Roots of the Great Depression

GUIDING QUESTION *What were the underlying conditions that led to the collapse of the U.S. economy?*

The stock market crash played a major role in putting the economy into a recession. Yet the crash would not have led to a long-lasting depression if other forces had not been at work. The roots of the Great Depression were deeply entangled in the economy of the 1920s.

The Uneven Distribution of Income

Overproduction was a factor leading to the onset of the Great Depression. More efficient machinery increased the production capacity of factories and farms. Most Americans did not earn enough to buy up the goods they helped produce. Manufacturing output per person-hour rose 32 percent, but the average worker's wage increased only 8 percent. In 1929, the top 5 percent of all American households earned 30 percent of the nation's income. In contrast, about two-thirds of families earned less than $2,500 a year, leaving them with little disposable income.

Farmers, in particular, did not share in the prosperity of the 1920s, as many had gone into debt to buy land or equipment during World War I, when demand for their products was high. When prices fell, they tried to produce even more to pay their debts, taxes, and living expenses. Prices dropped so low that many farmers went bankrupt and lost their farms.

During the 1920s, many Americans had purchased high-cost items, such as refrigerators and cars, on the **installment** plan. Purchasers could make small down payments and pay the remainder of the item's price in monthly installments. Paying off such debts eventually forced some buyers to stop making new purchases. Because of the decrease in demand for their products, manufacturers in turn cut production and laid off employees.

The slowdown in retail sales reverberated throughout the economy. When radio sales slumped, for example, orders for copper wire, wood cabinets, and glass radio tubes slowed. Montana copper miners, Minnesota lumberjacks, and Ohio glassworkers lost jobs. Jobless workers cut purchases, further reducing sales. This put even more Americans out of work.

NEXT GENERATION SUNSHINE STATE STANDARDS

Continued from page 291

MAFS.912.S-ID.1: Summarize, represent and interpret data on a single count or measurement variable.

SS.912.A.1.2: Utilize a variety of primary and secondary sources to identify author, historical significance, audience, and authenticity to understand a historical period.

SS.912.A.1.4: Analyze how images, symbols, objects, cartoons, graphs, charts, maps, and artwork may be used to interpret the significance of time periods and events from the past.

SS.912.A.5.11: Examine causes, course, and consequences of the Great Depression and the New Deal.

SS.912.A.5.12: Examine key events and people in Florida history as they relate to United States history.

bank run persistent and heavy demands by a bank's depositors, creditors, or customers to withdraw money

installment regular periodic payment made to pay off the cost of an item when buying it on credit

CHARTS/GRAPHS

1 *Identifying Central Ideas*
What basic economic principle underlay the cause of the Great Depression?
LAFS.1112.RH.3.7, SS.912.A.1.4, SS.912.A.5.11

2 *Analyzing Information*
What effect did the decline in automobile sales have on related industries?
LAFS.1112.RH.3.7, SS.912.A.1.4, SS.912.A.5.11

CAUSES OF THE GREAT DEPRESSION

What Caused the Economy to Collapse?

Low Interest Rates
Federal Reserve kept interest rates low; companies borrowed money and expanded more than necessary.

Overproduction
Companies made more goods than could be sold.

Uneven Distribution of Wealth
Not everyone who wanted consumer goods could afford them.

High Tariffs
Tariffs restricted foreign demand for American goods.

Falling Demand
With too many goods unsold, production was cut back and employees were laid off.

Stock Market Speculation
Low interest rates encouraged borrowing money to speculate, endangering bank solvency.

Automobile sales declined. This loss of demand meant less demand for: Textiles, Oil, Steel, Rubber

Cyclical Effect

Industry slowed, which caused: Unemployment, Lower wages, Which helped contribute further to:

Analyzing — PRIMARY SOURCES

Hoover Rejects Government Intervention

"You cannot extend the mastery of the government over the daily working life of a people without at the same time making it the master of the people's souls and thoughts. . . . Free speech does not live many hours after free industry and free commerce die. . . . Every step of bureaucratizing of the business of our country poisons the very roots of liberalism—that is, political equality, free speech, free assembly, free press, and equality of opportunity. It is the road not to more liberty, but to less liberty."

—Herbert Hoover, from a speech delivered October 22, 1928

DBQ *ANALYZING PRIMARY SOURCES* Why did Hoover refuse to support government intervention in the economy? LAFS.1112.RH.3.7, SS.912.A.1.2, SS.912.A.5.11

SKILLS PRACTICE

Work with a partner. Have your partner tell you something about life during the Great Depression. Listen carefully while your partner talks. Summarize or retell what your partner has told you. ELD.K12.ELL.SI.1, ELD.K12.ELL.SS.1

Unemployment insurance was nonexistent. Many families had little or no savings. Lost jobs often meant dire circumstances. In 1930 alone, about 26,000 businesses failed.

The Loss of Export Sales

Many jobs might have been saved if American manufacturers had sold more goods abroad. As the bull market of the 1920s sped up, however, U.S. banks made loans to speculators rather than loans to foreign companies. Loans from U.S. banks had helped European nations make war reparations and pay down war debts. They had also secured foreign markets for U.S. exports. Without these loans from U.S. banks, foreign companies purchased fewer American products.

In 1929, Hoover wanted to encourage overseas trade by lowering tariffs. Congress, however, decided to protect American industry from foreign competition by raising tariffs. The resulting legislation, the Hawley-Smoot Tariff, raised the average tariff rate to the highest level in American history. In the end, it failed to help American businesses, because foreign countries responded by raising their own tariffs. This meant fewer American products were sold overseas. By 1932, exports had fallen to less than half the level that they had been in 1929. A decrease in exports hurt both American companies and farmers.

Mistakes by the Federal Reserve

Just as consumers were able to buy more goods on credit, access to easy money propelled the stock market. Instead of raising interest rates to curb excessive speculation, the Federal Reserve Board kept its rates low throughout the 1920s.

The Board's failure to raise interest rates significantly helped cause the Depression in two ways. First, by keeping rates low, the Board encouraged member banks to make risky loans. Second, the low interest rates led business leaders to think that the economy was still expanding. As a result, they borrowed more money to expand production. This was a serious mistake because it led to overproduction when sales were falling. When the Depression finally hit, companies had to lay off workers to cut costs. Then the Federal Reserve made another mistake: it raised interest rates, thus tightening credit. The economy continued to spiral downward.

✓ READING PROGRESS CHECK

Determining Cause and Effect What were three existing economic conditions that contributed to the Depression?

LESSON 1 REVIEW

Reviewing Vocabulary

1. ***Contrasting*** What is the difference between buying on margin and a margin call? LAFS.1112.RH.2.4

2. ***Describing*** What occurs during a bank run? LAFS.1112.RH.2.4

3. ***Evaluating*** Why was buying stocks based on speculation a risk? LAFS.1112.RH.2.4

Using Your Notes

4. ***Identifying Cause and Effect*** Use the notes that you completed during the lesson to write a few sentences identifying the causes of the Great Depression. LAFS.1112.WHST.1.1

Answering the Guiding Questions

5. ***Evaluating*** What economic choices caused the economy to become unstable in the late 1920s? SS.912.A.5.11

6. ***Describing*** How did the stock market crash trigger a chain of events that led to the Depression? SS.912.A.5.11

7. ***Analyzing*** What were the underlying conditions that led to the collapse of the U.S. economy? SS.912.A.5.11

Writing Activity

8. **INFORMATIVE/EXPLANATORY** Write an essay for a financial magazine telling the chain of events leading to the Great Depression. Be sure to sequence the events correctly to make them easier for readers to understand. LAFS.1112.WHST.1.2, LAFS.1112.WHST.4.10

LESSON 2

Life During the Great Depression

ESSENTIAL QUESTIONS

- What causes changes in the economy over time?
- How do depressions affect societies?

READING HELPDESK

Academic Vocabulary

- suspend
- technique
- colleague

Content Vocabulary

- bailiff
- soap opera
- hobo

TAKING NOTES:

Key Ideas and Details

Organizing As you read, use a graphic organizer such as the one below to describe the effects of the Depression.
LAFS.1112.RH.3.7, SS.912.A.5.11

Effects of the Great Depression

NEXT GENERATION
SUNSHINE STATE STANDARDS

LAFS.1112.RH.2.4: Determine the meaning of words and phrases as they are used in a text, including analyzing how an author uses and refines the meaning of a key term over the course of a text (e.g., how Madison defines faction in Federalist No. 10).

LAFS.1112.RH.3.7: Integrate and evaluate multiple sources of information presented in diverse formats and media (e.g., visually, quantitatively, as well as in words) in order to address a question or solve a problem.

LAFS.1112.WHST.1.2: Write informative/ explanatory texts, including the narration of historical events, scientific procedures/ experiments, or technical processes.

Continued on page 297

IT MATTERS BECAUSE

Large numbers of people lost their jobs and homes during the Depression. To help people escape their troubles, popular entertainment offered humorous and optimistic movies and radio programs. Novelists and photographers created more realistic portrayals of American life.

The Depression Worsens

GUIDING QUESTION *How did economic changes affect everyday life during the 1930s?*

The Depression grew steadily worse during President Hoover's administration. In 1930, across the nation, 1,352 banks **suspended** operations, more than twice the number of bank failures in 1929. In 1932 alone, some 30,000 companies went out of business. By 1933, roughly one-fourth of the workforce was unemployed.

Struggling to Get By

The jobless often went hungry. When possible, they stood in breadlines for free food or lined up outside soup kitchens set up by private groups. People who could not pay their rent or mortgage lost their homes. Some, paralyzed by fear and humiliation, did not move and were evicted. Court officers called **bailiffs** ejected them and their belongings. Throughout the country, newly homeless people put up shacks on unused or public lands. They built shantytowns, which they called Hoovervilles after the president they blamed for their plight.

In search of work or a better life, many homeless, unemployed Americans began walking, hitchhiking, or, most often, "riding the rails" across the country. These wanderers, called **hoboes,** would sneak past railroad police to slip into open boxcars on freight trains. Hundreds of thousands of people, mostly boys and young men, wandered from place to place in this way.

The Depression also caused many immigrants to return to their native countries. In some cases, this repatriation was voluntary as jobs became scarce. In other cases, repatriation was forced. The federal

Many Americans abandoned their homes as windstorms and drought turned the Great Plains into a Dust Bowl.

▶ **CRITICAL THINKING**
Making Generalizations How does this photo illustrate the Depression experience of some Americans? LAFS.1112.RH.3.7, SS.912.A.1.4, SS.912.A.5.11

suspend to cease or stop

bailiff minor officer of the courts

hobo a homeless and usually penniless wanderer

Florida CONNECTION

Air Conditioning Changes the South

Before Willis Carrier invented air-conditioning, the world of the Deep South was a very different one. The intense summer heat deterred industries from opening there. Once movie theaters began to be air-conditioned in the 1920s, moviegoers flocked to theaters to escape the hot, sticky outside world. The cool air of theater interiors gave a glimpse of how Carrier's invention would change the South in years to come. SS.912.A.5.11, SS.912.A.5.12

government launched repatriation drives to send poor immigrants back to their home countries. It also stepped up efforts to deport immigrants who had violated the law. In the Southwest, federal officials rounded up Mexicans (often without regard to their citizenship status) and forcibly returned them to Mexico.

Although estimates vary, historians believe that the Mexican Repatriation resulted in somewhere between 500,000 and 2 million people of Mexican heritage, perhaps more than half of whom were American citizens, being forced to move to Mexico. Mexicans were probably targeted more than others, in part because of racism, and in part because of cost. Hispanics were one of the most highly visible immigrant minorities remaining after the immigration laws of the 1920s had restricted other immigrants, and deporting Hispanics was easier and less expensive than shipping hundreds of thousands of people back to Europe.

The Dust Bowl

Farmers soon faced a new disaster. The Great Plains were very dry with high winds. Topsoil was held in place by deep rooted prairie grasses that preserved moisture in times of low rainfall. The Homestead Act encouraged large-scale settlement of the region, and as the population grew, tractors and combines came into widespread use. Much of the Great Plains were extensively deep-plowed making the topsoil susceptible to rapid erosion.

Deep-plowing was not a problem for many decades, as the Great Plains experienced higher than normal rainfall from the late 1800s to the 1920s. But when crop prices dropped in the 1920s, many farmers left their fields uncultivated even as temperatures had begun to climb and rainfall had begun to decline. In the early 1930s, a severe drought hit, and there was nothing anchoring the soil or retaining moisture. The soil turned to dust. Human and physical geographic factors had combined to create a disaster.

Winds blew the arid earth aloft, blackening the sky for hundreds of miles. Dust buried crops and livestock. Humans and animals caught outdoors sometimes died of suffocation when the dust filled their lungs. During most of the 1930s, an average of 50 dust storms a year hit the Plains.

Some Great Plains farmers managed to hold on to their land, but others were not as lucky. If their land was mortgaged, they had to turn the property over to the banks. Then, nearly penniless, many families headed west, hoping for a better life in California. Because many migrants were from Oklahoma, they became known as "Okies." In California, their struggles continued:

Courtesy of USDA/National Resource Conservation Service

PRIMARY SOURCE

❝ [They have] one-room shacks usually about 10 by 12 feet, have no rug, no water, no bed. In one corner there is a little iron wood stove. Water must be carried from the faucet at the end of the street. **❞**

—John Steinbeck, from *The Harvest Gypsies, 1936*

✔ READING PROGRESS CHECK

Explaining What changes to daily life occurred for people affected by the economic hardships of the Great Depression?

Arts and Entertainment

GUIDING QUESTION *In what ways did culture reflect the Depression experience?*

The hard times of the 1930s led many Americans to want to escape their worries—if only for an hour or two—through entertainment. Most people could scrape together the money to go to the movies, or they could sit with their families and listen to one of the many radio programs broadcast across the country. Entertainment provided an escape from the difficult times. Movies and radio programs grew increasingly popular. During the 1930s, more than 60 million Americans went to the movies each week. Child stars delighted viewers, and comedies provided a relief from daily worries. The Marx Brothers amused audiences in such films as *Animal Crackers*. Moviegoers also loved cartoons. Walt Disney produced the first feature-length animated film, *Snow White and the Seven Dwarfs*, in 1937.

Serious films often celebrated ordinary people and the values of small-town America. In *Mr. Smith Goes to Washington*, Jimmy Stewart played a decent but naïve senator who refuses to compromise his principles and exposes the corruption of some of his **colleagues.** Although few movies portrayed the hard times of the era, dramas tended to show heroes, often regular people, standing up to corruption or powerful forces. These films resonated with Americans because they offset the feelings of helplessness the Depression had caused, and also reflected the belief of many people that they were victims of corruption among the wealthy and powerful.

In 1939, MGM produced *The Wizard of Oz*, a colorful musical that lifted viewers' spirits. That same year, Vivien Leigh and Clark Gable thrilled audiences in *Gone with the Wind,* a Civil War epic that won nine Academy Awards. Hattie McDaniel won Best Supporting Actress, becoming the first African American to win an Academy Award.

While movies captured the imagination, radio offered information and entertainment. Tens of millions of people listened to the radio daily. Comedians such as Jack Benny were popular, as were the adventures of superheroes such as the Green Hornet. Daytime dramas continued their story lines from day to day. Programs such as *The Guiding Light* presented the personal struggles of middle-class families. The sponsors were often makers of laundry soaps, so the shows were nicknamed **soap operas.** Radio also exposed listeners to a variety of musical styles. Americans enjoyed hit songs from movies and Broadway musicals to swing music to country.

Literature and the visual arts also flourished during the 1930s. Writers and artists tried to portray life around them, using the homeless and unemployed as their subjects in stories and pictures. Novelists developed new writing techniques. In *The Sound and the Fury*, William Faulkner shows what characters are thinking and feeling before they speak. Using this stream of consciousness **technique,** he exposes hidden attitudes of the residents of a fictional Mississippi county. Another Southern writer named

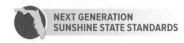

NEXT GENERATION SUNSHINE STATE STANDARDS

Continued from page 295

LAFS.1112.WHST.4.10: Write routinely over extended time frames (time for reflection and revision) and shorter time frames (a single sitting or a day or two) for a range of discipline-specific tasks, purposes, and audiences.

SS.912.A.1.2: Utilize a variety of primary and secondary sources to identify author, historical significance, audience, and authenticity to understand a historical period.

SS.912.A.1.4: Analyze how images, symbols, objects, cartoons, graphs, charts, maps, and artwork may be used to interpret the significance of time periods and events from the past.

SS.912.A.1.7: Describe various socio-cultural aspects of American life including arts, artifacts, literature, education, and publications.

SS.912.A.5.11: Examine causes, course, and consequences of the Great Depression and the New Deal.

SS.912.A.5.12: Examine key events and people in Florida history as they relate to United States history.

SS.912.H.1.1: Relate works in the arts (architecture, dance, music, theatre, and visual arts) of varying styles and genre according to the periods in which they were created.

SS.912.H.3.2: Identify social, moral, ethical, religious, and legal issues arising from technological and scientific developments, and examine their influence on works of arts within a culture.

colleague a person who works in the same, or a similar, profession

soap opera a serial drama on television or radio using melodramatic situations

technique a method of achieving a desired aim

BIOGRAPHY

Margaret Bourke-White (1904–1971)

Margaret Bourke-White was *Life* magazine's first female photojournalist. Her picture of the construction of Fort Peck Dam appeared on the magazine's first cover.

▶ CRITICAL THINKING
Making Generalizations Why do you think photojournalism became so influential? SS.912.H.1.1

Thomas Wolfe used the facts of his own life to examine the theme of artistic creation in his powerful novels, including *Look Homeward Angel*.

Perhaps no writer did more than reporter and novelist John Steinbeck to capture the characteristics and issues of the Depression. Steinbeck focused on the rural poor, particularly agricultural workers and farmers. He created a sense of realism with rich, detailed descriptions, showing how people said things and what they and their surroundings looked like. He focused on how their circumstances were partly the result of the economic system, but he also stressed the importance of friendship and family in helping people survive hardship.

Steinbeck's writings added flesh and blood to journalists' reports of poverty and misfortune and evoked both sympathy for his characters and indignation at social injustice. In *The Grapes of Wrath* (1939), Steinbeck tells the story of a family fleeing the Dust Bowl to find a new life in California. Steinbeck had visited the camps of migrant families and sympathized with their fears. In his novel, he describes the experiences of the Joad family who headed to California after losing their farm.

Images were also becoming more influential. Photographers roamed the nation with the new 35-millimeter cameras, seeking new subjects. In 1936, *TIME* magazine publisher Henry Luce introduced *LIFE,* a weekly photojournalism magazine that enjoyed instant success. The striking pictures of photojournalists Dorothea Lange and Margaret Bourke-White showed how the Great Depression affected average Americans.

Lange photographed homeless people in San Francisco and poor migrant agricultural workers in California's Central Valley. One of her most famous photos, entitled *"Migrant Mother"* (1936), exemplifies the Depression era's characteristics and issues. The photo depicts a sad, weary woman with seven children who had just sold her car's tires to buy food. Lange also traveled throughout the Dust Bowl states capturing images of the devastated region. When the images were collected in a best-selling book *An American Exodus* (1939), the state of California responded by setting up camps to shelter migrant workers.

Like Lange, Margaret Bourke-White was a master at using photography to capture the era's ironies and contrasts. In 1937, *LIFE* magazine carried one of her most famous photographs. It showed a line of poor African American flood victims waiting for help in front of a billboard which declared, "World's Highest Standard of Living" and showed a white family happily driving a car.

Painters of the 1930s included Thomas Hart Benton and Grant Wood, whose styles were referred to as the regionalist school. Their work emphasized traditional American values, especially those of the rural Midwest and South. Wood's best-known painting today is *American Gothic*, which portrays a stern farmer and his daughter in front of their humble farmhouse. The portrait pays tribute to no-nonsense Midwesterners while gently making fun of their severity.

✓ READING PROGRESS CHECK

Examining How did the Depression influence culture?

©Bettmann/Corbis

LESSON 2 REVIEW

Reviewing Vocabulary
1. ***Summarizing*** Why were the lives of hoboes difficult during the Depression? LAFS.1112.RH.2.4

Using Your Notes
2. ***Identifying*** How did some radio shows come to be nicknamed soap operas? LAFS.1112.RH.2.4

Answering the Guiding Questions
3. ***Evaluating*** How did economic changes affect everyday life during the 1930s? SS.912.A.5.11

4. ***Describing*** In what ways did culture reflect the Depression experience? SS.912.A.5.11

Writing Activity
5. INFORMATIVE/EXPLANATORY Write two to three paragraphs describing the Dust Bowl, its causes, its effect on people, and how it made the Great Depression worse for those living on the Great Plains. LAFS.1112.WHST.1.2, LAFS.1112.WHST.4.10

Determining Cause and Effect

Why Learn This Skill?

Why do we study history? We know things have happened in the past that have shaped the world we live in today. There are many things we appreciate and other things that we think are wrong. The purpose of history, perhaps more than anything else, is to explain why things happened and what changed as a result. In short, understanding history requires you to identify cause-and-effect relationships.

Learning the Skill

Determining cause and effect involves considering why an event occurred. A cause is an action, an event, a condition, or a decision that makes something else happen. What happens is the effect.

There are three kinds of causes. Necessary causes are causes that you have to have or the event cannot happen. A sufficient cause is a cause that all by itself can cause an event. But it is not the only possible cause. Contributory causes cannot cause an event by themselves, but they can help shape the conditions under which it happens.

To determine cause and effect, follow these steps:

- Ask why an event happened. List possible reasons for the event.
- Look at the list. Which causes are necessary? Are they all necessary? Which ones might be sufficient but not needed to explain the event? Which causes only contributed to shaping the event?
- Look at the timing of the causes. Which ones established conditions far in the past? These are long range causes. Which ones helped trigger an event once conditions were in place? These are short-term or immediate causes.
- To determine effects, ask "What happened because of this?" or "What were the results of this?"
- Examine which effects happened right away and which ones only developed slowly over time. These are short and long-range effects.
- Be sure you have causes and events in the correct sequence.
- Make sure there is a logical or reasonable connection between the causes and effects you have identified. Sometimes things happen close together, but that doesn't mean one caused the other. Writing history is all about explaining why your evidence proves a cause and effect relationship.

Practicing this Skill

Open the lesson "Life During the Great Depression." Read the section entitled "The Dust Bowl" and answer these questions:

1. What event is being explained in this section?
2. What causes are said to have explained the event?
3. Which causes are long-range causes? Which causes are short term causes?
4. Which causes are necessary? Which are contributory?
5. What were the effects of these causes?

Applying the Skill

Open the lesson "The Causes of the Great Depression." Reread the lesson and apply your skills at determining cause and effect. Write a brief essay describing the causes of the Great Depression. Be sure to identify short term and long term causes, and point out which causes led to effects that in turn led to even more causes that made the Depression worse. Identify which causes were necessary to the Depression, and which ones were contributory.

LESSON 3

Hoover's Response to the Depression

ESSENTIAL QUESTIONS

• What causes changes in the economy over time?
• How do depressions affect societies?

READING HELPDESK

Academic Vocabulary

• series   • community

Content Vocabulary

• public works   • foreclose
• relief

TAKING NOTES:

Key Ideas and Details

Organizing As you read about Herbert Hoover's response to the Depression, create a graphic organizer listing his major initiatives and their results.
LAFS.1112.RH.3.7, SS.912.A.5.11

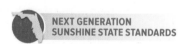

NEXT GENERATION SUNSHINE STATE STANDARDS

LAFS.1112.RH.2.4: Determine the meaning of words and phrases as they are used in a text, including analyzing how an author uses and refines the meaning of a key term over the course of a text (e.g., how Madison defines faction in Federalist No. 10).

LAFS.1112.RH.3.7: Integrate and evaluate multiple sources of information presented in diverse formats and media (e.g., visually, quantitatively, as well as in words) in order to address a question or solve a problem.

LAFS.1112.WHST.1.1: Write arguments focused on discipline-specific content.

LAFS.1112.WHST.4.10: Write routinely over extended time frames (time for reflection and revision) and shorter time frames (a single sitting or a day or two) for a range of discipline-specific tasks, purposes, and audiences.

Continued on page 302

IT MATTERS BECAUSE

President Hoover tried to fix the economy by providing loans to banks and corporations and by starting public works projects. Later, he reluctantly supported direct aid to impoverished families. By the early 1930s, more Americans were demanding the government's help.

Promoting Recovery

GUIDING QUESTION *How did President Hoover's governing philosophy influence his efforts to combat the Great Depression?*

On Friday, October 25, 1929, the day after Black Thursday, President Herbert Hoover declared that "the fundamental business of the country . . . is on a sound and prosperous basis." On March 7, 1930, he told the press that "the worst effects of the crash upon employment will have passed during the next sixty days." Critics derided his optimism as conditions worsened. Hoover hoped to downplay the public's fears and to avoid more bank runs and layoffs. He urged consumers and business leaders to make rational decisions. In the end, Hoover's efforts failed to inspire the public's confidence, and the economy continued its downward slide.

Hoover believed that American "rugged individualism" would keep the economy moving and that the government should not step in to help individuals. After World War I, many European countries implemented a form of socialism, which Hoover felt contributed to their lack of economic recovery. In 1922, Hoover had written a book, *American Individualism,* explaining why the American system of individualism was the best social, political, spiritual, and economic system. Thus, it was difficult for him to propose more government control.

Despite public statements that the economy was not in trouble, Hoover was worried. He organized a **series** of conferences, bringing together heads of banks, railroads, and other big businesses, as well as labor leaders and government officials, to strategize about solutions.

Industry leaders pledged to keep factories open and to stop slashing wages, but by 1931, they had broken those pledges. Hoover increased funding for **public works,** or government-financed building projects. The resulting construction jobs employed a small fraction of the millions of unemployed. The only way the government could create enough new jobs was through massive spending, which Hoover refused to do.

Someone had to pay for public works projects. If the government raised taxes, consumers would have less money to spend, hurting business. If the government kept taxes low and ran a budget deficit—spending more than it collected—it would have to borrow money, making less available for loans. As the 1930 congressional elections approached, most Americans blamed the party in power for the ailing economy. The Republicans lost 49 seats and their majority in the House of Representatives; they held on to the Senate by a single vote.

Trying to Rescue the Banks

To get the economy growing, Hoover wanted to increase the money supply to help banks make loans to corporations. They could then expand production and rehire workers. The president asked the Federal Reserve Board to put more currency into circulation, but the Board refused. To ease the money shortage, Hoover set up the National Credit Corporation (NCC) in October 1931. The NCC created a pool of money that allowed troubled banks to continue lending money in their **communities.** This program, however, failed to meet the nation's needs.

In 1932, Hoover requested Congress to set up the Reconstruction Finance Corporation (RFC) to make loans to businesses. By early 1932, the RFC had lent about $238 million to banks, railroads, and building-and-loan associations. Overly cautious, the RFC failed to increase its lending sufficiently. The economy continued its decline.

Direct Help for Citizens

Hoover strongly opposed the federal government's participation in **relief**—money given directly to impoverished families. He believed that only state and local governments should dole out relief, with any other needs being met by private charity. By the spring of 1932, however, state and local governments were running out of money, and private charities lacked the resources to handle the crisis.

Support for a federal relief measure increased, and Congress passed the Emergency Relief and Construction Act in July. Reluctantly, Hoover signed it.

Thinking Like a
HISTORIAN
Analyzing Secondary Sources

Historians debate whether Hoover's intervention after the stock market crash was too much or insufficient, premature, or tardy. It has been argued that Hoover's actions were responsible for the length of the Depression. Would you agree or disagree? Review the steps Hoover took to promote recovery and evaluate their effects, noting whether they were too severe or weak, or too early or late.
SS.912.A.1.1

series a number of events that come one after another

public works projects such as highways, parks, and libraries built with public funds for public use

community people with common characteristics living in the same area

relief aid in the form of money or supplies for those in need

CAN HOOVER FIGHT THE DEPRESSION?

While the Democratic Party donkey marches outside singing old songs, Hoover tries to deal with economic problems caused by high tariffs, depression, and drought.

Herbert Hoover reassures a farmer his scarecrow labeled "Farm Relief" will help.

POLITICAL CARTOONS

Like any president during a crisis, Hoover's actions were debated in the press.

1 **Drawing Conclusions** How are Hoover and the Democrats portrayed in the cartoon on the left?
LAFS.1112.RH.3.7, SS.912.A.1.4

2 **Interpreting** What does the cartoon on the right suggest about Hoover's plan to help farmers?
LAFS.1112.RH.3.7, SS.912.A.1.4, SS.912.H.1.2

(l)The Granger Collection, New York; (r)MPI/Archive Photos/Getty Images

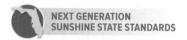

**NEXT GENERATION
SUNSHINE STATE STANDARDS**

Continued from page 300

SS.912.A.1.1: Describe the importance of historiography, which includes how historical knowledge is obtained and transmitted, when interpreting events in history.

SS.912.A.1.2: Utilize a variety of primary and secondary sources to identify author, historical significance, audience, and authenticity to understand a historical period.

SS.912.A.1.4: Analyze how images, symbols, objects, cartoons, graphs, charts, maps, and artwork may be used to interpret the significance of time periods and events from the past.

SS.912.A.5.11: Examine causes, course, and consequences of the Great Depression and the New Deal.

SS.912.H.1.2: Describe how historical events, social context, and culture impact forms, techniques, and purposes of works in the arts, including the relationship between a government and its citizens.

foreclose to take possession of a property from a mortgager because of defaults on payments

The new act called for $1.5 billion for public works and $300 million in emergency loans to the states for direct relief. For the first time in American history, the federal government was supplying direct relief funds. By this time, however, the new program could not reverse the damage that had been done.

✓ **READING PROGRESS CHECK**

Identifying What two major strategies did President Hoover use to promote economic recovery?

In an Angry Mood

GUIDING QUESTION *Why did citizens try to change government policy during the Depression's early years? How did they change it?*

In the months after the Wall Street crash, most Americans were resigned to bad economic news. By 1931, however, many were becoming increasingly discontent.

Hunger Marches and Protests by Farmers

In January 1931, about 500 residents of Oklahoma City looted a grocery store. The following month, hundreds of unemployed citizens smashed the windows of a Minneapolis grocery store and helped themselves to meat, produce, and canned goods. Crowds began showing up at rallies and "hunger marches" organized by the American Communist Party. On December 5, 1932, in Washington, D.C., a group of about 1,200 hunger marchers chanted, "Feed the hungry, tax the rich." Police herded them into a cul-de-sac and denied them food and water. Some members of Congress insisted on the marchers' right to petition their government. With that, the marchers made their way to Capitol Hill.

The hungry poor were not the only people who began to protest conditions during the Depression. During the agricultural boom that took place during World War I, many farmers had heavily mortgaged their land to pay for seed, equipment, and feed. After the war, prices sank so low that farmers began losing money. Creditors **foreclosed** on nearly one million farms between 1930 and 1934. They took ownership of the land and evicted families. Some farmers began destroying their crops, desperately trying to raise prices by reducing the supply. In Nebraska, farmers burned corn to heat their homes. Georgia dairy farmers blocked highways and stopped milk trucks, dumping the milk into ditches.

©Bettmann/Corbis

Farmers protest low dairy prices by destroying supply.

▶ **CRITICAL THINKING**
Analyzing Primary Sources
How do you think poor and hungry people might have responded to this photo?
LAFS.1112.RH.3.7, SS.912.A.1.4

The Bonus Marchers

After World War I, Congress had enacted a $1,000 bonus for each veteran, to be distributed in 1945. In 1929, Texas congressman Wright Patman introduced a bill that would authorize early payment of these bonuses. In May 1932, several hundred Oregon veterans began marching to Washington, D.C., to lobby for passage of the legislation. As they moved eastward, other veterans joined them until they numbered about 1,000. Wearing ragged military uniforms, they trudged along the highways or rode the rails, singing old war songs. The press termed the marchers the "Bonus Army."

Once in Washington, the veterans camped in Hoovervilles. More veterans joined them until the Bonus Army swelled to an estimated 15,000. President Hoover acknowledged the veterans' right to petition but refused to meet with them. When the Senate voted down the bonus bill, veterans outside the Capitol began to grumble. In a statement, Hoover said, "Congress made provision for the return home of the so-called bonus marchers who have for many weeks been given every opportunity of free assembly, free speech and free petition to the Congress." Many returned home, but some marchers stayed on. Some lived in the camps; others squatted in vacant buildings downtown.

In late July, Hoover ordered the buildings cleared. The police tried, but when an officer panicked and fired into a crowd, killing two veterans, the secretary of war asked if he could send in army troops. General Douglas MacArthur ignored Hoover's orders to clear the buildings but to leave the camps alone. MacArthur sent in cavalry, infantry, and tanks to clear the camps. Soon, unarmed veterans were running away, pursued by some 700 soldiers. The soldiers teargassed stragglers and burned the shacks. National press coverage of troops assaulting veterans further harmed Hoover's reputation and hounded him throughout the 1932 campaign.

Although Hoover failed to resolve the economic crisis, he did more than any prior president to expand the federal government's role in the economy. The Reconstruction Finance Corporation was the first federal agency created to stimulate the economy during peacetime. The rout of the Bonus Army marchers and the lingering Depression, however, tarnished Hoover's public image.

Guards clash with Bonus Army marchers.

▶ **CRITICAL THINKING**
Interpreting What do you observe about the Bonus Army's attempt to defend itself?
LAFS.1112.RH.3.7, SS.912.A.1.4

✓ **READING PROGRESS CHECK**

Identifying Between 1931 and 1932, what federal government programs and acts were created to promote economic recovery, and what was each intended to do?

New York Daily News/Getty Images

LESSON 3 REVIEW

Reviewing Vocabulary

1. *Evaluating* What was the purpose of the increased funding to public works? LAFS.1112.RH.2.4

2. *Summarizing* Why did creditors foreclose on so many farms during the Depression? LAFS.1112.RH.2.4

Using Your Notes

3. *Analyzing* Use the notes that you completed during the lesson to explain why the strategies that the Hoover administration used were successful or not successful. LAFS.1112.WHST.1.1

Answering the Guiding Questions

4. *Assessing* How did President Hoover's governing philosophy influence his efforts to combat the Great Depression? SS.912.A.5.11

5. *Describing* Why and how did citizens try to change government policy during the Depression's early years? SS.912.A.5.11

Writing Activity

6. **ARGUMENT** Suppose that you are a World War I veteran in 1932. Write a persuasive letter to your congressman explaining why you need your bonus now, not in 1945. LAFS.1112.WHST.1.1, LAFS.1112.WHST.4.10

STUDY GUIDE

THE CAUSES OF THE GREAT DEPRESSION
LESSON 1

 LOW INTEREST RATES — Federal Reserve kept interest rates low; companies borrowed money and expanded more than necessary.

 OVERPRODUCTION — Companies made more goods than could be sold.

 UNEVEN DISTRIBUTION OF WEALTH — Not everyone who wanted consumer goods could afford them.

 HIGH TARIFFS — Tariffs restricted foreign demand for American goods.

 FALLING DEMAND — With too many goods unsold, production was cut back and employees were laid off.

 STOCK MARKET SPECULATION — Low interest rates encouraged borrowing money to speculate, endangering bank solvency.

LIFE DURING THE GREAT DEPRESSION
LESSON 2

The Dust Bowl covered much of the Great Plains
- Overcultivated soil and drought exposed fragile topsoil
- 2.5 million left the Plains and migrated west

HOOVER'S RESPONSE TO THE DEPRESSION
LESSON 3

CAUTIOUS BEGINNINGS

National Credit Corporation
- Started in October 1931
- Increased money supply for banks to lend to business

Reconstruction Finance Corporation
- Begun in 1932
- over $230 milion loaned to lenders, railroads

RELUCTANT PUBLIC RELIEF

Emergency Relief and Construction Act
- Passed by Congress in July 1932; reluctantly signed by Hoover
- $1.5 billion in public works finances provided
- $300 million in emergency loans provided to state governments

Directions: On a separate sheet of paper, answer the questions below. Make sure you read carefully and answer all parts to the question.

Lesson Review

Lesson 1

1 *Describing* Describe the effect the stock market crash had on banks and identify how bank failures contributed to the coming of the Great Depression. LAFS.1112.WHST.3.9, SS.912.A.5.11

2 *Identifying* What is monetary policy and which organization controls monetary policy in the United States? What is the main tool the organization uses to try to regulate the American economy?

3 *Explaining* How did the uneven distribution of income, in combination with the use of installment plans and easy credit, help cause the Great Depression? SS.912.A.5.11

Lesson 2

4 *Describing* How were the characteristics and issues of the Great Depression reflected in the era's visual arts? What new visual art form rose to prominence during the Great Depression? Who were some of its best known practitioners? SS.912.A.5.11, SS.912.H.1.1

5 *Defining* What is repatriation? LAFS.1112.RH.2.4

6 *Identifying Cause and Effect* What impact did the Dust Bowl have on farmers living on the Great Plains? SS.912.A.5.11

7 *Describing* Many people were poor in the 1930s, yet 60 million people went to the movies each week. Why do you think they chose to spend their limited amount of money in that way? How were the movies of the 1930s a reaction to the issues and characteristics of the Depression? SS.912.A.5.11, SS.912.H.1.1

Lesson 3

8 *Interpreting Significance* What three major initiatives did President Hoover take to help the economy of the United States? SS.912.A.5.11

9 *Summarizing* Describe the measures some farmers took in an attempt to raise prices on agricultural goods.

10 *Specifying* What did the Emergency Relief and Construction Act offer, and what was its impact? SS.912.A.5.11

11 *Identifying Cause and Effect* What did World War I veterans do to try to get their service bonuses early, and how did the public react to it?

Exploring the Essential Questions

12 *Analyzing* Write an essay that identifies factors that contribute to change in the economy over time. The essay should be supported with your knowledge of the booming 1920s economy and Great Depression of the 1930s. LAFS.1112.WHST.2.4, SS.912.A.5.4, SS.912.A.5.11

13 *Synthesizing* How do depressions affect societies? Use your knowledge of the Great Depression to explain your answer. SS.912.A.5.11

Critical Thinking

14 *Drawing Conclusions* Why did the Depression lead to the forced deportation of immigrants and especially large numbers of Mexican immigrants? SS.912.A.5.11

15 *Identifying Cause and Effect* How did runs on banks contribute to the high rate of bank failures during the Great Depression? SS.912.A.5.11

16 *Analyzing* What were the effects of widespread unemployment during the Great Depression? SS.912.A.5.11

17 *Economics* Explain the purpose of the Reconstruction Finance Corporation (RFC) created by President Hoover. Who benefited from this program? SS.912.A.5.11

21st Century Skills

18 *Categorizing Information* Many people traveled around, relocated within, or permanently left the United States during the Great Depression. Categorize the kinds of movement and groups of people. Analyze how groups were similar or different from one another. SS.912.A.5.11, SS.912.G.4.2, SS.912.G.4.3

Need Extra Help?

If You've Missed Question	1	2	3	4	5	6	7	8	9	10	11	12	13	14	15	16	17	18
Go to Lesson	1	1	1	2	2	2	2	3	3	3	3	1, 2, 3	2	2	1	3	3	2

19 *Applying Relative Chronology By Sequencing* Research popular movies of the 1930s, either online or at the library. Create a time line listing popular movies produced in the 1930s. Identify each movie's theme or basic plot. What patterns do you see? What do the popular movies suggest to you about the mood of the American public? LAFS.1112.RH.3.7, LAFS.1112.SL.1.3, LAFS.1112.WHST.3.7, SS.912.A.1.3, SS.912.A.1.4, SS.912.A.5.11, SS.912.H.1.1, SS.912.H.1.5

DBQ Analyzing Primary Sources

Read the excerpt below from a speech by Herbert Hoover, then answer the following questions.

PRIMARY SOURCE

"You cannot extend the mastery of the government over the daily working life of a people without at the same time making it the master of the people's souls and thoughts. . . . Free speech does not live many hours after free industry and free commerce die. . . . Every step of bureaucratizing of the business of our country poisons the very roots of liberalism—that is, political equality, free speech, free assembly, free press, and equality of opportunity. It is the road not to more liberty, but to less liberty."

—Herbert Hoover, from a speech delivered October 22, 1928

20 *Finding the Main Idea* What is Hoover's main idea? Why does he think government should not interfere in the economy? Do you agree with his main idea? Write a paragraph explaining your point of view. LAFS.1112.RH.1.1, LAFS.1112.RH.1.2, LAFS.1112.RH.3.8, LAFS.1112.RH.4.10, LAFS.1112.WHST.2.4, LAFS.1112.WHST.4.10, SS.912.A.5.11

21 *Identifying Frame of Reference* When did Hoover make this speech? Explain why that date is significant given what would happen later. Why did Hoover have reason to think he was correct at the time he gave his speech? Think about both the date and Hoover's previous experiences. LAFS.1112.RH.1.3, LAFS.1112.RH.3.7, LAFS.1112.RH.3.8, LAFS.1112.RH.4.10, SS.912.A.5.11

Analyzing Visuals

Use the map to answer the following questions.

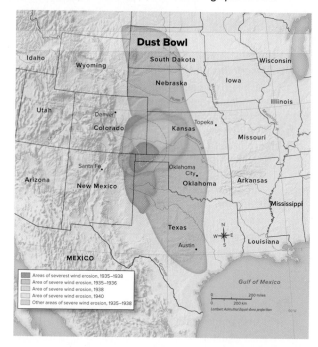

22 *Analyzing Geographic Patterns and Distributions* When you look at the severity and the length of time, which regions in which states suffered the worst effects of the Dust Bowl for the longest period of time? SS.912.G.2.1, SS.912.G.2.5

23 *Posing Questions about Geographic Patterns* Although many farmers moved to nearby cities to escape the Dust Bowl, a large number migrated to California. What questions do you need to pose to identify the route most of them followed and to explain why they made such a long trip? Using a map of the United States, roughly estimate how many miles farmers had to migrate if they went to California's Central Valley. SS.912.G.1.3, SS.912.G.2.1, SS.912.G.2.5, SS.912.G.4.3

Extended Response Question

24 *Summarizing* Write a summary of how the Great Depression affected the U.S. economy. Be sure to describe new government programs that were implemented, as well as the Depression's effects on workers and businesses. LAFS.1112.WHST.1.2, LAFS.1112.WHST.4.10, SS.912.A.5.11

Need Extra Help?

If You've Missed Question	**19**	**20**	**21**	**22**	**23**	**24**
Go to Lesson	2	1	1	2	2	1, 2, 3

◀ Franklin D. Roosevelt, a Democrat, shared a progressive attitude with his famous cousin, President Theodore Roosevelt, a Republican.

FROM 1933 TO 1941

Roosevelt and the New Deal

THE STORY MATTERS ...

The Great Depression had changed the lives of many Americans. Millions had lost their jobs, their savings, and their homes. Democrat Franklin Delano Roosevelt offered hope and relief in the presidential election of 1932. In his first hundred days in office, he sent bill after bill to Congress. This legislation became known as the New Deal. It included an array of programs and laws designed to rejuvenate the American economy and prevent such an economic disaster from reoccurring.

ESSENTIAL QUESTIONS

- Can the government fix the economy?
- Is government responsible for the economic well-being of its citizens?

Place & Time: United States 1931–1941

Franklin D. Roosevelt and his administration had a monumental task in 1933. The Great Depression had affected millions of Americans. People began to demand help from the federal government. Promising a "New Deal" for the American people, President Roosevelt took immediate steps to put people back to work, strengthen the economy, and establish a safety net for the nation. Roosevelt's critics challenged his plan because never before had the federal government intervened so directly in the economy.

Step Into the Place

Read the quotes and look at the information presented on the map.

Analyzing Historical Documents What different perspectives do these excerpts reveal about the role of government in the economy?

PRIMARY SOURCE

"So, first of all, let me assert my firm belief that the only thing we have to fear is fear itself—nameless, unreasoning, unjustified terror which paralyzes needed efforts to convert retreat into advance. . . .

Our greatest primary task is to put people to work. This is no unsolvable problem if we face it wisely and courageously. It can be accomplished in part by direct recruiting by the Government itself, treating the task as we would treat the emergency of a war, but at the same time, through this employment, accomplishing greatly needed projects to stimulate and reorganize the use of our natural resources."

—President Franklin D. Roosevelt, from his first Inaugural Address, March 4, 1933

PRIMARY SOURCE

"Now what would I have my party do? I would have them re-declare the principles that they put forth in that 1932 platform [reduce the size of government, balance the federal budget]. . . .

Just get the platform of the Democratic party and get the platform of the Socialist party and . . . make your mind up to pick up the platform that more nearly squares with the record, and you will have your hand on the Socialist platform.

[I]t is all right with me, if they want to disguise themselves as Karl Marx or Lenin or any of the rest of that bunch, but I won't stand for their allowing them to march under the banner of Jackson or Cleveland."

—Alfred E. Smith, former Democratic presidential candidate, from a speech delivered January 25, 1936

(t)The Granger Collection, New York; (tr)Library of Congress, Prints & Photographs Division [LC-USZ62-26759]; (bl & br)detail/White House Collection/The White House Historical Association

Step Into the Time

PREDICTING CONSEQUENCES

Choose an event from the time line and write a paragraph describing how that event might have influenced Roosevelt's New Deal policies.

Hoover 1929–1933

1933 Unemployment peaks at 24.9%

F. Roosevelt 1933–1945

1934 Securities and Exchange Commission is created

U.S. PRESIDENTS

UNITED STATES

WORLD

1931

1933

January 1933 Hitler becomes German chancellor during economic turmoil

1933 World Economic Conference fails to reduce tariffs

1934 Britain passes the Unemployment Assistance Act

NEXT GENERATION SUNSHINE STATE STANDARDS
Students will understand the following benchmarks from the Florida NGSSS

LAFS.1112.RH.3.7: Integrate and evaluate multiple sources of information presented in diverse formats and media (e.g., visually, quantitatively, as well as in words) in order to address a question or solve a problem.

LAFS.1112.RH.3.9: Integrate information from diverse sources, both primary and secondary, into a coherent understanding of an idea or event, noting discrepancies among sources.

SS.912.A.1.2: Utilize a variety of primary and secondary sources to identify author, historical significance, audience, and authenticity to understand a historical period.

SS.912.A.1.3: Utilize timelines to identify the time sequence of historical data.

SS.912.A.1.4: Analyze how images, symbols, objects, cartoons, graphs, charts, maps, and artwork may be used to interpret the significance of time periods and events from the past.

SS.912.A.5.11: Examine causes, course, and consequences of the Great Depression and the New Deal.

Public Works Projects of the New Deal

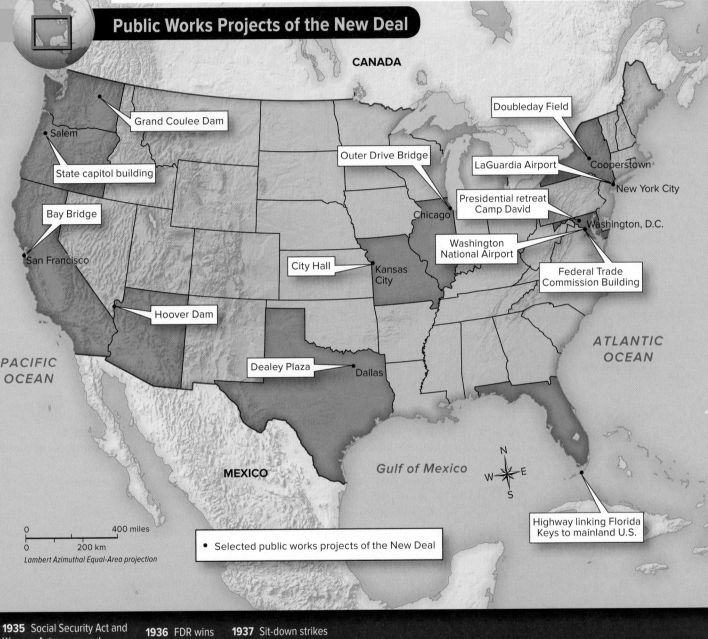

CANADA

Grand Coulee Dam

Salem

State capitol building

Bay Bridge

San Francisco

Hoover Dam

PACIFIC OCEAN

Outer Drive Bridge

LaGuardia Airport

Doubleday Field

Cooperstown

New York City

Presidential retreat Camp David

Chicago

Washington, D.C.

Washington National Airport

City Hall

Kansas City

Federal Trade Commission Building

ATLANTIC OCEAN

Dealey Plaza

Dallas

MEXICO

Gulf of Mexico

N W E S

Highway linking Florida Keys to mainland U.S.

0   400 miles
0   200 km
Lambert Azimuthal Equal-Area projection

• Selected public works projects of the New Deal

1935 Social Security Act and Wagner Act are passed

May 1935 Supreme Court strikes down NRA

1936 FDR wins reelection as president for a second term

1937 Sit-down strikes force General Motors to recognize the United Auto Workers (UAW)

1938 Fair Labor Standards Act sets minimum wage and 44-hour workweek

1940 First Social Security checks are mailed

1941 United States enters World War II

1935   **1937**   **1939**   **1941**

1936 Wave of sit-down strikes in France leads to 40-hour workweek

February 1936 British economist John Maynard Keynes's *The General Theory of Employment, Interest, and Money* is published

1938 Oil is discovered in Saudi Arabia

1939 World War II begins

LESSON 1
The First New Deal

ESSENTIAL QUESTIONS

• Can government fix the economy?
• Is government responsible for the economic well-being of its citizens?

READING HELPDESK

Academic Vocabulary

• apparent
• ideology
• fundamental

Content Vocabulary

• polio
• gold standard
• bank holiday
• fireside chats

TAKING NOTES

Key Ideas and Details

Sequencing As you read about Roosevelt's first three months in office, complete a time line to record the major problems he addressed during this time. LAFS.1112.RH.3.7, SS.912.A.1.3, SS.912.A.5.11

March 5, 1933 ____ June 16, 1933

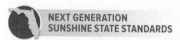

**NEXT GENERATION
SUNSHINE STATE STANDARDS**

ELD.K12.ELL.SI.1 English language learners communicate for social and instructional purposes within the school setting.

ELD.K12.ELL.SS.1: English language learners communicate information, ideas and concepts necessary for academic success in the content area of Social Studies.

LAFS.1112.RH.2.4: Determine the meaning of words and phrases as they are used in a text, including analyzing how an author uses and refines the meaning of a key term over the course of a text (e.g., how Madison defines faction in Federalist No. 10).

Continued on page 312

IT MATTERS BECAUSE

Franklin Delano Roosevelt was elected president in 1932, following his promise of a "New Deal" for Americans. In his first hundred days in office, he introduced a flood of legislation designed to rescue banks, industry, and agriculture, and provide jobs for the unemployed.

Roosevelt's Rise to Power

GUIDING QUESTION *What qualities make an effective leader?*

Franklin Delano Roosevelt, a distant cousin of Theodore Roosevelt, grew up in Hyde Park, New York. In his youth, Franklin learned to hunt, ride horses, and sail; he also developed a lifelong commitment to conservation and a love of rural areas in the United States. Roosevelt was educated at Harvard and then at Columbia Law School. While at Harvard, he became friends with Theodore Roosevelt's niece, Eleanor, whom he later married.

Intensely competitive, Roosevelt liked to be in control. He also liked being around people. His charming personality, deep rich voice, and wide smile expressed confidence and optimism. In short, his personality seemed made for a life in politics.

Roosevelt began his political career in 1910 when he was elected to the New York State Senate. He earned a reputation as a progressive reformer. Three years later, he became assistant secretary of the navy in the Wilson administration. In 1920, his reputation (and famous surname) helped him win the vice presidential nomination on the unsuccessful Democratic ticket.

After losing the election, Roosevelt temporarily withdrew from politics. The next year, he caught the dreaded paralyzing disease **polio.** Although there was no cure, Roosevelt refused to give in. He began a vigorous exercise program to restore muscle control. With heavy steel braces on his legs, he was able to walk short distances by leaning on a cane and someone's arm and swinging his legs forward from his hips.

While recovering from polio, Roosevelt depended on his wife and his aide, Louis Howe, to keep his name prominent in the New York Democratic Party. Eleanor Roosevelt became an effective public speaker, and her efforts kept her husband's political career alive.

By the mid-1920s, Roosevelt was again active in the Democratic Party. In 1928, he ran for governor of New York. He campaigned hard to show that his illness had not slowed him down, and he narrowly won the election. In 1930, he was reelected in a landslide. As governor, Roosevelt oversaw the creation of the first state relief agency to aid the unemployed.

Roosevelt's popularity in New York paved the way for his presidential nomination in 1932. Americans saw in him an energy and optimism that gave them hope despite the tough economic times. After Roosevelt became president, his serenity and confidence amazed people. When one aide commented on his attitude, Roosevelt replied, "If you had spent two years in bed trying to wiggle your big toe, after that anything else would seem easy."

In mid-June 1932, when the country was deep in the Depression, Republicans gathered in Chicago and nominated Herbert Hoover to run for a second term as president. Later that month, the Democrats also held their national convention in Chicago. When Roosevelt won the nomination, he broke with tradition by flying to Chicago to accept it in person. His speech set the tone for his campaign:

PRIMARY SOURCE

❝Let it be from now on the task of our Party to break foolish traditions. . . . [I]t is inevitable that the main issue of this campaign should revolve about . . . a depression so deep that it is without precedent. . . . Republican leaders not only have failed in material things, they have failed in national vision, because in disaster they have held out no hope. . . . I pledge you, I pledge myself, to a new deal for the American people.❞

—speech delivered to the Democratic National Convention, July 2, 1932

From that point forward, Roosevelt's policies for ending the Depression became known as the New Deal. Roosevelt's confidence that he could make things better contrasted sharply with Herbert Hoover's **apparent** failure to do anything effective. On Election Day, Roosevelt won in a landslide, winning the electoral vote in all but six states.

✓ **READING PROGRESS CHECK**

Interpreting What characteristics did Roosevelt have that made him popular with Americans?

(t)Library of Congress, Prints & Photographs Division [LC-USZ62-25812]; (b)©Underwood & Underwood/Bettmann/Corbis

BIOGRAPHY

Eleanor Roosevelt (1884–1962)

Eleanor Roosevelt transformed the role of First Lady. She traveled, toured factories and coal mines, and met with workers, then told her husband what people were thinking. She was a strong supporter of civil rights and urged him to stop discrimination in New Deal programs. After President Roosevelt's death, she was appointed a delegate to the United Nations in 1946, where she helped draft the Universal Declaration of Human Rights.

▶ **CRITICAL THINKING**
Predicting Consequences
How might Franklin Roosevelt's political career have been different if Eleanor had not been his wife?
LAFS.1112.RH.3.7, SS.912.A.6.9

polio abbreviated term for poliomyelitis, an acute infectious disease affecting the skeletal muscles, often resulting in permanent disability and deformity

apparent appearing to be fact as far as can be understood

Franklin Roosevelt delivers his first Inaugural Address.

▶ **CRITICAL THINKING**
Interpreting Why was it important that Franklin Roosevelt inspired optimism among so many Americans? LAFS.1112.RH.3.7, SS.912.A.1.4, SS.912.A.5.11

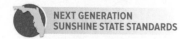

**NEXT GENERATION
SUNSHINE STATE STANDARDS**

Continued from page 310

LAFS.1112.RH.3.7: Integrate and evaluate multiple sources of information presented in diverse formats and media (e.g., visually, quantitatively, as well as in words) in order to address a question or solve a problem.

LAFS.1112.WHST.1.1: Write arguments focused on discipline-specific content.

LAFS.1112.WHST.4.10: Write routinely over extended time frames (time for reflection and revision) and shorter time frames (a single sitting or a day or two) for a range of discipline-specific tasks, purposes, and audiences.

SS.912.A.1.2: Utilize a variety of primary and secondary sources to identify author, historical significance, audience, and authenticity to understand a historical period.

SS.912.A.1.4: Analyze how images, symbols, objects, cartoons, graphs, charts, maps, and artwork may be used to interpret the significance of time periods and events from the past.

SS.912.A.5.11: Examine causes, course, and consequences of the Great Depression and the New Deal.

SS.912.A.6.9: Describe the rationale for the formation of the United Nations, including the contribution of Mary McLeod Bethune.

SS.912.G.1.2: Use spatial perspective and appropriate geographic terms and tools, including the Six Essential Elements, as organizational schema to describe any given place.

SS.912.G.2.1: Identify the physical characteristics and the human characteristics that define and differentiate regions.

gold standard a monetary standard in which one ounce of gold equals a set number of dollars

bank holiday closing of banks during the Great Depression to avoid bank runs

ideology a system of thought that is held by an individual, group, or culture

SKILLS PRACTICE

As you read about the First New Deal, use a graphic organizer of your choice to take notes about the different approaches to ending the Depression. After completing the lesson, use your notes to write a summary of what you read. ELD.K12.ELL.SI.1, ELD.K12.ELL.SS.1

The Hundred Days

GUIDING QUESTION *Why are the first hundred days so important for a president?*

Roosevelt won the presidency in November 1932, but the situation grew worse between the election and his inauguration. Unemployment continued to rise and bank runs increased. People feared that Roosevelt would abandon the **gold standard** and reduce the value of the dollar to fight the Depression. Under the gold standard, one ounce of gold equaled a set number of dollars. To reduce the value of the dollar, the United States would have to stop exchanging dollars for gold. Many Americans and foreign investors with deposits in American banks decided to take their money out of the banks and convert it to gold before it lost its value.

Across the nation, people stood in long lines with paper bags and suitcases, waiting to withdraw their money from banks. By March 1933, more than 4,000 banks had collapsed, wiping out nine million savings accounts. In 38 states, governors declared **bank holidays**—closing the remaining banks before bank runs could put them out of business.

By the day of Roosevelt's inauguration, most of the nation's banks were closed. One in four workers was unemployed. Roosevelt knew he had to restore the nation's confidence. "First of all," he declared in his Inaugural Address, "let me assert my firm belief that the only thing we have to fear is fear itself. . . . This nation asks for action, and action now!"

The New Deal Begins

Roosevelt and his advisers came into office bursting with ideas about how to end the Depression. Roosevelt had no clear agenda, nor did he have a strong political **ideology.** He argued, "The country needs bold, persistent experimentation. . . . Above all, try something."

The new president sent bill after bill to Congress. Between March 9 and June 16, 1933—which came to be called the Hundred Days—Congress passed 15 major acts to resolve the economic crisis. These programs made up what would be called the First New Deal.

A Divided Administration

Although he alone made the final decision about what policies and programs to pursue, Roosevelt depended on his advisers for new ideas. He deliberately chose advisers who disagreed with one another because he wanted to hear many different points of view.

One influential group of President Roosevelt's advisers supported the belief that if the government agencies worked with businesses to regulate wages, prices, and production, they could lift the economy out of the Depression. A second group of advisers, who distrusted big business and felt business leaders had caused the Depression, wanted government planners to run key parts of the economy. A third group of advisers supported former president Woodrow Wilson's "New Freedom" philosophy. They wanted Roosevelt to break up big companies and allow competition to set wages, prices, and production levels. This group of advisers also thought that the government should impose regulations to keep economic competition fair.

☑ READING PROGRESS CHECK

Summarizing What were the key accomplishments during Roosevelt's first hundred days in office?

Banks and Debt Relief

GUIDING QUESTION *Why did Roosevelt broadcast "fireside chats"?*

Roosevelt knew that very few of the new programs would work as long as the nation's banks remained closed. Before he did anything else, he had to restore people's confidence in the banking system. Within a week of his taking office, the Emergency Banking Relief Act was passed. The new law required federal examiners to survey the nation's banks and issue Treasury Department licenses to those that were financially sound.

On March 12, Roosevelt addressed the nation by radio. Sixty million people listened to this first of many **"fireside chats."** He said, "I assure you that it is safer to keep your money in a reopened bank than under the mattress." When banks opened on March 13, deposits far outweighed withdrawals. The banking crisis was over.

With confidence in the banking system restored, Roosevelt then proceeded to use powers granted in the Emergency Banking Relief Act to take the dollar off the gold standard. In June, Congress went further by passing a law that made all contracts payable only in legal tender. No one could demand gold in payment or use gold to pay for things.

Almost immediately, inflation began. This was exactly what the president wanted. The purpose of going off the gold standard was to cause inflation, what Roosevelt called "reflation" because he believed the dollar was overvalued from decades of deflation. Roosevelt wanted to cause inflation to help people in debt.

When money inflates, it loses value. Debts become easier to pay because the money owed is not worth as much. At the same time, inflation causes prices to go up. As Roosevelt had hoped, the increase in prices earned more money for farmers and others who were suffering from low prices for their goods. The United States stayed off the gold standard for about nine months, until the president thought the dollar's value had fallen far enough. In early 1934, Roosevelt set a new price for the gold standard, in which one ounce of gold equaled 35 U.S. dollars.

fireside chats radio broadcasts made by Roosevelt to the American people to explain his initiatives

The FDIC and SEC

Many of Roosevelt's advisers wanted to go further, pushing for new regulations for banks and the stock market. Roosevelt agreed, supporting the Securities Act of 1933 and the Banking Act of 1933, commonly known as the Glass-Steagall Act. The Securities Act required companies that sold stocks and bonds to provide complete and truthful information to investors. The Securities and Exchange Commission (SEC) was created to regulate the stock market and stop fraud. The Glass-Steagall Act separated commercial banking from investment banking. Commercial banks that handled everyday transactions could no longer risk depositors' money through stock speculation. The act also created the Federal Deposit Insurance Corporation (FDIC) to provide government insurance for bank deposits. The creation of the FDIC increased public confidence in the banking system.

In creating the FDIC and the SEC, Congress changed the historical role of state and federal governments in financial matters. Until the New Deal, the regulation of banks had been the responsibility of state governments. Today banks can have a federal charter or a state charter, and be subject to both federal and state regulations. Similarly, up until 1933, the operation of stock markets had been generally unregulated. Under the laissez-faire ideas of the late 1800s, the idea that the federal government should impose rules on a market where people met to buy and sell stocks was never seriously considered. The great crash of 1929 changed people's thinking.

The FDIC still exists today. It guarantees bank deposits up to $250,000 for all member banks and is funded by insurance premiums paid by the banks, not by taxpayer money. The FDIC supervises the operations of over 4,500 banks nationwide making sure they are sound, and comply with all financial regulations and consumer protection laws. You can tell if a bank is FDIC insured by looking for the "Member FDIC" logo on bank windows, paper documents, and websites.

The SEC also still exists, regulating the operations of the nation's stock markets. It inspects stock brokers, investment advisors, and agencies that rate stocks. It investigates reports of fraud, insider trading, and works to prevent companies from misleading investors with false information. The SEC does not insure investments. Investing in companies always carries risk and investors can lose their money. The SEC's role is not to protect investments, but to prevent fraud and make sure investors are given correct information so they can make good investment decisions.

Mortgage and Debt Relief

Terrified of losing their homes and farms, many Americans cut back on spending to make sure they could pay their mortgages. Roosevelt responded by introducing policies to help Americans with their debts. For example, the Home Owners' Loan Corporation (HOLC) bought the mortgages of home owners who were behind in their payments. It then restructured the loans with longer repayment terms and lower interest rates.

The Farm Credit Administration (FCA) helped farmers refinance their mortgages. These loans saved millions of farms from foreclosure. Although the FCA may have slowed economic recovery by making less money available to lend to more efficient businesses, it did help many desperate and impoverished people hold onto their land.

Both the HOLC and the FCA represented a dramatic expansion of the federal government's role in the economy. Never before had the federal government been involved in helping people with their mortgages.

✓ READING PROGRESS CHECK

Summarizing How did the government restore confidence in the banking system?

Farms and Industry

GUIDING QUESTION *How did New Deal legislation try to stabilize agriculture and industry?*

Many of Roosevelt's advisers believed that both farmers and businesses were suffering because prices were too low and production too high. To help the nation's farmers, Congress passed the Agricultural Adjustment Act. The act was based on a simple idea that prices for farm goods were low because farmers grew too much food. Under this act, the government's Agricultural Adjustment Administration (AAA) would pay farmers not to raise certain livestock, grow certain crops, and produce dairy products. Over the next two years, farmers withdrew millions more acres from cultivation and received more than $1 billion in support payments. The program met its goal, although raising food prices in a depression drew harsh criticism. Also, not all farmers benefited. Thousands of tenant farmers, many of them African Americans, lost their jobs and homes when landlords took their fields out of production.

The government turned its attention to manufacturing in June 1933, with the National Industrial Recovery Act (NIRA). Once passed, this law authorized the National Recovery Administration (NRA) to suspend antitrust laws and

The TVA 1940

The Tennessee Valley Authority (TVA) was a New Deal project that produced great results. The TVA built dams to control floods, conserve forestlands, and bring electricity to rural areas.

Today, TVA power facilities include 17,000 miles of transmission lines, 29 hydroelectric dams, 11 fossil-fuel plants, 4 combustion-turbine plants, 3 nuclear power plants, and a pumped-storage facility. These combine to bring power to nearly 8 million people in a seven-state region.

Since 1998, the TVA has been working to reduce air pollution. Projects are designed to cut harmful emissions released into the air. The TVA is committed to developing programs that protect the environment.

Area served by TVA

Major dam

Power plant

GEOGRAPHY CONNECTION

1 THE WORLD IN SPATIAL TERMS *What states other than Tennessee benefited from the TVA projects?* SS.912.A.1.4, SS.912.A.5.11

2 PLACES AND REGIONS *Why do you think the majority of the projects were located in eastern Tennessee?* SS.912.A.5.11

allowed business, labor, and government to cooperate with rules, or codes of fair competition, for each industry. Codes set prices, established minimum wages, shortened workers' hours to create more jobs, permitted unionization, and helped businesses develop industry-wide rules of fair competition. The NRA revived a few industries, but the codes were difficult to administer. Employers disliked that the NRA allowed workers to form unions. They also argued that paying minimum wages forced them to raise prices. After the NRA was instituted, industrial production fell. The NRA was declared unconstitutional in 1935.

✓ READING PROGRESS CHECK

Specifying How was the Agricultural Adjustment Act intended to stabilize the agricultural industry?

Relief Programs

GUIDING QUESTION *How did New Deal programs differ from President Hoover's attempts to combat the Depression?*

Many of President Roosevelt's advisers emphasized tinkering with prices and providing debt relief to solve the Depression. Others maintained that the Depression's **fundamental** cause was low consumption. They thought getting money into the hands of needy individuals would be the fastest remedy. Because neither Roosevelt nor his advisers wanted to give money to the unemployed, they supported work programs for the unemployed.

The decision to create federal work programs marked yet another change in the historical roles of state and federal government. Before the Depression, government relief programs had been rare and, when set up, had always been funded and managed by state and local governments. The first time relief aid had been sent from the federal government to state governments to help them

fundamental being of central importance

fund programs for jobs was during the Hoover administration. But the New Deal went even further, creating several federally managed job programs that bypassed the state governments entirely.

The CCC

The most highly praised New Deal work relief program was the Civilian Conservation Corps (CCC). The CCC offered unemployed young men, 18–25 years old, the opportunity to work under the direction of the forestry service planting trees, fighting forest fires, and building reservoirs. To prevent a repeat of the Dust Bowl, the workers planted a line of more than 200 million trees, known as a Shelter Belt, from north Texas to North Dakota.

The young men lived in camps near their work areas and earned $30 a month, $25 of which was sent directly to their families. The average CCC worker returned home after six to twelve months, better nourished and with greater self-respect. CCC programs also taught more than 40,000 of their recruits to read and write. By the time the CCC closed down in 1942, it had put 3 million young men to work outdoors—including 80,000 Native Americans, who helped reclaim land they had once owned. After a second Bonus Army march on Washington in 1933, Roosevelt added some 250,000 veterans to the CCC as well.

FERA and the PWA

A few weeks after authorizing the CCC, Congress established the Federal Emergency Relief Administration (FERA). Roosevelt chose Harry Hopkins, a former social worker, to run FERA. Initially, it did not create projects for the unemployed. Instead, it gave money to state and local agencies to fund their relief projects.

After meeting with Roosevelt to discuss his new job, Hopkins spent $5 million on relief projects. When critics charged that some of the projects did not make sense in the long run, Hopkins replied, "People don't eat in the long run—they eat every day."

In June 1933, Congress authorized another relief agency, the Public Works Administration (PWA). One-third of the nation's unemployed were in the construction industry. To put them back to work, the PWA began building highways, dams, schools, and other government facilities.

The PWA awarded contracts to construction companies. By insisting that contractors not discriminate against African Americans, the agency broke down some of the racial barriers in the construction trades.

The CWA

By the fall of 1933, neither FERA nor the PWA had reduced unemployment significantly, and Hopkins realized that unless the federal government acted quickly, a huge number of unemployed citizens would be in severe distress once winter began. After Hopkins explained the situation, President Roosevelt authorized him to set up the Civil Works Administration (CWA).

Hiring workers directly, the CWA employed 4 million people, including 300,000 women. The agency built or improved 1,000 airports, 500,000 miles of roads, 40,000 school buildings, and 3,500 playgrounds and parks. The program spent nearly $1 billion in just five months. Although the CWA helped many people get through the winter, President Roosevelt was alarmed by how quickly the agency was spending money, and did not want Americans to get used to the federal government providing them with jobs. Warning that the Civil Works Administration would "become a habit with the country," Roosevelt insisted that it be shut down the following spring. Hopkins summarized what the CWA had accomplished:

This poster for the Civilian Conservation Corps (CCC) expresses the optimism of the New Deal.

▶ **CRITICAL THINKING**

Drawing Conclusions How did the CCC provide opportunities for work, play, study, and health?
HE.912.C.2.7, SS.912.A.1.4, SS.912.A.5.11

A YOUNG MAN'S OPPORTUNITY

CCC

FOR WORK PLAY STUDY & HEALTH

APPLICATIONS TAKEN BY
ILLINOIS EMERGENCY RELIEF COMMISSION
ILLINOIS SELECTING AGENCY

Library of Congress, Prints & Photographs Division [LC-DIG-ppmsca-12896]

This political cartoon from 1933 depicts the efforts made by President Roosevelt to end the Great Depression with his New Deal.

President Roosevelt tries to "prime" the economic pump using taxpayer dollars to get the economy going again.

1 *Analyzing Primary Sources* How does the artist feel about the New Deal? SS.912.A.1.2

2 *Analyzing Visuals* What symbols are used to convey the artist's message? SS.912.A.1.4

The Granger Collection, New York

PRIMARY SOURCE

❝Long after the workers of CWA are dead and gone and these hard times are forgotten, their effort will be remembered by permanent useful works in every county of every state.❞

—from *Spending to Save: The Complete Story of Relief,* 1936

Success of the First New Deal

During his first year in office, Roosevelt convinced Congress to pass an astonishing array of legislation. The First New Deal did not restore prosperity, but it reflected Roosevelt's zeal for action and his willingness to experiment. Banks were reopened, many more people retained their homes and farms, and more people were employed. Perhaps the most important result of the First New Deal was a change in the spirit of the American people. Roosevelt's actions had inspired hope and restored Americans' faith in their nation.

✓ **READING PROGRESS CHECK**

Identifying How did the relief programs help combat the Depression?

─ *Connections to* ─
TODAY

Emergency Economic Stabilization Act

Government relief programs and legislation to help banks and other financial institutions are still enacted today. In 2008, the Emergency Economic Stabilization Act became law. It provided up to $700 billion to the secretary of the treasury to buy mortgages and other troubled assets from the country's banks "to promote financial market stability."

LESSON 1 REVIEW

Reviewing Vocabulary

1. *Defining* How did polio affect President Roosevelt's character and physical abilities? LAFS.1112.SL.2.4

2. *Explaining* What did people fear would happen if the nation went off the gold standard? LAFS.1112.RH.2.4, SS.912.A.5.11

Using Your Notes

3. *Summarizing* Use the notes you completed during the lesson to write a short paragraph summarizing how Roosevelt addressed the major problems during his first three months in office. LAFS.1112.WHST.1.2

Answering the Guiding Questions

4. *Identifying* What qualities make an effective leader? LAFS.1112.WHST.3.9

5. *Making Inferences* Why are the first hundred days so important for a president? SS.912.A.5.11

6. *Describing* Why did Roosevelt broadcast "fireside chats"? SS.912.A.5.11

7. *Analyzing* How did New Deal legislation try to stabilize agriculture and industry? LAFS.1112.WHST.3.9, SS.912.A.5.11

8. *Contrasting* How did New Deal programs differ from President Hoover's attempts to combat the Depression? SS.912.A.5.11

Writing Activity

9. ARGUMENT If you were an adviser to President Roosevelt, what ideas would you suggest to end the Depression? Provide an argument for why your ideas would work. LAFS.1112.WHST.1.1, LAFS.1112.WHST.4.10, SS.912.A.5.11

LAFS.1112.RH.1.1, LAFS.1112.RH.1.2, LAFS.1112.RH.1.3, LAFS.1112.RH.2.5, LAFS.1112.SL.1.3, SS.912.A.1.1, SS.912.A.1.6, SS.912.A.5.11

The First New Deal

When FDR took office in 1933, the economy had been getting worse for more than three years. During the first one hundred days of his presidency, he oversaw 15 major pieces of legislation that attempted to revive the nation's economy and provide relief to the unemployed. Never before had the federal government intervened so directly in the economy. Key to stopping the economic downslide was FDR's ability to inspire confidence that the nation's economic problems could be solved.

INAUGURAL ADDRESS, 1933

"I am certain that my fellow Americans expect that on my **induction** into the Presidency I will address them with a candor and a decision which the present situation of our nation impels. This is preeminently the time to speak the truth, the whole truth, frankly and boldly. . . .

So, first of all, let me assert my firm belief that the only thing we have to fear is fear itself—nameless, unreasoning, unjustified terror which paralyzes needed efforts to convert retreat into advance. In every dark hour of our national life a leadership of frankness and **vigor** has met with that understanding and support of the people themselves which is essential to victory. I am convinced that you will again give that support to leadership in these critical days. . . .

This Nation asks for action, and action now.

Our greatest primary task is to put people to work. This is no unsolvable problem if we face it wisely and courageously. It can be accomplished in part by direct recruiting by the Government itself, treating the task as we would treat the emergency of a war, but at the same time, through this employment, accomplishing greatly needed projects to simulate and reorganize the use of our natural resources."

—President Franklin D. Roosevelt, first inaugural address, delivered March 4, 1933, excerpted from *The Public Papers and Addresses of Franklin D. Roosevelt*

VOCABULARY

induction
process of placing someone in office

vigor
strength or force

revival
a renewal, coming alive again

framework
a basic supporting part or structure

shiftless
lacking in ambition, lazy

laissez-faire
idea that government should not regulate the economy

ORAL HISTORY INTERVIEW

"During the whole '33 one-hundred days, Congress, people didn't know what was going on, the public couldn't understand these things that were being passed so fast. They knew something was happening, something good for them. They began investing and working and hoping again. . . .

The bank rescue of 1933 was probably the turning point of the Depression. When people were able to survive the shock of having all the banks closed, and then see the banks open up . . . there began to be confidence. The public helped itself, after it got confidence. It marked the **revival** of hope. . . . A Depression is much like a run on a bank. It's a crisis of confidence."

—Raymond Moley, original member of FDR's "Brains Trust"

ORAL HISTORY INTERVIEW

"What Roosevelt and the New Deal did was to turn around and face the realities. . . . A hundred years from now, when historians look back on it, they will say a big corner was turned. People agreed that old things didn't

PHOTO: ©Underwood & Underwood/Bettmann/Corbis; TEXT: (r)Hard Times (1986) by Studs Terkel. Used by Permission. All rights reserved work. What ran through the whole New Deal was finding a way to make things work.

Before that, Hoover would loan money to farmers to keep their mules alive, but wouldn't loan money to keep their children alive. This was perfectly right within the **framework** of classical thinking. If an individual couldn't get enough to eat, it was because he wasn't on the ball. It was his responsibility. The New Deal said: Anybody who is unemployed isn't necessarily unemployed because he's **shiftless**. . . .

Great quantities [of letters] came pouring in, letters from everywhere. . . They were proposals from people, solutions to all sorts of problems. Some of them crackpot, some of them quite good. Everybody had suggestions. The country was aware, as it never was before, that it was on the edge of something. . .

Laissez-faire as such certainly did not come to an end with the New Deal. We still have a tremendous amount of freedom of decision making in the individual corporate enterprise. The new element is the government's positive responsibility for making our economy run."

—Economist Gardiner C. Means, economic adviser in the Roosevelt administration

PHOTO: Library of Congress, Prints & Photographs Division [LC–USZ62-13060 j]; TEXT: (t) Hard Times (1986) by Studs Terkel. Used by permission. All rights reserved. (b) From The Challenge to Liberty (1936) by Herbert Hoover, published by Charles Scribner's Sons © 7736, 3362 by permission of the Herbert Hoover Foundation.

"Even if the government conduct of business could give us the maximum of efficiency instead of least efficiency, it would be purchased at the cost of freedom. It would increase rather than decrease abuse and corruption, stifle initiative and invention, undermine the development of leadership, cripple the mental and spiritual energies of our people and the forces which make progress. . . .

The nation seeks for solution of its many difficulties. These solutions can come alone through the constructive forces from the system built upon Liberty. They cannot be achieved by the destructive forces of Regimentation. The purification of Liberty from abuses, the restoration of confidence in the rights of men, the release of the dynamic forces of initiative and enterprise are alone the methods by which these solutions can be found and the purpose of American life assured. . . ."

—Former president Herbert Hoover in his book, *The Challenge to Liberty* (1934)

◄ *A crowd confronts police at the locked gates of a bank shortly after Roosevelt's inauguration*

DBQ Analyzing Historical Documents

1. **Acquiring Information** What is the "present situation" that President Roosevelt references in the first paragraph? What does President Roosevelt claim is the "greatest primary task"?

2. **Evaluating Language and Context** What words and phrases does Roosevelt use in this speech to build confidence and trust, and to convince people help is coming and that they do not have to be afraid anymore?

3. **Finding the Main Idea** What appears to be the main idea of Hoover's book based on this excerpt?

4. **Analyzing Historical Questions** Critics of Roosevelt at the time and later suggested he was undermining the free enterprise system. What do Gardiner Means' comments suggest was the administration's viewpoint on free enterprise? What does he say is different from a laissez-faire approach?

5. **Answering Historical Questions** Look at the photo of the bank holiday. What do you think was the effect when people arrived at the bank to find they could not get their money out? Why does Raymond Moley think their reaction was a good thing in the long run?

6. **Corroborating** Based on Roosevelt's speech, what does he appear to think is the biggest obstacle facing his administration? How do the two interviews corroborate what Roosevelt said in his inaugural speech?

7. **Evaluating Frame of Reference** What are Herbert Hoover's basic assumptions about the government and the economy? How does his frame of reference affect your opinion about the validity of his ideas? Why else might you question the validity of his arguments?

LESSON 2
The Second New Deal

ESSENTIAL QUESTIONS
• Can government fix the economy?
• Is government responsible for the economic well-being of its citizens?

READING HELPDESK

Academic Vocabulary

• benefit   • thereby
• finance

Content Vocabulary

• deficit spending
• binding arbitration
• sit-down strike

TAKING NOTES

Key Ideas and Details

Organizing As you read about President Roosevelt's Second New Deal, complete a graphic organizer similar to the one below by filling in his main legislative successes during this period.
LAFS.1112.RH.3.7, SS.912.A.5.11

Legislation	Provisions

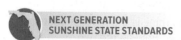

**NEXT GENERATION
SUNSHINE STATE STANDARDS**

LAFS.1112.RH.2.4: Determine the meaning of words and phrases as they are used in a text, including analyzing how an author uses and refines the meaning of a key term over the course of a text (e.g., how Madison defines faction in Federalist No. 10).

LAFS.1112.RH.3.7: Integrate and evaluate multiple sources of information presented in diverse formats and media (e.g., visually, quantitatively, as well as in words) in order to address a question or solve a problem.

Continued on page 321

320

IT MATTERS BECAUSE

Criticism of the New Deal led President Roosevelt to introduce new legislation in 1935. These laws created the Works Progress Administration, the National Labor Relations Board, and the Social Security Administration.

Launching the Second New Deal

GUIDING QUESTION *Why did President Roosevelt decide to introduce new legislation to fight the Depression?*

President Roosevelt was tremendously popular during his first two years in office, but opposition to his policies began to grow. New Deal programs had created more than 2 million new jobs. More than 10 million workers remained unemployed, however, and the nation's total income was about half of what it had been in 1929.

Criticism From Right and Left

Roosevelt faced hostility from both the political right and the left. The right wing had long believed that the New Deal regulated business too tightly. Opponents thought that it gave the federal government too much power over the states. By late 1934, the right wing increased its opposition as Roosevelt started **deficit spending**, abandoning a balanced budget and borrowing money to pay for his programs. Many business leaders became alarmed at the growing deficit.

Some on the left, however, believed that the New Deal had not gone far enough. They wanted even more economic intervention to shift wealth from the rich to middle-income and poor Americans. One outspoken critic was Huey Long. As governor of Louisiana, Long had championed the poor. He improved schools, colleges, and hospitals, and built roads and bridges. These **benefits** made him popular, and he built a powerful but corrupt political machine. In 1930, Long was elected to the U.S. Senate. In 1934, he established the Share Our Wealth Society to "pull down these huge piles of gold until there shall be a real job, not a little old sow-belly, black-eyed pea job but a real spending money, beef-steak and gravy. . . Ford in the garage . . . red, white, and blue job for every man." Long planned to run for president in 1936.

Roosevelt also faced a challenge from Catholic priest and popular radio host Father Charles Coughlin. Once an ardent New Deal supporter, the Detroit resident had grown impatient with its moderate reforms. He called for inflating the currency and nationalizing the banking system. In 1934, he organized the National Union for Social Justice, which some Democrats feared would become a new political party.

A third challenge came from California physician Francis Townsend. He proposed that the federal government pay citizens over age 60 a pension of $200 a month. Recipients would have to retire and spend the entire check each month. Townsend believed that the plan would increase spending and free up jobs for the unemployed. His proposal attracted millions of supporters, especially older Americans, who mobilized as a political force for the first time. Together, Long, Coughlin, and Townsend had supporters around the country. Roosevelt faced the possibility of a coalition that would prevent his reelection.

The WPA

In 1935, Roosevelt launched a series of programs, now known as the Second New Deal, to generate greater economic recovery. Among these new programs was the Works Progress Administration (WPA), the New Deal's largest public works program. Between 1935 and 1941, the WPA employed 8.5 million workers and spent $11 billion to construct about 650,000 miles of roadways, 125,000 public buildings, 853 airports, more than 124,000 bridges, and more than 8,000 parks. One WPA program, called Federal Project Number One, **financed** artists, musicians, theater people, and writers. Artists created murals and sculptures for public buildings; musicians set up orchestras and smaller musical groups; playwrights, actors, and directors wrote and staged plays; and writers recorded the stories of those who had once been enslaved and others whose voices had not often been heard.

The Supreme Court's Role

In May 1935, in *Schechter Poultry Corporation* v. *United States,* the Supreme Court struck down the authority of the National Recovery Administration. The Schechter brothers had been convicted of violating the NRA's poultry code. The Court ruled that the Constitution did not allow Congress to delegate its legislative powers to the executive branch, and therefore the NRA's codes were unconstitutional. Roosevelt worried that the ruling suggested the Supreme Court could strike down the rest of the New Deal.

Roosevelt knew he needed a new series of programs to keep voters' support. He called congressional leaders to a White House conference and thundered that Congress could not go home until it passed his new bills. That summer, Congress passed Roosevelt's programs.

✓ READING PROGRESS CHECK

Synthesizing What factors encouraged Roosevelt to introduce the Second New Deal?

©Bettmann/Corbis

NEXT GENERATION
SUNSHINE STATE STANDARDS

Continued from page 320

LAFS.1112.WHST.1.1: Write arguments focused on discipline-specific content.

LAFS.1112.WHST.4.10: Write routinely over extended time frames (time for reflection and revision) and shorter time frames (a single sitting or a day or two) for a range of discipline-specific tasks, purposes, and audiences.

SS.912.A.1.2: Utilize a variety of primary and secondary sources to identify author, historical significance, audience, and authenticity to understand a historical period.

SS.912.A.1.4: Analyze how images, symbols, objects, cartoons, graphs, charts, maps, and artwork may be used to interpret the significance of time periods and events from the past.

SS.912.A.5.11: Examine causes, course, and consequences of the Great Depression and the New Deal.

deficit spending
government practice of spending borrowed money rather than raising taxes, usually in an attempt to boost the economy

benefit something that promotes well-being or is a useful aid

finance to provide money for a project

Some, including Dr. Francis Townsend, criticized the New Deal for not going far enough to relieve the economic troubles of poor and middle-class Americans.

▶ CRITICAL THINKING
Comparing and Contrasting
How did the political left's criticisms of the New Deal differ from those of the political right?
SS.912.A.1.4, SS.912.A.5.11

THE TOWNSEND PLAN
$200. PER MONTH FOR THOSE OVER 60 YRS OF AGE — THE SPENDING OF THIS MONEY WILL PUT THE CONTROL OF CREDIT IN THE HANDS OF THE PEOPLE — PREVENTING ECONOMIC CHAOS

The New Deal

Some opponents of the New Deal believed it was undermining American society. Others thought it did not go far enough.

❝It is not easy for me to stand up here tonight and talk to the American people against the Democratic Administration. This is not easy . . . during my whole public life I put patriotism above partisanship. And when I see danger, I say danger— What are these dangers that I see? The first is the arraignment of class against class . . . In my time I have met some good and bad industrialists. I have met some good and bad financiers, but I have also met some good and bad laborers, and this I know, that permanent prosperity is dependent upon both capital and labor alike.

And I also know that there can be no permanent prosperity in this country until industry is able to employ labor, and there certainly can be no permanent recovery upon any governmental theory of 'soak the rich' or 'soak the poor.'❞

—"Betrayal of the Democratic Party," Alfred E. Smith, keynote address to the American Liberty League, 1936

Al Smith was elected governor of New York four times. He was the Democratic Party's nominee for president in 1928.

❝So now, ladies and gentlemen, we come to that plan of mine . . . for the redistribution of wealth and for guaranteeing comforts and conveniences to all humanity out of this abundance in our country. I hope none will be horror-stricken when they hear me say that we must limit the size of the big man's fortune in order to guarantee a minimum of fortune, life and comfort to the little man; but, if you are, think first that such is the declaration on which Roosevelt rode into the nomination and election of President. While my urgings are declared by some to be the average of a madman . . . if you will listen to me you will find that it is restating the laws handed down by God to man; you will find that it was the exact provision of the contract and law of the Pilgrim Fathers who landed at Plymouth in 1620.❞

—from "Share Our Wealth," Huey Long radio address, 1935

Huey Long was a United States senator from Louisiana.

DBQ Document Based Questions

1 *Comparing and Contrasting* In what ways are Huey Long's and Alfred E. Smith's concerns exactly the opposite of each other? LAFS.1112.RH.2.6, LAFS.1112.SL.1.3, SS.912.A.1.2, SS.912.A.5.11

2 *Analyzing* Do you agree with Long or with Smith? Or do you disagree with them both? Explain your opinion. LAFS.1112.RH.2.6, LAFS.1112.SL.1.3, SS.912.A.1.2, SS.912.A.5.11

Reforms for Workers and Senior Citizens

GUIDING QUESTION *How did the Wagner Act and the Social Security Act affect Americans?*

When the Supreme Court struck down the NRA, it also invalidated the section of the NIRA that gave workers the right to organize. Democrats knew that the working-class vote was key to winning reelection in 1936. They also believed that unions could help end the Depression because high union wages would give workers more money to spend, **thereby** boosting the economy. Opponents disagreed, arguing that high wages forced companies to charge higher prices and hire fewer people. Despite these concerns, Congress pushed ahead with new labor legislation.

The Wagner Act

In July 1935, Congress passed the National Labor Relations Act, also called the Wagner Act. This act guaranteed workers the right to unionize and bargain collectively. It also established the National Labor Relations Board (NLRB), which organized factory elections by secret ballot to determine whether workers wanted a union. The NLRB could also investigate employers' actions and stop unfair practices. The Wagner Act also set up a process called **binding arbitration,** whereby dissatisfied union members took their complaints to a neutral party who would listen to both sides and decide on the issues.

(l)The Granger Collection, New York; (r)Library of Congress, Prints & Photographs Division [LC-DIG-hec-38169]

The Wagner Act led to a burst of labor activity. In 1935 John L. Lewis, leader of the United Mine Workers, helped form the Committee for Industrial Organization (CIO), which set out to organize unions that included all workers, skilled and unskilled, in a particular industry. First, it focused on the automobile and steel industries, two of the largest industries in which workers were not yet unionized. Organizers used new tactics to get employers to recognize the unions. For example, during **sit-down strikes,** employees stopped work inside the factory and refused to leave. This technique prevented management from sending in replacement workers. It was a common CIO tactic for several years.

In late December 1936, the United Auto Workers (UAW), a CIO union, began a sit-down strike at General Motor's plant in Flint, Michigan. Family, friends, and others passed food and other provisions to them through windows. Violence broke out when police launched a tear gas assault on strikers, wounding 13, but the strike held. On February 11, 1937, General Motors recognized the UAW as its employees' sole bargaining agent. The UAW became one of the most powerful unions in the United States.

U.S. Steel, the nation's largest steel producer and a long-standing opponent of unionizing, decided it did not want a repeat of GM's experience. In March 1937, the company recognized the CIO's steelworkers union. Smaller steel producers did not follow suit and suffered bitter strikes. By 1941, however, the steelworkers union had won contracts throughout the industry.

In the late 1930s, employees in other industries worked hard to gain union recognition from their employers. Union membership tripled from roughly 3 million in 1933 to about 9 million in 1939. In 1938, the CIO changed its name to the Congress of Industrial Organizations and became a federation of industrial unions.

Social Security

After passing the Wagner Act, Congress began work on one of the United States's most important pieces of legislation. This was the Social Security Act, which provided some financial security for older Americans, unemployed workers, and others. Roosevelt and his advisers viewed the bill primarily as an insurance measure. Workers earned the right to receive benefits because they paid special taxes to the federal government, just as they paid premiums in buying a life insurance policy. The legislation also provided modest welfare payments to others in need, including people with disabilities and poor mothers with dependent children.

Some critics did not like the fact that the money came from payroll taxes imposed on workers and employers, but to Roosevelt these taxes were crucial:

©Bettmann/Corbis

Analyzing
PRIMARY SOURCES

The GM Strike

❝Beds were made up on the floor of each car, the seats being removed if necessary. . . . I could not see—and I looked for it carefully—the slightest damage done anywhere to the General Motors Corporation. The nearly completed car bodies, for example, were as clean as they would be in the salesroom, their glass and metal shining.❞

—Bruce Bliven, from "Sitting Down in Flint," the *New Republic*, January 27, 1937

DBQ **DRAWING CONCLUSIONS** How do the strikers seem to have acted during the strike?
SS.912.A.1.2, SS.912.A.5.11

thereby because of that

binding arbitration
process in which a neutral party hears arguments from two opposing sides and makes a decision that both must accept

sit-down strike
method of boycotting work by sitting down at work and refusing to leave the establishment

Sit-down strikers at the GM Fisher body plant in Flint, Michigan, took over the plant in late December 1936. Their action led to a national strike that lasted until February 11, 1937.

▶ CRITICAL THINKING
Analyzing Primary Sources
What did the atmosphere within the GM Fisher plant seem to be during the strike? SS.912.A.1.2, SS.912.A.5.11

The Social Security Act provided a small income to millions of Americans who were unable to work through no fault of their own.

▶ CRITICAL THINKING
Predicting Consequences How might Social Security have changed Americans' sense of personal economic security?
SS.912.A.5.11

AP Images

❝We put those payroll contributions there so as to give the contributors a legal, moral, and political right to collect their pensions and their unemployment benefits. With those taxes in there, no . . . politician can ever scrap my social security program.❞

—quoted in "Memorandum on Conference with FDR Concerning Social Security Taxation," 1941

What Roosevelt did not anticipate was that Congress would later borrow from the Social Security fund to pay for other programs without raising payroll taxes.

The core of Social Security was the monthly retirement benefit, which people collected when they stopped working at age 65. Unemployment insurance supplied a temporary income to workers who had lost their jobs.

Social Security continues to be a part of American life today. When Americans find themselves unemployed, they can draw on their unemployment insurance from Social Security for many weeks while they look for a new job. In addition, of course, Americans who have contributed to the Social Security system are eligible for a pension benefit when they retire. In 2013, the government paid out over $1.3 trillion in Social Security payments, approximately 37 percent of all federal government spending that year.

Social Security dramatically changed the role of the federal government. It was the first example of what came to be called "entitlement" programs. An entitlement program is not simply a form of welfare or relief. It is a payment from the government that Americans are entitled to receive, in part because they have paid into the system regularly with deductions from their paychecks, and in part because the law imposes a requirement on the government to make the payments.

Social Security was controversial at the time it was passed, and remains a source of political debate today, in part because even though Americans are entitled to their Social Security payments, the federal government has borrowed against the Social Security fund in the past, and is now forced to borrow more money to pay its Social Security obligations. With the federal government deeply in debt and continuing to use deficit spending in almost every budget, concerns have arisen as to whether Social Security can remain solvent and the U.S. government will be able to meet its obligations. Social Security established the principle that the federal government should be responsible for those who, through no fault of their own, are unable to work.

✓ READING PROGRESS CHECK

Evaluating What were some benefits of the Wagner Act and the Social Security Act for the American public?

LESSON 2 REVIEW

Vocabulary Review
1. *Defining* What happens when the federal government starts a policy of deficit spending? LAFS.1112.RH.2.4

2. *Explaining* What was one unique feature of sit-down strikes? LAFS.1112.RH.2.4, SS.912.A.5.11

Using Your Notes
3. *Summarizing* Review the notes that you completed during the lesson, and then summarize the provisions of Roosevelt's major legislation of the Second New Deal. LAFS.1112.SL.2.4, SS.912.A.5.11

Answering the Guiding Questions
4. *Identifying Cause and Effect* Why did President Roosevelt decide to introduce new legislation to fight the Depression? SS.912.A.5.11

5. *Analyzing* How did the Wagner Act and the Social Security Act affect Americans? LAFS.1112.WHST.3.9, SS.912.A.5.11

Writing Activity
6. ARGUMENT Choose a person or group who criticized the New Deal. Write an editorial to the local newspaper expressing why readers should be in support of, or in opposition to, that viewpoint. LAFS.1112.WHST.1.1, LAFS.1112.WHST.4.10

LESSON 3
The New Deal Coalition

ESSENTIAL QUESTIONS
- Can government fix the economy?
- Is government responsible for the economic well-being of its citizens?

READING HELPDESK

Academic Vocabulary
- recovery • mediate

Content Vocabulary
- court-packing
- broker state
- safety net

TAKING NOTES

Key Ideas and Details

Outlining As you read, create an outline similar to the one below.
LAFS.1112.RH.3.7

> The New Deal Coalition
> I. Roosevelt's Second Term
>   A.
>   B.
>   C.

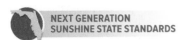

**NEXT GENERATION
SUNSHINE STATE STANDARDS**

LAFS.1112.RH.2.4: Determine the meaning of words and phrases as they are used in a text, including analyzing how an author uses and refines the meaning of a key term over the course of a text (e.g., how Madison defines faction in Federalist No. 10).

LAFS.1112.RH.3.7: Integrate and evaluate multiple sources of information presented in diverse formats and media (e.g., visually, quantitatively, as well as in words) in order to address a question or solve a problem.

LAFS.1112.WHST.1.1: Write arguments focused on discipline-specific content.

LAFS.1112.WHST.4.10: Write routinely over extended time frames (time for reflection and revision) and shorter time frames (a single sitting or a day or two) for a range of discipline-specific tasks, purposes, and audiences.

Continued on page 326

IT MATTERS BECAUSE

President Roosevelt was reelected in a landslide in 1936. Early in his second term, however, his court-packing plan and a new recession hurt him politically. The Fair Labor Standards Act, the last significant piece of New Deal legislation, provided new protections for workers.

Roosevelt's Second Term

GUIDING QUESTION *Why do you think Roosevelt easily won reelection?*

In 1936, millions of voters owed their jobs, mortgages, and bank accounts to the New Deal. Many African Americans, who had reliably voted Republican since Reconstruction, switched their allegiance to the Democratic Party. Women and African Americans had made modest gains, thanks to the support of Eleanor Roosevelt, who toured the country and recounted her experiences to her husband. She persuaded him to address some of their problems in his New Deal programs. A Democratic Party coalition emerged, including not just the white South, but also African Americans, farmers, workers, immigrants, women, progressives, and intellectuals.

The Election of 1936

The Republicans nominated Kansas governor Alfred Landon as their presidential challenger. He wanted to "free the spirit of American enterprise," but could not convince most voters that change was needed. Roosevelt won more than 60 percent of the popular vote.

The Court-Packing Plan

Although the New Deal was popular, the Supreme Court saw things differently. In January 1936, it declared the Agricultural Adjustment Act unconstitutional. Cases pending on Social Security and the Wagner Act meant that the Court might strike down other New Deal programs.

Roosevelt was furious. After his reelection, he tried to change the Court's political balance. He sent Congress a bill that would increase the number of justices and allow the president to appoint an additional

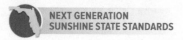

NEXT GENERATION SUNSHINE STATE STANDARDS

Continued from page 325

SS.912.A.1.2: Utilize a variety of primary and secondary sources to identify author, historical significance, audience, and authenticity to understand a historical period.

SS.912.A.1.4: Analyze how images, symbols, objects, cartoons, graphs, charts, maps, and artwork may be used to interpret the significance of time periods and events from the past.

SS.912.A.5.10: Analyze support for and resistance to civil rights for women, African Americans, Native Americans, and other minorities.

SS.912.A.5.11: Examine causes, course, and consequences of the Great Depression and the New Deal.

court-packing the act of a leader to change the political balance of power in a nation's judiciary system by appointing judges who will rule in favor of his or her policies

recovery an economic upturn, as after a depression

Mary McLeod Bethune, shown with Eleanor Roosevelt, became the first African American woman to head a federal agency.

▶ **CRITICAL THINKING**
Comparing and Contrasting
What mood does the photograph convey? **SS.912.A.1.2**

justice if a sitting justice who had served 10 years did not retire within six months of reaching age 70. The bill, if passed, would have allowed Roosevelt to appoint up to six new justices.

The **court-packing** plan, as it was called, was a major political mistake. Many Southern Democrats feared new justices would overturn segregation. African American leaders worried future justices might oppose civil rights. Many Americans thought the plan gave the president too much power. The Court appeared to back down, narrowly upholding the constitutionality of both the Wagner Act and the Social Security Act. Soon after, a conservative justice's resignation allowed Roosevelt to appoint a justice who supported the New Deal.

Although the bill was quietly killed and Roosevelt achieved his goal of changing the Court's view of the New Deal, the court-packing plan hurt his reputation. Moreover, it caused conservative Democrats to work with Republicans to block any further New Deal proposals.

The Recession of 1937

Roosevelt's problems continued. In early 1937, the economy seemed to be on the verge of **recovery**. Industrial output was almost back to pre-Depression levels, and many people believed the worst was over. Concerned about rising debt, Roosevelt ordered the WPA and the PWA to be cut significantly. Unfortunately, he cut spending just as the first Social Security payroll taxes took $2 billion out of the economy. By the end of 1937, about two million people were out of work.

A debate over the value of government spending arose within the administration. The leaders of the WPA and the PWA cited a new economic theory called Keynesianism (KAYN • zee • uh • nih • zuhm), which held that government should spend heavily in a recession to jump-start the economy.

At first, Roosevelt was reluctant to begin deficit spending again. Some critics believed the recession proved the public was becoming too dependent on government spending. But in early 1938, with no recovery in sight, Roosevelt asked Congress for $3.75 billion for the PWA, the WPA, and other programs.

☑ **READING PROGRESS CHECK**

Determining Cause and Effect What factors helped Roosevelt win a landslide victory in 1936?

The New Deal Ends

GUIDING QUESTION *What impact has New Deal legislation had on federal and state governments?*

In his second Inaugural Address, Roosevelt pointed out that despite progress in climbing out of the Depression, many Americans were still poor:

PRIMARY SOURCE

❝I see one-third of a nation ill-housed, ill-clad, ill-nourished. . . . The test of our progress is not whether we add more to the abundance of those who have much; it is whether we provide enough for those who have too little.❞

—from *The Public Papers and Addresses of Franklin D. Roosevelt: The Constitution Prevails*, 1937

The Last New Deal Reforms

One of the president's goals for his second term was to provide better housing for the nation's poor. Eleanor Roosevelt, who had toured poverty-stricken Appalachia and the rural South, strongly urged the president to do something. Roosevelt responded with the passage of the National Housing Act, which established the United States Housing Authority. This organization received $500 million to subsidize loans to builders willing to construct low-cost housing.

©Bettmann/Corbis

Roosevelt also sought to help the nation's tenant farmers. About 150,000 white and 195,000 African American tenant farmers were expelled from farms when landlords took their land out of production under the AAA. To stop this trend, Congress created the Farm Security Administration to give loans to tenants so they could purchase farms.

The last major piece of New Deal reform was the Fair Labor Standards Act, which abolished child labor, limited the workweek to 44 hours for most workers, and set the first federal minimum wage at 25 cents an hour. The recession of 1937 enabled Republicans to win seats in Congress in the midterm elections of 1938. Together with conservative Southern Democrats, they began blocking further New Deal legislation. By 1939, the New Deal era had come to an end.

The New Deal's Legacy

The onset of the Great Depression in 1929 was a major turning point in American history. The economic crisis of the Depression led to the New Deal, which fundamentally changed the relationship between the American people and the federal government. As a result of the Depression, the power of the federal government to intervene in the economy significantly increased.

At the same time, the historical role of state governments and their relationship to the federal government began to shift as well. Increasingly the federal government took on a regulatory role that had previously been left to state governments. In addition, state governments began to look to the federal government as a source of additional funds to help them afford state programs and provide aid in difficult economic circumstances.

The New Deal did not end the Depression, but it did give many Americans a stronger sense of security and stability. As a whole, the New Deal tended to balance competing economic interests. Supreme Court decisions in 1937 and 1942 further increased federal power over the economy and allowed it to **mediate** between competing groups.

In taking on this mediating role, the New Deal established what some have called the **broker state,** in which the government works out conflicts among different interests. This broker role has continued under the administrations of both parties ever since. The New Deal also brought about a new public attitude toward government. Roosevelt's programs had succeeded in creating a **safety net**—safeguards and relief programs that protected people against economic disaster. Throughout the hard times of the Depression, most Americans maintained a surprising degree of confidence in the American system.

 READING PROGRESS CHECK

Evaluating How did the New Deal change how government worked?

Florida CONNECTION

Marjorie Kinnan Rawlings (1896–1953)

Marjorie Kinnan Rawlings published a story in the *Washington Post* in 1912 and won a national magazine contest when she was 16. Rawlings attended the University of Wisconsin and worked as a newspaper reporter, but truly found her voice as a writer after she bought an orange grove in Florida. Most of her novels deal with the people of Florida and the challenges they face, celebrating their regional humor and capturing their dialect. Her most famous book, *The Yearling*, received the Pulitzer Prize in 1939.
SS.912.A.5.12

mediate to attempt to resolve conflict between hostile people and groups

broker state role of government to work out conflicts among competing interest groups

safety net something that provides security against misfortune; specifically, government relief programs intended to protect against economic disaster

---

LESSON 3 REVIEW

Reviewing Vocabulary

1. *Stating* What was Roosevelt's court-packing plan?
LAFS.1112.RH.2.4, SS.912.A.5.11
2. *Defining* What is a broker state? LAFS.1112.RH.2.4
3. *Explaining* How does a safety net work? LAFS.1112.RH.2.4

Using Your Notes

4. *Summarizing* Review the notes that you completed during the lesson. What were the key events of the final years of the New Deal? SS.912.A.5.11

Answering the Guiding Questions

5. *Synthesizing* Why do you think Roosevelt easily won reelection?
LAFS.1112.WHST.3.9
6. *Evaluating* What impact has New Deal legislation had on federal and state governments? SS.912.A.5.11

Writing Activity

7. ARGUMENT Do you think that Roosevelt's solution to the 1937 recession was the best one? Write a short essay in which you give your opinions about Roosevelt's actions and describe your own ideas to ease the crisis. LAFS.1112.WHST.1.1, LAFS.1112.WHST.4.10

STUDY GUIDE

THE FIRST NEW DEAL
LESSON 1

THE FIRST NEW DEAL	
Aims	**Result**
Help banking industry	Securities Act of 1933
	The Glass-Steagall Act
Support farmers	Farm Credit Administration
	Agricultural Adjustment Act
Create more jobs	National Industrial Recovery Act
	Civilian Conservation Corps
	Civil Works Administration
Provide funding to companies and individuals	Federal Emergency Relief Administration
	Public Works Administration
Aid home owners	Home Owners' Loan Corporation

THE SECOND NEW DEAL
LESSON 2

THE SECOND NEW DEAL	
Aims	**Result**
Create more jobs	Works Progress Administration
Provide funding to companies and individuals	Social Security Act
Reform labor standards	The Wagner Act The Fair Labor Standards Act of 1938

THE NEW DEAL COALITION
LESSON 3

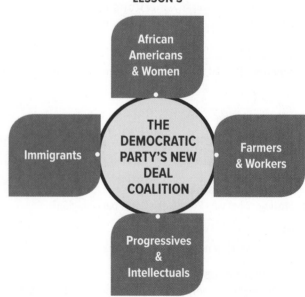

THE DEMOCRATIC PARTY'S NEW DEAL COALITION

- African Americans & Women
- Immigrants
- Farmers & Workers
- Progressives & Intellectuals

Directions: On a separate sheet of paper, answer the questions below. Make sure you read carefully and answer all parts to the question.

Lesson Review

Lesson 1

1 *Identifying Central Issues* What were the Hundred Days? SS.912.A.5.11

2 *Describing* Explain why Roosevelt asked Congress to abandon the gold standard, and then later restored it. How did these decisions reflect his administration's monetary policy? SS.912.A.5.11

3 *Identifying* Describe the different perspectives on government regulation of business among Roosevelt's advisors. Why did Roosevelt assemble an administration made up of so many people with differing viewpoints? SS.912.A.5.11

Lesson 2

4 *Summarizing* What did Roosevelt's opponents think about the work and policies established in the first two years of his presidency? SS.912.A.5.11

5 *Identifying Cause and Effect* Why was the Wagner Act enacted? SS.912.A.5.11

6 *Summarizing* Explain the idea of the Social Security system, why it was passed, and how it is supposed to function. SS.912.A.5.11

Lesson 3

7 *Evaluating* Why was the court-packing plan so controversial? Explain the implications of the plan on the relationship between the legislative, executive, and judicial branches of government. SS.912.A.5.11

8 *Identifying* What decisions by Roosevelt may have contributed to the Recession of 1937? SS.912.A.5.11

9 *Explaining* Think about all of the changes that occurred during the New Deal, and then explain why 1929 and the onset of the Great Depression is a turning point in American history. SS.912.A.5.11

Exploring the Essential Questions

10 *Presenting a Point of View* Imagine you are running for Congress during the Great Depression and that you are preparing for a political debate with a member of the opposing party. Prepare your opening statement by answering the question: "Is government responsible for the economic well-being of its citizens?" Revise your statement as needed to make sure you are communicating effectively with your audience. LAFS.1112.SL.2.4, LAFS.1112.WHST.2.4, LAFS.1112.WHST.2.5, LAFS.1112.WHST.4.10, SS.912.A.5.11

Critical Thinking

11 *Drawing Conclusions* What conclusions can you draw about the decision to establish the Works Progress Administration (WPA)? What were some of the long-term effects of WPA projects? SS.912.A.5.11

12 *Evaluating* What constitutional issues were raised by the federal government's efforts to end the Great Depression? Describe how the Supreme Court responded to the New Deal. Did its rulings reflect a strict construction of the Constitution? Explain why or why not. SS.912.A.5.11

13 *Identifying* What financial protection do Americans have today because of the Federal Deposit Insurance Corporation that they did not have before Roosevelt's New Deal Program? Why is this protection significant? SS.912.A.5.11

21st Century Skills

14 *Explaining Continuity and Change* Why did large numbers of African Americans shift from supporting the traditional support of the Republican Party and begin voting for Roosevelt and other Democratic candidates? SS.912.A.5.11

Need Extra Help?

If You've Missed Question	**1**	**2**	**3**	**4**	**5**	**6**	**7**	**8**	**9**	**10**	**11**	**12**	**13**	**14**
Go To Lesson	1	1	1	2	2	2	3	3	3	1, 2	2	2	1	3

15 *Applying Chronology and Sequencing* Using the library, or online sources, research the programs created during the first 100 days of Roosevelt's administration. Create a time line of the programs. List each of the major acts and programs passed by Congress in order and identify the date they passed. Then use the time line to explain which groups of people were targeted for help in the first 100 days of the administration. LAFS.1112.RH.3.9, LAFS.1112.WHST.3.7, SS.912.A.1.3, SS.912.A.5.11

DBQ Analyzing Primary Sources

Read the excerpt from Eleanor Roosevelt's autobiography, and then answer the questions that follow.

PRIMARY SOURCE

"This trip to the mining areas was my first contact with the work being done by the Quakers. I liked the idea of trying to put people to work to help themselves. The men were started on projects and taught to use their abilities to develop new skills. The women were encouraged to revive any household arts they might once have known but which they had neglected in the drab life of the mining village. This was only the first of many trips into the mining districts but it was the one that started the homestead idea [placing people in communities with homes, farms, and jobs]. . . . It was all experimental work, but it was designed to get people off relief, to put them to work building their own homes and to give them enough land to start growing food."

—*The Autobiography of Eleanor Roosevelt*, 1937

16 *Drawing Conclusions* According to Eleanor Roosevelt, what were benefits of the Quaker project and the homestead idea? LAFS.1112.RH.3.8, LAFS.1112.RH.4.10

17 *Making Connections* What does this say about Eleanor Roosevelt's views on government aid to the poor? LAFS.1112.RH.1.2, LAFS.1112.RH.3.8, LAFS.1112.RH.4.10

Analyzing Visuals

Use the graph to answer the following questions.

Source: *Average Employment Rates Based on Non-Depression Era 1923–1925 figures*

18 *Analyzing Graphs* What does the zero line represent on the graph? Based on the graph's pattern, what was the state of the economy in 1941? MAFS.912.S-IC.2, MAFS.912.S-ID.1, SS.912.A.5.11

19 *Explaining* Based on what you know about the New Deal and the events of the era, what caused the dramatic decline in employment in late 1937? What is significant about the decline? Make sure to communicate your analysis as clearly as possible. MAFS.912.S-IC.2, MAFS.912.S-ID.1, MAFS.K12.MP.3.1, MAFS.K12.MP.6.1, SS.912.A.5.11

Extended Response Questions

20 *Expository* Look up the full text of Roosevelt's first Inaugural Address to the nation on March 4, 1933, either online or at a library. Imagine that you are a newspaper reporter who covered the inauguration and is now looking back at Roosevelt's first 100 days in office. Write a news article describing the mood of the nation at the time and the promises that Roosevelt made to the nation. Describe what Roosevelt was trying to do in the speech. Use evidence from the speech and from the chapter to explain what Roosevelt accomplished in his first 100 days and whether he lived up to his promises in the speech. LAFS.1112.RH.1.1, LAFS.1112.SL.1.2, LAFS.1112.RH.1.2, LAFS.1112.RH.3.8, LAFS.1112.RH.3.9, LAFS.1112.RH.4.10, LAFS.1112.SL.1.3, LAFS.1112.WHST.2.4, LAFS.1112.WHST.3.7, LAFS.1112.WHST.4.10, SS.912.A.5.11

Need Extra Help?

If You've Missed Question	**15**	**16**	**17**	**18**	**19**	**20**
Go To Lesson	1	1	1	1, 3	1, 3	1

networks
There's More Online!

U.S. Navy serviceman Dorie Miller was a cook on the USS *West Virginia* docked at Pearl Harbor, Hawaii, on December 7, 1941. He heroically took over an antiaircraft gun when his commanding officer was fatally wounded. He later won the Navy Cross for his courageous actions during the battle. On November 25, 1944, Miller was officially listed as "presumed dead" a year after his escort cruiser was torpedoed in the Pacific.

FROM 1931 TO 1941

A World in Flames

Library of Congress, Prints & Photographs Division [LC-USZC4-2328]

THE STORY MATTERS ...

After Japanese forces attacked American forces at Pearl Harbor on December 7, 1941, thousands of men and women volunteered to serve in the U.S. military. With the U.S. declaration of war, American soldiers were thrown into a fight to the death between fascism and democracy.

ESSENTIAL QUESTIONS

- Could World War II have been prevented?
- Why do some people fail to respond to injustice while others try to prevent injustice?

LESSON 1
The Origins of World War II

LESSON 2
From Neutrality to War

LESSON 3
The Holocaust

Place & Time: United States 1931–1941

After the experience of World War I, many Americans and Europeans did not want to be involved in such a war ever again. Many Americans believed that some European nations would always be fighting one another and there was no reason for the United States to step in. As another war brewed overseas during the 1930s, Americans were torn between ignoring it or using their influence to maintain peace. When war finally erupted, the nation remained supportive of its traditional allies, if reluctant to enter the fray itself. After the conflict reached U.S. soil, however, Americans devoted themselves to victory.

Step Into the Place

Read the quotes and look at the information presented on the map.

 DBQ **Analyzing Historical Documents** How are these two quotes similar in their description of the Japanese attack on Pearl Harbor and the outbreak of war? How are they different?

PRIMARY SOURCE

❝We saw a lot of planes diving down and we thought that the army air force was practicing again. We didn't know what it was. . . . [T]wo planes came over us and they were so low that you could see the pilots in the plane. They dropped bombs on each side of us, but missed. Then we saw the big red ball, which signified they were Japanese planes. Well then we knew we were at war.❞

—Will Lehner, a sailor aboard the USS *Ward* during the attack on Pearl Harbor, from an interview, 2004

PRIMARY SOURCE

❝Yesterday, December 7, 1941—a date which will live in infamy—the United States of America was suddenly and deliberately attacked by naval and air forces of the Empire of Japan. . . . No matter how long it may take us to overcome this premeditated invasion, the American people in their righteous might will win through to absolute victory. . . . I ask that the Congress declare that since the unprovoked and dastardly attack by Japan on Sunday, December 7, 1941, a state of war has existed between the United States and the Japanese Empire.❞

—President Franklin D. Roosevelt, from his speech to Congress, December 8, 1941

Step Into the Time

MAKING CONNECTIONS
Choose an event from the time line and describe how the event reflects the state of the world leading up to 1941.

F. Roosevelt
1933–1945

1934 Nye Committee holds hearings on causes of World War I

U.S. PRESIDENTS

UNITED STATES

WORLD

1931

1933

1931 Japan invades Manchuria

1933 Hitler becomes chancellor of Germany

1934 Hitler denounces Treaty of Versailles

NEXT GENERATION SUNSHINE STATE STANDARDS
Students will understand the following benchmarks from the Florida NGSSS

LAFS.1112.RH.2.6: Evaluate authors' differing points of view on the same historical event or issue by assessing the authors' claims, reasoning, and evidence.

LAFS.1112.RH.3.7: Integrate and evaluate multiple sources of information presented in diverse formats and media (e.g., visually, quantitatively, as well as in words) in order to address a question or solve a problem.

SS.912.A.1.2: Utilize a variety of primary and secondary sources to identify author, historical significance, audience, and authenticity to understand a historical period.

SS.912.A.1.3: Utilize timelines to identify the time sequence of historical data.

SS.912.A.1.4: Analyze how images, symbols, objects, cartoons, graphs, charts, maps, and artwork may be used to interpret the significance of time periods and events from the past.

SS.912.A.6.1: Examine causes, course, and consequences of World War II on the United States and the world.

The Attack on Pearl Harbor   December 7, 1941

The first of nearly 200 Japanese planes began dropping bombs on Pearl Harbor just before 8:00 in the morning.

← 1st Wave (7:40 AM)
← 2nd Wave (8:40 AM)

0 ——————— 10 miles
0 ——————— 10 km

Oahu

• *Wheeler Field*

Kaneohe Naval Air Station

Pearl Harbor

• *Hickam Field*

• Honolulu

Sunk
Damaged
Undamaged

Pearl Harbor

Detroit
Raleigh
Medusa   Utah
Tangier
Curtiss

Solace
Allen   Chew

Ford Island

Arizona
Tennessee   Vestal
Maryland   West Virginia
Neosho   Oklahoma
California   Argonne
Sacramento   Ramapo
Avocet   Helena   New Orleans
Oglala   San Francisco
St. Louis
Cachalot   Bagley
Shaw   Honolulu
Pennsylvania
Cassin   Downes

Nevada

Pelias
Sumner
Castor

N
W ✦ E
S

Because Hawaii is located thousands of miles from Japan, U.S. military officials had doubted that the Japanese would attempt an attack there—leaving Pearl Harbor an open and inviting target.

Kauai   *Hawaiian Islands*
Niihau
Oahu   *Molokai*
PACIFIC OCEAN   *Lanai*   *Maui*
Kahoolawe

0 ——————— 100 miles   *Hawaii*
0 ——————— 100 km

The Origins of World War II

There's More Online!

READING HELPDESK

Academic Vocabulary

- exploit
- command
- dominate

Content Vocabulary

- fascism
- appeasement
- collective

TAKING NOTES

Key Ideas and Details

Organizing As you read about the events in Europe and Asia after World War I, complete a graphic organizer similar to the one below, using the major headings of the lesson to create an outline. LAFS.1112.RH.3.7, SS.912.A.6.1

> The Origins of World War II
> I. The Rise of Dictators
>   A.
>   B.
>   C.
>   D.
> II.

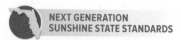
NEXT GENERATION SUNSHINE STATE STANDARDS

LAFS.1112.RH.2.4: Determine the meaning of words and phrases as they are used in a text, including analyzing how an author uses and refines the meaning of a key term over the course of a text (e.g., how Madison defines faction in Federalist No. 10).

LAFS.1112.WHST.1.2: Write informative/ explanatory texts, including the narration of historical events, scientific procedures/ experiments, or technical processes.

Continued on page 335

ESSENTIAL QUESTIONS

- Could World War II have been prevented?
- Why do some people not respond to injustice while others try to prevent injustice?

IT MATTERS BECAUSE

In the years following World War I, aggressive and expansionist governments took power in Europe and Asia. Meanwhile, most Americans did not want to get involved in another foreign war.

The Rise of Dictators

GUIDING QUESTION *What economic and political conditions following World War I encouraged dictatorships?*

The Treaty of Versailles, along with the economic depression that followed, contributed to the rise of antidemocratic governments in both Europe and Asia. These antidemocratic states would eventually break the peace agreement that ended World War I.

Mussolini and Fascism in Italy

One of Europe's first dictatorships arose in Italy. In 1919, Benito Mussolini founded Italy's Fascist movement. **Fascism** was an aggressive nationalistic movement that considered the nation more important than the individual. Fascists believed that order in society and national greatness came through a dictator who led a strong government and built an empire.

Mussolini's fascism was also strongly anticommunist. After the Russian Revolution, many Europeans feared that Communists, allied with labor unions, were trying to bring down their governments. Mussolini **exploited** these fears by portraying fascism as a bulwark against communism, protecting private property and the middle class. He pledged to return Italy to the glories of the Roman Empire.

Backed by the Blackshirts, a Fascist militia, Mussolini threatened to march on Rome in 1922, claiming he was defending Italy against a communist revolution. Liberal members of the Italian parliament insisted that the king declare martial law. When he refused, the cabinet resigned. Conservative advisers then persuaded the king to appoint Mussolini as the premier. Once in office, Mussolini—who took the title of Il Duce, or "The Leader"—embarked on an ambitious program of bringing order to Italy.

Stalin Takes Over the Soviet Union

After the Russian Revolution, the Communist Party, led by Vladimir Lenin, created the Union of Soviet Socialist Republics (USSR) in 1922. The Communists instituted one-party rule, suppressed individual liberties, and punished opponents.

After Lenin died in 1924, Joseph Stalin came to power. By 1926, Stalin was the new Soviet dictator. He began a massive effort to industrialize his country using Five-Year Plans. Steel production increased, but industrial wages declined by 43 percent from 1928 to 1940. Family farms were combined and turned into **collectives,** or government-owned farms. Peasants who resisted by killing livestock or hoarding crops faced show trials or death from starvation. As many as 10 million peasants died in famines during 1932 and 1933. Stalin also sought to expand Soviet influence beyond its borders, proclaiming, "[W]orld dictatorship can be established only when the victory of socialism has been achieved in certain countries or groups of countries . . . [growing into] a World Union of Soviet Socialist Republics uniting the whole of mankind. . . ."

Stalin tolerated no opposition, targeting political enemies along with artists and intellectuals. He used concentration camps, which held nearly two million people by 1935. Prisoners were used as slave labor. Between 15 and 20 million people died under Stalin's rule, which lasted until his death in 1953.

Hitler and Nazi Germany

Adolf Hitler was a fervent nationalist who hated both the victorious Allies and the German government that had accepted their peace terms ending World War I. He became the leader of the National Socialist German Workers' Party, or Nazi Party. The Nazis were one of many political parties that arose out of postwar Germany's political and economic chaos. The party called for Germany to expand its territory and to reject the terms of the Treaty of Versailles. It also was anti-Semitic. In November 1923, the Nazis tried to seize power by marching on city hall in Munich, Germany. The plan failed, the Nazi Party was banned for a time, and Hitler was arrested.

While in prison, Hitler wrote *Mein Kampf* ("My Struggle"), in which he claimed that Germans, particularly blond, blue-eyed Germans, belonged to a "master race" called Aryans. He argued that the Slavic peoples of Eastern Europe belonged to an inferior race, which Germans should enslave. However, Hitler's racism was strongest toward Jews. Hitler blamed the Jews for many of the world's problems, especially for Germany's defeat in World War I.

After his release, Hitler changed his tactics. He focused on getting Nazis elected to the Reichstag, the lower house of the German parliament. When the Depression struck Germany, many desperate Germans began to vote for radical parties, including the Nazis and Communists. By 1932, the Nazis were the largest party in the Reichstag. The following year, the German president appointed Hitler as chancellor.

After taking office, Hitler called for new elections. Storm troopers, as the Nazi paramilitary units were called, began intimidating voters. After the election, the Reichstag, **dominated** by the Nazis and other right-wing parties, voted to give Hitler dictatorial powers. In 1934, Hitler became president, which gave him control of the army. He then gave himself the new title of Der Führer, or "The Leader."

fascism a political system headed by a dictator that calls for extreme nationalism and often racism and no tolerance of opposition

exploit to take unfair advantage of

collective a farm, especially in Communist countries, formed from many small holdings collected into a single unit for joint operation under governmental supervision

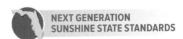

NEXT GENERATION SUNSHINE STATE STANDARDS

Continued from page 334

LAFS.1112.WHST.4.10: Write routinely over extended time frames (time for reflection and revision) and shorter time frames (a single sitting or a day or two) for a range of discipline-specific tasks, purposes, and audiences.

LAFS.1112.RH.3.7: Integrate and evaluate multiple sources of information presented in diverse formats and media (e.g., visually, quantitatively, as well as in words) in order to address a question or solve a problem.

SS.912.A.1.4: Analyze how images, symbols, objects, cartoons, graphs, charts, maps, and artwork may be used to interpret the significance of time periods and events from the past.

SS.912.A.6.1: Examine causes, course, and consequences of World War II on the United States and the world.

dominate to be in a state or position of command or control over all others

Mussolini (left), Hitler (center), and Stalin (right) rose to power during times of political and economic instability.

▶ CRITICAL THINKING

Making Inferences Why would political and economic instability lead to a rise of dictatorships?
LAFS.1112.RH.3.7, SS.912.A.6.1

(l)Library of Congress, Prints & Photographs Division [LC-DIG-sgbain-37518]; (c)Hugo Jaeger/Time & Life Pictures/Getty Images; (r)FPG/Taxi/Getty Images

Hideki Tōjō became prime minister of Japan in 1941 and supported an aggressive military policy.

▶ CRITICAL THINKING
Predicting Consequences What might be a result of Tōjō's aggressive leadership?
LAFS.1112.RH.3.7, SS.912.A.6.1

command to be in control of, to have full power

Militarists Control Japan

In Japan, as in Germany, difficult economic times helped undermine the political system. Japanese industries had to import nearly all of the resources they needed to produce goods. When the Depression struck, other countries raised their tariffs, making things worse. Many Japanese military officers blamed the country's problems on corrupt politicians. They believed that Japan was destined to dominate East Asia and that straying from traditional beliefs corrupted the country.

The military leaders argued that seizing territory was the only way Japan could get the resources it needed. In September 1931, the Japanese army invaded Manchuria, a resource-rich region of northern China. In October, hoping to avoid conflict with the United States, Emperor Hirohito's prime minister asked Minister of War Hideki Tōjō to withdraw some troops from China. Tōjō refused, threatening to bring down the government. The military was in **command** of the country. The Japanese army swept through China, and in 1937 invaded Nanking (now Nanjing), destroying the city and killing as many as 300,000 of its residents. The incident became known as the "Rape of Nanking." In October 1941, Tōjō took over as prime minister.

✔ READING PROGRESS CHECK

Examining How did postwar conditions contribute to the rise of dictatorships in Europe?

World War II Begins

GUIDING QUESTION *How did European nations try to prevent war?*

In 1935, Hitler began to defy the Treaty of Versailles that had ended World War I. He announced that Germany would build a new air force and begin a military draft that would greatly expand its army—actions in direct violation of the treaty. Rather than enforce the treaty by going to war, European leaders tried to negotiate with Hitler.

Europe's leaders had several reasons for believing—or wanting to believe—that a deal could be reached with Hitler to avoid war. First, they wanted to avoid a repeat of World War I. Second, some thought most of Hitler's demands were reasonable, including his demand that all German-speaking regions be united. Third, many people assumed that the Nazis would want peace once they gained more territory.

The Austrian *Anschluss*

In late 1937, Hitler again called for the unification of all German-speaking people, including those in Austria and Czechoslovakia. He believed that Germany could expand its territory only by force.

In February 1938, Hitler threatened to invade German-speaking Austria unless Austrian Nazis were given important government posts. Austria's chancellor gave in to this demand, but then tried to put the matter of unification with Germany to a democratic vote. Fearing the outcome, Hitler sent troops into Austria in March and announced the *Anschluss*, or unification, of Austria and Germany.

The Munich Crisis

Hitler next announced German claims to the Sudetenland, an area of Czechoslovakia with a large German-speaking population. The Czechs strongly resisted Germany's demands. France threatened to fight if Germany attacked Czechoslovakia, and the Soviet Union also promised aid. Prime Minister Neville Chamberlain pledged Britain's support to France, its ally.

LIBRARY OF CONGRESS, PRINTS & PHOTOGRAPHS DIVISION [LC-DIG-PPMSCA-13329]

Representatives of Britain, France, Italy, and Germany met in Munich, Germany, to decide Czechoslovakia's fate. At the Munich Conference, on September 29, 1938, Britain and France agreed to Hitler's demands, a policy that came to be known as **appeasement.** In other words, they made concessions and believed that if they gave Hitler what he wanted, they could avoid war. Czechoslovakia had to give up the Sudetenland or fight Germany on its own. When Chamberlain returned home, he stated, "My good friends, for the second time in our history, a British Prime Minister has returned from Germany bringing peace with honor. I believe it is 'peace for our time.' Go home and get a nice quiet sleep."

Appeasement, however, failed to preserve the fragile peace. In March 1939, Germany sent troops into Czechoslovakia and divided the country. Slovakia became independent in name, but it was actually under German control. The Czech lands became a German protectorate.

Hitler Demands Danzig

A month after the Munich Conference, Hitler demanded that the city of Danzig be returned to German control. Danzig was more than 90 percent German, and it had been part of Poland since World War I. Hitler also requested a highway and railroad across the Polish Corridor.

Hitler's new demands convinced Britain and France that war was inevitable. On March 31, 1939, Britain announced that if Poland went to war to defend its territory, Britain and France would come to its aid. This declaration encouraged Poland to refuse Hitler's demands. In May 1939, Hitler ordered the German army to prepare to invade Poland. He also ordered his foreign minister to begin negotiations with the Soviet Union. If Germany was going to fight Britain and France, Hitler did not want to have to fight the Soviets too.

The Nazi-Soviet Pact

When German officials proposed a non-aggression treaty to the Soviets, Stalin agreed. He believed the best way to protect the Soviet Union was to turn the capitalist nations against each other. If the treaty worked, Germany would go to war against Britain and France.

The non-aggression pact, signed by Germany and the Soviet Union on August 23, 1939, shocked the world. Communism and Nazism were supposed to be opposed to each other. Leaders in Britain and France understood, however, that Hitler had made the deal to free himself for war against their countries and Poland. They did not know that the treaty called for the division of Poland between Germany and the Soviet Union.

The Invasion of Poland and the Fall of France

On September 1, 1939, Germany invaded Poland. Two days later, Britain and France declared war on Germany. World War II had begun. The Germans used a new type of warfare called blitzkrieg, or "lightning war." Blitzkrieg used massed tanks, combined with waves of aircraft and paratroopers, to break through and encircle enemy positions. By October 5, 1939, the Germans had defeated the Polish military.

Meanwhile, Western Europe remained quiet. British and French troops in France waited for a German attack. On May 10, 1940, Hitler launched a new blitzkrieg. While German troops parachuted into the Netherlands, tanks rolled into Belgium and Luxembourg. British and French forces raced north into Belgium. The Germans crossed the Ardennes Mountains of Luxembourg and eastern Belgium. German tanks smashed through the French lines and moved west across northern France. The British and French were trapped in Belgium.

Hulton Archive/Getty Images

Neville Chamberlain (1869–1940)

After serving at top levels of the British government since the end of World War I, Neville Chamberlain became prime minister in 1937. Chamberlain's term was dominated by growing tension with Nazi Germany. He signed the Munich Agreement with Hitler in 1938 as part of an appeasement policy. Wildly popular as the man who avoided another war, Chamberlain quickly fell from favor when Hitler invaded Poland a year later. Chamberlain resigned, and died of cancer just six months later.

▶ **CRITICAL THINKING**
Drawing Conclusions Why did opinions of Chamberlain change so quickly after Hitler invaded Poland?
LAFS.1112.RH.3.7, SS.912.A.6.1

appeasement giving in to unjust demands in order to avoid all-out conflict

Britain's Neville Chamberlain (third from left), Mussolini (center), and Hitler (third from right) agreed to prevent war at the Munich Conference in 1938. To appease Hitler, representatives at the conference agreed that Czechoslovakia would give up the Sudetenland to Germany. Less than a year later, Germany occupied all of Czechoslovakia, invaded Poland, and was at war with Britain and France.

► CRITICAL THINKING
Drawing Conclusions Why do you think that the policy of appeasement failed?
LAFS.1112.RH.3.7, SS.912.A.6.1

The Miracle at Dunkirk

German troops drove Allied forces toward the English Channel. The port of Dunkirk became the Allies' only way out. As German forces moved in on Dunkirk, Hitler ordered them to stop. Historians think that Hitler was nervous about risking his tank forces. Whatever his reasons, Hitler's orders provided a three-day delay that allowed Allied forces to evacuate. When the evacuation ended on June 4, an estimated 338,000 British and French troops had been saved during the "Miracle at Dunkirk."

Less than three weeks later, on June 22, 1940, France surrendered. To govern the rest of France, Germany set up a puppet government at the town of Vichy and made Marshal Philippe Pétain the leader, but gave him no power. French general Charles de Gaulle led the Free French resistance forces from the French colony of Algiers. He worked with Allied leaders and refused to recognize the defeat of France.

Britain Remains Defiant

Hitler expected Britain to negotiate peace after France surrendered. He was mistaken. On June 4, 1940, British prime minister Winston Churchill delivered a defiant speech, vowing that Britain would never surrender:

PRIMARY SOURCE

"Even though large tracts of Europe and many old and famous States have fallen or may fall into the grip of the Gestapo and all the odious apparatus of Nazi rule, we shall not flag or fail, we shall go on to the end. . . . [W]e shall defend our island, whatever the cost may be . . . we shall never surrender. . . . "

—Winston Churchill, from his speech to Parliament, June 4, 1940

That same month, Hitler ordered the German air force, the *Luftwaffe*, to begin attacking British ships in the English Channel. Then, in August and September, the *Luftwaffe* battled the British Royal Air Force in what became known as the Battle of Britain. After London was bombed accidentally, Britain retaliated by bombing Berlin. The *Luftwaffe* then began targeting its attacks on London and other cities. Britain's use of radar gave it the advantage. After major losses on both sides, Hitler canceled the planned invasion of Britain. Churchill praised the sacrifices of the pilots who saved Britain, saying, "Never in the field of human conflict was so much owed by so many to so few."

✓ READING PROGRESS CHECK

Evaluating How was Britain able to prevent Germany from invading?

LESSON 1 REVIEW

Reviewing Vocabulary

1. *Explaining* How did fascism put Europe on the path to war?
LAFS.1112.RH.2.4, SS.912.A.6.1
2. *Stating* How was the Soviet collectivization of agriculture an example of a dictatorial government? LAFS.1112.RH.2.4, SS.912.A.6.1

Using Your Notes

3. *Summarizing* Use your notes from the lesson to write a paragraph explaining how dictators came to power during this era. LAFS.1112.RH.3.7, SS.912.A.6.1

Answering the Guiding Questions

4. *Evaluating* What economic and political conditions following World War I encouraged dictatorships? SS.912.A.6.1

5. *Synthesizing* How did European nations try to prevent war?
SS.912.A.6.1

Writing Activity

6. INFORMATIVE/EXPLANATORY Write a short essay explaining why the Nazi-Soviet Non-Aggression Pact was such a surprise to the world. LAFS.1112.WHST.1.2, LAFS.1112.WHST.4.10, SS.912.A.6.1

LESSON 2
From Neutrality to War

ESSENTIAL QUESTIONS
- Could World War II have been prevented?
- Why do some people fail to respond to injustice while others try to prevent injustice?

READING HELPDESK

Academic Vocabulary
- revise
- underestimate
- purchase

Content Vocabulary
- internationalism
- strategic materials

TAKING NOTES

Key Ideas and Details

Organizing As you read about U.S. efforts to stay neutral, complete a graphic organizer similar to the one below by identifying events that shifted American involvement in the war.
LAFS.1112.RH.3.7, SS.912.A.6.2

```
┌─────────────────────┐
│ Events That Shifted │
│ American Involvement │
└─────────────────────┘
   │       │       │
┌────┐  ┌────┐  ┌────┐
└────┘  └────┘  └────┘
```

**NEXT GENERATION
SUNSHINE STATE STANDARDS**

ELD.K12.ELL.SI.1: English language learners communicate for social and instructional purposes within the school setting.

ELD.K12.ELL.SS.1: English language learners communicate information, ideas and concepts necessary for academic success in the content area of Social Studies.

LAFS.1112.RH.1.2: Determine the central ideas or information of a primary or secondary source; provide an accurate summary that makes clear the relationships among the key details and ideas.

LAFS.1112.RH.2.4: Determine the meaning of words and phrases as they are used in a text, including analyzing how an author uses and refines the meaning of a key term over the course of a text (e.g., how Madison defines faction in Federalist No. 10).

Continued on page 340

IT MATTERS BECAUSE
Although Americans wanted to avoid fighting in another foreign war, they sent aid when their allies were threatened. The attack on Pearl Harbor convinced the United States to declare war.

American Neutrality

GUIDING QUESTION *Why did many Americans support isolationism? Why did President Roosevelt support internationalism?*

The rise of dictatorships and militarism in Europe discouraged many Americans. The sacrifices they had made during World War I seemed pointless. In addition, during the Depression, most European nations announced they would no longer repay their war debts to the United States. In response, many Americans once again began supporting isolationism and trying to avoid involvement in international conflicts.

The Nye Committee
Meanwhile, accusations emerged that arms manufacturers had tricked the United States into entering World War I. In 1934, Senator Gerald P. Nye held hearings to investigate these allegations. The Nye Committee report documented the huge profits that arms factories had made during the war and created the impression that these businesses influenced the decision to go to war, causing even more Americans to turn toward isolationism.

Legislating Neutrality
In response to growing Italian and German aggression in Europe, Congress passed the Neutrality Act of 1935. This legislation—reflecting a response to the Nye report—made it illegal for Americans to sell arms to any country at war.

In October 1935, as part of his dream to build a new Roman empire, Mussolini ordered the Italian military to invade Ethiopia, then known as Abyssinia. The war was short, the Abyssinian forces

HELPING HANDS—BUT NOT ARMS

By 1940, many Americans joined Roosevelt in wanting to help Britain and France in their struggle against Hitler. Isolationists, however, still wished to keep the country from directly entering the conflict.

This political cartoon shows Uncle Sam extending a helping hand to Britain but refusing to sell arms to Britain and France.

1 *Making Inferences*
According to the cartoon, why should the United States refuse to sell arms overseas? SS.912.A.1.4, SS.912.A.6.2, SS.912.H.1.5

2 *Analyzing Primary Sources*
What does this cartoon try to persuade the viewer to believe? LAFS.1112.RH.1.2, LAFS.1112.SL.1.3

SKILLS PRACTICE

Work with a partner. Point to a picture in this lesson about the United States entering World War II. Retell in your own words the part of the text that goes with the picture. ELD.K12.ELL.SI.1, ELD.K12.ELL.SS.1

NEXT GENERATION SUNSHINE STATE STANDARDS

Continued from page 339
LAFS.1112.RH.3.7: Integrate and evaluate multiple sources of information presented in diverse formats and media (e.g., visually, quantitatively, as well as in words) in order to address a question or solve a problem.

LAFS.1112.SL.1.3: Evaluate a speaker's point of view, reasoning, and use of evidence and rhetoric, assessing the stance, premises, links among ideas, word choice, points of emphasis, and tone used.

LAFS.1112.WHST.1.2: Write informative/explanatory texts, including the narration of historical events, scientific procedures/experiments, or technical processes.

LAFS.1112.WHST.4.10: Write routinely over extended time frames (time for reflection and revision) and shorter time frames (a single sitting or a day or two) for a range of discipline-specific tasks, purposes, and audiences.

Continued on page 342

internationalism
a national policy of actively trading with foreign countries to foster peace and prosperity

were no match for the Italian troops, and the emperor, Haile Selassie, was forced into exile.

Knowing that the American people and Congress would not support action to stop Italy, Roosevelt supported the passage of a new law, the Neutrality Act of 1936, which extended the ban on arms sales imposed by the Neutrality Act of 1935, and also banned loans to nations at war. The 1936 act was far more likely to hurt Italy than Abyssinia, which would not have been able to borrow much money anyway.

In 1936, another conflict began, this time in Europe, when the Spanish Civil War erupted. On one side were the rebel Nationalists led by General Franco, and supported by Germany and Italy. On the other side were the Republicans, supported both by the Soviet Union and by thousands of volunteers from Europe and the United States who went to Spain to fight against Franco.

The Spanish Civil War was widely portrayed as the first clash between the forces of fascism and the forces of western democracy and it greatly contributed to growing tensions in Europe and to the fear that another world war was coming. Franco's forces eventually won the civil war, and Franco became the leader of Spain until his death in 1975.

Soon after the Spanish Civil War began, Hitler and Mussolini pledged to cooperate on several international issues, and Japan aligned itself with Germany and Italy. Together, the three nations became known as the Axis Powers. As European tensions worsened, Congress passed the Neutrality Act of 1937, continuing the ban on selling arms to warring nations and also requiring them to buy all nonmilitary supplies from the United States on a "cash-and-carry" basis. Countries had to send their own ships to pick up goods and had to pay in cash. Loans were not allowed. Isolationists knew that attacks on American ships had helped bring the country into World War I. They wanted to prevent such attacks that could bring the nation into another European war.

Roosevelt's Internationalism

Despite the government's stand on neutrality, President Roosevelt supported **internationalism,** the idea that trade between nations creates prosperity and helps prevent war. He warned that the neutrality acts "might drag us into war instead of keeping us out," but he did not veto the bills. When Japan invaded China in July 1937 without declaring war, Roosevelt claimed the Neutrality Act of 1937 did not apply. He authorized the sale of weapons to China, warning that the nation should not let an "epidemic of lawlessness" infect the world:

Chicago History Museum/http://www.chicagohs.org

PRIMARY SOURCE

"There is no escape through mere isolation or neutrality.... When an epidemic of physical disease starts to spread, the community ... joins in a quarantine of the patients in order to protect the health of the community against the spread of the disease.... War is a contagion, whether it be declared or undeclared."

—from *The Public Papers and Addresses of Franklin D. Roosevelt*

✓ **READING PROGRESS CHECK**

Explaining What steps did the supporters of United States isolationism take to ensure that the country remained neutral in an international conflict?

Neutrality Tested

GUIDING QUESTION *How did President Roosevelt assist Britain while maintaining U.S. neutrality?*

Roosevelt wanted to help Britain and France in their struggle and asked Congress to **revise** the neutrality laws to allow the sale of weapons to warring nations. Congress passed the Neutrality Act of 1939, permitting the sale of weapons but only on a "cash-and-carry" basis.

In the spring of 1940, the United States faced the first test of its neutrality. Britain asked Roosevelt for old American destroyers to replenish its fleet, and the president used a loophole in the cash-only requirement for **purchases.** He sent 50 ships to Britain in exchange for America's use of British bases in the Atlantic. Because the deal did not involve an actual sale, the Neutrality Act did not apply.

Widespread acceptance of the Destroyers-for-Bases deal indicated a change in public opinion. By July 1940, most Americans favored offering limited aid to the Allies, but debate continued over the scope of that aid. The Fight for Freedom Committee wanted the repeal of neutrality laws and stronger actions against Germany. On the other side, the America First Committee opposed any intervention to help the Allies.

After winning reelection in 1940, Roosevelt expanded the nation's role in the war. Speaking to Congress, he listed the Four Freedoms for which both the United States and Britain stood: freedom of speech, freedom of worship, freedom from want, and freedom from fear.

The Lend-Lease Act

By December 1940, Great Britain had run out of funds to fight the war. Roosevelt proposed the Lend-Lease Act, which allowed the United States to lend or lease arms to any country considered "vital to the defense of the United States." Britain could receive weapons, then return them or pay rent for them after the war. Congress passed the Lend-Lease Act by a wide margin. Lend-lease aid eventually went to the Soviet Union as well, when in June 1941, Hitler invaded the Soviet Union. Roosevelt followed Britain's lead in supporting any state fighting the Nazis.

A Hemispheric Defense Zone

The problem of getting American arms and supplies to Britain remained. German submarines in the Atlantic sank hundreds of thousands of tons of cargo each month. The British Navy lacked the ships to stop them.

Because the United States was still officially neutral, Roosevelt could not order the navy to protect British cargo ships. Instead, he developed the idea of a hemispheric defense zone, declaring that the entire western half of the Atlantic was part of the Western Hemisphere and therefore neutral.

BIOGRAPHY

Winston Churchill (1874–1965)

British leader Winston Churchill first won election to Parliament in 1900, rising to become head of the British Navy in 1911. In the years leading up to World War II, he spoke out repeatedly against Hitler's aggression, and after becoming prime minister committed the nation to intense efforts to defeat Germany. Churchill became known for his public speaking skills and for his tenacious patriotism during the war. His Conservative Party lost power after the war, but Churchill again served as Britain's prime minister from 1951 until his retirement in 1955.

▶ **CRITICAL THINKING**
Drawing Conclusions Why might Roosevelt have particularly wanted to help Churchill?
LAFS.1112.RH.3.7, SS.912.A.6.1, SS.912.A.6.2

revise to make changes to an original work

purchase something obtained especially for a price in money or its equivalent

©Bettmann/Corbis

He then ordered the U.S. Navy to patrol the western Atlantic and reveal the location of German submarines to the British.

The Atlantic Charter

In August 1941, Roosevelt and Churchill met and developed the Atlantic Charter, which committed both nations to a postwar world of democracy, nonaggression, free trade, economic advancement, and freedom of the seas. Churchill later said that FDR "made it clear that he would look for an 'incident' which would justify him in opening hostilities" with Germany.

In early September, a German submarine, or U-boat, fired on an American destroyer that had been radioing the U-boat's position to the British. Roosevelt promptly responded by ordering American ships to follow a "shoot-on-sight" policy toward German submarines. The Germans escalated hostilities the following month, targeting two American destroyers. One of them, the Reuben James, sank after being torpedoed, killing over 100 sailors. As the end of 1941 drew near, Germany and the United States continued a tense standoff.

✓ **READING PROGRESS CHECK**

Summarizing What indications were there that public opinion was shifting away from American isolationism?

Japan Attacks Pearl Harbor

GUIDING QUESTION *How did the United States try to slow Japan's advances in the Pacific?*

Despite the growing tensions in Europe, it was the Japanese attack on Pearl Harbor that finally brought the United States into World War II. Ironically, Roosevelt's efforts to help Britain fight Germany resulted in Japan's decision to attack the United States.

America Embargoes Japan

As German submarines sank British ships in the Atlantic, the British began moving warships from Southeast Asia, leaving India and other colonial possessions vulnerable to Japanese attack. To hinder Japanese aggression, Roosevelt began applying economic pressure. Japan depended on the United States for many key materials, including scrap iron, steel, and especially oil. In July 1940, Congress gave the president the power to restrict the sale of **strategic materials**—items important for fighting a war. Roosevelt then blocked the sale of airplane fuel and scrap iron to Japan. Furious, the Japanese signed an alliance with Germany and Italy, becoming a member of the Axis.

In 1941, Roosevelt began sending lend-lease aid to China, hoping to enable the Chinese to tie down the Japanese and prevent them from attacking elsewhere. The strategy failed. By July 1941, Japan had sent military forces into southern Indochina, directly threatening the British Empire. In response, Roosevelt froze all Japanese assets in the United States, reduced oil shipments to Japan, and sent General Douglas MacArthur to the Philippines to build up American defenses there.

Despite Roosevelt's support for the British and French, many Americans believed that fighting another war overseas was against the nation's interests.

▶ **CRITICAL THINKING**
Predicting Consequences
How would you expect isolationists' feelings to change if the United States suffered a direct attack? LAFS.1112.RH.3.7, SS.912.A.1.4, SS.912.A.6.2

NEXT GENERATION SUNSHINE STATE STANDARDS

Continued from page 340

SS.912.A.1.2: Utilize a variety of primary and secondary sources to identify author, historical significance, audience, and authenticity to understand a historical period.

SS.912.A.1.4: Analyze how images, symbols, objects, cartoons, graphs, charts, maps, and artwork may be used to interpret the significance of time periods and events from the past.

SS.912.A.6.1: Examine causes, course, and consequences of World War II on the United States and the world.

SS.912.A.6.2: Describe the United States response in the early years of World War II (Neutrality Acts, Cash and Carry, Lend Lease Act).

SS.912.H.1.5: Examine artistic response to social issues and new ideas in various cultures.

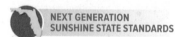

strategic materials
items needed for fighting a war

Thomas D. McAvoy/Time & Life Pictures/Getty Images

With its war against China in jeopardy because of a lack of resources, the Japanese military planned to attack the resource-rich British and Dutch colonies in Southeast Asia. They also decided to seize the Philippines and to attack the American fleet at Pearl Harbor. Negotiations with the Americans continued, but neither side would back down. In late November 1941, six Japanese aircraft carriers, two battleships, and several other warships set out for Hawaii.

Surprise Attack

The Japanese government appeared to be continuing negotiations with the United States in good faith. American intelligence, however, had decoded Japanese messages that made it clear that Japan was preparing to go to war against the United States. On November 27, American commanders at the Pearl Harbor naval base received a war warning from Washington D.C., but it did not mention Hawaii as a possible target. Because of its great distance from Japan, officials doubted that Japan would attack Hawaii.

The U.S. military's inability to interpret the intelligence correctly left Pearl Harbor an open target. Japan's surprise attack on December 7, 1941, was devastating. Eight battleships, three cruisers, three destroyers, and four other vessels were sunk or damaged. The attack destroyed over 180 aircraft and killed 2,403 Americans. Another 1,178 were injured.

That night, a gray-faced Roosevelt met with his cabinet, telling them the country faced the most serious crisis since the Civil War. The next day, he asked Congress to declare war: The Senate voted 82 to 0 and the House 388 to 1 to declare war on Japan.

Germany Declares War

Hitler had hoped that Japan would attack the United States so that the majority of U.S. forces would be sent to the Pacific front. He expected the United States to enter the European war as incidents between German submarines and the United States mounted in the Atlantic.

Hitler **underestimated** the strategy of the United States, which was to view Germany as the larger threat yet fight the Japanese with the U.S. Navy. By helping Japan, he hoped for Japanese support against the Soviet Union after they had defeated the Americans. On December 11, Germany and Italy both declared war on the United States.

✔ READING PROGRESS CHECK

Sequencing What sequence of events led the United States to a declaration of war?

Because American officials did not expect it, the attack on Pearl Harbor was particularly devastating.

▶ CRITICAL THINKING
Determining Cause and Effect
What was the immediate result of the attack on Pearl Harbor?
LAFS.1112.RH.3.7, SS.912.A.1.4, SS.912.A.6.1

underestimate to estimate lower than the real amount or number

Time & Life Pictures/Getty Images

LESSON 2 REVIEW

Reviewing Vocabulary

1. *Contrasting* How does internationalism differ from isolationism? LAFS.1112.RH.2.4, SS.912.A.6.1

2. *Explaining* How did restricting the sale of strategic materials hinder Japan's aggression in the Pacific? LAFS.1112.RH.2.4, SS.912.A.6.2

Using Your Notes

3. *Determining Cause and Effect* Use the notes you completed during the lesson to write a paragraph identifying the events that moved the United States from neutrality to war. SS.912.A.6.2

Answering the Guiding Questions

4. *Evaluating* Why did many Americans support isolationism? Why did President Roosevelt support internationalism? SS.912.A.6.2

5. *Synthesizing* How did President Roosevelt assist Britain while maintaining U.S. neutrality? SS.912.A.6.2

6. *Explaining* How did the United States try to slow Japan's advances in the Pacific? SS.912.A.6.2

Writing Activity

7. INFORMATIVE/EXPLANATORY Write a short essay in which you discuss why the United States had taken action against the Japanese before the attack. LAFS.1112.WHST.1.2, LAFS.1112.WHST.4.10, SS.912.A.6.2

LESSON 3

The Holocaust

ESSENTIAL QUESTIONS

• Could World War II have been prevented?
• Why do some people not respond to injustice while others try to prevent injustice?

READING HELPDESK

Academic Vocabulary

• prohibit   • virtually
• assume

Content Vocabulary

• concentration camp
• extermination camp

TAKING NOTES

Key Ideas and Details

Organizing As you read about the Holocaust, complete a graphic organizer similar to the one below, by listing examples of Nazi persecution of European Jews. LAFS.1112.RH.3.7, SS.912.A.6.3

```
Examples
   of
Persecution
```

**NEXT GENERATION
SUNSHINE STATE STANDARDS**

LAFS.1112.RH.1.1: Cite specific textual evidence to support analysis of primary and secondary sources, connecting insights gained from specific details to an understanding of the text as a whole.

LAFS.1112.RH.2.4: Determine the meaning of words and phrases as they are used in a text, including analyzing how an author uses and refines the meaning of a key term over the course of a text (e.g., how Madison defines faction in Federalist No. 10).

LAFS.1112.RH.3.7: Integrate and evaluate multiple sources of information presented in diverse formats and media (e.g., visually, quantitatively, as well as in words) in order to address a question or solve a problem.

LAFS.1112.WHST.1.1: Write arguments focused on discipline-specific content.

Continued on page 345

IT MATTERS BECAUSE
Nazis first acted upon their racist ideology when they imposed restrictions on Jews and stripped them of basic rights. Eventually, Nazi Germany created concentration camps and systematically attempted to kill all European Jews.

Nazi Persecution of the Jews

GUIDING QUESTION *Why did many Jews remain in Nazi Germany and within Axis-controlled areas of Europe?*

During the Holocaust, the Nazis murdered nearly six million Jews, two-thirds of the Jews in Europe. The Nazis also murdered millions of people from other groups they considered inferior. The Hebrew term for the Holocaust is Shoah, meaning "catastrophe," but it is often used specifically to refer to the Nazi campaign to exterminate the Jews during World War II. The Holocaust was a genocide, the systematic murder of members of a group with the intent to destroy the existence of the group.

The Nuremberg Laws
Although the Nazis persecuted anyone who dared oppose them, as well as people with disabilities, Gypsies (now known as Roma), homosexuals, and Slavic peoples, they reserved their strongest hatred for the Jews. This loathing went far beyond the European anti-Semitism that was common at the time. In the Middle Ages, Jews had been subjected to discrimination and sometimes to mob violence and expulsions. But in nineteenth- and twentieth-century Western and Central Europe, both the frequency and intensity of anti-Jewish government policies diminished.

After the Nazis took power, however, they quickly moved to deprive German Jews of many established rights. In September 1935, the Nuremberg Laws took citizenship away from Jewish Germans and banned marriage between Jews and other Germans. Two months later, another decree barred Jews from holding public office or voting. Another law compelled Jews with German-sounding names to adopt "Jewish" names. Soon the passports of Jews were marked with a red J to identify them as Jewish.

By the summer of 1936, at least half of Germany's Jews were jobless, having lost the right to work as civil servants, journalists, farmers, and actors. In 1938, the Nazis also banned Jews from practicing law and medicine and from operating businesses. With no source of income, life for Jews became very difficult.

Despite worsening conditions, many Jews chose to remain in Germany during the early years of Nazi rule. Well integrated into German society before this time, they were reluctant to leave and give up the lives they had built there. Many also thought that conditions would surely improve after a time. In fact, conditions soon became worse.

Kristallnacht

On November 7, 1938, a young Jewish refugee named Herschel Grynszpan shot and killed a German diplomat in Paris. Grynszpan's parents and more than 14,000 other Polish Jews had been deported from Germany to Poland, and the distraught young man was seeking revenge for this act and for the persecution of the Jews in general.

Using this as a pretext, Hitler ordered his minister of propaganda, Joseph Goebbels, to stage attacks against the Jews that would seem like a spontaneous popular reaction to news of the murder. On the night of November 9, this plan played out in a spree of destruction. In Vienna, a Jewish child named Frederic Morton watched in terror that night as Nazi storm troopers broke into his family's apartment:

PRIMARY SOURCE

"They yanked out every drawer in every one of our chests and cupboards, and tossed each in the air. They let the cutlery jangle across the floor, the clothes scatter, and stepped over the mess to fling the next drawer. Their exuberance was amazing. . . . 'We might be back,' the leader said. On the way out he threw our mother-of-pearl ashtray over his shoulder, like confetti. We did not speak or move or breathe until we heard their boots against the pavement."

—quoted in *Facing History and Ourselves*

The anti-Jewish violence that erupted throughout Germany and Austria that night came to be called *Kristallnacht,* or "night of broken glass," because broken glass littered the streets afterward. By the following morning, more than ninety Jews were dead, hundreds were badly injured, and thousands more were terrorized. The Nazis had forbidden police to interfere while roving bands of thugs destroyed 7,500 Jewish businesses and hundreds of synagogues.

The lawlessness of *Kristallnacht* continued. Following the initial night of violence, the Gestapo, the government's secret police, arrested about 30,000 Jewish men.

Mary Evans Picture Library/Weimer Archive

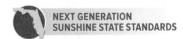

NEXT GENERATION
SUNSHINE STATE STANDARDS

Continued from page 344

LAFS.1112.WHST.2.4: Produce clear and coherent writing in which the development, organization, and style are appropriate to task, purpose, and audience.

LAFS.1112.WHST.4.10: Write routinely over extended time frames (time for reflection and revision) and shorter time frames (a single sitting or a day or two) for a range of discipline-specific tasks, purposes, and audiences.

SS.912.A.1.2: Utilize a variety of primary and secondary sources to identify author, historical significance, audience, and authenticity to understand a historical period.

SS.912.A.1.4: Analyze how images, symbols, objects, cartoons, graphs, charts, maps, and artwork may be used to interpret the significance of time periods and events from the past.

Continued on page 346

On *Kristallnacht,* November 9, 1938, Nazi storm troopers destroyed Jewish property, such as this burned-out synagogue, and terrorized Jewish families across the Third Reich.

▶ CRITICAL THINKING

Making Generalizations How do you think publication of the photograph of the synagogue would have affected world opinion toward the Nazis?
LAFS.1112.RH.3.7, SS.912.A.1.4, SS.912.A.6.3

After weeks of fierce resistance, Jews in the Warsaw ghetto in Poland are rounded up for deportation to concentration camps in May 1943.

▶ **CRITICAL THINKING**

Predicting Consequences What details in the photograph suggest what might happen when these people reach the concentration camps? LAFS.1112.RH.1.1, LAFS.1112.RH.3.7, SS.912.A.1.4, SS.912.A.6.3

prohibit to make illegal by an authority

assume to take for granted or as true

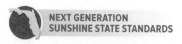

NEXT GENERATION SUNSHINE STATE STANDARDS

Continued from page 345

SS.912.A.6.3: Analyze the impact of the Holocaust during World War II on Jews as well as other groups.

SS.912.G.1.2: Use spatial perspective and appropriate geographic terms and tools, including the Six Essential Elements, as organizational schema to describe any given place.

SS.912.G.2.1: Identify the physical characteristics and the human characteristics that define and differentiate regions.

The state also confiscated insurance payments owed to Jewish owners of ruined businesses.

Jewish Refugees Try to Flee

Kristallnacht and its aftermath marked a significant escalation of Nazi persecution against the Jews. Many Jews, including Frederic Morton's family, decided that it was time to leave and fled to the United States. Between 1933, when Hitler took power, and the start of World War II in 1939, some 250,000 Jews escaped Nazi-controlled Germany. These emigrants included prominent scientists, such as Albert Einstein, and business owners like Otto Frank, who resettled his family in Amsterdam in 1933. Otto's daughter Anne kept a diary of her family's life in hiding after the Nazis overran the Netherlands. The "secret annex," as she called their hiding place, has become a museum.

Limits on Jewish Immigration By 1938, one U.S. consulate in Germany had a backlog of more than 100,000 visa applications from Jews trying to leave for the United States. Following the Nazi *Anschluss,* some 3,000 Austrian Jews applied for U.S. visas each day. Most never received visas to the United States or to the other countries where they applied. As a result, millions of Jews remained trapped in Nazi-dominated Europe.

Several factors limited Jewish immigration to the United States. Nazi orders **prohibited** Jews from taking more than about four dollars out of Germany. United States' immigration law, however, forbade granting a visa to anyone "likely to become a public charge." Customs officials tended to **assume** that this description applied to Jews, because Germany had forced them to leave behind any wealth. High unemployment rates in the 1930s also made immigration unpopular. Few Americans wanted to raise immigration quotas, even to accommodate European refugees. Others did not want to admit Jews because they held anti-Semitic attitudes. The existing immigration policy allowed only 150,000 immigrants annually, with a fixed quota from each country. The law permitted no exceptions for refugees or victims of persecution.

International Response At an international conference on refugees in 1938, several European countries, the United States, and Latin America stated their regret that they could not take in more of Germany's Jews without raising their immigration quotas. Meanwhile, Nazi propaganda chief Joseph Goebbels announced, "[I]f there is any country that believes it has not enough Jews, I shall gladly turn over to it all our Jews." Hitler also declared himself "ready to put all these criminals at the disposal of these countries . . . even on luxury ships."

As war loomed in 1939, many ships departed from Germany crammed with Jews desperate to escape. Some of their visas, however, had been forged or sold illegally, and Mexico, Paraguay, Argentina, and Costa Rica all denied access to Jews with such documents. So, too, did the United States.

The *St. Louis* Affair On May 27, 1939, the SS *St. Louis* entered the harbor in Havana, Cuba, with 930 Jewish refugees on board. Most of these passengers hoped to go to the United States eventually, but they had certificates improperly issued by Cuba's director of immigration giving them permission to

Yivo Institute for Jewish Research

land in Cuba. When the ships arrived in Havana, the Cuban government refused to let the refugees come ashore. For several days, the ship's captain steered his ship in circles off the coast of Florida, awaiting official permission to dock at a U.S. port. Denied permission, the ship turned back toward Europe, disembarking in France, Holland, Belgium, and Great Britain. Within two years, the first three of these countries fell under Nazi domination. Many of the refugees brought to these countries perished in the Nazis' "final solution."

✓ **READING PROGRESS CHECK**

Explaining What factors made it difficult for Jewish people to leave Europe?

The Final Solution

GUIDING QUESTION *How did the Nazis try to exterminate Europe's Jewish population?*

On January 20, 1942, Nazi leaders met at the Wannsee Conference to coordinate the "final solution of the Jewish question." Previous "solutions" had included rounding up Jews, Roma, Slavs, and others from conquered areas, shooting them, and piling them into mass graves. Another method forced Jews and other "undesirables" into trucks and then piped in exhaust fumes to kill them. These methods, however, had proven too slow and inefficient for the Nazis.

At Wannsee, the Nazis made plans to round up Jews from the vast areas of Nazi-controlled Europe. Jews were taken to detention centers known as **concentration camps.** There, healthy individuals would work as slave laborers until they dropped dead of exhaustion, disease, or malnutrition. Most others, including the elderly, young children, and the infirm (among them laborers who could no longer work) would be sent to **extermination camps,** attached to many of the concentration camps, to be executed in massive gas chambers.

Concentration Camps

The Nazis had established their first concentration camps in 1933 to jail political opponents. After the war began, the Nazis built concentration camps throughout Europe.

concentration camp
a camp where persons are detained or confined

extermination camp
a camp where men, women, and children were sent to be executed

Men, women, and children are packed onto cattle cars for transport to extermination camps.

▶ CRITICAL THINKING
Making Generalizations What does the fact that Jews were transported on cattle cars indicate about Nazi attitudes toward them? LAFS.1112.RH.3.7, SS.912.A.1.4, SS.912.A.6.3

Yad Vashem Photo Archives, courtesy of USHMM

The Holocaust 1939–1945

Legend:
- Concentration camp
- Extermination camp
- Location of *Einsatzgruppen* (paramilitary death squads)
- International boundary, January 1938

Map labels: NORWAY, FINLAND, SWEDEN, North Sea, ESTONIA, DENMARK, Baltic Sea, LATVIA, Moscow, UNITED KINGDOM, Bergen-Belsen, LITHUANIA, EAST PRUSSIA (Ger.), Ravensbrück, UNION OF SOVIET SOCIALIST REPUBLICS, NETH., GERMANY, Treblinka, POLAND, BELG., Buchenwald, Chelmno, Sobibor, Majdanek, Paris, LUX., Auschwitz-Birkenau, Belzec, Dachau, CZECHOSLOVAKIA, FRANCE, SWITZ., AUSTRIA, HUNGARY, ROMANIA, Black Sea, ITALY, Adriatic Sea, YUGOSLAVIA, BULGARIA, Rome, ALBANIA, GREECE, Mediterranean Sea

Scale: 400 miles / 400 km
Lambert Azimuthal Equal-Area projection

Jewish Losses: 1939–1945

Baltic States	228,000
Belgium	40,000
Bulgaria	14,000
Byelorussian SSR	245,000
Czechoslovakia	155,000
Denmark	500
France	90,000
Germany and Austria	210,000
Greece	54,000
Hungary	450,000
Italy	8,000
Netherlands	195,000
Poland	3,000,000
Romania	300,000
Russian SSR	107,000
Ukrainian SSR	900,000
Yugoslavia	26,000

GEOGRAPHY CONNECTION

Nazi concentration camps and extermination camps extended across several countries.

1 **THE WORLD IN SPATIAL TERMS** *Where were most of the extermination camps located?* SS.912.A.1.4, SS.912.A.6.3, SS.912.G.1.2

2 **PLACES AND REGIONS** *Which three nations had the highest number of Jewish losses?* SS.912.A.1.4, SS.912.A.6.3, SS.912.G.1.2, SS.912.G.2.1

As one of the largest concentration camps, Buchenwald had more than 200,000 prisoners working 12-hour shifts as slave laborers in nearby factories. Although Buchenwald had no gas chambers, hundreds of prisoners died there every month from exhaustion and horrible living conditions. As a U.S. Army chaplain wrote in his diary in 1945:

PRIMARY SOURCE

"One thousand Weimar citizens toured the Buchenwald camp in groups of 100. They saw blackened skeletons and skulls in the ovens of the crematorium. In the yard outside, they saw a heap of white human ashes and bones. . . . Those who were dead were stripped of their clothing and lay naked, many stacked like cordwood waiting to be burned in the crematory. At one time, 5,000 had been stacked on the vacant lot next to the crematory."

—from the diary of Captain Luther D. Fletcher, quoted in *World War II: From the Battle Front to the Home Front*

Leon Bass, a young American soldier, saw Buchenwald at the end of the war. A room built to hold 50 people had housed more than 150, with bunk beds built almost to the ceiling. Bass recalled:

PRIMARY SOURCE

"I looked at a bottom bunk and there I saw one man. He was too weak to get up; he could just barely turn his head. He was skin and bones. He looked like a skeleton; and his eyes were deep set. He didn't utter a sound; he just looked at me with those eyes, and they still haunt me today."

—quoted in *Facing History and Ourselves*

TEXT: Leon Bass quoted in Elements of Time: Holocaust Testimonies, 83-84. Copyright © 2011 by Facing History and Ourselves National Foundation. Reprinted by permission.

Extermination Camps

In late 1941, the Nazis built extermination facilities at the Chelmno and Auschwitz camps in Poland. After the Wannsee Conference, extermination facilities were built at four other camps in Poland. At these camps, including the infamous Treblinka, Jews were the Nazis' main victims. Auschwitz alone housed about 100,000 people in 300 prison barracks. Its gas chambers, built to kill 2,000 people at a time, could gas 12,000 people in a day. Of the estimated 1,600,000 people who died at Auschwitz, about 1,300,000 were Jews. Most of the others were Poles, Soviet prisoners of war, or Roma.

Upon arrival at Auschwitz, healthy prisoners were selected for slave labor. Elderly or disabled people, the sick, and mothers and children went immediately to the gas chambers, after which their bodies were burned in giant crematoriums.

In only a few years, Jewish culture, which had existed in Europe for more than 1,000 years, had been **virtually** obliterated by the Nazis in the lands they conquered. Despite exhaustive debate, there is still great controversy about why and how an event so horrifying as the Holocaust could have occurred. No consensus has been reached, but most historians point to a number of factors: the German people's sense of injury after World War I; severe economic problems; Hitler's control over the German nation; the lack of a strong tradition of representative government in Germany; German fear of Hitler's secret police; and a long history of anti-Jewish prejudice and discrimination in Europe.

☑ **READING PROGRESS CHECK**

Explaining What was the purpose and outcome of the Wannsee Conference?

American soldiers force German civilians to view bodies after the liberation of the Buchenwald concentration camp.

▶ **CRITICAL THINKING**
Drawing Conclusions Why did American soldiers force German civilians to view the atrocities at the concentration camp?
LAFS.1112.RH.3.7, SS.912.A.1.4, SS.912.A.6.3

virtually almost entirely; nearly

United States Holocaust Memorial Museum, courtesy of Harold Royall

---

LESSON 3 REVIEW

Reviewing Vocabulary

1. *Defining* What was the purpose of the concentration camps? LAFS.1112.RH.2.4, SS.912.A.6.3

2. *Identifying* How was the Buchenwald concentration camp different from Treblinka and Auschwitz? LAFS.1112.RH.2.4, SS.912.A.6.3

Using Your Notes

3. *Making Connections* Review the notes you completed during the lesson, and then identify an anti-Jewish policy or action that should have warned the world that the Nazis needed to be stopped immediately. SS.912.A.6.3

Answering the Guiding Questions

4. *Evaluating* Why did many Jews remain in Nazi Germany and within Axis-controlled areas of Europe? SS.912.A.6.3

5. *Explaining* How did the Nazis try to exterminate Europe's Jewish population? SS.912.A.6.3

Writing Activity

6. ARGUMENT Imagine that you are living in the United States during the 1930s. You believe that more Jewish immigrants should be allowed to come into the country. Write a letter to your representative or senator in Congress to express your point of view. LAFS.1112.WHST.1.1, LAFS.1112.WHST.2.4, LAFS.1112.WHST.4.10, SS.912.A.6.3

LAFS.1112.RH.1.1, LAFS.1112.RH.1.2, LAFS.1112.RH.1.3, LAFS.1112.RH.2.5, LAFS.1112.RH.3.7, LAFS.1112.RH.3.9, LAFS.1112.RH.4.10, SS.912.A.1.2, SS.912.A.1.4, SS.912.A.6.3

The Holocaust

As the Allies liberated areas from German control in the spring of 1945, they discovered horrifying scenes in Nazi concentration camps. The Nazi regime had systematically murdered six million Jews and killed another six million Poles, Slavs, Roma, homosexuals, communists, and persons who were mentally disabled. Photographs of the newly liberated camps shocked the American public, although the Roosevelt administration and the State Department had evidence of the death camps as early as 1942.

VOCABULARY

prohibited
to forbid by authority

horde
a large disorganized group or crowd

facilitate
to make easier

malignant
evil in nature or influence, vicious

vengeance
revenge, getting even

vindicate
prove true or correct

NAZI DECREE, 1941

I. (1) Jews over six years of age are **prohibited** from appearing in public without wearing a Jewish star.

(2) The Jewish star is a yellow piece of cloth with a black border, in the form of a six-pointed star the size of a palm of the hand. The inscription reads 'JEW' in black letters. It shall be worn visibly, sewn on the left chest side of the garment.

II. Jews are forbidden:

(a) to leave their area of residence without written permission of the local police, carried on their person.

(b) to wear medals, decorations or other insignia.

—Nazi decree issued September 1, 1941 from *Nazism 1919–1945, Volume 3: Foreign Policy, War and Racial Extermination—A Document Reader*

EYEWITNESS ACCOUNT

"[There] were two barracks: the men stood on one side, the women on the other. They were addressed in a very polite and friendly way: 'You have been on a journey. You are dirty. You will take a bath. Get undressed quickly.' Towel and soap were handed out, and then suddenly the brutes woke up and showed their true faces: this **horde** of people, these men and women were driven outside with hard blows and forced both summer and winters to go the few hundred metres to the 'Shower Room.' Above the entry door was the word 'Shower'. One could even see shower heads on the ceiling which were cemented in but never had water flowing through them.

These poor innocents were crammed together, pressed against each other. Then panic broke out, for at last they realized the fate in store for them. But blows with rifle butts and revolver shots soon restored order and finally they all entered the death chamber. The doors were shut and, ten minutes later, the temperature was high enough to **facilitate** the condensation of the hydrogen cyanide for the condemned were gassed with hydrogen cyanide. This was the so-called 'Zyklon B' . . . which was used by the German barbarians. . . . One could hear fearful screams, but a few moments later there was complete silence."

—André Lettich, Jewish prisoner assigned to remove bodies from the gas chambers at Birkenau from *Nazism 1919–1945, Volume 3: Foreign Policy, War and Racial Extermination—A Document Reader*

TEXT: (l)Nazism 1919-1945 Volume 3 Foreign Policy, War and Racial Extermination: A Documentary Reader, Edited by J. Noakes and G. Pridham, new edition with index, 2001; (r)From The New York Times, November 10, 1978 © 1978 The New York Times. All rights reserved. Used by permission and protected by the Copyright Laws of the United States.

AMERICAN SOLDIER'S DIARY, 1945

"One thousand Weimar citizens toured the Buchenwald camp in groups of 100. They saw blackened skeletons and skulls in the ovens of the crematorium. In the yards outside, they saw a heap of white human ashes and bones . . .

Often . . . the SS wished to make an example of someone in killing him. They hung him on the lot adjacent to the crematory, and all the three sections of the camp witnessed the sight—some 30,000 prisoners . . ."

—diary of Captain Luther D. Fletcher, from *World War II: From the Battle Front to the Home Front*

PROSECUTION STATEMENT

The wrongs which we seek to condemn and punish have been so calculated, so **malignant**, and so devastating, that civilization cannot tolerate their being ignored, because it cannot survive their being repeated. That four great nations, flushed with victory and stung with injury stay the hand of **vengeance** and voluntarily submit their captive enemies to the judgment of the law is one of the most significant tributes that Power has ever paid to Reason.

This Tribunal, while it is novel and experimental, is not the product of abstract speculations nor is it created to **vindicate** legalistic theories. This inquest represents the practical effort of four of the most mighty of nations, with the support of 17 more, to utilize international law to meet the greatest menace of our times—aggressive war.

. . . What makes this inquest significant is that these prisoners represent sinister influences that will lurk in the world long after their bodies have returned to dust. We will show them to be living symbols of racial hatreds, of terrorism and violence, and of the arrogance and cruelty of power. . . . Civilization can afford no compromise with the social forces which would gain renewed strength if we deal ambiguously or indecisively with the men in whom those forces now precariously survive.

—Robert H. Jackson, Chief of Counsel for the United States, Opening Statement before the International Military Tribunal, Nuremberg, Germany, November 21, 1945

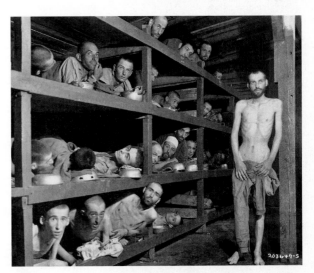

▲ *These survivors of Buchenwald concentration camp, liberated in 1945, show the horrifying conditions under which they lived.*

DBQ Analyzing Historical Documents

1. **Evaluating Text Evidence** In his eyewitness account, André Lettich describes the Germans as "barbarians." What evidence does he provide in his account to support this accusation? Why does the language of Lettich's account help to validate the source?

2. **Finding the Main Idea** What do all these primary sources have in common?

3. **Acquiring Information** What restrictions did the Nazis impose on Jews in 1941?

4. **Corroborating** How does the photo of Buchenwald corroborate the American soldier's diary?

5. **Analyzing Historical Questions** Study the photo, then read the excerpt from the American soldier's diary, and the excerpt from Robert Jackson's opening statement. What impact did the liberation of the concentration camps have on soldiers and the world? How did the Allies respond to the discovery of the camps?

6. **Answering Historical Questions** Why does Jackson say the war crimes trials were necessary?

7. **Evaluating Sources** Given that Jackson was Chief of Counsel for the United States at Nuremberg, how would you evaluate him as a source of information?

©Pvt. H. Miller/Corbis

STUDY GUIDE

THE ORIGINS OF WORLD WAR II
LESSON 1

March 1938
Anschluss of Austria

February 1938
Hitler demands German control of Sudetenland

September 1938
Britain & France appease Hitler at Munich Conference

October 1938
Hitler demands control over Danzig

August 1939
Nazi-Soviet Non-Aggression signed

September 1939
Nazi troops invade Poland

FROM NEUTRALITY TO WAR
LESSON 2

Restricted sale of strategic material
- Airplane fuel
- Scrap iron
- Steel
- Oil

Lend-Lease aid to China

Freezing Japanese assets in U.S.

MacArthur relocated to Philippines

THE HOLOCAUST
LESSON 3

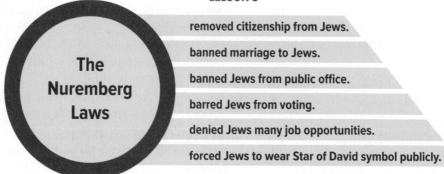

The Nuremberg Laws

removed citizenship from Jews.

banned marriage to Jews.

banned Jews from public office.

barred Jews from voting.

denied Jews many job opportunities.

forced Jews to wear Star of David symbol publicly.

Directions: On a separate sheet of paper, answer the questions below. Make sure you read carefully and answer all parts to the question.

Lesson Review

Lesson 1

1 *Comparing* What did Hitler, Mussolini, and Stalin have in common? SS.912.A.6.1

2 *Identifying* Explain how the borders of Europe changed as a result of the Anschluss and the Munich Conference. Why was the policy adopted by British and French leaders at Munich known as appeasement? SS.912.A.6.1

3 *Explaining* What famous battle saved Britain from being invaded by Germany, and why was it critical in preventing an invasion? Who fought this battle and what new technology enabled the British to win the battle even though they were outnumbered? SS.912.A.6.1

Lesson 2

4 *Identifying Central Issues* By the mid-1930s, why did many Americans have bitter feelings about World War I? SS.912.A.6.2

5 *Summarizing* When Japan invaded China in 1937, what justification did Roosevelt use to authorize the sale of arms to the Chinese even though the Neutrality Act of 1937 made it illegal to sell arms to countries fighting a war? SS.912.A.6.2

Lesson 3

6 *Evaluating* Why were Jews, Roma, and Slavs persecuted by the Nazis? SS.912.A.6.3

7 *Identifying Significance* What was the Wannsee Conference, and what happened as a result of decisions made at that conference? SS.912.A.6.3

8 *Explaining* Why did the United States not waive its immigration quotas to allow more Jewish refugees into the country?

Exploring the Essential Questions

9 *Conducting an Historical Inquiry* Could World War II have been prevented? Write a brief essay that reviews the historical evidence presented in the chapter about the causes of World War II. Use that evidence to explain whether or not you think World War II could have been prevented. LAFS.1112.RH.3.9, LAFS.1112.WHST.3.9, LAFS.1112.WHST.4.10, SS.912.A.1.1, SS.912.A.6.1

10 *Making an Oral Presentation* Use the library or online sources, as well as the information in the text, to prepare a speech about the Holocaust. Be sure to use authoritative sources, follow citation conventions, and organize your research to effectively communicate your findings. If possible, use presentation software to create a slideshow with images and quotes to accompany your speech. Be sure to trace the ideas of anti-Semitism and events in Germany that led to the Holocaust and discuss why it was able to happen. Explain why it is important to learn about the Holocaust and not forget that it happened. LAFS.1112.RH.3.9, LAFS.1112.SL.1.2, LAFS.1112.SL.2.4, LAFS.1112.WHST.2.6, LAFS.1112.WHST.3.7, LAFS.1112.WHST.3.8, LAFS.1112.WHST.3.9, SS.912.A.1.2, SS.912.A.1.5, SS.912.A.6.3

Critical Thinking

11 *Analyzing* When Germany invaded France in World War I, the fighting quickly bogged down in trench warfare. What advancements and changes in conventional weapons enabled Germany to quickly break through French lines and force France to surrender? Identify the type of warfare that Germany introduced and explain why it allowed the German military to conquer so much of Europe in such a short time. SS.912.A.6.1

21st Century Skills

12 *Sequencing using Absolute and Relative Chronology* Create a time line showing the sequence of events that began with Japan's decision to build an empire in Asia and ended with Japan's decision to attack Pearl Harbor, triggering America's entry into World War II. Include dates for events on the time line as well as captions for each event that explains its significance to the coming of the war. SS.912.A.1.3, SS.912.A.6.1

13 *Discussing* Prepare for a class discussion by answering the question: What were the similarities and differences between the Japanese and German drives to build an empire? During discussion, make sure to further the dialogue by asking thoughtful questions and by responding to your classmates' questions. LAFS.1112.SL.1.1, SS.912.A.6.1

Need Extra Help?

If You've Missed Question	**1**	**2**	**3**	**4**	**5**	**6**	**7**	**8**	**9**	**10**	**11**	**12**	**13**
Go to Lesson	1	1	1	2	2	3	3	3	1	3	1	2	1, 2

DBQ Analyzing Primary Sources

Use the quotation to answer the following questions.

In May 1941 President Roosevelt declared a national emergency because of concerns that the war in Europe was likely to spill over into the western hemisphere. Read the excerpt below from his speech proclaiming the emergency:

PRIMARY SOURCE

❝The first and fundamental fact is that what started as a European war has developed, as the Nazis always intended it should develop, into a world war for world domination. . . . It is unmistakably apparent to all of us that, unless the advance of Hitlerism is forcibly checked now, the Western Hemisphere will be within range of the Nazi weapons of destruction. . . . To the people of the Americas, a triumphant Hitler would say, as he said after the seizure of Austria, and as he said after Munich, and as he said after the seizure of Czechoslovakia: 'I am now completely satisfied. This is the last territorial readjustment I will seek.' And he would of course add: 'All we want is peace, friendship, and profitable trade relations with you in the New World.' . . . Nobody can foretell tonight just when the acts of the dictators will ripen into attack on this hemisphere and us. But we know enough by now to realize that it would be suicide to wait until they are in our front yard.❞

—Radio Address, May 27, 1941

14 *Interpreting Speeches* What parts of the speech demonstrate how German aggression contributed to the United States' entry into the war? LAFS.1112.RH.1.1, LAFS.1112.RH.3.8, LAFS.1112.RH.4.10, SS.912.A.6.1

15 *Finding the Main Idea* In justifying the declaration of emergency, what does Roosevelt say to counter the arguments of Americans who supported neutrality and isolationism? LAFS.1112.RH.3.8, LAFS.1112.RH.4.10, LAFS.1112.SL.1.3, SS.912.A.6.1, SS.912.A.6.2

Analyzing Visuals

Use the image to answer the following questions.

On May 22, 1941, cartoonist Theodor Geisel (later to be known as Dr. Seuss) published this political cartoon criticizing U.S. isolationism in the face of the Nazi threat.

"Ho hum! When he's finished pecking down that last tree he'll quite likely be tired."

16 *Analyzing Visuals* What do the trees and each of the two birds represent? LAFS.1112.RH.1.1, SS.912.A.1.4, SS.912.A.6.1, SS.912.A.6.2

17 *Identifying Central Ideas* Using what you know about U.S. isolationism and Roosevelt's internationalism, analyze Geisel's message. How does the cartoon support his claim? LAFS.1112.RH.1.2, LAFS.1112.RH.3.7, LAFS.1112.RH.3.8, SS.912.A.1.4, SS.912.A.6.1, SS.912.A.6.2

18 *Making Inferences* If a reader saw this cartoon in 1941 and agreed with its message, what policies might that person have supported? LAFS.1112.RH.3.7, SS.912.A.1.4, SS.912.A.6.1, SS.912.A.6.2

Extended Response Questions

19 *Understanding Relationships Among Events* Write an essay identifying Hitler's ideas and describing the actions that he and the German government took that contributed to the United States becoming involved in World War II. To help you write clearly, plan out the points you will cover before writing, and revise after you are done with your first draft. LAFS.1112.WHST.1.2, LAFS.1112.WHST.2.4, LAFS.1112.WHST.2.5, LAFS.1112.WHST.4.10, SS.912.A.6.1, SS.912.A.6.2

Need Extra Help?

If You've Missed Question	**14**	**15**	**16**	**17**	**18**	**19**
Go to Lesson	1, 2	1, 2	1, 2	1, 2	1, 2	1

◄ "Rosie the Riveter" is a fictional character that came to symbolize women in the workforce during World War II. Images such as this one encouraged women to participate in the war effort.

FROM 1941 TO 1945

America and World War II

THE STORY MATTERS ...

During World War II, millions of Americans enlisted in the armed forces, risking their lives in the struggle. On the home front, Americans also helped the war effort by giving up goods needed by the military and by buying war bonds. Read the chapter to learn how Americans sacrificed during World War II in the hopes of achieving a better future.

ESSENTIAL QUESTION
- What kinds of sacrifices does war require?

The Granger Collection, New York

Place & Time: The World 1941–1945

After Germany invaded Poland, President Roosevelt expanded the army and built up the country's defenses. After the bombing of Pearl Harbor, the United States was at war. The United States increased the defense budget and rapidly increased production of aircraft, ships, and equipment. The nation was now fighting a war that involved Europe, Africa, and the Pacific.

Step Into the Place

Read the quote and look at the information presented on the map.

 DBQ How did the scale of World War II influence Roosevelt's feelings about democracy?

PRIMARY SOURCE

"The preservation of the spirit and faith of the nation does, and will, furnish the highest justification for every sacrifice that we may make in the cause of national defense.

In the face of great perils never before encountered, our strong purpose is to protect and to perpetuate the integrity of democracy.

For this we muster the spirit of America, and the faith of America.

We do not retreat. We are not content to stand still. As Americans, we go forward, in the service of our country. . . ."

—Franklin D. Roosevelt, Third Inaugural Address, January 20, 1941

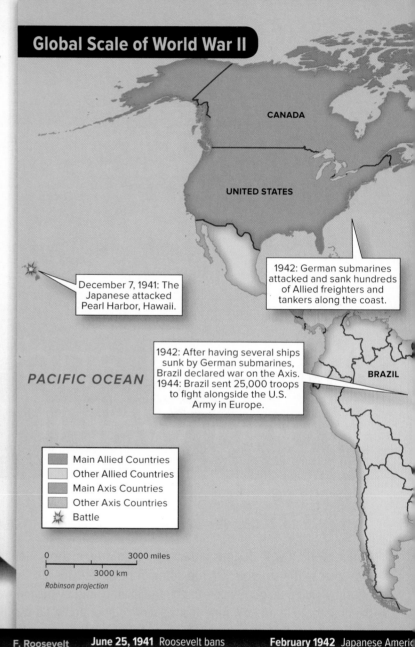

Global Scale of World War II

CANADA

UNITED STATES

December 7, 1941: The Japanese attacked Pearl Harbor, Hawaii.

1942: German submarines attacked and sank hundreds of Allied freighters and tankers along the coast.

1942: After having several ships sunk by German submarines, Brazil declared war on the Axis. 1944: Brazil sent 25,000 troops to fight alongside the U.S. Army in Europe.

PACIFIC OCEAN

BRAZIL

Main Allied Countries
Other Allied Countries
Main Axis Countries
Other Axis Countries
Battle

| 0 | | 3000 miles |
| 0 | | 3000 km |

Robinson projection

Step Into the Time

DETERMINING CAUSE AND EFFECT Choose a WWII event from the time line and write a paragraph explaining how this event impacted Americans on the home front.

F. Roosevelt
1933–1945

June 25, 1941 Roosevelt bans discrimination in defense industries

December 8, 1941 United States enters World War II

February 1942 Japanese American relocation ordered

May 1942 Women's Army Auxilia Corps established

U.S. PRESIDENTS

UNITED STATES

WORLD

1941

1942

December 7, 1941 Japan attacks Pearl Harbor

May 1942 Japan captures the Philippin

June 1942 United States wins Battle of Midway

NEXT GENERATION SUNSHINE STATE STANDARDS
Students will understand the following benchmarks from the Florida NGSSS

LAFS.1112.RH.3.7: Integrate and evaluate multiple sources of information presented in diverse formats and media (e.g., visually, quantitatively, as well as in words) in order to address a question or solve a problem.

LAFS.1112.RH.3.9: Integrate information from diverse sources, both primary and secondary, into a coherent understanding of an idea or event, noting discrepancies among sources.

SS.912.A.1.2: Utilize a variety of primary and secondary sources to identify author, historical significance, audience, and authenticity to understand a historical period.

SS.912.A.1.3: Utilize timelines to identify the time sequence of historical data.

SS.912.A.1.4: Analyze how images, symbols, objects, cartoons, graphs, charts, maps, and artwork may be used to interpret the significance of time periods and events from the past.

SS.912.A.6.1: Examine causes, course, and consequences of World War II on the United States and the world.

ARCTIC OCEAN

GREAT BRITAIN
GERMANY
FRANCE
ITALY

UNION OF SOVIET SOCIALIST REPUBLICS

CHINA

JAPAN

ATLANTIC OCEAN

PACIFIC OCEAN

INDIAN OCEAN

February 1943: The Germans defeated American forces at the Battle of Kasserine Pass.

November 1942: The British defeated German forces in the Egyptian coastal city of El Alamein, securing the Suez Canal.

1937: Japanese troops moved against Chinese units near Beijing, which led to war between the two countries. The Japanese went on to take and pillage the Chinese capital, Nanking.

1942: The Japanese took Burma and closed the Burma Road, a vital supply line into China.

European colonies in Africa supplied resources and, in some cases, troops to both the Axis and Allies.

N
W-E
S

left page: (t)Library of Congress, Prints & Photographs Division [LC-USZ62-26759]; (b)detail/White House Collection/The White House Historical Association; **right page:** detail/White House Collection/The White House Historical Association

June 1943 Race riots in Detroit and "zoot suit" riots in Los Angeles

December 1944 Supreme Court rules in *Korematsu* v. *United States* that Japanese American relocation is constitutional

April 1945 Franklin Roosevelt dies in office and Harry S. Truman becomes president

Truman 1945–1953

1943

1944

1945

February 1943 Germans defeated at Stalingrad

July 1943 Allied forces land in Italy

June 6, 1944 Eisenhower leads D-Day invasion

October 1944 MacArthur's forces land in the Philippines

February 1945 U.S. Marines capture Iwo Jima

August 1945 United States drops atomic bombs on Japan

LESSON 1
Wartime America

ESSENTIAL QUESTION
• What kinds of sacrifices does war require?

READING HELPDESK

Academic Vocabulary

- draft
- justify
- coordinate

Content Vocabulary

- disenfranchised
- cost-plus
- Sunbelt
- zoot suit
- victory suit
- rationing
- victory garden

TAKING NOTES

Key Ideas and Details

Organizing Use the following graphic organizer to list changes for women and minorities during the war. LAFS.1112.RH.3.7, SS.912.A.6.4

	Changes
Women	
African Americans	
Native Americans	
Hispanic Americans	
Japanese Americans	

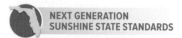
NEXT GENERATION SUNSHINE STATE STANDARDS

ELD.K12.ELL.SI.1: English language learners communicate for social and instructional purposes within the school setting.

Continued on page 359

IT MATTERS BECAUSE

After World War I, America returned to isolationism. When the nation entered World War II in 1941, its armed forces ranked nineteenth in might, behind the tiny European nation of Belgium. Three years later, the United States was producing 40 percent of the world's arms.

Building the Military

GUIDING QUESTION *What roles did minorities and women play in the armed forces during World War II?*

Within days of Germany's attack on Poland in 1939, President Roosevelt expanded the army to 227,000 soldiers. Before the spring of 1940, many Americans had opposed a peacetime **draft.** Opinions changed after France surrendered to Germany in June 1940. In September of that year, Congress approved the Selective Training and Service Act—a plan for the first peacetime draft in American history—by a wide margin.

The man responsible for taking the flood of recruits and building a large modern army capable of engaging the armed forces of Germany and Japan was General George C. Marshall, chief of staff of the U.S. Army and Roosevelt's chief military advisor. Marshall would guide the largest expansion of the army in American history from fewer than 190,000 men at the time the war began in Europe in 1939 to over 8 million men by the war's end.

You're in the Army Now

More than 60,000 men enlisted in the month after the attack on Pearl Harbor. At first, the flood of recruits overwhelmed the army's training facilities and equipment supplies. In 1940 the Department of Agriculture had transferred over 350,000 acres to the War Department. New bases such as the Naval Air Station in Jacksonville, Florida, were built, and existing ones such as Eglin Air Force Base were expanded. Many recruits lived in tents rather than barracks, carried sticks representing guns, and practiced maneuvers with trucks labeled "TANK."

New recruits were given physical exams and injections against smallpox and typhoid. Then they were issued uniforms, boots, and available equipment, and sent to basic training for eight weeks. Trainees drilled and exercised constantly and learned how to work as a team. Basic training helped break down barriers between soldiers. Recruits came from all over the country, and training together created tight relationships among the troops.

A Segregated Military

Although basic training promoted unity, most recruits did not encounter Americans from every part of society. At the start of the war, the U.S. military was segregated. African Americans were organized into their own units, but white officers generally commanded them. Military leaders typically assigned them to construction and supply units.

Pushing for "Double V" Not all African Americans wanted to support the war. As one African American college student noted: "The Army jim-crows us. . . . Employers and labor unions shut us out. Lynchings continue. We are **disenfranchised** . . . [and] spat upon. What more could Hitler do to us than that?" Nevertheless, most agreed that they should support their country. One leading African American newspaper, the *Pittsburgh Courier,* launched the "Double V" campaign to urge readers to support the war to win a double victory over Hitler's racism abroad and racism at home.

African Americans in Combat Under pressure from African American leaders, President Roosevelt ordered the armed services to recruit African Americans and to put them into combat. He also promoted Colonel Benjamin O. Davis, Sr., the highest-ranking African American officer, to the rank of brigadier general.

In early 1941, the air force created its first African American unit, the 99th Pursuit Squadron. Trained in Tuskegee, Alabama, the pilots became known as the Tuskegee Airmen. Commanded by Lt. Colonel Benjamin O. Davis, Jr., the squadron helped win the Battle of Anzio in Italy. Three other Tuskegee squadrons protected American bombers as they flew to their targets. Known as the 332nd Fighter Group, these squadrons flew 200 such missions without losing a single member to enemy aircraft. Also, the African American 761st Tank Battalion was commended for service during the Battle of the Bulge.

Other Minorities in the Military Although Japanese Americans were not allowed to serve at first, as the war progressed second-generation Japanese Americans served in the 100th Infantry Battalion and the 442nd Regimental Combat Team. Almost half had been in internment camps in

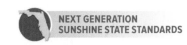

NEXT GENERATION SUNSHINE STATE STANDARDS

Continued from page 358

ELD.K12.ELL.SS.1: English language learners communicate information, ideas and concepts necessary for academic success in the content area of Social Studies.

MAFS.912.S-ID.1: Summarize, represent and interpret data on a single count or measurement variable.

LAFS.1112.RH.2.4: Determine the meaning of words and phrases as they are used in a text, including analyzing how an author uses and refines the meaning of a key term over the course of a text (e.g., how Madison defines faction in Federalist No. 10).

LAFS.1112.RH.3.7: Integrate and evaluate multiple sources of information presented in diverse formats and media (e.g., visually, quantitatively, as well as in words) in order to address a question or solve a problem.

LAFS.1112.WHST.1.2: Write informative/ explanatory texts, including the narration of historical events, scientific procedures/ experiments, or technical processes.

LAFS.1112.WHST.3.9: Draw evidence from informational texts to support analysis, reflection, and research.

LAFS.1112.WHST.4.10: Write routinely over extended time frames (time for reflection and revision) and shorter time frames (a single sitting or a day or two) for a range of discipline-specific tasks, purposes, and audiences.

SS.912.A.1.1: Describe the importance of historiography, which includes how historical knowledge is obtained and transmitted, when interpreting events in history.

SS.912.A.1.2: Utilize a variety of primary and secondary sources to identify author, historical significance, audience, and authenticity to understand a historical period.

SS.912.A.1.4: Analyze how images, symbols, objects, cartoons, graphs, charts, maps, and artwork may be used to interpret the significance of time periods and events from the past.

Continued on page 360

draft a system used for choosing people from the population to serve in the military

disenfranchise to deprive of the right to vote

SKILLS PRACTICE

When you hear new academic vocabulary words, be sure to use them to help build your understanding of them. This section uses the academic terms "draft," "coordinate," and "justify." Include these words in sentences you write and in discussions with your classmates.
ELD.K12.ELL.SI.1, ELD.K12.ELL.SS.1

U.S. ARMED FORCES, 1939–1946 — CHARTS/GRAPHS

Military personnel (millions)
10, 8, 6, 4, 2
Army
Navy
Marines
Year: 1939, 1940, 1941, 1942, 1943, 1944, 1945, 1946

Source: *Historical Statistics of the United States.*

1 *Comparing and Contrasting*
In which years were the armed forces at their highest and lowest levels? MAFS.912.S-ID.1

2 *Drawing Conclusions*
Between which two years was there the greatest increase in the armed services? What happened during this time period that might account for the increase? MAFS.912.S-ID.1, LAFS.1112.SL.2.4

Broadened Perspectives

❝ Entrance into the Army in August, 1942, widened my horizons literally as well as experientially: for the first time I travelled beyond a 200 mile radius from Newark. I marveled at the flatness of the prairie in Illinois. . . . Stops at posts in Miami Beach, Florida, and Richmond, Virginia, were my introduction to the American South.❞

—Carl Degler, from *The History Teacher*, vol. 23, 1990

DBQ DRAWING CONCLUSIONS

Why might entering the army have changed a person's perspective? SS.912.A.1.2

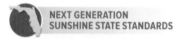

NEXT GENERATION SUNSHINE STATE STANDARDS

Continued from page 359

SS.912.A.6.1: Examine causes, course, and consequences of World War II on the United States and the world.

SS.912.A.6.4: Examine efforts to expand or contract rights for various populations during World War II.

SS.912.A.6.5: Explain the impact of World War II on domestic government policy.

SS.912.A.6.15: Examine key events and peoples in Florida history as they relate to United States history.

the Southwest. Together these units became the most decorated in the history of the United States military. Approximately 500,000 Hispanic Americans served in the armed forces despite racial hostility against them. By the end of the war, 17 Hispanic Americans had received the Medal of Honor.

About one-third of all able-bodied Native American men aged 18–50 served in the military during the war. More than 400 Navajo marines served as "code talkers," relaying critical information and orders over field radios as spoken messages coded in their own language.

Of the half million Jewish Americans who served in the military, approximately 52,000 were decorated for bravery. Because so many European Jews died as a result of the Holocaust, American Jews took on increased leadership in the worldwide Jewish community.

Although the military did not end all segregation during the war, it did integrate military bases in 1943 and steadily expanded the role of African Americans within the armed forces. These successes paved the way for President Truman's decision to fully integrate the military in 1948.

Women Join the Armed Forces

Women also joined the armed forces. The army enlisted them for the first time but barred them from combat. Many army jobs were administrative and clerical. Filling these jobs with women freed more men for combat.

Congress first allowed women in the military in May 1942 by creating the Women's Army Auxiliary Corps (WAAC). It appointed War Department official Oveta Culp Hobby as WAAC's first director. Many women were unhappy that WAAC was not part of the regular army, however. About a year later, the army replaced the WAAC with the Women's Army Corps (WAC), and Hobby became a colonel.

The coast guard, navy, and marines followed suit and set up women's units. Another 68,000 women served as nurses in the army and navy. About 300 women serving as Women Airforce Service Pilots (WASPs) made more than 12,000 flights to deliver planes to the war effort.

✓ **READING PROGRESS CHECK**

Summarizing How did the status of women and minorities in the armed forces change during the war?

©Bettmann/Corbis

CHARTS/GRAPHS

1. *Determining Cause and Effect* When did tank production begin to drop? Why might this be so?
MAFS.912.S-ID.1, LAFS.1112.WHST.3.9

2. *Predicting Consequences* How might the changes in industrial production toward the end of the war have affected employment in the late 1940s? LAFS.1112.WHST.3.9

MOBILIZING INDUSTRY

Source: The Big 'L': American Logistics in World War II.

Industrial workers watch as new tanks roll out of the factory.

American Economy in Wartime

GUIDING QUESTION *How did the U.S. government mobilize the economy for war?*

Fighting a global war troubled President Roosevelt, but not British prime minister Winston Churchill who knew that victory depended on industry. He compared the American economy to a gigantic boiler: "Once the fire is lighted under it there is no limit to the power it can generate."

Converting the Economy

War production increased rapidly after the attack on Pearl Harbor, helped by existing government plans to build thousands of warplanes and a "Two-Ocean" navy. Roosevelt believed that government and business had to work together to prepare for war. He created the National Defense Advisory Committee and asked business leaders to serve on the committee. The president and his advisers believed that giving industry incentives to produce goods quickly was the best way to rapidly mobilize the economy.

Normally, the government asked companies to bid on contracts to produce military equipment, a slow process. Instead, the government signed **cost-plus** contracts, agreeing to pay a company the cost to make a product plus a guaranteed percentage as profit. Under the cost-plus system, the more—and faster—a company produced, the more money it made. Although not cheap, the system got war materials produced quickly and in quantity. Cost-plus convinced many companies to convert to war production, and Congress authorized the Reconstruction Finance Corporation (RFC) to make loans to companies wanting to convert.

cost-plus a government contract to pay a manufacturer the cost to produce an item plus a guaranteed percentage

American Industry Gets the Job Done

By the fall of 1941, much had already been done to prepare the economy for war, but it was still only partially mobilized. The attack on Pearl Harbor changed everything. By the summer of 1942, almost all major industries and some 200,000 companies had converted to war production. Together they made the nation's wartime "miracle" possible.

ANALYZING PRIMARY SOURCES

The Value of Vehicles

PRIMARY SOURCE

"The greatest advantage . . . the United States has enjoyed on the ground in the fighting so far [was] . . . the jeep and the two-and-a-half-ton truck. These are the instruments which moved and supplied United States troops in battle, while the German Army . . . depended heavily on animal transport. . . . The United States, profiting from the mass production achievements of its automotive industry . . . had mobility that completely outclassed the enemy.**"**

—General George C. Marshall, chief of staff for the U.S. Army, quoted in *Miracle of World War II*

DBQ Analyzing Historical Documents

Making Inferences Why was U.S. mobility such an important advantage? **SS.912.A.1.2**

Library of Congress, Prints & Photographs Division [LC-USZ62-61397]

During World War II, millions of American women took jobs in wartime factories.

▶ **CRITICAL THINKING**
Making Connections What was the long-term impact of women's wartime participation in the labor force? SS.912.A.1.4, SS.912.A.6.5

 Florida
CONNECTION

The Mosquito Fleet

During the war, the U.S. Coast Guard was placed under the command of the U.S. Navy. The Coast Guard was responsible for patrolling the nation's coastlines, including Florida's 1,100 mile coast. Beginning in 1942, the "Mosquito Fleet"—a collection of private vessels outfitted with machine guns and radios—helped patrol this coast. As the war continued, regular Coast Guard ships took over this responsibility. SS.912.A.6.15

Tanks Replace Cars The automobile industry was uniquely suited to mass-producing military goods. Automobile plants began making trucks, jeeps, and tanks. Mass production was critical because the country that could move troops and supplies most quickly usually won the battle.

Automobile factories produced rifles, helmets, artillery, and dozens of other pieces of military equipment along with vehicles. Henry Ford created an assembly line near Detroit for the enormous B-24 "Liberator" bomber. The factory went on to build more than 8,600 aircraft. Overall, the auto industry made nearly one-third of all wartime military equipment.

Building Liberty Ships Ford's remarkable achievement in aircraft production was more than matched by Henry Kaiser's shipyards. German submarines were sinking American cargo ships at a terrifying rate. The United States had to find a way to build cargo ships as quickly as possible. Kaiser's method emphasized speed and results. Instead of building an entire ship in one place from the keel up, parts were prefabricated and brought to the shipyard for assembly.

Kaiser's shipyards built many kinds of ships, but they were best known for basic cargo ships called Liberty ships. When the war began, it took 244 days to build the first Liberty ship. After Kaiser shipyards applied their mass-production techniques, average production time dropped to 41 days. Kaiser's shipyards built 30 percent of all American ships constructed during the war.

As war production grew, controversies between business leaders, government agencies, and the military increased. President Roosevelt created the War Production Board (WPB) to direct priorities and production goals. Later he set up the Office of War Mobilization to settle disputes among the different agencies.

✔ READING PROGRESS CHECK

Explaining How did the government work to quickly prepare the American economy for the war effort?

Life on the Home Front

GUIDING QUESTION *How did World War II change life for women and minorities in the United States?*

The war dramatically changed American society. Unlike much of Europe and Asia, which experienced devastation, America benefited somewhat from the war. Mobilizing the economy finally ended the Great Depression, creating almost 19 million new jobs and nearly doubling the average family's income. As an Ohio worker noted, "[O]ne of the important things that came out of World War II was the arrival of the working class at a new status level in this society. . . . The war integrated into the mainstream a whole chunk of society that had been living on the edge."

Library of Congress, Prints & Photographs Division [LC-USZ62-97395]

The improvement in the economy did not come without cost. Families had to move to where the defense factories were located. Housing conditions were terrible. The pressures and prejudices of the era led to strikes, race riots, and rising juvenile delinquency. Goods were rationed and taxes were higher. Workers earned more money, but also worked longer hours.

When the war began, American defense factories wanted to hire white men. With so many men in the military, however, there simply were not enough white men to fill all of the jobs. Under pressure to produce, employers began to recruit women and minorities.

Women in Defense Plants

During the Great Depression, many people believed married women should not work outside the home, especially if they took jobs that could go to men trying to support their families. Most working women were young, single, and employed in traditional female jobs such as domestic work or teaching. The wartime labor shortage, however, forced factories to recruit married women for industrial jobs traditionally reserved for men.

Although the government hired nearly 4 million women, primarily for clerical jobs, the women working in the factories captured the public's imagination. The great symbol of the campaign to hire women was "Rosie the Riveter," a character from a popular song by the Four Vagabonds. The lyrics told of Rosie, who worked in a factory while her boyfriend served in the marines. Images of Rosie appeared on posters, in newspapers, and in

Florida CONNECTION

The "Double V" Campaign

In Florida, the "Double V" campaign spurred the growth of the NAACP. The National Urban League investigated employment discrimination. Harry T. Moore and the NAACP challenged pay discrimination against teachers and encouraged voter registration. By 1946, African American voter registration in Florida had reached 13 percent. SS.912.A.6.15

ANALYZING SUPREME COURT CASES

KOREMATSU v. *UNITED STATES*, 1944

Background to the Case

During World War II, President Roosevelt's Executive Order 9066 and other legislation gave the military the power to exclude people of Japanese descent from areas that were deemed important to U.S. national defense and security. In 1942 Toyosaburo Korematsu refused to leave San Leandro, California, which had been designated as a "military area" based on Executive Order 9066. Korematsu was found guilty in federal district court of violating Civilian Exclusion Order No. 34. Korematsu petitioned the Supreme Court to review the federal court's decision.

Japanese American women and their children talk together at the Heart of the Mountain Relocation Camp.

How the Court Ruled

In their decision, the majority of the Supreme Court, with three dissenting, found that, although exclusion orders based on race are constitutionally suspect, the government is justified in time of "emergency and peril" to suspend citizens' civil rights. A request for a rehearing of the case in 1945 was denied.

❶ Drawing Conclusions Why did the Supreme Court find in favor of the government in this case, even though the justices were suspicious of exclusion based on race? LAFS.1112.WHST.3.9

❷ Suggesting a Solution Under what circumstances, if any, do you think the government should be able to suspend civil liberties of all or specific groups of American citizens? SS.912.A.1.6

National Archives/Time & Life Pictures/Getty Images

Sunbelt a new industrial region in southern California and the Deep South that developed during World War II

coordinate to harmonize or bring into common action, movement, or condition

Thinking Like a
HISTORIAN

Distinguishing Fact from Opinion

When *In Defense of Internment: The Case for "Racial Profiling" in World War II and the War on Terror* was published in 2004, many historians were outraged. Author Michelle Malkin supported the decision to put Japanese Americans in internment camps. The Historians' Committee for Fairness said it was "contradicted by several decades of scholarly research." Malkin wrote that Roosevelt had evidence that some spying was taking place on the West Coast, and that Roosevelt was protecting national security.
SS.912.A.1.1

zoot suit men's clothing of extreme cut typically consisting of a thigh-length jacket with wide padded shoulders and baggy, pleated pants with narrow cuffs

magazines. Eventually 2.5 million women worked in shipyards, aircraft factories, and other manufacturing plants.

By the end of the war, the number of working women had increased from 12.9 million to 18.8 million. Although most women were laid off or left their jobs voluntarily after the war, their success permanently changed American attitudes about women in the workplace.

African Americans Demand War Work

Factories hired women, but they resisted hiring African Americans. Frustrated by the situation, A. Philip Randolph, the head of the Brotherhood of Sleeping Car Porters—a major union for African American railroad workers—decided to act. He informed President Roosevelt that he was organizing a march on Washington "in the interest of securing jobs . . . in the national defense and . . . integration into the . . . military and naval forces."

On June 25, 1941, Roosevelt issued Executive Order 8802, which stated, "there shall be no discrimination in the employment of workers in defense industries or government because of race, creed, color, or national origin." To enforce the order, he created the Fair Employment Practices Commission, the first federal civil rights agency since Reconstruction.

Mexican Farmworkers

The wartime economy also benefited Mexicans. In 1942, the federal government arranged for Mexican farmworkers to help harvest crops in the Southwest as part of the Bracero Program, which continued until 1964. More than 200,000 Mexicans came to work during the war. Many also helped build and maintain railroads. Migrant workers thus became important to the Southwest's economic system.

✅ **READING PROGRESS CHECK**

Describing What changes did women and minorities experience as a result of economic mobilization?

A Nation on the Move

GUIDING QUESTION *How did the wartime relocation of many Americans affect U.S. government and society?*

The wartime economy created millions of new jobs, leading 15 million Americans to move to find work. The growth of southern California and cities in the Deep South created a new industrial region—the **Sunbelt.** Cities with war industries had to find room for the thousands of arriving workers. Tent cities and parks filled with tiny trailers sprang up. Congress authorized $150 million for housing in 1940. In 1942, Roosevelt created the National Housing Agency (NHA) to **coordinate** government housing programs.

Racism Leads to Violence

Many African Americans left the South for jobs in war factories in the North and West. However, African Americans often faced suspicion and intolerance. Racial violence erupted in Detroit on Sunday, June 20, 1943. Fighting between white and African American teens triggered a citywide riot that left 25 African Americans and 9 whites dead.

In Los Angeles, the fear of juvenile crime and racism against Mexican Americans became linked in the "zoot suit" riots. Popular with Mexican American teenagers, **zoot suits** had very baggy, pleated pants and an overstuffed, knee-length jacket with wide lapels. Most men, to conserve fabric for the war, wore a **"victory suit"** with no vest, no cuffs, a short jacket, and narrow lapels. In June 1943, after hearing rumors that zoot-suiters had attacked several sailors, some 2,500 soldiers and sailors attacked Mexican American neighborhoods in Los Angeles.

Japanese, German, and Italian American Relocation

When Japan attacked Pearl Harbor, many Americans turned their anger against Japanese immigrants and Japanese Americans. On February 19, 1942, President Roosevelt signed Executive Order 9066 allowing the War Department to declare any part of the United States a military zone and to remove people from that zone as needed. He must have felt **justified** four days later when a Japanese submarine surfaced north of Santa Barbara, California, and shelled an oil refinery. Most of the West Coast was declared a military zone, and people of Japanese ancestry were evacuated to 10 internment camps farther inland.

In 1988 President Ronald Reagan apologized to Japanese Americans on behalf of the U.S. government and signed legislation granting $20,000 to each surviving Japanese American who had been interned.

Thousands of people of German and Italian descent also had their freedom restricted. All unnaturalized residents of German and Italian descent aged 14 years or over were deemed enemy aliens and subject to regulations including travel restrictions and the seizure of personal property. More than 5,000 were arrested and sent to live in military internment camps.

✓ READING PROGRESS CHECK

Determining Cause and Effect How did both voluntary and forced movement during World War II change the United States?

Daily Life in Wartime

GUIDING QUESTION *What steps did the government take to stabilize wages and prices?*

Both wages and prices began to rise quickly during the war because of the high demand for workers and raw materials. Worried about inflation, Roosevelt created the Office of Price Administration and Civilian Supply (OPACS) and the Office of Economic Stabilization (OES) to regulate wages and certain prices. At the end of the war, prices had risen only about half as much as they had during World War I.

While OPACS and OES worked to control inflation, the War Labor Board (WLB) tried to prevent strikes. Most American unions issued a "no strike pledge," instead asking the WLB to mediate wage disputes. By the end of the war, the WLB had helped settle more than 17,000 disputes.

Support and Sacrifices

High demand for raw materials and supplies created shortages. OPACS began **rationing,** or limiting the purchase of, many products to make sure enough were available for military use. Households picked up a book of rationing coupons every month for different kinds of food. When people bought food, they had to have enough coupon points to cover their purchases. Meat, sugar, fats, oils, processed foods, coffee, shoes, and

Americans donated pots, tires, tin cans, car bumpers, broken radiators, and rusting bicycles to scrap drives held during World War II.

▶ CRITICAL THINKING
Drawing Conclusions How did holding scrap drives help the government prevent shortages?
LAFS.1112.WHST.3.9, SS.912.A.6.1

victory suit a men's suit with no vest, no cuffs, a short jacket, and narrow lapels, worn during World War II in order to save fabric for the war effort

justify to prove or to show to be just, right, or reasonable

rationing restricting the amount of an item an individual can have due to a limited supply

©Seattle Post-Intelligencer Collection; Museum of History and Industry/Historical/Corbis gasoline were all rationed. Driving distances were restricted, and the speed limit was set at 35 miles per hour to save gas and rubber.

Americans also planted gardens in backyards, schoolyards, city parks, and empty lots to produce more food for the war effort. The government encouraged **victory gardens** by praising them in film reels, pamphlets, and official statements. The government organized scrap drives to collect rubber, tin, aluminum, and steel.

victory garden garden planted by citizens during war to raise vegetables for home use, leaving more for the troops

The federal government spent more than $300 billion during World War II—more money than it had spent from Washington's administration to the end of Franklin Roosevelt's second term. Congress raised taxes, although not as high as what Roosevelt requested, due to public opposition to large tax increases. As a result, the extra taxes collected covered only 45 percent of the war's cost.

To make up the difference, the government issued war bonds. Buying bonds is a way to loan money to the government. In exchange for the money, the government promised to repay the bonds' purchase price plus interest at some future date. Individual Americans demonstrated their patriotism and commitment to winning the war by buying nearly $50 billion worth of war bonds. Banks, insurance companies, and other financial institutions bought the rest—more than $100 billion worth of bonds.

Despite the hardships, the overwhelming majority of Americans believed the war had to be fought. Although the war brought many changes to the United States, most Americans remained united behind one goal—winning the war.

Hollywood Goes to War

In 1942 President Roosevelt created the Office of War Information (OWI). The OWI's role was to improve the public's understanding of the war and to act as a liaison office with various media. The OWI established detailed guidelines for filmmakers, including a set of questions to be considered before making a movie, such as, "Will this picture help win the war?"

✓ **READING PROGRESS CHECK**

Evaluating How did the Office of Price Administration and Civilian Supply assure there were enough supplies for military use?

LESSON 1 REVIEW

Reviewing Vocabulary
1. *Explaining* How did cost-plus contracts help the United States prepare for war? LAFS.1112.RH.2.4, LAFS.1112.WHST.3.9

Using Your Notes
2. *Evaluating* Use the notes that you completed during the lesson to evaluate which groups benefited from the war, and how they did so. LAFS.1112.WHST.3.9

Answering the Guiding Questions
3. *Summarizing* What roles did minorities and women play in the armed forces during World War II? LAFS.1112.WHST.3.9, SS.912.A.6.4, SS.912.A.6.5
4. *Analyzing* How did the U.S. government mobilize the economy for war? LAFS.1112.WHST.3.9

5. *Assessing* How did World War II change life for women and minorities in the United States? LAFS.1112.WHST.3.9, SS.912.A.6.4, SS.912.A.6.5
6. *Making Connections* How did the wartime relocation of many Americans affect U.S. government and society? LAFS.1112.WHST.3.9, SS.912.A.6.4, SS.912.A.6.5
7. *Specifying* What steps did the government take to stabilize wages and prices? LAFS.1112.WHST.3.9, SS.912.A.6.5

Writing Activity
8. INFORMATIVE/EXPLANATORY Think about what you learned about women and minorities in the workforce during World War I. Write a short essay in which you compare the roles of women and minorities in the workforce during World War I and World War II. LAFS.1112.WHST.1.2, LAFS.1112.WHST.3.9

LESSON 2

The War in the Pacific

ESSENTIAL QUESTION
• What kinds of sacrifices does war require?

READING HELPDESK

Academic Vocabulary

• code

Content Vocabulary

• amphtrac
• kamikaze

TAKING NOTES

Key Ideas and Details

Organizing Use the following graphic organizer to record the major battles discussed and the victor in each.
LAFS.RH.3.7, SS.912.A.6.1

Major Pacific Battles

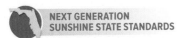

NEXT GENERATION SUNSHINE STATE STANDARDS

LAFS.1112.RH.2.4: Determine the meaning of words and phrases as they are used in a text, including analyzing how an author uses and refines the meaning of a key term over the course of a text (e.g., how Madison defines faction in Federalist No. 10).

LAFS.1112.RH.3.7: Integrate and evaluate multiple sources of information presented in diverse formats and media (e.g., visually, quantitatively, as well as in words) in order to address a question or solve a problem.

LAFS.1112.WHST.1.1: Write arguments focused on discipline-specific content.

Continued on page 368

IT MATTERS BECAUSE

The early battles of the war required changes in strategy from all sides. In the Pacific, the Battle of Midway was a major turning point against the Japanese. After that American victory, Admiral Nimitz and General MacArthur led American forces in a steady advance across the Pacific.

Holding the Line Against Japan

GUIDING QUESTION *Why was the Doolittle Raid important for U.S. forces in the Pacific?*

Admiral Chester Nimitz, the commander of the United States Navy in the Pacific, began planning operations against the Japanese navy. Although the Japanese had badly damaged the American fleet at Pearl Harbor, they had missed the American aircraft carriers, which were at sea on a mission. The United States had several carriers in the Pacific, and Nimitz was determined to use them. In the days just after Pearl Harbor, however, Nimitz could do little to stop Japan's advance into Southeast Asia.

The Fall of the Philippines

A few hours after bombing Pearl Harbor, the Japanese attacked American airfields in the Philippines. Two days later, they landed troops. The American and Filipino forces defending the Philippines were badly outnumbered. Their commander, General Douglas MacArthur, retreated to the Bataan Peninsula. Using the peninsula's rugged terrain, the troops held out for more than three months.

By March, in desperation, the troops ate cavalry horses and mules. The lack of food and supplies, along with diseases such as malaria, scurvy, and dysentery, took their toll. The women of the Army Nurse Corps worked on Bataan in primitive conditions. Patients slept in the open air. One nurse, Rose Meier, reported, "If we needed more room, we got our axes and chopped some bamboo trees down."

General Douglas MacArthur (1880–1964)

General Douglas MacArthur graduated from West Point in 1903. One of his first military assignments was in the Philippines, site of his later World War II defeat and subsequent victory. In 1904 he was appointed aide-de-camp to his father, General Arthur MacArthur, in Japan. Following his World War II success in the Pacific, he was appointed Supreme Commander, Allied Powers (SCAP) in Japan. There he decreased Japan's military and helped reestablish its economy.

▶ CRITICAL THINKING

Evaluating What is the significance of MacArthur's early military experience in the Philippines and Japan?

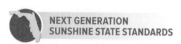

NEXT GENERATION SUNSHINE STATE STANDARDS

Continued from page 367

LAFS.1112.WHST.3.9: Draw evidence from informational texts to support analysis, reflection, and research.

LAFS.1112.WHST.4.10: Write routinely over extended time frames (time for reflection and revision) and shorter time frames (a single sitting or a day or two) for a range of discipline-specific tasks, purposes, and audiences.

SS.912.A.1.2: Utilize a variety of primary and secondary sources to identify author, historical significance, audience, and authenticity to understand a historical period.

SS.912.A.1.4: Analyze how images, symbols, objects, cartoons, graphs, charts, maps, and artwork may be used to interpret the significance of time periods and events from the past.

SS.912.A.6.1: Examine causes, course, and consequences of World War II on the United States and the world.

SS.912.A.6.15: Examine key events and peoples in Florida history as they relate to United States history.

Realizing MacArthur's capture would demoralize the American people, President Roosevelt ordered the general to evacuate to Australia. MacArthur promised, "I came through, and I shall return."

On April 9, 1942, the weary defenders of the Bataan Peninsula finally surrendered. Nearly 78,000 prisoners of war were forced to march—sick, exhausted, and starving—65 miles (105 km) to a Japanese prison camp. Almost 10,000 troops died on this march, which was later to be called the Bataan Death March. Private Leon Beck was taken prisoner when Bataan surrendered and took part in the Bataan Death March for 13 days before escaping. He later recalled:

PRIMARY SOURCE

"They'd halt us in front of these big artesian wells . . . so we could see the water and they wouldn't let us have any. Anyone who would make a break for water would be shot or bayoneted. Then they were left there. Finally, it got so bad further along the road that you never got away from the stench of death. There were bodies laying all along the road in various degrees of decomposition—swollen, burst open, maggots crawling by the thousands. . . ."

—from *Death March: The Survivors of Bataan*, 1981

Sixty-six women nurses were also captured and sent to the University of Santo Tomas in Manila. They remained there—with 11 navy nurses and some 3,000 Allied civilians—until early in 1945.

Although the troops in the Bataan Peninsula surrendered, a small force held out on the island of Corregidor in Manila Bay. Finally, in May 1942, Corregidor surrendered. The Philippines had fallen to the Japanese.

The Doolittle Raid on Tokyo

Even before the Philippines fell, President Roosevelt was searching for a way to raise the morale of the American people. He wanted to bomb Tokyo, but American planes could reach Tokyo only if an aircraft carrier brought them close enough. However, Japanese ships in the North Pacific prevented carriers from getting near Japan.

In early 1942, a military planner suggested replacing the carrier's usual short-range bombers with long-range B-25 bombers that could attack from farther away. The only problem was that, although B-25s could take off from a carrier, the bombers could not land on its short deck. After attacking Japan, they would have to land in China.

President Roosevelt put Lieutenant Colonel James Doolittle in command of the mission to bomb Tokyo. At the end of March, a crane loaded sixteen B-25s onto the aircraft carrier *Hornet*. The next day, the *Hornet* headed west across the Pacific. On April 18, American bombs fell on Japan for the first time.

Japan Changes Strategy

While Americans rejoiced in the air force's success, Japanese leaders were aghast at the raid. Those bombs could have killed Emperor Hirohito, who was revered as a god. The Doolittle Raid convinced Japanese leaders to change their strategy.

Before the raid, the Japanese navy had disagreed about the next step. The officers in charge of the navy's planning wanted to cut American supply lines to Australia by capturing the south coast of New Guinea. The commander of the fleet, Admiral Yamamoto, wanted to attack Midway Island—the last American base in the North Pacific west of Hawaii. Yamamoto believed that attacking Midway would lure the American fleet into battle and enable his fleet to destroy it.

Library of Congress, Prints & Photographs Division [LC-USZ62-210027]

These Navajo code talkers assigned to a Pacific-based marine regiment relay orders using a field radio.

▶ **CRITICAL THINKING**

Evaluating What advantages did the code talkers provide to American forces?
LAFS.1112.WHST.3.9, SS.912.A.1.4, SS.912.A.6.1

After Doolittle's raid, the Japanese war planners dropped their opposition to Yamamoto's idea. The American fleet had to be destroyed to protect Tokyo from bombing. The attack on New Guinea would still go ahead, but only three aircraft carriers were assigned to the mission. All of the other carriers were ordered to assault Midway.

The Battle of the Coral Sea

The Japanese believed that they could safely proceed with two attacks at once because they thought their operations were secret. What the Japanese did not know was that an American team of **code** breakers based in Hawaii had already broken the Japanese navy's secret code for conducting operations.

In March 1942, decoded Japanese messages alerted the United States to the Japanese attack on New Guinea. In response, Admiral Nimitz sent two carriers, the *Yorktown* and the *Lexington,* to intercept the Japanese in the Coral Sea. There, in early May, carriers from both sides launched all-out airstrikes against each other. Although the Japanese sank the *Lexington* and badly damaged the *Yorktown,* the American attacks prevented the Japanese from landing on New Guinea's south coast and kept the supply lines to Australia open.

The Navajo Code Talkers

When American marines stormed an enemy beach, they used radios to communicate. Using radios, however, meant that the Japanese could intercept and translate the messages. In the midst of the battle, there was no time to use a code-machine. Acting upon the suggestion of Philip Johnston, an engineer who had lived on a Navajo reservation as a child, the marines recruited Navajos to serve as "code talkers."

The Navajo language had no written alphabet and was known only to the Navajo and a few missionaries and anthropologists. The Navajo recruits developed code words, using their own language, that stood for military terms. For example, the Navajo word *jay-sho,* or "buzzard," was code for *bomber; lo-tso,* or "whale," meant *battleship;* and *ni-ma-si,* or "potatoes," stood for *grenades.*

Code talkers proved invaluable in combat. They could relay a message in minutes that would have taken a code-machine operator hours to encipher and transmit. During the Battle of Iwo Jima, code talkers transmitted more than 800 messages during the first 48 hours as the marines struggled to

code a signal or symbol used to represent something that is to be kept secret

The Navajo language is not a written language, and only a small number of people understand it.

▶ **CRITICAL THINKING**

Drawing Conclusions What was the advantage of having a code that the Japanese could not decipher? LAFS.1112.WHST.3.9, SS.912.A.6.1

(t)©Bettmann/Corbis;(b)©Ron Sachs/CNP/Corbis News/Corbis

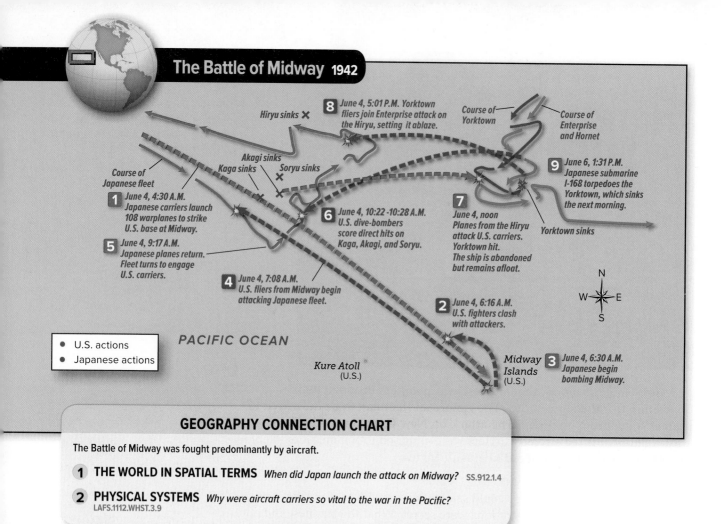

8 June 4, 5:01 P.M. Yorktown fliers join Enterprise attack on the Hiryu, setting it ablaze.

Hiryu sinks ✕

Course of Yorktown

Course of Enterprise and Hornet

Akagi sinks
Kaga sinks   Soryu sinks
✕   ✕

Course of Japanese fleet

9 June 6, 1:31 P.M. Japanese submarine I-168 torpedoes the Yorktown, which sinks the next morning.

1 June 4, 4:30 A.M. Japanese carriers launch 108 warplanes to strike U.S. base at Midway.

5 June 4, 9:17 A.M. Japanese planes return. Fleet turns to engage U.S. carriers.

6 June 4, 10:22 -10:28 A.M. U.S. dive-bombers score direct hits on Kaga, Akagi, and Soryu.

7 June 4, noon Planes from the Hiryu attack U.S. carriers. Yorktown hit. The ship is abandoned but remains afloat.

Yorktown sinks

4 June 4, 7:08 A.M. U.S. fliers from Midway begin attacking Japanese fleet.

2 June 4, 6:16 A.M. U.S. fighters clash with attackers.

N
W ✦ E
S

• U.S. actions
• Japanese actions

PACIFIC OCEAN

Kure Atoll
(U.S.)

Midway Islands
(U.S.)

3 June 4, 6:30 A.M. Japanese begin bombing Midway.

GEOGRAPHY CONNECTION CHART

The Battle of Midway was fought predominantly by aircraft.

1 **THE WORLD IN SPATIAL TERMS** *When did Japan launch the attack on Midway?* SS.912.1.4

2 **PHYSICAL SYSTEMS** *Why were aircraft carriers so vital to the war in the Pacific?*
LAFS.1112.WHST.3.9

get ashore under intense bombardment. Sworn to secrecy, their mission was not revealed until 1971. In 2001, Congress awarded code talkers the Congressional Gold Medal for their unique contribution during the war.

✓ READING PROGRESS CHECK

Explaining What did the Doolittle Raid on Tokyo accomplish?

Battle of Midway

GUIDING QUESTION *Why was the Battle of Midway a turning point in the war in the Pacific?*

Back at Pearl Harbor, the code-breaking team now learned of the plan to attack Midway. With so many ships at sea, Admiral Yamamoto transmitted the plans for the Midway attack by radio, using the same code the Americans had already cracked.

Admiral Nimitz had been waiting for the opportunity to ambush the Japanese fleet. He immediately ordered carriers to take up positions near Midway. Unaware that they were heading into an ambush, the Japanese launched their aircraft against Midway on June 4, 1942. The Americans were ready. The Japanese ran into a blizzard of antiaircraft fire, and 38 planes were shot down. As the Japanese prepared a second wave to attack Midway, aircraft from the American carriers *Hornet, Yorktown,* and *Enterprise* launched a counterattack. The American planes caught the Japanese carriers with fuel, bombs, and aircraft exposed on their flight decks. Within minutes, three Japanese carriers were reduced to burning wrecks.

A fourth was sunk a few hours later, and Admiral Yamamoto ordered his remaining ships to retreat.

The Battle of Midway was a turning point in the war. The Japanese navy lost four large carriers—the heart of its fleet. Just six months after Pearl Harbor, the United States had stopped the Japanese advance. The victory was not without cost, however. The battle killed 362 Americans and 3,057 Japanese.

✓ READING PROGRESS CHECK

Explaining Why was the United States able to ambush the Japanese at Midway and turn the tide of the war?

Driving Back Japan

GUIDING QUESTIONS *What was the military strategy behind "island-hopping"? Was it successful?*

The American plan to defeat Japan called for a two-pronged attack. The Pacific Fleet, commanded by Admiral Nimitz, would advance through the central Pacific by "hopping" from one island to the next, closer and closer to Japan. Meanwhile, General MacArthur's troops would advance through the Solomon Islands, capture the north coast of New Guinea, and then launch an invasion to retake the Philippines.

Island-Hopping in the Pacific

By the fall of 1943, the navy was ready to launch its island-hopping campaign, but the geography of the central Pacific posed a problem. Many of the islands were coral reef atolls. The water over the coral reef was not always deep enough

Analyzing
PRIMARY SOURCES

Sherrod on the Battle of Tarawa

❝Two more Marines scaled the seawall, [one] carrying a twin-cylindered tank strapped to his shoulders, the other holding the nozzle of the flamethrower. . . . [A] khaki-clad figure ran out the side entrance. The flamethrower . . . caught him in its withering stream of intense fire. As soon as it touched him, the [Japanese soldier] flared up like a piece of celluloid. He was dead instantly . . . charred almost to nothingness.❞

—Robert Sherrod, from *Tarawa: The Story of a Battle*

DBQ *DRAWING CONCLUSIONS*

Based on this excerpt, how do you think fighting continued?
SS.912.A.1.2

GEOGRAPHY CONNECTION

The Pacific Fleet gained control of the Pacific islands one by one on its way to defeat Japan.

1 **THE WORLD IN SPATIAL TERMS**
When Nimitz left Pearl Harbor, what was his destination? SS.912.A.1.4

2 **HUMAN SYSTEMS** *How does the map show the success of the island-hopping strategy?* LAFS.1112.WHST.3.9, SS.912.A.1.4

Island-Hopping in the Pacific 1942–1945

	Japanese Empire and conquests
—	Farthest extent of Japan's conquests, July 1942
←	Allied forces
✴	Major battle
◎	Atomic bombing

Other troops fighting in the Pacific included the American Volunteer Group (AVG), known as the Flying Tigers, who helped defend China against Japanese forces.

▶ **CRITICAL THINKING**
Analyzing Information How did aircraft help support the troops on the ground? LAFS.1112.WHST.3.9, SS.912.A.1.4

amphtrac an amphibious tractor used to move troops from ships to shore

to allow landing craft to get to the shore. If the landing craft ran aground on the reef, the troops would have to wade to the beach. As some 5,000 United States Marines learned at Tarawa Atoll, wading ashore could cause very high casualties. Tarawa, part of the Gilbert Islands, was the navy's first objective. The Japanese base there had to be captured in order to put air bases in the nearby Marshall Islands.

When the landing craft hit the reef, at least 20 ships ran aground. The marines had to plunge into shoulder-high water and wade several hundred yards to the beach. Raked by Japanese fire, only one marine in three made it ashore. Once the marines reached the beach, the battle was still far from over.

Although many troops died wading ashore, one vehicle had been able to cross the reef and deliver its troops onto the beaches. The vehicle was a boat with tank tracks, nicknamed the "Alligator." This amphibious tractor, or **amphtrac,** had been invented in the late 1930s to rescue people in Florida swamps. It had never been used in combat, and the navy decided to buy only 200 of them in 1941. If more had been available at Tarawa, American casualties probably would have been much lower.

More than 1,000 marines died on Tarawa. Photos of bodies lying crumpled next to burning landing craft shocked Americans back home. Many people began to wonder how many lives would be lost in defeating Japan.

The next assault—Kwajalein Atoll in the Marshall Islands—went much more smoothly. This time all of the troops went ashore in amphtracs. Although the Japanese resisted fiercely, the marines captured Kwajalein and nearby Eniwetok with far fewer casualties.

After the Marshall Islands, the navy targeted the Mariana Islands. American military planners wanted to use the Marianas as a base for a new heavy bomber, the B-29 Superfortress. The B-29 could fly farther than any other plane in the world. From airfields in the Marianas, B-29s could bomb Japan. Admiral Nimitz decided to invade three of the Mariana Islands: Saipan, Tinian, and Guam. Despite strong Japanese resistance, American troops captured all three by August 1944. A few months later, B-29s began bombing Japan.

MacArthur Returns

As the forces under Admiral Nimitz hopped across the central Pacific, General Douglas MacArthur's troops began their own campaign in the southwest Pacific. The campaign began by invading Guadalcanal in the Solomon Islands, east of New Guinea, in August 1942. It continued until early 1944, when MacArthur's troops finally captured enough islands to surround the main Japanese base in the region. In response, the Japanese withdrew their ships and aircraft from the base, although they left 100,000 troops behind to hold the island.

Worried that the navy's advance across the central Pacific was leaving him behind, MacArthur ordered his forces to leap nearly 600 miles (966 km) to capture the Japanese base at Hollandia on the north coast of New Guinea. Shortly after securing New Guinea, MacArthur's troops seized the island of Morotai—the last stop before the Philippines.

To take back the Philippines, the United States assembled an enormous invasion force. In October 1944, over 700 ships carrying more

©Bettmann/Corbis

than 160,000 troops sailed for Leyte Gulf in the Philippines. On October 20, the troops began to land on Leyte, an island on the eastern side of the Philippines. A few hours after the invasion began, MacArthur headed to the beach. Upon reaching the shore, he strode to a radio and spoke into the microphone: "People of the Philippines, I have returned. By the grace of Almighty God, our forces stand again on Philippine soil."

To stop the American invasion, the Japanese sent four aircraft carriers toward the Philippines from the north and secretly dispatched another fleet from the west. Believing the Japanese carriers were leading the main attack, most of the American carriers protecting the invasion left Leyte Gulf and headed north to stop them. Seizing their chance, the Japanese warships to the west raced through the Philippine Islands into Leyte Gulf and ambushed the remaining American ships.

The Battle of Leyte Gulf was the largest naval battle in history. It was also the first time that the Japanese used **kamikaze** attacks. *Kamikaze* means "divine wind" in Japanese. It refers to the great storm that destroyed the Mongol fleet during its invasion of Japan in the thirteenth century. Kamikaze pilots would deliberately crash their planes into American ships, killing themselves, but also inflicting severe damage. Luckily for the Americans, just as their situation was becoming desperate, the Japanese commander, believing more American ships were on the way, ordered a retreat.

Although the Japanese fleet had retreated, the campaign to recapture the Philippines from the Japanese was long and grueling. More than 80,000 Japanese were killed; fewer than 1,000 surrendered. MacArthur's troops did not capture Manila until March 1945. The battle left the city in ruins and more than 100,000 Filipino civilians dead. The remaining Japanese retreated into the rugged terrain north of Manila; they were still fighting in August 1945 when word came that Japan had surrendered.

✔ **READING PROGRESS CHECK**

Describing How did the United States Navy successfully drive back Japanese forces in the Pacific?

kamikaze during World War II, a Japanese suicide pilot whose mission was to crash into his target

Victory in the Battle of Leyte Gulf enables MacArthur to return to the Philippines.

▶ CRITICAL THINKING
Analyzing Visuals How does the photo represent the success of the island-hopping strategy? LAFS.1112.WHST.3.9

©Digital Stock/Corbis

LESSON 2 REVIEW

Reviewing Vocabulary
1. *Explaining* Explain how amphtracs helped the marines land more safely on Pacific islands. LAFS.1112.RH.2.4

Using Your Notes
2. *Explaining* Use your notes on major Pacific battles to explain the causes and effects of the effort to defeat the Japanese in 1942. LAFS.1112.WHST.3.9

Answering the Guiding Questions
3. *Assessing* Why was the Doolittle Raid important for U.S. forces in the Pacific? LAFS.1112.WHST.3.9, SS.912.A.6.1

4. *Drawing Conclusions* Why was the Battle of Midway a turning point in the war in the Pacific? LAFS.1112.WHST.3.9, SS.912.A.6.1

5. *Evaluating* What was the military strategy behind "island-hopping"? Was it successful? LAFS.1112.WHST.3.9, SS.912.A.6.1

Writing Activity
6. ARGUMENT Suppose you are a journalist in 1971 reporting on the government's disclosure about the Navajo code talkers. Write a newspaper article informing Americans how the code talkers assisted the marines at the Battle of Iwo Jima. LAFS.1112.WHST.1.1, LAFS.1112.WHST.3.9

LESSON 3
The War in Europe

• What kinds of sacrifices does war require?

READING HELPDESK

Academic Vocabulary

• target
• intense
• briefly

Content Vocabulary

• periphery
• convoy system

TAKING NOTES

Key Ideas and Details

Organizing Use the following graphic organizer to record the major battles discussed and when each was fought.
LAFS.1112.RH.3.7, SS.912.A.6.1

Major European and North African Battles

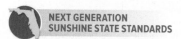

**NEXT GENERATION
SUNSHINE STATE STANDARDS**

ELD.K12.ELL.SI.1: English language learners communicate for social and instructional purposes within the school setting.

ELD.K12.ELL.SS.1: English language learners communicate information, ideas and concepts necessary for academic success in the content area of Social Studies.

LAFS.1112.RH.2.4: Determine the meaning of words and phrases as they are used in a text, including analyzing how an author uses and refines the meaning of a key term over the course of a text (e.g., how Madison defines faction in Federalist No. 10).

Continued on page 375

IT MATTERS BECAUSE
British and American troops won victories over the Axis powers in North Africa and Italy. Next, Allied leaders made plans for an invasion of Europe.

Halting the Germans

GUIDING QUESTION *Why did Churchill and Roosevelt want to attack German-controlled areas in North Africa before areas in Europe?*

Since 1940, U.S. military strategists had discussed with President Roosevelt the pressures of a two-front war. He wanted to get U.S. troops into battle in Europe, but Prime Minister Churchill did not believe the United States and Britain were ready to invade Europe. Instead, the prime minister wanted to attack the **periphery,** or edges, of the German empire. Roosevelt eventually agreed, and in July 1942, he ordered the invasion of Morocco and Algeria—two French territories indirectly under German control.

The Battle for North Africa

Roosevelt decided to invade for two reasons. The invasion would give the army some experience without requiring a lot of troops. It would also help the British troops fight the Germans in Egypt. Most of Britain's empire, including India, Hong Kong, Singapore, Malaya, and Australia, sent supplies to Britain through Egypt's Suez Canal.

German general Erwin Rommel, whose success earned him the nickname "Desert Fox," commanded the "Afrika Korps." After a 12-day battle at the Egyptian coastal city of El Alamein, the British secured the Suez Canal and forced Rommel to retreat in November 1942. Despite this defeat, German forces remained a serious threat in North Africa.

Later that month, American troops commanded by General Dwight D. Eisenhower invaded North Africa. When the Americans advanced into the mountains of western Tunisia, they fought the German army for the first time. At the Battle of Kasserine Pass, the Americans were outmaneuvered and outfought. They suffered roughly 7,000 casualties and lost nearly 200 tanks. Eisenhower fired the general who led the attack and put General George Patton in command. The American and British forces finally pushed the Germans back. On May 13, 1943, the last German troops in North Africa surrendered.

The Battle of the Atlantic

After Germany declared war on the United States, German submarines entered American coastal waters. American cargo ships were easy **targets,** especially at night when the glow from the cities in the night sky silhouetted the vessels. To protect the ships, citizens on the East Coast dimmed their lights every evening and put up special "blackout curtains." If they had to drive at night, they did so with their headlights off.

By August 1942, German submarines had sunk about 360 American ships along the East Coast, including many oil tankers. The loss of so many ships convinced the U.S. Navy to set up a **convoy system** in which cargo ships traveled in groups escorted by warships. The convoy system improved the situation dramatically, making it much more difficult for a submarine to torpedo a cargo ship and escape without being attacked.

The spring of 1942 marked the high point of the German submarine campaign. In May and June alone, more than 1.2 million tons of shipping were sunk. Yet in those same two months, American and British shipyards built more than 1.1 million tons of new shipping. At the same time, American airplanes and warships began to use new technology, including radar, sonar, and depth charges, to locate and attack submarines. As the new technology began to take its toll on German submarines, the Battle of the Atlantic turned in favor of the Allies.

The Battle of Stalingrad

Adolf Hitler was convinced that defeating the Soviet Union depended on destroying the Soviet economy. In May 1942, he ordered his army to capture strategic oil fields, factories, and farmlands in southern Russia and Ukraine. The city of Stalingrad, which controlled the Volga River and was a major railroad junction, was key to the attack. If the German army captured Stalingrad, they would cut off the Soviets from the resources they needed to stay in the war.

NEXT GENERATION SUNSHINE STATE STANDARDS

Continued from page 374

LAFS.1112.RH.3.7: Integrate and evaluate multiple sources of information presented in diverse formats and media (e.g., visually, quantitatively, as well as in words) in order to address a question or solve a problem.

LAFS.1112.WHST.3.9: Draw evidence from informational texts to support analysis, reflection, and research.

LAFS.1112.WHST.4.10: Write routinely over extended time frames (time for reflection and revision) and shorter time frames (a single sitting or a day or two) for a range of discipline-specific tasks, purposes, and audiences.

SS.912.A.1.2: Utilize a variety of primary and secondary sources to identify author, historical significance, audience, and authenticity to understand a historical period.

SS.912.A.1.4: Analyze how images, symbols, objects, cartoons, graphs, charts, maps, and artwork may be used to interpret the significance of time periods and events from the past.

SS.912.A.6.1: Examine causes, course, and consequences of World War II on the United States and the world.

SS.912.G.1.3: Employ applicable units of measurement and scale to solve simple locational problems using maps and globes.

periphery the outer boundary of something

target something or someone fired on or marked for attack

convoy system a system in which merchant ships travel with naval vessels for protection

A British tank successfully navigates a wide ditch in the desert outside a town in North Africa.

▶ **CRITICAL THINKING**
Analyzing Primary Sources How do you think the environment made combat in North Africa challenging? **SS.912.A.1.4**

The Art Archive

When German troops entered Stalingrad in mid-September, Stalin ordered his troops to hold the city at all costs. The Germans were forced to fight from house to house, losing thousands of soldiers in the process. Unlike the Soviets, they were not equipped to fight in the bitter cold. On November 23, Soviet reinforcements arrived and surrounded Stalingrad, trapping almost 250,000 German troops. When the battle ended in February 1943, some 91,000 Germans had surrendered. Only 5,000 of them survived the Soviet prison camps. Each side lost nearly half a million soldiers. The Battle of Stalingrad put the Germans on the defensive.

A Soviet gun crew fights against Nazi forces in Stalingrad. Only one day after the Nazis publicly boasted that the city would fall to them, the Red Army turned the tide of the battle.

▶ CRITICAL THINKING

Analyzing Images How do you think the environment made combat in Stalingrad difficult?
LAFS.1112.WHST.3.9, SS.912.A.1.4

✓ READING PROGRESS CHECK

Explaining What was Roosevelt's purpose in invading North Africa?

Striking Germany and Italy

GUIDING QUESTION *What were the goals of strategic bombing in Germany and the invasion of Sicily?*

The Allied invasion of North Africa in November 1942 had shown that a large-scale invasion from the sea was possible. The success of the landings convinced Roosevelt to meet again with Churchill to plan the next stage of the war. In January 1943, Roosevelt headed to Casablanca, Morocco, to meet the prime minister.

At the Casablanca Conference, Roosevelt and Churchill agreed to step up the bombing of Germany. The goal of this new campaign was "the progressive destruction of the German military, industrial, and economic system, and the undermining of the morale of the German people." The Allies also agreed to attack the Axis on the island of Sicily. Churchill called Italy the "soft underbelly" of Europe. He was convinced that the Italians would quit the war if the Allies invaded their homeland.

Strategic Bombing

The Allies had been bombing Germany even before the Casablanca Conference. Britain's Royal Air Force had dropped an average of 2,300 tons (2,093 t) of explosives on Germany every month for more than three years. The United States Eighth Army Air Force had dropped an additional 1,500 tons (1,365 t) of bombs during the last six months of 1942. These numbers were small, however, compared to the massive new campaign. Between January 1943 and May 1945, the Royal Air Force and the United States Eighth Army Air Force dropped approximately 53,000 tons (48,230 t) of explosives on Germany every month.

The bombing campaign did not destroy Germany's economy or undermine German morale, but it did cause a severe oil shortage and wrecked the railroad system. It also destroyed so many aircraft factories that Germany's air force could not replace its losses. By the time the Allies landed in France, they had control of the air, ensuring that their troops would not be bombed.

Striking the Soft Underbelly

As the bombing campaign against Germany intensified, plans to invade Sicily also moved ahead. General Dwight D. Eisenhower commanded the invasion, with General Patton and British general Bernard Montgomery

©Bettmann/Corbis

heading the ground forces. The invasion began before dawn on July 10, 1943. Despite bad weather, the Allied troops made it ashore with few casualties. A new amphibious truck delivered supplies and artillery to the soldiers on the beach.

Eight days after the troops came ashore, American tanks smashed through enemy lines and captured the western half of the island. Patton's troops then headed east, while the British attacked from the south. By August 17, the Germans had evacuated the island.

The attack on Sicily created a crisis within the Italian government. The king of Italy, Victor Emmanuel, and a group of Italian generals decided that it was time to depose Mussolini. On July 25, 1943, the king invited the dictator to his palace. "My dear Duce," the king began, "it's no longer any good. Italy has gone to bits. Army morale is at rock bottom. The soldiers don't want to fight anymore. . . . You can certainly be under no illusion as to Italy's feelings with regard to yourself. At this moment, you are the most hated man in Italy." The king then arrested Mussolini, and the new Italian government began negotiating a surrender to the Allies.

Following Italy's surrender, however, German troops seized control of northern Italy, including Rome, and returned Mussolini to power. The Germans then took up positions near the heavily fortified town of Cassino. The terrain near Cassino was steep, barren, and rocky. Rather

GEOGRAPHY CONNECTION

The war against Germany and Italy was fought on three fronts.

1 THE WORLD IN SPATIAL TERMS *How much west-to-east territory did the Axis control near the end of 1942?* SS.912.G.1.3, SS.912.G.4.9

2 PLACES AND REGIONS *What Allied victories are shown in North Africa?* SS.912.A.1.4

The War in Europe and North Africa 1942–1945

Extent of Axis control before World War II
Extent of Axis control, early Nov. 1942
Allies
Neutral nations
Allied victory
Axis victory

1 El Alamein, Nov. 1942. British forces defeated German forces commanded by Rommel, preventing German control of North Africa.
2 Stalingrad, Feb. 1943. A large German force was defeated at the city of Stalingrad, ending German hopes of defeating the Soviet Union.
3 Kasserine Pass, Feb.–Mar. 1943. American troops fought German forces for the first time and were beaten badly.
4 Leningrad, Sept. 1941–Jan. 1944. For 900 days the Soviets held off the Germans who were besieging the city.
5 Sicily, July–Aug. 1943. Allies landed in Sicily; began the liberation of Italy.
6 Anzio, Jan.–May 1944. U.S. forces landed near Rome behind German lines.
7 D-Day, June 1944. Allies landed at Normandy; began liberation of France.
8 Operation Market Garden, Sept. 1944. Allied troops parachuted into the Netherlands to seize bridges across the Rhine, but the attack failed.
9 Battle of the Bulge, Dec. 1944–Jan. 1945. Last large German counter-attack against American and British troops was halted.

**Vernon Baker
(1919–2010)
U.S. Army Company C,
370th Regiment,
92nd Infantry Division**

On April 5, 1945, First Lieutenant Vernon Baker and his platoon advanced toward Castle Aghinolfi, a German stronghold in the mountains near Viareggio, Italy. Baker and about 25 others moved ahead of the group, and Baker successfully destroyed an observation post, a dugout, and three machine gun positions. In 1996 his actions earned him a Medal of Honor "for conspicuous gallantry and intrepidity at the risk of his own life above and beyond the call of duty in action on 5 and 6 April 1945." This made Baker one of seven African American World War II veterans to receive belated recognition for their service.

▶ **CRITICAL THINKING**
Drawing Conclusions Why were Baker's actions so important to the assault on Castle Aghinolfi? **LAFS.1112.WHST.3.9**

than attack such difficult terrain, the Allies landed at Anzio, behind German lines. Instead of retreating, however, as the Allies had hoped, the Germans surrounded the Allied troops near Anzio.

It took the Allies five months to break through the German lines at Cassino and Anzio. Finally, in late May 1944, the Germans retreated. Less than two weeks later, the Allies captured Rome. Fighting in Italy continued, however, for another year. The Italian campaign was one of the bloodiest in the war, with more than 300,000 Allied casualties.

The Tehran Conference

Roosevelt wanted to meet with Stalin before the Allies invaded France. In late 1943, Stalin agreed, proposing that Roosevelt and Churchill meet him in Tehran, Iran.

The leaders reached several agreements. Stalin promised to launch a full-scale offensive against the Germans when the Allies invaded France in 1944. Roosevelt and Stalin then agreed to divide Germany after the war so that it would never again threaten world peace. Stalin promised that once Germany was defeated, the Soviet Union would help the United States against Japan. He also accepted Roosevelt's proposal of an international peacekeeping organization after the war. Part of the agreement proclaimed:

PRIMARY SOURCE

"The common understanding which we have here reached guarantees that victory will be ours. And as to peace—we are sure that our concord will win an enduring Peace. We recognize fully the supreme responsibility . . . to make a peace which will command the goodwill of the overwhelming mass of the peoples of the world and banish the scourge and terror of war for many generations."

—from the Tehran Declaration, December 1, 1943

☑ **READING PROGRESS CHECK**

Evaluating What did Roosevelt and other leaders hope to accomplish by attacking Germany and Italy?

The D-Day Invasion

GUIDING QUESTION *What if D-Day had failed and Germany had defeated the Allies in Europe?*

After the conference in Tehran, Roosevelt headed to Cairo, Egypt, where he and Churchill continued planning an invasion of France that would force Germany to again fight the war on two fronts. One major decision, however, still had to be made. The president had to choose the commander for Operation Overlord—the code name for the invasion. Roosevelt selected General Eisenhower.

Planning Operation Overlord

Hitler had fortified the French coast along the English Channel, but he did not know when or where the Allies would land. The Germans believed the landing would be in Pas-de-Calais—the area of France closest to Britain. The Allies encouraged this belief by placing dummy equipment along the coast across from Calais. The real target was farther south, a 60-mile stretch of five beaches along the Normandy coast.

The selection of a site for the largest amphibious landing in history was one of the biggest decisions of World War II. Allied planners considered coastlines from Denmark to Portugal in search of a sheltered location with firm flat beaches within range of friendly fighter planes in England. There

Army Courtesy Photo

also had to be enough roads and paths to move jeeps and trucks off the beaches and to accommodate the hundreds of thousands of American, Canadian, and British troops set to stream ashore following the invasion. An airfield and a seaport that the Allies could use were also needed. Most important was a reasonable expectation of achieving the element of surprise.

Planners also discussed who should lead France after the invasion. General Eisenhower had informed Charles de Gaulle that the French Resistance forces would assist in the liberation of Paris, but President Roosevelt was not sure he trusted de Gaulle and refused to recognize him as the official French leader.

By the spring of 1944, more than 1.5 million American soldiers, 12,000 airplanes, and 5 million tons (4.6 million t) of equipment had been sent to England. Only setting the invasion date and giving the command to go remained. The invasion had to begin at night to hide the ships crossing the English Channel. The ships had to arrive at low tide so that they could see the beach obstacles. The low tide had to come at dawn so that gunners bombarding the coast could see their targets. Paratroopers, who would be dropped behind enemy lines, needed a moonlit night to see where to land. Perhaps most important of all was good weather. A storm would ground the airplanes, and high waves would swamp landing craft.

Given all these requirements, there were only a few days each month to begin the invasion. The first opportunity was from June 5 to 7, 1944. Eisenhower's planning staff referred to the day any operation began by the letter *D*. The invasion date, therefore, came to be known as D-Day. Heavy cloud cover, strong winds, and high waves made June 5 impossible. The weather was forecast to improve **briefly** a day later. The Channel

briefly for a short time

Allied troops from various parts of the British coast headed for Normandy beaches for the D-Day invasion.

▶ **CRITICAL THINKING**
Determining Cause and Effect
How did the D-Day invasion turn the tide of World War II?
LAFS.1112.WHST.3.9, SS.912.6.1

©Bettmann/Corbis

Fighting at Omaha Beach

"Two hundred yards out, we took a direct hit. . . . Somehow or other, the ramp door opened up . . . and the men in front were being struck by machine gun fire. Everyone started to jump off into the water. . . . The tide was moving us so rapidly. . . . We would grab out at some of those underwater obstructions and mines built on telephone poles and girders, and hang on. We'd take cover, then make a dash through the surf to the next one, fifty feet beyond.**"**

—Lieutenant John Bentz Carroll, from *D-Day: Piercing the Atlantic Wall*, 1994

DBQ *MAKING INFERENCES*

Based on this description, what can you infer about the manner of the landing on Omaha Beach?
LAFS.1112.WHST.3.9, SS.912.A.1.2

intense existing in an extreme degree

SKILLS PRACTICE

Explain the events of one of the major battles in World War II. Before you start, think about interesting and specific details of the battle. Include as many of these details as you can in your explanation. ELD.K12.ELL.SI.1, ELD.K12.ELL.SS.1

---

would still be rough, but the landing ships and aircraft could operate. After looking at forecasts one last time, shortly after midnight on June 6, 1944, Eisenhower gave the final order: "OK, we'll go."

The Longest Day

Nearly 7,000 ships carrying more than 100,000 soldiers headed for Normandy's coast. At the same time, 23,000 paratroopers were dropped inland, east and west of the beaches. Allied fighter-bombers raced up and down the coast, hitting bridges, bunkers, and radar sites. At dawn, Allied warships began a tremendous barrage. Thousands of shells rained down on the beaches, code-named "Utah," "Omaha," "Gold," "Sword," and "Juno."

The American landing at Utah Beach went well. The German defenses were weak, and in less than three hours, the troops had captured the beach and moved inland, suffering fewer than 200 casualties. On the eastern flank, the British and Canadian landings also went well. By the end of the day, British and Canadian forces were several miles inland.

Omaha Beach, however, was a different story. Surrounded at both ends by cliffs that rose wall-like from the sea, Omaha Beach was only four miles long. A 150-foot high bluff overlooked the entire beach, and there were only five ravines leading from the beach to the top of the bluff. The Germans had made full use of the geographic advantage the high bluff gave them. They dug trenches and built concrete bunkers for machine guns at the top of the cliffs and positioned them to guard the ravines leading from the bluff to the beach. Under **intense** German fire, the American assault almost disintegrated.

General Omar Bradley, commander of the American forces landing at Omaha and Utah, began making plans to evacuate. Slowly, however, the American troops began to knock out the German defenses. More landing craft arrived, ramming their way through the obstacles to get to the beach. Nearly 2,500 Americans were either killed or wounded on Omaha, but by early afternoon, Bradley received this message: "Troops formerly pinned down on beaches . . . [are] advancing up heights behind beaches." By the end of the day, nearly 35,000 American troops had landed at Omaha, and another 23,000 had landed at Utah. More than 75,000 British and Canadian troops were on shore as well. The invasion had succeeded.

✓ READING PROGRESS CHECK

Summarizing Why was it so important that all of the conditions be met before Eisenhower could order D-Day to begin? What would have happened if the invasion had failed?

LESSON 3 REVIEW

Reviewing Vocabulary

1. *Explaining* Explain how using the convoy system helped the United States begin winning the Battle of the Atlantic. LAFS.1112.RH.2.4

Using Your Notes

2. *Sequencing* Review the notes you completed during the lesson and use them to sequence the major Allied victories. LAFS.1112.WHST.3.9

Answering the Guiding Questions

3. *Analyzing* Why did Churchill and Roosevelt want to attack German-controlled areas in North Africa before areas in Europe? LAFS.1112.WHST.3.9, SS.912.A.6.1

4. *Determining Cause and Effect* What were the goals of strategic bombing in Germany and the invasion of Sicily? LAFS.1112.WHST.3.9, SS.912.A.6.1

5. *Speculating* What if D-Day had failed and Germany had defeated the Allies in Europe? LAFS.1112.WHST.3.9, SS.912.A.6.1

Writing Activity

6. **NARRATIVE** American soldiers invading Normandy on D-Day showed extreme bravery in the face of enormous difficulties. Imagine that you are one of the first soldiers approaching Omaha Beach by water. Write a description of the beach and the atmosphere at that moment. Be sure to include sensory words. LAFS.1112.WHST.3.9, LAFS.1112.WHST.4.10

networks
There's More Online!

LESSON 4
The War Ends

ESSENTIAL QUESTION

• What kinds of sacrifices does war require?

READING HELPDESK

Academic Vocabulary

• despite   • nuclear

Content Vocabulary

• hedgerow
• napalm

TAKING NOTES

Key Ideas and Details

Organizing As you read, create an outline of the section similar to the one below, using the major headings as the main points. LAFS.1112.RH.3.7, SS.912.A.6.6, SS.912.A.6.7

> The War Ends
> I. The Third Reich Collapses
>   A.
>   B.
> II.
>   A.
>   B.

**NEXT GENERATION
SUNSHINE STATE STANDARDS**

LAFS.1112.RH.2.4: Determine the meaning of words and phrases as they are used in a text, including analyzing how an author uses and refines the meaning of a key term over the course of a text (e.g., how Madison defines faction in Federalist No. 10).

LAFS.1112.RH.3.7: Integrate and evaluate multiple sources of information presented in diverse formats and media (e.g., visually, quantitatively, as well as in words) in order to address a question or solve a problem.

LAFS.1112.WHST.3.9: Draw evidence from informational texts to support analysis, reflection, and research.

Continued on page 382

IT MATTERS BECAUSE

Fierce fighting in both Europe and the Pacific during 1945 led to the defeat of the Axis powers. As the war ended, the Allies began war-crimes trials as part of a plan to build a better world.

The Third Reich Collapses

GUIDING QUESTION *Why was the Battle of the Bulge so important to the Allied forces?*

Although D-Day had been a success, it was only the beginning. Surrounding many fields in Normandy were **hedgerows**—dirt walls, several feet thick, covered in shrubbery—built to fence in cattle and crops. They also enabled the Germans to fiercely defend their positions. The battle of the hedgerows ended on July 25, 1944, when 2,500 U.S. bombers blew a hole in the German lines, enabling U.S. tanks to race through the gap.

As the Allies broke out of Normandy, the French Resistance—French civilians who had secretly organized to resist the German occupation—staged a rebellion in Paris. When the Allies liberated Paris on August 25, the streets were filled with French citizens celebrating their victory.

The Battle of the Bulge

As the Allies advanced toward the German border, Hitler decided to stage one last desperate offensive. His goal was to cut off Allied supplies coming through the port of Antwerp, Belgium. The attack began just before dawn on December 16, 1944. Six inches (15 cm) of snow covered the ground, and the weather was bitterly cold. Moving rapidly, the Germans caught the American defenders by surprise. As the German troops raced west, their lines bulged outward, and the attack became known as the Battle of the Bulge.

Eisenhower ordered General Patton to the rescue. Three days later, faster than anyone expected in the midst of a snowstorm, Patton's troops slammed into the German lines. As the weather cleared, Allied aircraft began hitting German fuel depots.

hedgerow an enclosure made of dirt walls covered in shrubbery built to fence in cattle and crops

On Christmas Eve, out of fuel and weakened by heavy losses, the German troops driving toward Antwerp were forced to halt. Two days later, Patton's troops broke through to the German line. Fighting continued for three weeks, but the United States had won the Battle of the Bulge. On January 8, the Germans began to withdraw, having suffered more than 100,000 casualties. They had very few resources left to prevent the Allies from entering Germany.

American troops march through the snow on January 31, 1945, during the Battle of the Bulge.

▶ **CRITICAL THINKING**

Making Inferences Looking at the photo, what can you infer about the conditions during the Battle of the Bulge? LAFS.1112.WHST.3.9, SS.912.A.1.4, SS.912.A.6.1

NEXT GENERATION SUNSHINE STATE STANDARDS

Continued from page 381

LAFS.1112.WHST.4.10: Write routinely over extended time frames (time for reflection and revision) and shorter time frames (a single sitting or a day or two) for a range of discipline-specific tasks, purposes, and audiences.

SS.912.A.1.2: Utilize a variety of primary and secondary sources to identify author, historical significance, audience, and authenticity to understand a historical period.

SS.912.A.1.4: Analyze how images, symbols, objects, cartoons, graphs, charts, maps, and artwork may be used to interpret the significance of time periods and events from the past.

Continued on page 383

The War Ends in Europe

While American and British forces fought to liberate France, the Soviets attacked German troops in Russia. By the end of the Battle of the Bulge, the Soviets had driven Hitler's forces out of Russia and across Poland. By February 1945, the Soviets were only 35 miles (56 km) from Germany's capital, Berlin.

Soviet troops crossed Germany's eastern border, while American forces attacked its western border. By the end of February 1945, American troops had reached the Rhine River, Germany's last major line of defense in the west. On March 7, American tanks crossed the Rhine. As German defenses crumbled, American troops raced east to within 70 miles (113 km) of Berlin. On April 16, Soviet troops finally smashed through the German defenses and reached the outskirts of Berlin five days later.

Deep in his Berlin bunker, Adolf Hitler knew the end was near. On April 30, 1945, he committed suicide. On May 7, 1945, Germany accepted the terms for an unconditional surrender. The next day—May 8, 1945—was proclaimed V-E Day, for "Victory in Europe."

☑ **READING PROGRESS CHECK**

Explaining Why was the Battle of the Bulge such a disastrous defeat for Germany?

Japan Is Defeated

GUIDING QUESTION *Do you agree or disagree with President Truman's decision to drop the atomic bomb? Explain your reasons.*

Unfortunately, President Roosevelt did not live to see the defeat of Germany. On April 12, 1945, while vacationing in Warm Springs, Georgia, he died of a stroke. His vice president, Harry S. Truman, became president during this difficult time.

The next day, Truman told reporters: "Boys, if you ever pray, pray for me now. . . . When they told me yesterday what had happened, I felt like the

The Granger Collection, New York

moon, the stars, and all the planets had fallen on me." **Despite** his feelings, Truman began at once to make decisions about the war. Although Germany surrendered a few weeks later, the war with Japan continued, and Truman was forced to make some of the most difficult decisions of the war during his first six months in office.

The Battle of Iwo Jima

On November 24, 1944, bombs fell on Tokyo. Above the city flew eighty B-29 Superfortress bombers that had traveled more than 1,500 miles (2,414 km) from new American bases in the Mariana Islands. By the time the B-29s reached Japan, however, they did not have enough fuel left to fix their navigational errors or to adjust for high winds. Many of their bombs missed the targets. The pilots needed an island closer to Japan so the B-29s could refuel. American military planners chose Iwo Jima.

Iwo Jima was perfectly located, roughly halfway between the Marianas and Japan, but its geography was formidable. It had a dormant volcano at its southern tip and rugged terrain with rocky cliffs, jagged ravines, and dozens of caves. Volcanic ash covered the ground. Even worse, the Japanese had built a vast network of concrete bunkers connected by miles of tunnels.

On February 19, 1945, some 60,000 marines landed on Iwo Jima. As the troops leaped from the amphtracs, they sank up to their ankles in the soft ash and were pounded by Japanese artillery. The marines crawled inland, attacking the Japanese bunkers with flamethrowers and explosives. More than 6,800 marines were killed capturing the island. Admiral Nimitz later wrote that, on Iwo Jima, "uncommon valor was a common virtue."

Firebombing Japan

While American engineers prepared airfields on Iwo Jima, General Curtis LeMay, commander of the B-29s based in the Marianas, changed strategy. To help the B-29s hit their targets, he ordered them to drop bombs filled with napalm—a type of jellied gasoline. The bombs would not only explode but would also start fires. Even if the B-29s missed their targets, the fires they started would spread to the intended targets.

The use of firebombs was very controversial because the fires would also kill civilians; however, LeMay could think of no other way to destroy Japan's war production quickly. Loaded with firebombs, B-29s attacked Tokyo on March 9, 1945. As strong winds fanned the flames, the firestorm grew so intense that it sucked the oxygen out of the air, asphyxiating thousands. As one survivor later recalled:

©Digital Stock/Corbis

NEXT GENERATION
SUNSHINE STATE STANDARDS

Continued from page 382

SS.912.A.6.1: Examine causes, course, and consequences of World War II on the United States and the world.

SS.912.A.6.3: Analyze the impact of the Holocaust during World War II on Jews as well as other groups.

SS.912.A.6.6: Analyze the use of atomic weapons during World War II and the aftermath of the bombings.

SS.912.A.6.7: Describe the attempts to promote international justice through the Nuremberg Trials.

despite in spite of

napalm a type of jellied gasoline

U.S. Marines raise the American flag after the capture of Iwo Jima. More than 6,800 marines were killed before the island was captured.

▶ CRITICAL THINKING
Determining Cause and Effect How might the Battle of Iwo Jima have been a factor in President Truman's decision to drop the atomic bomb? SS.912.A.6.1

*"*The fires were incredible . . . with flames leaping hundreds of feet into the air. . . . With every passing moment the air became more foul . . . the noise was a continuing crashing roar. . . . Fire-winds filled with burning particles rushed up and down the streets. I watched people . . . running for their lives. . . . The flames raced after them like living things, striking them down. . . . Wherever I turned my eyes, I saw people . . . seeking air to breathe.*"*

—quoted in American Heritage *New History of World War II*

The firebombing of Tokyo killed more than 80,000 people and destroyed more than 250,000 buildings. By the end of June 1945, Japan's six key industrial cities had been firebombed. By the end of the war, the B-29s had firebombed 67 Japanese cities.

The Invasion of Okinawa

Despite the massive damage that firebombing caused, there were few signs in the spring of 1945 that Japan was ready to quit. Many American officials believed the Japanese would not surrender until Japan had been invaded. To prepare for the invasion, the United States needed a base near Japan to stockpile supplies and build up troops. Iwo Jima was small and still too far away. Military planners chose Okinawa—only 350 miles (563 km) from mainland Japan.

American troops landed on Okinawa on April 1, 1945. Instead of defending the beaches, the Japanese troops took up positions in the island's rugged mountains. To dig the Japanese out of their caves and bunkers, the American troops had to fight their way up steep slopes against constant machine gun and artillery fire. More than 12,000 American soldiers, sailors, and marines died during the fighting, but by June 22, 1945, Okinawa had finally been captured.

The Terms for Surrender

Shortly after the United States captured Okinawa, the Japanese emperor, Hirohito, urged his government to find a way to end the war. The biggest problem was the American demand for unconditional surrender. Many Japanese leaders were willing to surrender, but on one condition: Hirohito had to stay in power.

American officials knew that the fate of Hirohito was the most important issue for the Japanese. Most Americans, however, blamed the emperor for the war and wanted him removed from power. President Truman was reluctant to go against public opinion. Furthermore, he knew the United States was almost ready to test a new weapon that might force Japan to surrender without any conditions. The new weapon was the atomic bomb.

The Manhattan Project

In 1939 Leo Szilard, a Jewish physicist who had fled Nazi persecution, learned that German scientists had split the uranium atom. Szilard had been the first scientist to suggest that splitting the atom might release enormous energy. Worried that the Nazis were working on an atomic bomb, Szilard convinced the world's best-known physicist, Albert Einstein, to sign a letter Szilard had drafted and send it to President Roosevelt. In the letter, Einstein warned that by using uranium, "extremely powerful bombs of a new type may . . . be constructed."

Roosevelt responded by setting up a scientific committee to study the issue. In 1941 the committee met with British scientists who were already working on an atomic bomb. The Americans then convinced Roosevelt to begin a program to build an atomic bomb.

The secret American program to build an atomic bomb was code-named the Manhattan Project and was headed by General Leslie R. Groves. The first breakthrough came in 1942, when Szilard and Enrico Fermi, another physicist, built the world's first **nuclear** reactor at the University of Chicago. Groves then organized a team of engineers and scientists to build an atomic bomb at a secret laboratory in Los Alamos, New Mexico. Physicist J. Robert Oppenheimer led the team. On July 16, 1945, they detonated the world's first atomic bomb in New Mexico.

Hiroshima and Nagasaki

Even before the bomb was tested, American officials began debating how to use it. Admiral William Leahy, chairman of the Joint Chiefs of Staff, opposed using the bomb because it would kill civilians. He believed an economic blockade and conventional bombing would convince Japan to surrender. Secretary of War Henry Stimson wanted to warn the Japanese about the bomb and tell them their emperor could stay in power if they surrendered. Secretary of State James Byrnes, however, wanted to drop the bomb on Japan without any warning.

President Truman later wrote that he "regarded the bomb as a military weapon and never had any doubts that it should be used." His advisers had warned him to expect massive casualties if the United States invaded Japan. Truman believed it was his duty as president to use every weapon available to save American lives.

nuclear relating to the nucleus of an atom

A key figure of the nuclear age, Enrico Fermi proved a nuclear reaction could be initiated, controlled, and stopped.

▶ **CRITICAL THINKING**
Identifying Central Ideas Why was Enrico Fermi's work on nuclear reactions so important?
SS.912.A.6.6

ANALYZING PRIMARY SOURCES

Should America Drop the Atomic Bomb on Japan?

People continue to debate whether President Truman's decision to drop atomic bombs on Japan was the best way to end World War II.

❞The world will note that the first atomic bomb was dropped on Hiroshima, a military base. . . . If Japan does not surrender, bombs will have to be dropped on her war industries and, unfortunately, thousands of civilian lives will be lost. . . .

Having found the bomb we have used it. We have used it against those who attacked us without warning at Pearl Harbor, against those who have starved and beaten and executed American prisoners of war, against those who have abandoned all pretense of obeying international laws of warfare. We have used it in order to shorten the agony of war, in order to save the lives of thousands and thousands of young Americans.**❞**

—Harry S. Truman, radio report to the American people, August 9, 1945

Harry S. Truman
President of the United States

❞It is my opinion that the use of this barbarous weapon at Hiroshima and Nagasaki was of no material assistance in our war against Japan. The Japanese were already defeated and ready to surrender because of the effective sea blockade and the successful bombing with conventional weapons. . . .

The lethal possibilities of atomic warfare in the future are frightening. My own feeling was that in being the first to use it, we had adopted an ethical standard common to the barbarians of the Dark Ages. I was not taught to make war in that fashion, and wars cannot be won by destroying women and children.**❞**

—William Leahy, from *I Was There*, 1950

William Leahy
Chairman of the Joint
Chiefs of Staff

DBQ **Analyzing Historical Documents**

❶ ***Identifying Points of View*** What reasons does Truman offer to justify the use of the atomic bomb?
SS.912.A.1.2, SS.912.A.6.6

❷ ***Summarizing*** Why does Leahy say he was against using the bomb? SS.912.A.1.2, SS.912.A.6.6

(l)Oxford Science Archive/Print Collector/Getty Images; (br)Myron Davis/Time Life Pictures/Getty Images; (b)The Art Archive/Culver Pictures

The United States dropped an atomic bomb that destroyed the Japanese city of Hiroshima.

▶ CRITICAL THINKING
Analyzing Primary Sources What details in the picture illustrate the effect of the atomic bomb? SS.912.A.1.4, SS.912.A.6.6

The Allies threatened Japan with "prompt and utter destruction" if the nation did not surrender, but the Japanese did not reply. Truman then ordered the military to drop the bomb. On August 6, 1945, a B-29 bomber named *Enola Gay* dropped an atomic bomb, code-named "Little Boy," on Hiroshima, an important industrial city.

The bomb destroyed about 63 percent of the city. Between 80,000 and 120,000 people died instantly, and thousands more died later from burns and radiation sickness. Three days later, on August 9, the Soviet Union declared war on Japan. Later that day, the United States dropped another atomic bomb, code-named "Fat Man," on the city of Nagasaki, killing between 35,000 and 74,000 people. Faced with such massive destruction and the shock of the Soviets joining the war, Hirohito ordered his government to surrender. On August 15, 1945—V-J Day—Japan surrendered. The long war was over.

Putting the Enemy on Trial

In August 1945, the United States, Britain, France, and the Soviet Union created the International Military Tribunal (IMT) to punish German and Japanese leaders for war crimes. The tribunal held trials in Nuremberg, Germany, where Hitler had staged Nazi Party rallies.

Twenty-two German leaders were prosecuted at the Nuremberg Trials. Three were acquitted, 7 were given prison sentences, and 12 were sentenced to death. Trials of lower-ranking leaders continued until April 1949, leading to 24 more executions and 107 prison sentences.

Similar trials were held in Tokyo. The IMT for the Far East charged 25 Japanese leaders with war crimes. The Allies did not indict Hirohito, fearing that any attempt to put the emperor on trial would lead to an uprising. Eighteen Japanese defendants were sentenced to prison. The rest were sentenced to death by hanging.

©Bettmann/Corbis

The trials punished many of the people responsible for World War II and the Holocaust, but they were also part of the American plan for building a better world. As Robert Jackson, chief counsel for the United States at Nuremberg, said in his opening statement to the court: "The wrongs we seek to condemn and punish have been so calculated, so malignant and so devastating, that civilization cannot tolerate their being ignored because it cannot survive their being repeated."

World War II: A Turning Point

The years 1939–1945 were a major turning point in world history. By the end of World War II, large areas of the world's great powers—Britain, France, Germany, Japan and the Soviet Union—lay devastated. Germany and Japan were occupied by foreign armies. Some 25 million people had been killed. Two-thirds of European Jews were murdered in the Holocaust. This increased international support for the establishment of a Jewish state. Japan's empire was gone and the European empires would never fully recover. Over the next three decades, nearly all of the subject peoples of the British, French, and Dutch empires would gain their independence. New countries in Africa, Asia, and the Middle East were born. The Middle Eastern conflict between the new nation of Israel and the Arab nations was itself a direct result of World War II.

The war also opened a new era in American history. The American economy was undamaged, and by the mid-1940s it was producing over 35 percent of the entire world's gross domestic product. A vast American military force was deployed in Europe and Asia, and it also controlled the world's first nuclear weapons. The United States had emerged as the world's strongest economic and military power. It was in a position of such strength and dominance that a new term—superpower—was later coined to describe its relationship to the rest of the world.

Only one other country had the potential to rival the United States at the end of the war. The Soviet Union, although devastated from Germany's invasion, had built its own enormous army and industrial capacity. Soviet troops were in control of Eastern Europe, and communist ideas posed the only real ideological challenge to American ideas of democracy, free enterprise, and limited government. Although World War II had put an end to Nazism, the struggle had left Europe divided, and the resulting tensions between former allies would soon lead to a new international conflict known as the Cold War.

✓ READING PROGRESS CHECK

Analyzing What arguments did Truman consider when deciding whether to use the atomic bomb?

LESSON 4 REVIEW

Reviewing Vocabulary

1. *Explaining* Explain why napalm bombs are highly destructive.
LAFS.1112.RH.2.4

Using Your Notes

2. *Summarizing* Using the notes you completed during the lesson on factors that led to the end of World War II, explain how the Allies achieved victory in Europe and over Japan.
LAFS.1112.WHST.3.9

Answering the Guiding Questions

3. *Analyzing* Why was the Battle of the Bulge so important to the Allied forces? LAFS.1112.WHST.3.9

4. *Defending* Do you agree or disagree with President Truman's decision to drop the atomic bomb? Explain your reasons. LAFS.1112.WHST.3.9, SS.912.A.1.2, SS.912.A.6.6

Writing Activity

5. NARRATIVE Suppose that you are in a large U.S. city when news of victory over Japan comes. Describe the celebrations and the mood of the people. LAFS.1112.WHST.4.10

SKILLBUILDER

LAFS.1112.RH.1.1, LAFS.1112.RH.1.2, LAFS.1112.RH.1.3, LAFS.1112.RH.2.6, LAFS.1112.RH.3.7, LAFS.1112.RH.3.8, LAFS.1112.RH.3.9, LAFS.1112.RH.4.10, LAFS.1112.SL.1.3, LAFS.1112.WHST.3.8, MAFS.K12.MP.3.1, SS.912.A.1.1, SS.912.A.1.2, SS.912.A.1.5

Using Secondary Sources

Why Learn This Skill?

Secondary sources are everywhere. Every history book is a secondary source, including this textbook. Any book, article, document, website, or other presentation of information that discusses or describes information that originates somewhere else is a secondary source. Primary sources are where scholars get information: primary sources include data, facts, documents, letters, quotes, interviews, original photos, art, speeches, transcripts, and other materials that people create as part of their activities. Secondary sources are efforts by people to comment on primary sources to try to understand what they mean and what those sources tell us about people's activities. Learning to use secondary sources will help you figure out whether those sources are presenting a complete and accurate picture of a topic or event, and whether you can rely on the information they present.

Learning the Skill

When writing a secondary source, historians typically combine many primary sources and other secondary sources together to create the historical narrative. The goal of a secondary source is to analyze and interpret primary sources, then synthesize, or combine, them so that generalizations and evaluations about history are possible. Secondary sources are what stitch all the evidence together into a presentation of events that we call history.

The reason you analyze a secondary source is to figure out what an author's main ideas and argument are, and to determine whether you agree with them or not, and why.

Follow these steps:

1. First, ask yourself what you are trying to accomplish with the secondary source. Are you trying to acquire information? Or are you trying to analyze or answer historical questions?

2. Who is the author? What are his or her credentials? Do they have training or a background that makes you think you can trust their work?

3. Who published the secondary source? Does that indicate any possible bias and special motive for the work that might make you suspicious of its conclusions?

4. Look at the secondary source. When was it written? Examine its title and table of contents. What clues does it provide as to the topic of the work and the approach the author is taking?

5. Does the secondary source have footnotes or endnotes where it cites the primary sources it uses to prove its ideas? Does it have a bibliography listing all of the sources of evidence used to prepare the work?

6. What kind of sources are being used? Is the secondary source using mostly other secondary sources, or is it using many primary sources? This is important if you want to use the secondary source to acquire information. You have to be sure the information is reliable.

7. If it is using primary sources, what kind are being used? Are they reliable? Does the author generally rely on one particular kind of primary source to support his or her conclusions? Are there any weaknesses or biases in the types of primary sources being used? Might the author be led to the wrong conclusion by relying on one type of source too much?

8. Figure out the author's argument. This is important if you are using the secondary source to analyze or answer historical questions. Look at the work's introduction and conclusion. What are the major questions or issues the author is trying to explain? Is the author trying to be objective, clearly separating facts from opinions? Or is the author making a strong emotional argument with a very clear opinion, and all the facts seem to support that opinion?

9. Think about the author's conclusions. Do they make sense to you? What kind of evidence could be used to disprove them? Did the author examine sources that challenge his ideas and explain how they fit into the work?

Practicing this Skill

Practice this skill with this text you are using. This text is a secondary source. Let's analyze your textbook.

1. Can the textbook be used to acquire information? Can the textbook be used to analyze and answer historical questions? Explain.
2. Who are the authors of this program? What are their credentials? What else have they written? Do you think they can be trusted to be professional?
3. Who published your textbook? What is their purpose? Is there likely to be a bias in what they publish?
4. Does the textbook use primary sources? What kinds?
5. Does your textbook have one single argument or focus on only one major issue? Why or why not?
6. Pick one chapter in your textbook and analyze it as a secondary source. Try to identify its main argument and how it analyzes and explains the historical questions of the time period the chapter covers.

© Image Source, all rights reserved

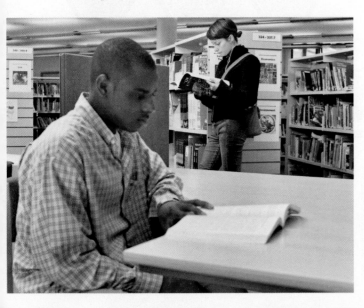

Applying the Skill

There has been much controversy over the years about the American decision to drop the atomic bomb on Japan. Different historians have viewed the decision differently, and have come to different conclusions. Here are several secondary sources about the decision:

Gar Alperovitz, *The Decision to Use the Atomic Bomb* (1995)

Herbert Feis, *Japan Subdued* (1961)

Gregg Herken, *The Winning Weapon* (1981)

Robert James Maddox, *Weapons For Victory* (1995)

Martin Sherwin, *A World Destroyed* (1975)

Look up two of these secondary sources and apply the skills you have learned for analyzing secondary sources. Then answer these historical questions:

1. *Acquiring Information* What are the major opinions of historians concerning Truman's decision?

2. *Analyzing Historical Questions* Write a brief report on the kinds of evidence being used by historians analyzing the decision to drop the bomb. How might the sources used affect their interpretation?

3. *Answering Historical Questions* Based on what you have learned, why do you think President Truman dropped the atomic bomb on Japan? Do you agree with the decision?

STUDY GUIDE

WARTIME AMERICA
LESSON 1

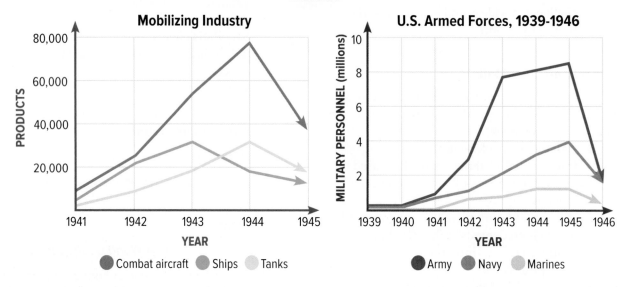

Mobilizing Industry

Combat aircraft • Ships • Tanks

U.S. Armed Forces, 1939-1946

Army • Navy • Marines

THE WAR IN THE PACIFIC
LESSON 2

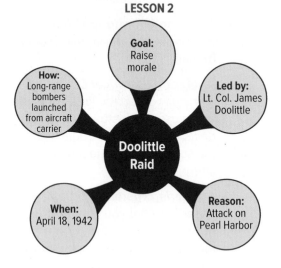

Doolittle Raid

Goal: Raise morale

How: Long-range bombers launched from aircraft carrier

Led by: Lt. Col. James Doolittle

When: April 18, 1942

Reason: Attack on Pearl Harbor

THE WAR IN EUROPE
LESSON 3
Operation Overlord

1.5 million American soldiers

12,000 aircraft

5 million tons of equipment

THE WAR ENDS
LESSON 4

Nazis on Trial
• Nuremberg, Germany
• August 1945: 22 Germans prosecuted—3 acquitted, 7 jailed, 12 sentenced to death
• Later prosecutions (April 1949)—24 sentenced to death, 107 jailed

Japanese on Trial
• Tokyo, Japan
• 25 war criminals put on trial
• 18 sentenced to jail
• 7 sentenced to death

Directions: On a separate sheet of paper, answer the questions below. Make sure you read carefully and answer all parts to the question.

Lesson Review

Lesson 1

1 ***Describing*** What was the "Double V" campaign? Which African American leader took steps to expand economic opportunities for African Americans in industry? What did he begin to organize and how did President Roosevelt respond? SS.912.A.6.1, SS.912.A.6.4

2 ***Summarizing*** Explain how the war affected the American economy and home front. As industries mobilized for war, how did people respond? What government agencies were set up to regulate the economy and what practices were encouraged or enforced in order to monitor food purchases, gasoline use, and recycling? SS.912.A.6.1, SS.912.A.6.5

Lesson 2

3 ***Describing*** What was the Bataan Death March? Why did the march take place? SS.912.A.6.1

4 ***Identifying Cause and Effect*** What was the Doolittle Raid, and what was its impact on the war? SS.912.A.6.1

5 ***Evaluating*** Why was the Battle of Midway a turning point in the war? SS.912.A.6.1

Lesson 3

6 ***Specifying*** What tactic did the United States use to prevent huge shipping losses in the Atlantic? SS.912.A.6.1

7 ***Describing*** Why was the awarding of the Congressional Medal of Honor to Vernon Baker especially significant? SS.912.A.6.1

8 ***Analyzing*** Why was the invasion of Normandy important? SS.912.A.6.1

Lesson 4

9 ***Making Connections*** What was the significance of the Battle of the Bulge? SS.912.A.6.1

10 ***Summarizing*** Why did the United States want to invade the island of Okinawa? SS.912.A.6.1

Exploring the Essential Questions

11 ***Categorizing*** Design a booth for a history conference that is titled "The Sacrifices of World War II." The booth should contain three charts, each listing a different category of sacrifice: Economic, Military/Civilian, and Social. Consider the most important points you wish to communicate. Then use text, maps, and illustrations to show the information you would include in this booth. LAFS.1112.SL.1.2, LAFS.1112.WHST.1.2, LAFS.1112.WHST.2.4, LAFS.1112.WHST.4.10, LAFS.1112.WHST.2.5, SS.912.A.1.1, SS.912.A.1.4, SS.912.A.1.7, SS.912.A.6.1, SS.912.A.6.2, SS.912.G.1.2, SS.912.G.2.1

Critical Thinking

12 ***Analyzing*** Identify the purpose of Executive Order 9066, and explain the constitutional issues raised by the forced relocation and internment of Japanese Americans and some German and Italian Americans during the war. Explain the Supreme Court's decisions in the cases of *Korematsu* and *Ex Parte Endo*. SS.912.A.6.1, SS.912.A.6.4

13 ***Evaluating*** Discuss the exceptional bravery and contributions of Navajo code talkers during the war. SS.912.A.6.1

14 ***Analyzing*** Analyze the historical significance of the Holocaust and the liberation of concentration camps at the end of the war. How did the Allies react to the discovery of the Holocaust after the war? SS.912.A.1.1, SS.912.A.6.1, SS.912.A.6.3

21st Century Skills

15 ***Explaining Continuity and Change*** World War II created many opportunities for women, both in the military and the economy, but they faced many obstacles as well. What contributions did women make to the military effort and the wartime economy? What obstacles did they face? LAFS.1112.RH.3.8, SS.912.A.6.1, SS.912.A.6.4

Need Extra Help?

If You've Missed Question	❶	❷	❸	❹	❺	❻	❼	❽	❾	❿	⓫	⓬	⓭	⓮	⓯
Go to Lesson	1	1	2	2	2	3	3	3	4	4	1	1	2	4	1

DBQ Analyzing Primary Sources

Read the two secondary sources below, and then answer the questions that follow.

Historian Gar Alperovitz argues that Truman had alternatives to the atomic bomb, but chose to use the weapon in order to pressure Stalin and force Japan's surrender before the Soviet Union could join the war and invade Japan:

"Quite simply, it is not true that the atomic bomb was used because it was the only way to save the 'hundreds of thousands' or 'millions' of lives as was subsequently claimed. The readily available options were to modify the surrender terms and/or await the shock of the Russian attack. Perhaps it is here, most poignantly, that we confront our own reluctance to ask the difficult questions—for even if one were to accept the most inflated estimates of lives saved by the atomic bomb, the fact remains that it was an act of violent destruction aimed at large concentrations of noncombatants."

—from *The Decision to Use the Atomic Bomb*

Historian Herbert Feis argues that Truman's desire to avoid an invasion of Japan, thus saving thousands of lives on both sides, motivated his decision to drop the bomb.

PRIMARY SOURCE

"Our right, legal and historical, to use the bomb may thus well be defended; but those who made the decision to use it were not much concerned over these considerations, taking them for granted. Their thoughts about its employment were governed by one reason which was deemed imperative: that by using the bomb, the agony of war might be ended more quickly. The primary and sustaining aim from the start of the great exertion to make the bomb was military, and the impelling reason for the decision to use it was military— to end the war victoriously as soon as possible."

—from *Japan Subdued*

16 **Using Secondary Sources to Analyze History** Write a brief report explaining why Alperovitz thinks the use of the bomb was unnecessary, and why Feis disagrees. What do both historians seem to agree is true about the decision to drop the bomb? What questions do you need to answer to be able to judge which historian has a better argument? LAFS.1112.RH.1.3, LAFS.1112.RH.2.6, LAFS.1112.RH.3.7, LAFS.1112.RH.3.8, LAFS.1112.RH.3.9, LAFS.1112.RH.4.10, SS.912.A.1.1, LAFS.1112.WHST.1.2, LAFS.1112.WHST.2.4, LAFS.1112.WHST.3.9, LAFS.1112.WHST.4.10, SS.912.A.6.1

17 **Answering Historical Questions** Write an essay explaining the controversy surrounding the use of the atomic bomb on Japan. Use historical evidence from the chapter to describe both sides of the argument, and then explain your point of view on the issue. Was dropping the bomb the correct decision? LAFS.1112.RH.3.7, LAFS.1112.RH.3.8, LAFS.1112.RH.3.9, LAFS.1112.RH.4.10, LAFS.1112.WHST.3.9, LAFS.1112.WHST.4.10, SS.912.A.1.1, SS.912.A.6.1

Analyzing Visuals

Use the map to answer the following questions.

18 **Analyzing** Examine the map of World War II in the Pacific. Why did the U.S. Navy adopt an "island hopping" strategy in the Pacific as part of its plan to defeat Japan? SS.912.A.1.4, SS.912.A.6.1, SS.912.G.2.1

Extended Response Question

19 **Evaluating** Research and then write an essay analyzing Franklin Roosevelt's domestic and international leadership during World War II. Explain the approach he and his administration took to rapidly mobilize American industry and discuss its effectiveness. Then examine Roosevelt's conferences with American allies, his objectives, and how successful he was in achieving his goals. Use authoritative sources and evaluate the authenticity of any resources you find online, use relevant details to support your analysis, and cite your sources properly. LAFS.1112.RH.1.1, LAFS.1112.RH.3.7, LAFS.1112.RH.3.9, LAFS.1112.RH.4.10, LAFS.1112.WHST.2.4, LAFS.1112.WHST.4.10, SS.912.A.1.5, SS.912.A.6.1, SS.912.A.6.2, SS.912.A.6.5

Need Extra Help?

If You've Missed Question	16	17	18	19
Go to Lesson	2	2	2	2, 3

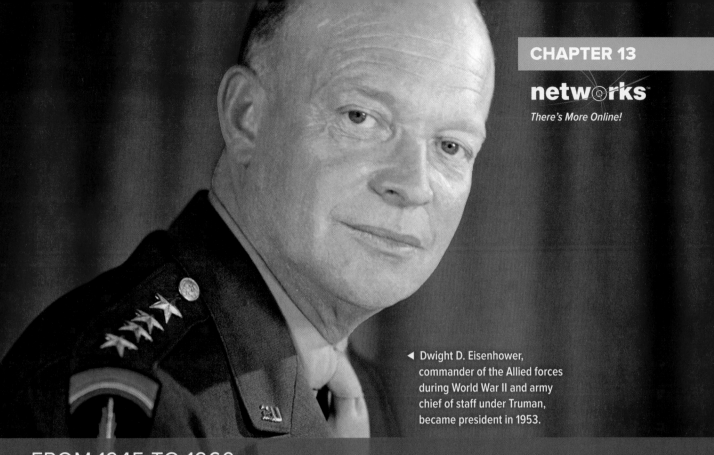

◀ Dwight D. Eisenhower, commander of the Allied forces during World War II and army chief of staff under Truman, became president in 1953.

FROM 1945 TO 1960

The Cold War Begins

THE STORY MATTERS ...

The destruction caused by the atomic bomb raised the stakes of military conflict. American concerns about the lack of freedom in countries controlled by the Soviet Union created a growing tension between the two nations. The United States and the Soviet Union would continue in a state of political conflict, military tension, and economic competition for almost 45 years. Conflict broke out in 1950 when Communist North Korea invaded South Korea, expanding the Cold War.

ESSENTIAL QUESTIONS
- How did the Cold War shape postwar international relations?
- How did Cold War tensions affect American society?

LESSON 1
The Origins of the Cold War

LESSON 2
The Early Cold War Years

LESSON 3
The Cold War and American Society

LESSON 4
Eisenhower's Cold War Policies

CHAPTER 13

Place & Time: United States 1945–1960

Relations between the Soviet Union and the other Allies soured as the Soviets established Communist governments in Eastern Europe. President Truman authorized billions of dollars of American aid to devastated European nations as well as to the Allies' former enemies, Germany and Japan. Americans grew fearful of the possibility of Communists infiltrating the U.S. government, while others feared an attack with nuclear weapons. By the early 1950s, Americans were looking for someone or something that would make them feel secure.

Step Into the Place

Read the quotes and look at the information presented on the map.

 Analyzing Historical Documents How do the United States and the Soviet Union each seem to be interpreting the intentions of the other nation?

PRIMARY SOURCE

> [The] USSR still [believes] in antagonistic 'capitalist encirclement' with which in the long run there can be no permanent peaceful coexistence. . . . In summary, we have here a political force committed fanatically to the belief that . . . it is desirable and necessary that the internal harmony of our society be disrupted, our traditional way of life be destroyed, the international authority of our state be broken, if Soviet power is to be secure.
>
> —George F. Kennan, American diplomat, from "The Long Telegram," February 22, 1946

PRIMARY SOURCE

> The more the war recedes into the past, the more distinct becomes . . . the division of the political forces operating on the international arena into two major camps. . . . The principal driving force of the imperialist camp is the U.S.A. . . . The cardinal purpose of the imperialist camp is to strengthen imperialism, to hatch a new imperialist war, to combat socialism and democracy, and to support reactionary and antidemocratic profascist regimes.
>
> —Andrey Zhdanov, adviser to Stalin, from *For a Lasting Peace for a People's Democracy*, no. 1, November 1947

left page: (tl)©Hulton-Deutsch Collection/Corbis; (tr)©Bettmann/Corbis; (tr)©Bettmann/Corbis; (b)detail/White House Collection/The White House Historical Association; right page: detail/White House Collection/The White House Historical Association

Step Into the Time

MAKING CONNECTIONS
Research an individual featured on the time line. Use your research to explain how this person might have influenced American society or international relations.

U.S. PRESIDENTS

Truman 1945–1953

UNITED STATES

1945 Franklin Roosevelt dies

1947 Truman Doctrine declared

1948 Berlin Airlift begins

1949 U.S. and Western European nations form NATO

1950 Senator McCarthy charges U.S. State Department contains Communists

1945   1947   1949

WORLD

1945 Potsdam Conference discusses terms of surrender and postwar boundaries

1948 Communist coup in Czechoslovakia

1950 North Korea invades South Korea

NEXT GENERATION SUNSHINE STATE STANDARDS
Students will understand the following benchmarks from the Florida NGSSS

LAFS.1112.RH.3.7: Integrate and evaluate multiple sources of information presented in diverse formats and media (e.g., visually, quantitatively, as well as in words) in order to address a question or solve a problem.

LAFS.1112.RH.3.9: Integrate information from diverse sources, both primary and

secondary, into a coherent understanding of an idea or event, noting discrepancies among sources.

SS.912.A.1.2: Utilize a variety of primary and secondary sources to identify author, historical significance, audience, and authenticity to understand a historical period.

SS.912.A.1.3: Utilize timelines to identify the time sequence of historical data.

SS.912.A.1.4: Analyze how images, symbols, objects, cartoons, graphs, charts, maps, and artwork may be used to interpret the significance of time periods and events from the past.

SS.912.A.6.10: Examine causes, course, and consequences of the early years of the Cold War (Truman Doctrine, Marshall Plan, NATO, Warsaw Pact).

The Global Cold War 1947–1955

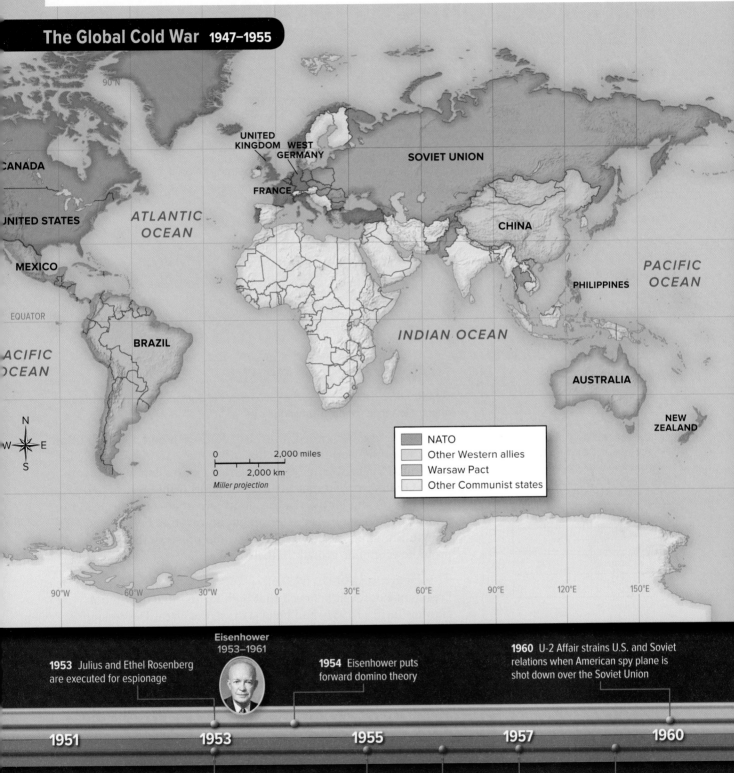

Legend:
- NATO
- Other Western allies
- Warsaw Pact
- Other Communist states

Scale: 2,000 miles / 2,000 km — Miller projection

Eisenhower 1953–1961

1953 Julius and Ethel Rosenberg are executed for espionage

1954 Eisenhower puts forward domino theory

1960 U-2 Affair strains U.S. and Soviet relations when American spy plane is shot down over the Soviet Union

Timeline: 1951 — 1953 — 1955 — 1957 — 1960

1953 Soviet leader Joseph Stalin dies

1955 Soviet Union and Communist nations in Eastern Europe form Warsaw Pact

1956 Soviet leader Nikita Khrushchev delivers speech denouncing Stalin

1957 Soviet Union launches *Sputnik*

1959 Fidel Castro takes power in Cuba

There's More Online!

The Origins of the Cold War

ESSENTIAL QUESTIONS
- How did the Cold War shape postwar international relations?
- How did Cold War tensions affect American society?

READING HELPDESK

Academic Vocabulary

- liberate
- equipment

Content Vocabulary

- charter
- satellite nations
- Iron Curtain

TAKING NOTES

Key Ideas and Details

Organizing As you read, complete a graphic organizer similar to the one below by filling in the names of the conferences held during the last days of World War II and the outcomes of each.
LAFS.1112.RH.3.7, SS.912.A.6.1, SS.912.A.6.9

Conferences	Outcomes

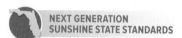

**NEXT GENERATION
SUNSHINE STATE STANDARDS**

LAFS.1112.RH.2.4: Determine the meaning of words and phrases as they are used in a text, including analyzing how an author uses and refines the meaning of a key term over the course of a text (e.g., how Madison defines faction in Federalist No. 10).

LAFS.1112.RH.3.7: Integrate and evaluate multiple sources of information presented in diverse formats and media (e.g., visually, quantitatively, as well as in words) in order to address a question or solve a problem.

LAFS.1112.WHST.3.9: Draw evidence from informational texts to support analysis, reflection, and research.

Continued on page 397

IT MATTERS BECAUSE

As World War II was coming to an end, the Allied powers set up a peacekeeping organization to prevent future wars. Soon, however, tensions arose over the amount of freedom the Soviets would allow the nations they controlled.

Building a New World

GUIDING QUESTION *How did the conferences at Dumbarton Oaks and Yalta attempt to shape the postwar world?*

Well before the war ended, President Roosevelt had begun to think about what the world would be like after the war. Many people in the United States worried that the Great Depression would come back. Others worried that the United States would return to isolationism, and let the rivalries between other countries lead to new wars. Roosevelt was determined, however, to build a new economic and political system that would preserve the peace and promote economic growth in the world.

The Bretton Woods System

President Roosevelt believed that high tariffs—like the Smoot-Hawley Tariff of 1931—had helped cause the Great Depression. He and his advisors were convinced that the best way to generate prosperity and economic growth after the war was to increase the amount of trade between countries and to create institutions that would keep the trade system stable.

In July 1944, Roosevelt organized a conference for the world's nations except those that belonged to the Axis. The conference was held at Bretton Woods, New Hampshire and established many international economic institutions that are still part of the world's economic system today.

The first organization set up at Bretton Woods was the World Bank. Its purpose was to help rebuild Europe after the war, and help nations in Asia, Africa, and Latin America develop their economies.

The World Bank still performs this role today, loaning money to help nations with their economic development. The second institution set up was the International Monetary Fund (IMF). Its purpose was to help countries with trade deficits. A trade deficit is when a country imports more than it exports. Countries with trade deficits have more of their money flowing out to buy foreign goods than they have flowing in from other countries who are buying their goods. The IMF was to use its funds to avoid trade wars and to prevent each country's money from changing too much in value. The IMF continues to perform this function today.

In addition to these two institutions, the nations set up a new currency system. The U.S. dollar became the world's reserve currency. All nations set an exchange rate between their currency and the dollar. The dollar in turn was put on a gold standard. One ounce of gold would equal 35 U.S. dollars, and the United States pledged to always keep enough gold in reserve so that anyone with dollars could convert them into gold on demand.

One of the benefits of the Bretton Woods system was that it would prevent nations from using inflation to escape their debts. Everyone remembered that Germany had used inflation to make its currency almost worthless after World War I as a way to avoid paying its reparations debts. The Bretton Woods system would keep the world's currencies stable and help keep the world at peace. The weakness of the system was that a gold standard limited the use of monetary policy to fight inflation or get out of a recession. By setting exchange rates, it also meant trade between nations could become unbalanced if the exchange rate did not accurately reflect the market value of goods being traded across borders.

Creating the United Nations

Roosevelt not only wanted to create a new global economic system, he also wanted a new political system to help prevent another world war. He believed one cause of World War II had been the American decision to stay out of the League of Nations after World War I. He wanted the United States and its allies to create a new international organization that would take an active role in preserving the peace.

In 1944, at the Dumbarton Oaks estate in Washington, D.C., delegates from 39 countries met to discuss the new organization, which was to be called the United Nations (UN). The delegates at the conference agreed that the UN would have a General Assembly, in which every member nation in the world would have one vote. The UN would also have a Security Council with 11 members. Five countries would be permanent members of the Security Council: Britain, France, China, the Soviet Union, and the United States. These five permanent members would each have veto power.

The advantage of the United Nations was that it put all of the great powers that had helped to defeat the Axis in the Security Council. This would force them to consult with each other and work together whenever the United Nations took action. The weakness of the United Nations was that the veto allowed any one member of the Security Council to stop the UN from taking action.

On April 25, 1945, representatives from 50 countries came to San Francisco to officially organize the United Nations and design its **charter.** The General Assembly was given the power to vote on resolutions and to choose the non-permanent members of the Security Council. The Security Council was responsible for international peace and security. It could ask its members to use military force to uphold a UN resolution.

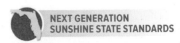

NEXT GENERATION SUNSHINE STATE STANDARDS

Continued from page 396

LAFS.1112.WHST.4.10: Write routinely over extended time frames (time for reflection and revision) and shorter time frames (a single sitting or a day or two) for a range of discipline-specific tasks, purposes, and audiences.

SS.912.A.1.2: Utilize a variety of primary and secondary sources to identify author, historical significance, audience, and authenticity to understand a historical period.

SS.912.A.1.4: Analyze how images, symbols, objects, cartoons, graphs, charts, maps, and artwork may be used to interpret the significance of time periods and events from the past.

SS.912.A.6.1: Examine causes, course, and consequences of World War II on the United States and the world.

SS.912.A.6.9: Describe the rationale for the formation of the United Nations, including the contribution of Mary McLeod Bethune.

SS.912.A.6.10: Examine causes, course, and consequences of the early years of the Cold War (Truman Doctrine, Marshall Plan, NATO, Warsaw Pact).

SS.912.A.6.13: Analyze significant foreign policy events during the Truman, Eisenhower, Kennedy, Johnson, and Nixon administrations.

SS.912.G.1.2: Use spatial perspective and appropriate geographic terms and tools, including the Six Essential Elements, as organizational schema to describe any given place.

SS.912.G.4.9: Use political maps to describe the change in boundaries and governments within continents over time.

Florida CONNECTION

Mary McLeod Bethune (1875–1955)

Mary McLeod Bethune was an educator, reformer, and civil rights leader. In 1904 she founded a school for African American girls in Daytona Beach, Florida, that is now part of Bethune-Cookman College. In the 1930s, Bethune was the director of the Division of Negro Affairs in the National Youth Administration. She was a delegate to the conference that organized the United Nations in 1945. At that conference she served as an adviser on interracial relations and supported independence from colonial rule for people in Africa and Asia. SS.912.A.6.9

charter a constitution

The Division of Germany 1945

North Sea

Baltic Sea

POLAND

NETHERLANDS

BELGIUM

Elbe R.

Berlin

inset

Rhine R.

FRANCE

Danube R.

CZECHOSLOVAKIA

AUSTRIA

SWITZ.

UN. KING.

Allied Occupation Zones, 1945–1949
- American
- British
- French
- Soviet
- —— Present-day Germany
- ---- Uncertain border

0   6 mi.
0   6 km

West Berlin

East Berlin

0   200 miles
0   200 km
Lambert Azimuthal Equal-Area projection

GEOGRAPHY CONNECTION

Germany and its capital Berlin were divided into four zones.

1. **PLACES AND REGIONS** *Which country controlled the smallest region of Germany?* SS.912.A.6.10, SS.912.G.1.2

2. **THE WORLD IN SPATIAL TERMS** *In what zone in the divided Germany was Berlin located?* SS.912.A.6.10, SS.912.G.1.2, SS.912.G.4.9

liberate to set free

Left to right: Churchill, Roosevelt, and Stalin. Leaders of the "Big Three" Allied nations met at the Yalta Conference to determine how to organize postwar Europe.

▶ CRITICAL THINKING

Predicting Consequences How might allowing Stalin to influence the political landscape of Eastern Europe affect that region's later foreign policy? SS.912.6.10

The Yalta Conference

In February 1945, with the war in Europe nearly over, Roosevelt, Churchill, and Stalin met at Yalta—a Soviet resort on the Black Sea—to plan the postwar world. Several agreements reached at Yalta later played an important role in causing the Cold War.

A key issue discussed at Yalta was Poland. Shortly after the Germans had invaded Poland in 1939, the Polish government fled to Britain. In 1944, however, Soviet troops drove back the Germans and entered Poland. As they **liberated** Poland from German control, the Soviets encouraged Polish Communists to set up a new government. As a result, two governments claimed the right to govern Poland: one Communist and one non-Communist. President Roosevelt and Prime Minister Churchill both argued that the Poles should be free to choose their own government.

Stalin, however, quickly pointed out that every time invaders had entered Russia from the west, they had come through Poland. Eventually, the three leaders compromised. Roosevelt and Churchill agreed to recognize the Polish government set up by the Soviets. Stalin agreed it would include members of the prewar Polish government, and free elections would be held as soon as possible.

The Declaration of Liberated Europe

After reaching a compromise on Poland, the three leaders agreed to issue the Declaration of Liberated Europe. The declaration echoed the Atlantic Charter, asserting "the right of all people to choose the form of government under which they will live." The Allies promised that the people of Europe would be allowed "to create democratic institutions of their own choice" and to create temporary governments that represented "all democratic elements." They pledged "the earliest possible establishment through free elections of governments responsive to the will of the people."

Dividing Germany

The conference then focused on Germany. Roosevelt, Churchill, and Stalin agreed to divide Germany into four zones. Great Britain, the United States, the Soviet Union, and France

The Granger Collection, New York

would each control one zone. The same four countries would also divide the German capital city of Berlin into four zones, even though it was in the Soviet zone.

Although pleased with the decision to divide Germany, Stalin also demanded that Germany pay heavy reparations for the war damages it had caused. An agreement was reached that Germany could pay war reparations with trade goods and products, half of which would go to the Soviet Union. The Allies would remove industrial machinery, railroad cars, and other **equipment** from Germany as reparations. Later arguments about reparations greatly increased tensions between the United States and the Soviet Union.

equipment the articles or physical resources prepared or furnished for a specific task

Rising Tensions

The Yalta decisions shaped the expectations of the United States. Two weeks after Yalta, the Soviets pressured the king of Romania into appointing a Communist government. The United States accused the Soviets of violating the Declaration of Liberated Europe. Soon afterward, the Soviets refused to allow more than three non-Communist Poles to serve in the 18-member Polish government. There was also no indication that they intended to hold free elections in Poland as promised. On April 1, President Roosevelt informed the Soviets that their actions in Poland were not acceptable.

Yalta marked a turning point in Soviet-American relations. President Roosevelt had hoped that an Allied victory and the creation of the United Nations would lead to a more peaceful world. Instead, as the war came to an end, the United States and the Soviet Union became increasingly hostile toward each other. The Cold War, an era of confrontation and competition between the nations, lasted from about 1946 to about 1990.

Soviet Concerns

As the war ended, Soviet leaders became concerned about security. They wanted to keep Germany weak and make sure that the countries between Germany and the Soviet Union were under Soviet control. Soviet leaders also believed that communism was a superior economic system that would eventually replace capitalism. They accepted Lenin's theory that capitalist countries would eventually try to destroy communism. This made them suspicious of capitalist nations.

American Economic Issues

While Soviet leaders focused on securing their borders, American leaders focused on economic problems. They believed that the Great Depression became so severe because nations reduced trade. They also believed that when nations stop trading, they are forced into war to get resources. By 1945, Roosevelt and his advisers were convinced that economic growth through world trade was the key to peace. They also thought that the free enterprise system, with private property rights and limited government intervention in the economy, was the best route to prosperity.

UN Responses to the War

In response to the atrocities of World War II, the United Nations held a General Assembly in December 1946. It passed a resolution that made genocide punishable internationally. The text of the Convention on the Prevention and Punishment of the Crime of Genocide became the first UN human rights treaty. Former First Lady Eleanor Roosevelt chaired a UN Commission on Human Rights in 1948. The commission drafted the Universal Declaration of Human Rights, promoting the inherent dignity of every human being and committing to end discrimination.

✓ READING PROGRESS CHECK

Identifying What agreements at the Yalta Conference contributed to the rise of the Cold War?

The Iron Curtain in Europe 1948

Legend:
- Communist countries
- Non-communist countries
- Iron Curtain

GEOGRAPHY CONNECTION

The "Iron Curtain" separated Communist nations in Eastern Europe controlled by the Soviet Union from non-Communist nations to the West.

1 THE WORLD IN SPATIAL TERMS *With which countries did East Germany share a border?* SS.912.A.6.10, SS.912.G.1.2

2 PLACES AND REGIONS *How did the amount of territory controlled by the Soviets compare with that of the rest of Europe?* SS.912.A.6.10, SS.912.G.1.2

Truman Takes Control

GUIDING QUESTION *Why did the Potsdam Conference further increase tensions between the United States and the Soviet Union?*

Eleven days after confronting the Soviets on Poland, President Roosevelt died and Harry S. Truman became president. Truman was strongly anti-Communist. He believed World War II had begun because Britain had tried to appease Hitler. He did not intend to make that mistake with Stalin. "We must stand up to the Russians," he told Secretary of State Edward Stettinius the day he took office.

Ten days later, Truman did exactly that at a meeting with Soviet foreign minister Molotov. Truman immediately brought up Poland and demanded that Stalin hold free elections as he had promised at Yalta. Molotov took the unexpectedly strong message back to Stalin. The meeting marked an important shift in Soviet-American relations and set the stage for further confrontations.

The Potsdam Conference

In July 1945, with the war against Japan still raging, Truman finally met Stalin at Potsdam, near Berlin. Both men had come to Potsdam to work out a deal on Germany. Truman was now convinced that industry was critical to Germany's survival. Unless its economy was allowed to revive, the rest of Europe would never recover, and the German people might turn to communism out of desperation.

Stalin and his advisers were convinced they needed reparations from Germany. The war had devastated the Soviet economy. Soviet troops had begun stripping their zone in Germany of its machinery and equipment for use back home, but Stalin wanted Germany to pay much more.

At the conference, Truman took a firm stand against heavy reparations. He insisted that Germany's industry had to be allowed to recover. Truman suggested the Soviets take reparations from their zone, while the Allies

satellite nations nations politically and economically dominated or controlled by another more powerful country

TEXT: Winston Churchill and the Sinews of Peace Address, March 5, 1946, Westminster College, Fulton, Missouri. Reproduced with permission of Curtis Brown, London on behalf of the Estate of Sir Winston Churchill. Copyright © Winston S. Churchill.

allowed industry to revive in the other zones. Stalin opposed this idea since the Soviet zone was mostly agricultural. To get the Soviets to accept the agreement, Truman offered Stalin a small amount of industrial equipment from the other zones, but required the Soviets to pay for part of it with food shipments. He also offered to accept the new German-Polish border the Soviets had established.

Stalin did not like the proposal. At Potsdam, Truman learned of the successful U.S. atomic bomb tests. He hinted to Stalin that the United States had a new, powerful weapon. Stalin suspected Truman of trying to bully him. He thought the Americans wanted to limit reparations to keep the Soviets weak. Despite his suspicions, Stalin had to accept the terms. American and British troops controlled Germany's industrial heartland, and there was no way for the Soviets to get reparations without cooperating. The Potsdam Conference marked yet another increase in tensions.

The Iron Curtain Descends

Although Truman had won the argument over reparations, he had less success on other issues at Potsdam. The Soviets refused to make stronger commitments to uphold the Declaration of Liberated Europe.

The presence of the Soviet army in Eastern Europe ensured that pro-Soviet Communist governments would eventually be established in the nations of Poland, Romania, Bulgaria, Hungary, and Czechoslovakia. The Communist countries of Eastern Europe came to be called **satellite nations** because they were controlled by the Soviets, as satellites are tied by gravity to the planets they orbit. Although not under direct Soviet control, these nations had to remain Communist and friendly to the Soviet Union. They also had to follow policies that the Soviets approved.

After watching the Communist takeover in Eastern Europe, the former British prime minister Winston Churchill coined a phrase to describe what had happened. On March 5, 1946, in a speech delivered in Fulton, Missouri, Churchill referred to an "iron curtain" falling across Eastern Europe. The press picked up the term, and for the next 43 years, it described the Communist nations of Eastern Europe and the Soviet Union. With the **Iron Curtain** separating Eastern Europe from the West, the World War II era had come to an end. The Cold War was about to begin.

✓ READING PROGRESS CHECK

Determining Cause and Effect How did the Potsdam Conference lead to greater tensions between the Americans and the Soviets?

Analyzing PRIMARY SOURCES

Churchill on the Iron Curtain

❝A shadow has fallen upon the scenes so lately lighted by the Allied victory. . . . From Stettin in the Baltic to Trieste in the Adriatic, an iron curtain has descended across the continent. Behind that line lie all the capitals of the ancient states of Central and Eastern Europe. Warsaw, Berlin, Prague, Vienna, Budapest, Belgrade, Bucharest and Sofia, all these famous cities and the populations around them lie in what I must call the Soviet sphere, and all are subject in one form or another, not only to Soviet influence, but to a very high and, in some cases, increasing measure of control from Moscow.❞

—Winston Churchill, from an address to Westminster College, Fulton, Missouri, March 5, 1946

DBQ ***ANALYZING PRIMARY SOURCES*** What words and phrases does Churchill use to convey his negative view of what is happening? LAFS.1112.RH.2.4, SS.912.A.1.2, SS.912.A.6.10

Iron Curtain the political and military barrier that isolated Soviet-controlled countries of Eastern Europe after World War II

LESSON 1 REVIEW

Reviewing Vocabulary
1. ***Describing*** What was the geographic relationship between Soviet satellite nations and the Iron Curtain? LAFS.1112.RH.2.4, SS.912.G.1.2, SS.912.A.6.10

Using Your Notes
2. ***Determining Cause and Effect*** Use your notes to write a few sentences about the effects of the major conferences of World War II. LAFS.1112.WHST.3.9, SS.912.A.6.10, SS.912.A.6.13

Answering the Guiding Questions
3. ***Summarizing*** How did the conferences at Dumbarton Oaks and Yalta attempt to shape the postwar world? LAFS.1112.WHST.3.9, SS.912.A.6.9, SS.912.A.6.10

4. ***Explaining*** Why did the Potsdam Conference further increase tensions between the United States and the Soviet Union? LAFS.1112.WHST.3.9, SS.912.A.6.13

Writing Activity
5. **NARRATIVE** Suppose that you were a student who saw Churchill deliver his famous "iron curtain" speech. Write a letter to a friend summarizing Churchill's ideas and giving your own opinions about the rising tensions between the Soviet Union and the West. LAFS.1112.WHST.4.10

LESSON 2
The Early Cold War Years

ESSENTIAL QUESTIONS

• How did the Cold War shape postwar international relations?
• How did Cold War tensions affect American society?

READING HELPDESK

Academic Vocabulary

• insecurity   • initially

Content Vocabulary

• containment
• limited war

TAKING NOTES

Key Ideas and Details

Organizing As you read, use a graphic organizer similar to the one below to list early conflicts between the Soviet Union and the United States. LAFS.1112.RH.3.7, SS.912.A.6.10

Conflicts Between the USSR and the U.S.

NEXT GENERATION SUNSHINE STATE STANDARDS

LAFS.1112.RH.2.4: Determine the meaning of words and phrases as they are used in a text, including analyzing how an author uses and refines the meaning of a key term over the course of a text (e.g., how Madison defines faction in Federalist No. 10).

LAFS.1112.RH.3.7: Integrate and evaluate multiple sources of information presented in diverse formats and media (e.g., visually, quantitatively, as well as in words) in order to address a question or solve a problem.

Continued on page 404

402

IT MATTERS BECAUSE
President Truman worked to contain communism by supporting Greece, Iran, and West Germany. When Communist North Korea invaded South Korea, Truman and the United Nations sent troops to aid South Korea.

Containing Communism

GUIDING QUESTION *What was the policy of containment?*

Despite growing tensions with the Soviet Union, many American officials continued to believe cooperation with the Soviets was possible. In late 1945, the foreign ministers of the former Allies met first in London, then in Moscow, to discuss the future of Europe and Asia. Although both British and American officials pushed for free elections in Eastern Europe, the Soviets refused to budge.

The Long Telegram
Increasingly exasperated by the Soviets' refusal to cooperate, officials at the U.S. State Department asked the American Embassy in Moscow to explain Soviet behavior. On February 22, 1946, diplomat George Kennan responded with what became known as the Long Telegram—a message, thousands of words long, explaining his views of the Soviets. According to Kennan, the Soviets' view of the world came from a traditional "Russian sense of **insecurity**" and fear of the West, intensified by the communist ideas of Lenin and Stalin. Because Communists believed they were in a historical struggle against capitalism, Kennan argued, it was impossible to reach any permanent settlement with them.

Kennan proposed what became basic American policy throughout the Cold War: "a long-term, patient but firm and vigilant **containment** of Russian expansive tendencies." In Kennan's opinion, the Soviet system had major economic and political weaknesses. If the United States could keep the Soviets from expanding their power, it would only be a matter of time before their system would fall apart, beating communism without going to war. The Long Telegram circulated widely in Truman's administration and became the basis for the administration's policy of containment—keeping communism within its present territory through diplomatic, economic, and military actions.

Crisis in Iran

While Truman's administration discussed Kennan's ideas, a series of crises erupted during the spring and summer of 1946. These crises seemed to prove that Kennan was right about the Soviets. The first crisis began in Iran.

During World War II, the United States had troops in southern Iran while Soviet troops held northern Iran to secure a supply line from the Persian Gulf. After the war, instead of withdrawing as promised, the Soviet troops remained in northern Iran. Stalin then began demanding access to Iran's oil supplies. To increase the pressure, Soviet troops helped local Communists in northern Iran establish a separate government.

American officials saw these actions as a Soviet push into the Middle East. The secretary of state sent Stalin a strong message demanding that Soviet forces withdraw. At the same time, the battleship USS *Missouri* sailed into the eastern Mediterranean. The pressure seemed to work. Soviet forces withdrew, having been promised a joint Soviet-Iranian oil company, although the Iranian parliament later rejected the plan.

The Truman Doctrine

Frustrated in Iran, Stalin turned northwest to Turkey. There, the straits of the Dardanelles were a vital route from Soviet ports on the Black Sea to the Mediterranean. Russia had wanted to control this strategic route for centuries. In August 1946, Stalin demanded joint control of the Dardanelles with Turkey.

Presidential adviser Dean Acheson saw this move as part of a Soviet plan to control the Middle East. He advised Truman to make a show of force. The president ordered the new aircraft carrier *Franklin D. Roosevelt* to join the *Missouri* in protecting Turkey and the eastern Mediterranean.

Meanwhile, Britain tried to help Greece. In August 1946, Greek Communists launched a guerrilla war against the Greek government. British troops helped fight the guerrillas, but in February 1947, Britain informed the United States that it could no longer afford to help Greece due to Britain's weakened postwar economy.

Shortly after, Truman went before Congress to ask for $400 million to fight Communist aggression in Greece and Turkey. His speech outlined a policy that became known as the Truman Doctrine. Its goal was to aid those who worked to resist being controlled by others. In the long run, it pledged the United States to fight the spread of communism worldwide.

PRIMARY SOURCE

❝The peoples of a number of countries of the world have recently had totalitarian regimes forced upon them against their will. The Government of the United States has made frequent protests against coercion and intimidation, in violation of the Yalta agreement in Poland, Romania, and Bulgaria. At the present moment in world history nearly every nation must choose between alternative ways of life. The choice is too often not a free one. . . . I believe that it must be the policy of the United States to support free peoples who are resisting attempted subjugation by armed minorities or by outside pressures. I believe that we must assist free peoples to work out their own destinies in their own way.❞

—President Truman, from his address to Congress, March 12, 1947

The Marshall Plan

Meanwhile, postwar Western Europe faced grave problems. Economies were ruined, people faced starvation, and political chaos was at hand. In June 1947, Secretary of State George C. Marshall proposed the European

insecurity the state of not being confident or sure

containment the policy or process of preventing the expansion of a hostile power

President Truman signs the Foreign Aid Assistance Act, providing aid to Greece and Turkey. The policy of supporting nations resisting Communist pressure became known as the Truman Doctrine.

▶ CRITICAL THINKING
Identifying Central Ideas What was the main purpose of the Truman Doctrine? LAFS.1112.WHST.3.9, SS.912.A.6.10

MPI/Archive Photos/Getty Images

1 *Posing Questions About Geographic Distributions*
Britain (the U.K.) received the largest amount of Marshall Plan aid. What questions do you need to ask to explain why the British received so much more aid? What would you predict is the reason?
MAFS.912.S-ID.1, SS.912.A.6.10

2 *Posing Questions About Geographic Patterns*
Based on the chart, which three countries' economies would you expect to recover most quickly? Why might that not be true? Write two questions you need to ask to know if your prediction is accurate. MAFS.912.S-ID.1, SS.912.A.6.10

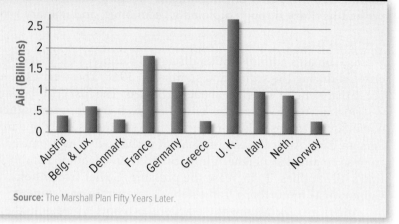

Source: The Marshall Plan Fifty Years Later.

NEXT GENERATION SUNSHINE STATE STANDARDS

Continued from page 402

LAFS.1112.SL.2.4: Present information, findings, and supporting evidence, conveying a clear and distinct perspective, such that listeners can follow the line of reasoning, alternative or opposing perspectives are addressed, and the organization, development, substance, and style are appropriate to purpose, audience, and a range of formal and informal tasks.

LAFS.1112.WHST.3.9: Draw evidence from informational texts to support analysis, reflection, and research.

LAFS.1112.WHST.1.1: Write arguments focused on discipline-specific content.

MAFS.912.S-ID.1: Summarize, represent and interpret data on a single count or measurement variable.

SS.912.A.1.2: Utilize a variety of primary and secondary sources to identify author, historical significance, audience, and authenticity to understand a historical period.

SS.912.A.1.4: Analyze how images, symbols, objects, cartoons, graphs, charts, maps, and artwork may be used to interpret the significance of time periods and events from the past.

SS.912.A.6.10: Examine causes, course, and consequences of the early years of the Cold War (Truman Doctrine, Marshall Plan, NATO, Warsaw Pact).

SS.912.A.6.12: Examine causes, course, and consequences of the Korean War.

SS.912.A.6.13: Analyze significant foreign policy events during the Truman, Eisenhower, Kennedy, Johnson, and Nixon administrations.

SS.912.G.1.2: Use spatial perspective and appropriate geographic terms and tools, including the Six Essential Elements, as organizational schema to describe any given place.

SS.912.G.4.9 : Use political maps to describe the change in boundaries and governments within continents over time.

Recovery Program, or Marshall Plan, which would give European nations American aid to rebuild their economies. Truman saw both the Marshall Plan and the Truman Doctrine as essential for containment. Marshall offered help to all nations planning a recovery program.

Although the Marshall Plan was offered to the Soviet Union and its satellite nations, the Soviets rejected it and developed their own economic program. This action further separated Europe into competing regions. The Marshall Plan pumped billions of dollars in supplies, machinery, and food into Western Europe. The region's recovery weakened the appeal of communism and opened new markets for trade.

In his 1949 inaugural address, Truman proposed assistance for underdeveloped countries outside the war zone. The Point Four Program aimed to provide them with "scientific advances and industrial progress" for their improvement and growth. The Department of State administered the program until its merger with other foreign aid programs in 1953.

The Berlin Airlift

Truman and his advisers believed Western Europe's prosperity depended on Germany's recovery. The Soviets, however, still wanted Germany to pay reparations. This dispute brought the nations to the brink of war. By early 1948, American officials had concluded that the Soviets were trying to undermine Germany's economy. In response, the United States, Britain, and France merged their German zones and allowed the Germans to have their own government, creating the Federal Republic of Germany, which became known as West Germany. They also agreed to merge their zones in Berlin and make West Berlin part of West Germany. The Soviet zone became the German Democratic Republic, or East Germany. West Germany was mostly independent but not allowed to have a military.

The creation of West Germany convinced the Soviets they would never get the reparations they wanted. In June 1948, Soviet troops blockaded West Berlin, hoping to force the United States to reconsider its decision or abandon West Berlin. Truman sent bombers capable of carrying atomic weapons to bases in Britain. Hoping to avoid war with the Soviets, he ordered the air force to fly supplies into Berlin rather than troops.

The Berlin Airlift began in June 1948 and continued through the spring of 1949, bringing in more than two million tons of supplies to the city. Stalin finally lifted the blockade on May 12, 1949. The airlift symbolized American determination to contain communism and not give in to Soviet demands.

The Creation of NATO

The Berlin blockade convinced many Americans that the Soviets were bent on conquest. The public began to support a military alliance with Western Europe. By April 1949, an agreement had been made to form the North Atlantic Treaty Organization (NATO)—a mutual defense alliance.

NATO **initially** included 12 countries: the United States, Canada, Britain, France, Italy, Belgium, Denmark, Portugal, the Netherlands, Norway, Luxembourg, and Iceland. NATO members agreed to come to the aid of any member who was attacked. For the first time, the United States had committed itself to maintaining peace in Europe. Six years later, NATO allowed West Germany to rearm and join its organization. This decision alarmed Soviet leaders. They responded by organizing a military alliance in Eastern Europe known as the Warsaw Pact.

initially of or relating to the beginning; to start with

☑ **READING PROGRESS CHECK**

Identifying Central Issues What was the main idea behind containment?

Developments in Asia and the Korean War

GUIDING QUESTION *Why was the Korean War a major turning point in the Cold War?*

The Cold War eventually spread beyond Europe. Conflicts also emerged in Asia, where events in China and Korea brought about a new attitude toward Japan and sent American troops back into battle in Asia less than five years after World War II had ended.

The Chinese Revolution

In China, Communist forces led by Mao Zedong had been struggling against the Nationalist government led by Chiang Kai-shek since the late 1920s. During World War II, the two sides suspended their war to resist Japanese occupation. With the end of World War II, however, civil war broke out again. Although Mao and the Communist forces made great gains, neither side could win nor agree to a compromise.

GEOGRAPHY CONNECTION

NATO was formed as an alliance to defend against an outside attack. In response, the Soviet Union created its own alliance known as the Warsaw Pact.

1 HUMAN SYSTEMS
Which nations are the founding members of NATO? SS.912.A.6.10, SS.912.G.1.2

2 PLACES AND REGIONS
Why was West Germany not a part of the original group of NATO nations? SS.912.A.6.10, SS.912.G.4.9

NATO Is Born 1949

Founding NATO member

NORTH KOREA

P'yŏngyang

Sea of Japan (East Sea)

38th Parallel

Inch'ŏn Seoul

Yellow Sea

SOUTH KOREA

Pusan

125°E   130°E   135°E

0   200 miles
0   200 km
Miller projection

— Boundary 1950
— Boundary 1953

▶ CRITICAL THINKING

Analyzing What geographical feature forms the border between China and North Korea? SS.912.G.1.2

To prevent a communist revolution in Asia, the United States sent the Nationalist government $2 billion in aid beginning in the mid-1940s. The Nationalists, however, squandered this advantage through poor military planning and corruption. By 1949, the Communists had captured the Chinese capital of Beijing, while support for the Nationalists declined.

In August 1949, the U.S. State Department discontinued aid to the Chinese Nationalists. The defeated Nationalists then fled to the small island of Formosa (now called Taiwan). The victorious Communists established the People's Republic of China in October 1949.

China's fall to communism shocked Americans. To make matters worse, in September 1949, the Soviet Union announced that it had successfully tested its first atomic weapon. Then, early in 1950, the People's Republic of China and the Soviet Union signed a treaty of friendship and alliance. Many Western leaders feared that China and the Soviet Union would support communist revolutions in other nations.

The United States kept formal diplomatic relations with only the Nationalist Chinese in Taiwan. It used its veto power in the UN Security Council to keep representatives of the new Communist People's Republic of China out of the UN, allowing the Nationalists to retain their seat.

New Policies in Japan

The Chinese revolution brought about a significant change in American policy toward Japan. At the end of World War II, General Douglas MacArthur had taken charge of occupied Japan. His mission was to introduce democracy and keep Japan from threatening war again. Once the United States lost China as its chief ally in Asia, it adopted policies to encourage the rapid recovery of Japan's industrial economy. Just as the United States viewed West Germany as the key to defending all of Europe against communism, it saw Japan as the key to defending Asia.

The Korean War

At the end of World War II, American and Soviet forces entered Korea to disarm the Japanese troops stationed there. The Allies divided Korea at the 38th parallel of latitude. Soviet troops controlled the north, while American troops controlled the south.

As the Cold War began, talks to reunify Korea broke down. A Communist Korean government was organized in the north, while an American-backed government controlled the south. Both governments claimed authority over Korea, and border clashes were common. The Soviets provided military aid to the North Koreans, who quickly built an army. On June 25, 1950, North Korean troops invaded the south, driving back the poorly equipped South Korean forces.

Truman saw the Communist invasion of South Korea as a test of the containment policy and ordered American naval and air power into action. He then called on the United Nations to act. Because the Soviet Union was boycotting the Security Council over its China policy, Truman succeeded. With the pledge of UN troops, he ordered General MacArthur to send American troops from Japan to Korea.

The American and South Korean troops were driven back into a small pocket of territory near the port of Pusan. Inside the "Pusan perimeter," troops stubbornly resisted the North Koreans, buying time for MacArthur to organize reinforcements.

On September 15, 1950, MacArthur ordered a daring invasion behind enemy lines at the port of Inchon. The Inchon landing took the North Koreans by surprise. Within weeks they were in full retreat back across the 38th parallel. Truman then gave the order to pursue the North Koreans beyond the 38th parallel. MacArthur pushed the North Koreans north to the Yalu River, the border with China.

China Enters the War The Communist People's Republic of China saw the advancing UN troops as a threat and warned them to halt their advance. When warnings were ignored, Chinese forces crossed the Yalu River in November. Hundreds of thousands of Chinese troops flooded across the border, driving the UN forces back across the 38th parallel.

As his troops fell back, an angry MacArthur demanded approval to expand the war against China. He asked for a blockade of Chinese ports, the use of Chiang Kai-shek's Nationalist forces, and the bombing of Chinese cities with atomic weapons.

Truman Fires MacArthur President Truman refused MacArthur's demands because he did not want to expand the war into China or to use the atomic bomb. MacArthur persisted, publicly criticizing the president and arguing that it was a mistake to keep the war limited. "There is no substitute for victory," MacArthur insisted, by which he meant that if the United States was going to go to war, it should use all of its power to win. A limited war was a form of appeasement, he argued, and appeasement "begets new and bloodier war."

Determined to maintain control of policy and show that he commanded the military, an exasperated Truman fired MacArthur for insubordination in April 1951. Later, in private conversation, Truman explained: "I was sorry to have to reach a parting of the way with the big man in Asia, but he asked for it and I had to give it to him."

MacArthur, who remained popular despite being fired, returned home to parades and a hero's welcome. Many Americans criticized the president. Congress and military leaders, however, supported his decision and his Korean strategy. American policy in Asia remained committed to **limited war**—a war fought to achieve a limited objective, such as containing communism. Truman later explained his position:

Soldiers of the U.S. 2nd Infantry Division man a machine gun near the Chongchon River in Korea, November 20, 1950.

▶ **CRITICAL THINKING**
Identifying Central Ideas What was the objective of the United States during the Korean War?
LAFS.1112.WHST.3.9, SS.912.A.6.12

limited war a war fought with limited commitment of resources to achieve a limited objective, such as containing communism

PRIMARY SOURCE

❞The Kremlin [Soviet Union] is trying, and has been trying for a long time, to drive a wedge between us and the other nations. It wants to see us isolated. It wants to see us distrusted. It wants to see us feared and hated by our allies. Our allies agree with us in the course we are following. They do not believe we should take the initiative to widen the conflict in the Far East. If the United States were to widen the conflict, we might well have to go it alone.❞
—from an address to the Civil Defense Conference, May 7, 1951

Armistice Ends Fighting By mid-1951, UN forces had pushed the Chinese and North Korean forces back across the 38th parallel. The war settled into a series of relatively small battles over hills and other local objectives. In July 1951, peace negotiations began at Panmunjom. As talks continued, the war became increasingly unpopular in the United States. After Dwight D. Eisenhower was elected to the presidency in 1952, the former general traveled to Korea to talk with commanders and their troops. He became determined to bring the war to an end.

©Bettmann/Corbis

In 1951 President Truman fired General Douglas MacArthur over disagreements about how to conduct the Korean War.

This cartoon suggests that General MacArthur had overstepped his authority in Korea.

1 **Making Inferences** What does the cartoon imply MacArthur was trying to do in Asia? SS.912.A.1.4, SS.912.A.6.12

2 **Analyzing Primary Sources** Is this cartoon supportive of General MacArthur or critical of him? Explain. SS.912.A.1.4, SS.912.A.6.12

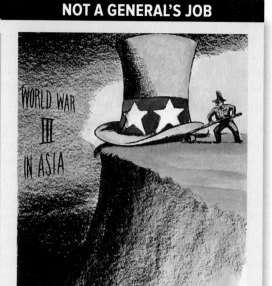

WORLD WAR III IN ASIA

The Granger Collection, New York

SKILLS PRACTICE

Work with a partner. Take turns asking one another questions about the causes of the Cold War. Answer one another's questions about the Long Telegram, the Truman Doctrine, the Marshall Plan, the Berlin Airlift, and other important events.

ELD.K12.ELL.SI.1, ELD.K12.ELL.SS.1

Eisenhower quietly hinted to the Chinese that the United States might use a nuclear attack in Korea. The threat seemed to work. In July 1953, negotiators signed an armistice. The battle line between the two sides in Korea, which was very near the prewar boundary, became the border between North Korea and South Korea. A "demilitarized zone" (DMZ) separated them. American troops are still based in Korea, helping to defend South Korea's border. There has never been a peace treaty to end the war. More than 33,600 American soldiers died in action, and over 20,600 died in accidents or from disease.

Changes in Policy The Korean War marked a turning point in the Cold War. Until 1950, the United States had preferred to use political pressure and economic aid to contain communism. After the Korean War began, the United States embarked on a major military buildup. The war also helped expand the Cold War to Asia. Before 1950, American efforts to contain communism focused on Europe. With the Korean War, the nation became more militarily involved in Asia. By 1954, the United States had signed defense agreements with Japan, South Korea, and Taiwan. The United States also formed the Southeast Asia Treaty Organization (SEATO) in 1954. Aid also began flowing to French forces fighting Communists in Vietnam.

✓ READING PROGRESS CHECK

Analyzing How did the Korean War change the course of the Cold War?

LESSON 2 REVIEW

Reviewing Vocabulary
1. *Defining* What is the defining feature of limited war?
   LAFS.1112.RH.2.4, SS.912.A.6.12

Using Your Notes
2. *Summarizing* Review the notes you completed during the lesson to write a paragraph summarizing the major conflicts between the Soviet Union and the United States during the early years of the Cold War. LAFS.1112.SL.2.4, SS.912.A.6.10

Answering the Guiding Questions
3. *Explaining* What was the policy of containment?
   LAFS.1112.RH.2.4, SS.912.A.6.10
4. *Describing* Why was the Korean War a major turning point in the Cold War? LAFS.1112.WHST.3.9, SS.912.A.6.12

Writing Activity
5. **ARGUMENT** Write a letter to the editor of a newspaper explaining why you agree or disagree with President Truman's firing of General MacArthur. LAFS.1112.WHST.1.1, SS.912.A.6.12

Using A Decision-Making Process

Why Learn This Skill?

Life is full of choices. It seems that almost all the time we are being asked to make decisions. While some decisions, such as what color of socks to wear, are not that important, others, such as whether or not to go to university, or what job to take, can affect the rest of your life. History is also full of choices. Much of the work of historians is looking at the decisions people have made and trying to figure out why they made them and whether they had other choices. Learning a good decision-making process will help you make better choices for yourself, and help you understand historical choices made by others.

Learning the Skill

Follow these five steps to help you through the process of making good decisions.

1. Identify the problem. What are you being asked to choose?
2. Gather information about the problem, and clearly identify your options and the various alternatives that are possible.
3. Try to predict the consequences for each option. Identify both positive and negative things that might happen for each option. Consider both short-term and long-term consequences. Sometimes short-term hardships can lead to long-term benefits that make the difficulties getting there worthwhile.
4. Evaluate the consequences. This is the hardest step. How important are each of the positive and negative consequences, sometimes referred to as the costs and benefits, when weighed against each other?
5. Make your decision. Know that once you make a decision and act on it, it causes new things to happen, possibly things you did not predict. Be prepared to stick to your decision if it is leading to something you want, even if it is hard to follow through. But if the decision leads to negative consequences you did not

expect, be prepared to start a new decision-making process.

Practicing the Skill

Decisions throughout history have affected the outcome of events and created the world we live in today. Each of the following events took place as a result of a decision made by a person or a group of people during the Cold War. Identify the alternatives and describe their consequences.

1. The United States begins the Berlin Airlift after Stalin cuts off surface transportation bringing supplies from the West.
2. The Marshall Plan for rebuilding war-torn Western Europe is approved.
3. President Truman relieves General Douglas MacArthur of his command for insubordination.

Applying the Skill

Making Decisions Do research at the library or online at a news website and identify a current issue facing the United States. Identify the issue, then review the facts and what you already know about the issue. Identify various alternatives and determine the consequences for each. Use this information to evaluate both positive and negative consequences. Make a sound decision about which alternative would be best for you, and write a paragraph defending your decision.

Tony Vaccaro/Archive Photos/Getty Images

LESSON 3

The Cold War and American Society

ESSENTIAL QUESTIONS

• How did the Cold War shape postwar international relations?
• How did Cold War tensions affect American society?

READING HELPDESK

Academic Vocabulary

• manipulate   • convince

Content Vocabulary

• subversion
• loyalty review program
• perjury
• censure
• fallout

TAKING NOTES

Key Ideas and Details

Organizing As you read, summarize the lesson content by using the major headings to create an outline similar to the one below. LAFS.1112.RH.3.7, SS.912.A.5.2, SS.912.A.6.8

> The Cold War and
> American Society
> I. A New Red Scare
>   A. The Truman Loyalty
>   Review Program
>   B.
>   C.

NEXT GENERATION SUNSHINE STATE STANDARDS

LAFS.1112.RH.2.4: Determine the meaning of words and phrases as they are used in a text, including analyzing how an author uses and refines the meaning of a key term over the course of a text (e.g., how Madison defines faction in Federalist No. 10).

LAFS.1112.RH.3.7: Integrate and evaluate multiple sources of information presented in diverse formats and media (e.g., visually, quantitatively, as well as in words) in order to address a question or solve a problem.

Continued on page 411

IT MATTERS BECAUSE

Fearing subversive activity, the government tried to root out Communists in government, Hollywood, and labor unions, while Americans learned to live with the threat of nuclear attack.

A New Red Scare

GUIDING QUESTION *How did the post–World War II Red Scare compare and contrast with the one that followed World War I?*

During the 1950s, rumors and accusations spawned fears that Communists were trying to take over the world. The Red Scare began in September 1945, when a clerk named Igor Gouzenko walked out of the Soviet Embassy in Ottawa, Canada, and defected. Gouzenko carried documents showing a Soviet effort to infiltrate government agencies in Canada and the United States, with the specific goal of obtaining information about the atomic bomb. The case stunned Americans. It implied that spies had infiltrated the American government. Soon the search for spies escalated into a general fear of Communist **subversion,** or effort to weaken a society and overthrow its government.

The Truman Loyalty Review Program

In early 1947, President Truman established a **loyalty review program** to screen all federal employees. Truman's action seemed to confirm suspicions that Communists had infiltrated the government and so added to fears that communism was sweeping the nation. Between 1947 and 1951, more than six million federal employees were screened for loyalty—a term difficult to define. A person might become a suspect for reading certain books, belonging to various groups, traveling overseas, or seeing certain foreign films. The Federal Bureau of Investigation (FBI) scrutinized some 14,000 people. About 2,000 quit their jobs, many under pressure. Another 212 were fired for "questionable loyalty," despite a lack of actual evidence.

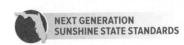
HUAC and Anti-Communist Investigations

FBI director J. Edgar Hoover remained unsatisfied. In 1947, he went before the House Un-American Activities Committee (HUAC). Formed in 1938 to investigate subversive activities in the United States, HUAC had been a minor committee before Hoover's involvement. He urged HUAC to hold public hearings on Communist subversion to expose not just Communists but also "Communist sympathizers" and "fellow travelers." Under Hoover's leadership, the FBI sent agents to infiltrate groups suspected of subversion and wiretapped thousands of telephones.

Hollywood on Trial One of HUAC's first hearings in 1947 focused on the film industry as a cultural force that Communists might **manipulate** to spread their ideas and influence. Future American president Ronald Reagan was head of the Screen Actors Guild at the time and, when called before HUAC, he testified that there were Communists in Hollywood. During the hearings, ten screenwriters, known as the "Hollywood Ten," used their Fifth Amendment right to protect themselves from self-incrimination and refused to testify. The incident led producers to blacklist, or agree not to hire, anyone who was believed to be a Communist or who refused to cooperate with the committee. The blacklist created an atmosphere of distrust and fear.

Alger Hiss In 1948, Whittaker Chambers, a magazine editor and former Communist Party member, told HUAC that several government officials were also former Communists or spies. One official Chambers named was Alger Hiss, a diplomat who had served in Roosevelt's administration, attended the Yalta Conference, and helped organize the United Nations. Hiss sued Chambers for libel, but Chambers testified that, in 1937 and 1938, Hiss had given him secret State Department documents. Hiss denied being either a spy or a member of the Communist Party, and he also denied ever having known Chambers.

The committee was ready to drop the investigation until California representative Richard Nixon **convinced** his colleagues to continue the hearings to determine who had lied. Chambers produced copies of secret documents, along with microfilm that he had hidden in a hollow pumpkin. These "pumpkin papers," Chambers claimed, proved Hiss was lying. A jury agreed and convicted Hiss of **perjury,** or lying under oath.

The Rosenbergs Another spy case centered on accusations that American Communists had sold secrets about the atomic bomb to the Soviets to help them produce a bomb in 1949. In 1950, the hunt for spies led the FBI to arrest Julius and Ethel Rosenberg, a New York couple who were members of the Communist Party. The government charged them with spying for the Soviets.

The Rosenbergs denied the charges but were condemned to death for espionage. Many people believed that they were simply victims caught in the wave of anti-Communist frenzy. Appeals and pleas for clemency failed, however, and the Rosenbergs were executed in June 1953.

Project Venona In 1946, American and British cryptographers, working for a project code-named "Venona," cracked the Soviet Union's spy code, enabling them to read approximately 3,000 messages between Moscow and the United States collected during the Cold War. These messages confirmed extensive Soviet spying and ongoing efforts to steal nuclear secrets. The government did not reveal Project Venona's existence until 1995. The Venona documents provided strong evidence that the Rosenbergs were indeed guilty.

Continued from page 410

LAFS.1112.RH.4.10: By the end of grade 12, read and comprehend history/social studies texts in the grades 11–CCR text complexity band independently and proficiently.

LAFS.1112.SL.2.4: Present information, findings, and supporting evidence, conveying a clear and distinct perspective, such that listeners can follow the line of reasoning, alternative or opposing perspectives are addressed, and the organization, development, substance, and style are appropriate to purpose, audience, and a range of formal and informal tasks.

Continued on page 412

subversion a systematic attempt to overthrow a government by using persons working secretly from within

loyalty review program a policy established by President Truman that authorized the screening of all federal employees to determine their loyalty to the U.S. government

manipulate to operate or arrange manually to achieve a desired effect

convince to bring to belief, consent, or a course of action

perjury lying when one has sworn under oath to tell the truth

Although he had led the effort to develop the atomic bomb, scientist J. Robert Oppenheimer's left-wing views and opposition to the hydrogen bomb led to the suspension of his security clearance and controversial public hearings.

▶ CRITICAL THINKING
Drawing Conclusions Why were people suspicious of Oppenheimer?
SS.912.A.6.8

©Bettmann/Corbis

BIOGRAPHY

Joseph McCarthy (1908–1957)

When Wisconsin politician Joseph McCarthy first ran for Senate in 1946, he claimed his opponent was "communistically inclined." His later accusations of Communist subversion made him a national figure. Between 1950 and 1954, McCarthy made headlines for his investigations of government departments and figures, despite his inability to build a solid case against anyone. His often wild accusations became the hallmark of McCarthyism.

▶ **CRITICAL THINKING**
Identifying Central Ideas What was the larger threat behind allowing McCarthyism to spread?
LAFS.1112.RH.4.10, SS.912.A.6.8

NEXT GENERATION SUNSHINE STATE STANDARDS

Continued from page 411
LAFS.1112.WHST.1.1: Write arguments focused on discipline-specific content.

LAFS.1112.WHST.3.9: Draw evidence from informational texts to support analysis, reflection, and research.

MAFS.912.S-ID.1: Summarize, represent and interpret data on a single count or measurement variable.

SS.912.A.1.1: Describe the importance of historiography, which includes how historical knowledge is obtained and transmitted, when interpreting events in history.

SS.912.A.1.2: Utilize a variety of primary and secondary sources to identify author, historical significance, audience, and authenticity to understand a historical period.

SS.912.A.1.4: Analyze how images, symbols, objects, cartoons, graphs, charts, maps, and artwork may be used to interpret the significance of time periods and events from the past.

SS.912.A.5.2: Explain the causes of the public reaction (Sacco and Vanzetti, labor, racial unrest) associated with the Red Scare.

Continued on page 414

The Red Scare Spreads

Many state and local governments, universities, businesses, unions, churches, and private groups also began efforts to find Communists. The University of California required its faculty to take loyalty oaths and fired 157 who refused. Many Catholic groups became anti-Communist and urged members to identify Communists within the Church. The Taft-Hartley Act of 1947 required union leaders to take oaths saying that they were not Communists. Many union leaders did not object. Instead, they launched efforts to purge their own organizations, eventually expelling 11 unions that refused to remove Communist leaders.

☑ **READING PROGRESS CHECK**

Comparing and Contrasting What was one way that the Red Scare of the 1950s and the Red Scare of the 1920s were similar?

McCarthyism

GUIDING QUESTION *Why did many Americans believe Senator McCarthy's accusations?*

In 1949, the Red Scare intensified as the Soviet Union successfully tested an atomic bomb, and China fell to communism. To many Americans, these events seemed to prove that the United States was losing the Cold War.

In February 1950, little-known senator Joseph R. McCarthy gave a speech to a Republican women's group in West Virginia. Halfway through his speech, McCarthy made a surprising statement when he claimed:

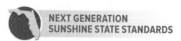

PRIMARY SOURCE

❝While I cannot take the time to name all the men in the State Department who have been named as members of the Communist Party and members of a spy ring, I have here in my hand a list of 205 that were known to the Secretary of State as being members of the Communist Party and who nevertheless are still working and shaping the policy of the State Department.❞

—quoted in *The Fifties*, 1993

The Associated Press sent the statement nationwide. Reporters at an airport asked McCarthy to see his list. McCarthy replied that he would be happy to show it to them, but unfortunately, it was in his bag on the plane. In fact, the list never appeared. McCarthy, however, continued making charges.

McCarthy proclaimed that Communists were a danger at home and abroad. He distributed a booklet accusing Democratic Party leaders of corruption and of protecting Communists. McCarthy often targeted Secretary of State Dean Acheson, calling him incompetent and a tool of Stalin. He also accused George C. Marshall, former army chief of staff and secretary of state, of disloyalty. The prevailing anxiety about communism made many Americans willing to accept McCarthy's claims.

The McCarran Act

In 1950, with McCarthy and others arousing fears of Communist spies, Congress passed the Internal Security Act, also called the McCarran Act. The act made it illegal to attempt to establish a totalitarian government in the United States, and required all Communist-related organizations to publish their records and register with the United States attorney general. Communists could not have passports and, in cases of a national emergency, could be arrested and detained. Unwilling to punish people for their opinions, Truman vetoed the bill, but Congress easily overrode his veto in 1950. Later Supreme Court cases limited the act's scope.

©Bettmann/Corbis

McCarthy's Rise and Fall

In 1953, McCarthy became chairman of the Senate subcommittee on investigations, which forced government officials to testify about alleged Communist influences. Investigations became witch-hunts—searches for disloyalty based on weak evidence and irrational fears. McCarthy's tactic of damaging reputations with vague, unfounded charges became known as McCarthyism.

McCarthy's sensational accusations put him in the headlines, and the press quoted him often and widely. He badgered witnesses and then refused to accept their answers. His tactics left a cloud of suspicion that he and others interpreted as guilt. People were afraid to challenge him.

In 1954, McCarthy began to look for Soviet spies in the United States Army. During weeks of televised hearings, millions of Americans watched McCarthy question and bully officers, harassing them about trivial details and accusing them of misconduct. His popular support began to fade.

Finally, to strike back at the army's lawyer, Joseph Welch, McCarthy brought up the past of a young lawyer in Welch's firm who had been a member of a Communist-front organization while in law school. Welch, who was fully aware of the young man's past, exploded at McCarthy for possibly ruining the young man's career: "Until this moment, I think I never really gauged your cruelty or your recklessness. . . . You have done enough. Have you no sense of decency, sir, at long last? Have you left no sense of decency?"

Spectators cheered. Welch had said what many Americans had been thinking. Later that year, the Senate passed a vote of **censure,** or formal disapproval, against McCarthy. Although he remained in the Senate, McCarthy had lost all influence. He died in 1957.

☑ READING PROGRESS CHECK

Assessing Why were people prepared to accept McCarthy's claims?

Life During the Early Cold War

GUIDING QUESTION *How did fears of nuclear war affect American society?*

The Red Scare and the spread of nuclear weapons had a profound impact on American life in the 1950s. Fears of communism and war affected both ordinary Americans and government leaders.

Facing the Bomb

Americans were shocked when the Soviets successfully tested the more powerful hydrogen bomb, or H-bomb, in 1953. The United States had tested its own H-bomb less than a year earlier. Americans prepared for a surprise Soviet attack. Schools created bomb shelters and held bomb drills to teach students to "duck-and-cover" to protect themselves from a nuclear bomb blast.

©Bettmann/Corbis

Analyzing
SUPREME COURT CASES

Watkins v. United States, 1957

In 1954, labor organizer John Watkins testified before HUAC. He agreed to discuss his connections with the Communist Party and to identify people who were still members, but refused to talk about those who were no longer members. Watkins received a misdemeanor conviction for refusing to answer questions "pertinent to the question under inquiry." In 1957, he appealed his case to the Supreme Court. In a 6-to-1 decision, the Supreme Court held that the activities of HUAC during its investigations were beyond the scope of the stated aims of the committee, as well as the authority of congressional powers.

DBQ *DEFENDING* What argument would you make in support of John Watkins's position? LAFS.1112.RH.4.10, SS.912.A.6.8

Some Americans invested in personal bomb shelters stocked with food, believing it would allow them to survive a bomb blast.

▶ CRITICAL THINKING

Interpreting Study the facial expressions of the members of this family. What can you interpret about the likely significance of the bomb shelter for this family? SS.912.A.1.4, SS.912.A.6.8

CANNED FOOD

censure to express a formal disapproval of an action

fallout radioactive particles dispersed by a nuclear explosion

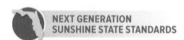

Thinking Like a
HISTORIAN

Determining Cause and Effect

The United States experienced two major Red Scares during the twentieth century: one during the 1920s, and one during the 1950s. Both of these scares occurred shortly after a major nation—first Russia, and later China—adopted a Communist form of government. As a historian, find the effect these scares had on American society and determine if they can be related.
SS.912.A.1.1, SS.912.A.6.8

NEXT GENERATION SUNSHINE STATE STANDARDS

Continued from page 412

SS.912.A.6.8: Analyze the effects of the Red Scare on domestic United States policy.

SS.912.H.1.1: Relate works in the arts (architecture, dance, music, theatre, and visual arts) of varying styles and genre according to the periods in which they were created.

SS.912.H.1.5: Examine artistic response to social issues and new ideas in various cultures.

Although "duck-and-cover" might have made people feel safer, it would not have protected them from nuclear radiation. Experts have noted that for every person killed outright by a nuclear blast, four more would die later from **fallout,** the radiation left over after a blast. To protect themselves, some families built backyard fallout shelters.

Popular Culture in the Cold War

As worries about nuclear war and Communist infiltration filled the public imagination, Cold War themes soon appeared in films, plays, television, the titles of dance tunes, and popular fiction. Matt Cvetic, an FBI undercover informant who secretly infiltrated the Communist Party, captivated readers with reports in the *Saturday Evening Post* in 1950. His story was later made into the movie *I Was a Communist for the FBI* (1951). Another film, *Walk East on Beacon* (1952), features the FBI's activities in a spy case. In 1953, Arthur Miller's thinly veiled criticism of the Communist witch-hunts, *The Crucible,* appeared on Broadway. The play remains popular today as a cautionary tale about how hysteria can lead to false accusations.

In 1953, a weekly television series, *I Led Three Lives,* about an undercover FBI counterspy who was also a Communist Party official, debuted. Popular tunes such as "Atomic Boogie" and "Atom Bomb Baby" played on the radio. The next year, author Philip Wylie published *Tomorrow!,* a novel describing the horrific effects of nuclear war on an unprepared American city. Wylie wrote his novel to educate the public about the horrors of atomic war.

One of the most famous and enduring works of this period is John Hersey's nonfiction book *Hiroshima*. Originally published as the August 1946 edition of *The New Yorker* magazine, the book provides six firsthand accounts of the United States dropping the atomic bomb on Hiroshima, Japan. Not only did it make some Americans question the use of the bomb, but *Hiroshima* also underscored the real, personal horrors of a nuclear attack.

At the same time, the country was enjoying postwar prosperity and optimism. That spirit, combined with McCarthyism, fears of Communist infiltration, and the threat of atomic attack, made the early 1950s a time of contrasts. As the 1952 election approached, Americans were looking for someone or something that would make them feel more secure.

☑ **READING PROGRESS CHECK**

Analyzing How did the Cold War affect popular culture in the 1950s?

LESSON 3 REVIEW

Reviewing Vocabulary

1. *Evaluating* What was the significance of Truman's loyalty review program? LAFS.1112.RH.2.4, SS.912.A.6.8

2. *Identifying Cause and Effect* What was the effect of the Senate's vote of censure against McCarthy?
LAFS.1112.RH.2.4, SS.912.A.6.8

Using Your Notes

3. *Summarizing* Use the notes you completed during the lesson to write a paragraph summarizing how the early years of the Cold War affected American society.
LAFS.1112.SL.2.4, SS.912.A.6.8

Answering the Guiding Questions

4. *Comparing and Contrasting* How did the post–World War II Red Scare compare and contrast with the one that followed World War I? LAFS.1112.WHST.1.1, SS.912.A.6.8

5. *Drawing Inferences* Why did many Americans believe Senator McCarthy's accusations? LAFS.1112.WHST.1.1, SS.912.A.6.8

6. *Describing* How did fears of nuclear war affect American society? LAFS.1112.WHST.1.1, SS.912.A.6.8

Writing Activity

7. ARGUMENT Consider the historical events surrounding the early Cold War era. Were HUAC and Senator McCarthy justified in investigating people who were suspected of being Communists? LAFS.1112.WHST.1.1, SS.912.A.6.8

LESSON 4

Eisenhower's Cold War Policies

ESSENTIAL QUESTIONS
• How did the Cold War shape postwar international relations?
• How did Cold War tensions affect American society?

READING HELPDESK

Academic Vocabulary
• imply   • response

Content Vocabulary
• massive retaliation
• brinkmanship
• covert
• developing nation
• military-industrial complex

TAKING NOTES

Key Ideas and Details

Organizing As you read, complete a concept web similar to the one below by filling in aspects of Eisenhower's Cold War policies. LAFS.1112.RH.3.7, SS.912.A.6.13

Eisenhower's Cold War Policies

NEXT GENERATION
SUNSHINE STATE STANDARDS

LAFS.1112.RH.2.4: Determine the meaning of words and phrases as they are used in a text, including analyzing how an author uses and refines the meaning of a key term over the course of a text (e.g., how Madison defines faction in Federalist No. 10).

LAFS.1112.RH.3.7: Integrate and evaluate multiple sources of information presented in diverse formats and media (e.g., visually, quantitatively, as well as in words) in order to address a question or solve a problem.

Continued on page 416

IT MATTERS BECAUSE

President Eisenhower believed developing new technology to deliver nuclear weapons would help prevent war. He also directed the CIA to use covert operations in the struggle to contain communism.

Massive Retaliation

GUIDING QUESTION *How were the policies of massive retaliation and brinkmanship different from previous military policies?*

By the end of 1952, many Americans were ready for a change in leadership. The Cold War had much to do with that attitude. Many people believed that Truman's foreign policy was not working. The Soviet Union had tested an atomic bomb and consolidated its hold on Eastern Europe. China had fallen to communism, and American troops were fighting in Korea.

Tired of the criticism and uncertain he could win, Truman decided not to run again. The Democrats nominated Adlai Stevenson, governor of Illinois. The Republicans chose Dwight D. Eisenhower, the general who had organized the D-Day invasion. Stevenson had little chance against a national hero who had helped win World War II. Americans wanted someone they could trust to lead the nation in the Cold War. Eisenhower won by a landslide.

"More Bang for the Buck"

The Cold War shaped Eisenhower's thinking from the moment he took office. He was convinced that the key to victory was not simply military might but also a strong economy. The United States had to show the world that the free enterprise system could produce a better society than communism. At the same time, economic prosperity would prevent Communists from gaining support in the United States and protect society from subversion.

As a professional soldier, Eisenhower knew the costs associated with large-scale conventional war. Preparing for that kind of warfare, he believed, was too expensive. "We cannot defend the

In 1955 the U.S. Air Force unveiled the huge B-52 bomber, which could fly across continents to drop nuclear bombs. The B-52 is still in use today.

▶ CRITICAL THINKING
Determining Cause and Effect
How did Eisenhower's nuclear strategy lead to the development of new aircraft technology?
SS.912.A.6.13

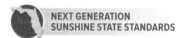 **massive retaliation** a policy of threatening a massive response, including the use of nuclear weapons, against a Communist state trying to seize a peaceful state by force

NEXT GENERATION SUNSHINE STATE STANDARDS

Continued from page 415

LAFS.1112.RH.4.10: By the end of grade 12, read and comprehend history/social studies texts in the grades 11–CCR text complexity band independently and proficiently.

LAFS.1112.SL.2.4: Present information, findings, and supporting evidence, conveying a clear and distinct perspective, such that listeners can follow the line of reasoning, alternative or opposing perspectives are addressed, and the organization, development, substance, and style are appropriate to purpose, audience, and a range of formal and informal tasks.

LAFS.1112.WHST.1.2: Write informative/explanatory texts, including the narration of historical events, scientific procedures/experiments, or technical processes.

LAFS.1112.WHST.3.9: Draw evidence from informational texts to support analysis, reflection, and research.

SS.912.A.1.2: Utilize a variety of primary and secondary sources to identify author, historical significance, audience, and authenticity to understand a historical period.

SS.912.A.1.4: Analyze how images, symbols, objects, cartoons, graphs, charts, maps, and artwork may be used to interpret the significance of time periods and events from the past.

Continued on page 417

nation in a way which will exhaust our economy," the president declared. Instead of maintaining a large and expensive army, the nation "must be prepared to use atomic weapons in all forms." Nuclear weapons, he said, gave "more bang for the buck."

The Korean War had convinced Eisenhower that the United States could not contain communism by fighting a series of small wars. Such wars were unpopular and too expensive. Instead, wars had to be prevented in the first place. The best way to do that seemed to be to threaten to use nuclear weapons. This policy came to be called **massive retaliation.**

Eisenhower's emphasis on nuclear weapons required new technology to deliver them. The president wanted to make sure that the United States could wage nuclear war even if the Soviets destroyed American bases in Europe or Asia. This required technology that would allow the U.S. to strike the USSR without needing bases overseas. At the same time, American forces had to be very difficult to destroy in one attack. If massive retaliation was to be an effective strategy, American nuclear weapons had to be deployed in a way that an enemy could not eliminate them all at once in a surprise attack. For this reason, the United States began to build what would later be referred to as the nuclear triad, a three part system made up of long-range bombers, land-based missiles, and missile-carrying submarines.

In 1955, the U.S. air force unveiled the first part of the triad, the huge B-52 bomber which could fly across continents to drop nuclear bombs. The B-52 is still in use today. But because bombers could be shot down, Eisenhower also approved the development of intercontinental ballistic missiles (ICBMs) that could reach anywhere in the world in less than 30 minutes. The Atlas missile was the first American ICBM. It was also used to launch the first seven U.S. astronauts in the early 1960s. A modified version of the Atlas is still used today to launch satellites.

For the third part of the triad, Eisenhower also began a program to build submarines capable of launching nuclear missiles from underwater. The Polaris submarine was the first submarine ever built to launch long-range missiles. The first Polaris submarine was deployed in 1960 and carried 16 nuclear missiles.

The new policy enabled Eisenhower to cut military spending from around $50 billion to about $34 billion by reducing the size of the army, which was expensive to maintain. He then increased the U.S. nuclear arsenal from about 1,000 bombs in 1953 to about 18,000 bombs in 1961.

©Randy Jolly/Aero Graphics, Inc./Terra/Corbis

One result of the decision to focus on massive retaliation was the emergence of a new arms race. The United States and the Soviet Union began to compete in the development of missiles and bombers, and steadily expanded the size and power of their nuclear arsenal.

Brinkmanship

President Eisenhower's willingness to threaten nuclear war to maintain peace worried some people. Critics called this **brinkmanship**—the willingness to go to the brink of war to force the other side to back down—and argued that it was too dangerous. During several crises, however, President Eisenhower felt compelled to threaten nuclear war.

The Taiwan Crisis Shortly after the Korean War ended, a new crisis erupted in Asia. Although Communists had taken power in mainland China, Chinese Nationalists still controlled Taiwan and several small islands along China's coast. In the fall of 1954, China threatened to seize two of the islands. Eisenhower saw Taiwan as part of the "anti-Communist barrier" in Asia that needed to be protected at all costs.

When China began shelling the islands and announced that Taiwan would be liberated, Eisenhower asked Congress to authorize the use of force to defend Taiwan. He then warned that an attack on Taiwan would be resisted by U.S. naval forces and hinted that they would use nuclear weapons to stop an invasion. Soon afterward, China backed down.

The Suez Crisis The following year, a serious crisis erupted in the Middle East. Eisenhower wanted to prevent Arab nations from aligning with the Soviet Union. To build support among Arabs, Secretary of State Dulles offered to help Egypt finance the construction of a dam on the Nile River.

The deal ran into trouble in Congress, however, because Egypt had bought weapons from Communist Czechoslovakia. Dulles was forced to withdraw the offer. A week later, Egyptian troops seized control of the Suez Canal from the Anglo-French company that had controlled it. The Egyptians intended to use the canal's profits to pay for the dam.

In October 1956, British and French troops invaded Egypt. Eisenhower was furious with Britain and France. The situation became even more dangerous when the Soviet Union threatened rocket attacks on Britain and France and offered to send troops to help Egypt. Eisenhower immediately put U.S. nuclear forces on alert, noting, "if those fellows start something, we may have to hit 'em—and, if necessary, with *everything* in the bucket."

Pressured by the United States, the British and French called off the invasion. The Soviet Union had won a major diplomatic victory by supporting Egypt. Soon other Arab nations began accepting Soviet aid.

☑ **READING PROGRESS CHECK**

Contrasting How did Eisenhower's military policies contrast with those of Truman?

Analyzing
PRIMARY SOURCES

Secretary of State Dulles on Brinkmanship

❝You have to take chances for peace, just as you must take chances in war. Some say that we were brought to the verge of war. Of course we were brought to the verge of war. The ability to get to the verge without getting into the war is the necessary art.... If you try to run away from it, if you are scared to go to the brink, you are lost. We've had to look it square in the face.... We walked to the brink and we looked it in the face. We took strong action.❞

—John Foster Dulles, quoted in *Rise to Globalism*

DBQ **ANALYZING PRIMARY SOURCES**

Why did Dulles believe that brinkmanship strengthened U.S. foreign policy?
SS.912.A.1.2, SS.912.A.6.11

brinkmanship the practice of pushing a dangerous situation to the limit to force an opponent to back down

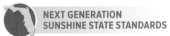

NEXT GENERATION SUNSHINE STATE STANDARDS

Continued from page 416
SS.912.A.6.11: Examine the controversy surrounding the proliferation of nuclear technology in the United States and the world.
SS.912.A.6.13: Analyze significant foreign policy events during the Truman, Eisenhower, Kennedy, Johnson, and Nixon administrations.

An Atlas rocket lifts off carrying a payload to orbit. The Atlas missile was the first American intercontinental ballistic missile (ICBM). First developed in the 1950s, intercontinental ballistic missiles can deliver a nuclear warhead to any target in the world in less than 30 minutes. The Atlas rocket is still used today to launch satellites into orbit.

The Cold War Begins **417**

Covert Operations

GUIDING QUESTION *Why did President Eisenhower want to use covert operations to combat the spread of communism?*

President Eisenhower relied on brinkmanship on several occasions, but he knew it could not work in all situations. It could prevent war, but it could not prevent Communists from staging revolutions within countries. To do this, Eisenhower decided to use **covert,** or hidden, operations conducted by the Central Intelligence Agency (CIA).

Many of the CIA's operations took place in **developing nations**—nations with primarily agricultural economies. Many of these countries blamed European imperialism and American capitalism for their problems. Their leaders looked to the Soviet Union as a model of how to industrialize their countries. They often threatened to nationalize, or put under government control, foreign businesses operating in their countries.

One way to stop developing nations from moving into the Communist camp was to provide them with financial aid, as Eisenhower had tried to do in Egypt. In some cases, however, in which the threat of communism seemed stronger, the CIA ran covert operations to overthrow anti-American leaders and replace them with pro-American leaders.

Iran and Guatemala

Two examples of covert operations that achieved American objectives took place in Iran and Guatemala. By 1953, Iranian prime minister Mohammed Mossadegh had nationalized the Anglo-Iranian Oil Company. He seemed ready to make an oil deal with the Soviet Union. The pro-American shah of Iran tried to force Mossadegh out of office, but the shah failed and fled into exile. The CIA quickly sent agents to organize street riots and arrange a coup that ousted Mossadegh and returned the shah to power.

The following year, the CIA intervened in Guatemala. In 1950, with Communist support, Jacobo Arbenz Guzmán was elected president of Guatemala. After Arbenz Guzmán assumed office in 1951, his land-reform program took over large estates and plantations, including those of the American-owned United Fruit Company. In May 1954, Communist Czechoslovakia delivered arms to Guatemala. The CIA responded by arming the Guatemalan opposition and training them at secret camps in Nicaragua and Honduras. Shortly after these CIA-trained forces invaded Guatemala, Arbenz Guzmán left office.

Trouble in Eastern Europe

Covert operations did not always work as Eisenhower hoped. Stalin died in 1953, and a power struggle began in the Soviet Union. By 1956, Nikita Khrushchev had emerged as the Soviet leader. That year, Khrushchev delivered a secret speech to Soviet officials. He attacked Stalin's policies and insisted that there were many ways to build a communist society. Although the speech was secret, the CIA obtained a copy of it and distributed copies of it throughout Eastern Europe and the world.

Many Eastern Europeans had long been frustrated with Communist rule. Hearing Khrushchev's speech further discredited communism. In June 1956, riots erupted in Eastern Europe. By late October, a full-scale uprising had begun in Hungary. Although Khrushchev was willing to tolerate greater freedom in Eastern Europe, he had never meant to **imply** that the Soviets would tolerate an end to communism in the region. Soon after the uprising began, Soviet tanks rolled into the capital of Hungary and crushed the rebellion.

covert not openly shown or engaged in; secret

developing nation a nation whose economy is primarily agricultural

SKILLS PRACTICE

Write new vocabulary words from this lesson on cards. Include the words *imply, response, retaliation, brinkmanship,* and *covert* as well as others that are new to you. Review your cards often until you can read the words quickly on sight.

ELD.K12.ELL.SI.1, ELD.K12.ELL.SS.1, LAFS.1112.RH.2.4

imply to express indirectly

The New York Times.

"All the News That's Fit to Print"

LATE CITY EDITION
U. S. Weather Bureau Report (Page 33) forecasts.
Cloudy and cool today and tonight.
Mostly fair tomorrow.
Temp. range: 65—53. Yesterday: 62.4—49.2.

VOL. CVII..No. 36,414.   © 1957, by The New York Times Company. Times Square, New York 36, N. Y.   NEW YORK, SATURDAY, OCTOBER 5, 1957.   10¢ beyond 100-mile zone from New York City   FIVE CENTS

SOVIET FIRES EARTH SATELLITE INTO SPACE; IT IS CIRCLING THE GLOBE AT 18,000 M. P. H.; SPHERE TRACKED IN 4 CROSSINGS OVER U. S.

Sputnik was the world's first artificial satellite. It made news around the world and launched the space race.

Scientists prepare the first U.S. satellite, *Explorer I*, for launch in 1958.

Sputnik II, launched only a month after *Sputnik*, carried the first living creature into orbit—an "astro" dog named Laika.

Sputnik Launches the Space Race

As the United States began to develop ICBMs, Americans were stunned to discover that the Soviet Union already had them. On October 4, 1957, the Soviets demonstrated this technology by launching Sputnik, the first artificial satellite to orbit Earth. Less than four months later, the United States launched its first satellite, Explorer 1. Determined not to be beaten by the Soviets, Eisenhower established the National Aeronautics and Space Administration, or NASA, in late 1958 to begin developing a civilian space program for the United States.

Sputnik marked a turning point in history and the beginning of a new era—the use of satellites in space. Both nations in the Cold War began launching satellites to assist in communications and to spy on other nations. Today, satellites are a vital part of modern communications and

(t)The Granger Collection, New York; (c)NSSDC/NASA; (cr)Donald Unbrock/Time & Life Pictures/Getty Images; (bl)©Bettmann/Corbis

President Eisenhower addressed ▶ concerns about communist activity in the Middle East by asking Congress to authorize military force to assist nations resisting a communist threat. This policy became known as the Eisenhower Doctrine.

travel. They transmit television, radio, and cell phone signals, and the satellites of the Global Positioning System (GPS) help drivers and pilots navigate.

The Eisenhower Doctrine

The United States was not the only nation using covert means to support its foreign policy. President Gamal Abdel Nasser of Egypt had emerged from the Suez crisis as a hero to the Arab people, and by 1957 he had begun working with Jordan and Syria to spread pan-Arabism—the idea that all Arab people should be united into one nation.

Eisenhower and Dulles worried about Nasser's links to the Soviets and feared he was laying the groundwork to take control of the Middle East. In late 1957, Eisenhower asked Congress to authorize the use of military force whenever the president thought it necessary to assist Middle East nations resisting Communist aggression. The policy came to be called the Eisenhower Doctrine. It essentially extended the Truman Doctrine and the policy of containment to the Middle East.

In July 1958, Eisenhower's concerns appeared to be confirmed when left-wing rebels, believed to be backed by Nasser and the Soviets, seized power in Iraq. Fearing his government was next, the president of Lebanon sought help. Eisenhower ordered 5,000 marines to Beirut, the Lebanese capital. Once the situation stabilized, the U.S. forces withdrew.

Soviet leader Nikita Khrushchev rose to power in the mid-1950s, following the death of longtime dictator Joseph Stalin.

▶ **CRITICAL THINKING**

Drawing Conclusions How did covert operations around the world contribute to tensions between the United States and the Soviet Union? LAFS.1112.WHST.3.9, SS.912.A.6.13

A Spy Plane Is Shot Down

After the Hungarian uprising, Khrushchev reasserted Soviet power and the superiority of communism. Although he had supported "peaceful coexistence" with capitalism, he began accusing the "capitalist countries" of starting a "feverish arms race." In 1957, after the launch of *Sputnik,* Khrushchev boasted, "We will bury capitalism. . . . Your grandchildren will live under communism."

Late the following year, Khrushchev demanded the withdrawal of Allied troops from West Berlin. Secretary of State Dulles rejected Khrushchev's demands. If the Soviets threatened Berlin, Dulles announced, NATO would respond, "if need be by military force." Brinkmanship worked again, and Khrushchev backed down. Eisenhower invited Khrushchev to visit the United States in late 1959. The visit's success led the two leaders to agree to hold a summit in Paris.

Shortly before the summit was to begin in 1960, the Soviet Union shot down an American U-2 spy plane. At first Eisenhower claimed that the aircraft was a weather plane that had strayed off course. Then Khrushchev dramatically produced the pilot, Francis Gary Powers. Eisenhower refused to apologize, saying

(t)Library of Congress, Prints & Photographs Division [LC-USZ62-117123]; (b)©Bettmann/Corbis the flights had protected American security. In **response,** Khrushchev broke up the summit.

In this climate of heightened tension, Eisenhower prepared to leave office. In January 1961, he delivered a farewell address to the nation in which he pointed out that a new relationship had developed between the military establishment and the defense industry. He warned Americans to be on guard against the influence of this **military-industrial complex** in a democracy.

Although he had avoided war and contained communism, Eisenhower was frustrated. He had sent military advisers to South Vietnam to train a South Vietnamese army and also saw Fidel Castro establish a communist regime in Cuba. Eisenhower stated, "I confess that I lay down my official responsibilities in this field with a definite sense of disappointment. As one who has witnessed the horror and the lingering sadness of war . . . I wish I could say tonight that a lasting peace is in sight."

☑ READING PROGRESS CHECK

Identifying Why did Eisenhower direct the CIA to use covert operations?

response something said or done as a reaction

military-industrial complex an informal relationship that some people believe exists between the military and the defense industry to promote greater military spending and influence government policy

The U-2 was America's most sophisticated spy plane. It was able to fly higher than any other plane at the time.

▶ CRITICAL THINKING
Making Inferences Why was the U-2 used as a spy plane?
LAFS.1112.WHST.3.9, SS.912.A.6.13

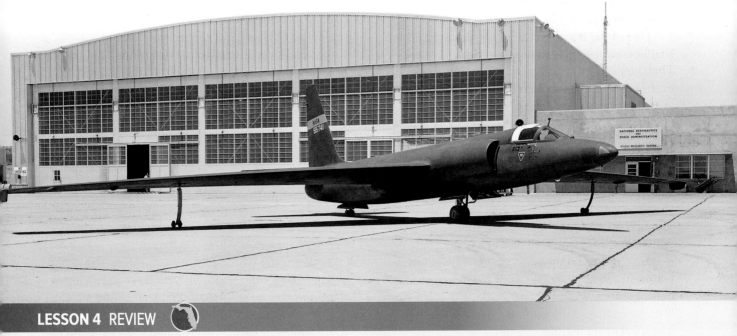

NASA

LESSON 4 REVIEW

Reviewing Vocabulary
1. **Explaining** What was the policy of brinkmanship?
LAFS.1112.RH.2.4 , LAFS.1112.WHST.3.9, SS.912.A.6.13
2. **Contrasting** How are developing nations primarily different from industrial nations? LAFS.1112.RH.2.4 , LAFS.1112.WHST.3.9

Using Your Notes
3. **Evaluating** Use the notes you completed during the lesson to consider Eisenhower's strategies for containing communism. Write a paragraph evaluating whether these strategies were successful. Explain your response.
LAFS.1112.SL.2.4, SS.912.A.6.13

Answering the Guiding Questions
4. **Contrasting** How were the policies of massive retaliation and brinkmanship different from previous military policies?
LAFS.1112.WHST.1.1, SS.912.A.6.8
5. **Describing** Why did President Eisenhower want to use covert operations to combat the spread of communism?
LAFS.1112.WHST.3.9, SS.912.A.6.13

Writing Activity
6. **INFORMATIVE/EXPLANATORY** Write a short essay in which you explain Eisenhower's foreign policy goals and practices. Be sure to include details about how these policies influenced historical events. LAFS.1112.WHST.1.2, SS.912.A.6.13

LAFS.1112.RH.3.9, SS.912.A.1.1, SS.912.A.1.2, LAFS.1112.WHST.2.5, LAFS.1112.WHST.4.10

Understanding How Historians Interpret the Past

Why Learn This Skill?

As you have read about the history of the United States, you probably have realized that historians do not always agree about why things happened or agree about how events affected things that happened later. When you study history, it is easy to become confused unless you have some idea of how historians interpret the past and the different approaches they use.

Learning the Skill

The study of how historians approach history is called **historiography.** It is in some ways the history of historians and their different approaches to interpreting the past.

One of the important things to understand is that how people view history changes over time. This happens for several reasons. Sometimes an event has to happen before people realize a past event was important and needs to be studied. Historical interpretations also change over time because new information becomes available. For example, a country may open its archives. Another reason interpretations change over time is because historians look at different kinds of evidence.

There are three big questions for historians. The first is *causation:* historians want to explain why something happened or why people made certain choices. The second issue is *outcome:* historians want to explain what happened because of an event or choices people made. The third issue is *meaning:* historians want to explain why a historical event matters.

There are several approaches historians take to answer these questions. The first is sometimes called *intentionalism,* or *volitionalism.* It has also been nicknamed "The Great Man" approach to history. It focuses on leaders, especially political leaders. It looks at who made key choices, and tries to figure out why they made those choices.

A second approach to history is *structuralism.* A structural approach looks at the way things are organized, the rules and structures of the political system, the economy, and society. For example, instead of focusing on a president and his goals, ambitions, and choices, a structuralist might look at how the Constitution structures the president's role and forces him to make certain choices and limits his ability to make other choices.

A third approach to history is *intellectualism.* Intellectual historians assume that ideas are the most important cause of things. They look at ideas, ideology, culture, and people's perceptions, so as to understand what happened.

As you might expect, these three approaches can lead to very different histories of the same event. And within these approaches, historians narrow their emphasis even further. Some structuralists, for example, emphasize the role of the economy alone, or the role of social classes. Others focus just on the political system. Among intellectual historians, some focus on ideology, while others stress the role of culture.

Practicing the Skill

Read the following paragraphs, and then answer the questions that follow about interpreting the causes of the Cold War.

Over the years there have been many different arguments put forward for why the Cold War began. Historians have suggested Roosevelt made mistakes at Yalta, and did not stand up to Stalin soon enough. Some think Truman was too aggressive and unwilling to compromise. Some argue that Stalin was authoritarian and paranoid and determined to control everything he could. Others have suggested Stalin was a committed communist and determined to do everything he could to spread communism into Europe. Some have suggested the Cold War was partly Churchill's responsibility. They suggest Britain maneuvered the United States into taking over Britain's role of balancing power in Europe so as to protect the British Empire.

Historians have also argued that American capitalism and its desire for overseas markets led to the clash with the Soviets. Others think the fundamental clash was between a democratic republic based on individual rights versus a totalitarian communist system. Another group of historians point out that the Russians knew their history of being invaded from the West and just wanted a buffer zone on their border to protect themselves. Others think the American military was determined to avoid another Pearl Harbor and pushed for alliances and overseas bases to make sure America remained safe.

1. In which of the theories above are historians practicing a volitional or intentionalist approach to the Cold War?
2. What would a structuralist emphasize in trying to understand the causes of the Cold War?
3. What theories about the Cold War would intellectual historians favor?

Roosevelt, Churchill, and Stalin at the Yalta Conference in 1945

Applying the Skill

Conducting a Historical Inquiry Now that you understand the basic approaches historians take to history, conduct your own historical inquiry into some aspect of the Cold War. Identify a question about the Cold War you would like to answer. Write it down.

Gather sources that talk about the history related to your question. Collect a variety of sources: gather works by historians, as well as collections of primary sources that include speeches and government documents from the Cold War. If possible, use a local library or online resources to examine old magazines and newspapers from the time you are studying. After gathering your sources, analyze them, making notes as to what they tell you. Write down a hypothesis, or possible explanation, for your original question. Ask yourself if you are taking an intentional, structural, or intellectual approach to the question. Does thinking about the question that way suggest other sources to examine? Test your hypothesis against your sources. Do any of them contradict your idea? Do you need other sources to confirm your idea? Once you are confident that you have a good answer to your question, prepare an article for a historical journal identifying your question, outlining your sources and findings, and presenting your conclusions.

STUDY GUIDE

THE ORIGINS OF THE COLD WAR
LESSON 1

Bretton Woods:
Improving global economy
- World Bank
- International Monetary Fund
- U.S. dollar becomes benchmark currency for foreign exchange

Dumbarton Oaks:
Improving global security
- defined structure of United Nations

Yalta Conference:
Allied cooperation
- Soviet control of Poland accepted by Great Britain & United States
- Declaration of Liberated Europe promotes new democratic governments
- Germany & Berlin divided into four Allied-controlled zones

Potsdam Conference:
Cold War tensions
- German reparations softened
- Stalin weakened Declaration of Liberated Europe
- Soviet satellite nations formed in Eastern Europe

THE EARLY COLD WAR YEARS
LESSON 2

Founding NATO nations, 1949
- Canada
- Belgium
- United States
- United Kingdom
- Portugal
- Norway
- Netherlands
- Denmark
- France
- Iceland
- Italy
- Luxembourg

THE COLD WAR AND AMERICAN SOCIETY
LESSON 3

- Alger Hiss Trial
- Julius & Ethel Rosenberg
- House Un-American Activities Committee
- Project Venona
- The Red Scare

EISENHOWER'S COLD WAR POLICIES
LESSON 4

The Early Space Race

October 4, 1957 — Soviet Union launches *Sputnik* satellite

February 1, 1958 — U.S. launches first satellite, *Explorer I*

July 29, 1958 — President Eisenhower approves creation of NASA

Directions: On a separate sheet of paper, answer the questions below. Make sure you read carefully and answer all parts to the question.

Lesson Review

Lesson 1

1 *Identifying Central Issues* What decisions were made at Yalta, and what role did they play in the emergence of the Cold War? SS.912.A.6.10

2 *Describing* Describe the manner in which Germany was divided by Great Britain, the United States, the Soviet Union, and France. SS.912.A.6.1

3 *Evaluating* What were the pros and cons of the United States joining the United Nations? What elements of the UN charter help the United States protect its interests? What were the potential weaknesses of the United Nations? SS.912.A.6.1

Lesson 2

4 *Identifying Central Issues* What was the policy of containment? How did it affect President Truman's decision to send troops to fight in the Korean War? SS.912.A.6.10, SS.912.A.6.12

5 *Making Connections* How was American aid to Western Europe a key to containing communism? What was the legislation that proposed such aid? SS.912.A.6.10

6 *Determining Cause and Effect* Explain the causes of the Korean War, the reasons the United States became involved, and the outcome of U.S. involvement. SS.912.A.6.12

Lesson 3

7 *Drawing Inferences* How did Senator McCarthy's accusations of Communist influence affect domestic life and intensify Cold War tensions? SS.912.A.6.8

8 *Describing* In the early 1950s, in what ways did literature and films about the H-bomb and Communist spies reflect the characteristics and issues of the era? SS.912.A.1.7, SS.912.A.6.8, SS.912.H.1.1, SS.912.H.1.5

Lesson 4

9 *Explaining* What was the role of brinkmanship in Eisenhower's foreign policy? Why was it controversial? SS.912.A.6.13

10 *Sequencing Events* Describe the events that followed as a result of the distribution of Khrushchev's secret speech. SS.912.A.6.11

11 *Comparing* Compare the Eisenhower Doctrine with the Truman Doctrine. What action took place following the establishment of the Eisenhower Doctrine? SS.912.A.6.13

Exploring the Essential Questions

12 *Synthesizing* Design a website describing the origins of the Cold War and its effects on 1950s society. On a sheet of paper, describe the website and the way you would organize the site's information. Include maps, biographies, and accounts of historic events to show ways Cold War tensions affected postwar international relations. Present a visual presentation of your website to the class. LAFS.1112.RH.3.9, LAFS.1112.WHST.2.4, LAFS.1112.WHST.2.6, SS.912.A.1.4, SS.912.A.1.7, SS.912.A.6.10, SS.912.A.6.11, SS.912.A.6.13

Critical Thinking

13 *Analyzing* Describe the Truman Doctrine and the Marshall Plan. Explain how these policies were intended to prevent further Soviet aggression in Europe after World War II. SS.912.A.6.10

14 *Describing* Explain the events that led to the creation of NATO, and outline the terms of the NATO treaty. What were some of the pros and cons of signing the NATO treaty and becoming a member of this international organization? SS.912.A.6.10

15 *Interpreting* Describe the relationship between U.S. international trade polices at the end of World War II and the U.S. free enterprise system. Describe the pros and cons of international trade treaties. SS.912.A.6.10

21st Century Skills

16 *Using a Decision Making Process* Imagine you work for President Eisenhower. The president has explained that the country needs a strong military because of the threat from the Soviet Union and

Need Extra Help?

If You've Missed Question	1	2	3	4	5	6	7	8	9	10	11	12	13	14	15	16
Go to Lesson	1	1	1	2	2	2	3	3	4	4	4	1, 3	2	2	2	4

the United States is committed to containing communism. At the same time, the president is worried about the economy. He is concerned that a lot of government spending on the military will weaken the economy. Write a briefing paper for the president recommending the policy of massive retaliation. In the paper, apply a decision-making process that explains why you are recommending this decision. Make sure to revise to ensure clarity and persuasiveness. LAFS.1112.WHST.1.1, LAFS.1112.WHST.2.4, LAFS.1112.WHST.2.5, LAFS.1112.WHST.4.10, SS.912.A.6.10, SS.912.A.6.13

DBQ Analyzing Primary Sources

Read the excerpt below, and answer the questions that follow.

In 1950 Margaret Chase Smith, the only woman in the Senate, was upset by Senator McCarthy's behavior. She had hoped that her colleagues would reprimand him. They failed to do so, and Smith then made her "Declaration of Conscience" speech.

PRIMARY SOURCE

"As a United States Senator, I am not proud of the way in which the Senate has been made a publicity platform for irresponsible sensationalism. I am not proud of the reckless abandon in which unproved charges have been hurled. . . . As an American, I am shocked at the way Republicans and Democrats alike are playing directly into the Communist design of 'confuse, divide, and conquer'. . . . I want to see our nation recapture the strength and unity it once had when we fought the enemy instead of ourselves."

—Margaret Chase Smith, speech to Congress, June 1, 1950

17 *Making Connections* What is the connection between Smith's point of view and the views of McCarthyism during the Red Scare? LAFS.1112.RH.3.8, LAFS.1112.RH.4.10, SS.912.A.6.8

18 *Interpreting Speeches* Why did Smith use the phrase "confuse, divide, and conquer"? LAFS.1112.RH.2.4, LAFS.1112.RH.2.5, LAFS.1112.RH.3.8, LAFS.1112.RH.4.10, LAFS.1112.SL.1.3, SS.912.A.6.8

Analyzing Visuals

Use the map to answer the following questions.

19 *Identify Central Issues* Identify and explain the reasons for the changes in Germany's political boundaries after World War II. SS.912.A.6.10, SS.912.G.4.9

20 *Interpreting Geographic Distributions* Based on the geography and control of the zones, what challenges would have existed for each of the Allied countries, and would any country have been more or less affected? SS.912.A.6.10, SS.912.G.2.1

21 *Posing Questions About Geographic Distributions* What questions would you need to ask about the geographic distribution on the map in order to understand why the Soviet Union was unwilling to take reparations from their zone only? SS.912.A.6.10, SS.912.G.1.2

Extended Response Question

22 *Comparing and Contrasting* Write an essay comparing and contrasting the international leadership of Franklin Roosevelt at the Yalta Conference with Harry Truman's leadership at the Potsdam Conference. Compare the United States' relationship with its allies at both conferences, identify the goals of Roosevelt and Truman, and evaluate their success in achieving their goals. To help you cover all the relevant points, create an outline before you write. LAFS.1112.WHST.1.2, LAFS.1112.WHST.2.4, LAFS.1112.WHST.2.5, LAFS.1112.WHST.4.10, SS.912.A.6.1, SS.912.A.6.10, SS.912.A.6.13

Need Extra Help?

If You've Missed Question	**17**	**18**	**19**	**20**	**21**	**22**
Go to Lesson	3	3	1	1	1	1

netw⊙rks

There's More Online!

�N Elvis Presley, born poor in Mississippi, rose to fame in the 1950s and became widely known as the "King of Rock 'n' Roll."

FROM 1945 TO 1960

Postwar America

©Sunset Boulevard/Historical/Corbis

THE STORY MATTERS ...

The 1950s was a time of tremendous change in America. New advances in technology planted the seeds of today's computerized world, and developments in medicine saved thousands of lives. A population explosion called the baby boom produced a generation that would change the world. Americans—young and old—also experienced a new genre of music called rock 'n' roll.

ESSENTIAL QUESTION

- How does prosperity change the way people live?

Place & Time: Postwar America 1945–1960

After World War II, the United States experienced years of strong economic growth, as well as advances in science, technology, medicine, and transportation. Although the prosperity did not reach everyone, the economic boom meant most Americans enjoyed more prosperity than earlier generations, and a new consumer culture emerged.

Step Into the Place

Look at the information presented on the map to identify where most of the interstate highways were built.

 Analyzing Historical Documents The creation of the interstate highway system had a tremendous impact on the nation's economy. What were its main effects?

Road Culture Interstate travel encouraged the development of hotels, stores, and restaurants near interstate exits.

left page (t)©Marvin Koner/Historical Premium/Corbis, (b)detail/White House Collection/The White House Historical Association; **right page** (t)Ralph Morse/Time Life Pictures/Getty Images, (c)J. R. Eyerman/Time & Life Pictures/Getty Images, (b)detail/White House Collection/The White House Historical Association

The Interstate Highway System

Olympia
Salem
Helena
Boise
Carson City
Sacramento
Salt Lake City
Cheyenne
Denver
Los Angeles
Santa Fe
Phoenix

0   400 miles
0   400 km
Lambert Azimuthal Equal-Area projection

Honolulu

Step Into the Time

PREDICTING CONSEQUENCES
Choose an event from the time line and write a paragraph predicting how the event would have made life in America more prosperous than life for earlier generations.

U.S. PRESIDENTS

UNITED STATES

WORLD

1944 GI Bill gives financial aid to veterans

1946 ENIAC becomes the first electronic computer

Truman
1945–1953

1950 David Riesman publishes *The Lonely Crowd*

1945   1947   1949

1949 George Orwell publishes *Nineteen Eighty-Four*

1950 Octavio Paz publishes *The Labyrinth of Solitude*

NEXT GENERATION SUNSHINE STATE STANDARDS
Students will understand the following benchmarks from the Florida NGSSS

LAFS.1112.RH.3.7: Integrate and evaluate multiple sources of information presented in diverse formats and media (e.g., visually, quantitatively, as well as in words) in order to address a question or solve a problem.

LAFS.1112.RH.3.9: Integrate information from diverse sources, both primary and

secondary, into a coherent understanding of an idea or event, noting discrepancies among sources.

SS.912.A.1.2: Utilize a variety of primary and secondary sources to identify author, historical significance, audience, and authenticity to understand a historical period.

SS.912.A.1.3: Utilize timelines to identify the time sequence of historical data.

SS.912.A.1.4: Analyze how images, symbols, objects, cartoons, graphs, charts, maps, and artwork may be used to interpret the significance of time periods and events from the past.

SS.912.A.7.1: Identify causes for Post-World War II prosperity and its effects on American society.

SS.912.G.4.7: Use geographic terms and tools to explain cultural diffusion throughout places, regions, and the world.

★ State capital
● Top ten city (population, 1950)
— Interstate highway

Commercial Trucking Interstate highways made distribution of goods by transport trucks fast and efficient.

Rise of Suburbs Interstate highways contributed to the growth of suburbs and urban sprawl.

1951 *I Love Lucy* debuts on television

Eisenhower 1953–1961

1955 Salk polio vaccine becomes widely available

1956 Congress passes Federal Highway Act

1958 John Kenneth Galbraith publishes *The Affluent Society*

1959 Lorraine Hansberry's *A Raisin in the Sun* opens on Broadway

1951   1953   1955   1957   1959

1953 Soviet Union detonates hydrogen bomb

1957 Six nations found the European Economic Community

1958 People's Republic of China launches Great Leap Forward

1959 St. Lawrence Seaway opens, linking the Great Lakes to the Atlantic Ocean

1960 British rock group adopts the name "The Beatles"

LESSON 1
Truman and Eisenhower

ESSENTIAL QUESTION

• How does prosperity change the way people live?

READING HELPDESK

Academic Vocabulary

• legislator   • abandon

Content Vocabulary

• **closed shop**
• **right-to-work laws**
• **union shop**
• **dynamic conservatism**

TAKING NOTES

Key Ideas and Details

Organizing As you read, complete a graphic organizer like this one by listing characteristics of the postwar economy.
LAFS.1112.RH.3.7, SS.912.A.7.1

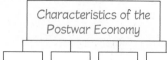

Characteristics of the Postwar Economy

NEXT GENERATION SUNSHINE STATE STANDARDS

LAFS.1112.RH.2.4: Determine the meaning of words and phrases as they are used in a text, including analyzing how an author uses and refines the meaning of a key term over the course of a text (e.g., how Madison defines faction in Federalist No. 10).

LAFS.1112.RH.3.7: Integrate and evaluate multiple sources of information presented in diverse formats and media (e.g., visually, quantitatively, as well as in words) in order to address a question or solve a problem.

LAFS.1112.WHST.1.1: Write arguments focused on discipline-specific content.

LAFS.1112.WHST.3.9: Draw evidence from informational texts to support analysis, reflection, and research.

Continued on page 431

IT MATTERS BECAUSE

In the postwar era, Congress limited the power of unions and rejected most of President Truman's plan for a "Fair Deal." When Eisenhower became president, he cut back some government programs but approved billions of dollars for the expansion of the interstate highway system.

Return to a Peacetime Economy

GUIDING QUESTION *What happened when the nation returned to a peacetime economy, and how did government try to ease the transition?*

After the war, many Americans feared the return to a peacetime economy. They worried about unemployment and a recession because military production had stopped and millions of former soldiers needed work. Despite such worries, the economy continued to grow after the war. Increased consumer spending helped ward off a recession. After so many years of economic depression and wartime shortages, Americans rushed out to buy consumer goods.

The Servicemen's Readjustment Act of 1944, popularly called the GI Bill, also boosted the economy. The act provided funds to help veterans establish businesses, buy homes, and attend college. The postwar economy did have problems in the early years after the war. A greater demand for goods led to higher prices. The resulting inflation soon triggered labor unrest. As the cost of living rose, workers in the automobile, steel, electrical, and mining industries went on strike for better pay.

Truman was afraid that the miners' strikes would drastically reduce the nation's energy supply. He ordered the government to take control of the mines. He also pressured mine owners to grant the union most of its demands. Truman even stopped a strike that shut down the nation's railroads by threatening to draft the striking workers into the army.

Labor unrest and high prices prompted many Americans to call for a change. The Republicans seized on these feelings during the 1946 congressional elections, and won control of both houses of Congress for the first time since 1930.

The new conservative Congress quickly set out to limit the power of organized labor. In 1947 **legislators** passed the Taft-Hartley Act, which outlawed the **closed shop,** or the practice of forcing business owners to hire only union members. This law also allowed states to pass **right-to-work laws,** which outlawed **union shops** (shops requiring new workers to join the union). It prohibited featherbedding, or limiting work output in order to create more jobs. It also banned using union money to support political campaigns. Truman, however, vetoed the bill, arguing that it was a mistake:

PRIMARY SOURCE

❝[It would] reverse the basic direction of our national labor policy, inject the Government into private economic affairs on an unprecedented scale, and conflict with important principles of our democratic society. Its provisions would cause more strikes, not fewer.❞
—from a message to the U.S. House of Representatives, June 20, 1947

Despite President Truman's concerns, Congress passed the Taft-Hartley Act in 1947 over his veto. Supporters of the act claimed that the law held irresponsible unions in check. Labor leaders, however, called the act a "slave labor" law, insisting that it erased many of the gains that unions had made since 1933.

✓ **READING PROGRESS CHECK**

Explaining How did the GI Bill help the nation transition from a wartime economy to a peacetime economy?

Truman's Program

GUIDING QUESTION *How did the Truman administration seek to continue New Deal goals?*

The Democratic Party's loss of control in Congress in the 1946 elections did not dampen President Truman's plans. After taking office, Truman had proposed domestic measures to continue the work of Franklin Roosevelt's New Deal. He worked to push this agenda through Congress.

Truman's Legislative Agenda

Truman's proposals included expanding Social Security benefits and raising the minimum wage. He also proposed public housing and slum clearance, a program to ensure full employment through federal spending and investment, a system of national health insurance, and long-range environmental and public works planning.

In February 1948, Truman also boldly asked Congress to pass a broad civil rights bill. The bill would protect African Americans' right to vote. It would also abolish poll taxes and make lynching a federal crime. He issued an executive order barring discrimination in federal employment and ending segregation in the armed forces. Most of Truman's legislative efforts failed as a coalition of Republicans and conservative Southern Democrats defeated many of his proposals.

There's More Online! connected.mcgraw-hill.com

©Bettmann/Corbis

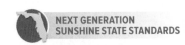

NEXT GENERATION SUNSHINE STATE STANDARDS

Continued from page 430

SS.912.A.1.2: Utilize a variety of primary and secondary sources to identify author, historical significance, audience, and authenticity to understand a historical period.

SS.912.A.1.4: Analyze how images, symbols, objects, cartoons, graphs, charts, maps, and artwork may be used to interpret the significance of time periods and events from the past.

SS.912.A.7.1: Identify causes for Post-World War II prosperity and its effects on American society.

SS.912.A.7.2: Compare the relative prosperity between different ethnic groups and social classes in the post-World War II period.

SS.912.A.7.17: Examine key events and key people in Florida history as they relate to United States history.

legislator one who makes laws as a member of a legislative body for a political unit

closed shop an agreement in which a company agrees to hire only union members

right-to-work law a law making it illegal to require employees to join a union

union shop a business that requires employees to join a union

The GI Bill provided funds for veterans to attend college after the war. By 1947, nearly half of all those attending college were veterans.

▶ **CRITICAL THINKING**
Making Inferences Why were so many college students veterans in 1947? SS.912.A.7.1

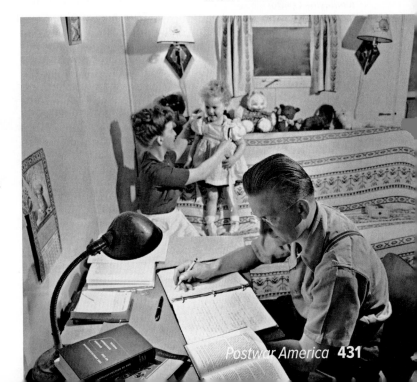

ELECTORAL VOTE
TOTAL: 531

7.3%
39

35.6%
189

57.1%
303

POPULAR VOTE
TOTAL: 48,793,826

2.41%
1,176,125

2.97%
1,447,065

45.07%
21,991,291

49.55%
24,179,345

- Truman (Democrat)
- Dewey (Republican)
- Thurmond (States' Rights)
- Other
- Mixed

* Eleven electors in Tennessee voted for Truman and one voted for Thurmond

Map state electoral votes:
WA 8, OR 6, CA 25, NV 3, ID 4, MT 4, WY 3, UT 4, AZ 4, NM 4, CO 6, ND 4, SD 4, NE 6, KS 8, OK 10, TX 23, MN 11, IA 10, MO 15, AR 9, LA 10, WI 12, IL 28, MI 19, IN 13, OH 25, KY 11, TN 12, MS 9, AL 11, GA 12, FL 8, WV 8, VA 11, NC 14, SC 8, PA 35, NY 47, NJ 16, DE 3, MD 8, CT 8, RI 4, MA 16, VT 3, NH 4, ME 5

GEOGRAPHY CONNECTION

Key states give Truman the electoral victory.

1 **THE WORLD IN SPATIAL TERMS** *In which state did one elector not vote with the rest of the state's electors?* SS.912.A.1.4

2 **PLACES AND REGIONS** *In which region did Thurmond enjoy the most electoral support?* LAFS.1112.WHST.3.9

abandon to withdraw protection, support, or help

Harry Truman gleefully shows the incorrect headline declaring his election defeat.

▶ **CRITICAL THINKING**
Identifying Central Ideas
What made Truman's victory such a surprise? LAFS.1112.RH.3.7, LAFS.1112.WHST.3.9

The Election of 1948

As the 1948 presidential election approached, most observers gave Truman little chance of winning. Some viewed his administration as inept. In addition, fractures in the Democratic Party seemed to doom his campaign. Two groups **abandoned** the party at that summer's convention. A group of Southern Democrats, angry at Truman's support of civil rights, formed the States' Rights, or Dixiecrat, Party. They nominated South Carolina governor Strom Thurmond for president. Liberal Democrats who were frustrated by Truman's ineffective domestic policies and critical of his anti-Soviet foreign policy formed a new Progressive Party. Henry A. Wallace was their presidential candidate. Besides these two new challengers, Truman faced his Republican opponent, New York governor Thomas Dewey. Dignified and popular, Dewey seemed unbeatable.

Truman remained confident of reelection, however. He traveled more than 20,000 miles by train and made more than 200 speeches. He attacked the majority Republican Congress as "do-nothing, good-for-nothing" for refusing to enact his legislative agenda. However, his attacks were not entirely accurate. The "Do-Nothing Congress" had passed his aid program to Greece and Turkey and the Marshall Plan. Congress had passed the law that created the Department of Defense, the National Security Council, and the CIA. It had permanently established the Joint Chiefs of Staff and set up the air force as an independent branch of the military. It also had passed the Twenty-second Amendment, which limited

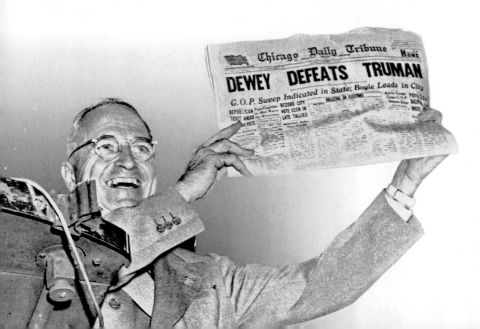

©Frank Cancellare/Bettmann Premium/Corbis

a president to two terms in office. But because Congress's actions were in areas that did not affect most Americans directly, Truman's charges began to stick.

Supported by laborers, African Americans, and farmers, Truman won a narrow but stunning victory over Dewey. In addition, the Democratic Party regained control of both houses of Congress.

The Fair Deal

Truman's 1949 State of the Union address repeated his previous domestic agenda. "Every segment of our population and every individual," he declared, "has a right to expect from our Government a fair deal." Whether intentional or not, the president had coined a name—the Fair Deal—to set his program apart from the New Deal.

The 81st Congress did not completely support Truman's Fair Deal. Legislators did raise the legal minimum wage to 75¢ an hour. They increased Social Security benefits by over 75 percent and extended them to 10 million additional people. Congress also passed the National Housing Act of 1949, which provided for the construction of low-income housing and for long-term rent subsidies. Congress refused, however, to pass national health insurance or to provide aid for farmers or schools. Led by conservative Republicans and Dixiecrats, legislators also opposed Truman's civil rights legislation.

✓ READING PROGRESS CHECK

Making Connections What components of the New Deal did Truman adopt as part of his legislative agenda?

The Eisenhower Years

GUIDING QUESTION *How did Eisenhower's presidency signal a more conservative direction for the government?*

In 1950 the United States went to war in Korea. The war consumed the nation's attention and resources, ending Truman's Fair Deal. By 1952, with the war at a bloody stalemate and his approval rating dropping quickly, Truman decided not to run again.

With no Democratic incumbent to face, Republicans pinned their hopes on a popular World War II hero: Dwight Eisenhower, former commander of the Allied Forces in Europe. The Democrats nominated Illinois governor Adlai Stevenson.

The Republicans adopted the slogan "It's time for a change!" The warm and friendly Eisenhower, known as "Ike," promised to end the war in Korea. "I like Ike" became the Republican rallying cry. Eisenhower won the election in a landslide. The Republicans also gained an eight-seat majority in the House, while the Senate became evenly divided between Democrats and Republicans.

Eisenhower and "Dynamic Conservatism"

President Eisenhower had two favorite phrases. "Middle of the road" described his political beliefs, and **"dynamic conservatism"** meant balancing economic conservatism with activism that would benefit the country. Under the guidance of a cabinet filled with business leaders, Eisenhower ended government price and rent controls. Many conservatives viewed these as unnecessary federal regulations of the economy. Eisenhower's administration believed business growth was vital to the nation. His secretary of defense, the former president of General Motors, declared that "what is good for our country is good for General Motors, and vice versa."

Analyzing
PRIMARY SOURCES

Truman's Fair Deal

❝As we look around the country, many of our shortcomings stand out. . . . Our minimum wages are far too low. . . . Our farmers still face an uncertain future. And too many of them lack the benefits of our modern civilization. Some of our natural resources are still being wasted. We are acutely short of electric power. . . . Five million families are still living in slums and firetraps. . . . Proper medical care is so expensive that it is out of the reach of the great majority of our citizens. Our schools . . . are utterly inadequate. Our democratic ideals are often thwarted by prejudice and intolerance. . . . [E]very individual has a right to expect from our Government a fair deal.❞

—from his State of the Union address, January 5, 1949

DBQ **ANALYZING** Why did Truman believe that reforms were needed? SS.912.A.1.2, SS.912.A.7.2

dynamic conservatism
a policy of balancing economic conservatism with some activism in other areas

The expansion of the federal highway system eased commuter traffic.

▶ **CRITICAL THINKING**

Analyzing Information How did the construction of the interstate highway system demonstrate Eisenhower's dynamic conservatism? LAFS.1112.WHST.3.9, SS.912.A.7.1

 Florida
CONNECTION

The Interstates

The National Interstate System created by the Federal Highway Act connected the entire country together. The increased ease of Interstate travel encouraged more long distance vacations by automobile. Many chose to drive south for Florida vacations, increasing the tourism industry in the state. Today Florida has over 17,000 miles of Interstate. SS.912.A.7.17

To cut federal spending, Eisenhower vetoed a school construction bill and agreed to slash aid to public housing. He also targeted aid to businesses, or what he called "creeping socialism." Shortly after taking office, he abolished the Reconstruction Finance Corporation (RFC), which loaned money to banks, railroads, and other large institutions in financial trouble. Another agency, the Tennessee Valley Authority (TVA), also came under Eisenhower's scrutiny. During his presidency, federal spending for the TVA fell from $185 million to $12 million. Eisenhower also supported some modest tax cuts.

In some areas, Eisenhower took an activist role. He especially pushed for two large government projects. As more Americans owned cars, the need for better roads increased. In 1956 Congress passed the Federal Highway Act, the largest public works program in American history. The act provided for a $25 billion, 10-year project to build more than 40,000 miles (64,400 km) of interstate highways. Congress also authorized the construction of the St. Lawrence Seaway. This project included building a series of locks along the St. Lawrence River that would allow ships to travel from the Great Lakes to the Atlantic Ocean. The three previous administrations had failed to accomplish this feat because of differences with Canada over the waterway.

Extending Social Security

Despite cutting federal spending and attempting to limit the government's role in the economy, President Eisenhower agreed to extend the Social Security system to an additional 10 million people. He also extended unemployment payments to 4 million more citizens. Eisenhower even agreed to raise the minimum wage and to continue to provide some government aid to farmers.

By the time Eisenhower ran for a second term in 1956, the nation had successfully shifted back to a peacetime economy. The battles between liberals and conservatives over whether to continue New Deal policies would continue. In the meantime, most Americans focused their energy on enjoying what had become a decade of tremendous prosperity.

 READING PROGRESS CHECK

Explaining What conservative measures did Eisenhower take during his administration?

Three Lions/Hulton Archive/Getty Images

LESSON 1 REVIEW

Reviewing Vocabulary

1. ***Contrasting*** How does a closed shop differ from a union shop? LAFS.1112.RH.2.4
2. ***Defining*** What is meant by the term *dynamic conservatism*? LAFS.1112.RH.2.4

Using Your Notes

3. ***Summarizing*** Use the notes you completed to write a paragraph summarizing the state of the U.S. economy after World War II. LAFS.1112.WHST.3.9, SS.912.A.7.1

Answering the Guiding Questions

4. ***Identifying*** What happened when the nation returned to a peacetime economy, and how did government try to ease the transition? LAFS.1112.WHST.3.9, SS.912.A.7.1

5. ***Describing*** How did the Truman administration seek to continue New Deal goals? LAFS.1112.WHST.3.9, SS.912.A.7.1

6. ***Analyzing*** How did Eisenhower's presidency signal a more conservative direction for the government? LAFS.1112.WHST.3.9, SS.912.A.7.1

Writing Activity

7. ***ARGUMENT*** Suppose that you are a member of Congress who heard Truman deliver his speech on the Fair Deal. Write a speech convincing your fellow members of Congress to pass or defeat Truman's Fair Deal measures. LAFS.1112.SL.2.6, LAFS.1112.WHST.1.1, LAFS.1112.WHST.3.9

LESSON 2
The Affluent Society

ESSENTIAL QUESTION

• How does prosperity change the way people live?

READING HELPDESK

Academic Vocabulary
• phenomenon
• conform

Content Vocabulary
• baby boom
• white-collar job
• blue-collar worker
• multinational corporation
• franchise
• rock 'n' roll
• generation gap

TAKING NOTES

Key Ideas and Details

Sequencing As you read, use a time line to record major events of science, technology, and popular culture during the late 1940s and 1950s. LAFS.112.3.7, SS.912.A.1.3

**NEXT GENERATION
SUNSHINE STATE STANDARDS**

LAFS.1112.RH.2.4: Determine the meaning of words and phrases as they are used in a text, including analyzing how an author uses and refines the meaning of a key term over the course of a text (e.g., how Madison defines faction in Federalist No. 10).

LAFS.1112.RH.3.7: Integrate and evaluate multiple sources of information presented in diverse formats and media (e.g., visually, quantitatively, as well as in words) in order to address a question or solve a problem.

LAFS.1112.WHST.1.1: Write arguments focused on discipline-specific content.

LAFS.1112.WHST.3.9: Draw evidence from informational texts to support analysis, reflection, and research.

Continued on page 436

IT MATTERS BECAUSE

For many Americans, the 1950s was a time of affluence, with many new technological breakthroughs. In addition, new forms of entertainment created a generational divide between young people and adults.

American Abundance

GUIDING QUESTION *How did the lives of Americans change after World War II?*

The 1950s was a decade of incredible prosperity. Between 1940 and 1955, the average income of U.S. families roughly tripled. People in all income brackets were experiencing a rapid rise in income, although the abundance was not distributed equally. In 1958 economist John Kenneth Galbraith published *The Affluent Society,* in which he claimed that the nation's postwar prosperity was a new **phenomenon.** Galbraith suggested that whereas past societies had an "economy of scarcity" with limited economic productivity, the United States had now created an "economy of abundance." New business techniques and technology enabled the production of abundant goods and services. They dramatically raised the U.S. standard of living.

With more disposable income than ever, Americans began spending on new consumer goods. Advertising helped fuel the spending spree. It became the United States's fastest-growing industry. Manufacturers employed new, carefully planned marketing techniques to create consumer demand for their products.

The Growth of Suburbia

Advertisers targeted consumers with money to spend, many of whom lived in new mass-produced suburbs that grew up around cities in the 1950s. Levittown, New York, was one of the earliest of the mass-produced suburbs. It was the brainchild of Bill Levitt, who mass-produced hundreds of simple, similar-looking homes 10 miles east of New York City. Between 1947 and 1951, families rushed to buy the inexpensive homes. Similar suburbs multiplied throughout the nation. The suburban population doubled, while the population of cities rose only 10 percent.

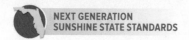
Continued from page 435

MAFS.912.S-ID.1: Summarize, represent and interpret data on a single count or measurement variable.

SS.912.A.1.2: Utilize a variety of primary and secondary sources to identify author, historical significance, audience, and authenticity to understand a historical period.

SS.912.A.1.4: Analyze how images, symbols, objects, cartoons, graphs, charts, maps, and artwork may be used to interpret the significance of time periods and events from the past.

SS.912.A.1.7: Describe various socio-cultural aspects of American life including arts, artifacts, literature, education, and publications.

SS.912.A.7.1: Identify causes for Post-World War II prosperity and its effects on American society.

SS.912.A.7.2: Compare the relative prosperity between different ethnic groups and social classes in the post-World War II period.

SS.912.A.7.3: Examine the changing status of women in the United States from post-World War II to present.

SS.912.A.7.17: Examine key events and key people in Florida history as they relate to United States history.

SS.912.H.1.1: Relate works in the arts (architecture, dance, music, theatre, and visual arts) of varying styles and genre according to the periods in which they were created.

SS.912.H.1.3: Relate works in the arts to various cultures.

SS.912.H.1.6: Analyze how current events are explained by artistic and cultural trends of the past.

Continued on page 438

phenomenon an event or occurrence that is exceptional or unusual

baby boom a marked rise in birthrate, such as occurred in the United States following World War II

white-collar job a job in a field not requiring work clothes or protective clothing, such as sales

blue-collar worker a worker who performs manual labor, particularly work that requires protective clothing

multinational corporation large corporation with overseas investments

franchise the right or license to market a company's goods or services in an area, such as a store of a chain operation

CHARTS/GRAPHS — THE BIRTHRATE, 1940–1970

1 *Analyzing* In what year was there the greatest increase in the number of live births? Why might this be? **MAFS.912.S-ID.1**

2 *Drawing Conclusions* What economic consequences does a society with a "baby boom" have to face when that generation reaches retirement age? **LAFS.1112.RH.3.7, SS.912.A.1.7**

*per 1,000 population for women 15–44 years old.

Source: Historical Statistics of the United States.

Reasons for suburban growth varied. Some people wished to escape the crime and congestion of the city. Others believed suburbs offered a better life and were more affordable. The GI Bill and the government's decision to give income tax deductions for mortgage and property tax payments made home ownership more attractive than ever. Between 1940 and 1960, the percentage of Americans who owned their homes rose from about 41 percent to about 61 percent.

The Baby Boom

The U.S. birthrate exploded after World War II. From 1945 to 1961, more than 65 million children were born in the United States. At the height of this **baby boom,** a child was born every seven seconds. Many factors contributed to the baby boom. First, young couples who had put off getting married during World War II and the Korean War could finally begin their families. Also, the government encouraged the growth of families by offering generous GI benefits for home purchases. Finally, popular culture celebrated pregnancy, parenthood, and large families.

The Changing Workplace

As the economy grew, ongoing mechanization of farms and factories meant more Americans began working in offices in what came to be called **white-collar jobs.** These employees typically wore a white dress shirt and a tie to work instead of the blue denim work shirts of factory workers and laborers. In 1956, white-collar workers outnumbered **blue-collar workers** for the first time.

The shift to white-collar jobs was partly the result of both new technology and management innovations introduced into the workplace. In the 1950s, the first business computers came on the market. Payroll, billing, inventory, record-keeping, and scientific and engineering calculations could all be done by computers. As companies began to use computers, managers were able to consolidate clerical tasks across departments. This meant fewer clerical workers were needed and these tasks could be done faster and more reliably. People could focus on management tasks.

Many white-collar employees worked for large corporations. To be more competitive, some corporations expanded overseas. They became **multinational corporations,** locating near raw materials and benefiting from a cheap labor pool. Also during this time, another management innovation— the **franchise**—became popular. In a franchise, a person owns and runs one or more stores of a larger chain. Believing that consumers valued dependability and familiarity, the owners of chain operations required their franchises to conform to a uniform look and style. Doing so made each store's operations more efficient and consistent and helped to reduce costs.

Many other corporate leaders also expected conformity rather than freethinking. Sociologist David Riesman and others criticized this trend. In his 1950 book *The Lonely Crowd,* Riesman argued that conformity was changing people. He claimed that people used to judge themselves on the basis of their own values and the esteem of their families. But now, he said, "The American is said to be shallower, freer with his money, friendlier, more uncertain of himself and his values, more demanding of approval. . . . [This attitude of] other-direction is becoming the typical character of the 'new' middle class." In his 1956 book *The Organization Man,* William H. Whyte, Jr., attacked the similarity many businesses cultivated in their employees to keep any individual from dominating.

✔ READING PROGRESS CHECK

Describing How did corporations change the lives of Americans?

Scientific Advances

GUIDING QUESTION *How did technological advances change society?*

As the United States experienced social changes during the postwar era, it also witnessed important scientific advances. During the 1950s, scientists broke new ground in electronics, aviation, and medicine.

Advances in Electronics and Aviation

The electronics industry advanced rapidly after World War II. In 1947 three U.S. physicists developed the transistor, a tiny electric generator that made it possible to create small portable radios.

The computer age also dawned in the postwar era. In 1946 scientists developed one of the nation's earliest computers, ENIAC (Electronic Numerical Integrator and Computer), to make military calculations. Several years later, a newer model, UNIVAC (Universal Automatic Computer), processed business data and started the computer revolution.

Aviation progressed rapidly as well. Aircraft designers used more plastics and light metals, swept-back wings, and new jet engine technology to build planes that could fly farther on the same amount of fuel. These advances made airline travel affordable for more people.

Medical Breakthroughs

Prior to the 1950s, there were few effective treatments for cancer and heart attacks. Medical breakthroughs in the 1950s changed that. The development of radiation treatments and chemotherapy helped many cancer patients survive. Cardiopulmonary resuscitation (CPR), developed in 1950, helped many people survive heart attacks. Doctors also learned to replace worn-out heart valves with artificial valves, and implanted the first pacemakers in 1952.

Tuberculosis and polio had frightened Americans for decades. Tuberculosis patients were isolated in sanatoriums to prevent the spread of this highly contagious lung disease. During the 1950s, a blood test for the disease and new antibiotics helped end fears. In 1956 tuberculosis fell from the list of the top ten fatal diseases.

Polio epidemics typically left their victims dead or paralyzed. Parents frantically tried to protect their children from the disease. Some sent them to the country to avoid excessive contact with

BIOGRAPHY

Dr. Jonas Salk (1914–1995)

Jonas Salk enrolled in college as a prelaw student but soon changed his mind. He switched his major to premed and went on to become a research scientist. Sometimes he made rounds in the overcrowded polio wards of a hospital near his lab, where nurses described their feelings of helpless rage. One nurse said, "I can remember how the staff used to kid Dr. Salk— kidding in earnest—telling him to hurry up and do something." Salk became famous for the polio vaccine he developed in 1952.

▶ CRITICAL THINKING

Analyzing What character traits do you think made Dr. Salk a successful research scientist?

conform to change in a way that fits a standard or authority

Charitable donations funded the medical research that helped cure or control many childhood diseases.

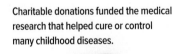

YOU CAN WALK!! GIVE TO POLIO BUILDING FUND

(t)©Bettmann/Corbis, (b)Martha Holmes/Time & Life Pictures/Getty Images

SKILLS PRACTICE

Keep a list of words you hear often during class lessons and discussion. Pay attention to common words the teacher uses when asking questions or giving instructions and common words other students use when responding. Use these words when asking questions in class or during class discussions.
ELD.K12.ELL.SI.1, ELD.K12.ELL.SS.1, LAFS.1112.RH.2.4

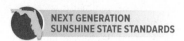

NEXT GENERATION SUNSHINE STATE STANDARDS

Continued from page 436

SS.912.H.3.1: Analyze the effects of transportation, trade, communication, science, and technology on the preservation and diffusion of culture.

SS.912.H.2.5: Describe how historical, social, cultural, and physical settings influence an audience's aesthetic response.

SS.912.H.3.2: Identify social, moral, ethical, religious, and legal issues arising from technological and scientific developments, and examine their influence on works of arts within a culture.

others. Public swimming pools and beaches were closed. Parks and playgrounds were deserted. In 1952 a record 58,000 new cases were reported. Finally, research scientist Jonas Salk developed an injectable polio vaccine, which became available to the public in 1955. Researcher Albert Sabin then developed an oral polio vaccine. Safer and more convenient than Salk's vaccine, the Sabin vaccine helped the threat of polio nearly disappear.

☑ **READING PROGRESS CHECK**

Evaluating What technological advancements helped treat cancer?

The New Mass Media

GUIDING QUESTION *How did the new mass media reflect the characteristics of the time?*

Regular television broadcasts had begun in the early 1940s, but there were few stations and sets were expensive. In 1946 no more than 8,000 televisions were in use across the nation. By 1957, though, nearly 40 million sets had been sold, and more than 80 percent of families owned at least one television.

The Rise of Television

Early television programs included comedies, variety shows, and action programs. In 1953 Lucille Ball and her husband, Desi Arnaz, starred in one of the medium's most popular shows ever, a comedy called *I Love Lucy.* One episode attracted an audience of 44 million viewers—more than for the presidential inauguration the following day.

Many early comedy shows, such as those starring Bob Hope and Jack Benny, were adapted from radio programs. Variety shows, such as Ed Sullivan's *Toast of the Town,* provided a mix of comedy, music, dance, and acrobatics. Quiz shows also drew large audiences after the 1955 debut of *The $64,000 Question.* Westerns such as *The Lone Ranger* and *Gunsmoke* grew quickly in popularity. Viewers also enjoyed police shows such as *Dragnet.* Television news and sports broadcasts grew in popularity as well.

Hollywood Adapts

As television's popularity grew, movies lost viewers. Attendance plunged from 82 million in 1946 to 36 million by 1950. By 1960, one-fifth of the nation's movie theaters had closed. Hollywood used contests, door prizes, and advertising to attract audiences, but failed. Hollywood tried 3-D movies that required the audience to wear special glasses. Viewers quickly tired of the glasses and the films' often-silly plots.

However, Cinemascope—a process that showed movies on large, panoramic screens—finally gave Hollywood something television could not match. Full-color spectacles like *The Robe* and *Around the World in 80 Days* cost a great deal to make, but drew huge audiences and profits.

Hollywood's new approach to movie-making with big investments in special effects, elaborate costumes, glamorous movie stars, exciting storylines, exotic locales, and huge marketing campaigns also gave the industry an edge in other parts of the world. As television spread in Europe, it cost European movie studios their audiences, just as it had American movie studios. But because television had spread across the United States sooner than Europe, the Hollywood studios had already adapted, and they quickly won over large European audiences. As a result, Hollywood began to play an important role in diffusing American culture across the globe—a role that continues to the present day.

Radio Draws Them In

Television also forced the radio industry to change. Television made radio comedies, dramas, and soap operas obsolete. Radio stations responded by broadcasting recorded music, news, weather, sports, and talk shows.

Radio had one audience that television could not reach—people traveling in their cars. People commuting from the suburbs, running errands, or traveling on long road trips relied on radio for news and entertainment. As a result, the number of radio stations more than doubled between 1948 and 1957.

✔ **READING PROGRESS CHECK**

Making Connections Why is television considered part of the new mass media?

rock 'n' roll popular music usually played on electronically amplified instruments and characterized by a persistent, heavily accented beat, much repetition of simple phrases, and often country, folk, and blues elements

generation gap a cultural separation between parents and their children

New Music and Poetry

GUIDING QUESTIONS *Why did young people in the 1950s develop their own popular culture? Why were the results different from those in previous generations?*

Teens in every generation seek to separate themselves from their parents. In that respect, the 1950s were just like earlier decades, but the results were different for two reasons. First, teens had disposable income that could be spent on entertainment designed specifically for them. Second, the new mass media meant that teens around the country could hear the same music or see the same television shows. The new youth culture became an independent market for the entertainment and advertising industries.

Rock 'n' Roll

In 1951, at a record store in downtown Cleveland, Ohio, radio disc jockey Alan Freed noticed white teenagers buying African American rhythm-and-blues records and dancing to the music in the store. Freed convinced his manager to put the music on the air, and listeners went crazy for it. Soon, white artists began making music that stemmed from these African American sounds, creating a new form of music, **rock 'n' roll.**

With a loud and heavy beat that made it ideal for dancing, and lyrics about themes that appealed to young people, rock 'n' roll became wildly popular. Teens bought recordings from artists such as Buddy Holly, Chuck Berry, and Bill Haley and the Comets. In 1956 teenagers found their first rock 'n' roll hero in music and movie star Elvis Presley. At first, popular television host Ed Sullivan refused to invite Presley to appear on his variety show. He insisted that rock 'n' roll music was not fit for a family-oriented show. After another show featuring Presley upset Sullivan's high ratings, however, he relented.

Presley owed his popularity as much to his moves as to his music, swinging his hips and dancing during his performances in ways that shocked many people. Many adults condemned rock 'n' roll as loud, mindless, and dangerous. The city council of San Antonio, Texas, banned rock 'n' roll from the jukeboxes at public swimming pools.

The rock 'n' roll hits that teens bought in record numbers united them in a world their parents did not share. Thus, in the 1950s, this new music helped to create what became known as the **generation gap,** or the cultural separation between children and their parents.

During the 1950s, teens around the nation eagerly bought rock 'n' roll records. The music was popular at dances called hops and even on television programs like *American Bandstand.*

▶ **CRITICAL THINKING**
Predicting Consequences
How might the rise of youth culture during the 1950s affect teens of later generations?
LAFS.1112.WHST.3.9, SS.912.A.7.1, SS.912.H.1.6

Library of Congress, Prints & Photographs Division [LC-USZ62-126069]

The Beat Movement

A group of mostly white writers and artists who called themselves *beats,* or *beatniks,* highlighted a values gap in 1950s America. Beat poets, writers, and artists criticized American culture for its sterility, conformity, and emptiness. In 1956, 29-year-old poet Allen Ginsberg published a long poem titled "Howl" blasting American life. It began, "I saw the best minds of my generation destroyed by madness, starving hysterical naked . . . burning for the ancient heavenly connection to the starry dynamo in the machinery of night." Beat author Jack Kerouac's book *On the Road* (1957), about his freewheeling adventures with a car thief and con artist, shocked some readers. Although the beat movement remained small, it laid the foundations for the widespread youth cultural rebellion of the 1960s.

African American Entertainers

African American entertainers struggled to find acceptance. With a few notable exceptions, television tended to shut out African Americans. In 1956 NBC gave popular African American singer Nat King Cole a 15-minute musical variety show. However, NBC was unable to find a national sponsor for a show hosted by an African American, so it canceled the show two years later.

African American rock 'n' roll singers faced fewer obstacles. Chuck Berry, Little Richard, and Ray Charles all recorded hit songs. The same era also saw the rise of several female African American groups, including the Shirelles and the Ronettes. The music of these early rock 'n' roll artists profoundly influenced popular music around the world. Little Richard and Chuck Berry, for example, inspired the Beatles, whose music swept Britain and the world in the 1960s.

Despite the advances in music and the economic boom of the 1950s, not all Americans were part of the new society. For many minorities and rural poor, the American Dream remained well out of reach.

Chuck Berry was one of the leading popular music performers of the 1950s.

► **CRITICAL THINKING**
Determining Cause and Effect
How did Berry's popularity influence later generations of musicians? SS.912.H.1.3

☑ READING PROGRESS CHECK

Determining Cause and Effect What made rock 'n' roll part of the new culture of the 1950s?

PHOTO: ©Michael Ochs Archives/Historical/Corbis ; TEXT: L. 1-2, 3 (from "burning") -5 from "HOWL" FROM COLLECTED POEMS 1947-1980 by ALLEN GINSBERG. Copyright © 1955 by Allen Ginsberg. Reprinted by permission of HarperCollins Publishers.

LESSON 2 REVIEW

Reviewing Vocabulary

1. *Contrasting* How did white-collar jobs and blue-collar jobs differ? LAFS.1112.RH.2.4

2. *Defining* What is the generation gap? LAFS.1112.WHST.1.1, LAFS.1112.WHST.3.9

Using Your Notes

3. *Explaining* Use the notes you completed during the lesson to write a short paragraph explaining some of the major changes that took place during the 1950s. LAFS.1112.WHST.3.9

Answering the Guiding Questions

4. *Describing* How did the lives of Americans change after World War II? LAFS.1112.WHST.3.9, SS.912.A.7.1

5. *Analyzing Cause and Effect* How did technological advances change society? LAFS.1112.WHST.3.9, SS.912.A.7.1

6. *Making Connections* How did the new mass media reflect the characteristics of the time? LAFS.1112.WHST.3.9, SS.912.H.1.1, SS.912.H.3.2

7. *Evaluating* Why did young people in the 1950s develop their own popular culture? LAFS.1112.RH.2.4, LAFS.1112.WHST.3.9, SS.912.H.1.1, SS.912.H.2.5

Writing Activity

8. ARGUMENT Think about U.S. youth culture today. Consider how it is similar to and different from the youth culture of the 1950s. Then write a short essay in which you give your opinions about how youth culture can influence society, and whether youth culture is as important as adult culture. LAFS.1112.WHST.1.1, LAFS.1112.WHST.3.9, SS.912.H.1.6

LESSON 3

The Other Side of American Life

ESSENTIAL QUESTION

• How does prosperity change the way people live?

READING HELPDESK

Academic Vocabulary

• income   • entity

Content Vocabulary

• poverty line
• urban renewal
• termination policy
• juvenile delinquency

TAKING NOTES

Key Ideas and Details

Organizing As you read, use the major headings of this section to create an outline similar to the one below.
LAFS.1112.RH.3.7

> The Other Side of American Life
> I. Poverty Amid Prosperity
>   A.
>   B.

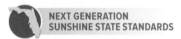

NEXT GENERATION
SUNSHINE STATE STANDARDS

MAFS.912.S-ID.1: Summarize, represent and interpret data on a single count or measurement variable.

SS.912.A.1.2: Utilize a variety of primary and secondary sources to identify author, historical significance, audience, and authenticity to understand a historical period.

SS.912.A.1.4: Analyze how images, symbols, objects, cartoons, graphs, charts, maps, and artwork may be used to interpret the significance of time periods and events from the past.

SS.912.A.1.6: Use case studies to explore social, political, legal, and economic relationships in history.

Continued on page 442

IT MATTERS BECAUSE

During the 1950s, about 20 percent of the American population—particularly people of color and those living in the inner cities and Appalachia—did not share in the general prosperity. Experts also worried about the rise in juvenile delinquency.

Poverty Amid Prosperity

GUIDING QUESTION *Are the people and regions most affected by poverty today the same as in the 1950s?*

The 1950s saw a large expansion of the middle class. At least one in five Americans, or about 30 million people, however, lived below the **poverty line.** This is an arbitrary figure the government sets to reflect the minimum **income** required to support a family. Many Americans mistakenly thought that the country's prosperity had provided for everyone.

The poor included single mothers and the elderly; minorities such as Puerto Ricans and Mexican immigrants; rural Americans—both African American and white; and inner-city residents, who remained stuck in crowded slums. Many Native Americans endured poverty whether they stayed on reservations or migrated to cities.

The Decline of the Inner City

Poverty was most apparent in the nation's urban centers. As middle-class families moved to the suburbs, they left behind the poor and less educated. Many city centers deteriorated because they no longer received taxes from their former middle-class residents. Cities could no longer provide adequate public transportation, housing, and other services.

When government tried to help inner-city residents, it often made matters worse. **Urban renewal** programs tried to eliminate poverty by tearing down slums and building new high-rises for poor residents. Yet these crowded projects often created an

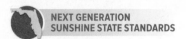
Continued from page 441

SS.912.A.7.1: Identify causes for Post–World War II prosperity and its effects on American society.

SS.912.A.7.2: Compare the relative prosperity between different ethnic groups and social classes in the post-World War II period.

SS.912.H.1.3: Relate works in the arts to various cultures.

SS.912.H.1.5: Examine artistic response to social issues and new ideas in various cultures.

poverty line a level of personal or family income below which one is classified as poor by the federal government

income a gain or recurrent benefit usually measured in money derived from capital or labor

urban renewal government programs that attempt to eliminate poverty and revitalize urban areas

termination policy a government policy to bring Native Americans into mainstream society by withdrawing recognition of Native American groups as legal entities

entity something having independent, separate, or self-contained existence

Eight family members lived in this three-room house lined with newspaper in Appalachia in the 1950s.

▶ **CRITICAL THINKING**
Drawing Conclusions Besides inadequate housing, what other effects did poverty have on people?
LAFS.1112.WHST.3.9, SS.912.A.1.4, SS.912.A.7.2

atmosphere of violence. The government also unwittingly created a condition supporting poverty with a rule that evicted residents of public housing as soon as they began earning a higher income.

African Americans

Although more than 3 million African Americans had migrated from the South to Northern cities, long-standing patterns of racial discrimination kept many of them poor. In 1958 African Americans' salaries, on average, were only 51 percent of what whites earned.

In 1959 the play *A Raisin in the Sun,* written by African American author Lorraine Hansberry, opened on Broadway. The play told the story of a working-class African American family struggling against poverty and racism. Hansberry wrote: "The ghettos are killing us; not only our dreams . . . but our very bodies."

Hispanics

Much of the nation's Hispanic population also struggled with poverty. Nearly 5 million Mexicans had come to the United States through the Bracero Program to work on farms and ranches in the Southwest. Braceros were temporary contract workers. Many later returned home, but some 350,000 settled permanently in the United States. They worked long hours, for little pay, in conditions that were often unbearable. The migrant workers' list of grievances included "poor food . . . substandard housing, prejudice and discrimination, physical mistreatment and exposure to pesticides . . . and unsatisfactory earnings," according to one Bracero Program history.

Native Americans

By the middle of the 1900s, Native Americans—who made up less than one percent of the population—were the poorest ethnic group in the nation. After World War II, the United States government launched a program to bring Native Americans into mainstream society. Under the plan, which became known as the **termination policy,** the federal government withdrew all official recognition of the Native American groups as legal **entities** and made them subject to the same laws as white citizens. Another program encouraged Native Americans to relocate from their reservations to cities.

For many Native Americans, relocation was a disaster. For example, in the mid-1950s, the Welfare Council of Minneapolis said of Native American living conditions: "One Indian family of five or six, living in two rooms, will take in relatives and friends who come from the reservations seeking jobs until perhaps fifteen people will be crowded into the space." During the 1950s, Native Americans in Minneapolis could expect to live only 37 years, compared to 68 years for other Minneapolis residents. Benjamin Reifel, a Sioux, described the despair the termination policy produced: "The Indians believed that when the dark clouds of war passed from the skies overhead, their rising tide of expectations, though temporarily stalled, would again reappear. Instead they were threatened by termination. . . . Soaring expectations began to plunge."

Appalachia

The mountainous region of Appalachia, stretching from New York to Georgia, often kept poverty hidden. Coal mining, long the backbone of the Appalachian economy, mechanized in the 1950s, causing soaring unemployment.

PHOTO: National Archives and Records Administration, Records of the Solid Fuels Administration for War [245-MS-2134]; TEXT: "Indian Affairs - Report - The Minnesota Indian in Minneapolis 1956", Box 121, Folder 1, United Way of Minneapolis Records, Social Welfare History Archives, University of Minnesota.

Some 1.5 million people left Appalachia to seek a better life in the cities. Appalachia had fewer doctors than the rest of the country, and rates of nutritional deficiency and infant mortality were high. Because of the area's poverty, education also suffered.

☑ READING PROGRESS CHECK

Identifying What are two regions where poverty was most prevalent in the 1950s, and why was their level of prosperity so low?

Juvenile Delinquency

GUIDING QUESTION *What factors were blamed for the rise in juvenile delinquency?*

During the 1950s, many middle-class white Americans found it easy to ignore poverty and racism. Some social problems, however, became impossible to ignore. **Juvenile delinquency**—antisocial or criminal behavior of young people—became one of those problems when the United States saw a 45 percent rise in juvenile crime rates between 1948 and 1953.

Americans disagreed on what had triggered the rise. Experts blamed television, movies, comic books, racism, busy parents, a rising divorce rate, lack of religion, and anxiety over the military draft. Some cultural critics claimed that young people were rebelling against the conformity of their parents. Others blamed a lack of discipline. Bishop Fulton J. Sheen complained that parents had raised bored children who sought new thrills, such as "alcohol, marijuana, even murder." Still others pointed at social causes, blaming teen violence on poverty. Most teens stayed clear of gangs, drugs, and crime. Still, the public stereotyped young people as juvenile delinquents, especially those who had long hair or used street slang.

Concerned about their children, many parents focused on the schools as a possible solution. When baby boomers began entering the school system in the 1950s, enrollments increased by 13 million, and school districts struggled to pay for new buildings and hire more teachers. In 1957 the Soviet Union's launch of *Sputnik I* and *Sputnik II*, the world's first space satellites, caused more panic about education. Many felt that the nation had fallen behind its Cold War enemy. They blamed what they saw as a lack of technical education. Efforts to improve math and science education began. Yet fears about the nation's young people lingered at the end of the decade.

☑ READING PROGRESS CHECK

Evaluating Why do you think schools were a possible solution for juvenile delinquency?

juvenile delinquency
antisocial or criminal behavior of young people

— *Connections to* —
TODAY

Juvenile Delinquency

Teens are more involved in crime, drugs, and gangs today than they were in the 1950s. There are four times as many juvenile court cases as there were in 1960. In the late 1990s, about 2 million juveniles (ages 10–17) were arrested, mostly for drug-related crimes. Many of these crimes were committed by juveniles in gangs. The number of juvenile cases has dropped in the past decade, but gang crimes are on the rise. SS.912.A.1.6

SKILLS PRACTICE

There are many words and phrases from the 1950s you still hear today. As you listen to the teacher's lesson, take notes about the definition and meaning of key words and phrases, such as *poverty line, urban renewal,* and *juvenile delinquency.*
ELD.K12.ELL.SI.1, ELD.K12.ELL.SS.1, LAFS.1112.RH.2.4

LESSON 3 REVIEW

Reviewing Vocabulary
1. *Defining* If someone is living below the poverty line, what does that mean? LAFS.1112.RH.2.4
2. *Explaining* Why did some people stereotype certain young people as juvenile delinquents? LAFS.1112.RH.2.4, LAFS.1112.WHST.3.9

Using Your Notes
3. *Making Connections* Use your notes from the lesson to determine what caused some young people to become juvenile delinquents and how society responded with solutions. LAFS.1112.RH.3.7

Answering the Guiding Questions
4. *Evaluating* Are the people and regions most affected by poverty today the same as in the 1950s? LAFS.1112.WHST.3.9, SS.912.A.7.2
5. *Identifying* What factors were blamed for the rise in juvenile delinquency? LAFS.1112.WHST.3.9, SS.912.A.7.1

Writing Activity
6. **NARRATIVE** You are a writer for your school newspaper. This month's paper is featuring a throwback to the 1950s. Write an article that highlights a social problem affecting your generation that parallels problems in the 1950s.
LAFS.1112.WHST.1.2, SS.912.A.1.6

STUDY GUIDE

TRUMAN AND EISENHOWER
LESSON 1

ECONOMICS
- Greater postwar demand caused inflation
- Labor rumblings against inflated costs
- Truman asked for government control of mines to prevent strikes and loss of energy sources

GI BILL
- Aimed to boost economy
- Helped veterans establish businesses or attend college
- Helped veterans buy houses

POLITICS
- Republicans campaigned against economic and labor unrest
- GOP won control of both houses of Congress in 1946 election
- Achieved passage of Taft-Hartley Act in 1947

THE AFFLUENT SOCIETY
LESSON 2

Rise of New Mass Media

Television
- Attracted large audiences
- Early shows adapted from radio program formats
- Forced other mediums, such as movies and radio, to adapt

Movies
- Had to adapt to changing culture
- Innovations like Cinemascope tried to win back audiences from television
- Transmitted American culture globally

Radio
- Competed with television for audiences
- Tapped into new commuters driving from suburbs

THE OTHER SIDE OF AMERICAN LIFE
LESSON 3

Poverty Amid Prosperity
- Single mothers
- Elderly
- Immigrants
- Rural Americans: both African American and white
- Inner-city Residents
- Native Americans

Directions: On a separate sheet of paper, answer the questions below. Make sure you read carefully and answer all parts to the question.

Lesson Review

Lesson 1

1 **Describing** What impact did the decrease in military spending have on the economy and business cycle after World War II? SS.912.A.7.1

2 **Explaining** What impact did the Taft-Hartley Act have on organized labor?

3 **Analyzing** How did the GI Bill boost the postwar economy? SS.912.A.7.1

4 **Summarizing** Summarize the actions by the Eisenhower administration that improved transportation both on land and waterways. SS.912.A.7.1

Lesson 2

5 **Describing** Identify the new popular music of the 1950s and some of the most popular performers. How did this music reflect both the characteristics and issues of the era? What was its positive and negative impact? SS.912.A.1.7, SS.912.A.7.1, SS.912.H.1.1, SS.912.H.1.3, SS.912.H.2.5, SS.912.H.3.2

6 **Evaluating** In what ways did Beat poets express the characteristics and issues of the 1950s? What was the positive and negative impact of the Beat movement? SS.912.A.1.7, SS.912.A.7.1, SS.912.H.1.1, SS.912.H.1.3, SS.912.H.2.5

7 **Explaining** What contributions did women performers make to the shaping of American culture in the 1950s? SS.912.A.1.7, SS.912.A.7.1, SS.912.A.7.2, SS.912.H.1.1, SS.912.H.1.3

8 **Identifying** Which significant medical breakthroughs were made in the 1950s? SS.912.A.7.1

9 **Explaining** How did African American singers contribute to American culture in the 1950s? What obstacles did they face? SS.912.A.1.7, SS.912.A.7.1, SS.912.A.7.2, SS.912.H.1.1, SS.912.H.1.3

Lesson 3

10 **Comparing and Contrasting** Explain how the lives of minorities differed from those of white middle-class Americans during the 1950s. SS.912.A.7.2

11 **Economics** What factors negatively affected the economy of Appalachia in the 1950s? SS.912.A.7.2

12 **Describing** Describe the conditions for Native Americans in the mid-1900s, as well as the government policies implemented and the struggles that followed implementation. SS.912.A.7.2

13 **Analyzing** What were some factors that people believed contributed to a rise in juvenile delinquency, and how did they try to solve the problem? SS.912.A.7.2

Exploring the Essential Questions

14 **Presenting Information** Design a poster titled "Prosperity in the 1950s." Gather and use relevant text, graphs, and illustrations to show how prosperity of the era affected the lives of many Americans, and how it did not benefit others. LAFS.1112.WHST.3.7, SS.912.A.1.4, SS.912.A.7.1, SS.912.A.7.2

Critical Thinking

15 **Making Connections** The rise of large corporations increased white-collar jobs, and some sociologists thought it increased conformity, as well. Why might a culture of conformity result from the rise of large, multi-national corporations? What types of business or fields of work would be less likely to develop a culture of conformity? SS.912.A.7.1

16 **Making Generalizations** What generalizations can you make about televised entertainment and the American public's interests based on the popularity of early television shows? SS.912.A.1.7, SS.912.H.1.1, SS.912.H.1.3, SS.912.H.1.5, SS.912.H.3.2

17 **Describing** How did the management's introduction of the business computer impact the workplace, and enhance productivity for both business and workers? SS.912.A.7.1

18 **Analyzing** What impact did American popular culture in the 1950s have on the rest of the world? What contributed to the diffusion of American culture around the globe? SS.912.A.1.7, SS.912.A.7.1, SS.912.G.4.7, SS.912.H.1.1, SS.912.H.3.1

Need Extra Help?

If You've Missed Question	1	2	3	4	5	6	7	8	9	10	11	12	13	14	15	16	17	18
Go to Lesson	1	1	1	1	2	2	2	2	2	3	3	3	3	2	2	2	2, 3	2

19 *Identifying Central Issues* What action did President Truman take to address the rights of minorities in the military? SS.912.A.7.2

21st Century Skills

20 *Understanding Relationships Among Events* What conditions in the postwar United States contributed to the baby boom? How did the baby boom contribute to the prosperity of the era? SS.912.A.7.1

21 *Sequencing* Make a time line of important events of the 1950s postwar America, as reflected in the chapter. SS.912.A.1.3, SS.912.A.7.1

DBQ Analyzing Primary Sources

Read the excerpt below and then answer the questions that follow.

PRIMARY SOURCE

"[It would] reverse the basic direction of our national labor policy, inject the Government into private economic affairs on an unprecedented scale, and conflict with important principles of our democratic society. Its provisions would cause more strikes, not fewer."

—Harry S. Truman, message to the U.S. House of Representatives, June 20, 1947

22 *Interpreting Primary Sources* What legislation is Truman opposing in the message above? What argument is he making that he thinks will appeal to Republicans and conservative Democrats? LAFS.1112.RH.1.2, LAFS.1112.RH.3.7, LAFS.1112.RH.3.8, LAFS.1112.SL.1.3, SS.912.A.7.1

23 *Drawing Inferences* Taking into account the date of the message and the groups that made up the New Deal coalition, what political factors do you think influenced Truman's message above? LAFS.1112.RH.3.7, LAFS.1112.RH.3.8, LAFS.1112.RH.4.10, SS.912.A.7.1

Analyzing Visuals

Use the graph showing percent of suburban population to answer the following questions.

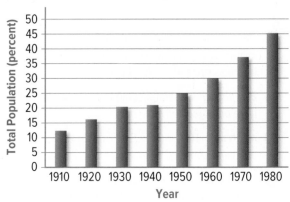

Source: *The First Measured Century.*

24 *Geographic Distributions and Patterns* Approximately what percentage of the total population lived in the suburbs in 1910? How long did it take for the percentage of suburban dwellers to double, compared to what it had been in 1910? MAFS.912.S-ID.1, MAFS.K12.MP.1.1, SS.912.G.2.1

25 *Making Predictions* Consider the graph and what you've learned in this chapter. What developments in the 1950s contributed to this geographic pattern and what consequences can you predict would happen in the future? MAFS.912.S-IC.2, MAFS.912.S-ID.1, MAFS.K12.MP.1.1, MAFS.K12.MP.3.1, SS.912.A.7.1, SS.912.G.2.1, SS.912.G.4.2, SS.912.G.4.3

26 *Posing Questions About Geographic Patterns* What questions do you need to answer to know if the trend shown above resulted in the predictions you made? Write a report identifying the questions that you need to answer. Conduct research to find out if what you predicted actually occurred between the 1990s and the 2010s. Add the results to your report. LAFS.1112.RH.3.9, LAFS.1112.WHST.3.7, LAFS.1112.WHST.3.8, LAFS.1112.WHST.3.9, MAFS.912.S-ID.1, MAFS.K12.MP.1.1, MAFS.K12.MP.3.1, MAFS.K12.MP.5.1, SS.912.A.1.6, SS.912.A.7.1, SS.912.G.2.1, SS.912.G.4.2, SS.912.G.4.3

Extended Response Question

27 *Comparing and Contrasting* Write an expository essay comparing and contrasting the postwar domestic agendas of Presidents Truman and Eisenhower. Categorize how their ideas and approaches to domestic issues were similar and different. Revise and rewrite as necessary to communicate your ideas effectively. LAFS.1112.WHST.1.2, LAFS.1112.WHST.2.4, LAFS.1112.WHST.2.5, LAFS.1112.WHST.4.10, SS.912.A.7.1

Need Extra Help?

If You've Missed Question	**19**	**20**	**21**	**22**	**23**	**24**	**25**	**26**	**27**
Go to Lesson	1	2	1, 2, 3	1	1	2	2	2	1

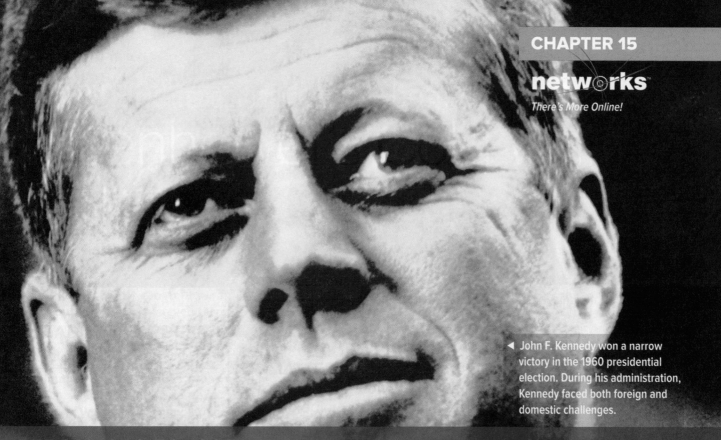

◄ John F. Kennedy won a narrow victory in the 1960 presidential election. During his administration, Kennedy faced both foreign and domestic challenges.

FROM 1960 TO 1968
The New Frontier and the Great Society

THE STORY MATTERS ...

When U.S. intelligence discovered Soviet nuclear missile silos in Cuba, just 90 miles from the United States, the bright New Frontier that President Kennedy had promised Americans seemed very far away. During the 13-day standoff between the United States and the Soviet Union, there was increasing fear that nuclear strikes would occur. The crisis was resolved when President Kennedy helped negotiate both nations away from the brink of nuclear war.

ESSENTIAL QUESTIONS

- Can government fix society's problems?
- How do you think Presidents Kennedy and Johnson changed American society?

Place & Time: United States 1960–1968

The 1960s began with great optimism in the United States, as President John F. Kennedy seemed ready to lead the way from the fear and accusations of the 1950s to a New Frontier—and to the moon itself. The threat of nuclear war and the assassination of Kennedy could not derail the drive for change. President Lyndon B. Johnson presided over landmark legislation meant to create a Great Society of wealth and equality for all.

Step Into the Place

Read the quotes and look at the information presented on the map.

DBQ **Analyzing Historical Documents** Compare and contrast the tone in President Kennedy's speech and Premier Khrushchev's letter. What clues does this give you about each author's point of view?

PRIMARY SOURCE

"Our goal is not the victory of might, but the vindication of right—not peace at the expense of freedom, but both peace and freedom, here in this hemisphere, and, we hope, around the world. God willing, that goal will be achieved."

—President John F. Kennedy, from a speech delivered October 22, 1962

PRIMARY SOURCE

"If, however, you have not lost your self-control and sensibly conceive what this might lead to, then, Mr. President, we and you ought not now to pull on the ends of the rope in which you have tied the knot of war, because the more the two of us pull, the tighter that knot will be tied. And a moment may come when that knot will be tied so tight that even he who tied it will not have the strength to untie it, and then it will be necessary to cut that knot. . . ."

—Soviet premier Nikita Khrushchev, from a letter to President Kennedy, October 26, 1962

left page (tl)©Bettmann/Corbis, (tr)Hank Walker/Time & Life Pictures/Getty Images, (bl)SuperStock/SuperStock, (br)detail/White House Collection/The White House Historical Association; right page AP Images

Step Into the Time

PREDICTING CONSEQUENCES

Choose an event from the time line that you think influenced the relationship between the United States and the Soviet Union. Write a paragraph that predicts the political impact that this event might have had on the two countries.

U.S. PRESIDENTS

UNITED STATES

WORLD

Kennedy 1961–1963

L. Johnson 1963–1969

March 1961 Peace Corps is created

April 17, 1961 Bay of Pigs invasion

Oct. 1962 Cuban missile crisis

Nov. 1963 Kennedy is assassinated

| | 1960 | 1961 | 1962 | 1963 |

August 1961 Construction of Berlin Wall begins

April 1961 Soviet astronaut Yury Gagarin becomes first person to orbit Earth

1963 Beijing receives grain from the West during a severe famine under Mao's policies

NEXT GENERATION SUNSHINE STATE STANDARDS
Students will understand the following benchmarks from the Florida NGSSS

LAFS.1112.RH.2.6: Evaluate authors' differing points of view on the same historical event or issue by assessing the authors' claims, reasoning, and evidence.
LAFS.1112.SL.1.3: Evaluate a speaker's point of view, reasoning, and use of evidence and rhetoric, assessing the stance, premises, links among ideas, word choice, points of emphasis, and tone used.
SS.912.A.1.2: Utilize a variety of primary and secondary sources to identify author, historical significance, audience, and authenticity to understand a historical period.

SS.912.A.1.3: Utilize timelines to identify the time sequence of historical data.
SS.912.A.1.4: Analyze how images, symbols, objects, cartoons, graphs, charts, maps, and artwork may be used to interpret the significance of time periods and events from the past.

SS.912.A.6.13: Analyze significant foreign policy events during the Truman, Eisenhower, Kennedy, Johnson, and Nixon administrations.
SS.912.G.2.3: Use geographic terms and tools to analyze case studies of regional issues in different parts of the world that have critical economic, physical, or political ramifications.

Cuban Missile Ranges   October 1962

The discovery by American intelligence agencies that the Soviet Union had placed long-range missiles in Cuba led to one of the most intense situations of the Cold War. The proximity of the missile bases to the United States posed a serious and immediate threat.

CANADA

2,000 miles, 17 minutes

1,500 miles, 15 minutes

UNITED STATES

New York City

Washington, D.C.

Denver

1,748 miles

1,000 miles, 12 minutes

1,136 miles

1,309 miles

Atlanta

PACIFIC OCEAN

Dallas

743 miles

ATLANTIC OCEAN

1,101 miles

- • City
- ← Distance (miles) from Cuba
- ◀ Physical/Temporal distance from missile launch origin

Gulf of Mexico

Miami

228 miles

0   400 miles
0   400 km
Lambert Azimuthal Equal-Area projection

MEXICO

Havana   CUBA

N W E S

1965 Congress establishes Medicare and Medicaid

1966 Congress passes the Child Nutrition Act

1968 Lyndon Johnson decides not to run for reelection

1964 — 1965 — 1966 — 1967 — 1968

1964 Soviet premier Nikita Khrushchev is forced to resign

March 18, 1965 Cosmonaut Aleksey Leonov spacewalks for 10 minutes before returning to *Voskhod 2*

1966 South Africa prime minister Hendrik Verwoerd is assassinated

LESSON 1
The New Frontier

ESSENTIAL QUESTIONS

• Can government fix society's problems?
• How do you think Presidents Kennedy and Johnson changed American society?

READING HELPDESK

Academic Vocabulary

• commentator   • arbitrary

Content Vocabulary

• missile gap
• reapportionment
• due process

TAKING NOTES

Key Ideas and Details

Categorizing As you read, complete a graphic organizer similar to the one below by listing domestic successes and setbacks of the Kennedy administration.
LAFS.1112.RH.3.7, SS.912.A.7.4

Successes	Setbacks

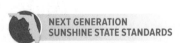

NEXT GENERATION SUNSHINE STATE STANDARDS

LAFS.1112.WHST.3.9: Draw evidence from informational texts to support analysis, reflection, and research.

SS.912.A.1.1: Describe the importance of historiography, which includes how historical knowledge is obtained and transmitted, when interpreting events in history.

SS.912.A.1.4: Analyze how images, symbols, objects, cartoons, graphs, charts, maps, and artwork may be used to interpret the significance of time periods and events from the past.

SS.912.A.1.6: Use case studies to explore social, political, legal, and economic relationships in history.

Continued on page 451

IT MATTERS BECAUSE

In the presidential election campaign of 1960, John F. Kennedy promised to move the nation into "the New Frontier." After narrowly winning the election, Kennedy succeeded in getting only part of his agenda enacted.

The Election of 1960

GUIDING QUESTION *How did the election of 1960 change the way candidates ran their campaigns?*

On September 26, 1960, at 9:30 P.M. Eastern Standard Time, an estimated 75 million people sat indoors and focused on their television sets. They were watching the first televised presidential debate. The debate marked a new era of television politics.

During the 1960 presidential race, both parties made substantial use of television. The Democrats spent more than $6 million on television and radio spots, while the Republicans spent more than $7.5 million. Television news **commentator** Eric Sevareid complained that the candidates had become "packaged products." He declared that the "Processed Politician has finally arrived."

The candidates differed in many ways. John F. Kennedy, the Democratic nominee and a senator, was a Catholic from a wealthy Massachusetts family. Richard M. Nixon, the Republican nominee and current vice president, was a Quaker from California. He had grown up in a family that struggled financially. Kennedy seemed outgoing and relaxed. Nixon struck many as formal and stiff.

Although the candidates presented different styles, they differed little on key issues. Both promised to boost the economy, and both portrayed themselves as "Cold Warriors," determined to stop the forces of communism. Kennedy expressed concern about a suspected **"missile gap,"** claiming the United States lagged behind the Soviets in weaponry. Nixon warned that the Democrats' fiscal policies would boost inflation and that only he had the foreign policy experience needed for the nation.

Kennedy's Catholic faith became an issue, just as Al Smith's Catholicism had in 1928. The United States had never had a Catholic president, and many Protestants had concerns about Kennedy. Kennedy decided to confront this issue openly in a speech: "I believe in an America where the separation of church and state is absolute—where no Catholic prelate would tell the President (should he be a Catholic) how to act and no Protestant minister would tell his parishioners for whom to vote."

The series of four televised debates influenced the election's close outcome. Kennedy won the popular vote by 118,574 out of more than 68 million votes cast, and the Electoral College by 303 votes to 219. Despite his narrow victory, Kennedy captured the imagination of the American public as few presidents had before him. During the campaign, many had been taken with Kennedy's youth and optimism. His Inaugural Address reinforced this impression. In the speech, Kennedy declared that "the torch has been passed to a new generation" and called on citizens to take a more active role in making the nation better. "My fellow Americans," he exclaimed, "ask not what your country can do for you—ask what you can do for your country."

✔ READING PROGRESS CHECK

Explaining How was the presidential election of 1960 different from earlier campaigns?

Kennedy Takes Office

GUIDING QUESTION *What were some domestic policies initiated when Kennedy took office?*

Upon entering office, President Kennedy set out to implement a legislative agenda that became known as the New Frontier. He hoped to increase aid to education, provide health insurance to the elderly, and create a Department of Urban Affairs. He would soon find that passing such legislation was no easy task on Capitol Hill. Although the Democrats had majorities in both houses of Congress, Kennedy was unable to push through many of his programs. His narrow victory had not helped many Democrats get elected. Those who did win, therefore, felt that they owed him nothing. In

commentator one who comments, discusses, or reports in an expository manner, especially news on radio or television

missile gap a supposed shortage in the number of nuclear weapons possessed by the United States compared to the number the Soviet Union had

©Bettmann/Corbis

The Kennedy-Nixon debates were the first presidential debates to be televised.

NEXT GENERATION
SUNSHINE STATE STANDARDS

Continued from page 450

SS.912.A.7.3: Examine the changing status of women in the United States from post-World War II to present.

SS.912.A.7.4: Evaluate the success of 1960s era presidents' foreign and domestic policies.

SS.912.A.7.8: Analyze significant Supreme Court decisions relating to integration, busing, affirmative action, the rights of the accused, and reproductive rights.

SS.912.A.7.17: Examine key events and key people in Florida history as they relate to United States history.

Continued on page 453

The Presidential Election 1960

ELECTORAL VOTE
TOTAL: 537

2.8%
15
40.8%
219
56.4%
303

POPULAR VOTE
TOTAL: 68,838,219

0.73%
503,331
49.72%
34,226,731
49.55%
34,108,157

Kennedy (Democrat)
Nixon (Republican)
Byrd (Democrat)
Mixed

WA 9
OR 6
ID 4
MT 4
ND 4
SD 4
WY 3
NE 6
MN 11
WI 12
MI 20
IA 10
NV 3
UT 4
CO 6
KS 8
CA 32
AZ 4
NM 4
OK 8*
TX 24
IL 27
IN 13
OH 25
MO 13
AR 8
LA 10
KY 10
TN 11
MS 8
AL 11**
GA 12
SC 8
NC 14
WV 8
VA 12
MD 9
DE 3
NJ 16
PA 32
NY 45
CT 8
RI 4
MA 16
ME 5
NH 4
VT 3
FL 10
AK 3
HI 3

* Seven electors in Oklahoma voted for Nixon and one voted for Byrd.
** Six electors in Alabama voted for Byrd and five voted for Kennedy.

GEOGRAPHY CONNECTION

Senator John F. Kennedy of Massachusetts narrowly defeated Vice President Richard Nixon in the 1960 presidential election.

1 **THE WORLD IN SPATIAL TERMS**
Which states gave one or more electoral votes to Harry Byrd? SS.912.G.1.2

2 **PLACES AND REGIONS**
What region of the nation went most solidly Republican? SS.912.G.1.2

Thinking Like a
HISTORIAN

Determining Cause and Effect

When the Kennedy administration created the Presidential Commission on the Status of Women in 1961, its stated goal was to examine employment policies for women. The reasons for the formation of the commission, however, were not as clear. At the time, the Equal Rights Amendment (ERA) was considered politically dangerous and opposed by some labor leaders. The ERA was stuck in Congress because some thought it was too extreme a step in women's rights. Some believe Kennedy created the commission to address the status of women, appeal to women voters, and avoid the politically-sensitive issue of the ERA. Others believe it was created to pay a political debt to Women's Bureau leader Esther Peterson, a supporter of Kennedy.
SS.912.A.1.1, SS.912.A.7.3

Florida
CONNECTION

The Pork Chop Gang

The Florida legislature was once dominated by the Pork Chop Gang, a group of mostly conservative Democrats from the rural counties of northern Florida. The population of southern Florida had grown dramatically, but state legislative districts did not reflect this shift. In the early 1960s, a Dade County senate district included 311,000 people, while a northern Florida senate district included only 17,000 people. The "one person, one vote" reapportionment principle greatly weakened the Pork Chop Gang's power. SS.912.A.7.17

addition, Southern Democrats—a large part of the Democrats in Congress—saw Kennedy's program as too expensive and, together with Republicans, were able to defeat many of Kennedy's proposals.

Successes and Setbacks

President Kennedy achieved some victories, particularly in improving the economy. Although the economy had soared through much of the 1950s, it had slowed by the end of the decade. To increase economic growth and create jobs, Kennedy advocated deficit spending and investing more funds in defense and space exploration. Such spending did indeed create jobs and stimulate economic growth.

Kennedy also asked businesses to hold down prices and labor leaders to hold down pay increases. The labor unions in the steel industry agreed to reduce their demands for higher wages, but several steel companies raised prices sharply. Kennedy responded by threatening to have the Department of Defense buy cheaper foreign steel. He asked the Justice Department to investigate whether the steel industry was fixing prices. The steel companies backed down and cut their prices, but the victory caused strained relations with the business community.

In addition, the president pushed for tax cuts. When opponents argued that a tax cut would help only the wealthy, Kennedy asserted that lower taxes meant businesses would have more money to expand. This, in turn, would create new jobs and benefit everybody. However, Congress refused to pass the tax cut because of fears that it would cause inflation. Congress also blocked his plans for health insurance for senior citizens and federal aid to education. Congress did agree to Kennedy's request to raise the minimum wage, his proposal for the Area Redevelopment Act, and the Housing Act. These acts helped create jobs and build low-income housing in poor areas.

Expanding Women's Rights

In 1961, Kennedy created the Presidential Commission on the Status of Women. The commission called for federal action against gender discrimination and affirmed the right of women to equally paid employment. The commission proposed the Equal Pay Act, which Kennedy signed in 1963. Kennedy never appointed a woman to his cabinet. A number of women, however, worked in other prominent positions in the administration, including Esther Peterson, assistant secretary of labor and director of the Women's Bureau of the Department of Labor.

A New Focus on the Disabled

In 1961, Kennedy convened the President's Panel on Mental Retardation. The panel's first report called for funding of research into developmental disabilities and educational and vocational programs for people with developmental disabilities. It also called for a greater reliance on residential, rather than institutional, treatment centers.

Responding to the report, Congress enacted the Mental Retardation Facilities and Community Mental Health Centers Construction Act of 1963. This legislation provided grants to build research centers and grants to states to construct mental health centers. It also provided funds to train educational personnel to work with people with developmental disabilities.

In 1962, Eunice Kennedy Shriver, the president's sister, began a day camp at her home for children with developmental disabilities. Camp Shriver, as it was first known, offered people with disabilities a chance to be physically competitive. That effort later grew into the Special Olympics program. The first Special Olympics Games were held in Chicago in 1968.

☑ READING PROGRESS CHECK

Identifying What were the economic initiatives introduced by Kennedy after taking office?

Warren Court Reforms

GUIDING QUESTION *How important are some of the Warren Court rulings for today's society?*

In 1953, Earl Warren, governor of California, became chief justice of the United States. Under Warren's leadership, the Supreme Court issued several rulings that dramatically reshaped American politics and society.

"One Person, One Vote"

Some of the Court's more notable decisions concerned **reapportionment.** By 1960, more Americans resided in urban than in rural areas, but many states' electoral districts did not reflect this shift. In Tennessee, for example, a rural county with only 2,340 voters had one state representative, while an urban county with 133 times more voters had only seven. Thus, rural voters had far more political influence than urban ones. Some Tennessee voters took the matter to court, and their case, *Baker* v. *Carr* (1962), went to the Supreme Court. The Court ruled that federal courts had jurisdiction to hear lawsuits seeking to force states to redraw electoral districts. In *Reynolds* v. *Sims* (1964), the Court ruled that states must reapportion electoral districts along the principle of "one person, one vote," so that all citizens' votes would have equal weight, rather than giving **arbitrary** power to rural voters. The decision shifted political power from rural and often conservative areas to urban areas, where more liberal voters lived. It also boosted the political power of African Americans and Hispanics, who typically lived in cities.

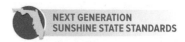

NEXT GENERATION SUNSHINE STATE STANDARDS

Continued from page 451

SS.912.G.1.2: Use spatial perspective and appropriate geographic terms and tools, including the Six Essential Elements, as organizational schema to describe any given place.

reapportionment
the method states use to draw up political districts based on changes in population

arbitrary existing or coming about seemingly at random or as an unfair or unreasonable act of will

---

🏛 ANALYZING SUPREME COURT CASES

BAKER v. *CARR*, 1962
REYNOLDS v. *SIMS*, 1964

Background of the Cases

Although many more Americans were living in urban areas, most states had not redrawn their political districts to reflect this shift. This gave rural voters more political influence than urban voters. In *Baker* v. *Carr*, the Supreme Court ruled on whether federal courts had jurisdiction in lawsuits seeking to force states to redraw their electoral districts. In *Reynolds* v. *Sims*, the Court decided whether uneven electoral districts violated the equal protection clause of the Fourteenth Amendment.

How the Court Ruled

In *Baker* v. *Carr*, the Supreme Court ruled that federal courts can hear lawsuits seeking to force state authorities to redraw electoral districts. In *Reynolds* v. *Sims*, the Court ruled that the inequality of representation in the Alabama legislature did violate the equal protection clause. These rulings forced states to reapportion their political districts according to the principle of "one person, one vote."

The 1962 Supreme Court. Seated, left to right: Associate Justices Tom Clark and Hugo Black, Chief Justice Earl Warren, Associate Justices William O. Douglas and John Harlan; standing, left to right: Associate Justices Byron White, William Brennan, Potter Stewart, and Arthur Goldberg. Justices Byron White and Arthur Goldberg were appointed by Kennedy.

DBQ Document Based Questions

1. **Identifying Central Ideas** What is the primary problem at issue in the *Reynolds* v. *Sims* case?
   LAFS.1112.WHST.3.9, SS.912.A.1.6, SS.912.A.7.8

2. **Making Inferences** How do you think reapportionment according to "one person, one vote" changed state politics? LAFS.1112.RH.2.4, LAFS.1112.WHST.3.9, SS.912.A.1.6, SS.912.A.7.8

©Bettmann/Corbis

In the Supreme Court case *Miranda* v. *Arizona*, attorneys argued that Ernesto Miranda (right) had no idea of his legal rights and should have been told that he had the right to a lawyer.

▶ CRITICAL THINKING

Drawing Conclusions What can you conclude about what police told suspects before the establishment of Miranda rights?
LAFS.1112.WHST.3.9, SS.912.A.7.8

due process a judicial requirement that laws may not treat individuals unfairly, arbitrarily, or unreasonably, and that courts must follow proper procedures and rules when trying cases

Extending Due Process

The Supreme Court began to use the Fourteenth Amendment to extend the Bill of Rights to the states. Originally, the Bill of Rights applied only to the federal government. Many states had their own bills of rights, but some federal rights did not exist at the state level. The Fourteenth Amendment states that "no state shall . . . deprive any person of life, liberty, or property without due process of law." **Due process** means that the law may not treat individuals unfairly, arbitrarily, or unreasonably.

The Court ruled in several cases that due process meant applying the federal Bill of Rights to the states. In 1961, the Supreme Court ruled in *Mapp* v. *Ohio* that state courts could not consider evidence obtained in violation of the U.S. Constitution. In *Gideon* v. *Wainwright* (1963), the Court ruled that a defendant in a state court had the right to a lawyer, regardless of his or her ability to pay. In *Escobedo* v. *Illinois* (1964), the Court ruled that suspects must be allowed access to a lawyer and informed of their right to remain silent before being questioned. *Miranda* v. *Arizona* (1966) went further, requiring authorities to inform suspects of their right to remain silent; that anything they say can and will be used against them in court; and that they have a right to a lawyer. These warnings are known as Miranda rights.

Prayer and Privacy

The Supreme Court also reaffirmed the separation of church and state. The Court applied the First Amendment to the states in *Engel* v. *Vitale* (1962), ruling that states could not compose official prayers and require those prayers to be recited in public schools. In *Abington School District* v. *Schempp* (1963), it ruled against state-mandated Bible readings in public schools. The Court ruled in *Griswold* v. *Connecticut* (1965) that prohibiting the sale and use of birth control devices violated citizens' constitutional right to privacy. As with most rulings of the Warren Court, some people supported these decisions and others did not. What most people did agree upon, however, was the Court's pivotal role in shaping national policy. These decisions continue to shape the way Americans act and behave today.

☑ READING PROGRESS CHECK

Making Connections Which Warren Court rulings continue to be important today? Why?

©Bettmann/Corbis

LESSON 1 REVIEW

Reviewing Vocabulary

1. *Drawing Conclusions* Why would Americans have worried about a potential "missile gap"? LAFS.1112.RH.2.4, SS.912.A.7.4

2. *Explaining* What is the purpose of due process? LAFS.1112.RH.2.4

Using Your Notes

3. *Making Generalizations* Review the notes that you completed during the lesson. Describe why some parts of the Kennedy administration's agenda were refused by Congress, and why others were passed. LAFS.1112.SL.2.4, SS.912.A.7.4

Answering the Guiding Questions

4. *Analyzing* How did the election of 1960 change the way candidates ran their campaigns? LAFS.1112.WHST.3.9

5. *Identifying* What were some domestic policies initiated when Kennedy took office? LAFS.1112.WHST.3.9, SS.912.A.7.4

6. *Evaluating* How important are some of the Warren Court rulings for today's society? LAFS.1112.WHST.3.9, SS.912.A.7.8

Writing Activity

7. INFORMATIVE/EXPLANATORY Select one of the Supreme Court rulings from this lesson as a case study. Using the Internet, research additional background information about the case and the long-term impact of the ruling. Then write an essay presenting your findings. Essays should include an introduction, supporting paragraphs, and a conclusion. LAFS.1112.WHST.1.2, LAFS.1112.WHST.4.10

LESSON 2
JFK and the Cold War

ESSENTIAL QUESTIONS
• Can government fix society's problems?
• How do you think Presidents Kennedy and Johnson changed American society?

READING HELPDESK

Academic Vocabulary

• conventional   • remove
• institute

Content Vocabulary

• flexible response
• space race

TAKING NOTES

Key Ideas and Details

Sequencing As you read the lesson, complete a graphic organizer similar to the one below to record the major events of the Cold War between 1959 and 1963.
LAFS.1112.RH.3.7, SS.912.A.1.3, SS.912.A.6.10, SS.912.A.6.13

NEXT GENERATION
SUNSHINE STATE STANDARDS

LAFS.1112.RH.2.4: Determine the meaning of words and phrases as they are used in a text, including analyzing how an author uses and refines the meaning of a key term over the course of a text (e.g., how Madison defines faction in Federalist No. 10).

LAFS.1112.RH.3.7: Integrate and evaluate multiple sources of information presented in diverse formats and media (e.g., visually, quantitatively, as well as in words) in order to address a question or solve a problem.

Continued on page 456

IT MATTERS BECAUSE
During the Kennedy administration, ongoing tensions with the Soviet Union led to crises over Cuba and West Berlin. To contain communism and stay ahead in technology, President Kennedy created aid programs for developing nations and expanded the space program.

Containing Communism

GUIDING QUESTION *How were President Kennedy's programs to combat communism different from the programs of previous administrations?*

When John F. Kennedy entered the White House in 1961, the Cold War with the Soviet Union dominated all other concerns. He used a range of programs to try to stop the spread of communism. These included a **conventional** weaponry program to give the nation's military more flexibility. The programs also included economic aid to Latin America and the creation of the Peace Corps to help developing nations.

A More Flexible Response
Kennedy took office at a time of growing global instability. Resentment at wealthy Western nations was on the rise in the developing world, often encouraged by the Soviet Union. Kennedy felt that Eisenhower had relied too heavily on nuclear weapons. To allow for a **"flexible response"** to resist Communist movements, the president pushed for a buildup of troops and conventional weapons. He also expanded the Special Forces, an elite army unit used in limited conflicts.

Despite his commitment to flexible response, Kennedy had warned against a "missile gap" during his campaign. Although no gap actually existed, the United States began a massive build-up of intercontinental ballistic missiles (ICBMs) armed with nuclear warheads. At the time Kennedy took office, less than 20 ICBMS were deployed by the United States, and only 50 new Minuteman missiles were planned. The Soviet Union had less than 10 ICBMs

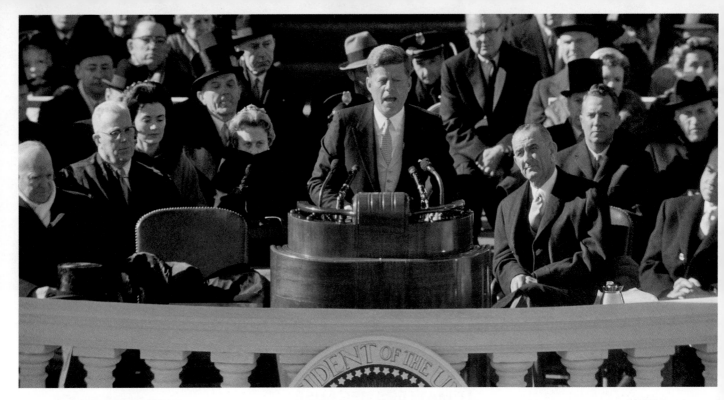

John F. Kennedy delivered his inaugural speech on January 20, 1961. He spoke of his generation's obligation to defend liberty. Seated at right is incoming Vice President Lyndon Johnson.

▶ **CRITICAL THINKING**
Identifying Central Ideas Why do you think that President Kennedy chose to speak of defending liberty during his inaugural speech? LAFS.1112.WHST.3.9

conventional nonnuclear

flexible response the buildup of conventional troops and weapons to allow a nation to fight a limited war without using nuclear weapons

space race the Cold War competition over dominance of space exploration capability

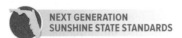

NEXT GENERATION SUNSHINE STATE STANDARDS

Continued from page 455

LAFS.1112.SL.2.4: Present information, findings, and supporting evidence, conveying a clear and distinct perspective, such that listeners can follow the line of reasoning, alternative or opposing perspectives are addressed, and the organization, development, substance, and style are appropriate to purpose, audience, and a range of formal and informal tasks.

LAFS.1112.WHST.1.2: Write informative/ explanatory texts, including the narration of historical events, scientific procedures/ experiments, or technical processes.

Continued on page 458

ready to fire at the United States. Nonetheless, Kennedy decided to build 1000 Minutemen ICBMS. The decision continued the arms race for the remainder of the 1960s and into the 1970s. Tensions increased as the Soviets began their own mass production of missiles, and began to look for other ways to ensure they could match the firepower of the United States.

Aid to Other Countries

Kennedy wanted to renew diplomatic focus on Latin America, where governments were often in the hands of the wealthy few and many people lived in extreme poverty. In some countries, these conditions spurred the growth of left-wing movements aimed at overthrowing their governments. In his Inaugural Address, President Kennedy said, "To our sister republics south of our border, we offer a special pledge—to convert our good words into good deeds—in a new alliance for progress. . . ."

When the United States became involved in Latin America, it was usually to help existing governments stay in power and to prevent Communist movements from flourishing. Poor Latin Americans resented this intrusion, just as they resented American corporations, whose presence was seen as a kind of imperialism.

The Alliance for Progress To improve relations between the United States and Latin America, Kennedy proposed the Alliance for Progress, a series of cooperative aid projects with Latin American governments. The Alliance was designed to create a "free and prosperous Latin America" that would be more stable and less likely to support Communist-inspired revolutions.

Over a 10-year period, the United States pledged $20 billion to help Latin American countries establish better schools, housing, health care, and fairer land distribution. The results were mixed. In some countries, the Alliance did promote real reform. In others, local rulers used the money to keep themselves in power.

The Peace Corps Another program aimed at helping developing nations fight poverty was the Peace Corps. This program sent Americans to provide humanitarian services in developing nations. After rigorous training,

George Silk/Time Life Pictures/Getty Images

volunteers spent two years in countries that requested assistance. Among other projects, Peace Corps volunteers built roads, taught English, laid out sewage systems, and trained medical technicians.

The Cold War in Space

In 1961, Yury Gagarin (YUR•ee guh•GAHR•uhn), a Soviet astronaut, became the first person to orbit Earth. Again, as in 1957 with the launch of *Sputnik,* the first satellite, the Soviets had beaten the United States in the **space race.** Kennedy worried that Soviet successes in space might convince the world that communism was better than capitalism. Less than six weeks after the Soviet flight, the president went before Congress and declared: "I believe this Nation should commit itself to achieving the goal, before this decade is out, of landing a man on the Moon." Kennedy's speech set in motion a massive effort to develop the necessary technology. In 1962, John Glenn became the first American to orbit Earth. Six years later, the United States sent three men into orbit in a capsule called *Apollo.* The capsule was launched using the Saturn V, the most powerful rocket ever built. The Saturn V gave both *Apollo* and its lunar module—which astronauts would use to land on the moon—enough velocity to reach the moon.

On July 16, 1969, a Saturn V lifted off in Florida, carrying three American astronauts: Neil Armstrong, Edwin "Buzz" Aldrin, and Michael Collins. On July 20, Armstrong and Aldrin boarded the lunar module, named *Eagle,* and headed down to the moon. Minutes later, Armstrong radioed NASA's flight center in Texas: "Houston . . . the *Eagle* has landed." Armstrong became the first human being to walk on the moon. As he set foot on the lunar surface, he announced: "That's one small step for a man, one giant leap for mankind." The United States had demonstrated its technological superiority over the Soviet Union.

In addition, the moon landing represented a potential turning point in human history. For the first time, human beings had walked on the surface of another world. Although no one has gone any further from home in the nearly 50 years that have passed since the first moon landing, the success of the mission demonstrated that human beings might one day set out to colonize other worlds.

The space program also set in motion an enormous wave of technological innovation that continues to shape the world today. The requirement for clear communications with the astronauts led to improved transmission technology, making possible the use of satellites to transmit

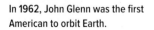

In 1962, John Glenn was the first American to orbit Earth.

▶ **CRITICAL THINKING**
Making Generalizations In addition to being explorers, what other role did the U.S. astronauts play? LAFS.1112.WHST.3.9, SS.912.A.6.15

Florida CONNECTION

The Kennedy Space Center

In 1958 President Eisenhower created the National Aeronautics and Space Administration (NASA), establishing its Launch Operations Center on Florida's east coast. In 1961 NASA announced an 80,000 acre expansion of the center for the lunar missions. Today about 1.5 million people visit the Space Center annually, making it the state's fourth most popular tourist attraction. Now NASA is transitioning from the Space Shuttle to new, lower-cost exploration methods. NASA also provides classroom materials to help educate students about its discoveries. SS.912.A.7.17

Neil Armstrong was the first person to walk on the moon. To reach the moon, NASA developed the giant Saturn V rocket, which lifted a three-person capsule, called Apollo, and a landing craft, called the Lunar Module, into space. Once Apollo and the Lunar Module entered orbit around the moon, the Lunar Module carried two astronauts from the Apollo capsule down to the moon's surface.

(t)©John Glenn/Historical/Corbis; (bl)©Neil Armstrong/Bettmann/Corbis, (br)NASA

The New Frontier and the Great Society **457**

Florida
CONNECTION

Impact of the Cuban Revolution

When Fidel Castro overthrew the government of Fulgencio Batista in Cuba in 1959, the impact on Florida was powerful and immediate. About 200,000 people left Cuba between 1960 and 1962, with Miami as the main destination. Cuban immigrants in Florida stimulated economic growth and provided a large labor force. In the span of one generation, Miami went from a declining tourist and retirement center with few foreigners to the capital of the Caribbean with proportionately more foreigners than any other U.S. city. SS.912.A.6.15

NEXT GENERATION SUNSHINE STATE STANDARDS

Continued from page 456

LAFS.1112.WHST.3.9: Draw evidence from informational texts to support analysis, reflection, and research.

LAFS.1112.WHST.4.10: Write routinely over extended time frames (time for reflection and revision) and shorter time frames (a single sitting or a day or two) for a range of discipline-specific tasks, purposes, and audiences.

SS.912.A.1.4: Analyze how images, symbols, objects, cartoons, graphs, charts, maps, and artwork may be used to interpret the significance of time periods and events from the past.

SS.912.A.6.10: Examine causes, course, and consequences of the early years of the Cold War (Truman Doctrine, Marshall Plan, NATO, Warsaw Pact).

SS.912.A.6.13: Analyze significant foreign policy events during the Truman, Eisenhower, Kennedy, Johnson, and Nixon administrations.

Continued on page 459

GEOGRAPHY CONNECTION

The Cuban Missile Crisis brought the United States and the Soviet Union to the brink of war.

1 **THE WORLD IN SPATIAL TERMS**
Where in Cuba did the Bay of Pigs invasion begin? SS.912.A.1.4, SS.912.G.1.2

2 **PLACES AND REGIONS**
Approximately how close were the Soviet Union's nuclear missiles in Cuba to the mainland United States? SS.912.A.1.4, SS.912.G.1.2, SS.912.G.2.3

radio, phone, and television signals. It also led to the first wireless headsets. Power requirements so far from home led to advances in battery technology and solar cell technology. Navigational concerns led to improvements in computer technology, particularly involving the use of integrated circuits to build computers that could fit in the space available.

Other inventions resulting from the space program that have improved our way of life include water filters, new types of insulation, flame resistant fabrics, the CAT scanner, memory foam for beds and chairs, and new types of rubber, now used in running shoes and hiking boots. Innovations in robotics for the space program went on to benefit manufacturers around the world and helped drive down the price of goods.

In general, the moon landing boosted the confidence of Americans and enhanced the nation's stature abroad. If the United States could put men on the moon, what could it not do? Three years later, in the wake of the success of the Apollo missions, President Nixon approved the development of a new reusable spacecraft that would later be known as the Space Shuttle.

☑ READING PROGRESS CHECK

Analyzing Why do you think the space race was a part of President Kennedy's programs to combat communism?

Crises of the Cold War

GUIDING QUESTION *What was the most important foreign policy event of the Kennedy administration? Why was it the most important event?*

President Kennedy's efforts to combat Communist influence in other countries led to some of the most intense crises of the Cold War. At times, these crises left Americans and people in many other nations wondering whether the world would survive.

The Bay of Pigs

The first crisis occurred in Cuba, only 90 miles (145 km) from American shores. There, Fidel Castro had overthrown the corrupt Cuban dictator

The Cuban Missile Crisis October 1962

- ✪ Capital city
- • Other city
- ▬ American quarantine zone
- Soviet missile sites

UNITED STATES

Gulf of Mexico — Miami

BAHAMAS

TROPIC OF CANCER

October 27, 1962: U-2 spy plane shot down

Havana

ATLANTIC OCEAN

CUBA

April 17, 1961: Bay of Pigs Invasion

Guantánamo

Caribbean Sea

JAMAICA

HAITI

0 — 200 miles
0 — 200 km

85°W   80°W   75°W

25°N   20°N

Fulgencio Batista in 1959. At once, Castro established ties with the Soviet Union, **instituted** drastic land reforms, and seized foreign-owned businesses, many of which were American. Cuba's alliance with the Soviets worried many Americans. Soviet premier Nikita Khrushchev was also expressing his hope to strengthen Cuba's military.

Fearing that the Soviets would use Cuba as a base from which to spread revolution, President Eisenhower had authorized the CIA to secretly train and arm a group of Cuban exiles, known as *La Brigada,* to invade the island. His goal was to set off a popular uprising against Castro. When Kennedy became president, his advisers approved the plan. Kennedy agreed to the operation with some changes. On April 17, 1961, about 1,400 armed Cuban exiles landed at the Bay of Pigs on the south coast of Cuba. The invasion was a disaster. *La Brigada*'s boats ran aground on coral reefs. Then Kennedy canceled their air support to keep the United States's involvement a secret. The expected popular uprising never happened. Within two days, Castro's forces killed or captured almost all the members of *La Brigada.*

The Bay of Pigs was a dark moment for the Kennedy administration. The incident exposed an American plot to overthrow a neighbor's government. The disastrous outcome made the United States look weak and disorganized.

The Berlin Wall Goes Up

In June 1961, Kennedy faced another foreign policy challenge when he met with Soviet premier Nikita Khrushchev in Vienna, Austria. To stop Germans from leaving Communist East Germany for West Berlin, Khrushchev demanded that the Western powers recognize East Germany and withdraw from Berlin. Berlin was a city lying completely within East Germany. Kennedy refused and reaffirmed the West's commitment to West Berlin.

Khrushchev retaliated by building a wall through Berlin, blocking movement between the Soviet sector and the rest of the city. Guards along the wall shot at people who tried to cross from East Berlin to West Berlin. The Berlin Wall stood as a symbol of Cold War divisions.

The Cuban Missile Crisis

During the summer of 1962, American intelligence learned that Soviet technicians and equipment had arrived in Cuba and that military construction was in progress. On October 22, Kennedy announced that the Soviet Union had placed long-range nuclear missiles in Cuba. This location made them a clear threat to the United States.

Kennedy ordered a naval quarantine to stop the delivery of more missiles, and demanded the existing missile sites be dismantled. He warned that if attacked, the United States would respond fully against the Soviet Union. Still, work on the missile sites continued. Nuclear warfare seemed more possible than ever.

Then, after a flurry of secret negotiations, the Soviet Union offered to **remove** the missiles if the United States promised not to invade Cuba. The United States also agreed to remove its missiles from Turkey near the Soviet border.

In reality, neither Kennedy nor Khrushchev wanted nuclear war. "Only lunatics or suicides, who themselves want to perish and to destroy the whole world before they die, could do this," wrote Khrushchev. "We . . . want to live and do not at all want to destroy your country." On October 28, the leaders reached an agreement. The world could breathe again.

---

institute to initiate or establish

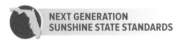

**NEXT GENERATION
SUNSHINE STATE STANDARDS**

Continued from page 458

SS.912.A.6.15: Examine key events and peoples in Florida history as they relate to United States history.

SS.912.A.7.4: Evaluate the success of 1960s era presidents' foreign and domestic policies.

SS.912.A.7.11: Analyze the foreign policy of the United States as it relates to Africa, Asia, the Caribbean, Latin America, and the Middle East.

SS.912.A.7.17: Examine key events and key people in Florida history as they relate to United States history.

SS.912.G.2.1: Identify the physical characteristics and the human characteristics that define and differentiate regions.

SS.912.G.2.3: Use geographic terms and tools to analyze case studies of regional issues in different parts of the world that have critical economic, physical, or political ramifications.

SKILLS PRACTICE

When you are speaking, think about how the ideas connect. This is very important when explaining history. Describe the events of the Cuban Missile Crisis. Choose connecting words to show cause, comparison, contrast, sequence, or other connections. ELD.K12.ELL.SI.1, ELD.K12.ELL.SS.1, SS.912.A.7.4

remove to take away or change the location of

The Cuban missile crisis forced the United States and the Soviet Union to consider the consequences of nuclear war. In August 1963, the two countries agreed to a treaty that banned testing nuclear weapons in the atmosphere. In the long run, however, the missile crisis had consequences. Soviet leadership saw Khrushchev as having agreed to a humiliating retreat, and he fell from power in 1964. The crisis also exposed the Soviets' military inferiority and prompted a dramatic Soviet arms buildup, which the United States matched.

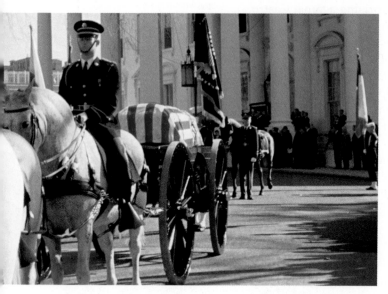

President Kennedy's funeral procession and burial service were broadcast live over all three television networks.

▶ CRITICAL THINKING
Predicting Consequences What effect do you think Kennedy's assassination had on how his presidency is remembered?
LAFS.1112.WHST.3.9

Death of a President

Soon after the Senate ratified the test ban treaty, John F. Kennedy's presidency ended shockingly and tragically. On November 22, 1963, Kennedy and his wife traveled to Texas. As the presidential motorcade rode slowly through the crowded streets of Dallas, gunfire rang out. Someone had shot the president twice. Government officials sped Kennedy to a nearby hospital, where he was pronounced dead moments later.

Lee Harvey Oswald, the man accused of killing Kennedy, appeared to be a confused and embittered Marxist who had spent time in the Soviet Union. He himself was shot to death while in police custody two days after Kennedy's assassination. The bizarre situation led some to speculate that the second gunman, local nightclub owner Jack Ruby, killed Oswald to protect others involved in the crime. In 1964, a national commission headed by Chief Justice Warren concluded that Oswald was the lone assassin. The report of the Warren Commission left some questions unanswered. Theories about a conspiracy to kill the president have persisted, though none has gained wide acceptance.

In the wake of the assassination, the United States and much of the world went into mourning. Kennedy was president for little more than 1,000 days. Yet he made a profound impression on most Americans. Kennedy's successor, Vice President Lyndon Baines Johnson, set out to promote many of the programs that Kennedy left unfinished.

☑ READING PROGRESS CHECK

Interpreting Significance How do you think the assassination of President Kennedy affected the nation?

©Bettmann/Corbis

LESSON 2 REVIEW

Reviewing Vocabulary
1. ***Explaining*** How was Kennedy's "flexible response" different from Eisenhower's strategy for containing communism? LAFS.1112.RH.2.4, SS.912.A.6.13

2. ***Summarizing*** Why was the space race so important to the United States? LAFS.1112.RH.2.4, SS.912.A.6.13

Using Your Notes
3. ***Making Generalizations*** Use the notes you completed during the lesson to describe which areas the Kennedy administration succeeded in, and which areas posed setbacks to the president's drive to win the Cold War. SS.912.A.6.13, SS.912.A.7.4

Answering the Guiding Questions
4. ***Analyzing*** How were President Kennedy's programs to combat communism different from the programs of previous administrations? LAFS.1112.WHST.3.9, SS.912.A.6.13, SS.912.A.7.4

5. ***Synthesizing*** What was the most important foreign policy event of the Kennedy administration? Why was it the most important event? LAFS.1112.RH.2.4, SS.912.A.6.13, SS.912.A.7.4, SS.912.A.7.11

Writing Activity
6. **INFORMATIVE/EXPLANATORY** Write two to three descriptive paragraphs explaining how President Kennedy's programs affected the world and the American people, both in his leadership and in his death. LAFS.1112.WHST.1.2, LAFS.1112.WHST.4.10, SS.912.A.6.13, SS.912.A.7.4, SS.912.A.7.11

LAFS.1112.WHST.3.7, LAFS.1112.WHST.3.8, MAFS.K12.MP.1.1, SS.912.A.7.4, SS.912.A.7.11

Using a Problem Solving Process

Why Learn This Skill?

Life is full of choices. Imagine that you have just done poorly on a chemistry exam. You wonder why you cannot do better since you always go to class, take notes, and study for exams. In order to improve your grades, you need to identify the specific problem and then take actions to solve it.

Learning the Skill

There are six key steps you should follow that will help you through the problem-solving process.

1. Identify the problem. Be specific. Problems can be too big to be solved, but when broken into smaller problems, each in turn may be solvable. Focus on exactly one specific thing that is a problem and should be fixed.

2. Gather information. This is critical. Many problems are the result of poor communication or a lack of facts. Be sure you have collected all the facts you need, that the facts are accurate, and that you have a clear understanding of what everyone involved has said or done before.

3. List and consider possible solutions. As much as possible, keep emotion out of your thinking. People often are inclined to support a solution that makes them feel better or is in their interest, forgetting all of the other people who will be affected by the solution that is put in place.

4. Consider the advantages and disadvantages of each solution. Look at both short-term and long-term outcomes. A quick fix that does not take enough facts into account will just break down and cause new problems in the future.

5. Now that you have listed and considered the possible options, choose the best solution to your problem and put it into effect.

6. Evaluate the effectiveness of the solution. Did it work? Is the problem solved? Has solving the problem created new problems? If so, return to the problem solving process.

Practicing the Skill

Go to the lesson "The New Frontier" and reread the section, "Kennedy Takes Office." Use that information and the steps listed on this page to answer the following questions.

1. What problem did Kennedy encounter in the summer of 1962 when American intelligence studied photos of Cuba?

2. What options were available to the president to deal with the situation? What were the advantages and disadvantages of each solution?

3. Explain the solution Kennedy implemented to solve his problem.

4. Evaluate the effectiveness of Kennedy's solution. Was it successful? How do you determine this?

Applying the Skill

Problem Solving Do research at the library or online at a news website and identify a significant problem facing your local community. Gather information and be sure you have accurate data and a clear understanding of the situation. Write a comment that you could send to a newspaper or post online that describes the problem, lists the options and their advantages and disadvantages. Propose a solution, and give your evaluation of the chosen solution.

LESSON 3
The Great Society

ESSENTIAL QUESTIONS
• Can government fix society's problems?
• How do you think Presidents Kennedy and Johnson changed American society?

READING HELPDESK

Academic Vocabulary
• confine   • subsidy

Content Vocabulary
• consensus

TAKING NOTES

Key Ideas and Details

Organizing As you read, complete a graphic organizer similar to the one below to list the social and economic programs started during Lyndon Johnson's administration. LAFS.1112.RH.3.7, SS.912.A.7.13

Johnson's Programs

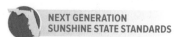

NEXT GENERATION SUNSHINE STATE STANDARDS

LAFS.1112.RH.2.4: Determine the meaning of words and phrases as they are used in a text, including analyzing how an author uses and refines the meaning of a key term over the course of a text (e.g., how Madison defines faction in Federalist No. 10).

LAFS.1112.RH.3.7: Integrate and evaluate multiple sources of information presented in diverse formats and media (e.g., visually, quantitatively, as well as in words) in order to address a question or solve a problem.

Continued on page 463

IT MATTERS BECAUSE

Lyndon B. Johnson had decades of experience in Congress and was skilled in getting legislation enacted. When he became president, he moved quickly to push for passage of civil rights and antipoverty bills.

Johnson Takes the Reins

GUIDING QUESTION *How did President Johnson's experience in Congress help him get legislation passed?*

Just hours after President Kennedy had been pronounced dead, Lyndon B. Johnson took the oath of office in the cabin of *Air Force One*. Days later, Johnson appeared before Congress and urged the nation to build on Kennedy's legacy. Although the nation was booming, not all Americans shared in its prosperity. In his 1962 book *The Other America,* Michael Harrington claimed that almost 50 million poor Americans lived largely hidden in slums, Appalachia, the Deep South, and Native American reservations. Soon after taking office, Johnson decided to launch an antipoverty crusade.

Johnson's Leadership Style

Lyndon Baines Johnson was born and raised in the "hill country" of central Texas, near the banks of the Pedernales River. Johnson remained a Texan in his heart, and his style posed a striking contrast with Kennedy's. He was a man of impressive stature who spoke directly, convincingly, and even roughly at times. He earned a reputation as a man who got things done. He did favors, twisted arms, bargained, flattered, and threatened in order to find **consensus,** or general agreement. His ability to build coalitions had made him one of the most effective and powerful leaders in Senate history.

Why was Johnson concerned about the poor? He had known hard times growing up, and had seen extreme poverty firsthand in a brief career as a teacher in a low-income area. He also believed that a wealthy, powerful government should try to improve the lives of its citizens. Finally, there was Johnson's ambition. He wanted history to portray him as a great president.

A War on Poverty

consensus general agreement

Before his death, Kennedy had plans for an antipoverty program and a civil rights bill. Continuing these efforts seemed logical. Johnson knew that any program linked to the slain president would be popular. In his State of the Union address in 1964, he said: "Unfortunately, many Americans live on the outskirts of hope—some because of their poverty, and some because of their color, and all too many because of both. Our task is to help replace their despair with opportunity. This administration . . . declares unconditional war on poverty in America."

By the summer of 1964, Johnson had convinced Congress to pass the Economic Opportunity Act, which attacked inadequate public services, illiteracy, and unemployment. The act established 10 new programs within a new agency, the Office of Economic Opportunity (OEO). Many of the new programs were directed at young, inner-city Americans.

The Neighborhood Youth Corps provided work-study programs to help the underprivileged earn a high school diploma or college degree. The Job Corps helped unemployed people ages 16–21 acquire job skills. One of the more dramatic programs introduced was VISTA (Volunteers in Service to America), which was essentially a domestic Peace Corps. VISTA put young people with skills and community-minded ideals to work in poor neighborhoods and rural areas to help people overcome poverty. Additional programs included Upward Bound, which offered tutoring to high school students, and a Work Experience Program, which provided day care and other support for those in poor households to enable them to work.

The Election of 1964

Johnson quickly won public approval, but just as quickly had to run for the office he first gained through tragedy. The Republican candidate in the 1964 election was Senator Barry Goldwater of Arizona, known for his strong conservatism. "Extremism in the defense of liberty is no vice. Moderation in the pursuit of justice is no virtue," Goldwater declared when accepting the nomination. Few Americans were ready to embrace Goldwater's message, which seemed too aggressive for a nation nervous about nuclear war. On Election Day, Johnson won in a landslide, gaining more than 61 percent of the popular vote and winning all but six states in the Electoral College.

✔️ **READING PROGRESS CHECK**

Explaining What parts of Johnson's congressional background helped him get his legislation approved?

NEXT GENERATION SUNSHINE STATE STANDARDS

Continued from page 462

LAFS.1112.SL.2.4: Present information, findings, and supporting evidence, conveying a clear and distinct perspective, such that listeners can follow the line of reasoning, alternative or opposing perspectives are addressed, and the organization, development, substance, and style are appropriate to purpose, audience, and a range of formal and informal tasks.

LAFS.1112.WHST.1.2: Write informative/explanatory texts, including the narration of historical events, scientific procedures/experiments, or technical processes.

LAFS.1112.WHST.3.9: Draw evidence from informational texts to support analysis, reflection, and research.

LAFS.1112.WHST.4.10: Write routinely over extended time frames (time for reflection and revision) and shorter time frames (a single sitting or a day or two) for a range of discipline-specific tasks, purposes, and audiences.

MAFS.912.S-ID.1: Summarize, represent and interpret data on a single count or measurement variable.

SS.912.A.1.2: Utilize a variety of primary and secondary sources to identify author, historical significance, audience, and authenticity to understand a historical period.

SS.912.A.1.4: Analyze how images, symbols, objects, cartoons, graphs, charts, maps, and artwork may be used to interpret the significance of time periods and events from the past.

SS.912.A.7.4: Evaluate the success of 1960s era presidents' foreign and domestic policies.

SS.912.A.7.13: Analyze the attempts to extend New Deal legislation through the Great Society and the successes and failures of these programs to promote social and economic stability.

POVERTY RATE IN AMERICA, 1960–2000

CHARTS/GRAPHS

Source: U.S. Census Bureau.

At left, an unemployed miner and his family posed on the porch of their Kentucky home in 1964.

1 *Making Generalizations* Based on the data in the chart, what decade had the greatest decrease in the poverty rate? Why do you think this was the case? **MAFS.912.S-ID.1, SS.912.A.1.4**

2 *Analyzing Information* Based on the data in the chart, how successful was Johnson's War on Poverty? **MAFS.912.S-ID.1, SS.912.A.7.4**

John Dominis/Time Life Pictures/Getty Images

Health and Welfare	Education	The War on Poverty	Consumer and Environmental Protection
Medicare (1965) established a comprehensive health insurance program for all senior citizens; financed through the Social Security system.	**Elementary and Secondary Education Act** (1965) targeted aid to students and funded related activities such as adult education and education consulting.	**Office of Economic Opportunity** (1964) oversaw many programs to improve life in inner cities, including Job Corps, an education and job training program for at-risk youth.	**Clean Air Act** (1963) **and Water Quality Act** (1965) supported development of standards and goals for water and air quality.
Medicaid (1965) provided health and medical assistance to low-income families; funded through federal and state governments.	**Higher Education Act** (1965) supported college tuition scholarships, student loans, and work-study programs for low- and middle-income students.	**Housing and Urban Development Act** (1965) established new housing subsidy programs and made federal loans and public housing grants easier to obtain.	**Highway Safety Act** (1966) improved federal, state, and local coordination and created training standards for emergency medical technicians.
Child Nutrition Act (1966) established a school breakfast program and expanded the school lunch and milk programs to improve nutrition.	**Project Head Start** (1965) funded a preschool program for disadvantaged children.	**Demonstration Cities and Metropolitan Development Act** (1966) revitalized urban areas through a variety of social and economic programs.	**Fair Packaging and Labeling Act** (1966) required all consumer products to have true and informative labels.

CHARTS/GRAPHS

1 *Identifying Central Ideas*
What was the purpose of the Water Quality Act and Clean Air Act? SS.912.A.1.4 , SS.912.A.7.13

2 *Analyzing Information*
Which Great Society program do you think had the most effect on American life? Why do you think so? SS.912.A.7.13

confine to limit or restrict

SKILLS PRACTICE

Work with a partner. Take turns telling each other the information you learned in this lesson about the War on Poverty and the Great Society. ELD.K12.ELL.SI.1, ELD.K12.ELL.SS.1

subsidy money granted by the government to achieve a specific goal that is beneficial to society

The Great Society

GUIDING QUESTION *How does Great Society legislation influence current government programs and philosophies?*

After his election, Johnson began working with Congress to create the "Great Society" he had promised during his campaign. His goals reflected the times. The civil rights movement had brought racial inequalities to the forefront, and the strong economy encouraged people to believe that poverty could be reduced. Johnson noted the Great Society's goals during a speech in May 1964, aiming not to **confine** government efforts but to form a society "where the city of man serves not only the needs of the body and the demands of commerce but the desire for beauty and the hunger for community."

Johnson's ambitious vision encompassed more than 60 programs initiated between 1965 and 1968, including Medicare and Medicaid. Medicare had strong support because it was offered to all senior citizens, about half of whom lacked health insurance. Medicare's twin program, Medicaid, financed health care for welfare recipients living below the poverty line. These programs reflected New Deal ideals by entitling categories of Americans to benefits.

Great Society programs also strongly supported education. The Elementary and Secondary Education Act of 1965 granted millions of dollars to public and private schools. Education efforts also extended to preschoolers through Project Head Start, for disadvantaged children who had "never looked at a picture book or scribbled with a crayon."

Johnson also urged Congress to act on several pieces of legislation addressing urban issues. One created a new cabinet agency, the Department of Housing and Urban Development, in 1965. Its first secretary, Robert Weaver, was the first African American to serve in the cabinet. A broad-based program informally called "Model Cities" authorized federal **subsidies** to many cities to improve transportation, health care, housing, and policing.

One notable Great Society measure changed the composition of the American population: the Immigration Act of 1965. This act ended the system established in the 1920s that gave preference to northern European immigrants. The new law opened wider the door of the United States to immigrants from all parts of Europe, Asia, and Africa.

The Great Society's Legacy

Great Society programs touched nearly every aspect of American life and improved many lives. In the years since Johnson left office, however, debate has continued over whether the Great Society was truly a success. In many ways, the impact of the Great Society was limited. Some programs did not work as well as hoped. In many cases, the programs grew so quickly they became unmanageable and difficult to evaluate.

Cities, states, and groups eligible for aid began to expect immediate and life-changing benefits. Other Americans opposed the massive growth of federal programs. When Johnson attempted to fund both his grand domestic agenda and the increasingly costly war in Vietnam, the Great Society eventually suffered. Some Great Society initiatives have survived, however, including Medicare and Medicaid, the Department of Transportation, the Department of Housing and Urban Development (HUD), and Project Head Start. Overall, the programs provided some important benefits to poor communities and gave political and administrative experience to minority groups.

The Great Society's attempt to create more economic opportunity did have some unintended consequences. The cost of Medicare began to expand rapidly, in part because of the rising costs of medical care and new medical technology, and in part because of the tendency of Congress to add more and more items to what Medicare covered. In addition, as baby boomers aged, the number of people signing up for Medicare became a greater proportion of the population. Because Medicare is an entitlement program, the government is obligated to make payments, and this has contributed to deficit spending and the rise in the national debt.

Critics of the Great Society have also argued that far from ending poverty, the various programs of the War on Poverty and Great Society actually fostered a culture of dependency and a new permanent "underclass." According to this argument, people in the underclass were trapped, unable to improve their economic circumstances, because they had become too reliant on government programs.

✓ READING PROGRESS CHECK

Making Connections What government programs carry on the ideals of the Great Society?

Analyzing PRIMARY SOURCES

The Challenge of Poverty

❝The walls of the ghettos are not going to topple overnight, nor is it possible to wipe out the heritage of generations of social, economic and educational deprivation by the stroke of a Presidential pen. The war against poverty is a long-range undertaking. It requires staying power as well as a sense of urgency.❞

—*New York Times* editorial, January 1, 1967

DBQ *USING CONTEXT CLUES*

Based on its use in the passage above, what is the meaning of deprivation? LAFS.1112.RH.2.4

LESSON 3 REVIEW

Reviewing Vocabulary

1. *Explaining* Why is the ability to build a consensus an important skill for a leader? LAFS.1112.RH.2.4

Using Your Notes

2. *Categorizing* Use the notes you completed during the lesson to group the programs Johnson created into categories. LAFS.1112.RH.3.7, SS.912.A.7.13

Answering the Guiding Questions

3. *Analyzing* How did President Johnson's experience in Congress help him get legislation passed? LAFS.1112.WHST.3.9, SS.912.A.7.4

4. *Synthesizing* How does Great Society legislation influence current government programs and philosophies? LAFS.1112.WHST.3.9, SS.912.A.7.4

Writing Activity

5. **INFORMATIVE/EXPLANATORY** What connections can you make between the ideals of the New Deal and those of the Great Society? Write a short essay in which you analyze efforts to extend New Deal goals through the Great Society, and evaluate the successes and failures of those efforts. LAFS.1112.WHST.1.2, LAFS.1112.WHST.4.10, SS.912.A.7.4

STUDY GUIDE

THE NEW FRONTIER
LESSON 1

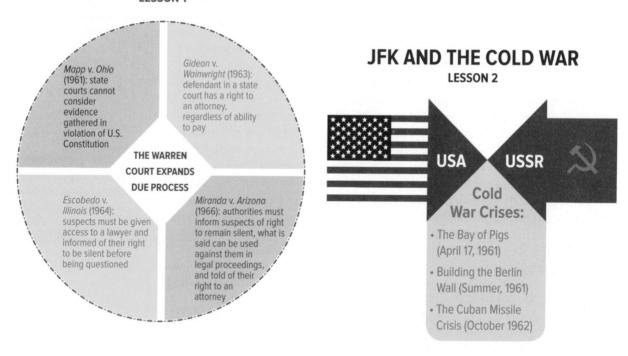

THE WARREN COURT EXPANDS DUE PROCESS

Mapp v. *Ohio* (1961): state courts cannot consider evidence gathered in violation of U.S. Constitution

Gideon v. *Wainwright* (1963): defendant in a state court has a right to an attorney, regardless of ability to pay

Escobedo v. *Illinois* (1964): suspects must be given access to a lawyer and informed of their right to be silent before being questioned

Miranda v. *Arizona* (1966): authorities must inform suspects of right to remain silent, what is said can be used against them in legal proceedings, and told of their right to an attorney

JFK AND THE COLD WAR
LESSON 2

USA   **USSR**

Cold War Crises:

- The Bay of Pigs (April 17, 1961)
- Building the Berlin Wall (Summer, 1961)
- The Cuban Missile Crisis (October 1962)

THE GREAT SOCIETY
LESSON 3

HEALTH AND WELFARE	**Medicare:** a health insurance program for senior citizens
	Medicaid: health and medical assistance for low-income families
	Child Nutrition Act: school breakfast program and expanded school lunch and milk programs
EDUCATION	**Elementary and Secondary Education Act:** aid to students and adult education funding
	Higher Education Act: college tuition scholarships, student loans, work-study programs
	Project Head Start: preschool program for disadvantaged children
WAR ON POVERTY	**Office of Economic Opportunity:** improved life in inner cities with efforts such as Job Corps
	Housing and Urban Development Act: new housing subsidy and eased access to federal and public housing programs
	Demonstration Cities and Metropolitan Development Act: revitalized urban areas
CONSUMER AND ENVIRONMENTAL PROTECTION	**Clean Air Act & Water Quality Act:** created standards and goals for water/air quality improvements
	Highway Safety Act: improved federal, state, and local coordination of driver- and road-related issues and created training for emergency medical technicians
	Fair Packaging and Labeling Act: required all consumer products to have accurate labeling

Directions: On a separate sheet of paper, answer the questions below. Make sure you read carefully and answer all parts to the question.

Lesson Review

Lesson 1

1 *Analyzing* Even though Democrats controlled Congress, why was President Kennedy unable to pass all of the New Frontier programs he had proposed? SS.912.A.7.4

2 *Describing* What was the conflict between President Kennedy and the steel companies? SS.912.A.7.4

3 *Explaining* Explain the imbalance that existed in electoral districts prior to redrawing districts in 1964. What phrase did the Supreme Court use in the case of *Reynolds* v. *Sims* to explain why courts could force states to redraw voting districts? SS.912.A.7.8

Lesson 2

4 *Analyzing* How did the arms race contribute to events in Cuba and intensify the Cold War? SS.912.A.6.13, SS.912.A.7.4, SS.912.A.7.11

5 *Making Connections* What was the purpose of the Berlin Wall, and what did it come to symbolize? SS.912.A.6.13, SS.912.A.7.4

6 *Identifying* What events and decisions propelled the end of Khrushchev's leadership in the Soviet Union? SS.912.A.6.13, SS.912.A.7.4

7 *Evaluating* Describe how Cold War tensions were intensified by the space race. SS.912.A.6.13, SS.912.A.7.4

Lesson 3

8 *Assessing* How did the creation of Medicare reflect the ideals and goals of President Johnson's Great Society? SS.912.A.7.4, SS.912.A.7.13

9 *Analyzing Issues* Why did President Johnson try to help Americans living in poverty? SS.912.A.7.4, SS.912.A.7.13

10 *Specifying* How did the Immigration Act of 1965 begin to change the demographic characteristics of the American population? SS.912.A.7.4, SS.912.A.7.13

11 *Explaining* Why did programs of the Great Society harken back to Roosevelt's New Deal and Truman's Fair Deal? SS.912.A.7.4, SS.912.A.7.13

Exploring the Essential Questions

12 *Preparing Oral Presentations* Write a two-minute speech answering the question "Can government fix society's problems?" Take a clear position for or against the idea, and cite evidence from the chapter to support your position. LAFS.1112.RH.1.1, LAFS.1112.SL.2.4, LAFS.1112.SL.2.6, LAFS.1112.WHST.1.1, LAFS.1112.WHST.2.4, LAFS.1112.WHST.3.9, SS.912.A.7.4, SS.912.A.7.13

Critical Thinking

13 *Evaluating* Explain the concept of "due process" in the Fourteenth Amendment. How did the Warren Court interpret this concept in the 1960s? Describe how the Court's decisions marked a shift from a strict construction of the Constitution and brought about constitutional change. SS.912.A.7.8

14 *Analyzing* What programs of the War on Poverty and the Great Society were intended to increase economic opportunities for Americans? What were the unintended consequences of those programs? SS.912.A.7.4, SS.912.A.7.13

21st Century Skills

15 *Using a Problem Solving Process* Imagine you work for President Kennedy. The president has explained that the Soviets seem to be far ahead in space technology. Their success in putting the first satellite, and then the first man into orbit seems to be showing the world that communism is a better system than free enterprise and democracy. The president asks for ideas on how the United States can beat the Soviet Union in the space race. Prepare a briefing paper for the president recommending the United States begin work to put the first man on the moon. In the paper, apply a problem-solving process that walks the president through your thinking and explains why you are recommending this plan. After you have written your first draft, make sure that you revise your briefing to clarify your arguments for the president. LAFS.1112.RH.3.7, LAFS.1112.RH.3.9, LAFS.1112.WHST.1.1, LAFS.1112.WHST.2.4, LAFS.1112.WHST.2.5, LAFS.1112.WHST.4.10, SS.912.A.7.4

Need Extra Help?

If You've Missed Question	1	2	3	4	5	6	7	8	9	10	11	12	13	14	15
Go to Lesson	1	1	1	2	2	2	2	3	3	3	3	3	1	3	2

16 *Explaining Continuity and Change* Explain the reasons why the United States helped organize and support the Bay of Pigs invasion. Describe the outcome of the invasion. SS.912.A.7.4, SS.912.A.7.11

17 *Creating Graphs* Conduct research at the library or online. Create a new graph from 1948 to the present showing which years the United States was in recession and which presidents were in power for which years on the graph. Then add a line showing the poverty rate from 1948 to the present. What conclusions can you draw from your graph? LAFS.1112.WHST.3.7, MAFS.912.S-IC.2, MAFS.912.S-ID.1, MAFS.K12.MP.3.1, MAFS.K12.MP.5.1, MAFS.K12.MP.6.1, SS.912.A.7.4

DBQ Analyzing Primary Sources

Read the excerpt below from President Kennedy's Inaugural Address, and then answer the questions that follow.

PRIMARY SOURCE

"Let every nation know, whether it wishes us well or ill, that we shall pay any price, bear any burden, meet any hardship, support any friend, oppose any foe, to assure the survival and the success of liberty . . .

In the long history of the world, only a few generations have been granted the role of defending freedom in its hour of maximum danger. I do not shrink from this responsibility—I welcome it. I do not believe that any of us would exchange places with any other people or any other generation. The energy, the faith, the devotion which we bring to this endeavor will light our country and all who serve it. And the glow from that fire can truly light the world.

And so, my fellow Americans, ask not what your country can do for you; ask what you can do for your country."

—John F. Kennedy, Inaugural Address, January 20, 1961

18 *Analyzing Speeches* What concerns is President Kennedy responding to in this speech? What is endangered? And what is he committing the nation to do? In addition to American citizens, what audience Kennedy is addressing? LAFS.1112.RH.1.1, LAFS.1112.RH.1.2, LAFS.1112.RH.2.4, LAFS.1112.RH.3.7, LAFS.1112.RH.3.8, LAFS.1112.RH.4.10, LAFS.1112.SL.1.3, SS.912.A.7.4

19 *Evaluating Language* What words and phrases does Kennedy use to evoke patriotism and encourage Americans to support his position? Given the language used, how would you interpret the validity of the president's comment we shall "pay any price?" LAFS.1112.RH.1.1, LAFS.1112.RH.1.3, LAFS.1112.RH.3.8, LAFS.1112.RH.3.9, LAFS.1112.RH.4.10, LAFS.1112.SL.1.3, SS.912.A.7.4

Analyzing Visuals

Use the cartoon to answer the following questions.

HERBLOCK'S CARTOON

"Kindly Move Over A Little, Gentlemen"

20 *Analyzing Visuals* What does the boy represent, and why do you think the cartoonist made him so small? LAFS.1112.RH.2.5, SS.912.A.1.4, SS.912.A.7.4, SS.912.H.1.5

21 *Making Inferences* According to the cartoon, what is Johnson trying to do? SS.912.A.1.4, SS.912.A.7.4, SS.912.H.1.5

Extended Response Questions

22 *Explaining* Imagine you are a reporter shortly after the Cuban Missile crisis has ended. Write an article describing Soviet actions in Cuba and President Kennedy's role in resolving the crisis. Research some articles from the time to help you write in a style and tone appropriate to the historical period, and revise as necessary. LAFS.1112.SL.1.3, LAFS.1112.WHST.1.2, LAFS.1112.WHST.2.4, LAFS.1112.WHST.2.5, LAFS.1112.WHST.3.7, LAFS.1112.WHST.4.10, SS.912.A.7.4, SS.912.A.7.11

A 1965 Herblock Cartoon, copyright by The Herb Block Foundation

Need Extra Help?

If You've Missed Question	**16**	**17**	**18**	**19**	**20**	**21**	**22**
Go to Lesson	2	2, 3	2	2	3	3	2

netw✦rks
There's More Online!

◀ Rosa Parks's refusal to give up her seat on a Montgomery, Alabama, bus was the spark that launched the Montgomery bus boycott in 1955.

FROM 1954 TO 1968

The Civil Rights Movement

THE STORY MATTERS ...

The civil rights movement gained momentum rapidly after World War II. Supreme Court rulings, massive protests by civil rights groups, and new federal legislation all combined to make racial segregation illegal in the United States.

ESSENTIAL QUESTIONS

- Why do you think the civil rights movement made gains in postwar America?
- What motivates a society to make changes?

LESSON 1
The Movement Begins

LESSON 2
Challenging Segregation

LESSON 3
New Civil Rights Issues

©Bettmann/Corbis

Place & Time: United States 1954–1968

Rosa Parks made a decision in December 1955 that ignited a movement to end segregation and achieve civil liberties for all Americans. A young pastor by the name of Martin Luther King, Jr., spearheaded efforts to reach these goals. By the mid-1960s, civil rights activists had gained two important pieces of legislation: the Civil Rights Act of 1964 and the Voting Rights Act of 1965.

Step Into the Place

Read the quotes and look at the information presented on the map.

 Analyzing Historical Documents Daisy Bates and Orval Faubus both describe the situation in Little Rock, Arkansas, in 1957. How do the two quotes reflect different perspectives?

PRIMARY SOURCE

❝Suddenly I realized that this calm I had so taken for granted was only the calm before the storm, that this was war, and that as State President of the National Association for the Advancement of Colored People I was in the front-line trenches. Was I ready for war? . . . Who was I really and what did I stand for? . . . [M]y mind ranged over these questions and over the whole course of my life. Toward dawn I knew I had found the answer. I was ready. I drifted off into the sleep of a mind no longer torn by doubt or indecision.❞

—Daisy Bates, from *The Long Shadow of Little Rock: A Memoir*, 1962

PRIMARY SOURCE

❝Malice, envy, hate is deplorable, in any place or in any circumstances, but as President Eisenhower has said himself, you can't change the hearts of people by law. Now, in view of the progress that we have made, all I ask for in this situation, and all I've ever asked for, is some time for the situation to change for it to become acceptable, so that there would not be disorder and violence. . . . So, why should we be so impatient as to want to force it, because force begets force, hate begets hate, malice begets malice. But, if time was given for an adjustment of the attitudes and the feelings of people, then it can be peacefully accomplished, which would be better for all concerned.❞

—Orval Faubus, from an interview with news commentator Mike Wallace, September 15, 1957

left page (t)Library of Congress, Prints & Photographs Division [LC-USZ62-115050]; (c)©Bettmann/Corbis; (b)detail/White House Collection/The White House Historical Association; **right page** (t)©Casey Mison/Bettmann/Corbis; (b)©Flip Schulke/Historical/Corbis; (b)©SuperStock/SuperStock; (b)Harul/White House

Step Into the Time

MAKING CONNECTIONS
Research an individual featured on the time line. Write a paragraph describing their role in the civil rights movement.

U.S. PRESIDENTS

Eisenhower 1953–1961

UNITED STATES

WORLD

1956

1959

May 17, 1954 *Brown v. Board of Education* ruling is issued

December 1955 Montgomery, Alabama, bus boycott begins

September 1957 Eisenhower sends federal troops to ensure integration of a Little Rock high school

1960 Greensl sit-in begins

February 1959 European Court of Human Rights holds first session in Strasbourg, France

1960 Nigeria gains independence

NEXT GENERATION SUNSHINE STATE STANDARDS
Students will understand the following benchmarks from the Florida NGSSS

LAFS.1112.RH.3.7: Integrate and evaluate multiple sources of information presented in diverse formats and media (e.g., visually, quantitatively, as well as in words) in order to address a question or solve a problem.

LAFS.1112.RH.3.9: Integrate information from diverse sources, both primary and secondary, into a coherent understanding of an idea or event, noting discrepancies among sources.

SS.912.A.1.2: Utilize a variety of primary and secondary sources to identify author, historical significance, audience, and authenticity to understand a historical period.

SS.912.A.1.3: Utilize timelines to identify the time sequence of historical data.

SS.912.A.1.4: Analyze how images, symbols, objects, cartoons, graphs, charts, maps, and artwork may be used to interpret the significance of time periods and events from the past.

SS.912.A.7.5: Compare nonviolent and violent approaches utilized by groups (African Americans, women, Native Americans, Hispanics) to achieve civil rights.

SS.912.A.7.6: Assess key figures and organizations in shaping the Civil Rights Movement and Black Power Movement.

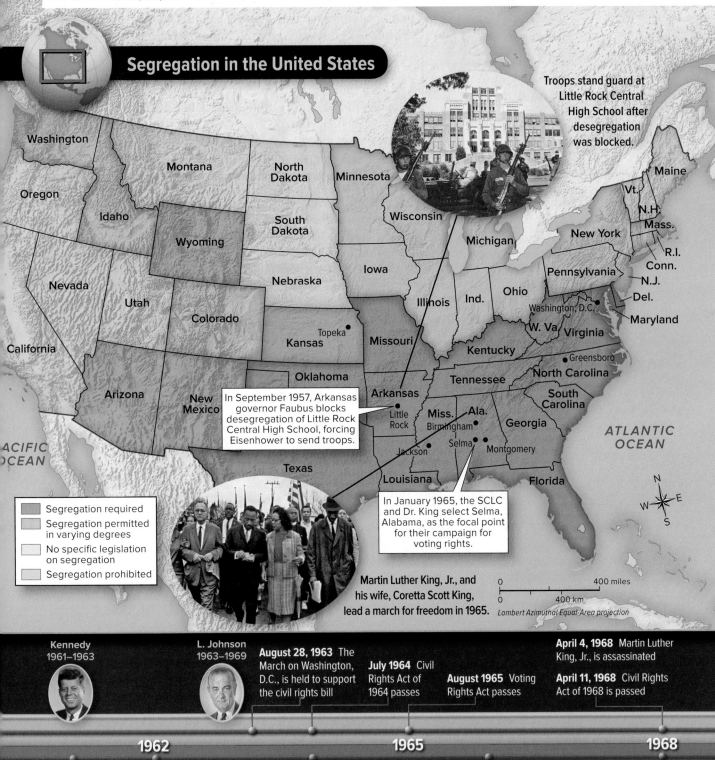

Segregation in the United States

Troops stand guard at Little Rock Central High School after desegregation was blocked.

In September 1957, Arkansas governor Faubus blocks desegregation of Little Rock Central High School, forcing Eisenhower to send troops.

In January 1965, the SCLC and Dr. King select Selma, Alabama, as the focal point for their campaign for voting rights.

Martin Luther King, Jr., and his wife, Coretta Scott King, lead a march for freedom in 1965.

Segregation required
Segregation permitted in varying degrees
No specific legislation on segregation
Segregation prohibited

0   400 miles
0   400 km
Lambert Azimuthal Equal-Area projection

Kennedy 1961–1963

L. Johnson 1963–1969

August 28, 1963 The March on Washington, D.C., is held to support the civil rights bill

July 1964 Civil Rights Act of 1964 passes

August 1965 Voting Rights Act passes

April 4, 1968 Martin Luther King, Jr., is assassinated

April 11, 1968 Civil Rights Act of 1968 is passed

1962

1965

1968

March 1961 South Africa withdraws from British Commonwealth, adhering to its policy of apartheid

August 1962 Nelson Mandela is arrested in South Africa for stance against apartheid

October 1962 Cuban missile crisis erupts

1964 Tokyo Olympic Games ban South Africa for its apartheid policy

1966 China's Cultural Revolution begins

April 11, 1968 At Mexico Summer Olympics, U.S. sprinters Tommie Smith and John Carlos give black power salute and are suspended from the team

LESSON 1
The Movement Begins

ESSENTIAL QUESTIONS

• Why do you think the civil rights movement made gains in postwar America?
• What motivates a society to make changes?

READING HELPDESK

Academic Vocabulary

• facility

Content Vocabulary

• "separate but equal"
• de facto segregation

TAKING NOTES

Key Ideas and Details

Organizing As you read, complete a graphic organizer similar to the one below by listing the techniques used to challenge segregation. LAFS.1112.RH.3.7, SS.912.A.7.5, SS.912.A.7.6

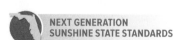

Civil Rights Movement

**NEXT GENERATION
SUNSHINE STATE STANDARDS**

LAFS.1112.RH.2.4: Determine the meaning of words and phrases as they are used in a text, including analyzing how an author uses and refines the meaning of a key term over the course of a text (e.g., how Madison defines faction in Federalist No. 10).

LAFS.1112.RH.3.7: Integrate and evaluate multiple sources of information presented in diverse formats and media (e.g., visually, quantitatively, as well as in words) in order to address a question or solve a problem.

LAFS.1112.SL.2.4: Present information, findings, and supporting evidence, conveying a clear and distinct perspective, such that listeners can follow the line of reasoning, alternative or opposing perspectives are addressed, and the organization, development, substance, and style are appropriate to purpose, audience, and a range of formal and informal tasks.

Continued on page 475

IT MATTERS BECAUSE

After World War II, African Americans and other civil rights supporters challenged segregation in the United States. Their efforts were strongly opposed by Southern segregationists. Eventually, the federal government began to take a firmer stand for civil rights.

The Origins of the Movement

GUIDING QUESTION *What techniques did the civil rights movement use to challenge segregation?*

On December 1, 1955, Rosa Parks left her job as a seamstress in Montgomery, Alabama, and boarded a bus to go home. In 1955, buses in Montgomery reserved seats in the front for whites and seats in the rear for African Americans. Seats in the middle were available to African Americans only if there were few whites on the bus. Parks took a seat just behind the white section, and soon all of the seats on the bus were filled. When the driver noticed a white man standing, he told Parks and three other African Americans in her row to get up so the white man could sit down. When Parks did not move, the driver called the police.

News of Parks's arrest reached the National Association for the Advancement of Colored People (NAACP), which asked Parks whether her case could be used to challenge segregation. Parks replied, "If you think it will mean something to Montgomery and do some good, I'll be happy to go along with it."

Parks's decision would spark a new era in the civil rights movement. The struggle would not be easy. In 1896, the Supreme Court had declared segregation to be constitutional in *Plessy* v. *Ferguson*, which established the **"separate but equal"** doctrine. Laws that segregated African Americans were permitted as long as equal **facilities** were provided. The facilities provided for African Americans, however, were usually of poorer quality than those provided for whites. Areas without laws requiring segregation often had **de facto segregation**—segregation by custom and tradition.

Court Challenges Begin

The civil rights movement had been building for a long time. Since 1909, the NAACP had supported court cases aimed at overturning segregation. Over the years, the NAACP had achieved some victories. In 1935, for example, the Supreme Court ruled in *Norris* v. *Alabama* that exclusion of African Americans from juries violated their rights to equal protection under the law.

New Political Power

African Americans also enjoyed increased political power. Northern politicians increasingly sought their votes and listened to their concerns. During the 1930s, many African Americans benefited from New Deal programs and began supporting the Democratic Party. This gave the party new strength in the North. The northern wing of the party was now able to counter Southern Democrats, who often supported segregation.

The Push for Desegregation

During World War II, African American leaders began to use their political power to help end discrimination in wartime factories. They also increased opportunities for African Americans in the military.

In 1942, James Farmer and George Houser founded the Congress of Racial Equality (CORE) in Chicago. CORE began using sit-ins, a form of protest first popularized by union workers in the 1930s, to desegregate restaurants that refused to serve African Americans. Using the sit-in strategy,

"separate but equal" a doctrine established by the 1896 Supreme Court case *Plessy* v. *Ferguson* that permitted laws segregating African Americans as long as equal facilities were provided

facility something that is built, installed, or established to serve a particular purpose

de facto segregation segregation by custom and tradition

🏛 ANALYZING SUPREME COURT CASES

BROWN v. *BOARD OF EDUCATION* (1954)

Background of the Case

One of the most important Supreme Court cases in American history began in 1952, when the Supreme Court agreed to hear the NAACP's case *Brown* v. *Board of Education of Topeka, Kansas,* and three other cases. They all dealt with the question of whether the principle "separate but equal," established in *Plessy* v. *Ferguson,* was constitutional with regard to public schools.

How the Court Ruled

In a unanimous decision in 1954, the Court ruled in favor of Linda Brown and the other plaintiffs. In doing so, it overruled *Plessy* v. *Ferguson.* It rejected the idea that equivalent but separate schools for African American and white students were constitutional. The Court held that racial segregation in public schools violated the Fourteenth Amendment's equal protection clause. Chief Justice Earl Warren summed up the Court's decision, declaring: "[I]n the field of public education, the doctrine of 'separate but equal' has no place. Separate educational facilities are inherently unequal." The Court's rejection of "separate but equal" was a major victory for the civil rights movement. It led to the overturning of laws requiring segregation in other public places.

The children involved in the *Brown* v. *Board of Education* case are shown in this 1953 photograph. They are, from front to back, Vicki Henderson, Donald Henderson, Linda Brown (of the case title), James Emanuel, Nancy Todd, and Katherine Carper. Together, their cases led to the Supreme Court decision that public schools could not be segregated on the basis of race.

DBQ Analyzing Historical Documents

❶ *Explaining* Why did the Supreme Court find in favor of Linda Brown? LAFS.1112.WHST.3.9, SS.912.A.1.6, SS.912.A.7.8

❷ *Examining* Why was the ruling in *Brown* v. *Board of Education* so important? LAFS.1112.WHST.3.9, SS.912.A.1.6, SS.912.A.7.8

Carl Iwasaki/Time Life Pictures/Getty Images

Library of Congress, Prints & Photographs Division [LC-US262-111163]

Florida CONNECTION

Tallahassee Bus Boycott

On May 26, 1956, Wilhelmina Jakes Street and Carrie Patterson, students at Florida A&M University, boarded a bus in Tallahassee, Florida. They took two open seats next to a white passenger. Even though the white woman did not complain, the bus driver asked the African American women to move to the back of the bus. When they refused, the driver called the police. They were arrested and charged with "inciting a riot." Their arrest led to a boycott of the bus system. Led by Reverend C. K. Steele, the boycott ended the segregation of public transit in Tallahassee and advanced the civil rights movement in Florida.
SS.912.A.7.7

Dr. Martin Luther King, Jr., used his position as a minister to preach his message of nonviolent resistance.

▶ **CRITICAL THINKING**
Drawing Conclusions Why do you think Dr. King was effective in getting his message across?
SS.912.A.7.6

members of CORE went to segregated restaurants. They sat down and refused to leave. The sit-ins were intended to shame managers into integrating their restaurants. CORE successfully integrated many public facilities in Northern cities, including Chicago, Detroit, Denver, and Syracuse.

Brown v. Board of Education

After World War II, the NAACP continued to challenge segregation in the courts. From 1939 to 1961, the NAACP's chief counsel and director of its Legal Defense and Educational Fund was African American attorney Thurgood Marshall. After the war, Marshall focused his efforts on ending segregation in public schools.

In 1954, the Supreme Court decided to combine several cases and issue a general ruling on segregation in schools. One of the cases involved a young African American girl named Linda Brown, who was denied admission to her neighborhood school in Topeka, Kansas, because of her race. She was told to attend an all-black school across town. With the help of the NAACP, her parents sued the Topeka school board. On May 17, 1954, the Supreme Court ruled unanimously in *Brown* v. *Board of Education of Topeka, Kansas,* that segregation in public schools was unconstitutional.

Southern Resistance

The *Brown* decision marked a dramatic reversal of the precedent established in the *Plessy* v. *Ferguson* case in 1896. *Brown* v. *Board of Education* applied only to public schools, but the ruling threatened the entire system of segregation. Although it convinced many African Americans that the time had come to challenge segregation, it also angered many white Southerners. Some became even more determined to defend segregation, regardless of what the Supreme Court ruled.

Although some school districts in the Upper South integrated their schools, anger and opposition was a far more common reaction. Senator Harry F. Byrd of Virginia called on Southerners to adopt "massive resistance" against the ruling. Across the South, hundreds of thousands of white Americans joined citizens' councils to pressure their local governments and school boards into defying the Supreme Court. Many states adopted pupil assignment laws, which established elaborate requirements other than race that schools could use to prevent African Americans from attending white schools.

The Supreme Court inadvertently encouraged white resistance when it followed up its decision in *Brown* v. *Board of Education* a year later. The Court ordered school districts to proceed "with all deliberate speed" to end school segregation. The wording was vague enough that many districts were able to keep their schools segregated for many more years.

Massive resistance also appeared in Congress. In 1956, a group of 101 Southern members of Congress signed the "Southern Manifesto." It denounced the Supreme Court's ruling as "a clear abuse of judicial power" and pledged to use "all lawful means" to reverse the decision. Not until 1969 did the Supreme Court order all school systems to desegregate "at once" and operate integrated schools "now and hereafter."

✔ **READING PROGRESS CHECK**

Examining What two types of segregation were practiced in the South?

The Civil Rights Movement Begins

GUIDING QUESTION *Why was the Montgomery bus boycott successful?*

In the midst of the uproar over the *Brown* v. *Board of Education* case, Rosa Parks made her decision to challenge segregation of public transportation. Jo Ann Robinson, head of a local group called the Women's Political Council, called on African Americans to boycott Montgomery's buses on the day Rosa Parks appeared in court. The boycott marked the start of a new era of the civil rights movement among African Americans.

The Montgomery Bus Boycott

The Montgomery bus boycott had a successful outcome. Several African American leaders formed the Montgomery Improvement Association to run the boycott and to negotiate with city leaders. They elected a 26-year-old pastor named Martin Luther King, Jr., to lead them.

Dr. King encouraged the people to continue their protest, but cautioned that the protest had to be peaceful:

PRIMARY SOURCE

❝Now let us say that we are not advocating violence. . . . The only weapon that we have in our hands this evening is the weapon of protest. . . . If we were incarcerated behind the iron curtains of a communistic nation—we couldn't do this. If we were trapped in the dungeon of a totalitarian regime—we couldn't do this. But the great glory of American democracy is the right to protest for right.❞

—quoted in *Parting the Waters: America in the King Years*, 1989

King had earned a Ph.D. in theology from Boston University. He believed that the only moral way to end segregation and racism was through nonviolent passive resistance. African Americans, he urged, must say to racists, "[W]e will soon wear you down by our capacity to suffer. And in winning our freedom we will so appeal to your heart and conscience that we will win you in the process."

King's powerful words stirred African Americans in Montgomery to continue their boycott for over a year. In November 1956, the Supreme Court declared Alabama's laws requiring segregation on buses unconstitutional. After the Court's ruling, the Montgomery boycott was ended. Many other cities in the South, however, successfully resisted integrating their public transportation systems for years.

African American Churches

Martin Luther King, Jr., was not the only local minister involved in the bus boycott. Many of the other leaders were African American ministers. African American churches served as forums for protests and planning meetings, and mobilized volunteers.

The Montgomery bus boycott had demonstrated that nonviolent protest could be successful. Dr. King, Rev. Fred Shuttlesworth of Birmingham, Alabama, and other African American ministers and civil rights activists established the Southern Christian Leadership Conference (SCLC) in 1957. The SCLC set out to eliminate segregation and to encourage African Americans to register to vote. Dr. King served as the SCLC's first president. The organization challenged segregation at voting booths and in public transportation, housing, and accommodations.

✔ READING PROGRESS CHECK

Drawing Conclusions How did the bus boycott create a mass movement for change?

African Americans walk to work during the third month of the Montgomery bus boycott.

▶ CRITICAL THINKING
Determining Cause and Effect
Consider the number of people you see walking in this photograph. Why do you think the bus boycott was effective? SS.912.A.1.4, SS.912.A.7.7

NEXT GENERATION
SUNSHINE STATE STANDARDS

Continued from page 472
LAFS.1112.WHST.1.1: Write arguments focused on discipline-specific content.
LAFS.1112.WHST.3.9: Draw evidence from informational texts to support analysis, reflection, and research.
LAFS.1112.WHST.4.10: Write routinely over extended time frames (time for reflection and revision) and shorter time frames (a single sitting or a day or two) for a range of discipline-specific tasks, purposes, and audiences.
SS.912.A.1.2: Utilize a variety of primary and secondary sources to identify author, historical significance, audience, and authenticity to understand a historical period.
SS.912.A.1.4: Analyze how images, symbols, objects, cartoons, graphs, charts, maps, and artwork may be used to interpret the significance of time periods and events from the past.
SS.912.A.1.6: Use case studies to explore social, political, legal, and economic relationships in history.
SS.912.A.7.4: Evaluate the success of 1960s era presidents' foreign and domestic policies.
SS.912.A.7.5: Compare nonviolent and violent approaches utilized by groups (African Americans, women, Native Americans, Hispanics) to achieve civil rights.
SS.912.A.7.6: Assess key figures and organizations in shaping the Civil Rights Movement and Black Power Movement.
SS.912.A.7.7: Assess the building of coalitions between African Americans, whites, and other groups in achieving integration and equal rights.
SS.912.A.7.8: Analyze significant Supreme Court decisions relating to integration, busing, affirmative action, the rights of the accused, and reproductive rights.
SS.912.A.7.17: Examine key events and key people in Florida history as they relate to United States history.

The Heirs to the Estate of Martin Luther King Jr., c/o Writers House as agent for the proprietor New York, NY. Copyright 1963 Dr. Martin Luther King Jr. c/o Writers House as agent for the proprietor New York, NY. Copyright renewed 1991 Coretta Scott King; (b) Martin Luther King, Jr., The Papers of Martin Luther King, Jr., Volume IV: Symbol of the Movement, January 1957–December 1958. (Berkeley, University of California Press, 2000) Pg 341. Reprinted by arrangement with The Heirs to the Estate of Martin Luther King Jr., c/o Writers House as agent for the proprietor New York, NY. Copyright 1963 Dr. Martin Luther King Jr. copyright renewed 1991 Coretta Scott King.

Eisenhower Responds

GUIDING QUESTION *How did President Eisenhower respond to the civil rights movement?*

President Eisenhower sympathized with the civil rights movement, yet he feared the possible effect of a court ruling overturning segregation. Following the precedent set by President Truman, he ordered navy shipyards and veterans' hospitals to desegregate. At the same time, Eisenhower disagreed with using protests and court rulings. He believed segregation and racism would end gradually, as values changed. With the nation in the midst of the Cold War, he worried that challenging white Southerners might divide the nation. Publicly, he refused to endorse the *Brown* v. *Board of Education* decision, remarking, "I don't believe you can change the hearts of men with laws or decisions." Regardless, Eisenhower knew he had to uphold the authority of the federal government. As a result, he became the first president since Reconstruction to send troops into the South to protect the rights of African Americans.

Crisis in Little Rock

In September 1957, the school board in Little Rock, Arkansas, was under a federal court order requiring that nine African American students be admitted to Central High. The governor of Arkansas, Orval Faubus, was determined to win reelection. He began to campaign as a defender of

white supremacy. He ordered troops from the Arkansas National Guard to prevent the nine students from entering the school. As the National Guard troops surrounded the school, an angry white mob gathered to intimidate students.

Faubus had used the armed forces of a state to oppose the federal government—the first such challenge to the Constitution since the Civil War. Eisenhower knew that he could not allow Faubus to defy the federal government. After a conference between Eisenhower and Faubus proved fruitless, the district court ordered the governor to remove the troops. Instead of ending the crisis, however, Faubus simply left the school to the mob. After the African American students entered the building, angry whites beat at least two African American reporters and broke many windows.

The violence finally convinced President Eisenhower that he had to act. Federal authority had to be upheld. He immediately ordered the U.S. Army to send troops to Little Rock and federalized the Arkansas National Guard. By nightfall, more than 1,000 soldiers of the 101st Airborne Division had arrived. By 5:00 A.M., the troops had encircled the school, bayonets ready. A few hours later, the nine African American students arrived in an army station wagon and walked into the high school. Federal authority had been upheld, but the troops had to stay in Little Rock for the rest of the school year.

Arkansas governor Orval Faubus is shown holding up a paper arguing that the federal government was abusing its power by forcibly integrating Central High.

▶ CRITICAL THINKING
Identifying Central Ideas Why did President Eisenhower send troops to Little Rock? SS.912.A.1.4, SS.912.A.7.6

New Civil Rights Legislation

In the same year that the Little Rock crisis began, Congress passed the first civil rights law since Reconstruction. The Civil Rights Act of 1957 was intended to protect the right of African Americans to vote. Eisenhower believed firmly in the right to vote, and he viewed it as his responsibility to protect voting rights. He also knew that if he sent a civil rights bill to Congress, conservative Southern Democrats would try to block the

©Bettmann/Corbis

In 1957 Elizabeth Eckford (left center) was one of the "Little Rock Nine," those African American students determined to integrate Central High School in Little Rock.

▶ CRITICAL THINKING
Making Inferences Why do you think the crowd is shouting at Elizabeth Eckford? SS.912.A.1.4, SS.912.A.7.6

legislation. In 1956, he did send the bill to Congress, hoping not only to split the Democratic Party but also to convince more African Americans to vote Republican.

Several Southern senators did try to stop the Civil Rights Act of 1957. Senate majority leader Democrat Lyndon Johnson, however, put together a compromise that enabled the act to pass. Although its final form was much weaker than originally intended, the act still brought the power of the federal government into the civil rights debate. It created a Civil Rights Division within the Department of Justice and gave it the authority to seek court injunctions against anyone interfering with the right to vote. It also created the United States Commission on Civil Rights to investigate any denial of voting rights. After the bill passed, the SCLC announced a campaign to register 2 million new African American voters.

✓ READING PROGRESS CHECK

Explaining Why did Eisenhower intervene in the Little Rock controversy?

Florida CONNECTION

Harry T. Moore (1905–1951)

Harry T. Moore has been called the civil rights movement's first martyr. Moore began his career as a teacher in Brevard County, Florida. In 1933 he joined the NAACP and later established a local chapter. His civil rights activism ultimately cost him his job in 1946. Moore then devoted himself full time to the NAACP. In the role of executive secretary, he helped increase the membership of the Florida NAACP to some 10,000. On the evening of December 25, 1951, a bomb placed under his home exploded. He and his wife, Harriette, were killed by the blast. Their murderers were never conclusively identified or punished. SS.912.A.7.17

LESSON 1 REVIEW

Reviewing Vocabulary
1. *Explaining* Why was the struggle for civil rights more difficult because of the "separate but equal" doctrine established in the *Plessy* v. *Ferguson* case? LAFS.1112.RH.2.4, SS.912.A.7.8

Using Your Notes
2. *Explaining* Use the notes you completed during the lesson to write a paragraph explaining the different tactics used during civil rights protests and why they were successful. LAFS.1112.RH.3.7, SS.912.A.7.5

Answering the Guiding Questions
3. *Interpreting* What techniques did the civil rights movement use to challenge segregation? LAFS.1112.WHST.3.9, SS.912.A.7.5

4. *Analyzing* Why was the Montgomery bus boycott successful? LAFS.1112.WHST.3.9, SS.912.A.7.7

5. *Summarizing* How did President Eisenhower respond to the civil rights movement? LAFS.1112.WHST.3.9, SS.912.A.7.4

Writing Activity
6. ARGUMENT Assume the role of an African American soldier returning from World War II. Write a letter to the editor of a newspaper describing your expectations of civil rights and why you should have those rights. LAFS.1112.WHST.1.1, LAFS.1112.WHST.4.10

©Bettmann/Corbis

LAFS.1112.RH.1.1, LAFS.1112.RH.1.2, LAFS.1112.RH.1.3, LAFS.1112.RH.2.5, LAFS.1112.SL.1.3, SS.912.A.7.5, SS.912.A.7.6

The Civil Rights Movement

Although major figures of the civil rights movement such as Martin Luther King, Jr., are widely remembered today, the movement drew its strength from the dedication of grassroots supporters. In rural and urban areas across the South, ordinary individuals advanced the movement through their participation in marches, boycotts, and voter registration drives. Those who dared to make a stand against discrimination risked being fired from their job, evicted from their home, and becoming the target of physical violence.

VOCABULARY

plantation
an agricultural estate worked by laborers

decent
agreeing with standards of proper behavior, good taste, or morality

testifying
making a statement based on personal knowledge or belief

canvassers
a person who asks for votes, contributions, or support to determine public opinion

adjoining
to sit next to or in contact with

incurable
unable to cure

PUBLIC TESTIMONY, 1964

"[M]y husband came, and said the **plantation** owner was raising Cain because I had tried to register and before he quit talking the plantation owner came, and said, 'Fannie Lou, do you know—did Pap tell you what I said?' And I said, 'Yes sir.' He said, 'I mean that . . . If you don't go down and withdraw . . . well— you might have to go because we are not ready for that.' . . .

And I addressed him and told him and said, 'I didn't try to register for you. I tried to register for myself.'

I had to leave that same night.

On the 10th of September, 1962, 16 bullets were fired into the home of Mr. and Mrs. Robert Tucker for me. That same night two girls were shot in Ruleville, Mississippi. Also Mr. Joe McDonald's house was shot in. And in June, the 9th, 1963, I had attended a voter registration workshop, was returning back to Mississippi. . . . I stepped off the bus . . . and somebody screamed . . . 'Get that one there,' and when I went to get in the car, when the man told me I was under arrest, he kicked me.

I was carried to the county jail. . . . [The patrolmen] left my cell and it wasn't too long before they came back. He said, 'You are from Ruleville all right,' and he used a curse word, he said 'We are going to beat you until you wish you were dead.'

. . . All of this on account we want to register, to become first-class citizens, and if the freedom Democratic Party is not seated now, I question America, is this America, the land of the free and the home of the brave where we have to sleep with our telephones off the hooks because our lives be threatened daily because we want to live as **decent** human beings, in America?"

—Fannie Lou Hamer **testifying** before the Credentials Committee of the Democratic National Convention, August 22, 1964

STRATEGY MEMO, APRIL 1960

"The choice of the non-violent method, 'the sit-in,' symbolizes both judgment and promise. It is a judgment upon middle-class conventional, half-way efforts to deal with radical social evil. It is specifically a judgment upon contemporary civil rights attempts. As one high school student from Chattanooga exclaimed, 'We started because we were tired of waiting for you to act. . . .'"

—James M. Lawson, Jr., "From a Lunch-Counter Stool", April 1960, Student Nonviolent Coordinating Committee Papers

Text: ((l and r) Republished with permission of Greenwood Publishing Group, Inc. from Documentary History of the Modern Civil Rights Movement by Peter B. Levy, © 1992 by Peter B. Levy; permission conveyed through Copyright Clearance Center, Inc.

"All during the years, while the NAACP conducted a boycott of the downtown stores in Jackson, I had been one of [John] Salter's most faithful **canvassers** and church speakers. During the last week of school, he told me that sit-in demonstrations were about to start in Jackson and that he wanted me to be the spokesman for a team that would sit-in at Woolworth's lunch counter.

. . . Seconds before 11:15 we were occupying three seats at the previously segregated Woolworth's lunch counter. In the beginning the waitresses seemed to ignore us, as if they really didn't know what was going on. Our waitress walked past us a couple of times before she noticed we had started to write our own orders down and realized we wanted service. She asked us what we wanted. We began to read to her from our order slips. She told us that we would be served at the back counter, which was for Negroes.

'We would like to be served here,' I said.

The waitress started to repeat what she had said, then stopped in the middle of the sentence. She turned the lights out behind the counter, and she and the other waitresses almost ran to the back of the store, deserting all their white customers.

I guess they thought that violence would start immediately after the whites at the counter realized what was going on. . . .

At noon, students from a nearby white high school started pouring in to Woolworth's. When they first saw us they were sort of surprised. . . . [T]he white students started chanting all kinds of anti-Negro slogans. We were called a little bit of everything. . . .

A man rushed forward, threw Memphis from his seat, and slapped my face. Then another man who worked in the store threw me against an **adjoining** counter. . . . The mob started smearing us with ketchup, mustard, sugar, pies, and everything on the counter. . . . About ninety policemen were standing outside the store; they had been watching the whole thing through the windows, but had not come in to stop the mob or do anything. . . .

After the sit-in, all I could think of was how sick Mississippi whites were. . . . Now I knew it was impossible for me to hate sickness. The whites had a disease, an **incurable** disease in its final stages. What were our chances against such a disease?"

—Anne Moody, *Coming of Age in Mississippi*

DBQ Analyzing Historical Documents

1. **Comparing and Contrasting** Compare and contrast the accounts of Fannie Lou Hamer and Anne Moody. What do they have in common? How do they differ? What do the similarities of their accounts help corroborate?

2. **Evaluating** How do these documents affect your perspective on the civil rights movement? As a historian studying this period, what other sources would you look for to help broaden your understanding?

3. **Acquiring Information** Who does James Lawson indicate were the leaders of the sit-in movement? What explanation does he give for the start of the sit-in movement?

4. **Analyzing Historical Questions** Combine the information from all three sources. Explain why segregation remained in place for so long in the American South? Who resisted change?

5. **Making Generalizations** Martin Luther King, Jr., in his "Letter from Birmingham Jail" said that "segregation distorts the soul and damages the personality." In her final paragraph, Moody states that "The whites had a disease, an incurable disease in its final stages." What are King and Moody trying to say about how people behave when they believe a law is unjust? Why might people act irrationally?

6. **Transferring Information** Moody and Hamer describe how people reacted to their civil rights activities. Take their descriptions, and your impressions of their experiences, and transfer them to a visual form. There are many historical photos from the civil rights movement available online. Locate appropriate images and use presentation software to show visually the kind of reactions African American civil rights protestors such as Moody and Hamer experienced.

LESSON 2
Challenging Segregation

ESSENTIAL QUESTIONS

• Why do you think the civil rights movement made gains in postwar America?
• What motivates a society to make changes?

READING HELPDESK

Academic Vocabulary

• register

Content Vocabulary

• filibuster
• cloture

TAKING NOTES

Key Ideas and Details

Organizing As you read about the struggle for civil rights, use the following graphic organizer to identify challenges to segregation in the South. LAFS.1112.RH.3.7, SS.912.A.7.5

Challenge	Result
Sit-in Movement	
Freedom Riders	

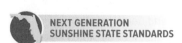

NEXT GENERATION SUNSHINE STATE STANDARDS

LAFS.1112.RH.2.4: Determine the meaning of words and phrases as they are used in a text, including analyzing how an author uses and refines the meaning of a key term over the course of a text (e.g., how Madison defines faction in Federalist No. 10).

LAFS.1112.RH.3.7: Integrate and evaluate multiple sources of information presented in diverse formats and media (e.g., visually, quantitatively, as well as in words) in order to address a question or solve a problem.

LAFS.1112.SL.2.4: Present information, findings, and supporting evidence, conveying a clear and distinct perspective, such that listeners can follow the line of reasoning, alternative or opposing perspectives are addressed, and the organization, development, substance, and style are appropriate to purpose, audience, and a range of formal and informal tasks.

Continued on page 481

IT MATTERS BECAUSE

In the early 1960s, the struggle for civil rights intensified. African American citizens and white supporters created organizations that directed protests, targeted inequalities, and attracted the attention of the mass media and the government.

The Sit-in Movement

GUIDING QUESTION *What were the goals of the Student Nonviolent Coordinating Committee?*

In the fall of 1959, four young African Americans—Joseph McNeil, Ezell Blair, Jr., David Richmond, and Franklin McCain—enrolled at North Carolina Agricultural and Technical College, an African American college in Greensboro. The four freshmen often talked about the civil rights movement. In January 1960, McNeil suggested a sit-in. "All of us were afraid," Richmond later recalled. "But we went and did it."

On February 1, 1960, the four friends entered the nearby Woolworth's department store. They purchased school supplies and then sat at the whites-only lunch counter and ordered coffee. When they were refused service, Blair asked, "I beg your pardon, but you just served us at [the checkout] counter. Why can't we be served at the counter here?" The students stayed at the counter until it closed. They then stated that they would sit there daily until they got the same service as white customers. They left the store excited. McNeil recalled, "I just felt I had powers within me, a superhuman strength that would come forward." McCain noted, "I probably felt better that day than I've ever felt in my life."

News of the daring sit-in spread quickly. The following day, 29 African American students arrived at Woolworth's determined to sit at the counter until served. By the end of the week, more than 300 students were taking part. A new mass movement for civil rights had begun. Within two months, sit-ins had spread to 54 cities in nine states. They were staged at segregated stores, restaurants, hotels, and movie theaters. By 1961, sit-ins had been held in more than 100 cities.

The sit-in movement brought large numbers of idealistic and energized college students into the civil rights struggle. Many were discouraged by the slow pace of desegregation. Sit-ins offered them a way to dictate the pace of change.

At first, the leaders of the NAACP and the SCLC were nervous about the sit-in campaign. Those conducting sit-ins were heckled, punched, kicked, beaten with clubs, and burned with cigarettes, hot coffee, and acid. Most did not fight back.

Urged on by former NAACP official and SCLC executive director Ella Baker, students established the Student Nonviolent Coordinating Committee (SNCC) in 1960. African American college students from all across the South made up the majority of SNCC's members. Many whites also joined. SNCC became an important civil rights group.

Volunteer Robert Moses urged the SNCC to start helping rural Southern African Americans, who often faced violence if they tried to **register** to vote. Many SNCC volunteers, including Moses, bravely headed south as part of a voter education project. During a period of registration efforts in 1964 known as Freedom Summer, the Ku Klux Klan brutally murdered three SNCC workers with the complicity of local officials.

SNCC organizer and sharecropper Fannie Lou Hamer was evicted from her farm after registering to vote. Police arrested her in Mississippi as she was returning from a voter registration workshop in 1963. They beat her while she was in jail. She still went on to help organize the Mississippi Freedom Democratic Party and challenged the legality of the state's segregated Democratic Party at the 1964 national convention.

✔ **READING PROGRESS CHECK**

Making Inferences Why were SNCC organizers willing to put themselves at such personal risk?

The Freedom Riders

GUIDING QUESTION *How did the Kennedy administration's Justice Department help the civil rights movement?*

Despite rulings outlawing segregation in interstate bus service, bus travel remained segregated in much of the South. Alabama was one state where many bus terminals were still segregated. Alabama's governor, John Patterson, was known to be in favor of segregation. As attorney general of the state, he had banned the NAACP from being active in Alabama, and he had fought the bus boycotts.

In early May 1961, teams of African American and white volunteers who became known as Freedom Riders boarded several southbound interstate buses. Buses were met by angry white mobs in Anniston, Birmingham, and Montgomery, Alabama. The mobs slit bus tires and threw rocks at the windows. In Anniston, someone threw a firebomb into one bus. Fortunately, no one was killed.

In Birmingham, riders emerged from a bus to face a gang of young m[en] armed with baseball bats, chains, and lead pipes. The gang beat the rid[ers] viciously. Birmingham public safety commissioner Theophilus Eugen[e] "Bull" Connor claimed that there had been no police at the bus sta[tion] because it was Mother's Day and he had given many officers the da[y off]

register to file personal information in order to become eligible for an official event

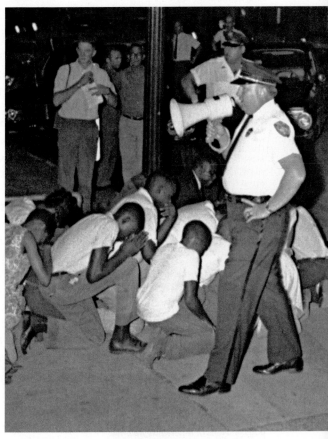

Nonviolent protests, such as this pray-in in Albany, Georgia, in 1962, spread across the nation as the civil rights movement gained momentum.

▶ **CRITICAL THINKING**
Drawing Conclusions What details in this photograph suggest that it was an effective form of protest? SS.912.A.1.4, S[...]

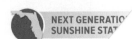

NEXT GENERATION SUNSHINE STAT[E]

Continued from page [...]

LAFS.1112.WHST.1[...] explanatory text[...] historical eve[...]tinely over experimen[...] for reflection and
LAFS.1[...]me frames (a single infor[...] two) for a range of [...]ecific tasks, purposes, and [...]es.

[...].912.A.1.2: Utilize a variety of primary and secondary sources to identify author, historical significance, audience, and authenticity to understand a historical period.

Continued on page 482

There's More Online! connected.mcgraw-hill.com

AP Images

Continued from page 481

SS.912.A.1.4: Analyze how images, symbols, objects, cartoons, graphs, charts, maps, and artwork may be used to interpret the significance of time periods and events from the past.

SS.912.A.7.3: Examine the changing status of women in the United States from post-World War II to present.

SS.912.A.7.4: Evaluate the success of 1960s era presidents' foreign and domestic policies.

SS.912.A.7.5: Compare nonviolent and violent approaches utilized by groups (African Americans, women, Native Americans, Hispanics) to achieve civil rights.

SS.912.A.7.6: Assess key figures and organizations in shaping the Civil Rights Movement and Black Power Movement.

SS.912.A.7.7: Assess the building of coalitions between African Americans, whites, and other groups in achieving integration and equal rights.

SS.912.A.7.13: Analyze the attempts to extend New Deal legislation through the Great Society and the successes and failures of these programs to promote social and economic stability.

A young protester in Birmingham, Alabama, is attacked by police dogs. Millions of Americans watched the graphic violence on televised nightly news.

▶ **CRITICAL THINKING**

Conclusions In what ways violent images have il rights movement?
.A.7.5

FBI evidence later showed that Connor had told the local Klan to beat the riders until "it looked like a bulldog got a hold of them." The violence made national news, shocking many Americans and drawing the federal government's attention to the plight of African Americans in the South.

Kennedy and Civil Rights

While campaigning for the presidency in 1960, John F. Kennedy had promised to support civil rights. Civil rights leaders such as NAACP executive director Roy Wilkins urged Kennedy to support civil rights legislation after taking office. However, Kennedy knew he needed the support of Southern senators to get other programs through Congress and any new civil rights legislation would anger them.

Kennedy did, however, bring approximately 40 African Americans into high-level government positions. He appointed Thurgood Marshall to a federal judgeship on the Second Circuit Appeals Court in New York. Kennedy also created the Committee on Equal Employment Opportunity (CEEO). He allowed the Justice Department, run by his brother Robert, to actively support the civil rights movement. The department tried to help African Americans register to vote by filing lawsuits across the South.

After the attacks on the Freedom Riders in Montgomery, both Kennedys publicly urged them to have a "cooling off" period. CORE leader James Farmer rejected the idea and announced that the riders would head into Mississippi. To stop the violence, President Kennedy made a deal with Mississippi senator James Eastland. No violence occurred when buses arrived in Jackson, but Kennedy did not protest the riders' arrests.

The cost of bailing the Freedom Riders out of jail used up most of CORE's funds. When Thurgood Marshall learned of the situation, he offered Farmer the use of the NAACP Legal Defense Fund's huge bail-bond account to keep the rides going. When President Kennedy found that the Freedom Riders were still active, he ordered the Interstate Commerce Commission (ICC) to tighten its regulations against segregated bus terminals. Robert Kennedy ordered the Justice Department to take legal action against Southern cities that maintained segregated bus terminals. By late 1962, segregation in interstate bus travel had virtually ended.

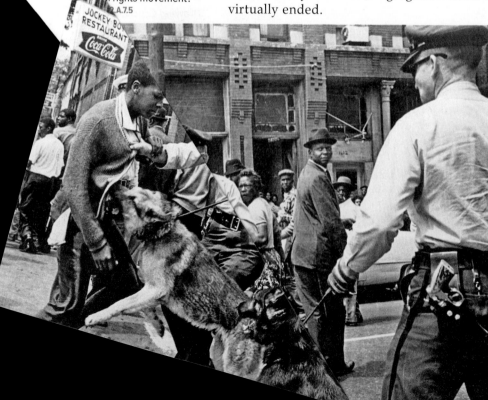

Violence in Birmingham

Martin Luther King, Jr., decided in the spring of 1963 to launch demonstrations in Birmingham, Alabama. He knew they would provoke a violent response, but he believed it was the only way to get the president to actively support civil rights. Eight days after the protests began, King was arrested. While in jail, he began writing the "Letter from Birmingham Jail." It was an eloquent defense of nonviolent protest. In his letter, King argued that "there are two types of laws:

PHOTO: Bill Hudson/AP Images; TEXT: Martin Luther King, Jr., "Letter from Birmingham Jail, 16 April 1963. Reprinted by arrangement with The Heirs to the Estate of Martin Luther King Jr., c/o Writers House as agent for the proprietor New York, NY. Copyright 1963 Dr. Martin Luther King Jr.; copyright renewed 1991 Coretta Scott King just and unjust . . . [and] one has a moral responsibility to disobey unjust laws. . . . Any law that uplifts human personality is just. Any law that degrades human personality is unjust. All segregation statutes are unjust because segregation distorts the soul and damages the personality."

After King was released, the protests began to grow again. Public Safety Commissioner Connor responded with force. He ordered police to use clubs, police dogs, and high-pressure fire hoses on the demonstrators.

One powerful demonstration was called the Children's March. On May 2, heroic young people marched in groups from churches to downtown businesses. Many were attacked by police, and many were arrested. On September 15, 1963, the Ku Klux Klan bombed Birmingham's Sixteenth Street Baptist Church, killing four young girls. News reports of these attacks on children led to greater support for the civil rights movement.

✔ READING PROGRESS CHECK

Explaining Why do you think there was such a violent reaction to the civil rights movement?

The Civil Rights Act of 1964

GUIDING QUESTION *How did the Civil Rights Act of 1964 allow the federal government to fight racial discrimination?*

Events in Alabama grew more and more tragic. At his inauguration as Alabama's governor, George Wallace had stated, "I draw a line in the dust . . . and I say, Segregation now! Segregation tomorrow! Segregation forever!" On June 11, 1963, federal marshals ordered Wallace to move from where he stood in front of the University of Alabama's admissions office to block two African Americans from enrolling. The next day, a white segregationist murdered civil rights activist Medgar Evers in Mississippi. Evers had been the NAACP's first field secretary, and had focused his efforts on voter registration and boycotts. His death made him a martyr of the civil rights movement. Amid these events, President Kennedy announced a civil rights bill.

The March on Washington

Civil rights leaders kept the pressure on legislators and the president by planning a large-scale march on Washington. On August 28, 1963, more than 250,000 demonstrators, African American and white, gathered near the Lincoln Memorial. They heard speeches and sang songs. Dr. King then delivered a powerful speech calling for freedom and equality for all Americans.

PHOTO: Francis Miller/TimePix/Getty Images; TEXT: Martin Luther King, Jr., "I Have a Dream," August 28, 1963. Reprinted by arrangement with The Heirs to the Estate of Martin Luther King Jr., c/o Writers House as agent for the proprietor New York, NY. Copyright 1963 Dr. Martin Luther King Jr.; copyright renewed 1991 Coretta Scott King.

Analyzing
PRIMARY SOURCES

"I Have A Dream" Speech

" I have a dream that one day this nation will rise up and live out the true meaning of its creed: 'We hold these truths to be self-evident, that all men are created equal.' . . .

I have a dream that one day on the red hills of Georgia, the sons of former slaves and the sons of former slave owners will be able to sit down together at the table of brotherhood.

I have a dream that my four little children will one day live in a nation where they will not be judged by the color of their skin but by the content of their character.**"**

—Martin Luther King, Jr., from the "Address in Washington," August 28, 1963

DBQ **ANALYZING PRIMARY SOURCES** What is the dream King refers to in his speech?
SS.912.A.1.2, SS.912.A.7.7

Martin Luther King, Jr., speaks to the assembled crowd in Washington, D.C.

▶ CRITICAL THINKING

Making Inferences What details about the March on Washington encouraged more public support for the civil rights movement and put pressure on Congress to act on the civil rights bill? LAFS.1112.WHST.3.9, SS.912.A.1.4, SS.912.A.7.7

The Civil Rights Movement **483**

The Bill Becomes Law

Kennedy tried and failed to win passage of civil rights legislation. After his assassination in November 1963, Lyndon Johnson—former leader of the Senate Democrats—became president. He had helped pass the Civil Rights Acts of 1957 and 1960, but had done so by weakening their provisions and by compromising with other Southern senators.

Nevertheless, Johnson worked to get Kennedy's civil rights legislation through Congress. The bill passed the House of Representatives in February 1964. Then it stalled in the Senate for several weeks. Its opponents used a **filibuster,** a tactic in which senators speak continuously to prevent a vote. In June the Senate voted for **cloture**—to end debate and take a vote— with a vote of 71 for and 29 against. The Senate then easily passed the bill. On July 2, 1964, Johnson signed the Civil Rights Act of 1964 into law.

The Civil Rights Act of 1964 was the most comprehensive civil rights law Congress had ever enacted. The law made segregation illegal in most places of public accommodation, and it gave citizens of all races and nationalities equal access to public facilities. The law gave the U.S. attorney general more power to bring lawsuits to force school desegregation and required private employers to end discrimination in the workplace. It also established the Equal Employment Opportunity Commission (EEOC) as a permanent federal agency.

The law also went further than simply banning discrimination based on race. It also banned discrimination based on religion, gender, and national origin. For religious minorities, for immigrants, and for women, the act represented a dramatic step forward in expanding their political rights and economic opportunities as well.

The passage of the Civil Rights Act of 1964 immediately raised constitutional issues. The act banned racial discrimination in facilities and businesses that served the general public. It specifically banned any type of hotel, restaurant, theater, or entertainment venue from discrimination. Yet it was unclear whether the federal government had jurisdiction under the Constitution to regulate these businesses.

Article 1, section 8, gives Congress the power to regulate interstate commerce, but prior to 1964, hotels, restaurants, and theaters had been regulated by state governments, and few would have argued that they were engaged in interstate commerce. As a result, challenges to the law's constitutionality began immediately. The owner of the Heart of Atlanta Motel

filibuster an attempt to kill a bill by having a group of senators take turns speaking continuously so that a vote cannot take place

cloture a motion that ends debate and calls for an immediate vote

---

CHARTS/GRAPHS

Marchers in Selma, Alabama, hoped to build support for a new voting rights law.

1 Identifying Central Ideas How did the Civil Rights Act of 1964 work to end segregation? LAFS.1112.WHST.3.9, SS.912.A.1.4, SS.912.A.7.4

2 Drawing Conclusions Why do you think counties where less than half of all adults were registered to vote were a focus of the Voting Rights Act of 1965? LAFS.1112.WHST.3.9, SS.912.A.1.4

MARCHING FOR FREEDOM, SELMA, 1965

The Civil Rights Act of 1964
- Gave the federal government power to prevent racial discrimination and established the Equal Employment Opportunity Commission (EEOC).
- Made segregation illegal in most places of public accommodation.
- Gave the U.S. attorney general more power to bring lawsuits to force school desegregation.
- Required employers to end workplace discrimination.

The Voting Rights Act of 1965
- Authorized the U.S. attorney general to send federal examiners to register qualified voters.
- Suspended discriminatory devices, such as literacy tests, in counties where less than half of all adults were registered to vote.

PHOTO: Steve Schapiro; TEXT: Martin Luther King, Jr., "Selma March," January 2, 1965. Reprinted by arrangement with The Heirs to the Estate of Martin Luther King Jr., c/o Writers House as agent for the proprietor New York, NY. Copyright 1965 Dr. Martin Luther King Jr; copyright renewed 1991 Coretta Scott King.

refused to allow African Americans to stay at his hotel, and filed suit in federal court. The case rapidly advanced to the Supreme Court. In December 1964, in the case *Heart of Atlanta Motel* v. *United States,* the Supreme Court ruled that the interstate commerce clause did indeed give Congress the power to ban discrimination in facilities serving the public.

✓ READING PROGRESS CHECK

Assessing Did government support for civil rights come from the federal or state level?

The Struggle for Voting Rights

GUIDING QUESTION *Why was the passage of the Voting Rights Act of 1965 a turning point in the civil rights movement?*

Despite the passage of the Civil Rights Act of 1964, voting rights remained an issue. The Twenty-fourth Amendment, ratified in 1964, helped somewhat. It eliminated poll taxes in federal (but not state) elections. African Americans still faced hurdles, however, when they tried to vote. As the SCLC and the SNCC stepped up their voter registration efforts in the South, their members were often attacked and beaten, and several were murdered. Convinced that a new law was needed to protect African American voting rights, Dr. King decided to hold another dramatic protest.

President Johnson signs the Voting Rights Act into law on August 6, 1965.

▶ CRITICAL THINKING
Comparing and Contrasting How were the Civil Rights Act of 1964 and the Voting Rights Act of 1965 similar and different?
LAFS.1112.WHST.3.9, SS.912.A.7.4

The Selma March

In December 1964, Dr. King received the Nobel Peace Prize in Oslo, Norway, for his work in the civil rights movement. A few weeks later, he announced, "We are not asking, we are demanding the ballot."

In January 1965, the SCLC and Dr. King selected Selma, Alabama, as the focal point for their campaign for voting rights. Although African Americans made up a majority of Selma's population, they made up only 3 percent of registered voters. To prevent African Americans from registering to vote, Sheriff Jim Clark had deputized and armed dozens of white citizens. His posse terrorized African Americans. On one occasion, they even used clubs and cattle prods on them. King's demonstrations in Selma led to the arrest of more than 3,000 African Americans, including schoolchildren, by Sheriff Clark.

To keep pressure on the president and Congress to act, Dr. King joined with SNCC activists and organized a "march for freedom" from Selma to the state capitol in Montgomery, a distance of about 50 miles (80 km). On Sunday, March 7, 1965, the march began. The SCLC's Hosea Williams and SNCC's John Lewis led some 600 protesters toward Montgomery.

As the protesters approached the Edmund Pettus Bridge, which led out of Selma, Sheriff Clark ordered them to disperse. Many protesters were beaten in full view of television cameras. This brutal attack, known later as "Bloody Sunday," left 70 marchers hospitalized and another 70 injured.

The nation was stunned as it viewed the shocking footage of law enforcement officers beating peaceful demonstrators. Watching the events

AP Images

from the White House, President Johnson became furious. Eight days later, he appeared before a nationally televised joint session of Congress to propose a new voting rights law.

The Voting Rights Act of 1965

On August 3, 1965, the House of Representatives passed the voting rights bill by a wide margin. The following day, the Senate also passed the bill. The Voting Rights Act of 1965 authorized the U.S. attorney general to send federal examiners to register qualified voters, bypassing local officials who often refused to register African Americans. The law also suspended discriminatory devices, such as literacy tests, in counties where less than half of all adults had been registered to vote.

The results were dramatic. By the end of the year, almost 250,000 African Americans had registered as new voters. The number of African American elected officials in the South also increased. In 1960, for example, no African American from the South held a seat in the U.S. Congress. By 2011, there were 44 African American members of Congress.

The passage of the Voting Rights Act of 1965 marked a turning point in the civil rights movement. The movement had now achieved two major legislative goals. Segregation had been outlawed, and new federal laws were in place to prevent discrimination and protect voting rights. After 1965, the movement began to shift its focus. It turned its attention to the problems of African Americans trapped in poverty and living in ghettos in many of the nation's major cities.

The Voting Rights Act of 1965, like the Civil Rights Act of 1964, immediately raised constitutional questions. Historically, each state had been allowed to set the rules regarding eligibility to vote. Article 1 section 2 of the Constitution only specifies that each state has to use the same rules for choosing members of Congress as it uses for choosing members of its state legislature. Article 2 section 1 specifies that each state gets to choose how to select the electors who vote for the president. By banning literacy tests, Congress was imposing a rule on voting, and it was unclear whether this violated the rights of the states to set voting rules. In 1966, in *Katzenbach v. Morgan,* the Supreme Court ruled that the Fourteenth Amendment gave Congress the authority to ban literacy tests and impose voting rules on the state governments.

☑ READING PROGRESS CHECK

Summarizing What was the positive outcome of the brutal response of police to civil rights protests?

LESSON 2 REVIEW

Reviewing Vocabulary

1. *Explaining* How did opponents of the Civil Rights Act of 1964 use the filibuster to try to block its passage? LAFS.1112.RH.2.4

Using Your Notes

2. *Summarizing* Use the notes you completed during the lesson on challenges to segregation to write a paragraph summarizing how the Freedom Riders helped the civil rights movement. LAFS.1112.RH.3.7, LAFS.1112.WHST.3.9, SS.912.A.7.7

Answering the Guiding Questions

3. *Identifying* What were the goals of the Student Nonviolent Coordinating Committee? LAFS.1112.WHST.3.9, SS.912.A.7.6

4. *Analyzing* How did the Kennedy administration's Justice Department help the civil rights movement? LAFS.1112.WHST.3.9, SS.912.A.7.4

5. *Interpreting* How did the Civil Rights Act of 1964 allow the federal government to fight racial discrimination? LAFS.1112.WHST.3.9, SS.912.A.7.4

6. *Evaluating* Why was the passage of the Voting Rights Act of 1965 a turning point in the civil rights movement? LAFS.1112.WHST.3.9, SS.912.A.7.4

Writing Activity

7. INFORMATIVE/EXPLANATORY Assume the role of a journalist working for a college newspaper in 1960. Write an article for the newspaper describing the sit-in movement, including its participants, goals, and achievements. LAFS.1112.WHST.1.2, LAFS.1112.WHST.4.10

LESSON 3
New Civil Rights Issues

ESSENTIAL QUESTIONS
- Why do you think the civil rights movement made gains in postwar America?
- What motivates a society to make changes?

READING HELPDESK

Academic Vocabulary
- enforcement

Content Vocabulary
- racism
- black power

TAKING NOTES

Key Ideas and Details

Organizing As you read, use the following graphic organizer to list major violent events in the civil rights movement and their results. LAFS.1112.RH.3.7, SS.912.A.7.5

Event	Result

NEXT GENERATION SUNSHINE STATE STANDARDS

LAFS.1112.RH.2.4: Determine the meaning of words and phrases as they are used in a text, including analyzing how an author uses and refines the meaning of a key term over the course of a text (e.g., how Madison defines faction in Federalist No. 10).

LAFS.1112.RH.3.7: Integrate and evaluate multiple sources of information presented in diverse formats and media (e.g., visually, quantitatively, as well as in words) in order to address a question or solve a problem.

Continued on page 488

IT MATTERS BECAUSE

By the mid-1960s, much progress had been made in the area of civil rights. However, leaders of the movement began to understand that merely winning political rights for African Americans would not completely solve their economic problems. African American leaders would continue to try to end economic inequality.

Urban Problems

GUIDING QUESTION *Why did riots break out in dozens of U.S. cities in the late 1960s?*

Despite the passage of civil rights laws in the 1950s and 1960s, racism was still common in American society. Changing the law could not change people's attitudes, nor did it end urban poverty.

In 1965, approximately 70 percent of African Americans lived in large cities. Even if African Americans had been allowed to move into white neighborhoods, many were stuck in low-paying jobs with little chance of advancement. In 1960, only 15 percent of African Americans held professional, managerial, or clerical jobs, compared to 44 percent of whites. The average income of African American families was only 55 percent of that of the average income for white families. Almost half of African Americans lived in poverty, with an unemployment rate typically twice that of whites.

Poor neighborhoods in the nation's major cities were overcrowded and dirty, leading to higher rates of illness and infant mortality. Juvenile delinquency rates rose, as did the rate of young people dropping out of school. Complicating matters even more was a rise in the number of single-parent households.

The Watts Riot

Just five days after President Johnson signed the Voting Rights Act, a riot erupted in Watts, an African American neighborhood in Los Angeles. Allegations of police brutality served as the catalyst for this uprising. It lasted for six days and required more than 14,000 members of the National Guard and 1,500 law officers to restore

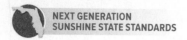
Continued from page 487

LAFS.1112.SL.2.4: Present information, findings, and supporting evidence, conveying a clear and distinct perspective, such that listeners can follow the line of reasoning, alternative or opposing perspectives are addressed, and the organization, development, substance, and style are appropriate to purpose, audience, and a range of formal and informal tasks.

LAFS.1112.WHST.1.2: Write informative/explanatory texts, including the narration of historical events, scientific procedures/experiments, or technical processes.

LAFS.1112.WHST.3.9: Draw evidence from informational texts to support analysis, reflection, and research.

LAFS.1112.WHST.4.10: Write routinely over extended time frames (time for reflection and revision) and shorter time frames (a single sitting or a day or two) for a range of discipline-specific tasks, purposes, and audiences.

SS.912.A.1.2: Utilize a variety of primary and secondary sources to identify author, historical significance, audience, and authenticity to understand a historical period.

SS.912.A.1.4: Analyze how images, symbols, objects, cartoons, graphs, charts, maps, and artwork may be used to interpret the significance of time periods and events from the past.

SS.912.A.7.4: Evaluate the success of 1960s era presidents' foreign and domestic policies.

Continued on page 489

racism prejudice or discrimination against a person because of his or her race

order. Riots broke out in dozens of other American cities between 1964 and 1968. In Detroit, burning, looting, and conflicts with police and the National Guard resulted in 43 deaths and more than 1,000 wounded in 1967. Property loss was estimated at almost $200 million.

The Kerner Commission

In the same year, President Johnson appointed the National Advisory Commission on Civil Disorders—headed by Governor Otto Kerner of Illinois—to study the causes of the urban riots and to make recommendations. The Kerner Commission, as it became known, blamed racism for most inner-city problems. "Our nation is moving toward two societies, one black, one white—separate and unequal," it concluded. The commission recommended the creation of inner-city jobs and the construction of new public housing, but with the spending for the Vietnam War, Johnson never endorsed the recommendations of the commission.

The Shift to Economic Rights

In the mid-1960s, Dr. Martin Luther King, Jr., decided to focus on the economic problems that African Americans faced. To call attention to deplorable housing conditions, Dr. King and his wife Coretta moved into a slum apartment in an African American neighborhood in Chicago. He and the SCLC hoped to improve the economic status of African Americans in poor neighborhoods.

The Chicago Movement, however, made little headway. When Dr. King led a march through the all-white suburb of Marquette Park to demonstrate the need for open housing, he was met by angry white mobs more hostile than those in Birmingham and Selma. Mayor Richard J. Daley met with Dr. King and discussed a new program to clean up the slums. Associations of realtors and bankers also agreed to promote open housing. In theory, mortgages and rental property would be available to everyone, regardless of race. In practice, little changed.

☑ **READING PROGRESS CHECK**

Identifying In what way did poverty contribute to the racial divide?

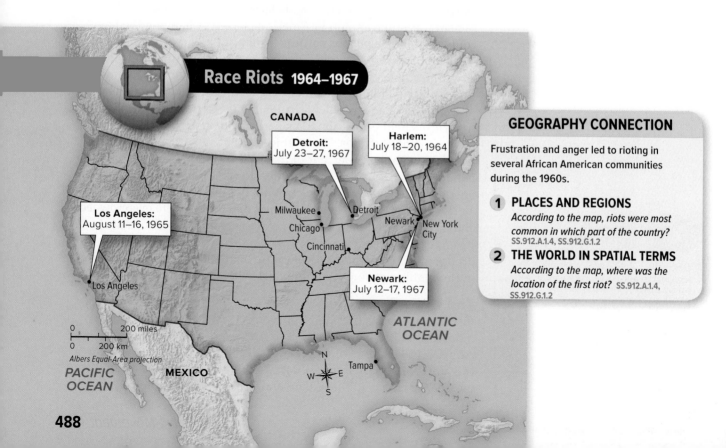

Race Riots 1964–1967

Detroit: July 23–27, 1967

Harlem: July 18–20, 1964

Los Angeles: August 11–16, 1965

Newark: July 12–17, 1967

CANADA

Milwaukee · · Detroit

Chicago · · Newark · New York City

Cincinnati

Los Angeles

ATLANTIC OCEAN

0   200 miles
0   200 km
Albers Equal-Area projection

PACIFIC OCEAN   MEXICO   Tampa ·

GEOGRAPHY CONNECTION

Frustration and anger led to rioting in several African American communities during the 1960s.

1 PLACES AND REGIONS
According to the map, riots were most common in which part of the country? SS.912.A.1.4, SS.912.G.1.2

2 THE WORLD IN SPATIAL TERMS
According to the map, where was the location of the first riot? SS.912.A.1.4, SS.912.G.1.2

Stokely Carmichael (1941–1998)

Stokely Carmichael was the founder of the 1960s Black Power movement. As a "Freedom Rider," he traveled to the South to ride on buses in protest of interstate transportation segregation laws. In 1964 Carmichael traveled to Alabama, where he organized an independent political party called the Lowndes County Freedom Organization. The organization's symbol was a black panther. In 1966 he first spoke of a new "Black Power" movement, which both promoted African American pride and advocated the necessity of self-defense in violent situations. Eventually, Carmichael relocated to Guinea, West Africa, where he changed his name to Kwame Ture. He died of cancer in Guinea in 1998.

Malcolm X (1925–1965)

Malcolm X was one of the most controversial black activists of the mid-twentieth century. He converted to the Nation of Islam while imprisoned in the 1940s. Paroled in 1952, he became an anti-white Muslim activist, calling himself "Malcolm X." Distancing himself from the Nation of Islam, he created his own group called the Organization of Afro-American Unity. During a pilgrimage, he began to rethink his social policies. He decided that white people were not inherently evil and that African Americans could enact change through traditional means. Malcolm X's new viewpoints drew harsh criticism from the Nation of Islam. On February 21, 1965, three African American gunmen assassinated him.

Black Power

GUIDING QUESTION *Why did many young African Americans join the black power movement?*

Dr. King's lack of progress in Chicago seemed to show that nonviolent protests could do little to solve economic problems. After 1965, many African Americans, especially urban young people, began to turn away from King. Some leaders called for more aggressive forms of protest. Some organizations, including CORE and SNCC, believed that African Americans alone should lead their struggle. Many young African Americans called for **black power,** a term that had many meanings. A few, including Robert F. Williams and H. Rap Brown, interpreted black power to mean that physical self-defense was acceptable.

To most, including Stokely Carmichael, the leader of SNCC in 1966, the term meant that African Americans should control the social, political, and economic direction of their struggle:

PRIMARY SOURCE

❝This is the significance of black power as a slogan. For once, black people are going to use the words they want to use—not just the words whites want to hear. . . . The need for psychological equality is the reason why SNCC today believes that blacks must organize in the black community. Only black people can . . . create in the community an aroused and continuing black consciousness.❞

—from "What We Want," the *New York Review of Books,* September 1966

Black power stressed pride in the African American cultural group. It emphasized racial distinctiveness rather than adapting to the dominant culture. African Americans showed pride in their racial heritage by adopting new "Afro" hairstyles and African-style clothing. Many also took

black power the mobilization of the political and economic power of African Americans, especially to compel respect for their rights and to improve their condition

NEXT GENERATION SUNSHINE STATE STANDARDS

Continued from page 488

SS.912.A.7.5: Compare nonviolent and violent approaches utilized by groups (African Americans, women, Native Americans, Hispanics) to achieve civil rights.

SS.912.A.7.6: Assess key figures and organizations in shaping the Civil Rights Movement and Black Power Movement.

SS.912.A.7.13: Analyze the attempts to extend New Deal legislation through the Great Society and the successes and failures of these programs to promote social and economic stability.

SS.912.G.1.2: Use spatial perspective and appropriate geographic terms and tools, including the Six Essential Elements, as organizational schema to describe any given place.

African names. Dr. King and some other leaders criticized black power as a philosophy of hopelessness and despair.

Malcolm X

By the early 1960s, a young man named Malcolm X had become a symbol of the black power movement. Born Malcolm Little in Omaha, Nebraska, he experienced a difficult childhood and adolescence. In 1946, he was sent to prison for burglary. Prison transformed Malcolm. He educated himself and played an active role in the prison debate society.

Eventually, he joined the Nation of Islam, commonly known as the Black Muslims. Despite the name, the Nation of Islam is very different from mainstream Islam. The Nation of Islam preached black nationalism. After joining the Nation of Islam, Malcolm Little changed his name to Malcolm X. The *X* symbolized the family name of his enslaved African ancestors. He declared that his true name had been stolen from him by slavery, and he would no longer use the name white society had given him. Malcolm X's criticisms of white society and the mainstream civil rights movement gained national attention for the Nation of Islam.

By 1964, Malcolm X had broken with the Black Muslims. Discouraged by scandals involving the Nation of Islam's leader, he went to the Muslim holy city of Makkah (Mecca) in Saudi Arabia. After seeing Muslims from many races worshipping together, he no longer promoted separatism. After Malcolm X broke with the Nation of Islam, he continued to criticize the organization. Because of this, organization members shot and killed him in February 1965.

Malcolm X's speeches and ideas influenced a new generation of militant African American leaders who preached black power, black nationalism, and economic self-sufficiency. In 1966, in Oakland, California, Huey P. Newton and Bobby Seale organized the Black Panthers. Black Panther leaders called for an end to racial oppression and for control of major institutions in the African American community, such as schools, law **enforcement,** housing, and hospitals.

enforcement the act of urging or carrying out by force

✅ READING PROGRESS CHECK

Summarizing How did the black power movement lead African Americans away from Dr. King's message of nonviolent disobedience and the goal of integration?

Dr. King Is Assassinated

GUIDING QUESTION *How did Martin Luther King, Jr.'s death affect the civil rights movement?*

In March 1968, Dr. King went to Memphis, Tennessee, to support a strike of African American sanitation workers. At the time, the SCLC had been planning a national Poor People's Campaign to promote economic advancement for impoverished Americans. The purpose of this campaign was to lobby the federal government to commit billions of dollars to end poverty and unemployment in the United States. People of all races and nationalities were to converge on Washington, D.C., where they would camp out until both Congress and President Johnson agreed to pass the requested legislation to fund the proposal.

On April 4, 1968, as he stood on his hotel balcony in Memphis, Dr. King was assassinated by a sniper. In a speech the previous night, he had told a gathering at a local church, "I've been to the mountaintop. . . . I've looked over. And I've seen the promised land. I may not get there with you, but I want you to know tonight that we as a people will get to the promised land."

Dr. King's death touched off both national mourning and riots in more than 100 cities, including Washington, D.C. The Reverend Ralph Abernathy, who had served as a trusted assistant to Dr. King for many years, led the Poor People's Campaign in King's absence. However, the demonstration did not achieve any of the major objectives that either King or the SCLC had hoped it would.

In the wake of Dr. King's death, Congress did pass the Civil Rights Act of 1968. This law, sometimes known as the Fair Housing Act of 1968, outlawed discrimination on the basis of race, color, religion, or national origin when selling, renting, or financing housing. In many communities across the nation, racism had led to an informal segregation. People would simply refuse to sell their homes or rent property to people based on their race. Sometime banks would not approve loans because of racist attitudes or assumptions that affected the thinking of the loan officers. The Civil Rights Act of 1968 put an end to these practices.

The law also benefited immigrants and religious minorities. Historically, in many places in the United States, Jewish Americans had encountered rules preventing them from buying or renting property in certain neighborhoods. The Civil Rights Act of 1968 expanded their economic opportunities as well.

The assassination of Dr. King in 1968 marked a turning point in the civil rights movement. After his death, the movement began to fragment. With formal laws in place banning segregation and discrimination, and guaranteeing voting rights, the movement lost some of its unity of purpose and the vision he had given it. The shift to economic rights was already underway at the time of his death, and it was clear that the struggle to end poverty and provide more economic opportunity would be very difficult and would have to involve very different approaches than the movement had used in the past.

The assassination of Dr. Martin Luther King, Jr., shocked the nation. On April 9, 1968, the country joined in sorrow to mourn his death.

▶ **CRITICAL THINKING**
Predicting Consequences How do you think the violence that erupted after Dr. King's death affected the civil rights movement? SS.912.A.1.4, SS.912.A.7.6

 READING PROGRESS CHECK

Explaining In what way was Dr. King's "mountaintop" speech prophetic?

PHOTO: Lynn Pelham/Time & Life Pictures/Getty Images; TEXT: Dr. Martin Luther King, Jr., I've Been to the Mountaintop delivered April 3, 1968, Mason Temple. Reprinted by arrangement with The Heirs to the Estate of Martin Luther King Jr. c/o Writers House as agent for the proprietor New York, NY. Copyright 1968 Dr. Martin Luther King Jr.; copyright renewed 1991 Coretta Scott King

LESSON 3 REVIEW

Reviewing Vocabulary
1. *Explaining* Explain how the findings and recommendations of the Kerner Commission related to racism. LAFS.1112.RH.2.4, SS.912.A.7.4

Using Your Notes
2. *Assessing* Use your notes on violent events during the civil rights movement to write a paragraph assessing the result of each event. LAFS.1112.RH.3.7, LAFS.1112.WHST.3.9

Answering the Guiding Questions
3. *Identifying* Why did riots break out in dozens of American cities in the late 1960s? LAFS.1112.WHST.3.9, SS.912.A.7.5

4. *Analyzing* Why did many young African Americans join the black power movement? LAFS.1112.WHST.3.9, SS.912.A.7.6

5. *Making Connections* How did Dr. Martin Luther King, Jr.'s death affect the civil rights movement? LAFS.1112.WHST.3.9, SS.912.A.7.6

Writing Activity
6. INFORMATIVE/EXPLANATORY Assume the role of a reporter in the late 1960s. Suppose that you have interviewed both a follower of Dr. King and a member of the Black Panthers. Write a transcript of each interview. LAFS.1112.WHST.1.2, LAFS.1112.WHST.4.10, SS.912.A.7.5, SS.912.A.7.6

Sequencing and Reading a Time Line

Why Learn This Skill?

Many people complain that history is just a bunch of dates they have to memorize. In fact, it is the relationship between events that really matters to historians. They want to explain what caused something to happen, or how something affected something else over time.

History is a series of causes and effects that happen over time in a sequence. Unlike science, where you can repeat an experiment, in history, everything happens once in a particular order. If you want to know what caused something, you have to know the sequence of events.

Learning the Skill

Sequencing is simply putting things in the correct order. What came first? What came next? Did an event happen before or after another event? Putting historical events in the correct sequence will often reveal a possible relationship between them. Historians then look at the historical evidence to see if they can prove that there is a cause-and-effect relationship in the sequence.

Sequencing involves two types of chronology—absolute chronology and relative chronology. **Absolute chronology** is when something happened. Generally we use a specific date and time to establish absolute chronology. **Relative chronology** tells when something happened compared to something else. If you give the year President Obama was first elected, you are using absolute chronology. If you are asked whether President Reagan came before or after President Clinton, you use relative chronology to answer.

A very common way to present a sequence of related historical events and teach their relative and absolute chronology is to use a time line. A **time line** is a kind of chart that can be presented on a horizontal or vertical line. It lists events that occurred in order between specific dates. The

Key Events of the Civil Rights Movement, 1954–1965

October 1955 After a lengthy legal battle, Autherine Lucy becomes the first African American student to attend the University of Alabama. On February 1, 1956, Lucy enrolled as a graduate student in library science. However, she was denied entry after the school claimed it could not offer her enough protection from the angry mobs she encountered on campus. She was expelled after she and her attorneys accused the university of conspiring with the mob. The school reversed Lucy's expulsion in 1988, and she went on to receive her master's degree in 1992.

December 1956 Supreme Court decision in *Browder* v. *Gayle* making segregation illegal on public buses takes effect and the Montgomery Bus Boycott ends

September 1957 Arkansas governor Faubus blocks desegregation of Little Rock High School, forcing Eisenhower to send troops to the school

1955

1957

1959 **February 1960**

May 1954 In *Brown* v. *Board of Education*, the Supreme Court declares segregated schools to be unconstitutional

December 1955 Rosa Parks is arrested and the Montgomery Bus Boycott begins

Janurary 1957 Martin Luther King, Jr., and other Southern ministers create SCLC

February 1960 Students in Greensboro, North Carolina, stage a sit-in at a local lunch counter; student leaders form SNCC in April number of years between these dates is called the time span. For example, a time line that begins in 1400 and ends in 1500 has a time span of 100 years. Time lines are usually divided into smaller segments, or time intervals. Intervals can be vast, each interval being an entire historical era, or they can be small, a year, a month, a day—whatever is needed to sequence the events.

A time line is a visual aid; it helps you remember the correct order of events and people, and also the dates associated with them. It often includes captions with each event giving a quick summary of what happened.

Practicing this Skill

Look at the time line on key events of the civil rights movement, and then answer the questions that follow:

1. What is the time span of this time line?
2. What intervals is the time line using?
3. When did Martin Luther King deliver his "I Have a Dream" speech? What major legislation was passed the year after the speech?
4. Use the time line to put these people and events in the correct relative chronology: Freedom Summer, James Farmer, Greensboro sit-ins, Rosa Parks.

5. What major event happened just before Congress passed the Voting Rights Act? What relationship is there between the two events?
6. What possible cause and effect sequence does the time line show between court decisions, protests, and legislation?

Applying the Skill

Sequencing Using Absolute and Relative Chronology Now that you understand sequencing, time lines, and absolute and relative chronology, read through Lesson 3, New Civil Rights Issues. Then go to the lesson New Approaches to Civil Rights in the chapter Politics and Economics, 1968–1980. Create a time line sequencing the events of the civil rights movement from 1968–1980. Be sure to include dates and brief one-sentence captions identifying key events and individuals.

May 1961 James Farmer organizes the first Freedom Riders to desegregate interstate bus travel

May 1963 Martin Luther King, Jr., leads protests in Birmingham, Alabama; police assault the protestors and King is jailed

August 1963 King delivers his "I Have a Dream" speech during the March on Washington in support of the new civil rights act

July 1964 Johnson signs the Civil Rights Act of 1964 into law

March 1965 King leads a march in Selma, Alabama, to build support for a new voting rights law; police brutally attack members

August 3, 1965 Congress passes the Voting Rights Act of 1965

1961   1963   1965

September 1962 James Meredith tries to register at University of Mississippi; riots force Kennedy to send troops

May 1963 On May 2, hundreds of African American schoolchildren march through Birmingham, Alabama, in a protest called the Children's Crusade; many of these children are arrested

June 1964 Campaign called "Freedom Summer" begins, with the goal of allowing African Americans to register to vote in Mississippi, a state that heavily excluded black votes; "Freedom Schools" teach literacy and African American history and encourage voter registration

August 1964 The Mississippi Freedom Democratic Party was a nondiscriminatory political party created to challenge the status of the whites-only Democratic Party. Their efforts to participate at the Democratic National Convention were televised. As cochair of the MFDP, Civil Rights activist Fannie Lou Hamer campaigned heavily for equal voting rights. Despite being falsely imprisoned and savagely beaten, she maintained her efforts for the civil rights movement. During her testimony for the MFDP at the Democratic National Convention, she spoke of her arrest: "All of this is on account we want to register, to become first-class citizens, and if the Freedom Democratic Party is not seated now, I question America. Is this America, the land of the free and the home of the brave where we have to sleep with our telephones off the hooks because our lives be threatened daily because we want to live as decent human beings—in America?"

STUDY GUIDE

THE MOVEMENT BEGINS
LESSON 1

Origins of the Civil Rights Movement

Growing Political Influence

Court Challenges

public actions, such as boycotts

formed Congress of Racial Equality

NAACP

Brown v. Board of Education

CHALLENGING SEGREGATION
LESSON 2

Freedom Rides begin (May 1961)

March on Washington (Aug. 28, 1963)

Sit-ins begin (Feb. 1, 1960)

Public protests begin in Birmingham (spring of 1963)

Civil Rights Act passed (July 2, 1964)

Voting Rights Act passed (August, 1965)

SNCC Forms (1960)

Sixteenth Street church bombing (Sept. 15, 1963)

Selma March (Mar 7, 1965)

NEW CIVIL RIGHTS ISSUES
LESSON 3

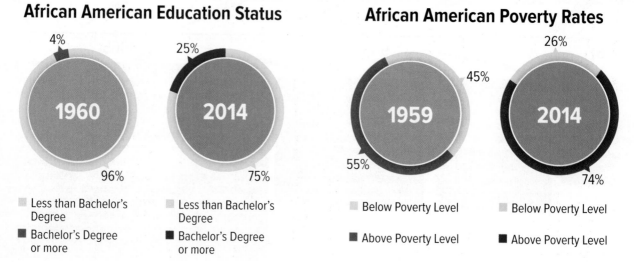

African American Education Status

1960 — 4% / 96%

2014 — 25% / 75%

Less than Bachelor's Degree

Bachelor's Degree or more

African American Poverty Rates

1959 — 45% / 55%

2014 — 26% / 74%

Below Poverty Level

Above Poverty Level

Directions: On a separate sheet of paper, answer the questions below. Make sure you read carefully and answer all parts to the question.

Lesson Review

Lesson 1

1 *Summarizing* Explain the events leading up to the *Brown* v. *Board of Education* decision and summarize the Supreme Court's ruling. SS.912.A.7.8

2 *Analyzing Cause and Effect* What role did Rosa Parks play in the bus boycott in Montgomery, Alabama? SS.912.A.7.5, SS.912.A.7.6

3 *Describing* How did many white southerners react to the *Brown* v. *Board* ruling? What actions did they take in response? Identify two southern governors who sought to preserve the status quo in southern schools. What did they do? SS.912.A.7.8

4 *Describing* What actions did President Eisenhower take to address minority rights? Be sure to discuss direct presidential actions as well as legislation he supported. Be sure to explain the obstacles he faced in Congress and explain why he was able to get legislation passed. SS.912.A.7.4

Lesson 2

5 *Evaluating* What made the sit-in strategy an effective form of protest? SS.912.A.7.5

6 *Identifying Cause and Effect* How did the arrests of Freedom Riders in Mississippi begin a chain of decisions and actions that ultimately led to the collapse, or near collapse, of segregated busing? SS.912.A.7.5, SS.912.A.7.7

7 *Describing* Who tried to stop the Civil Rights Act of 1964 from passing the United States Senate and what tactic was used? How was their opposition overcome? SS.912.A.7.5, SS.912.A.7.7

8 *Describing* Why was it so difficult for African Americans in Southern states to register to vote?

9 *Evaluating* What was the significance of the Selma march of 1965, and how did it help to increase participation of minorities in the political process? SS.912.A.7.5

10 *Analyzing* Why was the Twenty-fourth Amendment passed? How did the amendment expand the right to participate in the democratic process and help ensure equal political rights for African Americans and others?

Lesson 3

11 *Explaining* What conditions led to riots in urban African American communities in the 1960s? SS.912.A.7.5

12 *Identifying and Describing* How did Malcolm X's speeches and ideas influence a new generation of African American leaders? SS.912.A.7.6

13 *Identifying Central Issues* What were the main ideas of black power? SS.912.A.7.6

14 *Drawing Conclusions* Why was 1968, the year of Dr. Martin Luther King's death, a turning point for the civil rights movement? SS.912.A.7.6

15 *Explaining* How did the Civil Rights Act of 1968 expand economic opportunities for religious minorities? SS.912.A.7.7

Exploring the Essential Questions

16 *Conducting an Historical Inquiry* Segregation began in the United States in the late 1800s. African Americans began resisting it soon after. But from 1900 to 1950, only small gains were made in their efforts to roll back segregation and regain their civil rights. What changed in the 1950s and 1960s? Why was the civil rights movement able to make gains in post-war America? Conduct research at the library or online. Identify the types of evidence you need and prepare an essay answering these questions. Your paper should follow proper essay form with an introduction, argument and presentation of evidence, and a conclusion. Sources should be cited, and a bibliography attached. LAFS.1112.WHST.2.4, LAFS.1112.WHST.3.7, LAFS.1112.WHST.3.8, SS.912.A.7.5, SS.912.A.7.7

17 *Analyzing* Identify the different types of non-violent protest used during the civil rights movement and explain what each group was trying to achieve with their protest. SS.912.A.7.5

Need Extra Help?

If You've Missed Question	1	2	3	4	5	6	7	8	9	10	11	12	13	14	15	16	17
Go to Lesson	1	1	1	1	2	2	2	2	2	2	3	3	3	3	3	1, 2, 3	1, 2

Critical Thinking

18 *Analyzing Effects* Why was the Supreme Court's decision in *Brown v. Board of Education* significant? SS.912.A.7.8

19 *Identifying* Describe Martin Luther King, Jr.'s, role in the civil rights movement. What were his successes, and what qualities made him an effective leader? SS.912.A.7.6

20 *Analyzing* Describe the role litigation played in protecting minority rights during the civil rights movement and expanding the right to participate in the democratic process. How effective were lawsuits in bringing about change? SS.912.A.7.8

21 *Evaluating* What changes resulted from the civil rights movement? Did these changes increase minority participation in the political process?

22 *Explaining* What constitutional issues were raised by the passage of the Civil Rights Act of 1964 and the Voting Rights Act of 1965? Name the two important cases from the 1960s in which the Supreme Court addressed the issues raised and explain the reason the Court upheld both laws. SS.912.A.7.8

21st Century Skills

23 *Organizing* Make a chart listing each of the major pieces of legislation passed by Congress during the civil rights movement of the 1950s and 1960s. Summarize what each piece of legislation contributed toward achieving equal political rights for African Americans.

24 *Using Absolute and Relative Chronology* Create a time line listing the following people and their role in the civil rights movement in the correct chronological sequence. Beside each name or event, write the year when the person made his or her contribution.

- President Eisenhower sends troops to Little Rock
- Martin Luther King, Jr., helps organize the Montgomery Bus Boycott
- Rosa Parks is arrested
- The Freedom Riders begin their trips into the South
- Thurgood Marshall wins *Brown v. Board of Education*
- James Farmer founds Congress on Racial Equality

- President Johnson signs the Voting Rights Act
- Four men begin the sit-in movement in Greensboro, North Carolina
- The March on Washington takes place
- Dr. King is assassinated
- Filibuster by Southern senators is shut down allowing a new civil rights act to pass
- African Americans march on Selma
  SS.912.A.1.3, SS.912.A.7.5, SS.912.A.7.6, SS.912.A.7.7, SS.912.A.7.8

DBQ Analyzing Primary Sources

Read the excerpt below from Martin Luther King, Jr.'s, "Letter from Birmingham Jail," and then answer the questions that follow:

PRIMARY SOURCE

❝One may well ask: "How can you advocate breaking some laws and obeying others?" The answer lies in the fact that there are two types of laws: just and unjust. . . . [and] one has a moral responsibility to disobey unjust laws. I would agree with St. Augustine that 'an unjust law is no law at all.'

. . . Any law that uplifts human personality is just. Any law that degrades human personality is unjust. All segregation statutes are unjust because segregation distorts the soul and damages the personality.❞

—Dr. Martin Luther King, Jr., from "Letter from Birmingham Jail," 1963

25 *Generalizing* How did the philosophy Dr. King describes in his letter shape the civil rights movement? LAFS.1112.RH.3.8, LAFS.1112.RH.4.10, SS.912.A.7.6

26 *Interpreting Primary Sources* What do you think Dr. King meant when he wrote that an unjust law degrades human personality? LAFS.1112.RH.1.2, LAFS.1112.RH.3.8, LAFS.1112.RH.4.10, SS.912.A.7.6

Extended Response Question

27 *Summarizing* Identify each of the following organizations: NAACP, SNCC, SCLC, and CORE. Write a paragraph about each organization, describing its contribution to the civil rights movement and describing its approach to expanding the civil rights of African Americans. LAFS.1112.WHST.2.4, LAFS.1112.WHST.3.9, LAFS.1112.WHST.4.10, SS.912.A.7.6

Need Extra Help?

If You've Missed Question	**18**	**19**	**20**	**21**	**22**	**23**	**24**	**25**	**26**	**27**
Go to Lesson	1	1, 2, 3	1, 2	1, 2, 3	2	1, 2, 3	1, 2, 3	2	2	1, 2

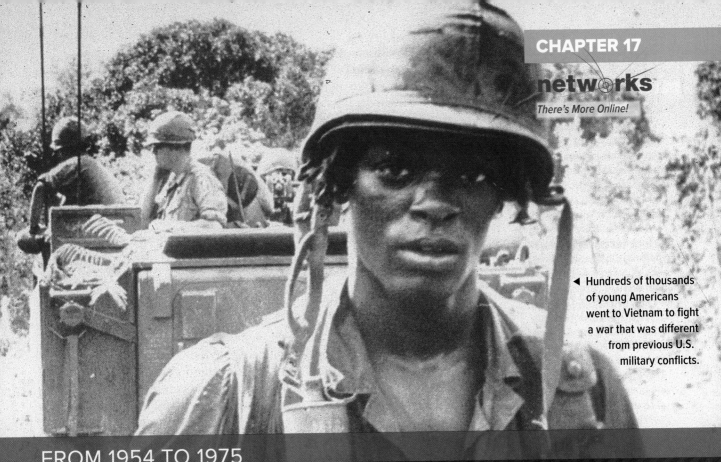

netw⚹rks
There's More Online!

◄ Hundreds of thousands of young Americans went to Vietnam to fight a war that was different from previous U.S. military conflicts.

FROM 1954 TO 1975

The Vietnam War

THE STORY MATTERS ...

Americans had supported their government's war efforts and helped win a decisive victory in World War II. The war in Vietnam, however, was different; people questioned whether the United States should be involved at all. As more Americans came to believe their leaders were not being truthful about the war, the country changed in a profound way.

ESSENTIAL QUESTIONS
- How does military conflict divide people within cultures?
- Should citizens support the government during wartime?

LESSON 1
Going to War in Vietnam

LESSON 2
Vietnam Divides the Nation

LESSON 3
The War Winds Down

©Doug Wilson/Historical/Corbis

Place & Time: Vietnam 1954–1975

The United States wanted to stop the spread of communism after the French defeat by Communist forces in 1954. American involvement in Vietnam would result in eight years of war and the loss of thousands of American lives.

Step Into the Place

Read the quotes and look at the information presented on the map.

Analyzing Historical Documents How do these statements by Ho Chi Minh and General William Westmoreland demonstrate the varying beliefs regarding how Vietnam should be controlled?

PRIMARY SOURCE

"[W]e, members of the Provisional Government of the Democratic Republic of Viet-Nam, solemnly declare to the world that Viet-Nam has the right to be a free and independent country—and in fact it is so already. The entire Vietnamese people are determined to mobilize all their physical and mental strength, to sacrifice their lives and property in order to safeguard their independence and liberty."

—Ho Chi Minh, from the *Declaration of Independence of Vietnam*, 1945

PRIMARY SOURCE

"The objective of the United States government in Vietnam was made clear by the Truman Doctrine of 1947. The Truman Doctrine came after World War II had been concluded, the fighting had stopped, and international arrangements were in disarray. It became very clear that the Soviet Union was going to grab as much real estate as possible in the aftermath of that great war. Thus, the Truman Doctrine said in essence: 'We will not allow a little country to be pushed around and be taken over by the communists. Somebody has to come to their rescue and we will do that.'"

—General William C. Westmoreland, from *Vietnam in Perspective*, 1987

left page: (tl)©Bettmann/Corbis; (cr)Dennis Oulds/Hulton Archive/Getty Images; (bl)detail/White House Collection/The White House Historical Association; (br)SuperStock/SuperStock;
right page (l & r)detail/White House Collection/The White House Historical Association

Step Into the Time

PREDICTING CONSEQUENCES

Choose an event from the time line and write a paragraph that predicts how the event may have influenced public opinion about involvement in Vietnam.

Eisenhower 1953–1961

Kennedy 1961–1963

U.S. PRESIDENTS

UNITED STATES

WORLD

1955 U.S. military aid and advisers are sent to South Vietnam

1955

1960

1954 France leaves Indochina

1956 Diem refuses to participate in nationwide elections in Vietnam

1958 U.S. troops land in Lebanon

1960 U-2 spy plane is shot down in the Soviet Union

NEXT GENERATION SUNSHINE STATE STANDARDS
Students will understand the following benchmarks from the Florida NGSSS

LAFS.1112.RH.3.7: Integrate and evaluate multiple sources of information presented in diverse formats and media (e.g., visually, quantitatively, as well as in words) in order to address a question or solve a problem.

LAFS.1112.RH.3.9: Integrate information from diverse sources, both primary and secondary, into a coherent understanding of an idea or event, noting discrepancies among sources.

SS.912.A.1.2: Utilize a variety of primary and secondary sources to identify author, historical significance, audience, and authenticity to understand a historical period.

SS.912.A.1.3: Utilize timelines to identify the time sequence of historical data.

SS.912.A.1.4: Analyze how images, symbols, objects, cartoons, graphs, charts, maps, and artwork may be used to interpret the significance of time periods and events from the past.

SS.912.A.6.14: Analyze causes, course, and consequences of the Vietnam War.

SS.912.A.7.10: Analyze the significance of Vietnam and Watergate on the government and people of the United States.

The War in Vietnam 1965–1973

CHINA

Dien Bien Phu

Hanoi

Gulf of Tonkin

LAOS

NORTH VIETNAM

South China Sea

March 30, 1972: More than 20,000 North Vietnamese troops crossed the border between North Vietnam and South Vietnam, which led to a major retreat by the South Vietnamese army.

Vientiane

Con Thien 1967

Khe Sanh 1968

February 8–March, 1971: Invasion of Laos

Hue 1968

THAILAND

Mekong R.

HO CHI MINH TRAIL

Vinh Huy 1967

Dak To 1967

Cu Nghi 1966

Ia Drang 1965

200 miles
200 km
Miller projection

CAMBODIA

SOUTH VIETNAM

← Major U.S. and South Vietnamese troop movement

← Major North Vietnamese supply line

✳ Major battle

May 1–June 29, 1970: Invasion of Cambodia

Phnom Penh

Saigon

April 30, 1975: The last Americans left the U.S. Embassy, and South Vietnam officially surrendered to the North.

Timeline:

L. Johnson 1963–1969

1964 Congress passes Gulf of Tonkin Resolution

1965 U.S. combat troops land in Vietnam

January 1968 Tet Offensive begins

August 1968 Antiwar protest in Chicago

Nixon 1969–1974

April 1970 Nixon orders invasion of Cambodia

May 1970 National Guard troops kill student protesters at Kent State University

1973 Last U.S. troops leave Vietnam

1965

1970

1975

1965 Military leaders oust civilian government in South Vietnam

1973 Paris Peace Accords signed to establish peace in Vietnam

1975 Saigon falls to North Vietnamese invasion

The Vietnam War **499**

LESSON 1
Going to War in Vietnam

- How does military conflict divide people within cultures?
- Should citizens support the government during wartime?

READING HELPDESK

Academic Vocabulary

- strategic
- traditional

Content Vocabulary

- domino theory
- napalm
- guerrilla
- Agent Orange

TAKING NOTES

Key Ideas and Details

Organizing Complete a graphic organizer similar to the one below by providing the reasons the United States aided France in Vietnam. **LAFS.1112.RH.3.7, SS.912.A.6.14**

Reasons for U.S. Support of France →

NEXT GENERATION SUNSHINE STATE STANDARDS

LAFS.1112.RH.2.4: Determine the meaning of words and phrases as they are used in a text, including analyzing how an author uses and refines the meaning of a key term over the course of a text (e.g., how Madison defines faction in Federalist No. 10).

LAFS.1112.SL.2.4: Present information, findings, and supporting evidence, conveying a clear and distinct perspective, such that listeners can follow the line of reasoning, alternative or opposing perspectives are addressed, and the organization, development, substance, and style are appropriate to purpose, audience, and a range of formal and informal tasks.

LAFS.1112.WHST.1.1: Write arguments focused on discipline-specific content.

Continued on page 501

IT MATTERS BECAUSE

In the late 1940s and early 1950s, most Americans knew little about Indochina, France's colony in Southeast Asia. During the Cold War, however, American officials became concerned that the region might fall to communism.

American Involvement in Vietnam

GUIDING QUESTION *Why did the United States provide military aid to the French in Indochina?*

In 1940, Japan invaded Vietnam, becoming one of a series of foreign nations to rule the Asian country. The Chinese had controlled the region for hundreds of years. Then, from the late 1800s until World War II, the French ruled Vietnam, Laos, and Cambodia—a region then known as French Indochina.

The Growth of Vietnamese Nationalism

By the early 1900s, nationalism had become a powerful force in Vietnam. Several political parties pushed for independence or for reform of French colonial rule. Among the leaders of the nationalist movement was Nguyen That Thanh—better known by his assumed name, Ho Chi Minh. After years in Europe, China, and the Soviet Union, he returned to Southeast Asia. There, he helped found the Indochinese Communist Party in 1930 and worked for independence.

Ho Chi Minh's activities forced him to flee Indochina and spend several years in exile in the Soviet Union and China. In 1941, he returned to Vietnam. By then, Japan had seized control of the country. Ho Chi Minh organized a nationalist group called the Vietminh, which united Communists and non-Communists in the effort to expel the Japanese. Soon afterward, the United States began sending aid to the Vietminh.

America Aids the French

When Japan surrendered to the Allies in 1945, it gave up control of Indochina. Ho Chi Minh quickly declared Vietnam's independence. France had no intention of losing its former colony, however. French troops returned to Vietnam in 1946 and drove the Vietminh into hiding.

The Vietminh fought back against the French-dominated regime and slowly gained control of large areas of the country. As the fighting escalated, France appealed to the United States for help. The request put American officials in a difficult position. The United States opposed colonialism. It had pressured the Dutch to give up their empire in Indonesia and supported the British decision to give India independence in 1947. American officials, however, did not want Vietnam to be Communist.

China's fall to communism and the outbreak of the Korean War helped convince President Truman to aid France. President Eisenhower continued Truman's policy and defended his decision with what became known as the **domino theory**—the idea that if Vietnam fell to communism, the rest of Southeast Asia would follow, like a line of dominoes falling over.

Defeat at Dien Bien Phu

Despite aid from the United States, the French continued to struggle against the Vietminh, who used hit-and-run and ambush tactics. These are the tactics of **guerrillas,** irregular troops who blend into the civilian population and are difficult for regular armies to fight. Rising casualties and a lack of victories made the war unpopular with the French public.

The turning point came in the mountain town of Dien Bien Phu. By seizing the town, the French planned to cut the Vietminh's supply lines and force them into open battle. Soon afterward, a huge Vietminh force surrounded Dien Bien Phu and began bombarding the town. On May 7, 1954, the French forces fell to the Vietminh. The defeat convinced the French to make peace and withdraw from Indochina.

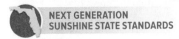

NEXT GENERATION SUNSHINE STATE STANDARDS

Continued from page 500

LAFS.1112.WHST.3.9: Draw evidence from informational texts to support analysis, reflection, and research.

Continued on page 502

domino theory the belief that if one nation in Asia fell to the Communists, neighboring countries would follow

guerrilla member of an armed band that carries out surprise attacks and sabotage rather than open warfare

GEOGRAPHY CONNECTION

Several factors contributed to American involvement in Vietnam.

1. **PLACES AND REGIONS** *What aspects of a Communist Vietnam threatened Japan's economy?* SS.912.A.1.4, SS.912.A.6.14, SS.912.G.1.2, SS.912.G.4.9

2. **THE USES OF GEOGRAPHY** *What was the threat to world shipping if Vietnam became a Communist country?* SS.912.A.1.4, SS.912.A.6.14, SS.912.G.1.2

Why Did Vietnam Matter to the United States?

Food for Japan
Japan was a key U.S. ally helping to contain communism in Asia. Japan had to import food, and South Vietnam was a major supplier of rice for the region.

Malaysian Rubber and Tin
Malaysia produced large amounts of tin and rubber needed by western industries. If it fell to communism, the supplies might be cut off.

Oil from Indonesia
Japan also depended on imported oil. If Southeast Asia fell to communism, oil supplies might have been cut off.

Strait of Malacca
Much of the world's shipping passed through this narrow strait. If Vietnam became communist, bombers would have been in range to threaten to block this strait.

Ho Chi Minh, Communist leader of North Vietnam, was determined to reunite Vietnam and began arming Vietcong guerrillas to seize power in South Vietnam.

▶ CRITICAL THINKING

Analyzing Why did American involvement in Vietnam grow after the Geneva Accords? LAFS.1112.RH.3.7, SS.912.A.6.13, SS.912.A.6.14

strategic important to the conduct or success of a larger plan

traditional set by custom; handed down from one generation to another

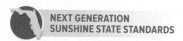

NEXT GENERATION SUNSHINE STATE STANDARDS

Continued from page 501

LAFS.1112.WHST.4.10: Write routinely over extended time frames (time for reflection and revision) and shorter time frames (a single sitting or a day or two) for a range of discipline-specific tasks, purposes, and audiences.

SS.912.A.1.2: Utilize a variety of primary and secondary sources to identify author, historical significance, audience, and authenticity to understand a historical period.

SS.912.A.1.4: Analyze how images, symbols, objects, cartoons, graphs, charts, maps, and artwork may be used to interpret the significance of time periods and events from the past.

SS.912.A.6.13: Analyze significant foreign policy events during the Truman, Eisenhower, Kennedy, Johnson, and Nixon administrations.

SS.912.A.6.14: Analyze causes, course, and consequences of the Vietnam War.

SS.912.A.7.10: Analyze the significance of Vietnam and Watergate on the government and people of the United States.

SS.912.G.1.2: Use spatial perspective and appropriate geographic terms and tools, including the Six Essential Elements, as organizational schema to describe any given place.

SS.912.G.4.9: Use political maps to describe the change in boundaries and governments within continents over time.

Geneva Accords

Negotiations to end the conflict were held in Geneva, Switzerland. The resulting Geneva Accords provided for a temporary division of Vietnam along the 17th parallel. Ho Chi Minh and the Vietminh controlled North Vietnam, and a pro-Western regime led by the fiercely anti-Communist Ngo Dinh Diem (ehn•GOH DIHN deh•EHM) held the South. French troops soon left, and the United States became the principal protector of the new government in South Vietnam.

The accords called for elections to be held in 1956 to reunite the country under a single government. Diem refused to permit the elections, however, fearing Ho Chi Minh would win. Eisenhower approved of Diem's actions and increased American aid to South Vietnam.

☑ **READING PROGRESS CHECK**

Analyzing Why did the United States protect South Vietnam?

American Involvement Deepens

GUIDING QUESTION *How did American involvement in Vietnam change during the Kennedy and Johnson administrations?*

After Ngo Dinh Diem refused to hold national elections, Ho Chi Minh and the Communists began an armed struggle to reunify the nation. They organized a new guerrilla army of South Vietnamese Communists, which became known as the Vietcong. Eisenhower sent hundreds of military advisers to train South Vietnam's army, but the Vietcong continued to grow more powerful because many Vietnamese opposed Diem's government. By 1961, the Vietcong had established control over much of the countryside.

Kennedy Takes Over

When President Kennedy took office in 1961, he continued to support South Vietnam, believing the country was vital in the battle against communism. From 1961 to late 1963, the number of U.S. military personnel in South Vietnam jumped from about 2,000 to around 15,000. Yet they failed to shore up the floundering Diem regime. For example, the South Vietnamese created special fortified villages known as **strategic** hamlets. They then moved villagers to these hamlets, despite the peasants' resentment at being uprooted from their villages. The program proved to be extremely unpopular.

The Overthrow of Diem

American officials blamed Diem. He made himself even more unpopular by discriminating against Buddhism, one of the country's most widely practiced religions. In the spring of 1963, he banned the **traditional** religious flags for the Buddha's birthday. When Buddhists protested in the streets, Diem's police killed nine people. In response, a Buddhist monk poured gasoline over his robes and set himself on fire, the first of several to do so. Images of their self-destruction horrified Americans as they watched the footage on television news reports.

In August 1963, U.S. ambassador Henry Cabot Lodge arrived in Vietnam. He learned that several Vietnamese generals were plotting to overthrow the unpopular Diem. When Lodge expressed U.S. sympathy for their cause, the generals launched a military coup, seizing power on November 1, 1963. They executed Diem soon after. Despite his unpopularity, Diem had been a respected nationalist. After his death, South Vietnam's government weakened.

Johnson and Vietnam

Just three weeks after Diem's death, Kennedy was assassinated. The presidency—and the growing problem of Vietnam—now belonged to President Lyndon B. Johnson. Although he approached Vietnam

RDA/Hulton Archive/Getty Images

cautiously at first, Johnson wanted to keep the country from falling to the Communists. Additionally, some had blamed Democrats when China became a Communist country in 1949. Should the Democrats "lose" Vietnam, Johnson feared, it might "shatter my Presidency, kill my administration, and damage our democracy."

On August 2, 1964, Johnson announced that North Vietnamese torpedo boats had fired on two U.S. destroyers in the Gulf of Tonkin. Two days later, he reported another attack. Insisting that these were unprovoked, he ordered American aircraft to attack North Vietnamese ships and naval facilities.

Johnson then asked Congress for the authority to defend American forces and allies in Southeast Asia. Congress readily agreed, and on August 7, 1964, it passed the Gulf of Tonkin Resolution. This authorized the president to "take all necessary measures to repel any armed attack against the forces of the United States and to prevent further aggression." Soon after, the Vietcong began to attack bases where American advisers were stationed in South Vietnam. After one particularly damaging attack, Johnson sent American aircraft to bomb North Vietnam.

ANALYZING PRIMARY SOURCES

Should America Fight in Vietnam?

As the war in Vietnam dragged on, Americans became increasingly divided over the nation's role in the conflict. In January 1966, George W. Ball delivered an address to indicate "how we got [into Vietnam] and why we must stay." George F. Kennan, a former ambassador to the Soviet Union, argued that American involvement in Vietnam was "something we would not choose deliberately if the choice were ours to make all over again today."

———— NO ————

" Vietnam is not a region of major military-industrial importance. . . . [E]ven a situation in which South Vietnam was controlled exclusively by the Vietcong . . . would not present, in my opinion, dangers great enough to justify our direct military intervention.

George F. Kennan
Former diplomat

And to attempt to crush North Vietnamese strength to a point where Hanoi could no longer give any support for Vietcong political activity in the South would . . . have the effect of bringing in Chinese forces at some point. . . .

Our motives are widely misinterpreted; and the spectacle of Americans inflicting grievous injury on the lives of a poor and helpless people . . . produces reactions among millions of people throughout the world profoundly detrimental to the image we would like them to hold of this country. **"**

—from testimony before the Senate Foreign Relations Committee, February 10, 1966

———— YES ————

" [T]he conflict in Viet-Nam is a product of the great shifts and changes triggered by the Second World War. . . . [T]he Soviet Union under Stalin exploited the confusion to push out the perimeter of its power and influence in an effort to extend the outer limits of Communist domination by force or the threat of force. . . .

George W. Ball
Undersecretary of State

The bloody encounters in [Vietnam] . . . are thus in a real sense battles and skirmishes in a continuing war to prevent one Communist power after another from violating internationally recognized boundary lines fixing the outer limits of Communist dominion. . . .

In the long run our hopes for the people of South Viet-Nam reflect our hopes for people everywhere. What we seek is a world living in peace and freedom. **"**

—from a speech delivered January 30, 1966

> **DBQ** **Analyzing Historical Documents**
>
> **1** *Identifying Central Ideas* Why does Ball believe that the United States is justified in fighting in Vietnam?
> SS.912.A.1.2, SS.912.A.6.13, SS.912.A.6.14
>
> **2** *Comparing and Contrasting* What is the fundamental difference between the views of Ball and Kennan?
> SS.912.A.1.2, SS.912.A.6.13, SS.912.A.6.14

(l)Rolls Press/Popperfoto/Getty Images; (r)©Bettmann/Corbis

Roy P. Benavidez (1935–1998)

Roy P. Benavidez received the Medal of Honor, the nation's highest award for heroism, for action in the Vietnam War. In May 1968, Benavidez went to the aid of Special Forces team members who were wounded and surrounded, unable to get to a helicopter. Benavidez ran 80 yards through enemy fire. Wounded three times in getting to the men, he stayed with them some eight hours, preparing an evacuation. During that time, he was wounded two more times. While carrying men to the rescue helicopter, he was attacked from behind, but managed to kill his attacker in hand-to-hand combat. Only after loading all the dead and wounded, did Benavidez board the helicopter. His actions saved the lives of at least eight other men.

Helicopters allowed U.S. troops to get in and out of jungles and mountainous areas in Vietnam.

▶ **CRITICAL THINKING**
Determining Cause and Effect How did the Vietnamese landscape make troop movements difficult? LAFS.1112.WHST.3.9, SS.912.A.1.4, SS.912.A.6.14

Both the American public and Johnson's advisers generally supported these actions. Some officials disagreed, however. Undersecretary of State George Ball initially supported involvement in Vietnam, but later turned against it. He warned that if the United States got too involved, it would be difficult to get out. "Once on the tiger's back," he warned, "we cannot be sure of picking the place to dismount."

Other advisers, such as National Security Advisor McGeorge Bundy, believed that success in Vietnam was important to protect American interests and maintain stability in Southeast Asia. In a memo to the president, he argued:

PRIMARY SOURCE

"The stakes in Vietnam are extremely high. The American investment is very large, and American responsibility is a fact of life which is palpable in the atmosphere of Asia, and even elsewhere. The international prestige of the U.S. and a substantial part of our influence are directly at risk in Vietnam."

—quoted in *The Best and the Brightest,* 1972

In March 1965, Johnson again expanded American involvement by ordering a sustained bombing campaign against North Vietnam. That same month, he sent the first U.S. combat troops into Vietnam.

☑ **READING PROGRESS CHECK**

Describing What event weakened the government of South Vietnam?

A Bloody Stalemate

GUIDING QUESTION *What military tactics were used by the Vietcong, and how did American troops respond?*

By the end of 1965, more than 180,000 U.S. combat troops were fighting in Vietnam. That number doubled in 1966. The U.S. military entered Vietnam with great confidence. "America seemed omnipotent then," wrote one of the first marines to arrive, Philip Caputo, in his prologue to *A Rumor of War.* "[W]e saw ourselves as the champions of 'a cause that was destined to triumph.'"

Lacking the firepower of the American forces, the Vietcong used ambushes, booby traps, and other guerrilla tactics. These techniques could be greatly destructive. Ronald J. Glasser, an American army doctor, described the devastating effects of one booby trap:

PRIMARY SOURCE

"Three quarters of the way through the tangle, a trooper brushed against a two-inch vine, and a grenade slung at chest high went off, shattering the right side of his head and body. . . . Nearby troopers took hold of the unconscious soldier and, half carrying, half dragging him, pulled him the rest of the way through the tangle."

—quoted in *Vietnam, A History,* 1997

The Vietcong also frustrated American troops by blending in with the general population and then quickly vanishing. "It was a sheer physical impossibility to keep the enemy from slipping away whenever he wished," explained one American general.

"Search and Destroy"

To counter these tactics, American troops tried to find enemy troops, bomb their positions, destroy their

MPI/Archive Photos/Getty Images

supply lines, and force them out into the open for combat. American planes dropped **napalm,** a jellied gasoline that explodes on contact. They also used **Agent Orange,** a chemical that strips leaves from trees and shrubs, turning farmland and forest into wasteland.

American military leaders underestimated the Vietcong's strength. They also misjudged the enemy's stamina and the support they had among the South Vietnamese. American generals believed that bombing and killing large numbers of Vietcong would destroy their morale and lead them to surrender. The guerrillas, however, had no intention of surrendering, and they were willing to accept huge losses to achieve their goals.

The Ho Chi Minh Trail

In the Vietcong's war effort, North Vietnamese support was a major factor. Although the Vietcong included many South Vietnamese, North Vietnam provided arms, advisers, and leadership. As Vietcong casualties mounted, North Vietnam began sending North Vietnamese Army units to fight. North Vietnam sent arms and supplies south by way of a network of jungle paths known as the Ho Chi Minh Trail. The trail wound through Cambodia and Laos, bypassing the border between North Vietnam and South Vietnam.

North Vietnam itself received weapons and other support from the Soviet Union and China. Johnson feared that directly attacking North Vietnam would bring China into the war, as had happened in Korea. Yet Johnson's limits made winning the war very difficult. Instead of conquering territory, American troops had to fight a war of attrition—defeating enemy forces by wearing them down. This strategy led troops to conduct grisly body counts after battles to determine how many enemy soldiers had been killed. The American military began measuring "progress" in the war by the number of enemy dead.

Bombing from American planes killed many thousands of Vietnamese. American soldiers were also dying in increasing numbers. The notion of a quick and decisive victory grew increasingly remote. As a result, many citizens back home began to question the nation's involvement in the war.

Chemicals such as napalm and Agent Orange devastated the landscape of Vietnam.

▶ CRITICAL THINKING
Drawing Conclusions How might the use of chemical weapons have encouraged the South Vietnamese populace to support the Vietcong?
LAFS.1112.WHST.3.9, SS.912.A.1.4, SS.912.A.6.14

napalm a jellied gasoline used for bombs

Agent Orange a chemical defoliant used to clear Vietnamese jungles during the Vietnam War

 READING PROGRESS CHECK

Explaining What two chemical weapons did the United States use in Vietnam?

©Bettmann/Corbis

LESSON 1 REVIEW

Reviewing Vocabulary

1. ***Explaining*** What are guerrilla tactics? LAFS.1112.RH.2.4

2. ***Defining*** What was the "domino theory"? LAFS.1112.RH.2.4

Using Your Notes

3. ***Summarizing*** Use the notes you completed during the lesson to summarize the reasons the United States aided France in Vietnam. LAFS.1112.WHST.3.9, SS.912.A.6.14

Answering the Guiding Questions

4. ***Evaluating*** Why did the United States provide military aid to the French in Indochina? LAFS.1112.WHST.3.9, SS.912.A.6.14

5. ***Describing*** How did U.S. involvement in Vietnam change during the Kennedy and Johnson administrations? LAFS.1112.WHST.3.9, SS.912.A.6.13, SS.912.A.6.14

6. ***Analyzing*** What military tactics were used by the Vietcong, and how did U.S. troops respond? LAFS.1112.WHST.3.9, SS.912.A.6.14

Writing Activity

7. **ARGUMENT** Take on the role of a member of Congress in 1964. Write a statement supporting or opposing the Gulf of Tonkin Resolution. LAFS.1112.WHST.1.1, LAFS.1112.WHST.4.10, SS.912.A.6.13, SS.912.A.6.14

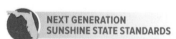

LESSON 2
Vietnam Divides the Nation

networks
There's More Online!

READING HELPDESK

Academic Vocabulary

- media
- disproportionate

Content Vocabulary

- credibility gap
- teach-in
- dove
- hawk

TAKING NOTES

Key Ideas and Details

Organizing Fill in a graphic organizer similar to the one below, listing reasons for opposition to the Vietnam War.
LAFS.1112.RH.37, SS.912.A.6.14

Reasons for Opposition to Vietnam War

NEXT GENERATION SUNSHINE STATE STANDARDS

LAFS.1112.RH.2.4: Determine the meaning of words and phrases as they are used in a text, including analyzing how an author uses and refines the meaning of a key term over the course of a text (e.g., how Madison defines faction in Federalist No. 10).

LAFS.1112.WHST.1.1: Write arguments focused on discipline-specific content.

LAFS.1112.WHST.3.9: Draw evidence from informational texts to support analysis, reflection, and research.

LAFS.1112.WHST.4.10: Write routinely over extended time frames (time for reflection and revision) and shorter time frames (a single sitting or a day or two) for a range of discipline-specific tasks, purposes, and audiences.

Continued on page 507

ESSENTIAL QUESTIONS

- How does military conflict divide people within cultures?
- Should citizens support the government during wartime?

IT MATTERS BECAUSE

As casualties mounted in Vietnam, many Americans began to protest the war. The conflict over the war, increasing violence, and the apparent lack of progress in Vietnam led President Johnson to decide not to run again.

The Antiwar Movement Emerges

GUIDING QUESTION *Why did Americans disagree about the Vietnam War?*

When the first U.S. combat troops arrived in Vietnam in the spring of 1965, about 66 percent of Americans approved of U.S. policy in Vietnam. As the war dragged on, however, public support began to wane. **Media** accounts seemed to contradict government reports. For example, the American commander in South Vietnam, General William Westmoreland, reported that the "enemy's hopes are bankrupt" and "the end begins to come into view." Yet millions of people saw images of American casualties on television in their living rooms each day as Vietnam became the first "television war." For many people, a **credibility gap** had developed—they had a hard time believing what the Johnson administration said about the war.

Congress, which in the Gulf of Tonkin Resolution had granted Johnson a great deal of power to conduct the war, began to seek greater involvement. Beginning in February 1966, the Senate Foreign Relations Committee held "educational" hearings on Vietnam. They called in policy makers and critics to discuss the administration's military strategy.

Teach-ins Begin

In March 1965, a group of faculty members and students at the University of Michigan joined together in a **teach-in.** They discussed the issues surrounding the war and reaffirmed their reasons for opposing it. In May 1965, 122 colleges held a "National Teach-In" by radio for more than 100,000 antiwar demonstrators.

People opposed the war for different reasons. Some saw the conflict as a civil war in which the United States should not interfere. Others saw South Vietnam as a corrupt dictatorship and believed defending it was immoral.

Anger at the Draft

Thousands of demonstrators held protests against the war. Students for a Democratic Society (SDS) organized a march on Washington, D.C., that drew more than 20,000 people. A rally at the Lincoln Memorial drew tens of thousands of protesters as well.

Many protesters focused on what they saw as an unfair draft system. Until 1969, college students could often defer military service until after graduation. Young people from working-class families unable to afford college were more likely to be drafted. Draftees were most likely to be assigned to combat units, and they commonly made up more than half of the casualties. Most who served in Vietnam, however, enlisted voluntarily.

Nevertheless, a **disproportionate** number of working-class and minority youths went to war. Between 1961 and 1966, African Americans constituted about 10 percent of military personnel. Because African Americans were more likely to be assigned to combat units, however, they accounted for almost 20 percent of combat-related deaths. This skewed death rate angered African American leaders. In April 1967, Dr. Martin Luther King, Jr., publicly condemned the conflict: "I speak for the poor of America who are paying the double price of smashed hopes at home, and death and corruption in Vietnam. . . . The great initiative in this war is ours. The initiative to stop it must be ours." In response, military officials tried to reduce African American casualties. By war's end, African Americans made up about 12 percent of America's dead.

As the war escalated, an increased draft call put many college students at risk of being drafted. An estimated 500,000 draftees refused to go. Some burned their draft cards, did not show up for induction, or fled the country. From 1965 to 1968, officials prosecuted over 3,000 Americans who refused to serve. In 1969, a lottery system was instituted, so only those with low numbers were subject to the draft. Many draftees argued that if they were old enough to fight, they were old enough to vote. In 1971, the Twenty-sixth Amendment to the Constitution was ratified, giving all citizens age 18 and older the right to vote in all state and federal elections.

Hawks and Doves

In the face of growing opposition to the war, President Johnson remained determined to continue fighting, recognizing the effort as resistance to communism. He assailed his critics in Congress as "selfish men who want to

---

Analyzing
SUPREME COURT
CASES

Tinker v. Des Moines

In 1965, students in Des Moines, Iowa, expressed their opposition to the Vietnam War by wearing black armbands to school. The school district then banned the wearing of black armbands and subsequently expelled three students who violated the policy. The students challenged their expulsion as a violation of their First Amendment right to free speech. In 1969, the Supreme Court ruled 7 to 2 in favor of the students, holding that the wearing of black armbands was a form of "symbolic expression" covered by the First Amendment. As long as their symbolic protest was not disruptive, they had a right to express their opinion.

DBQ **INTERPRETING SIGNIFICANCE** How does the *Tinker* decision affect your right to wear a T-shirt supporting a cause you believe in? SS.912.A.1.6

NEXT GENERATION SUNSHINE STATE STANDARDS

Continued from page 506

MAFS.912.S-ID.1: Summarize, represent and interpret data on a single count or measurement variable.

SS.912.A.1.4: Analyze how images, symbols, objects, cartoons, graphs, charts, maps, and artwork may be used to interpret the significance of time periods and events from the past.

SS.912.A.1.6: Use case studies to explore social, political, legal, and economic relationships in history.

SS.912.A.6.13: Analyze significant foreign policy events during the Truman, Eisenhower, Kennedy, Johnson, and Nixon administrations.

SS.912.A.6.14: Analyze causes, course, and consequences of the Vietnam War.

SS.912.A.7.1: Identify causes for Post-World War II prosperity and its effects on American society.

SS.912.A.7.4: Evaluate the success of 1960s era presidents' foreign and domestic policies.

SS.912.A.7.9: Examine the similarities of social movements (Native Americans, Hispanics, women, anti-war protesters) of the 1960s and 1970s.

SS.912.A.7.10: Analyze the significance of Vietnam and Watergate on the government and people of the United States.

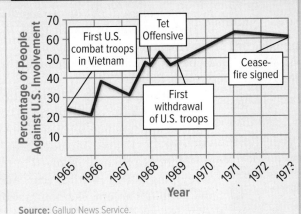

CHARTS/GRAPHS | **OPPOSITION TO THE VIETNAM WAR**

As the Vietnam War progressed, opposition to the conflict generally increased.

1 **Analyzing** During which two years was opposition to the war lowest? What event occurred around that time? MAFS.912.S-ID.1, SS.912.A.6.14, SS.912.A.7.10

2 **Predicting Consequences** In what year did opposition to the war peak? What consequence might you expect this to have? MAFS.912.S-ID.1, SS.912.A.6.14, SS.912.A.7.10

Source: Gallup News Service.

---

media a means of expression or communication, especially in reference to the agencies of mass communication—newspapers, radio, television, and the Internet

credibility gap lack of trust or believability

teach-in an extended meeting or class held to discuss a social or political issue

disproportionate being out of proportion; lacking in proper relation

dove a person in favor of the United States withdrawing from the Vietnam War

hawk someone who believed the United States should continue its military efforts in Vietnam

Antiwar demonstrators protest in New York City in 1969.

▶ **CRITICAL THINKING**
Analyzing Information What can you learn about war protesters from this photograph? SS.912.A1.4, SS.912.A.7.10

advance their own interests" and was dismissive of the college protesters. Johnson was not alone in his views. In time, the nation seemed to be divided into two camps. **Doves** wanted the United States to leave Vietnam. **Hawks**, however, wanted the nation to stay and fight. Some saw communism as a threat and challenged the patriotism of the doves. As the two groups debated, the war appeared to take a dramatic turn for the worse.

☑ **READING PROGRESS CHECK**

Explaining What was the effect of the Vietnam War being a "television war"?

1968: The Pivotal Year

GUIDING QUESTION *Why was 1968 considered the most turbulent year of the 1960s?*

The most turbulent year of the chaotic 1960s was 1968. The year saw a shocking political announcement, two traumatic assassinations, and a political convention held amid strident antiwar demonstrations. First, however, the United States endured a surprise attack in Vietnam.

The Tet Offensive

On January 30, 1968, during Tet, the Vietnamese New Year, the Vietcong and North Vietnamese launched a massive surprise attack. In what was called the Tet Offensive, guerrilla fighters attacked most American airbases in South Vietnam and most of the South's major cities. Vietcong even blasted their way into the American embassy in Saigon.

After about a month of fighting, U.S. and South Vietnamese soldiers repelled the enemy troops, inflicting heavy losses on them. But less tangible damage had been done. The American people were shocked that an enemy supposedly on the verge of defeat could launch such a large-scale attack. The media openly criticized the war. "The American people should be getting ready to accept, if they haven't already, the prospect that the whole Vietnam effort may be doomed," declared the *Wall Street Journal*. Television newscaster Walter Cronkite said that it seemed "more certain than ever that the bloody experience in Vietnam is to end in a stalemate."

Johnson Leaves the Race

Both Johnson and the war had become increasingly unpopular. With the presidential election of 1968 on the horizon, some Democratic politicians made surprising moves. In November 1967, Eugene McCarthy—a little-known liberal senator from Minnesota—declared that he would challenge Johnson for the Democratic presidential nomination. At first, his candidacy was mostly dismissed, but he attracted support from those who opposed the war. In March 1968, McCarthy made a strong showing in the New Hampshire primary, winning more than 40 percent of the vote. Realizing that Johnson was vulnerable, Senator Robert Kennedy, who also opposed the war, quickly entered the race for the Democratic nomination.

With both the country and his own party deeply divided, Johnson appeared on television on March 31, 1968. He announced, "I have concluded that I should not permit the presidency to become involved in the partisan divisions that are developing in this political year. Accordingly, I shall not seek, and I will not accept, the nomination of my party for another term as your President."

Bernard Gotfryd/Premium Archive/Getty Images

A Season of Violence

More shocking events followed Johnson's announcement. On April 4, Dr. Martin Luther King, Jr., was assassinated in Memphis by James Earl Ray. On June 5, Robert Kennedy, who appeared likely to win the Democratic nomination, was gunned down by Sirhan Sirhan, an Arab nationalist.

The violence that seemed to plague the country in 1968 culminated with a chaotic and well-publicized clash between antiwar protesters and police at the Democratic National Convention in Chicago. Thousands of young activists surrounded the convention center to protest the war. Despite these protests, the delegates selected Vice President Hubert Humphrey as the Democratic nominee. Meanwhile, in a park not far from the convention hall, protesters and police began fighting. Demonstrators taunted police with the chant, "The whole world is watching!" as the officers tried to force them to disperse. Violence between protesters and police aired on national television.

Protests at the Democratic National Convention in 1968 were nationally televised.

▶ CRITICAL THINKING
Drawing Conclusions How might the protests at the convention have affected voters' opinions of Democrats? SS.912.A.1.4, SS.912.A.7.10

Nixon Wins the Presidency

At a much more sedate convention, Republicans selected former vice president and 1960 presidential hopeful Richard Nixon as their candidate. A third candidate, Governor George Wallace of Alabama, decided to run in 1968 as an independent. An outspoken segregationist, Wallace sought to attract Americans who felt threatened by the civil rights movement and urban social unrest.

Public opinion polls gave Nixon a wide lead over Humphrey and Wallace. Nixon's campaign promise to unify the nation and restore law and order appealed to Americans who feared their country was spinning out of control. He claimed to represent a silent majority of Americans who sought to maintain law and order but had been overshadowed in recent years by social and political turmoil. He promised that he had a "secret plan" to bring "peace with honor" in Vietnam.

Humphrey's campaign faced significant challenges, but by October 1968, his increasingly antiwar stance and strong campaigning helped turn his numbers around. A week before the election, President Johnson announced that the bombing of North Vietnam had halted and that a cease-fire would follow. These boosts came too late for Humphrey, however. Nixon defeated him by more than 100 electoral votes, although he only won the popular vote by a slim margin of 43 percent to 42 percent.

©Arthur Rothstein/Historical/Corbis

SKILLS PRACTICE

Look at the protest signs in the pictures in this lesson. Look for words you know on the signs. Think about what the words mean. ELD.K12.ELL.SI.1, ELD.K12.ELL.SS.1

✓ READING PROGRESS CHECK

Evaluating Why was the Tet Offensive a turning point in the Vietnam War?

LESSON 2 REVIEW

Reviewing Vocabulary

1. *Defining* What was the credibility gap? LAFS.1112.RH.2.4

2. *Contrast* How did doves and hawks differ? LAFS.1112.RH.2.4

Using Your Notes

3. *Summarizing* Use the notes you completed during the lesson to write a paragraph that summarizes the reasons why many people opposed the Vietnam War. LAFS.1112.WHST.3.9, SS.912.A.7.10

Answering the Guiding Questions

4. *Identifying* Why did Americans disagree about the Vietnam War? LAFS.1112.WHST.3.9, SS.912.A.6.14, SS.912.A.7.10

5. *Describing* Why was 1968 considered the most turbulent year of the 1960s? LAFS.1112.WHST.3.9, SS.912.A.6.14, SS.912.A.7.10

Writing Activity

6. ARGUMENT Suppose that you were living in 1968. Write an article for a student newspaper in which you present opposing views of the Vietnam War. LAFS.1112.SL.1.1, LAFS.1112.WHST.4.10, SS.912.A.6.14, SS.912.7.10

LESSON 3
The War Winds Down

ESSENTIAL QUESTIONS
• How does military conflict divide people within cultures?
• Should citizens support the government during wartime?

READING HELPDESK

Academic Vocabulary
• generation
• unresolved

Content Vocabulary
• linkage
• Vietnamization

TAKING NOTES

Key Ideas and Details

Organizing As you read, use the following graphic organizer to list the steps that President Nixon took to end American involvement in Vietnam.
LAFS.1112.RH.3.7, SS.912.A.6.13, SS.912.A.6.14

Steps Nixon Took

**NEXT GENERATION
SUNSHINE STATE STANDARDS**

LAFS.1112.RH.2.4: Determine the meaning of words and phrases as they are used in a text, including analyzing how an author uses and refines the meaning of a key term over the course of a text (e.g., how Madison defines faction in Federalist No. 10).

LAFS.1112.RH.3.7: Integrate and evaluate multiple sources of information presented in diverse formats and media (e.g., visually, quantitatively, as well as in words) in order to address a question or solve a problem.

Continued on page 511

IT MATTERS BECAUSE
Shortly after taking office, President Nixon moved to end the nation's involvement in Vietnam. The final years of the conflict yielded more bloodshed and turmoil, as well as growing cynicism.

Nixon Moves to End the War

GUIDING QUESTION *What policies did Nixon employ to end the war?*

As a step toward ending the war, Nixon appointed Henry Kissinger as special assistant for national security affairs. Kissinger embarked upon a policy called **linkage,** or improving relations with the Soviet Union and China, to try to persuade them to reduce their aid to North Vietnam. In August 1969, Kissinger also entered into secret negotiations with North Vietnam's representative, Le Duc Tho.

Meanwhile, Nixon began **Vietnamization.** This process involved the gradual withdrawal of U.S. troops while the South Vietnamese assumed more of the fighting. He announced the withdrawal of 25,000 soldiers on June 8, 1969. At the same time, however, Nixon increased air strikes against North Vietnam and began secretly bombing Vietcong sanctuaries in neighboring Cambodia.

Turmoil at Home Continues
In late 1969, Americans learned that in the spring of 1968 an American platoon under the command of Lieutenant William Calley had massacred unarmed South Vietnamese civilians in the hamlet of My Lai. Most of the victims were old men, women, and children. Calley eventually went to prison for his role in the killings. Jan Barry, a founder of the Vietnam Veterans Against the War, viewed My Lai as a symbol of the dilemma his **generation** faced in the conflict:

PRIMARY SOURCE

❝To kill on military orders and be a criminal, or to refuse to kill and be a criminal is the moral agony of America's Vietnam war generation. It is what has forced upward of sixty thousand young Americans, draft resisters and deserters, to Canada, and created one hundred thousand military deserters a year. . . .❞
—quoted in *Who Spoke Up?: American Protest Against the War in Vietnam, 1963–1975,* 1984

In April 1970, Nixon announced that American troops had invaded Cambodia to destroy Vietcong bases there. Many believed this invasion expanded the war, which set off many protests. On May 4, Ohio National Guard soldiers armed with tear gas and rifles fired on demonstrators at Kent State University, killing four students. Days later, police killed two student demonstrators at Jackson State College in Mississippi.

An angry Congress began to work to end the president's control of the war. In December 1970, it repealed the Gulf of Tonkin Resolution, which had given the president nearly complete power in directing the conflict.

The following year, a former employee of the Department of Defense, Daniel Ellsberg, leaked what became known as the Pentagon Papers to the *New York Times*. The documents contained details about decisions to expand the war, and confirmed what many Americans had long believed: the government had not been honest with them.

The U.S. invasion of Cambodia led to mass protests and to the tragic killing of four students by National Guard troops at Kent State University in May 1970.

▶ **CRITICAL THINKING**

Determining Cause and Effect
How did the invasion of Cambodia lead to the shootings at Kent State University? SS.912.A.1.4, SS.912.A.7.10

linkage policy of improving relations with the Soviet Union and China in hopes of persuading them to cut back their aid to North Vietnam

Vietnamization the process of making South Vietnam assume more of the war effort by slowly withdrawing American troops from Vietnam

generation a group of individuals who were born and who live during the same period of time

The United States Pulls Out

Americans were increasingly ready for the war to end as the presidential election of 1972 approached. Nixon faced Democratic challenger George McGovern, an outspoken critic of the war. Less than a month before the election, however, Kissinger emerged from his secret talks with Le Duc Tho to announce that "peace is at hand." Nixon soundly defeated McGovern.

Soon, Kissinger's peace negotiations broke down over disagreements about the presence of North Vietnamese troops in the South. In December 1972, to force North Vietnam to resume negotiations, the Nixon administration began the most destructive air raids of the war. In what became known as the "Christmas bombings," American B-52s dropped thousands of tons of bombs on North Vietnamese targets for 11 straight days. Then negotiations resumed. On January 27, 1973, the warring sides signed an agreement "ending the war and restoring the peace in Vietnam." The United States promised to withdraw its troops, and both sides agreed to exchange prisoners of war. After almost eight years of war, the nation ended its direct involvement in Vietnam.

The Domino Effect

Peace did not last. In January 1975, Cambodia fell under the control of the Communist group the Khmer Rouge. In March 1975, the North Vietnamese army invaded South Vietnam. Nixon had resigned in August 1974 following Watergate, a scandal that broke as the war was winding down. When the new president, Gerald Ford, asked for funds to aid the South Vietnamese, Congress refused. On April 30, the North Vietnamese captured Saigon, South Vietnam's capital. They then renamed the city Ho Chi Minh City. Laos, another country in the region, was also greatly affected by the Vietnam War. Though Laos was run by a neutral coalition government during most of the war, the constant effects of bombings on the parts of the Ho Chi Minh Trail in Laos destabilized that neutrality. Communists took over in Laos after the fall of Saigon. Thus, the domino effect played out as predicted.

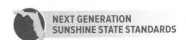

NEXT GENERATION SUNSHINE STATE STANDARDS

Continued from page 510
LAFS.1112.WHST.3.9: Draw evidence from informational texts to support analysis, reflection, and research.

LAFS.1112.WHST.4.10: Write routinely over extended time frames (time for reflection and revision) and shorter time frames (a single sitting or a day or two) for a range of discipline-specific tasks, purposes, and audiences.

Continued on page 512

✔ **READING PROGRESS CHECK**

Sequencing How did the "Christmas bombings" help to put an end to U.S. involvement in the Vietnam War?

John Filo

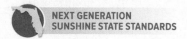
Continued from page 511

SS.912.A.1.2: Utilize a variety of primary and secondary sources to identify author, historical significance, audience, and authenticity to understand a historical period.

SS.912.A.1.4: Analyze how images, symbols, objects, cartoons, graphs, charts, maps, and artwork may be used to interpret the significance of time periods and events from the past.

SS.912.A.1.6: Use case studies to explore social, political, legal, and economic relationships in history.

SS.912.A.6.13: Analyze significant foreign policy events during the Truman, Eisenhower, Kennedy, Johnson, and Nixon administrations.

SS.912.A.6.14: Analyze causes, course, and consequences of the Vietnam War.

SS.912.A.7.4: Evaluate the success of 1960s era presidents' foreign and domestic policies.

SS.912.A.7.9: Examine the similarities of social movements (Native Americans, Hispanics, women, anti-war protesters) of the 1960s and 1970s.

SS.912.A.7.10: Analyze the significance of Vietnam and Watergate on the government and people of the United States.

The Legacy of Vietnam

GUIDING QUESTION *How was the political and cultural aftermath of the Vietnam War different from previous international conflicts?*

"The lessons of the past in Vietnam," President Ford declared in 1975, "have already been learned—learned by Presidents, learned by Congress, learned by the American people—and we should have our focus on the future." Vietnam had a profound effect on America.

The War's Human Toll

America paid a heavy price for its involvement in Vietnam, far more than the estimated $173 billion in direct costs. Approximately 58,000 young Americans died, and some 300,000 were injured. An estimated 1 million North Vietnamese and South Vietnamese soldiers died, as did millions more civilians. Back home, some soldiers had trouble readjusting. Army Specialist Doug Johnson recalled:

PRIMARY SOURCE

❝It took a while for me to recognize that I did suffer some psychological problems in trying to deal with my experience in Vietnam. . . . One evening . . . I went to see a movie on post. I don't recall . . . what it was about, but I remember there was a sad part, and that I started crying uncontrollably. It hadn't dawned on me before this episode that I had . . . succeeded in burying my emotions.❞

—quoted in *Touched by the Dragon,* 1998

Because many people considered the war a defeat and wanted to put it behind them, the veterans' sacrifices often went unrecognized. They received relatively few welcome-home parades and celebrations.

🏛 ANALYZING SUPREME COURT CASES

NEW YORK TIMES v. *UNITED STATES,* 1971

Background to the Case

In 1971, Daniel Ellsberg leaked classified documents, known as the Pentagon Papers, to the *New York Times* and the *Washington Post*. When the newspapers attempted to publish these documents, the Nixon administration argued that publication would threaten national security. The case centered on the First Amendment guarantee of a free press.

How the Court Ruled

In a 6-to-3 per curiam opinion—*per curiam* meaning that the decision was issued by the whole Court and not specific justices—the Court found that the Nixon administration had failed to prove that publication of the Pentagon Papers would imperil the nation in any way. The *New York Times* and the *Washington Post* could publish the Pentagon Papers.

Daniel Ellsberg leaked the classified documents known as the Pentagon Papers. The New York Times *went to court to battle for its right to print the Pentagon Papers.*

DBQ **Analyzing Historical Documents**

❶ *Drawing Conclusions* Why do you think Daniel Ellsberg leaked the Pentagon Papers to the press? **SS.912.A.1.6, SS.912.A.7.10**

❷ *Defending* Do you think the government can ever justify media censorship, even based on national security concerns? **SS.912.A.1.6, SS.912.A.7.10**

©Bettmann/Corbis

The war remained **unresolved** for the American families whose relatives and friends were classified as prisoners of war (POWs) or missing in action (MIA). Despite many official investigations, these families were not convinced that the government had told the truth about POW/MIA policies.

Vietnam remained on the nation's mind nearly a decade later. In 1982 the nation dedicated the Vietnam Veterans Memorial in Washington, D.C., a large black granite wall inscribed with the names of those killed and missing in action in the war.

The War's Impact on the Nation

The war also left a mark on national politics. In 1973, Congress passed the War Powers Act as a way to reestablish some limits on executive power. The act required the president to inform Congress of any commitment of troops abroad within 48 hours, and to withdraw them in 60 to 90 days, unless Congress explicitly approved the troop commitment. No president has recognized this limitation, however, and the courts have tended to avoid the issue.

Nonetheless, every president since the law's passage has asked Congress to authorize the use of military force before committing ground troops to combat. In general, the war shook the nation's confidence and made some begin to question American foreign policies.

On the domestic front, the Vietnam War increased Americans' cynicism about their government. Together with Watergate, Vietnam made many Americans feel that the nation's leaders had misled them.

☑ READING PROGRESS CHECK

Assessing How did the American public treat returning Vietnam veterans?

The Vietnam Veterans Memorial is inscribed with the names of the more than 58,000 people killed or missing in Vietnam.

▶ **CRITICAL THINKING**
Making Generalizations How does the Vietnam Veterans Memorial symbolize U.S. involvement in the war? SS.912.A.1.4, SS.912.A.7.10

unresolved not cleared up; not dealt with successfully

Alex Wong/Getty Images News/Getty Images

SKILLS PRACTICE

Make a speech to your class giving your opinion about the Vietnam War. As you prepare the speech, make a list of the academic vocabulary words and content vocabulary words used in this chapter. Use at least eight of these words in the speech.
ELD.K12.ELL.SI.1, ELD.K12.ELL.SS.1, LAFS.1112.RH.2.4, LAFS.1112.SL.2.4

LESSON 3 REVIEW

Reviewing Vocabulary

1. *Defining* What was Vietnamization? LAFS.1112.RH.2.4

2. *Explaining* What was the goal of the linkage policy? LAFS.1112.RH.2.4

Using Your Notes

3. *Assessing* Use the notes you completed during the lesson to write a short essay assessing the effectiveness of the various strategies Nixon pursued in Vietnam. LAFS.1112.RH.3.7, SS.912.A.7.4

Answering the Guiding Questions

4. *Identifying* What policies did Nixon employ to end the war? LAFS.1112.WHST.3.9, SS.912.A.6.13, SS.912.A.7.4

5. *Contrasting* How was the political and cultural aftermath of the Vietnam War different from previous international conflicts? LAFS.1112.WHST.3.9, SS.912.A.7.10

Writing Activity

6. NARRATIVE Suppose you are a college student in 1970. Write a journal entry expressing your thoughts and feelings about the events at Kent State University and Jackson State College. LAFS.1112.WHST.4.10, SS.912.A.7.10

STUDY GUIDE

GOING TO WAR IN VIETNAM
LESSON 1

Why Did Vietnam Matter?

Malaysian Rubber and Tin
- large amounts of this natural resource found in region
- was needed by western industries

Food for Japan
- Japan was a key U.S. ally in Asia
- South Vietnam was a major source of rice

Strait of Malacca
- important global shipping route

Indonesian Oil
- Japan needed imported oil

VIETNAM DIVIDES THE NATION
LESSON 2

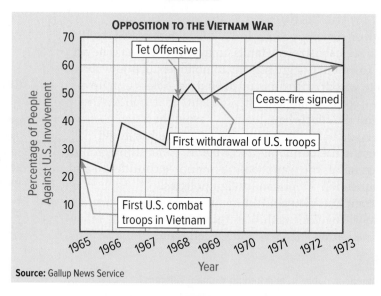

OPPOSITION TO THE VIETNAM WAR

Percentage of People Against U.S. Involvement

- Tet Offensive
- Cease-fire signed
- First withdrawal of U.S. troops
- First U.S. combat troops in Vietnam

Year: 1965 1966 1967 1968 1969 1970 1971 1972 1973

Source: Gallup News Service

THE WAR WINDS DOWN
LESSON 3

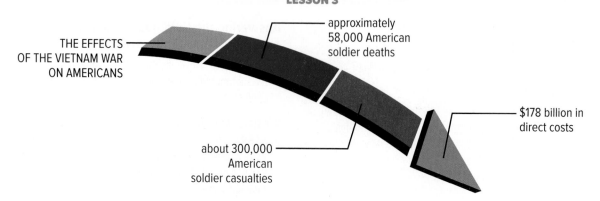

THE EFFECTS OF THE VIETNAM WAR ON AMERICANS

- approximately 58,000 American soldier deaths
- about 300,000 American soldier casualties
- $178 billion in direct costs

Directions: On a separate sheet of paper, answer the questions below. Make sure you read carefully and answer all parts to the question.

Lesson Review

Lesson 1

1 *Identifying Long Range Causes* Who controlled Vietnam prior to 1954, and how did this affect the coming of the Vietnam War? SS.912.A.6.14

2 *Explaining* Explain the difference between the two groups in Vietnam—North Vietnam under Ho Chi Minh and South Vietnam under Ngo Dinh Diem. SS.912.A.6.14

3 *Describing* What was the Vietcong? Why was its influence significant to what President Eisenhower was trying to do near the beginning of U.S. involvement in the Vietnam War? SS.912.A.6.14

4 *Explaining* What military tactics did the Vietminh use in Vietnam? SS.912.A.6.14

5 *Identifying Cause and Effect* How did the Gulf of Tonkin incident and the subsequent congressional resolution contribute to U.S. involvement in Vietnam? SS.912.A.6.14, SS.912.A.7.10

6 *Describing* What was the Ho Chi Minh Trail, and what was its importance in the Vietnam War? SS.912.A.6.14

Lesson 2

7 *Describing* What were the "teach-ins," and what viewpoints were represented among war protestors? SS.912.A.6.14, SS.912.A.7.9

8 *Identifying Perspectives* Why did many Americans question the fairness of the military draft during the Vietnam War? SS.912.A.6.14, SS.912.A.7.10

9 *Identifying Cause and Effect* What political rights were conferred by the Twenty-sixth Amendment? Explain why this amendment was introduced, and how it expanded the rights of certain people to participate in the democratic process. SS.912.A.7.10

10 *Analyzing* In what way did the Vietnam War shape the American presidential election in 1968? SS.912.A.6.13, SS.912.A.6.14, SS.912.A.7.10

Lesson 3

11 *Analyzing* What was Vietnamization? What was its purpose? SS.912.A.6.13, SS.912.A.6.14

12 *Understanding Relationships* What was the effect of the "Christmas bombings" of 1972 on the peace negotiations? SS.912.A.6.13, SS.912.A.6.14, SS.912.A.7.4

13 *Identifying Cause and Effect* What news triggered additional protests against the war, including the Kent State University demonstration, which resulted in student deaths? SS.912.A.6.14, SS.912.A.7.10

14 *Identifying Cause and Effect* How did the Pentagon Papers increase support for the antiwar movement? SS.912.A.6.14, SS.912.A.7.4, SS.912.A.7.10

Exploring the Essential Questions

15 *Analyzing* Why did the Vietnam War trigger such a massive anti-war movement compared to other American wars? Be sure to include the credibility gap and the issue of escalation in your answer. SS.912.A.6.14, SS.912.A.7.10

Critical Thinking

16 *Drawing Conclusions* Explain the domino theory and how it contributed to the political decision to become involved in the Vietnam War. SS.912.A.6.14

17 *Identifying Central Issues* Even though the United States initially supported Diem and South Vietnam, why did the United States support a military coup against Diem in 1963? SS.912.A.6.14

18 *Evaluating* Why did President Johnson want to avoid directly attacking North Vietnam, and how did U.S. military tactics create a different type of war? SS.912.A.6.14

19 *Finding the Main Idea* What was decided in the Supreme Court case *Tinker* v. *Des Moines*? SS.912.A.7.10

20 *Analyzing* Explain why the United States was unable to achieve its goals in Vietnam. SS.912.A.6.14, SS.912.A.7.10, LAFS.1112.WHST.3.8

21st Century Skills

21 *Sequencing* Create a time line that identifies the key events and dates of the Vietnam War, including events that helped to cause the war, events that shaped the American role in South Vietnam, and

Need Extra Help?

If You've Missed Question	**1**	**2**	**3**	**4**	**5**	**6**	**7**	**8**	**9**	**10**	**11**	**12**	**13**	**14**	**15**	**16**	**17**	**18**	**19**	**20**
Go to Lesson	1	1	1	1	1	1	2	2	2	2	3	3	3	3	2	2	1	1	2	1, 2, 3

events that shaped the outcome of the war, leading up to, during, and after the Vietnam War. SS.912.A.1.3, SS.912.A.6.14, SS.912.A.7.10

22 *Preparing a Speech* Should citizens support the government during wartime? Take a point of view on this issue and write a short speech explaining your opinion. Support your point of view with historical evidence. LAFS.1112.SL.2.4, LAFS.1112.WHST.1.1, LAFS.1112.WHST.2.4, LAFS.1112.WHST.4.10, SS.912.A.7.10

23 *Comparing and Contrasting* Explain the difference between Johnson's and Nixon's attitudes toward attacking Cambodia. SS.912.A.6.13, SS.912.A.6.14

DBQ Analyzing Primary Sources

Read the excerpt below, and then answer the questions that follow.

PRIMARY SOURCE

❝I read a lot of pacifist literature to determine whether or not I was a conscientious objector. I finally concluded that I wasn't. . . . The one clear decision I made in 1968 about me and the war was that if I was going to get out of it, I was going to get out in a legal way. I was not going to defraud the system in order to beat the system. I wasn't going to leave the country, because the odds of coming back looked real slim. . . . With all my terror of going into the Army . . . there was something seductive about it, too. I was seduced by World War II and John Wayne movies. . . . I had been, as we all were, victimized by a romantic, truly uninformed view of war.❞

—*Nam: The Vietnam War in the Words of the Men and Women Who Fought There*, 1981

24 *Evaluating* Explain how you could use corroboration to evaluate the validity of this source as a good example of the experiences of Vietnam veterans. LAFS.1112.RH.2.6, LAFS.1112.RH.3.8, LAFS.1112.RH.3.9, LAFS.1112.SL.1.3, SS.912.A.1.1, SS.912.A.6.14

25 *Drawing Conclusions* What does this source tell you about the role of the media before Vietnam? How did the way Americans remembered World War II shape the soldier's frame of reference and help him overcome his fear of being drafted? LAFS.1112.RH.3.8, LAFS.1112.RH.4.10, SS.912.A.1.1, SS.912.A.1.7, SS.912.A.6.1, SS.912.A.6.14, SS.912.A.7.10

Analyzing Visuals

Use the map below to answer the questions that follow.

26 *Posing Questions About Geographic Distributions* What questions do you need to ask to be able to explain why South Vietnam was strategically important to the United States military? SS.912.A.6.14, SS.912.G.1.2, SS.912.G.2.1, SS.912.G.4.9

27 *Identifying Cause and Effect* Using this map, as well as what you have learned in the chapter, explain the reasons why the United States government decided to support France and get involved in Vietnam. SS.912.A.6.14, SS.912.G.1.2, SS.912.G.2.1, SS.912.G.4.9

Extended Response Questions

28 *Analyzing* The conflict in Vietnam has been called the first "television war." Write a brief essay describing how television changed the way Americans viewed war in the 1960s, and how media coverage affected the nation's response to the war in Vietnam. Your essay should have an introduction, at least two paragraphs, and a conclusion. LAFS.1112.WHST.2.4, LAFS.1112.WHST.4.10, SS.912.A.1.7, SS.912.A.6.14, SS.912.A.7.10

29 *Summarizing* Either online, or at the library, research the details of the events that led to Roy Benavidez winning the Medal of Honor. Write a brief newspaper article summarizing his story, and identifying the most remarkable elements of his heroism and character. LAFS.1112.WHST.2.4, LAFS.1112.WHST.2.6, LAFS.1112.WHST.3.7, LAFS.1112.WHST.4.10, SS.912.A.6.14

Need Extra Help?

If You've Missed Question	21	22	23	24	25	26	27	28	29
Go to Lesson	1, 2, 3	2	1, 2, 3	1	1	1	1	2	1

Betty Friedan wrote her 1963 book *The Feminine Mystique* to describe a dissatisfaction many women felt about their social roles. The book also inspired many women to fight for equal rights.

FROM 1960 TO 1980

The Politics of Protest

THE STORY MATTERS ...

The civil rights movement that began in the 1950s inspired other groups in American society to stage protests in the 1960s and 1970s. Students, women, and Latinos all formed organizations and began demanding changes in how American society treated them.

ESSENTIAL QUESTIONS

- What did students, women, and Latinos learn from the civil rights movement and apply to their protest actions?
- How has society changed for students, women, and Latinos?

©Bettmann/Corbis

Place & Time: United States 1960–1980

In 1968, Shirley Chisholm became the first African American woman elected to Congress, as a representative for New York. In the House of Representatives, Chisholm supported equality of opportunity for all and the Equal Rights Amendment. Phyllis Schlafly was an attorney who unsuccessfully ran for Congress in 1952. She became a conservative political activist and formed the organization Stop ERA, which campaigned to defeat the Equal Rights Amendment.

Step Into the Place

Read the quotes and look at the information presented on the map.

DBQ **Analyzing Historical Documents** How is the focus of Chisholm's argument general and how is Schlafly's specific?

PRIMARY SOURCE

"Discrimination against women . . . is so widespread that it seems to many persons normal, natural, and right. . . .

. . . It is time we act to assure full equality of opportunity . . . to women.

The argument that this amendment will not solve the problem of sex discrimination is not relevant. . . . Of course laws will not eliminate prejudice from the hearts of human beings. But that is no reason to allow prejudice to continue to be enshrined in our laws."

—Representative Shirley Chisholm, from a speech before Congress, August 10, 1970

PRIMARY SOURCE

"This amendment will absolutely and positively make women subject to the draft. Why any woman would support such a ridiculous and un-American proposal as this is beyond comprehension. . . .

Another bad effect of the Equal Rights Amendment is that it will abolish a woman's right to child support and alimony. . . .

Under present American laws, the man is *always* required to support his wife and each child he has caused to be brought into the world. Why should women abandon these good laws . . . ?"

—Phyllis Schlafly, from the *Phyllis Schlafly Report*, February 1972

left page: (tl & tr)/AP Images; (bl & br)/detail/White House Collection/The White House Historical Association; (bc)SuperStock/SuperStock; right page: (bl to br)/detail/White House Collection/The White House Historical Association

Step Into the Time

MAKING CONNECTIONS
Research an individual or event from the time line. Write a paragraph describing the impact this person or event had on the civil rights movement.

U.S. PRESIDENTS

UNITED STATES

WORLD

Eisenhower 1953–1961

Kennedy 1961–1963

1962 César Chávez and Dolores Huerta found National Farm Workers Association

L. Johnson 1963–1969

1966 National Organization for Women founded

1960

1965

1961 Construction of Berlin Wall begins

1964 South Africa's Nelson Mandela sentenced to life in prison

1966 Indira Gandhi becomes prime minister of India

NEXT GENERATION SUNSHINE STATE STANDARDS
Students will understand the following benchmarks from the Florida NGSSS

LAFS.1112.RH.3.7: Integrate and evaluate multiple sources of information presented in diverse formats and media (e.g., visually, quantitatively, as well as in words) in order to address a question or solve a problem.

LAFS.1112.RH.3.9: Integrate information from diverse sources, both primary and secondary, into a coherent understanding of an idea or event, noting discrepancies among sources.

SS.912.A.1.2: Utilize a variety of primary and secondary sources to identify author, historical significance, audience, and authenticity to understand a historical period.

SS.912.A.1.3: Utilize timelines to identify the time sequence of historical data.

SS.912.A.1.4: Analyze how images, symbols, objects, cartoons, graphs, charts, maps, and artwork may be used to interpret the significance of time periods and events from the past.

SS.912.A.7.3: Examine the changing status of women in the United States from post-World War II to present.

ERA Ratification, 1972–1982

YEAR RATIFIED

- 1972
- 1973
- 1974
- 1975
- 1977
- Did not ratify
- Ratified, then rescinded

1968 American Indian Movement founded

Nixon 1969–1974

1970 United Farm Workers wins contract with grape growers

January 1973 *Roe* v. *Wade* decision on abortion

February 1973 Native Americans clash with FBI at Wounded Knee

Ford 1974–1977

Carter 1977–1981

1970

1975

1980

1967 The Biafran Civil War begins in Nigeria

1968 Soviet Union invades Czechoslovakia

1969 Golda Meir becomes prime minister of Israel

February 1979 Ayatollah Khomeini returns to Iran to lead Islamic republic

May 1979 Margaret Thatcher elected Britain's prime minister

LESSON 1

Students and the Counterculture

ESSENTIAL QUESTIONS

• What did students, women, and Latinos learn from the civil rights movement and apply to their protest actions?
• How has society changed for students, women, and Latinos?

READING HELPDESK

Academic Vocabulary

• conformity   • rationality

Content Vocabulary

• counterculture
• hippies
• communes

TAKING NOTES

Key Ideas and Details

Organizing As you read about the rise of youth culture and activism, use the major headings of this lesson to create an outline similar to the one below. LAFS.1112.RH.3.7, SS.912.A.7.5, SS.912.A.7.9

> Students and the Counterculture
> I. The Rise of the Youth
>   Movement
>   A.
>   B.
> II.
>   A.
>   B.

NEXT GENERATION SUNSHINE STATE STANDARDS

LAFS.1112.RH.1.2: Determine the central ideas or information of a primary or secondary source; provide an accurate summary that makes clear the relationships among the key details and ideas.

LAFS.1112.RH.2.4: Determine the meaning of words and phrases as they are used in a text, including analyzing how an author uses and refines the meaning of a key term over the course of a text (e.g., how Madison defines faction in Federalist No. 10).

Continued on page 521

IT MATTERS BECAUSE

The 1960s was one of the most tumultuous decades in American history. The decade also gave birth to a youth movement that challenged the American political system and conventional middle-class values.

The Rise of the Youth Movement

GUIDING QUESTION *How were the protest techniques used by student protesters similar to and different from those of the civil rights movement?*

The roots of the 1960s youth movement stretched back to the 1950s. In the decade after World War II, the country had enjoyed a time of peace and prosperity. Prosperity did not extend to all, however. Some, especially the artists and writers of the beat movement, openly criticized American society. They believed American society had come to value **conformity** over independence and financial gain over spiritual and social advancement. At the same time, the civil rights movement raised serious questions about racism in American society. The nuclear arms race between the United States and the Soviet Union made many of the nation's youth fear for the future. For many young people, the events of the 1950s had called into question the wisdom of their parents and their political leaders.

The youth movement originated with the baby boomers, the huge generation born after World War II. By 1970, 58.2 percent of the American population was under 35 years old. The economic boom of the 1950s meant more families could afford to send their children to college. College life gave young people a sense of freedom and independence. It was on college campuses across the nation that youth protest movements began and reached their peak.

Students for a Democratic Society

Young people were concerned about the injustices they saw in the nation's political and social system. In their view, a small, wealthy elite controlled politics, and wealth was unfairly divided. These young people formed what came to be known as the New Left.

A prominent organization within the New Left was Students for a Democratic Society (SDS). It defined its views in a 1962 declaration known as the Port Huron Statement. Written largely by Tom Hayden, editor of the University of Michigan's student newspaper, the declaration called for an end to apathy and urged citizens to stop accepting a country run by big corporations and big government.

PRIMARY SOURCE

❝ . . . [H]uman degradation, symbolized by the Southern struggle against racial bigotry . . . the Cold War, symbolized by the presence of the Bomb, brought awareness that we ourselves, and our friends, and millions of abstract 'others' . . . might die at any time. . . .

Our work is guided by the sense that we may be the last generation in the experiment with living. ❞

—from the *Port Huron Statement*, 1962

SDS chapters focused on protesting the Vietnam War and other issues, including poverty, campus regulations, nuclear power, and racism.

The Free Speech Movement

Another movement that captured the nation's attention in the 1960s was the free speech movement, led by Mario Savio and others at the University of California at Berkeley. The movement began in the fall of 1964, when the university decided to restrict students' rights to distribute literature and to recruit volunteers for political causes on campus.

Like many college students, those at Berkeley were dissatisfied with practices at their university. Huge classes were divided into sections and taught by graduate students. Many professors claimed they were too busy with research to meet with students. Faceless administrators made rules that were not always easy to obey and imposed punishments for violations. Feeling isolated in this impersonal environment, many Berkeley students rallied to support the free speech movement.

The struggle between Berkeley's students and administrators peaked on December 2, 1964, with a sit-in and powerful speech by Savio. Early the next morning, 600 police officers entered the campus and arrested more than 700 protesters. The arrests set off an even larger protest movement. Within days, a campus-wide strike had stopped classes. Many members of the faculty

©Bettmann/Corbis

NEXT GENERATION SUNSHINE STATE STANDARDS

Continued from page 520

LAFS.1112.RH.3.7: Integrate and evaluate multiple sources of information presented in diverse formats and media (e.g., visually, quantitatively, as well as in words) in order to address a question or solve a problem.

LAFS.1112.WHST.1.2: Write informative/ explanatory texts, including the narration of historical events, scientific procedures/ experiments, or technical processes.

LAFS.1112.WHST.3.9: Draw evidence from informational texts to support analysis, reflection, and research.

LAFS.1112.WHST.4.10: Write routinely over extended time frames (time for reflection and revision) and shorter time frames (a single sitting or a day or two) for a range of discipline-specific tasks, purposes, and audiences.

SS.912.A.1.2: Utilize a variety of primary and secondary sources to identify author, historical significance, audience, and authenticity to understand a historical period.

SS.912.A.1.4: Analyze how images, symbols, objects, cartoons, graphs, charts, maps, and artwork may be used to interpret the significance of time periods and events from the past.

SS.912.A.6.14: Analyze causes, course, and consequences of the Vietnam War.

SS.912.A.7.1: Identify causes for Post-World War II prosperity and its effects on American society.

SS.912.A.7.5: Compare nonviolent and violent approaches utilized by groups (African Americans, women, Native Americans, Hispanics) to achieve civil rights.

SS.912.A.7.9: Examine the similarities of social movements (Native Americans, Hispanics, women, anti-war protesters) of the 1960s and 1970s.

SS.912.H.1.5: Examine artistic response to social issues and new ideas in various cultures.

conformity agreement in form, manner, or character

SKILLS PRACTICE

Pick a partner. Read the lesson on Students and Counterculture together. Take turns reading aloud bold-faced words, or other words in the lesson that you do not know. When your partner reads a word tell them what it means. When you read a word, have them tell you what it means. If you need help, ask your teacher. **ELD.K12.ELL.SI.1, ELD.K12.ELL.SS.1, LAFS.1112.RH.2.4**

Members of SDS protest the Vietnam War.

▶ **CRITICAL THINKING**

Identifying Central Ideas What are two issues that led to the activism of the members of SDS? **LAFS.1112.WHST.3.9, SS.912.A.1.4, SS.912.A.7.5, SS.912.A.7.9**

The Politics of Protest **521**

voiced their support for the free speech movement. In the face of this growing opposition, the administration gave in to the students' demands.

Soon afterward, the Supreme Court upheld students' rights to freedom of speech and assembly on campuses. In a unanimous vote, the Court upheld the section of the Civil Rights Act assuring these rights in places offering public accommodations, which, by definition, included college campuses. The Berkeley revolt became a model for other student protests in the 1960s. The tactics used by the Berkeley protesters were soon being used in college demonstrations across the country.

☑ READING PROGRESS CHECK

Comparing and Contrasting What techniques did the students on the Berkeley campus use to protest for free speech?

The Counterculture

GUIDING QUESTION *How did the counterculture movement affect the nation?*

While many young Americans in the 1960s sought to reform the system, others rejected it entirely. They tried to create a new lifestyle based on flamboyant dress, rock music, drug use, and communal living. They created what became known as the **counterculture,** and the people were commonly called **"hippies."**

Hippie Culture

Originally, hippies rejected **rationality,** order, and traditional middle-class values. They wanted to build a utopia—a society that was freer, closer to nature, and full of love, tolerance, and cooperation. Many hippies wanted to drop out of society by leaving home. They wanted to live together in **communes**—group living arrangements in which members shared everything and worked together. Much of this was a reaction to the 1950s stereotype of the white-collar "man in the gray flannel suit" who led a constricted and colorless life. Singer-songwriter Bob Dylan expressed the counterculture beliefs through his lyrics:

PRIMARY SOURCE

❝ Come mothers and fathers throughout the land/and don't criticize what you can't understand/Your sons and your daughters are beyond your command/Your old road is rapidly agin'/Please get out of the new one if you can't lend your hand/for the times they are a-changin' ❞

—from "The Times They Are A-Changin'," 1964

counterculture a culture with values and beliefs different from those of the mainstream

hippies name for young Americans, especially during the 1960s, who rejected the conventions of established society

rationality the quality or state of being agreeable to reason

communes group living arrangements in which members share everything and work together

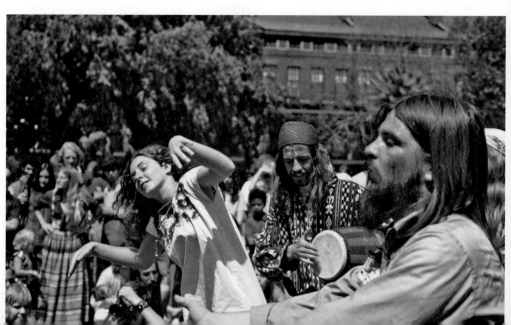

Members of the counterculture often rejected the expectations of mainstream society.

▶ CRITICAL THINKING
Making Inferences How does the style of dress shown express the counterculture's way of thinking? LAFS.1112.WHST.3.9, SS.912.A.1.5

PHOTO: ©Vince Streano/Encyclopedia/Corbis; TEXT: The Times they Are A-Changin', by Bob Dylan. Copyright © 1963; renewed 1996 Special Rider Music.

This political cartoon depicts the skepticism many Americans had toward the counterculture and the hippie movement.

▶ **CRITICAL THINKING**

1 *Analyzing Primary Sources* What is the cartoonist saying is wrong with the counterculture? LAFS.1112.RH.1.2, LAFS.1112.WHST.3.9, SS.912.A.1.4

2 *Analyzing Visuals* How does the cartoonist focus the reader's attention on some hippie stereotypes? LAFS.1112.WHST.3.9, SS.912.A.1.4

Cartoonists critical of the counterculture and "hippies" often used humor to present their views. Exaggerations in clothing, facial expressions, and other characteristics help the cartoonist make his or her point.

How does the cartoonist focus the reader's attention on some hippie stereotypes? What does the cartoonist imply with this cartoon?

Jack Knox Collection, The Ohio State University Billy Ireland Cartoon Library & Museum

The Impact of the Counterculture

After a few years, the counterculture movement began to decline. The fashion and music of the counterculture, however, continued to affect American culture. More individualized dressing, including strands of beads, ragged blue jeans, and long hair for men, became generally accepted. Counterculture musicians made use of folk music and the rhythms of rock 'n' roll. They wrote heartfelt lyrics that expressed the hopes and fears of their generation. Folk singers included Bob Dylan, who became an important voice of the movement, as did singers Joan Baez and Pete Seeger. Rock musicians included Jimi Hendrix, Janis Joplin, and The Who. The music and innovations of these artists continue to influence musicians today.

✓ **READING PROGRESS CHECK**

Making Connections What kind of society did the counterculture want to build?

LESSON 1 REVIEW

Reviewing Vocabulary

1. *Naming* Why were young people who rebelled against mainstream society called the "counterculture"? LAFS.1112.RH.2.4

2. *Summarizing* What did "conformity" mean to hippies in the 1960s? LAFS.1112.RH.2.4, LAFS.1112.WHST.3.9

Using Your Notes

3. *Making Connections* Use the notes that you completed during the lesson to describe the relationship between student protesters and the hippies. LAFS.1112.RH.3.7, LAFS.1112.WHST.3.9

Answering the Guiding Questions

4. *Comparing and Contrasting* How were the protest techniques used by student protesters similar to and different from those of the civil rights movement? LAFS.1112.WHST.3.9, SS.912.A.7.9

5. *Synthesizing* How did the counterculture movement affect the nation? LAFS.1112.WHST.3.9, SS.912.A.1.5

Writing Activity

6. INFORMATIVE/EXPLANATORY Suppose that you are a mainstream journalist in the late 1960s. Write a newspaper article about hippies. Describe their hair, clothes, values, and living arrangements. LAFS.1112.WHST.1.2, LAFS.1112.WHST.4.10

LESSON 2
The Feminist Movement

ESSENTIAL QUESTIONS
• What did students, women, and Latinos learn from the civil rights movement and apply to their protest actions?
• How has society changed for students, women, and Latinos?

READING HELPDESK

Academic Vocabulary
• gender
• compatible

Content Vocabulary
• feminism

TAKING NOTES

Key Ideas and Details

Organizing As you read about the feminist movement, complete a graphic organizer similar to the one below by listing the main arguments for and against the Equal Rights Amendment (ERA). **LAFS.1112.RH.3.7, SS.912.A.7.5**

Arguments For and Against the ERA	
For ERA	Against ERA

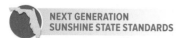

NEXT GENERATION SUNSHINE STATE STANDARDS

LAFS.1112.RH.2.4: Determine the meaning of words and phrases as they are used in a text, including analyzing how an author uses and refines the meaning of a key term over the course of a text (e.g., how Madison defines faction in Federalist No. 10).

LAFS.1112.RH.3.7: Integrate and evaluate multiple sources of information presented in diverse formats and media (e.g., visually, quantitatively, as well as in words) in order to address a question or solve a problem.

LAFS.1112.WHST.1.1: Write arguments focused on discipline-specific content.

LAFS.1112.WHST.3.9: Draw evidence from informational texts to support analysis, reflection, and research.

Continued on page 525

IT MATTERS BECAUSE
By the 1960s, many women had become dissatisfied with society's perception of women and what their proper roles should be. Some women began to join organizations dedicated to expanding opportunities for women. The Equal Rights Amendment stirred a national debate.

A Renewed Women's Movement

GUIDING QUESTION *What events revitalized the women's movement?*

African Americans and college students were not the only groups seeking to change American society in the 1960s. By the middle of the decade, a new movement had emerged: the feminist, or women's liberation, movement. **Feminism** is the belief that men and women should be equal politically, economically, and socially. The onset of World War II provided women with greater opportunity. After the war, however, many women returned to traditional roles. The new postwar emphasis on establishing families discouraged women from seeking employment.

Despite the popular emphasis on homemaking, the number of women who held jobs outside the home actually increased during the 1950s. Many women went to work outside the home to make ends meet, or to help their families maintain comfortable lifestyles. By 1960, about one-third of all married women were part of the paid workforce. Yet many people at the time continued to believe that women could better serve society by remaining in the home to influence the next generation of men.

Origins of the Movement
By the early 1960s, many women were increasingly resentful of a world where newspaper ads separated jobs by **gender,** banks denied women credit, and female employees often were paid less for the same work. Nearly half of American women worked by the mid-1960s, but three-fourths of these women worked in lower-paying clerical, sales, or factory jobs, or as janitors and hospital attendants.

One stimulus that invigorated the women's movement was the President's Commission on the Status of Women. Its report highlighted the problems women faced in the workplace and helped create a network of feminist activists who lobbied for women's legislation. In 1963, they won passage of the Equal Pay Act, which in most cases outlawed paying men more than women for the same job.

Many women who had stayed home were also discontented. Betty Friedan tried to describe the reasons for this in her 1963 book *The Feminine Mystique*. Friedan had interviewed women who had graduated with her from Smith College in 1942. She reported that while most had everything they could want in life, they felt unfulfilled. As the book became a best seller, women began reaching out to one another. They poured out their anger and sadness in what came to be known as consciousness-raising sessions. While they talked about their unhappiness, they were also building the base for a nationwide mass movement.

Congress gave the women's movement another boost by including gender in the 1964 Civil Rights Act. Title VII of the act outlawed job discrimination not only on the basis of race, color, religion, and national origin, but also on the basis of gender. This provided a strong legal basis for the changes the women's movement later demanded.

But simply having the law on the books was not enough. Even the agency charged with administering the Civil Rights Act—the Equal Employment Opportunity Commission (EEOC)—ruled in 1965 that gender-segregated help-wanted ads were legal.

The Time is NOW

By June 1966, Betty Friedan had returned to an idea that she and other women had been considering—the need for an organization to promote feminist goals. Friedan and others then set out to form the National Organization for Women (NOW). In October 1966, a group of about 30 women and men held the founding conference of NOW.

PRIMARY SOURCE

❝[T]he time has come to confront, with concrete action, the conditions that now prevent women from enjoying the equality of opportunity and freedom of choice which is their right, as individual Americans, and as human beings.❞

—from *NOW Statement of Purpose*, 1966

The new organization responded to their members' growing frustration by demanding greater educational and career opportunities for women. NOW leaders denounced the exclusion of women from certain professions and from most levels of politics. NOW also was against the practice of paying women less than men for equal work. This had been prohibited by the Equal Pay Act, but was still commonplace.

When NOW set out to pass an Equal Rights Amendment to the Constitution, its membership rose to over 200,000. By July 1972, the movement had its own magazine, *Ms.* A key editor of *Ms.* was Gloria Steinem, an author who became one of the movement's leading figures.

✔ **READING PROGRESS CHECK**

Synthesizing What were two of the forces that helped to bring the women's movement to life in the 1960s?

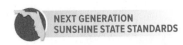

Continued from page 524

LAFS.1112.WHST.4.10: Write routinely over extended time frames (time for reflection and revision) and shorter time frames (a single sitting or a day or two) for a range of discipline-specific tasks, purposes, and audiences.

MAFS.912.S-IC.2: Make inferences and justify conclusions from sample surveys, experiments, and observational studies.

MAFS.912.S-ID.1: Summarize, represent and interpret data on a single count or measurement variable.

SS.912.A.1.2: Utilize a variety of primary and secondary sources to identify author, historical significance, audience, and authenticity to understand a historical period.

SS.912.A.1.4: Analyze how images, symbols, objects, cartoons, graphs, charts, maps, and artwork may be used to interpret the significance of time periods and events from the past.

SS.912.A.5.7: Examine the freedom movements that advocated civil rights for African Americans, Latinos, Asians, and women.

Continued on page 527

feminism the belief that men and women should be equal politically, economically, and socially

gender term applied to the characteristics of a male or female

A group of men and women march together holding signs while participating in a 1976 ERA protest in Pittsburgh, Pennsylvania.

▶ **CRITICAL THINKING**
Drawing Conclusions How might the success of the civil rights movement have encouraged women to organize?
LAFS.1112.WHST.3.9, SS.912.A.1.4, SS.912.A.7.9

Barbara Freeman/Hulton Archive/Getty Images

Feminist and writer Gloria Steinem drew attention to the problems facing women and fought for the ratification of the Equal Rights Amendment.

▶ CRITICAL THINKING

Determining Cause and Effect
What was one effect that Gloria Steinem had on the feminist movement? SS.912.A.7.3

Thinking Like a
HISTORIAN

Comparing and Contrasting

The emergence of social movements in the 1960s and 1970s has deep roots in American history. Social movements, historians contend, often share common goals—quality of life issues, political and democratic processes, economic and environmental issues. The significance of the two decades is the concentration of all such issues in a small time span: gender equality at home and at work; political issues and processes; labor and civil rights causes; and environmental and health concerns. SS.912.A.1.7, SS.912.A.7.9

Successes and Failures

GUIDING QUESTION *What political and economic gains did women make during this time?*

During the late 1960s and early 1970s, the women's movement fought to amend the Constitution and enforce Title VII of the Civil Rights Act. It also worked to repeal laws against abortion and pass legislation against gender discrimination in employment, housing, and education. As a leading voice in the women's movement, Steinem explained the need for such legislation.

PRIMARY SOURCE

❝ The truth is that all our problems stem from the same sex based myths. We may appear before you as white radicals or the middle-aged middle class or black soul sisters, but we are all sisters in fighting against these outdated myths. Like racial myths, they have been reflected in our laws. ❞

—Gloria Steinem, from testimony before a Senate subcommittee in support of the ERA, May 1970

The Equal Rights Amendment

The women's movement seemed to be off to a strong start when Congress passed the Equal Rights Amendment (ERA) in March 1972. The amendment specified: "Equality of rights under the law shall not be denied or abridged by the United States or by any State on account of sex." To become part of the Constitution, the amendment had to be ratified by 38 states. Many states did so—35 by 1979—but then significant opposition to the amendment began to build.

Opponents argued that it would take away some women's rights. These included the right to alimony in divorce cases and the right to have single-gender colleges. They feared it would eliminate women's exemption from the draft and do away with laws that provided special protection for women in the workforce.

One outspoken opponent was Phyllis Schlafly, organizer of the Stop ERA campaign. By the end of 1979, five states had voted to rescind their approval. Many people had become worried that the amendment would give federal courts too much power to interfere with state laws. Unable to achieve ratification by three-fourths of the states by the deadline set by Congress, the ERA finally failed in 1982.

Equality in Education

One major achievement of the movement came in the area of education. Kathy Striebel's experience illustrated the discrimination female students often faced in the early 1970s. In 1971, Striebel, a junior high school student in St. Paul, Minnesota, wanted to compete for her school's swim team, but the school did not allow girls to join. Kathy's mother, Charlotte Striebel, was a member of the local NOW chapter. Through it, she learned that St. Paul had recently banned gender discrimination in education. She filed a grievance with the city's human rights department, and officials required the school to allow Kathy to swim.

Shortly after joining the team, Kathy beat out one of the boys and earned a spot at a meet. As she stood on the block waiting to swim, the opposing coach declared that she was ineligible because the meet was outside St. Paul and thus beyond the jurisdiction of its laws.

In response, leaders of the women's movement lobbied to ban gender discrimination in education. In 1972, Congress responded by passing a law known collectively as the Educational Amendments. One section, Title IX,

Library of Congress, Prints & Photographs Division [LC-U9-25332-25]

prohibited federally funded schools from discriminating against women in nearly all aspects of school operations, from admissions to athletics.

Title IX increased opportunities for women. Within just a few years, the number of women attending college surged, and by 1978 the majority of people attending college were women. By 2014, women made up approximately 58 percent of all college students.

Title IX also created new opportunities for women in college athletics. It required that women and men have equal opportunities to participate in sports and receive sports-related scholarships. Women's participation in sports grew dramatically as a result. The demand generated by the growing number of women's sports teams, as well as increased funding and prestige, drew many new coaches, including men, to the women's sports.

Right to Privacy and *Roe* v. *Wade*

The feminist movement worked to secure the right to make private decisions, including reproductive decisions. A constitutional right to marital privacy was introduced in 1965 when the Supreme Court outlawed state bans on contraceptives for married couples in *Griswold* v. *Connecticut*.

The right to privacy was expanded beyond married couples when activists began challenging laws against abortion. Until 1973, the right to regulate abortion was reserved to the states. The original plan of the Constitution gave states most of the authority to enact laws impinging on personal or property rights in the interest of safety, health, welfare, and morality. Early in the country's history, some abortions were permitted in the early stages of pregnancy. By the mid-1800s, however, states had passed laws prohibiting abortion, except to save the life of the mother. In the late 1960s, some states began adopting more liberal abortion laws. For example, several states allowed abortion if carrying a pregnancy to term might endanger the woman's mental health or if she was a victim of rape or incest.

The big change came with the 1973 Supreme Court decision in *Roe* v. *Wade*. The decision stated that state governments could not regulate abortion during the first three months of pregnancy, a time that was ruled to be within a woman's constitutional right to privacy. During the second three months of pregnancy, states could regulate abortions on the basis of the health of the mother. States could ban abortion in the final three months except in cases of a medical emergency. Those in favor of abortion rights cheered *Roe* v. *Wade* as a victory, but the issue was far from settled politically. The decision gave rise to the right-to-life movement, whose members consider abortion morally wrong and work toward its total ban.

After the *Roe* v. *Wade* ruling, the two sides began an impassioned battle that continues today. In the 1992 case *Planned Parenthood* v. *Casey*, the Supreme Court modified *Roe* v. *Wade*. The Court decided that states could place some restrictions on abortions. For example, doctors could be required to explain the risks and have patients give "informed consent." Underage girls might now be required to inform their parents before getting an abortion, although the Court did strike down laws requiring women to notify their husbands before having an abortion. It also abandoned the rule that states could ban abortion only in the final trimester. Technology had enabled a fetus to be viable outside the womb much earlier in a pregnancy. States could now restrict abortion based on the viability of the fetus.

Tennis great Billie Jean King was a trailblazer in the effort to gain equality for women in sports. In 1972, Title IX banned educational discrimination against women in fields ranging from admissions to extracurricular activities.

▶ **CRITICAL THINKING**

Predicting Consequences
What consequence might Title IX have had on girls' involvement in school sports?
SS.912.A.7.3

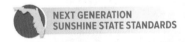

NEXT GENERATION SUNSHINE STATE STANDARDS

Continued from page 525

SS.912.A.7.3: Examine the changing status of women in the United States from post-World War II to present.

SS.912.A.7.5: Compare nonviolent and violent approaches utilized by groups (African Americans, women, Native Americans, Hispanics) to achieve civil rights.

SS.912.A.7.8: Analyze significant Supreme Court decisions relating to integration, busing, affirmative action, the rights of the accused, and reproductive rights.

SS.912.A.7.9: Examine the similarities of social movements (Native Americans, Hispanics, women, anti-war protesters) of the 1960s and 1970s.

SS.912.A.7.13: Analyze the attempts to extend New Deal legislation through the Great Society and the successes and failures of these programs to promote social and economic stability.

Focus On Sport/Getty Images Sport/Getty Images

compatible capable of existing in harmony

The number of women in the workforce climbed steadily from the 1950s through the 1990s.

1 Comparing and Contrasting By how much did the percentage of working women increase between 1950 and 2000? MAFS.912.S-IC.2, MAFS.912.S-ID.1, SS.912.A.1.4

2 Making Generalizations What general trend do you see in women's participation in the workforce? MAFS.912.S-ID.1, SS.912.A.1.4, SS.912.A.7.3

Source: *Historical Statistics of the United States: Earliest Times to the Present, Volume 2.*

More women are working outside the home today in the United States than ever before.

▶ **CRITICAL THINKING**
Making Connections How does the women's movement of the 1960s and 1970s help working women today? SS.912.A.7.3

The Impact of the Feminist Movement

The women's movement profoundly changed society. Since the 1970s, many women have pursued college degrees and careers outside of the home. Since the women's movement began, two-career families are much more common than they were in the 1950s and 1960s—although a need for greater family income may also be a factor in that increase. Mothers working outside the home are more accepted and more common than they were in the 1950s and 1960s. Many employers now offer options to help women make work life more **compatible** with family life, including flexible hours, on-site child care, and job sharing.

Even with those changes, a significant income gap between men and women still exists. About one-third of the wage gap is due to the uneven distribution of men and women among various occupations. For example, more men than women tend to work in higher-paying construction and engineering trades. Likewise, more women than men tend to work in lower-paying household service and office occupations.

Women have made the most dramatic gains in professional jobs since the 1970s. By 2000, women made up more than 40 percent of the nation's graduates receiving medical or law degrees.

☑ **READING PROGRESS CHECK**

Explaining Why were *Roe* v. *Wade*, Title IX, and the Equal Pay Act cornerstones in the women's rights movement?

Thomas Barwick/Getty Images

LESSON 2 REVIEW

Reviewing Vocabulary

1. *Explaining* What was the main goal of the feminist movement? LAFS.1112.WHST.3.9

Using Your Notes

2. *Comparing and Contrasting* Review the notes that you completed during the lesson to compare and contrast the arguments for and against the Equal Rights Amendment. LAFS.1112.RH.3.7, LAFS.1112.WHST.3.9

Answering the Guiding Questions

3. *Analyzing Cause and Effect* What events revitalized the women's movement? LAFS.1112.WHST.3.9, SS.912.7.3, SS.912.7.9

4. *Identifying* What political and economic gains did women make during this time? LAFS.1112.WHST.3.9, SS.912.A.7.3

Writing Activity

5. **ARGUMENT** Take a position either for or against the ratification of the Equal Rights Amendment. Then write a newspaper editorial convincing readers to support your position. LAFS.1112.WHST.1.1, LAFS.1112.WHST.4.10

LESSON 3

Latino Americans Organize

There's More Online!

READING HELPDESK

Academic Vocabulary

- likewise
- adequate

Content Vocabulary

- repatriation
- bilingualism

TAKING NOTES

Key Ideas and Details

Sequencing Complete a time line similar to the one below by recording major events in the struggle of Latinos for equal civil and political rights.
LAFS.1112.RH.3.7, SS.912.A.1.3, SS.912.A.7.5, SS.912.A.7.9

1947	1954	1956

1967	1968	1969

NEXT GENERATION SUNSHINE STATE STANDARDS

LAFS.1112.RH.2.4: Determine the meaning of words and phrases as they are used in a text, including analyzing how an author uses and refines the meaning of a key term over the course of a text (e.g., how Madison defines faction in Federalist No. 10).

LAFS.1112.RH.3.7: Integrate and evaluate multiple sources of information presented in diverse formats and media (e.g., visually, quantitatively, as well as in words) in order to address a question or solve a problem.

LAFS.1112.WHST.1.2: Write informative/explanatory texts, including the narration of historical events, scientific procedures/experiments, or technical processes.

LAFS.1112.WHST.3.9: Draw evidence from informational texts to support analysis, reflection, and research.

Continued on page 531

ESSENTIAL QUESTIONS

- What did students, women, and Latinos learn from the civil rights movement and apply to their protest actions?
- How has society changed for students, women, and Latinos?

IT MATTERS BECAUSE

Most Mexican Americans and Mexican immigrants lived in the Southwest. By the mid-twentieth century, more immigrants arrived from various parts of Latin America. Latinos formed civil rights organizations to challenge discrimination.

Latinos Migrate North

GUIDING QUESTION *Why did many Mexicans migrate to the United States from the early to the mid-1900s, and how did this affect American society?*

Americans of Mexican heritage have lived in what is now the United States since before the founding of the republic. In the twentieth century, Mexican immigration to the United States rose greatly, partly due to the turmoil of the Mexican Revolution that began in 1910. During the 1920s, half a million Mexicans immigrated to the United States through official channels. An unknown number entered the country through other means.

While some people of Mexican heritage moved to northern states, most remained concentrated in the areas that were once the northern provinces of Mexico. In 1930, 90 percent of ethnic Mexicans in the United States lived in areas of the West and Southwest. As a result of heavy Mexican immigration, the ethnic Mexican population in Texas grew from 71,062 in 1900 to 683,681 in 1930. **Likewise,** Southern California had a large Spanish-speaking population.

Mexicans Face Discrimination

Across the Southwest, most Mexican Americans lived in barrios. Barrios were the product of a combination of the region's history and discrimination against Latinos. Los Angeles was founded as a Spanish town in 1781. A century later when English-speaking settlers arrived, they built around the older Spanish-speaking district. From 1900 to 1930, Mexican immigration increased the ethnic Mexican population of the city from as many as 5,000 to around 150,000. By then, the Spanish-speaking population was segregated in the eastern

❝For the Mexicans the barrio was a colony of refugees. We came to know families from Chihuahua, Sonora, Jalisco, and Durango. . . .

As poor refugees, their first concern was to find a place to sleep, then to eat and find work. In the barrio they were most likely to find all three, for not knowing English, they needed something that was even more urgent than a room, a meal, or a job, and that was information in a language they could understand.❞

—from *Barrio Boy*, 1971

DBQ *MAKING INFERENCES*

What was the most important benefit that the barrio offered new immigrants? SS.912.A.1.2

likewise in the same way; similarly

repatriation being restored or returned to the country of origin, allegiance, or citizenship

part of the city. Most lived in dilapidated housing and suffered high rates of infant mortality and disease.

In California and across the Southwest, employment discrimination meant that most ethnic Mexicans could find work only in low-paying jobs. Many worked as agricultural laborers. During the Great Depression, many Mexican Americans faced increased hostility and discrimination as unemployment rates soared. About one-third of the nation's Mexican population returned to Mexico. Some left voluntarily, believing it would be easier to get by in Mexico. Others left as part of the **repatriation**—a series of deportations launched by federal officials. This included not only immigrants but often their American-born children as well.

During World War II, labor shortages in the Southwest led to the creation of the Bracero Program. Under this arrangement, Mexican workers entered into short-term labor contracts, mostly as low-wage farmworkers. Meanwhile, illegal immigration also increased. In 1954, Eisenhower's administration launched a program intended to deport undocumented Latino immigrants. Police swept through barrios seeking undocumented immigrants. As a result, more than 3.7 million Mexicans were deported over the next three years.

The raids were criticized in the United States and in Mexico for intimidating people for simply "looking Mexican." In addition, the program often failed to distinguish between individuals legally in the country—including U.S. citizens—and those who had entered illegally.

Other Latinos Arrive

Although Mexicans remained the largest group of Spanish-speaking newcomers in the 1950s, large numbers of Puerto Ricans arrived as well. American citizens since 1917, Puerto Ricans may move freely within American territory. After World War II, economic troubles prompted more than a million Puerto Ricans to move to the U.S. mainland. The majority settled in New York City, where they faced racial discrimination and high poverty levels.

The nation became home to more than 350,000 Cuban immigrants in the decade after the Cuban Revolution of 1959. Many were professionals and business owners who settled in the Miami, Florida, area. They were typically welcomed as refugees fleeing Communist oppression. By 1970, more than 9 million Latinos lived in the United States.

☑ READING PROGRESS CHECK

Determining Cause and Effect What international events encouraged Latinos to move to the United States, and how did this migration affect the nation?

©Bettmann/Corbis

| **CHARTS/GRAPHS** | **GROWTH OF LATINO POPULATION IN THE UNITED STATES** |

Shown here is a family of Mexican migrant workers who came to the United States as part of the Bracero Program during World War II.

1 *Analyzing Information* How has the overall Latino population changed since 1950? MAFS.912.S-ID.1

2 *Making Inferences* Based on the chart, what can you infer about the Latino population in the United States? MAFS.912.S-ID.1

Legend:
- Mexicans
- Puerto Ricans
- Cubans
- Other Latinos
- Total Latinos

Y-axis: Population (millions), 0 to 36

X-axis: Year — 1910 1920 1930 1940 1950 1960 1970 1980 1990 2000

Source: *Historical Statistics of the United States: Earliest Times to the Present, Volume 1.*

Every member of a migrant worker family had to work to survive. Here, Mexican children pick cotton in Texas.

▶ CRITICAL THINKING
Making Inferences What does this photograph indicate about economic opportunity for migrant farmworkers? SS.912.A.1.4, SS.912.A.7.2

SKILLS PRACTICE

After you have read the lesson on Latino Americans, pick a partner. Work with your partner to check and deepen each other's understanding of the text. Take turns asking each other questions to see if you both understood the lesson. Ask questions about why Latinos moved north and south of the border. Ask why they formed protest groups. Ask what they achieved. ELD.K12.ELL.SI.1, ELD.K12.ELL.SS.1, SS.912.A.7.9

Latinos Organize

GUIDING QUESTION *How was the Latino approach to gaining civil rights similar to and different from the African American civil rights movement?*

Regardless of their citizenship status, people of Mexican heritage were often treated as outsiders by the English-speaking majority. Latinos formed organizations to work for equal rights and fair treatment.

In 1929, a number of Mexican American organizations came together to create the League of United Latin American Citizens (LULAC). The organization's purpose was to fight discrimination against persons of Latin American ancestry. Membership was limited to those of Latin American heritage who were U.S. citizens. LULAC encouraged assimilation into American society and adopted English as its official language.

In *Mendez* v. *Westminster* (1947), a group of Mexican parents won a lawsuit that challenged school segregation in California. Two years after the *Mendez* case, LULAC filed a similar lawsuit that aimed to end the practice of segregating Spanish-speaking children into "Mexican schools" in the state of Texas. During the 1950s, the organization was also a vocal critic of the abuses of deportation authorities. In 1954, the Supreme Court's ruling in *Hernandez* v. *Texas* extended more rights to Latino citizens. The case ended the exclusion of Mexican Americans from juries in Texas.

Another Latino organization, the American GI Forum, was founded by Dr. Hector P. Garcia. The purpose of the GI Forum was to protect the rights of Mexican American veterans. After World War II, Latino veterans were excluded from veterans' organizations. They were also denied medical services by the Veterans Administration.

The GI Forum's first effort to combat racial injustice involved a Mexican American soldier killed during World War II. A funeral home refused to hold his funeral because he was Mexican American. The GI Forum drew national attention to the incident, and the soldier's remains

NEXT GENERATION SUNSHINE STATE STANDARDS

Continued from page 529

LAFS.1112.WHST.4.10: Write routinely over extended time frames (time for reflection and revision) and shorter time frames (a single sitting or a day or two) for a range of discipline-specific tasks, purposes, and audiences.

MAFS.912.S-ID.1: Summarize, represent and interpret data on a single count or measurement variable.

SS.912.A.1.2: Utilize a variety of primary and secondary sources to identify author, historical significance, audience, and authenticity to understand a historical period.

SS.912.A.1.4: Analyze how images, symbols, objects, cartoons, graphs, charts, maps, and artwork may be used to interpret the significance of time periods and events from the past.

SS.912.A.5.7: Examine the freedom movements that advocated civil rights for African Americans, Latinos, Asians, and women.

SS.912.A.7.2: Compare the relative prosperity between different ethnic groups and social classes in the post-World War II period.

SS.912.A.7.5: Compare nonviolent and violent approaches utilized by groups (African Americans, women, Native Americans, Hispanics) to achieve civil rights.

SS.912.A.7.9: Examine the similarities of social movements (Native Americans, Hispanics, women, anti-war protesters) of the 1960s and 1970s.

SS.912.A.7.16: Examine changes in immigration policy and attitudes toward immigration since 1950.

©Jim Sugar/Encyclopedia/Corbis

BIOGRAPHY

**César Chávez
(1927–1993)**

An Arizona native, labor leader César Chávez grew up a Mexican American migrant farm laborer. He was a community organizer during the 1950s before founding the National Farm Workers Association, a forerunner of the United Farm Workers. A strong supporter of nonviolence, he led peaceful strikes and boycotts that were usually successful. His contributions earned Chávez a Presidential Medal of Freedom the year following his death.

▶ **CRITICAL THINKING**
Making Inferences Why might Chávez have cared so much about farm laborers' rights?
LAFS.1112.WHST.3.9, SS.912.A.7.5

adequate sufficient for a specific requirement; completed to its minimum requirements

bilingualism the practice of teaching immigrant students in their own language

were buried in Arlington National Cemetery. Under Dr. Garcia's leadership, the organization broadened its scope and began to challenge discrimination against all Latinos. It helped pay the poll taxes of poor Hispanics so that they could vote, fought against segregated schools, helped fund the attorneys arguing *Hernandez* v. *Texas*, and worked to register Latino voters. In 1968, Garcia was appointed to the United States Commission on Civil Rights. Today the GI Forum has nearly 160,000 members across the United States.

☑ READING PROGRESS CHECK

Identifying What were the goals of Latino civil rights organizations?

Protests and Progress

GUIDING QUESTION *How did groups such as the United Farm Workers and* La Raza Unida *promote Latino civil rights?*

As the 1960s began, Latino Americans continued to face prejudice and limited access to **adequate** education, employment, and housing. Encouraged by the African American civil rights movement, Latinos launched a series of campaigns to improve their economic situation and end discrimination.

In the early 1960s, César Chávez and Dolores Huerta organized two groups that fought for farmworkers. In 1965, the groups went on strike in California to demand union recognition, increased wages, and better benefits. When employers resisted, Chávez organized a national boycott of table grapes. Between 14 and 17 million citizens stopped buying grapes, and industry profits tumbled. In 1966, Chávez and Huerta merged their two organizations into the United Farm Workers (UFW). Chávez held a hunger strike in 1968 to support the effort. A UFW spokesman described the impact the hunger strike had on Chávez and the farmworkers: "After twenty-five days, César was carried to a nearby park where the fast ended during a mass with thousands of farmworkers. He had lost thirty-five pounds, but there was no more talk about violence among the farmworkers." The new union kept the boycott going until 1970, when the grape growers finally agreed to raise wages and improve working conditions.

Young Latinos also became involved in civil rights. In 1967, college students in San Antonio, Texas, led by José Angel Gutiérrez, founded the Mexican American Youth Organization (MAYO). MAYO organized walkouts and demonstrations to protest discrimination. One Texas walkout led to the creation of bilingual education at a local high school.

MAYO's success and the spread of protests across the West and Southwest convinced Gutiérrez to found a new political party in 1969. It was called *La Raza Unida,* or "the United People." *La Raza Unida* mobilized Mexican American voters with calls for job-training programs and greater access to financial institutions. By the early 1970s, it had elected Latinos to local offices in several cities with large Latino populations. A larger civil rights movement among Mexican Americans, many of whom began calling themselves Chicanos, emerged. The movement fought against discrimination and celebrated Latino pride.

In the late 1960s, many Latino leaders promoted **bilingualism**—the practice of teaching immigrant students in their own language while they also learned English. Congress supported this movement by passing the Bilingual Education Act in 1968, which directed school districts to set up classes for immigrants in their own language while they were learning English. This became politically controversial. Beginning in the 1980s, an

Arthur Schatz/Time & Life Pictures/Getty Images

This mural by Martin Travers, titled *Naya Bihana*, shows the distinctive style of Chicano Murals.

English-only movement began. By the 2000s, more than half of the nation's state legislatures had passed laws or amendments making English the official language of their state.

The Chicano Mural Movement

Efforts by Hispanic Americans to defend their civil rights and promote economic opportunity within their community were encouraged by a renewed sense of their ethnic and cultural identity. In the 1960s, a new art movement began in the urban southwest, particularly in the Mexican-American barrios of Texas and southern California. Artists, often working with teams of volunteers from local communities, began creating large brightly colored murals on the walls of city buildings, schools, churches, highway overpasses, and apartment buildings.

The style of the murals was inspired by the works of artists Diego Rivera and José Orozco. The murals depicted Mexican American culture, which is why the movement came to be known as the Chicano Mural Movement. The style of the murals resembled the styles of art in ancient Mexico, but reflected the characteristics and issues of the 1960s and 1970s.

The murals reminded Latinos of their cultural heritage and religion, portrayed economic and social problems, especially those facing farm workers and domestic workers, and challenged the racism of the era. Murals also included portraits of Cesar Chavez, famous Latino heroes from American, Mexican, and Texan history, pictures of missions, and religious scenes. An important impact of the Chicano Mural Movement was that it helped remind Hispanics of their identity and their contributions to the United States, and encouraged them to support the struggle for their rights.

 READING PROGRESS CHECK

Explaining How did Latinos work for the rights of farmworkers?

(l)John Flournoy/McGraw-Hill Education; (r)Cathy Murphy/Hulton Archive/Getty Images

BIOGRAPHY

Dolores Huerta (1930–)

In 1955, Dolores Huerta helped found the Stockton chapter of the Community Service Organization (CSO). The group fought for Mexican American civil rights. Huerta led voter registration drives and worked for improved public services for farmworkers and other community residents.

In 1962, Huerta joined with César Chávez to form the National Farm Workers Association (NWFA). When the NWFA became the United Farm Workers (UFW), Huerta continued her activism on behalf of farmworkers by lobbying in Sacramento and Washington, D.C., against the farm owners' use of toxic pesticides that harmed workers, organizing strikes of field workers, and campaigning for candidates favorable to the farmworkers' causes.

LESSON 3 REVIEW

Reviewing Vocabulary

1. *Defining* What was the repatriation? LAFS.1112.RH.2.4

2. *Summarizing* How has the bilingualism movement changed over time? LAFS.1112.RH.2.4, LAFS.1112.WHST.3.9

Using Your Notes

3. *Making Generalizations* Review the notes that you completed throughout the lesson, and then describe the successes and setbacks of Latino activists in the twentieth century. LAFS.1112.WHST.3.9, SS.912.A.7.9

Answering the Guiding Questions

4. *Analyzing Cause and Effect* Why did many Mexicans migrate to the United States from the early to mid-1900s, and how did this affect American society? LAFS.1112.WHST.3.9

5. *Synthesizing* How was the Latino approach to gaining civil rights similar to and different from the African American civil rights movement? LAFS.1112.WHST.3.9, SS.912.A.7.9

6. *Synthesizing* How did groups such as the United Farm Workers and *La Raza Unida* promote Latino civil rights? LAFS.1112.WHST.3.9, SS.912.A.7.9

Writing Activity

7. INFORMATIVE/EXPLANATORY Write an essay explaining the purpose of the strike against table-grape growers in the 1960s and how strikers planned to achieve their goals. LAFS.1112.WHST.1.2, LAFS.1112.WHST.4.10

STUDY GUIDE

STUDENTS AND THE COUNTERCULTURE
LESSON 1

The Youth Movement

Students for a Democratic Society

The Free Speech Movement

The Counterculture

THE FEMINIST MOVEMENT
LESSON 2

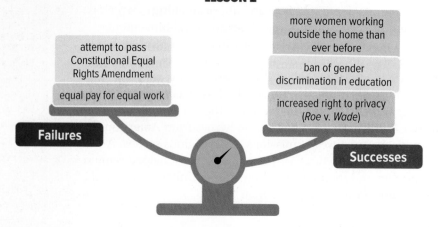

attempt to pass Constitutional Equal Rights Amendment

equal pay for equal work

Failures

more women working outside the home than ever before

ban of gender discrimination in education

increased right to privacy (*Roe v. Wade*)

Successes

LATINO AMERICANS ORGANIZE
LESSON 3

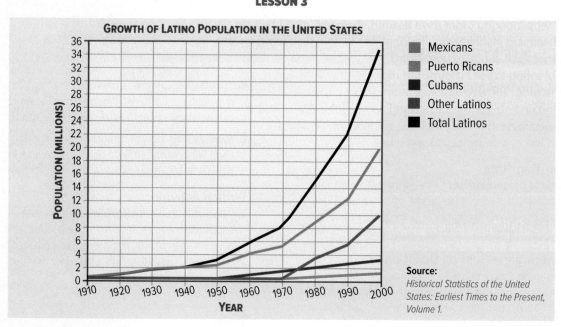

GROWTH OF LATINO POPULATION IN THE UNITED STATES

POPULATION (MILLIONS)

YEAR

- Mexicans
- Puerto Ricans
- Cubans
- Other Latinos
- Total Latinos

Source:
Historical Statistics of the United States: Earliest Times to the Present, Volume 1.

Directions: On a separate sheet of paper, answer the questions below. Make sure you read carefully and answer all parts to the question.

Lesson Review

Lesson 1

1 ***Making Connections*** Describe the connection between American prosperity, college attendance, and youth protest movements. SS.912.A.7.1, SS.912.A.7.2

2 ***Identifying Central Issues*** What was the major belief about society that drove many people into the counterculture? SS.912.A.7.1

3 ***Defining*** What aspects of the counterculture were expressed in the rock 'n' roll music of the 1960s? What are some of the positive impacts of counterculture rock 'n' roll music? What are some of its negative impacts? SS.912.A.1.7, SS.912.A.7.1, SS.912.H.1.1, SS.912.H.1.5

Lesson 2

4 ***Describing*** What role did Betty Friedan play in the women's rights movement? SS.912.A.5.7, SS.912.A.7.3, SS.912.A.7.9

5 ***Summarizing*** What were the Educational Amendments, and how did school athletics tie to these amendments? SS.912.A.7.3

6 ***Comparing*** What strategies and techniques did the feminist movement adopt from the civil rights movement? SS.912.A.7.3, SS.912.A.7.5, SS.912.A.7.9

Lesson 3

7 ***Comparing and Contrasting*** Describe the roles of LULAC, MAYO, and *La Raza Unida* in the Chicano civil rights movement. How are these groups similar? How are they different? SS.912.A.5.7, SS.912.A.7.9

8 ***Identifying Cause and Effect*** How did a national grape boycott impact workers' rights? What role did César Chávez play in the boycott? SS.912.A.5.7, SS.912.A.7.5, SS.912.A.7.9

9 ***Making Inferences*** What organizations did César Chávez and Dolores Huerta create? Why do you think they chose to merge their unions to form the UFW? What was the role of UFW? SS.912.A.5.7, SS.912.A.7.5, SS.912.A.7.9

Exploring the Essential Questions

10 ***Drawing Conclusions*** What actions did women's groups and Latinos use to expand their economic opportunities and political rights? SS.912.A.5.7, SS.912.A.7.5, SS.912.A.7.9

Critical Thinking

11 ***Theorizing*** Theorize about why music and musicians held such a significant place within the counterculture movement of the 1960s. Does music remain as significant to the youth of today? SS.912.A.1.7, SS.912.A.7.1, SS.912.H.1.1., SS.912.H.1.3, SS.912.H.1.5

12 ***Describing*** What role did Phyllis Schlafly play in the defeat of the Equal Rights Amendment? What were some of her reasons for opposing this amendment? SS.912.S.5.7, SS.912.A.7.3

13 ***Evaluating*** Write a brief description of the Chicano Mural Movement. How did this movement reflect some of the characteristics and issues of the time and help shape American culture? LAFS.1112.WHST.4.10, SS.912.A.1.7, SS.912.A.5.7, SS.912.A.7.5, SS.912.A.7.16, SS.912.H.1.1, SS.912.H.1.5

21st Century Skills

14 ***Categorizing*** Refer to the various amendments, acts, or rights gained during this period and categorize them according to the group in society whom they most impacted. Analyze the information noting balances or imbalances, or whether or not the change is still significant today. LAFS.1112.RH.3.7, SS.912.A.7.1, SS.912.A.7.2, SS.912.A.7.3, SS.912.A.7.5, SS.912.A.7.8, SS.912.A.7.9

15 ***Evaluating Decisions*** What new movement arose from the *Roe* v. *Wade* decision, and how does that movement influence politics today? Explain whether the Supreme Court's decision was based on strict construction or a judicial interpretation of the Constitution. SS.912.A.7.8

16 ***Identifying Central Issues*** What was one of the major issues that led to the growth of the feminist movement in the 1960s? SS.912.A.5.7, SS.912.A.7.3

Need Extra Help?

If You've Missed Question	**1**	**2**	**3**	**4**	**5**	**6**	**7**	**8**	**9**	**10**	**11**	**12**	**13**	**14**	**15**	**16**
Go to Lesson	1	1	1	2	2	2	3	3	3	2, 3	1	2	3	1, 2, 3	2	2

17 *Creating Written Presentations* Conduct research to learn the impact on students of the Educational Amendments passed in 1972. Focus on how they changed the opportunities for girls and young women. Assemble a report describing landmark events and specific stories you find during your research. Be sure to evaluate your sources for validity and bias. LAFS.1112.RH.3.9, LAFS.1112.WHST.3.7, LAFS.1112.WHST.3.8, LAFS.1112.WHST.4.10, SS.912.A.1.2, SS.912.A.1.5, SS.912.A.5.7, SS.912.A.7.3

18 *Creating Maps* In the late 1960s, states near the United States-Mexico border had a strong Latino rights' movement presence. Research the cities in the United States with high Latino populations during the late 1960s and early 1970s. Compare with populations today. Present this information in a map, citing your sources. Analyze whether there has or has not been a shift in regions of the United States with a strong Latino presence. LAFS.1112.RH.3.9, LAFS.1112.WHST.3.7, LAFS.1112.WHST.3.8, SS.912.A.7.2, SS.912.G.1.2, SS.912.G.1.3, SS.912.G.2.1, SS.912.G.4.3

DBQ Analyzing Primary Sources

Use the photo to answer the following questions.

This photo was published in *Life* magazine in 1965. It shows feminist leader and future cofounder of *Ms.* magazine Gloria Steinem holding a sign with a phrase made popular by the civil rights movement: "We Shall Overcome."

19 *Making Connections* How does the message of this photo relate to the work that Steinem did to help promote Title VII of the 1964 Civil Rights Act and make it popular with the public? LAFS.1112.RH.3.7, LAFS.1112.RH.3.9, SS.912.A.5.7, SS.912.A.7.3, SS.912.A.7.5, SS.912.H.1.5

20 *Analyzing Visuals* In this photo, Steinem is seated indoors against a white background. How does this setting affect the message and impact of the photo? LAFS.1112.SL.1.3, SS.912.A.5.7, SS.912.A.7.3, SS.912.A.7.5, SS.912.H.1.5

Analyzing Visuals

Use the graph to answer the following questions.

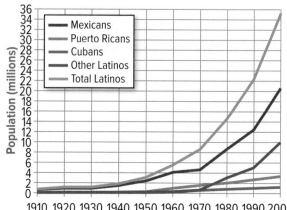

Source: *Historical Statistics of the United States: Earliest Times to the Present, Volume 1*

21 *Analyzing Geographic Distributions* Which nationality makes up the majority of Latino Americans? What questions would you need to ask in order to explain the national origins of Latinos other than those from Mexico and Cuba? SS.912.A.7.16, SS.912.G.1.2, SS.912.G.2.1, SS.912.G.4.2, SS.912.G.4.3

22 *Analyzing Geographic Patterns* Why did the number of people of Cuban nationality begin to rise in the 1960s? Why did the growth of the Mexican population slow between 1960 and 1970? What questions do you need to pose to explain why Latino numbers in general began to rise rapidly from 1970 onward? SS.912.A.7.16, SS.912.G.2.1, SS.912.G.1.2, SS.912.G.4.2, SS.912.G.4.3

Extended Response Question

23 *Analyzing Changing Demographics* Write an essay describing the causes and effects of legal and illegal immigration to the United States and explain how it has changed the demographics of the United States. The essay should have an introduction, at least three paragraphs, and a conclusion. Be sure to use correct social studies terminology when discussing key concepts about immigration and changes in American society. LAFS.1112.RH.3.7, LAFS.1112.WHST.2.4, LAFS.1112.WHST.2.6, LAFS.1112.WHST.4.10, MAFS.912.S-IC.2, SS.912.A.7.16

Need Extra Help?

If You've Missed Question	**17**	**18**	**19**	**20**	**21**	**22**	**23**
Go to Lesson	2	3	2	2	3	3	3

Yale Joel/Time & Life Pictures/Getty Images

◀ Henry Kissinger won the Nobel Peace Prize in 1973 for negotiating the Paris Peace Accords, which aimed to bring about a cease-fire in the Vietnam War and a withdrawal of American forces.

©Bettmann/Corbis

FROM 1968 TO 1980

Politics and Economics

THE STORY MATTERS ...

Henry Kissinger and President Nixon reshaped U.S. foreign policy. As President Nixon's national security advisor, Kissinger assisted with diplomatic negotiations with the Soviet Union and the People's Republic of China, building bridges where there had previously been hostility.

ESSENTIAL QUESTIONS

- How do you think the Nixon administration affected people's attitudes toward government?
- How does society change the shape of itself over time?

Place & Time: United States 1970–1979

When President Nixon took office, he decided to take a new approach to American relations with the Soviet Union and the People's Republic of China. The United States had been at odds with these Communist countries for decades. Nixon's new approach was one of détente, or easing of tensions, with the two nations. The Cold War was still on, but Nixon believed that only by redefining American foreign policy and forming partnerships with his "opponents" could anything be gained.

Step Into the Place

Read the quote and look at the information presented on the map.

DBQ **Analyzing Historical Documents** How do the quote and the information on the map confirm President Nixon's role in establishing relations with China?

PRIMARY SOURCE

‖ Now, with regard to the situation we now face, what is it that brings China and the U.S. together? For example, we have differences on Taiwan, not in my opinion so significant over the long run but difficult in the short run. We have differences over Southeast Asia. We have different attitudes toward Japan. We have different attitudes toward Korea. Now we say, and most of our rather naive American press buys this line, that the new relationship between China and America is due to the fact we have a basic friendship between our peoples. ‖

—President Richard Nixon, from a meeting with Chinese leader Zhou Enlai, February 22, 1972

left page (l)©Bettmann Premium/Corbis; (b) detail/White House Collection/The White House Historical Association; right page (l & r)detail/White House Collection/The White House Historical Association

Détente: U.S. Relations with the Soviet Union and China

60°N

UNITED STATES
Washington, D.C. ✪

30°N

0°

PACIFIC OCEAN

30°S

0   4,000 miles
0   4,000 km
Miller projection

150°W   120°W   90°W
60°S

Step Into the Time

PREDICTING CONSEQUENCES

Choose an event from the time line and write a paragraph predicting the general social, political, and economic consequences that event might have on political power, civil rights, or the environment.

Nixon
1969–1974

April 22, 1970 First Earth Day observed

December 1970 Environmental Protection Agency established

1972 Nixon visits China and the Soviet Union

June 1972 Watergate burglars are arrested

U.S. PRESIDENTS

UNITED STATES

WORLD

1968   1970   1972

1971 People's Republic of China admitted to UN

NEXT GENERATION SUNSHINE STATE STANDARDS
Students will understand the following benchmarks from the Florida NGSSS

LAFS.1112.RH.3.7: Integrate and evaluate multiple sources of information presented in diverse formats and media (e.g., visually, quantitatively, as well as in words) in order to address a question or solve a problem.

LAFS.1112.RH.3.9: Integrate information from diverse sources, both primary and secondary, into a coherent understanding of an idea or event, noting discrepancies among sources.

SS.912.A.1.2: Utilize a variety of primary and secondary sources to identify author, historical significance, audience, and authenticity to understand a historical period.

SS.912.A.1.3: Utilize timelines to identify the time sequence of historical data.

SS.912.A.1.4: Analyze how images, symbols, objects, cartoons, graphs, charts, maps, and artwork may be used to interpret the significance of time periods and events from the past.

SS.912.A.6.13: Analyze significant foreign policy events during the Truman, Eisenhower, Kennedy, Johnson, and Nixon administrations.

SS.912.A.7.4: Evaluate the success of 1960s era presidents' foreign and domestic policies.

ARCTIC OCEAN

In 1969, a longstanding territorial dispute resulted in armed clashes along the Soviet–Chinese border. Tensions remained throughout the 1970s.

• Moscow

SOVIET UNION

PACIFIC OCEAN

In May 1972, President Richard M. Nixon visited the Soviet Union and signed the first Strategic Arms Limitation Treaty (SALT).

Beijing ⊕

CHINA

In February 1972, Richard M. Nixon visited China, the first U.S. president to do so while in office.

TLANTIC OCEAN

INDIAN OCEAN

N
W · E
S

30°W   0°   30°E   60°E   90°E   120°E   150°E

February 1973 AIM and government clash at Wounded Knee, South Dakota

May 1973 Senate Watergate hearings begin

August 9, 1974 Nixon resigns

August 1, 1975 President Ford signs Helsinki Accords, easing Cold War tensions.

Ford 1974–1977

Carter 1977–1981

November 1979 Iranian revolutionaries seize U.S. embassy in Tehran

1974   1976   1978   1980

1973 Britain, Ireland, and Denmark join Common Market

1974 India becomes world's sixth nuclear power

1977 Human rights manifesto is signed by 241 Czech activists and intellectuals

July 1979 Sandinista guerrillas overthrow Nicaraguan dictator Anastasio Somoza

December 1979 Soviet Union invades Afghanistan

Politics and Economics **539**

LESSON 1
The Nixon Administration

ESSENTIAL QUESTIONS

• How do you think the Nixon administration affected people's attitudes toward government?
• How does society change the shape of itself over time?

READING HELPDESK

Academic Vocabulary

• welfare   • liberal

Content Vocabulary

• revenue sharing
• impound
• détente
• summit

TAKING NOTES

Key Ideas and Details

Organizing As you read, complete a graphic organizer similar to the one below by listing Nixon's domestic and foreign policies. LAFS.1112.RH.3.7, SS.912.A.6.13, SS.912.A.7.4

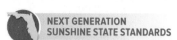

NEXT GENERATION SUNSHINE STATE STANDARDS

LAFS.1112.RH.1.2: Determine the central ideas or information of a primary or secondary source; provide an accurate summary that makes clear the relationships among the key details and ideas.

LAFS.1112.RH.2.4: Determine the meaning of words and phrases as they are used in a text, including analyzing how an author uses and refines the meaning of a key term over the course of a text (e.g., how Madison defines faction in Federalist No. 10).

LAFS.1112.RH.3.7: Integrate and evaluate multiple sources of information presented in diverse formats and media (e.g., visually, quantitatively, as well as in words) in order to address a question or solve a problem.

Continued on page 541

540

IT MATTERS BECAUSE

After he won the 1968 election, President Richard Nixon sought to restore law and order at home. His greatest accomplishments, however, were in foreign policy, where he worked to ease Cold War tensions with China and the Soviet Union.

Appealing to Middle America

GUIDING QUESTION *What were Nixon's keys to victory in the 1968 presidential election?*

Many Americans longed for an end to the turmoil that seemed to be plaguing the nation. In 1968, these frustrated citizens turned to Republican presidential candidate Richard Nixon. He aimed his campaign messages at this group, whom he referred to as "Middle America" and the "silent majority." Nixon promised "peace with honor" in Vietnam and law and order at home. He also promised a more streamlined government and a return to more traditional values.

In the election, Nixon faced President Johnson's vice president, Democrat Hubert Humphrey. He also went up against a strong third-party candidate, George Wallace, an experienced Southern politician and avowed supporter of segregation. Wallace captured 13.5 percent of the popular vote. Yet Nixon managed to win with 43.4 percent of the popular vote to Humphrey's 42.7, and 301 electoral votes to Humphrey's 191.

The Southern Strategy

Nixon partially owed his victory to a surprisingly strong showing in the South. The South had long been a Democratic stronghold, but Nixon worked hard to get its support. He had met with powerful South Carolina senator Strom Thurmond and won his support by promising several things. Nixon agreed to appoint only conservatives to the federal courts and to name a Southerner to the Supreme Court. He also promised to oppose court-ordered busing and to choose a vice-presidential candidate that the South could support. (Nixon chose Spiro Agnew, governor of the state of Maryland.)

Nixon's efforts paid off on Election Day. Large numbers of white Southerners left the Democratic Party. Humphrey's only Southern victory was in Lyndon Johnson's home state of Texas. Wallace claimed most of the states in the Deep South, but Nixon captured Virginia, Tennessee, Kentucky, and North Carolina. Thurmond's support delivered his state of South Carolina for the Republicans as well.

After his victory, Nixon set out to attract more Southerners to the Republican Party. This effort became known as the Southern strategy. He took steps to slow desegregation and worked to overturn civil rights policies. He also reversed a program that had cut off funds for racially segregated schools.

A Law-and-Order President

Nixon had promised to uphold law and order, and his administration went after antiwar protesters. Attorney General John Mitchell warned that he stood ready to prosecute anyone who crossed state lines to start riots. His deputy, Richard Kleindienst, declared, "We're going to enforce the law against draft evaders, against radical students, against deserters, against civil disorders, against organized crime, and against street crime."

President Nixon also attacked the recent Supreme Court rulings that expanded the rights of accused criminals. Nixon openly criticized the Court and its chief justice, Earl Warren. The president promised to fill vacancies on the Court with judges who would support the rights of law enforcement over the rights of suspected criminals.

Warren retired soon after Nixon took office. The president replaced him with respected conservative judge Warren Burger. He placed three other conservative justices on the Court, including one from the South. The Burger Court did not reverse Warren Court rulings on suspects' rights, but it refused to expand those rights. For example, in *Stone* v. *Powell* (1976), it limited defendants' rights to appeal state convictions to the federal judiciary. The Burger Court also reaffirmed capital punishment.

NEXT GENERATION SUNSHINE STATE STANDARDS

Continued from page 540

LAFS.1112.WHST.1.2: Write informative/ explanatory texts, including the narration of historical events, scientific procedures/ experiments, or technical processes.

LAFS.1112.WHST.3.9: Draw evidence from informational texts to support analysis, reflection, and research.

LAFS.1112.WHST.4.10: Write routinely over extended time frames (time for reflection and revision) and shorter time frames (a single sitting or a day or two) for a range of discipline-specific tasks, purposes, and audiences.

SS.912.A.1.2: Utilize a variety of primary and secondary sources to identify author, historical significance, audience, and authenticity to understand a historical period.

SS.912.A.1.4: Analyze how images, symbols, objects, cartoons, graphs, charts, maps, and artwork may be used to interpret the significance of time periods and events from the past.

SS.912.A.6.13: Analyze significant foreign policy events during the Truman, Eisenhower, Kennedy, Johnson, and Nixon administrations.

SS.912.A.6.14: Analyze causes, course, and consequences of the Vietnam War.

SS.912.A.7.4: Evaluate the success of 1960s era presidents' foreign and domestic policies.

SS.912.A.7.11: Analyze the foreign policy of the United States as it relates to Africa, Asia, the Caribbean, Latin America, and the Middle East.

GEOGRAPHY CONNECTION

Republican Richard Nixon defeated Democrat Hubert Humphrey and third-party candidate George Wallace in the election of 1968.

1 **PLACES AND REGIONS** *In which region did Nixon receive the most support?* SS.912.A.1.4

2 **THE WORLD IN SPATIAL TERMS** *Which states' electoral votes went wholly or in part to Wallace?* SS.912.A.1.4

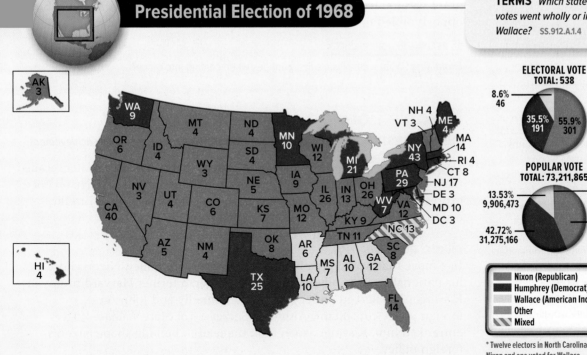

Presidential Election of 1968

ELECTORAL VOTE
TOTAL: 538

8.6% 46
35.5% 191
55.9% 301

POPULAR VOTE
TOTAL: 73,211,865

13.53% 9,906,473
0.33% 244,746
42.72% 31,275,166
43.42% 31,785,480

- Nixon (Republican)
- Humphrey (Democrat)
- Wallace (American Independent)
- Other
- Mixed

* Twelve electors in North Carolina voted for Nixon and one voted for Wallace.

revenue sharing federal tax money that is distributed among the states

impound to take possession of

welfare aid in the form of money or necessities for those in need, especially disadvantaged social groups

liberal a person who generally believes the government should take an active role in the economy and in social programs but should not dictate social behavior

The New Federalism

Nixon had also promised to reduce the size of the federal government. He planned to end several federal programs and give more control to state and local governments. Nixon called this the "New Federalism." He argued that such an approach would make government more effective. "I reject the patronizing idea that government in Washington, D.C., is inevitably more wise, more honest and more efficient than government at the local or State level," Nixon declared. "The idea that a bureaucratic elite in Washington knows what's best for people . . . is really a contention that people cannot govern themselves."

Under Nixon's New Federalism plan, Congress passed a series of **revenue-sharing** bills granting federal funds to state and local agencies. As states came to depend on federal funds, the federal government could impose conditions on states. Unless states met those conditions, funds would be cut off.

As part of the New Federalism, Nixon wanted to end many of Johnson's Great Society programs. He vetoed funding for the Department of Housing and Urban Development. He eliminated the Office of Economic Opportunity, and tried unsuccessfully to shut down the Job Corps. When Congress appropriated money for programs he opposed, Nixon **impounded,** or refused to release, the funds. By 1973, it was estimated that he had impounded as much as $18 billion. The Supreme Court eventually declared the practice of impoundment unconstitutional.

The Family Assistance Plan

One federal program Nixon wanted to reform was the nation's **welfare** system—Aid to Families with Dependent Children (AFDC). The program had many critics. In 1969, Nixon proposed replacing the AFDC with the Family Assistance Plan. The plan called for providing needy families a yearly grant of $1,600, which could be supplemented by outside earnings. Many **liberals** applauded the plan as a significant step toward expanding federal responsibility for the poor.

Although the program won approval in the House in 1970, it soon came under harsh attack. Welfare recipients complained that the federal grant was too low. Conservatives disapproved of guaranteed income. Such opposition led to the program's defeat in the Senate.

✓ READING PROGRESS CHECK

Explaining What were Nixon's first priorities when coming into office?

Nixon's Foreign Policy

GUIDING QUESTION *What do you think was Nixon's greatest foreign policy achievement?*

Despite Nixon's domestic initiatives, a State Department official later recalled that Nixon had a "monumental disinterest in domestic policies." Nixon once expressed his hope that a "competent cabinet" of advisers could run the country, allowing him to focus on foreign affairs.

Nixon and Kissinger

In a move that would greatly influence his foreign policy, Nixon chose as his national security advisor Henry Kissinger, a former Harvard professor. Kissinger had served under Presidents Kennedy and Johnson as a foreign policy consultant. Although Secretary of State William Rogers outranked him, Kissinger soon took the lead in helping shape Nixon's foreign policy.

SKILLS PRACTICE

Write down vocabulary terms your teacher uses when teaching about President Nixon. Look up those terms in the text. Write down words that have similar meanings to help you remember the terms. Draw a picture if it helps you remember the vocabulary. Think of the words and pictures the next time you hear or see one of the new vocabulary words.
ELD.K12.ELL.SI.1, ELD.K12.ELL.SS.1, LAFS.1112.RH.2.4

The Nixon Doctrine Nixon and Kissinger shared many views. Both believed abandoning the war in Vietnam would damage the nation's position in the world. Thus, they worked toward a gradual withdrawal while also training the South Vietnamese to defend themselves.

This policy of Vietnamization, as it was called, was extended globally in what came to be known as the Nixon Doctrine. In July 1969, only six months after taking office, Nixon announced that the United States would honor all of the alliances it had signed. The nation would continue to provide military aid and training to allies. Yet, it would no longer "conceive all the plans, design all the programs, execute all the decisions and undertake all the defense of the free nations of the world." America's allies would have to take responsibility for maintaining peace and stability in their own areas of the world.

The New Policy of Détente The Soviet Union was not pleased when Nixon became president. He was known to be strongly anti-Communist. Yet Nixon and Kissinger believed the United States needed to adjust to the growing role of China, Japan, and Western Europe. This emerging "multipolar" world demanded a different approach to American foreign policy.

Both Nixon and Kissinger wanted to continue to contain communism, but they believed that negotiation with Communists was a better way for the United States to achieve its international goals. They developed a new approach called **détente,** or relaxation of tensions, between the United States and its two major Communist rivals, the Soviet Union and China. Nixon said that the nation had to build a better relationship with its main rivals for world peace:

PRIMARY SOURCE

❝We must understand that détente is not a love fest. It is an understanding between nations that have opposite purposes, but which share common interests, including the avoidance of a nuclear war. Such an understanding can work—that is, restrain aggression and deter war—only as long as the potential aggressor is made to recognize that neither aggression nor war will be profitable.❞

—quoted in *The Limits of Power*, 1992

The successes of détente were diminished due to upheavals in smaller nations. In Chile, President Salvador Allende was killed during a coup supported by the American CIA. Similarly, the Angolan Civil War, which began in 1975, featured secret aid from the United States. The conflicts in Chile and Angola were examples of proxy wars—conflicts during the Cold War that did not directly involve the United States and the Soviet Union but pursued Cold War aims of the two superpowers.

Nixon Visits China

Détente began with an effort to improve American-Chinese relations. Since 1949, when Communists took power in China, the United States had refused to recognize the Communists as the legitimate rulers. Instead, the U.S. government recognized the exiled regime on the island of Taiwan as the Chinese government. Having long supported this policy, Nixon now set out to reverse it.

Removal of U.S. Troops from Iraq

Just as Vietnamization called for the South Vietnamese military to take over duties from American troops, the gradual close of American involvement in Iraq has seen American troops give increased responsibility to Iraqi security forces. Although American combat troops officially left Iraq in August 2010, some 50,000 soldiers remained in the country. Their primary duty was to help the Iraqi army as it assumed full control over the nation's security.

détente a policy that attempts to relax or ease tensions between nations

Mao Zedong, leader of China, greets President Nixon in Beijing on February 21, 1972.

▶ **CRITICAL THINKING**
Identifying Central Ideas What was the primary goal of the policy of détente? LAFS.1112.WHST.3.9, SS.912.A.1.4, SS.912.A.7.4

AFP/Getty Images

Henry Kissinger (1923–)

Henry Kissinger and his family left Germany for the United States in 1938 to escape Nazi anti-Jewish restrictions. Kissinger served in U.S. military intelligence during World War II, then attended Harvard University, later joining its faculty. He was a consultant on national security under Presidents Kennedy and Johnson, before becoming Nixon's national security advisor and later secretary of state. He helped establish the policy of détente with the Soviet Union and China. Kissinger negotiated the cease-fire with North Vietnam and was awarded the Nobel Peace Prize in 1973. In 1977, Kissinger received the Presidential Medal of Freedom.

▶ **CRITICAL THINKING**
Drawing Conclusions How did Henry Kissinger influence foreign policy in the 1970s? SS.912.A.6.13

summit a meeting between heads of government

After a series of highly secret negotiations between Kissinger and Chinese leaders, Nixon announced that he would visit China in February 1972. During the historic trip, the leaders of both nations agreed to establish "more normal" relations between their countries. In a statement Nixon made to his Chinese hosts during a banquet toast:

PRIMARY SOURCE

❝[S]o let us, in these next five days, start a long march together. Not in lockstep, but on different roads leading to the same goal: the goal of building a world structure of peace and justice in which all may stand together with equal dignity.❞
—quoted in the *New York Times*, February 22, 1972

United States–Soviet Tensions Ease

Nixon's strategy toward the Soviet Union worked. Shortly after the public learned of American negotiations with China, the Soviets proposed an American-Soviet **summit,** or high-level diplomatic meeting, to be held in May 1972. On May 22, President Nixon flew to Moscow for a weeklong summit. Nixon was the first American president since World War II to visit the Soviet Union.

During the historic Moscow summit, the two superpowers signed the first Strategic Arms Limitation Treaty, or SALT I, a plan the two nations had been working on for years. The treaty temporarily froze the number of strategic nuclear weapons. Nixon and Soviet premier Leonid Brezhnev also agreed to increase trade and the exchange of scientific information. Détente had helped ease tensions between the two countries. One Soviet official admitted that by the end of Nixon's presidency, "the United States and the Soviet Union had their best relationship of the whole Cold War period."

Another highlight of détente was a series of meetings that created the Helsinki Accords. In 1975, the United States, Canada, and most of the countries of Eastern and Western Europe committed to three sets of recommendations focusing on security, economic, and human rights issues. In one section, the signing states agreed to "respect human rights and fundamental freedoms, including the freedom of thought, conscience, religion or belief, for all without distinction as to race, sex, language or religion."

President Nixon indeed had made his mark on the world stage. However, a scandal was about to engulf his presidency and plunge the nation into one of its greatest constitutional crises.

☑ **READING PROGRESS CHECK**

Defining What was the policy of Vietnamization, and how did it relate to the Nixon Doctrine?

©Bettmann/Corbis

LESSON 1 REVIEW

Reviewing Vocabulary
1. *Explaining* How does revenue sharing work? LAFS.1112.RH.2.4

2. *Identifying* What takes place at a summit? LAFS.1112.RH.2.4

Using Your Notes
3. *Summarizing* Review the notes that you completed throughout the lesson to summarize Nixon's major domestic and foreign policy initiatives. LAFS.1112.RH.3.7, SS.912.A.6.13, SS.912.A.7.4

Answering the Guiding Questions
4. *Stating* What were Nixon's keys to victory in the 1968 presidential election? LAFS.1112.WHST.3.9, SS.912.A.7.4

5. *Evaluating* What do you think was Nixon's greatest foreign policy achievement? LAFS.1112.WHST.3.9, SS.912.A.6.13, SS.912.A.7.4

Writing Activity
6. INFORMATIVE/EXPLANATORY Take on the role of a journalist assigned to cover the 1972 Moscow summit. Write a newspaper article about the events and outcomes of this meeting. LAFS.1112.WHST.1.2, LAFS.1112.WHST.4.10

LESSON 2
The Watergate Scandal

- How do you think the Nixon administration affected people's attitudes toward government?
- How does society change the shape of itself over time?

READING HELPDESK

Academic Vocabulary

- incident
- challenger

Content Vocabulary

- executive privilege
- special prosecutor

TAKING NOTES

Key Ideas and Details

Outlining Use the headings in this lesson to create an outline similar to the one below by recording information about the Watergate scandal.
LAFS.1112.RH.3.7, SS.912.A.7.10

> The Watergate Scandal
> I. The Roots of Watergate
>   A.
>   B.
> II.
>   A.
>   B.

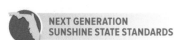

**NEXT GENERATION
SUNSHINE STATE STANDARDS**

LAFS.1112.RH.2.4: Determine the meaning of words and phrases as they are used in a text, including analyzing how an author uses and refines the meaning of a key term over the course of a text (e.g., how Madison defines faction in Federalist No. 10).

LAFS.1112.RH.3.7: Integrate and evaluate multiple sources of information presented in diverse formats and media (e.g., visually, quantitatively, as well as in words) in order to address a question or solve a problem.

LAFS.1112.WHST.1.1: Write arguments focused on discipline-specific content.

Continued on page 546

IT MATTERS BECAUSE

Despite a successful first term, Richard Nixon and his supporters worried about reelection. The tactics they resorted to led to the Watergate scandal, one of the nation's great constitutional crises.

The Roots of Watergate

GUIDING QUESTION *Why did Nixon's advisers order a break-in at the Democratic Party's headquarters?*

The Watergate scandal led to the only time in the nation's history when the president of the United States was forced to resign from office. It began on the morning of June 17, 1972, when a young *Washington Post* reporter named Bob Woodward was assigned to cover a seemingly insignificant but bizarre **incident.** Early that morning, five men had broken into the Democratic National Committee (DNC) headquarters in the city's Watergate apartment office complex. Woodward attended the arraignment. He was asked to go to see if there was a story worth reporting.

As Woodward sat near the back of the courtroom listening to the bail proceedings for the five defendants, the judge asked each man his occupation. One of the men, James McCord, answered that he was retired from government service. "Where in government?" asked the judge. "CIA," McCord whispered. Woodward sprang to attention. Why was a former CIA agent involved in what seemed to be just a burglary? Over the next two years, Woodward and another reporter, Carl Bernstein, investigated this question. They uncovered a scandal that helped trigger a constitutional crisis and eventually forced Nixon to resign.

Mounting a Reelection Fight

The Watergate scandal directly involved the Nixon administration's efforts to cover up its involvement in the break-in at the Democratic National Committee headquarters. It also included other illegal actions. Many scholars believe the roots of the scandal, however, lay in Nixon's character and the atmosphere of the White House.

NEXT GENERATION
SUNSHINE STATE STANDARDS

Continued from page 545

LAFS.1112.WHST.3.9: Draw evidence from informational texts to support analysis, reflection, and research.

LAFS.1112.WHST.4.10: Write routinely over extended time frames (time for reflection and revision) and shorter time frames (a single sitting or a day or two) for a range of discipline-specific tasks, purposes, and audiences.

SS.912.A.1.4: Analyze how images, symbols, objects, cartoons, graphs, charts, maps, and artwork may be used to interpret the significance of time periods and events from the past.

SS.912.A.1.5: Evaluate the validity, reliability, bias, and authenticity of current events and Internet resources.

SS.912.A.1.6: Use case studies to explore social, political, legal, and economic relationships in history.

SS.912.A.7.10: Analyze the significance of Vietnam and Watergate on the government and people of the United States.

incident single occurrence of a happening or situation

challenger one who enters a competition

James McCord shows the Senate Watergate Committee the bugging device he installed.

▶ **CRITICAL THINKING**
Identifying Central Ideas
What made the Watergate scandal so damaging to the Nixon administration? **LAFS.1112.WHST.3.9, SS.912.A.1.4, SS.912.A.7.10**

Richard Nixon had fought hard to become president, battling back from numerous political defeats. Along the way, he had grown defensive, secretive, and often resentful of his critics. He became president amid race riots, war protests, and other turmoil. He became so consumed with his opponents that he made an "enemies list" of people whom he considered a threat to his presidency.

As the 1972 presidential election approached, Nixon's reelection prospects seemed promising, but not certain. He had just finished triumphant trips to China and the Soviet Union. Former governor George Wallace had dropped out of the race after an assassin's bullet paralyzed him. And many considered Democratic **challenger** Senator George McGovern too liberal. But the Vietnam War still raged, and staffers remembered the close 1968 election. Determined to win, they began spying on opposition rallies and spreading rumors about opponents.

Trying to help the president, Nixon's advisers ordered five men to break into the Democratic Party's headquarters at the Watergate complex and steal sensitive campaign information. They were also to place wiretaps on the office telephones. While the burglars worked, a security guard spotted a piece of tape holding a door lock. The guard removed the tape, but when he passed the door later, he saw that it had been replaced. He quickly called police, who arrived shortly and arrested the men.

The Cover-Up Begins

After the break-in, the media discovered that one burglar, James McCord, was not only an ex-CIA officer but also a member of the Committee for the Re-election of the President (CRP). Reports surfaced that the burglars had been paid from a secret CRP fund controlled by the White House.

Nixon may not have ordered the break-in, but he did order a cover-up. White House officials destroyed incriminating documents and gave investigators false testimony. With Nixon's consent, administration officials asked the CIA to stop the FBI from investigating the source of money paid to the burglars. The CIA told the FBI that the investigation threatened national security. FBI deputy director W. Mark Felt then secretly leaked information about Watergate to the *Washington Post*.

Meanwhile, Nixon's press secretary dismissed the incident, and the president told the American public, "The White House has had no involvement whatever in this particular incident." It worked. Most Americans believed Nixon. Despite efforts by the media to keep the story alive, few people paid much attention during the 1972 presidential campaign. Nixon won reelection by one of the largest margins in history.

☑ READING PROGRESS CHECK

Explaining What effect did the CIA have on the FBI's investigation of the burglars in the Watergate break-in?

The Cover-Up Unravels

GUIDING QUESTION *How much power can a president wield to ensure national security?*

In early 1973, the Watergate burglars went on trial. Under relentless prodding from federal judge John J. Sirica, McCord agreed to cooperate with the grand jury investigation and to testify before the newly created Senate Select Committee on Presidential Campaign Activities. The chairman of the committee was Democratic senator Sam J. Ervin from North Carolina.

A Summer of Shocking Testimony

McCord's testimony opened a floodgate of confessions. Presidential counsel John Dean, who had testified in June 1973, confessed that former attorney general John Mitchell had ordered the Watergate break-in and that Nixon had taken part in the cover-up.

The Nixon administration strongly denied the charges. Dean had no evidence, and the Senate committee spent weeks trying to determine who was telling the truth. The answer appeared on July 16. White House aide Alexander Butterfield testified that Nixon had ordered a taping system installed in the White House to record all conversations to help him write his memoirs after leaving office. The tapes would tell the committee what Nixon knew and when he knew it—if the president released them.

The Case of the Tapes

At first, Nixon refused to hand over the tapes, pleading **executive privilege,** the principle that White House conversations should remain confidential to protect national security. **Special Prosecutor** Archibald Cox took Nixon to court in October 1973 to make him give up the tapes. Nixon ordered Attorney General Elliot Richardson to fire Cox, but Richardson refused and resigned. Nixon then ordered Richardson's deputy to fire Cox, but he, too, resigned. Nixon's solicitor general, Robert Bork, finally fired Cox, but the incident badly damaged Nixon's reputation.

The fall of 1973 proved disastrous for other reasons as well. Vice President Spiro Agnew resigned in disgrace after investigators found that he had taken

executive privilege
principle stating that communications of the executive branch should remain confidential to protect national security

special prosecutor a lawyer from outside the government

🏛 ANALYZING SUPREME COURT CASES

UNITED STATES v. *NIXON,* 1974

Background to the Case

In 1974, Special Prosecutor Leon Jaworski issued a subpoena to gain access to audio tape recordings President Nixon had made of conversations. Jaworski believed that the tapes would prove the active involvement of the president in the Watergate cover-up. Nixon filed a motion to prevent the subpoena, claiming executive privilege. The case went to district court, but that court withheld judgment pending the decision of the Supreme Court.

The Senate committee overseeing the Watergate investigation, chaired by Senator Sam Ervin (fourth from left at the table), wanted access to Nixon's White House tape recordings.

How the Court Ruled

In a unanimous 8-to-0 decision (Justice Rehnquist did not take part), the Supreme Court found that executive privilege did not protect Nixon's tape recordings. The ruling stated that while the president has a right to protect military secrets and other sensitive material and has a right to some confidentiality, the needs of a criminal trial must take precedence. In the Court's opinion Chief Justice Warren Burger wrote, "We conclude that when the ground for asserting privilege as to subpoenaed materials sought for use in a criminal trial is based only on the generalized interest in confidentiality, it cannot prevail over the fundamental demands of due process of law in the fair administration of criminal justice. . . ."

DBQ Document Based Questions

❶ *Identifying Central Ideas* What was the purpose or central issue of the case? SS.912.A.1.6, SS.912.A.7.10

❷ *Defending* Do you agree with the Supreme Court's decision in this case? Explain. SS.912.A.1.6

Rose Mary Woods was Nixon's personal secretary. She claimed that an 18½ minute gap in the Watergate tapes was the result of an accidental erasure.

▶ **CRITICAL THINKING**

Drawing Conclusions Why might Woods's explanation of the gap in the tapes have been doubted? LAFS.1112.WHST.3.9, SS.912.A.1.4, SS.912.A.7.10

bribes while governor of Maryland and while serving in office in Washington. Gerald Ford, Republican leader of the House of Representatives, became the new vice president.

Nixon Resigns

Nixon tried to quell outrage by appointing a new special prosecutor, Leon Jaworski, who also proved determined to obtain the tapes. In July the Supreme Court ruled that Nixon had to surrender them. He complied. Days later, the House Judiciary Committee voted to impeach Nixon, or officially charge him with misconduct. Charges included obstructing justice, misusing federal agencies to violate the rights of citizens, and defying the authority of Congress. Then new evidence emerged: a tape revealed that Nixon had ordered the CIA to stop the FBI probe into the Watergate burglary on June 23, 1972. Impeachment and conviction were inevitable. On August 9, 1974, Nixon resigned in disgrace.

Vice President Gerald Ford took office as president of the United States after Nixon's resignation. He urged Americans to put the scandal behind them, saying, "Our long national nightmare is over." On September 8, 1974, Ford announced a full pardon for Nixon. Ford's pardon of Nixon drew public criticism and diminished his popularity.

The Impact of Watergate

The constitutional crisis led to new laws intended to limit the power of the executive branch. The Federal Campaign Act Amendments of 1974 limited campaign contributions and set up an independent agency to enforce strict election laws. The Ethics in Government Act required financial disclosure by high government officials throughout all branches of government. The FBI Domestic Security Investigation Guidelines Act restricted the FBI's political intelligence-gathering activities. Congress also laid out a means to appoint an independent counsel to investigate and prosecute wrongdoing by high government officials.

Many Americans developed a distrust of public officials. Others, such as Bob Woodward, believed the affair proved that no one is above the law: "Watergate was probably a good thing for the country. . . . The problem with kings, and prime ministers, and presidents, is that they think . . . that they have some special rights. . . . We have our laws and believe them, and they apply to everyone, [which] is a very good thing."

☑ **READING PROGRESS CHECK**

Assessing What role did the Nixon tapes play in discovering the truth about the Watergate scandal?

LESSON 2 REVIEW

Reviewing Vocabulary

1. Defining What is executive privilege? LAFS.1112.RH.2.4

2. Stating What do special prosecutors do? LAFS.1112.RH.2.4, LAFS.1112.WHST.3.9

Using Your Notes

3. Sequencing Use your notes to write a description of the major events of the Watergate scandal in order. LAFS.1112.RH.3.7

Answering the Guiding Questions

4. Explaining Why did Nixon's advisers order a break-in at the Democratic Party's headquarters? LAFS.1112.WHST.3.9, SS.912.A.7.10

5. Analyzing Ethical Issues How much power can a president wield to ensure national security? LAFS.1112.WHST.3.9, SS.912.A.7.10

Writing Activity

6. ARGUMENT Shortly after taking office, President Ford granted Nixon a full pardon for any crimes he may have been involved in or committed. Use the Internet to find two or more reactions to this action and identify the author and time period when the reaction was written. Evaluate the validity, reliability, and bias of the reactions, and write a paragraph comparing which is the best source to use to understand Ford's actions. LAFS.1112.WHST.1.1, LAFS.1112.WHST.4.10, SS.912.A.1.5, SS.912.A.7.10

AP Images

LESSON 3
Ford and Carter

ESSENTIAL QUESTIONS

- How do you think the Nixon administration affected people's attitudes toward government?
- How does society change the shape of itself over time?

READING HELPDESK

Academic Vocabulary

- theory
- deregulation

Content Vocabulary

- inflation
- stagflation
- embargo

TAKING NOTES

Key Ideas and Details

Determining Cause and Effect
As you read, complete a graphic organizer similar to the one below by listing the causes of economic problems in the 1970s. LAFS.1112.RH.3.7, SS.912.A.7.14

**NEXT GENERATION
SUNSHINE STATE STANDARDS**

LAFS.1112.RH.2.4: Determine the meaning of words and phrases as they are used in a text, including analyzing how an author uses and refines the meaning of a key term over the course of a text (e.g., how Madison defines faction in Federalist No. 10).

LAFS.1112.RH.3.7: Integrate and evaluate multiple sources of information presented in diverse formats and media (e.g., visually, quantitatively, as well as in words) in order to address a question or solve a problem.

LAFS.1112.WHST.3.9: Draw evidence from informational texts to support analysis, reflection, and research.

Continued on page 551

IT MATTERS BECAUSE
By the time Richard Nixon resigned, the postwar economic boom period Americans had experienced was ending. Presidents Gerald R. Ford and Jimmy Carter attempted to lead the United States through both domestic and foreign crises.

The Economic Crisis of the 1970s

GUIDING QUESTION *What economic conditions or problems led to a stagnant economy during the 1970s?*

After World War II, American prosperity seemed normal. It relied on easy access to global raw materials and a strong manufacturing base at home. In the 1970s, however, prosperity gave way to a decade of hard times.

A Mighty Economic Machine Slows
Economic troubles began in the mid-1960s. President Johnson increased deficit spending to fund the Vietnam War and the Great Society without raising taxes. This pumped money into the economy, but by the 1970s, this spending caused rapid **inflation.**

Rising oil prices dealt another blow. By 1970, the United States had become dependent on imported oil. In 1973, the Arab members of the Organization of the Petroleum Exporting Countries (OPEC) used oil as a political weapon when war erupted between Israel and its Arab neighbors. Arab members announced an **embargo,** or trade ban, on petroleum to countries that supported Israel. They raised the price of crude oil by 70 percent and then by another 130 percent a few months later. After the embargo ended, oil prices continued to rise, from $3 per barrel in 1973 to $30 per barrel in 1980. This meant that Americans had less money for other goods, which contributed to a recession.

Historians can examine economic data when they are trying to analyze history and to better understand the actions and choices made during a particular period of history. They can draw conclusions from comparing and contrasting the price of oil from two different time periods. They can evaluate how global or local historic events or changes in supply and demand may have contributed to a decline or rise in oil prices. For example, in 1981 crude oil prices for refiners hit a high of about $39 per barrel. They declined slowly and then sharply until the early 2000s. Then, in 2008, oil prices rose dramatically, to about $131 per barrel. In order to analyze the similar data for oil prices in 1981 and 2008, historians might look at related local and world events that could have affected this soar in prices in both years.

Transferring Information Use the information above, as well as research from the library or online, to create a visual presentation of oil prices from 1970 to today. Use spreadsheet software that lets you create graphs. Add captions identifying major political or economic events that occurred when prices were high. LAFS.1112.WHST.3.7, MAFS.K12.MP.5.1, SS.912.A.1.1

inflation the loss of value of money

embargo a government ban on trade with other countries

stagflation persistent inflation combined with stagnant consumer demand and relatively high unemployment

theory a hypothesis meant for argument or investigation

A Stagnant Economy

Declining manufacturing was another economic problem. By 1970, many American factories were old and less efficient than those in competing countries. In 1971, the nation imported more than it exported for the first time since 1889. Many factories closed. Millions of workers lost their jobs. In the early 1970s, Nixon thus faced a new economic problem nicknamed **"stagflation"**—a combination of inflation and a stagnant economy with high unemployment.

Because some economists supported the **theory** that inflation could only occur when demand for goods was high, they were not sure what fiscal policy the government should follow in order to fight inflation and the recession. Nixon wanted to control inflation. The government first tried to cut spending and raise taxes, and then tried to get the Federal Reserve to raise interest rates. When these methods failed, Nixon decided to end the gold standard.

After World War II, as part of the Bretton Woods system, the U.S. dollar was made convertible to gold at the rate of 35 dollars for one ounce of gold. Other currencies in the world were then pegged to the U.S. dollar at agreed upon exchange rates. The United States maintained gold reserves equal to the amount of currency in circulation. Anytime someone wanted to convert their dollars into gold they could do so.

The problem with the system was that it limited monetary policy. If the United States wanted to put more money into circulation, it had to make sure there was an equivalent amount of gold in reserve. When inflation began in the late 1960s, many people thought part of the problem was that foreign nations were gouging, or charging high unfair prices, to American consumers. OPEC seemed to be an example of this. If the dollar's value changed, however, the cost of imported goods could be brought down.

No major trading partner of the United States, however, wanted to change its exchange rate. Americans were buying lots of imported goods, and foreign countries were earning a lot of U.S. dollars that they could convert to gold. So Nixon decided to "close the gold window," announcing that dollars could no longer be redeemed for gold. The president also imposed a 90-day freeze on wages and prices to try to prevent the end of the gold standard from making inflation even worse.

Nixon's actions became known as the New Economic Policy, or the Nixon Shock. The plan was supposed to be temporary, to force other countries to renegotiate their exchange rates. But by early 1973, the system had collapsed and the gold standard came to an end. The United States moved to a true fiat currency. Fiat currency is money that has value because the government says it has value and requires people to accept it for payment of goods and services.

Because it was no longer tied to gold or any other physical thing that has value, the dollar began to "float" or rise or fall in value compared to other nation's currencies. The end of the gold standard gave the Federal Reserve the ability to use monetary policy without many limitations. It could now freely pump money into the economy to help overcome recessions or slow the expansion of the money supply to control inflation. But critics have argued that it makes the international economy less stable, encourages deficit spending, and has led to sudden swings in the world's stock markets.

☑ READING PROGRESS CHECK

Determining Cause and Effect Why were some economists unsure of how to fight stagflation?

Ford and Carter Battle the Economic Crisis

GUIDING QUESTION *How did Ford and Carter try to resolve the nation's domestic issues?*

When Nixon resigned in 1974, inflation was still high. Meanwhile, the unemployment rate was over 5 percent. It would now be up to the new president, Gerald Ford, to confront stagflation.

Ford Tries to "Whip" Inflation

By 1975, unemployment had risen to nearly 9 percent. Ford launched a plan called WIN—"Whip Inflation Now"—but it had little impact on the economic situation. He tried other measures to reduce inflation, including keeping taxes low, but these plans also failed to revive the economy.

Ford's Foreign Policy

Ford continued Nixon's general foreign policy strategy. He kept Kissinger on as secretary of state and continued to pursue détente. In August 1975, Ford met with leaders of NATO and the Warsaw Pact to sign the Helsinki Accords. Under the accords, the parties recognized the post–World War II borders of Eastern Europe. The Soviets promised to uphold certain human rights, although this did not always happen.

In May 1975, soon after Communists seized power in Cambodia, Cambodian forces captured the *Mayaguez,* an American cargo ship. Ford sent U.S. Marines to retrieve the ship, but Cambodia had already secretly released the crew. Unaware of the crew's safety, the marines recaptured the ship, and 41 servicemen died in the battle.

The Election of 1976

The presidential race pitted Ford against former Georgia governor Jimmy Carter, who had no experience in Washington. Carter ran as an outsider promising to restore honesty to the federal government. He also promised to create or reform several domestic programs. Carter's image as a moral and upstanding individual attracted many voters, and he narrowly defeated Ford.

Carter's Economic Policies

Carter tried to use domestic policies to fix the economy. At first he tried to end the recession and reduce unemployment by increasing government spending and cutting taxes. Then he tried to ease inflation by reducing the money supply and raising interest rates. These measures did not work.

Although Jimmy Carter's outsider status had made him an appealing candidate, his inexperience in Washington proved problematic.

▶ CRITICAL THINKING
Drawing Conclusions How might a lack of experience in Washington have made it difficult for Carter to achieve his goals? LAFS.1112.WHST.3.9

NEXT GENERATION
SUNSHINE STATE STANDARDS

Continued from page 549

LAFS.1112.WHST.4.10: Write routinely over extended time frames (time for reflection and revision) and shorter time frames (a single sitting or a day or two) for a range of discipline-specific tasks, purposes, and audiences.

Continued on page 552

deregulation the act or process of removing restrictions or regulations

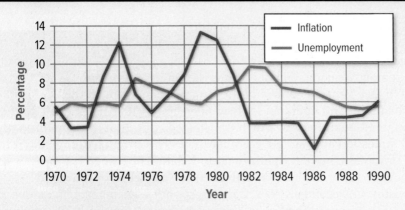

INFLATION AND UNEMPLOYMENT RATES

— Inflation
— Unemployment

Percentage / Year

Source: U.S. Department of Labor; Bureau of Labor Statistics.

CHARTS/GRAPHS

President Ford failed to solve the nation's lingering economic problems.

1 *Analyzing Information*
What was the trend for both unemployment and inflation in the late 1970s? MAFS.912.S-ID.1

2 *Drawing Conclusions* What effect do you think levels of inflation and unemployment had on Ford's presidential bid in 1976? LAFS.1112.WHST.3.9, MAFS.912.S-ID.1

Library of Congress, Prints & Photographs Division [LC-USZC2-10]

//He looked exhausted and careworn, sitting behind the big wooden desk in the Oval Office as he spoke. 'It was my decision to attempt the rescue operation. It was my decision to cancel it when problems developed. . . . The responsibility is fully my own.'

The mood at the senior staff meeting was somber and awkward. I sensed that we were all uncomfortable, like when a loved one dies and friends don't know quite what to say.**//**

—Chief of Staff Hamilton Jordan, *Crisis*, 1982

DBQ ***ANALYZING PRIMARY SOURCES*** Why did Carter consider the rescue operation's failure his responsibility? LAFS.1112.RH.3.7, SS.912.A.1.2

SKILLS PRACTICE

The text on Presidents Ford and Carter can be challenging. Before reading, look through the lesson. Look at the headings, the vocabulary terms, the charts and graphs, and the photos. Write down what they are telling you about the 1970s. As you read, refer to your notes to remind you of the context. ELD.K12.ELL.SI.1, ELD.K12.ELL.SS.1, LAFS.1112.RH.3.7

NEXT GENERATION SUNSHINE STATE STANDARDS

Continued from page 551

MAFS.912.S-ID.1: Summarize, represent and interpret data on a single count or measurement variable.

MAFS.K12.MP.5.1: Use appropriate tools strategically. Mathematically proficient students consider the available tools when solving a mathematical problem.

SS.912.A.1.1: Describe the importance of historiography, which includes how historical knowledge is obtained and transmitted, when interpreting events in history.

SS.912.A.1.2: Utilize a variety of primary and secondary sources to identify author, historical significance, audience, and authenticity to understand a historical period.

Continued on page 553

Carter believed that the nation's most serious economic problem was its dependence on foreign oil. He asked Americans to fight against rising energy consumption. He also proposed a national energy program to conserve oil and to promote the use of coal and renewable energy sources. Carter even convinced Congress to create a Department of Energy, and asked Americans to reduce energy consumption. Some argued that Carter should deregulate the domestic oil industry to decrease dependence on imported oil. Carter agreed to support **deregulation** but called for a special tax to keep oil companies from overcharging.

In the summer of 1979, instability in the Middle East produced a second major fuel shortage. Under pressure, Carter spoke in a televised address. He warned about a "crisis of confidence" that had struck "at the very heart and soul and spirit of our national will." The address became known as the "malaise" speech, although Carter had not used that word. Many Americans felt that Carter was blaming them for his failures.

President Carter's difficulties in solving the nation's economic problems lay partly in his inexperience and inability to work with Congress. He made little effort to reach out to Washington's legislative leaders, and many of his energy proposals failed. By 1979, public opinion polls showed that Carter's popularity had dropped.

✔ **READING PROGRESS CHECK**

Summarizing How did President Carter try to change the domestic oil industry?

Carter's Foreign Policy

GUIDING QUESTION *What were President Carter's greatest foreign policy success and his greatest failure?*

A man of strong religious beliefs, President Carter argued that the United States must try to be "right and honest and truthful and decent" in dealing with other nations. Yet it was on the international front that Carter suffered a devastating defeat.

Morality in Foreign Policy

In his Inaugural Address, Carter gave his foreign policy a focus by saying:

PRIMARY SOURCE

//Our commitment to human rights must be absolute . . . the powerful must not persecute the weak, and human dignity must be enhanced. . . . We pledge perseverance and wisdom in our efforts to limit the world's armaments to those necessary for each nation's own domestic safety.**//**

—from his Inaugural Address, January 20, 1977

Carter and his foreign policy team—including Andrew Young, the first African American ambassador to the United Nations—strove to achieve these goals.

To remove a major symbol of American interventionism, Carter agreed to give Panama control of the Panama Canal, which the United States had built and operated for over 60 years. In 1978, the Senate ratified two Panama Canal treaties, which transferred control of the canal from the United States to Panama on December 31, 1999. Carter also singled out the Soviet Union as a human rights violator. Relations between the two superpowers suffered a further setback when Soviet troops invaded Afghanistan in December 1979. Carter responded by imposing an embargo on the sale of grain to the Soviet Union and boycotting the 1980 Summer Olympic Games in Moscow. Détente was crumbling.

Triumph and Failure in the Middle East

In 1978, Carter helped broker peace between Israel and Egypt through the Camp David Accords. The treaty, signed in 1979, established peace between Israel and Egypt—two nations that had been bitter enemies for decades. This was the first time Israel traded land and removed settlements for peace. Although many Arab nations did not support the treaty, it helped begin the slow peace process in the Middle East.

Just months after the treaty was signed in 1979, Carter faced a crisis in Iran. The United States had long supported Iran's monarch, the shah, because Iran was a major oil supplier and a buffer against Soviet expansion. The shah had grown increasingly unpopular in Iran due to his repressive rule and Westernizing reforms. The Islamic clergy opposed the shah's reforms. In January 1979, protesters forced him to flee. An Islamic republic was then declared.

Led by religious leader Ayatollah Khomeini, this new regime distrusted the United States because of its support of the shah. In November 1979, revolutionaries stormed the American embassy in Tehran and took 52 Americans hostage. The Carter administration unsuccessfully tried to negotiate the hostages' release. In April 1980, Carter approved a daring rescue attempt that failed when several helicopters malfunctioned and one crashed in the desert. Eight servicemen died in the accident.

The crisis continued. Every night, news programs reminded viewers how many days the hostages had been held. Carter's inability to free them cost him support in the 1980 election. On January 20, 1981, the day Carter left office, Iran released the Americans, ending their 444 days in captivity.

President Anwar El Sadat of Egypt, President Jimmy Carter of the United States, and Prime Minister Menachem Begin of Israel sign the Camp David Accords in 1978. The agreement led to a treaty between Israel and Egypt that has kept the two nations at peace for over 35 years.

NEXT GENERATION SUNSHINE STATE STANDARDS

Continued from page 552

SS.912.A.7.11: Analyze the foreign policy of the United States as it relates to Africa, Asia, the Caribbean, Latin America, and the Middle East.

SS.912.A.7.12: Analyze political, economic, and social concerns that emerged at the end of the 20th century and into the 21st century.

SS.912.A.7.14: Review the role of the United States as a participant in the global economy (trade agreements, international competition, impact on American labor, environmental concerns).

 READING PROGRESS CHECK

Evaluating How would you describe the philosophy of Carter's foreign policy?

LESSON 3 REVIEW

Reviewing Vocabulary

1. *Stating* What are the pros and cons of an embargo? LAFS.1112.RH.2.4
2. *Contrasting* How does inflation differ from stagflation? LAFS.1112.RH.2.4

Using Your Notes

3. *Making Generalizations* Use your notes to write a generalization about the causes of economic problems in the 1970s. LAFS.1112.RH.3.7

Answering the Guiding Questions

4. *Analyzing Cause and Effect* What economic conditions or problems led to a stagnant economy during the 1970s? LAFS.1112.RH.2.4, LAFS.1112.WHST.3.9

5. *Explaining* How did Ford and Carter try to resolve the nation's domestic issues? LAFS.1112.WHST.3.9

6. *Assessing* What were Carter's greatest foreign policy success and his greatest failure? Why? LAFS.1112.WHST.3.9, SS.912.A.7.11

Writing Activity

7. NARRATIVE Assume the role of a journalist during the conclusion of the Iran hostage crisis. Write a script for a radio broadcast, recapping the events of the crisis, to be aired the day of the hostages' release. LAFS.1112.WHST.4.10

©David Rubinger/Historical/Corbis

LESSON 4

New Approaches to Civil Rights

ESSENTIAL QUESTIONS

• How do you think the Nixon administration affected people's attitudes toward government?
• How does society change the shape of itself over time?

READING HELPDESK

Academic Vocabulary

• criteria   • appropriate

Content Vocabulary

• busing
• affirmative action

TAKING NOTES

Key Ideas and Details

Sequencing Complete a time line similar to the one below by recording groups in the civil rights movement and their actions. **LAFS.1112.RH.3.7, SS.912.A.1.3, SS.912.A.7.5, SS.912.A.7.6, SS.912.A.7.8**

NEXT GENERATION SUNSHINE STATE STANDARDS

LAFS.1112.RH.2.4: Determine the meaning of words and phrases as they are used in a text, including analyzing how an author uses and refines the meaning of a key term over the course of a text (e.g., how Madison defines faction in Federalist No. 10).

LAFS.1112.RH.3.7: Integrate and evaluate multiple sources of information presented in diverse formats and media (e.g., visually, quantitatively, as well as in words) in order to address a question or solve a problem.

LAFS.1112.WHST.1.2: Write informative/explanatory texts, including the narration of historical events, scientific procedures/experiments, or technical processes.

LAFS.1112.WHST.3.9: Draw evidence from informational texts to support analysis, reflection, and research.

Continued on page 555

IT MATTERS BECAUSE

Throughout the 1960s and 1970s, minority groups such as African Americans, Native Americans, and persons with disabilities began to develop new ways to expand opportunities and assert their civil rights.

African Americans Seek Greater Opportunity

GUIDING QUESTION *How did African American civil rights leaders change their reform focus?*

Although various forms of racial discrimination had become illegal, many African Americans saw little improvement in their daily lives. Access to good jobs and schooling remained issues. Civil rights leaders began to focus on these problems.

Equal Access to Education

In the 1970s, African Americans began to push harder for improvements in public education and access to good schools. In the 1954 case *Brown* v. *Board of Education,* the Supreme Court had ordered an end to segregated public schools. In the 1960s, however, many schools remained segregated as communities moved slowly to comply with the Court. Since children usually attended a school in their neighborhood, segregation in public schools reflected the racial segregation of neighborhoods.

In many cases where such de facto segregation existed, the white schools were superior, as Ruth Baston of the NAACP noted in 1965 after visiting Boston schools:

PRIMARY SOURCE

"When we would go to white schools, we'd see . . . a small number of children in each class. The teachers were permanent. We'd see wonderful materials. When we'd go to our schools, we would see overcrowded classrooms, children sitting out in the corridors, and so forth. And so then we decided that where there were a large number of white students, that's where the care went. That's where the books went. That's where the money went."

—quoted in *Voices of Freedom,* 1990

Courts began ordering local governments to bus children to schools outside their neighborhoods to achieve greater racial balance. The practice led to protests and even riots in several white communities. The Supreme Court, however, upheld the constitutionality of **busing** in the 1971 case *Swann v. Charlotte-Mecklenburg Board of Education.*

In response, many white parents took their children out of public schools or moved to districts with no busing. For example, thousands of white students left Boston's public school system to attend parochial and private schools. By late 1976, minorities made up the majority of Boston's public school students. This "white flight" also occurred in other cities. Detroit tried to bus students from one district to another in 1974. The plan was challenged, however, and the Court ruled in *Milliken* v. *Bradley* that busing across district lines was unconstitutional unless districts had been purposely drawn to create segregation.

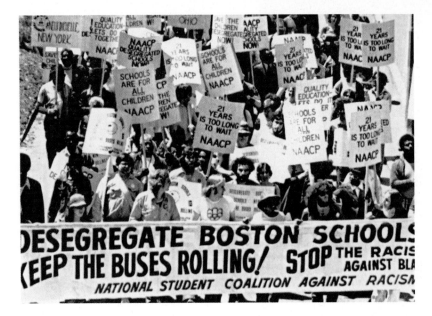

The National March on Boston in 1975 marked the anniversary of the *Brown* v. *Board of Education* decision.

▶ **CRITICAL THINKING**
Making Inferences Why are protesters holding signs that read "21 years is too long to wait"? SS.912.A.1.4

busing a policy of transporting children to schools outside their neighborhoods to achieve greater racial balance

affirmative action an active effort to improve employment or educational opportunities for minorities and women

Affirmative Action

In addition to supporting busing, civil rights leaders began advocating **affirmative action** as a new way to solve discrimination. Affirmative action was enforced through executive orders and federal policies. It called for companies, schools, and institutions doing business with the federal government to recruit African Americans. The hope was that this would lead to improved social and economic status. Officials later expanded affirmative action to include other minority groups and women.

Through affirmative action, Atlanta witnessed a significant increase in minority job opportunities. In 1974, Maynard Jackson took office as Atlanta's first African American mayor. When Jackson was elected, African Americans made up a large part of Atlanta's population. Few city contracts went to African American companies, however. Jackson worked to change this imbalance. Through his efforts, small companies and minority firms took on a higher percentage of all city contracts.

The *Bakke* Case

Critics argued that an unintended consequence of affirmative action programs was reverse discrimination. They claimed that instead of reducing racism, affirmative action had resulted in the use of quotas, and that qualified white men were kept from jobs, promotions, and places in schools because slots were set aside for minorities or women on the basis of race or gender. In 1978, the Supreme Court addressed affirmative action in *Regents of the University of California* v. *Bakke.* Officials at the University of California at Davis medical school had twice turned down the application of a white applicant named Allan Bakke. When Bakke learned that slots had been set aside for minorities, he sued the school. Bakke pointed out that the school had admitted minority applicants with lower exam scores than his. He claimed that the school had discriminated against him based on his race.

NEXT GENERATION SUNSHINE STATE STANDARDS

Continued from page 554

LAFS.1112.WHST.4.10: Write routinely over extended time frames (time for reflection and revision) and shorter time frames (a single sitting or a day or two) for a range of discipline-specific tasks, purposes, and audiences.

SS.912.A.1.2: Utilize a variety of primary and secondary sources to identify author, historical significance, audience, and authenticity to understand a historical period.

SS.912.A.1.4: Analyze how images, symbols, objects, cartoons, graphs, charts, maps, and artwork may be used to interpret the significance of time periods and events from the past.

SS.912.A.7.5: Compare nonviolent and violent approaches utilized by groups (African Americans, women, Native Americans, Hispanics) to achieve civil rights.

SS.912.A.7.6: Assess key figures and organizations in shaping the Civil Rights Movement and Black Power Movement.

SS.912.A.7.8: Analyze significant Supreme Court decisions relating to integration, busing, affirmative action, the rights of the accused, and reproductive rights.

Continued on page 556

Scherl/SV-Bilderdienst/The Image Works

BIOGRAPHY

Ben Nighthorse Campbell (1933–)

A member and chief of the Northern Cheyenne tribe, Ben Nighthorse Campbell entered politics in the early 1980s as a Colorado state legislator. He was elected to the U.S. Senate in 1992, serving as the governing body's only Native American member until he chose not to run for reelection in 2004. In addition to his political career, Campbell has also been a successful jewelry designer, rancher, and horse trainer.

▶ **CRITICAL THINKING**
Explaining Why was Campbell's election to the U.S. Senate significant?

criteria standards on which a judgment or action may be based

NEXT GENERATION SUNSHINE STATE STANDARDS

Continued from page 555

SS.912.A.7.9: Examine the similarities of social movements (Native Americans, Hispanics, women, anti-war protesters) of the 1960s and 1970s.

SS.912.A.7.12: Analyze political, economic, and social concerns that emerged at the end of the 20th century and into the 21st century.

SS.912.A.7.13: Analyze the attempts to extend New Deal legislation through the Great Society and the successes and failures of these programs to promote social and economic stability.

In a 5-to-4 ruling, the Supreme Court declared that the university had violated Bakke's civil rights. It added, though, that schools had an interest in having racial diversity and could consider race as part of their admissions **criteria.** They could not, however, use "fixed quotas," or slots reserved for minority students.

New Political Leaders

New political leaders emerged in the African American community in the 1970s. For the first time since Reconstruction, African Americans became more influential in national politics. Jesse Jackson, a former aide to Martin Luther King, Jr., was among this new generation of activists. In 1971, Jackson founded Operation PUSH (People United to Save Humanity). Operation PUSH was dedicated to developing African American businesses, educational opportunities, and social and political development. In 1984 and 1988, Jackson sought the Democratic presidential nomination and lost. Yet he won over millions of voters.

In 1971, African American members of Congress organized the Congressional Black Caucus (CBC) to more clearly represent their concerns. One of the CBC's founding members was Shirley Chisholm of New York, the first African American woman to serve in Congress. In 1977, another former assistant to Dr. King, U.S. Representative Andrew Young, became the first African American to serve as U.S. ambassador to the United Nations. He later served as the mayor of Atlanta. By the mid-1980s, African American mayors had been elected in Atlanta, Detroit, Chicago, Los Angeles, New Orleans, Philadelphia, and Washington, D.C.

Another leader who emerged in the 1980s was Louis Farrakhan, a prominent minister of the Nation of Islam. He organized the Million Man March on October 16, 1995. His goal for the march was to promote self-reliance and responsibility among African American men. Speakers at the event included Jesse Jackson and poet Maya Angelou.

In 1990, Virginia voters elected L. Douglas Wilder, who became the first African American governor of a state. That same year, David Dinkins took office as the first African American mayor of New York City.

✓ **READING PROGRESS CHECK**

Explaining What was the goal of affirmative action?

Native Americans Raise Their Voices

GUIDING QUESTION *What civil rights gains have Native Americans achieved since the 1960s?*

In 1970, Native Americans were one of the nation's smallest minority groups, yet they faced enormous problems. The unemployment rate for Native Americans was ten times the national rate. Unemployment was particularly high on reservations, where nearly half of all Native Americans lived. Little education or training was available. Their average annual family income was $1,000 less than that of African Americans. In addition, statistics showed that the life expectancy of Native Americans was seven years below that of whites.

A Protest Movement Emerges

In 1961, more than 400 members of 67 Native American groups gathered in Chicago to discuss their problems. They developed a Declaration of Indian Purpose which asked for federal programs to create greater economic opportunities for all Native Americans. In 1968, Congress passed the Indian Civil Rights Act. The legislation guaranteed reservation residents the protections of the Bill of Rights while still recognizing tribal courts.

©Dave Bartruff/Documentary/Corbis

The American Indian Movement, with leaders Russell Means (left) and Dennis Banks, staged a protest at Wounded Knee, South Dakota, in 1973.

▶ CRITICAL THINKING

Comparing and Contrasting How were the goals of the Native American movement similar to the goals of other movements in the 1960s and 1970s? SS.912.A.7.9

Native Americans who viewed the government's efforts as too modest formed more militant groups, such as the American Indian Movement (AIM). In 1969, Native Americans occupied the closed federal prison on Alcatraz Island in San Francisco Bay for 19 months, claiming ownership "by right of discovery."

AIM's most famous protest took place at Wounded Knee, South Dakota. U.S. troops had killed hundreds of Sioux there in 1890. In February 1973, AIM members seized the town for 70 days. They demanded that the government honor its past treaty obligations, insisting on changes in reservation administration. Before the siege between AIM and the FBI ended, two Native Americans were killed and both sides suffered injuries.

Other groups, such as the Hopi and the Navajo, objected to land leases to mining companies that scoured the land, displaced families, and posed a threat to sacred places. They wrote letters of protest to the government.

Native American Gains

By the mid-1970s, the Native American movement had begun to achieve some of its goals. In 1975, Congress passed the Indian Self-Determination and Educational Assistance Act. This act encouraged tribal participation in and management of federal programs, such as social services, law enforcement, and health services, which the Bureau of Indian Affairs and Health and Human Services' Indian Health Service had previously administered. It also increased funds for Native American education.

Native Americans won several court cases involving land and water rights. The Pueblo of Taos, New Mexico, regained property rights to Blue Lake, a place sacred to their religion. In 1980, the government paid the Passamaquoddy and the Penobscot peoples $81.5 million to give up their claim to land in Maine. Other court decisions gave tribal governments the power to tax businesses on reservations.

Since Native Americans began to organize, many reservations have improved their economic conditions. Businesses such as electric plants,

Analyzing
PRIMARY SOURCES

Letter Protesting Mining on Hopi Lands

"Today the sacred lands where the Hopi live are being desecrated by men who seek coal and water from our soil that they may create more power for the white man's cities. This must not be allowed to continue. . . . The Great Spirit said not to take from the Earth. . . . Your government has almost destroyed our basic religion which is actually a way of life for all our people in this land of the Great Spirit."

—quoted in *Touch the Earth*, 1971

DBQ **ANALYZING PRIMARY SOURCES** Why do the Hopi claim that coal mining on their lands is wrong? SS.912.A.1.2

AP Images

resorts, cattle ranches, and oil and gas wells have been developed. More recently, gambling casinos have become a successful activity. Rulings on sovereignty have allowed some Native Americans to operate casinos under their own laws even though state laws prevent others from doing so.

In addition to economic gains, Native Americans expanded their political rights as a religious minority. In 1978, Congress passed the American Indian Religious Freedom Restoration Act. The act was intended to protect the rights of American Indians, as well as Native Hawaiians, and the native peoples of Alaska, to practice their traditional religions and to be given access to sacred sites for purposes of religious ceremonies.

In the 1980s, however, in a series of cases, the Supreme Court ruled that laws that burdened a person's religion were not violating the First Amendment as long as those laws were applicable to all people. For example, when Native Americans tried to stop the Forest Service from building a road through sacred land claiming it violated their First Amendment rights, the Court held that the road was not an infringement on their beliefs. Similarly, when Native Americans were denied state unemployment benefits because they tested positive for drugs, the Court upheld the decision, even though the positive test was because the Native Americans had eaten peyote, a type of cactus used in Native American religious ceremonies.

In response to the Court's ruling, a coalition of civil rights and religious organizations pressured Congress to pass a new Religious Freedom Restoration Act in 1993. The new law stated that government laws could not impose burdens on a person's religion, regardless of whether the laws were general in nature, and not aimed at a person's religious beliefs. The law strengthened the rights of Native Americans and other religious groups.

✓ READING PROGRESS CHECK

Summarizing Why did Native Americans protest for their civil rights to be recognized?

The Disability Rights Movement

GUIDING QUESTION *How did federal legislation protect the civil rights of people with disabilities?*

The struggle for disability rights had its early expression in the independent living movement that began at the University of California at Berkeley in the early 1970s. The movement advocated for the right of people of all levels of abilities to choose to live freely in society. This was part of a new attitude that encouraged people who had disabilities to move out of institutions and live independently.

People with disabilities also looked to the federal government to protect their civil rights. They sought access to public facilities. They also demanded bans on discrimination in employment. One victory was the 1968 Architectural Barriers Act. This act required that new buildings constructed with federal funds be accessible to persons with disabilities. The Rehabilitation Act of 1973 was even more significant. Section 504 states that no person with a disability can be discriminated against in any way by an entity that receives federal funding.

Passage of the Rehabilitation Act meant little, however, until procedures for enforcing it were established. As of 1977, the Department of Health, Education, and Welfare (HEW) had no such procedures. Frustrated, the American Coalition of Citizens with Disabilities organized protests. On April 5, 1977, some 2,000 persons with disabilities in 10 cities

Section 504 of the Rehabilitation Act and, later, the Americans with Disabilities Act specified that people with disabilities must have equal access to public facilities, such as transportation and parking.

▶ **CRITICAL THINKING**

Identifying Central Ideas What rights did people with disabilities struggle for in the 1970s? SS.912.A.7.5

©Ed Kashi/Corbis News/Corbis

began sit-ins at regional HEW offices. Protesters in San Francisco kept up their sit-in for over three weeks, until HEW's director signed the regulations banning discrimination.

Changes also occurred in special education. In 1966, Congress created the Bureau for the Education of the Handicapped, which provided grants to develop programs for educating children with disabilities. In 1975, the Education for All Handicapped Children Act required that all students with disabilities receive a free, **appropriate** education. One trend was to mainstream, or bring into the regular classroom, students with disabilities.

In 1990, Congress enacted the Americans with Disabilities Act. This far-reaching legislation banned discrimination against persons with disabilities in employment, transportation, public education, and telecommunications. Today, technologies such as closed-captioned television broadcasts, devices for telephones, and screen readers help people with disabilities access information in new ways.

appropriate especially suitable or compatible

✓ **READING PROGRESS CHECK**

Explaining What tactics did people with disabilities use to protest that were also used by other minority groups? Were they effective? Explain.

LESSON 4 REVIEW

Reviewing Vocabulary
1. ***Identifying*** What was the purpose of busing? LAFS.1112.RH.2.4, LAFS.1112.WHST.3.9

Using Your Notes
2. ***Comparing*** Use your notes to write a paragraph identifying similarities among the gains made by African Americans, Native Americans, and people with disabilities. LAFS.1112.RH.3.7, LAFS.1112.WHST.3.9

Answering the Guiding Questions
3. ***Evaluating*** How did African American civil rights leaders change their reform focus? LAFS.1112.WHST.3.9, SS.912.A.7.5

4. ***Describing*** What civil rights gains have Native Americans achieved since the 1960s? LAFS.1112.WHST.3.9, SS.912.A.7.5

5. ***Summarizing*** How did federal legislation protect the civil rights of people with disabilities? LAFS.1112.WHST.3.9, SS.912.A.7.5

Writing Activity
6. **INFORMATIVE/EXPLANATORY** Write a paragraph in which you summarize the issues involved in the Supreme Court cases of *Swann* v. *Charlotte-Mecklenburg Board of Education* and *Regents of the University of California* v. *Bakke*. LAFS.1112.WHST.1.2, LAFS.1112.WHST.4.10, SS.912.A.7.8

LESSON 5
Environmentalism

ESSENTIAL QUESTIONS

• How do you think the Nixon administration affected people's attitudes toward government?
• How does society change the shape of itself over time?

READING HELPDESK

Academic Vocabulary

• intensify   • alternative

Content Vocabulary

• smog   • fossil fuel

TAKING NOTES

Key Ideas and Details

Organizing As you read, complete a graphic organizer similar to the one below by including actions taken to combat the nation's environmental problems in the 1960s and 1970s.
LAFS.1112.RH.3.7, SS.912.A.7.14

Actions Taken

NEXT GENERATION SUNSHINE STATE STANDARDS

LAFS.1112.RH.2.4: Determine the meaning of words and phrases as they are used in a text, including analyzing how an author uses and refines the meaning of a key term over the course of a text (e.g., how Madison defines faction in Federalist No. 10).

LAFS.1112.RH.3.7: Integrate and evaluate multiple sources of information presented in diverse formats and media (e.g., visually, quantitatively, as well as in words) in order to address a question or solve a problem.

LAFS.1112.WHST.1.2: Write informative/explanatory texts, including the narration of historical events, scientific procedures/experiments, or technical processes.

Continued on page 562

IT MATTERS BECAUSE

Americans became increasingly aware of the damage being done to the environment. Soon, environmental issues became national concerns, and individuals, local groups, and the government acted to address the damage and protect natural resources.

The Origins of Environmentalism

GUIDING QUESTION *What concerns inspired the environmental movement?*

In 1966, Carol Yannacone of Patchogue, a small community on Long Island, New York, learned that officials were using the powerful pesticide DDT as part of a mosquito control operation at a local lake. Yannacone and her husband Victor, an attorney, were concerned that the pesticide might be poisonous. They decided to contact local scientists, who confirmed their suspicions.

The Yannacones then successfully sued to halt the use of the pesticide. In so doing, they had discovered a new strategy for addressing environmental concerns. Shortly after the Yannacones' court victory, the scientists involved in the case established the Environmental Defense Fund. They used its contributions for a series of legal actions across the country to halt DDT spraying. Along with those of other environmental organizations, their efforts led to a nationwide ban on DDT in 1972.

The effort to ban DDT was only one part of a new environmental movement that took shape in the 1960s and 1970s. The person who helped trigger this new movement was a soft-spoken marine biologist named Rachel Carson. Carson's 1962 book *Silent Spring* assailed the increasing use of pesticides, particularly DDT. She argued that while pesticides curbed insect populations, they also killed birds, fish, and other creatures that might ingest them. Carson warned Americans of a "silent spring," in which there would be no birds left to usher spring in with their songs. "No . . . enemy action had silenced the rebirth of new life in this stricken world. The people had done it themselves. . . . A grim specter has crept upon us almost unnoticed, and this imagined tragedy may easily become a stark reality we all shall know," she warned.

Silent Spring became a best seller and one of the most controversial and influential books of the 1960s. The chemical industry was outraged and began an intense campaign to discredit Carson and her arguments. Many Americans believed Carson's warnings, however, largely because of what they were seeing around them and reading in news reports.

Rivers across the nation were no longer safe for fishing or swimming. In the Northwest, timber companies were cutting down acres of forest. In 1969, a major oil spill off Santa Barbara, California, ruined miles of beach and killed many birds and aquatic animals. Land development in Florida's Everglades contributed to the destruction of much of the original natural area. Pollution and garbage caused many fish to die in Lake Erie. And all across the country major cities were suffering from increasingly severe smog.

Smog, or fog made heavier and darker by smoke and chemical fumes, was the one environmental problem that the majority of Americans could see and experience every day. In a few locations, such as the Los Angeles region, smog was the result of a very large population living in a small area surrounded by mountains and a warm desert and using millions of motor vehicles. The geography of the region trapped the automobile exhaust over the city. Elsewhere, smog was simply the result of a growing population and its distribution into dense urban areas. By 1970, approximately 75 percent of Americans lived in cities. As they watched the air quality grow steadily worse, many citizens became convinced it was time to do something about protecting the environment.

A Grassroots Effort Begins

Many observers point to April 1970 as the unofficial beginning of the environmentalist movement. That month, the nation first observed Earth Day, a day devoted to environmental concerns. The national response was overwhelming. On college campuses, in secondary schools, and in communities, Americans actively showed their environmental awareness.

After Earth Day, many citizens formed local environmental groups, adding new voices to those of organizations such as the Audubon Society, the Sierra Club, and the Wilderness Society. These organizations worked to protect the environment and promote the conservation of natural resources. In 1970, activists started the Natural Resources Defense Council to coordinate a nationwide network of scientists, lawyers, and activists.

Many communities and businesses responded to these organizations. They tried to make communities and buildings more environmentally friendly, and worked to restore damaged natural spaces.

✓ READING PROGRESS CHECK

Determining Cause and Effect How did the environmental movement affect the rise of smaller grassroots efforts?

The Environmental Movement Blossoms

GUIDING QUESTION *How did new laws passed in this time period protect the environment?*

As the environmental movement gained support, the federal government took action. In 1970, President Nixon signed the National Environmental

Alfred Eisenstaedt/Time & Life Pictures/Getty Images

Florida
CONNECTION

Use of DEET

After the pesticide DDT was banned in 1972, people living in mosquito-filled areas of Florida turned to other ways to protect themselves from bites. The most common mosquito deterrent today is DEET, a chemical that repels insects such as mosquitoes and biting flies. Scientists have not found evidence that using DEET at normal levels harms people, and the level required for it to significantly damage wildlife such as freshwater fish is much higher than that typically found in wastewater and streams.
SS.912.A.7.17

smog fog made heavier and darker by smoke and chemical fumes

The publication of *Silent Spring* made biologist Rachel Carson one of the early environmental movement's important figures. The book's warnings about the dangers of pollution drew fire from the chemical industry but won over many readers.

▶ CRITICAL THINKING
Making Generalizations
What was Carson's greatest contribution to the environmental movement? SS.912.A.7.14

Smog heavily polluted the air around major cities, heightening residents' awareness of environmental problems.

▶ CRITICAL THINKING
Analyzing Primary Sources
Based on this photograph, what might be a main contributor to the problem of smog? SS.912.A.1.4, SS.912.A.7.14

Policy Act, which created the Environmental Protection Agency (EPA). The EPA set and enforced pollution standards, promoted research, and directed antipollution activities with state and local governments.

In 1970, President Nixon signed a new Clean Air Act into law. This act established emissions standards for factories and automobiles. It aimed to improve national air quality within five years, and set guidelines and timetables for states and cities to meet.

In the following years, Congress passed two more pieces of significant environmental legislation. The Clean Water Act of 1972 restricted the discharge of pollutants into the nation's lakes and rivers. The other act was the Endangered Species Act of 1973, which established measures for saving threatened animal and plant species. These laws succeeded in reducing smog, and the pollution of many lakes, streams, and rivers declined.

The Endangered Species Act did pose a constitutional question. Because it imposed restrictions on the use of land where endangered species existed, did the act interfere with the Fifth Amendment property rights of individuals, businesses, or communities? The Constitution specifies that private property cannot be taken for public use without just compensation. In the years since the act has passed, many cases have gone to court but no general rule has emerged. Each case is examined on its own merits, and in some cases courts have required the government to compensate property owners for the losses they have suffered when the Endangered Species Act is applied to their property.

Love Canal

Despite increasing federal legislation, Americans also worked for change at the community level throughout the 1970s. One of the most powerful displays of community activism occurred in a housing development near Niagara Falls, New York, known as Love Canal.

During the 1970s, residents of Love Canal began to notice an increasingly high number of health problems in their community. The people in the community were suffering from nerve damage, blood diseases, cancer, miscarriages, and birth defects. The residents soon learned that their community sat atop a decades-old toxic waste dump. Over time, its hazardous contents had spread through the ground. Led by a local woman, Lois Gibbs, the residents joined together and demanded that the government take steps to address these health threats. Gibbs later wrote about the importance of organizing to protect the environment:

PRIMARY SOURCE

❝ It will take a massive effort to move society from corporate domination, in which industry's rights to pollute and damage human health and the environment supersede the public's right to live, work, and play in a safe environment. This is a political fight, since the science is already there showing that people's health is being placed at risk. To win the political fight, we need to continue to build the movement, to network with one another, and to plan, strategize, and keep moving forward. ❞

—from *Love Canal: The Story Continues . . .*, 1998

NEXT GENERATION SUNSHINE STATE STANDARDS

Continued from page 560

LAFS.1112.WHST.3.9: Draw evidence from informational texts to support analysis, reflection, and research.

LAFS.1112.WHST.4.10: Write routinely over extended time frames (time for reflection and revision) and shorter time frames (a single sitting or a day or two) for a range of discipline-specific tasks, purposes, and audiences.

SS.912.A.1.2: Utilize a variety of primary and secondary sources to identify author, historical significance, audience, and authenticity to understand a historical period.

SS.912.A.1.4: Analyze how images, symbols, objects, cartoons, graphs, charts, maps, and artwork may be used to interpret the significance of time periods and events from the past.

SS.912.A.7.12: Analyze political, economic, and social concerns that emerged at the end of the 20th century and into the 21st century.

SS.912.A.7.14: Review the role of the United States as a participant in the global economy (trade agreements, international competition, impact on American labor, environmental concerns).

SS.912.A.7.17: Examine key events and key people in Florida history as they relate to United States history.

Designpics.com/PunchStock

Residents struggled against uncooperative officials and worked to increase awareness of their plight. The state finally relocated more than 200 families in 1978.

The same year, President Carter declared Love Canal a limited disaster area. In 1980, he called for emergency aid and moved approximately 500 families who remained to new locations. In 1983, Love Canal residents sued the company that had created the dump site and settled the case for around $20 million. The site was cleaned up by sealing the waste within an underground bunker and demolishing homes located above the dumping ground.

Concerns About Nuclear Energy

Also during the 1970s, a number of citizens became concerned about the use of nuclear reactors to generate electricity. As nuclear power plants began to dot the nation's landscape, the debate over their use **intensified.** Supporters of nuclear energy hailed it as a cleaner and less expensive **alternative** to **fossil fuels,** such as coal, oil, and natural gas, which are in limited supply. Opponents warned of the risks nuclear energy posed, particularly the devastating consequences of radiation released into the air.

The nuclear debate gained national attention in a shocking fashion in 1979. In the early hours of March 28, one of the reactors at the Three Mile Island nuclear facility outside Harrisburg, Pennsylvania, overheated. The problem occurred after its cooling system failed. That night, as plant officials scrambled to fix the problem, low levels of radiation began to escape from the reactor.

Officials evacuated many nearby residents, while others fled on their own. Citizens and community groups expressed outrage at protest rallies. Officials closed down the reactor and sealed the leak. The Nuclear Regulatory Commission, the federal agency that regulates the nuclear power industry, eventually declared that the plant was safe. President Carter even arranged a visit to the site to allay the public's concerns.

The accident at Three Mile Island had a powerful impact politically. It left much of the public with grave doubts about the safety of nuclear energy. Such doubts have continued.

intensify to become more frequent and powerful

alternative another choice

fossil fuel a fuel formed in the Earth from decayed plant or animal remains

✓ READING PROGRESS CHECK

Evaluating Was the national government's response to the environmental movement effective? Why?

LESSON 5 REVIEW

Reviewing Vocabulary
1. *Describing* What is smog? LAFS.1112.RH.2.4

2. *Listing* What are some examples of fossil fuels? LAFS.1112.RH.2.4

Using Your Notes
3. *Naming* Review the notes that you completed throughout the lesson to list some environmental protection initiatives that were begun during this period. LAFS.1112.RH.3.7, SS.912.A.7.14

Answering the Guiding Questions
4. *Identifying* What concerns inspired the environmental movement? SS.912.A.7.14

5. *Assessing* How did new laws passed during this time period protect the environment? SS.912.A.7.14

Writing Activity
6. INFORMATIVE/EXPLANATORY Take on the role of an investigative reporter, and describe the environmental disaster at either Love Canal or Three Mile Island. Explain how community activism brought the issue to the nation's attention. LAFS.1112.WHST.1.2, LAFS.1112.WHST.4.10, LAFS.1112.RH.3.7, SS.912.A.7.14

STUDY GUIDE

THE NIXON ADMINISTRATION
LESSON 1

NEW FEDERALISM
- reduce federal government's size
- more authority at state government level

FOREIGN POLICY
- Nixon Doctrine—shifting control back to Vietnam
- détente—relaxing of tension between U.S. and Soviets

THE WATERGATE SCANDAL
LESSON 2

June 1972
Break-in of the Democratic Party election headquarters occurs at Watergate building complex.

October 1972
The FBI establishes that the break-in is part of Nixon's re-election spying effort.

November 1972
Richard Nixon is re-elected president.

January 1973
Former Nixon aides are convicted of conspiracy, burglary, and wiretapping in the Watergate event.

May 1973
Senate Watergate Committee begins televised hearings.

July 1973
Testimony reveals that Nixon has recorded conversations in the White House; the president refuses to turn over audio tapes.

August 1974
Nixon becomes first president to resign office; Gerald Ford assumes the executive office.

FORD AND CARTER
LESSON 3

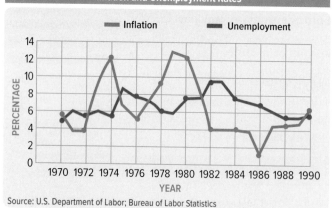

Inflation and Unemployment Rates

Source: U.S. Department of Labor; Bureau of Labor Statistics

NEW APPROACHES TO CIVIL RIGHTS
LESSON 4

New Civil Rights Expansions

Accelerating School Integration

Affirmative Action

Busing into new schools for better racial balance

Negatives: riots and white flight into suburbs

Bakke case

ENVIRONMENTALISM
LESSON 5

DDT

A pesticide used to control mosquitos was later found to be poisonous to other animals. Public pressure eliminated the chemical's use and demonstrated a new method for achieving change.

Directions: On a separate sheet of paper, answer the questions below. Make sure you read carefully and answer all parts to the question.

Lesson Review

Lesson 1

1 ***Analyzing*** How were both federal and state governments affected by Nixon's New Federalism? SS.912.A.7.4

2 ***Explaining*** Explain the policy that is known as the "Nixon Doctrine." SS.912.A.6.13, SS.912.A.7.4

3 ***Explaining*** How was détente a factor in Nixon's decision to visit China? What were Nixon's goals in planning this visit? SS.912.A.6.13, SS.912.A.7.4, SS.912.A.7.11

Lesson 2

4 ***Explaining*** Explain the reason behind the taping system in the White House and Nixon's request for executive privilege. SS.912.A.7.10

5 ***Describing*** What role did James McCord play in the Watergate scandal? SS.912.A.7.10

6 ***Identifying Cause and Effect*** How was the FBI Domestic Security Investigation Guidelines Act a result of the Watergate scandal? SS.912.A.7.10

Lesson 3

7 ***Summarizing*** Summarize the state of the American economy in the 1970s including the recession and "stagflation." SS.912.A.7.12, SS.912.A.7.14

8 ***Explaining*** Explain the significance of the Camp David Accords for U.S policy in the Middle East. SS.912.A.7.11

9 ***Identifying Economic Consequences*** Why did the Nixon administration decide to abandon the gold standard in 1971? How did this change American currency? What impact did this decision have on the economy at the time, and what implications did it have for American monetary policy? SS.912.A.7.12, SS.912.A.7.14

10 ***Describing*** What effect did President Johnson's increased deficit spending have on the economy by the 1970s? Why was President Johnson increasing spending? What action might he have taken to produce a different economic outcome? SS.912.A.7.12, SS.912.A.7.14

Lesson 4

11 ***Identifying Cause and Effect*** When and why did a Supreme Court ruling revise affirmative action practices? SS.912.A.7.8

12 ***Explaining*** What were the goals of the American Coalition of Citizens with Disabilities? What did the disabilities rights movement eventually achieve? SS.912.A.7.12

13 ***Making Connections*** What event made Wounded Knee, South Dakota, an important location for the American Indian Movement (AIM) in 1973? Describe what change occurred as a result of the event and the actions of the group. SS.912.A.7.9

Lesson 5

14 ***Identifying Perspectives*** What were the political outcomes of Rachel Carson's book *Silent Spring*? SS.912.A.1.7 , SS.912.H.1.5

15 ***Describing*** What were two key acts of legislation enacted in 1970 to help protect the environment? SS.912.A.7.12

16 ***Explaining*** Explain the argument for nuclear energy as an alternative to fossil fuels, and explain the incident that amplified the public's concerns over nuclear energy. SS.912.A.7.12

Exploring the Essential Questions

17 ***Drawing Conclusions*** Give an oral presentation describing the political turmoil of the 1970s. The presentation should answer the question: How did the Nixon administration's actions affect people's attitudes toward government? LAFS.1112.SL.2.4, SS.912.A.7.10

18 ***Creating a Written Presentation*** Write an essay to answer the question: How did society change during the 1970s? LAFS.1112.WHST.4.10, SS.912.A.7.3, SS.912.A.7.4, SS.912.A.7.8, SS.912.A.7.9, SS.912.A.7.1

Critical Thinking

19 ***Synthesizing*** How did affirmative action create economic opportunities for minorities? How has affirmative action produced some unintended consequences? SS.912.A.7.8

Need Extra Help?

If You've Missed Question	1	2	3	4	5	6	7	8	9	10	11	12	13	14	15	16	17	18	19
Go to Lesson	1	1	1	2	2	2	3	3	3	3	4	4	4	5	5	5	2	1, 2, 3, 4, 5	4

20 *Analyzing Information* How did the American Indian Religious Freedom Act expand the political rights of a religious minority? SS.912.A.7.5

21 *Identifying Central Issues* Explain the debate over capital punishment that emerged in the 1970s. Explain whether the Burger Court appointed by Nixon used a strict construction or judicial interpretation of the Constitution to make their decision about the issue. SS.912.A.1.6, SS.912.A.7.8

22 *Sequencing* Create a time line of events that describe the presidencies of Richard Nixon, Gerald Ford, and Jimmy Carter. Include dates and descriptions of at least three events surrounding each president. SS.912.A.1.3, SS.912.A.7.10, SS.912.A.7.11, SS.912.A.7.12

23 *Identifying Cause and Effect* What were the effects of population growth and distribution on smog in the Los Angeles basin in the 1960s and 1970s? Explain how the lobbying of environmentalists helped improve the situation. SS.912.A.7.12

21st Century Skills

24 *Identifying Perspectives and Differing Interpretations* Explain why you think Nixon used the term "silent majority." LAFS.1112.RH.2.4, SS.912.A.7.4

25 *Identifying Cause and Effect* What motivated people to break into the Watergate apartment complex? LAFS.1112.RH.3.7, SS.912.A.7.10

26 *Understanding Relationships Among Events* What effect did the 1973 OPEC oil embargo have on the free enterprise system in the United States? How did the embargo impact Americans' energy use over time? SS.912.A.7.11, SS.912.A.7.14

27 *Explaining Continuity and Change* Explain the role that Carol and Victor Yannacone played in the origins of environmentalism. SS.912.A.7.12

28 *Identifying Cause and Effect* What is the role of the EPA in managing the environment? How do private citizens participate in managing the environment? How might the actions of the EPA come to affect the Fifth Amendment property rights of individuals and industries? SS.912.A.7.12

DBQ **Analyzing Primary Sources**

Use the cartoon to answer the following questions.

Ranan Lurie 1970

29 *Analyzing Visuals* What do the two men wearing hats represent? LAFS.1112.RH.1.1, LAFS.1112.RH.3.7, LAFS.1112.RH.3.8, SS.912.H.1.5

30 *Analyzing Visuals* What message does this cartoon convey about taxpayers and the buildup of weapons? LAFS.1112.RH.1.1. LAFS.1112.RH.3.7, LAFS.1112.RH.3.8, SS.912.H.1.5

Extended Response Question

31 *Informative/Explanatory* Write an essay explaining how the Watergate scandal challenged people's ideas about executive privilege and trust of government leaders. Your essay should contain an introduction and at least two paragraphs. LAFS.1112.WHST.2.6, LAFS.1112.WHST.4.10

Need Extra Help?

If You've Missed Question	20	21	22	23	24	25	26	27	28	29	30	31
Go to Lesson	4	1	1, 2, 3	5	1	2	3	5	5	1	1	2

Ranan R. Lurie, Cartoonews International Syndicate, New York City

Ronald Reagan was hailed by many Americans as a conservative hero who would lead the country to prosperity after two decades of social change and turmoil.

FROM 1980 TO 1992

The Resurgence of Conservatism

THE STORY MATTERS ...

After several decades in which progressive and liberal ideas dominated American politics, conservatism began making a comeback in the 1970s. In 1980, voters elected the conservative Ronald Reagan as president. Reagan's commitment to less government regulation, a stronger military, and uncompromising anticommunism seemed to meet voters' concerns.

ESSENTIAL QUESTION

• How do you think the resurgence of conservative ideas has changed society?

©Tony Korody/Sygma/Corbis

Place & Time: Eastern Europe 1979–1991

In the 1980s, President Ronald Reagan took a tough stance against the Soviet Union and Eastern Bloc nations by building up weapons and supporting anticommunist movements. By the end of the 1980s, the Soviet Union was greatly weakened, fell, and broke apart into separate republics. Other Communist governments in the Eastern Bloc fell as well. The Cold War was over. With his successor George H. W. Bush calling for a "new world order," the United States prepared to take on a leading role in a complicated world of new alliances.

Step Into the Place

Read the quotes and look at the information presented on the map.

 Analyzing Historical Documents What do the quotes and the information on the map indicate about democratic movements in Eastern Europe and the political climate that resulted?

PRIMARY SOURCE

"We are witnessing most profound social change. Whether in the East or the South, the West or the North, hundreds of millions of people, new nations and States, new public movements and ideologies have moved to the forefront of history. Broad-based and frequently turbulent popular movements have given expression . . . to a longing for independence, democracy and social justice. The idea of democratizing the entire world order has become a powerful socio-political force."

—Mikhail Gorbachev, from a speech to the UN General Assembly, December 7, 1988

PRIMARY SOURCE

"This is an historic moment. We have in this past year made great progress in ending the long era of conflict and cold war. We have before us the opportunity to forge for ourselves and for future generations a new world order—a world where the rule of law, not the law of the jungle, governs the conduct of nations."

—George H. W. Bush, from a televised broadcast to the nation, January 16, 1991

left page (tl)U.S. Department of Defense; (tr)Georges DeKeerle/Hulton Archive/Getty Images; (b)detail/White House Collection/The White House Historical Association; (br)U.S. Department of Defense; right page detail/White House Collection/The White House Historical Association

Step Into the Time

MAKING CONNECTIONS
Choose an event from the time line and write a paragraph that predicts the economic consequences that event might have on the resurgence of conservatism.

U.S. PRESIDENTS

Carter 1977–1981

Reagan 1981–1989

1981 American hostages released from Iran

1982 Boland Amendment keeps the U.S. from giving aid to the contras

UNITED STATES

1978   **1980**   **1982**

WORLD

April 1979 Islamic Republic of Iran declared

December 1979 Soviets invade Afghanistan

1980 War begins between Iran and Iraq

LAFS.1112.RH.3.7: Integrate and evaluate multiple sources of information presented in diverse formats and media (e.g., visually, quantitatively, as well as in words) in order to address a question or solve a problem.

LAFS.1112.RH.3.9: Integrate information from diverse sources, both primary and secondary, into a coherent understanding of an idea or event, noting discrepancies among sources.

SS.912.A.1.2: Utilize a variety of primary and secondary sources to identify author, historical significance, audience, and authenticity to understand a historical period.

SS.912.A.1.3: Utilize timelines to identify the time sequence of historical data.

SS.912.A.1.4: Analyze how images, symbols, objects, cartoons, graphs, charts, maps, and artwork may be used to interpret the significance of time periods and events from the past.

SS.912.A.7.12: Analyze political, economic, and social concerns that emerged at the end of the 20th century and into the 21st century.

Revolutions in Eastern Europe

- 1. Democratic elections, 1989
- 2. Non-Communist governments created, 1989
- 3. Berlin Wall torn down, Nov. 1989
- 4. Germany reunited, 1990
- 5. Slovenia and Croatia independent, 1991; Bosnia and Herzegovina independent, 1992
- 6. Baltic States became independent, 1991
- 7. Czechoslovakia divided, 1993

Union of Soviet Socialist Republics
Warsaw Pact countries
Other Communist countries

March 23, 1983 Reagan announces his Star Wars program

October 23, 1983 U.S. Marine barracks bombed in Lebanon

1986 Iran-Contra scandal enters the news

1987 INF Treaty signed between U.S. and Soviet Union

G. H. W. Bush 1989–1993

1991 Persian Gulf War occurs between Iraq and UN coalition

1984 **1986** **1988** **1990**

1985 Mikhail Gorbachev becomes leader of Soviet Union

April 1989 Tiananmen Square protest in China begins

1989 Communist governments collapse across Eastern Europe

1990 East and West Germany reunite as one nation

1991 Soviet Union dissolves

LESSON 1

The New Conservatism

READING HELPDESK

Academic Vocabulary

- indicate
- stability

Content Vocabulary

- liberal
- televangelist
- conservative

TAKING NOTES

Key Ideas and Details

Outlining As you read about the resurgence of conservatism, complete a graphic organizer similar to the one below. Use the major headings of this section to outline information about the rise of the new conservatism in the United States. LAFS.1112.RH.3.7, SS.912.A.7.12

> The New Conservatism
> I. Liberalism and Conservatism
>   A.
>   B.
> II.
>   A.

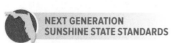

NEXT GENERATION SUNSHINE STATE STANDARDS

LAFS.1112.RH.1.2: Determine the central ideas or information of a primary or secondary source; provide an accurate summary that makes clear the relationships among the key details and ideas.

LAFS.1112.RH.2.4: Determine the meaning of words and phrases as they are used in a text, including analyzing how an author uses and refines the meaning of a key term over the course of a text (e.g., how Madison defines faction in Federalist No. 10).

Continued on page 571

- How do you think the resurgence of conservative ideas has changed society?

IT MATTERS BECAUSE

By the 1980s, new levels of discontent with government and society had left many Americans concerned about the direction of the nation. Some began to call for a return to more conservative approaches and values.

Liberalism and Conservatism

GUIDING QUESTION *Do you consider yourself liberal or conservative?*

Conservative writer Midge Decter was appalled at the looting and arson that rocked New York City during a blackout on the night of July 13, 1977. City officials and the media blamed the events on the anger and despair of youth in neglected areas. Decter disagreed:

PRIMARY SOURCE

❝[T]hose young men went on their spree of looting because they had been given permission to do so. They had been given permission to do so by all the papers and magazines, movies and documentaries—all the outlets for the purveying of enlightened liberal attitude and progressive liberal policy—which had for years and years been proclaiming that race and poverty were sufficient excuses for lawlessness.❞

—from "Looting and Liberal Racism," *Commentary,* September 1977

Midge Decter's article blaming liberalism for the New York riots illustrates one side of a debate in American politics that still continues. On one side are people who call themselves **liberals;** on the other side are those who identify as **conservatives.** In the 1960s, liberal ideas dominated U.S. politics. Conservative ideas gained support in the 1970s. In 1980, conservative Ronald Reagan was elected president.

Liberalism

In general, modern liberals believe that government should regulate the economy to protect people from the power of corporations and wealthy elites. Liberals also believe that the federal government should help disadvantaged Americans through social programs and by putting more of society's tax burden on wealthier people. They believe that those with greater assets should take on more of the costs of government.

Although liberals favor government intervention in the economy, they do not support the government regulating social behavior. They are opposed to the government supporting or endorsing religious beliefs, no matter how indirectly. They believe that a society with ethnic and cultural diversity tends to be more creative and energetic.

Conservatism

Conservatives distrust the power of government and wish to limit it. They also believe that government regulation makes the economy less efficient, and that free enterprise is the best economic system. They argue that increased economic regulation could lead to regulation in every aspect of people's behavior. Conservatives fear the government will so restrict people's economic freedom that Americans will no longer be able to improve their standard of living. They generally oppose high taxes and government programs that redistribute wealth.

Many conservatives believe that most social problems result from issues of morality and character. They argue that such issues are best addressed through commitment to a religious faith and through the private efforts of churches, individuals, and communities to help those in need. Despite this general belief, conservatives often support the use of police powers to regulate social behavior.

✔ **READING PROGRESS CHECK**

Contrasting How do liberals and conservatives view government?

Conservatism Revives

GUIDING QUESTION *Why are some regions of the country more conservative or liberal than other areas?*

During the New Deal era of the 1930s, conservative ideas lost influence in national politics. After World War II, however, conservatism began to revive.

The Role of the Cold War

The Cold War helped revive support for conservative ideas. First, the struggle against communism revived the debate about the role of the government in the economy. Some Americans believed that liberal economic ideas were slowly leading the United States toward communism and set out to stop this trend. They also thought the United States had failed to stop the spread of Soviet power because liberals did not fully understand the need for a strong anticommunist foreign policy. At the same time, some Americans viewed the Cold War in religious terms, seeing the struggle against communism as a struggle between good and evil. Liberalism gradually lost the support of these Americans as they increasingly turned to conservatism.

Conservatives Organize

In 1955, a young conservative, William F. Buckley, founded a magazine called *National Review,* which helped revive conservative ideas in the United States. Buckley worked to spread conservative ideas to a wider audience. In 1960, some 90 young conservative leaders met at Buckley's family estate and founded Young Americans for Freedom (YAF). This independent conservative group pushed for their ideas and supported conservative candidates. By 1964, the new conservative movement had achieved enough influence within the Republican Party to enable the conservative Barry Goldwater to win the nomination for president. President Lyndon Johnson defeated him and won by a landslide.

The Rise of the Sunbelt

In the 1950s and early 1960s, the South and the West were more conservative than other regions. Southern conservatives, however, generally voted for the Democrats, while conservatives in the West voted for the Republicans.

liberal a person who generally believes the government should take an active role in the economy and in social programs but should not dictate social behavior

conservative a person who believes government power, particularly in the economy, should be limited in order to maximize individual freedom

NEXT GENERATION SUNSHINE STATE STANDARDS

Continued from page 570

LAFS.1112.RH.3.7: Integrate and evaluate multiple sources of information presented in diverse formats and media (e.g., visually, quantitatively, as well as in words) in order to address a question or solve a problem.

LAFS.1112.WHST.3.9: Draw evidence from informational texts to support analysis, reflection, and research.

Continued on page 572

Thinking Like a HISTORIAN

Contrasting

Throughout history, the terms *liberal* and *conservative* have not always had the same sense as they do today. Culture and history have influenced their meanings. For example, after the Napoleonic Wars, European leaders met at the Congress of Vienna (1814–1815) to reconstruct Europe. Conservatives included monarchs, nobles, and church leaders who supported the idea that Europe should return to its pre-Napoleonic political and social order, a hierarchical one in which the lower class submitted to the rule of the upper class. There was fear that democratic "rule by many" would lead to rule by an uneducated mob. On the other hand, liberals represented the middle class and advocated a separation of powers, natural rights, and a republic. Understanding that a word's definition may change over time is important for a clear reading of history. LAFS.1112.RH.2.4, SS.912.A.1.1

The Rise of the Sunbelt 1950–1980

CANADA

74% Wash. 2,378,963 4,132,156

73% Ore. 1,521,341 2,633,105

60% 400%

Mont.

N. Dak.

Minn.

Wis.

Mich.

Me.

Vt.

N.H.

Mass.

N.Y.

R.I.

Conn.

124%

Idaho 588,637 943,935

Wyo. 290,176 469,557

62%

S. Dak.

Iowa

Pa.

N.J.

Del.

Nev. 160,083 800,493

112%

Utah 688,862 1,461,037

Colo. 1,325,089 2,889,964

118%

Nebr.

Ill.

Ind.

Ohio

Md.

61%

Calif. 10,586,223 23,667,902

262%

Kans.

Mo.

W. Va.

Va. 3,318,680 5,346,818

ATLANTIC OCEAN

Ariz. 749,587 2,718,215

N. Mex. 681,187 1,333,241

96%

Okla.

Ark.

Tenn.

59%

N.C.

S.C.

120°W

30°N

PACIFIC OCEAN

85%

Texas 7,711,194 14,229,191

57%

La. 2,683,516 4,205,900

Miss. Ala.

Ga. 3,444,578 5,463,105

252%

70°W

Fla. 2,771,305 9,746,324

MEXICO

Gulf of Mexico

90°W

80°W

0 _____ 400 miles
0 _____ 400 km
Lambert Azimuthal Equal-Area projection

60°W

50°N

40°N

	Sunbelt states
3,444,578	Population (1950)
5,463,105	Population (1980)
59%	Percent growth

Population shown only for states having 50% or more population growth between 1950 and 1980

GEOGRAPHY CONNECTION

Warm climates and job opportunities contributed to population growth in the Sunbelt.

1 THE WORLD IN SPATIAL TERMS *Which Sunbelt states had more than 8 million residents in 1980?* SS.912.A.1.4, SS.912.A.7.17

2 ENVIRONMENT AND SOCIETY *What factors may explain why some Sunbelt states experienced strong growth while others did not?* LAFS.1112.WHST.3.9, SS.912.G.2.3, SS.912.G.4.2

NEXT GENERATION SUNSHINE STATE STANDARDS

Continued from page 571

LAFS.1112.WHST.4.10: Write routinely over extended time frames (time for reflection and revision) and shorter time frames (a single sitting or a day or two) for a range of discipline-specific tasks, purposes, and audiences.

SS.912.A.1.2: Utilize a variety of primary and secondary sources to identify author, historical significance, audience, and authenticity to understand a historical period.

Continued on page 573

Thus, the party that won the populous Northeast would win the presidential election. Since the Northeast strongly supported liberal ideas, both parties leaned toward liberal policies.

This pattern began to change during World War II, when large numbers of Americans moved south and west for jobs in war factories. These Sunbelt states experienced dramatic population growth. For instance, Census Bureau data showed Florida's population growing every year from 1946 until 2009. The movement was fueled by warmer climates and increasing job opportunities; Florida's weather and expanding tourist industry met both criteria. As the Sunbelt's economy expanded, these residents began thinking differently about the government than people in the Northeast did.

Sunbelt and Suburban Conservatism

Industry in the Northeast was in decline, leading to the region's nickname, the Rust Belt. Northeasterners looked to the government to help them solve problems of unemployment, congestion, and pollution. In contrast, many Americans in the Sunbelt opposed high taxes and federal regulations that might interfere with their region's growth. Many white Southerners were also angry with the Democrats for supporting civil rights, which they saw as the federal government's effort to impose its policies on the South.

When Barry Goldwater argued that the federal government was becoming too strong, many Southerners agreed. For the first time since Reconstruction, they began voting Republican in large numbers. Although Goldwater lost, he showed that supporting conservative policies attracted Southern voters.

Americans living in the West also responded to conservative criticism of the government. Westerners resented federal environmental regulations that limited ranching, controlled water use, and restricted the development of natural resources. By 1980, the Sunbelt's population had surpassed that of the Northeast, giving these conservative regions more electoral votes.

During the 1960s and 1970s, many Americans moved to suburbs to escape urban chaos. Even there, however, they found the middle-class lifestyle they desired was in danger. Rapid inflation had caused their buying power to shrink while taxes remained high. Tax cuts became a national issue. As conservatives called for tax cuts, middle-class voters flocked to their cause.

The Religious Right

Some people were drawn to conservatism because they feared that American society had lost touch with its traditional values. Some Americans with conservative religious faith were shocked by Supreme Court decisions protecting the right to an abortion, limiting prayer in public schools, and expanding protections for people accused of crimes. In addition, student protesters' contempt for authority seemed to **indicate** a general breakdown in American values and morality. These concerns helped expand the conservative cause into a mass movement. The feminist movement's push for the Equal Rights Amendment (ERA) also upset some religious conservatives because it challenged aspects of the traditional family. Phyllis Schlafly's efforts to oppose the Equal Rights Amendment played an important role in the conservative resurgence. In 1972, Schlafly founded the Eagle Forum, a political interest group whose purpose was to educate voters and lobby the government on behalf of conservative social issues, particularly issues involving the family and women's role in society.

Protestant evangelicals were the largest group of religious conservatives. After World War II, a religious revival began in the United States among this group. Ministers such as Billy Graham and Oral Roberts built national followings, and some owned their own newspapers, magazines, radio stations, and television networks. With television, evangelical ministers reached a nationwide audience. These **televangelists** included Marion "Pat" Robertson and Jerry Falwell, who founded a group called the Moral Majority. The Moral Majority built up a network of ministers to register new voters who backed conservative candidates and issues. The group registered 2 million new voters in the 1980 election.

Gun Control and the NRA

For many Christians, the single defining issue that brought them into the conservative movement was the *Roe* v. *Wade* decision upholding the right to abortion. For another group of Americans, particularly in the south and west, the passage of the Gun Control Act of 1968 became the focus of their concern about growing federal power.

Rising crime rates in the 1960s convinced Congress to impose additional regulations and controls on gun sales and ownership. For many Americans, the law seemed to be a step toward taking away their Second Amendment rights to own a gun. In response, the National Rifle Association (NRA) began to focus on politics.

The NRA was formed in 1871 to help improve people's skills in the use of firearms. It did not engage in extensive lobbying until the 1970s, when conservatives within the organization took control and began an intensive effort to lobby Congress whenever legislation involving gun control and Second Amendment rights was proposed. The NRA's large membership and

NEXT GENERATION SUNSHINE STATE STANDARDS

Continued from page 572

SS.912.A.1.4: Analyze how images, symbols, objects, cartoons, graphs, charts, maps, and artwork may be used to interpret the significance of time periods and events from the past.

SS.912.A.7.1: Identify causes for Post-World War II prosperity and its effects on American society.

SS.912.A.7.12: Analyze political, economic, and social concerns that emerged at the end of the 20th century and into the 21st century.

SS.912.A.7.17: Examine key events and key people in Florida history as they relate to United States history.

SS.912.G.2.3: Use geographic terms and tools to analyze case studies of regional issues in different parts of the world that have critical economic, physical, or political ramifications.

SS.912.G.4.2: Use geographic terms and tools to analyze the push/pull factors contributing to human migration within and among places.

indicate to point out, point to, or demonstrate the necessity of

televangelist an evangelist who conducts regularly televised religious programs organizational skills have continued to play an important role in the electoral success of conservative political leaders since the 1970s.

A New Coalition

As a result of all of these different political, economic, and social concerns, a new conservative coalition came together in American politics. Conservatives began to believe that society had lost its way. Political scandal, economic worries, growing federal power, and ongoing social turmoil seemed to plague the nation. International events such as the withdrawal from Vietnam seemed to make the nation look weak. Many Americans were tired of upheaval. They wanted **stability** and a return to what they remembered as better times.

The Rise of Think Tanks

Despite the rising support for conservative ideas, and the emergence of a new conservative political coalition, many conservative leaders in the 1970s worried that there was no mechanism for taking broad conservative ideas and turning them into specific policy ideas and solutions that the government could actually implement. Many conservatives had been disappointed with Richard Nixon. Nixon had used conservative rhetoric in his speeches, but often supported liberal approaches to governing. Nixon had backed the Family Assistance Plan, the New Economic Policy, and the creation of the EPA, in part because those were the only solutions to specific problems being proposed.

In 1973, several leading conservatives established the Heritage Foundation, the first in a series of new think tanks that conservatives created in the 1970s and 1980s. The purpose of the Heritage Foundation, and think tanks in general, is to provide political leaders with research papers, policy ideas, and concrete recommendations on how to change the law in support of the think tank's values and beliefs.

In 1981, the Heritage Foundation published a report with 2000 specific suggestions on how to reduce the size of the federal government and move government in a more conservative direction. President Ronald Reagan's administration implemented many of these proposals, and many people at the Heritage Foundation were chosen for positions in the Reagan administration.

Think tanks have continued to proliferate in the years since. There are dozens of conservative and liberal think tanks today where researchers develop policy proposals and ideas for legislation.

✓ READING PROGRESS CHECK

Making Connections How did economic factors cause a shift in ideas about the government among residents in the Sunbelt?

Jerry Falwell related to the concerns of conservative Christians and organized them into a conservative voting bloc.

▶ CRITICAL THINKING
Making Connections How might the Cold War have encouraged Americans to join the religious right? LAFS.1112.WHST.3.9, SS.912.A.7.12

stability a state of peace; condition resistant to change or upheaval

Diana Walker/Time & Life Pictures/Getty Images

LESSON 1 REVIEW

Reviewing Vocabulary
1. *Listing* What are some core ideas of conservatives? LAFS.1112.RH.2.4, LAFS.1112.WHST.3.9
2. *Identifying* Where would you expect to see the message of a televangelist? LAFS.1112.RH.2.4, LAFS.1112.WHST.3.9

Using Your Notes
3. *Identifying Cause and Effect* Use your notes to write a paragraph describing the factors that led to the revival of conservatism. LAFS.1112.RH.3.7, LAFS.1112.WHST.3.9

Answering the Guiding Questions
4. *Classifying* Do you consider yourself liberal or conservative? LAFS.1112.RH.2.4, LAFS.1112.WHST.3.9
5. *Analyzing Cause and Effect* Why are some regions of the country more conservative or liberal than other areas? LAFS.1112.WHST.3.9, SS.912.A.7.12

Writing Activity
6. NARRATIVE Suppose that you are a magazine journalist. Write a narrative article about the revival of conservatism from the period after World War II to 1980. LAFS.1112.WHST.4.10, SS.912.A.7.12

LESSON 2
The Reagan Years

ESSENTIAL QUESTION

• How do you think the resurgence of conservative ideas has changed society?

READING HELPDESK

Academic Vocabulary

• confirmation   • visible

Content Vocabulary

• supply-side economics
• deficit
• mutual assured destruction

TAKING NOTES

Key Ideas and Details

Organizing As you read about the resurgence of conservatism, complete a graphic organizer similar to the one below by filling in the major points of the supply-side theory of economics.
LAFS.1112.RH.3.7, SS.912.A.3.10, SS.912.A.7.12

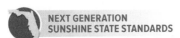

NEXT GENERATION SUNSHINE STATE STANDARDS

LAFS.1112.RH.1.2: Determine the central ideas or information of a primary or secondary source; provide an accurate summary that makes clear the relationships among the key details and ideas.

LAFS.1112.RH.2.4: Determine the meaning of words and phrases as they are used in a text, including analyzing how an author uses and refines the meaning of a key term over the course of a text (e.g., how Madison defines faction in Federalist No. 10).

LAFS.1112.RH.3.7: Integrate and evaluate multiple sources of information presented in diverse formats and media (e.g., visually, quantitatively, as well as in words) in order to address a question or solve a problem.

Continued on page 577

IT MATTERS BECAUSE

In 1981, Ronald Reagan became president. He cut taxes, deregulated several industries, and appointed conservative justices. He began a massive military buildup that greatly increased the deficit and sent aid to insurgent groups fighting communism.

The Road to the White House

GUIDING QUESTION *How did Reagan's early personal experiences influence his political beliefs?*

At age 15, Ronald Reagan worked as a lifeguard on the Rock River in Illinois. Reagan later wrote that this experience taught him quite a bit about human nature:

PRIMARY SOURCE

"Lifeguarding provides one of the best vantage points in the world to learn about people. During my career at the park, I saved seventy-seven people. I guarantee you they needed saving—no lifeguard gets wet without good reason. . . . Not many thanked me, much less gave me a reward. . . . They felt insulted. . . . I got to recognize that people hate to be saved."
—from *Where's the Rest of Me?*, 1965

Along with a philosophy of self-reliance and independence, Reagan took the belief that people do not want to be saved to the White House.

Becoming a Conservative

Reagan's adult experiences also swayed him toward conservative views. After graduating from Eureka College in 1932, he worked as a radio broadcaster and became a Hollywood actor in the late 1930s. In 1947, Reagan became the president of the Screen Actors Guild—the actors' union. As president of the Screen Actors Guild, he testified before the House Un-American Activities Committee. Reagan had been a liberal Democrat, but dealing with Communists in the union shifted him toward conservative Republican ideas.

In the 1950s, Reagan traveled the nation to promote a television program that he hosted. During these travels, he said, he met many people who complained about big government. By the time he ran

Reagan's First Inaugural Address

❝ We have every right to dream heroic dreams. . . . You can see heroes every day going in and out of factory gates. Others, a handful in number, produce enough food to feed all of us. . . . You meet heroes across a counter. . . . There are entrepreneurs with faith in themselves and faith in an idea who create new jobs, new wealth and opportunity. . . . Their patriotism is quiet but deep. Their values sustain our national life. ❞

—Ronald Reagan, January 20, 1981

DBQ *MAKING INFERENCES*

According to Reagan, how does capitalism relate to patriotism? SS.912.A.1.2

supply-side economics
economic theory that lower taxes will boost the economy as businesses and individuals invest their money, thereby creating prosperity and economic growth that will offset the tax cuts

for governor of California in 1966, Reagan was a committed conservative. Reagan won the election and was reelected in 1970. Ten years later, he won the Republican presidential nomination.

The Election of 1980

Reagan's campaign appealed to frustrated Americans by promising to cut taxes and increase defense spending. He won the support of social conservatives by calling for a constitutional amendment banning abortion. Reagan won the election easily. For the first time since 1954, Republicans also gained control of the Senate.

✅ READING PROGRESS CHECK

Assessing How did Reagan's travels around the country affect his political beliefs?

Domestic Policies

GUIDING QUESTION *If you were president, how would you fight stagflation?*

Ronald Reagan believed that the key to restoring the economy and overcoming problems in society was to get Americans to believe in themselves again. "In this present crisis," he claimed, "government is not the solution to our problem; government is the problem."

Reaganomics

Reagan first turned to the lingering problem of stagflation. Conservative economists offered two competing ideas for fixing the economy. One group supported raising interest rates to combat inflation. The other group supported **supply-side economics.** They believed that high taxes took too much money away from investors, and that tax cuts could provide extra money to expand businesses and create new jobs. The result would be a larger supply of goods for consumers, who would now have more money to spend because of the tax cuts.

Reagan adopted supply-side economics. He encouraged the Federal Reserve to keep interest rates high and asked Congress to pass a massive 25 percent tax cut. Critics called his approach Reaganomics or "trickle-down economics." They believed Reagan's policy would help corporations and wealthy Americans, but little wealth would "trickle down" to middle-class or poor Americans.

CHARTS/GRAPHS

As a result of Reagan's economic policies, the national debt increased rapidly.

1 *Drawing Conclusions*
Many think the federal deficit rose in the 1980s because of military spending. Based on the chart, what conclusion can you draw about the increase in the deficit? MAFS.912.S-ID.1

2 *Making Inferences* Why do you think the federal debt rose faster than total expenses? SS.912.A.1.4

3 *Creating a Thematic Graph* Research the federal debt since 1992. Create a graph showing how the debt has changed between 1992 and today. MAFS.912.S-IC.2

THE BUDGET DEFICIT

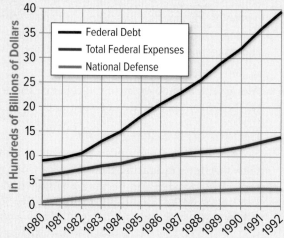

- Federal Debt
- Total Federal Expenses
- National Defense

In Hundreds of Billions of Dollars

40, 35, 30, 25, 20, 15, 10, 5, 0

1980 1981 1982 1983 1984 1985 1986 1987 1988 1989 1990 1991 1992

Source: Departments of Commerce and Treasury; Office of Management and Budget.

Mark Lennihan/AP Images

Cutting Programs Lower taxes increased the budget **deficit**—the amount by which expenditures exceed income. To keep the deficit under control, Reagan proposed cuts to social programs, including food stamps, school lunches, Medicare payments, unemployment compensation, and student loans.

After a struggle, Congress passed most of these cuts, but the fight convinced Reagan that Congress would never cut spending enough to balance the budget. He decided that cutting taxes and building up the military were more important than balancing the budget.

Deregulation Reagan believed that excessive government regulation was another cause of the economy's problems. His first act as president was to sign an executive order to end price controls on oil and gasoline. Other deregulation in broadcasting, banking, and automotive industries soon followed. Increased oil drilling, mining, and logging on public land angered environmentalists, as did EPA decisions to ease regulations on pollution-control equipment and to reduce safety checks on chemicals and pesticides.

Reagan Wins Reelection By 1984, the nation had begun the biggest economic expansion in its history. Incomes climbed and unemployment fell. The recovery made Reagan very popular, and he won the 1984 presidential election in a landslide against Democrats Walter Mondale and Representative Geraldine Ferraro, the first woman nominated to run for vice president for a major party.

Shifting the Judicial Balance

Reagan tried to bring a strict constructionist outlook to the federal judiciary, wanting judges there who followed the original intent of the

deficit the amount by which expenses exceed income

SKILLS PRACTICE

Before you read the rest of the lesson, look through the lesson at visuals, headings, and the bold-faced terms. Write down predictions about President Reagan's policies. When you come to these features as you read, check to see if your predictions are correct.
ELD.K12.ELL.SI.1, ELD.K12.ELL.SS.1

NEXT GENERATION SUNSHINE STATE STANDARDS

Continued from page 575

LAFS.1112.WHST.1.1: Write arguments focused on discipline-specific content.

LAFS.1112.WHST.3.9: Draw evidence from informational texts to support analysis, reflection, and research.

LAFS.1112.WHST.4.10: Write routinely over extended time frames (time for reflection and revision) and shorter time frames (a single sitting or a day or two) for a range of discipline-specific tasks, purposes, and audiences.

Continued on page 578

ANALYZING PRIMARY SOURCES

Debating Tax Cuts

During the 1984 presidential campaign, President Ronald Reagan and Democratic candidate Walter Mondale presented opposing ideas about taxes, government spending, and the budget deficit.

❝[T]he plan that we have had and that we are following is a plan that is based on growth in the economy. . . . Our tax cut, we think, was very instrumental in bringing about this economic recovery. . . . So, we believe that as we continue to reduce the level of government spending . . . and, at the same time, as the growth in the economy increases the revenues the government gets, without raising taxes, those two lines will meet. . . . The deficit is the result of excessive government spending. . . . I don't believe that Mr. Mondale has a plan for balancing the budget; he has a plan for raising taxes. . . . And for the 5 years previous to our taking office, taxes doubled in the United States, and the budgets increased $318 billion. So, there is no ratio between taxing and balancing a budget.**❞**

—Ronald Reagan, from the presidential debate, October 7, 1984

❝[E]ven with historically high levels of economic growth, we will suffer a $263 billion deficit. . . . Real interest rates—the real cost of interest—will remain very, very high, and many economists are predicting that we're moving into a period of very slow growth. . . . I proposed over a hundred billion dollars in cuts in federal spending over 4 years, but I am not going to cut it out of Social Security and Medicare and student assistance and things . . . that people need. . . . The rate of defense spending increase can be slowed. . . . And there are other ways of squeezing this budget without constantly picking on our senior citizens and the most vulnerable in American life.**❞**

—Walter Mondale, from the presidential debate, October 7, 1984

DBQ Analyzing Historical Documents

❶ **Specifying** How does Reagan propose to balance the federal budget? LAFS.1112.WHST.3.9, SS.912.A.1.2

❷ **Summarizing** How does Mondale respond to Reagan's plan? What effects does he foresee from that course? LAFS.1112.WHST.3.9, SS.912.A.1.2

Ronald Reagan (1911–2004)

During his two terms as president, Reagan used the charm and communication skills he learned as a Hollywood actor to gain a great deal of popularity with voters. Reagan's legacy as president includes his negotiations with Mikhail Gorbachev and the Soviet Union that contributed to the end of the Cold War. Reagan's popularity and his administration's policies have served as a basis for much of today's Republican Party philosophy.

▶ **CRITICAL THINKING**
Drawing Conclusions How might Reagan's legacy have been different had communism not fallen in the Soviet Union shortly after his tenure as president?

confirmation the formal approval of an executive act by a legislature

visible what can be seen

NEXT GENERATION SUNSHINE STATE STANDARDS

Continued from page 577

MAFS.912.S-IC.2: Make inferences and justify conclusions from sample surveys, experiments, and observational studies.

MAFS.912.S-ID.1: Summarize, represent and interpret data on a single count or measurement variable.

SS.912.A.1.2: Utilize a variety of primary and secondary sources to identify author, historical significance, audience, and authenticity to understand a historical period.

SS.912.A.1.4: Analyze how images, symbols, objects, cartoons, graphs, charts, maps, and artwork may be used to interpret the significance of time periods and events from the past.

Continued on page 579

Constitution. He changed the Supreme Court by nominating moderate conservative Sandra Day O'Connor, who became the first female justice in 1981. In 1986, Reagan chose conservative associate justice William Rehnquist to succeed retiring chief justice Warren Burger, and named conservative judge Antonin Scalia to fill Rehnquist's vacancy. After the Senate denied the **confirmation** of conservative Robert Bork in 1987, Reagan nominated moderate Anthony Kennedy as a new associate justice.

✓ **READING PROGRESS CHECK**

Expressing What factors led to the reelection of President Reagan?

Reagan Oversees a Military Buildup

GUIDING QUESTION *Why did Reagan build up the military?*

Reagan also adopted a new foreign policy that rejected both containment and détente. He called the Soviet Union "an evil empire." In his view, the United States should try to defeat evil, not contain or negotiate with it.

"Peace Through Strength"

In Reagan's opinion, the only option in dealing with the Soviet Union was "peace through strength," a phrase he used during his campaign. Reagan launched a $1.5 trillion military buildup meant to bankrupt and destroy the Soviet Union if it tried to keep up. The United States also tried to stop nations from supporting terrorism. After Libya backed a terrorist bombing in Berlin, the United States launched an air attack on Libya on April 14, 1986.

Reagan's military buildup created new jobs in defense industries. Supply-side economists had predicted that, despite the spending, lower taxes and cuts in government programs would generate enough revenue growth to balance the budget. Although tax revenues rose, Reagan could not cut popular programs significantly. The annual budget deficit went from $80 billion to more than $200 billion.

The Reagan Doctrine

Reagan believed that the United States should support guerrilla groups who were fighting to overthrow Communist or pro-Soviet governments. This policy became known as the Reagan Doctrine.

Aid to Afghan Rebels Perhaps the most **visible** example of the Reagan Doctrine was in Afghanistan. In 1979, Soviet troops had invaded Afghanistan. Reagan sent hundreds of millions of dollars in covert military aid to Afghan guerrillas who were fighting the Soviets. As casualties mounted, the war strained the Soviet economy, and in 1988 the Soviets decided to withdraw.

Nicaragua and Grenada Reagan was also concerned about Soviet influence in Nicaragua. Rebels known as the Sandinistas had overthrown a pro-American dictator in Nicaragua in 1979, set up a socialist government, and accepted Cuban and Soviet aid. The Reagan administration responded by secretly arming an anti-Sandinista guerrilla force known as the contras. When Congress learned of this policy, it banned further aid to the contras. In Grenada, radical Marxists overthrew the left-wing government in 1983. Reagan sent in troops, who quickly defeated the Grenadian and Cuban soldiers, and a new anti-Communist government was put in place.

The Iran-Contra Scandal Despite the congressional ban, individuals in Reagan's administration illegally continued to support the Nicaraguan rebels. They also secretly sold weapons to Iran, considered an enemy and sponsor of terrorism, in exchange for the release of American hostages in the Middle East.

U.S. Department of Defense

Profits from the weapons sales were then sent to the contras. News of these operations broke in November 1986. U.S. Marine colonel Oliver North and senior National Security Council members and CIA officials admitted before Congress to covering up their actions. President Reagan had approved the sale of arms to Iran, but the congressional investigation concluded that he had had no direct knowledge about the diversion of the money to the contras.

Arms Control

As part of the military buildup, Reagan decided to place missiles in Western Europe to counter Soviet missiles. When protest erupted worldwide, he offered to cancel the new missiles if the Soviets removed their missiles from Eastern Europe. He also proposed Strategic Arms Reduction Talks (START) to cut the number of missiles on both sides in half. The Soviets refused.

"Star Wars" Reagan disagreed with the military strategy known as nuclear deterrence, sometimes called **"mutual assured destruction."** He knew that if nuclear war did begin, there would be no way to defend the United States. In March 1983, he proposed the Strategic Defense Initiative (SDI), nicknamed "Star Wars," to develop weapons that could intercept incoming missiles.

A New Soviet Leader In 1985, Mikhail Gorbachev became the leader of the Soviet Union and agreed to resume arms-control talks. Gorbachev believed that the Soviet Union could not afford another arms race with the United States. Reagan and Gorbachev met in a series of summits. The first ended in a stalemate, as Gorbachev promised to cut back nuclear forces if Reagan gave up SDI, but Reagan refused. Reagan then challenged Gorbachev to make reforms. In West Berlin, Reagan stood at the Brandenburg Gate of the Berlin Wall—the symbol of divided Europe—and declared: "General Secretary Gorbachev, if you seek peace, if you seek prosperity for the Soviet Union and Eastern Europe . . . tear down this wall!"

Relations Improve In December 1987, the two leaders signed the Intermediate Range Nuclear Forces (INF) Treaty. With an arms control deal in place, Gorbachev pushed ahead with economic and political reforms, which eventually led to the collapse of the Soviet Union. In the United States, the economy was booming, the military was strong, and relations with the Soviet Union rapidly improving as Ronald Reagan's second term came to an end.

✓ **READING PROGRESS CHECK**

Explaining Why did President Reagan not favor a policy of détente?

The B-52 Stratofortress can carry nuclear or precision-guided conventional weapons, including air-launched cruise missiles.

▶ **CRITICAL THINKING**
Making Inferences How could an arms control agreement benefit both the United States and the Soviet Union?

mutual assured destruction the strategy assuming that, as long as two countries can destroy each other with nuclear weapons, they will be afraid to use them

NEXT GENERATION SUNSHINE STATE STANDARDS

Continued from page 578

SS.912.A.3.10: Review different economic and philosophic ideologies.

SS.912.A.7.11: Analyze the foreign policy of the United States as it relates to Africa, Asia, the Caribbean, Latin America, and the Middle East.

SS.912.A.7.12: Analyze political, economic, and social concerns that emerged at the end of the 20th century and into the 21st century.

LESSON 2 REVIEW

Reviewing Vocabulary

1. *Making Connections* Why did supply-side economics appeal to conservatives? LAFS.1112.RH.2.4

2. *Determining Cause and Effect* Why did the budget deficit rise during the Reagan presidency? LAFS.1112.WHST.3.9, SS.912.A.7.12

Using Your Notes

3. *Explaining* Use your notes to write a paragraph explaining the theory of supply-side economics. LAFS.1112.RH.3.7

Answering the Guiding Questions

4. *Making Connections* How did Reagan's early personal experiences influence his political beliefs? LAFS.1112.WHST.3.9

5. *Hypothesizing* If you were president, how would you fight stagflation? LAFS.1112.RH.2.4, LAFS.1112.WHST.3.9

6. *Summarizing* Why did Reagan build up the military? LAFS.1112.RH.2.4, SS.912.A.7.12

Writing Activity

7. ARGUMENT Do you think that the benefits of supply-side economics outweighed the costs? Write a short essay in which you present your opinion about the question. Be sure to defend your opinion with facts and information from the lesson. LAFS.1112.WHST.1.1, LAFS.1112.WHST.4.10

Tech. Sgt. Robert J. Horstman/U.S. Air Force

LESSON 3
Life in the 1980s

READING HELPDESK

Academic Vocabulary
- via
- orientation

Content Vocabulary
- yuppie
- discount retailing

TAKING NOTES

Key Ideas and Details

Organizing Complete a graphic organizer similar to the one below by listing the kinds of social issues that Americans faced in the 1980s.
LAFS.1112.RH.3.7, SS.912.A.7.12

**NEXT GENERATION
SUNSHINE STATE STANDARDS**

LAFS.1112.RH.1.2: Determine the central ideas or information of a primary or secondary source; provide an accurate summary that makes clear the relationships among the key details and ideas.

LAFS.1112.RH.2.4: Determine the meaning of words and phrases as they are used in a text, including analyzing how an author uses and refines the meaning of a key term over the course of a text (e.g., how Madison defines faction in Federalist No. 10).

LAFS.1112.RH.3.7: Integrate and evaluate multiple sources of information presented in diverse formats and media (e.g., visually, quantitatively, as well as in words) in order to address a question or solve a problem.

Continued on page 581

ESSENTIAL QUESTION
- How do you think the resurgence of conservative ideas has changed society?

IT MATTERS BECAUSE
The 1980s was a period of increased wealth for many, as areas of the economy improved and new technologies appeared. Cuts in social programs, however, left many Americans in need, leading to new activism.

A Booming Economy

GUIDING QUESTION *How did discount retailing and new forms of media contribute to the economic boom of the 1980s?*

By late 1983, stagflation had largely ended and stock prices soared as many companies reported record profits. Stockbrokers, speculators, and real estate developers made multimillion-dollar deals. Many of the new moneymakers were young, ambitious, and hardworking. They were nicknamed **yuppies,** short for "young urban professionals."

The rapid economic growth and emphasis on accumulating wealth in the 1980s was partly caused by the baby boom. By then, most baby boomers had finished college, entered the job market, and begun building their careers. Because baby boomers were so numerous, their concerns tended to shape the culture.

The strong economic growth of the 1980s mostly benefited middle- and upper-class Americans. As a result, the emphasis on acquiring wealth had another effect on society. From 1967 to 1986, the amount of money earned by the top 5 percent of Americans fluctuated between 14.4 and 16.5 percent of the nation's aggregate family income. In the late 1980s, their share of the nation's income began to rise. By the mid-1990s, the top 5 percent of Americans earned over 20 percent of the nation's income.

A Retail Revolution

In addition to the booming real estate and stock markets, the economy witnessed a revolution in retail sales with the growth of **discount retailing.** This type of selling had actually begun to emerge in the 1960s, but did not have a major impact on the economy until the 1980s. Discount retailers sell large quantities at very low prices, trying to sell the goods fast to turn over their entire inventory in a short period.

Source: *Statistical Abstract of the United States*, 1995.

The U.S. economy grew rapidly in the 1980s for several reasons—lower taxes spurred investment and spending, new methods of retailing lowered prices, and new technology led to new businesses and the creation of many new jobs.

1 *Analyzing Information* In what year of the 1980s did the Dow Jones sharply decline? **MAFS.912.S-ID.1, SS.912.A.1.4**

2 *Making Connections* How might a change in stock prices relate to the economy? **LAFS.1112.WHST.3.9, SS.912.A.7.12**

yuppie a young, college-educated adult employed in a well-paying profession and living in or near a large city

discount retailing selling large quantities of goods at very low prices and trying to sell the goods quickly to turn over the entire inventory in a short period of time

via by way of or through

Discount retailers could make more money than traditional retailers who sold fewer products at higher prices. The most successful discount retailer was Sam Walton, the founder of Wal-Mart. Annual sales at Wal-Mart increased from about $2 billion in 1980 to over $20 billion by 1988. By 1985, he was the richest person in the United States.

Walton was one of the first retailers to track inventory and sales with a computer database. He also used a system of distribution centers to resupply stores. Others soon copied this approach. By the late 1970s, discount retailers such as Home Depot and Best Buy had begun to build "superstores." Their innovations created millions of new jobs in the 1980s and helped fuel the era's rapid economic growth.

A Revolution in Media

In the 1980s, other entrepreneurs began changing the news and entertainment industries. Until the late 1970s, television viewers were limited to three national networks, local stations, and the public television network. In 1970, a businessman named Ted Turner bought a failing television station in Atlanta, Georgia. He pioneered a new type of broadcasting by creating WTBS in 1975. WTBS was the first "superstation"—a television station that sold low-cost sports and entertainment programs **via** satellite to cable companies across the nation.

The Rise of Cable Television Turner's innovation changed broadcasting and helped spread cable television. Other new cable networks focused on specific audiences, such as churchgoers, shoppers, or minorities. In 1980, entrepreneur Robert Johnson created Black Entertainment Television (BET). In 1981 ,music and technology merged when Music Television (MTV) went on the air to broadcast performances of songs and images, or music videos. Although the videos were often criticized for their content, MTV was a hit. Music videos boosted the careers of artists such as Madonna and Michael Jackson.

Rap music was the new sound of the 1980s. Originating in local clubs in New York City's South Bronx, rap emphasized heavy bass and rhythmic sounds and lyrics that frequently focused on the African American experience in the inner city. Its rapid rise in popularity made rap into a multimillion-dollar industry.

Florida
CONNECTION

Walt Disney World

In October 1971, the Walt Disney World Resort opened in Lake Buena Vista, Florida, near Orlando. Its first theme park, the Magic Kingdom, quickly made Disney World one of the most popular tourist attractions in the United States. In 1982 EPCOT (Experimental Prototype Community of Tomorrow) opened as a theme park featuring technologies of the future and international cultures. Two other theme parks, Disney's Hollywood Studios and Disney's Animal Kingdom, were later added. By the early 2000s, Walt Disney World Resort was attracting approximately 17 million visitors annually. **SS.912.A.7.17**

NEXT GENERATION SUNSHINE STATE STANDARDS

Continued from page 580

LAFS.1112.WHST.1.2: Write informative/explanatory texts, including the narration of historical events, scientific procedures/experiments, or technical processes.

LAFS.1112.WHST.3.9: Draw evidence from informational texts to support analysis, reflection, and research.

LAFS.1112.WHST.4.10: Write routinely over extended time frames (time for reflection and revision) and shorter time frames (a single sitting or a day or two) for a range of discipline-specific tasks, purposes, and audiences.

MAFS.912.S-ID.1: Summarize, represent and interpret data on a single count or measurement variable.

SS.912.A.1.4: Analyze how images, symbols, objects, cartoons, graphs, charts, maps, and artwork may be used to interpret the significance of time periods and events from the past.

Continued on page 582

BIOGRAPHY

Oprah Winfrey (1954–)

Oprah Winfrey entered the media as a news reporter for an African American radio station. In 1978, she moved to Baltimore to coanchor the news on a local TV station. Six years later, she moved to Chicago to host the show that became *The Oprah Winfrey Show*. By 1986, her show was syndicated on more than 100 channels nationwide. Winfrey expanded her reach with Oprah's Book Club and launched Oxygen Media in 1998, *O Magazine* in 2000, and the Oprah Winfrey Network (OWN) in 2011.

▶ **CRITICAL THINKING**
Drawing Conclusions Why might Winfrey be so influential?

NEXT GENERATION SUNSHINE STATE STANDARDS

Continued from page 581

SS.912.A.7.12: Analyze political, economic, and social concerns that emerged at the end of the 20th century and into the 21st century.

SS.912.A.7.17: Examine key events and key people in Florida history as they relate to United States history.

SS.912.H.1.5: Examine artistic response to social issues and new ideas in various cultures.

SS.912.H.3.1: Analyze the effects of transportation, trade, communication, science, and technology on the preservation and diffusion of culture.

SS.912.H.3.2: Identify social, moral, ethical, religious, and legal issues arising from technological and scientific developments, and examine their influence on works of arts within a culture.

Technology and Media Technology also transformed how people accessed entertainment. Until the 1980s, most people listened to music on large stereo systems that played records in their homes and relied on the car radio when they were driving. The new Sony Walkman made music portable, marking the beginning of a new way for people to access music. In the 1990s, portable compact disc (CD) players replaced the Walkman, and in the early 2000s, digital audio players, such as the iPod and MP3 players, advanced the technology even further.

Videocassette recorders (VCRs) allowed people to tape television shows or watch taped films whenever they wished. By the early 2000s, digital video disk (DVD) recorders began replacing VCRs.

Initially, the entertainment industry worried that VCRs would lead to copyright violations, but when the Supreme Court ruled in *Sony Corp. of America v. Universal City Studios* that people could record television shows and movies for home use, Hollywood quickly adapted. Studios soon realized that the VCR had created a demand for home video editions of movies, and that a lot of additional money could be made selling videos.

The new technology also helped to accelerate the diffusion of American culture around the globe. By the 1980s, Hollywood movies were often making more money overseas than they were in the United States. The VCR accelerated that trend, particularly in nations in Asia and Africa, where other forms of media were less accessible. In places where there were few movie theaters or local television offerings, VCR recordings of American movies and television shows often served as the main source of entertainment.

Technology also brought about a new form of entertainment—the video game. Early video games grew out of military computer technology. The first video arcade game was a game called *Pong,* released in 1972. Home video games developed quickly. In the early 1980s, sales reached about $3 billion with the popularity of games such as *Pac-Man* and *Space Invaders.* By the mid-1980s, home video games competed with arcade games in graphics and speed. Video games have continued to grow in popularity to the present day.

GPS is Launched Another major technology that began to be deployed in the 1980s and which plays an important role in improving the quality of life today is the Global Positioning System, or GPS. The GPS is composed of a series of satellites in low earth orbit that allow users to precisely determine their location on earth and navigate more accurately.

The system was proposed in the 1970s by the U.S. military as a way to improve military navigation. But in 1983, a civilian airliner, Korean Air Lines Flight 007, made the mistake of crossing into Soviet airspace and was shot down. Soon afterward, President Reagan issued an order that GPS be made available for civilian use as soon as the system came online.

The first GPS satellite was placed in orbit in 1989, and the system was completed in 1994. Since then, the use of GPS has grown exponentially. It was quickly and widely adopted for air and sea navigation. And as the computer revolution took hold, technology companies found ways to build inexpensive GPS units that drivers could use in their cars. By the early 2000s, cell phones had begun to incorporate GPS signals, allowing anyone with a smart phone the ability to use GPS to navigate. The GPS system is a dramatic example of how space technology has improved safety and the quality of life around the world.

✓ **READING PROGRESS CHECK**

Comparing and Contrasting Of the new media and technology that emerged in the 1980s, which are still in use today?

Mark Mainz/Getty Images Entertainment/Getty Images

AIDS quilts became ways for people to share the story and the loss of their loved ones to the disease. Typically, the names of AIDS victims are sewn onto the quilt squares.

▶ **CRITICAL THINKING**
Analyzing Primary Sources
What is the impact of having the names of victims on AIDS quilts?
SS.912.A.1.4, SS.912.A.7.12, SS.912.H.1.5

New Social Activism

GUIDING QUESTION *Why did new activist groups form in the 1980s?*

The 1980s was a decade of wealth and prosperity. Yet social problems, such as drugs, poverty, homelessness, and disease, continued.

Social Problems

Drug abuse in the 1980s made many city neighborhoods dangerous. Drug users often committed crimes in order to get money for drugs. Drug use spread from cities to suburbs, small towns, and rural areas.

Fighting Drugs and Alcohol In an effort to reduce teen drug use, some schools began searching student bags and lockers for drugs. In 1984, one teen who had been arrested for selling drugs challenged the school's right to search her purse without a warrant. In 1985, the Supreme Court case *New Jersey* v. *T.L.O.* upheld the school's right to search without a warrant if it had probable cause. Similarly, the 1995 case of *Vernonia School District* v. *Acton* held that random drug tests do not violate students' Fourth Amendment rights.

Abuse of alcohol was also a serious concern. In 1980, Mothers Against Drunk Driving (MADD) was founded to try to stop underage drinking and drunk driving in general, and "[t]o aid the victims of crimes performed by individuals driving under the influence of alcohol or drugs, to aid the families of such victims and to increase public awareness of the problem of drinking and drugged driving." In 1984, Congress cut highway funds to any state that did not raise the legal drinking age to 21.

The AIDS Epidemic In 1981, researchers identified a deadly disease that they named "acquired immunodeficiency syndrome," or AIDS. AIDS weakens the immune system. In the United States, AIDS was first noticed among homosexual men. Soon, though, it spread among heterosexual men and women. Many people were infected by sexual partners. Between 1981 and 1988, the Centers for Disease Control and Prevention identified more than 100,000 cases in the United States.

New Activist Groups

AIDS increased the visibility of the country's gay and lesbian community, but some homosexuals had been engaged in efforts to defend their civil rights since the 1960s. On June 27, 1969, New York City police raided a nightclub called the Stonewall Inn. The police had often raided the nightclub because of the sexual **orientation** of its patrons. Frustration among the gay and lesbian onlookers led to a riot. The Stonewall Riot marked the beginning of the gay activist movement. Soon after, organizations such as the Gay Liberation Front began efforts to increase tolerance of homosexuality.

Rock 'n' Rollers Become Activists Many musicians and entertainers in the 1980s began using their celebrity to raise awareness about social issues. To help starving people in Ethiopia, Irish rocker Bob Geldof organized musicians in England to present "Band Aid" concerts in 1984. In the next year, the event grew into "Live Aid." People in some 100 countries watched benefit concerts televised from London, Philadelphia, and Sydney, Australia. The organization's theme song, "We Are the World," was a best seller. In the same year, country singer Willie Nelson organized "Farm Aid" to help American farmers who were going through hard times. Musicians also publicized efforts to end the segregated apartheid social system in South Africa. By the late 1980s, the United States and other nations were attempting to end apartheid in South Africa by imposing economic sanctions against the country.

Senior Citizens Begin To Lobby Another group that became politically active in the 1980s was senior citizens. Decades of improvements in medicine had resulted in more Americans surviving to an older age. In addition, the birthrate had declined, so younger people represented a comparatively smaller proportion of the population. The fact that more Americans were receiving Social Security payments created budget pressures for the government. Older Americans became very vocal in the political arena, opposing cuts in Social Security or Medicare. Because they tend to vote in large numbers, senior citizens are an influential interest group. Their major lobbying organization is AARP (which originally stood for the American Association of Retired Persons).

☑ READING PROGRESS CHECK

Explaining What role did the government take in supporting efforts to remedy social problems?

---

orientation a position relative to a standard

Florida CONNECTION

Advocate for the Elderly

When Claude Pepper died in April 1989, he was then the oldest living member of Congress. He was first elected as a senator for Florida during Franklin Roosevelt's second term. Throughout his time as an elected public servant, he spoke out for the needs of elderly Americans. In the 1970s, Pepper became the chair of the House Select Committee on Aging. From this influential position, he supported legislation that aimed to improve the quality of life for the elderly. SS.912.A.7.17

LESSON 3 REVIEW

Reviewing Vocabulary

1. *Listing* What were the characteristics of yuppies?
LAFS.1112.RH.2.4

2. *Classifying* What are some major discount retailers?
LAFS.1112.RH.2.4, LAFS.1112.RH.3.9

Using Your Notes

3. *Contrasting* Use your notes to write a description of the main tensions in American society during the 1980s.
LAFS.1112.RH.3.7, LAFS.1112.RH.3.9

Answering the Guiding Questions

4. *Making Connections* How did discount retailing and new forms of media contribute to the economic boom of the 1980s?
LAFS.1112.RH.3.9, SS.912.A.7.12

5. *Analyzing Cause and Effect* Why did new activist groups form in the 1980s? LAFS.1112.RH.3.9, SS.912.A.7.12

Writing Activity

6. INFORMATIVE/EXPLANATORY Select one technological innovation from the 1980s and describe how it continues to have an influence on life today. Be sure to include descriptive words to show how that innovation affects modern life.
LAFS.1112.WHST.1.2, LAFS.1112.WHST.4.10, SS.912.A.7.12

LESSON 4
The End of the Cold War

ESSENTIAL QUESTION

• How do you think the resurgence of conservative ideas has changed society?

READING HELPDESK

Academic Vocabulary

• repress   • retain

Content Vocabulary

• perestroika
• glasnost
• downsizing
• capital gains tax
• grassroots movement

TAKING NOTES

Key Ideas and Details

Categorizing As you read, complete a graphic organizer similar to the one below by describing U.S. foreign policy in each of the places listed. LAFS.1112.RH.3.7, SS.912.A.7.11

Place	Foreign Policy
Soviet Union	
China	
Panama	
Middle East	

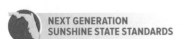

NEXT GENERATION SUNSHINE STATE STANDARDS

LAFS.1112.RH.1.2: Determine the central ideas or information of a primary or secondary source; provide an accurate summary that makes clear the relationships among the key details and ideas.

LAFS.1112.RH.2.4: Determine the meaning of words and phrases as they are used in a text, including analyzing how an author uses and refines the meaning of a key term over the course of a text (e.g., how Madison defines faction in Federalist No. 10).

Continued on page 586

IT MATTERS BECAUSE

In the late 1980s, the United States faced a series of international crises. The Cold War came to an end in Europe, but events in the Middle East soon led the United States into its first major war since Vietnam.

The Soviet Union Collapses

GUIDING QUESTION *How did Gorbachev's attempts to revive the Soviet Union's economy lead to a revolution?*

When Ronald Reagan left office, many Americans wanted his domestic policies to be continued. In 1988, Republicans nominated George H. W. Bush, who reassured Americans that he would do just that:

PRIMARY SOURCE

❝My opponent won't rule out raising taxes. But I will. And the Congress will push me to raise taxes and I'll say 'no.' And they'll push, and I'll say 'no,' and they'll push again, and I'll say to them: 'Read my lips: no new taxes.'❞

—from his acceptance address at the Republican National Convention, August 18, 1988

The Democrats hoped to regain the White House in 1988 by promising to help minorities as well as working-class and poor Americans. Civil rights leader Jesse Jackson tried to create a "rainbow coalition" of those groups, and although unsuccessful, he became the first African American to make a serious run for the presidential nomination. The Democrats nominated Michael Dukakis, who was the governor of Massachusetts, but with Reagan's endorsement and a strong economy, Bush easily won the general election. Though voters had focused on domestic issues during the election campaign, President Bush had to focus on foreign policy soon after taking office.

Revolution in Eastern Europe

As president, Bush continued Reagan's policy of cooperation with Soviet leader Mikhail Gorbachev. By the late 1980s, the Soviet economy was suffering from years of inefficient central planning and huge

perestroika a policy of economic and government restructuring instituted by Mikhail Gorbachev in the Soviet Union in the 1980s

glasnost a Soviet policy permitting open discussion of political and social issues and freer dissemination of news and information

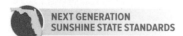

NEXT GENERATION SUNSHINE STATE STANDARDS

Continued from page 585

LAFS.1112.RH.3.7: Integrate and evaluate multiple sources of information presented in diverse formats and media (e.g., visually, quantitatively, as well as in words) in order to address a question or solve a problem.

LAFS.1112.WHST.1.1: Write arguments focused on discipline-specific content.

LAFS.1112.WHST.3.9: Draw evidence from informational texts to support analysis, reflection, and research.

LAFS.1112.WHST.4.10: Write routinely over extended time frames (time for reflection and revision) and shorter time frames (a single sitting or a day or two) for a range of discipline-specific tasks, purposes, and audiences.

Continued on page 587

The Tiananmen Square protests ended in bloodshed when the Chinese government sent in the army to crush the demonstrations.

▶ **CRITICAL THINKING**
Comparing and Contrasting
How did the results of the Tiananmen Square protests differ from those of the revolutions in Eastern Europe?

repress to curb or prevent an activity

expenditures on the arms race. To save the economy, Gorbachev instituted **perestroika,** or "restructuring," which allowed some private enterprise and profit making.

Gorbachev also established **glasnost,** or "openness," to allow more freedom of religion and speech. Glasnost spread to Eastern Europe, and in 1989 revolutions replaced Communist rulers with democratic governments in Bulgaria, Czechoslovakia, Hungary, Poland, and Romania. At midnight on November 9, 1989, guards at the Berlin Wall opened the gates. Soon, bulldozers began leveling the symbol of Communist repression. East Germany and West Germany soon reunited.

The End of the Soviet Union

As Eastern Europe abandoned communism, Gorbachev faced mounting criticism at home. In August 1991, a group of Communist Party officials and army officers tried to stage a coup. They arrested Gorbachev and sent troops into Moscow. In Moscow, Russian president Boris Yeltsin defied the coup leaders from his offices in the Russian Parliament. President Bush telephoned Yeltsin to express U.S. support. The coup soon collapsed and Gorbachev returned to Moscow. All 15 Soviet republics declared their independence from the Soviet Union. In late December 1991, Gorbachev announced the end of the Soviet Union. Most of the former Soviet republics joined in a federation called the Commonwealth of Independent States (CIS). Although member states remained independent, they formed a common economic zone in 1993.

☑ **READING PROGRESS CHECK**

Explaining Why do you think glasnost spread to Eastern Europe?

A New World Order

GUIDING QUESTION *How did the end of the Cold War lead to more global U.S. military conflicts?*

After the Cold War, President Bush noted that a "new world order" was emerging. As he told Congress in a speech, "We stand today at a unique and extraordinary moment. . . . Out of these troubled times . . . a new world order . . . can emerge: a new era—freer from the threat of terror, stronger in the pursuit of justice, and more secure in the quest for peace." The new world order introduced new military challenges around the globe. For example, U.S. troops led Operation Restore Hope, providing humanitarian assistance and famine relief to refugees in Somalia. Western aid had supported that country during the 1980s due to its strategic location near Middle Eastern oil fields, but with the end of the Cold War, its importance—and U.S. aid—had waned.

Tiananmen Square

Despite the collapse of communism elsewhere, China's Communist leaders were determined to stay in power. China's government had relaxed controls on the economy, but continued to **repress** political speech. In April and May 1989, Chinese students and workers held pro-democracy demonstrations at Tiananmen Square in Beijing, China's capital. In early June, government tanks and soldiers crushed the protests. Many people were killed. Hundreds of pro-democracy activists were arrested and later sentenced to death. Shocked, the United States and several European countries halted arms sales and reduced diplomatic contacts with China. The World Bank suspended loans. Bush resisted harsher sanctions. He thought that trade and diplomacy would change China's behavior.

©David Turnley/Turnley/Corbis

Panama

In 1978, the United States had agreed to give Panama control over the Panama Canal by the year 2000. Because of the canal's importance, American officials wanted to make sure Panama's government was both stable and pro–United States. But by 1989, Panama's dictator, General Manuel Noriega, was aiding drug traffickers and harassing American military personnel defending the canal. In December 1989, Bush ordered U.S. troops to invade Panama. The troops seized Noriega, who was sent to the United States to stand trial on drug charges. The troops then helped the Panamanians hold elections and organize a new government.

The Persian Gulf War

President Bush faced perhaps his most serious crisis in the Middle East. In August 1990, Iraqi dictator Saddam Hussein sent his army to invade oil-rich Kuwait. U.S. officials feared that the invasion might be only the first step and that Iraq's ultimate goal was to capture Saudi Arabia and its vast oil reserves. President Bush persuaded other United Nations member countries from Europe, the Middle East, and Canada to join a coalition to stop Iraq. The United Nations set a deadline for Iraqi withdrawal from Kuwait, after which the coalition would use force to remove them. Congress voted to authorize the use of force if Iraq did not withdraw.

On October 31, 1990, General Colin Powell, chairman of the Joint Chiefs of Staff, Secretary of Defense Dick Cheney, and other high-ranking officials met with President Bush. It was clear that Iraq would not obey the UN deadline. Powell presented the plan for attacking Iraq. "Mr. President," Powell began, "[w]e've gotta take the initiative out of the enemy's hands if

NEXT GENERATION SUNSHINE STATE STANDARDS

Continued from page 586

SS.912.A.1.4: Analyze how images, symbols, objects, cartoons, graphs, charts, maps, and artwork may be used to interpret the significance of time periods and events from the past.

SS.912.A.7.11: Analyze the foreign policy of the United States as it relates to Africa, Asia, the Caribbean, Latin America, and the Middle East.

SS.912.A.7.12: Analyze political, economic, and social concerns that emerged at the end of the 20th century and into the 21st century.

SS.912.G.2.3: Use geographic terms and tools to analyze case studies of regional issues in different parts of the world that have critical economic, physical, or political ramifications.

GEOGRAPHY CONNECTION

After its invasion of Kuwait, Iraq was defeated by a U.S.-led coalition of troops.

1 PLACES AND REGIONS
Why do you think that Allied troops staged their invasion of Iraq from Saudi Arabia? SS.912.A.1.4, SS.912.A.7.11, SS.912.G.2.3

2 THE WORLD IN SPATIAL TERMS *What nations did Iraq attack with SCUD missiles during the war?* SS.912.A.1.4

The Persian Gulf War 1991

3. Allied ground war against Iraqi troops, February 23–26, 1991

2. Operation Desert Storm began, January 16, 1991

1. Buildup of Allied troops along Saudi Arabia–Iraq border, August 1990–February 1991

4. Cease-fire declared by President Bush, February 27, 1991

	Iraqi SCUD attacks	Allied troop buildup
Iraq and occupied territory	Allied air attacks	Allied troop movement
Allied against Iraq	Iraqi troop placements	Major oil fields
Neutral countries		

Lambert Azimuthal Equal-Area projection

As you listen to the language spoken in the classroom to explain the end of the Cold War and the problems of the 1990s, make a list of the words you do not know. Use a dictionary to look them up after the lesson. Write down what the words mean to make sure you remember them. ELD.K12.ELL.SI.1, ELD.K12.ELL.SS.1

we're going to go to war." Cheney later recalled that Bush "never hesitated." He looked up from the plans and simply said, "Do it."

On January 16, 1991, coalition forces launched Operation Desert Storm. Cruise missiles and laser-guided bombs fell on Iraq, destroying its air defenses, bridges, artillery, and other military targets. After about six weeks, the coalition launched a massive ground attack. Thousands of Iraqi soldiers died. Fewer than 300 coalition troops were killed. Just 100 hours after the ground war began, Bush declared Kuwait to be liberated. Iraq accepted the cease-fire terms, and American troops returned home to cheering crowds.

☑ READING PROGRESS CHECK

Assessing Why did President Bush persuade United Nation members to join together to stop Iraq's invasion of Kuwait?

Domestic Challenges

GUIDING QUESTION *Why did President George H. W. Bush lose his bid for reelection in 1992?*

President Bush spent much of his time dealing with foreign policy, but he could not ignore domestic issues. He inherited a growing deficit and a slowing economy. With the Persian Gulf crisis, the economy plunged into a recession and unemployment rose.

The Economy Slows

The recession that began in 1990 was partly caused by the end of the Cold War. As the Soviet threat faded, the nation cut back on military spending. Soldiers and defense industry workers were laid off. Other companies also began **downsizing**, or laying off workers to become more efficient. The nation's high level of debt made the recession worse.

The huge deficit forced the government to borrow money to pay for its programs, keeping money from being available to businesses. The government also had to pay interest on its debt, using money that might otherwise have helped fund programs or boost the economy.

Many savings and loan institutions had collapsed, making the deficit worse. After President Reagan allowed them to be deregulated, many had made risky or even dishonest investments. When these investments failed, depositors collected from federal programs that insured deposits. The cost to the public may have reached $500 billion.

Gridlock in the Government

President Bush tried to improve the economy. He called for a cut in the **capital gains tax**—the tax paid by businesses and investors when they sell stocks or real estate for a profit. Bush believed that the tax cut would encourage businesses to expand. Calling the idea a tax break for the rich, Democrats in Congress defeated it.

Aware that the growing federal deficit was hurting the economy, Bush broke his "no new taxes" campaign pledge. After meeting with congressional leaders, he agreed to a tax increase in exchange for cuts in spending. This decision turned many voters against Bush.

The 1992 Election

Although the recession had hurt his popularity, Bush won the Republican nomination. Bush promised to address voters' economic concerns. He blamed congressional Democrats for the government's gridlock.

downsizing reducing a company in size by laying off workers and managers to become more efficient

capital gains tax a federal tax paid by businesses and investors when they sell stocks or real estate

Many businesses laid off workers as the economy slowed for the first time in almost a decade.

▶ CRITICAL THINKING

Predicting Consequences How would you expect the downsizing trend to affect Bush's reelection prospects? SS.912.A.7.12

©John A. Giordano/Corbis News/Corbis SABA

Ross Perot's inclusion in the televised presidential debate was unusual for a third-party candidate.

This cartoon makes reference to frequent third-party presidential candidate Ralph Nader as well as a Clinton campaign catchphrase, "It's the economy, stupid."

The election of 1992 marked the first time since 1968 that no candidate won at least 50 percent of the popular vote, and for a similar reason: in 1992 a strong third-party challenger, Ross Perot, took votes from both major candidates.

1 *Analyzing Primary Sources* What does the cartoon suggest about independent candidates? SS.912.A.1.4

2 *Making Connections* From which candidate was Perot more likely to take votes? Why? LAFS.1112.WHST.3.9, SS.912.A.7.12

The Democrats nominated Arkansas governor William Jefferson Clinton, despite stories that questioned his character and his evasion of military service. Calling himself a "New Democrat," Clinton promised to cut middle-class taxes, reduce government spending, and reform the nation's health care and welfare programs. His campaign repeatedly blamed Bush for the recession.

An independent candidate, billionaire Texas businessman H. Ross Perot, also made a strong challenge. He stressed the need to end deficit spending. His no-nonsense style appealed to many Americans, and a **grassroots movement**—groups of people organizing at the local level— put Perot on the ballot in all 50 states.

Clinton won the election with 43 percent of the popular vote and 370 electoral votes. Bush won 37 percent of the popular vote, and Perot 19 percent. The Democrats also **retained** control of Congress.

The 46-year-old Clinton was the first person from the baby boomer generation to occupy the White House. It was his task to revive the economy and guide the United States in a rapidly changing world.

grassroots movement
a group of people organizing at the local or community level, away from political or cultural centers

retain to keep in possession

✓ **READING PROGRESS CHECK**

Identifying What campaign promise did Bush break? Why?

LESSON 4 REVIEW

Reviewing Vocabulary
1. *Defining* What was perestroika? LAFS.1112.RH.2.4
2. *Determining Cause and Effect* What was one effect of glasnost? LAFS.1112.RH.2.4, LAFS.1112.WHST.3.9
3. *Locating* Where does a grassroots movement begin?

Using Your Notes
4. *Describing* Use your notes to write a paragraph describing the role the United States played in world affairs during the Bush presidency. LAFS.1112.RH.3.7

Answering the Guiding Questions
5. *Making Connections* How did Gorbachev's attempts to revive the Soviet Union's economy lead to a revolution? LAFS.1112.WHST.3.9, SS.912.A.7.12
6. *Analyzing Cause and Effect* How did the end of the Cold War lead to more global U.S. military conflicts? LAFS.1112.WHST.3.9, SS.912.A.7.12
7. *Explaining* Why did President George H. W. Bush lose his bid for reelection in 1992? LAFS.1112.WHST.3.9

Writing Activity
8. ARGUMENT Suppose that you are a television political commentator. Write a short speech persuading viewers to support Bush, Clinton, or Perot in the 1992 presidential election. LAFS.1112.WHST.1.1, LAFS.1112.WHST.4.10

(l)©Wally McNamee/Corbis News/Corbis; (r)Mike Lane/Cagle Cartoons

STUDY GUIDE

THE NEW CONSERVATISM
LESSON 1

CONSERVATISM

- want to limit the federal government's power
- government regulation & high taxes makes the economy less efficient
- free enterprise is the best economic system

LIBERALISM

- economic regulation protects consumers from powerful corporate interests
- the federal government needs to protect the disadvantaged
- social behavior should not be regulated

THE REAGAN YEARS
LESSON 2

FEDERAL DEBT

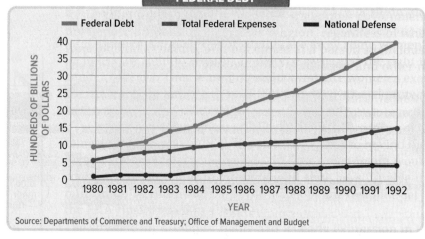

— Federal Debt — Total Federal Expenses — National Defense

HUNDREDS OF BILLIONS OF DOLLARS

40
35
30
25
20
15
10
5
0

1980 1981 1982 1983 1984 1985 1986 1987 1988 1989 1990 1991 1992

YEAR

Source: Departments of Commerce and Treasury; Office of Management and Budget

LIFE IN THE 1980s
LESSON 3

- Expanding economy
- Expanding media and cable television
- New discount retail store model
- Growing emphasis on computers and digital information

THE END OF THE COLD WAR
LESSON 4

End of the Soviet Union

- the fifteen Soviet republics declare independence
- glasnost allows more freedom of speech
- perestroika increases private enterprise and profit in economy
- Communist Party leader coup fails
- Eastern European revolutions

Directions: On a separate sheet of paper, answer the questions below. Make sure you read carefully and answer all parts to the question.

Lesson Review

Lesson 1

1 *Describing* What were the causes of the conservative resurgence of the 1980s and the 1990s? SS.912.A.7.12

2 *Comparing and Contrasting* How are the ideas of liberals different from those of conservatives? SS.912.A.7.12

Lesson 2

3 *Interpreting Significance* What were the economic and foreign policies that Reagan was committed to achieving? Which goals did he decide not to push for in order to achieve his other priorities? SS.912.A.7.11, SS.912.A.7.12

4 *Identifying Cause and Effect* What was the purpose of Reagan's Peace Through Strength policy? What was its effect on the spread of communism? What impact did this buildup have on the American economy? SS.912.A.7.11, SS.912.A.7.12

5 *Draw Conclusions* Draw conclusions about the collaboration of Ronald Reagan and Mikhail Gorbachev, including the reduction in arms, the collapse of the Soviet Union, and the dismantling of the Berlin Wall in 1989. SS.912.A.7.11, SS.912.A.7.12

6 *Interpreting* Offer an interpretation of Reagan's words to Gorbachev when he said, ". . . if you seek peace, if you seek prosperity for the Soviet Union and Eastern Europe . . . tear down this wall!" How are the words an example of negotiation? LAFS.1112.SL.1.3, SS.912.A.7.11, SS.912.A.7.12

Lesson 3

7 *Explaining* How did entrepreneurs such as Robert L. Johnson help transform the news and entertainment industries? SS.912.A.7.12

8 *Comparing and Contrasting* How did activist groups such as the Gay Liberation Front, MADD, and AARP address social issues in the 1980s? SS.912.A.7.12

9 *Identifying Cause and Effect* How did senior citizens create budget pressures for the U.S. government? SS.912.A.7.12

Lesson 4

10 *Analyzing* Describe the reasons for the United States' involvement in the Persian Gulf War. SS.912.A.7.11

11 *Identifying Cause and Effect* Why might the year 1991 be considered a turning point in history? SS.912.A.7.12

12 *Analyzing* How did the United States contribute to the end of the Cold War? SS.912.A.7.12

13 *Summarizing* How and why did the United States intervene in Panama to ultimately remove Panama's dictator, General Manuel Noriega? SS.912.A.7.11

14 *Describing* What role did U.S. General Colin Powell play in the United States-Iraq conflict? SS.912.A.7.12

Exploring the Essential Questions

15 *Making Observations* How do you think the resurgence of conservative ideas has changed society since the 1980s? SS.912.A.7.12

Critical Thinking

16 *Identifying* Briefly describe the roles of the following organizations in the conservative resurgence of the 1980s: the Heritage Foundation, the Moral Majority, and the National Rifle Association. SS.912.A.7.12

17 *Explaining* What space exploration technology resulted in a revolution in mass media? How did American entrepreneurs apply this technology to the marketplace? How does access to these technological innovations improve the standard of living in the United States? SS.912.H.3.1, SS.912.H.3.2

18 *Evaluating* Write a short essay evaluating the political and social contributions of the following conservative leaders: Billy Graham, Barry Goldwater, Sandra Day O'Connor, and Phyllis Schlafly. LAFS.1112.WHST.4.10, SS.912.A.7.12

19 *Describing* Explain the impact of technological innovations in music and video recording in the 1980s. SS.912.A.7.12, SS.912.H.3.1, SS.912.H.3.2

20 *Explaining* What management innovations using new technology led to a retail revolution in the 1980s, and what impact did it have on the economy and standard of living? SS.912.H.3.2

Need Extra Help?

If You've Missed Question	1	2	3	4	5	6	7	8	9	10	11	12	13	14	15	16	17	18	19	20
Go to Lesson	1	1	2	2	2	2	3	3	3	4	4	4	4	4	1	1	3	1	3	3

21 *Making Arguments* What qualities of effective leadership did President Ronald Reagan demonstrate? Choose a quality of leadership you believe he demonstrated and defend your choice in an argument. LAFS.1112.WHST.1.1, SS.912.A.7.12

22 *Analyzing* Compare the technology launched in the 1980s for entertainment with technology designed for entertainment in the last five to ten years. Analyze the impact of both sets of innovations, and consider any connections between the two eras. SS.912.H.1.6, SS.912.H.3.1, SS.912.H.3.2

21st Century Skills

23 *Explaining Demographic Patterns* What caused population shifts in the Rustbelt and Sunbelt, and how did it affect the rise of the conservative movement? SS.912.A.7.12, SS.912.G.2.3, SS.912.G.4.3

24 *Speculating* How has American culture spread to the rest of the world through popular music? What impact has this form of American popular media had on other cultures? SS.912.H.3.1

25 *Research Skills* Research the experience of veterans of Operation Desert Storm. Refer to reliable primary and secondary sources. Share your information through writing and images. LAFS.1112.WHST.3.9, LAFS.1112.WHST.4.10, SS.912.A.1.4, SS.912.A.7.12

26 *Creating Presentations* Develop a multi-media presentation that depicts the cultural and historical moments of the 1980s. Use video clips, photographs, illustrations, newspaper headlines, and articles to provide a full depiction. LAFS.1112.RH.3.7, LAFS.1112.RH.3.9, LAFS.1112.SL.2.5, LAFS.1112.WHST.2.6, LAFS.1112.WHST.3.7, SS.912.H.1.1, SS.912.H.3.1

DBQ **Analyzing Primary Sources**

President Ronald Reagan addressed the American people at the end of his presidency. The following is an excerpt from that address:

PRIMARY SOURCE

❝The way I see it, there were two great triumphs, two things that I'm proudest of. One is the economic recovery, in which the people of America created—and filled—19 million new jobs. The other is the recovery of our morale. America is respected again. . . . Common sense told us that when you put a big tax on something, the people will produce less of it. So, we cut the people's tax rates, and the people produced more than ever before. The economy bloomed. . . . Common sense told us that to preserve the peace, we'd have to become strong again after years of weakness and confusion. So, we rebuilt our defenses, and this New Year we toasted the new peacefulness around the globe.❞

—from his farewell address to the nation, January 11, 1989

27 *Analyzing Primary Sources* Summarize what Reagan believed were his greatest accomplishments. LAFS.1112.RH.1.2, LAFS.1112.RH.4.10, SS.912.A.7.12

28 *Making Inferences* In Reagan's opinion, how did his administration preserve peace? What evidence does he cite to support his claim? LAFS.1112.RH.3.8, LAFS.1112.RH.4.10, SS.912.A.7.12

29 *Interpreting* What economic viewpoint does Reagan offer in this excerpt? LAFS.1112.RH.3.8, LAFS.1112.RH.4.10

Analyzing Visuals

Use the political cartoon to answer the following question.

30 *Interpreting Images* What conservative opinion about liberals does this cartoon reflect? What details support this reading? LAFS.1112.RH.1.1, LAFS.1112.RH.3.8, SS.912.A.1.4, SS.912.A.7.12, SS.912.H.1.5

Extended Response Question

31 *Argument* Write an essay expressing your opinion about the effectiveness of Reagan's revolution. Was Reagan's conservative revolution that began in 1980 successful or unsuccessful in meeting its goals of shrinking the federal government, restoring U.S. military prestige, and electing conservative politicians? Remember to revise your essay as needed to clearly communicate your point. LAFS.1112.WHST.1.1, LAFS.1112.WHST.2.4, LAFS.1112.WHST.2.5, LAFS.1112.WHST.3.9, LAFS.1112.WHST.4.10, SS.912.A.7.12

Gary McCoy/Cagle Cartoons

Need Extra Help?

If You've Missed Question	21	22	23	24	25	26	27	28	29	30	31
Go to Lesson	2	3	1	3	4	1, 2, 3, 4	2	2	2	1	2

◀ Los Angeles Dodgers pitcher Fernando Valenzuela became a symbol of Hispanic success, winning Rookie of the Year and the Cy Young Award in 1981.

FROM 1980 TO 2000

A Time of Change

THE STORY MATTERS ...

Immigration made the United States increasingly interconnected with the rest of the world. It also brought a growing awareness of Hispanic influence on American culture, as immigration from Latin America began to swell in the 1980s. Rookie pitcher for the Los Angeles Dodgers Fernando Valenzuela, a recent immigrant from Mexico, attracted an unprecedented number of fans to Dodgers games and became a cultural icon in the Latino community.

ESSENTIAL QUESTIONS
- How have improvements in science and technology helped change society?
- How have immigration, technology, and global trade changed the world?

©Vince Streano/Corbis

Place & Time: United States 1981–1999

The economic growth and technological innovations experienced by the United States under the Reagan administration were soon surpassed by those that took place under President Bill Clinton. As the economy became more global and less segmented, cheaper labor in other countries made it more challenging for American companies to compete with goods made overseas that were sold at a lower price. With an interconnected world and a new wave of immigration, the United States continued to change.

Step Into the Place

Read the quote and look at the information presented on the map.

 Analyzing Historical Documents President Clinton's address and the information on the map indicate a trend toward globalization in the late twentieth century. What do we learn from the speech that can't be learned by studying the map?

PRIMARY SOURCE

" . . . Even as people take pride in their national independence, we know we are becoming more and more interdependent. The movement of people, money, and ideas across borders, frankly, breeds suspicion among many good people in every country. They are worried about globalization because of its unsettling and unpredictable consequences.

Yet, globalization is not something we can hold off or turn off. It is the economic equivalent of a force of nature, like wind or water. We can harness wind to fill a sail. We can use water to generate energy. We can work hard to protect people and property from storms and floods. But there is no point in denying the existence of wind or water, or trying to make them go away. The same is true for globalization. We can work to maximize its benefits and minimize its risks, but we cannot ignore it and it is not going away."

—President Bill Clinton, from an address at Vietnam National University, November 17, 2000

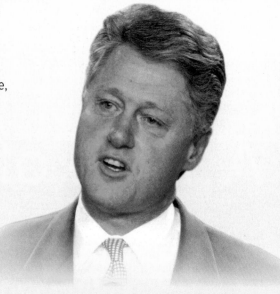

left page (t)Diana Walker/Getty Images News/Getty Images, (b)U.S. Department of Defense; right page (l (c)detail/White House Collection/The White House Historical Association, (r)Eric Draper, White House/U.S. Department of Defense

Step Into the Time

MAKING CONNECTIONS
Choose an event from the time line and write a paragraph suggesting the ways that event might reflect or influence how the countries of the world became increasingly connected during the last decades of the twentieth century.

Reagan 1981–1989

U.S. PRESIDENTS

UNITED STATES

WORLD

1981 IBM introduces its version of the PC or personal computer

1984 Apple's Macintosh introduces the mouse and on-screen icons

1986 Immigration Reform and Control Act passed

1981   1984   1987

1983 Finnish company Nokia begins concentrating on producing cell phones

1987 Soviet Union and United States sign INF treaty

NEXT GENERATION SUNSHINE STATE STANDARDS
Students will understand the following benchmarks from the Florida NGSSS

LAFS.1112.RH.3.7: Integrate and evaluate multiple sources of information presented in diverse formats and media (e.g., visually, quantitatively, as well as in words) in order to address a question or solve a problem.

LAFS.1112.RH.3.9: Integrate information from diverse sources, both primary and secondary, into a coherent understanding of an idea or event, noting discrepancies among sources.

SS.912.A.1.2: Utilize a variety of primary and secondary sources to identify author, historical significance, audience, and authenticity to understand a historical period.

SS.912.A.1.3: Utilize timelines to identify the time sequence of historical data.

SS.912.A.1.4: Analyze how images, symbols, objects, cartoons, graphs, charts, maps, and artwork may be used to interpret the significance of time periods and events from the past.

SS.912.A.7.12: Analyze political, economic, and social concerns that emerged at the end of the 20th century and into the 21st century.

SS.912.A.7.14: Review the role of the United States as a participant in the global economy (trade agreements, international competition, impact on American labor, environmental concerns).

Globalization of the Economy

The impact of globalization can be seen in the production of computers. Although computers are made in the United States, the materials for their parts come from around the world.

G. H. W. Bush
1989–1993

1993 Mosaic, the first popular Web browser, is released

Clinton
1993–2001

1994 NAFTA takes effect

1995 Timothy McVeigh bombs federal building in Oklahoma City

1998 House of Representatives impeaches President Clinton

1999 Senate acquits Clinton

G. W. Bush
2001–2009

| 1990 | 1993 | 1996 | 1999 |

1990 The World Wide Web is developed in Switzerland

1992 The Bosnian conflict begins

1993 Israeli-Palestinian peace accord signed

1995 The World Trade Organization is established

1997 Slobodan Milošević becomes president of the Federal Republic of Yugoslavia

LESSON 1
The Clinton Years

ESSENTIAL QUESTIONS

• How have improvements in science and technology helped change society?
• How have immigration, technology, and global trade changed the world?

READING HELPDESK

Academic Vocabulary

• modify
• unprecedented
• participant

Content Vocabulary

• perjury
• ethnic cleansing

TAKING NOTES

Key Ideas and Details

Outlining As you read about the administration of President Clinton, use the headings of the section to create an outline similar to the one below.
LAFS.1112.RH.3.7

> The Clinton Years
> I. Clinton's Agenda
>   A.
>   B.
>   C.
>   D.
> II.

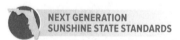
NEXT GENERATION SUNSHINE STATE STANDARDS

HE.912.C.2.7: Analyze how culture supports and challenges health beliefs, practices, and behaviors.
LAFS.1112.RH.1.2: Determine the central ideas or information of a primary or secondary source; provide an accurate summary that makes clear the relationships among the key details and ideas.

Continued on page 598

IT MATTERS BECAUSE

When William Jefferson Clinton was elected in 1992, he became the first Democrat to win the presidency in 12 years. After achieving only part of his agenda, he faced a Republican Congress that had very different plans.

Clinton's Agenda

GUIDING QUESTION *During his first presidential term, what domestic policy areas did Clinton focus on?*

Just 46 years old when he took office, Bill Clinton was the first baby boomer to reach the Oval Office. He set out an ambitious domestic agenda focusing on the economy, the family, education, crime, and health care.

Raising Taxes, Cutting Spending

Clinton first focused on the economy. He saw the massive federal deficit as the main source of the economy's weakness. It forced the government to borrow heavily, which helped drive up interest rates. Clinton believed that lowering interest rates would enable businesses and consumers to borrow more money for business investment and increased consumer purchasing, which would then promote growth.

About half of all government spending went to entitlement programs—such as Social Security and veterans' benefits—that could not easily be cut because so many people relied on them. Facing these constraints, Clinton's 1993 plan for reducing the deficit proposed raising taxes on middle and upper incomes and placing new taxes on gasoline, heating oil, and natural gas. Congressional Republicans refused to support the unpopular tax increases. Clinton pressured Democrats, however, and after many amendments, a **modified** version of the plan narrowly passed.

Stumbling on Health Care

During his campaign, Clinton had promised to reform the health care system. Some 40 million Americans, or roughly 15 percent of the nation, did not have health insurance. The president created a task force and appointed his wife, Hillary Rodham Clinton, to head it—an **unprecedented** role for a First Lady. The task force developed a plan that put much of the burden of paying for the benefits on employers. Small business owners feared they could not afford it. The insurance industry and doctors' organizations mounted a nationwide advertising campaign to build public opposition to the plan. Republican opposition and a divided Democratic Party led to the death of the plan without a vote.

Families and Education

During his campaign, Clinton had stressed the need to help American families. His first success was the Family Medical Leave Act. This law gave workers up to 12 weeks per year of unpaid leave for the birth or adoption of a child or for the illness of a family member. He also persuaded Congress to create the AmeriCorps program. This program puts students to work improving low-income housing, teaching children to read, and cleaning up the environment. AmeriCorps incorporated the VISTA program that John F. Kennedy had created. AmeriCorps volunteers earn a salary and are awarded a scholarship to continue their education. In September 1994, some 20,000 AmeriCorps volunteers began serving in more than 1,000 communities.

Crime and Gun Control

Clinton strongly endorsed new gun-control laws. Despite opposition from many Republicans and the National Rifle Association (NRA), Congress passed a gun-control law known as the Brady Bill. This law established a waiting period and required a criminal background check before selling someone a handgun. The following year, Clinton introduced another bill to fund new prisons and add 100,000 more police officers. It also banned 19 kinds of assault weapons and funded crime prevention programs.

The Rise of Advocacy Groups

The debates that erupted over Clinton's agenda in the 1990s demonstrated the growing influence and power of political and social advocacy groups. In one sense, advocacy groups have always been part of American history. Whenever citizens join together in a formal organization to push for new laws or changes to society, they have formed an advocacy group. In the 1800s, abolitionists formed political advocacy groups as did supporters of woman suffrage. The civil rights movement was made up of many political and social advocacy groups as well.

After the turmoil of the 1960s and 1970s, however, the United States witnessed the rise of a large number of new advocacy groups. This was in part because politics had become so polarized, and in part because of highly controversial decisions by the Supreme Court. Increasingly, the nation found itself divided, with liberals and progressives aligned with the Democratic party, and conservatives and libertarians aligned with the Republican party. Both sides began to form organizations to advocate for their issues.

Advocacy groups use a variety of methods to bring about change. They lobby politicians, and donate money to political campaigns. They try to educate voters and change their opinions; their leaders write blogs, produce videos, appear on news shows, and engage in public debates. Advocacy groups also file lawsuits and write briefs to influence court decisions, and of course, they stage protests, organize marches, and conduct public events to raise awareness of their causes and issues.

modify to make changes or alter

unprecedented having no earlier occurrence of something similar

President Clinton explains the proposed Health Security card in a speech to Congress in October 1993.

▶ CRITICAL THINKING
Determining Cause and Effect What factors contributed to the failure of Clinton's health care plan? LAFS.1112.WHST.3.9, SS.912.A.7.12

SKILLS PRACTICE

Pick a partner. Read the lesson on the Clinton administration together. When you do not understand the content, ask your partner to explain it to you. If they do not understand the content, they should ask you for help. Ask the teacher for help if both of you have trouble understanding the content. ELD.K12.ELL.SI.1, ELD.K12.ELL.SS.1

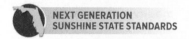

**NEXT GENERATION
SUNSHINE STATE STANDARDS**

Continued from page 596

LAFS.1112.RH.2.4: Determine the meaning of words and phrases as they are used in a text, including analyzing how an author uses and refines the meaning of a key term over the course of a text (e.g., how Madison defines faction in Federalist No. 10).

LAFS.1112.RH.3.7: Integrate and evaluate multiple sources of information presented in diverse formats and media (e.g., visually, quantitatively, as well as in words) in order to address a question or solve a problem.

LAFS.1112.WHST.1.1: Write arguments focused on discipline-specific content.

LAFS.1112.WHST.3.9: Draw evidence from informational texts to support analysis, reflection, and research.

LAFS.1112.WHST.4.10: Write routinely over extended time frames (time for reflection and revision) and shorter time frames (a single sitting or a day or two) for a range of discipline-specific tasks, purposes, and audiences.

SS.912.A.1.2: Utilize a variety of primary and secondary sources to identify author, historical significance, audience, and authenticity to understand a historical period.

SS.912.A.1.4: Analyze how images, symbols, objects, cartoons, graphs, charts, maps, and artwork may be used to interpret the significance of time periods and events from the past.

SS.912.A.6.15: Examine key events and peoples in Florida history as they relate to United States history.

SS.912.A.7.11: Analyze the foreign policy of the United States as it relates to Africa, Asia, the Caribbean, Latin America, and the Middle East.

SS.912.A.7.12: Analyze political, economic, and social concerns that emerged at the end of the 20th century and into the 21st century.

SS.912.A.7.13: Analyze the attempts to extend New Deal legislation through the Great Society and the successes and failures of these programs to promote social and economic stability.

SS.912.A.7.15: Analyze the effects of foreign and domestic terrorism on the American people.

SS.912.H.1.2: Describe how historical events, social context, and culture impact forms, techniques, and purposes of works in the arts, including the relationship between a government and its citizens.

Political Advocacy Groups

Political issues involving taxation, economic policy, and government programs have always been contentious and have led to a host of advocacy groups across the political spectrum. Prominent conservative advocacy groups include the Heritage Foundation, as well as Americans for Tax Reform (ATR), led by Grover Norquist. The ATR opposes tax increases and advocates reducing the amount of money collected by the government.

The United States Chamber of Commerce serves as a powerful advocacy group on economic issues. Representing many of the nation's businesses, the Chamber is one of the largest lobbying groups in the United States. Perhaps the best-known of all the conservative political advocacy groups is the National Rifle Association (NRA). It became well known in part because a Hollywood actor, Charlton Heston, was elected president of the NRA in 1998. After Heston's death, Wayne LaPierre became the NRA's primary spokesman for defending the right of gun ownership.

The American Association of Retired Persons (AARP) has fought to prevent cuts in Social Security and Medicare spending and has lobbied for healthcare reforms. With approximately 40 million members, the AARP is one of the most powerful advocacy groups in the United States.

Advocacy groups who support liberal and progressive positions on political and economic issues include People for the American Way, founded by the television producer Norman Lear, in response to the rise of the religious right. Other major progressive organizations include MoveOn.org, founded in 1998 by Joan Blades and Wes Boyd in response to Bill Clinton's impeachment, and the Center for American Progress, founded by John Podesta as a liberal alternative to the Heritage Foundation. Liberal advocacy groups are also prominent in pushing for environmental laws. The most prominent environmental advocacy groups include Greenpeace, the Sierra Club, and the National Defense Resources Council.

Social Advocacy Groups

Social issues, including abortion rights, have generated their own group of social advocacy organizations. On the liberal side of the spectrum are the National Abortion Rights Action League (NARAL) and Planned Parenthood, which defend the right to choose abortion. From 1996 to 2006, Gloria Feldt led Planned Parenthood. Since then, the organization has been led by Cecile Richards. On the opposite side of the issue is the National Right to Life Committee (NRLC). The NRLC was led by Wanda Franz from 1991 to 2011, then Carol Tobias became the organization's president.

Other social issues and concerns about the nation's values have led to a range of advocacy organizations. The Human Rights Campaign is the largest social and political advocacy group working to expand rights for gay and lesbian individuals. On the opposite side of many of these issues have been organizations such as Focus on the Family, led by James Dobson, and the Family Research Council, led by Tony Perkins, both of which advocate for traditional family values.

Another important aspect to the rise of political and social advocacy groups has been the role of extremely wealthy Americans in supporting them. Because campaign finance laws limit the amount of money people can give directly to candidates, many wealthy Americans donate heavily to advocacy groups in order to promote political and social issues that matter to them. Some of the more controversial billionaires who have helped finance advocacy groups, and whose names are often in the news are

George Soros, who supports progressive causes, and Charles and David Koch, whose foundations support conservative causes.

By the 1990s, there were literally thousands of political and social advocacy groups in the United States advocating on every issue, and their numbers have continued to grow. When studying the history of the United States from Bill Clinton's presidency to the present, an important part of the analysis should always be to look at the advocacy groups on both sides of the issue, and determine how they have influenced the democratic process.

☑ READING PROGRESS CHECK

Summarizing How did Clinton help stimulate the economy and handle the massive federal deficit?

Republicans Gain Control of Congress

GUIDING QUESTION *How did the Republican Party respond to their victory in the 1994 midterm elections?*

Clinton's popularity was low by late 1994. He had raised taxes and failed to fix health care. The economy was improving, but many companies were still downsizing. Personal issues involving Clinton further weakened public confidence in him. In response, many Americans decided to vote Republican.

The Contract With America

In the 1994 midterm elections, congressional Republicans, led by Representative Newt Gingrich of Georgia, proposed the "Contract with America." This program proposed changes including lower taxes, welfare reform, tougher anticrime laws, and a balanced budget amendment. Republicans won a majority in both houses of Congress for the first time in 40 years. House Republicans quickly passed almost the entire program, but the Senate defeated several proposals, and the president vetoed others.

The Budget Battle

In 1995, Republicans and Clinton clashed over the new federal budget. Clinton vetoed several Republican budget proposals, saying they cut into social programs too much. Gingrich believed if Republicans stood firm, Clinton would approve the budget rather than let the government shut down for lack of funds. Clinton, however, allowed the federal government to close.

By standing firm, Clinton regained much of the support he had lost. Congressional Republicans realized that they needed to work with the president to pass legislation. Soon afterward, they reached an agreement with Clinton to balance the budget. The next year, Congress passed the Health Insurance Portability Act to improve health coverage for people who changed jobs and to reduce discrimination against those with pre-existing illnesses. Congress also passed the Welfare Reform Act, which limited people to no more than two consecutive years on welfare and required them to work to receive benefits. The law also increased child-care spending and gave tax breaks to companies hiring new employees who had been on welfare.

Clinton Wins Reelection

The economic boom of the 1990s was the longest sustained peacetime expansion in American history, and Clinton took credit for it. Inflation and unemployment fell to their lowest levels in 40 years. A booming economy helped Clinton's popularity climb rapidly.

In April 1995, however, an act of domestic terrorism shocked the nation. Timothy McVeigh, formerly a soldier in the U.S. Army, planted a massive homemade bomb in a rental truck near a federal building in Oklahoma

City. The explosion killed 168 people and injured more than 500 others. As a result, American officials began investigating right-wing militant groups who shared views like McVeigh's, and membership in those groups declined.

In 1996, Republicans nominated Senator Bob Dole to run against Clinton. H. Ross Perot also ran again. Despite two opponents, Clinton won reelection with more than 49 percent of the popular vote and 379 electoral votes. Republicans, however, retained control of Congress.

✓ READING PROGRESS CHECK

Drawing Conclusions What were the political consequences of the budget battle?

Clinton's Second Term

GUIDING QUESTION *Why was President Clinton's domestic agenda less aggressive during his second term?*

During Clinton's second term, the economy continued to expand. In 1997, he submitted a balanced budget to Congress. In 1998, the government began to run a surplus—that is, it collected more money than it spent. Despite these achievements, Clinton devoted much of his second term to foreign policy and struggling against personal scandal.

ANALYZING PRIMARY SOURCES

Is a Balanced Budget Amendment a Good Idea?

One of the ideas that congressional Republicans put forth in the "Contract with America" was a balanced budget amendment to the Constitution. Would such an amendment force Congress to be more responsible in how it spends the taxpayers' money? Or would it dangerously limit Congress's ability to respond to economic and national security emergencies?

——— YES ———

Strom Thurmond
U.S. Senator

❝While Congress could achieve a balanced budget by statute, past efforts . . . have failed. It is simply too easy for Congress to change its mind. . . . The constitutional amendment is unyielding in its imposition of discipline on Congress to make the tough decisions necessary to balance the federal budget. Over the past half-century, Congress has demonstrated a total lack of fiscal discipline evidenced by an irrational and irresponsible pattern of spending. This reckless approach has seriously jeopardized the Federal government and threatens the very future of this Nation. As a result, I believe we must look to constitutional protection from a firmly entrenched fiscal policy which threatens the liberties and opportunities of our present and future citizens.❞

—statement to the Judiciary Committee, February 16, 1994

——— NO ———

Mark Hatfield
U.S. Senator

❝And I thought the amendment simply a political ploy to erroneously make Americans think we were actually doing something about the deficit. In fact, we knew how to truly balance the budget but lacked the political courage to do so. Instead, this amendment had a hidden escape valve, saying we could all ignore it with a three-fifth Congressional vote. And . . . this [amendment] could have taken up to seven years to be adopted. We didn't have that long. . . . I wanted a balanced budget with all these kinks worked out. I've been quoted as saying, 'I pray for the integrity, justice, and courage to vote the correct vote, not the political vote,' and this was no time for change.❞

—from *Against the Grain: Reflections of a Rebel Republican*, 2001

DBQ Analyzing Historical Documents

❶ *Analyzing Primary Sources* How might an "irresponsible pattern of spending" by Congress threaten the nation's future? LAFS.1112.WHST.3.9, SS.912.A.1.2, SS.912.A.7.12

❷ *Drawing Conclusions* Which argument do you find more convincing? Why? SS.912.A.1.2, SS.912.A.7.12

(l)Terry Ashe/Time Life Pictures/Getty Images; (r)Georgia General Assembly

BATTLE OVER A BALANCED BUDGET

In 1995, a clash between congressional Republicans and President Clinton over the federal budget led to a shutdown of the federal government.

1 *Identifying Central Ideas* Why do you think the cartoonist says that both Clinton and Gingrich might be non-essential federal employees? LAFS.1112.WHST.3.9, SS.912.A.1.4, SS.912.H.1.2

2 *Making Inferences* What is the significance of depicting rain and puddles in the cartoon? SS.912.A.1.4

Putting Children First

During Clinton's second term, one area of domestic policy he focused on was helping the nation's children. He asked Congress for a $500 per child tax credit. He also signed the Adoption and Safe Families Act and asked Congress to ban cigarette advertising aimed at children. In August 1997, Clinton signed the Children's Health Insurance Program to provide health insurance for children whose parents could not afford it.

Clinton also focused on students. "I came from a family where nobody had ever gone to college before. . . . When I became President, I was determined to do what I could to give every student that chance. I am well aware, if it hadn't been for that chance . . . I wouldn't be standing here today," he told graduating college students. Clinton asked for a tax credit, a large increase in student grants, and expansion of Head Start for disadvantaged preschoolers.

Clinton Is Impeached

Clinton's popularity soon faltered, however. During his first term, he was accused of arranging illegal loans for Whitewater Development, an Arkansas real estate company, as governor of that state. Attorney General Janet Reno called for an independent counsel to investigate. A three-judge panel appointed former federal judge Kenneth Starr to this role.

In early 1998, new allegations emerged about Clinton's relationship with a White House intern. Some evidence suggested that he had committed **perjury,** or had lied under oath, about the relationship. In September 1998, Starr argued that Clinton had obstructed justice, abused his power as president, and committed perjury. Starr found no evidence to formally charge Clinton regarding the Whitewater accusations, however.

Clinton's supporters argued that Starr was playing politics. Opponents claimed Clinton should face charges if he had committed a crime. On December 19, 1998, the House of Representatives passed two articles of impeachment, one for perjury and one for obstruction of justice. The vote split along party lines, and the case moved to the Senate. On February 12, 1999, the senators voted 55 to 45 that Clinton was not guilty of perjury, and 50–50 on obstruction of justice. Both votes fell short of the two-thirds needed to remove Clinton from office, but his reputation suffered.

perjury lying when one has sworn under oath to tell the truth

— *Thinking Like a* —
HISTORIAN
Comparing and Contrasting

Bill Clinton became only the second American president to be impeached. The first was Andrew Johnson, the Reconstruction-era president who succeeded Abraham Lincoln. In both cases, political opposition to the president by Congress played a role in bringing the Chief Executive to trial. Unlike Clinton's case, however, Johnson's crisis stemmed from a political, rather than personal, scandal: he fired the secretary of war without Senate approval, a violation of the Tenure of Office Act. Although Congress failed to remove either leader, historians generally agree that political motivations contributed to their trials.

✓ READING PROGRESS CHECK

Examining What impact did impeachment have on Clinton's second term?

Library of Congress, Prints & Photographs Division [LC-USZ62-120083]

Clinton's impeachment trial captured the attention of the nation.

► CRITICAL THINKING
Predicting Consequences What influence might public opinion have on the outcome of an impeachment trial?

ethnic cleansing the expulsion, imprisonment, or killing of ethnic minorities by a dominant majority group

participant one who takes part or shares in something

Haitians gather outside the fence of the U.S. camp to talk to American peacekeepers.

► CRITICAL THINKING
Making Inferences What can you conclude about the Haitian people's hope for peace from the way they are clustered at the fence? SS.912.A.1.4, SS.912.A.7.11

Clinton's Foreign Policy

GUIDING QUESTION *How did the Clinton administration provide foreign aid to areas of conflict around the world?*

Although Clinton's domestic policies became bogged down in struggles with Congress, he was able to engage in a series of major foreign policy initiatives. Several times he used force to try to resolve regional conflicts.

The Haitian Intervention

In 1991, military leaders in Haiti overthrew democratically elected president Jean-Bertrand Aristide. Seeking to restore democracy, the Clinton administration convinced the United Nations to impose a trade embargo on Haiti. The embargo caused a severe economic crisis in that country, and many Haitians fled to the United States. Clinton then ordered an invasion of Haiti. However, former president Carter convinced Haiti's rulers to step aside, and American troops landed to serve as peacekeepers.

Bosnia and Kosovo

The United States also was concerned about mounting tensions in southeastern Europe. During the Cold War, Yugoslavia had been a nation of many ethnic groups under a strong Communist government. In 1991, Yugoslavia began to split apart. In the new republic of Bosnia and Herzegovina, a civil war erupted among Orthodox Christian Serbs, Catholic Croatians, and Bosnian Muslims. The Serbs began what they called **ethnic cleansing**—the brutal expulsion of non-Serbs from a geographic area. In some cases, Serbian troops slaughtered Bosnian Muslims instead of moving them.

The United States convinced its NATO allies to take military action. NATO warplanes attacked the Serbs in Bosnia, forcing them to negotiate. The Clinton administration arranged peace talks in Dayton, Ohio, where the **participants** signed a peace plan known as the Dayton Accords. In 1996, about 60,000 NATO troops entered Bosnia to enforce the plan.

In 1998, another war erupted, this time in the Serbian province of Kosovo. Kosovo has two major ethnic groups—Serbs and Albanians. Many Albanians wanted Kosovo to separate from Serbia. To keep Kosovo in Serbia, Serbian leader Slobodan Milošević ordered a crackdown. Worried by Serbian violence against Albanian civilians, Clinton asked European leaders to intervene. In March 1999, NATO began bombing Serbia, and Serbia pulled its troops out of Kosovo.

Peacemaking in the Middle East

Although Iraq was defeated in the Persian Gulf War, Iraqi president Saddam Hussein was determined to hang onto power. In 1996, Iraqi forces attacked the Kurds, an ethnic group whose homeland lies in northern Iraq. To stop the attacks, the United States fired cruise missiles at Iraqi military targets.

Relations between Israel and the Palestinians were even more volatile. In 1993, Israeli Prime Minister Yitzhak Rabin and Palestine Liberation Organization (PLO) leader Yasir Arafat reached an agreement. This was the first direct agreement between Israel and the PLO, the first time the PLO recognized Israel's right to exist, and the first time Israel recognized the PLO as the representative of the Palestinians. President Clinton then invited Arafat and Rabin to the White House, where they signed the Declaration of Principles—a plan for

(t)Peter Lennihan/AP Images; (b)©Peter Turnley/Corbis

©Les Stone/Sygma/Corbis

Israeli Prime Minster Yitzhak Rabin (left) and Palestinian leader Yasir Arafat shake hands after signing the 1993 Declaration of Principles.

▶ **CRITICAL THINKING**

Defending Do you think that the United States should intervene in world conflicts? Why or why not? SS.912.A.7.11

creating a Palestinian government. Extremist opposition to the peace plan emerged on both sides. Radical Palestinians terrorists exploded bombs in Israel, killing 256 civilians. In 1995, a right-wing Israeli assassinated Prime Minister Rabin.

In 1994, with help from the United States, Jordan and Israel signed a peace treaty. In 1998, Israeli and Palestinian leaders met with President Clinton at the Wye River Plantation in Maryland. The agreement they reached, however, did not address the contested status of Jerusalem or the ultimate dimensions of a projected Israeli withdrawal from the West Bank and Gaza.

In July 2000, President Clinton invited Arafat and Israeli Prime Minister Ehud Barak to Camp David to discuss unresolved issues. Barak agreed to the creation of a Palestinian state in all of Gaza and over 90 percent of the West Bank, but Arafat rejected the deal. In late September 2000, a Palestinian uprising began. The region was as far from peace as ever.

☑ **READING PROGRESS CHECK**

Drawing Conclusions Why did the Clinton administration intervene in conflicts such as Haiti, the former Yugoslavia, and the Middle East?

LESSON 1 REVIEW

Reviewing Vocabulary

1. ***Defining*** How is perjury different from lying? LAFS.1112.RH.2.4

2. ***Identifying*** For what purpose did Bosnian Serbs practice ethnic cleansing? LAFS.1112.RH.2.4, LAFS.1112.WHST.3.9, SS.912.A.7.12

Using Your Notes

3. ***Evaluating*** Review the notes you took during the lesson. Write a paragraph telling whether President Clinton was more successful in domestic policy or in foreign policy. Support your opinion with specific details from the lesson. LAFS.1112.WHST.3.9, SS.912.A.7.11, SS.912.A.7.12

Answering the Guiding Questions

4. ***Identifying*** During his first presidential term, what domestic policy areas did Clinton focus on? LAFS.1112.WHST.3.9, SS.912.A.7.12

5. ***Describing*** How did the Republican Party respond to their victory in the 1994 midterm elections? LAFS.1112.WHST.3.9, SS.912.A.7.12

6. ***Assessing*** Why was President Clinton's domestic agenda less aggressive during his second term? LAFS.1112.WHST.3.9, SS.912.A.7.12

7. ***Explaining*** How did the Clinton administration provide foreign aid to areas of conflict around the world? LAFS.1112.WHST.3.9, SS.912.A.7.11

Writing Activity

8. **ARGUMENT** Suppose that you are a member of Congress. Write a speech in which you attempt to persuade other lawmakers to vote for or against Clinton's impeachment. LAFS.1112.WHST.1.1, LAFS.1112.WHST.4.10, SS.912.A.7.12

LESSON 2

A New Wave of Immigration

ESSENTIAL QUESTIONS

• How have improvements in science and technology helped change society?
• How have immigration, technology, and global trade changed the world?

READING HELPDESK

Academic Vocabulary

• **illegal**
• **resident**
• **allocate**

Content Vocabulary

• **migration chains**
• **refugee**
• **amnesty**

TAKING NOTES

Key Ideas and Details

Determining Cause and Effect As you read the lesson, complete a graphic organizer similar to the one below to list the effects of the Immigration Act of 1965. SS.912.A.7.16

Effects of the
Immigration Act of 1965

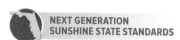

**NEXT GENERATION
SUNSHINE STATE STANDARDS**

MAFS.912.S-ID.1: Summarize, represent and interpret data on a single count or measurement variable.

SS.912.A.1.2: Utilize a variety of primary and secondary sources to identify author, historical significance, audience, and authenticity to understand a historical period.

Continued on page 606

IT MATTERS BECAUSE

In the late twentieth century, the number of immigrants to the United States hit an all-time high. Large numbers of non-European immigrants changed the nation's ethnic composition. Immigration, both legal and illegal, became a difficult political issue.

Changes in Immigration Law

GUIDING QUESTION *How have important immigration laws affected legal and illegal immigration to the United States?*

After the introduction of the national origins quota system in the 1920s, the sources and character of immigration to the United States changed dramatically. For the next few decades, the total number of immigrants arriving annually remained markedly lower. The quota system, which favored immigrants from northern and western Europe, remained largely unchanged until the mid-1960s.

The Immigration Act of 1965 abolished the national origins quota system. It gave preference to skilled persons and persons with close relatives who are U.S. citizens—policies that remain in place today. The preference given to the children, spouses, and parents of U.S. citizens meant that **migration chains** were established. As newcomers became citizens, they could send for relatives in their home country. Also, the legislation introduced the first limits on immigration from the Western Hemisphere. The act further provided that immigrants could apply for U.S. citizenship after five years of legal residency.

At the time of its passage, few people expected that the new law would cause much change in the pattern or volume of immigration to the United States. Supporters of the law presented it as an extension of America's growing commitment to equal rights for all people, regardless of race or ethnicity. As U.S. Representative Philip Burton of California explained:

PRIMARY SOURCE

"Just as we sought to eliminate discrimination in our land through the Civil Rights Act, today we seek by phasing out the national origins quotas to eliminate discrimination in immigration to this Nation composed of the descendants of immigrants."

—from a speech before Congress, August 25, 1965

Supporters of the new law also assumed that the new equal quotas for non-European nations would generally go unfilled. In fact, immigration from non-European countries soared. Some newcomers arrived in the United States as **refugees.** Beginning in 1948, refugees from countries ravaged by World War II were admitted, although they were counted as part of their nation's quota. The Cold War brought more refugees. According to the McCarran-Walter Act of 1952, anyone who was fleeing a Communist regime could be admitted as a refugee. The Refugee Act of 1980 further broadened U.S. policy by defining a refugee as anyone leaving his or her country due to a "well-founded fear of persecution on account of race, religion, nationality, membership in a particular group, or political opinion."

The growing problem of **illegal** immigration also prompted changes in immigration law. During the Reagan administration, Congress passed the Immigration Reform and Control Act of 1986, which established penalties for employers who knowingly hired unauthorized immigrants. This law strengthened border controls to prevent illegal entry into the United States. It also set up a process to grant **amnesty,** or a pardon, to any undocumented alien who could prove that he or she had entered the country before January 1, 1982, and had since lived in the United States.

migration chains the process by which immigrants who have acquired U.S. citizenship can send for relatives in their home country to join them

refugee someone leaving his or her country due to a well-founded fear of persecution on account of race, religion, nationality, membership in a particular group, or political opinion

illegal not according to or authorized by law

amnesty the act of granting a pardon to a large group of people

GEOGRAPHY CONNECTION

In 2000, there were an estimated 8.4 million unauthorized residents in the United States.

1 **PLACES AND REGIONS** *According to the map, which states have the largest numbers of unauthorized residents?* SS.912.G.4.3

2 **HUMAN SYSTEMS** *What are some geographic factors that could explain why some states attract more immigrants than others?* SS.912.G.4.2

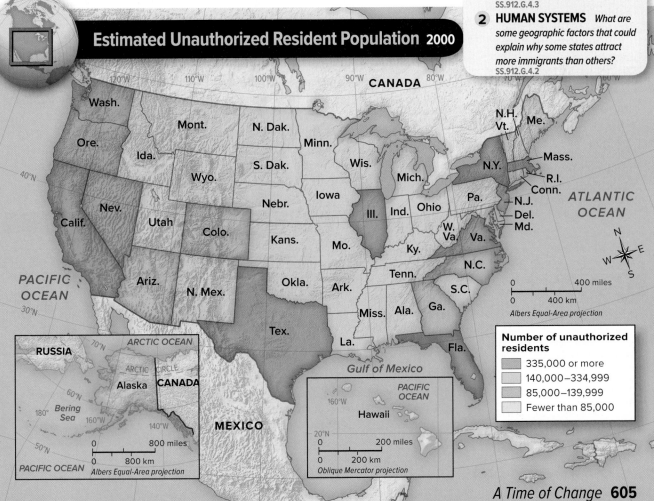

Estimated Unauthorized Resident Population 2000

Number of unauthorized residents
- 335,000 or more
- 140,000–334,999
- 85,000–139,999
- Fewer than 85,000

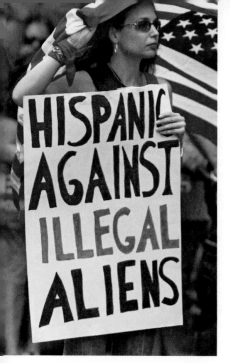

Illegal immigration has long been a divisive issue.

▶ **CRITICAL THINKING**
Using Context Clues In what sense is this woman using the term *aliens*? LAFS.1112.RH.2.4

allocate to set apart for something specific

resident one who lives in a place for some length of time

SKILLS PRACTICE

Before reading this lesson on Immigration, look through the lesson and write down all the bold-faced terms. Find their definitions, either in the text or in the glossary. Then use a thesaurus to find and write down other meanings for the words. ELD.K12.ELL.SI.1, ELD.K12.ELL.SS.1

NEXT GENERATION SUNSHINE STATE STANDARDS

Continued from page 604

SS.912.A.7.12: Analyze political, economic, and social concerns that emerged at the end of the 20th century and into the 21st century.

SS.912.A.7.16: Examine changes in immigration policy and attitudes toward immigration since 1950.

SS.912.A.6.15: Examine key events and peoples in Florida history as they relate to United States history.

Despite these changes, illegal immigration persisted, and the number of unauthorized immigrants grew. By 1990, an estimated 3.5 million unauthorized immigrants resided in the United States. By the mid-1990s, Congress was debating new ways to combat illegal immigration. It passed the Illegal Immigration Reform and Immigrant Responsibility Act of 1996, which made several changes to American immigration law.

First, it required families sponsoring an immigrant to have an income above the poverty level. Second, it **allocated** more resources to stop illegal immigration, authorizing an additional 5,000 U.S. Border Patrol agents and calling for the construction of a 14-mile fence along the border near San Diego. Third, the law toughened penalties for smuggling people or providing fraudulent documents. Finally, the law made it easier for immigration authorities to deport undocumented aliens.

Another change in immigration law was spurred by the terrorist attacks of September 11, 2001. The USA PATRIOT Act of 2001 put immigration under the control of the newly created Department of Homeland Security. It also tripled the number of Border Patrol agents, Customs Service inspectors, and Immigration and Naturalization Service inspectors along the Canadian border.

☑ READING PROGRESS CHECK

Sequencing How did the Immigration Reform and Control Act of 1986 attempt to control illegal immigration?

Recent Immigration

GUIDING QUESTION *How has the federal government addressed immigration reform in the twenty-first century?*

Certain states experienced a larger influx of immigrants than others. In 1990, California, Texas, New York, New Jersey, and Florida had the largest populations of foreign-born **residents.** High numbers of immigrants also increased the ethnic diversity of these states, as their Latino and Asian populations grew. Among the immigrants who arrived during the 1990s, just over 10 percent came from Europe. More than half of new immigrants came from Latin America, while about another 25 percent came from Asia. By 2001, the top five countries of origin for legal immigrants to the United States were Mexico, India, China, the Philippines, and Vietnam.

Refugees added to the growing immigrant population. In the 25 years following the Cuban Revolution of 1959, more than 800,000 Cubans arrived in the United States. So many settled in the Miami, Florida, area that the only city that is home to more Cubans is Havana, Cuba. Also, the Vietnam

CHARTS/GRAPHS	ILLEGAL BORDER CROSSING DEATHS

After the attacks of September 11, 2001, border security became a greater concern for many Americans.

Number of deaths: 500, 400, 300, 200, 100, 0
Years: 1998 1999 2000 2001 2002 2003 2004 2005 2006 2007 2008 2009

Source: United States Government Accountability Office. Congressional Research Service.

1 *Analyzing Information* What year saw the most people die while crossing the border illegally? MAFS.912.S-ID.1, SS.912.A.1.4

2 *Determining Cause and Effect* Why do you think the government's attempts to control border crossings have not reduced the number of deaths? SS.912.A.7.16

Stanley Rogouski

War created refugees. Some 600,000 immigrants from Vietnam, Laos, and Cambodia arrived in the decade after 1974.

Other immigrants arrived without official permission. The largest number of unauthorized immigrants came from Mexico, El Salvador, and Guatemala. The amnesty program established in 1986 had been designed to solve the problem of illegal immigration. Yet, over the next 20 years, the number of unauthorized immigrants more than tripled. Americans were divided over whether unauthorized immigrants should be able to obtain driver's licenses or send their children to public schools and receive other government services.

Some believed that unauthorized immigrants should be deported. Others favored allowing them to apply for temporary work visas so the government could keep track of them. Some supported permitting them to earn permanent residence if they learned English, paid back taxes, and had no criminal record.

In 2006, President George W. Bush made immigration reform a top priority, but members of Congress strongly disagreed over how to solve the problem. A bipartisan majority of the Senate favored legislation that blended tougher enforcement of immigration laws with some form of earned citizenship.

The Senate bill included a provision that allowed undocumented aliens who grew up in the United States and graduated from high school to apply for citizenship. Conservative Republicans who held the majority in the House objected that this would reward illegal behavior. "Granting amnesty to people who broke the law penalizes the millions of people who are waiting to come to America legally," argued Republican senator Phil Gramm of Texas.

The House rejected any form of amnesty and called for the United States to build a wall along its Mexican border. By this time, the United States had already tripled the size of its border patrol without reducing illegal immigration. As Congress debated a bill that would subject undocumented aliens to criminal prosecution, Latinos held rallies across the country, carrying signs that read: "We are not criminals."

Advocates of immigration reform promoted alternatives such as expanding quotas through a guest-worker program and establishing a legalization process for those already in the country. Some undocumented immigrants had lived in the United States for years and had raised families. Deporting them would mean separating husbands, wives, and children. Some had arrived as children and had lived in the United States most of their lives. Their own children, born in the United States, were native-born citizens even though their parents lacked legal status. Among those who became legal citizens, most wanted other family members to join them.

✔ READING PROGRESS CHECK

Hypothesizing How would you solve the problem of illegal immigration?

Florida CONNECTION

Cuban Migration

Cuban migration to the United States has a history that goes back almost 200 years. The first significant wave of Cubans were cigar makers who came to Key West in the early nineteenth century to avoid high American tariffs on imported cigars. Throughout the first half of the twentieth century many Cubans who were opposed to Cuba's political leadership settled in Florida, especially the Miami area. Often these activists stayed until leaders changed and then they returned to the island. Fidel Castro's Communist revolution in 1959 changed the tone of these temporary migrations. More Cubans began migrating to Florida and staying, as Castro's power held decade after decade. Cold War tensions between the United States and Cuba made the arrival of Cubans more difficult to resolve. This was made worse when an economic decline in Cuba during the 1990s spurred a new flood of illegal emigrants. During the Clinton administration, the United States and Cuba formally agreed to work together to regulate Cuban migration to the United States. SS.912.A.6.15, SS.912.A.7.17

LESSON 2 REVIEW

Reviewing Vocabulary

1. **Defining** Why were people who came to the United States as a result of World War II and the Cold War considered refugees? LAFS.1112.RH.2.4, LAFS.1112.WHST.3.9

2. **Explaining** How might migration chains affect the immigration patterns or numbers of immigrants entering the country? LAFS.1112.RH.2.4, LAFS.1112.WHST.3.9

Using Your Notes

3. **Summarizing** Review the notes that you completed during the lesson. Then write a paragraph summarizing the effects of the Immigration Act of 1965. LAFS.1112.WHST.3.9, SS.912.A.7.16

Answering the Guiding Questions

4. **Evaluating** How have important immigration laws affected legal and illegal immigration to the United States? LAFS.1112.WHST.3.9, SS.912.A.7.16

5. **Describing** How has the federal government addressed immigration reform in the twenty-first century? LAFS.1112.WHST.3.9, SS.912.A.7.12, SS.912.A.7.16

Writing Activity

6. **ARGUMENT** After reading about the problem of illegal immigration, write a letter to your representative in Congress explaining what you feel he or she should do about the problem. LAFS.1112.WHST.1.1, LAFS.1112.WHST.4.10

The New Immigrants

In the decades since the Immigration Act of 1965 was enacted, the number of immigrants in the United States has risen dramatically. By 2010, immigrants comprised more than 12 percent of the population. The largest group of these new immigrants came from Latin America and Asia. Immigration has become a topic of political debate. Should the United States make it easier to immigrate legally? Should the United States decrease the number of persons allowed to immigrate? How should unauthorized immigrants be treated?

VOCABULARY

buzzword
a trendy or popular word or phrase

illegals
foreign people living in a country without having official permission to live there

mesa
a flat hill or plateau with steep sides

maneuverability
moves around objects easily

smuggled
to take or bring in secretly

upheaval
a time of violent disorder or change

ORAL INTERVIEW

On our third attempt, my wife, children, and I escaped by boat from Vietnam and arrived in Hong Kong, where we remained for three months. Then my brother, who came to America in 1975, sponsored us, and we arrived in America in 1978. . . .

Neither I nor anyone in our family spoke any English before our arrival in America. I realized that I must study to communicate. . . . For nine months we lived in one town, where my children went to school. My wife and I also attended school to learn English. . . .

[W]e still have the need to return to Vietnam one day. This is our dream. In Vietnam, before the Communists came, we had a sentimental life, more [mentally] comfortable and cozy, more joyful. . . .

Here in America, we have all the material comforts, very good. But . . . In Vietnam . . . when we were out from the home, we laughed, we jumped. And we had many relatives and friends to come to see us at home. Here in America, I only know what goes on in my home; my neighbor knows only what goes on in his home. We have a saying, 'One knows only one's home.' In America, when we go to work, we go in our cars. When we return, we leave our cars and enter our homes [and do not meet neighbors]. . . . That's why we do not have the kind of being at ease that we knew in Vietnam.

Everything is very smooth for us in America, and we have quickly adapted to our new life here. . . . This is our fourth home. When we left our previous place, our neighbors cried, for they liked us very much. We used to visit one another and exchange gifts at Christmas. When we came to this place, two or three of our neighbors came to see us. Since that day, they like us. Thanks to God, I have that thing, that kind of nature.

—Vietnamese immigrant

ORAL INTERVIEW

The **buzzword** is diversity. It's on TV, politics, and this school [university], but then people like me are seen as foreigners and worst, **illegals**. The logic is if you look Mexican you are an immigrant, don't speak English and are illegal. I get tired of saying that's not me, oh well, except for the Mexican part. I don't look at an Anglo with an Italian name and say, 'Hey, do you speak Italian and when did you come to the United States?'

—Diana, second-generation Mexican American

TEXT: (l) Excerpts from HEARTS OF SORROW: VIETNAMESE-AMERICAN LIVES by James M. Freeman. Copyright © 1993 by the Board of Trustees of the Leland Stanford Jr. University. With the permission of Stanford University Press, www.sup.org.. (r) Narratives of Mexican American Women: Emergent Identitites of the Second Generation by Alma M. Garcia, published by AltaMira Press. © 2004 by AltaMira Press. Used with Permission.

Usually we catch young men, who are looking for work to support their families back in Mexico. But more and more we are seeing entire families. They start coming around 7:30 P.M. over the **mesa** near Cristo Rey Mountain. A steady stream of people all night. We use our night vision "infrared" equipment to spot a lot of **illegals** who would otherwise go unnoticed.

Sometimes border patrolmen ride horseback to patrol these hills. It's an interesting contrast—high-tech infrared machines directing cowboys on horseback. Other times we patrol in small trucks, which provide **maneuverability.** Before we begin using night-vision equipment, aliens had an easier time coming through this area without getting caught. Now we can sit on top of a hill, spot undocumented aliens, then radio for patrol vehicles to come apprehend the groups or individuals after they enter into Texas or New Mexico.

This time of year, in late winter, the aliens try to find work on farms in the Upper Rio Grande Valley. This is the time when farm laborers start pulling weeds and preparing the ground for planting. Between New Year and June . . . many of the aliens we apprehend are usually agricultural workers or people heading for cities further north, like Denver or Chicago.

Perhaps our greatest concern is the trafficking of drugs tied to the smuggling of illegal aliens. Smuggling of all sorts has become big business in the border regions. . . .

We catch illegal immigrants who come from as many as eighty-five countries around the world. Even people from Eastern Europe, who are **smuggled** in for large fees through South America and Mexico City.

It's a pretty lonesome feeling out here at night, alone or with a partner. We do get the feeling that we're outnumbered. . . . I've jumped into a boxcar or a freight-train gondola, turned on my flashlight, and seen twenty-five or thirty aliens. What can I do? Surround them? I can only tell them to get off the train. If they want to fight, I'm in trouble. That does happen from time to time but, fortunately, not very often. Most of the freight-yarders are from farther down south in Mexico. They're real docile. There have been times I've jumped off a moving train while chasing people, stepped in a hole, and fallen face down. The guy I was chasing stopped and came back to help me. He said, 'Gee, did you hurt yourself? I'm sorry.'

. . . The great majority of them are decent people coming here to look for work. Their families' economics conditions are pretty bad in Mexico. You have to sympathize with them to a point. But if you open the border wide up, you're going to invite political and social **upheaval.** Our job is to prevent illegal entry to our country, but we know that they're going to keep coming as long as our grass is greener. And we also know that we can't catch them all."

—Michael Teague, U.S. Border Patrol

DBQ Analyzing Historical Documents

1. **Answering Historical Questions** Based on the information provided in these excerpts, why are the new immigrants coming to the United States?

2. **Evaluating Validity** What are the contradictions in the Vietnamese immigrant's story? How would you explain them?

3. **Making Inferences** By looking at her use of language, how might you infer that Diana is second-generation?

4. **Acquiring Information** According to Michael Teague, what is the greatest concern for the border patrol concerning illegal activity?

5. **Evaluating Frames of Reference** How would you evaluate Michael Teague's perspective on immigration? How does his frame of reference affect his reliability as a source?

SKILLBUILDER

LAFS.1112.WHST.3.7, MAFS.K12.MP.1.1, MAFS.K12.MP.5.1, MAFS.K12.MP.6.1, SS.912.G.2.1, SS.912.G.4.2, SS.912.G.4.3, SS.912.G.4.7

Using a Database

Why Learn This Skill?

Do you have a large collection of MP3 music files or a collection of digital photos? Do you have a list of email addresses, phone numbers, or SMS contacts on your phone or computer? If so, you have created a database. In the world today, there are literally millions of databases and if you want to be successful, you will almost certainly need to know how to use a database.

Learning the Skill

A database is simply information that has been collected and arranged so that it is easy to find information. A database can hold any kind of information—photos, maps, text, data, music, etc. A database is not the same thing as the Internet. The information in a database is usually more reliable and better organized because it is "curated." Someone reviewed the data to make sure it was accurate and appropriate.

A database can be created entirely on paper. An old printed phone book is a database. But the term is generally used to refer to information stored on a computer. Programmers create software called database management systems (DBMS) that let people store, organize, search, and retrieve data. Modern database software allows users to display the data visually. Instead of just presenting lists of facts and numbers, the software takes the information you want from the database and presents it as a graph, or chart, or table, or even sets it as a layer over top of a map so you can see the relationship between the data and geographical locations. Database software also allows users to easily add, delete, change, or update information.

When searching a database, it helps to understand how a database is structured. A database is made up of records. A record represents one item of data, such as a photo, or a song, or an article, etc. Each record has standard fields of information. For example, there is usually a title field, a subject field, and a field with a date, and usually there are many other fields as well. Think of a database as a giant table of information made up of columns and rows. The words used to describe each item in the cells of the table are the fields. The words put into fields and the words used to label the columns and rows are called metadata. Metadata is what the computer searches when you ask it to find information in a database.

Follow these steps to use a database:

1. Determine what information you want to access. Be as specific as possible.
2. Databases typically have a number of fields where you can select words or categories for a specific search. Think about what you already know about the information. Use that knowledge to decide what terms you want in the fields for your search.
3. If there is not a field that fits with what you want to find, you often can use a keyword search. This is similar to using a search engine on the Internet. Keyword searching allows you to combine terms and concepts to find exactly what you are looking for. Most databases let you use Boolean operators. Boolean operators are connecting words that give commands to the computer. Boolean operators are the words "AND" "OR" and "NOT." They let you combine search words and shape your search more effectively.
4. Create a search string with keywords using Boolean operators that matches what you are trying to find.
5. Review the records or information retrieved from the database to determine if it is what you wanted. If not, try a new search.

Practicing this Skill

In recent years, databases have become an extremely popular way to display geographic information. The databases take the geographic information requested and draw it on a map so that it is easy to visualize. These kind of databases can be used to see geographic distributions and geographic patterns. A **geographic distribution** shows where things are located and how much is located in each area. A **geographic pattern** shows how things change geographically over time or over distance.

The United States Census Bureau now has online many database systems for looking up geographic information. Go to www.census.gov. Locate the Census Data Mapper and launch it. Select "Population and Race" for the data theme field, "Percent Hispanic" for the data table field, and 5 classes. Have the database make your map, then answer the following questions:

1. **Analyzing Geographic Distributions** What states have the highest percentage of Hispanics?

2. **Analyzing Geographic Patterns** What pattern do you see in how Hispanic Americans are distributed in the United States?

3. **Posing Questions about Geographic Distributions** Based on the areas where Hispanic populations are highest, what three countries do you think might be the source for most Hispanic immigrants? What questions do you need to ask about the geographic distribution to be able to know for sure where most Hispanic immigrants originated?

4. **Posing Questions about Geographic Patterns** Now change the data table field to "Percent Asian." How is the geographic pattern of Asian Americans similar to Hispanic Americans? How is it different? What questions do you need to ask to understand why the Asian pattern is different from the Hispanic pattern?

Applying the Skill

Now change the fields on the Data Mapper. Select Age and Sex for a data theme and median age for a data table. Keep the setting at 5 classes. Make your map, then answer the following questions:

1. What parts of the country have the oldest average age? Which parts have the youngest average age? Write down some possible reasons for the distribution and pattern. Write down the questions you need answered to know if your reasons are correct.

John Flournoy/McGraw-Hill Education

LESSON 3

Technology and Globalization

ESSENTIAL QUESTIONS

• How have improvements in science and technology helped change society?
• How have immigration, technology, and global trade changed the world?

READING HELPDESK

Academic Vocabulary

• cited
• awareness

Content Vocabulary

• telecommute
• euro
• global warming

TAKING NOTES

Key Ideas and Details

Organizing As you read the lesson, complete the graphic organizer below to show ways new technology and trade brought the world closer together during the 1990s. LAFS.1112.RH.3.7

Globalism

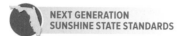

NEXT GENERATION SUNSHINE STATE STANDARDS

LAFS.1112.RH.2.4: Determine the meaning of words and phrases as they are used in a text, including analyzing how an author uses and refines the meaning of a key term over the course of a text (e.g., how Madison defines faction in Federalist No. 10).

LAFS.1112.RH.3.7: Integrate and evaluate multiple sources of information presented in diverse formats and media (e.g., visually, quantitatively, as well as in words) in order to address a question or solve a problem.

LAFS.1112.WHST.3.9: Draw evidence from informational texts to support analysis, reflection, and research.

Continued on page 606

IT MATTERS BECAUSE

Since the 1980s, computer technology has advanced greatly, with the creation of home computers and the expansion of the Internet. Trade barriers have fallen, and the environment has become a global concern.

The Computer Changes Society

GUIDING QUESTION *How did the computer revolution change the workplace?*

The first electronic digital computer began operation in 1946 and was the size of a small house. In 1959, Robert Noyce designed the first integrated circuit—a whole electronic circuit on a single silicon chip. In 1968, Noyce's company, Intel, put several integrated circuits on a single chip. This made circuits much smaller and easy to manufacture. By the late 1960s, manufacturers were making microprocessors, or single chips with many integrated circuits containing both memory and computing functions. These microprocessors made computers even smaller and faster.

Using microprocessor technology, Steve Jobs and Stephen Wozniak set out to build a small computer suitable for personal use. They founded Apple Computer in 1976. The following year they launched the Apple II, the first practical and affordable home computer. In 1981, International Business Machines (IBM) introduced the "Personal Computer," or PC. In 1984, Apple put out the Macintosh, which used on-screen icons that users could manipulate with a mouse.

As Jobs and Wozniak were creating Apple, Bill Gates cofounded Microsoft with Paul Allen. In 1980, IBM hired Microsoft to make an operating system for its new PC. The system was called MS-DOS. Microsoft came out with the "Windows" operating system in 1985. Computers became essential tools in almost all businesses. By the late 1990s, many workers were able to **telecommute,** or work from home via computer.

Telecommunications also underwent a revolution. In 1996, Congress passed a law allowing phone companies to compete with one another and to send television signals. It also allowed cable companies to offer telephone service. Soon wireless digital technology made it possible to make small, inexpensive satellite dishes for home use. Cell phones, invented in the 1940s, became popular as wireless digital technology made phones smaller and service cheaper. As this technology became more advanced, companies developed interconnectable digital music players, cameras, radios, televisions, and music and video recorders.

✓ READING PROGRESS CHECK

Describing What advantage did microprocessors give to computers?

The Rise of the Internet

GUIDING QUESTION *How have advances in telecommunications and the rise of the Internet affected the U.S. standard of living?*

The Internet began as a system of networked computers of a U.S. Defense Department agency that linked to a system of networked supercomputers of the National Science Foundation. Similar networks grew across the world, and this communications system became known as the Internet. As personal computer ownership rose, individuals—rather than just government agencies—began connecting to the Internet. By 2007, more than 1 billion people around the world were regularly using the Internet.

Birth of the World Wide Web

In 1990, researchers in Switzerland developed a new way to present information on Internet-linked computers. Known as the World Wide Web, this system used hypertext, or "links," and was accessed with Web browser software. Users could post information on Web pages and use links to move between sites.

Enthusiasm for the World Wide Web spawned a "dot-com" economy. The stock of Internet-related companies helped fuel the prosperity of the 1990s. It fell dramatically in 2000 when many unprofitable online companies failed. A few "dot-com" companies were very successful. This new economy also required American workers to acquire new skills. This retraining increased productivity as well as the nation's GDP. Driven by the information technology industry, the GDP rose more than 20 percent during the mid- to late 1990s.

The Internet Changes Society

For many people, the World Wide Web builds a sense of community. People with common interests visit the same Web sites to post comments and interact with one another. They share stories and photos about themselves on blogs—short for Web logs. "People read and publish blogs because they recognize that there is a way to put themselves into this virtual world and interact within it. With every new sign-up . . . our world gets a little smaller—and the web gets more character," explained Internet entrepreneur Biz Stone.

✓ READING PROGRESS CHECK

Analyzing How has digital technology affected the U.S. economy?

The New Global Economy

GUIDING QUESTION *How did NAFTA and other regional trading blocs affect the global economy?*

In the 1990s, economies of individual nations were becoming more interdependent as new technology helped link the world together economically and culturally. Also, many world leaders were convinced that free trade and the global exchange of goods contributed to prosperity and economic growth. This idea that the world is becoming increasingly interconnected is called globalism, and the process is globalization.

telecommute to work at home by means of an electronic linkup with a central office

Florida
CONNECTION

The Global Citrus Industry

Orange juice may not just be for breakfast anymore, but it seems like the world cannot get enough of one of Florida's signature crops. The state produces more oranges than any place else in the world, save Brazil. The entire citrus industry generates almost $10 billion for Florida every year.
SS.912.A.7.17

NEXT GENERATION SUNSHINE STATE STANDARDS

Continued from page 606

LAFS.1112.WHST.4.10: Write routinely over extended time frames (time for reflection and revision) and shorter time frames (a single sitting or a day or two) for a range of discipline-specific tasks, purposes, and audiences.

SS.912.A.1.2: Utilize a variety of primary and secondary sources to identify author, historical significance, audience, and authenticity to understand a historical period.

SS.912.A.1.4: Analyze how images, symbols, objects, cartoons, graphs, charts, maps, and artwork may be used to interpret the significance of time periods and events from the past.

SS.912.A.7.12: Analyze political, economic, and social concerns that emerged at the end of the 20th century and into the 21st century.

SS.912.A.7.14: Review the role of the United States as a participant in the global economy (trade agreements, international competition, impact on American labor, environmental concerns).

SS.912.A.7.17: Examine key events and key people in Florida history as they relate to United States history.

SS.912.G.2.5: Use geographic terms and tools to analyze case studies of debates over how human actions modify a selected region.

SS.912.H.3.1: Analyze the effects of transportation, trade, communication, science, and technology on the preservation and diffusion of culture.

SS.912.H.3.2: Identify social, moral, ethical, religious, and legal issues arising from technological and scientific developments, and examine their influence on works of arts within a culture.

Selling American-made goods abroad had long been important to U.S. prosperity. American businesses make money selling goods abroad, and consumers benefit by having the option to buy cheaper imported goods. Opponents, however, argued that global trade could cost American workers jobs. The debate became an important part of American politics.

Regional Blocs

Regional trade pacts, like the North American Free Trade Agreement (NAFTA), increase international trade. Approved by Congress in 1993, NAFTA linked Canada, the United States, and Mexico in a free-trade zone. Many Americans feared that NAFTA would cause industrial jobs to move to Mexico, where labor costs were lower. Although some jobs were lost, the U.S. unemployment rate fell as wages rose. Many American businesses upgraded their technology, and workers shifted to more skilled jobs or to the service industry.

In 1993, the European Union (EU) was created to promote economic and political cooperation among many European nations. It created a common bank, encouraged free trade, and created a common currency called the **euro.** The Asia-Pacific Economic Cooperation (APEC) came together in 1989 to promote economic cooperation and lower trade barriers. Major political differences, however, kept its members from acting together.

The World Trade Organization

In 1995, the World Trade Organization (WTO) formed to represent some 120 nations in efforts to negotiate international trade agreements and trade disputes. Supporters of the WTO **cited** benefits for American consumers, including cheaper imports, new markets, and copyright protection. Opponents argued that the United States would have to accept the WTO's rulings in trade disputes even if they hurt the American economy.

euro the basic currency shared by the countries of the European Union since 1999

cite to point out as an example in an argument or debate

GEOGRAPHY CONNECTION

Global trading blocs have formed to increase international trade.

1. **THE WORLD IN SPATIAL TERMS** *What large countries make up the Asia-Pacific Economic Cooperation?* SS.912.A.1.4, SS.912.A.7.14

2. **HUMAN SYSTEMS** *Why might it be beneficial for countries within a region to join in a free-trade agreement?* SS.912.A.1.4, SS.912.A.7.14

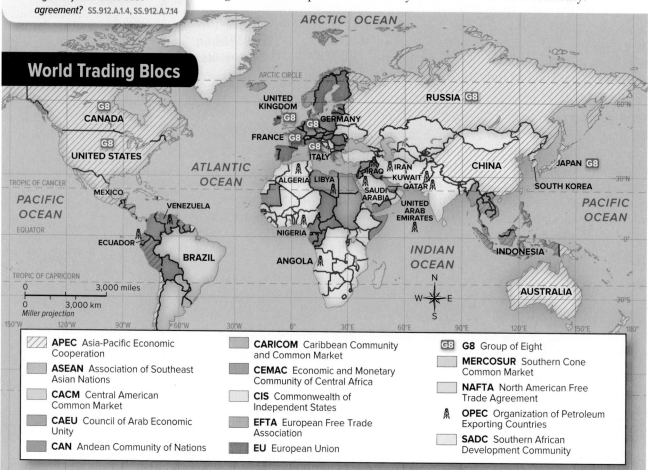

World Trading Blocs

APEC Asia-Pacific Economic Cooperation	**CARICOM** Caribbean Community and Common Market	**G8** Group of Eight
ASEAN Association of Southeast Asian Nations	**CEMAC** Economic and Monetary Community of Central Africa	**MERCOSUR** Southern Cone Common Market
CACM Central American Common Market	**CIS** Commonwealth of Independent States	**NAFTA** North American Free Trade Agreement
CAEU Council of Arab Economic Unity	**EFTA** European Free Trade Association	**OPEC** Organization of Petroleum Exporting Countries
CAN Andean Community of Nations	**EU** European Union	**SADC** Southern African Development Community

Trade With China

China presented a huge potential market for American goods, but some were wary of trading with China due to its poor record on human rights. President Clinton urged Congress to grant China permanent normal trade relation status to bring it into the world community. Although many groups objected, Congress passed the bill in late 2000.

✓ **READING PROGRESS CHECK**

Identifying What trade agreements and organizations promoted globalization?

Global Environmentalism

GUIDING QUESTION *How have the United States and other nations responded to global environmental concerns?*

The rise of a global economy also increased **awareness** of environmental issues. Environmentalists began thinking of the environment as a global system and addressing issues they believed were of global concern. In the 1980s, scientists discovered that chlorofluorocarbons (CFCs) were affecting the layer of ozone in Earth's atmosphere. Ozone blocks many of the sun's ultraviolet rays. At that time, CFCs were widely used in air conditioners and refrigerators. In that same decade, scientists documented a large hole in the ozone layer over Antarctica. In 1987, the United States and many other nations agreed to phase out CFCs and other chemicals that might be weakening the ozone layer.

During this time, another environmental issue emerged when some scientists warned that **global warming** could lead to more droughts and other forms of extreme weather. Many experts concluded that carbon dioxide emissions from factories and power plants caused global warming, but others disagreed. The issue became controversial because of the cost of controlling emissions. Industries would have to pay the cost of reducing emissions, and these costs would be passed on to consumers. Developing nations trying to industrialize would be hurt the most. Economic growth in wealthier nations would be hurt as well. Concern about global warming led the EU and many other nations to sign the Kyoto Protocol in 1997, promising to reduce emissions. President Clinton did not submit the protocol for ratification because most senators opposed it. President George W. Bush withdrew the United States from the agreement entirely, citing flaws in the treaty.

awareness the state of having or showing realization, perception, or knowledge

global warming an increase in average world temperatures over time

✓ **READING PROGRESS CHECK**

Describing What scientific data encouraged nations to protect the environment?

LESSON 3 REVIEW

Reviewing Vocabulary

1. *Defining* How can telecommuting be an easier option for some employees? LAFS.1112.RH.2.4, SS.912.H.3.2

2. *Explaining* Why are scientists concerned about the effects of global warming? LAFS.1112.RH.2.4, LAFS.1112.WHST.3.9

Using Your Notes

3. *Explaining* Review the notes you took during the lesson and explain why many people felt that the world came closer together during the 1990s. LAFS.1112.RH.3.7

Answering the Guiding Questions

4. *Analyzing* How did the computer revolution change the workplace? LAFS.1112.WHST.3.9, SS.912.A.7.12, SS.912.H.3.2

5. *Determining Cause and Effect* How have advances in telecommunications and the rise of the Internet affected the U.S. standard of living? LAFS.1112.WHST.3.9, SS.912.A.7.12, SS.912.H.3.2

6. *Making Connections* How did NAFTA and other regional trading blocs affect the global economy? LAFS.1112.WHST.3.9, SS.912.A.7.14

7. *Describing* How have the United States and other nations responded to global environmental concerns? LAFS.1112.WHST.3.9, SS.912.A.7.14, SS.912.G.2.5

Writing Activity

8. NARRATIVE Imagine what your life would be like without technological developments such as the Internet and the cell phone. Write a short narrative in which you describe how your typical day would be different without this type of technology. LAFS.1112.WHST.4.10, SS.912.H.3.2

STUDY GUIDE

THE CLINTON YEARS
LESSON 1

Clinton's Domestic Agenda
1. raising taxes on wealthiest and reducing spending
2. passage of Brady Bill

+

Republicans Gain Control
1. passage of the Contract with America
2. government shutdown

Cooperative Achievements
1. Welfare Reform Act
2. Health Insurance Portability Act

A NEW WAVE OF IMMIGRATION
LESSON 2

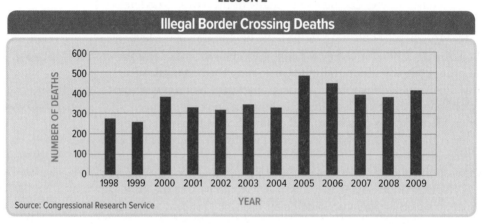

Illegal Border Crossing Deaths

Source: Congressional Research Service

TECHNOLOGY AND GLOBALIZATION
LESSON 3

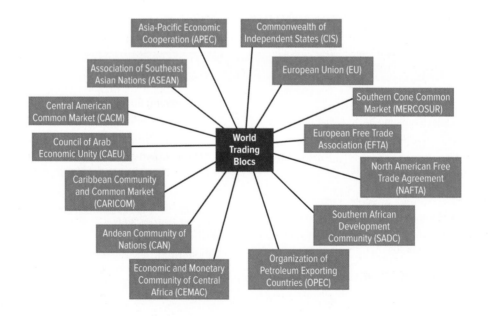

Asia-Pacific Economic Cooperation (APEC)

Commonwealth of Independent States (CIS)

Association of Southeast Asian Nations (ASEAN)

European Union (EU)

Central American Common Market (CACM)

Southern Cone Common Market (MERCOSUR)

Council of Arab Economic Unity (CAEU)

European Free Trade Association (EFTA)

World Trading Blocs

North American Free Trade Agreement (NAFTA)

Caribbean Community and Common Market (CARICOM)

Southern African Development Community (SADC)

Andean Community of Nations (CAN)

Economic and Monetary Community of Central Africa (CEMAC)

Organization of Petroleum Exporting Countries (OPEC)

Directions: On a separate sheet of paper, answer the questions below. Make sure you read carefully and answer all parts to the question.

Lesson Review

Lesson 1

1 **Summarizing** Summarize the legislation during Clinton's term that impacted families and communities. SS.912.A.7.12, SS.912.A.7.13

2 **Explaining** Why might the political situation in Clinton's second term be referred to as "divided government?" SS.912.A.7.12

3 **Interpreting Significance** What was the significance of the Brady Bill? SS.912.A.7.12

4 **Identifying Cause and Effect** How did the United States respond to the process of ethnic cleansing in the Balkan Crisis? SS.912.A.7.11

Lesson 2

5 **Summarizing** What were two key points of the Illegal Immigration Reform and Immigrant Responsibility Act of 1996? How do the measures of this act reflect changing views on the societal issue of illegal immigration since the Immigration Act of 1965? SS.912.A.7.16

6 **Analyzing** Why did many refugees from Europe come to the United States in the late 1940s and early 1950s? SS.912.A.7.16, SS.912.G.4.2, SS.912.G.4.3

7 **Explaining** Why was a grant of amnesty so important to the immigrant community? SS.912.A.7.16

Lesson 3

8 **Explaining** How have innovations in computer technology since the 1980s improved the standard of living in the United States? How have different technology companies continued to drive these innovations? SS.912.A.1.7

9 **Evaluating** How has the involvement of the United States in trade agreements and globalization affected the average American? SS.912.A.7.14

10 **Analyzing** In what way has the Internet shifted the way people participate in and think of communities? How has it affected the nation's economic development? SS.912.A.7.14

Exploring the Essential Questions

11 **Exploring Issues** Write a short report that could be published as a Web page. The report should explain the global impact of technology, immigration, or international trade. Underline four words that could be made into hypertext links. Include four footnotes to describe what the viewer would see by clicking on the hypertext. Trade your report with a classmate, and give each other feedback. LAFS.1112.WHST.2.4, LAFS.1112.WHST.2.5, LAFS.1112.WHST.2.6, LAFS.1112.WHST.4.10, SS.912.A.7.12, SS.912.A.7.16

Critical Thinking

12 **Evaluating** What were the contributions of Newt Gingrich to the Contract with America? Explain the social and political impact of this conservative pledge. SS.912.A.7.12

13 **Identifying Perspectives** How did the Immigration Act of 1965 reflect the issues and concerns of the time? SS.912.A.7.16

14 **Identifying Cause and Effect** What was the effect of an increase of unauthorized immigrants on efforts that both limited and supported immigrants? SS.912.A.7.16

15 **Researching** Research one social advocacy organization and one political advocacy organization of the 1990s. Include a description of the group, its leader, and its methods of gaining public support. LAFS.1112.WHST.3.7, SS.912.A.7.12

21st Century Skills

16 **Analyzing Geographic Distributions on a Database** Go to the U.S. Census Bureau online, locate the Thematic Map database, and then choose the Census Data Mapper link. Launch the database and select the "Population and Race" theme and "Percent Hispanic" for the data table field. Have the database make your map, and then answer the following questions: What areas of the country have the lowest distribution of Hispanics? What questions do you need to ask to be able to explain why Hispanics have not migrated to these regions? Make a prediction as to what you expect to learn. MAFS.912.S-IC.2, MAFS.K12.MP.1.1, MAFS.K12.MP.5.1, SS.912.A.7.16, SS.912.G.2.1, SS.912.G.4.3

Need Extra Help?

If You've Missed Question	1	2	3	4	5	6	7	8	9	10	11	12	13	14	15	16
Go to Lesson	1	1	1	1	2	2	2	3	3	3	1, 2, 3	1	2	2	1	2

17 *Analyzing Geographic Patterns on a Database* Go to the U.S. Census Bureau online, and locate the Census Data Mapper database. Launch the database and select "Age and Sex" and "Percent Male" for the data table field. Have the database make your map, and then answer the following questions: Are the number of men and women equally distributed in the United States? What pattern do you notice about the percentage of men? What questions do you need to ask to be able to explain the pattern? MAFS.912.S-IC.2, MAFS.912.S-ID.1, MAFS.K12.MP.1.1, MAFS.K12.MP.3.1, SS.912.G.2.1

18 *Creating a Thematic Map* Create a map that shows national borders of Yugoslavia prior to 1991, during the civil war in Bosnia and Herzegovina, and the region as it is today. Include a key that indicates information about the ethnic groups in that region. SS.912.G.1.2, SS.912.G.1.3, SS.912.G.2.1

19 *Research Skills* Use multiple sources to learn about how the Internet is both open internationally and restricted nationally. Make sure that you evaluate the sources you use before incorporating information from them. Then, present how Europe, Africa, Asia, and North and South America participate in the global exchange by means of the Internet and social networks. What restrictions exist, who is impacted by such restrictions, and what are the prospects for an even freer Internet? LAFS.1112.WHST.3.7, SS.912.A.1.2, SS.912.A.1.5, SS.912.A.7.12, SS.912.H.3.1

DBQ Analyzing Primary Sources

Use the quotation by Bill Clinton to answer the following question.

❝ . . . Even as people take pride in their national independence, we know we are becoming more and more interdependent. The movement of people, money, and ideas across borders, frankly, breeds suspicion among many good people in every country. They are worried about globalization because of its unsettling and unpredictable consequences.❞

—Bill Clinton in 2000

20 *Analyzing Primary Sources* What impact do agreements such as NAFTA have on the free enterprise system in the United States? What are the pros and cons of U.S. participation in free trade treaties? LAFS.1112.RH.3.7, LAFS.1112.RH.3.8, LAFS.1112.RH.4.10, SS.912.A.7.12

21 *Understanding Relationships Among Events* How was the onset of globalization a by-product of new technology and business innovations, and why might it have signaled the course for future international economic relationships? LAFS.1112.RH.3.7, LAFS.1112.RH.3.8, LAFS.1112.RH.4.10, SS.912.A.7.12

DBQ Analyzing Visuals

Use the graph to answer the following questions.

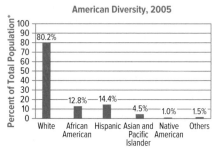

American Diversity, 2005

Percent of Total Population*

White 80.2%, African American 12.8%, Hispanic 14.4%, Asian and Pacific Islander 4.5%, Native American 1.0%, Others 1.5%

* Percentages add to more than 100 percent because Hispanics may be of any race.
Source: U.S. Census Bureau.

22 *Analyzing Visuals* Which group accounted for the smallest percentage of the total population in 2005? MAFS.912.S-ID.1, SS.912.A.7.16

23 *Making Predictions* How are increases in legal immigration changing demographic patterns in the United States? How will these changes impact the United States? MAFS.912.S-IC.2, SS.912.A.7.16, SS.912.G.2.1, SS.912.G.4.3

24 *Posing Questions* Make a chart that represents the data in the graph. Then use the Internet to research the geographic distribution of each group at any time during the 21st century. Record the information in your chart. Use the chart to write your own three-question quiz about the distribution patterns, and include the corresponding answers. LAFS.1112.WHST.3.7, MAFS.912.S-IC.2, MAFS.912.S-ID.1, MAFS.K12.MP.5.1, SS.912.A.7.16, SS.912.G.2.1, SS.912.G.4.3

Extended Response Question

25 *Informative/Explanatory* Television commentators often use this expression: "The world is getting smaller." Write an essay explaining how globalization, computer technology, and immigration have made the world seem like a "smaller" place. Use examples from the chapter to support your argument. LAFS.1112.WHST.2.4, LAFS.1112.WHST.3.9, SS.912.A.1.2, SS.912.H.3.1, SS.912.H.3.2

Need Extra Help?

If You've Missed Question	**17**	**18**	**19**	**20**	**21**	**22**	**23**	**24**	**25**
Go to Lesson	2	3	1	1	3	2	2	2	3

◄ The terrorist attacks of September 11, 2001 was a turning point in modern United States history. The goals of the George W. Bush administration had to quickly adjust and define new roles for the federal government in a time of global uncertainty.

FROM 2001 TO 2008

America's Challenges for a New Century

THE STORY MATTERS ...

As the United States entered the twenty-first century, a new collection of challenges emerged. Terrorists launched devastating attacks on September 11, 2001 that led to wars in Afghanistan and Iraq. President Bush's administration focused on maintaining the American people's safety at home and around the world. President Bush faced domestic problems such as Hurricane Katrina and the complicated foreign policy decisions caused by the fight against terrorism.

ESSENTIAL QUESTIONS

- How is American culture shaped by a set of common values and practices?
- How have disputes over ideas, values, and politics resulted in change?

Anthony Correia/Getty Images News/Getty Images

Place & Time: United States 2000–2009

The 2000 presidential election was one of the closest elections in the nation's history. Neither Al Gore or George W. Bush won a majority of the popular votes cast. Bush won across the South and throughout the Great Plains states. Gore won in the northeast, the Great Lakes states, and the west coast. The election turned on the outcome of many contested votes in the state of Florida. How to count confusing ballot data was the result of several court challenges and much debate. Several weeks after Election Day, the U.S. Supreme Court called a halt to further ballot counting and declared that the most recent official data awarded Florida and the election to George W. Bush.

Step Into the Place

Read the quote and look at the information presented on the map.

 Analyzing Historical Documents What is the main point that Florida Chief Justice Wells and Supreme Court Justice Stevens are discussing in their legal opinions?

PRIMARY SOURCE

❝In [the four days remaining], all questionable ballots must be reviewed by the judicial officer appointed to discern the intent of the voter in a process open to the public. Fairness dictates that a provision be made for either party to object to how a particular ballot is counted. Additionally, this short time period must allow for judicial review. I respectfully submit this cannot be completed [in the provided time], creating the very real possibility of disenfranchising those nearly six million voters who are able to correctly cast their ballots on election day.❞

—Florida Supreme Court Chief Justice Charles Wells,
in *Gore* v. *Harris* (2000)

PRIMARY SOURCE

❝In the interest of finality . . . the majority effectively orders the disenfranchisement of an unknown number of voters whose ballots reveal their intent—and are therefore legal votes under state law—but were for some reason rejected by ballot-counting machines.❞

—U.S. Supreme Court Justice John Paul Stevens,
in *Bush* v. *Gore* (2000)

PHOTO: (t) Getty Images/Staff/Getty Images; (c)Mark Wilson/Staff/Getty Images; (c)The White House Historical Association and Decatur House, a National Trust Site

Step Into the Time

PREDICTING CONSEQUENCES

Choose an event from the time line and explain how that event might contribute to America's challenges.

November 2000 A close vote in Florida causes a contested presidential election

G. W. Bush 2001–2009

September 11, 2001 Terrorists attack the World Trade Center, the Pentagon, and cause a plane crash in Pennsylvania

U.S. PRESIDENTS

UNITED STATES 2000

WORLD 2002

December 2001 Terrorists attack the Indian Parliament

NEXT GENERATION SUNSHINE STATE STANDARDS
Students will understand the following benchmarks from the Florida NGSSS

LAFS.1112.RH.3.7: Integrate and evaluate multiple sources of information presented in diverse formats and media (e.g., visually, quantitatively, as well as in words) in order to address a question or solve a problem.

LAFS.1112.RH.3.9: Integrate information from diverse sources, both primary and secondary, into a coherent understanding of an idea or event, noting discrepancies among sources.

SS.912.A.1.2: Utilize a variety of primary and secondary sources to identify author, historical significance, audience, and authenticity to understand a historical period.

SS.912.A.1.3: Utilize timelines to identify the time sequence of historical data.

SS.912.A.1.4: Analyze how images, symbols, objects, cartoons, graphs, charts, maps, and artwork may be used to interpret the significance of time periods and events from the past.

SS.912.A.7.17: Examine key events and key people in Florida history as they relate to United States history.

Presidential Election, 2000

Legend:
- Bush (Republican)
- Gore (Democrat)
- Nader (Green)
- Other

* One Gore elector from Washington, D.C., abstained from casting an electoral vote.

Lambert Azimuthal Equal-Area projection

Strength of Victory in Florida
Strong Democrat Win ← Neutral → Strong Republican Win

- **B** Bush (Republican) won the county
- **G** Gore (Democrat) won the county

ELECTORAL VOTE
TOTAL: 538
- 49.4% 266
- 50.4% 271

POPULAR VOTE
TOTAL: 105,396,466
- 2.74% 2,882,738
- 1.01% 1,066,237
- 47.87% 50,455,156
- 48.38% 50,992,335

Timeline:

March 2003 The United States invades Iraq

August 2005 Hurricane Katrina devastates parts of Louisiana and Mississippi, causing flooding of New Orleans

October 2008 Emergency Economic Stabilization Act passed in response to mortgage crisis

November 2008 Barack Obama elected as first African American president

2004 — **2006** — **2008**

May 2003 Terrorist bombings in Casablanca, Morocco

March 2004 Terrorists bomb trains in Spain

December 2004 Tsunami in Indian Ocean devastates Indonesia and surrounding regions

July 2005 Terrorists bomb London subway system

July 2006 Israel invades Lebanon in response to Hezbollah attack

November 2008 Terrorists attack downtown Mumbai, India

LESSON 1

Bush's Global Challenges

* How is American culture shaped by a set of common values and practices?
* How have disputes over ideas, values, and politics resulted in change?

READING HELPDESK

Academic Vocabulary

* resolve
* interpretation
* obtain

Content Vocabulary

* chad
* terrorism
* state-sponsored terrorism
* anthrax

TAKING NOTES

Key Ideas and Details

Organizing Use the following graphic organizer to show causes of terrorism.
LAFS.1112.RH.3.9

Causes of Terrorism

NEXT GENERATION SUNSHINE STATE STANDARDS

LAFS.1112.RH.1.2: Determine the central ideas or information of a primary or secondary source; provide an accurate summary that makes clear the relationships among the key details and ideas.

LAFS.1112.RH.2.4: Determine the meaning of words and phrases as they are used in a text, including analyzing how an author uses and refines the meaning of a key term over the course of a text (e.g., how Madison defines faction in Federalist No. 10).

LAFS.1112.RH.3.7: Integrate and evaluate multiple sources of information presented in diverse formats and media (e.g., visually, quantitatively, as well as in words) in order to address a question or solve a problem.

Continued on page 623

IT MATTERS BECAUSE

After a disputed outcome in the election of 2000, George W. Bush became president. On September 11, 2001, terrorists attacked the United States. In response, Bush and Congress launched a war on terrorism.

The Election of 2000

GUIDING QUESTION *Why was the presidential election of 2000 controversial?*

In the election of 2000, the division between liberals and conservatives widened. The election itself was one of the closest in American history.

The Candidates Campaign

The Democrats nominated Vice President Al Gore for president. For his running mate, Gore chose Senator Joseph Lieberman, the first Jewish American to run for vice president on a major party ticket. The Republican candidate was Texas governor George W. Bush, son of former president George H. W. Bush. For his vice-presidential candidate, Bush chose Dick Cheney, who had served as George H. W. Bush's secretary of defense. Well-known consumer advocate Ralph Nader also entered the race on the Green Party ticket.

The election campaign revolved around the question of what to do with surplus tax revenues. Both Bush and Gore agreed that Social Security needed reform, but they disagreed on the details. Both promised to cut taxes, to improve public education, and to support plans to help senior citizens pay for prescription drugs.

A Close Vote

No candidate won a majority in the 2000 election, but Gore received the most votes, with 48.4 percent of the popular vote compared to 47.9 percent for Bush. To win the presidency, however, candidates must win a majority of votes in the Electoral College.

The election came down to the results in Florida—both men needed its 25 electoral votes to win. The counts in Florida were so close that state law required a recount of the ballots using vote-counting machines. There were, however, thousands of ballots the machines could not read. Gore then asked for a recount of ballots in several strongly Democratic counties. After the machine recount showed Bush still ahead, a battle began over the manual recounts.

Most Florida ballots required voters to cast a vote by punching a small piece of cardboard out of the ballot beside the candidate's name. This small piece is called a **chad.** Vote counters had to determine how to count a ballot if the chad was still partially attached. On some, the chad was still in place, and the voter had left only a dimple on the ballot's surface. Vote counters thus had to determine what the voter intended—and different counties used different standards.

Under state law, Florida officials had to certify the results by a certain date. When it became clear that not all of the recounts could be finished in time, Gore went to court to challenge the deadline. The Florida Supreme Court agreed to set a new deadline. At Bush's request, the U.S. Supreme Court intervened to decide whether the Florida Supreme Court had acted constitutionally. The hand recounts continued, but not all of the counties were able to meet the new deadline. On November 26, Florida officials certified Bush the winner by 537 votes.

NEXT GENERATION SUNSHINE STATE STANDARDS

Continued from page 622

LAFS.1112.WHST.1.1: Write arguments focused on discipline-specific content.

LAFS.1112.WHST.3.9: Draw evidence from informational texts to support analysis, reflection, and research.

LAFS.1112.WHST.4.10: Write routinely over extended time frames (time for reflection and revision) and shorter time frames (a single sitting or a day or two) for a range of discipline-specific tasks, purposes, and audiences.

SS.912.A.1.2: Utilize a variety of primary and secondary sources to identify author, historical significance, audience, and authenticity to understand a historical period.

Continued on page 624

chad a small piece of cardboard produced by punching a data card

ANALYZING SUPREME COURT CASES

BUSH v. GORE, 2000

Background of the Case

The outcome of the 2000 presidential election hinged on Florida's 25 electoral votes. When the polls closed on November 7, the vote in Florida was so close that it triggered an automatic recount. Bush led by only 1,784 out of more than 6 million votes cast. When ballots were again run through tabulation machines, Bush's lead shrank to fewer than 200 votes. Gore requested hand recounts of ballots in four predominantly Democratic counties where thousands of punch-card ballots had recorded no vote for president. Bush asked the U.S. District Court to block any further recounts.

While the manual recount was still in progress, the Florida secretary of state certified Bush as the winner by 537 votes. Gore appealed this action, and the Florida Supreme Court authorized manual recounts of disputed ballots to begin immediately. Bush appealed the ruling to the U.S. Supreme Court, which ordered the recount to stop.

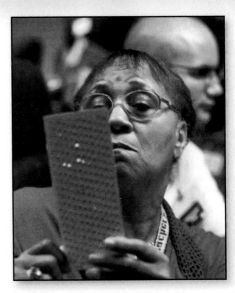

An election worker inspects a ballot during the Florida recount.

How the Court Ruled

The Florida Supreme Court ordered any recounts to use a general standard set forth in Florida law to discern the "clear intent of the voter." In a 7-2 ruling, the U.S. Supreme Court declared that because different vote counters used different standards, the recount did not treat all voters equally.

In addition, both federal law and the Constitution require the electoral votes for president to be cast on a certain day. If Florida missed that deadline, its electoral votes would not count. The Court ruled 5-4 that there was not enough time left to conduct a manual recount that would pass constitutional standards.

DBQ Analyzing Historical Documents

❶ *Identifying Central Ideas* If it is the electoral votes that count in the election of the president, why is it important to count the popular vote?
SS.912.A.1.6, SS.912.A.7.12

❷ *Drawing Conclusions* What made the decision in *Bush* v. *Gore* controversial? LAFS.1112.WHST.3.9, SS.912.A.7.12

Robert King/Getty Images News/Getty Images

NEXT GENERATION SUNSHINE STATE STANDARDS

Continued from page 623

SS.912.A.1.4: Analyze how images, symbols, objects, cartoons, graphs, charts, maps, and artwork may be used to interpret the significance of time periods and events from the past.

SS.912.A.1.6: Use case studies to explore social, political, legal, and economic relationships in history.

SS.912.A.7.11: Analyze the foreign policy of the United States as it relates to Africa, Asia, the Caribbean, Latin America, and the Middle East.

SS.912.A.7.12: Analyze political, economic, and social concerns that emerged at the end of the 20th century and into the 21st century.

SS.912.A.7.15: Analyze the effects of foreign and domestic terrorism on the American people.

SS.912.A.7.17: Examine key events and key people in Florida history as they relate to United States history.

resolve fixity of purpose, or resoluteness

terrorism the use of violence by nongovernmental groups against civilians to achieve a political goal by instilling fear and frightening governments into changing policies

interpretation the act or process of explaining or telling the meaning of

President George W. Bush visits the site of the collapsed World Trade Center, in the days after September 11, 2001.

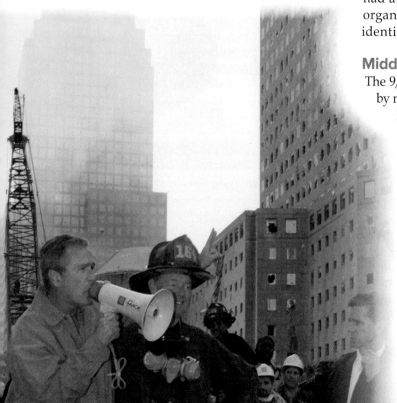

Bush v. Gore

Gore's lawyers returned to court, arguing that thousands of ballots remained uncounted. The Florida Supreme Court ordered all state counties to begin a hand recount of ballots rejected by the machines. As counting began, the U.S. Supreme Court ordered the recount to stop until it had issued its ruling. On December 12 in *Bush v. Gore*, the U.S. Supreme Court ruled 7–2 that because identical ballots might be treated differently by different vote counters, the recount violated the U.S. Constitution's equal protection clause. Bush remained the certified winner in Florida.

✓ **READING PROGRESS CHECK**

Expressing Do you think that Gore winning the popular vote but not the electoral vote is controversial? Why?

September 11, 2001

GUIDING QUESTION *What contributed to the rise in terrorist groups, and why did these groups resort to violent attacks?*

On September 11, 2001, two passenger jets slammed into the two towers of the World Trade Center in New York City. Soon afterward, a third plane crashed into the Pentagon in Washington, D.C. Within about two hours, the World Trade Center collapsed in a billow of dust and debris, killing nearly 3,000 people. The airplanes did not crash accidentally. Hijackers deliberately flew them into the buildings. Hijackers had also seized a fourth airplane. Passengers on that flight had learned of the earlier attacks. Four passengers decided to fight the hijackers, and the plane crashed in a field in Pennsylvania.

A National Emergency

The attacks shocked Americans. Citizens donated food, money, supplies, and their own time toward the recovery effort. They rallied together to show their unity and **resolve.** On September 14, President Bush declared a national emergency. Congress authorized the use of force to fight whoever had attacked the nation. Osama bin Laden and his organization, al-Qaeda (al KY•duh), were soon identified as the plotters behind the attacks.

Middle East Terrorism and the United States

The 9/11 attacks were acts of **terrorism,** the use of violence by nongovernmental groups to achieve a political goal. Most terrorist attacks on Americans since World War II have been carried out by Middle Eastern groups.

In the 1920s, the United States invested in Middle East oil. The ruling families in some kingdoms grew wealthy, but most other people remained poor. Many Muslims feared their traditional values were weakening as the oil industrialists also brought Western ideas into the region. New movements arose calling for a strict **interpretation** of the Quran—the Muslim holy book—and a return to traditional religious laws. Some militant supporters began using terrorism to achieve their goals.

Paul J. Richards/AFP/Getty Images

Major Terrorist Attacks 1993–Present

1. **1993** Bomb at the World Trade Center in New York City killed 6

13. **2011** Bombing at Coptic Christian church in Alexandria, Egypt, killed 32

9. **2003** Attacks against coalition troops and civilians in Iraq begin.

3. **1996** Bombing of Khobar Towers barracks in Dhahran, Saudi Arabia, killed 19 Americans

14. **2015** Over 128 are killed in a terrorist attack in Paris.

12. **2005** Bombs on the London subway killed 52

2015 A terrorist couple kill 14 coworkers at a Christmas party in San Bernardino, California

8. **2003** Attacks against coalition troops and civilians in Afghanistan begin.

10. **2004** Bombing of commuter trains in Madrid, Spain, killed 191

16. **2016** Suicide bombers in Brussels, Belgium kill over 30 and injure almost 300.

6. **2001** Hijacked airliners crashed into the World Trade Center, the Pentagon, and a field in Pennsylvania, killing nearly 3,000

11. **2004** Attack on the U.S. Consulate in Jedda, Saudi Arabia, killed 5

2. **1995** Bombs at a U.S.-Saudi facility in Riyadh killed 7 Americans.

4. **1998** Bombings at U.S. embassies in Kenya and Tanzania killed more than 200

5. **2000** Attack on the USS *Cole* killed 17 American sailors

7. **2002** Bombing in Bali, Indonesia, killed more than 200

NORTH AMERICA · SOUTH AMERICA · EUROPE · ASIA · AFRICA · AUSTRALIA · PACIFIC OCEAN · ATLANTIC OCEAN · INDIAN OCEAN

0 — 4,000 miles
0 — 4,000 km
Miller projection

GEOGRAPHY CONNECTION

Terrorism is a worldwide threat that usually occurs without any warning and harms innocent people.

1 **THE WORLD IN SPATIAL TERMS** *On what continents have attacks occurred?* SS.912.A.1.4

2 **HUMAN SYSTEMS** *What can you infer about terrorist networks by the many targets that have been attacked?* LAFS.1112.WHST.3.9, SS.912.A.1.4

The United States's support of Israel also angered many in the Middle East. In 1947, as a response to global outrage over the Holocaust, the UN proposed to divide the British Mandate of Palestine into an Arab state and a Jewish state. The Jews accepted the UN plan and established Israel in 1948. Arab states responded by attacking Israel. The territory that the UN had proposed as an Arab state came under the control of Israel, Jordan, and Egypt. In the 1950s, Palestinians began staging guerrilla raids and terrorist attacks against Israel. Since the United States gave aid to Israel, it became the target of Muslim hostility. In the 1970s, several Middle Eastern nations realized they could fight Israel and the United States by providing terrorists with money, weapons, and training. This is called **state-sponsored terrorism.** The governments of Libya, Syria, Iraq, and Iran have all sponsored terrorists.

state-sponsored terrorism violent acts against civilians that are secretly supported by a government in order to attack other nations without going to war

The Rise of Al-Qaeda

In 1979, the Soviet Union invaded Afghanistan, and Muslims from across the world headed there to help fight the Soviets. Among them was Osama bin Laden. In 1988, bin Laden founded the organization called al-Qaeda or "the Base." This organization carried out attacks on U.S. embassies and other targets in the years leading up to the 9/11 attacks.

☑ **READING PROGRESS CHECK**

Determining Cause and Effect Why did Muslim hostility grow against the United States in the Middle East?

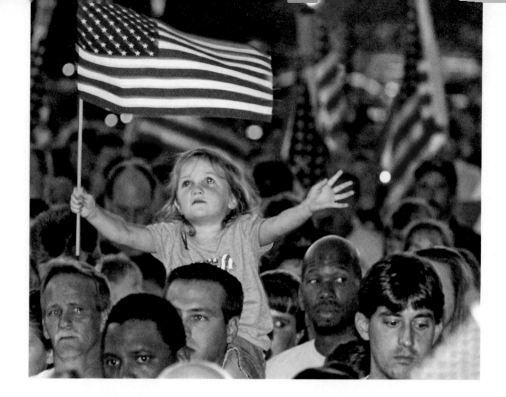

Three-year old Alana Milawski waves the flag at a candlelight vigil in Las Vegas on September 12, 2001. In the weeks following the 9/11 attacks, Americans all across the nation held prayer vigils, put up flags, donated blood, raised money, and collected food, blankets and supplies for victims of the attacks.

The War on Terrorism Begins

GUIDING QUESTION *What major actions marked the beginning of the United States's war on terrorism?*

On September 20, 2001, President Bush demanded that the Taliban regime in Afghanistan turn over bin Laden and his supporters and shut down all terrorist camps. The United States began building international support against terrorism and began deploying troops to the Middle East. The war would not end quickly, but it was a war the nation had to fight:

PRIMARY SOURCE

❝ Great harm has been done to us. We have suffered great loss. And in our grief and anger we have found our mission and our moment. . . . Our Nation—this generation—will lift a dark threat of violence from our people and our future. ❞

—President George W. Bush, *Address to Joint Session of Congress,* September 20, 2001

Homeland Security and the USA PATRIOT Act

One effective way to fight terrorist groups is to cut off their funding. On September 24, President Bush issued an executive order freezing the financial assets of individuals and groups suspected of terrorism. He asked other nations to help, and soon some 80 nations had issued orders freezing the assets of the organizations and individuals on the American list.

To protect against further attacks, Bush created the Office of Homeland Security and asked Congress to pass legislation to help law enforcement agencies locate terrorist suspects. Congress had to balance Fourth Amendment protections against unreasonable search and seizure with the need to increase security, but in October 2001, Bush signed into law the antiterrorist bill called the USA PATRIOT Act. The law made it easier to wiretap suspects, track Internet communications, and seize voice mail. Authorities were permitted to conduct secret searches and were allowed to **obtain** a nationwide search warrant usable in any jurisdiction. In June 2002, Bush asked Congress to combine the agencies responsible for public safety into a new cabinet department, the Department of Homeland Security. This agency worked to coordinate efforts to fight terrorism.

obtain to gain possession of

©Reuters/Corbis

Bioterrorism Strikes the United States On October 5, 2001, a new threat arose when a newspaper editor in Florida died from an anthrax infection. **Anthrax,** a type of bacteria, has been used to create biological weapons. Antibiotics can cure anthrax, but if left untreated, it can quickly become lethal. Anthrax was also found in offices in New York and Washington, D.C. It became clear that these anthrax attacks were being delivered via the postal service. As a result of these attacks, 5 people died and 17 were sickened.

The War in Afghanistan Begins On October 7, 2001, the United States began bombing al-Qaeda camps and Taliban military forces in Afghanistan. Addressing the nation, Bush explained that Islam and the Afghan people were not the enemy, and that the United States would send aid to refugees. He also declared that the war on terrorism would continue until victory was achieved.

An Economic Crisis

Even before the terrorist attack on September 11, the American economy had been weakening. The attacks triggered an economic crisis. Stock markets plunged and the Dow Jones Industrial Average suffered its biggest one week loss in history up to that point. Unemployment, which had already begun to rise, became even worse.

With the United States facing a new war and a great deal of uncertainty, President Bush knew he had to act quickly to prevent the mild recession that had already begun from turning into a serious economic downturn. In his address to the nation on September 20, he asked Americans for their "continued participation and confidence in the American economy" and he stressed that while "terrorists attacked a symbol of American prosperity; they did not touch its source."

Three months earlier, the president had convinced Congress to pass a major tax cut in order to help the economy. The Bush tax cuts reduced tax rates for all Americans and cut the capital gains tax. The economy remained weak throughout 2002, however, in part because of the uncertainty caused by the war on terror. Bush pushed Congress to pass a second tax cut in 2003 that accelerated the tax cuts passed in the first bill. By mid-2003, the economy was in full recovery and unemployment had begun to fall. Critics argued that cutting taxes while funding the war on terrorism helped turn the budget surpluses of the late 1990s into a deficit by the end of 2002. Supporters argued that the tax cuts prevented the recession from becoming much worse and causing even greater deficits.

☑ READING PROGRESS CHECK

Identifying What was the purpose of the Office of Homeland Security?

Although many people were sickened and some died from a bioterrorist anthrax attack, no suspects were ever arrested.

▶ **CRITICAL THINKING**
Making Inferences Why did law enforcement officials determine that the appearance of anthrax was a terrorist attack?
LAFS.1112.WHST.3.9, SS.912.A.7.15

anthrax a bacteria causing serious infection or death used to create biological weapons

Greg Mathieson/Mai/Time & Life Pictures/Getty Images

LESSON 1 REVIEW

Reviewing Vocabulary
1. *Stating* Why is anthrax a bioterrorism threat? LAFS.1112.RH.2.4

Using Your Notes
2. *Explaining* Review the notes that you took during this lesson and write a paragraph explaining why some groups in the Middle East disagree with U.S. foreign policy. LAFS.1112.RH.3.7

Answering the Guiding Questions
3. *Interpreting* Why was the presidential election of 2000 controversial? LAFS.1112.WHST.3.9, SS.912.A.7.12

4. *Listing* What contributed to the rise in terrorist groups, and why did these groups resort to violent attacks? LAFS.1112.WHST.3.9, SS.912.A.7.15
5. *Identifying* What major actions marked the beginning of the United States's war on terrorism? LAFS.1112.WHST.3.9, SS.912.A.7.15

Writing Activity
6. **ARGUMENT** The USA PATRIOT Act gave law enforcement new ways to fight terrorism. Write a letter to a newspaper explaining why you are either for or against giving up some freedoms in exchange for increased security. LAFS.1112.WHST.1.1, LAFS.1112.WHST.4.10, SS.912.A.7.15

LESSON 2

Focusing on Afghanistan and Iraq

ESSENTIAL QUESTIONS

• How is American culture shaped by a set of common values and practices?
• How have disputes over ideas, values, and politics resulted in change?

READING HELPDESK

Academic Vocabulary

• inspectors   • eliminate
• significantly

Content Vocabulary

• weapons of mass destruction (WMD)
• sect

TAKING NOTES

Key Ideas and Details

Organizing As you read, use the following graphic organizer to show the different groups in Iraq. LAFS.1112.RH.3.7

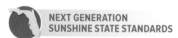

NEXT GENERATION SUNSHINE STATE STANDARDS

LAFS.1112.RH.1.2: Determine the central ideas or information of a primary or secondary source; provide an accurate summary that makes clear the relationships among the key details and ideas.

LAFS.1112.RH.2.4: Determine the meaning of words and phrases as they are used in a text, including analyzing how an author uses and refines the meaning of a key term over the course of a text (e.g., how Madison defines faction in Federalist No. 10).

LAFS.1112.RH.3.7: Integrate and evaluate multiple sources of information presented in diverse formats and media (e.g., visually, quantitatively, as well as in words) in order to address a question or solve a problem.

LAFS.1112.WHST.1.2: Write informative/explanatory texts, including the narration of historical events, scientific procedures/experiments, or technical processes.

Continued on page 630

IT MATTERS BECAUSE
After the attacks of September 11, 2001, U.S. forces invaded Afghanistan, the Central Asian nation that had sheltered many al-Qaeda members. In 2003, troops invaded Iraq and toppled the regime of Saddam Hussein.

Afghanistan and the Taliban

GUIDING QUESTION *Why did the United States want to overthrow the Taliban regime?*

Soon after the September 11 attacks, the United States launched a war in Afghanistan to bring down the Taliban regime that had sheltered Osama bin Laden and other members of al-Qaeda. U.S. warplanes bombed Taliban forces as the United States began sending military aid to the Northern Alliance, a coalition of Afghan groups that had been fighting the Taliban for several years. The U.S. bombing campaign quickly shattered the Taliban's defenses, and the Northern Alliance launched a massive attack. In December 2001, the Taliban government fell, and surviving members fled to the mountains of Afghanistan. Afghanistan slowly began to recover from decades of war.

Rebuilding Afghanistan
After the Taliban fled, the United States and its allies helped local Afghan leaders create a new government. Meanwhile, thousands of U.S. and allied troops arrived to act as peacekeepers. In 2003 NATO took command of the peacekeeping. Afghanistan held its first nationwide democratic election in December 2004, and Hamid Karzai was elected president. One year later, the Afghan people elected a National Assembly. Despite these successes, Afghanistan continued to suffer from violence. The U.S. military has remained in Afghanistan in an effort to help stabilize the country.

The Continuing Fight Against Terror
During the George W. Bush and the Barack Obama administrations, U.S. troops remained in Afghanistan. The continuing goal was to maintain peace in the country, fight the remaining Taliban members,

and create a stable Afghan-led nation. When he arrived in the White House, President Obama expanded the American combat role in Afghanistan.

U.S. intelligence agencies believed that Osama bin Laden had fled to Pakistan, which shares a border with Afghanistan. Reports in the summer of 2010 suggested that the mastermind of the September 11 terrorist attacks was hiding north of Pakistan's capital city of Islamabad. In May 2011, bin Laden's exact location was verified and President Obama ordered U.S. troops to attack. Bin Laden was killed after a brief fight and DNA tests confirmed his identity. President Obama announced to the nation that "justice has been done." Former President George W. Bush responded to bin Laden's death by reminding the nation that "the fight against terror goes on, but . . . [n]o matter how long it takes, justice will be done."

During the almost decade-long search for bin Laden, the U.S. and its allies captured or killed hundreds of al-Qaeda members. Between 2002 and 2006, the U.S. government believed it prevented at least 10 major al-Qaeda attacks, including at least three on the United States and two on Great Britain. But the American people were also growing more cautious about endless military deployments. President Obama planned to reduce U.S. troops in Afghanistan to under 10,000 beginning in 2015 and a further reduction to approximately 4,500 in 2016. Total troop removal from Afghanistan was to be accomplished in 2017.

☑ READING PROGRESS CHECK

Summarizing What progress has the U.S. made in its efforts to fight terrorism in Afghanistan?

Confronting Iraq

GUIDING QUESTION *What factors led to the U.S. invasion of Iraq?*

The terrorist attacks of September 11 showed that groups such as al-Qaeda were determined to kill as many Americans as possible. President Bush and his advisers were deeply concerned that terrorists might acquire **weapons of mass destruction (WMD)**—including nuclear, chemical, and biological weapons—that could kill large numbers of people all at once.

During the Cold War, the United States relied upon a policy of deterrence to prevent the use of such weapons. The rise of state-sponsored terrorism created a new problem. If a nation secretly gave weapons to terrorists who then used them against the United States, the U.S. military might not know whom to attack in response to their use.

The "Axis of Evil"

In his 2002 State of the Union address, President Bush warned that an "axis of evil" made up of Iraq, Iran, and North Korea posed a grave threat. Each nation had been known to sponsor terrorism and was suspected of developing weapons of mass destruction. Bush warned that the United States "will not permit the world's most dangerous regimes to threaten us with the world's most destructive weapons."

The president and his advisers believed Iraq to be the most immediate danger. It had used chemical weapons against the Kurds, an ethnic group in northern Iraq. After the 1991 Gulf War, UN **inspectors** found evidence that Iraq had developed biological weapons and had been working on a nuclear bomb. Between 1991 and 1998, Iraq appeared to be hiding weapons of mass destruction from UN inspectors. In 1998 the Iraqi government expelled the inspectors. In response, President Clinton ordered a massive bombing attack on Iraq to destroy its ability to make such weapons. Despite the attack, intelligence agencies continued to believe Iraq was hiding weapons of mass destruction.

PHOTO: David Guttenfelder/AP Images; TEXT: Statement by President George W. Bush on bin Laden's Death, May 1, 2011.

BIOGRAPHY

Hamid Karzai (1957–)

Hamid Karzai was elected president in Afghanistan's first democratic election on October 9, 2004. He worked to remove the Taliban and its supporters from Afghanistan. In 2001, participants of the UN-sponsored Bonn Conference elected him Chairman of the Interim Administration. He was then elected President of the Transitional Government on June 13, 2002, by members of the Emergency Loya Jirga (grand council). Karzai has been a strong proponent of establishing a Loya Jirga, believing it to be the only way to resolve the differences among the various Afghan factions. Though there have been charges of corruption in his administration, as president, Karzai has been an advocate of human rights and has appointed several women to his cabinet.

▶ CRITICAL THINKING
Drawing Conclusions Why do you think Hamid Karzai was elected president of Afghanistan? SS.912.A.7.12

weapons of mass destruction (WMD) weapons—including nuclear, chemical, and biological—capable of killing large numbers of people all at once

inspector a person appointed to examine facilities, usually in search of specific items, in regard to safety or quality

NEXT GENERATION
SUNSHINE STATE STANDARDS

Continued from page 628

LAFS.1112.WHST.3.9: Draw evidence from informational texts to support analysis, reflection, and research.

LAFS.1112.WHST.4.10: Write routinely over extended time frames (time for reflection and revision) and shorter time frames (a single sitting or a day or two) for a range of discipline-specific tasks, purposes, and audiences.

SS.912.A.1.2: Utilize a variety of primary and secondary sources to identify author, historical significance, audience, and authenticity to understand a historical period.

SS.912.A.1.4: Analyze how images, symbols, objects, cartoons, graphs, charts, maps, and artwork may be used to interpret the significance of time periods and events from the past.

Continued on page 632

significantly in a way that is important enough to have an effect

The war in Iraq relied heavily on advanced technology. U.S. forces used new tools such as remote-controlled drone bombers and laser-guided pointers to precisely target enemy bunkers.

▶ **CRITICAL THINKING**

Interpreting What advantages does this soldier seem to have over the enemy? **SS.A.1.4, SS.A.7.15**

An Ultimatum to Iraq

In 2002 President Bush decided to deal with Iraq. On September 12, he asked the United Nations for a new resolution against Iraq. If Iraq's dictator, Saddam Hussein, wanted peace, he would have to give up Iraq's weapons of mass destruction, readmit the UN weapons inspectors, stop supporting terrorism, and stop oppressing his people. Although he was asking the United Nations to pass a resolution, the president made it clear that the United States would act with or without UN support. Bush asked Congress to authorize the use of force against Iraq, which it did. Later, the United Nations approved a new resolution against Iraq that threatened "serious consequences" if Iraq did not comply.

In November 2002, Iraq agreed to readmit UN weapons inspectors. It then submitted a statement admitting it had weapons of mass destruction before the Gulf War, but denying it currently had them. Secretary of State Colin Powell said that Iraq's declaration contained lies and was in "material breach" of the UN resolution.

As the United States and a coalition of some 30 nations prepared for war with Iraq, others in the UN Security Council argued that the inspectors should be given more time to find evidence of Iraq's WMD programs. By March 2003, inspectors still had found nothing, and the United States began pressing the United Nations to authorize the use of force.

France and Russia, two UN Security Council members with veto power, refused to back such a resolution. As war became imminent, world opinion divided between those who supported the United States and those who opposed an attack on Iraq. Around the world, antiwar protesters staged rallies and marches. Several nations that had supported the United States in its war on terror and had sent troops to Afghanistan—including France, Germany, and Canada—refused to join the coalition against Iraq. Saudi Arabia and Turkey—both American allies—refused to allow the United States to attack Iraq from their territories. The only nation bordering Iraq that granted permission to use its territory was Kuwait.

The Invasion Begins

On March 20, 2003, the U.S.-led coalition forces attacked Iraq. More than 150,000 U.S. troops, some 45,000 British troops, and a few hundred special forces from Australia and Poland took part in the invasion. Much of the Iraqi army dissolved as soldiers refused to risk their lives for Saddam Hussein. A few fierce battles took place, but the Iraqis were unable to slow the coalition advance **significantly.** On May 1, President Bush declared that the major combat was over. About 140 Americans and several thousand Iraqis had died. Hussein was captured in late 2003. After a prolonged trial, an Iraqi court found him guilty of ordering mass executions. He was executed in 2006.

Insurgents and Reconstruction

Soon after the coalition took control of the country, small groups of Iraqis began staging bombings, sniper attacks, and sporadic battles against coalition forces. Some carrying out the attacks were former members of Saddam Hussein's military. Others were affiliated with al-Qaeda and other radical Muslim groups who believed the invasion offered a chance to build support in the Muslim world by organizing resistance to the United States. Militias belonging to the different religious and ethnic groups in Iraq also carried out some attacks.

Scott Nelson/Getty Images News/Getty Images

(t)ALI YUSSEF/AFP/Getty Images; (b)Wathiq Khuzaie/Getty Images

Despite problems of lingering violence and uncertainty, many began to rebuild a shattered Iraq.

▶ **CRITICAL THINKING**
Defending What was the most important U.S. accomplishment in Iraq? Why? SS.912.A.1.4

The majority of Iraq's population is Shia Muslim, but there is also a large Sunni Muslim minority. The Sunni were themselves divided between Sunni Arabs, who ruled the country under Saddam Hussein's leadership, and Sunni Kurds. The collapse of Hussein's dictatorship renewed old hostilities among these groups, known as **sects**, forcing coalition troops to protect them from attacks from each other's militias.

sect a subgroup within a religious community whose beliefs differ from the larger group

Having aimed to overthrow a tyrant and **eliminate** the possibility of weapons of mass destruction being given to terrorists, the United States found itself trying to suppress an insurgency, prevent a civil war, and establish a new Iraqi government. The United States and its allies spent more than $30 billion to improve infrastructure, but insurgent attacks slowed these efforts. Despite the problems, Iraq's economy began to grow rapidly and living standards substantially improved.

eliminate to remove or get rid of

U.S. policy makers faced a dilemma. If they pulled troops out too soon, Iraq might fall into civil war and provide a safe haven and breeding ground for terrorist groups. At the same time, the longer the United States stayed, the more its presence might stir resentment and support for terrorist groups. The best solution seemed to be to get a functioning, democratic Iraqi government in place as quickly as possible and then train its forces to take over the country's security. To set up their democratic government, in January 2005, the Iraqi people went to the polls in huge numbers for the first free elections in their country's history. After much debate, voters then overwhelmingly approved a new constitution in October 2005.

Problems in Iraq

Many Americans were encouraged when large numbers of Iraqis turned out to vote in democratic elections, but hope for peace in Iraq soon faded. Many Americans had expected the war to end quickly, but between 2003 and 2006, insurgents killed more than 3,000 U.S. soldiers. As the fighting dragged on, support for the war began to decline. Also, the failure to find any WMD added to growing controversy as to whether the war had been a mistake.

The elections were followed by a rise in sectarian violence as Sunni and Shia militias turned against each other. Ongoing suicide bombings, kidnappings, and attacks on U.S. soldiers set a majority of Americans against the war. As a *New York Times* editorial argued:

In 2005 Iraqis were able to vote in their first free elections. The ink on this woman's finger is to show that she voted, and became a symbol of hope during the election.

▶ **CRITICAL THINKING**
Predicting Consequences Will regular elections lead to a more stable national government in Iraq? SS.912.A.7.12

PRIMARY SOURCE

❝Iraq is becoming a country that America should be ashamed to support, let alone occupy. The nation as a whole is sliding closer to open civil war. In its capital, thugs kidnap and torture innocent civilians with impunity, then murder them for their religious beliefs. . . . The stories about innocent homeowners and storekeepers who are dragged from their screaming families and killed by . . . militias are heartbreaking, as is the thought that the United States, in its hubris, helped bring all this to pass.❞

—from the *New York Times*, April 2, 2006

A U.S. Army soldier plays soccer with Iraqi children while on patrol in Baghdad.

▶ **CRITICAL THINKING**

Defending Was Operation Iraqi Freedom a success? Why or why not? LAFS.1112.WHST.3.9, SS.912.A.1.4, SS.912.A.7.15

NEXT GENERATION SUNSHINE STATE STANDARDS

Continued from page 630

SS.912.A.7.11: Analyze the foreign policy of the United States as it relates to Africa, Asia, the Caribbean, Latin America, and the Middle East.

SS.912.A.7.12: Analyze political, economic, and social concerns that emerged at the end of the 20th century and into the 21st century.

SS.912.A.7.13: Analyze the attempts to extend New Deal legislation through the Great Society and the successes and failures of these programs to promote social and economic stability.

SS.912.A.7.15: Analyze the effects of foreign and domestic terrorism on the American people.

Democrats demanded the president set a timetable for withdrawing U.S. troops, a policy that President Bush described as "cut and run."

Troops Surge to Iraq

In 2006, Secretary of Defense Donald Rumsfeld resigned, and President Bush appointed Robert Gates to replace him. Bush then announced a plan to send a "surge" of some 20,000 more troops to Iraq to restore order in Baghdad, where the violence was concentrated. With the additional surge of troops, General David Petraeus began clearing and holding areas of Baghdad that had been plagued by crime and insurgent attacks. His forces also reached out to Sunni groups in western Iraq that had been opposed to the American presence.

In the western province of Anbar, a militant group known as al-Qaeda in Iraq (AQI) tried to impose a militant version of Islam through murder and intimidation. The Sunni groups in that area began working with U.S. forces to fight AQI. These actions helped change the course of the war.

By the fall of 2008, violence in Iraq had been dramatically reduced. Coalition forces had handed over control of 12 of Iraq's 18 provinces to the Iraqi government and coalition casualties were lower than at any time since the war began in 2003. In August 2010, Operation Iraqi Freedom officially ended as the number of U.S. troops remaining in Iraq was reduced to about 50,000. Their job was primarily to train Iraqi troops.

☑ READING PROGRESS CHECK

Summarizing What dilemmas did the United States face if troops were pulled out of Iraq too soon?

Murad Sezer/AP Images

LESSON 2 REVIEW

Reviewing Vocabulary

1. ***Defining*** What are weapons of mass destruction? LAFS.1112.RH.2.4
2. ***Comparing and Contrasting*** What is the difference between terrorism and state-sponsored terrorism? LAFS.1112.RH.2.4, LAFS.1112.WHST.3.9

Using Your Notes

3. ***Explaining*** Review the notes you have taken describing the different groups in Iraq. Then explain why the fighting continued in Iraq after President Bush declared the major combat was over. LAFS.1112.RH.3.7

Answering the Guiding Questions

4. ***Summarizing*** Why did the United States want to overthrow the Taliban regime? LAFS.1112.WHST.3.9, SS.912.A.7.15

5. ***Identifying*** What factors led to the U.S. invasion of Iraq? LAFS.1112.WHST.3.9, SS.912.A.7.15

Writing Activity

6. **NARRATIVE** Suppose that you are an Iraqi who has recently voted in your first election. Write a journal entry that explains how you feel following your vote. LAFS.1112.WHST.1.2, LAFS.1112.WHST.4.10

LESSON 3
Domestic Challenges

READING HELPDESK

Academic Vocabulary

- controversial

Content Vocabulary

- swing vote

TAKING NOTES

Key Ideas and Details

Outlining Use the following graphic organizer to create an outline using the major headings of the lesson. LAFS.1112.RH.3.7

> Domestic Challenges
> I. Security vs. Liberty
>   A.
>   B.
> II.

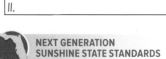

**NEXT GENERATION
SUNSHINE STATE STANDARDS**

LAFS.1112.RH.1.2: Determine the central ideas or information of a primary or secondary source; provide an accurate summary that makes clear the relationships among the key details and ideas.

LAFS.1112.RH.2.4: Determine the meaning of words and phrases as they are used in a text, including analyzing how an author uses and refines the meaning of a key term over the course of a text (e.g., how Madison defines faction in Federalist No. 10).

LAFS.1112.RH.3.7: Integrate and evaluate multiple sources of information presented in diverse formats and media (e.g., visually, quantitatively, as well as in words) in order to address a question or solve a problem.

LAFS.1112.WHST.1.2: Write informative/ explanatory texts, including the narration of historical events, scientific procedures/ experiments, or technical processes.

Continued on page 634

ESSENTIAL QUESTIONS

- How is American culture shaped by a set of common values and practices?
- How have disputes over ideas, values, and politics resulted in change?

IT MATTERS BECAUSE

After a close campaign, President Bush was reelected in 2004, but scandals and continued difficulties in Iraq helped Democrats win control of Congress in 2006.

Security vs. Liberty

GUIDING QUESTION *How did the September 11th terrorist attacks and the wars in Afghanistan and Iraq increase tension between the need for national security and protecting civil liberties?*

In early 2004, President Bush's approval ratings began to fall. The ongoing war in Iraq and the failure of inspectors to find any weapons of mass destruction weakened his support, as did the scandal at the Iraqi prison of Abu Ghraib, where some prisoners were abused by American soldiers. These events gave Democrats the opportunity to mount a serious challenge in the 2004 election.

President Bush and Vice President Cheney were renominated by the Republicans. The Democrats nominated Massachusetts senator John Kerry for president and North Carolina senator John Edwards for vice president. Despite the problems in Iraq, voters felt it safer to stay with the incumbent. Nationwide, Bush won both the popular and the electoral vote.

Prisoners at Guantanamo

The war on terror heightened the tension between national security and civil liberties. People questioned whether terrorist attacks justified limits on civil liberties and whether captured terrorists had any rights at all.

In 2004, President Bush decided to hold captured members of al-Qaeda at the American military base in Guantanamo Bay, Cuba, where they could be interrogated. This decision was very **controversial.** Some people argued that the prisoners should have the right to a lawyer, formal charges, and a proper trial. The Bush administration insisted that the prisoners were enemy combatants, not suspects charged with a crime, and did not have the right to appeal their detentions to an American court. The administration also declared that the procedures regarding the treatment of prisoners, as

Hamdan v. Rumsfeld

Al-Qaeda associate Salim Ahmed Hamdan was captured in 2001 and was moved to Guantanamo Bay in 2002. President Bush later determined that Hamdan was eligible for a military trial on counts of committing war crimes. Writing for the Supreme Court, Justice John Paul Stevens argued that the military commission created to conduct the trial violated the Uniform Code of Military Justice and the Geneva Conventions. Stevens stated: "It is not evident why the danger posed by international terrorism . . . should require . . . any variance from the courts-martial rules."

▶ CRITICAL THINKING

Drawing Conclusions How did the ruling affect the policy on detainees? SS.912.A.1.6, SS.912.A.7.15

controversial given to controversy, disputable

NEXT GENERATION SUNSHINE STATE STANDARDS

Continued from page 633

LAFS.1112.WHST.3.9: Draw evidence from informational texts to support analysis, reflection, and research.

LAFS.1112.WHST.4.10: Write routinely over extended time frames (time for reflection and revision) and shorter time frames (a single sitting or a day or two) for a range of discipline-specific tasks, purposes, and audiences.

SS.912.A.1.2: Utilize a variety of primary and secondary sources to identify author, historical significance, audience, and authenticity to understand a historical period.

Continued on page 635

President Bush's second term was marked by several disputes over the nation's domestic policy goals, such as how to operate national security investigations.

▶ CRITICAL THINKING

Making Inferences What civil liberties did opponents of the national security program believe were being violated? SS.912.A.1.4, SS.912.A.7.12

specified in the Geneva Conventions, did not apply to terrorists since they were not part of any nation's armed forces.

The Supreme Court disagreed. In *Rasul* v. *Bush* (2004), the Court ruled that foreign prisoners who claimed that they were unlawfully imprisoned had the right to have their cases heard in court. In response, the Bush administration created military tribunals to hear detainee cases. The Supreme Court struck this plan down in 2006 in *Hamdan* v. *Rumsfeld.*

Bush then asked Congress to establish new tribunals that met the Court's objections. Congress passed the Military Commissions Act, which stated that noncitizens captured as enemy combatants had no right to file writs of habeas corpus. In 2008, in *Boumediene* v. *Bush,* the Supreme Court ruled that the detainees had a right to habeas corpus and declared that section of the Military Commissions Act unconstitutional.

Domestic Surveillance

As part of the war on terror, the National Security Agency (NSA) began wiretapping domestic telephone calls made to overseas locations when they believed one party in the call was a member of al-Qaeda or affiliated with al-Qaeda. When the monitoring program became public in 2005, it created a controversy. Civil rights groups argued that the program violated the Fourth Amendment. In 2006 a federal judge declared the wiretapping to be unconstitutional, but the following year an appeals court overturned the judge's decision. When Congress began drafting legislation to address the issue, the Bush administration suspended the program and announced that future wiretaps would require a warrant from the Foreign Intelligence Surveillance Court.

☑ READING PROGRESS CHECK

Reasoning Do you agree with the Supreme Court's decision about the rights of detainees at Guantanamo Bay? Why or why not?

A Stormy Second Term

GUIDING QUESTION *What were the successes and failures of President George W. Bush's second term?*

President Bush's reelection convinced him that he had a mandate to continue his policies. He explained in a press conference: "[W]hen you win, there is a feeling that the people have spoken and embraced your point of

Mark Wilson/Getty Images News/Getty Images

view. And that's what I intend to tell the Congress. . . . I earned capital in the campaign, political capital. And now I intend to spend it."

Debating Social Security

One priority of Bush's second term domestic policy was Social Security reform. He proposed that workers be allowed to put 4 percent of their income in private accounts rather than in Social Security. He believed that private accounts would grow rapidly and help cover the expected shortfall in Social Security accounts. Democrats argued that privatizing any part of Social Security was dangerous. With the public unenthusiastic, the plan was never brought to a vote in Congress. Although this plan failed, Bush did convince Congress to enact a new prescription drug program for seniors. Under the new program, provided by Medicare, people age 65 and older can sign up for insurance that helps cover the cost of prescription drugs.

Hurricane Katrina

On August 29, 2005, Hurricane Katrina smashed into the Gulf Coast of the United States, spreading devastation from Florida to Louisiana. The fierce winds, rain, high tides, and storm surges destroyed buildings, roads, and electrical lines, left thousands of people homeless, and cost at least 1,200 lives. After the hurricane had passed, rising waters breached levees protecting New Orleans and flooded the low-lying city, causing thousands to flee to rooftops and for shelter in the convention center and at the Superdome. Waiting for days with little food, clean water, or information from authorities, survivors were shown on television news in deplorable conditions.

Reporters asked why the government was not responding more quickly. The mayor of New Orleans was faulted for not issuing a mandatory evacuation until the storm was less than a day away and for having failed to provide public transportation. The Federal Emergency Management Agency (FEMA) seemed unprepared in its response. With polls showing a sharp drop in confidence in his administration, President Bush fired the head of FEMA and traveled to New Orleans to pledge federal funds for rebuilding the city. Congress approved $200 billion for the massive task.

Hurricane Katrina ravaged New Orleans, Louisiana. During the flooding, people wrote messages on their roofs in the hope that rescuers would see them.

▶ **CRITICAL THINKING**

Identifying Central Ideas Why were Americans angered over President Bush's response to Hurricane Katrina? LAFS.1112.WHST.3.9, SS.912.A.1.4, SS.912.A.7.12

NEXT GENERATION SUNSHINE STATE STANDARDS

Continued from page 634

SS.912.A.1.4: Analyze how images, symbols, objects, cartoons, graphs, charts, maps, and artwork may be used to interpret the significance of time periods and events from the past.

SS.912.A.1.5: Evaluate the validity, reliability, bias, and authenticity of current events and Internet resources.

SS.912.A.1.6: Use case studies to explore social, political, legal, and economic relationships in history.

SS.912.A.7.12: Analyze political, economic, and social concerns that emerged at the end of the 20th century and into the 21st century.

SS.912.A.7.13: Analyze the attempts to extend New Deal legislation through the Great Society and the successes and failures of these programs to promote social and economic stability.

SS.912.A.7.14: Review the role of the United States as a participant in the global economy (trade agreements, international competition, impact on American labor, environmental concerns).

SS.912.A.7.15: Analyze the effects of foreign and domestic terrorism on the American people.

SS.912.A.7.17: Examine key events and key people in Florida history as they relate to United States history.

(t)Andrea Booher/FEMA, (inset)AFP/Getty Images

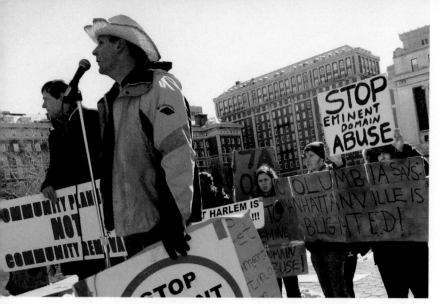

▲ The use of eminent domain has angered many people across the country.

Kelo v. *City of New London*

The Fifth Amendment states that the government cannot take property for public use without giving property owners just compensation. In 2000, the city of New London, Connecticut, seized property from several homeowners and gave the land to a corporation in order to have it redeveloped as part of a plan to rejuvenate the city's economy. The homeowners challenged the taking of their land, arguing that it was not being seized for public use, as specified in the Constitution.

In 2005, in a 5-4 decision, the Supreme Court interpreted the term "public use" in a broad way. The Court interpreted the phrase "public use" to mean the government can take property if it serves a public purpose, even if it is not truly for public use. In other words, if government wants to promote development in a community so as to create new jobs, or increase tax revenue, it can take property from one private owner and give it to another.

The case outraged people across the political spectrum. Many conservatives saw it as example of the Court violating rights by going beyond what they believed was the actual meaning of the Constitution. Many liberals were outraged that government could take land from individual homeowners and give it to large corporations. After the decision, more than 40 states passed laws restricting the ability of state and local jurisdictions to take land away from homeowners for "economic development" by businesses.

swing vote a vote that may sometimes lean conservative and other times liberal

New Supreme Court Judges

In 2005 President Bush filled two vacancies on the Supreme Court. In the spring of 2005, Justice Sandra Day O'Connor announced her retirement. Although appointed by President Reagan, Justice O'Connor had been a pivotal **swing vote** on the Court, sometimes siding with conservatives, sometimes with liberals. As her replacement, Bush nominated federal judge John G. Roberts, Jr., a conservative who was well regarded in the Senate. Before the Senate could act, however, Chief Justice William Rehnquist died. Bush then named Roberts to replace him. Again attempting to fill Justice O'Connor's vacancy, President Bush nominated federal judge Samuel Alito, Jr., a well-known conservative justice. Roberts and Alito were confirmed by the Senate.

The 2006 Midterm Elections

The first two years of President Bush's second term had not gone well. At the same time, Americans had also grown frustrated with Congress. The Republican majority seemed awash in scandals. Two Republicans had resigned from Congress after being convicted of corruption, and House majority leader Tom DeLay had resigned after being indicted for violating campaign finance laws. Congress seemed unable to control spending, partly because Republicans and Democrats had been adding an increasing number of special funding requests to spending bills.

Voters expressed their unhappiness with the president and the Republican Congress in 2006. The Democrats won a majority in both the House and the Senate for the first time since 1992. House Democrats then

Thinking Like a
HISTORIAN

Evaluating Information

Suppose you needed to write a report about an election. The Internet might be the first place you would look for information. How do you evaluate if the information you find is valid and unbiased? You should check to see if the organization or author is identified. If you are unable to verify the creator of the site, be wary of trusting the information. If a site refers to sources, that is a clue that the information is reliable. Also, the information should be presented factually and objectively, without bias.

SS.912.A.1.5

Michael Appleton/NY Daily News Archive/Getty Images

elected California representative Nancy Pelosi to be the first female Speaker of the House of Representatives. She summed up Democrats' interpretation of their victory:

PRIMARY SOURCE

❝The election of 2006 was a call to change, not merely to change the control of Congress, but for a new direction for our country. . . . Our Founders envisioned a new America driven by optimism, opportunity, and courage. . . . Now it is our responsibility to carry forth that vision of a new America into the 21st century.❞

—from a speech to the House of Representatives, January 4, 2007

Despite promises to end the war and change how Congress operated, Speaker Pelosi and other Democrats were not able to get enough votes to cut funding, set a deadline for pulling troops out of Iraq, or reduce spending. The American economy was on a downturn.

The weak economy caused many people to struggle financially. As a result, many Americans either sold their homes or lost them to foreclosure.

Economic Recession

By 2008, the American economy was in crisis. In 2007 many people with low incomes or poor credit began defaulting on their mortgage payments. At the same time, housing prices began to fall. People could no longer borrow against their home values, and banks across the country that had relied on mortgage-backed investments did not know what their investments were worth. Without adequate "real" funds to lend, banks reduced the amounts they lent, and many businesses feared they could not borrow enough money to keep operating. This led to a long recession and caused a number of well-known investment banking firms to face bankruptcy and collapse. Companies began laying off workers in response to the financial crisis. By January 2009, the unemployment rate was up to 7.2%. The country was in an economic recession.

 READING PROGRESS CHECK

Making Inferences What effect did Hurricane Katrina have on the Bush administration?

Florida
CONNECTION

Hurricane Andrew

On August 24, 1992, Hurricane Andrew, one of the most destructive hurricanes in recent history, hit southern Florida. It caused the most damage in Miami-Dade County. This storm brought winds over 160 miles an hour. It caused $40 billion worth of damages, destroyed over 25,000 homes, and killed 65 people. Andrew's winds were stronger than Hurricane Katrina, but it did not cause the levee failure and flooding that made Katrina so deadly. SS.912.A.7.17

LESSON 3 REVIEW

Reviewing Vocabulary
1. *Explaining* What is meant by the term *swing vote*? LAFS.1112.RH.2.4

Using Your Notes
2. *Summarizing* Review your notes and write a summary of the major domestic events of President Bush's second term. LAFS.1112.RH.3.7, LAFS.1112.WHST.3.9

Answering the Guiding Questions
3. *Making Connections* How did the September 11th terrorist attacks and the wars in Afghanistan and Iraq increase tension between the need for national security and protecting civil liberties? LAFS.1112.WHST.3.9, SS.912.A.7.12, SS.912.A.7.15

4. *Evaluating* What were the successes and failures of President George W. Bush's second term? LAFS.1112.WHST.3.9, SS.912.A.7.12

Writing Activity
5. **NARRATIVE** Write a journal entry describing President Bush's second term that will be read by students 50 years in the future. Be clear and concise with your descriptions of these events. LAFS.1112.WHST.1.2, LAFS.1112.WHST.4.10

©Tannen Maury/epa/Corbis

STUDY GUIDE

BUSH'S GLOBAL CHALLENGES
LESSON 1

Selected Terrorist Attacks Involving al-Qaeda

1996	Bombing of Khobar Towers, Saudi Arabia
1998	Bombing of U.S. embassies in Kenya and Tanzania
2000	Attack on U.S.S. *Cole*
2001	September 11th attacks
2004	Bombing of commuter trains in Madrid, Spain

FOCUSING ON AFGHANISTAN AND IRAQ
LESSON 2

Nov. 2002
UN Resolution demands that Iraq allow weapons inspectors back in.

Mar. 2003
Coalition forces begin Iraq invasion.

Oct. 2004
Report concludes Iraq did not have WMDs.

Jan. 2005
Iraqis participate in first free elections.

Jan. 2007
President Bush orders troop surge to restore order in Baghdad.

DOMESTIC CHALLENGES
LESSON 3

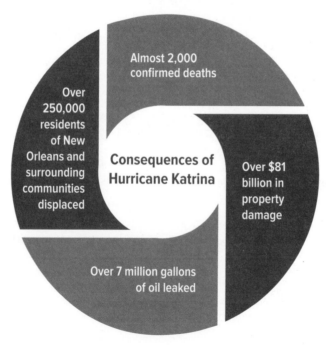

Almost 2,000 confirmed deaths

Over 250,000 residents of New Orleans and surrounding communities displaced

Consequences of Hurricane Katrina

Over $81 billion in property damage

Over 7 million gallons of oil leaked

Directions: On a separate sheet of paper, answer the questions below. Make sure you read carefully and answer all parts to the question.

Lesson Review

Lesson 1

1 *Explaining* Why might the year 2001 be considered a turning point in American history? SS.912.A.7.11, SS.912.A.7.12, SS.912.A.7.15

2 *Describing* What was the military response to September 11 called? What Middle Eastern nation was the primary focus of this war? Why was it chosen as the war's focus? SS.912.A.7.11, SS.912.A.7.15

3 *Analyzing* What was the impact of the September 11 attack on the U.S. economy? What policies did President Bush push through Congress in response? SS.912.A.7.12, SS.912.A.7.15

Lesson 2

4 *Explaining* Why did the United States invade Iraq? SS.912.A.7.11, SS.912.A.7.15

5 *Describing* Describe the conflicting viewpoints regarding the United States' entry into war with Iraq in 2003 without United Nations' confirmation of weapons of mass destruction. What were the positions of other nations? SS.912.A.7.11, SS.912.A.7.15

Lesson 3

6 *Analyzing* Why did the National Security Agency wiretap domestic phone calls, and why was this action controversial in the global War on Terror? SS.912.A.7.12, SS.912.A.7.15

7 *Listing* Which members of the Supreme Court were added during President Bush's second term as president?

8 *Stating* What was the outcome of the Supreme Court case *Kelo* v. *City of New London*? How does the decision impact Fifth Amendment property rights of individuals, businesses, and communities? SS.912.A.7.12

Exploring the Essential Questions

9 *Evaluating Counterarguments* Write the text for a short debate on a political or legal issue. Describe two conflicting views on the issue, and present counterarguments. LAFS.1112.WHST.1.1, LAFS.1112.WHST.4.10, SS.912.A.7.12

10 *Evaluating* Write a paragraph about the role of disputes in creating change, and the ways in which American culture is shaped by a set of common values and practices. LAFS.1112.WHST.1.2, LAFS.1112.WHST.4.10, SS.912.A.7.12

Critical Thinking

11 *Evaluating* Identify a significant social leader and a significant political leader and describe the central issue concerning your selections. SS.912.A.7.12

12 *Identifying Central Issues* What were key issues tied to the experience of and response to Hurricane Katrina? SS.912.A.7.12

13 *Drawing Conclusions* Discuss the solvency of long-term entitlement programs such as Social Security and how they are affected by problems such as long-term unemployment during the twenty-first century recession. SS.912.A.7.13

14 *Identifying* What did the *Hamdan* v. *Rumsfeld* case state about the right of political detainees at Guantanamo Bay?

21st Century Skills

15 *Explaining Continuity and Change* How did the September 11 attacks lead to the USA PATRIOT Act, and how did it lead to the expansion of the NSA? What constitutional issues have been raised by these developments? SS.912.A.7.12, SS.912.A.7.15

16 *Explaining* How did the constitutional roles of the executive, legislative, and judicial branches of the federal government impact the outcome of the presidential election of 2000? SS.912.A.7.8, SS.912.A.7.12

17 *Creating and Analyzing Arguments* How was the levee failure in New Orleans after Hurricane Katrina due to factors of physical geography? How were the failures due to factors of human geography? SS.912.A.7.12, SS.912.G.2.1

Need Extra Help?

If You've Missed Question	1	2	3	4	5	6	7	8	9	10	11	12	13	14	15	16	17
Go to Lesson	1	1	1	2	2	3	3	3	3	3	1, 2, 3	3	3	3	1	3	3

DBQ Analyzing Primary Sources

Use the comments below about the controversial USA PATRIOT Act to answer the following questions.

PRIMARY SOURCE

"If we were to take the position, reflected in provisions in the USA PATRIOT Act, that the government can invade our privacy and gather evidence that can be used against us based on no suspicion whatsoever that we've done anything wrong, but simply because the government wants to gather evidence . . . then we will have rendered that Fourth Amendment principle essentially meaningless."

—Congressman Bob Barr (R-GA), from "Problems with the USA PATRIOT Act," December 6, 2005

PRIMARY SOURCE

"Zero. That's the number of substantiated USA PATRIOT Act civil liberties violations. Extensive congressional oversight found no violations."

—Congressman James Sensenbrenner (R-WI), from "No rights have been violated," March 1, 2006

18 *Analyzing Primary Sources* Compare the quotes. Which Congressman is most successful in defending his position? Why? LAFS.1112.RH.2.6, LAFS.1112.SL.1.3, LAFS.1112.RH.3.8, SS.912.A.7.12, SS.912.A.7.15

19 *Evaluating Arguments* What is Congressman Sensenbrenner's response to the accusation that the PATRIOT Act violates civil rights? LAFS.1112.RH.2.6, LAFS.1112.RH.3.8, SS.912.A.7.12, SS.912.A.7.15

Extended Response Question

20 *Informative/Explanatory* Write an essay that describes upheaval in U.S. domestic and foreign policy in the twenty-first century. How have controversial events challenged both political leaders and the general public? Edit your essay to ensure you communicated your point clearly. LAFS.1112.WHST.1.2, LAFS.1112.WHST.2.4, LAFS.1112.WHST.2.5, LAFS.1112.WHST.4.10, SS.912.A.7.12, SS.912.A.7.15

Analyzing Visuals

Use the map to answer the following questions.

21 *Evaluating Information* Based on the information shown on the map, identify which region of the world has been attacked most often by al-Qaeda terrorism. SS.912.A.7.15, SS.912.G.2.1

22 *Understanding Visuals* Which attacks shown on the map are not directly related to retaliation against the United States? LAFS.1112.RH.3.7, SS.912.A.7.15, SS.912.G.2.1

Major Terrorist Attacks 1993–Present

Need Extra Help?

If You've Missed Question	18	19	20	21	22
Go to Lesson	1	1	2, 3	1	1

◀ Barack Obama took office in January 2008 as the nation's first African American president.

FROM 2008 TO PRESENT

Obama and Beyond

THE STORY MATTERS ...

President Barack Obama began his administration after the economic crash of 2008. This was but one of the challenges he faced, following a campaign that promised the American people hope and change. President Obama also had to lead American soldiers still fighting in Afghanistan and Iraq, navigate the tension-filled partisan politics of Washington, D.C., and confront the ongoing fight against terrorism around the world.

ESSENTIAL QUESTIONS
- How is American culture shaped by a set of common values and practices?
- How have disputes over ideas, values, and politics resulted in change?

Place & Time: United States 2008–Present

In the first decade of the twenty-first century, the growth of the nation's urban population (at a 12.1 percent increase) was faster than the overall increase of the nation's population as a whole (a 9.7 percent increase). Today, the United States is over 80 percent urban. The U.S. Census Bureau defines urbanized areas as places with 50,000 or more residents. As far back as the 1920s, the majority of Americans lived in urban areas. However, in the decades after World War II, many Americans relocated to expanding suburban areas around the nation's primary cities, and suburbs became the dominant residential location in the 1990s. In the 2010 national census, 486 areas were identified as urbanized and, according to the same census, 36 new urban areas have appeared since 2000.

Step Into the Place

Read the quote and look at the information presented on the map.

 Analyzing Historical Documents Read the statement written by Drs. Glaeser and Kahn about the history of American urbanization. List factors not mentioned in the quoted text that have contributed to the expansion of urban areas in the United States.

PRIMARY SOURCE

"In the early part of the 20th century, cities grew upward. Tenements and luxury apartment buildings replaced brownstones. Skyscrapers came to adorn urban landscapes. But at the end of the 20th century, urban growth has pushed cities further and further out. The compact urban areas of 1900 have increasingly been replaced by unending miles of malls, office parks, and houses on larger and larger lots. At first, people continued to work in cities but lived in sprawling suburbs. But the jobs followed the people and now metropolitan areas are characterized by decentralized homes and decentralized jobs. In [modern] America, urban growth and sprawl are almost synonymous and edge cities have become the dominant urban form."

—Dr. Edward L. Glaeser and Dr. Matthew E. Kahn, "Sprawl and Urban Growth," May 2003

(c)©Reed Hutchinson, (cr) Photo: Martha Stewart, (b)©Pete Souza/Obama Transition Team/Handout/Corbis News/Corbis

Step Into the Time

PREDICTING CONSEQUENCES

Choose an event from the time line and explain how that event might shape America's challenges.

November 2008 Barack Obama elected as first African American president

2009 U.S. economic recession pushes poverty level over 14%, its highest point in 15 years

Obama 2009–2017

March 2010 The Affordable Care Act becomes law

August 2010 U.S. withdraws all but 50,000 troops from Iraq

November 2010 Tea Party shakes up congressional midterm elections

U.S. PRESIDENTS

UNITED STATES   2008   2010

WORLD

November 2008 Terrorists attack downtown Mumbai, India

December 2009 Greece's economic credit rating is downgraded

January 2010 Earthquake in Haiti causes major destruction and loss of life

NEXT GENERATION SUNSHINE STATE STANDARDS
Students will understand the following benchmarks from the Florida NGSSS

LAFS.1112.RH.3.7: Integrate and evaluate multiple sources of information presented in diverse formats and media (e.g., visually, quantitatively, as well as in words) in order to address a question or solve a problem.

LAFS.1112.RH.3.9: Integrate information from diverse sources, both primary and secondary, into a coherent understanding of an idea or event, noting discrepancies among sources.

SS.912.A.1.2: Utilize a variety of primary and secondary sources to identify author, historical significance, audience, and authenticity to understand a historical period.

SS.912.A.1.3: Utilize timelines to identify the time sequence of historical data.

SS.912.A.1.4: Analyze how images, symbols, objects, cartoons, graphs, charts, maps, and artwork may be used to

interpret the significance of time periods and events from the past.

SS.912.A.7.1: Identify causes for Post-World War II prosperity and its effects on American society.

Percent Population Residing in Urbanized Areas by County, 2010

Urbanized Population
- 80.0–100.0%
- 50.0–79.9%
- 20.0–49.9%
- 0.1–19.9%
- No Urbanized Population

★ Top 10 Urban Areas
4,586,770 Population of Urban Area
(3470.3) Population Density of Urban Area (persons per square mile)
• New Urbanized Area

Albers Equal-Area Conic projection

SOURCE: U.S. Census Bureau, 2010

May 2011 U.S. special forces locate and kill Osama bin Laden

November 2012 Barack Obama wins reelection

August 2014 Protests begin in Ferguson, Missouri after the police shooting death of Michael Brown

June 2015 Same sex marriage protected by Supreme Court ruling in *Obergefell* v. *Hodges*

June 2015 Affordable Care Act survives latest Supreme Court challenge

2011 A series of popular uprisings in the Middle East—the Arab Spring—topples existing governments in Egypt, Libya, and Tunisia

September 2012 U.S. Embassy in Benghazi, Libya attacked; four Americans killed

February 2014 Russian forces invade parts of Ukraine

May 2014 Islamic State (ISIS) forces begin invading areas of Turkey, Syria, and Iraq

August 2014 Targeted U.S. airstrikes in the Middle East attempt to push back advance of Islamic State troops

November 2015 Terrorist attacks kill hundreds in Paris, France, and Beirut, Lebanon

Obama and Beyond **643**

LESSON 1
Obama's First Term

ESSENTIAL QUESTIONS

• How is American culture shaped by a set of common values and practices?
• How have disputes over ideas, values, and politics resulted in change?

READING HELPDESK

Academic Vocabulary

• monitor
• procedure

Content Vocabulary

• earmark

TAKING NOTES

Key Ideas and Details

Organizing As you read about key events in the Obama candidacy and presidency, use the major headings of the lesson to create an outline similar to the one below. LAFS.1112.RH.3.7

> The Obama Presidency
> I. The Election of 2008
>   A.
>   B.
> II.
>   A.
>   B.

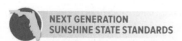

**NEXT GENERATION
SUNSHINE STATE STANDARDS**

LAFS.1112.RH.2.4: Determine the meaning of words and phrases as they are used in a text, including analyzing how an author uses and refines the meaning of a key term over the course of a text (e.g., how Madison defines faction in Federalist No. 10).

LAFS.1112.RH.3.7: Integrate and evaluate multiple sources of information presented in diverse formats and media (e.g., visually, quantitatively, as well as in words) in order to address a question or solve a problem.

LAFS.1112.WHST.1.1: Write arguments focused on discipline-specific content.

Continued on page 645

IT MATTERS BECAUSE

The election of Barack Obama was a historic moment for the United States. Yet the challenges he and the nation faced in the new century resulted in more and more political disagreements and party polarization.

The Election of 2008

GUIDING QUESTION *What issues and events attracted support for Barack Obama's presidential campaign?*

In 2007, a major financial crisis peaked. Millions of Americans found themselves unable to make payments on their home mortgages. Financial institutions failed. As the 2008 election approached, the economy replaced the war in Iraq as the most important issue for voters.

Choosing the Candidates

Senator John McCain of Arizona, a widely admired hero of the Vietnam War, won the Republican nomination for president. He chose Sarah Palin, the conservative governor of Alaska, as his running mate.

Illinois senator Barack Obama bested New York senator Hillary Clinton to win the Democratic nomination. Obama's delivery of the keynote address at the 2004 Democratic National Convention impressed Democrats and made him a national political figure. Senator Joe Biden was Obama's running mate, and his 35 years in the Senate helped balance criticism of Obama's relative inexperience.

Obama Wins

In October 2008, President Bush and Congress passed a $700 billion bailout for the nation's financial institutions, intended to help the worsening crisis. Many Americans opposed it because it seemed to reward those who had been responsible for the crisis. With the approval ratings of the president and Congress at all-time lows, McCain and Obama both promised change. Obama made good use of the Internet and formed a strong grassroots network of young supporters.

Barack Obama waves to the crowd at Chicago's Grant Park on election night in November 2008.

On Election Day, Obama won 53 percent of the popular vote and 365 electoral votes. It was the biggest victory for a Democratic candidate since 1964. Obama, the first African American to win the presidency, exulted:

PRIMARY SOURCE

❝This is our moment . . . to put our people back to work and open doors of opportunity for our kids; to restore prosperity and promote the cause of peace; to reclaim the American Dream and reaffirm that fundamental truth—that out of many, we are one; that . . . where we are met with . . . those who tell us that we can't, we will respond with that timeless creed that sums up the spirit of a people: Yes We Can.❞

—from the *Address at Grant Park*, November 4, 2008

✓ READING PROGRESS CHECK

Analyzing How did the passing of the $700 billion bailout affect the 2008 election?

Financial Meltdown

GUIDING QUESTION *How did the economic recession and housing crisis affect Obama's domestic goals?*

When Americans voted President Obama into office, many expected an immediate improvement in the shaky economy. Obama's domestic agenda proposed to create jobs, relieve the suffering of families, assist home owners, and ease the financial crisis. Yet as the economy worsened, Obama's specific plans to solve the nation's problems drew criticism. Some people believed he was not doing enough, while others argued that he was misusing government authority by doing too much. Despite the Bush administration's bailout of financial institutions and insurance companies, the American economy continued to weaken. More Americans lost their homes, and banks closed. Many large companies reported record losses and laid off workers, contributing to a spike in unemployment. As the crisis spread worldwide, global trade lessened and the world economy shrank.

Obama's Economic Response

In response to the failing economy, Obama signed the American Recovery and Reinvestment Act in February 2009. The act aimed to stimulate the economy by providing tax cuts to working families and small businesses. It

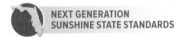

NEXT GENERATION SUNSHINE STATE STANDARDS

Continued from page 644

LAFS.1112.WHST.4.10: Write routinely over extended time frames (time for reflection and revision) and shorter time frames (a single sitting or a day or two) for a range of discipline-specific tasks, purposes, and audiences.

SS.912.A.1.2: Utilize a variety of primary and secondary sources to identify author, historical significance, audience, and authenticity to understand a historical period.

SS.912.A.1.4: Analyze how images, symbols, objects, cartoons, graphs, charts, maps, and artwork may be used to interpret the significance of time periods and events from the past.

SS.912.A.7.11: Analyze the foreign policy of the United States as it relates to Africa, Asia, the Caribbean, Latin America, and the Middle East.

SS.912.A.7.12: Analyze political, economic, and social concerns that emerged at the end of the 20th century and into the 21st century.

SS.912.A.7.14: Review the role of the United States as a participant in the global economy (trade agreements, international competition, impact on American labor, environmental concerns).

SS.912.A.7.15: Analyze the effects of foreign and domestic terrorism on the American people.

Chris McGrath/Getty Images

Foreclosures averaged between 4%–6% for many years.

1 *Evaluating* What was the percentage increase in foreclosures between 2007 and 2009?

2 *Making Generalizations* Why was there a steady rise in foreclosures beginning in 2007?
LAFS.1112.RH.3.7, SS.912.A.1.4

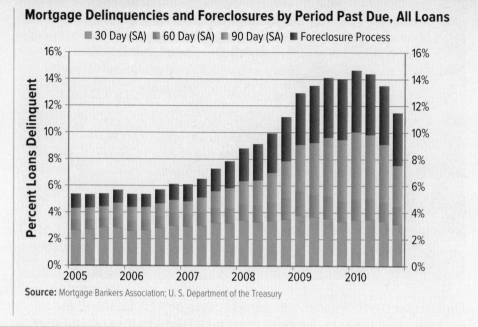

Mortgage Delinquencies and Foreclosures by Period Past Due, All Loans

■ 30 Day (SA) ■ 60 Day (SA) ■ 90 Day (SA) ■ Foreclosure Process

Source: Mortgage Bankers Association; U. S. Department of the Treasury

---

monitor to observe, oversee, or regulate

allocated federal funds for growth and investment, as well as for education, health, and other entitlement programs. The Act also set up a system to **monitor** how the recovery money was spent. In July 2010, Obama pushed additional legislation through the Democrat-controlled Congress that provided protection for consumers and called for more government oversight of financial institutions and large companies.

There were some early signs that Obama's measures were working. The nation's gross domestic product (GDP) had climbed. Some of the large businesses that had accepted stimulus funds were reporting gains. The unemployment rate, however, continued to rise, as did the federal deficit. And many Americans were uncomfortable with what they viewed as a rapidly growing role of the federal government in the economy.

☑ READING PROGRESS CHECK

Identifying Central Ideas Do you think the American Recovery and Reinvestment Act helped stimulate the economy?

Health Care Reform and the Midterm Elections

GUIDING QUESTION *What other major domestic events defined Obama's first years as president?*

As a candidate and president-elect, Obama stressed many other domestic issues. One main priority was to reform and expand the health care system. The results of the midterm elections reflected some people's dissatisfaction with this.

Health Care Reform

procedure a particular way of conducting, engaging, or implementing an activity

Obama's health care reform plan aimed to lower health care costs, introduce better **procedures** for delivering care, and insure all Americans. In a speech delivered to Congress in 2009, he said, "We are the only advanced democracy on Earth—the only wealthy nation—that allows such hardships for millions of its people. There are now more than thirty million American citizens who cannot get coverage."

Obama wanted to pay for the plan through higher taxes on the wealthy and by reducing wasteful spending. Yet some Americans opposed this as another expensive government intrusion. Months of heated partisan debate took place in Congress. No Republican voted for the final bill that passed in March 2010, and many vowed to overturn it. Though Obama had promised to reform the system of **earmarks**, the bill contained many. The bill extended health care coverage to about 32 million more Americans who could not previously afford it. It prevented insurers from denying insurance to people who had preexisting medical conditions. It allowed young adults to remain on their family's health insurance until they were 26 years old. It also gave tax credits to small businesses that provide health care to their employees. According to the White House, the plan would lower costs, strengthen the Medicare program, and expand the Medicaid program.

2010 Midterm Elections

As the 2010 midterm elections approached, Obama's approval rating was at a low point. Conservatives felt that the stimulus and health care bills had been too expensive and had not strengthened the economy. A grassroots movement called the "Tea Party" sprang up to protest the Obama administration. The movement took its name from a reference to the Boston Tea Party protests against British taxation. Most in the movement opposed what they called "big government"—including taxes, the health care program, and the economic stimulus plans of Bush and Obama. Yet they disagreed on many other issues.

Republicans reveled in a rousing win in the midterm elections. In the greatest shift in power in over 60 years, the party gained 63 House seats and regained control of that House of Congress. The Republicans also captured six Senate seats, though the Democrats maintained the majority. In a White House conference the day after the election, President Obama said, "Over the last two years, we've made progress. But, clearly, too many Americans haven't felt that progress yet, and they told us that yesterday." The United States still had obstacles to overcome: the worst economic depression in 70 years and continuing foreign conflicts.

✔ READING PROGRESS CHECK

Synthesizing What issues were raised by the Tea Party movement?

Political and Economic Issues

GUIDING QUESTION *Why was it so difficult for Congress and the president to reach agreement on ways to improve the economy?*

Despite the president's stimulus plan, the national economy suffered from persistent high rates of unemployment. At the same time that federal funding expanded to try to stimulate the economy, many state and local governments cut back on their spending and laid off teachers and other public workers. Young people who were just entering the workforce found it to be the worst job market since the Great Depression.

The National Debt, Spending, and Taxes

The national debt grew alarmingly high. Among the causes of the increased debt were President Obama's stimulus plan, President George W. Bush's tax cuts, the two wars in Iraq and Afghanistan, an expansion of Medicare to cover prescription drugs, the housing crisis, and the recession. Unemployment was a significant factor because those who lost their jobs, or who took lower-paying employment, paid less in taxes. Federal deficits required more borrowing, which meant that the government had to pay more for the interest on its debts.

Thinking Like a
HISTORIAN

Interpreting Significance

When President Obama chose Sonia Sotomayor and Elena Kagan to fill vacancies on the U. S. Supreme Court, he became the first president to successfully nominate two women to the nation's highest court. These women are now the third and fourth female justices in the nation's history.

Born and raised in a Puerto Rican family in the Bronx, New York, Sotomayor is the nation's first justice of Latin American descent. Determining the significance and influence of both women's service to the Supreme Court will be based on their interpretations of the legal questions that come before the Court.

earmarks specifications added by members of Congress from both parties for the expenditure of federal money for particular projects

The issues of deficit spending, the national debt, and taxes, served to drive the two traditional political parties further apart. The president appointed a commission to reach a compromise, but its proposed solutions of cutting spending and raising taxes won little support in Congress. Rather than directly confronting economic problems, Congress delayed addressing these problems, shelving them for future consideration.

Significant Supreme Court Decisions

Like Congress, the Supreme Court was deeply divided over issues facing the nation, and it reached major decisions with 5-to-4 margins. In the case of *Citizens United* v. *the Federal Elections Commission* (2010), the Supreme Court lifted many of the limits Congress had set on campaign financing calling them restrictions on freedom of speech. As a result, corporations could make political contributions, and wealthy individuals were free to make unlimited donations. This ruling sent both political parties scrambling to raise campaign finances. The ruling also allowed non-party groups to spend massive amounts on media advertising. The resulting onslaught of negative political advertising further propelled political polarization.

Since conservative justices held a narrow majority on the Supreme Court, there were doubts that it would uphold President's Obama's health care law as constitutional. Four of the justices believed that the government could not mandate that individuals purchase health insurance or face a penalty. Four of the justices believed equally strongly that the government had constitutional authority to require insurance under its power to regulate interstate commerce. Chief Justice John Roberts cast the deciding vote in 2012. In another 5-to-4 decision, the Court determined that Congress could not legally command people to buy insurance, but the federal government did have the power to tax those who did not buy insurance.

The 21st Century Economy

Despite the wars and recessions that have created division and affected the world since 2001, globalization continues and the world's economy is increasingly interconnected. The primary reason for this is the ongoing revolution in digital technology and communications. The use of cell phones, the Internet, and the computer has converged in a way that allows people to connect, interact, research, create, and work from anywhere, at any time, using a wide range of devices.

The members of the Supreme Court in 2014, bottom: Clarence Thomas, Antonin Scalia, John G. Roberts, Jr., Anthony Kennedy, Ruth Bader Ginsburg; top: Sonia Sotomayor, Stephen G. Breyer, Samuel Anthony Alito, Jr., Elena Kagan

Steven Petteway, Collection of the Supreme Court of the United States

This new level of interactivity, sometimes called hyperconnectivity, is transforming society and the economy. As Christine Lagarde, the head of the International Monetary Fund observed: "If the previous revolutions were about using machines for brawn, this is about using machines for brains."

Multinational corporations quickly adopted the new information and communications technology, allowing them to integrate their operations worldwide to a degree that was not possible in previous decades. Global financial corporations also used this technology to enable the world's capital to flow swiftly to new opportunities. Yet these interconnections also posed a danger. The world learned in 2008 that economic problems in one part of the globe could have a sweeping affect in other parts of the world.

Several new corporations driven by innovative entrepreneurs found ways to profit from the new interconnectivity. Steve Jobs led Apple, Inc. to enormous success through the introduction of new digital devices, including the iPhone, introduced in 2007, and the iPad, introduced in 2010. Another key entrepreneur in the early 21st century was Jeff Bezos, who founded Amazon.com in 1995 as an online bookstore. Amazon revolutionized online retailing and rapidly became one of the top 500 companies in the world selling almost any product through its website. Amazon has also helped drive the adoption of eBook readers and tablets. Google is another major multinational corporation that arose because of the Internet. Founded in 1998 by Sergey Brin and Larry Page, Google began as a search engine for the Internet. The company had the goal of organizing the world's information, and making it accessible and useful. Google quickly became the most widely used search engine in the world, and as the company grew, it expanded its research and development into other areas of software. Google Maps revolutionized online map use and navigation. Google also financed, and later acquired, the Android operating system, widely used on smart phones and tablets. Google continues to fund research into new applications of digital technology, including artificial intelligence, self-driving cars, robotics, translation software, renewable energy, and biotechnology.

Although the digital revolution has led to the rise of many new technology companies, many of the largest multinational corporations shaping the world's economy predate the digital revolution. Of the 25 largest companies in the world in 2013, eleven were oil companies, and four were car companies, underscoring that the need for energy and transportation continues to drive much of the world's economic growth.

The primary sources of the world's energy remain fossil fuels: oil, coal, and natural gas. In the 1990s, hydraulic fracturing, also known as fracking, was developed to extract gas from shale. The technology triggered what has been called the "shale boom"—the rapid growth of the gas and oil industry in parts of the United States where large shale formations exist. Fracking technology has helped reduce American dependence on foreign energy, and has played an important role in the economy's recovery from the recession of 2008. After critics raised concerns about its environmental impact, political debates erupted in several states as to whether or not to allow fracking operations to proceed.

✓ READING PROGRESS CHECK

Identifying Central Issues What economic solutions did liberals and conservatives propose?

Winning a Second Term

GUIDING QUESTION *What issues defined the political campaign of Barack Obama versus the Republican Party's platform?*

Having been elected president in 2008 by promising hope and change, President Obama found his reelection jeopardized by the economy's slow recovery from the recession. After Republicans won control of the House of

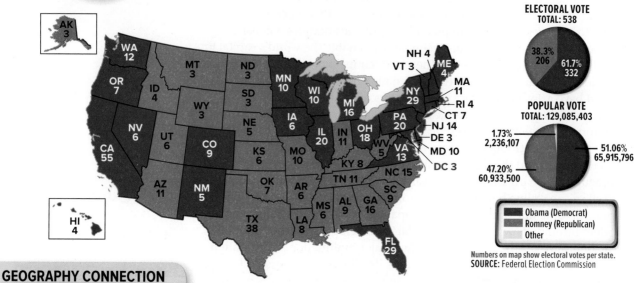

ELECTORAL VOTE
TOTAL: 538

38.3%
206

61.7%
332

POPULAR VOTE
TOTAL: 129,085,403

1.73%
2,236,107

51.06%
65,915,796

47.20%
60,933,500

Obama (Democrat)
Romney (Republican)
Other

Numbers on map show electoral votes per state.
SOURCE: Federal Election Commission

GEOGRAPHY CONNECTION

1. **THE WORLD IN SPATIAL TERMS** *What commonalities can you identify that united the states that voted for Mitt Romney?*

2. **PLACES AND REGIONS** *Why do you think President Obama won Upper Midwest states such as Ohio and Michigan?* SS.912.A.1.4

Representatives in 2010, the party's chances of defeating President Obama seemed stronger. Former Massachusetts Governor Mitt Romney promised to apply his business leadership skills to improve the economy and put more people back to work. He captured the nomination after defeating party rivals who tried appealing to the Tea Party protest movement.

Politics and New Media

The Internet increasingly played a role in American politics. By the 2012 elections, two-thirds of all Americans were using social networks. Unlike the traditional media, social networks created more interaction by encouraging people to respond and to share information. Studies showed that many people were likely to vote if they learned through social networks that their friends voted. Political parties recognized that social networking had become a new way of getting their messages out.

The parties also relied heavily on websites and e-mail for fundraising, to recruit volunteers, and provided lengthier discussions of their positions on the issues. Independent bloggers, commentators, and satirists were also active participants in the campaign conversation. The posting and sharing of online videos by average citizens created more democracy in the media.

After an expensive and hard-fought campaign, President Obama defeated Romney to win a second term. The polls showed that the weakened economy remained the leading issue for the voters, but they credited the president's efforts to rebuild the economy and restore employment.

More Partisan Struggles

The election left Congress divided between a Republican majority in the House of Representatives and a Democratic majority in the Senate. Major issues of deficits, taxes, immigration, and the environment remained unresolved. Citizens challenged both parties to break the partisan divide and legislative gridlock.

During the next two years of President Obama's second term, the president and Congress wrestled over issues. Obama argued for raising the federal minimum wage and reforming immigration laws, but the division in Congress prevented any significant legislative action. Republicans continued to criticize

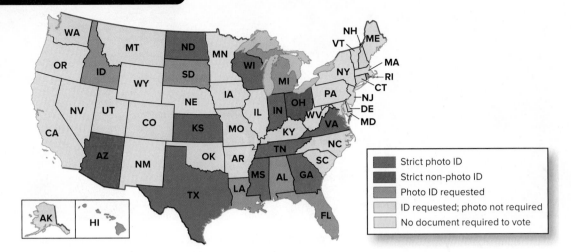

Voter ID Laws, 2016

Legend:
- Strict photo ID
- Strict non-photo ID
- Photo ID requested
- ID requested; photo not required
- No document required to vote

the Affordable Care Act, attacked the president's foreign policy, and launched investigations into a series of scandals in Obama's administration.

All of these factors combined in the midterm election of 2014 to give the Republicans the largest majority in the House of Representatives since the 1920s. The Republicans also took control of the Senate for the first time since 2007. With Congress back under their control beginning in January 2015, Republicans hoped to move the nation in a direction they were comfortable supporting. Democrats in Congress considered whether or not to block legislation as Republicans had done. President Obama was determined to focus on his party's goals while working with his political opponents.

PRIMARY SOURCE

❝While I'm sure we'll continue to disagree on some issues that we're passionate about, I'm eager to work with Congress over the next two years to get the job done. The challenges that lay ahead of us are far too important to allow partisanship or ideology to prevent our progress as a nation.❞

—President Barack Obama, November 5, 2014

The challenges that the nation faced were more than just those of political disagreements within its borders, the United States also faced many challenges around the world.

☑ **READING PROGRESS CHECK**

Summarizing What role did the Internet play in the 2012 elections?

▶ **CRITICAL THINKING**

One of the key differences between the Republican and the Democratic parties in recent years has been their stances on the use of Voter IDs during elections. Given the location of the strictest voting laws and what you have learned about recent national election results, can you determine which political party tends to support stronger voter ID laws? SS.912.A.1.4

LESSON 1 REVIEW

Reviewing Vocabulary
1. *Making Inferences* Why did Obama sign a bill with earmarks when he had opposed them? LAFS.1112.RH.2.4

Using Your Notes
2. *Summarizing* Use your notes to write a paragraph summarizing the first term domestic issues faced by the Obama administration. SS.912.A.7.12

Answering the Guiding Questions
3. *Identifying Central Issues* What issues and events attracted support for Barack Obama's presidential campaign? SS.912.A.7.11, SS.912.A.7.12

4. *Identifying Cause and Effect* How did the economic recession and housing crisis affect Obama's domestic goals? SS.912.A.7.12, SS.912.A.7.14
5. *Specifying* What other major domestic events defined Obama's first years as president? SS.912.A.7.12, SS.912.A.7.14

6. *Interpreting* What did the results of the midterm election say about the mood of the country at that time? SS.912.A.7.12

Writing Activity
7. **NARRATIVE** Write a journal entry describing events of these years that will be read by students 50 years in the future. Be clear and concise with your description of these events. LAFS.1112.WHST.1.1, LAFS.1112.WHST.4.10

LESSON 2

A Troubled World

ESSENTIAL QUESTIONS

• How is American culture shaped by a set of common values and practices?
• How have disputes over ideas, values, and politics resulted in change?

READING HELPDESK

Academic Vocabulary

• asylum

Content Vocabulary

• migrant

TAKING NOTES

Key Ideas and Details

Organizing Use the following graphic organizer to show areas of crisis in U.S. foreign policy. **LAFS.1112.RH.3.7**

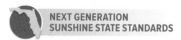

NEXT GENERATION SUNSHINE STATE STANDARDS

LAFS.1112.RH.2.4: Determine the meaning of words and phrases as they are used in a text, including analyzing how an author uses and refines the meaning of a key term over the course of a text (e.g., how Madison defines faction in Federalist No. 10).

LAFS.1112.RH.3.7: Integrate and evaluate multiple sources of information presented in diverse formats and media (e.g., visually, quantitatively, as well as in words) in order to address a question or solve a problem.

LAFS.1112.WHST.1.1: Write arguments focused on discipline-specific content.

Continued on page 653

IT MATTERS BECAUSE

In the twenty-first century, the United States faces a number of foreign policy and economic challenges. The fight against terrorism continues, and there are debates at home about how involved our armed forces must be in foreign wars. Beyond military and national safety questions, the U.S. economy remains a key player in global monetary shifts with the keen awareness that U.S. government actions and positions cause ripple effects around the world.

A World of Conflicts

GUIDING QUESTION *How did international issues affect the United States?*

President Obama's first years in office saw a great deal of conflict and disagreement between his administration and members of the Republican party. The political parties had different ideas about how to strengthen the economy and how to keep the nation safe.

The United States also faced a great deal of global conflict. President Obama worked to protect the nation from more terrorist attacks and strived to find a way to bring American soldiers back home as quickly and effectively as possible.

U.S. Wars in Iraq and Afghanistan

President Obama came to office determined to follow a more international approach to foreign policy. His foreign policy, therefore, relied more on the United Nations and sought to build consensus among American allies. The Obama administration ended the American combat mission in Iraq and reduced the number of U.S. troops stationed there. The U.S. also increased its use of remote-controlled drone aircraft to track and eliminate militant leaders of al-Qaeda. While the drones reduced the chances of American and NATO casualties, protests arose when the crafts caused injury and death to innocent civilians near targets. Critics warned that drone attacks worked against U.S. policy by alienating civilians who felt threatened by them. Between the Iraq and

©Ayman Oghanna/Corbis

Arab citizens in several North African nations conducted political protests against their dictator governments during President Obama's first term. This resulted in several regime changes in the regions, raising some hopes that democracy might take hold in parts of the Middle East.

▶ **CRITICAL THINKING**

Analyzing Information Identify whether or not President Obama was supportive of the popular protests that occurred in the Middle East during the Arab Spring movement. LAFS.1112.RH.3.7, SS.912.A.1.4, SS.912.A.7.11

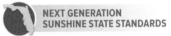

NEXT GENERATION SUNSHINE STATE STANDARDS

Continued from page 652

LAFS.1112.WHST.4.10: Write routinely over extended time frames (time for reflection and revision) and shorter time frames (a single sitting or a day or two) for a range of discipline-specific tasks, purposes, and audiences.

SS.912.A.1.2: Utilize a variety of primary and secondary sources to identify author, historical significance, audience, and authenticity to understand a historical period.

SS.912.A.1.4: Analyze how images, symbols, objects, cartoons, graphs, charts, maps, and artwork may be used to interpret the significance of time periods and events from the past.

SS.912.A.7.11: Analyze the foreign policy of the United States as it relates to Africa, Asia, the Caribbean, Latin America, and the Middle East.

SS.912.A.7.12: Analyze political, economic, and social concerns that emerged at the end of the 20th century and into the 21st century.

SS.912.A.7.15: Analyze the effects of foreign and domestic terrorism on the American people.

Afghanistan wars—including military operations, foreign aid, and wounded veterans' health care costs—the United States paid more than a trillion dollars a year. These costs helped fuel the deficits and national debt.

The Arab Spring

The wars in Iraq and Afghanistan heightened tension between the United States and some Muslim countries around the world, and violent extremists sought to exploit the situation. In 2009, President Obama went to Egypt to speak at Cairo University. There he called for a "new beginning" between the United States and the Muslim world, based on mutual respect. He pledged to pursue a peaceful settlement of the long dispute between Israelis and Palestinians, and also to promote democracy and human rights in the face of ruthless governments.

In 2011, popular unrest in the Middle East led to a series of revolutions against oppressive governments. The movement, known as the "Arab Spring," overthrew dictators in Tunisia, Libya, and Egypt. Since American troops were engaged in combat in Afghanistan, Obama was reluctant to provide American military support to the rebels in these nations. Instead, he relied on other NATO nations to provide the air support that helped rebels remove Muammar Qaddafi from power in Libya. Overthrowing dictators caused widespread political instability that posed serious problems for U.S. policy in the Middle East. Some of the governments that fell had been security partners with the U.S. There was a risk that religious extremists might gain power, which would complicate relations with the U.S., make compromise with Israel more difficult, and jeopardize the supply of oil and other commerce from the Middle East. Another unsettling danger was the possibility that Iran had the capability to develop nuclear weapons.

Fighting the Islamic State

After President Obama completed the withdrawal of U.S. troops from Iraq in 2011, another problem in the Middle East drew the U.S. back once again. A splinter group of al-Qaeda known as the Islamic State in Iraq and Syria (ISIS), or the Islamic State, assembled an army and set out to create a new Muslim state ruled by Sunni Muslims and guided by sharia law. ISIS ignored international borders, and its forces rapidly seized control of large areas of northern Iraq and eastern Syria. ISIS targeted Christians, non-Sunni Muslims, and various religious minorities. Its forces destroyed churches and Shia Muslim shrines and committed brutal public executions. Large numbers of refugees fled from ISIS-controlled areas.

The invasion of ISIS troops into Syria and Iraq has been a significant threat to the citizens of the region.

▶ **CRITICAL THINKING**
Determining Cause and Effect How does the formation and actions of the Islamic State relate to the United States' previous involvement in Iraq and the Middle East? LAFS.1112.RH.3.7, SS.912.A.1.4, SS.912.A.7.11

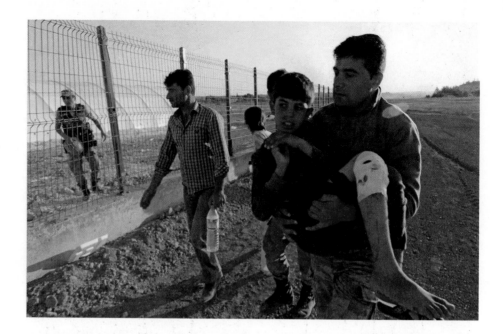

Abu Bakr al-Baghdadi emerged as the leader of the Islamic State in 2010. He had earlier been part of al-Qaeda in Iraq (AQI) that fought the Iraqi government and attacked Iraq's Shia Muslims.

In 2014, ISIS militants kidnapped over 100 Kurdish schoolboys in Syria and forced them to study radical Islamic teachings. This pattern of religious conversion and forced cooperation was repeated as ISIS moved through Syria and northern Iraq, taking over the Iraqi towns of Mosul and Tikrit. The United Nations estimated that because of ISIS over 1 million Iraqi citizens had fled from their homes. The Pentagon agreed to increase U.S. advisory troops in Iraq to 800. These military advisers aided the Iraqi forces fighting against ISIS and guarded the U.S. Embassy and airport in Baghdad.

President Obama also authorized targeted airstrikes within Iraq to push back ISIS forces and to provide protection for religious minorities targeted by ISIS. When ISIS released public videos of the execution of captured American and British journalists, President Obama pledged to increase the number of U.S. troops in Iraq to over 1,000, and to continue air and drone strikes against ISIS-controlled areas.

Crisis in Ukraine

At the same time, another crisis developed in Eastern Europe. In 2013, Ukraine's president, Viktor Yanukovych announced that Ukraine would back out of efforts to strengthen ties with the European Union and would instead cooperate with Russia. Russian President Vladimir Putin said that his country would buy billions of dollars in Ukraine's government bonds and cut the price Ukrainians pay for Russia's imported natural gas. In 2014, Ukrainians who feared their nation was losing its independence to Russia held public protests in Kiev's Independence Square. More than 20 protesters died during the demonstrations and hundreds were injured through clashes with the police. Soon after these events, Ukraine's prime minister resigned.

Pro-Russian protestors began their own demonstrations in the southern Ukrainian peninsula of Crimea, where 60 percent of the population was ethnically Russian. In response to the Crimean protests, Putin ordered military activity in western Russia. On that same day, U.S. Secretary of State John Kerry promised $1 billion in aid to Ukraine. In February 2014, Russian military took control of airports in Crimea and the Sevastopol naval base. The United States criticized Russia's aggressive actions and, along with the European Union, imposed a series of economic sanctions on Russia. President Putin responded

Mehmet Akif Parlak/Anadolu Agency/Getty Images

that he would not fight the Ukrainian people, but did not reverse Russia's actions in Crimea. Crimea's local parliament voted to join Russia in a Referendum.

Western observers regarded the vote for secession as a sham. Fighting continued in eastern Ukraine between Ukrainian armed forces and Russian-backed separatists who wanted their region of Ukraine to join Russia. In July 2014, as the fighting raged, a Malaysian passenger jet passing over Ukraine was accidentally shot down, killing all 298 people aboard.

✔ READING PROGRESS CHECK

Identifying Themes What are the similar issues found in the varied unrest in the Middle East and Ukraine?

Europe's Financial and Humanitarian Crisis

GUIDING QUESTION *What role does the U.S. play in the problems faced in Europe?*

A European debt crisis affected the American economy. Like the United States, European nations had experienced a collapse of their real estate markets, bank failures, and recession. Some of these governments, including Greece, Spain, Portugal, Italy, and Ireland, struggled with high deficits and national debt. High unemployment in these countries diminished their ability to trade with the U. S., which, in turn, further slowed the American recovery.

The Euro Crisis

Many European countries share a common currency—the euro—so nations in the euro bloc that had economic problems looked for loans from other nations with stronger economies. Germany boasted the most prosperous economy in Europe, but Germans were unhappy about "bailing out" those nations that had mismanaged their finances. In order to get financial support from the wealthier nations, the debtor governments had to agree to reduce their government spending, even though this triggered higher unemployment and further depressed their economies.

Trade and investments closely connected the United States economy to Europe. Uncertainties over Europe's economic future worried American investors. American officials encouraged European leaders to stabilize their economies.

The Refugee Crisis

Just as European nations began the process of stabilizing their common economic system, the actions of ISIS in the Middle East created a new problem. People living in areas of Syria, Turkey, Iraq, and other nations in the Middle East were driven out of their homes by Islamic State military action. Hundreds of thousands of these displaced peoples turned to European nations as places to recover and rebuild their lives. These refugees hoped to find a safe place for themselves and their children.

By the end of 2015, an estimated 750,000 people had been displaced and were in search of safety and stability. The arrival of these people in need caused economic, political, and social challenges to many European nations, as well as to the United States. Part of the controversy centered around whether receiving nations considered the displaced as refugees. Some governments wanted to call the people fleeing these conflicts in the Middle East **migrants**—people who choose to move from one location to another, especially to find employment—because refugees have more protections against deportation under the international **asylum** laws. Nations that grant asylum to refugees agree not to deport them back to their place of origin. But a country can define its own rules about denying border crossing to migrants. Among the European nations, Germany had received almost

▶ CRITICAL THINKING
Drawing Conclusions How did the European euro crisis affect economic events in the United States? LAFS.1112.RH.3.7, SS.912.A.1.4, SS.912.A.7.12

migrant people who choose to move from one location to another, especially to find employment

asylum protection granted to refugees against deportation

Dimitrios Sotiriou/Pacific Press/LightRocket/Getty Images

half of those seeking asylum, yet it had granted asylum to less than 50,000 individuals. Some of this reluctance came from the economic weaknesses across Europe following the height of the euro economic crisis. But many nations also feared that terrorists might blend in with the refugee population, using crowds to sneak past border securities to plan and conduct attacks against the West.

Attacks in Paris

Such fears seemed to be legitimate when a series of suicide bombings and gunfire attacks ripped through Paris, France, in November 2015. Over 120 people died and at least 400 were injured as a result of the attacks, which were planned and carried out by Abdelhamid Abaaoud and other ISIS supporters. Abaaoud was a Belgian citizen who moved to Syria in 2014 to work and train with ISIS. He took advantage of Europe's open border policies to move back to Europe and coordinate with other terrorists.

Reactions in the United States

President Obama and the American people responded with sympathy to the French people after the attacks and renewed the United States's commitment to aid the international effort to end the ISIS threat. U.S. military strikes were carried out alongside French forces the day after the Paris attacks. In addition, the U.S. pledged to continue the humanitarian efforts needed to aid refugees fleeing ISIS attacks in Syria, Lebanon, Iraq, and throughout the Middle East. The United States pledged over $4 billion for Syrian aid and over $600 million for similar assistance in Iraq.

President Obama called the ISIS terrorists "thugs and killers," not a true representation of Muslims around the globe. In a televised address to the nation on December 6, a few days after new terrorist-driven gun violence in San Bernardino, California, Obama warned against making snap judgments about all Muslims.

PRIMARY SOURCE

❝[I]t is the responsibility of all Americans—of every faith—to reject discrimination . . . to reject proposals that Muslim Americans should somehow be treated differently. Because when we travel down that road, we lose. . . . Muslim Americans are our friends and our neighbors, our co-workers, our sports heroes—and, yes, they are our men and women in uniform who are willing to die in defense of our country. We have to remember that.❞

—President Barack Obama, address to the nation, December 6, 2015

✓ **READING PROGRESS CHECK**

Understanding Terms Why are some European nations reluctant to categorize displaced peoples from the Middle East as refugees?

LESSON 2 REVIEW

Reviewing Vocabulary

1. *Explaining* What is the importance of the word *asylum*?
LAFS.1112.RH.2.4

Using Your Notes

2. *Summarizing* Use your notes to write a paragraph summarizing the main foreign policy problems faced by the Obama administration. SS.912.A.7.11, SS.912.A.7.12

Answering the Guiding Questions

3. *Identifying Central Issues* What events caused the European refugee crisis? SS.912.A.7.11, SS.912.A.7.12, SS.912.A.7.15

4. *Identifying Cause and Effect* How did Europe's economic problems contribute to concerns about refugees? SS.912.A.7.11, SS.912.A.7.12

5. *Specifying* What sequence of events led to Russia's intervention in the Ukrainian region? SS.912.A.7.12

6. *Explaining* How did the United States respond to the problems being faced in Europe as a result of ISIS activity? SS.912.A.7.11, SS.912.A.7.12, SS.912.A.7.15

Writing Activity

7. **PERSUASIVE** Imagine that you are a Republican presidential candidate preparing for a debate on foreign policy. Write an "opening statement" for the debate that describes how the Obama administration has failed to properly meet the challenges of the events described in this lesson.
LAFS.1112.WHST.1.1, LAFS.1112.WHST.4.10

LESSON 3

Obama's Domestic Policy Challenges

ESSENTIAL QUESTIONS

• How is American culture shaped by a set of common values and practices?
• How have disputes over ideas, values, and politics resulted in change?

READING HELPDESK

Academic Vocabulary

• deprive

Content Vocabulary

• deadlock
• hate crime
• indict

TAKING NOTES

Key Ideas and Details

Categorizing As you read, complete a graphic organizer similar to the one below by describing the U.S. domestic issues listed. LAFS.1112.RH.3.7

Issue	Main Points
Occupy Wall Street	
Tea Party	
Racial Inequality	
Gun Control	

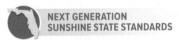

**NEXT GENERATION
SUNSHINE STATE STANDARDS**

LAFS.1112.RH.2.4: Determine the meaning of words and phrases as they are used in a text, including analyzing how an author uses and refines the meaning of a key term over the course of a text (e.g., how Madison defines faction in Federalist No. 10).

LAFS.1112.RH.3.7: Integrate and evaluate multiple sources of information presented in diverse formats and media (e.g., visually, quantitatively, as well as in words) in order to address a question or solve a problem.

LAFS.1112.WHST.1.1: Write arguments focused on discipline-specific content.

Continued on page 658

IT MATTERS BECAUSE

Politics and government in twenty-first century America is characterized by strongly opposing sides. A great deal of the debate in the media and in our hometowns centers around broad groups of conservatives and liberals who differ over how much problem-solving authority to give the federal government. The United States faces a great deal of social and economic changes, creating new challenges for all levels of government.

Polarized Politics

GUIDING QUESTION *How did Americans react to the slow economic recovery from the recession?*

There is always some income inequality in a free enterprise economic system. But during times of recession, when the economy slows dramatically, the inequality gap grows wider and a broader base of the population feels the pinch of the nation's economic weakness.

The Income Gap

The recession widened the gap between income levels in America. The economy improved, but slow wage growth and lingering unemployment hit those in middle and lower incomes the hardest. As wealthier individuals recovered from the recession faster, their share of the nation's total income increased. Middle-income families' share of income fell from 62 precent in 1970 to 45 percent in 2010. The share of income for the wealthiest rose from 29 percent in 1970 to 46 percent in 2010.

Middle income Americans cut back on their spending, which further restrained recovery. The decline in manufacturing jobs hit these families hardest. The family home was usually their biggest investment. When housing values fell sharply during the recession, some people found themselves paying for home mortgages that were worth more than their homes. Rising costs of health care and college tuition also battered those in the middle incomes.

Occupy Wall Street protestors claimed that high salaries and bonuses for corporate and banking executives were excessive. Social media coverage helped the protest in New York gain support, spawning similar protest movements that spread to a dozen major cities.

▶ **CRITICAL THINKING**
Identifying Central Ideas What was the main goal of the Occupy movement? LAFS.1112.RH.3.7, SS.912.A.1.4, SS.912.A.7.12

NEXT GENERATION SUNSHINE STATE STANDARDS

Continued from page 657

LAFS.1112.WHST.4.10: Write routinely over extended time frames (time for reflection and revision) and shorter time frames (a single sitting or a day or two) for a range of discipline-specific tasks, purposes, and audiences.

SS.912.A.1.2: Utilize a variety of primary and secondary sources to identify author, historical significance, audience, and authenticity to understand a historical period.

SS.912.A.1.4: Analyze how images, symbols, objects, cartoons, graphs, charts, maps, and artwork may be used to interpret the significance of time periods and events from the past.

SS.912.A.7.11: Analyze the foreign policy of the United States as it relates to Africa, Asia, the Caribbean, Latin America, and the Middle East.

SS.912.A.7.12: Analyze political, economic, and social concerns that emerged at the end of the 20th century and into the 21st century.

SS.912.A.7.15: Analyze the effects of foreign and domestic terrorism on the American people.

deadlock to be at a standstill and unable to progress because of equal and opposite forces

hate crime a category of crime that targets victims based upon race, creed, gender, or religious affiliation

Occupy Wall Street

The widening gap between income groups helped spark a movement called "Occupy Wall Street." Protesters claimed that they represented "the 99 percent" of the population against the wealthiest 1 percent. They began by occupying a park in New York City's financial district. Occupy Wall Street drew attention to economic inequality, tax breaks for the wealthy, and corporate greed. Most of the protesters were young and identified themselves as political independents who were critical of both major parties. President Obama acknowledged that the movement expressed people's frustration with the financial crisis. After police moved demonstrators out of the parks they had occupied, the movement dwindled. Although the Occupy Wall Street movement expressed popular anger, it suffered from a lack of leadership and specific solutions to the nation's economic problems.

The Tea Party in Congress

Public anxiety over the rising national debt was expressed by a protest group known as the Tea Party. Their goal was to cut federal spending and fight for lower taxes. Some Tea Party-endorsed candidates won seats in Congress in 2010. These new congresspersons favored confrontation over cooperation. When House Speaker John Boehner attempted to negotiate a budget compromise with the president, Tea Party conservatives rejected the agreement. A **deadlock** between Republicans and Democrats ensured little progress from Washington, D.C., and rising public disapproval for the government. This frustration grew throughout Obama's time in Washington and played a role in the 2016 presidential election.

New Civil Rights Issues

The first decades of the twenty-first century saw several different civil rights issues emerge. In 2009, President Obama signed the Matthew Shepard and James Byrd, Jr., Hate Crimes Prevention Act of 2009, a new federal law prompted by the 1998 murders of Matthew Shepard, a gay man, and James Byrd, Jr., an African American. In both cases, the savage nature of the murders attracted national attention. The law expanded the definition of hate crimes, provided funds to state and local authorities to encourage investigation of **hate crimes**, and gave federal authorities greater power to examine possible hate crimes when local authorities chose not to follow up.

The gay and lesbian civil rights movement also began to promote the right to same-sex marriage. In 2003, Massachusetts became the first state to legalize same-sex marriage. Laws regulating marriage have historically been a responsibility of state governments. As a result, the campaign for same-sex marriage took place largely at the state level.

Spencer Platt/Getty Images News/Getty Images

The *Obergefell* v. *Hodges* decision marked a dramatic shift in the interpretation of marriage rights and the meaning of the Constitution.

▶ **CRITICAL THINKING**
Understanding Consequences
How did critics of the *Obergefell* decision respond to the Supreme Court's ruling? LAFS.1112.RH.3.7, SS.912.A.1.4, SS.912.A.7.12

The problem facing gay and lesbian couples was that while their marriage might be legal in one state, if they moved to another state with different laws, their marriage might not be recognized. In 1996 Congress, with the support of President Clinton, had passed the Defense of Marriage Act (DOMA), defining marriage for federal purposes as a union between one man and one women and specifying that states could refuse to recognize same-sex marriages allowed in other states.

In 2012, in *Windsor* v. *United States*, the Supreme Court struck down part of DOMA, saying that the federal government could not limit marriage to one man and one woman. The Court ruled that limiting marriage **deprived** people of their Fifth Amendment rights under the due process clause because it meant treating people from different states in different ways. The Court's decision, however, did not overturn state laws regarding marriage. Thirty states had previously amended their constitutions to define marriage as between one man and one woman, but by 2015, same-sex marriage had become legal in 37 states and the District of Columbia.

In June 2015, the Supreme Court ruled in *Obergefell* v. *Hodges* that the Fourteenth Amendment's equal protection clause meant that the if a same sex couple were married in a state where it was legal, that marriage must be officially recognized in all states. The *Obergefell* ruling also overruled the 1996 DOMA law. While many Americans publically celebrated the ruling, critics complained that members of the Supreme Court had stretched the constitutional rights of gays and lesbians too far. Among those critics was dissenting Chief Justice John Roberts, who wrote "[the Court] is not a legislature. Whether same-sex marriage is a good idea should be of no concern to us."

deprive to take something away from someone

Clarifying Second Amendment Rights

Another major development involving the Bill of Rights came in 2008, in the case of *District of Columbia* v. *Heller*. For the first time, the Supreme Court ruled that the Second Amendment of the Constitution gives individuals the right to own firearms. The Second Amendment states: "A well regulated militia, being necessary to the security of a free state, the right of the people to keep and bear arms, shall not be infringed." For decades, supporters of gun control had cited the reference to a well-regulated militia as evidence that the right extended only to militias organized by state and federal governments. In *Heller*, the Supreme Court found for the first time that an individual's right to bear arms exists.

Andrew Harrer/Bloomberg/Getty Images

In 2010, in *McDonald* v. *Chicago*, the Court ruled that the Second Amendment also applies to the states, and that state laws must recognize the right of individuals to bear arms. For many conservatives, and organizations such as the National Rifle Association (NRA), the decisions represented a major victory in their decades-long effort to assert individual rights under the Second Amendment.

✓ READING PROGRESS CHECK

Identifying Central Issues What were the causes of disagreement over setting economic policies?

Social and Racial Unrest

GUIDING QUESTION *Were there any common threads that connected the various protests and protest groups together?*

In the summer of 2014, a police officer shot and killed a young African American man named Michael Brown in Ferguson, Missouri, a suburb of St. Louis. Brown's death sparked weeks of racial protest in Ferguson and in other urban areas across the country. Mass protests about the unequal treatment of African Americans by local police departments revealed a great deal of anger.

The Black Lives Matter Movement

Brown had robbed a convenience store and fled the scene. When local police responded to a 911 call and encountered Brown, there was a struggle. Officer Darren Wilson testified that Brown assaulted him and then tried to escape. Wilson pursued and fired his weapon multiple times. Brown, who was unarmed, was hit and later died. His death angered Ferguson residents and people around the country.

indict to charge someone with a criminal offense

When Officer Wilson was not **indicted** for the death of Brown, the public protests in Ferguson turned violent. Curfews attempted to maintain peace, but a great deal of property damage occurred, much of it to businesses. President Obama made a public statement that urged calm.

PRIMARY SOURCE

❝I join Michael [Brown's] parents in asking anyone who protests this decision to do so peacefully. Let me repeat Michael's father's words: 'Hurting others or destroying property is not the answer. . . . I do not want my son's death to be in vain. I want it to lead to incredible change, positive change. . . .' As [local police] do their jobs in the coming days, they need to work with the community . . . to distinguish [violent individuals] from the vast majority who just want their voice heard around legitimate issues. . . .❞

—President Barack Obama, statement on the Ferguson Grand Jury's decision, November 24, 2014

A series of social protests in 2015 brought new discussion on the actions of police officers during arrests.

▶ **CRITICAL THINKING**
Identifying Cause and Effect How did the Michael Brown arrest result in a series of protests across urban areas in the United States? LAFS.1112.RH.3.7, SS.912.A.1.4, SS.912.A.7.12

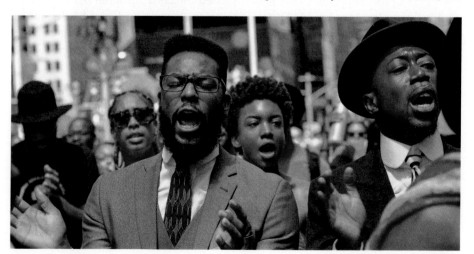

Albin Lohr-Jones/Pacific Press/LightRocket/Getty Images

An organization of ordinary citizens formed to protest these events. This grassroots movement called itself #BlackLivesMatter, using the hashtag symbol of a popular social media Web site. They organized public rallies in Ferguson and in several other cities across the country to draw attention to the incidents of police violence and to emphasize the economic and social inequality of African Americans in society and within the criminal justice system. The arrest-related death of Freddie Gray in Baltimore, Maryland in April 2015 further motivated protesters. Gray suffered a spinal injury during his arrest and died a week later. Public riots followed Gray's funeral.

Then, in June, more violence shocked the nation in Charleston, South Carolina. A white supremacist who had posted his racist beliefs online killed nine African Americans at a church prayer meeting. The resulting protests motivated the state government to take down the Confederate battle flag, which had flown on the capital building grounds since the 1950s. President Obama stated that this action and some changes in Ferguson, such as increased use of body cameras by police, was "a signal of good will and healing, and a meaningful step towards a better future."

Gun Violence and Public Safety

Gun violence repeatedly stunned the nation. In December 2012, a 20-year-old gunman killed 20 elementary school children and six staff members at the Sandy Hook elementary school in Newtown, Connecticut. The following month, the Obama administration called on Congress to strengthen gun control legislations, including better background checks during gun purchases to identify those with criminal records, a history of violent mental problems, or known terrorist ties.

Obama also wanted to ban the commercial sale of assault weapons that use high-capacity bullet magazines. The supporters of such restrictions claimed that reducing the number of bullets a shooter could carry would reduce the possibility of mass violence. Critics contended that people intent on enacting public shootings were not law-abiding citizens in the first place and would not be deterred by tougher laws.

When further shootings occurred, President Obama held several press conferences deploring each incident of violence, and asked the Republican and Democratic members of the House and the Senate to come together to pass stronger gun control legislation. Still, Congress did not pass any legislation. Some members of Congress strongly supported the right to own guns and the protections of the Second Amendment. Other members may have feared voters penalizing them in the next election by not voting them back in office.

In December 2015, there was a mass shooting in San Bernardino, California. A married couple entered the husband's office Christmas party and killed 14 coworkers and injured 7 others before they were killed by the police. At first, investigators were reluctant to blame the attacks on terrorist influences, but as the FBI examined the couple more carefully, evidence suggested that the attacks had been influenced by radical Islamic terrorist beliefs.

What was certain from the beginning was that the couple had a large collection of weapons and ammunition. Opponents of gun control argued that this incident showed that gun ownership could have provided protection from this violence, arguing that someone with a gun could have stopped the shooters before they had killed so many. Supporters of gun control countered that stronger laws could prevent violent people from acquiring the weapons and ammunition needed to carry out such deadly actions.

☑ READING PROGRESS CHECK

Identifying Central Issues How did members of Congress respond to President Obama's comments on the need for stronger gun control legislation?

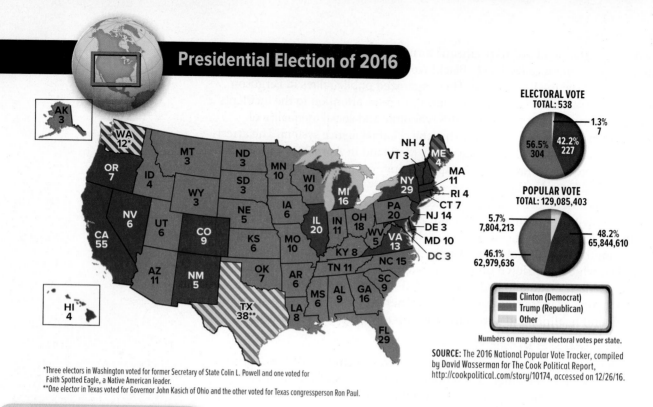

ELECTORAL VOTE
TOTAL: 538

56.5% 304 — 42.2% 227 — 1.3% 7

POPULAR VOTE
TOTAL: 129,085,403

5.7% 7,804,213 — 48.2% 65,844,610 — 46.1% 62,979,636

■ Clinton (Democrat)
■ Trump (Republican)
■ Other

Numbers on map show electoral votes per state.

SOURCE: The 2016 National Popular Vote Tracker, compiled by David Wasserman for The Cook Political Report, http://cookpolitical.com/story/10174, accessed on 12/26/16.

*Three electors in Washington voted for former Secretary of State Colin L. Powell and one voted for Faith Spotted Eagle, a Native American leader.
**One elector in Texas voted for Governor John Kasich of Ohio and the other voted for Texas congressperson Ron Paul.

GEOGRAPHY CONNECTION

In a surprise victory, Republican candidate Donald Trump defeated Democratic candidate Hillary Clinton.

1 **PLACES AND REGIONS** *What conclusions can you draw about the election based on what regions voted Republican and what regions voted Democrat?*

2 **THE WORLD IN SPATIAL TERMS** *Who won the most electoral votes? Who won the most popular votes? What effect could that result have on the perception of the election?*

President-elect Trump gives his victory speech on Election Night.

The 2016 Presidential Election

GUIDING QUESTION *What circumstances explained the outcome of the presidential election?*

The 2016 presidential election revealed a deep national divide over political, economic, and social issues. In 2015, a large number of men and women announced their candidacy. During the state primary phase of the campaign, 17 Republican candidates and 5 Democratic candidates ran for their party's official nomination.

Surprising Primary Results

Obama's Secretary of State Hillary Clinton fought and won a tight primary race against Vermont senator Bernie Sanders for the Democratic Party nomination. Clinton was expected to win the nomination but faced a real challenge from Sanders, who energized young voters by protesting economic imbalances and lack of opportunity that made daily life challenging for many Americans.

For Republicans, the biggest surprise was the candidacy of businessman and reality TV star Donald Trump. Trump's blunt rhetoric against Mexican and Muslim immigrants sparked outrage. But a growing number of Americans responded to Trump's promise to "Make America Great Again." Throughout the spring and summer of 2016, Trump's campaign won more and more Republican state primaries. He secured the Republican nomination by defeating challengers that included experienced senators and governors.

A Bitter Campaign with a Dramatic Result

The general election campaign included Green Party nominee Jill Stein and Libertarian Gary Johnson. But most of the media focus and national conversation centered on Donald Trump versus Hillary Clinton. The differences between the

Mark Wilson/Getty Images

two candidates were abundant. Clinton was the first woman major party nominee to run for president. She had decades of experience in government—as a state and national first lady, as a senator, and as secretary of state. Trump had no government or military experience.

The battle between Clinton and Trump was deeply personal and less focused on traditional political issues. The Republican kept his supporters angry over several events in Clinton's past government service—especially improper use of State Department emails. Though the FBI investigated and cleared Clinton of criminal wrong-doing, Trump supporters loved to chant "Lock her up!" at their candidate's rallies. The Clinton campaign described Trump as a man with a history of abuse toward women and an angry personality.

Clinton's message was one of cooperation and unity, both within the nation and with foreign allies. Her campaign highlighted her lifetime commitment to public service and government participation. It warned of Trump's unpredictability and portrayed him as unsuitable to represent the United States. Trump promised to restore American global influence, ignite the economy, provide needed jobs, and protect the nation from foreign threats.

The results on Election Night shocked many, from politicians to pollsters. Trump's aggressive America-first message appealed to Americans who could not get good jobs and felt ignored by Washington, D.C. Clinton appealed to women, minorities, and more educated voters—but not to the same levels of enthusiasm that had elected Barack Obama. Although Clinton won the popular vote, the Electoral College total swung on close vote counts in Wisconsin, Michigan, and Pennsylvania—propelled by voters that had suffered from years of industrial economic decline before and during the recession and who yearned for change. Once the victory was assured, Trump spoke to a crowd of happy supporters in New York City:

PRIMARY SOURCE

"I promise you that I will not let you down. We will do a great job. We will do a great job. I look very much forward to being your president, . . . and I can only say that while the campaign is over, our work on this movement is now really job beginning."

—President-elect Donald Trump, November 10, 2016

✓ READING PROGRESS CHECK

Identifying What were the main themes of Donald Trump's White House campaign?

LESSON 3 REVIEW

Reviewing Vocabulary

1. *Explaining* What political conditions resulted in so much government *deadlock*? LAFS.1112.RH.2.4

Using Your Notes

2. *Summarizing* Use your notes to write a paragraph summarizing the causes and consequences of the social protests of the summer of 2014. SS.912.A.7.12

Answering the Guiding Questions

3. *Identifying Central Issues* What were the main political concerns of Americans during Barack Obama's second term as president? SS.912.A.7.12, SS.912.A.7.15

4. *Identifying Cause and Effect* What event triggered the rise of the #BlackLivesMatter movement? SS.912.A.7.12

5. *Specifying* Describe the events of the 2016 presidential nomination campaign. SS.912.A.7.12

Writing Activity

6. **NARRATIVE** Imagine that you are a Republican Party member examining the progress of the 2016 presidential election campaign. Write a summary paragraph or two that describes what the focal points of the party nominee candidates were at the end of 2015 and into the primary and caucus races. Who were the main candidates and what were their main issue positions? LAFS.1112.WHST.1.1, LAFS.1112.WHST.4.10

STUDY GUIDE

OBAMA'S FIRST TERM
LESSON 1

HOME FORECLOSURES

Mortgage Delinquencies and Foreclosures by Period Past Due, All Loans

■ 30 Day (SA)* ■ 60 Day (SA) 90 Day (SA) Foreclosure Process

Source: Mortgage Bankers Association; U. S. Department of the Treasury
*(SA) stands for seasonally adjusted

A TROUBLED WORLD
LESSON 2

CONTINUED MIDDLE EAST UNREST

Arab Spring launches uprisings in Tunisia, Libya, and Egypt

Islamic State begins seizing land in Iraq and Syria

| 2011 | 2011 | 2014 | 2014 |

Almost all U.S. troops withdraw from Afghanistan and Iraq

New drone air attacks led by U.S. military try to push back at Islamic State troop movement

CHALLENGES AT HOME
LESSON 3

IMPORTANT SUPREME COURT CASES	
District of Columbia v. *Heller* (2008)	Ruled that the Second Amendment gives individuals the right to own firearms.
McDonald v. *Chicago* (2010)	Followed from *Heller* case that the Second Amendment right applies not only to federal law, but also state law.
Windsor v. *United States* (2012)	Eliminated part of the Defense of Marriage Act that limited definition of marriage to one man and one woman.
Obergefell v. *Hodges* (2015)	Recognized same-sex marriages as legal across all 50 states and overruled the Defense of Marriage Act.

Directions: On a separate sheet of paper, answer the questions below. Make sure you read carefully and answer all parts to the question.

Lesson Review

Lesson 1

1 *Making Connections* What are two aspects of the recession that the American Recovery and Reinvestment Act of 2009 was designed to combat, and how did it affect the private sector? SS.912.A.7.12

2 *Evaluating* What is the significance of Sonia Sotomayor's appointment to the Supreme Court?

3 *Analyzing* What compromises were required to pass healthcare reform in March 2010? How might those compromises affected public perception of the bill? SS.912.A.7.12

4 *Summarizing* Why did the national debt grow at an alarming rate, and what affect did the national debt have on politics? SS.912.A.7.12

Lesson 2

5 *Sequencing* Create a time line of the Ukrainian Crisis. SS.912.A.1.3, SS.912.A.7.12

6 *Defining* What was the Arab Spring, and what sort of changes did it cause? SS.912.A.7.12

7 *Evaluating* Why did the economic problems in some European Union countries have such a widespread impact? SS.912.A.7.12, SS.912.A.7.14

8 *Making Connections* What events led up to the refugee crisis? What events affected how Europe responded to the crisis? SS.912.A.7.12

Lesson 3

9 *Identifying* What were the goals and concerns of the Tea Party movement and the Occupy Wall Street movement? Which movement has had more success? Explain why. SS.912.A.7.12

10 *Describing* Pick a Supreme Court case from this lesson and describe what legal question it answered. What were the ideas, values, and politics that were debated in that case? SS.912.A.7.12

Exploring the Essential Questions

11 *Exploring Issues* How has social media changed how people participate and relate to politics and social issues? SS.912.A.7.12

12 *Summarizing* Given what you know about American history, how are the current disputes over ideas, values, and politics a continuation of larger historical debates? SS.912.A.7.12

Critical Thinking

13 *Identifying Cause and Effect* Why is 2008 a turning point in American political history? SS.912.A.7.12

14 *Exploring Issues* Describe some of the civil rights struggles of the twenty-first century. SS.912.A.7.12

15 *Sequencing* Identify and sequence key events of the war on terror from the end of President Bush's administration through President Obama's terms of office. SS.912.A.7.15

16 *Organizing* Create a chart listing major multinational corporations and individual entrepreneurs who have shaped the twenty-first century economy and the contributions each has made. SS.912.A.7.14

17 *Making Connections* How has the growth of technology affected America's role in the global economy? SS.912.A.7.12, SS.912.A.7.14

21st Century Skills

18 *Explaining* What were the major political issues of President Obama's first term? Identify the policies the president supported to address these issues. SS.912.A.7.11

19 *Economics* Explain the connection between credit and the housing crisis that began in 2007. SS.912.A.7.12, SS.912.A.7.14

20 *Identifying Cause and Effect* How did the financial crises in Greece and the European Union affect the United States economy? SS.912.A.7.12, SS.912.A.7.14

Need Extra Help?

If You've Missed Question	1	2	3	4	5	6	7	8	9	10	11	12	13	14	15	16	17	18	19	20
Go to Lesson	1	1	1	1	2	2	2	2	3	3	2,3	1,2,3	1	3	1	1	1	1	1	2

㉑ *Research Skills* Pick an activist movement from the last ten years in the United States. Research the arguments the activists make and any counter arguments that may have been around in that time. Then, present your findings to your classmates. As a class, discuss what common themes appear throughout the various different activist groups researched. LAFS.1112.SL.1.1, LAFS.1112.WHST.3.7, LAFS.1112.SL.2.4, SS.912.A.7.12

DBQ Analyzing Primary Sources

Read the excerpt below from Barack Obama's victory speech from 2008 and then answer the questions that follow:

PRIMARY SOURCE

"This is our moment . . . to put our people back to work and open doors of opportunity for our kids; to restore prosperity and promote the cause of peace; to reclaim the American Dream and reaffirm that fundamental truth—that out of many, we are one; that . . . where we are met with . . . those who tell us that we can't, we will respond with that timeless creed that sums up the spirit of a people: Yes We Can."

—from the Address at Grant Park, November 4, 2008

㉒ *Analyzing Primary Sources* What issues are being referenced in this excerpt? SS.912.A.7.12

㉓ *Evaluating Arguments* What is the tone of this speech? What aspects of American culture is Obama evoking and why? LAFS.1112.RH.1.1, LAFS.1112.RH.1.2, LAFS.1112.RH.3.8, LAFS.1112.SL.1.3

Analyzing Visuals

Use the image to answer the following questions.

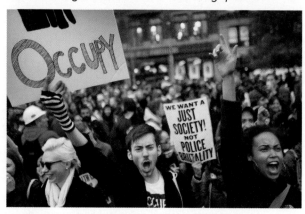

㉔ Which of the following answer choices agrees with that you can see about this photo of the Occupy Movement?

A The Occupy Movement was based primarily in the Great Plains states.

B The Occupy Movement appealed to a wide variety of American citizens.

C The Occupy Movement fought against the notion of equality for all Americans.

D The Occupy Movement drew its base of influence from rural areas.

㉕ Why did this protest movement take up the word "Occupy" as its movement name? Think about what you see in the picture and what you know from your study to answer the question.

Extended Response Question

㉖ *Analyzing* Using the material in this chapter and your own research, write an essay analyzing how the threat of terrorism has affected American politics. LAFS.1112.WHST.1.2, LAFS.1112.WHST.3.7, LAFS.1112.WHST.4.10, SS.912.A.7.15

Spencer Platt/Getty Images News/Getty Images

Need Extra Help?

If You've Missed Question	㉑	㉒	㉓	㉔	㉕	㉖
Go to Lesson	3	1	1	3	3	2, 3

CONTENTS

PRESIDENTS OF THE UNITED STATES

**The first Republican Party became toda... Democratic Party. Today's Republican Pa... began in 1854.

1. GEORGE WASHINGTON

Presidential term: 1789–1797
Lived: 1732–1799
Born in: Virginia
Elected from: Virginia
Occupations: Soldier, Planter
Party: None
Vice President: John Adams

2. JOHN ADAMS

Presidential term: 1797–1801
Lived: 1735–1826
Born in: Massachusetts
Elected from: Massachusetts
Occupations: Teacher, Lawyer
Party: Federalist
Vice President: Thomas Jefferson

3. THOMAS JEFFERSON

Presidential term: 1801–1809
Lived: 1743–1826
Born in: Virginia
Elected from: Virginia
Occupations: Planter, Lawyer
Party: Republican**
Vice Presidents: Aaron Burr,
                 George Clinton

4. JAMES MADISON

Presidential term: 1809–1817
Lived: 1751–1836
Born in: Virginia
Elected from: Virginia
Occupation: Planter
Party: Republican**
Vice Presidents: George Clinton,
                 Elbridge Gerry

5. JAMES MONROE

Presidential term: 1817–1825
Lived: 1758–1831
Born in: Virginia
Elected from: Virginia
Occupation: Lawyer
Party: Republican**
Vice President: Daniel D.
                Tompkins

6. JOHN QUINCY ADAMS

Presidential term: 1825–1829
Lived: 1767–1848
Born in: Massachusetts
Elected from: Massachusetts
Occupation: Lawyer
Party: Republican**
Vice President: John C. Calhoun

7. ANDREW JACKSON

Presidential term: 1829–1837
Lived: 1767–1845
Born in: South Carolina
Elected from: Tennessee
Occupations: Lawyer, Soldier
Party: Democratic
Vice Presidents: John C. Calhoun,
                 Martin Van Buren

8. MARTIN VAN BUREN

Presidential term: 1837–1841
Lived: 1782–1862
Born in: New York
Elected from: New York
Occupation: Lawyer
Party: Democratic
Vice President: Richard M.
                Johnson

9. WILLIAM H. HARRISON

Presidential term: 1841
Lived: 1773–1841
Born in: Virginia
Elected from: Ohio
Occupations: Soldier, Planter
Party: Whig
Vice President: John Tyler

The White House Historical Association

10 JOHN TYLER

Presidential term: 1841–1845
Lived: 1790–1862
Born in: Virginia
Elected as V.P. from: Virginia
 Succeeded Harrison
Occupation: Lawyer
Party: Whig
Vice President: None

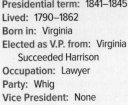

11 JAMES K. POLK

Presidential term: 1845–1849
Lived: 1795–1849
Born in: North Carolina
Elected from: Tennessee
Occupation: Lawyer
Party: Democratic
Vice President: George M. Dallas

12 ZACHARY TAYLOR

Presidential term: 1849–1850
Lived: 1784–1850
Born in: Virginia
Elected from: Louisiana
Occupation: Soldier
Party: Whig
Vice President: Millard Fillmore

13 MILLARD FILLMORE

Presidential term: 1850–1853
Lived: 1800–1874
Born in: New York
Elected as V.P. from: New York
 Succeeded Taylor
Occupation: Lawyer
Party: Whig
Vice President: None

14 FRANKLIN PIERCE

Presidential term: 1853–1857
Lived: 1804–1869
Born in: New Hampshire
Elected from: New Hampshire
Occupation: Lawyer
Party: Democratic
Vice President: William R. King

15 JAMES BUCHANAN

Presidential term: 1857–1861
Lived: 1791–1868
Born in: Pennsylvania
Elected from: Pennsylvania
Occupation: Lawyer
Party: Democratic
Vice President: John C.
 Breckinridge

16 ABRAHAM LINCOLN

Presidential term: 1861–1865
Lived: 1809–1865
Born in: Kentucky
Elected from: Illinois
Occupation: Lawyer
Party: Republican
Vice Presidents: Hannibal Hamlin,
 Andrew Johnson

17 ANDREW JOHNSON

Presidential term: 1865–1869
Lived: 1808–1875
Born in: North Carolina
Elected as V.P. from: Tennessee
 Succeeded Lincoln
Occupation: Tailor
Party: Democratic; National
Unionist
Vice President: None

18 ULYSSES S. GRANT

Presidential term: 1869–1877
Lived: 1822–1885
Born in: Ohio
Elected from: Illinois
Occupations: Farmer, Soldier
Party: Republican
Vice Presidents: Schuyler Colfax,
 Henry Wilson

The White House Historical Association

19 RUTHERFORD B. HAYES

Presidential term: 1877–1881
Lived: 1822–1893
Born in: Ohio
Elected from: Ohio
Occupation: Lawyer
Party: Republican
Vice President: William A.
        Wheeler

20 JAMES A. GARFIELD

Presidential term: 1881
Lived: 1831–1881
Born in: Ohio
Elected from: Ohio
Occupations: Laborer, Professor
Party: Republican
Vice President: Chester A.
        Arthur

21 CHESTER A. ARTHUR

Presidential term: 1881–1885
Lived: 1830–1886
Born in: Vermont
Elected as V.P. from: New York
        Succeeded Garfield
Occupations: Teacher, Lawyer
Party: Republican
Vice President: None

22 GROVER CLEVELAND

Presidential term: 1885–1889
Lived: 1837–1908
Born in: New Jersey
Elected from: New York
Occupation: Lawyer
Party: Democratic
Vice President: Thomas A.
        Hendricks

23 BENJAMIN HARRISON

Presidential term: 1889–1893
Lived: 1833–1901
Born in: Ohio
Elected from: Indiana
Occupation: Lawyer
Party: Republican
Vice President: Levi P. Morton

24 GROVER CLEVELAND

Presidential term: 1893–1897
Lived: 1837–1908
Born in: New Jersey
Elected from: New York
Occupation: Lawyer
Party: Democratic
Vice President: Adlai E. Stevenson

25 WILLIAM MCKINLEY

Presidential term: 1897–1901
Lived: 1843–1901
Born in: Ohio
Elected from: Ohio
Occupations: Teacher, Lawyer
Party: Republican
Vice Presidents: Garret Hobart,
        Theodore
        Roosevelt

26 THEODORE ROOSEVELT

Presidential term: 1901–1909
Lived: 1858–1919
Born in: New York
Elected as V.P. from: New York
        Succeeded McKinley
Occupations: Historian, Rancher
Party: Republican
Vice President: Charles W. Fair-
        banks

27 WILLIAM H. TAFT

Presidential term: 1909–1913
Lived: 1857–1930
Born in: Ohio
Elected from: Ohio
Occupations: Lawyer
Party: Republican
Vice President: James S.
        Sherman

The White House Historical Association

28 WOODROW WILSON

Presidential term: 1913–1921
Lived: 1856–1924
Born in: Virginia
Elected from: New Jersey
Occupation: College Professor
Party: Democratic
Vice President: Thomas R.
Marshall

29 WARREN G. HARDING

Presidential term: 1921–1923
Lived: 1865–1923
Born in: Ohio
Elected from: Ohio
Occupations: Newspaper
Editor, Publisher
Party: Republican
Vice President: Calvin Coolidge

30 CALVIN COOLIDGE

Presidential term: 1923–1929
Lived: 1872–1933
Born in: Vermont
Elected as V.P. from: Massachusetts, Succeeded Harding
Occupation: Lawyer
Party: Republican
Vice President: Charles G. Dawes

31 HERBERT C. HOOVER

Presidential term: 1929–1933
Lived: 1874–1964
Born in: Iowa
Elected from: California
Occupation: Engineer
Party: Republican
Vice President: Charles Curtis

32 FRANKLIN D. ROOSEVELT

Presidential term: 1933–1945
Lived: 1882–1945
Born in: New York
Elected from: New York
Occupation: Lawyer
Party: Democratic
Vice Presidents: John N. Garner,
Henry A. Wallace, Harry S.Truman

33 HARRY S. TRUMAN

Presidential term: 1945–1953
Lived: 1884–1972
Born in: Missouri
Elected as V.P. from: Missouri
Succeeded Roosevelt
Occupations: Clerk, Farmer
Party: Democratic
Vice President: Alben W. Barkley

34 DWIGHT D. EISENHOWER

Presidential term: 1953–1961
Lived: 1890–1969
Born in: Texas
Elected from: New York
Occupation: Soldier
Party: Republican
Vice President: Richard M.
Nixon

35 JOHN F. KENNEDY

Presidential term: 1961–1963
Lived: 1917–1963
Born in: Massachusetts
Elected from: Massachusetts
Occupations: Author, Reporter
Party: Democratic
Vice President: Lyndon B.
Johnson

36 LYNDON B. JOHNSON

Presidential term: 1963–1969
Lived: 1908–1973
Born in: Texas
Elected as V.P. from: Texas
Succeeded Kennedy
Occupation: Teacher
Party: Democratic
Vice President: Hubert H.
Humphrey

The White House Historical Association

PRESIDENTS OF THE UNITED STATES

37 RICHARD M. NIXON

Presidential term: 1969–1974
Lived: 1913–1994
Born in: California
Elected from: New York
Occupation: Lawyer
Party: Republican
Vice Presidents: Spiro T. Agnew,
    Gerald R. Ford

38 GERALD R. FORD

Presidential term: 1974–1977
Lived: 1913–2006
Born in: Nebraska
    Appointed as V.P. upon Agnew's
    resignation; succeeded Nixon
Occupation: Lawyer
Party: Republican
Vice President: Nelson A.
    Rockefeller

39 JAMES E. CARTER, JR.

Presidential term: 1977–1981
Lived: 1924–
Born in: Georgia
Elected from: Georgia
Occupations: Business, Farmer
Party: Democratic
Vice President: Walter F. Mondale

40 RONALD W. REAGAN

Presidential term: 1981–1989
Lived: 1911–2004
Born in: Illinois
Elected from: California
Occupations: Actor, Lecturer
Party: Republican
Vice President: George H.W.
    Bush

41 GEORGE H.W. BUSH

Presidential term: 1989–1993
Lived: 1924–
Born in: Massachusetts
Elected from: Texas
Occupation: Business
Party: Republican
Vice President: J. Danforth
    Quayle

42 WILLIAM J. CLINTON

Presidential term: 1993–2001
Lived: 1946–
Born in: Arkansas
Elected from: Arkansas
Occupation: Lawyer
Party: Democratic
Vice President: Albert Gore, Jr.

43 GEORGE W. BUSH

Presidential term: 2001–2009
Lived: 1946–
Born in: Connecticut
Elected from: Texas
Occupation: Business
Party: Republican
Vice President: Richard B.
    Cheney

44 BARACK H. OBAMA

Presidential term: 2009–2017
Lived: 1961–
Born in: Hawaii
Elected from: Illinois
Occupation: Lawyer
Party: Democratic
Vice President: Joseph R.
    Biden, Jr.

45 DONALD J. TRUMP

Presidential term: 2017 –
Lived: 1946–
Born in: New York
Elected from: New York
Occupation: Business,
Entertainer
Party: Republican
Vice President: Michael R. Pence

(left to right, top to bottom)White House Historical Association; (8)Brooks Kraft/CORBIS; (9)Dan Hallman/AP Images

U.S. Territories

Puerto Rico
Population: 3,725,789
Land area: 3,425 sq. mi.

Guam
Population: 159,358
Land area: 209 sq. mi.

U.S. Virgin Islands
Population: 106,405
Land area: 134 sq. mi.

American Samoa
Population: 55,519
Land area: 77 sq. mi.

Northern Mariana Islands
Population: 53,883
Land area: 184 sq. mi.

Washington, D.C.
Population: 601,723
Land area: 61 sq. mi.

The states are listed in the order they were admitted to the Union. Population figures are based on U.S. Bureau of the Census for 2010. House of Representatives figures are from the Clerk of the House of Representatives. States are not drawn to scale.

1 Delaware
Year Admitted: 1787
Population: 897,934
Land area: 1,949 sq. mi.
Representatives: 1

2 Pennsylvania
Year Admitted: 1787
Population: 12,702,379
Land area: 44,743 sq. mi.
Representatives: 19

3 New Jersey
Year Admitted: 1787
Population: 8,791,894
Land area: 7,354 sq. mi.
Representatives: 13

4 Georgia
Year Admitted: 1788
Population: 9,687,653
Land area: 57,513 sq. mi.
Representatives: 13

5 Connecticut
Year Admitted: 1788
Population: 3,574,097
Land area: 4,842 sq. mi.
Representatives: 5

6 Massachusetts
Year Admitted: 1788
Population: 6,547,629
Land area: 7,800 sq. mi.
Representatives: 10
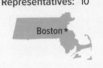

7 Maryland
Year Admitted: 1788
Population: 5,773,552
Land area: 9,707 sq. mi.
Representatives: 8

8 South Carolina
Year Admitted: 1788
Population: 4,625,364
Land area: 30,061 sq. mi.
Representatives: 6

9 New Hampshire
Year Admitted: 1788
Population: 1,316,470
Land area: 8,953 sq. mi.
Representatives: 2

10 Virginia
Year Admitted: 1788
Population: 8,001,024
Land area: 39,490 sq. mi.
Representatives: 11

11 New York
Year Admitted: 1788
Population: 19,378,102
Land area: 47,126 sq. mi.
Representatives: 29

12 North Carolina
Year Admitted: 1789
Population: 9,535,483
Land area: 48,618 sq. mi.
Representatives: 13

13 Rhode Island
Year Admitted: 1790
Population: 1,052,567
Land area: 1,034 sq. mi.
Representatives: 2

14 Vermont
Year Admitted: 1791
Population: 625,741
Land area: 9,217 sq. mi.
Representatives: 1

15 Kentucky
Year Admitted: 1792
Population: 4,339,367
Land area: 39,486 sq. mi.
Representatives: 6

16 Tennessee
Year Admitted: 1796
Population: 6,346,105
Land area: 41,235 sq. mi.
Representatives: 9

17 Ohio
Year Admitted: 1803
Population: 11,536,504
Land area: 40,861 sq. mi.
Representatives: 18

18 Louisiana
Year Admitted: 1812
Population: 4,533,372
Land area: 43,204 sq. mi.
Representatives: 7

19 Indiana
Year Admitted: 1816
Population: 6,483,802
Land area: 35,826 sq. mi.
Representatives: 9

20 Mississippi
Year Admitted: 1817
Population: 2,967,297
Land area: 46,923 sq. mi.
Representatives: 4

21 Illinois
Year Admitted: 1818
Population: 12,830,632
Land area: 55,519 sq. mi.
Representatives: 19

★ Springfield

22 Alabama
Year Admitted: 1819
Population: 4,779,736
Land area: 50,645 sq. mi.
Representatives: 7

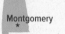
Montgomery
★

23 Maine
Year Admitted: 1820
Population: 1,328,361
Land area: 30,843 sq. mi.
Representatives: 2

★ Augusta

24 Missouri
Year Admitted: 1821
Population: 5,988,927
Land area: 68,742 sq. mi.
Representatives: 9

Jefferson City
★

25 Arkansas
Year Admitted: 1836
Population: 2,915,918
Land area: 52,035 sq. mi.
Representatives: 4

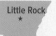
Little Rock
★

26 Michigan
Year Admitted: 1837
Population: 9,883,640
Land area: 56,539 sq. mi.
Representatives: 15

Lansing
★

27 Florida
Year Admitted: 1845
Population: 18,801,310
Land area: 53,625 sq. mi.
Representatives: 25

★Tallahassee

28 Texas
Year Admitted: 1845
Population: 25,145,561
Land area: 261,232 sq. mi.
Representatives: 32

Austin
★

29 Iowa
Year Admitted: 1846
Population: 3,046,355
Land area: 55,857 sq. mi.
Representatives: 5

★ Des Moines

30 Wisconsin
Year Admitted: 1848
Population: 5,686,986
Land area: 54,158 sq. mi.
Representatives: 8

Madison
★

31 California
Year Admitted: 1850
Population: 37,253,956
Land area: 155,779 sq. mi.
Representatives: 53

★
Sacramento

32 Minnesota
Year Admitted: 1858
Population: 5,303,925
Land area: 79,627 sq. mi.
Representatives: 8

Saint Paul
★

33 Oregon
Year Admitted: 1859
Population: 3,831,074
Land area: 95,988 sq. mi.
Representatives: 5

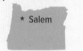
★ Salem

34 Kansas
Year Admitted: 1861
Population: 2,853,118
Land area: 81,759 sq. mi.
Representatives: 4

Topeka ★

35 West Virginia
Year Admitted: 1863
Population: 1,852,994
Land area: 24,038 sq. mi.
Representatives: 3

★ Charleston

36 Nevada
Year Admitted: 1864
Population: 2,700,551
Land area: 109,781 sq. mi.
Representatives: 3

★ Carson City

37 Nebraska
Year Admitted: 1867
Population: 1,826,341
Land area: 76,824 sq. mi.
Representatives: 3

Lincoln ★

38 Colorado
Year Admitted: 1876
Population: 5,029,196
Land area: 103,642 sq. mi.
Representatives: 7

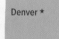
Denver ★

39 North Dakota
Year Admitted: 1889
Population: 672,591
Land area: 69,001 sq. mi.
Representatives: 1

Bismarck
★

40 South Dakota
Year Admitted: 1889
Population: 814,180
Land area: 75,811 sq. mi.
Representatives: 1

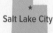
Pierre
★

41 Montana
Year Admitted: 1889
Population: 989,415
Land area: 145,546 sq. mi.
Representatives: 1

★ Helena

42 Washington
Year Admitted: 1889
Population: 6,724,540
Land area: 66,456 sq. mi.
Representatives: 9

★ Olympia

43 Idaho
Year Admitted: 1890
Population: 1,567,582
Land area: 82,643 sq. mi.
Representatives: 2

★ Boise

44 Wyoming
Year Admitted: 1890
Population: 563,626
Land area: 97,093 sq. mi.
Representatives: 1

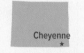
Cheyenne
★

45 Utah
Year Admitted: 1896
Population: 2,763,885
Land area: 82,170 sq. mi.
Representatives: 3

★
Salt Lake City

46 Oklahoma
Year Admitted: 1907
Population: 3,751,351
Land area: 68,595 sq. mi.
Representatives: 5

Oklahoma City
★

47 New Mexico
Year Admitted: 1912
Population: 2,059,179
Land area: 121,298 sq. mi.
Representatives: 3

★
Santa Fe

48 Arizona
Year Admitted: 1912
Population: 6,392,017
Land area: 113,594 sq. mi.
Representatives: 8

Phoenix
★

49 Alaska
Year Admitted: 1959
Population: 710,231
Land area: 570,641 sq. mi.
Representatives: 1

Juneau ★

50 Hawaii
Year Admitted: 1959
Population: 1,360,301
Land area: 6,422 sq. mi.
Representatives: 2

Honolulu ★

CONTENTS

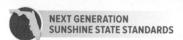

NEXT GENERATION SUNSHINE STATE STANDARDS

LAFS.1112.RH.1.1, LAFS.1112.RH.1.2,
LAFS.1112.RH.2.4, LAFS.1112.RH.2.5,
LAFS.1112.RH.4.10, LAFS.1112.SL.1.3,
LAFS.1112.WHST.3.9, SS.912.A.1.2

The Magna Carta, *signed by King John of England in 1215, marked a decisive step forward in the development of English constitutional government. Later, it served as a model for the colonists, who carried the Magna Carta's guarantees of political rights to America.*

" John, by the grace of God, king of England, lord of Ireland, duke of Normandy and Aquitaine, and count of Anjou; to the archbishops, bishops, abbots, earls, barons, justiciaries, foresters, sheriffs, reeves, ministers, and all bailiffs, and others his faithful subjects, greeting. . . . "

1. We have, in the first place, granted to God, and by this our present charter, confirmed for us and our heirs forever that the English church shall be free. . . .

9. Neither we nor our bailiffs shall seize any land or rent for any debt so long as the debtor's **chattels** are sufficient to discharge the same. . . .

12. No **scutage** or aid shall be imposed in our kingdoms unless by the common counsel thereof. . . .

14. For obtaining the common counsel of the kingdom concerning the assessment of aids . . . or of scutage, we will cause to be summoned, severally by our letters, the archbishops, bishops, abbots, earls, and great barons; we will also cause to be summoned generally, by our sheriffs and bailiffs, all those who hold lands directly of us, to meet on a fixed day . . . and at a fixed place. . . .

20. A free man shall be **amerced** for a small fault only according to the measure thereof, and for a great crime according to its magnitude. . . . None of these achievements shall be imposed except by the oath of honest men of the neighborhood.

21. Earls and barons shall be amerced only by their peers and only in proportion to the measure of the offense. . . .

38. In the future no bailiff shall upon his own unsupported accusation put any man to trial without producing credible witnesses to the truth of the accusation.

39. No free man shall be taken, imprisoned, **disseised**, outlawed, banished, or in any way destroyed, nor will we proceed against or prosecute him, except by the lawful judgment of his peers and by the law of the land.

40. To no one will we sell, to none will we deny or delay, right or justice. . . .

42. In the future it shall be lawful . . . for anyone to leave and return to our kingdom safely and securely by land and water, saving his fealty to us. Excepted are those who have been imprisoned or outlawed according to the law of the land. . . .

61. Whereas we, for the honor of God, and the amendment of our realm, and in order the better to allay the discord arisen between us and our barons, have granted all these things aforesaid. . . .

63. Wherefore we will, and firmly charge that all men in our kingdom shall have and hold all the aforesaid liberties, rights, and concessions . . . fully, and wholly to them and their heirs . . . in all places ever. . . . It is moreover sworn, as well on our part as on the part of the barons, that all these matters aforesaid will be kept in good faith and without deceit. Witness the above named and many others. Given by our hand in the meadow which is called Runnymeade. . . .

VOCABULARY

chattels
a piece of property other than real estate

scutage
tax

amerced
punished

disseised
seized

DBQ Analyzing Historical Documents

1 Identifying Which paragraph discusses the idea of a punishment "fitting" a crime?

2 Citing Text Evidence What are the similarities between the Magna Carta and the Bill of Rights? Provide at least one specific example from the text of the Magna Carta to support your comparison.

3 Assessing Which paragraphs address an individual's right to a trial by jury?

NEXT GENERATION SUNSHINE STATE STANDARDS

LAFS.1112.RH.1.1, LAFS.1112.RH.1.2,
LAFS.1112.RH.2.4, LAFS.1112.RH.2.5,
LAFS.1112.RH.4.10, LAFS.1112.SL.1.3,
LAFS.1112.WHST.3.9, SS.912.A.1.2

The Mayflower Compact, *On November 21, 1620, 41 colonists drafted the Mayflower Compact while still aboard the Mayflower. It was the first self-government plan ever put into effect in the English colonies. The compact was drawn up under these circumstances, as directed by Governor William Bradford:*

" This day, before we came to harbor, observing some not well affected to unity and **concord**, but gave some appearance of faction, it was thought good there should be an association and agreement that we should combine together in one body, and to submit to such government and governors as we should by common consent agree to make and choose, and set our hands to this that follows word for word. "

In the Name of God, Amen. We, who names are underwritten, the Loyal Subjects of our dread Sovereign Lord King James, by the Grace of God, of Great Britain, France, and Ireland, King, Defender of the Faith, etc.

Having undertaken for the Glory of God, and Advancement of the Christian Faith, and the honor of our King and Country, a Voyage to plant the first Colony in the northern Parts of Virginia. Do by these Presence of God and one another, covenant and combine ourselves together into a civil Body Politick, for our better Ordering and Preservation, and Furtherance of the Ends aforesaid; And by Virtue hereof do enact, constitute, and frame, such just and equal Laws, Ordinances, Acts, Constitutions, and Offices, from time to time, as shall be thought most **meet** and convenient for the general Good of the Colony; unto which we promise all due Submission and Obedience. In Witness, whereof we have hereunder subscribed our names at Cape Cod the eleventh of November, in the Reign of our Sovereign Lord King James of England, France, and Ireland, the eighteenth and of Scotland, the fifty-fourth. Anno Domini, 1620.

VOCABULARY

meet
suitable

concord
in agreement

DBQ Analyzing Historical Documents

❶ *Specifying* Why did the conditions aboard the *Mayflower* prompt Governor Bradford to draft the *Mayflower Compact?*

❷ *Identifying* Based on Bradford's statement, which three countries do you think were represented by the passengers aboard the *Mayflower?*

❸ *Recognizing Bias* Based on Bradford's use of the word "dread" to describe King James, what can be determined about his opinion of the king?

NEXT GENERATION SUNSHINE STATE STANDARDS

LAFS.1112.RH.1.1, LAFS.1112.RH.1.2,
LAFS.1112.RH.2.4, LAFS.1112.RH.2.5,
LAFS.1112.RH.4.10, LAFS.1112.SL.1.3,
LAFS.1112.WHST.3.9, SS.912.A.1.2

The Fundamental Orders of Connecticut,

In January 1639, settlers in Connecticut, led by Thomas Hooker, drew up the Fundamental Orders of Connecticut—America's first written constitution. It is essentially a body of laws and a compact among the settlers.

" Foreasmuch as it has pleased the Almighty God by the wide disposition of His Divine Providence so to order and dispose of things that we, the inhabitants and residents of Windsor, Hartford, and Wethersfield are now cohibiting and dwelling in and upon the river of Conectecotte and the lands thereunto adjoining; and well knowing where a people are gathered together the Word of God requires that, to maintain the peace and union of such a people, there should be an orderly and decent government established according to God, . . . do therefore associate and conjoin ourselves to be as one public state or commonwealth. . . . As also in our civil affairs to be guided and governed according to such laws, rules, orders, and decrees as shall be made, ordered, and decreed, as follows:

1. It is ordered . . . that there shall be yearly two general assemblies or courts; . . . The first shall be called the Court of Election, wherein shall be yearly chosen . . . so many magistrates and other public officers as shall be found **requisite**. Whereof one to be chosen governor . . . and no other magistrate to be chosen for more than one year; provided always there be six chosen beside the governor . . . by all that are admitted freemen and have taken the oath of fidelity, and do cohabit within this jurisdiction. . . .

4. It is ordered . . . that no person be chosen governor above once in two years, and that the governor be always a member of some approved congregation, and formerly of the magistracy within this jurisdiction; and all the magistrates freemen of this Commonwealth. . . .

5. It is ordered . . . that to the aforesaid Court of Election the several towns shall send their deputies. . . . Also, the other General Court . . . shall be for making of laws, and any other public occasion which concerns the good of the Commonwealth. . . .

7. It is ordered . . . that . . . the **constable** or constables of each town shall forthwith give notice distinctly to the inhabitants of the same . . . that . . . they meet and assemble themselves together to elect and choose certain deputies to be at the General Court then following to [manage] the affairs of the Commonwealth; . . .

10. It is ordered . . . that every General Court . . . shall consist of the governor, or someone chosen to moderate the Court, and four other magistrates, at least, with the major part of the deputies of the several towns legally chosen. . . . In which said General Courts shall consist the supreme power of the Commonwealth, and they only shall have power to make laws or repeal them, to grant levies, to admit of freemen, dispose of lands undisposed of to several towns or person, and also shall have power to call either Court or magistrate or any other person whatsoever into question for any misdemeanor. . . . "

VOCABULARY

requisite
needed for reaching a goal or achieving a purpose

constable
a police officer usually of a village or small town

DBQ Analyzing Historical Documents

❶ *Identifying* How many years in a row can a person serve as governor?

❷ *Explaining* What were the powers of the General Court?

❸ *Making Connections* In what ways do you think the settlers' past experience with government influenced the scope of the Fundamental Orders of Connecticut? Explain.

The English Bill of Rights,

In 1689 William of Orange and his wife Mary became joint rulers of England after accepting a list of conditions that later became known as the English Bill of Rights. This document assured the English people of certain basic civil rights and limited the power of the English monarchy.

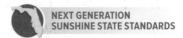

NEXT GENERATION
SUNSHINE STATE STANDARDS

LAFS.1112.RH.1.1, LAFS.1112.RH.1.2,
LAFS.1112.RH.2.4, LAFS.1112.RH.2.5,
LAFS.1112.RH.4.10, LAFS.1112.SL.1.3,
LAFS.1112.WHST.3.9, SS.912.A.1.2

❝ An act declaring the rights and liberties of the subject and settling the succession of the crown. Whereas the lords spiritual and temporal and commons assembled at Westminster lawfully, fully, and freely representing all the estates of the people of this realm did upon the thirteenth day of February in the year of our Lord one thousand six hundred eighty-eight [-nine] present unto their majesties . . . William and Mary prince and princess of Orange . . . . a certain declaration in writing made by the said lords and commons in the words following viz [namely]:

> Whereas the late king James the second, by the assistance of **divers** evil counsellors, judges and ministers employed by him did endeavor to subvert and **extirpate** the Protestant religion and the laws and liberties of this kingdom.
> By assuming and exercising a power of dispensing with and suspending of laws and the execution of laws without consent of parliament. . . .
> By levying money for and to the use of the crown by pretence of **prerogative** for other time and in other manner than the same was granted by parliament.
> By raising and keeping a standing army within this kingdom in time of peace without consent of parliament and quartering soldiers contrary to law. . . .
> By violating the freedom of election of members to serve in parliament. . . .
> And excessive bail hath been required of persons committed in criminal cases to elude the benefit of the laws made for the liberty of the subjects.
> And excessive fines have been imposed.
> And illegal and cruel punishments inflicted. . .
> And thereupon the said lords spiritual and temporal and commons . . . do . . . declare that the pretended power of suspending of laws or the execution of laws by regal authority without consent of parliament is illegal.
> That levying money for or to the use of the crown . . . without grant of parliament for longer time or in other manner than the same is or shall be granted is illegal.
> That it is the right of the subjects to petition the king and all commitments and protections for such petitioning are illegal.
> That the raising or keeping a standing army within the kingdom in time of peace unless it be with consent of parliament is against law. . . .
> That election of members of parliament ought to be free. . . .
> That excessive bail ought not to be required nor excessive fines imposed nor cruel and unusual punishments inflicted. . . .
> The said lords . . . do resolve that William and Mary, prince and princess of Orange, be declared king and queen of England, France, and Ireland. . . . ❞

VOCABULARY

divers
various

extirpate
to destroy

prerogative
a special right or privilege given because of one's rank or position

DBQ Analyzing Historical Documents

① Defending The document states that King James II "raised a standing army . . . and quartered soldiers contrary to law." What was unlawful about these actions?

② Recognizing Bias How does the author's point of view affect the tone of the document?

③ Determining Meaning How did the English Bill of Rights settle "the succession of the crown"?

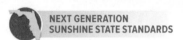

NEXT GENERATION SUNSHINE STATE STANDARDS

LAFS.1112.RH.1.1, LAFS.1112.RH.1.2,
LAFS.1112.RH.2.4, LAFS.1112.RH.2.5,
LAFS.1112.RH.4.10, LAFS.1112.SL.1.3,
LAFS.1112.WHST.3.9, SS.912.A.1.2

Second Treatise of Government,

English philosopher John Locke wrote Two Treatises of Government *in the early 1680s. Published in 1690, the* Second Treatise of Government *argues that government should be based on an agreement between the people and their ruler, and that if the ruler violates the agreement, a rebellion by the people may be justified.*

" *Of the State of Nature*

To understand Political Power right, and to derive it from its Original, we must consider what State all Men are naturally in, and that is, a State of perfect Freedom to order their Actions, and dispose of their Possessions, and Persons as they think fit, within the bounds of the Law of Nature, without asking leave, or depending upon the Will of any other Man.

Of the Beginning of Political Societies

Men being, as has been said, by Nature, all free, equal and independent, no one can be put out of this Estate, and subjected to the Political Power of another, without his own Consent. The only way whereby any one **divests** himself of his Natural Liberty and puts on the bounds of Civil Society is by agreeing with other Men to Joyn and unite into a Community, for their comfortable, safe, and peaceable living one amongst another, in a secure Enjoyment of their properties, and a greater Security against any that are not of it. This any number of Men may do, because it injures not the Freedom of the rest; they are left as they were in the Liberty of the State of Nature. . . .

Whosoever therefore out of a state of Nature unite into a Community, must be understood to give up all the power, necessary to the ends for which they unite into Society, to the majority of the Community. . . .

Of the Dissolution of Government

Governments are dissolved from within . . . when the Legislative is altered. . . . First, that when such a single Person or Prince sets up his own **Arbitrary** Will in place of the Laws, which are the Will of the Society, declared by the Legislative, then the Legislative is changed. . . . Secondly, when the Prince hinders the legislative from . . . acting freely, pursuant to those ends, for which it was Constituted, the Legislative is altered. . . . Thirdly, When by the Arbitrary Power of the Prince, the Electors, or ways of Election are altered, without the Consent, and contrary to the common Interest of the People, there also the Legislative is altered. . . .

In these and the like Cases, when the Government is dissolved, the People are at liberty to provide for themselves, by erecting a new Legislative, differing from the other, by the change of Persons, or Form, or both as they shall find it most for their safety and good. For the Society can never by the fault of another, lose the Native and Original Right it has to preserve itself. . . . "

VOCABULARY

divests
taking something off or away from

arbitrary
based on or determined by a person's preference or opinion

DBQ Analyzing Historical Documents

① Citing Text Evidence
According to Locke, what is the natural state of man?

② Determining Cause and Effect
What happens to a man's rights when he becomes a member of a community?

③ Identifying What three reasons does Locke give for the justified dissolution of government?

The Virginia Statute for Religious Freedom,

This statute, excerpted below, was the basis for the religion clauses in the Bill of Rights. Thomas Jefferson drafted the statute, and James Madison guided it through the Virginia legislature in 1786. The issue it addresses arose when the new state considered whether citizens should continue to support the Anglican Church, as they had in colonial times, or whether they should support any or all other denominations.

NEXT GENERATION SUNSHINE STATE STANDARDS

LAFS.1112.RH.1.1, LAFS.1112.RH.1.2, LAFS.1112.RH.2.4, LAFS.1112.RH.2.5, LAFS.1112.RH.4.10, LAFS.1112.SL.1.3, LAFS.1112.WHST.3.9, SS.912.A.1.2

Whereas Almighty God hath created the mind free; that all attempts to influence it by temporal punishments . . . tend only to beget habits of hypocrisy and meanness, and are a departure from the plan of the Holy author of our religion; . . . that the **impious** presumption of legislators and rulers, civil as well as ecclesiastical, who being themselves but fallible and uninspired men, have assumed dominion over the faith of others, setting up their own opinions and modes of thinking as the only true and infallible, and as such endeavoring to impose them to other, hath established and maintained false religions over the greatest part of the world, and through all time; . . . that to compel a man to furnish contributions of money for the propagation of opinions which he disbelieves, is sinful and tyrannical; . . . that our civil rights have no dependence on our religious opinions, any more than our opinions in physics or geometry; that therefore the **proscribing** any citizen as unworthy the public confidence by laying upon him an incapacity of being called to offices of trust . . . unless he profess or renounce this or that religious opinion, is depriving him injuriously of those privileges and advantages to which in common with his fellow-citizens he has a natural right; that it tends only to corrupt the principles of that religion it is meant to encourage, by bribing with a monopoly of worldly honours and **emoluments**, those who will externally profess and conform to it . . . :

Be it enacted by the General Assembly, That no man shall be compelled to frequent or support any religious worship, place, or ministry whatsoever, nor shall be enforced, restrained, molested, or burthened in his body or goods, nor shall otherwise suffer on account of his religious opinions, or belief; but that all men shall be free to profess, and by argument to maintain, their opinion in matters of religion, and that the same shall in no wise diminish, enlarge, or affect their civil capacities. . . .

VOCABULARY

impious
irreverent

proscribing
to prohibit

emoluments
to make money or profit from an office held

DBQ Analyzing Historical Documents

1 *Describing* How does the statute portray politicians and religious leaders of the time? What words are used to describe these men?

2 *Making Connections* Madison is known as the "Father of the Constitution." What similarities exist between this statute and the Constitution? How do they differ?

3 *Identifying Points of View* How might have Madison's and Jefferson's experiences during the Revolutionary War shaped their opinions on civil rights and religion?

**NEXT GENERATION
SUNSHINE STATE STANDARDS**

LAFS.1112.RH.1.1, LAFS.1112.RH.1.2,
LAFS.1112.RH.2.4, LAFS.1112.RH.2.5,
LAFS.1112.RH.4.10, LAFS.1112.SL.1.3,
LAFS.1112.WHST.3.9, SS.912.A.1.2

The Federalist, No. 10, *James Madison wrote several articles for a New York newspaper supporting ratification of the Constitution. In the excerpt below, he argues for the idea of a federal republic as a guard against factions, or overzealous parties, in governing the nation.*

" The latent causes of **faction** are thus sown in the nature of man; and we see them everywhere. . . . A zeal for different opinions concerning religion, concerning government, and many other points; . . . an attachment to different leaders ambitiously contending for pre-eminence and power . . . have, in turn, divided mankind into parties. . . . But the most common and durable source of factions has been the various and unequal distribution of property. Those who hold and those who are without property have ever formed distinct interests in society. Those who are creditors, and those who are debtors, fall under a like discrimination. A landed interest, a manufacturing interest, a mercantile interest, a moneyed interest, with many lesser interests, grow-up of necessity in civilized nations, and divide them into different classes, actuated by different **sentiments** and views. The regulation of these various and interfering interests forms the principal task of modern legislation. . . .

The inference to which we are brought is that the causes of faction cannot be removed and relief is only to be sought in the means of controlling its effects. . . .

By what means is this object attainable? Evidently by one of two only. Either the existence of the same passion or interest in a majority at the same time must be prevented, or the majority, having such coexistent passion or interest, must be rendered, by their number and local situation, unable to concert and carry into effect schemes of oppression. . . .

From this . . . it may be concluded that a pure democracy, by which I mean a society consisting of a small number of citizens, who assemble and administer the government in person, can admit of no cure for the mischief's of faction. A common passion or interest will, in almost every case, be felt by a majority of the whole; a communication and concert results from the form of government itself; and there is nothing to check the **inducements** to sacrifice the weaker party or an obnoxious individual. Hence it is that such democracies have ever been spectacles of turbulence and contention. . . .

A republic, by which I mean a government in which the scheme of representation takes place, opens a different prospect and promises the cure for which we are seeking. . . .

The two great points of difference between a democracy and a republic are: first, the delegation of the government in the latter to a small number of citizens elected by the rest; secondly the greater number of citizens and great sphere of country over which the latter may be extended. "

VOCABULARY

faction
a group acting together within a larger body

sentiments
thoughts or attitudes influenced by feeling

inducements
something that persuades

DBQ Analyzing Historical Documents

1 *Explaining* According to Madison's description, what are three causes of factions?

2 *Comparing* How does Madison's assessment of political parties compare to modern-day politics?

3 *Using Context Clues* Which word does Madison use in the first paragraph to support his argument that political parties divide people over **emotional** issues?

4 *Identifying* What form of government does Madison say is the "cure?"

The Federalist, No. 51,

The author of this Federalist paper is not known. It may have been either James Madison or Alexander Hamilton. The author argues that the Constitution's federal system and separation of powers will protect the rights of the people.

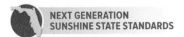

NEXT GENERATION SUNSHINE STATE STANDARDS

LAFS.1112.RH.1.1, LAFS.1112.RH.1.2,
LAFS.1112.RH.2.4, LAFS.1112.RH.2.5,
LAFS.1112.RH.4.10, LAFS.1112.SL.1.3,
LAFS.1112.WHST.3.9, SS.912.A.1.2

" In order to lay a due foundation for that separate and distinct exercise of the different powers of government, which to a certain extent is admitted on all hands to be essential to the preservation of liberty, it is **evident** that . . . the great security against a gradual concentration of the several powers in the same department, consists in giving to those who administer each department the necessary constitutional means and personal motives to resist encroachments of the others. . . .

Ambition must be made to **counteract** ambition. . . . A dependence on the people is, no doubt, the primary control on the government; but experience has taught mankind the necessity of auxiliary precautions. . . . The constant aim is to divide and arrange the several offices in such a manner as that each may be a check on the other. . . . In the compound republic of America, the power surrendered by the people is first divided between two distinct governments, and then the portion allotted to each subdivided among distinct and separate departments. . . .

In a free government the security for civil rights must be the same as that for religious rights. It consists in the one case in the **multiplicity** of sects. . . . In the extended republic of the United States, and among the great variety of interests, parties, and sects which it embraces, a coalition of a majority of the whole society could seldom take place on any other principles than those of justice and the general good. . . . It is no less certain than it is important . . . that the larger the society, provided it lie within a practical sphere, the more duly capable it will be of self-government. "

VOCABULARY

evident
clear, obvious

counteract
to lessen the force, action, or influence of something or someone

multiplicity
a great number

DBQ Analyzing Historical Documents

❶ Citing Text Evidence What does the author say is "essential to the preservation of liberty"?

❷ Identifying Points of View What "experience" is the author referring to in the second paragraph? How does this experience shape the tone of the message?

❸ Predicting Consequences What might happen without the system of checks and balances?

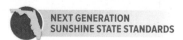

NEXT GENERATION SUNSHINE STATE STANDARDS

LAFS.1112.RH.1.1, LAFS.1112.RH.1.2,
LAFS.1112.RH.2.4, LAFS.1112.RH.2.5,
LAFS.1112.RH.4.10, LAFS.1112.SL.1.3,
LAFS.1112.WHST.3.9, SS.912.A.1.2

The Federalist, No. 68,

The Electoral College is one of the most enduringly controversial elements of the U.S. Constitution. In this excerpt from Federalist 68, written by Alexander Hamilton, the justification for this body of Electors is outlined.

" It was desirable that the sense of the people should operate in the choice of the person [the executive] to whom so important a trust was to be confided. This end will be answered by committing the right of making it, not to any preestablished body, but to men chosen by the people for the special purpose, and at the particular **conjuncture**.

It was equally desirable, that the immediate election should be made by men most capable of analyzing the qualities adapted to the station, and acting under circumstances favorable to deliberation, and to a judicious combination of all the reasons and inducements which were proper to govern their choice. A small number of persons, selected by their fellow-citizens from the general mass, will be most likely to possess the information and discernment requisite to such complicated investigations. . . .

The choice of SEVERAL, to form an intermediate body of electors, will be much less apt to convulse the community with any extraordinary or violent movements, than the choice of ONE who was himself to be the final object of the public wishes. And as the electors, chosen in each State, are to assemble and vote in the State in which they are chosen, this detached and divided situation will expose them much less to heats and **ferments**, which might be communicated from them to the people, than if they were all to be convened at one time, in one place. . . .

. . . [T]he people of each State shall choose a number of persons as electors, equal to the number of senators and representatives of such State in the national government, who shall assemble within the State, and vote for some fit person as President. Their votes, thus given, are to be transmitted to the seat of the national government, and the person who may happen to have a majority of the whole number of votes will be the President. But as a majority of the votes might not always happen to centre in one man, and as it might be unsafe to permit less than a majority to be conclusive, it is provided that, in such a contingency, the House of Representatives shall select out of the candidates who shall have the five highest number of votes, the man who in their opinion may be best qualified for the office. "

VOCABULARY

conjuncture
a combination of circumstances or events usually producing a crisis

ferments
to be or cause to be in a state of unrest or excitement

DBQ Analyzing Historical Documents

1 *Identifying* In which paragraph does Hamilton list the characteristics individuals should possess to become electors?

2 *Citing Text Evidence* According to Hamilton, how many electors should each state have?

3 *Predicting Consequences* What does Hamilton imply might happen if one person were to choose the president?

The Federalist, No. 78,

This portion of Federalist 78, also written by Alexander Hamilton, describes the important role of the judicial branch, especially its role of interpreting legislation to avoid conflicting with the meaning of the Constitution.

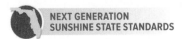

**NEXT GENERATION
SUNSHINE STATE STANDARDS**

LAFS.1112.RH.1.1, LAFS.1112.RH.1.2,
LAFS.1112.RH.2.4, LAFS.1112.RH.2.5,
LAFS.1112.RH.4.10, LAFS.1112.SL.1.3,
LAFS.1112.WHST.3.9, SS.912.A.1.2

" The Executive not only dispenses the honors, but holds the sword of the community. The legislature not only commands the purse, but prescribes the rules by which the duties and rights of every citizen are to be regulated. The judiciary, on the contrary, has no influence over either the sword or the purse; no direction either of the strength or of the wealth of the society; and can take no active resolution whatever. It may truly be said to have neither FORCE nor WILL, but merely judgment; and must ultimately depend upon the aid of the executive arm even for the efficacy of its judgments. . . .

Some perplexity respecting the rights of the courts to pronounce legislative acts void, because **contrary** to the Constitution, has arisen from an imagination that the doctrine would imply a superiority of the judiciary to the legislative power. It is urged that the authority which can declare the acts of another void, must necessarily be superior to the one whose acts may be declared void. As this doctrine is of great importance in all the American constitutions, a brief discussion of the ground on which it rests cannot be unacceptable.

There is no position which depends on clearer principles, than that every act of a delegated authority, contrary to the tenor of the commission under which it is exercised, is void. No legislative act, therefore, contrary to the Constitution, can be valid. To deny this, would be to affirm, that the deputy is greater than his principal; that the servant is above his master; that the representatives of the people are superior to the people themselves; that men acting by virtue of powers, may do not only what their powers do not authorize, but what they forbid. . . .

The interpretation of the laws is the proper and peculiar **province** of the courts. A constitution is, in fact, and must be regarded by the judges, as a fundamental law. It therefore belongs to them to ascertain its meaning, as well as the meaning of any particular act proceeding from the legislative body. If there should happen to be an irreconcilable variance between the two, that which has the superior obligation and validity ought, of course, to be preferred; or, in other words, the Constitution ought to be preferred to the statute, the intention of the people to the intention of their agents. "

VOCABULARY

contrary
opposite

province
proper or appropriate or area of skill, knowledge, or interest

DBQ Analyzing Historical Documents

1 *Expressing* What does Hamilton mean when he says the executive "holds the sword of the community" and the legislature "commands the purse"?

2 *Comparing* Hamilton compares the relationship between the legislature and the Constitution to a servant and its master. How are these two relationships similar?

3 *Stating* According to Hamilton, what is the responsibility of the judges with regard to the Constitution?

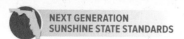

**NEXT GENERATION
SUNSHINE STATE STANDARDS**

LAFS.1112.RH.1.1, LAFS.1112.RH.1.2,
LAFS.1112.RH.2.4, LAFS.1112.RH.2.5,
LAFS.1112.RH.4.10, LAFS.1112.SL.1.3,
LAFS.1112.WHST.3.9, SS.912.A.1.2

VOCABULARY

apprise
to give notice

edifice
large building or structure

baneful
causing destruction or harm

felicity
great happiness

DBQ Analyzing Historical Documents

1 *Speculating* Would George Washington approve or disapprove of the current political culture in America? Why or why not?

2 *Giving Examples* President Washington warns about the "alternate domination of one faction over another, sharpened by the spirit of revenge." What did he mean? Provide one example of how this "alternate domination" has affected our nation's ability to accomplish change.

3 *Defending* George Washington warned about having connections with foreign countries. Did his predecessors heed this warning? Write a paragraph defending your opinion of whether this policy has helped or hurt the United States.

Washington's Farewell Address,

Washington arranged to have this Address printed in a Philadelphia newspaper on September 19, 1796. Designed in part to remove him from consideration for a third presidential term, the address also especially warned of the dangers of political parties and sectionalism.

" Friends and Fellow Citizens:
The period for a new election of a citizen to administer the executive government of the United States being not far distant . . . I should now **apprise** you of the revolution I have formed to define being considered. . . .

The unity of government which constitutes you one people is . . . a main pillar in the **edifice** of your real independence; the support of your tranquility at home, your peace abroad; of your safety; of your prosperity in every shape; of that very liberty which you so highly prize. But as it is easy to foresee that, from different causes and from different quarters, much pains will be taken, many artifices employed to weaken in your minds the conviction of this truth. . . .

The name of American, which belongs to you, in your national capacity, must always exhalt the just pride of patriotism more than any appellation derived from local discriminations. . . .

In contemplating the causes which may disturb our Union, it occurs as matter of serious concern that any ground should have been furnished for characterizing parties by geographic discriminations: Northern and Southern; Atlantic and Western; whence designing men may endeavor to excite a belief that there is a real difference to local interests and views. . . .

Let me now take a more comprehensive view and warn you in the most solemn manner against the **baneful** effects of the spirit of party generally. . . . The alternate domination of one faction over another, sharpened by the spirit of revenge natural to party dissention . . . is itself a frightful despotism. . . .

Of all the dispositions and habits which lead to political prosperity, religion and morality are indispensable supports. . . . A volume could not trace all their connections with private and public **felicity**. . . . And let us with caution indulge the supposition, that morality can be maintained without religion. Whatever may be conceded to the influence of refined education on minds of peculiar structure—reason and experience both forbid us to expect that national morality can prevail in exclusion of religious principle.

The great rule of conduct for us, in regard to foreign nations, is in extending our commercial relations to have with them as little political connection as possible. . . .

In offering you, my countrymen, these counsels of an old and affectionate friend, I dare not hope that they will make the strong and lasting impression I could wish. . . . But if I may even flatter myself that they may be productive of some partial benefit. . . . "

The Kentucky Resolution, *The Alien and Sedition*

Acts of 1798 made it easier for the government to suppress criticism and to arrest political enemies. This Federalist legislation inspired fierce opposition among Republicans, who looked to the state governments to reverse the acts. Two states, Kentucky and Virginia, passed resolutions stating their right to, in effect, disregard federal legislation. The resolutions laid the groundwork for the states' rights often cited during the Civil War. Thomas Jefferson wrote the Kentucky Resolution, excerpted below, which was adopted in 1799.

❝ RESOLVED, . . . that if those who administer the general government be permitted to **transgress** the limits fixed by that compact, by a total disregard to the special delegations of power therein contained, annihilation of the state governments, and the erection upon their ruins, of a general consolidated government, will be the inevitable consequence; that the principle and construction contended for by **sundry** of the state legislatures, that the general government is the exclusive judge of the extent of the power delegated to it, stop nothing short of despotism; . . . that the several states who forced that instrument, being sovereign and independent, have the unquestionable right to judge of its infraction; and that a **nullification**, by those sovereignties, of all unauthorized acts done under colour of that instrument, is the rightful remedy; . . . ❞

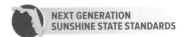
NEXT GENERATION SUNSHINE STATE STANDARDS

LAFS.1112.RH.1.1, LAFS.1112.RH.1.2, LAFS.1112.RH.2.4, LAFS.1112.RH.2.5, LAFS.1112.RH.4.10, LAFS.1112.SL.1.3, LAFS.1112.WHST.3.9, SS.912.A.1.2

VOCABULARY

transgress
to violate a law or command

sundry
various

nullification
the action of a state blocking or attempting to prevent the enforcement within its territory of a federal law of the U.S.

DBQ Analyzing Historical Documents

1 *Describing* What does Jefferson argue will happen to state governments if the federal government intrudes?

2 *Explaining* What does Jefferson propose is the "rightful remedy" to the Alien and Sedition Acts?

3 *Determining Word Meanings* Using context clues, what would you determine is the connotation of the word despotism?

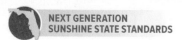

**NEXT GENERATION
SUNSHINE STATE STANDARDS**

LAFS.1112.RH.1.1, LAFS.1112.RH.1.2,
LAFS.1112.RH.2.4, LAFS.1112.RH.2.5,
LAFS.1112.RH.4.10, LAFS.1112.SL.1.3,
LAFS.1112.WHST.3.9, SS.912.A.1.2

"The Star-Spangled Banner,"

During the British bombardment of Fort McHenry during the War of 1812, a young Baltimore lawyer named Francis Scott Key was inspired to write the words to "The Star-Spangled Banner." Although it became popular immediately, it was not until 1931 that Congress officially declared "The Star-Spangled Banner" as the national anthem of the United States.

❞ O! say can you see, by the dawn's early light,

What so proudly we hail'd at the twilight's last gleaming,

Whose broad stripes and bright stars through the **perilous** fight,

O'er the ramparts we watch'd, were so gallantly streaming?

And the Rockets' red glare, the Bombs bursting in air,

Gave proof through the night that our Flag was still there;

O! say, does that star-spangled Banner yet wave,

O'er the Land of the free, and the home of the brave? ❞

This watercolor shows an American flag flying over Fort McHenry. The attack upon this fort inspired Francis Scott Key's "The Star Spangled Banner."

VOCABULARY

perilous
full of danger

indivisible
impossible to separate or divide

DBQ Analyzing Historical Documents

❶ **Making Connections** What do the Pledge of Allegiance and "The Star-Spangled Banner" have in common? How do they differ?

❷ **Paraphrasing** Using your own words, explain what happened the night of the attack on Fort McHenry.

❸ **Making Inferences** Why do you think President Eisenhower urged Congress to add the words "under God" to the Pledge of Allegiance?

The Pledge of Allegiance,

In 1892 the nation celebrated the 400th anniversary of Columbus's landing in America. In connection with this celebration, Francis Bellamy, a magazine editor, wrote and published the Pledge of Allegiance. The words "under God" were added by Congress in 1954 at the urging of President Dwight D. Eisenhower.

❞ I pledge allegiance to the Flag of the United States of America and to the Republic for which it stands, one Nation under God, **indivisible**, with liberty and justice for all. ❞

The Monroe Doctrine,

When Spain's power in South America began to weaken, other European nations seemed ready to step in. The United States was developing trade and diplomatic relations with South America, and it wanted to curb European influence there. The following is a statement President Monroe made on the subject in his annual message to Congress on December 2, 1823.

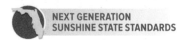

NEXT GENERATION SUNSHINE STATE STANDARDS

LAFS.1112.RH.1.1, LAFS.1112.RH.1.2, LAFS.1112.RH.2.4, LAFS.1112.RH.2.5, LAFS.1112.RH.4.10, LAFS.1112.SL.1.3, LAFS.1112.WHST.3.9, SS.912.A.1.2

" The occasion has been judged proper for asserting, as a principle in which the rights and interests of the United States are involved, that the American continents, by the free and independent condition which they have assumed and maintain, are henceforth not to be considered as subjects for future colonization by any European powers. . . .

. . . We owe it, therefore, to **candor** and to the amicable relations existing between the United States and those [European] powers to declare that we should consider any attempt on their part to extend their system to any portion of this hemisphere as dangerous to our peace and safety. With the existing colonies or dependencies of any European power we have not interfered and shall not interfere. But with the Governments who have declared their independence and maintain it, and whose independence we have, on great consideration and on just principles, acknowledged, we could not view any **interposition** for the purpose of oppressing them, or controlling in any other manner their destiny, by any European power in any other light than as the manifestation of an unfriendly disposition toward the United States. . . .

Our policy in regard to Europe, which was adopted at an early stage of the wars which have so long agitated that quarter of the globe, nevertheless remains the same, which is, not to interfere in the internal concerns of any of its powers; to consider the government de facto as the legitimate government for us; to cultivate friendly relations with it, and to preserve those relations by a frank, firm, and manly policy, meeting in all instances the just claims of every power, submitting to injuries from none. "

VOCABULARY

curb
to control

candor
sincere, honest expression

interposition
to step in between opposing parties or governments

DBQ Analyzing Historical Documents

❶ *Recognizing Bias* Why did President Monroe refer to the "American continents" in his address?

❷ *Stating* What action by European countries would be deemed as an "unfriendly disposition toward the United States"?

❸ *Interpreting* According to President Monroe, what approach is taken toward Europe? Do you agree or disagree with this statement?

NEXT GENERATION
SUNSHINE STATE STANDARDS

LAFS.1112.RH.1.1, LAFS.1112.RH.1.2,
LAFS.1112.RH.2.4, LAFS.1112.RH.2.5,
LAFS.1112.RH.4.10, LAFS.1112.SL.1.3,
LAFS.1112.WHST.3.9, SS.912.A.1.2

The Seneca Falls Declaration,

One of the first documents to call for equal rights for women was the Declaration of Sentiments and Resolutions, issued in 1848 at the Seneca Falls Convention in Seneca Falls, New York. Led by Lucretia Mott and Elizabeth Cady Stanton, the delegates at the convention used the language of the Declaration of Independence to call for women's rights.

We hold these truths to be self-evident; that all men and women are created equal; that they are endowed by their Creator with certain inalienable rights; that among these are life, liberty, and the pursuit of happiness; that to secure these rights governments are instituted, **deriving** their just powers from the consent of the governed. Whenever any form of government becomes destructive of these ends, it is the right of those who suffer from it to refuse allegiances to it, and to insist upon the institution of a new government. . . .

The history of mankind is a history of repeated injuries and **usurpations** on the part of man toward women, having in direct object the establishment of an absolute tyranny over her.

Now, in view of this entire disfranchisement . . . we insist that they have immediate administration to all the rights and privileges which belong to them as citizens of the United States. . . .

VOCABULARY

deriving
to come from a certain source or basis

usurpations
the act of seizing and holding by force or without right

DBQ Analyzing Historical Documents

1 ***Making Connections*** Why do Stanton and Mott reapply the language of the *Declaration of Independence* to their cause? In your opinion, is this an effective use of rhetoric?

2 ***Determining Word Meanings*** Based on the context clues provided, how would you define *disfranchisement*?

3 ***Comparing*** By using the *Declaration of Independence*, Stanton and Mott draw a comparison between men and an unpopular leader. To whom are men being compared?

4 ***Integrating Visual Information*** Study the illustrations of Elizabeth Cady Stanton and Lucretia Mott. How do these illustrations convey a sense of struggle and commitment?

Lucretia Mott (center) is threatened by an anti-suffragette mob.

Elizabeth Cady Stanton speaks at the first Women's Rights Convention, held in Seneca Falls, New York.

Lincoln's First Inaugural Address,

In March 1861, as the nation moved ever closer to a civil war, Abraham Lincoln took office as president. In Lincoln's view, the southern states could not claim to leave the Union and become its own country. Therefore, Lincoln vowed to work to maintain the connection between the two dividing regions by the powers granted him within the Constitution.

NEXT GENERATION
SUNSHINE STATE STANDARDS

LAFS.1112.RH.1.1, LAFS.1112.RH.1.2,
LAFS.1112.RH.2.4, LAFS.1112.RH.2.5,
LAFS.1112.RH.4.10, LAFS.1112.SL.1.3,
LAFS.1112.WHST.3.9, SS.912.A.1.2,
SS.912.A.2.1

" I have no purpose, directly or indirectly, to interfere with the institution of slavery in the States where it exists. I believe I have no lawful right to do so, and I have no inclination to do so. . . .

I hold that in contemplation of universal law and of the Constitution the Union of these States is **perpetual**. . . . Continue to execute all the express provisions of our National Constitution, and the Union will endure forever, it being impossible to destroy it except by some action not provided for in the instrument itself. . . .

Descending from these general principles, we find the proposition that in legal contemplation the Union is perpetual confirmed by the history of the Union itself. The Union is much older than the Constitution. It was formed, in fact, by the Articles of Association in 1774. It was matured and continued by the Declaration of Independence in 1776. It was further matured, and the faith of all the then thirteen States expressly **plighted** and engaged that it should be perpetual, by the Articles of Confederation in 1778. And finally, in 1787, one of the declared objects for ordaining and establishing the Constitution was "to form a more perfect Union."
But if destruction of the Union by one or by a part only of the States be lawfully possible, the Union is less perfect than before the Constitution, having lost the vital element of **perpetuity**. . . .

I therefore consider that in view of the Constitution and the laws the Union is unbroken, and to the extent of my ability, I shall take care, as the Constitution itself expressly enjoins upon me, that the laws of the Union be faithfully executed in all the States. . . .

That there are persons in one section or another who seek to destroy the Union at all events and are glad of any pretext to do it I will neither affirm nor deny; but if there be such, I need address no word to them. To those, however, who really love the Union may I not speak?

. . . In your hands, my dissatisfied fellow-countrymen, and not in mine, is the **momentous** issue of civil war. The Government will not assail you. You can have no conflict without being yourselves the aggressors. You have no oath registered in heaven to destroy the Government, while I shall have the most solemn one to "preserve, protect, and defend it."

. . . We are not enemies, but friends. We must not be enemies. Though passion may have strained it must not break our bonds of affection. The mystic chords of memory, stretching from every battlefield and patriot grave to every living heart and hearthstone all over this broad land, will yet swell the chorus of the Union, when again touched, as surely they will be, by the better angels of our nature." "

VOCABULARY

perpetual
lasting forever

plighted
pledged

perpetuity
endless, forever

momentous
having importance or consequence

DBQ Analyzing Historical Documents

1 *Using Context Clues* Based on the tone of President Lincoln's address, how would you describe the political climate when he took office?

2 *Stating* How did President Lincoln say he would handle the issue of slavery in the southern states?

3 *Identifying Points of View* Which group of people is President Lincoln referring to as "aggressors" and how does he support his claims that only they can destroy the Union?

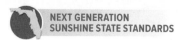
**NEXT GENERATION
SUNSHINE STATE STANDARDS**

LAFS.1112.RH.1.1, LAFS.1112.RH.1.2,
LAFS.1112.RH.2.4, LAFS.1112.RH.2.5,
LAFS.1112.RH.4.10, LAFS.1112.SL.1.3,
LAFS.1112.WHST.3.9, SS.912.A.1.2,
SS.912.A.2.1

VOCABULARY

aforesaid
said or named before

countervailing
to exert force against or counteract

vested
to be placed into the possession or
control of some person or authority

DBQ Analyzing Historical Documents

1 *Identifying* What resources
does President Lincoln say he will
use to protect those freed by his
proclamation?

2 *Predicting Consequences*
How would you expect the
southern states to react to the
president's actions?

3 *Making Connections* How
does President Lincoln's language
in the closing paragraph establish
a moral connection to the
proclamation?

The Emancipation Proclamation,

*On January 1, 1863, President Abraham Lincoln issued the Emancipation
Proclamation, which freed all enslaved persons to states under Confederate control.
The Proclamation was a significant step toward the passage of the Thirteenth
Amendment (1865), which ended slavery in the United States.*

" Whereas, on the 22nd day of September, in the year of our Lord 1862,
a proclamation was issued by the President of the United States,
containing, among other things, the following, to wit:

That on the 1st day of January, in the year of our Lord 1863, all persons
held as slaves within any state or designated part of a state, the people
whereof shall then be in rebellion against the United States, shall be
then, thenceforward, and forever free; and the executive government
of the United States, including the military and naval authority thereof,
will recognize and maintain the freedom of such persons and will do
no act or acts to repress such persons, or any of them, in any efforts
they may make for their actual freedom.

That the executive will, on the 1st day January **aforesaid**, by
proclamation, designate the states and parts of states, if any, in which
the people thereof, respectively, shall then be in rebellion against the
United States; and the fact that any state or the people thereof shall on
that day be in good faith represented in the Congress of the United
States by members chosen thereto at elections wherein a majority of
the qualified voters of such states shall have participated shall, in the
absence of strong **countervailing** testimony, be deemed conclusive
evidence that such state and the people thereof are not then in
rebellion against the United States.

Now, therefore, I, Abraham Lincoln, President of the United States, by
virtue of the power in me **vested** as commander in chief of the Army
and Navy of the United States, in time of actual armed rebellion
against the authority and government of the United States, and as a fit
and necessary war measure for suppressing said rebellion, do, on this
1st day of January, in the year of our Lord 1863, and in accordance
with my purpose so to do, publicly proclaimed for the full period of
100 days from the day first above mentioned, order, and designate as
the states and parts of states wherein the people thereof, respectively,
are this day in rebellion against the United States. . . .

And, by virtue of the power and for the purpose aforesaid, I do order
and declare that all persons held as slaves within said designated states
and parts of states are, and henceforward shall be, free; and that the
executive government of the United States, including the military and
naval authorities thereof, will recognize and maintain the freedom of
said persons. . . .
And upon this act, sincerely believed to be an act of justice, warranted
by the Constitution upon military necessity, I invoke the considerate
judgment of mankind and the gracious favor of Almighty God. . . . "

The Gettysburg Address, *President Abraham*

Lincoln delivered the Gettysburg Address on November 19, 1863, during the dedication of the Gettysburg National Cemetery. The dedication was in honor of the more than 7,000 Union and Confederate soldiers who died in the Battle of Gettysburg earlier that year. Lincoln's brief speech is often recognized as one of the finest speeches in the English language. It is also one of the most moving speeches in the nation's history.

There are five known manuscript copies of the address, two of which are in the Library of Congress. Scholars debate about which, if any, of the existing manuscripts comes closest to Lincoln's actual words that day.

" Four score and seven years ago our fathers brought forth on this continent a new nation, conceived in liberty and dedicated to the **proposition** that all men are created equal.

Now we are engaged in a great civil war, testing whether that nation or any nation so conceived and so dedicated can long endure. We are met on a great battlefield of that war. We have come to dedicate a portion of that field as a final resting place for those who here gave their lives that that nation might live. It is altogether fitting and proper that we should do this.

But in a larger sense, we cannot dedicate, we cannot **consecrate**, we cannot hallow this ground. The brave men, living and dead, who struggled here have consecrated it far above our poor power to add or detract. The world will little note nor long remember what we say here, but it can never forget what they did here. It is for us the living, rather, to be dedicated here to the unfinished work which they who fought here have thus far so nobly advanced. It is rather for us to be here dedicated to the great task remaining before us—that from these honored dead we take increased devotion to that cause for which they gave the last full measure of devotion—that we here highly resolve that these dead shall not have died in vain, that this nation under God shall have a new birth of freedom, and that government of the people, by the people, for the people, shall not perish from the earth. "

THE BATTLE OF GETTYSBURG, P? JULY 3? 1863.

More than 7,000 soldiers died at the Battle of Gettysburg.

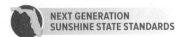

NEXT GENERATION SUNSHINE STATE STANDARDS

LAFS.1112.RH.1.1, LAFS.1112.RH.1.2,
LAFS.1112.RH.2.4, LAFS.1112.RH.2.5,
LAFS.1112.RH.4.10, LAFS.1112.SL.1.3,
LAFS.1112.WHST.3.9, SS.912.A.1.2,
SS.912.A.2.1

VOCABULARY

proposition
an idea offered to be thought about or accepted

consecrate
to make or declare sacred

DBQ Analyzing Historical Documents

❶ *Making Connections* Why do you think President Lincoln chose to deliver his speech on the battlefield?

❷ *Identifying* What is Lincoln referring to when he speaks of the "last full measure of devotion" and the "great task remaining?" How does he use the memory of the soldiers who have died at Gettysburg to advance this cause?

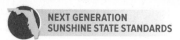

**NEXT GENERATION
SUNSHINE STATE STANDARDS**

LAFS.1112.RH.1.1, LAFS.1112.RH.1.2,
LAFS.1112.RH.2.4, LAFS.1112.RH.2.5,
LAFS.1112.RH.4.10, LAFS.1112.SL.1.3,
LAFS.1112.WHST.3.9, SS.912.A.1.2,
SS.912.A.4.2

President Harrison on Hawaiian Annexation,

An early expression of American imperialism came in the annexation of Hawaii. With the support of the American government, a small number of American troops overthrew the Hawaiian monarchy in January 1893. The excerpt below is from President Benjamin Harrison's written message to Congress. He sent the message along with the treaty for annexation to Congress on February 16, 1893.

" I do not deem it necessary to discuss at any length the conditions which have resulted in this decisive action. It has been the policy of the administration not only to respect but to encourage the continuance of an independent government in the Hawaiian Islands so long as it afforded suitable guarantees for the protection of life and property and maintained a stability and strength that gave adequate security against the domination of any other power. . . .

The overthrow of the monarchy was not in any way promoted by this government, but had its origin in what seems to have been a reactionary and revolutionary policy on the part of Queen Liliuokalani, which put in serious peril not only the large and **preponderating** interests of the United States . . . but all foreign interests. . . . It is quite evident that the monarchy had become effete and the queen's government is weak and inadequate as to be the prey of designing and **unscrupulous** persons. The restoration of Queen Liliuokalani . . . is undesirable . . . and unless actively supported by the United States would be accompanied by serious disaster and the disorganization of all business interests. The influence and interest of the United States in the islands must be increased and not diminished.

Only two courses are now open—one the establishment of a **protectorate** by the United States, and the other annexation, full and complete. I think the latter course, which has been adopted in the treaty, will be highly promotive of the best interests of the Hawaiian people and is the only one that will adequately secure the interests of the United States. These interests are not wholly selfish. It is essential that none of the other great powers shall secure these islands. Such a possession would not consist with our safety and with the peace of the world. This view of the situation is so apparent and conclusive that no protest has been heard from any government against proceeding looking to annexation. "

VOCABULARY

preponderating
to exceed in influence, power, or importance

unscrupulous
having no principles

protectorate
a small country that is ruled by a larger one

DBQ Analyzing Historical Documents

1 Using Context Clues Based on the context, what is the most likely definition for the word *effete*?

2 Identifying Evidence How does President Harrison defend the decision not to restore Queen Liliuokalani to power?

3 Determining Cause and Effect President Harrison explains how important it is that "none of the other great powers" secure the Hawaiian islands. Why?

The Fourteen Points, On January 8, 1918, President
Woodrow Wilson went before Congress to offer a statement of war aims called the
Fourteen Points. They reflected Wilson's belief that if the international community
accepted certain basic principles of conduct and set up institutions to carry them out,
there would be peace in the world.

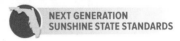
NEXT GENERATION
SUNSHINE STATE STANDARDS

LAFS.1112.RH.1.1, LAFS.1112.RH.1.2,
LAFS.1112.RH.2.4, LAFS.1112.RH.2.5,
LAFS.1112.RH.4.10, LAFS.1112.SL.1.3,
LAFS.1112.WHST.3.9, SS.912.A.1.2,
SS.912.A.4.5

"   We entered this war because violations of right had occurred. . . . What we
demand in this war, therefore, is . . . that the world be made fit and safe to live in. . . .

The only possible programme, as we see it, is this:

I. Open **covenants** of peace, openly arrived at, after which there shall be
no private international understandings of any kind but diplomacy
shall proceed always frankly and in the public view.

II. Absolute freedom of navigation upon the seas, outside territorial
waters, alike in peace and in war. . . .

III. The removal, so far as possible, of all economic barriers and the
establishment of an equality of trade conditions among all the
nations . . . .

IV. Adequate guarantees given and taken that national armaments will be
reduced to the lowest point consistent with domestic safety.

V. A free, open-minded, and absolutely **impartial** adjustment of all
colonial claims based upon a strict observance of the principle that in
determining all such questions of sovereignty the interests of the
populations concerned must have equal weight with the equitable
claims of the government whose title is to be determined.

VI. The evacuation of all Russian territory and . . . opportunity for the
independent determination of her own political development and
national polity. . . .

VII. Belgium . . . must be evacuated and restored. . . .

VIII. All French territory should be freed and the invaded portions restored,
and the wrong done to France by Prussia in 1871 in the matter of
Alsace-Lorraine should be righted. . . .

IX. A readjustment of the frontiers of Italy should be effected along dearly
recognizable lines of nationality.

X. The peoples of Austria-Hungary . . . should be accorded the freest
opportunity of autonomous development.

XI. Romania, Serbia, and Montenegro should be evacuated; occupied
territories restored . . . the relations of the several Balkan states to one
another determined by friendly counsel along historically established
lines of allegiance and nationality. . . .

XII. The Turkish portions of the present Ottoman Empire should be assured
a secure sovereignty. . . .

XIII. An independent Polish state should be erected which should include
the territories inhabited by **indisputably** Polish populations. . . .

XIV. A general association of nations must be formed under specific
covenants for the purpose of affording mutual guarantees of political
independence and territorial integrity. . . .   "

VOCABULARY

covenants
an agreement or contract

impartial
treating all things equally

indisputably
unquestionable

DBQ Analyzing Historical Documents

1 *Identifying Evidence* What
reason does President Wilson give
for entering into war?

2 *Examining* Which of the
Fourteen Points resulted in the
creation of Poland?

3 *Drawing Conlusions* President
Wilson's speech stresses the
restoration of borders and the
evacuation of countries. What are
some potential issues with border
disputes and occupation?

4 *Distinguishing Fact from
Opinion* President Wilson refers
to Italy's borders as "dearly
recognizable lines of neutrality."
Which word in this phrase
represents an opinion and is meant
to evoke emotion?

**NEXT GENERATION
SUNSHINE STATE STANDARDS**

LAFS.1112.RH.1.1, LAFS.1112.RH.1.2,
LAFS.1112.RH.2.4, LAFS.1112.RH.2.5,
LAFS.1112.RH.4.10, LAFS.1112.SL.1.3,
LAFS.1112.WHST.3.9, SS.912.A.1.2,
SS.912.A.6.5

VOCABULARY

acquiesce
to show acceptance or give consent through silence or lack of objection

armaments
supply of war materials

DBQ Analyzing Historical Documents

1 Paraphrasing What does President Roosevelt mean by "impressive expression of the public will and without regard to partisanship"? How does this give him more leverage before Congress?

2 Explaining What military support does President Roosevelt promise to democracies around the world? Does the United States continue to fulfill this promise today?

3 Visualizing President Roosevelt's "Four Freedoms" speech inspired artist Norman Rockwell to create a set of *Four Freedoms* paintings, which were published in *The Saturday Evening Post* in 1943. How does your generation express political opinions through art? Choose one example—music, painting, writing, or other form of art—and detail how it conveys a political message.

The Four Freedoms, *President Franklin D. Roosevelt delivered this address on January 6, 1941, in his annual message to Congress. In it, Roosevelt called for a world founded on "four essential human freedoms": freedom of speech and expression, freedom of worship, freedom from want, and freedom from fear.*

" Just as our national policy in internal affairs has been based upon a decent respect for the rights and dignity of all our fellow men within our gates, so our national policy in foreign affairs has been based on a decent respect for the rights and dignity of all nations, large and small. And the justice of morality must and will win in the end.

Our national policy is this:
First, by an impressive expression of the public will and without regard to partisanship, we are committed to all-inclusive national defense.

Second, by an impressive expression of the public will and without regard to partisanship, we are committed to full support of all those resolute peoples, everywhere, who are resisting aggression and are thereby keeping war away from our Hemisphere. . . .

Third . . . we are committed to the proposition that principles of morality and considerations for our own security will never permit us to **acquiesce** in a peace dictated by aggressors. . . .

Let us say to the democracies, "We Americans are vitally concerned in your defense of freedom. We are putting forth our energies, our resources, and our organizing powers to give you the strength to regain and maintain a free world. We shall send you, in ever increasing numbers, ships, planes, tanks, guns. This is our purpose and our pledge." In fulfillment of this purpose we will not be intimidated by the threats of dictators that they will regard as a breach of international law and as an act of war our aid to the democracies which dare to resist their aggression. . . .

In the future days, which we seek to make secure, we look forward to a world founded upon four essential human freedoms.

The first is freedom of speech and expression everywhere in the world.

The second is freedom of every person to worship God in his own way everywhere in the world.

The third is freedom from want, which, translated into world terms, means economic understandings which will secure to every nation a healthy peacetime life for its inhabitants everywhere in the world.

The fourth is freedom from fear—which, translated into world terms, means a worldwide reduction of **armaments** to such a point and in such a thorough fashion that no nation will be in a position to commit an act of physical aggression against any neighbor—anywhere in the world.. "

The Truman Doctrine, President Harry S. Truman

addressed a joint session of Congress on March 12, 1947, to request aid to fight Communist influence in Greece and Turkey. His message that communism had to be contained represents the central idea of American foreign policy during the Cold War.

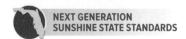

NEXT GENERATION SUNSHINE STATE STANDARDS

LAFS.1112.RH.1.1, LAFS.1112.RH.1.2,
LAFS.1112.RH.2.4, LAFS.1112.RH.2.5,
LAFS.1112.RH.4.10, LAFS.1112.SL.1.3,
LAFS.1112.WHST.3.9, SS.912.A.1.2,
SS.912.A.6.10

" The United States has received from the Greek Government an urgent appeal for financial and economic assistance. . . .

When forces of liberation entered Greece they found that the retreating Germans had destroyed virtually all the railways, roads, port facilities, communications, and merchant marine. More than a thousand villages had been burned. Eighty-five percent of the children were **tubercular**. Livestock, poultry, and draft animals had almost disappeared. Inflation had wiped out practically all savings. . . .

Greece is in desperate need of financial and economic assistance to enable it to resume purchases of food, clothing, fuel, and seeds. These are **indispensable** for the subsistence of its people and are obtainable only from abroad. Greece must have help to import the goods necessary to restore internal order and security, so essential for economic and political recovery. . . .

Greece must have assistance if it is to become a self-supporting and self-respecting democracy.

The United States must supply that assistance. We have already extended to Greece certain types of relief and economic aid but these are inadequate. There is no other country to which democratic Greece can turn. . . .

Greece's neighbor, Turkey, also deserves our attention. The future of Turkey as an independent and economically sound state is clearly no less important to the freedom-loving peoples of the world than the future of Greece. The circumstances in which Turkey finds itself today are considerably different from those of Greece. Turkey has been spared the disasters that have beset Greece. And during the war, the United States and Great Britain furnished Turkey with material aid. Nevertheless, Turkey now needs our support.

. . . To ensure the peaceful development of nations, free from coercion, the United States has taken a leading part in establishing the United Nations. The United Nations is designed to make possible lasting freedom and independence for all its members. We shall not realize our objectives, however, unless we are willing to help free peoples to maintain their free institutions . . . against aggressive movements that seek to impose upon them totalitarian regimes. . . .

This is an investment in world freedom and world peace. . . . The seeds of **totalitarian** regimes are nurtured by misery and want. They spread and grow in the evil soil of poverty and strife. They reach their full growth when the hope of a people for a better life has died. We must keep that hope alive. . . . If we falter in our leadership, we may endanger the peace of the world—and we shall surely endanger the welfare of our own nation. "

VOCABULARY

tubercular
related to or having tuberculosis

indispensable
necessary or essential

totalitarian
a government that has complete control over its people

DBQ Analyzing Historical Documents

1 Identifying Evidence What conditions does President Truman blame for a "militant minority . . . creating political chaos" in Greece?

2 Identifying Points of View President Truman is making a case for financial support for Greece and Turkey against communism. What reasons does he give to support his request?

3 Stating Why did the United States help create the United Nations?

4 Making Connections Is Truman's seed metaphor an effective portrayal of communism? Why or why not?

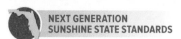

NEXT GENERATION SUNSHINE STATE STANDARDS

LAFS.1112.RH.1.1, LAFS.1112.RH.1.2, LAFS.1112.RH.2.4, LAFS.1112.RH.2.5, LAFS.1112.RH.4.10, LAFS.1112.SL.1.3, LAFS.1112.WHST.3.9, SS.912.A.1.2, SS.912.A.7.8

VOCABULARY

premised
to base on assumptions

segregation
he separation or isolation of a race, class, or minority group

hence
for this reason

compulsory
required by law

expenditures
money spent

DBQ Analyzing Historical Documents

❶ *Identifying* Which amendment do the plaintiffs use as their argument in the case?

❷ *Citing Text Evidence* The Court expresses the opinion that education is "perhaps the most important role of state and local governments". What two reasons does the Court use to support this claim?

❸ *Paraphrasing* Using your own words, write a paragraph explaining the Court's ruling and detail the points of the argument that led to the overturn of *Plessy v. Ferguson*.

Brown v. Board of Education, On May 17,

1954, the Supreme Court ruled in Brown v. Board of Education of Topeka, Kansas, that racial segregation in public schools was unconstitutional. This decision provided the legal basis for court challenges to segregation in every aspect of American life.

❝ These cases come to us from the States of Kansas, South Carolina, Virginia, and Delaware. They are **premised** on different facts and different local conditions, but a common legal question justifies their consideration together in this consolidated opinion.

In each instance, [Negro schoolchildren] had been denied admission to schools attended by white children under laws requiring or permitting **segregation** according to race. This segregation was alleged to deprive the plaintiffs of the equal protection of the laws under the Fourteenth Amendment.

The plaintiffs contend that segregated public schools are not "equal" and cannot be made "equal," and that **hence** they are deprived of the equal protection of the laws. . . .

Today, education is perhaps the most important function of state and local governments. **Compulsory** school attendance laws and the great **expenditures** for education both demonstrate our recognition of the importance of education to our democratic society . . . In these days, it is doubtful that any child may reasonably be expected to succeed in life if he is denied the opportunity of an education. . . .

We come then to the question presented: Does segregation of children in public schools solely on the basis of race, even though the physical facilities and other "tangible" factors may be equal, deprive the children of the minority group of equal educational opportunities? We believe that it does.

. . . We conclude that, in the field of public education, the doctrine of "separate but equal" has no place. Separate educational facilities are inherently unequal. Therefore, we hold that the plaintiff and others similarly situated for whom the actions have been brought are, by reason of the segregation complained of, deprived of the equal protection of the laws guaranteed by the Fourteenth Amendment. . . . ❞

Sitting on the steps of the U.S. Supreme Court, Nettie Hunt celebrates the Brown v. Board *ruling with her daughter Nickie.*

"I Have a Dream"

"I Have a Dream", *On August 28, 1963, on the steps of the Lincoln Memorial, King gave a stirring speech in which he **eloquently** spoke of his dreams for African Americans and for the United States.*

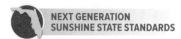

NEXT GENERATION
SUNSHINE STATE STANDARDS

LAFS.1112.RH.1.1, LAFS.1112.RH.1.2,
LAFS.1112.RH.2.4, LAFS.1112.RH.2.5,
LAFS.1112.RH.4.10, LAFS.1112.SL.1.3,
LAFS.1112.WHST.3.9, SS.912.A.1.2,
SS.912.A.7.6

" Five score years ago, a great American, in whose symbolic shadow we stand, signed the Emancipation Proclamation. This momentous decree came as a great beacon light of hope to millions of Negro slaves who had been seared in the flames of withering injustice. It came as a joyous daybreak to end the long night of captivity.

But one hundred years later, we must face the tragic fact that the Negro is still not free. One hundred years later, the life of the Negro is still sadly crippled by the manacles of segregation and the chains of discrimination.

There are those who are asking the devotees of civil rights, 'When will you be satisfied?'

We can never be satisfied as long as our bodies, heavy with the fatigue of travel, cannot gain lodging in the motels of the highways and the hotels of the cities.

We cannot be satisfied as long as the Negro's basic mobility is from a smaller ghetto to a larger one. . . .

We cannot be satisfied as long as a Negro in Mississippi cannot vote and a Negro in New York believes he has nothing for which to vote. . . .

I have a dream that one day this nation will rise up and live out the true meaning of its creed: 'We hold these truths to be self-evident that all men are created equal.'

I have a dream that one day on the red hills of Georgia, the sons of former slaves and the sons of former slaveowners will be able to sit down together at the table of brotherhood.

I have a dream that one day even the state of Mississippi, a state **sweltering** with the heat of injustice and oppression, will be transformed into an oasis of freedom and justice.

I have a dream that my four little children will one day live in a nation where they will not be judged by the color of their skin but by the content of their character. . . .

And when this happens, when we allow freedom to ring, when we let it ring from every village and every **hamlet**, from every state and every city, we will be able to speed up that day when all of God's children, black men and white men, Jews and Gentiles, Protestants and Catholics, will be able to join hands and sing in the words of that old Negro spiritual, 'Free at last! Free at last! Thank God Almighty, we are free at last!' "

VOCABULARY

eloquently
showing or using clear and forceful expression

sweltering
extremely hot

hamlet
a small village

DBQ Analyzing Historical Documents

1 *Making Connections* Martin Luther King, Jr. states that "Five score years ago, a great American, in whose symbolic shadow we stand, signed the Emancipation Proclamation." What two hints is the audience given to help identify this great American?

2 *Determining Word Meanings* What did Martin Luther King, Jr. mean by a "Negro's basic mobility is from a smaller ghetto to a larger one"?

3 *Summarizing* What phrase does King use to create a sense of rhythm in his speech and how does this affect the tone of his message?

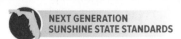
**NEXT GENERATION
SUNSHINE STATE STANDARDS**

LAFS.1112.RH.1.1, LAFS.1112.RH.1.2,
LAFS.1112.RH.2.4, LAFS.1112.RH.2.5,
LAFS.1112.RH.4.10, LAFS.1112.SL.1.3,
LAFS.1112.WHST.3.9, SS.912.A.1.2,
SS.912.A.7.15

President Bush's Address to Joint Session of Congress, September 20, 2001,

On September 11, 2001, terrorists crashed airplanes into the World Trade Center in New York City and the Pentagon in Washington, D.C. Thousands of people were killed. In his address, President George W. Bush announced a new kind of war against terrorism.

❝ On September the eleventh, enemies of freedom committed an act of war against our country. . . . Americans have known surprise attacks—but never before on thousands of civilians. . . .

The evidence we have gathered all points to a collection of loosely **affiliated** terrorist organizations known as al-Qaeda. . . . Our war on terror begins with al-Qaeda, but it does not end there. It will not end until every terrorist group of global reach has been found, stopped and defeated.

Americans are asking: Why do they hate us? They hate what we see right here in this chamber—a democratically elected government.

Their leaders are self-appointed. They hate our freedoms. . . . By sacrificing human life to serve their radical visions—by abandoning every value except the will to power—they follow in the path of **fascism**, and Nazism, and totalitarianism.

. . . We will direct every resource at our command—every means of diplomacy, every tool of intelligence, every instrument of law enforcement, every financial influence, and every necessary weapon of war—to the disruption and defeat of the global terror network.

I know there are struggles ahead, and dangers to face. But this country will define our times, not be defined by them. . . . Great harm had been done to us. We have suffered great loss. And in our grief and anger we have found our mission and our moment. . . . Our Nation—this generation—will lift a dark threat of violence from our people and our future. We will rally the world to this cause, by our efforts and by our courage. We will not tire, we will not **falter**, and we will not fail. ❞

President George W. Bush addresses a Joint Session of Congress following the September 11 terrorist attacks.

VOCABULARY

affliated
to connect closely with as a member or associate

fascism
a government led by a dictator that controls business and labor and opposition is not permitted

falter
to hesitate in action or purpose

DBQ Analyzing Historical Documents

① Explaining According to President Bush, why does al-Qaeda hate Americans?

② Interpreting What did President Bush mean when he said "night fell on a different world"?

③ Making Connections President Bush's speech was delivered on September 20, 2001. In your opinion, has the passage of time affected the political stance described here or the public's opinion of this tragic event? Write a paragraph explaining your thoughts.

Remarks by President Barack Obama on Osama bin Laden on May 1, 2011,

U.S. intelligence agencies believed Osama bin Laden had fled to Pakistan after coordinating the September 11, 2001 attacks on the United States. In May 2011, bin Laden's exact location was verified and President Obama ordered U.S. troops to attack. President Obama appeared on television to announce the successful military action.

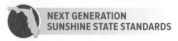

NEXT GENERATION SUNSHINE STATE STANDARDS

LAFS.1112.RH.1.1, LAFS.1112.RH.1.2, LAFS.1112.RH.2.4, LAFS.1112.RH.2.5, LAFS.1112.RH.4.10, LAFS.1112.SL.1.3, LAFS.1112.WHST.3.9, SS.912.A.1.2, SS.912.A.7.15

" It was nearly 10 years ago that a bright September day was darkened by the worst attack on the American people in our history. The images of 9/11 are seared into our national memory—hijacked planes cutting through a cloudless September sky; the Twin Towers collapsing to the ground; black smoke billowing up from the Pentagon; the wreckage of Flight 93 in Shanksville, Pennsylvania, where the actions of heroic citizens saved even more heartbreak and destruction.

. . . We quickly learned that the 9/11 attacks were carried out by al Qaeda—an organization headed by Osama bin Laden, which had openly declared war on the United States and was committed to killing innocents in our country and around the globe. And so we went to war against al Qaeda to protect our citizens, our friends, and our allies.

. . . last August, after years of **painstaking** work by our intelligence community, I was briefed on a possible lead to bin Laden . . . I met repeatedly with my national security team as we developed more information about the possibility that we had located bin Laden hiding within a compound deep inside of Pakistan.

. . . Today, at my direction, the United States launched a targeted operation against that compound in Abbottabad, Pakistan. A small team of Americans carried out the operation with extraordinary courage and capability. No Americans were harmed. They took care to avoid civilian casualties. After a firefight, they killed Osama bin Laden and took custody of his body.

. . . Over the years, I've repeatedly made clear that we would take action within Pakistan if we knew where bin Laden was. That is what we've done. But it's important to note that our **counterterrorism** cooperation with Pakistan helped lead us to bin Laden and the compound where he was hiding. Indeed, bin Laden had declared war against Pakistan as well, and ordered attacks against the Pakistani people.

Tonight, I called President Zardari, and my team has also spoken with their Pakistani counterparts. They agree that this is a good and historic day for both of our nations. And going forward, it is essential that Pakistan continue to join us in the fight against al Qaeda and its affiliates.

. . . The cause of securing our country is not complete. But tonight, we are once again reminded that America can do whatever we set our mind to. That is the story of our history, whether it's the pursuit of prosperity for our people, or the struggle for equality for all our citizens; our commitment to stand up for our values abroad, and our sacrifices to make the world a safer place. . . "

VOCABULARY

painstaking
taking great care

counterterrorism
political or military actions or policies designed to combat terrorism

DBQ Analyzing Historical Documents

1 Making Predictions Based on his statement, what concerns do you think President Obama might have about how the assassination of bin Laden might be perceived by some Muslims and Americans?

2 Citing Text Evidence Osama bin Laden was found—and killed—in Pakistan. Did this cause diplomatic issues between the two countries? Why or why not?

3 Making Connections How did the events of 9/11 affect your life? Does the death of bin Laden make you feel safer? Write a journal entry expressing your thoughts about these events.

ANALYZING SUPREME COURT CASES

CONTENTS

Schenck v. United States (1919)

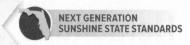
Background of the Case

When the United States entered World War I in 1917, the federal government passed the Espionage Act to protect itself against internal opposition to war.

Charles Schenck, who was general secretary of the Socialist Party in the United States, carried on a campaign encouraging young men to resist the wartime draft. He mailed thousands of circulars to men declaring that the draft was unconstitutional despotism and urging the men to assert their rights to resist the draft. Further, he claimed that the draft violated the Thirteenth Amendment, which banned involuntary servitude—or slavery—except as punishment for committing a crime.

For these actions Schenck was convicted of conspiracy to violate the Espionage Act by attempting to obstruct the recruitment of men into the U.S. armed forces. Schenck challenged his conviction on the grounds that his First Amendment rights had been violated.

Significance of the Case

The Court had to decide whether Schenck had been properly convicted and whether the Espionage Act was constitutional in the light of the free speech guarantees of the First Amendment. Was the broad limitation on the right of free speech as defined by the Espionage Act allowed? Or was the fact that the Espionage Act was designed to protect the nation's war effort sufficient reason for the Supreme Court to reject Schenck's First Amendment defense?

Oliver Wendell Holmes

HOW THE COURT RULED

The Court ruled unanimously that the Espionage Act was constitutional. Schenck was guilty of having violated the act. Justice Oliver Wendell Holmes, Jr., wrote the Court's opinion. The opinion was based on the idea that the First Amendment guarantees must be considered within the setting in which supposed violations occur.

Holmes stressed a principle that he felt defined the true scope of the First Amendment as it applies to political expression. "The question in every case," Holmes wrote, "is whether the words used are used in such circumstances and are of such a nature as to create a clear and present danger that they will bring about the substantive evils that Congress has a right to prevent."

The *Schenck* case clarified some limitations on free speech and supported the notion that the rights of the people are not absolute but must be balanced with national interests that are judged to be essential. The phrase "clear and present danger" would become the test for whether safety trumps First Amendment rights.

DBQ Document Based Questions

1 *Determining Word Meanings* Using context clues, how would you define the word despotism?

2 *Citing Text Evidence* What reasoning did the Supreme Court use to limit Schenck's First Amendment rights in this case?

3 *Making Connections* Justice Holmes cited that Schenk's actions presented a "clear and present danger" to the United States. Provide an example of another time in recent history that this principle may have been applied. Do you agree or disagree with this limitation to the First Amendment?

Hernandez *v.* Texas (1954)

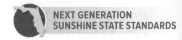

NEXT GENERATION
SUNSHINE STATE STANDARDS

SS.912.A.1.6

Background of the Case

Pete Hernandez lived and worked in the small town of Edna, Texas. While drinking with a friend at a bar, Pete got into a fight. After being asked to leave the bar, Hernandez went home and got a gun. He returned to the bar and shot and killed a man named Joe Espinoza. Hernandez was indicted on murder charges in September 1951.

His attorneys attempted to throw out the murder indictment. Most importantly, Hernandez and his defense counsel tried to disallow the petit jury panel on the grounds that Hernandez was denied equal protection under the Fourteenth Amendment, since Mexican Americans were excluded from the jury.

At the pre-trial hearing, Hernandez's attorneys made the case that despite the fact that Mexican Americans made up 14 percent of the population, no Mexican American had served on a jury in Jackson County, Texas, in more than 25 years. They claimed that citizens of Mexican ancestry were discriminated against in Jackson County.

The trial court denied the motions, and Hernandez was tried and found guilty of murder. An all-Anglo jury sentenced him to life in prison. On appeal, the Texas Court of Criminal Appeals affirmed the conviction but passed the legal question of equal protection on to the U.S. Supreme Court.

Significance of the Case

The Court agreed to hear the case in order to address the issue of the equal protection clause of the Fourteenth Amendment. Is it a violation of this right when a state tries a person of a particular race or ancestry in front of a jury that excludes people of the same race or ancestry? At question, also, was the state's claim that there were only two classes of people to consider: white and African American. The state contended that they did not have to consider race as an issue when determining the Hernandez jury.

HOW THE COURT RULED

In a unanimous 9-0 ruling, the Court ruled for Hernandez, reversing his murder conviction. Chief Justice Earl Warren delivered the opinion. He wrote that Jackson County, Texas, discriminated against Mexican Americans. He cited evidence of separate restrooms and diners. In addition, the juror statistics were overwhelming; no Mexican Americans had been assigned to a jury out of more than 6,000 jurors called in 25 years in Jackson County. Because Mexican Americans were considered a "special class," they were entitled to equal protection under the Fourteenth Amendment.

Earl Warren

DBQ Document Based Questions

1 *Identifying* What issue did Hernandez's attorney raise at his pre-trial hearing?

2 *Citing Text Evidence* What evidence did Justice Warren use as grounds to overturn the decision?

3 *Interpreting* Critics would argue that Hernandez should not have "walked" from the murder charges over a jury technicality. What were the greater implications of this case?

Mapp v. Ohio (1961)

NEXT GENERATION
SUNSHINE STATE STANDARDS

SS.912.A.1.6

Background of the Case

In May 1957, three police officers arrived at Dollree Mapp's home in Cleveland, Ohio, after receiving a tip that a suspect in a recent bombing was hiding there. After consulting her attorney, Mapp refused to allow the officers into her home.

Several officers arrived and forced their way into Mapp's house. When she demanded to see a search warrant, an officer held up a piece of paper, claiming it was a warrant. Mapp struggled with the officers over the alleged warrant, and she was handcuffed because she had been physical with the police. The police also refused Mapp's attorney—who had arrived to assist her—entrance into the home.

A search of the entire home turned up indecent books, pictures, and photographs that were deemed illegal by Ohio criminal law. Mapp was charged and convicted of violating this Ohio statute.

Although the prosecution failed to produce a search warrant at her trial, Mapp was convicted of having violated the Ohio law. On appeal, her attorney argued to the Ohio Supreme Court that the evidence against Mapp resulted from an illegal, warrantless search. The Ohio Supreme Court upheld the conviction, and Mapp appealed her case to the U.S. Supreme Court.

Significance of the Case

This case involves what the "exclusionary rule"—evidence seized in violation of a person's constitutional rights may not be used against that person in a trial. In *Wolf* v. *Colorado* (1949), a case similar to the *Mapp* case, the Supreme Court had recognized that the Fourth Amendment embodies the right of an individual to privacy, but it declined to forbid illegally seized evidence from being used at trial. Since the 1914 decision in *Weeks* v. *United States*, illegally seized evidence could not be used in federal courts. The issue in the *Mapp* case was whether or not the exclusionary rule of *Weeks*, applied to the states through the Fourteenth Amendment also prohibited illegally seized evidence in state courts.

HOW THE COURT RULED

Although Mapp won her case before the Court, the 5-3 decision produced conflicting opinions between justices Clark, Harlan, and Stewart. Justice Tom Clark's majority opinion was based on the fact that the Fourth Amendment is applied to both federal and state governments, which he argued should require equal enforcement at both levels. The decision forced states to obey the exclusionary rule.

Justice John Harlan's dissenting opinion argued that the Court focused on the wrong issue. He claimed that the Court should have considered whether or not the Ohio statute was "consistent with the rights of free thought and expression assured against state action by the Fourteenth Amendment."

Justice Potter Stewart wrote a separate opinion. He voted to reverse the Ohio Supreme Court's ruling based on the grounds that Mapp's First Amendment rights were violated.

Doll Ree Mapp

DBQ Document Based Questions

1 *Citing Text Evidence* At what point in their investigation did the police violate Mapp's Fourth Amendment rights?

2 *Defending* Which of the three justice's opinions do you agree with? Explain.

3 *Making Connections* How did the *Mapp* ruling differ from what the Court had decided in *Weeks*?

Engel *v.* Vitale (1962)

Background of the Case

Early in our country's history, prayer in school was considered a legitimate, even essential, part of education. As the country's population became more diversified, questions began to be raised as to the legality of this practice.

In 1951 the New York State Board of Regents, which supervises the state's public school system, approved a brief prayer at the start of each day. School districts were not required to use the prayer, and students were not required to recite it. In 1958 the New Hyde Park school board adopted the prayer and directed that it be recited each day in every class, although students could be excused from reciting it.

Steven Engel, the parent of two children in the New Hyde Park schools, objected to this practice. He asked a state court to order the prayer dropped. Engel directed his suit against the head of the school board, William J. Vitale, Jr. The state court and the New York Court of Appeals refused to prohibit reciting the prayer. Engel then appealed to the United States Supreme Court.

Significance of the Case

The question before the Court was whether the First Amendment, applied to the states through the due process clause of the Fourteenth Amendment, prohibits laws respecting the establishment of religion. Did the daily prayer of New York schools, although noncompulsory, violate the establishment clause?

HOW THE COURT RULED

The Court ruled in Engel's favor 6 to 1. Justice Hugo Black wrote the majority opinion. The Court disagreed with the school board's defense of what it called a "non-denominational prayer."

The Court called the practice of this prayer, even when it was not framed within a specific religious faith to be "inconsistent with the establishment clause." It held that a prayer "composed by government officials as part of a governmental program to further religious beliefs . . . breaches the constitutional wall of separation between Church and State."

Justice Potter Stewart dissented. He challenged the Court's reasoning in the case. He did not think that this example resulted in the establishment of an "official religion" and denied these school children a choice of religious practice.

The Court's decision provoked widespread controversy. Civil libertarians hailed it as a victory. Conservatives attacked it vigorously.

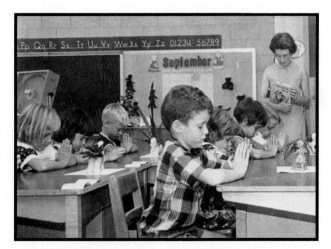

Prayer in the classroom has often been controversial.

DBQ Document Based Questions

1 *Determining Word Meanings* Using context clues, how would you define the words *nondenominational* and *noncompulsory*?

2 *Citing Text Evidence* According to Justice Black's majority opinion, how did the Regents' prayer violate the separation of church and state?

3 *Predicting Consequences* The school board and Justice Stewart argued that the prayer was constitutional since it was optional. Based on your experiences in school and among your peers, do you anticipate potential problems with this scenario? Explain.

Gideon v. Wainwright (1963)

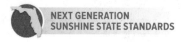
Background of the Case

In 1961, Clarence Earl Gideon—a petty thief who had served four prison terms—was arrested for breaking into the Bay Harbor poolroom in Panama City, Florida. He was accused of smashing a window, stealing wine, and breaking into a cigarette machine and jukebox to steal change.

Gideon asked the judge to appoint a lawyer for him since he could not afford to hire one himself. He argued that he was guaranteed an attorney under the Sixth Amendment. The judge refused, citing that under Florida law a lawyer could be provided only if the defendant was charged with a capital offense—one in which death was a possible penalty. Gideon was forced to defend himself, was found guilty, and was sentenced to five years in prison.

While in prison, Gideon submitted a handwritten petition to the U.S. Supreme Court to accept his case as a pauper. The Court may accept petitions from poverty-stricken individuals and appoint counsel to represent them. The Court appointed Abe Fortas—who would later become a Supreme Court justice—as Gideon's attorney.

Significance of the Case

The Court accepted Gideon's case in order to reconsider its decision in the case of *Betts* v. *Brady* (1942). In that case, the Court had ruled that, outside of special circumstances, the due process clause of the Fourteenth Amendment did not require the application of the Sixth Amendment's guarantee of counsel in criminal cases to state trials.

HOW THE COURT RULED

The Court's ruling was unanimous in Gideon's favor, overturning the 1942 decision in the *Betts* case.

Justice Hugo Black wrote the opinion for the Court. Black stressed that in order to provide due process, both wealthy and poor people are entitled to counsel. He stated that trained lawyers were seen by both the government and wealth defendants to be vital in criminal cases. Therefore it should not be allowed to force people to defend themselves.

The law that had allowed the Florida judge to deny Gideon counsel was changed. Poor defendants at both the state and federal levels—those accused of both noncapital and capital crimes— would be provided counsel. Gideon's letter, written from his prison cell, began a process resulting in a landmark decision that would ensure *all* defendants would be provided a fair trial.

Clarence Gideon (left) and his attorney Abe Fortas (right). Fortas would later become a member of the Supreme Court.

DBQ Document Based Questions

1 *Citing Text Evidence* Why did Gideon argue that he should be provided counsel?

2 *Analyzing* What evidence did Justice Black cite in his opinion to support the Court's decision that the right to an attorney is a basic, fundamental right afforded by the Constitution?

3 *Predicting Consequences* Suppose the Florida judge in Gideon's case had agreed to appoint him a lawyer. How would that have changed the outcome of Gideon's case? What might it mean for others?

Reynolds *v.* Sims (1964)

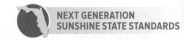

NEXT GENERATION
SUNSHINE STATE STANDARDS

SS.912.A.1.6

Background of the Case

In 1962, the Supreme Court ruled that it had the authority to review individual claims regarding redistricting, or redrawing electoral boundaries based on population. After this ruling, more than 30 lawsuits were filed against states accused of unconstitutional redistricting. Alabama was one of these states.

The case of *Reynolds* v. *Sims* questioned the constitutionality of the state's voting districts. The Alabama constitution of 1901 had established district boundaries based on the 1900 census, distributing senators and representatives, with each senatorial and house district being as equal as possible. As no reapportionment of voting districts had been made for 60 years, there was a vast discrepancy in the size of the population in the voting districts.

A group of citizens and taxpayers sued to have new reapportionment plans created. Their legal action was eventually appealed to the United States Supreme Court.

Significance of the Case

The question before the Court was whether or not the apportionment plans for the Alabama legislature violated the equal protection clause of the Fourteenth Amendment. The Court now had to decide whether the equal protection clause implied that both houses of a state legislature must reflect equal numbers of people in voting districts.

HOW THE COURT RULED

The Court ruled 8 to 1 that the equal protection clause had been violated.

Chief Justice Warren explained in his majority opinion that "legislators are elected by voters, not farms or cities or economic interests." If voters in one area have votes whose numbers would have an unusually large impact in the election of representatives, then the votes of people in other areas become that much less effective. Warren held that "full and effective participation by all citizens in state government requires, therefore, that each citizen have an equally effective voice in the election of members of his state legislature." He went on to explain that the weight of a vote cannot depend on whether the voter resides in a sparsely populated rural district or a thickly populated urban area.

Following this reasoning, the Court said, "We hold that, as a basic constitutional standard, the equal protection clause requires that seats in both houses of a bicameral state legislature must be apportioned on a population basis."

This decision by the Court is often described in abbreviated fashion as the "one person, one vote" principle.

African American voters in Alabama fill out their election ballots.

DBQ Document Based Questions

1 *Interpreting* What Constitutional standard did the Court uphold in Reynolds?

2 *Summarizing* Using your own words, explain what Chief Warren meant when he said "legislators are elected by voters, not farms or cities or economic interests"?

3 *Determining Cause and Effect* What impact do you think this ruling might have had on the 1966 election? Which party do you think benefitted from redistricting? Why?

Miranda *v.* Arizona (1966)

NEXT GENERATION
SUNSHINE STATE STANDARDS

SS.912.A.1.6

Background of the Case

In 1963, after a crime victim identified Ernesto Miranda in a police lineup, Miranda was arrested and taken into police custody. Miranda, a Mexican immigrant living in Phoenix, Arizona, did not have an attorney. He was questioned for two hours by two police officers. During this interrogation, Miranda confessed to the charges of kidnapping and rape. He signed a written confession. The police officers questioning him failed to inform him of his Fifth Amendment right against self-incrimination or of his Sixth Amendment right to an attorney.

Miranda was tried and found guilty. The prosecution used Miranda's confession as evidence in his trial. He was sentenced to 20 to 30 years in prison on each count. His defense attorney appealed to the Arizona Supreme Court, saying that Miranda's confession should not have been used at his trial because Miranda had not been informed of his rights. The Arizona Supreme Court denied the appeal and upheld Miranda's conviction.

Significance of the Case

The Fifth Amendment of the Constitution guarantees that "no person . . . shall be compelled in any criminal case to be a witness against himself. . . ." This right was made part of the Bill of Rights to prevent the government from forcing accused persons to confess to crimes they may or may not have committed. Miranda's case before the Supreme Court was based on this Fifth Amendment protection. The Court accepted the case in order to explore and clarify certain problems arising from earlier decisions related to the rights of individuals taken into police custody. The precise question that the Court explored was under what circumstances an interrogation may take place so that a confession made during the interrogation would be constitutionally admissible in a court of law.

HOW THE COURT RULED

The Supreme Court overturned Miranda's conviction in a 5-4 decision. Chief Justice Earl Warren wrote the majority opinion.

Warren noted that a suspect under interrogation faces strong mental and emotional pressures.

The Court wished to ease these pressures in order to avoid the possibility of self incrimination. An accused must be warned of their rights. Once these warnings are given, the individual in custody may choose to stop answering questions, or may halt the interrogation until his attorney is present. Otherwise, he may waive his exercise of these rights.

The *Miranda* ruling has led to the practice now followed routinely by law enforcement officials in which they read a suspect his or her *Miranda* rights.

Ernesto Miranda (right) and his attorney John J. Flynn (left)

DBQ Document Based Questions

1 *Citing Text Evidence* According to the *Miranda* ruling, at what point must an individual be read their rights?

2 *Analyzing* Chief Justice Warren claimed that suspects are subject to "great psychological pressures" during interrogation. How might this scenario lead to a forced confession?

Swann *v.* Charlotte-Mecklenburg Board of Education (1971)

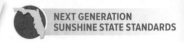

NEXT GENERATION
SUNSHINE STATE STANDARDS

SS.912.A.1.6

Background of the Case

The Supreme Court's ruling in *Brown* v. *Board of Education* in 1954 had declared segregation in schools unconstitutional. However, it left the process of desegregation up to the states. Nearly a decade after the *Brown* decision, less than 5 percent of African American children attended an integrated school.

This situation proved problematic for several reasons. Some states were deliberately disregarding the ruling, other states argued their cases in lower courts, and still others faced logistical challenges with busing. An example of this took place in a school district in Charlotte-Mecklenburg, North Carolina. In this district, roughly 14,000 black students attended schools that were 99 to 100 percent black.

The National Association for the Advancement of Colored People (NAACP) sued the school district on the behalf of Darius and Vera Swann, the parents of a six-year-old who wanted to attend an all-white elementary school closer to home. The Swanns won their case in federal district court, and the judge that presided over the case oversaw the busing strategy for the district. Swann was appealed to the Supreme Court.

Significance of the Case

The question at hand was whether or not federal courts were constitutionally authorized to provide supervision over and remedies for segregation policies that had been forced on the states in *Brown*.

HOW THE COURT RULED

In a unanimous 9-0 decision, the Court held that once schools violated the rules stated by the court opinion, the Equal Protection Clause gave the district courts' broad, flexible authority to correct these violations.

Justice Burger delivered the opinion for the Court, which stated that the technique of using bus transportation to introduce racial diversity to a segregated school district was a permissible use of the court's power to support the need for equality. Therefore, if school districts failed to implement segregation policies, the courts could step in.

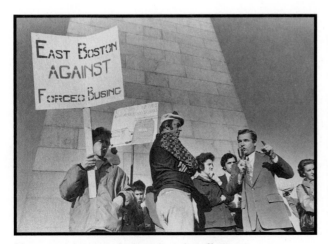

Many people protested against the efforts to desegregate with student busing.

DBQ Document Based Questions

1 *Describing* How would you describe the state's implementation of *Brown*?

2 *Making Connections* Why did the NAACP take interest in the Swanns' case?

3 *Predicting Consequences* What were some potential problems with busing? In your opinion, did these problems outweigh the purpose? Explain.

Wisconsin *v.* Yoder (1972)

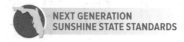
NEXT GENERATION
SUNSHINE STATE STANDARDS

SS.912.A.1.6

Background of the Case

The First Amendment to the Constitution states that Congress may pass no law regarding the establishment of religion or prohibiting the exercise of any religion. According to legal scholars who have interpreted the amendment, neither the national government nor state governments may pass laws that violate the beliefs of a religious group. The case of *Wisconsin* v. *Yoder* illustrates how the Supreme Court has extended the protection of the amendment to a particular religious group.

Wisconsin state law requires that all children attend high school until they are 16 years old. A group of Amish people feared that attending a public high school might threaten the beliefs of their young people and prevent them from learning valuable career skills necessary to their particular agricultural way of life. Therefore, they refused to obey this law. In 1968 the parents of three Amish teenagers who *had* attended public school through the eighth grade were fined by the Green County Circuit Court after refusing to enroll their children in New Glarus High School.

On appeal to the Wisconsin Supreme Court, the lower court's decision was reversed. The state ruled in favor of Yoder, citing that formal education for Amish children could legally end when students finish the eighth grade. The state appealed to the U.S. Supreme Court.

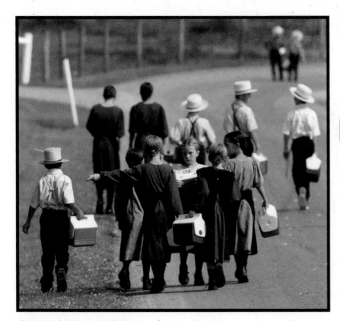

Amish children walk home from school.

Significance of the Case

The case affected Amish communities in 23 states; however, it had even wider implications, because it tested whether the First Amendment protects a group of people from being forced to send their children to public school if such attendance is contrary to their religious beliefs.

HOW THE COURT RULED

The Court affirmed the Wisconsin Supreme Court's decision, ruling 6 to 3 that the Amish, as a long-established religious group, may not be forced by the Wisconsin law to send their children to public high schools once they have completed the eighth grade. In its decision, the Court described the Amish as an identifiable religious group with a long history of demonstrated, sincerely held religious beliefs. In addition, the Court found that the Amish had introduced convincing evidence to show that sending Amish children to public high schools might impair their physical or mental health and make them less likely to discharge their duties and responsibilities in the Amish community.

The Court based its decision on the religious rights provision of the First Amendment and on the Fourteenth Amendment, which extends to the state level the protections granted to the national government by the Bill of Rights.

DBQ Document Based Questions

1 Stating What reasons did the Amish give for refusing to send their teenagers to public high school?

2 Explaining What other freedoms does the First Amendment protect? Provide at least one specific example.

3 Applying Does this ruling set the stage for future showdowns between religious groups and states over public education? Why or why not?

White *v.* Regester (1973)

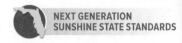

NEXT GENERATION
SUNSHINE STATE STANDARDS

SS.912.A.1.6

Background of the Case

The Supreme Court ruled on two cases in 1964 that involved redistricting at the state and national level. The Court's rulings in *Wesberry* v. *Sanders* and *Reynolds* v. *Sims* established that members of the U.S. House of Representatives and both houses of a state legislature must be chosen from districts approximately equal in population.

In 1970 the Texas legislature drafted a reapportionment plan based on the national census. The legislature established a new plan for the Texas house of representatives. The legislature could not agree on a reapportionment plan for the Texas senate, which led to a court battle challenging the constitutionality of both plans. The lawsuits claimed the plans were designed without regard to population in an attempt to discriminate against minorities based on race and ethnicity.

A three-judge district court upheld the reapportionment plan for the senate. It found the house plan unconstitutional. A deadline was established for the Texas legislature, giving it until July 1973 to reapportion the Texas house. The Texas legislature appealed to the Supreme Court.

Significance of the Case

The Court had two questions to consider in the case. First, were the districts unconstitutional because they varied too much in population size, violating the equal protection of the law clause of the Fourteenth Amendment? Second, were certain districts created for the purpose of discriminating against racial or ethnic minorities?

HOW THE COURT RULED

The Court ruled 6 to 3 to reverse the district court's judgment on the first question, which claimed the districts were not divided fairly with regard to population. Justice Byron White wrote the majority opinion. He cited that the population difference was 9.9 percent, which was an acceptable rate. White wrote that this amount of difference in the specific instances of these two congressional districts did not provide sufficient grounds for the basis of a widely sweeping decision of the Supreme Court.

With regards to the second question involving discrimination, the Court ruled unanimously. Justice White delivered this opinion as well. The Court ruled that the multi-member house districts created for certain counties were unconstitutional. The districts violated the Equal Protection Clause of the Fourteenth Amendment when it "invidiously excluded" African Americans and Mexican Americans from their right to participation in political life. Specifically their presence was not accurately reflected within their districts to give them an equal expectation of success in the election of representatives to the Texas house of representatives.

Congressional redistricting, sometimes described as gerrymandering, has been the subject of many court cases in the twentieth century. The term gerrymandering comes from this political cartoon image.

DBQ Document Based Questions

1 *Making Connections* Does the Court's ruling in White seem consistent with how it ruled in *Wesberry* and *Reynolds*? Explain.

2 *Defending* Why did the Court reverse the district court's decision regarding the first question, which claimed the districts were divided unfairly?

3 *Determining Word Meanings* Using the context clues from the text, what do you think the Court meant by "invidiously excluded?"

Regents of the University of California v. Bakke (1978)

NEXT GENERATION
SUNSHINE STATE STANDARDS

SS.912.A.1.6

Background of the Case

In 1973 the Medical School of the University of California at Davis admitted 16 minority students through a special affirmative action admissions process. This group of minority students collectively had substantially lower grade point averages and Medical College Aptitude Test scores than some of the other non-minority applicants. .

Alan Bakke, a white applicant, had a grade point average slightly below all the regular admission applicants, but his aptitude tests were much higher. When Bakke's 1973 and 1974 applications to the medical school were rejected, he sued the university's governing board. The California Superior Court found that the school's special admissions program violated the federal and state constitutions, Title VI, and the Civil Rights Act of 1964. The court did not order that Bakke be admitted, claiming that he had not proven he could be admitted if the special program were not in place.

Bakke appealed to the California Supreme Court, citing the equal protection clause of the Fourteenth Amendment. The higher court ordered his admission. The Regents took their case to the United States Supreme Court., arguing that their admission preferences battled the effects of discrimination, increased the number of physicians who practiced in poorer communities, and created an ethnically and racially diverse student body.

Significance of the Case

The Supreme Court had to resolve two questions. First, did the establishment of special admissions criteria for minority students violate the equal protection clause of the Fourteenth Amendment? Second, are racial preference considerations always unconstitutional?

HOW THE COURT RULED

The Court ruled for Bakke, holding that the university's special admissions program for minorities violated the equal protection clause of the Fourteenth Amendment.

Justice Lewis Powell stated in his ruling that if equal protection is not applied equally, regardless of a person's color, it is not equal. Bakke was not responsible for the discriminiatory harm being redressed by affirmative action and should not be punished. Powell did say the university could revise their admissions program to make race a factor among other considerations of admission.

The Court ruled that Bakke must be admitted to the Medical School of UC Davis. He graduated on June 6, 1982.

Allan Bakke graduated from the university in 1982.

DBQ Document Based Questions

1 *Expressing* What is reverse discrimination?

2 *Defending* Did Justice Powell effectively explain whether or not the establishment of special admissions criteria for minority students violated the equal protection clause of the Fourteenth Amendment? Explain.

3 *Predicting Consequences* What effect do you think the *Bakke* decision had on the civil rights movement?

Texas *v.* Johnson (1989)

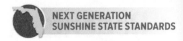

**NEXT GENERATION
SUNSHINE STATE STANDARDS**

SS.912.A.1.6

Background of the Case

In *Halter* v. *Nebraska (1907),* the Supreme Court established statutes that prohibited desecration of the U.S. flag. Following the decision, 48 states established similar laws. In 1989, while protesting outside the Republican National Convention in Dallas, Texas, Gregory Lee Johnson burned an American flag.

Johnson was arrested for violating a Texas flag desecration statute. He was convicted, fined $2,000, and sentenced to one year in prison. Johnson took his case to the Texas Fifth District Court of Appeals. This court supported his conviction. Johnson then appealed to the state's Supreme Court, which overturned the conviction. It said that Johnson's First Amendment right to free expression had been violated. The state of Texas appealed the case to the U.S. Supreme Court.

Significance of the Case

The Court had two important arguments to consider. First, could the government—and in this case, Texas— maintain the right to prevent "expressive speech" if it is considered a violation of the peace? Did Johnson's actions result in public unrest or disturbance?

Second, the Court had to consider the merits of the Texas law that prohibited flag burning for the sole purpose of protecting its symbolic value.

Many states had laws that protected the U.S. flag as a special symbol.

HOW THE COURT RULED

The Court ruled 5-4 in favor of Johnson. Justice William Brennan wrote the majority opinion,which said that Johnson's actions qualified as "expressive conduct," which would then be protected under the First Amendment.

With regards to the state's arguments, the Court determined that Johnson's actions did not result in public unrest or disturbance, which meant Texas did not have grounds to arrest Johnson.

Justice William Rehnquist wrote the dissenting opinion. Justice Rehnquist said that the Star Spangled Banner was a symbol that importantly represented the nation. Rehnquist argued that many Americans hold the flag in very high regard and with a strong place of honor.

He stated that a ban on flag burning does not violate the First Amendment. Justice Rehnquist reasoned that the ban was not meant to suppress particular ideas but instead to protect and preserve the flag as a sacred symbol of the United States.

The Court's ruling had far-reaching implications, reversing statutes in the 48 states that had banned the desecration of the American flag.

DBQ Document Based Questions

❶ *Determining Word Meanings* Using context clues, how would you define the word *desecration*?

❷ *Explaining* Why was it important that the Supreme Court defined Johnson's actions as expressive conduct?

❸ *Predicting Consequences* How would you expect individual states to react to this ruling?

©Bettmann/Corbis

Grutter v. Bollinger (2003)

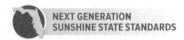
NEXT GENERATION
SUNSHINE STATE STANDARDS

SS.912.A.1.6

Background of the Case

In 1997, Barbara Grutter sued the University of Michigans Law School after it denied her admission. Barbara Grutter was a white resident of Michigan with a 3.8 undergraduate GPA and a very high admission test scores. Grutter claimed that the school's admissions process unfairly used race as a main factor in admissions. The University claimed that race was only one of many factors considered above and beyond test scores and GPA. A lower court ruled in favor of Grutter. On appeal, the decision was reversed in favor of the University. Grutter appealed her case to the Supreme Court.

That same year, Jennifer Gratz and Patrick Hammacher sued the University of Michigan's undergraduate school for denying them admission. The pair claimed that the undergraduate admissions program's 150-point scale was unconstitutional. Applicants with 100 or more points were usually guaranteed admission. Applicants from a historically discrinated against minority group received an automatic 20 points. A federal court ruled in favor of the applicants. The University of Michigan appealed to the U.S. Supreme Court.

Significance of the Case

Both *Grutter* and *Gratz* claimed that the University of Michigan's racial preferences used in admissions—within both its law school and its undergraduate school—violated the Equal Protection Clause of the Fourteenth Amendment.

HOW THE COURT RULED—A COMPARISON

In *Grutter* the Court ruled 5-4 in favor of the University of Michigan's Law School. Justice Sandra Day O'Connor wrote the opinion for the majority. The Court determined that the Equal Protection Clause does not prohibit the law school's "narrowly-tailored" use of race in admissions decisions. The Court ruled this way because the school proved its method to create a diverse student body was only one of many factors considered in admission.

In *Gratz* the Court ruled 6-3 in favor of the applicants Jennifer Gratz and Patrick Hammacher. In his opinion, Chief Justice William Rehnquist wrote that the undergraduate program's process involving race was "not narrowly-tailored enough." The Court claimed that the automatic bonus of 20 points was not a reasonable practice and that the undergraduate program placed too much weight solely on the racial characteristic of the applicant. Here, the Court found that the university had, in fact, violated the Equal Protection Clause of the Fourteenth Amendment.

The Grutter case was one of a pair of affirmative action cases heard by the Supreme Court.

DBQ Document Based Questions

1 *Specifying* What was the main difference between the way the law school and undergraduate school used race as a factor for admission?

2 *Determining Word Meanings* What phrase is used in both opinions by the justices in reference to the use of race in admissions? Based on your knowledge of the cases and the context clues provided, how would you define this word?

3 *Comparing and Contrasting* How are these cases similar? How are they different? Use a Venn diagram to compare and contrast these cases.

Citizens United *v.* Federal Election Commission (FEC) (2010)

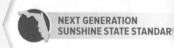

NEXT GENERATION
SUNSHINE STATE STANDAR

SS.912.A.1.6

Background of the Case

Federal election fundraising is a multi-billion dollar industry. Attempts to protect and regulate its influence on elections in the name of fair competition goes back to early 1880s. The Tilman Act (1907) was the first federal law that had an impact on campaign finance. The Taft-Hartley Act of 1947 expanded restrictions to include labor unions. These laws made it illegal for corporations and labor unions to directly contribute money to federal office campaigns. Political Action Committees (PACs) were created in response. The Federal Election Campaign Act (FECA) of 1971 and the Bipartisan Campaign Reform Act of 2002 (also called the McCain-Feingold Act) placed further limits on campaign contributions.

One restriction within the McCain-Feingold Act bans broadcast advertisements that mention a candidate for a specified amount of time before the General Election and a primary. In 2004, Citizens United, a conservative nonprofit group, filed a complaint with the Federal Election Commission (FEC), charging that ads for Michael Moore's film *Fahrenheit 9/11* violated this restriction. The FEC ruled in favor of Moore. Citizens Union then created a production company and made a movie, *Hillary: The Movie* in 2008, which the FEC deemed in violation of McCain-Feingold. The plaintiffs appealed and the case made its way to the Supreme Court.

Significance of the Case

Money has been an influencing factor in elections in this country since its earliest days. Some fear that large donations leads to corruption and encourages *Quid Pro Quo* through favorable legislation. Others believes that the First Amendment protects citizens for engaging in political speech, and that money equals "freedom of speech."

The influence of money in political campaigns was the focus of the Citizens United *case.*

HOW THE COURT RULED

The Court ruled 5-4 in favor of Citizens United, stating that while the government may regulate corporate political speech, it must not be allowed to suppress it altogether.

Justice Anthony Kennedy wrote the majority opinion, saying that protections of speech should not be based on the identity of speakers and that, "associations of individuals" should not be subject to restrictions. Limiting a corporation's ability to spend money was deemed unconstitutional because money was defined as freedom of speech.

Justice John Paul Stevens wrote the dissenting opinion, on behalf of four justices. The dissent warned that, "a democracy cannot function effectively when its constituent members believe that laws are being bought and sold." The conclusion of the dissent called the Court's opinion, "a rejection of the common sense of the American people. . . ."

DBQ Analyzing Historical Documents

❶ ***Determining Word Meanings*** Using context clues, how would you describe the phrase Quid Pro Quo?

❷ ***Citing Text Evidence*** Should corporations be considered "citizens"? Give one reason for and one against.

❸ ***Making Connections*** Legal scholars called *Citizens United* v. *FEC* "one of the most important First Amendment cases in years. It significantly impacted fundraising and political campaigning strategies in recent years. Provide at least one example from the 2012 election.

Charles Mann/Getty Images

Obergefell *v.* Hodges (2015)

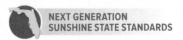
NEXT GENERATION
SUNSHINE STATE STANDARDS

SS.912.A.1.6

Background of the Case

The institution of marriage has a long and complicated history. What was once considered a system designed largely to safeguard wealth and property had turned into a strict definition of the union between a man and a woman. It wasn't until the 1970s that the issue was challenged in court. In 1971, the Supreme Court of Minnesota heard the case *Baker* v. *Nelson* and ruled that the state's law did not violate the Constitution.

The Defense of Marriage Act (DOMA) was a federal law signed in 1996 that defined marriage as "the union of one man and one woman." This legislation impacted around 1,100 federal laws and led to numerous legal challenges in federal court. The plaintiffs in *Obergefell* v. *Hodges* were made up of 14 same-sex couples and two men whose same-sex partners were deceased. The plaintiffs claimed that state officials (those named as defendants) had violated the Fourteenth Amendment by denying them the right to marry or refusing to recognize those marriages that had been previously performed in another state.

Significance of the Case

The Constitutional question the petitioners raised was two-fold: did the Fourteenth Amendment (which provides equal protection under the law) require a state to issue a marriage license for a same-sex couple; and also recognize a same-sex marriage legally licensed out of state? The decision would effectively invalidate all previous bans on gay marriage in 37 states.

HOW THE COURT RULED

The Court ruled 5 to 4 in favor of the plaintiffs, requiring states to license a marriage between two people of the same sex and to recognize legal same-sex marriages performed in a different state.

The majority opinion, written by Anthony Kennedy and representing the collective opinion of five justices, called the history of marriage, "one of both continuity and change." It determined that the fundamental right to marry applied to same-sex couples on the grounds of individual autonomy, the fact of a two-person union, safeguards for children and families, and that denial of the benefits of marriage makes their union unstable for no reason.

The four dissenting justices drafted individual opinions but generally shared the position that the ruling stretched the interpretation of the Constitution beyond its intended limits. Chief Justice Roberts said that the Supreme Court was not a legislator and that the issue of same-sex marriage should not have been left to the judiciary. Anthony Scalia said that previous public debate over same-sex marriage, "displayed American democracy at its best."

The *Obergefell* decision was a ruling that affected the entire nation almost immediately.

DBQ Analyzing Historical Documents

1 *Determining Word Meanings* Using context clues, how would you define the word autonomy?

2 *Citing Text Evidence* What reasoning did the Court use to determine how this ruling impacts "due process."

3 *Making Connections* Many landmark Supreme Court cases have involved the Fourteenth Amendment. Provide an example of at least one and describe its significance. Do you agree or disagree with the Court's interpretation of "individual fundamental rights."

American Literature Library

CONTENTS

"Bald Eagle Sends Mud-turtle to the End of the World",

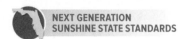

NEXT GENERATION
SUNSHINE STATE STANDARDS

LAFS.1112.RH.1.1, LAFS.1112.RH.2.4,
SS.912.H.1.1, SS.912.H.1.3

Native Americans had a highly developed civilization in place before European settlers arrived in America. They also had their own form of literature—not written, but handed down from generation to generation orally. A theme common to many Native American stories is their relationship to nature. Many are also parables—stories that use symbols or animals to teach lessons. "Bald Eagle Sends Mud-turtle to the End of the World," written down by Jeremiah Curtin, is an example of a parable.

" Once upon a time, a bald-headed old man . . . went down to fish in the lake. On his way home he stopped and gave some of the fish to his wife, and thus they lived well and happily. After they had passed many years in this manner, the old man became curious to know how large the world is.

Being chief of his people he called a council, and said, "I want to know how large the world is. I wish some man would volunteer to find out."' One young man said, "I will go and find out." "Very well," said the chief," How long will you be gone?"

"I can't tell, for I don't know how far I shall have to travel."

"Go," said the chief," and when you return you will tell us about your journey."

The young man started and after traveling two moons he came to a country where everything was white—the forests, the water, the grass. It hurt his feet to walk on the white ground, so he hurried back. When he reached home he notified the chief. The chief said, "I don't believe that he has been to the end of the world, but I will call a council and we will hear what he has to say."

When the people were assembled, the young man said: "I did not go very far, but l went as far as I was able." And he told all he knew of the White Country.

The chief said, "We must send another man." . . . Many men were sent, one after another, and each returned with a story a little different from that told by others, but still no one satisfied the chief. At last a man said, "I will start and I will go to the end of the world before I come back."

The chief looked at the man and saw that he was very **homely**, but very strong, and he said, "I think you will do as you promise. You may go." The chief called a council of the whole nation and each man agreed to make a journey by himself . . . The chief and his men went and were gone forty moons. When they came home a council was held and each told what he had seen. When the man came who had promised to go to the end of the world, he said, "I have been to the end of the world, I have seen all kinds of people, all kinds of game, all kinds of forests and rivers. I have seen things which no one else has ever seen."

The chief was satisfied. He said, "I am chief of all the people, you will be next to me. You'll be second chief." This was the pay the man got for his journey. He took his position as second chief.

The old chief was Bald Eagle. The first man sent out was Deer. His feet were tender, he could not endure the ice and snow of the White Country. The homely man who went to the end of the world was Mud-turtle. "

VOCABULARY

homely
not handsome

DBQ Analyzing Historical Documents

1 Identifying Points of View
What was the "white ground" that hurt the first young man's feet? What is this word choice meant to tell you about the people in the story?

2 Determining Cause and Effect
Why did the chief make the homely man his second chief?

NEXT GENERATION SUNSHINE STATE STANDARDS

LAFS.1112.RH.1.1, LAFS.1112.RH.2.4, SS.912.H.1.1, SS.912.H.1.3

VOCABULARY

scarcely
only just

quarrel
to argue about or find fault with

complexions
the hue or appearance of a person's skin, especially of the face

DBQ Analyzing Historical Documents

1 Describing According to the first paragraph, what has happened between Chief Red Jacket and his BROTHER?

2 Integrating Visual Information Why does Chief Red Jacket begin each paragraph with the word "BROTHER" in all uppercase letters?

3 Defending Chief Red Jacket is making the case to his "BROTHER" that he should be able to practice his own religion. What reasons does Chief Red Jacket give to support this case and is it effective?

Chief Red Jacket's Speech,

This selection is a portion of a famous speech given by Chief Red Jacket (Native American name Sagoyoweha). Red Jacket was an influential leader of the Seneca nation and the Iroquois confederation of tribes from the 1770s until the 1820s. He fought on the side of the British during the American Revolution, but in the War of 1812, he influenced his people to support the United States.

" BROTHER: Our seats were once large and yours were small. You have now become a great people, and we have **scarcely** a place left to spread our blankets. You have got our country, but you are not satisfied; you want to force your religion upon us. . . . You say that you are right and we are lost. How do we know this to be true? We understand that your religion is written in a book. If it was intended for us as well as you, why has not the Great Spirit given to us, and not only to us, but why did he not give to our forefathers, the knowledge of that book, with the means of understanding it rightly? We only know what you tell us about it. How shall we know when to believe, being so often deceived by the white people.

BROTHER: You say there is but one way to worship and serve the Great Spirit. If there is but one religion, why do you white people differ so much about it? Why not all agreed, as you can all read the book?

BROTHER: We do not understand these things. We are told that your religion was given to your forefathers, and has been handed down from father to son. We also have a religion, which was given to our forefathers, and has been handed down to us their children. We worship in that way. It teaches us to be thankful for all the favors we receive, to love each other, and to be united. We never **quarrel** about religion.

BROTHER: The Great Spirit has made us all, but He has made a great difference between his white and red children. He has given us different **complexions** and different customs. To you he has given the arts. To these He has not opened our eyes. . . . Since He has made so great a difference between us in other things, why may we not conclude that he has given us a different religion according to our understanding? The Great Spirit does right. He knows what is best for his children; we are satisfied. . . . We do not wish to destroy your religion, or take it from you. We only want to enjoy our own. "

from *A Midwife's Tale*,

Martha Ballard was born in 1735 in Massachusetts. She married Ephraim Ballard in 1754, and she moved to Maine, along the Kennebec River, to be with her husband in 1777. Martha kept an almost daily diary of her life and midwife work in Maine. Her diary tracks her visits to other families to assist with childbirth labor and the amount of money she was paid for these jobs. The "/" mark divides shillings and pence, so 1/6 means 1 shilling, 6 pence. Ballard's entries began with the day of the Month and the day of the week. The following entries are from January 1796. Misspellings and other abbreviations have been retained from the original document.

" 4 　 2 　 　 *At **ditoes** and other Neigbors.*
Clear and remarkable pleasant. I returnd home Early this morn. Was Calld in at Mr Kimballs to see a sick Child. It has the rash and Canker. I took Breakfast at Son Pollards. They are well. Calld at Mr. Lambarts. All well there. At Mr Densmores. Polly is more Comfortable than when I saw her last tho feeble yet. . . .

6 　 4 　 　 *At home. Had Company.*
Cloudy. I have been washing. Son Jonathan **dind** here. Mr. Livermore, his wife and Cousin, & Mrs Holdman took Tea. I feel some **fatagud** this Evening. I laid my Washing aside when my Company Came and finish it after they went away Except rinsing. . . .

9 　 7 　 　 *At Ditoes. Birth 2nt. Received 12/ and 4 lb Sugar*
Clear and Cold. I was Calld at 3 hour this morning to See Mrs. Gill again. Shee was safely delivered at 5 of a son (her first Child by Mr Gill) and is very Comfortable. Mr Gill bestowed 12/ as a reward for my service and I returnd home. . . .

10 　 D 　 　 *At home. Am not so well as I Could wish*
Clear and cold. Cyrus went to meeting. Harnon Barton went to Mr Pollards. Come here again before Cyrus returned from meeting. I have felt very unwell. Mr Burtun sent for me but I Could not go. Her youngest Child is Burnt. Phillip Bullin returned here. . . .

12 　 3 　 　 *At home*
Clear and pleasant. Mr Finny here giting wood ½ the day. Ezra Town went to see his Unkle and Aunt Gill. Laban Princes wife & Child sleep here. Mr Ballard returnd from surveying at Mr. Tabors. I have done my housework. Feel fatagud. . . .

15 　 6 　 　 *At ditoes. Birth 4th. This is the 612th Birth I have attended at Since the year 1777. The first I assisted was the wife of Petton Warrin in July 1778*
Cloudy. I was at Mr Mathews. His wife was delivered at 6 hour morning of a fine daughter after a severe illness. Her first Child. I received 9/. Made a present of 1/6 to the infant. I returnd home and find my house up in arms. How long God will preserve my strength to perform as I have done of late he only knows. May I trust in him at all times and do good and hee will fulfill his promis according to my Day. May he giv me strength and may I Conduct accordingly.
Birth William Mathews dagt. **X X** "

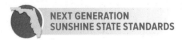

NEXT GENERATION
SUNSHINE STATE STANDARDS

LAFS.1112.RH.1.1, LAFS.1112.RH.2.4,
SS.912.H.1.1, SS.912.H.1.3

VOCABULARY

ditoes
Ballard uses this form of the word "ditto" to reference the repetition of a location that she visited in a previous diary entry.

dind
Ballard refers to the word "dined" here—to sit down and have a meal.

fatagud
spelled in a few different ways, Ballard is referring to the word "fatigued"—feeling tired or physically weak.

X X
a mark at the end of an entry indicates that a debt had been paid in full.

DBQ Analyzing Historical Documents

1 *Citing Text Evidence*
Approximately how many births has Martha attended?

2 *Using Context Clues* Martha Ballard states that after working all day as a midwife, she returned home to find her house "up in arms." Using context clues from the excerpt, what do you think is the meaning of this idiom?

3 *Identifying Points of View* How would you describe Martha Ballard's life? Write a paragraph that summarizes what you've learned about her. Compare your paragraph with her diary entries. How do these two sources compare, specifically what does Martha express through her point of view that your paragraph cannot express?

**NEXT GENERATION
SUNSHINE STATE STANDARDS**

LAFS.1112.RH.1.1, LAFS.1112.RH.2.4,
SS.912.H.1.1, SS.912.H.1.3

VOCABULARY

arduous
difficult, hard

particulars
areas of life

asinine
marked by failure to use intelligence
or good judgment

loath
unwilling

hobgoblin
a mischievious goblin, or ugly sprite

gazetted
announced in a periodical

DBQ Analyzing Historical Documents

1 *Citing Text Evidence*
According to the advice given by
Emerson in the second paragraph,
what must you to do to reinforce
yourself?

2 *Analyzing* Emerson writes
that "their sweet faces, have no
deep cause, but are put on and off
as the wind blows and a newspaper
directs." What did he mean?

3 *Making Connections*
Emerson uses the personification of
a rose to suggest how men should
live. Why might Emerson have used
personification to make his point?

"Self-Reliance" by Ralph Waldo Emerson, *Emerson's essay emphasizes the idea that everyone should rely upon their own instincts and individual beliefs when facing choices in life. This emphasis on individuality was one of Emerson's themes in much of his writings. He warns that conforming to the sometimes inappropriate expectations of society is not necessary.*

" What I must do is all that concerns me, not what the people think. This rule, equally **arduous** in actual and in intellectual life, may serve for the whole distinction between greatness and meanness. It is the harder, because you will always find those who think they know what is your duty better than you know it. It is easy in the world to live after the world's opinion; it is easy in solitude to live after our own; but the great man is he who in the midst of the crowd keeps with perfect sweetness the independence of solitude.

The objection to conforming to usages that have become dead to you is that it scatters your force. It loses your time and blurs the impression of your character. If you maintain a dead church, contribute to a dead Bible-society, vote with a great party either for the government or against it, spread your table like base housekeepers—under all these screens I have difficulty to detect the precise man you are. And, of course, so much force is withdrawn from your proper life. But do your work, and I shall know you. Do your work, and you shall reinforce yourself.

Well, most men have bound their eyes with one or another handkerchief, and attached themselves to someone of these communities of opinion. This conformity makes them not false in a few **particulars**, authors of a few lies, but false in all particulars. Their every truth is not quite true. . . . Meantime nature is not slow to equip us in the prison-uniforms of the party to which we adhere. We come to wear one cut of face and figure, and acquire by degrees the gentlest **asinine** expression . . . the forced smile which we put on in company where we do not feel at ease in answer to conversation which does not interest us. The muscles, not spontaneously moved, but moved by a low usurping willfulness, grow tight about the outline of the face with the most disagreeable sensation.

For nonconformity the world whips you with its displeasure. And therefore a man must know how to estimate a sour face. The by-standers look askance on him in the public street or in the friend's parlour. . . but the sour faces of the multitude, like their sweet faces, have no deep cause, but are put on and off as the wind blows and a newspaper directs.

The other terror that scares us from self-trust is our consistency; a reverence for our past act or word, because the eyes of others have no other data for computing our orbit than our past acts, and we are **loath** to disappoint them. but why . . . drag about this corpse of your memory . . .? Suppose you should contradict yourself, what then? It seems to be a rule of wisdom never to rely on your memory alone, scarcely even in acts of pure memory but to bring the past for judgment into the thousand-eyed present, and live ever in a new day.

A foolish consistency is the **hobgoblin** of little minds, adored by little statesmen and philosophers and divines. With consistency a great soul has simply nothing to do. He may as well concern himself with his shadow on the wall. Speak what you think now in hard words, and tomorrow speak what tomorrow thinks in hard words again, though it contradicts every thing you said today—'Ah, so you shall be sure to be misunderstood,'—Is it so bad, then, to be misunderstood? Pythagoras was misunderstood, and Socrates, and Jesus, and Luther, and Copernicus, and Galileo, and Newton, and every pure and wise spirit that ever took flesh. To be great is to be misunderstood.

I hope in these days we have heard the last of conformity and consistency. Let the words be **gazetted** and ridiculous henceforward. . . . Man is timid and apologetic; he is no longer upright; he dares not say 'I think,' 'I am,' but quotes some saint or sage. He is ashamed before the blade of grass or the blowing rose. These roses under my window make no reference to former roses or to better ones; they are for what they are; they exist with God to-day. There is no time to them. There is simply the rose; it is perfect in every moment of its existence. . . . But man postpones or remembers; he does not live in the present, but with reverted eye laments the past, or heedless of the riches that surround him, stands on tiptoe foresee the future. He cannot be happy and strong until he too lives with nature in the present, above time. **"**

**NEXT GENERATION
SUNSHINE STATE STANDARDS**

LAFS.1112.RH.1.1, LAFS.1112.RH.2.4,
SS.912.H.1.1, SS.912.H.1.3

Uncle Tom's Cabin by Harriet Beecher Stowe,

In this excerpt from Chapter 3, the enslaved George is visiting his wife, Eliza. They were sold to different slaveholders, but have been allowed to visit each other when not working. George had been hired out to a factory, where he was treated well and had invented a work-saving machine. But when the slaveholder saw George's pride in his accomplishment, he moved George back to the plantation and gave him mindless physical work in order to restore his humility.

"   'You are the handsomest woman I ever saw, and the best one I ever wish to see; but, oh, I wish I'd never seen you, nor you me!'

'O, George, how can you!'

'Yes, Eliza, it's misery, misery, misery! My life is bitter as **wormwood**; the very life is burning out of me. I'm a poor, miserable, forlorn **drudge**; I shall only drag you down with me, that's all. What's the use of our trying to do anything, trying to know anything, trying to be anything? What's the use of living? I wish I was dead!'

'O, now, dear George, that is really wicked! I know how you feel about losing your place in the factory, and you have a hard master; but pray be patient, and perhaps something—'

'Patient!' said he, interrupting her; 'haven't I been patient? Did I say a word when he came and took me away; for no earthly reason, from the place where everybody was kind to me? I'd paid him truly every cent of my earnings,—and they all say I worked well.'

'Well, it *is* dreadful,' said Eliza; 'but, after all, he is your master, you know.'

'My master! and who made him my master? That's what I think of—what right has he to me? I'm a man as much as he is. I'm a better man than he is. I know more about business than he does; I am a better manager than he is; I can read better than he can; I can write a better hand,—and I've learned it all myself, and no thanks to him,—I've learned it in spite of him; and now what right has he made a **drayhorse** of me?—to take me from things I can do, and do better than he can, and put me to work that any horse can do? He tries to do it; he says he'll bring me down and humble me, and he puts me to just the hardest, meanest, and dirtiest work, on purpose!'

'O, George! George! you frighten me! Why, I never heard you talk so; I'm afraid you'll do something dreadful. I don't wonder at your feelings, at all; but oh, do be careful—do, do—for my sake—for Harry's! . . . O, George, we must have faith. Mistress says that when all things go wrong to us, we must believe that god is doing the very best.'

'That's easy to say for people that are sitting on their sofas and riding in their carriages; but let 'em be where I am, I guess it would come some harder. I wish I could be good; but my heart burns, and

VOCABULARY

wormwood
something bitter or painful

drudge
a person who does dull or hard work

drayhorse
a horse used to pull heavy loads

smote
to affect like a sudden hard blow

DBQ Analyzing Historical Documents

① *Explaining* Why is George so upset with his master?

② *Using Context Clues* What context clues from George's story to Eliza help to identify the reason he was moved from the factory?

③ *Specifying* What does George plan to do?

can't be reconciled, anyhow. You couldn't in my place,—you can't now, if I tell you all I've got to say. You don't know the whole yet.'

'What can be coming now?'

'Well, lately Mas'r has been saying that he was a fool to let me marry off the place; that . . . I shall take a wife and settle down on his place . . .or he would sell me down the river.'

'Why—but you were married to *me* by the minister, as much as if you'd been a white man!' said Eliza, simply.

'Don't you know a slave can't be married? There is no law in this country for that; I can't hold you for my wife; if he chooses to part us. That's why I wish I'd never seen you, —why I wish I'd never been born; it would have been better for us both,—it would have been better for this poor child if he had never been born. All this may happen to him yet!'

'O, but [my] master is so kind!'

'Yes, but who knows?—he may die—and then [our son] may be sold to nobody knows who. What pleasure is it that he is handsome, and smart, and bright? I tell you, Eliza, that a sword will pierce through your soul for every good and pleasant thing your child is or has; it will make him worth too much for you to keep.'

The words **smote** heavily on Eliza's heart; the vision of the trader came before her eyes, and, as if some one had stuck her a deadly blow, she turned pale and gasped for breath.

'. . . So, Eliza, my girl,' said the husband, mournfully, 'bear up, now; and good-by, for I'm going.'

'George, George! Going where?'

'To Canada,' said he, straightening himself up; ' and when I'm there, I'll buy you; that's all the hope that's left us. You have a kind master, that won't refuse to sell you. I'll buy you and the boy;—God helping me, I will!'

'O, dreadful! if you should be taken?'

'I won't be taken, Eliza; I'll *die* first! I'll be free, or I'll die!' "

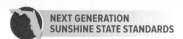

NEXT GENERATION
SUNSHINE STATE STANDARDS

LAFS.1112.RH.1.1, LAFS.1112.RH.2.4,
SS.912.H.1.1, SS.912.H.1.3

"Eating Rats" from *Co. Aytch* by Sam Watkins,

Sam Watkins of Columbia, Tennessee, enlisted in the Confederate Army in 1861. As a part of Company H of the First Tennessee Regiment, Watkins survived some of the most important battles of the Civil War. In 1864, Watkins was stationed near Chattanooga and his army was running low on food and supplies.

"   While stationed at this place, Chattanooga, rations were very scarce and hard to get, and it was, perhaps, economy on the part of our generals and commissaries to issue rather **scant** rations.

About this time we learned that Pemberton's army stationed at Vicksburg, were **subsisting** entirely on rats. Instead of the idea being horrid, we were glad to know that "necessity is the mother of invention," and that the idea had originated in the mind of genius. We at once acted upon the information, and started out rat hunting; but we couldn't find any rats. Presently we came to an old out-house that seemed a natural harbor for this kind of **vermin**. The house was quickly torn down and out jumped an old **residenter**, who was old and gray. I suppose that he had been chased before. But we had jumped him and were determined to catch him, or "burst a boiler." After chasing him backwards and forwards, the rat finally got tired of this foolishness and started for his hole. But a rat's tail is the last that goes in the hole, and as he went in we made a grab for his tail. Well, tail hold broke, and we held the skin of his tail in our hands. But we were determined to have that rat. After hard work we caught him. We skinned him, washed and salted him, buttered and peppered him, and fried him. He actually looked nice. The delicate aroma of the frying rat came to our hungry nostrils. We were **keen** to eat a piece of rat; our teeth were on edge; yea, even our mouth watered to eat a piece of rat. Well, after a while, he was said to be done. I got a piece of cold corn dodger, laid my piece of the rat on it, eat a little piece of bread, and raised the piece of rat to my mouth, when I happened to think of how that rat's tail did slip. I had lost my appetite for dead rat. I did not eat any rat. It was my first and last effort to eat dead rats. "

VOCABULARY

scant
barely enough

subsisting
to nourish oneself

vermin
small common harmful animals—like fleas or mice—that are hard to get rid of

residenter
inhabitant

keen
enthusiastic about something

DBQ Analyzing Historical Documents

❶ *Paraphrasing* Using your own words, explain what the phrase "necessity is the mother of invention" means.

❷ *Determining Cause and Effect* What reason did Sam Watkins give for his small rations and what does this scenario reveal about the state of the Confederate Army?

❸ *Narrative* Suppose you are a soldier in the Civil War. Your rations are running low. Write a letter to your family in which you describe your situation and ask for their help.

"Sanctuary" by Theodore Dreiser,

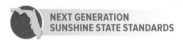
NEXT GENERATION
SUNSHINE STATE STANDARDS

LAFS.1112.RH.1.1, LAFS.1112.RH.2.4,
SS.912.A.3.8, SS.912.H.1.1, SS.912.H.1.3

This is an example of a muckracker publication. It exposed the scandals and corruption of urban American life at the turn of the twentieth century. Writers like Dreiser presented everyday life as it actually was, rather than in a romanticized style. The life of Madeleine, an impoverished young woman, is the theme of this selection from the short story "Sanctuary." In it we glimpse some of the urban conditions that inspired the work of many progressive reformers of the day.

" Primarily, there were the conditions under which [Madeleine] was brought to fifteen years of age: the crowded, scummy tenements; the narrow green-painted halls with their dim gas jets, making the entrance look more like that of a morgue than a dwelling place; the dirty halls and rooms with their green or blue or brown walls painted to save the cost of paper; the bare wooden floors, long since saturated with every type of grease and filth from oleomargarine and **suet** leaked from cheap fats or meats, to beer and whiskey and tobacco juice. . . .

And then the streets outside—any of the streets by which she had ever been surrounded—block upon block of other red, bare, commonplace tenements crowded to the doors with human life, the space before them sped over by noisy, gassy trucks and vehicles of all kinds. . . .

In this atmosphere were always longshoremen, wagon drivers, sweepers of floors, washers of dishes, waiters, janitors, workers in laundries, factories—mostly in indifferent or decadent or despairing conditions. And all of these people existed, in so far as she ever knew, upon that mysterious, **evanescent** and fluctuating something known as the weekly wage.

Always about her there had been drunkenness, fighting, complaining, sickness or death; the police coming in, and arresting one and another; the gas man, the rent man, the furniture man, hammering at doors for their due. . . .

It is not surprising that Madeleine came to her twelfth and thirteenth years without any real understanding of the great world about her and without any definite knowledge or skill. Her drunken mother was now more or less dependent upon her, her father having died of pneumonia and her brother and sister having disappeared to do for themselves. . . .

The child actually went hungry at times. . . . a neighbor perceiving her wretched state and suggesting that some extra helpers were wanted in a department store at Christmastime, she applied there, but so wretched were her clothes by now that she was not even considered. . . . she was able to get a place as a servant in a family.

Those who know anything of the life of a domestic know how thoroughly unsatisfactory it is—the leanness, the lack of hope. . . . she had only the kitchen for her chief chamber or a cubbyhole under the roof. . . .

VOCABULARY

suet
animal fat

evanescent
tending to vanish, impermanent

DBQ Analyzing Historical Documents

1 *Citing Text Evidence* What disadvantages did Madeleine face that made her life difficult?

2 *Analyzing* Where did Madeleine go to find her "sanctuary"?

And then, as was natural, love in the guise of youth, a rather sophisticated gallant somewhat above the world in which she was moving, appeared and paid his all but worthless court to her. . . .

A single trip to Wonderland, a single visit to one of its halls where music sounded to the splash of the waves and where he did his best to teach her to dance, a single meal in one of its gaudy, noisy restaurants . . . were given to hope, a new and seemingly realizable dream of happiness implanted in her young mind. The world was happier than she had thought, or could be made so; not all people fought and screamed at each other. There were such things as tenderness, soft words, sweet words.

But the way of so sophisticated a youth with a maid was brief and direct.

. . . Often in this hour she thought of the swift, icy waters of the river, glistening under a winter moon, and then again of the peace and quiet of the House of the Good Shepherd, its shielding remoteness from life, the only true home or sanctuary she had ever known. And so, brooding and repressing occasional sobs, she made her way toward it . . . thinking of the pathetically debasing love-life that was now over—the dream of love that never, ever could be again, for her.

***

The stark red walls of the institution stood as before, only dim and gray and cold. . . . She had come a long way, drooping, brooding, half-freezing and crying. More than once on the way the hopelessness of her life and her dreams had given her pause, causing her to turn again with renewed determination toward the river—only the vivid and reassuring picture she had retained of this same grim and homely place, its restricted peace and quiet, the sympathy of Sister St. Agnes and Mother St. Bertha, had carried her on . . . the face of Mother St. Bertha, wrinkled and aweary, appeared at the square opening.

'What is it, my child?' she asked. . . .

'It is Madeleine. I was here four years ago. I was in the girls' ward. I worked in the sewing room.'

She was so beaten by life . . . that even now and here she expected little more than an indifference which would send her away again. . . .

In a kind of dumbness of despair she . . . entered the warm, clean bath which had been provided. She stifled a sob as she did so, and others as she bathed. . . .

. . . 'Oh, Mother,' she sobbed as the Sister bent over her, 'don't ever make me go out in the world again, will you? You won't will you? I'm so tired! I'm so tired!'

'No, dear, no,' soothed the Sister . . . 'You need never go out in the world again unless you wish.' "

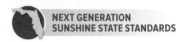

U.S.A., "Sacco and Vanzetti Must Die" by John Dos Passos,

*The story of Nicola Sacco and Bartolomeo Vanzetti, Italian immigrants convicted of murder in 1921, was the inspiration for this selection by John Dos Passos, written in 1936. Large demonstrations were held in support of Sacco and Vanzetti, who claimed they were convicted for being immigrants and anarchists—not for committing a crime. They were executed in 1927, inspiring this passage. In his **trilogy**, U.S.A., Dos Passos used an experimental form—fragments of songs, news headlines, and fragments from the lives of unrelated characters—to depict American **hypocrisy** and materialism. The lines in italics in the following passage from U.S.A. are from actual letters written by Sacco and Vanzetti.*

" Shall be the human race. Much I thought of you when I was lying on the death house—the singing, the kind tender voices of the children from the playground where there was life and the joy of liberty—just one step from the wall that contains the buried agony of three buried souls. It would remind me so often of you and of your sisters and I wish I could see you every moment, but I feel better that you will not come to the death house so that you could not see the horrible picture of three living in agony waiting to be electrocuted.

The Camera Eye

they have clubbed us off the street   they are stronger   they are rich

they hire and fire the politicians the newspapereditors the old judges the small men with reputations the collegepresidents the **wardheelers** (listen businessmen collegepresidents judges   America will not forget her betrayers) they hire the men with guns   the uniforms the policecars the patrolwagons

all rights you have won   you will kill the brave men our friends tonight

there is nothing left to do   we are beaten   we the beaten crowd together in these old dingy schoolrooms on Salem Street shuffle up and down the gritty creaking stairs sit hunched with bowed heads on benches and hear the old words of the haters of oppression   made new in sweat and agony tonight

our work is over   the scribbled phrases   the nights typing releases the smell of the printshop the shart reek of newsprinted leaflets   the rush for Western Union string words into wires the search for stinging words to make you feel who are your oppressors America

America our nation has been beaten by strangers who have turned our language inside out who have taken the clean words our fathers spoke and made them slimy and foul

VOCABULARY

trilogy
a work of fiction or nonfiction written in three separately published parts, or books

hypocrisy
acting in a way that contradicts what you say you believe in

wardheeler
a worker for a political boss in a ward or local area

DBQ Analyzing Historical Documents

1 Citing Text Evidence Why are the people who have "won" in the last paragraphs "afraid to be seen on the streets"?

2 Analyzing Who is "they" in the first few paragraphs under the heading The Camera Eye?

3 Making Connections What was the controversy surrounding the executions of Nicola Sacco and Bartolomeo Vanzetti?

their hired men sit on the judge's bench they sit back with their feet on the tables under the dome of the State House they are ignorant of our beliefs they have the dollars the guns the armed forces the powerplants

they have built the electricchair and hired the executioner to throw the switch

all right we are two nations

America our nation has been beaten by strangers who have bought the laws and fenced off the meadows and cut down the woods for pulp and turned our pleasant cities into slums and sweated the wealth of our people and when they want to they hire the executioner to throw the switch

but do they know that the old words of the immigrants are being renewed in blood and agony tonight do they know that the old American speech of the haters of oppression is new tonight in the mouth of an old woman from Pittsburgh of a husky boilermaker from Frisco who hopped freights clear from the Coast to come here in the mouth of a Back Bay socialworker in the mouth of an Italian printer of a hobo from Arkansas the language of the beaten nation is not forgotten in our ears tonigh

the men in the deathhouse made the old words new before they died

If it had not been for these things, I might have lived out my life talking at streetcorners to scourning men. I might have died unknown, unmarked, a failure. This is our career and our triumph. Never in our full life can we hope to do such work for tolerance, for justice, for man's understanding of man as now we do by an accident.

now their work is over   the immigrants haters of oppression lie quiet in black suits in the little understanding parlor in the North End   the city is quiet   the men of the conquering nation are not to be seen on the streets

they have won why are they scared to be seen on the streets? on the streets you see only the downcast faces of the beaten   the streets belong to the beaten nation   all the way to the cemetery where the bodies of the immigrants are to be burned   we line the curbs in the drizzling rain we crowd the wet sidewalks elbow to elbow silent pale looking with scared eyes at the coffins

we stand defeated America ❞

The Flivver King by Upton Sinclair,

Henry Ford did not invent the idea of an assembly line, but his automobiles established a modern method of industry and promoted mass production. It also put more pressure on the workers standing on the line, struggling to keep up with the growing demand.

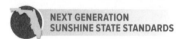

NEXT GENERATION SUNSHINE STATE STANDARDS

LAFS.1112.RH.1.1, LAFS.1112.RH.2.4, SS.912.A.5.4, SS.912.H.1.1, SS.912.H.1.3

" The manufacturers of automobiles were confronting a problem. The more men they had working, the more time these men wasted moving from one job to the next, and getting into another's way. . . . [S]omeone had a bright idea—instead of sending the man to the work, why not bring the work to the man?

The work of assembling the flywheel **magneto**, a small but complex part, was put on a sliding table, just high enough to be convenient for the workers, who sat on stools, each performing one operation upon a line of magnetos which crept slowly by. In the old way, a man doing the work of making a magneto could turn out one every twenty minutes; now the work was cut into twenty-nine operations, performed by twenty-nine different men, and the time per magneto was thirteen minutes and ten seconds. It was a revolution.

. . . Early in 1913, this revolution . . . [affected] an experiment in assembling a chassis, which is the car with its wheels before the body is put on. They had a platform on wheels, and a rope two hundred and fifty feet long, with a windlass to draw it. The materials to be used had been placed in piles along the route, and six assemblers were to travel with the platform and put a chassis together on the way, while men with stop-watches and notebooks kept record of every second it took them.

By the old method of building a car on one spot like a house, it had taken twelve hours and twenty-eight minutes of labor to assemble one chassis. By this new **crude** experiment they cut the time more than half. So very soon they set to work to rip out large sections of the plant and build them over. A moving platform was installed, and the various parts of the chassis came to it either on hooks handing from chains or on small motor-trucks travelling up the aisles. Presently they raised the line to waist-height, and before long they had two lines, one for tall men and one for short.

. . . Once this process was established, the irresistible tendency was to increase the speed of the "belt." . . . . There was always a **clamor** from the sales department for more cars. When the plant was turning out a thousand a day, those who had the job in hand knew that by increasing the speed of the assembly line one minute in an hour, they would get sixteen more cars that day. Why not try it? A couple of weeks later, after the workers on the line had accustomed themselves to the faster motions, why not try it again?

Never had there been such a device for speeding up labor. You simply moved a switch, and a thousand men jumped more quickly. . . . The worker cannot hold a stopwatch and count the number of cars which come to him in an hour. . . If he is a weakling, there are a dozen strong men waiting outside to take his place. Shut your mouth and do what you're told! "

VOCABULARY

Flivver
a small, cheap, old automobile

magneto
a small electric generator that uses permanent magnets to produce sparks in an internal-combustion engine

crude
performed in a rough or unskilled way

clamor
loud protest or demand

DBQ Analyzing Historical Documents

1 *Identifying* What production problem were automobile manufacturers hoping to fix with the assembly line?

2 *Determining Cause and Effect* What happened as a result of the assembly line's invention?

3 *Predicting Consequences* The desire to increase production—and make more money—put pressure on workers. Reread the last paragraph of the excerpt, and think about what labor problems might arise from the changes in the industry. Write a paragraph explaining the human consequences of the assembly line.

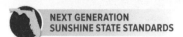

NEXT GENERATION SUNSHINE STATE STANDARDS

LAFS.1112.RH.1.1, LAFS.1112.RH.2.4,
SS.912.H.1.1, SS.912.H.1.3

Night by Elie Wiesel,

Many Jews who survived concentration camps during World War II found it too painful to speak or write about their experiences until many years later. Elie Wiesel waited for 10 years to write the story of his experiences of Auschwitz, where his family was killed. The first passage is from his 1960 novel, Night. *Wiesel was a teenager when the Nazis invaded his town of Sighet in Transylvania in 1944. He became a U.S. citizen in 1963, and he won the Nobel Peace Prize in 1986.*

World War II had shown the world an unprecedented scale of conflict. The science, technology, and industrialism—which were supposed to advance humanity—had been used instead for mass killing and devastation. It was not surprising that many postwar writers sought alternatives to traditional ways of thinking and writing.

VOCABULARY

expelled
to force someone to leave through an official action

deportees
people—who are not citizens of a country—who are forced to leave that country

Gestapo
the secret state police of Germany

haste
rapidity of motion or action

" And then, one day all foreign Jews were **expelled**. . . .

Crammed into cattle cars by the Hungarian police, they cried silently. Standing on the station platform we too were crying. The train disappeared over the horizon; all that was left was thick, dirty smoke.

Behind me, someone said, sighing, 'What do you expect? That's war. . . .'

The **deportees** were quickly forgotten. A few days after they left, it was rumored that they were in Galicia, working, and even that they were content with their fate.

Days went by. Then weeks and months. Life was normal again. A calm, reassuring wind blew through our homes. The shopkeepers were doing good business, the students lived among their books, and the children played in the streets.

One day, as I was about to enter the synagogue, I saw Moishe the Beadle sitting on a bench near the entrance.

He told me what had happened to him and his companions. The train with the deportees had crossed the Hungarian border and, once in Polish territory, had been taken over by the **Gestapo**. The train had stopped. The Jews were ordered to get off and onto waiting trucks. the trucks headed toward a forest. There everybody was ordered to get out. They were forced to dig huge trenches. When they had finished their work, the men from the Gestapo began theirs. Without passion or **haste**, they shot their prisoners, who were forced to approach the trench one by one and offer their necks. Infants were tossed into the air and used as targets for the machine guns. This took place in the Galician forest, near Kolomay. How had he, Moishe the Beadle, been able to escape? By a miracle. He was wounded in the leg and left for dead. "

DBQ Analyzing Historical Documents

❶ *Making Comparisons* How does the author use the phrase "crammed into cattle cars" to foreshadow the fate of the deportees?

❷ *Using Context Clues* Which phrases from the excerpt show a lack of sympathy or concern for the deportees? Identify at least two examples.

❸ *Describing* What happened once the train crossed into Polish territory?

On the Road by Jack Kerouac, The Beat

Generation was the first modern **subculture**, or "alternative" culture. It was a group of writers during the late 1950s and early 1960s that sought spontaneity, emotion, and engagement in real, gritty experiences.

In 1947, Kerouac and a friend took a road trip around the country, which inspired his most famous novel, On the Road. *It expresses the quest for experience and the pessimism of the Beats during the age of the atomic bomb.*

**NEXT GENERATION
SUNSHINE STATE STANDARDS**

LAFS.1112.RH.1.1, LAFS.1112.RH.2.4,
SS.912.A.7.1, SS.912.H.1.1, SS.912.H.1.3

" Later in the afternoon we went out and played baseball with the kids in the **sooty** field by the Long Island railyard. We also played basketball so frantically the younger boys said, 'Take it easy, you don't have to kill yourself.' They bounced smoothly all around us and beat us with ease. Dean and I were sweating. At one point Dean fell flat on his face on the concrete court. We huffed and puffed to get the ball away from the boys; they turned and flipped it away. Others darted in and smoothly shot over heads. We jumped at the basket like maniacs, and the younger boys just reached up and grabbed the ball from our sweating hand, and dribbled away. We were like hotrock blackbelly tenorman *Mad* of American back-alley go-music trying to play basketball against Stan Getz and Cool Charlie. They thought we were crazy. Dean and I went back home playing catch from each sidewalk of the street. We tried extra-special catches, diving over bushes and barely missing posts. When a car came by I ran alongside and flipped the ball to Dean just barely behind the vanishing bumper. He darted and caught it and rolled in the grass, and flipped it back for me to catch on the other side of a parked bread truck. I just made it with my meat hand and threw it back so Dean had to whirl and back up and fall on his back across the hedges. Back in the house Dean took his wallet, harrumphed, and handed my aunt the fifteen dollars he owed her from the time we got a speeding ticket in Washington. She was completely surprised and pleased. We had a big supper. 'Well, Dean,' said my aunt, 'I hope you'll be able to take care of your new baby that's coming and stay married this time.'

. . . 'You can't go all over the country having babies like that. Those poor little things'll grow up helpless. You've got to offer them a chance to live.' He looked at his feet and nodded. In the raw red dusk we said good-by, on a bridge over a superhighway.

. . . He took out a snapshot of Camille in Frisco with the new baby girl.

I realized these were all the snapshots which our children would look at someday with wonder, thinking their parents had lived smooth, well-ordered, stabilized-within-the-photo lives and got up in the morning to work proudly on the sidewalks of life, never dreaming the raggedy madness and riot of our actual lives, our actual night, the hell of it, the senseless nightmare road. All of it inside endless and beginningless emptiness. Pitiful forms of ignorance. "

VOCABULARY

subculture
a group that displays behavior different from that of society

sooty
soiled and dirty with black smoke particles

DBQ Analyzing Historical Documents

❶ *Analyzing* How does the author use juxtaposition in the passage to show that the men are unwilling to grow up?

❷ *Using Context Clues* Why did Kerouac use the verb "bent" when he wrote that Dean "bent to his life" and "walked quickly out of sight?"

❸ *Citing Text Evidence* What does the narrator hope for?

❹ *Making Connections* What imagery does Kerouac use in the passage that reminds the reader that the men are living in the shadow of the atomic bomb? Provide at least two examples.

NEXT GENERATION SUNSHINE STATE STANDARDS

LAFS.1112.RH.1.1, LAFS.1112.RH.2.4, SS.912.A.7.1, SS.912.H.1.1, SS.912.H.1.3

VOCABULARY

hierarchy
persons or things arranged in ranks or classes

jibe
to be in agreement

precepts
a principle meant to be a general rule of action

individualism
the belief that the interests of the individual are of the greatest importance

DBQ Analyzing Historical Documents

1 Finding the Main Idea Based on what you've read in the excerpt, what is the main idea of Whyte's book?

2 Citing Text Evidence According to Whyte, what do most Americans strive to achieve?

3 Making Connections Whyte's book *The Organization Man* was published in 1957. Reread the passage and think about the current state of society. Do you think Whyte's suspicions were justified? Write a paragraph explaining whether Whyte's arguments in *The Organization Man* are relevant in the world today. Provide at least two examples to support your claim.

The Organization Man by William H. Whyte, Jr.,

In post-World War II America, some social critics wrote about the effects of modern life on the character of Americans. William Whyte's "Organization Man" was a symbol of the suspicion that big business influence, suburban conformity, and perhaps Cold War concerns, were weakening the traditional view of an independent-minded American individual.

" [The Organization Man] are not the workers, nor are they the white-collar people in the usual, clerk, sense of the word. These people only work for The Organization. The ones I am talking about *belong* to it as well. They are the ones of our middle class who have left home, spiritually as well as physically, to take the vows of organization life, and it is they who are the mind and soul of our great self-perpetuating institutions. . . .

America has paid much attention to the economic and political consequences of big organization—the concentration of power in large corporations for example, the political power of the civil-service bureaucracies, the possible emergence of a managerial **hierarchy** that might dominate the rest of us. These are proper concerns, but no less important is the personal impact that organization life has had on the individuals within it. . . .

[T]here is almost always the thought that pursuit of individual salvation through hard work, thrift, and competitive struggle is the heart of the American achievement.

But the harsh facts of organization life simply do not **jibe** with these **precepts**. . . .

It is in America . . . that the contrast between the old ethic and current reality has been most apparent—and most poignant. Of all peoples it is we who have led in the public worship of **individualism**. . . . "

People of Plenty by David Potter,

For decades following World War II, the United States standard of living grew to levels it had not seen before. American industry was reawakened after the Great Depression and the rationing of wartime emergencies.

During this period of growth, the growing role of advertising in shaping the view of the American consumer was seen by some social observers as a concern. What might it mean for the nation's economy to be focused on steady consumption of goods rather than the purchase of necessities? In this excerpt, David Potter describes how the nation's economic goal became consumption.

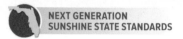

NEXT GENERATION SUNSHINE STATE STANDARDS

LAFS.1112.RH.1.1, LAFS.1112.RH.2.4,
SS.912.H.1.1, SS.912.H.1.3

" The quest for product **differentiation** became intensified as the industrial system became more mature, and as manufacturers had capacity to produce far beyond existing demand.'

In other words, advertising is not badly needed in an economy of scarcity, because total demand is usually equal or in excess of total supply, and every producer can normally sell as much as he produces. It is when potential supply outstrips demand—that is, when abundance **prevails**—that advertising begins to fulfill a really essential economic function. . . . [T]his means that the advertiser must distinguish his product, if not on essential grounds, then on trivial ones, and that he must drive home this distinction by employing a brand name and by keeping this name always before the public.

Let us consider this, however, not merely from the standpoint of the **enterpriser** but in terms of society as a whole. . . . [T]he most critical point in the functioning of society shifts from production to consumption, and, as it does so, the culture must be reoriented to convert the producer's culture into a consumer's culture. In a society of scarcity . . . the productive capacity has barely sufficed to supply the goods which people already desire and which they regard as essential to an adequate standard of living. Hence the social imperative has fallen upon increases in production. But in a society of abundance, the productive capacity can supply new kinds of goods faster than society in the mass learns to crave these goods or to regard them as necessities. If this new capacity is to be used, the imperative must fall upon consumption, and the society must be adjusted to a new set of desires and values in which consumption is paramount. "

VOCABULARY

differentiation
pointing out the difference or differences

prevails
to win against opposition

enterpriser
an individual willing to engage in daring or difficult action

DBQ Analyzing Historical Documents

❶ *Analyzing* What was Potter's opinion of advertising?

❷ *Identifying* According to Potter, society adjusted "to a new set of desires and values in which consumption is paramount." Do you agree or disagree with this statement? Why or why not?

❸ *Making Connections* Potter explains that, in an effort to promote consumption, advertisers must differentiate their products from the competition and create name brands that people recognize. Write a short essay expressing your opinion about advertising in America. How do name brands factor into your purchases? Do you think advertisers distinguish products on trivial grounds? Provide examples to defend your opinion.

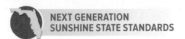

**NEXT GENERATION
SUNSHINE STATE STANDARDS**

LAFS.1112.RH.1.1, LAFS.1112.RH.2.4,
SS.912.A.7.16, SS.912.H.1.1, SS.912.H.1.3

Barrio Boy by Ernesto Galarza, *Ernesto Galarza was born in Mexico and moved to California when he was eight years old. After earning degrees from Stanford University and Columbia University, he returned to California and worked to improve the civil rights and labor conditions for Latinos.*

In this excerpt, Galarza described some of the cultural challenges he experienced as a young boy adjusting to a new life in the United States.

"   It took time to realize that when the Americans said "Sackmenna" they meant Sacra-men-to, or that "Kelly-phony" was their way of saying Cali-for-nia. Worse yet, the names of many of their towns could not be managed. . . .

    There was no authority . . . who could tell us the one proper way to pronounce a word and it would not have done much good if there had been. Try as they did the adults in my family could see no difference between "wood" and "boor." Words spelled the same way or nearly so in Spanish and English and whose meanings we could guess accurately—words like *principal* and *tomato*—were too few to help us in daily usage. The grown-ups adapted the most necessary words and managed to make themselves understood, words like the *French loff, yelly-rol, eppel pai, tee-kett,* and *kenn meelk.* . . .

    Our family conversations always occurred on our own kitchen porch, away from the **gringos**. One or the other of the adults would begin: *Se han filado?* Had we noticed—that the Americans do not ask permission to leave the room; that they had no respectful way of addressing an elderly person; that they spit brown over the railing of the porch into the yard; that when they laughed they roared; that they never brought *saludos* to everyone in your family from everyone in their family when they visited; that *General Delibree* was only a clerk; that *zopilotes* were not allowed on the streets to collect garbage; that the policemen did not carry lanterns at night; that Americans didn't keep their feet on the floor when they were sitting; that there was a special automobile for going to jail; that a rancho was not a rancho at all but a very small **hacienda**; that the saloons served their customers free eggs, pickles, and sandwiches; that instead of bullfighting, the gringos for sport tried to kill each other with gloves? "

VOCABULARY

gringos
slang term for a non-Hispanic person

saludos
greetings or best wishes

zopilotes
a crazy person, a fool

hacienda
a home

DBQ Analyzing Historical Documents

1 *Identifying* Which particular cultural challenge is this passage addressing?

2 *Identifying* What name does Ernesto call Americans? Based on the context clues, do you think this word has a positive of negative connotation? Explain your answer.

3 *Listing* Based on the "front porch" discussion mentioned in the last paragraph, what cultural norms do Latinos practice? List at least two.

Silent Spring by Rachel Carson,

Rachel Carson's Silent Spring *helped inspire the environmental movement. The book described how the use of insecticide chemicals was unwittingly killing animals and causing mysterious illness in people. Carson's book warned that our actions could have unexpected effects on the ecosystem. She suggested a more cautious, careful awareness of how we may change the world.*

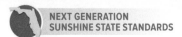

NEXT GENERATION SUNSHINE STATE STANDARDS

LAFS.1112.RH.1.1, LAFS.1112.RH.2.4, SS.912.A.7.12, SS.912.H.1.1, SS.912.H.1.3

" There was once a town in the heart of America where all life seemed to live in harmony with its surroundings. . . . Then a strange **blight** crept over the area and everything began to change. Some evil spell had settled on the community: mysterious maladies swept the flocks of chickens; the cattle and sheep sickened and died. Everywhere was a shadow of death. . . . There had been several sudden and unexplained deaths, not only among adults but even among children, who would be stricken suddenly while at play and die within a few hours.

There was a strange stillness. The birds, for example—where had they gone? Many people spoke of them, puzzled and disturbed. The feeding stations in the backyards were deserted. The few birds seen anywhere were **moribund**; they trembled violently and could not fly. It was a spring without voices. On the morning that had once throbbed with the dawn chorus of robins, catbirds, doves, jays, wrens, and scores of other bird voices there was now no sound; only silence lay over the fields and woods and marsh.

On the farms the hens brooded, but no chicks hatched. The farmers complained that they were unable to raise any pigs—the litters were small and the young survived only a few days. The apple trees were coming into bloom but no bees **droned** among the blossoms, so there was no pollination and there would be no fruit.

The roadsides, once so attractive, were now lined with browned and withered vegetation as though swept by fire. These, too, were silent, deserted by all living things. Even the streams were now lifeless. Anglers no longer visited them, for all the fish had died.

In the gutters under the eaves and between the shingles of the roofs, a white **granular** powder still showed a few patches; some weeks before it had fallen like snow upon the roofs and the lawns, the fields and streams.

No witchcraft, no enemy action had silenced the rebirth of new life in this stricken world. The people had done it themselves.

This town does not actually exist, but it might easily have a thousand counterparts in America or elsewhere in the world. I know of no community that has experienced all the misfortunes I describe. Yet every one of these disasters has actually happened somewhere. . . .

What has already silenced the voices of spring in countless towns in America? "

VOCABULARY

blight
something that harms or destroys

moribund
nearly dead

droned
to make a low dull monotonous humming sound

granular
having a grainy structure, feel, or appearance

DBQ Analyzing Historical Documents

1 *Explaining* What was the meaning of Rachel Carson's term "Silent Spring"?

2 *Identifying* What is the white granular powder on the rooftops?

3 *Using Context Clues* Rachel Carson explains at the end of the passage that "This town does not actually exist, but it might easily have a thousand counterparts in America or elsewhere in the world. I know of no community that has experienced all the misfortunes I describe." What fairytale-like phrase in the beginning of the excerpt signifies that this is perhaps a fictional scenario?

REFERENCE ATLAS

ATLAS KEY

SYMBOL KEY

.... Claimed boundary

——— International boundary
(political map)

——— International boundary
(physical map)

⊗ National capital

◦ State/Provincial capital

• Towns

▼ Depression

▲ Elevation

Dry salt lake

Lake

Rivers

Canal

UNITED STATES
STATES
POLITICAL

Lambert Azimuthal Equal-Area Projection

0   500 miles
0   500 kilometers

PACIFIC OCEAN

RUSSIA

St. Lawrence
Island

Bering Strait

Point Barrow   ARC

**Bering
Sea**

Seward
Peninsula

Brooks Range

**Beaufo.
Sea**

Norton
Sound

Yukon R.

ALASKA

Aleutian Islands

Nunivak
Island

Alaska Range

Fairbanks

ARCTIC C

*Bristol
Bay*

Alaska Peninsula

Anchorage

Kodiak I.

**Gulf of
Alaska**

Alexander
Archipelago

Juneau

Tacoma   Seattle
Olympia   Spokane   **MON**
Portland   **WASH.**   R
Salem   Cascade Range   He
Eugene   Snake R.   Butte
OREGON   **IDAHO**
Boise

Great
Salt Lake
Salt Lake   **WYO**
City

Sacramento   Reno
San Francisco   Carson City   **NEVADA**   **UTAH**
Sierra Nevada

Las
Vegas

CALIFORNIA   **ARIZONA**   Sa
Los Angeles   Albuqu
San Diego   Phoenix
Tucson   **ME**
El P

Honolulu

HAWAII

Hilo

TROPIC OF CANCER

40°N
170°E
180°
30°N
170°W
20°N
160°W
10°N
150°W   140°W   130°W   120°W   110°W

170°E   50°N   180°   60°N   170°W   70°N   160°W   150°W

GREENLAND
(KALAALLIT NUNAAT)
Den.

70°N

CANADA

NORTH
DAKOTA
Bismarck

MINNESOTA

Lake Superior

Pierre
SOUTH DAKOTA

Minneapolis   St. Paul

WISCONSIN

Sioux City   Madison   Milwaukee

NEBRASKA   IOWA
Omaha
Lincoln   Des Moines

Cheyenne

Denver

Kansas City
COLORADO   Topeka
KANSAS   MISSOURI   Jefferson
City

Oklahoma City   Tulsa

OKLAHOMA   ARKANSAS   Memphis
Little Rock

Fort Worth   Dallas

TEXAS   LOUISIANA
Baton Rouge
Austin   Houston   New Orleans
San Antonio

MEXICO

MICHIGAN

Lansing   Detroit

Chicago

ILLINOIS   IND.   Toledo   Cleveland

Indianapolis   Columbus   Pittsburgh

Springfield   Cincinnati   OHIO   W. VA.   Charleston
St. Louis   Frankfort   Louisville

KENTUCKY   VIRGINIA

Nashville   Raleigh

TENNESSEE   NORTH CAROLINA

Birmingham   Charlotte
Atlanta   Columbia
SOUTH
MISS.   ALABAMA   GEORGIA   CAROLINA

Jackson   Montgomery   Charleston

Savannah

Tallahassee   Jacksonville

FLORIDA

Tampa

Miami

Gulf of Mexico

Lake
Michigan   Huron

Lake
Ontario

Montpelier,   MAINE
VERMONT   Augusta

Portland

NEW   Concord, NEW HAMPSHIRE
YORK   Boston, MASSACHUSETTS
Albany   Providence, RHODE ISLAND
Buffalo   Hartford, CONNECTICUT

PA.   New York City

Harrisburg   Trenton, NEW JERSEY
Philadelphia

Baltimore   Dover, DELAWARE

Annapolis, MARYLAND
Washington, D.C.
Richmond
Virginia Beach

Erie

ATLANTIC OCEAN

Bermuda Is.
U.K.

BAHAMAS

Straits of Florida

CUBA

Caribbean
Sea

JAMAICA

HAITI   DOMINICAN
REPUBLIC

San Juan

PUERTO
RICO
U.S.

ANTIGUA
& BARBUDA

ST. KITTS
& NEVIS

DOMINICA

100°W   90°W   80°W   70°W   60°W

120°W   100°W   80°W   60°W   50°W   40°W   30°W   20°W   10°W   0°

OCEAN

N

60°N

50°N

40°N

30°N

20°N

10°W

20°W

30°W

40°W

50°W

UNITED STATES
PHYSICAL

Lake of
the Woods

Isle Royale
Lake Superior

Upper Peninsula

Lower Peninsula

Lake Michigan

Lake Huron

CENTRAL

LOWLAND

Minneapolis

Mississippi R.

Milwaukee

Chicago

Detroit

Lake Erie

Cleveland

Pittsburgh

Indianapolis

Wabash R.

St. Louis

Ohio R.

Cumberland R.

Tennessee R.

Ozark Plateau

Boston Mts.

Ouachita Mts.

Memphis

Red R.

Mississippi R.

COASTAL PLAIN

Houston

New Orleans

Mississippi
River Delta

Gulf of Mexico

Black Belt

Appalachian Plateau

Allegheny Mts.

Cumberland Plateau

Blue Ridge

APPALACHIAN MOUNTAINS

Mt. Mitchell
6,684 ft
2,037 m

Atlanta

Piedmont

Savannah R.

Jacksonville

Cape Canaveral

Lake
Okeechobee

The
Everglades

Miami

Florida Keys

Straits of Florida

Lake
Champlain

Green Mts.

Adirondack
Mts.

Lake Ontario

Niagara
Falls

White
Mts.

Gulf of
Maine

Boston

Cape Cod

Hudson R.

Long Island

New York City

Philadelphia

Baltimore

Delaware Bay

Washington, D.C.

Chesapeake Bay

Cape Hatteras

ATLANTIC
OCEAN

TROPIC OF CANCER

CUBA

PRINCIPAL HAWAIIAN ISLANDS

N

Kauai

Niihau

Oahu

Honolulu

Molokai

Lanai

Maui

Kahoolawe

Hawaii

Mauna Kea
13,796 ft
4,205 m

PACIFIC
OCEAN

0   100 miles
0   100 kilometers
Albers Equal-Area Conic Projection

N

D A

A New Nation, 1787

BRITISH NORTH AMERICA

Claimed by U.S. and Great Britain

Claimed by U.S. and Great Britain

Claimed by N.H. and N.Y.

Part of Mass.

Awarded to Pa. from Conn. 1782

Ceded by Mass. to N.Y. 1786

SPANISH NORTH AMERICA

Missouri R.

Mississippi R.

NORTHWEST TERRITORY

NEW HAMP

MASSACHU

RHODE

CONNECTI

Ceded by Mass. to U.S. 1785

Ceded by Va. to U.S. 1784

PENNSYLVANIA

New York City (1787-1790)

NEW JERSEY

SPANISH LOUISIANA

Ceded by Conn. to U.S. 1786 & 1800

Webash R.

Ohio R.

UNITED STATES

DELAWARE

MARYLAND

VIRGINIA

Arkansas R.

Ceded by New York to U.S. 1782

Claimed by Virginia

NORTH CAROLINA

ALTA CALIFORNIA

Claimed by North Carolina

SOUTH CAROLINA

Colorado R.

Gila R.

Ceded by S.C. to Ga. 1787

Claimed by Georgia

GEORGIA

Original 13 st

Land still clai by states 178

BAJA CALIFORNIA

Rio Grande

WESTERN INTERIOR PROVINCES

EASTERN INTERIOR PROVINCES

Claimed by Ga., Spain and U.S.

SPANISH FLORIDA

U.S. territory

British territo

Spanish terri

Disputed boundary

Coming of Age, 1821

BRITISH NORTH AMERICA

Claimed by U.S. and Great Britain

Columbia R.

U.S.-British treaty line of 1818

RED RIVER BASIN To U.S. 1818

MAINE 1820

OREGON COUNTRY U.S.-British agreement to joint occupation in 1818

Mississippi R.

MICHIGAN TERRITORY

Snake R.

UNORGANIZED TERRITORY

Adams-Onís Treaty line of 1819

Missouri R.

INDIANA 1816

Washington

ALTA CALIFORNIA

Arkansas R.

ILLINOIS 1818

Webash R.

Ohio R.

Colorado R.

MEXICO

MISSOURI 1821

ARKANSAS TERRITORY

Gila R.

Red R.

MISSISSIPPI 1817

ALABAMA 1819

UNITED STATES
TERRITORIAL GROWTH

Rio Grande

TEXAS

LOUISIANA 1812

FLORIDA To U.S. 1819

panding West of the Mississippi, 1803

BRITISH NORTH AMERICA

Claimed by U.S. and Great Britain

OREGON COUNTRY
Claimed by Great Britain, Russia, Spain, and United States

Claimed by U.S. and Great Britain

VERMONT 1791

NEW SPAIN (SPANISH MEXICO)

Mississippi R.

Missouri R.

INDIANA TERRITORY

OHIO 1803

Wabash R.

Ohio R.

Philadelphia (1790-1800)

Washington (new capital 1800)

LOUISIANA PURCHASE
Purchased by U.S. in 1803 from France

Arkansas R.

KENTUCKY 1792

TENNESSEE 1796

Red R.

Claimed by U.S. and Spain

Rio Grande

BAJA CALIFORNIA

Ceded by Georgia to U.S. 1802

MISSISSIPPI TERR.

SPANISH FLORIDA

Claimed by U.S. and Spain

	States previously in the Union
	States newly admitted

oast to Coast, 1850 and Beyond

BRITISH NORTH AMERICA

Treaty line of 1846

Treaty line of 1842

Treaty line of 1842

WASHINGTON 1889

OREGON TERRITORY
Added to U.S. in 1846

MONTANA 1889

NORTH DAKOTA 1889

MINNESOTA 1858

MICHIGAN 1837

OREGON 1859

IDAHO 1890

Snake R.

MINNESOTA TERRITORY

WISCONSIN 1848

Missouri R.

NEVADA 1864

WYOMING 1890

SOUTH DAKOTA 1889

UNORGANIZED TERRITORY

NEBRASKA 1867

IOWA 1846

UTAH TERRITORY

UTAH 1896

COLORADO 1876

Wabash R.

Ohio R.

W. VA. 1863

Washington

CALIFORNIA 1850

KANSAS 1861

Arkansas R.

Colorado R.

Gila R.

ARIZONA 1912

NEW MEXICO TERRITORY

OKLAHOMA 1907

ARKANSAS 1836

GADSDEN PURCHASE
To U.S. 1853

NEW MEXICO 1912

Red R.

Mississippi R.

RUSSIA

ALASKA 1959

Rio Grande

TEXAS 1845

Purchased by U.S. 1867

MEXICO

FLORIDA 1845

HAWAII 1959

Annexed by U.S. 1898

	States admitted after 1850

MIDDLE AMERICA
PHYSICAL / POLITICAL

UNITED STATES

Tijuana
Mexicali
Sonoran Desert
30°N
BAJA CALIFORNIA
Baja California
SONORA
Ciudad Juárez
CHIHUAHUA
Chihuahua
Gulf of California
Cape Falso
BAJA CALIFORNIA SUR
La Paz
Sierra Madre Occidental
SINALOA
DURANGO
COAHUILA
Nuevo Laredo
M
Monterrey
NUEVO LEÓN
Matamoros
Rio Bravo
ZACATECAS
E
Sierra Madre Oriental
TAMAULIPAS
Mazatlán
SAN LUIS POTOSÍ
X
San Luis Potosí
Ciudad Madero
Tampico
20°N
NAYARIT
X
AGUASCALIENTES
QUERÉTARO
Guadalajara
JALISCO
León
I
VERACRUZ
HIDALGO
MORELOS
GUANAJUATO
TLAXCALA
COLIMA
MICHOACÁN
MÉXICO
Mexico City
C
Veracruz
DISTRITO FEDERAL
Popocatépetl 17,887 ft. 5,450 m
PUEBLA
Orizaba 18,700 ft. 5,700 m
Bay of Campeche
Mérida
YUCAT
Yucatán Peninsula
QUIN RO
TABASCO
CAMPECHE
GUERRERO
Sierra Madre del Sur
OAXACA
Isthmus of Tehuantepec
O
Acapulco
CHIAPAS
Gulf of Mehuantepec
Sierra Madre
Belmopan
BELIZE
B
C
Gu Hon
GUATEMALA
HO
Guatemala
Tegucigal
San Salvador
EL SALVADOR
CENTRAL
AMERICA
Gulf of Me
Co Is
10°N
Revillagigedo Islands
Mex.
PACIFIC OCEAN
Cocos Is C.R.

110°W   100°W   90°W
120°W   110°W   100°W   90°W

9   10   11   12

80°N   40°W

ICELAND

GREENLAND (KALAALLIT NUNAAT) Den.

esmere sland

yon Island

Baffin Bay

• Arctic Bay

Ba ff i n I s l a n d

• Igloolik

Davis Strait

Melville Peninsula

Foxe Basin

V U T

• Repulse Bay

• Iqaluit

Southampton Island

esterfield et

Hudson Strait

Ungava Bay

Labrador Sea

CANADA

PHYSICAL / POLITICAL

Hudson Bay

Kuujjuaq •

• Nain

NEWFOUNDLAND AND LABRADOR

Cartwright •

Happy Valley-Goose Bay •

Schefferville •

Island of Newfoundland

Belcher Islands

Kuujjuarapik •

Smallwood Reservoir

Churchill Falls

• Fort Severn

Labrador City •

Q U E B E C

St. John's

Avalon Peninsula

James Bay

Manicouagan Reservoir

Anticosti I.

S H I E L D

Sept-Îles •

Gulf of St. Lawrence

St.-Pierre & Miquelon Fr.

O N T A R I O

Gaspé Pen.

PRINCE EDWARD ISLAND

Sydney •

Cape Breton I.

Chicoutimi •

Lake nipigon

Timmins •

Rouyn-Noranda •

Quebec •

NEW BRUNSWICK

Charlottetown

Thunder Bay •

Fredericton •

NOVA SCOTIA

ATLANTIC OCEAN

Lake Superior

North Bay •

Sudbury •

Montreal •

Saint John •

Halifax •

St. Lawrence

Lake Michigan

Ottawa ☆

Lake Huron

Bay of Fundy

Toronto •

L. Ontario

Niagara Falls

London •

Lake Erie

90°W   80°W   70°W   60°W

MIDDLE EAST
PHYSICAL / POLITICAL

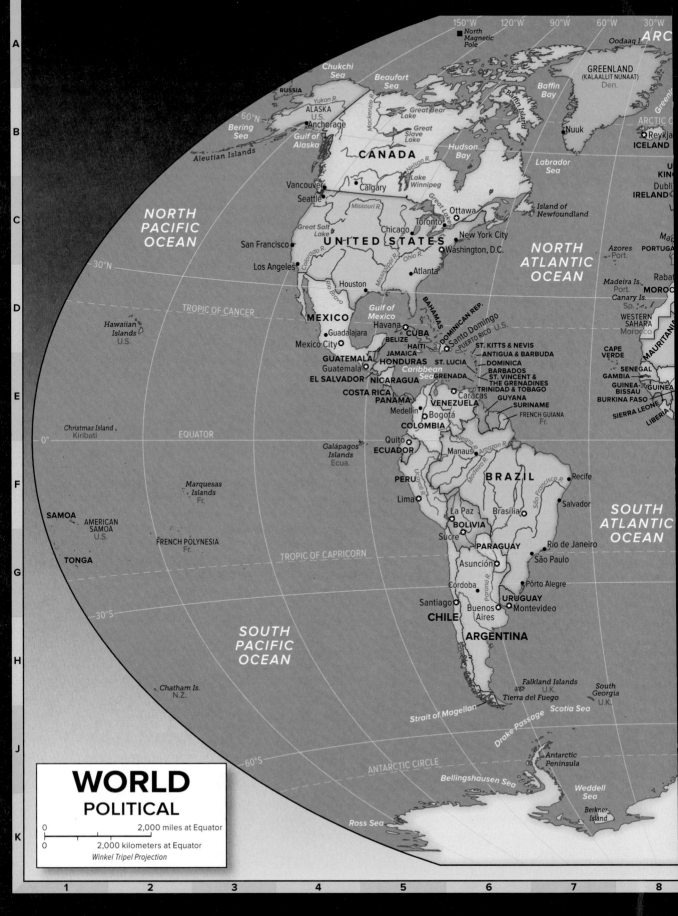

North
Magnetic
Pole

150°W   120°W   90°W   60°W   30°W

Oodaaq I.   ARC

A

*Chukchi
Sea*

*Beaufort
Sea*

GREENLAND
(KALAALLIT NUNAAT)
Den.

RUSSIA

*Baffin
Island*

*Baffin
Bay*

Greenl

60°N

ALASKA
U.S.

Anchorage

*Bering
Sea*

*Gulf of
Alaska*

Mackenzie R.

*Great Bear
Lake*

*Great
Slave
Lake*

*Hudson
Bay*

Nuuk

ARCTIC C

Reykja

ICELAND

B

Aleutian Islands

CANADA

Nelson R.

*Labrador
Sea*

U
KING

Dubli

IRELAND

NORTH
PACIFIC
OCEAN

Vancouver

Seattle

Calgary

*Lake
Winnipeg*

Missouri R.

Ottawa

Toronto

*Island of
Newfoundland*

C

30°N

San Francisco

*Great Salt
Lake*

UNITED STATES

Chicago

Great Lakes

New York City

Washington, D.C.

NORTH
ATLANTIC
OCEAN

*Azores
Port.*

Mad

PORTUGA

Los Angeles

Colorado R.

Ohio R.

Atlanta

*Madeira Is.
Port.*

Rabat

MORO

Houston

Mississippi R.

Rio Bravo

*Canary Is.
Sp.*

WESTERN
SAHARA
Morocco

D

TROPIC OF CANCER

*Hawaiian
Islands
U.S.*

MEXICO

*Gulf of
Mexico*

Havana

CUBA

BAHAMAS

DOMINICAN REP.

Santo Domingo

PUERTO RICO U.S.

CAPE
VERDE

MAURITANIA

Guadalajara

BELIZE

HAITI

ST. KITTS & NEVIS

Mexico City

JAMAICA

ANTIGUA & BARBUDA

SENEGAL

GUATEMALA

ST. LUCIA

DOMINICA

GAMBIA

Guatemala

HONDURAS

*Caribbean
Sea*

BARBADOS

GUINEA-
BISSAU

GUINEA

EL SALVADOR

NICARAGUA

GRENADA

ST. VINCENT &
THE GRENADINES

BURKINA FASO

COSTA RICA

TRINIDAD & TOBAGO

SIERRA LEONE

E

PANAMA

Caracas

GUYANA

LIBERIA

Medellin

VENEZUELA

SURINAME

Bogotá

FRENCH GUIANA
Fr.

COLOMBIA

Quito

Negro R.

ECUADOR

Manaus

Amazon R.

*Galápagos
Islands
Ecua.*

*Christmas Island
Kiribati*

0°

EQUATOR

F

*Marquesas
Islands
Fr.*

PERU

Madeira R.

BRAZIL

São Francisco R.

Recife

Ucayali R.

Lima

Salvador

SOUTH
ATLANTIC
OCEAN

SAMOA

AMERICAN
SAMOA
U.S.

FRENCH POLYNESIA
Fr.

La Paz

Brasília

BOLIVIA

TONGA

TROPIC OF CAPRICORN

Sucre

Rio de Janeiro

G

PARAGUAY

São Paulo

Asunción

Paraná R.

Pôrto Alegre

*Chatham Is.
N.Z.*

Cordoba

URUGUAY

30°S

Santiago

Buenos
Aires

Montevideo

CHILE

SOUTH
PACIFIC
OCEAN

ARGENTINA

H

*Falkland Islands
U.K.*

*South
Georgia
U.K.*

Tierra del Fuego

Strait of Magellan

Scotia Sea

J

60°S

ANTARCTIC CIRCLE

Drake Passage

*Antarctic
Peninsula*

Bellingshausen Sea

*Weddell
Sea*

K

Ross Sea

*Berkner
Island*

WORLD
POLITICAL

0   2,000 miles at Equator

0   2,000 kilometers at Equator

Winkel Tripel Projection

How do I study Geography?

Geographers have tried to understand the best way to teach and learn about geography. In order to do this, geographers created the *Five Themes of Geography*. The themes acted as a guide for teaching the basic ideas about geography to students like yourself.

People who teach and study geography, though, thought that the Five Themes were too broad. In 1994, geographers created 18 national geography standards. These standards were more detailed about what should be taught and learned. The Six Essential Elements act as a bridge connecting the Five Themes with the standards.

These pages show you how the Five Themes are related to the Six Essential Elements and the 18 standards.

5 Themes of Geography

1. Location
Location describes where something is. Absolute location describes a place's exact position on the Earth's surface. Relative location expresses where a place is in relation to another place.

2. Place
Place describes the physical and human characteristics that make a location unique.

3. Regions
Regions are areas that share common characteristics.

4. Movement
Movement explains how and why people and things move and are connected.

5. Human-Environment Interaction
Human-Environment Interaction describes the relationship between people and their environment.

6 Essential Elements

18 Geography Standards

I. The World in Spatial Terms

Geographers look to see where a place is located. Location acts as a starting point to answer "Where is it?" The location of a place helps you orient yourself as to where you are.

1. How to use maps and other tools.

2. How to use mental maps to organize information.

3. How to analyze the spatial organization of people, places, and environments.

II. Places and Regions

Place describes physical characteristics such as landforms, climate, and plant or animal life. It might also describe human characteristics, including language and way of life. Places can also be organized into regions. **Regions** are places united by one or more characteristics.

4. The physical and human characteristics of places.

5. How people create regions to interpret Earth's complexity.

6. How culture and experience influence people's perceptions of places and regions.

III. Physical Systems

Geographers study how physical systems, such as hurricanes, volcanoes, and glaciers, shape the surface of the Earth. They also look at how plants and animals depend upon one another and their surroundings for their survival.

IV. Human Systems

People shape the world in which they live. They settle in certain places, but not in others. An ongoing theme in geography is the movement of people, ideas, and goods.

V. Environment and Society

How does the relationship between people and their natural surroundings influence the way people live? Geographers study how people use the environment and how their actions affect the environment.

7. The physical processes that shape Earth's surface.

8. The distribution of ecosystems on Earth's surface.

9. The characteristics, distribution, and migration of human populations.

10. The complexity of Earth's cultural mosaics.

11. The patterns and networks of economic interdependence.

12. The patterns of human settlements.

13. The forces of cooperation and conflict.

14. How human actions modify the physical environment.

15. How physical systems affect human systems.

16. The meaning, use, and distribution of resources.

VI. The Uses of Geography

Knowledge of geography helps us understand the relationships among people, places, and environments over time. Applying geographic skills helps you understand the past and prepare for the future.

17. How to apply geography to interpret the past.

18. How to apply geography to interpret the present and plan for the future.

GEOGRAPHY SKILLS HANDBOOK

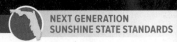

NEXT GENERATION
SUNSHINE STATE STANDARDS

SS.912.G.1.2

Throughout this text, you will discover how geography has shaped the course of events in history. Landforms, waterways, climate, and natural resources all have helped or hindered human activities. Usually people have learned either to adapt to their environments or to transform it to meet their needs. The resources in this Geography Skills Handbook will help you get the most out of your textbook—and provide you with skills you will use for the rest of your life.

Geographers use a wide array of tools to collect and analyze information to help them understand the Earth. The study of geography is more than knowing a lot of facts about places. Rather, it has more to do with asking questions about the Earth, pursuing their answers, and solving problems. Thus, one of the most important geographic tools is inside your head: the ability to think geographically.

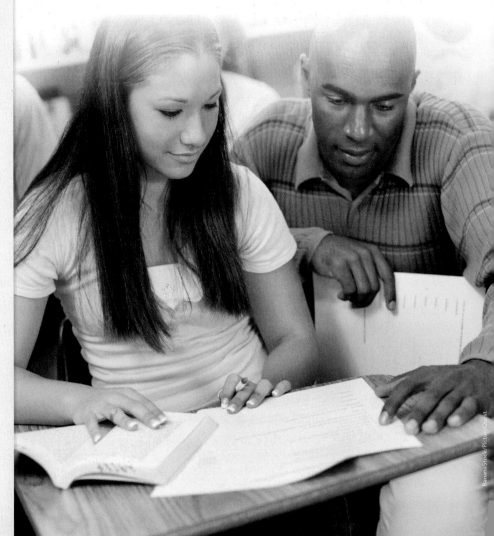

Globes and Maps

A **globe** is a scale model of the Earth. Because Earth is round, a globe presents the most accurate depiction of geographic information such as area, distance, and direction. However, globes show little close-up detail. A printed **map** is a symbolic representation of all or part of the planet. Unlike globes, maps can show small areas in great detail.

From 3-D to 2-D

Think about the surface of the Earth as the peel of an orange. To flatten the peel, you have to cut it into segments that are still connected as one piece. To create maps that are not interrupted, mapmakers, or **cartographers,** use mathematical formulas to transfer information from the three-dimensional globe to the two-dimenstional map. However, when the curves of a globe become straight lines on a map, distortion of size, shape, distance, or area occurs.

Great Circle Routes

A straight line of true direction—one that runs directly from west to east, for example,—is not always the shortest distance between two points. This is due to the curvature of the Earth. To find the shortest distance, stretch a piece of string around the globe from one point to the other. The string will form part of a *great circle,* an imaginary line that follows the curve of the Earth. Ship captains and airline pilots use these **great circle routes** to reduce travel time and conserve fuel.

The idea of a great circle route in an important difference between globes and maps. A round globe accurately shows a great circle route, as indicated on the top right map. However, the flat map below it shows the great circle distance (dotted line) between Tokyo and Los Angeles to be far longer than the true direction distance (solid line). In fact, the great circle distance is 315 miles (506 km) shorter.

SS.912.G.1.3

VOCABULARY

globe
a scale model of the Earth

maps
a symbolic representation of all or part of the planet

cartographers
mapmakers

great circle route
a straight line of true direction on a globe

GEOGRAPHY CONNECTION

1 *Explain* the significance of: globe, map, cartographer, great circle route.

2 *Describe* the problems that arise when the curves of a globe become straight lines on a map.

3 *Use* a Venn diagram like the one below to identify the similarities and differences between globes and maps.

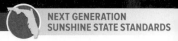

NEXT GENERATION SUNSHINE STATE STANDARDS

SS.912.G.1.3

Projections

To create maps, cartographers project the round Earth onto a flat surface—making a **map projection.** Distance, shape, direction, or size may be distorted by a projection. As a result, the purpose of the map usually dictates which projection is used. There are many kinds of map projections, some with general names and some named for the cartographers who developed them. Three basic categories of map projections are shown here: **planar, cylindrical,** and **conic.**

Planar Projection

A planar projection shows the Earth centered in such a way that a straight line coming from the center to any point represents the shortest distance. Also known as an azimuthal projection, it is most accurate at its center. As a result, it is often used for maps of the Poles.

Cylindrical Projection

A cylindrical projection is based on the projection of the globe onto a cylinder. This projection is most accurate near the Equator, but shapes and distances are distorted near the Poles.

Conic Projection

A conic projection comes from placing a cone over part of the globe. Conic projections are best suited for showing limited east-west areas that are not far from the Equator. For these uses, a conic projection can indicate distances and directions fairly accurately.

Common Map Projections

Each type of map projection has advantages and some degree of inaccuracy. Four of the most common projections are shown here.

Winkel Tripel Projection

Most general reference world maps are the Winkel Tripel projection. It provides a good balance between the size and shape of land areas as they are shown on the map. Even the polar areas are depicted with little distortion of size and shape.

Robinson Projection

The Robinson projection has minor distortions. The sizes and shapes near the eastern and western edges of the map are accurate, and outlines of the continents appear much as they do on the globe. However, the polar areas are flattened.

Goode's Interrupted Equal-Area Projection

An **interrupted projection** looks something like a globe that has been cut apart and laid flat. Goode's Interrupted Equal-Area projection shows the true size and shape of Earth's landmasses, but distances are generally distorted.

Mercator Projection

The Mercator projection increasingly distorts size and distance as it moves away from the Equator. However, Mercator projections do accurately show true directions and the shapes of landmasses, making these maps useful for sea travel.

VOCABULARY

map projection
the image of a round Earth onto a flat surface

planar
a map projection that is most accurate at the center

cylindrical
a map projection that is most accurate near the Equator

conic
a map projection that accurately shows east-west areas near the Equator

GEOGRAPHY CONNECTION

1 *Explain* the significance of: map projection, planar, cylindrical, conic, interrupted projection.

2 *How* does a cartographer determine which map projection to use?

3 *How* is Goode's Interrupted Equal-Area projection different from the Mercator projection?

4 *Which* of the four common projections described above is the best one to use when showing the entire world? Why?

5 *Use* a Venn diagram like the one below to identify the similarities and differences between the Winkel Tripel and Mercator projections.

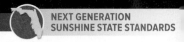

NEXT GENERATION
SUNSHINE STATE STANDARDS

SS.912.G.1.3

VOCABULARY

grid system
a pattern of lines on a map or globe that determines exact location on Earths' surface

hemisphere
one of the halves that geographers divide the Earth into

latitude
lines that circle the Earth parallel to the Equator

longitude
lines that circle the Earth from Pole to Pole

Prime Meridian
the line of longitude set at 0°

absolute location
a global address determined by the intersection of longitude and latitude lines

Determining Location

Geography is often said to begin with the question: Where? The basic tool for answering the question is location. Lines on globes and maps provide information that can help you locate places. These lines cross one another forming a pattern called a **grid system,** which helps you find exact places on the Earth's surface.

A **hemisphere** is one of the halves into which the Earth is divided. Geographers divide the Earth into hemispheres to help them classify and describe places on Earth. Most places are located in two of the four hemispheres.

Latitude

Lines of **latitude,** or parallels, circle the Earth parallel to the Equator and measure the distance north or south of the Equator in degrees. The Equator is measured at 0° latitude, while the Poles lie at latitudes 90°N (north) and 90°S (south). Parallels north of the Equator are called north latitude. Parallels south of the Equator are called south latitude.

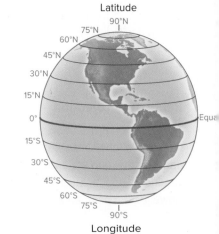

Longitude

Lines of **longitude,** or meridians, circle the Earth from Pole to Pole. These lines measure distance east or west of the **Prime Meridian** at 0° longitude. Meridians east of the Prime Meridian are known as east longitude. Meridian west of the Prime Meridian are known as west longitude. The 180° meridian on the opposite side of the Earth is called the International Date Line.

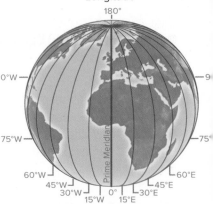

The Global Grid

Every place has a global address, or **absolute location.** You can identify the absolute location of a place by naming the latitude and longitude lines that cross exactly at that place. For example, Tokyo, Japan is located at 36°N latitude and 140°E longitude. For more precise readings, each degree is further divided into 60 units called minutes.

Northern and Southern Hemispheres

The diagram below shows that the Equator divides the Earth into the Northern and Southern Hemispheres. Everything north of the Equator is in the **Northern Hemisphere.** Everything south of the Equator is in the **Southern Hemisphere.**

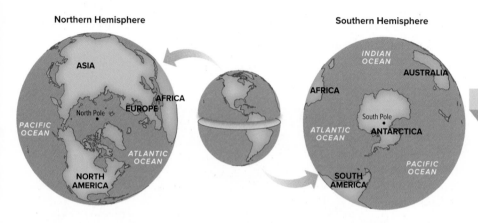

Eastern and Western Hemispheres

The Prime Meridian and the International Date Line divide the Earth into the Eastern and Western Hemispheres. Everything east of the Prime Meridian for 180° is in the **Eastern Hemisphere.** Everything west of the Prime Meridian for 180° is in the **Western Hemisphere.**

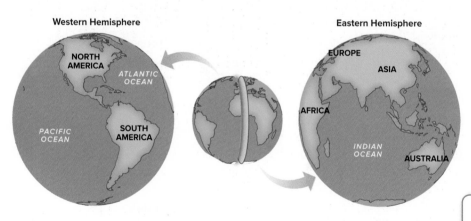

VOCABULARY

Northern Hemisphere
the half of the globe north of the Equator

Southern Hemisphere
the half of the globe south of the Equator

Eastern Hemisphere
the half of the globe east of the Prime Meridian for 180°

Western Hemisphere
the half of the globe west of the Prime Meridian for 180°

GEOGRAPHY CONNECTION

❶ *Explain* the significance of: location, grid system, hemisphere, Northern Hemisphere, Southern Hemisphere, Eastern Hemisphere, Western Hemisphere, latitude, longitude, Prime Meridian, absolute location.

❷ *Why* do all maps label the Equator 0° latitude and the Prime Meridian 0° longitude?

❸ *Which* lines of latitude and longitude divide the Earth into hemispheres?

❹ *Using* the Reference Atlas maps, fill in a chart by writing the latitude and longitude of three world cities. Have a partner try to identify the cities listed in your chart.

❺ *Use* a chart like the one below to identify the continents in each hemisphere. Some may be in more than one hemisphere.

Hemisphere	Continents
Northern	
Southern	
Eastern	
Western	

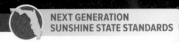

NEXT GENERATION SUNSHINE STATE STANDARDS

SS.912.G.1.3

Reading a Map

In addition to latitude and longitude, maps feature other important tools to help you interpret the information they contain. Learning to use these map tools will help you read the symbolic language of maps more easily.

Key

The key lists and explains the symbols, colors, and lines used on the map. The key is sometimes called a legend.

Title

The title tells you what kind of information the map is showing.

Boundary Lines

On political maps of large areas, boundary lines highlight the borders between different countries or states.

Compass Rose

The compass rose indicates directions. The four cardinal directions—north, south, east, and west—are usually indicated with arrows or the points of a star. The intermediate directions—northeast, northwest, southeast, and southwest—may also be shown.

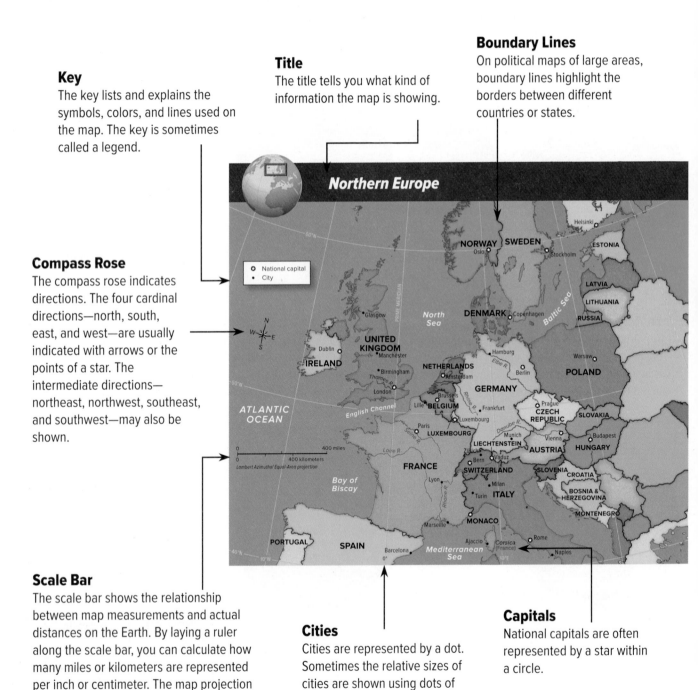

Scale Bar

The scale bar shows the relationship between map measurements and actual distances on the Earth. By laying a ruler along the scale bar, you can calculate how many miles or kilometers are represented per inch or centimeter. The map projection used to create the map is often listed near the scale bar.

Cities

Cities are represented by a dot. Sometimes the relative sizes of cities are shown using dots of different sizes.

Capitals

National capitals are often represented by a star within a circle.

SS.912.G.1.2

Using Scale

All maps are drawn to a certain scale. **Scale** is a consistent, proportional relationship between the measurements shown on the map and the measurement of the Earth's surface.

Small-Scale Maps A small-scale map, like this political map of France, can show a large area but little detail. Note that the scale bar on this map indicates that about 1 inch is equal to 200 miles.

Large-Scale Maps A large-scale map, like this map of Paris, can show a small area with a great amount of detail. Study the scale bar. Note that the map measurements correspond to much smaller distances than on the map of France.

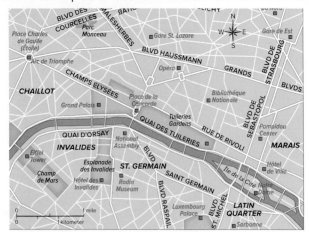

Absolute and Relative Location

As you learned on page 760, absolute location is the exact point where a line of latitude crosses a line of longitude. Another way to indicate location is by **relative location,** or the location of one place in relation to another. To find relative location, find a reference point—a location you already know—on a map. Then look in the appropriate direction for the new location. For example, locate Paris (your reference point) on the map of France above. The relative location of Lyon can be described as southeast of Paris.

VOCABULARY

Scale
a consistant, proportional relationship between measurements shown on a map and measurements of the Earth's surface

relative location
the location of one place in relation to another

GEOGRAPHY CONNECTION

❶ *Explain* the significance of: key, compass rose, cardinal directions, intermediate directions, scale bar, scale, relative location.

❷ *Describe* the elements of a map that help you interpret the information displayed on the map.

❸ *How* does the scale bar help you determine distances on the Earth's surface?

❹ *Describe* the relative location of your school in two different ways.

❺ *Use* a Venn diagram to identify the similarities and differences of small-scale maps and large-scale maps.

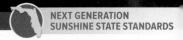

NEXT GENERATION SUNSHINE STATE STANDARDS

SS.912.G.1.3

Physical and Political Maps

Physical and political are the two main types of maps in this book. A **physical map** shows the location and the topography, or shape of the Earth's physical features. A study of an area's physical features often helps explain its historical development. A **political map** shows the boundaries and locations of political units such as countries, states, and cities. Non subject area is usually shown in a different color to set it apart from the main area of the map. This nonsubject area gives you a context for the region you are studying.

VOCABULARY

physical map
a map that shows the location and shape of the Earth's physical features

political map
a map that shows the boundaries and location of political units such as counties, state, and cities

Physical Maps

Physical maps use shading and texture to show general relief—the differences in elevation. or height, of landforms. Landforms are physical features such as plains, mountains, plateaus, and valleys. Physical maps show rivers, streams, lakes, and other water features.

Political Maps

Many features on a political map are human-made, or determined by humans rather than by nature. Some human-made features are boundaries, capital cities, and roads. Political maps may also show physical features such as mountains and rivers.

Thematic Maps

Maps that emphasize a particular kind of information or a single idea are called **thematic maps.** This textbook includes thematic maps that show civilizations, migrations, natural resources, war, trade, and exploration.

SS.912.G.1.3

VOCABULARY

thematic maps
maps focused on a kind of information or a single idea

Qualitative Maps

Maps that use colors, symbols, lines, or dots to show information related to a specific idea are called **qualitative maps.**

Flow-Line Maps

Maps that use arrows to show the movement of people, ideas, or physical systems are called **flow-line maps.**

GEOGRAPHY CONNECTION

❶ *Explain* the significance of: physical map, political map, thematic map, qualitative map, flow-line map.

❷ *Complete* a Venn diagram like the one to the right to compare physical and political maps.

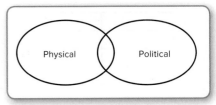

NEXT GENERATION
SUNSHINE STATE STANDARDS

SS.912.G.2.5

VOCABULARY

ecosystem
a community of plants and animals that depend upon one another and their surroundings for survival

biodiversity
the variations of lifeforms within an ecosystem

Ecosystems and Biodiversity

An **ecosystem** is a community of plants and animals that depend upon one another and their surroundings for survival. There are many different ecosystems on Earth. Plants, animals, and micro-organisms interact within an ecosystem. **Biodiversity** is the variation of life forms within an ecosystem.

Rain forests are one type of ecosystem. Nowhere is biodiversity more apparent than in tropical rain forests, which harbor at least half of all animal and plant species on Earth. Although the world's largest remaining tropical rain forests are in Brazil, there are temperate rain forests from North America to Australia, as seen in the photograph.

Desert climates occur in just under one-third of the Earth's total land area. The natural vegetation of a desert ecosystem consists of scrub and cactus, plants that tolerate low and unreliable precipitation, low humidity, and wide temperate ranges. This arid landscape is in Arizona.

GEOGRAPHY CONNECTION

❶ Explain the significance of: ecosystem, biodiversity.

❷ Complete a table like the one to the right to list some of the types of interactions in the physical systems.

	Interactions
Atmosphere	
Hydrosphere	
Lithosphere	

As the human communities expand, they threaten natural ecosystems. Because the Earth's land, air, and water are interrelated, what effects one part of the system affects all the other parts—including humans and other living things. The photograph shows deforestation, in this case clear-cutting of the Brazilian rain forest.

(t)Digital Vision/PunchStock; (c)MediaImages/PunchStock; (b)Digital Vision/Punchstock

Geographic Information Systems

Modern technology has changed the way maps are made. Most cartographers use computers with software programs called **geographic information systems (GIS).** A GIS is designed to accept data from different sources—maps, satellite images, printed text, and statistics. The GIS converts the data into a digital code, which arranges it in a database. Cartographers then program the GIS to process the data and produce maps. With GIS, each kind of information on a map is saved as a separate electronic layer.

VOCABULARY

geographic information systems
a software program that arranges a variety of data in a database and uses those data layers to produce maps

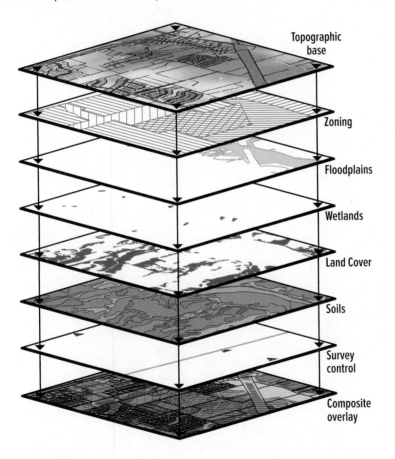

Topographic base

Zoning

Floodplains

Wetlands

Land Cover

Soils

Survey control

Composite overlay

GEOGRAPHY CONNECTION

❶ *How* does GIS allow cartographers to create maps and make changes to maps quickly and easily?

❷ *Complete* a chart like the one below by identifying the different types of layers available in a GIS to make more informative maps.

Layers

Ocean

Archipelago

Gulf

Reservoir

Volcano

Isthmus

Plateau

Highlands

Canyon

Cliff

Cape

Bay

Harbor

Reef

Island

Channel

Peninsula

archipelago a group of islands

basin area of land drained by a given river and its branches; area of land surrounded by lands of higher elevations

bay part of a large body of water that extends into a shoreline, generally smaller than a gulf

canyon deep and narrow valley with steep walls

cape point of land that extends into a river, lake, or ocean

channel wide strait or waterway between two landmasses that lie close to each other; deep part of a river or other waterway

cliff steep, high wall of rock, earth, or ice

continent one of the seven large landmasses on the Earth

delta flat, low-lying land built up from soil carried downstream by a river and deposited at its mouth

divide stretch of high land that separates river systems

downstream direction in which a river or stream flows from its source to its mouth

glacier large, thick body of slowly moving ice

gulf part of a large body of water that extends into a shoreline, generally larger and more deeply indented than a bay

harbor a sheltered place along a shoreline where ships can anchor safely

highland elevated land area such as a hill, mountain, or plateau

hill elevated land with sloping sides and rounded summit; generally smaller than a mountain

island land area, smaller than a continent, completely surrounded by water

isthmus narrow stretch of land connecting two larger land areas

lake a sizable inland body of water

lowland land, usually level, at a low elevation

mesa broad, flat-topped landform with steep sides; smaller than a plateau

mountain land with steep sides that rises sharply (1,000 feet or more) from surrounding land; generally larger and more rugged than a hill

Desert
Oasis
Mountain Peak
Basin
Sound
Mountain Range
Source of River
Glacier
Valley
Tributary
Hills
Strait
Upstream
Lake
Downstream
River
Mouth of River
Escarpment
Lowland
Plain
Delta
Seacoast

mountain peak pointed top of a mountain

mountain range a series of connected mountains

mouth (of a river) place where a stream or river flows into a larger body of water

oasis small area in a desert where water and vegetation are found

ocean one of the four major bodies of salt water that surround the continents

ocean current stream of either cold or warm water that moves in a definite direction through an ocean

peninsula body of land jutting into a lake or ocean, surrounded on three sides by water

physical feature characteristic of a place occurring naturally, such as a landform, body of water, climate pattern, or resource

plain area of level land, usually at low elevation and often covered with grasses

plateau area of flat or rolling land at a high elevation, about 300 to 3,000 feet (90 to 900 m) high

reef a chain of rocks, coral or sand at or near the surface of the water

river large natural stream of water that runs through the land

sea large body of water completely or partly surrounded by land

seacoast land lying next to a sea or an ocean

sound broad inland body of water, often between a coastline and one or more islands off the coast

source (of a river) place where a river or stream begins, often in highlands

strait narrow stretch of water joining two larger bodies of water

tributary small river or stream that flows into a large river or stream; a branch of the river

upstream direction opposite the flow of a river; toward the source of a river or stream

valley area of low land usually between hills or mountains

volcano mountain or hill created as liquid rock and ash erupt from inside the Earth

- Content vocabulary are words that relate to American history content.
- Words that have an asterisk (*) are academic vocabulary. They help you understand your school subjects.
- All vocabulary words are **boldfaced** or highlighted in yellow in your textbook.

ENGLISH	A	ESPAÑOL

Glossary/Glosario

*abandon to withdraw protection, support, or help (p. 432)

*abolition the immediate ending of slavery (p. 67)

*academic associated with higher learning at a scholarly institution (p. 220)

*access freedom or ability to obtain or make use of (p. 191)

*adapt to change in order to meet the demands of a certain environment or circumstance (p. 99)

*adequate sufficient for a specific requirement; completed to its minimum requirements (p. 532)

*adequately sufficiently; completed to its minimum requirements (p. 245)

*advocate to propose a certain position or viewpoint (p. 209)

affirmative action an active effort to improve employment or educational opportunities for minorities and women (p. 555)

Agent Orange a chemical defoliant used to clear Vietnamese jungles during the Vietnam War (p. 505)

*allocate to set apart for something specific (p. 606)

allotment a plot of land assigned to an individual or a family for cultivation (p. 111)

*alternative another choice (p. 563)

Americanization process of acquiring or causing a person to acquire American traits and characteristics (p. 160)

amnesty the act of granting a pardon to a large group of people (p. 605)

amphtrac an amphibious tractor used to move troops from ships to shore (p. 372)

anarchist a person who believes there should be no government (p. 271)

annuity money paid by contract at regular intervals (p. 107)

anthrax a bacteria used to create biological weapons (p. 627)

*abandonar retirar la protección, el apoyo o la ayuda (pág. 432)

*abolición el final inmediato de la esclavitud (pág. 67)

*académico asociado con el aprendizaje superior en una institución educativa (pág. 220)

*acceso libertad o capacidad de obtener o usar (pág. 191)

*adaptar cambiar para satisfacer las necesidades de un ambiente o circunstancia determinados (pág. 99)

*adecuado suficiente para un requisito específico; que cumple con los requisitos mínimos (pág. 532)

*adecuadamente suficientemente; que cumple con los requisitos mínimos (pág. 245)

*defender proponer una posición o un punto de vista determinados (pág. 209)

acción afirmativa esfuerzo activo por mejorar las oportunidades de empleo o de educación para las minorías y las mujeres (pág. 555)

Agente Naranja defoliante químico usado para limpiar las selvas vietnamitas durante la guerra de Vietnam (pág. 505)

*asignar reservar para algo específico (pág. 606)

parcela porción de terreno asignada a un individuo o familia para el cultivo (pág. 111)

*alternativa otra opción (pág. 563)

americanización proceso por el cual una e persona adquiere o hace que otra adquiera rasgos y características americanos (pág. 160)

amnistía acción de otorgar un perdón a un gran número de personas (pág. 605)

amtrac vehículo anfibio utilizado para trasladar tropas de los barcos hasta la orilla (pág. 372)

anarquista persona que cree que no debería haber gobierno (pág. 271)

anualidad dinero que se paga por contrato a intervalos regulares (pág. 107)

ántrax bacterias usadas para crear armas biológicas (pág. 627) *apparent appearing to be fact as far as can be understood (p. 311)

appeasement giving in to the unjust demands of a belligerent leader in order to avoid war (p. 337)

*appropriate especially suitable or compatible (p. 559)

*approximately an estimate of a figure that is close to the actual figure (p. 110)

*arbitrary existing or coming about seemingly at random or as an unfair or unreasonable act of will (p. 453)

arbitration settling a dispute by agreeing to accept the decision of an impartial outsider (pp. 135, 214)

armistice a temporary agreement to end fighting (p. 246)

assembly line a production system with machines and workers arranged so that each person performs an assigned task again and again as the item passes before him or her (p. 265)

assimilate to absorb a group into the culture of another population (p. 110)

*assume to take for granted or as true (p. 346)

*asylum deportation protection granted to refugees (p. 655)

*attrition the act of wearing down by constant harassment or attack (p. 79)

*authorities those who have control over determining and enforcing what is right or wrong (p. 253)

autonomy the quality of or state of being self-governing (p. 185)

*awareness the state of having or showing realization, perception, or knowledge (p. 615)

*aparente que parece ser un hecho hasta donde se puede entender (pág. 311)

apaciguamiento ceder a exigencias injustas de un líder beligerante para evitar la guerra (pág. 337)

*apropiado especialmente adecuado o compatible (pág. 559)

*aproximadamente estimado de una cifra que se acerca a la cifra real (pág. 110)

*arbitrario que existe o se produce al parecer por azar o como una acción injusta o poco razonable de la voluntad (pág. 453)

arbitraje resolución de una disputa mediante un acuerdo para aceptar la decisión de una tercera persona imparcial (págs. 135, 214)

armisticio acuerdo temporal para poner fin a una lucha (pág. 246)

cadena de montaje sistema de producción con máquinas y obreros dispuestos de manera que cada persona realiza una tarea asignada una y otra vez a medida que el producto pasa frente a ella (pág. 265)

asimilar incorporar a un grupo en la cultura de otra población (pág. 110)

*asumir dar por sentado o por cierto (pág. 346)

*asilo protección de ser deportado otorgada a los refugiados (pág. 655)

*atrición acto de desalentar par constantes ataques a acoso (pág. 79)

*autoridades personas que tienen el control para determinar qué está bien o mal y hacerlo cumplir (pág. 253)

autonomía calidad o estado de autogobernarse (pág. 185)

*conciencia tener o mostrar comprensión, percepción o conocimiento (pág. 615)

B

baby boom a marked rise in birthrate, such as occurred in the United States following World War II (p. 436)

bailiff minor officer of the courts (p. 295)

bank holiday closing of banks during the Great Depression to avoid bank runs (p. 312)

bank run persistent and heavy demands by a bank's depositors, creditors, or customers to withdraw money (p. 292)

barrios Spanish-speaking neighborhoods in a town or city (p. 101)

*benefit something that promotes well-being or is a useful aid (p. 320)

boom de natalidad marcado aumento en la tasa de nacimientos, como el que ocurrió en Estados Unidos después de la Segunda Guerra Mundial (pág. 436)

alguacil oficial inferior de las cortes (pág. 295)

cierre bancario cierre de bancos durante la Gran Depresión para evitar el pánico bancario (pág. 312)

pánico bancario demandas persistentes y considerables por parte de los depositantes, acreedores o clientes de un banco para retirar dinero (pág. 292)

barrios vecindarios de habla hispana en un pueblo o una ciudad (pág. 101)

*prestación algo que promueve el bienestar o es una ayuda útil (pág. 320)

Glossary/Glosario

ENGLISH	ESPAÑOL
bilingualism the practice of teaching immigrant students in their own language (p. 532)	**bilingüismo** práctica de enseñar a los estudiantes inmigrantes en su propio idioma (pág. 532)
bill a proposed law (p. 31)	**proyecto de ley** ley propuesta (pág. 31)
bill of rights a summary of fundamental rights and privileges guaranteed to a people against violation by the state (p.24)	**carta de derechos** resumen de los derechos y privilegios fundamentales que el estado garantiza al pueblo que no se violaran (pág. 24)
binding arbitration process whereby a neutral party hears arguments from two opposing sides and makes a decision that both must accept (p. 322)	**arbitraje obligatorio** proceso mediante el cual una parte neutral oye los argumentos de dos partes opuestas y toma una decisión que ambas partes deben aceptar (pág. 322)
black power the mobilization of the political and economic power of African Americans, especially to compel respect for their rights and to improve their condition (p. 489)	**poder negro** movilización del poder político y económico de los afroamericanos, en especial para exigir respeto a sus derechos y mejorar su situación (pág. 489)
blue-collar worker worker in the manual labor field, particularly those requiring protective clothing (p. 436)	**operarios** obreros que realizan actividades manuales, en particular aquellos que requieren usar ropa de protección (pág. 436)
blues style of music evolving from African American spirituals and noted for its melancholy sound (p. 280)	**blues** estilo de música que evoluciona a partir de la música espiritual afroamericana, caracterizado por su sonido melancólico (pág. 280)
bohemian a person (as an artist or a writer) leading an unconventional lifestyle (p. 275)	**bohemio** persona (por ejemplo un artista o un escritor) que lleva un estilo de vida poco convencional (pág. 275)
bonanza farm a large, highly profitable wheat farm (p. 104)	**granja en bonanza** granja de trigo extensa y de alta rentabilidad (pág. 104)
*****bond** a note issued by the government that promises to pay off a loan with interest (p. 165)	*****bono** título emitido por el gobierno en el que se compromete a pagar un préstamo con intereses (pág. 165)
*****briefly** for a short time (p. 379)	*****brevemente** por poco tiempo (pág. 379)
brinkmanship the willingness to go to the brink of war to force an opponent to back down (p. 417)	**política arriesgada** disposición de ir hasta el borde de una guerra para obligar al oponente a retractarse (pág. 417)
broker state role of the government to work out conflicts among competing interest groups (p. 327)	**estado intermediario** papel del gobierno para resolver conflictos entre grupos con conflictos de intereses (pág. 327)
bull market a long period of rising stock prices (p. 291)	**mercado alcista** periodo prolongado de alzas en el valor de las acciones (pág. 291)
busing a policy of transporting children to schools outside their neighborhoods to achieve greater racial balance (p. 555)	**transporte de escolares** política que consiste en trasladar a los niños a escuelas fuera de sus vecindarios para alcanzar mayor equilibrio racial (pág. 555)

C

capital gains tax a federal tax paid by businesses and investors when they sell stocks or real estate (p. 588)	**impuesto a las ganancias de capital** impuesto federal que pagan los comerciantes e inversionistas cuando venden acciones o bienes raíces (pág. 588)
carpetbagger name given to many Northerners who moved to the South after the Civil War and supported the Republicans (p. 85)	**explotador político** (*carpetbagger*) nombre dado a muchos norteños que se trasladaron al Sur después de la Guerra Civil y apoyaron a los Republicanos (pág. 85)

Glossary/Glosario

censure to express a formal disapproval of an action (p. 413)

chad a small piece of cardboard produced by punching a data card (p. 623)

*****challenger** one who enters a competition (p. 546)

charter a constitution (p. 397)

*****cite** to point out as an example in an argument or debate (p. 614)

closed shop an agreement in which a company agrees to hire only union members (pp. 136, 431)

cloture a motion that ends debate and calls for an immediate vote (p. 484)

*****code** a signal or symbol used to represent something that is to be kept secret (p. 369)

*****collapse** a sudden loss of force, value, or effect (p. 290)

*****colleague** a person who works in the same, or a similar, profession (p. 297)

collective a farm, especially in Communist countries, formed from many small holdings collected into a single unit for joint operation under governmental supervision (p. 335)

*****command** to be in control of; to have full power (p. 336)

*****commentator** one who explains, discusses, or reports in an expository manner, especially news on radio or television (p. 450)

committee of correspondence committee organized in each colony to communicate with and unify the colonies (p. 9)

communes group living arrangements in which members share everything and work together (p. 522)

*****community** people with common characteristics living in the same area (p. 301)

*****compatible** capable of existing in harmony (p. 528)

concentration camp a camp where persons are detained or confined (p. 347)

concurrent powers powers that both the national government and the states have (p. 29)

*****conference** a meeting of two or more persons for discussing matters of common concern (p. 213)

*****confine** to enclose or restrain (p. 464)

*****confirmation** the formal approval of an executive act by a legislative body (p. 578)

*****conform** to change in a way that fits a standard or authority (p. 437)

censura expresar formalmente la desaprobación de una acción (pág. 413)

confeti pequeño pedazo de cartulina que se produce al perforar una tarjeta de datos (pág. 623)

*****retador** persona que entra en una competencia (pág. 546)

carta constitucional una constitución (pág. 397)

*****citar** señalar como ejemplo en un argumento o debate (pág. 614)

taller cerrado acuerdo en el cual una compañía sólo contrata miembros del sindicato (págs. 136, 431)

clausura moción que pone fin a un debate y requiere una votación inmediata (pág. 484)

*****código** señal o símbolo usado para representar algo que se debe guardar en secreto (pág. 369)

*****colapso** pérdida repentina de fuerza, valor o efecto (pág. 290)

*****colega** persona que trabaja en la misma profesión o en una similar (pág. 297)

granja colectiva granja, especialmente en los países comunistas, formada por muchas propiedades pequeñas reunidas en una sola para operar conjuntamente bajo supervisión gubernamental (pág. 335)

*****mandar** tener el control, tener facultades plenas (pág. 336)

*****comentarista** persona que explica, analiza o informa de manera expositiva, en especial las noticias en la radio o la televisión (pág. 450)

comité de correspondencia comité organizado en cada colonia para comunicarse con las colonias y unificarlas (pág. 9)

comuna organización de vivienda en grupos, en la cual sus integrantes comparten todo y trabajan juntos (pág. 522)

*****comunidad** personas con características comunes que viven en la misma área (pág. 301)

*****compatible** que puede existir en armonía (pág. 528)

campo de concentración campo donde se detienen y confinan personas (pág. 347)

poderes concurrentes poderes que tienen ambos el gobierno nacional y los estados (pág. 29)

*****conferencia** reunión entre dos o más personas para analizar temas de interés común (pág. 213)

*****confinar** encerrar o restringir (pág. 464)

*****confirmación** aprobación formal de un acto legislativo por parte de la Asamblea Legislativa (pág. 578)

*****adecuar** cambiar de manera que se ajuste a un patrón o una autoridad (pág. 437)

Glossary/Glosario **773**

ENGLISH

ESPAÑOL

*conformity agreement in form, manner, or character (p. 520)

*conformidad acuerdo en la forma, el modo o el carácter (pág. 520)

conquistador Spanish for "conqueror"; the men who led the expeditions to conquer the Americas (p. 6)

conquistador hombre que lideraba las expediciones para la conquista de América (pág. 6)

consensus general agreement (p. 462)

consenso acuerdo general (pág. 462)

conservative a person who believes government power, particularly in the economy, should be limited in order to maximize individual freedom (p. 570)

conservador persona que cree que el poder del gobierno, particularmente en la economía, debe ser limitado para maximizar la libertad individual (pág. 570)

*constitute to be composed of, made up of, or formed from (p. 137)

*constituirse que está compuesto de, que consta o esta hecho de (pág. 137)

*consumer a person who buys what is produced by an economy (p. 128)

*consumidor persona que compra lo que produce una economía (pág. 128)

containment the policy or process of preventing the expansion of a hostile power (p. 402)

contención política o proceso para evitar la expansión de una potencia hostil (pág. 402)

contraband goods whose importation, exportation, or possession is illegal (p. 235)

contrabando bienes cuya importación, exportación o posesión es ilegal (pág. 235)

*controversial relating to a prolonged public dispute (p. 633)

*controvertido relativo a una disputa pública prolongada (pág. 633)

*controversy a prolonged public dispute (p. 62)

*controversia disputa pública prolongada (pág. 62)

*conventional nonnuclear (p. 455)

*convencional que no es de tipo nuclear (pág. 455)

*convince to bring to belief, consent, or a course of action (p. 411)

*convencer hacer que alguien crea algo, lo consienta, o realice una acción (pág. 411)

convoy a group that travels with something, such as a ship, to protect it (p. 245)

convoy grupo que viaja con algo, como un barco, para protegerlo (pág. 245)

convoy system a system in which merchant ships travel with naval vessels for protection (p. 375)

sistema de convoy sistema en el cual las embarcaciones comerciales viajan con naves de la armada para garantizar su protección (pág. 375)

cooperative a store where farmers buy products from each other; an enterprise owned and operated by those who use its services (p. 166)

cooperativa tienda donde los agricultores compran productos entre sí; empresa de propiedad de aquellos que usan sus servicios, quienes también la operan (pág. 166)

cooperative individualism President Hoover's policy of encouraging manufacturers and distributors to form their own organizations and volunteer information to the federal government in an effort to stimulate the economy (p. 263)

individualismo cooperativo política del presidente Hoover que estimulaba a los fabricantes y distribuidores a formar sus propias organizaciones y a dar información voluntaria al gobierno federal en un esfuerzo para estimular la economía (pág. 263)

*coordinate to harmonize or bring into common action, movement, or condition (p. 364)

*coordinar armonizar o realizar acciones o movimientos comunes, o tener las mismas condiciones (pág. 364)

corporation an organization that is authorized by law to carry on an activity but treated as though it were a single person (p. 127)

sociedad anónima organización autorizada por la ley para desarrollar una actividad, pero que recibe el tratamiento de un individuo particular (pág. 127)

cost of living the cost of purchasing goods and services essential for survival (p. 250)

costo de la vida costo de comprar bienes y servicios esenciales para la supervivencia (pág. 250)

cost-plus a government contract to pay a manufacturer the cost to produce an item plus a guaranteed percentage (p. 361)

contrato de margen fijo contrato del gobierno para pagar a un fabricante el costo de producir un artículo más un porcentaje garantizado (pág. 361)

counterculture a culture with values and beliefs different than those of the mainstream (p. 522)

contracultura cultura con valores y creencias que difieren de los de la cultura principal (pág. 522)

court-packing the act of changing the political balance of power in a nation's judiciary system whereby a national leader, such as the president of the United States, appoints judges who will rule in favor of his or her policies (p. 326)

reorganización de la corte acción de cambiar el equilibrio político del poder en el sistema judicial de una nación mediante la cual un líder nacional, como el presidente de Estados Unidos, nombra a los jueces que fallarán a favor de sus políticas (pág. 326)

covert not openly shown or engaged in; secret (p. 418)

encubierto que no se muestra o compromete abiertamente; secreto (pág. 418)

creationism the belief that God created the world and everything in it, usually in the way described in Genesis (p. 273)

creacionismo creencia de que Dios creó el mundo y todo lo que hay en él, por lo general de la manera en que se describe en el Génesis (pág. 273)

credibility gap lack of trust or believability (p. 506)

barrera de credibilidad falta de confianza (pág. 506)

*credit an amount or sum of money placed at a person's disposal by a bank on condition that it will be repaid with interest (p. 267)

*crédito suma de dinero que un banco pone a disposición de una persona con la condición de que ésta la pague con intereses (pág. 267)

*criteria standards on which a judgment or action may be based (p. 556)

*criterios estándares en los cuales se basa un juicio o una acción (pág. 556)

*culture the customary beliefs, social forms, and material traits of a racial, religious, or social group (p. 5)

*cultura creencias, formas sociales y rasgos materiales tradicionales de un grupo racial, religioso o social (pág. 5)

*currency paper money used as a medium of exchange (p. 165)

*moneda papel moneda usado como medio de cambio (pág. 165)

D

deadlock to be at a standstill and unable to progress because of equal and opposite forces (p. 658)

punto muerto estar en una paralización o imposibilidad de avance producto de fuerzas iguales y opuestas (pág. 658)

de facto segregation segregation by custom and tradition (p. 472)

segregación de facto segregación por costumbre y tradición (pág. 472)

deficit the amount by which expenses exceed income (p. 577)

déficit cantidad en la cual los gastos superan a los ingresos (pág. 577)

deficit spending government practice of spending borrowed money rather than raising taxes, usually in an attempt to boost the economy (p. 320)

gasto deficitario práctica gubernamental de gastar dinero prestado en lugar de aumentar los impuestos, por lo general en un esfuerzo por estimular la economía (pág. 320)

deflation a decline in the volume of available money or credit that results in lower prices, and, therefore, increases the buying power of money (pp. 132, 165)

deflación caída en el volumen de dinero disponible o crédito, que da lugar a precios más bajos y, en consecuencia, aumenta el poder adquisitivo del dinero (págs. 132, 165)

*deny to declare untrue (p. 273)

*negar declarar como falso (pág. 273)

deport to expel an individual from the country (p. 252)

deportar expulsar a un individuo de un país (pág. 252)

*deprive to take something away from someone (p. 659)

*privar quitarle algo a alguien (pág. 659)

*deregulation the act or process of removing restrictions or regulations (p. 552)

*desregulación acto o proceso de eliminar restricciones o regulaciones (pág. 552)

Glossary/Glosario

*despite in spite of (p. 383)

détente a policy that attempts to relax or ease tensions between nations (p. 543)

developing nation a nation whose economy is primarily agricultural (p. 418)

direct primary a vote held by all members of a political party to decide their candidate for public office (p. 204)

discount retailing selling large quantities of goods at very low prices and trying to sell the goods quickly to turn over the entire inventory in a short period of time (p. 580)

*discrimination different treatment or preference on a basis other than individual merit (p. 171)

disenfranchise to deprive of the right to vote (p. 359)

*disposable referring to the money remaining to an individual after deduction of taxes (p. 266)

*disproportionate lacking regularity or symmetry in size, degree, or intensity (p. 507)

*distribution the act or process of being given out or disbursed to clients, consumers, or members of a group (p. 127)

*diverse being different from one another (p. 275)

dollar diplomacy a policy of joining the business interests of a country with its diplomatic interests abroad (p. 194)

*dominate to be in a state or position of command or control over all others (p. 335)

domino theory the belief that if one nation in Asia fell to the Communists, neighboring countries would follow (p. 501)

dove a person in favor of the United States withdrawing from the Vietnam War (p. 508)

downsizing reducing a company in size by laying off workers and managers to become more efficient (p. 588)

*draft to select a person at random for mandatory military service (pp. 240, 358)

*draft a system used for choosing people from the population to serve in the military (p. 359)

dry farming a way of farming dry land in which seeds are planted deep in the ground where there is some moisture (p. 104)

due process a judicial requirement that laws may not treat individuals unfairly, arbitrarily, or unreasonably, and that courts must follow proper procedures and rules when trying cases (pp. 36, 454, 643)

*a pesar de pese a que (pág. 383)

distensión política orientada a suavizar o aliviar las tensiones entre las naciones (pág. 543)

nación en vías de desarrollo nación cuya economía es principalmente agrícola (pág. 418)

elección primaria votación de todos los miembros de un partido político para elegir su candidato a un cargo público (pág. 204)

venta al por menor con descuento vender grandes cantidades de bienes a precios muy bajos y tratar de hacerlo rápidamente para rotar todo el inventario en un corto periodo de tiempo (pág. 580)

*discriminación tratamiento diferente o preferencial por razones distintas al mérito individual (pág. 171)

privación del voto negar el derecho al voto (pág. 359)

*disponible relativo al dinero que le sobra a un individuo después de las deducciones de sus impuestos (pág. 266)

*desproporcionado que carece de regularidad o simetría en tamaño, grado o intensidad (pág. 507)

*distribución acción o proceso de entregar o desembolsar a los clientes, consumidores o integrantes de un grupo (pág. 127)

*diverso diferente uno de otro (pág. 275)

diplomacia del dólar política que une los intereses comerciales de un país con sus intereses diplomáticos en el extranjero (pág. 194)

*dominar hallarse en un estado o posición de mando o control sobre los demás (pág. 335)

teoría dominó creencia de que si una nación asiática caía ante los comunistas, los países vecinos también lo harían (pág. 501)

paloma persona que apoyaba el retiro de Estados Unidos de la guerra de Vietnam (pág. 508)

reducción de personal reducir el tamaño de una compañía despidiendo empleados y directivos para volverla más eficiente (pág. 588)

*conscribir elegir a una persona al azar para el servicio militar obligatorio (págs. 240, 358)

*conscripción sistema usado para elegir a una persona al azar para el servicio militar obligatorio (pág. 359)

agricultura de secano forma de cultivar terreno seco en la cual las semillas se plantan a grandes profundidades en el terreno donde hay un poco de humedad (pág. 104)

debido proceso requisito judicial según el cual las leyes no pueden tratar a los individuos de manera injusta, arbitraria o poco razonable, y los tribunales deben seguir los procedimientos y normas apropiados al ver las causas (págs. 36, 454, 643)

dynamic conservatism policy of balancing economic conservatism with some activism (p. 433)

conservadurismo dinámico política que consiste en equilibrar el conservadurismo económico con algún activismo (pág. 433)

E

earmark specifications added by both Republicans and Democrats for the expenditure of federal money for particular projects (p. 641)

asignación de fondos especificaciones de republicanos y demócratas para que el dinero federal se gaste en proyectos específicos (pág. 641)

economies of scale the reduction in the cost of a good brought about especially by increased production at a given facility (p. 127)

economías de escala reducción en el costo de un bien ocasionada por un aumento en la producción en un sector determinado (pág. 127)

*eliminate to remove or get rid of (p. 631)

*eliminar quitar o deshacerse de algo (pág. 631)

emancipate to free an enslaved person (p. 67)

emancipar dejar libre a una persona esclava (pág. 67)

embargo a government ban on trade with other countries (p. 549)

embargo prohibición gubernamental de comerciar con otras naciones (pág. 549)

*emphasis a special importance given to an object or idea (p. 233)

*énfasis importancia especial que se da a un objeto o a una idea (pág. 233)

empresario a person who arranged for the settlement of Texas in the early 1800s (p. 70)

empresario persona que hacía arreglos para el asentamiento de tierras en Texas en el siglo XIX (pág. 70)

*enforce to urge or carry out using force (pp. 9, 490)

*hacer cumplir instar o llevar a cabo por medio de la fuerza (págs. 9, 490)

*enforcement the act of urging or carrying out by force (p. 481)

*aplicación de la ley la acción de instar o llevar a cabo por medio de la fuerva (pág. 481)

*ensure to guarantee or make certain (p. 108)

*asegurar garantizar o cerciorarse de algo (pág. 108)

*entity something having independent, separate, or self-contained existence (p. 442)

*entidad algo que existe de manera independiente, separada o autónoma (pág. 442)

entrepreneur one who organizes, manages, and assumes the risks of a business or enterprise (p. 121)

emprendedor quien organiza, administra o asume los riesgos de un negocio o una empresa (pág. 121)

enumerated powers powers listed in the Constitution as belonging to the federal government (pp. 25, 29)

poderes enumerados poderes que se enumeran en la Constitución como pertenecientes al gobierno federal (págs. 25, 29)

*environmental relating to the environment; the complex system of plants, animals, water, and soil (p. 216)

*medioambiental relativo al medioambiente; el complejo sistema de plantas, animales, agua y suelo (pág. 216)

*equipment the articles or physical resources prepared or furnished for a specific task (p. 398)

*equipo artículos o recursos físicos preparados o suministrados para una tarea específica (pág. 398)

*erode to wear away at something until it fades (p. 235)

*erosionar desgastar algo hasta hacerlo desaparecer (pág. 235)

espionage spying, especially to gain government secrets (p. 239)

espionaje espiar, especialmente para conocer secretos del gobierno (pág. 239)

*ethnic relating to large groups of people classed according to common racial, national, tribal, religious, linguistic, or cultural origin or background (p. 145)

*étnico relativo a grandes grupos de personas clasificadas porque comparten el mismo origen o entorno racial, nacional, tribal, religioso, lingüístico o cultural (pág. 145)

ethnic cleansing the expulsion, imprisonment, or killing of ethnic minorities by a dominant majority group (p. 602)

limpieza étnica expulsión, encarcelamiento o asesinato de minorías étnicas por parte de una mayoría dominante (pág. 602)

Glossary/Glosario

ENGLISH	ESPAÑOL
euro the basic currency shared by the countries of the European Union since 1999 (p. 614)	**euro** moneda de todos los países de la Unión Europea desde 1999 (pág. 614)
*eventually at an unspecified time or day; in the end (p. 7)	***finalmente** en un momento o día no especificado; al final (pág. 7)
*evolution the scientific theory that humans and other forms of life have evolved over time (pp. 157, 273)	***evolución** teoría científica según la cual los seres humanos y otras formas de vida han evolucionado con el tiempo (págs. 157, 273)
executive privilege principle stating that communications of the executive branch should remain confidential to protect national security (p. 547)	**privilegio ejecutivo** principio que establece que las comunicaciones de la rama ejecutiva deben ser confidenciales para proteger la seguridad nacional (pág. 547)
*expansion the act or process of increasing or enlarging the extent, number, volume, or scope (p. 180)	***expansión** acción o proceso de aumentar o ampliar la extensión, el número, el volumen o el alcance (pág. 180)
*exploit to take unfair advantage of (p. 334)	***explotar** tomar una ventaja injusta (pág. 334)
extermination camp a camp where men, women, and children were sent to be executed (p. 347)	**campo de exterminio** campo adonde se enviaban hombres, mujeres y niños para que los ejecutaran (pág. 347)
*extract to remove by force (p. 97)	***arrancar** sacar por la fuerza (pág. 97)

F

ENGLISH	ESPAÑOL
*facility something that is built, installed, or established to serve a particular purpose (p. 472)	***instalación** algo que se construye, instala o establece con un propósito en particular (pág. 472)
fallout radioactive particles dispersed by a nuclear explosion (p. 414)	**lluvia radiactiva** partículas radiactivas dispersas debido a una explosión nuclear (pág. 414)
fascism a political system headed by a dictator that calls for extreme nationalism and often racism and no tolerance of opposition (p. 334)	**fascismo** sistema político encabezado por un dictador que llama al nacionalismo extremo y a menudo al racismo y a la falta de tolerancia hacia la oposición (pág. 334)
federalism political system in which power is divided between the national and state governments (p. 28)	**federalismo** sistema político en el cual el poder se divide entre los gobiernos nacional y estatal (pág. 28)
feminism the belief that men and women should be equal politically, economically, and socially (p. 524)	**feminismo** creencia según la cual hombres y mujeres deben ser iguales en lo político, lo económico y lo social (pág. 524)
filibuster an attempt to kill a bill by having a group of senators take turns speaking continuously so that a vote cannot take place (p. 484)	**obstruccionista** intento de impedir la aprobación de un proyecto de ley haciendo que un grupo de senadores se turnen para hablar continuamente para que la votación no pueda tener lugar (pág. 484)
*finance to provide money for a project (p. 321)	***financiar** proveer dinero para un proyecto (pág. 321)
fireside chats radio broadcasts made by FDR to the American people to explain his initiatives (p. 313)	**charlas íntimas** transmisiones de radio que hacía el presidente Roosevelt para explicar a los estadounidenses sus iniciativas (pág. 313)
flexible response the buildup of conventional troops and weapons to allow a nation to fight a limited war without using nuclear weapons (p. 455)	**respuesta flexible** concentración de tropas y armas convencionales para permitir que una nación participe en una guerra limitada sin emplear armas nucleares (pág. 455)

foreclose to take possession of a property from a mortgagor because of defaults on payments (p. 302)

ejecutar tomar posesión de una propiedad de un deudor hipotecario debido al incumplimiento en los pagos (pág. 302)

fossil fuel a fuel formed in the Earth from decayed plant or animal remains (p. 563)

combustible fósil combustible formado en la Tierra a partir de la descomposición de restos vegetales o animales (pág. 563)

*framework a set of guidelines to be followed (p. 21)

*estructura conjunto de directrices que se han de seguir (pág. 21)

franchise the right or license to market a company's goods or services in an area, such as a store of a chain operation (p. 436)

franquicia derecho o licencia para comercializar los bienes o servicios de una compañía en un área, por ejemplo una tienda de una cadena (pág. 436)

*fundamental being of central importance (p. 315)

*fundamental de importancia central (pág. 315)

G

*gender term applied to the characteristics of a male or female (p. 524)

*género término aplicado a las características masculinas o femeninas (pág. 524)

general strike a strike involving all the workers in a particular geographic location (p. 250)

huelga general huelga que involucra a todos los trabajadores de un punto geográfico en particular (pág. 250)

*generation a classification of people who share the same experience throughout their lives (p. 510)

*generación clasificación de personas que comparten las mismas experiencias durante su vida (pág. 510)

generation gap a cultural separation between parents and their children (p. 439)

brecha generacional separación cultural entre padres e hijos (pág. 439)

glasnost a Soviet policy permitting open discussion of political and social issues and freer dissemination of news and information (p. 586)

glasnost política soviética que permitió la discusión abierta de temas políticos y sociales y la libre difusión de noticias e información (pág. 586)

global warming an increase in average world temperatures over time (p. 615)

calentamiento global aumento en la temperatura promedio mundial a través del tiempo (pág. 615)

gold standard a monetary standard in which one ounce of gold equals a set number of dollars (p. 312)

patrón oro estándar monetario en el cual una onza de oro equivale a un número de dólares determinado (pág. 312)

graduated income tax a tax based on the net income of an individual or business and that taxes different income levels at different rates (p. 167)

impuesto graduado sobre la renta impuesto que se basa en los ingresos netos de un individuo o empresa, el cual grava con diferentes tasas niveles diferentes de ingreso (pág. 167)

graft the acquisition of money in dishonest ways, as in bribing a politician (p. 155)

corrupción adquisición de dinero en forma deshonesta, por ejemplo mediante un soborno a un político (pág. 155)

grassroots movement a group of people organizing at the local or community level, away from political or cultural centers (p. 589)

movimiento de base grupo de personas que se organiza a nivel local o comunitario, lejos de los centros políticos o culturales (pág. 589)

greenback unit of paper currency first issued by the federal government during the Civil War (p. 165)

greenback primer papel moneda emitido por el gobierno federal durante la Guerra Civil (pág. 165)

gross national product the total value of goods and services produced by a country during a year (p. 118)

producto nacional bruto valor total de los bienes y servicios que produce un país durante un año (pág. 118)

guerrilla a member of an armed band that carries out surprise attacks and sabotage rather than open warfare (pp. 195, 501)

guerrilla miembro de un grupo armado que lleva a cabo ataques sorpresivos y sabotajes en vez de entrar en una batalla abierta (págs. 195, 501)

Glossary/Glosario

H

ENGLISH	ESPAÑOL
hacienda a huge ranch (p. 100)	**hacienda** rancho grande (pág. 100)
hate crime a category of crime that targets victims based upon race, creed, gender, or religious affiliation (p. 659)	**crimen de odio** categoría de crimen que tiene como objetivo a víctimas según su raza, credo, género o afilicación religiosa (pág. 659)
hawk someone who believed the United States should continue its military efforts in Vietnam (p. 508)	**halcón** persona que creía que Estados Unidos debía continuar sus esfuerzos militares en Vietnam (pág. 508)
hedgerow an enclosure made of dirt walls built to fence in cattle and crops (p. 381)	**cerco de setos** cerco construido con muros de tierra para encerrar ganado y cultivos (pág. 381)
hippies refers to young Americans, especially during the 1960s, who rejected the conventions of established society (p. 522)	*hippies* relativo a los jóvenes estadounidenses que, especialmente de 1960 a 1970, rechazaron las convenciones establecidas por la sociedad (pág. 522)
hobo a homeless and usually penniless wanderer (p. 295)	**vagabundo** persona errante sin hogar y por lo general sin dinero (pág. 295)
holding company a company whose primary business is owning a controlling share of stock in other companies (p. 130)	**sociedad de cartera** compañía cuya actividad principal es poseer una participación accionaria mayoritaria en otras compañías (pág. 130)
homestead a piece of U.S. public land acquired by filing a record and living on and cultivating it (p. 104)	**posesión de tierras** una porción de terreno público estadounidense adquirió mediante la presentación y que viven en y cultivaria (pág. 104)
horizontal integration the combining of many firms engaged in the same type of business into one corporation (p. 132)	**integración horizontal** asociación de muchas firmas que tienen el mismo negocio dentro de una sociedad anónima (pág. 132)
hydraulic mining a method of mining by which water is sprayed at a very high pressure against a hill or mountain, washing away large quantities of dirt, gravel, and rock and exposing the minerals beneath the surface (p. 98)	**minería hidráulica** método de minería mediante el cual se riega con agua a elevadísima presión una colina o montaña; este lavado elimina grandes cantidades de suciedad, grava y roca, y expone los minerales que están bajo la superficie (pág. 98)

I

ENGLISH	ESPAÑOL
*ideology a system of thought that is held by an individual, group, or culture (p. 312)	*ideología sistema de pensamiento de un individuo, un grupo o una cultura (pág. 312)
*illegal not according to or authorized by law (p. 605)	*ilegal que no está de acuerdo o autorizado por la ley (pág. 605)
*immigrant one who enters and becomes established in a country other than that of his or her original nationality (p. 144)	*inmigrante persona que ingresa y se radica en un país diferente de aquel del cual es natural (pág. 144)
*impact a lasting impression upon an individual or group (p. 282)	*impacto impresión duradera en un individuo o grupo (pág. 282)
impeach to formally charge a public official with misconduct in office (p. 31)	**imputar** acusar formalmente a un funcionario publico por mala conducta en su cargo (pág. 31)
imperialism the actions used by one nation to exercise political or economic control over a smaller or weaker nation (p. 180)	**imperialismo** acciones que emplea una nación para ejercer control político o económico sobre una nación más pequeña o más débil (pág. 180)
implied powers powers not specifically listed in the Constitution but claimed by the federal government (p. 25)	**poderes implícitos** poderes que no están enumerados específicamente en la Constitución, pero que el gobierno federal reclama (pág. 25)
*imply to express indirectly (p. 419)	*implicar expresar en forma indirecta (pág. 419)
impound to take possession of (p. 542)	**incautar** tomar posesión (pág. 542)

Glossary/Glosario

*incentive something that motivates a person into action (p. 151)

*incident a single occurrence of a happening or situation (p. 545)

*income a gain or recurrent benefit usually measured in money derived from capital or labor (p. 441)

income tax a tax based on the net income of a person or business (p. 222)

indentured servant an individual who contracts to work for a colonist for a specified number of years in exchange for transportation to the colonies, food, clothing, and shelter (p. 8)

*indicate to point out, point to, or demonstrate the necessity of (p. 573)

indict to charge someone with a criminal offense (p. 660)

individualism the belief that no matter what a person's background is, the person can still become successful through effort (p. 156)

industrial union an organization of common laborers and craft workers in a particular industry (p. 133)

inflation an ongoing increase in prices and decrease in the value of money (pp. 165, 549)

*initially of or relating to the beginning (p. 405)

initiative the right of citizens to place a measure or issue before the voters or the legislature for approval (p. 204)

injunction a court order whereby one is required to do or to refrain from doing a specified act (p. 136)

*innovation a new idea or method (p. 104)

*insecurity the state of not being confident or sure (p. 402)

*inspector a person appointed to examine foreign facilities, usually in search of weapons (p. 629)

installment a monthly plan made to pay off the cost of an item when buying it on credit (p. 293)

*institute to initiate or establish something (p. 459)

insubordination disobedience to authority (p. 217)

*integrate to combine two previously separate things (p. 124)

*intense existing in an extreme degree (p. 380)

*intensify to become more frequent and powerful (p. 563)

internationalism a national policy of actively trading with foreign countries to foster peace and prosperity (p. 340)

*interpretation the act or process of explaining or telling the meaning of (p. 624)

*intervene to get involved in the affairs of another (p. 185)

*incentivo algo que motiva a una persona a actuar (pág. 151)

*incidente suceso o situación que ocurre una sola vez (pág. 545)

*ingreso ganancia o beneficio recurrente que por lo general se mide en dinero y proviene de capital o trabajo (pág. 441)

impuesto a la renta impuesto que se basa en los ingresos netos de una persona o negocio (pág. 222)

sirviente por contrato individuo que firma un contrato para trabajar para un colono durante un número específico de años a cambio de transporte a las colonias, alimentación, vestuario y vivienda (pág. 8)

*indicar señalar, describir o demostrar la necesidad de algo (pág. 573)

condenar acusar a alguien de un delito criminal (pág. 660)

individualismo creencia según la cual sin importar cuál sea el entorno de una persona, ésta puede llegar a tener éxito si se esfuerza (pág. 156)

sindicato industrial organización de obreros comunes y trabajadores calificados de una industria particular (pág. 133)

inflación aumento continuo de los precios y disminución del valor del dinero (págs. 165, 549)

*inicialmente relativo al principio (pág. 405)

iniciativa derecho que tienen los ciudadanos de presentar una propuesta o un tema ante los electores o la Asamblea Legislativa para su aprobación (pág. 204)

orden judicial orden judicial por la cual se le exige o prohíbe a alguien que realice una acción determinada (pág. 136)

*innovación idea o método nuevos (pág. 104)

*inseguridad no tener confianza o no estar seguro (pág. 402)

*inspector persona designada para examinar instalaciones extranjeras, por lo general en busca de armas (pág. 629)

cuota plan de pagos mensuales para cubrir el costo de un artículo que se compra a crédito (pág. 293)

*instituir iniciar o establecer algo (pág. 459)

insubordinación desobediencia a la autoridad (pág. 217)

*integrar unir dos cosas que antes estaban separadas (pág. 124)

*intenso que existe en grado extremo (pág. 380)

*intensificar volverse más frecuente y poderoso (pág. 563)

internacionalismo política nacional de comercio activo con países extranjeros para fomentar la paz y la prosperidad (pág. 340)

*interpretación acción o proceso de explicar o decir el significado de algo (pág. 624)

*intervenir involucrarse en los asuntos de otro (pág. 185)

Glossary/Glosario **781**

ENGLISH	ESPAÑOL
*invest to put money into a company in order to gain a future financial reward (p. 291)	***invertir** colocar dinero en una compañía para obtener una retribución financiera en el futuro (pág. 291)
*investigation a systematic examination or official inquiry (p. 261)	***investigación** examen sistemático o indagación oficial (pág. 261)
*investor one who puts money into a company in order to gain a future financial reward (p. 124)	***inversionista** quien invierte dinero en una compañía con el fin de obtener una retribución económica en el futuro (pág. 124)
Iron Curtain the political and military barrier that isolated Soviet-controlled countries of Eastern Europe after World War II (p. 401)	**Cortina de Hierro** barrera política y militar que aisló a los países controlados por la Unión Soviética de Europa del Este durante la Segunda Guerra Mundial (pág. 401)
*isolationism a national policy of avoiding involvement in world affairs (p. 263)	***aislacionismo** política nacional de evitar involucrarse en asuntos internacionales (pág. 263)

J

jazz American style of music that developed from ragtime and blues and that uses syncopated rhythms and melodies (p. 280)	*jazz* estilo de música estadounidense que se desarrolló a partir del *ragtime* y el *blues* y que usa ritmos y melodías sincopados (pág. 280)
Jim Crow laws statutes enacted to enforce segregation (p. 171)	leyes Jim Crow conjunto de leyes promulgadas para hacer cumplir políticas de segregación (pág. 171)
jingoism extreme nationalism marked by aggressive foreign policy (p. 185)	jingoísmo nacionalismo extremo marcado por una política exterior radical (pág. 185)
joint-stock company a form of business organization in which many investors pool funds to raise large amounts of money for large projects (p. 7)	sociedad comanditaria por acciones forma de organización empresarial en la cual muchos inversionistas hacen un fondo común para recaudar grandes sumas de dinero con el fin de realizar grandes proyectos (pág. 7)
judicial review power of the Supreme Court to determine whether laws of Congress are constitutional and to strike down those that are not (pp. 26, 35)	revisión judicial facultad de la Corte Suprema para determiner si las leyes expedidas por el Congreso son constitucionales y anular aquellas que no 10 son (págs. 26,35)
*justify to prove or to show to be just, right, or reasonable (p. 365)	*justificar probar o demostrar que algo es justo, correcto o razonable (pág. 365)
juvenile delinquency antisocial or criminal behavior of young people (p. 443)	delincuencia juvenil conducta antisocial o criminal de los adolescentes (pág. 443)

K

kamikaze during World War II, a Japanese suicide pilot whose mission was to crash into his target (p. 373)	kamikaze durante la Segunda Guerra Mundial, piloto suicida japonés cuya misión era estrellarse contra su objetivo (pág. 373)

Glossary/Glosario

L

labor union an organization of workers formed for the purpose of advancing its members' interests (p. 64)

laissez-faire a policy that government should interfere as little as possible in the nation's economy (p. 121)

land grant a grant of land by the federal government, especially for roads, railroads, or agricultural colleges (p. 124)

*legislation a proposed law to be voted on by a governing body (p. 204)

*legislator one who makes laws as a member of a political, legislative body (p. 431)

*liberal a person who generally believes the government should take an active role in the economy and in social programs but should not dictate social behavior (pp. 542, 570)

*liberate to set free (p. 398)

*likewise in the same way; similarly (p. 529)

limited war a war fought with limited commitment of resources to achieve a limited objective, such as containing communism (p. 407)

linkage the policy of improving relations with the Soviet Union and China in hopes of persuading them to cut back their aid to North Vietnam (p. 510)

lockout a company tool to fight union demands by refusing to allow employees to enter its facilities to work (p. 133)

loyalty review program a policy established by President Truman that authorized the screening of all federal employees to determine their loyalty to the U.S. government (p. 410)

lynch to execute, by hanging, without lawful approval (p. 172)

sindicato organización de trabajadores formada con el fin de promover los intereses de sus miembros (pág. 64)

laissez-faire política según la cual el gobierno debe intervenir lo menos posible en la economía de la nación (pág. 121)

concesión de tierras terrenos que el gobierno federal cede, especialmente para carreteras, vías férreas o escuelas agrarias (pág. 124)

*legislación ley propuesta para someterla a la votación de un órgano directivo (pág. 204)

*legislador quien hace las leyes, por ejemplo un miembro de un órgano legislativo o político (pág. 431)

*liberal persona que cree que el gobierno debe tener un papel activo en la economía y en los programas sociales, pero no debe dictar cuál debe ser la conducta social (págs. 542, 570)

*liberar poner en libertad (pág. 398)

*asimismo de la misma manera; de modo semejante (pág. 529)

guerra limitada guerra que en la que se participa comprometiendo pocos recursos para alcanzar un objetivo limitado, como contener el comunismo (pág. 407)

enlace política orientada a mejorar las relaciones con la Unión Soviética y China con la esperanza de persuadirlas de suspender sus ayudas a Vietnam del Norte (pág. 510)

cierre patronal estrategia de una compañía para frenar las exigencias de los sindicatos negándose a permitir que los empleados ingresen a trabajar en sus instalaciones (pág. 133)

programa de verificación de la lealtad política establecida por el presidente Truman que autorizaba investigar a todos los empleados federales para determinar si eran leales al gobierno de Estados Unidos (pág. 410)

linchar ejecutar en la horca sin autorización legal (pág. 172)

M

*manipulate to operate or arrange manually to achieve a desired effect (p. 411)

margin buying a stock by paying only a fraction of the stock price and borrowing the rest (p. 291)

margin call demand by a broker that investors pay back loans made for stocks purchased on margin (p. 291)

*manipular operar o acomodar manualmente para alcanzar un efecto deseado (pág. 411)

margen comprar acciones pagando sólo una fracción de su precio y pidiendo en préstamo el saldo (pág. 291)

margen de garantía exigencia de un corredor de bolsa para que los inversionistas paguen los préstamos hechos para la compra de acciones al margen (pág. 291)

Glossary/Glosario

ENGLISH	ESPAÑOL
massive retaliation a policy of threatening a massive response, including the use of nuclear weapons, against a Communist state trying to seize a peaceful state by force (p. 416)	**retaliación masiva** política consistente en amenazar con una respuesta masiva, incluido el uso de armas nucleares, contra un estado comunista que busca apoderarse de un estado pacífico por la fuerza (pág. 416)
mass media a medium of communication (as in television and radio) intended to reach a wide audience (p. 278)	**medios masivos de comunicación** medios de comunicación (como la televisión y la radio) que buscan llegar a una amplia audiencia (pág. 278)
mass production the production of large quantities of goods using machinery and often an assembly line (p. 265)	**producción masiva** producción de grandes cantidades de bienes usando maquinaria y a menudo una cadena de montaje (pág. 265)
***media** a means of expression or communication, especially in reference to the agencies of mass communication—newspapers, radio, television, and the Internet (p. 506)	***medios de comunicación** medios de expresión o comunicación, en especial las agencias de comunicación de masas: periódicos, radio, televisión e Internet (pág. 506)
***mediate** an attempt to resolve conflict between hostile people or groups (p. 327)	***mediar** intento de resolver conflictos entre grupos o personas hostiles (pág. 327)
***migrant** people who choose to move from one location to another, especially to find employment (p. 655)	***migrante** persona que elige mudarse de un lugar a otro, especialmente en busca de trabajo (pág. 655)
***migrate** to move from one location to another (p. 238)	***migrar** desplazarse de un lugar a otro (pág. 238)
migration chain the process by which immigrants who have acquired U.S. citizenship can send for relatives in their home country to join them (p. 604)	**cadena migratoria** proceso por el cual los inmigrantes que han obtenido la ciudadanía estadounidense pueden enviar por sus familiares en su ciudad natal para reunirse con ellos (pág. 604)
militarism a policy of aggressive military preparedness (p. 232)	**militarismo** política de preparación militar radical (pág. 232)
military-industrial complex an informal relationship that some people believe exists between the military and the defense industry to promote greater military spending and influence government policy (p. 421)	**complejo militar e industrial** relación informal que algunas personas creen que existe entre el ejército y la industria de defensa para incentivar el gasto militar e influir en las políticas del gobierno (pág. 421)
missile gap the belief that the Soviet Union had more nuclear weapons than the United States (p. 450)	**diferencia de misiles** creencia de que la Unión Soviética tenía más armas. nucleares que Estados Unidos (pág. 450)
Model T automobile built by the Ford Motor Company from 1908 until 1927 (p. 265)	**Modelo T** automóvil construido por la Compañía Automotriz Ford desde 1908 hasta 1927 (pág. 265)
***modify** to make changes or alter (p. 596)	***modificar** hacer cambios o alterar (pág. 596)
***monitor** to observe, oversee, or regulate (p. 640)	***monitorear** observar, supervisar o regular (pág. 640)
monopoly total control of a type of industry by one person or one company (p. 130)	**monopolio** control total de un tipo de industria por parte de una persona o compañía (pág. 130)
muckraker a journalist who uncovers abuses and corruption in a society (p. 203)	*muckracker* periodista que descubre abusos y corrupción en una sociedad (pág. 203)
multinational corporation large corporation with overseas investments (p. 436)	**multinacional** gran corporación con inversiones en el extranjero (pág. 436)
mutual-assured destruction the strategy assuming that, as long as two countries can destroy each other with nuclear weapons, they will be afraid to use them (p. 579)	**destrucción mutua asegurada** estrategia que asume que siempre y cuando dos países puedan destruirse entresí con armas nucleares, ambos estarán temerosos de usarlas (pág. 579)

Glossary/Glosario

N

napalm a jellied gasoline used for bombs (pp. 383, 505)

napalm gasolina gelatinosa usada para fabricar bombas (págs. 383, 505)

nationalism loyalty and devotion to a nation (p. 233)

nacionalismo lealtad y devoción a una nación (pág. 233)

national self-determination the free choice by the people of a nation of their own future political status (p. 247)

autodeterminación de los pueblos libre elección por parte de los habitantes de una nación de su situación política futura (pág. 247)

nativism hostility toward immigrants (pp. 146, 270)

nativismo hostilidad hacia los inmigrantes (págs. 146, 270)

*__network__ an interconnected system (p. 243)

*__red__ sistema interconectado (pág. 243)

nomad a person who continually moves from place to place, usually in search of food (p. 107)

nómada persona que se traslada continuamente de un lugar a otro, por lo general en busca de alimentos (pág. 107)

*__nuclear__ relating to the nucleus of an atom (p. 385)

*__nuclear__ relativo al núcleo de un átomo (pág. 385)

O

*__obtain__ to gain possession of (p. 626)

*__obtener__ lograr la posesión de algo (pág. 626)

*__ongoing__ being in process; continuing (p. 282)

*__en curso__ que se halla en proceso; que continúa (pág. 282)

Open Door policy a policy that allowed each foreign nation in China to trade freely in the other nations' spheres of influence (p. 191)

política de Puertas Abiertas política que permitía que toda nación extranjera en la China negociara libremente en la esfera de influencia de las otras naciones (pág. 191)

open range vast areas of grassland owned by the federal government (p. 99)

terreno abierto vastas áreas de praderas de propiedad del gobierno federal (pág. 99)

*__orientation__ a position relative to a standard (p. 584)

*__orientación__ posición con relación a un estándar (pág. 584)

*__outcome__ something that follows as a result or consequence (p. 79)

*__resultado__ algo que ocurre como producto o consecuencia (pág. 79)

P

Pan-Americanism the idea that the United States and Latin American nations should work together (p. 179)

Panamericanismo idea según la cual Estados Unidos y las naciones latinoamericanas deberían trabajar unidas (pág. 179)

*__participant__ one who takes part or shares in something (p. 602)

*__participante__ persona que toma parte en algo o lo comparte (pág. 602)

party boss the person in control of a political machine (p. 154)

jefe político persona que controla la maquinaria política (pág. 154)

*__perception__ comprehension or understanding influenced by observation, interpretation, and attitude (p. 76)

*__percepción__ comprensión o conocimiento influenciado por la observación, la interpretación y la actitud (pág. 76)

perestroika a policy of economic and government restructuring instituted by Mikhail Gorbachev in the Soviet Union in the 1980s (p. 586)

perestroika política de reestructuración económica y gubernamental instituida por Mijaíl Gorbachov en la Unión Soviética de 1980 a 1990 (pág. 586)

Glossary/Glosario

ENGLISH	ESPAÑOL
periphery the outer boundary of something (p. 374)	**periferia** límite exterior de algo (pág. 374)
perjury lying when one has sworn under oath to tell the truth (pp. 411, 601)	**perjurio** mentir cuando se ha jurado decir la verdad (págs. 411, 601)
***phenomenon** an exceptional, unusual, or abnormal person, thing, or occurrence (p. 435)	***fenómeno** persona, cosa o suceso excepcional, poco usual o anormal (pág. 435)
philanthropy providing money to support humanitarian or social goals (p. 157)	**filantropía** aportar dinero para apoyar causas humanitarias o sociales (pág. 157)
pillage to loot or plunder (p. 82)	**saquear** apoderarse de todo lo que se encuentra o robar (pág. 82)
polio abbreviated term for poliomyelitis, an acute infectious disease affecting the skeletal muscles, often resulting in permanent disability and deformity (p. 310)	**polio** abreviatura de poliomielitis, una enfermedad infecciosa aguda que afecta los músculos esqueléticos y a menudo produce discapacidad y deformidad permanentes (pág. 310)
political machine an organization linked to a political party that often controlled local government (p. 154)	**maquinaria política** organización vinculada a un partido político que a menudo es controlada por el gobierno local (pág. 154)
poll tax a tax of a fixed amount per person that had to be paid before the person could vote (p. 170)	**impuesto de capitación** impuesto de una cantidad fija por persona que debía pagarse para poder votar (pág. 170)
popular sovereignty before the Civil War, the idea that people living in a territory had the right to decide by voting if slavery would be allowed there (pp. 28, 72)	**soberanía popular** antes de la Guerra Civil, la idea de que las personas que vivían en un territorio tenían derecho a votar para decidir si se debía permitir la esclavitud ahí (págs. 28, 72)
populism a political movement founded in the 1890s representing mainly farmers that favored free coinage of silver and government control of railroads and other large industries (p. 165)	**populismo** movimiento político fundado en el siglo XIX que representaba principalmente a los agricultores que estaban a favor de la libre acuñación de plata y del control gubernamental de los ferrocarriles y otras grandes industrias (pág. 165)
poverty line a level of personal or family income below which one is classified as poor by the federal government (p. 441)	**límite de pobreza** nivel de ingresos personales o familiares por debajo del cual el gobierno federal lo clasifica como pobre (pág. 441)
***practice** to do something repeatedly so it becomes the standard (p. 122)	***practicar** hacer algo en repetidas ocasiones, de manera que se vuelva el estándar (pág. 122)
***predominantly** being most frequent or common (p. 64)	***predominantemente** con gran frecuencia o muy común (pág. 64)
***prior** happening before an event (p. 99)	***previo** que sucede antes de un evento (pág. 99)
***procedure** a particular way of conducting or engaging in an activity (p. 640)	***procedimiento** manera particular de realizar una actividad o participar en ella (pág. 640)
***prohibit** to make illegal by an authority (p. 346)	***prohibir** cuando una autoridad establece que algo es ilegal (pág. 346)
prohibition laws banning the manufacture, transportation, and sale of alcoholic beverages (p. 210)	**Prohibición** leyes que prohibían la fabricación, el transporte y la venta de bebidas alcohólicas (pág. 210)
propaganda the spreading of ideas about an institution or individual for the purpose of influencing opinion (p. 234)	**propaganda** difusión de ideas sobre una institución o un individuo con el propósito de influenciar a la opinión (pág. 234)
***prospective** to be likely to, or have intentions to, perform an act (p. 104)	***potencial** que es probable que, o tiene intenciones de, realizar una acción (pág. 104)

Glossary/Glosario

protective tariff a tax on imports designed to protect American manufacturers (p. 63)

arancel proteccionista impuesto sobre las importaciones diseñado para proteger a los fabricantes estadounidenses (pág. 63)

protectorate a country that is technically independent but is actually under the control of another country (p. 180)

protectorado país independiente desde el punto de vista técnico pero que en realidad está bajo el control de otro país (pág. 180)

public works projects such as highways, parks, and libraries built with public funds for public use (p. 301)

obras públicas proyectos como carreteras, parques y bibliotecas construidos con fondos públicos para uso público (pág. 301)

*publish to make a document available to the general public (p. 161)

*publicar hacer que un documento esté disponible al público (pág. 161)

*purchase something obtained especially for a price in money or its equivalent (p. 341)

*compra algo obtenido especialmente a cambio de un precio en dinero o su equivalente (pág. 341)

R

racism prejudice or discrimination against someone because of his or her race (p. 487)

racismo prejuicio o discriminación contra alguien por su raza (pág. 487)

*rationality the quality or state of being agreeable to reason (p. 522)

*racionalidad cualidad o condición de estar dispuesto a razonar (pág. 522)

rationing restricting the amount of an item an individual can have due to a limited supply (p. 365)

racionar restringir la cantidad de un artículo que un individuo puede tener, debido a la escasez de provisiones (pág. 365)

reapportionment the method states use to draw up political districts based on changes in population (p. 453)

redistribución método que usan los estados para conformar distritos políticos con base en los cambios demográficos (pág. 453)

recall the right that enables voters to remove unsatisfactory elected officials from office (p. 204)

revocatoria derecho que permite a los electores remover del cargo a funcionarios elegidos cuyo desempeño es insatisfactorio (pág. 204)

*recovery an economic upturn, as after a depression (p. 326)

*recuperación mejoría económica, por ejemplo después de una depresión (pág. 326)

referendum the practice of letting voters accept or reject measures proposed by the legislature (p. 204)

referendo práctica que permite a los electores aceptar o rechazar medidas propuestas por la Asamblea Legislativa (pág. 204)

refugee someone leaving his or her country due to a well-founded fear of persecution on account of race, religion, nationality, membership in a particular group, or political opinion (p. 605)

refugiado persona que deja su país debido a un temor bien fundado de persecución a causa de su raza, religión, nacionalidad, pertenencia a un grupo particular u opinión política (pág. 605)

*register to file personal information in order to become eligible for an official event (p. 481)

*inscribirse entregar información personal con el fin de ser elegible para un evento oficial (pág. 481)

*regulate to govern or direct according to rule (p. 215)

*regular gobernar o dirigir ciñéndose a las normas (pág. 215)

relief aid for the needy; welfare (p. 301)

auxilio ayuda para los necesitados; asistencia social (pág. 301)

*relocate to move to a new place (p. 107)

*trasladar pasar a un nuevo lugar (pág. 107)

*remove to change the location or position (p. 459)

*remover cambiar de ubicación o posición (pág. 459)

ENGLISH

ESPAÑOL

reparations the payment by the losing country in a war to the winner for the damages caused by the war (p. 247)

indemnización pago que el país perdedor en una guerra hace al ganador para compensar los daños ocasionados por la guerra (pág. 247)

repatriation being restored or returned to the country of origin, allegiance, or citizenship (p. 530)

repatriación acción por la cual se devuelve o regresa a una persona al país de origen, lealtad o ciudadanía (pág. 530)

*repress to stop something by force (p. 586)

*reprimir detener algo mediante el uso de la fuerza (pág. 586)

*requirement something essential to the existence or occurrence of something else (p. 83)

*requisito algo fundamental para la existencia o acontecimiento del algo más (pág. 83)

reserved powers powers that belong strictly to the states (p. 29)

poderes reservados poderes que pertenecen estrictamente a los estados (pág. 29)

*resident one who lives in a place for some length of time (p. 606)

*residente persona que vive en un lugar durante cierto tiempo (pág. 606)

*resolution a formal expression of opinion, will, or intent voted by an official body or assembly (p. 71)

*resolución expresión formal de una opinión, deseo o intención por la cual vota una asamblea u organismo oficial (pág. 71)

*resolve to come to an agreement (p. 247)

*resolver llegar a un acuerdo (pág. 247)

*resolve the fixity of purpose, or resoluteness (p. 624)

*determinación con un propósito fijo o resolución (pág. 624)

*resources materials used in the production process, such as money, people, land, wood, or steel (p. 118)

*recursos materiales utilizados en el proceso de producción, tales como dinero, personal, tierras, madera o acero (pág. 118)

*response something said or done as a reaction (p. 421)

*respuesta lo que se dice o se hace como reacción (pág. 421)

*restraint the act of limiting, restricting, or keeping under control (p. 105)

*restricción acción de limitar, restringir o mantener bajo control (pág. 105)

*retain to keep in possession (p. 589)

*retener mantener la posesión (pág. 589)

*revelation an act of revealing to view or making known (p. 262)

*revelación acción de revelar para ver o dar a conocer (pág. 262)

*revenue the total income produced by a given source (p. 25)

*renta ingresos totales producidos por una fuente determinada (pág. 25)

revenue sharing federal tax money that is distributed among the states (p. 542)

participación en los ingresos dinero proveniente de los impuestos federales que se distribuye entre los estados (pág. 542)

revenue tariff a tax on imports for the purpose of raising money (p. 63)

arancel financiero impuesto sobre las importaciones con el fin de recaudar dinero (pág. 63)

*revise to make changes to an original document (p. 341)

*modificar hacer cambios a un documento original (pág. 341)

right-to-work laws a law making it illegal to require employees to join a union (p. 431)

leyes de derecho al trabajo leyes que hacen ilegal exigir que los empleados se unan a un sindicato (pág. 431)

rock 'n' roll popular music usually played on electronically amplified instruments and characterized by a persistent, heavily accented beat, much repetition of simple phrases, and often country, folk, and blues elements (p. 439)

rock and roll música popular que por lo general se interpreta con instrumentos amplificados electrónicamente; se caracteriza por un compás persistente y bastante acentuado, muchas repeticiones de frases sencillas y, a menudo, elementos de música *country, folk* y *blues* (pág. 439)

S

safety net something that provides security against misfortune; specifically, government relief programs intended to protect against economic disaster (p. 327)

red de protección algo que brinda seguridad contra las calamidades; en particular, programas de ayuda del gobierno que buscan proteger contra un desastre económico (pág. 327)

satellite nations nations politically and economically dominated or controlled by another more powerful country (p. 401)

naciones satélite naciones que están bajo el dominio o control político y económico de un país más poderoso (pág. 401)

scalawag a name given to Southerners who supported Republican Reconstruction of the South (p. 85)

scalawag nombre dado a los sureños que apoyaban la Reconstrucción Republicana del Sur (pág. 85)

sect a subgroup within a religious community whose beliefs differ from the larger group (p. 631)

secta subgrupo en una comunidad religiosa, cuyas creencias difieren del grupo mayor (pág. 631)

segregation the separation or isolation of a race, class, or group (p. 171)

segregación separación o aislamiento de una raza, clase o grupo (pág. 171)

"separate but equal" a doctrine established by the 1896 Supreme Court case *Plessy* v. *Ferguson* that permitted laws segregating African Americans as long as equal facilities were provided (p. 472)

"separados pero iguales" doctrina establecida por la Corte Suprema en el caso *Plessy contra Ferguson* de 1896, que permitía las leyes que segregaban a la población afroamericana siempre que se brindaran instalaciones iguales (pág. 472)

separation of powers a government principle in which power is divided among different branches (p. 23)

separación de poderes principio de gobierno en el cual el poder está divido en diferentes ramas (pág. 23)

*series a number of events that come one after another (p. 300)

*serie conjunto de eventos que vienen uno después del otro (pág. 300)

settlement house an institution located in a poor neighborhood that provided numerous community services such as medical care, child care, libraries, and classes in English (p. 159)

centro comunitario institución localizada en un vecindario pobre que presta numerosos servicios a la comunidad, tales como atención médica, cuidado de niños, bibliotecas y clases en inglés (pág. 159)

siege a military blockade of a city or fortified place to force it to surrender (p. 89)

sitio bloqueo militar de una ciudad o lugar fortificado para obligarlo a rendirse (pág. 89)

*significantly in a manner likely to have influence or effect (p. 630)

*considerablemente de manera que puede influir o tener efecto (pág. 630)

sit-down strike a method of boycotting work by sitting down at work and refusing to leave the establishment (p. 323)

huelga de brazos caídos método de boicotear el trabajo sentándose en el puesto de trabajo y negándose a abandonar el establecimiento (pág. 323)

skyscraper a very tall building (p. 153)

rascacielos edificio muy alto (pág. 153)

smog fog made heavier and darker by smoke and chemical fumes (p. 561)

esmog niebla que se hace más densa y oscura debido al humo y a los vapores químicos (pág. 561)

soap opera a serial drama on television or radio using melodramatic situations (p. 297)

telenovela drama seriado en televisión o radio que presenta situaciones melodramáticas (pág. 297)

Social Darwinism a philosophy based on Charles Darwin's theories of evolution and natural selection, asserting that humans have developed through competition and natural selection with only the strongest surviving (pp. 157, 212)

Darwinismo Social filosofía basada en las teorías de Charles Darwin sobre la evolución y la selección natural, la cual afirma que los seres humanos se han desarrollado por la competencia y la selección natural y sólo los más fuertes han sobrevivido (págs. 157, 212)

sodbuster a name given to Great Plains farmers (p. 104)

rompeterreno nombre dado a los granjeros de las Grandes Llanuras (pág. 104)

*source the point at which something is provided (p. 271)

*fuente punto en el cual se proporciona algo (pág. 271)

Glossary/Glosario

ENGLISH	ESPAÑOL
space race refers to the Cold War competition over dominance of space exploration capability (p. 457)	**carrera espacial** relativo a la competencia que se dio durante la Guerra Fría por el dominio de la capacidad de exploración espacial (pág. 457)
speakeasy a place where alcoholic beverages are sold illegally (p. 274)	**clandestino** lugar en el que se venden bebidas alcohólicas ilegalmente (pág. 274)
special prosecutor a lawyer from outside the government (p. 547)	**fiscal especial** abogado externo al gobierno (pág. 547)
speculation the act of buying stocks at great risk with the anticipation that the prices will rise (p. 291)	**especulación** compra de acciones con gran riesgo con la expectativa de que los precios subirán (pág. 291)
sphere of influence a section of a country where a foreign nation enjoys special rights and powers (p. 191)	**esfera de influencia** sección de un país donde una nación extranjera goza de derechos y facultades especiales (pág. 191)
spoils system the practice of handing out government jobs to supporters; replacing government employees with the winning candidate's supporters (p. 65)	**sistema de sinecuras** práctica de dar trabajos gubernamentales a los partidarios; sustitución de los empleados del gobierno por partidarios del candidato ganador (pág. 65)
*__stability__ a state of peace; condition resistant to change or upheaval (p. 574)	*__estabilidad__ estado de paz, resistencia al cambio o la agitación (pág. 574)
stagflation persistent inflation combined with stagnant consumer demand and relatively high unemployment (p. 550)	**estanflación** inflación persistente en combinación con un estancamiento de la demanda y un desempleo relativamente alto (pág. 550)
state-sponsored terrorism violent acts against civilians that are secretly supported by a government in order to attack other nations without going to war (p. 625)	**terrorismo de Estado** actos violentos contra los civiles, que son apoyados en secreto por un gobierno con el fin de atacar a otras naciones sin entrar en guerra (pág. 625)
stock market a system for buying and selling stocks in corporations (p. 290)	**mercado de valores** sistema de compra y venta de acciones en las sociedades anónimas (pág. 290)
*__strategic__ related to long-term interests and how to achieve them (p. 502)	*__estratégico__ relacionado con intereses de largo plazo y cómo lograrlos (pág. 502)
strategic materials materials needed for fighting a war (p. 342)	**materiales estratégicos** materiales necesarios para participar en una guerra (pág. 342)
*__strategy__ a plan or method for achieving a goal (p. 166)	*__estrategia__ plan o método para alcanzar un objetivo (pág. 166)
*__subsidy__ money granted by the government to achieve a specific goal that is beneficial to society (p. 464)	*__subsidio__ dinero que el gobierno entrega para alcanzar un objetivo específico que beneficia a la sociedad (pág. 464)
subversion a systematic attempt to overthrow a government by using persons working secretly from within (p. 410)	**subversión** intento sistemático de derrocar un gobierno valiéndose de personas que trabajan en secreto dentro de ese gobierno (pág. 410)
suffrage the right to vote (p. 205)	**sufragio** derecho al voto (pág. 205)
*__sum__ a specified amount of money (p. 291)	*__suma__ cantidad específica de dinero (pág. 291)
summit a meeting between heads of government (p. 544)	**cumbre** reunión entre los jefes de gobierno (pág. 544)
Sunbelt a new industrial region in southern California and the Deep South, developing during World War II (p. 364)	**Cinturón del Sol** nueva región industrial al sur de California y el Bajo Sur, que se desarrolló durante la Segunda Guerra Mundial (pág. 364)
supply-side economics an economic theory that lower tax rates will boost the economy as businesses and individuals invest their money, thereby creating higher tax revenue (pp. 263, 576)	**economía de oferta** teoría económica según la cual los impuestos más bajos estimulan la economía en la medida que las empresas y los individuos invierten su dinero, en consecuencia se crea una renta tributaria más alta (págs. 263, 576)

*suspend to cease or stop (p. 295)

swing vote a vote that may sometimes lean conservative and other times liberal (p. 636)

*symbolize to represent, express, or identify by a symbol (p. 280)

*suspender cesar o detener (pág. 295)

voto flotante voto que unas veces puede ser conservador y otras veces liberal (pág. 636)

*simbolizar representar, expresar o identificar mediante un símbolo (pág. 280)

T

---

*target something or someone fired on or marked for attack (p. 375)

teach-in an extended meeting or class held to discuss a social or political issue (p. 506)

*technique a method of achieving a desired aim (p. 297)

telecommute to work at home by means of an electronic linkup with a central office (p. 612)

televangelist an evangelist who conducts regularly televised religious programs (p. 573)

temperance a moderation in or abstinence from alcohol (p. 66)

tenement multifamily apartments, usually dark, crowded, and barely meeting minimum living standards (p. 153)

*tension friction or opposition between groups (p. 192)

termination policy a government policy to bring Native Americans into mainstream society by withdrawing recognition of Native American groups as legal entities (p. 442)

terrorism the use of violence by non-governmental groups against civilians to achieve a political goal by instilling fear and frightening governments into changing policies (p. 624)

*theory a hypothesis meant for argument or investigation (p. 550)

*thereby because of that (p. 322)

time zone a geographic region in which the same standard time is kept (p. 98)

*traditional the usual way of doing things (p. 502)

*trigger to cause an action that causes a greater reaction (p. 154)

trust a combination of firms or corporations formed by a legal agreement, especially to reduce competition (p. 130)

*objetivo algo o alguien a quien se le dispara o se marca para atacar (pág. 375)

foro asamblea o clase prolongadas para tratar un tema social o político (pág. 506)

*técnica método para alcanzar un objetivo trazado (pág. 297)

teletrabajo trabajar en casa mediante una conexión electrónica con una oficina central (pág. 612)

telepredicador predicador que conduce habitualmente programas religiosos por televisión (pág. 573)

templanza moderación o abstinencia en el uso del alcohol (pág. 66)

casa de vecindad apartamentos multifamiliares, por lo general oscuros, hacinados y que apenas cumplen los estándares mínimos de vivienda (pág. 153)

*tensión fricción u oposición entre grupos (pág. 192)

política de terminación política gubernamental para incorporar a los indígenas americanos a la sociedad predominante cancelando el reconocimiento de los grupos indígenas americanos como entidades legales (pág. 442)

terrorismo uso de la violencia por parte de grupos no gubernamentales contra los civiles para alcanzar un objetivo político, atemorizando e intimidando a los gobiernos para que cambien sus políticas (pág. 624)

*teoría hipótesis planteada para argumentar o investigar (pág. 550)

*por consiguiente por esta razón (pág. 322)

huso horario región geográfica en la cual se mantiene la misma hora estándar (pág. 98)

*tradicional manera usual de hacer las cosas (pág. 502)

*desencadenar provocar una acción que provoca una reacción mayor (pág. 154)

trust asociación de firmas o sociedades anónimas formadas por un acuerdo legal, especialmente para reducir la competencia (pág. 130)

ENGLISH — U — ESPAÑOL

*unconstitutional not in accordance with or authorized by the constitution of a state or society (p. 224)

*inconstitucional no conforme con o autorizado por la Constitución de un Estado o la sociedad (pág. 224)

*underestimate to estimate lower than the real amount or number (p. 343)

*subestimar estimar en un valor más bajo que la cantidad o el número reales (pág. 343)

unfair trade practices trading practices that derive a gain at the expense of competition (p. 223)

prácticas comerciales desleales prácticas comerciales que generan ganancias a expensas del bienestar de la competencia (pág. 223)

*unify to bring a group together with a similar goal or thought pattern (p. 278)

*unificar juntar un grupo con un objetivo o un patrón de pensamiento similares (pág. 278)

union shop a business that requires employees to join a union (p. 431)

empresa de afiliación sindical obligatoria empresa que exige que los empleados se unan a un sindicato (pág. 431)

*unprecedented having no earlier occurrence of something similar (p. 597)

*sin precedentes que no ha ocurrido algo similar antes (pág. 597)

*unresolved not cleared up, or dealt with successfully (p. 513)

*sin resolver que no se ha aclarado, o tratado con buenos resultados (pág. 513)

urban renewal government programs that attempt to eliminate poverty and revitalize urban areas (p. 441)

renovación urbana programas gubernamentales que buscan eliminar la pobreza y revitalizar las áreas urbanas (pág. 441)

— V —

vertical integration the combining of companies that supply equipment and services needed for a particular industry (p. 129)

integración vertical asociación de compañías que abastecen equipo y servicios necesarios a una industria particular (pág. 129)

via to have come by of, or through (p. 581)

vía llegar por medio de o mediante (pág. 581)

victory garden a garden planted by civilians during war to raise vegetables for home use, leaving more of other foods for the troops (pp. 237, 366)

huerta de la victoria huerta plantada por los civiles durante la guerra con el fin de cultivar vegetales para uso doméstico, y dejar más de otros alimentos para las tropas (págs. 237, 366)

victory suit a men's suit with no vest, no cuffs, a short jacket, and narrow lapels, worn during World War II in order to save fabric for the war effort (p. 365)

traje de la victoria traje de hombre sin chaleco ni puños, con chaqueta corta y solapas pequeñas que se usó durante la Segunda Guerra Mundial con el fin de ahorrar tela para la guerra (pág. 365)

Vietnamization the process of making South Vietnam assume more of the war effort by slowly withdrawing American troops from Vietnam (p. 510)

vietnamización proceso por el cual se hizo que Vietnam del Sur asumiera mayor parte del esfuerzo bélico retirando lentamente las tropas estadounidenses de Vietnam (pág. 510)

vigilance committee a group of ordinary citizens formed by local law enforcement officers whose goal is to find criminals and bring them to justice (p. 97)

comité de vigilancia grupo de ciudadanos del común integrado por funcionarios locales que hacen cumplir las leyes, cuyo objetivo es hallar a los criminales y ponerlos a órdenes de la justicia (pág. 97)

*virtually almost entirely; nearly (p. 349)

*prácticamente casi todo; estrechamente (pág. 349)

*visible what can be seen (p. 578)

*visible que se puede ver (pág. 578)

*volunteer a person who joins the military by choice (p. 186)

*voluntario persona que elige enlistarse en la milicia (pág. 186)

W

weapons of mass destruction (WMD) weapons—including nuclear, chemical, and biological—that can kill large numbers of people all at once (p. 629)

armas de destrucción masiva (ADM) armas nucleares, químicas y biológicas, entre otras, que pueden matar a un gran número de personas a la vez (pág. 629)

*****welfare** aid in the form of money or necessities for those in need, especially disadvantaged social groups (p. 542)

*****asistencia social** ayuda en dinero o en especies para los necesitados, en especial para grupos en desventaja social (pág. 542)

white-collar job jobs in fields not requiring work clothes or protective clothing, such as sales (p. 436)

empleado de oficina trabajos en cargos que no requieren el uso de ropa de protección, como en ventas (pág. 436)

*****widespread** widely diffused or prevalent (p. 251)

*****extendido** ampliamente difundido o frecuente (pág. 251)

Y

yellow journalism type of sensational, biased, and often false reporting for the sake of attracting readers (p. 185)

prensa sensacionalista tipo de periodismo exagerado, tendencioso y a menudo falso con el fin de atraer lectores (pág. 185)

yuppie a young, college-educated adult employed in a well-paying profession and living in or near a large city (p. 580)

yupi adulto joven con educación universitaria que tiene una profesión bien remunerada y vive en una ciudad grande o cerca de ella (pág. 580)

Z

zoot suit men's clothing of extreme cut typically consisting of a thigh-length jacket with wide padded shoulders and baggy, pleated pants with narrow cuffs (p. 364)

traje *zoot* prenda de hombre de corte extremo que por lo general consta de una chaqueta larga y apretada con hombreras anchas y pantalones sueltos con pliegues y dobladillos angostos (pág. 364)

Glossary/Glosario

INDEX

Italicized page numbers refer to illustrations. The following abbreviations are used in the index: m = map; c = chart; p = photograph, painting, or picture; g = graph; crt = cartoon; q = quote

Index

Index

Index

Index

Index

Index

Index

Index

Index

Index

Index

Index

Index

Index

Index

Index

Index

Index